Every increase in elevation brings a decrease in air pressure, which results in a lower boiling point. At 7,000 feet, for example—the altitude of many towns in the Southwest—water boils at 199°F. This means slower cooking times (and makes a pressure cooker a more desirable appliance). Families who have been living in the mountains for years have already discovered, though trial and error, the best ways to adjust.

Newcomers to high altitudes must be patient and experiment to discover what works best. But here are some general rules for high-altitude cooking:

1. For stove-top cooking, use higher heat when practical; extend cooking times as necessary. Beans and grains will require significantly more time than at sea level.
2. Assume that batters and doughs will rise faster than at sea level.
3. Over 3,000 feet, increase baking temperatures by twenty-five degrees.
4. Over 3,000 feet, reduce baking powder (or other leavening) measurements by about ten percent; increase liquid in baked goods by the same percentage. You may want to reduce the amount of sugar slightly as well.
5. For every 2,000 foot increase in altitude above 3,000 feet, reduce leavening even further.

Imperial Measurements

Theoretically, both the United Kingdom and Canada use the metric system, but older recipes rely on the "imperial" measurement system, which differs from standard U.S. measurements in its liquid ("fluid") measurements:

$1/4$ cup = 2.5 ounces
$1/2$ cup ("gill") = 5 ounces
1 cup = 10 ounces
1 pint = 20 ounces
1 quart = 40 ounces

Measurement Conversions

Note that volume (i.e., cup) measures and weight (i.e., ounce) measures convert perfectly for liquids only. Solids are a different story; 1 cup of flour weighs only 4 or 5 ounces.

Dash or pinch = less than $1/4$ teaspoon
3 teaspoons = 1 tablespoon
2 tablespoons = 1 fluid ounce
4 tablespoons = $1/4$ cup = 2 fluid ounces
16 tablespoons = 1 cup = 8 fluid ounces
2 cups = 1 pint
2 pints = 1 quart
4 quarts = 1 gallon

Some Useful Substitutions

1 cup cake flour = $7/8$ cup all-purpose flour + $1/8$ cup cornstarch
1 tablespoon baking powder = 2 teaspoons baking soda + 1 teaspoon cream of tartar
1 cup buttermilk = 1 scant cup milk at room temperature + 1 tablespoon white vinegar
1 cup brown sugar = 1 cup white sugar + 2 tablespoons molasses
1 cup sour cream = 1 cup yogurt (preferably full fat)

Imperial vs. Metric

These are approximate, but are fine for all uses.

1 ounce = 28 grams
1 pound = 500 grams or $1/2$ kilo
2.2 pounds = 1 kilo
1 teaspoon = 5 milliliters (ml)
1 tablespoon = 15 milliliters
1 cup = $1/4$ liter
1 quart = 1 liter

Praise for *How to Cook Everything*:

"This is a cookbook whose pages are destined to become stuck together from constant use."
—*New York Times Book Review*

"An excellent glossary, temperature and measurement charts, menu suggestions, sources, and 250 black-and-white illustrations all make this nearly 1,000-page book worth much..."
—*Fine Cooking*

"Think of it as a more hip *Joy of Cooking*."
—*The Washington Post*

"The enormous breadth of recipes along with Bittman's engaging, straight-forward prose will appeal to cooks looking for reliable help with kitchen fundamentals."
—*Publishers Weekly*

"With sharp writing and nearly 1,000 pages of common-sense guidance, [Bittman] preaches the gospel of simple and delicious home cooking."
—*People Magazine*

"*How to Cook Everything* may become...the classic kitchen reference for a new generation of cooks."
—Knight Ridder News Service

"With Bittman's book in hand, cooks can toss those takeout menus and deliver home-cooked meals with a minimum of time and maximum flavor."
—*Syracuse Herald-Journal*

"Somewhere among the 1,500 recipes...there is something for everybody—repeat, everybody."
—*Dallas Morning News*

Other books by Mark Bittman:

Jean-Georges: Cooking at Home with a Four-Star Chef
(co-written by Jean-Georges Vongerichten)

Fish

Leafy Greens

How to Cook *Everything*

Simple Recipes for Great Food

MARK BITTMAN

Illustrations by Alan Witschonke

MACMILLAN · USA

Dedicated to Murray and Gertrude Bittman

IDG Books Worldwide, Inc.
An International Data Group Company
919 Hillsdale Boulevard
Suite 400
Foster City, CA 94404

For general information about IDG Books Worldwide's books in the United States, please call our Consumer Customer Service department at 800-762-2974. For reseller information, including discounts at previous sales, please call our Reseller Customer Service department at 800-434-3422.

Library of Congress Cataloging-in-Publication Data

Bittman, Mark.
    How to cook everything / by Mark Bittman.
       p. cm.
    Includes index.
    Book Only: ISBN 0-02-861010-5 (alk. paper)
    Book/CD: ISBN 0-7645-6258-4
    1. Cookery.   I. Title.
TX714.B573   1998
641.5—dc21   98-22959
                                           CIP

Printed in the United States of America

10 9 8 7

Book design by Nick Anderson

Contents

Acknowledgments

The author of a book as challenging as this owes thanks to literally hundreds of people—chefs, cookbook writers, friends, relatives, even casual acquaintances, who provided an unusual dish, a kind or insightful word, an idea, an inspiration. But through lack of space and time, and failure of memory, I can't include everyone who deserves mention. Which merely leaves a few dozen people whose influence, help, and often love have been and continue to be most powerful.

First, the people in publishing and the food world, many of whom have crossed the line from professional contact to friend, and all of whom have been there for me when I needed them (which in some cases was frequently): Pam Anderson, Eric Asimov, Harriet Bell, Fern Berman, Michalene Busico, Anna-Teresa Callen, Kerri Conan, Alan Davidson, Alice Fixx, Linda Giuca, Rozanne Gold, Maria Guarnaschelli,

Louise Kennedy, Stephanie Lyness, Priscilla Martel, Susan Quick, David Rosengarten, Rick Sandella, Arthur Schwartz, Cara de Silva, Phil Suarez, and Charlie Van Over. Rick Flaste, Trish Hall, and Chris Kimball have given me not only guidance and friendship but that rare gift of opportunity.

I owe special thanks to these colleagues and near-idols in the food-writing community from whom I have learned so much: Julia Child, Marcella Hazan, Lynne Rossetto Kasper, Hal McGee, Jacques Pepin, Julie Sahni, and Paula Wolfert. Dorie Greenspan and Barbara Kafka, who fall into this category, have also become good friends. Jane Grigson and Richard Sax, who are no longer cooking on earth, were kind to me while they were.

The following chefs and extraordinary single-subject experts have sustained me with food, information, instruction, and inspiration: Ignacio Blanco,

Daniel Boulud, Bill Bowers, Ken Coons, Wylie Dufresne, Johnny Earles, George Faison, Bob Feinn, Michael Lomonaco, Eberhard Mueller, Marion Nestle, Susan Parenti, Jon Rowley, Chris Schlesinger, and Kerry Simon. I must single out my good friend, Jean-Georges Vongerichten, for his extreme generosity and kindness.

Incredibly, I do retain a few friends outside of the food world, and I thank them for having me over for dinner when I couldn't bear the thought of cooking anymore, for sharing their family's recipes with me, and for their non-food support and love. These are Andrea Graziosi, Kathy and Allen Mathes, Mitch Orfuss, Sherry Slade, Bruna Soravia, Bob Spitz, and Fred Zolna. (I wish I could thank Phil Maniaci in person; maybe someday.) I am truly blessed to count Sally Connolly, Pamela Hort, David Paskin, and Semeon Tsalbins among my friends, and thank the stars that two of them happen to be world-class home cooks. Love, too, to my special friends and relatives Eli and Isabel Baar, Shari and Harry Suchecki, Ariel, Evan, Gaby, Sarah T., and Willa.

There are people, of course, who had a more direct impact on this book, and much of the credit (and none of the blame, if any) goes to them: Pam Hoenig—who holds a special place in my heart—Justin Schwartz, and Jane Sigal got the ball rolling. The book received an enormous boost from the work of Estelle Laurence, copy editor, and Melissa Moyal, production editor; Susan Clarey, publisher; Margaret Mirabile, Mike Freeland, and Nick Anderson, designers; photographer Dennis Gottleib, illustrator Alan Witschonke, and all the other folks who helped: Jim Willhite, Bozena Szwagulinski, Rebecca Payes, Michael Beacom, Brian Phair, Roland Elgey, Joan Ward, Selene Ahn, and Beth Jordan. Fern Berman and Robin Insley have done a magnificent job publicizing the book since its publication. Most of all, my sincere gratitude to my good friend Jack Bishop and the book's true (and final!) editor Jennifer Griffin, both of whom helped take this book to new heights, and each of whom gave up huge chunks of their lives to do so.

Finally, to Angela Miller, who changed my life, and John Willoughby, who brightens so many of my days, my love and thanks. To Kate and Emma Baar-Bittman, love, kisses, hugs, thanks, and a lifetime guarantee of soup with noodles anytime. As for my partner-in-life Karen Baar, you are a treasure.

—Woodbridge, Connecticut
April 1998

Introduction

Anyone can cook, and most everyone should. It's a sorry sign that many people consider cooking "from scratch" an unusual and even rare talent. In fact, cooking is a simple and rewarding craft, one that anyone can learn and even succeed at from the get-go.

Until the last half-century, every household had someone who cooked from scratch all the time. It was only during World War II that "convenience" began to drive the American food industry. And following the war, mass-produced canned goods, originally developed for the GI, were marketed to civilians; frozen foods became *de rigueur*; and manufactured foods, like oleomargarine, began to replace real ones, like butter.

More recently, the majority of women have joined the majority of men in the workforce, and few families have an individual whose full-time job is that of homemaker. Add to that the persuasive nature of contemporary marketing, which has convinced many people that fast food is not only quicker than home cooking but better and cheaper (it is neither, and in fact only marginally faster, if that), and you have a culinary crisis.

The result is that fine old American home cooking—a style which took advantage of the abundance of a bountiful land but always set aside extra for bad times—has largely been replaced by a style that might be called "the faster the better." Flavor, nutrition, tradition, and enjoyment are often sacrificed at the sacred altar of so-called convenience.

As far as I'm concerned, convenience is one of the two dirty words of American cooking, reflecting the part of our national character that is easily bored; the other is "gourmet." Convenience foods demonstrate our supposed disdain for the routine and the mundane: "I don't have time to cook." The gourmet phase, which peaked in the eighties, when food was seen as art, showed our ability to obsess about aspects of daily life that most other cultures take for granted. You might only cook once a week, but wow, what a meal.

Both of these tendencies are the enemies of good everyday cooking, one of the few simple, routine joys of daily life. The irony is that most "gourmet" foods and many "convenience" foods are equally difficult to prepare from scratch. Can you imagine what it takes to duplicate a Chicken McNugget with Sweet and Sour Sauce?

Luckily, several factors have combined in recent years to show us that good food could indeed be simple. In our search for "new" flavors, we began to look at the traditional regional cuisines of both the United States and the rest of the world. Equally important in the long run was the philosophy—now self-evident but first popularized in the seventies by pacesetting Berkeley chef Alice Waters and many others—that good ingredients were the basis of good cuisine.

These factors, combined with a seismic interest in Italian food, resulted in a more mature, healthier attitude among many eaters. Still, there remain several challenges: Many people never learned how to cook, an equal number believe they don't have the time, and some define cooking as heating up frozen food in a microwave oven. Much of this stems from the fact that many members of the last couple of generations— myself included—did not grow up witnessing their mothers carrying on the traditions of their grandmothers. The reasons for this do not fall within the scope of this book, but involve our national transience, our largely immigrant heritage, and the entrance of the majority of mothers into the workforce.

For all but the poorest Americans, there remains an embarrassment of riches when it comes to food. We are able to scorn leftovers, to buy almost every food preprepared—even salad!—to eat out daily, to rely heavily on frozen foods. Yet although we may gain marginal amounts of time by doing these things, we lose the delights of working in the kitchen, the wonders of creation, the pleasures of time spent in the honest pursuit of tradition and the nourishment of our bodies and those of our family.

We could all complain about the quality of ingredients at the supermarket. All mass-produced food is grown or raised for its hardiness, profitability, shelf life, and ability to withstand the rigors of transit, rather than for its flavor and nutritional values. Most of it comes to us from hundreds if not thousands of miles away; little of it is truly fresh; and it is sold to us not by the individuals who raised it or even selected it, but by anonymous corporations.

Nevertheless, even supermarket food is frequently of reasonably high quality, flavorful, and almost uniformly safe to eat. Furthermore, our world-beating distribution system delivers to us an incomparable variety of food—including imports that were once found only at the swankest shops—at prices that are so low that visitors from other countries are frequently shocked.

Home cooks, therefore, have the opportunity to create, simply and with a minimum of effort, a variety of food unparalleled in the history of the world. Not only can we buy extra-virgin olive oil, wood-aged soy sauce, genuine Parmesan, organic salad greens, Maine mussels, Montana lamb, and New Zealand apples without leaving our neighborhoods, but we have both the know-how and the tools to prepare these things in ways that are quick and authentic. "Convenience" foods should, by right, be a thing of the past. Both preboxed macaroni and cheese and Pasta with Butter, Sage, and Parmesan (page 140, in case you're curious) take 10 minutes to prepare from the time the water comes to a boil. Both provide decent fuel for the body. One provides a genuinely delicious eating experience and a link to traditions older than collective memory. Why would anyone not choose the real thing?

Similarly, turning a few pieces of leftover pita bread into a salad, converting less-than-perfect apples into a sauce—these are not only connections to an almost-forgotten past, but simple economies that not only save money but are a kind of alchemy: Gold from garbage!

Enough of the sales pitch; the fact that you have read this far indicates that you are interested in bettering your own cooking. It remains for me to convince you that the process is an easy one. There are no "secrets" to cooking—only good guidance combined with experience. To begin, you must consider five distinct elements. These are time, ingredients, recipes, equipment, and technique. The last two elements are given separate chapter headings of their own (pages 1–14). But to take the first three individually:

Time

You already make a commitment to cook, or at least to eat. Unless you are going to eat in restaurants all the time, you need to put food on the table, no matter what you do. And, as often as not, "convenience" food takes as long to get to the table as real food.

For example, it takes no more time to cook many meals than it does to call for a pizza and pick it up, or even wait for it to be delivered. Grilling a piece of meat or fish and steaming a vegetable or preparing a salad is a twenty-minute operation; so is making a simple pasta dish. These may not be meals that you look forward to, or meals that you will remember even a couple of days later. But they are meals in which the ingredients, flavors, and timing are entirely up to you: You know what you are eating and you know what it will taste like. It is a real experience.

Time is a precious commodity, no question about it. But there are few better ways to spend it than by preparing high-quality food for yourself and those you love. Set aside some time each day to cook dinner, and you will find it becomes a rewarding, energy-giving routine.

Ingredients

It's easy to have the makings of a meal or two on hand at all times just by maintaining the right mix of staples. Different people like to eat different ways, obviously, but certain foods belong in every kitchen all the time, and keep nearly indefinitely. To stock your pantry and refrigerator, make sure you have on hand:

- pasta and other grains, especially rice
- canned beans and other vegetables, especially tomatoes
- spices, and dried herbs when fresh are unavailable
- liquid seasonings such as olive oil, vinegar, and soy sauce
- eggs and butter
- flour, cornmeal, and the like
- nuts and dried fruits
- onions, potatoes, garlic, and other long-keeping vegetables
- non-fat dried milk (usually for emergencies)
- canned stock

With this list alone you will be equipped to make literally dozens of different meals, from pancakes to pasta. When you throw in the fresh ingredients that you're likely to have in the refrigerator as a result of weekly shopping jaunts—vegetables, herbs, fruit, meat, fish, milk, cheese, and other perishables—the result is that you'll be able to prepare most of the 1,500-odd recipes in this book without going out to search for special ingredients.

One thing you may find different about this cookbook when compared to most other large, general cookbooks: The recipes call for whole, fresh ingredients almost exclusively. I am not against the occasional use of canned stock, or frozen spinach, as part of a recipe where the ordinary-at-best nature of such products is disguised by the other ingredients in the recipe. But I do not believe in "miracle" recipes based on canned or dried soups, artificial mayonnaise, or powdered desserts. This is a cookbook, not a chemistry class; to cook good dishes you must start with real food.

Of course, you may become completely obsessed with ingredients, and understandably so. Combining the best ingredients simply is the easiest way to make brilliant food. An omelet made with farm-fresh eggs, a local chicken roasted with wonderful olive oil, sliced tomatoes straight from the garden—these are minimalist dishes that cannot be duplicated with supermarket ingredients. It pays to have a small variety of slightly unusual ingredients around—when you're improvising, if you come across a hunk of prosciutto, some good black olives, or some fresh herbs, your job will be easier. Buy a few extras at the supermarket and let them find their way into your cooking.

In general, the better the ingredients you have the simpler your cooking can be. If you garden, you already know this; your summer meals are probably nearly vegetarian (and you swear you'll eat more vegetables next winter). Same thing if you live near a pig farm: you probably eat lots of pork.

But becoming obsessed with ingredients is a full-time job, because the chase is endless—there's a saying I don't particularly like, but it fits here: Perfect is the enemy of good enough. If you spend your time looking for the perfect tomato, you won't eat any tomatoes at all. Do the best you can, and don't drive yourself nuts.

Of course, if you had perfect ingredients all the time you would hardly need a cookbook. But the story of contemporary cooking is often the story of compromise; you buy the best ingredients you can lay your hands on and combine them in ways that make sense. That's the thinking behind my recipes.

Recipes

Recipes, obviously, are the most important element in distinguishing one cookbook from another. All recipes have this in common: They combine a number of ingredients using a given set of techniques. This may seem self-evident, but the choice of ingredients and techniques, along with the clarity of the writing, is what defines a cookbook.

The single most important factor in determining whether you find a cookbook useful lies in its selection of recipes. There is a broad body of recipes from which an author may choose; some cookbooks contain four thousand, some CD-ROMS ten thousand, and there are many more in common use. The veritable explosion of international ingredients and techniques has brought us recipes—both traditional and contrived—that none of us had heard or conceived of just twenty years ago. Yet some of these recipes are simple, straightforward, and broadly appealing.

It is that phrase, in fact—simple, straightforward, and broadly appealing—that was my guideline in choosing the "mere" fifteen hundred recipes (more than enough to keep most people satisfied for a lifetime) best-suited for this basic cookbook. More accomplished cooks may find little new here. What everyone will find, I hope, is a sound selection of recipes for the home cook. When I have included older, well-established, traditional recipes, I have updated them by including modern flavors and cooking techniques. Those "newer" recipes I have included are almost all the older, well-established, traditional recipes of cultures whose cuisines were not a part of the American quilt until recently. These are largely Asian, but include some from other parts of the world as well.

Selection, of course, is only one step in determining the usefulness of a recipe to you. The others are the ease with which you can follow it, and the extent to which is it reliable. That is: Will it give you the results I intended, and are they the same as the results you wanted?

There are two factors involved here. One, quite simply, is the number of ingredients and techniques. The other is the language used in explaining the procedure. As I have said, I have chosen simple recipes, those that minimize the number of ingredients and techniques without compromising flavor. Whenever possible, I have established a basic recipe and used variations to demonstrate a number of different directions in which it can be taken; these variations may be low-fat, vegetarian, spicy, more elaborate, faster, or with completely different flavors but identical techniques. As you gain in experience and confidence you will begin creating your own variations. In any case, the basic recipe is always as straightforward as I can make it.

As for language, there is little I can say: I have done my best to spell things out clearly and simply, without jargon, and without taking anything for granted. I apologize in advance for any failures on my part.

A word about timing The timing for every recipe ever created is approximate. The rate at which food cooks is dependent on the moisture content and temperature of the food itself; measurements (which are rarely perfectly accurate); heat level (your medium-high heat may not be the same as mine or your oven may be off by 25 degrees); the kind of equipment (some pans conduct heat better than others); even the air temperature. Part of learning how to cook is judging doneness. As you're learning, poke at the food, peek inside it, taste it, and learn what each ingredient looks and feels like when it's done; the best cooks use time as a rough guideline, but judge doneness by touch, sight, and taste.

About Food Safety and Healthy Eating

Both of these subjects have been beaten to death, but the first, at least, is still worth discussing.

Food Safety

Most food-borne illnesses can be prevented and, since food sickens an estimated 6 million Americans each year (mostly from salmonella), and of those, about two thousand die (well under one percent of those who become ill), it's worth taking precautions.

Begin by keeping your hands and all food preparation surfaces and utensils perfectly clean; soap and hot water are good enough, although the new antibacterial kitchen soaps are probably even better. Wash cutting boards after using, and don't prepare food directly on your counters unless you wash them as well. Change sponges frequently too, and throw your sponges in the washing machine whenever you wash clothes in hot water. Or get into the routine of microwaving your sponge every day: Put it directly in the microwave and blast away until it's too hot to touch. Change your kitchen towel frequently also—at least once a day.

It should go without saying that your refrigerator functions well (35°F is about right, and 40°F is too warm) and that you use it. Food should be stored in the refrigerator until just before cooking (or removed for no more than an hour before cooking if you wish to bring it to room temperature first) or whenever you're not using it. Your freezer should be at 0°F or lower. Thaw foods in the refrigerator, or under cold running water. And never place cooked food on a plate that previously held raw food.

Those are the easy parts, which everyone should do without question. The other parts are more difficult. Of common foods, cooked vegetables and grains are the safest; next comes cooked fish; then comes cooked meat other than hamburger; then comes cooked chicken, eggs, and hamburger, with which most concerns are associated.

To be as safe as possible—and it will be clear to anyone reading this cookbook that I do not follow many of these rules (nor, to my knowledge, have I ever gotten sick from eating tainted food)—you should:

- Never eat raw meat or fish (in fact, one might say "Never eat raw food").
- Cook all foods, especially hamburger, eggs, and chicken, until well done.

With the exception of cooking chicken to absolute doneness, these rules go counter to the spirit of good cooking and good eating. A well-done hamburger is a hamburger better left uneaten, and, although a hard-boiled egg is a fine thing, it's the only time you want a yolk to reach the solid state. The decision is yours. As for me, I keep a spotlessly clean kitchen, wash my hands about forty times a day, and cook food so that it tastes as good as it can; that's how the recipes in this book are designed.

If you or someone in your family is at greater risk of serious food-borne illness—this includes children, pregnant women, the elderly, and people with compromised immune systems (from AIDS or cancer)—you should take every precaution possible, which probably means hard-cooking eggs and avoiding hamburger altogether. But this is a cookbook, not a prescriptive book; if you have any questions at all about your personal food safety, I suggest you speak with a doctor and a nutritionist.

Eating for Health

You're sick of this, I'm sure, so a quick summary of the current "wisdom," which may or may not be correct:

- Eat lots of fruit and vegetables.
- Minimize your intake of fat, especially fat that is solid at room temperature.
- Eat a wide variety of foods, all in moderation.

I eliminate nothing from my diet except bad food—by which I mean most "fast" food, most "convenience" food, and all "microwavable" food. I eat everything I'm offered at least once. My doctor assures me I'm going to live to be one hundred (and, although I hope he's right, I'm quite sure he's wrong). In any case, I doubt that it's food that is going to kill me. You make your own decisions. Bear in mind that I am not a scientist, just someone who enjoys cooking and eating, and believes that the preparation and consumption of good food improves mental well-being and therefore physical health.

The Last Word

People become obsessed with food and cooking; I have been obsessed with it for all of my adult life. But as time goes on I realize that—as one of my older daughter's bedtime books was titled—*Simple Things Are Best.*

It's true. Each year, I experiment less and less with complex dishes, and try to master the simple staples both of our widely divergent culture, and of other cultures from around the world. I look for good ingredients, and handle them minimally. I am usually satisfied with the food I prepare, but I am the first to admit that it is very rarely on the same level as that served in the world's best restaurants. (It's better, however, than that served in the vast majority of restaurants.)

Striving for brilliance in everyday cooking is a recipe for frustration. Rather, everyday cooking is about preparing good, wholesome, tasty, varied meals for the ones you love. This is a simple, satisfying pleasure. Your results need not be perfect to give you this gift, to which all humans are entitled.

Equipment

You can spend tens of thousands of dollars on kitchen equipment, or you can spend a couple of hundred bucks and be done with it. If you're lucky enough to inherit hand-me-downs from your parents or other friends or relatives, you probably have most of what you need already. This is not to say that some modern appliances are not worth having—if you're going to cook regularly, you will want a blender, a food processor, and an electric mixer. With the exception of an electric ice cream maker—which is a wonderful luxury—other appliances take up more room than they're worth for most people.

I recommend that you cook for a while with minimal equipment so that you can discover your preferences and therefore your priorities. Perhaps you need three or four skillets, a huge stockpot, and a springform pan, but have no use for cookie cutters or a pizza peel; it depends on what it is you want to eat.

Here, then, is a list—with highly personal comments—about what you ought to start with and what you might want to wait for. Items that I consider essential are in red.

The Basics of Knives

First of all, don't buy them from late-night TV. Go to a good department store or a kitchen supply store and look at those with high carbon-steel alloy blades. (The old-fashioned non-alloy blades take a wonderful edge but require more frequent sharpening and discolor immediately. Everyone—from master chefs to cookbook authors to experienced home cooks—uses high carbon-steel now.) The handles may be wood or plastic, although plastic handles are somewhat more durable and dishwasher-safe

1

(nevertheless, you're always better off washing a good knife by hand, since its blade may get nicked in the dishwasher), so I'd go with these. These knives are easily sharpened, and will last a lifetime if you don't whack too many chicken bones with them. A good **eight-inch chef's knife,** essentially an all-purpose blade that you will use for chopping and slicing, should set you back no more than thirty dollars, although you can spend many times that if you like; you may want a ten-inch one as well. Buy one that feels good in your hand.

Hold off, too, on a carving, or slicing knife—a long, thin blade that is not something you will use every day. In a pinch, you can carve or slice with your chef's knife, although not as precisely.

You also need two or three **paring knives,** for peeling, trimming, and other precise tasks—three or four inches long. Again, buy those that feel good in your hand, and don't spend more than five or six dollars on each. A thin-bladed boning knife is very useful, not only for boning but for piercing meat as it cooks to judge doneness; but you can wait for this. Serrated blades are best for cutting bread—unless you only eat presliced bread, buy a long, sturdy **bread knife;** this is a good place to economize, since even the ten-dollar models work fine.

You should consider buying a sharpening steel, which you use by drawing each side of the knife across it several times, holding the blade at a fifteen- to twenty-degree angle until the knife will cut the edge of a piece of paper held loosely in your hand. But many home cooks (including myself) have trouble maintaining a good edge with a steel.

The best and easiest (and unfortunately most expensive) way to keep knives sharp is with a good electric knife sharpener, which will set you back fifty to one hundred dollars, but is a worthwhile investment. Your other alternatives are to sharpen knives with a whetstone, which takes even more skill than a

steel (ask a handy friend, or an uncle, or the guy at the hardware store), or to bring knives to the local kitchen supply store or a good hardware store and get them sharpened professionally. Should you choose either of the latter options, you need a steel to maintain that edge in between sharpenings. (Steels do not sharpen knives, but they do keep the edge fine and straight.)

Remember this about all knives: Dull ones are dangerous. They slip off the food you're cutting and right onto the closest surface, which may be your finger. Although you must be extremely careful with sharp knives—casual contact will lead to a real cut—at least they go where you want them to. Respect your knives: Start with good ones, keep them sharp, and they will become your friends.

The Basics of Skillets and Sauté Pans

According to the manufacturers, a skillet (or frying pan) has curved, relatively shallow sides. A sauté pan has a flat bottom (hence usually more cooking surface), straight, deeper sides, and a lid—all of which make it much better for browning and braising. But the pans don't maintain those differences, and there are many hybrids. What you want is a flat bottom, and sides that angle out so that you can gain easy access to the food when you want to turn it.

As to material: Yes, copper is undeniably best, but you probably can't afford it. Cast iron is very, very good, and quite inexpensive, but it weighs a lot. When you transfer a skillet from the stove top to the oven, a common enough occurrence, you will wish it weren't cast iron (or that you'd spent more time at the gym). Another disadvantage of cast iron is that the metal can interact with acidic sauces, changing their flavor and color (this does no harm from a health perspective).

Since I can't afford copper either, I prefer heavy-duty aluminum skillets with a non-stick coating. They're lighter and cheaper than anything else, and they do a good job. (Some aluminum is "anodized" to make it stronger; these pans last longer, but are not necessarily better to cook with.) Non-stick coatings, while not perfect (they all wear out, regardless of manufacturers' claims), are extremely forgiving, a real bonus for less experienced cooks, especially in sautéing.

If aluminum pans are not good-looking enough for you (a real possibility), go with stainless steel, which is more expensive but attractive; be aware, though, that you'll probably be spending a lot more money for it. Do not be tempted by inexpensive stainless steel, which is a poor conductor of heat; all good stainless steel pans have a layer of copper or aluminum on their bottom and sides or sandwiched between two layers of steel.)

As for size: I recommend buying skillets as you need them, rather than in sets with saucepans. Start with two skillets: one **ten inches** in diameter (I call this "medium" throughout the book) and one **twelve inches** in diameter ("large"). The second will look huge in the store, but perfect once you start trying to brown chicken breasts in it. When you're ready to make omelets or crepes, or fry a single egg, you'll want an eight-inch pan ("small" to "medium") as well. There are new "sauté pans" with deep, rounded sides that are halfway between a traditional sauté pan and a saucepan; I like them very much, because they reduce spattering, which in turn reduces stove-top mess.

Pay attention to the handles, too: They should be riveted on and feel comfortable and sturdy. Although you can't judge this in the store, they should remain fairly cool when cooking on the stove top (if you find that the handles of a given brand become too hot during cooking, steer clear of that brand in the future). Also, you want handles that are ovenproof—you should be able to put any skillet in the oven, and you frequently will. This means no plastic.

Lids for skillets are extremely useful, and the advantage of aluminum is that the lids are quite inexpensive. Ultimately, many will be interchangeable; you need not buy a new lid for every pan you own.

The Basics of Saucepans and Pots

Here you have more leeway, because the non-stick issue is less important. (Since you cook mostly liquids in saucepans, preventing sticking is simply a matter of paying attention.) Stainless steel is a good choice, as are aluminum or cast iron with a baked-on porcelain coating. You can also use aluminum pans with non-stick coatings. (Never use uncoated aluminum, because the metal will react with acidic ingredients.)

You need at least one pot large enough to cook pasta, preferably a little oversized; an **eight-quart pot** is big enough for this and most tasks other than making stock. If you're going to make stock, get a sixteen-quart stockpot. Then get two or three **smaller saucepans** to start with—a small one (two or three cups), a medium one (one to $1^1/_2$ quarts), and a large one, around four quarts. Build from there—a large meal will use up all of your pots, so if you're going to cook regularly you'll eventually need at least six or eight. At some point you will also want a sturdy Dutch oven or covered casserole, of six to eight quarts. All of your pots and pans should have **lids,** although they may be interchangeable.

Although you may need a double-boiler arrangement at some point, don't rush out and buy one. Chances are you can rig one up with the equipment you have by setting one pot on top of another.

The Basics of Baking Dishes and Roasting Pans

There are two kinds here—metal and ceramic—and both are useful. Ceramic (or porcelain-coated metal) is best for bringing to the table; it looks good. But I recommend that you begin with a simple **eight by twelve-inch** or **nine by thirteen-inch metal roasting pan** and an **eight-inch square** or **nine-inch square metal baking pan.** They will meet most of your initial needs—you can roast a chicken, broil meat, bake quick breads or brownies, make macaroni and cheese, and more—and you can always add to your collection. Any metal except uncoated aluminum is fine; aluminum with a non-stick coating is also good.

Eventually, you will want an assortment of glass or ceramic baking dishes; soufflé molds; a larger metal baking dish (for turkey, browning large quantities of meat, and more). Buy them as you need them.

The Basics of Pastry Pans

This includes pie plates, bread pans, baking sheets, cake pans, tube pans, muffin tins, and the like. Because they're all for special uses, none of these is likely to be essential in your daily cooking, but all are critical when you need them. The sole exception is probably the **baking sheet**—it's great for broiling, especially if it has a small lip. Go with aluminum; for most purposes, uncoated will be okay here, but non-stick coating never hurts.

Let's take the others individually:

- **Pie plates:** Start with one, nine inches across. Oven-proof glass is very nice here. Add an eight-inch and a ten-inch when you have time. A ten-inch springform pan (with a removable rim) is great for cheesecake, but not much use otherwise. Wait.

- **Loaf pans:** You need two, nine by five inches or thereabouts. Non-stick aluminum is best; don't buy glass, which is less than ideal for bread.
- **Tube pans:** For angel cake, sponge cake, and the like. Buy as needed.
- **Muffin tins:** Cheap aluminum ones, with non-stick coating, are fine. Antiques of cast iron are much more attractive, but chances are your muffins will stick.
- **Cake pans:** For layer cakes, nine inches across. You need two or three.
- **Tart pan:** May be metal (removable rims are good) or ceramic; the latter is preferable because it will not interact with acidic tart ingredients, as will most made of metal.

The Basics of Bowls

I can't get enough of them, but you probably need only **small, medium,** and **large bowls** to start. Stainless steel bowls are cheap and extremely useful. Some people (like me) use them as serving bowls as well. If you want attractive serving bowls, buy them, but don't use them for mixing, because you will inevitably chip them. Eventually you'll need many, from those that are very small (for holding small bits of spices, herbs, etc., that you're about to cook with) to one that is very large (to fill with ice water, which you'll use to "shock" vegetables after cooking, or to cool down a smaller bowlful of custard). Add to your bowl collection whenever you see one that appeals to you.

The Basics of Cutting Boards

You do need a **cutting board;** whether it's of plastic or wood is your choice. Plastic can go in the dishwasher, wood is more attractive. You need more than one anyway, so try one of each until you determine your preference. Extremely heavy wood cutting boards are the best, but they also are costly.

To keep your cutting board from sliding around on the counter (annoying, isn't it?), place a damp towel under it.

The Basics of Spoons, Spatulas, and More

Wooden spoons have a pleasant feel and do not absorb much heat; they're best for stove-top use. **Large stainless steel spoons** are best for serving and transferring wet food from one container to another. A **slotted spoon** is essential, as is a **ladle.** Rubber spatulas are handy—especially the spoon-shaped ones. You need **two metal spatulas:** one narrow (for loosening all around the rim of cakes) and one wide (for turning pancakes). A large metal tongs (get the spring-loaded, rather than tension-driven, variety) is very useful. Asian-style skimmers are fantastic—even better than slotted spoons in some instances—for removing foods from simmering liquids or frying oils.

Again, these are a matter of taste. You'll accumulate many different utensils over the years; some will become your favorites, others will end up at a yard sale. Keep them all in an attractive jar, or in a used coffee can, right on your counter, next to the stove. You will want most of them handy.

The Basics of Measuring Devices

A set of **measuring spoons** is essential; two are even better, because one is always dirty at just the wrong moment. Same with measuring cups; two sets are better than one. Start with a **two-cup glass or plastic cup for liquids,** and a **set of one-quarter—to one-cup dry measures** (they're not the same thing). When you're ready, buy a four-cup glass measure, and another set of dry measures.

A scale is not essential, but as you progress in your cooking you will find it useful. (When cookbooks call for "one pound potatoes," you'll actually know what that means.) Electronic scales are overpriced; get a spring-loaded scale with an easily adjusted zero so you can readily compensate for the "tare" (the weight of the container holding your ingredient).

The Basics of Straining Devices

Anything with holes in it to drain liquid or force through pureed food is a strainer. You need more of these than you think, although it's fine to buy them as you need them. A **colander** is the first order of business, and you need it desperately, because you want to have pasta for dinner.

Soon, though, if not immediately, you'll also want a fine-meshed strainer as well, and probably two—one large, one small. A food mill is essential if you want to make applesauce or pureed tomato sauce, but you will be able to live without it if neither of those matter to you.

The Basics of Miscellaneous Tools

Some tools are too obvious to mention. But beyond a can opener:

- **Cheese grater:** This can be a small, handheld device for grating Parmesan directly onto pasta, as long as you have a food processor for heavy-duty grating. Otherwise buy a sturdy box grater.
- **Instant-read thermometer:** The most accurate way to determine whether food is done, especially for inexperienced cooks. You may never have cooked a leg of lamb in your life, but when that thermometer says 130°F, you know the inside is rare. This is a near-must. If you fry, you may want a frying thermometer, which will make your life a little easier. And if your baking times seem off, buy an oven thermometer, and use it.
- **Metal racks:** For cooling baked goods and roasting. Buy ones that will serve both purposes, by making sure they'll fit in your roasting pan.
- **Timer:** May be manual or electronic; some electronic types allow you to time several things at once, a definite plus if you can figure out how the things work.
- **Vegetable peeler:** The new U-shaped ones are best. Absolutely essential.
- **Whisks:** You need at least one stiff one, for keeping sauces smooth. But you may not need more than that if you plan to beat cream, egg whites, and so on electrically. Start with a medium-sized, stiff whisk, and build from there.
- **Baking stone:** If you're going to make pizzas or "boules" (page 227), you'll want one of these.
- **Brushes:** Great for spreading oil, melted butter, marinades, etc. Start with a one-inch brush, and buy it at the paint store, where it'll be much cheaper.
- **Citrus reamer:** You can cut a lemon in half, pick out the seeds with a knife, and squeeze. Or you an use one of these, and save twenty seconds each time.
- **Eggbeater:** You can use a whisk in most cases, but if you're not going to buy an electric mixer,

you will want this for those times when you must beat eggs until thick.
- **Funnel:** When you want it, you'll need it.
- **Mandoline:** There was a time when buying this brilliant slicing device would set you back two hundred dollars, and you can still spend that much on a heavy-duty French model. But the thirty-dollar Japanese mandolines are almost as good, and will last for years. Even if you're good with a knife, there's no way you can cut slices as quickly and uniformly as you can with a mandoline; there's a reason every good restaurant kitchen has a few lying around. I strongly recommend this tool, and just as strongly recommend that you be very, very careful when using it. Hold off on that second glass of wine until you're done slicing.
- **Melon baller:** Good for coring pears and apples, too. Buy one that has some heft to it, but don't rush out this minute.
- **Pizza peel:** If you have a baking stone, you'll want one. Good for large breads as well as pizza.
- **Ricer:** The best tool for making mashed potatoes, and therefore Gnocchi (page 165). Only if you care about these two dishes.
- **Rolling pin:** Try making a pie crust without one. Buy a straight rolling pin without ball bearings; it's lighter, more easily maneuvered, and unbreakable.
- **Salad spinner:** Nice item, and not only for drying salad greens. It's excellent for dunking anything that you want to rinse and drain repeatedly. Not essential but close.
- **Skewers:** Good not only for grilling but for testing for doneness. Not essential at first.
- **Steamer insert:** You can steam most foods on a plate or in a bowl, but collapsible aluminum steamers are useful.
- **Zester:** The easiest way to remove zest from lemons and other citrus, but not the only way;

you can remove zest with a vegetable peeler and mince it by hand.

There are other manual devices—like a pasta machine (page 155)—that you may never need. Again, it depends on what you wind up cooking (no one, or almost no one, cooks *everything*). My personal belief is that a time-saver you use once a year is probably not worth having. Because there are few kitchen tasks that cannot be accomplished with what you already have on hand, it doesn't really pay to make a fetish of gadgets.

The Basics of Appliances and Electric Gadgets

Now we're on to the big-ticket items. I'm going to assume that, like me, you're already stuck with an unsatisfactory stove and refrigerator and don't have thirty thousand dollars to remodel your kitchen. (If you have a choice, go with a gas range and an electric oven; if you don't have a choice, don't worry about it.) I'm also going to assume that you already know whether you want a waffle iron, and that you already have a toaster.

Still, your choices are staggering; there are so many appliances out there now that if you were to buy them all you'd have nowhere to stand. There are several that everyone should have, and several that no one should have, but most are judgment calls determined by what you cook. Here's a list of appliances in my order of priority. Note that I've omitted those—such as countertop grills and electric deep fryers—that I think are not even worth considering:

• **Food processor:** Hands down the most important electric tool in the kitchen. It can grate massive amounts of almost anything in seconds; it

can make bread dough, pie dough, even some cookie batters, in a minute; it can grind meat, puree vegetables, slice potatoes. If you have one, use it (I rely on it heavily, although not exclusively, in my recipes). If you don't, make the investment as soon as you can; there are very good ones available for less than two hundred dollars, and if you cook a lot you will use it daily. The small ones are valuable in their own right (not the "mini-choppers," but the three- to four-cup full-fledged food processors), but start with a large one, a model that can handle at least six cups of batter or dough.

Other than the instructions that come with the machine, there's only one trick in learning to use a food processor: Don't overprocess. If you want a puree, turn the machine on and walk away. But if you want to mince, use the "pulse" button, turning the machine on and off as many times as is necessary to get the texture you need. These are very powerful machines, capable of pureeing almost anything within seconds.

• **Electric mixer:** If you bake a lot, you will want both a powerful standing mixer and a small, handheld mixer. If you bake occasionally, you will want either. If you never bake, you still could use a hand mixer or an eggbeater for the occasional egg white or whipped cream.

• **Blender:** Perhaps not for everyone, but if you make a lot of soups and want to make some of them creamy, this is the tool. Also great for any blended drink (most food processors leak if loaded up with liquid) and for coconut milk. The new handheld immersion blenders are terrific for pureeing soups right in the pot.

• **Electric knife sharpener:** See The Basics of Knives. Few people, including chefs, can put a good edge on a knife with a whetstone. The new electric knife sharpeners turn a difficult craft into a no-brainer. Probably not the first investment you should make, but a good present for your wish list.

- **Ice cream maker:** Far from essential, but what a joy. If you like ice cream or sorbet, this is a worthwhile device, even if you use it only ten times a year. There are inexpensive manual machines, which contain an insert that you prefreeze, and these work fairly well. But the electric models with built-in refrigeration are divine; unfortunately, they cost several hundred dollars.

- **Electric juice extractor:** A nice item that you will only "need" if you're into drinking homemade juices. But an apple sorbet made from freshly juiced apples is a revelation, so this is worth thinking about. Good extractors are heavy and have large feed tubes so you don't have to chop fruits and veggies into tiny pieces first.

- **Pressure cooker:** For people in a hurry. Pressure cookers don't make anything better than regular cookware, they just make it faster. If you are short on time and big on stews, soups, stocks, or beans, it's a worthwhile investment. If you can take time to cook, or don't like slow-simmered foods, don't bother.

Pressure cookers have been improved enormously in recent years. They're safer than ever, and easy to use. If you want one, buy it new.

- **Coffee/spice grinder:** If you drink coffee, you probably have one of these. But even if you don't, consider it a wise ten-dollar investment. Freshly ground spices are a real joy, and this takes the work out of them.

- **Microwave:** Now that the fuss has died down, it turns out that this is a useful but hardly indispensable tool. I hardly ever cook in the microwave. But I use it to heat and warm, and for that it is of some value. Still, I will not replace my current machine when it goes; I'd rather have the counter space.

- **Bread machine:** As you'll see when you get to "Bread" (pages 217–253), I think that the combination of food processor and oven is a better way to bring fresh-baked bread to your house. But if you really have zero time, a bread machine is a good option.

Techniques

The most difficult of the factors involved in cooking, correct technique comes with good instruction (hopefully provided in the pages of this book) combined with practice. Sometimes good technique is everything. A skillet, for example, must be hot before butter is added in order for the butter to sizzle without burning, so that it can sear and crisp the food that is in turn added to it. This cannot be learned in an instant; you must get used to preheating the pan before adding the butter, you must judge the correct level of heat on your particular stove, you must learn to be ready at the right moment. If you haven't done this before, there's no reason to expect to be good at it right away, any more than you'd expect to serve aces the first time you played tennis.

On the other hand, your cooking can be plenty good while you are learning proper technique, and there are some techniques you can ignore altogether.

Most people who learned to cook from their parents, or from cookbooks, never learned the "correct" way to slice or dice an onion. Yet although this may mean that it takes them ten seconds longer to do it than it would otherwise, and that their pieces are not exactly uniform, it does not affect the flavor (or in most cases even the appearance) of their finished dishes.

We have designed this book to take advantage of the fact that people can learn many preparation techniques better through visual means than written ones. In the relevant sections, you'll find illustrations for using knives and other kitchen tools and for relatively complex procedures.

Cooking techniques—those that actually use heat to prepare food, such as grilling and sautéing—are a little different, because there is not much visual about them. Yet there are only a few basic, master techniques in cooking, and most have been the cornerstones of cuisine for centuries.

The Basics of Heat

Most beginning cooks fail to get sauté pans and ovens hot enough (this is not the case with grilling, where the biggest mistake is to make the grill too hot). Whether you're pan-grilling or sautéing, you should get used to preheating your skillet for a minute or two—longer if you have an electric range (see below)—before you start to cook. If you turn the heat on under your skillet, then start cooking, you're beginning with a cold pan and your food will never brown. And browning is important in developing flavor.

Likewise with an oven. Yes, preheating ovens is a common practice, and a good one. But 350°F is not hot enough to brown most meats in an oven; you need high heat, 450°F and higher, if you want to put a nice crust on the food you're cooking, whether it's bread or chicken. My recipes reflect that belief, but when you cook on your own, or with another cookbook, keep it in mind.

A note about electric ranges　If you have an electric range, you've probably been told that it's impossible to cook well with it. This is nonsense: Heat is heat. The disadvantage of an electric range is that its elements take time to respond—they're slow to heat up, and equally slow to cool down. All this means is that you have to plan ahead.

If you know you're going to want to start cooking over high heat, turn a burner to high a few minutes *before* you're ready to cook. If you know that you're going to want to transfer that skillet to low heat after an initial searing, have another burner ready at low, or medium-low heat, and simply move the skillet. It's as if you're cooking on a stove top that has hot and cold spots, rather than on an infinitely flexible burner.

Of course if the stove top is crowded and you don't have a spare burner, you'll have to anticipate: When your food is nearly done browning, for example, turn down the heat; the burner and skillet will retain enough heat to finish the process, and will have cooled off in time for you to proceed.

The Basics of Grilling and Broiling

Grilling is the oldest cooking method, and one that justifiably retains its popularity. It (and broiling) are the only methods that use direct heat—nothing but a thin layer of air separates the heat source from the food. This virtually guarantees a crisp crust quickly. (There is indirect "grilling" as well; see below.)

Although it can be easy, grilling is somewhat overrated. It isn't magic and, unless you use a wood fire or spice up your fire with wood chips, it does not "add" flavor. In fact, if you use a gas grill, grilling is identical to broiling—the only difference is that one puts the heat source on the bottom, the other on top. So there's no need to fire up that grill if it's cold outside—just turn on the broiler. (This assumes you have a reasonably efficient broiler; if you do not, your grill is probably more powerful and will generate more heat, so you will notice a difference in browning and cooking times.)

A couple of notes about the broiler:

- Always preheat it, but only for a few minutes. If your electric broiler requires the oven door to remain open in order to stay on, preheat the *oven* to 500°F, then preheat the broiler, and broil with the door open.
- If you are broiling food whose fat will render as it cooks—such as most chicken and meat—use a rack in a pan, so the fat can drip away from

the food. This is not necessary if you're broiling fish, vegetables, boneless chicken breasts, or anything that will remain in the broiler for just a few minutes.

- Generally, you will broil two to six inches away from the heat source, the closer distance for thin, quickly cooked foods, the greater distance for thick, slowly cooked foods. But this is detailed in each recipe, and you'll easily get the hang of it.

The main idea behind both of these techniques is to get a nice, slightly charred crust on the food's exterior while cooking the interior to the desired degree of doneness. Generally, the best foods to grill or broil are less than an inch thick; thicker foods tend to burn on the outside before they are fully cooked inside. Thin cuts of meat, poultry, fish, or vegetables are ideal for this, because the intense heat just about cooks the food through as it browns the outside.

But you can also grill or broil thicker cuts, with a couple of minor adjustments. In the broiler, just move the food farther from the heat source so it browns a little more slowly, turning occasionally and giving it time to cook through.

On the grill, start thicker cuts close to the flame and move them a few inches away after the initial browning. If you use hardwood charcoal or briquettes, you want to cook over glowing coals covered with ash. Right near those coals, the heat is in excess of 600°F, far too hot to cook anything. A couple of inches above, which is probably where your rack sits normally, the temperature is about 500°F, a great place to sear. (If you can hold your hand just above the rack for about two seconds, the temperature is just about right.) If you can raise the rack to four inches, you have effectively lowered the heat below 400°F, a good place to cook bone-in chicken. (Here, you will be able to hold your hand for as long as four seconds.) If you can't raise the rack, move the food to a cooler part of the grill.

Or, on many grills, you can use indirect heat to finish cooking larger pieces of meat. (This is no longer grilling, technically; rather it is a form of roasting—but never mind.) After an initial searing, bank the coals to one side (on a gas grill, lower the heat, or turn one of the burners off) and move the food to the cool side of the grill; then cover the grill. Now you have the food bathing in a pool of hot air, but removed from the searing direct heat of the flame. This technique also allows you to slow down the cooking, so you can place some soaked wood chips on the fire and add a little of their flavor to your food.

The chief drawback of broiling and grilling is that their intense heat can dry out many foods, especially those without a lot of internal fat. This is why broiled and grilled foods are often served with moist dipping sauces or dressings.

A word about grilling versus barbecue   Grilling, as defined above, is cooking food over direct heat. Barbecue means one of two things: long, slow, usually indirect cooking with smoke, or anything treated with a barbecue sauce.

The Basics of Roasting

Like grilling and broiling, roasting uses dry heat; the difference is that it does so in a closed environment, and the heat is indirect. Most roasting should be done at high heat—450°F or higher—and, at its best, crisps up the exterior of foods, whether vegetables, fish, or meat, without much danger of burning, while cooking the interior relatively slowly and avoiding overcooking. Flavors added during roasting may be in the form of solids or liquids, and the liquids left in the roasting pan after cooking may be used for a sauce.

Baking, also performed in the oven, is done at lower heat, and (in my book, at least) usually refers to the cooking of breads and pastries. Of course the oven can also be used for warming, or for heating foods in closed containers—in which case it is acting very much like your stove top.

Electric ovens tend to be more accurate than gas ovens, but both are notoriously unreliable. A difference of 25°F doesn't make much difference when you're roasting a large piece of meat (although it will affect your timing, of course), but it can be a killer when you're making a delicate dessert, such as a custard. Buy an oven thermometer, and use it.

The Basics of Sautéing

Sauté is French for "jump," and simply refers to food that is cooked, in a hot pan, with some amount of fat (some say that the pan "surprises" the food). Whether that fat is a half cup of butter or one tablespoon of olive oil, naturally, has an effect on the finished product. But regardless of the amount or type of fat you use, sautéing, like roasting, grilling, and broiling, can put a crust on food. And it has a couple of advantages: Properly done, sautéing does not dry food out, and it gives you a base on which you can easily build a sauce (see The Basics of Reduction Sauces, page 790).

The simplest, most straightforward sauté begins by dredging thin slices of meat or fish in flour, bread crumbs, or other seasonings; the food is then cooked over high heat, in hot fat, for ten minutes or less. (To sauté anything over an inch or so in thickness requires an initial browning followed by covering the pan; this is more like braising.) "Deglazing" the pan afterward—using a liquid to release the flavorful bits that remain after cooking—is a quick and easy way to make a sauce, known as a reduction. You can deglaze with lemon juice, vinegar, wine, stock, juice, cream, or a combination.

Traditionally, the fat used in sautéing served two purposes: to crisp the coating, and to prevent the food from sticking to the pan. Thanks to non-stick pans,

however, you can use just need enough fat to provide some sizzle if this is a concern.

Pan-grilling: Non-stick pans have led to an increase in what is best called "pan-grilling"—cooking over high heat, in a skillet, with no added fat. (With some very sturdy foods with even surfaces, such as steaks, pan-grilling can be done in a heavy cast-iron skillet as well.) You should only try pan-grilling with thin, quickly cooked foods (not, for example, with bone-in chicken), and you should only try it if you have a good exhaust fan.

Having said that, however, there is a fine combination of pan-grilling and roasting that will work for somewhat thicker foods, and contain the smoke: Before you start to cook, preheat the oven to 500°F. When it's hot, heat your skillet until it is very hot, then add the food. Sear it on one side, just for a minute; undoubtedly, it will become so smoky that you will wish you never began. Quickly transfer the pan to the oven, and finish the cooking in there, turning the food only once. You will brown both sides and have all the time you need to cook the interior. (Just be careful handling the pan—its handle will become as hot as its cooking surface.)

The Basics of Stir-Frying

Stir-frying is similar to sautéing in that food is cooked over high heat in a small amount of fat. There are, however, several differences. Food to be stir-fried is cut up before cooking, which further minimizes cooking time; liquid is added during the cooking; and stir-fries are most often associated with Asian flavorings, while sautés are European (although there is no binding reason for this, the tradition continues). Traditionally, stir-fries were prepared in woks, but you need not follow this tradition. In fact, the design of a wok is not well suited to most home ranges; a large, deep-sided skillet, with sloping sides is best. These are sometimes sold as woks with handles, or, as discussed in the skillet section (page 2), in one of the hybridized "sauté pans" with deep, rounded sides, sort of a combination sauté pan/saucepan.

To stir-fry successfully, you must have all your ingredients ready and at hand; once you begin cooking, there will be virtually no time to dig things out of the cabinet or refrigerator and begin measuring them. In addition, you must use very high heat; even more than sautéing, most stir-frying requires you set your burner on "high" and leave it there. (If, however, at any point during the cooking you feel that things have gotten out of control, turn off the heat and think for a minute. You will not ruin anything by doing so.)

Stir-fried food is fairly dry—in order to brown the little bits of meat, fish, chicken, and/or vegetables that you're cooking, you must keep moisture out of the skillet or wok. This usually means you will want to finish a stir-fry with some liquid, usually wine, stock, or water. In some traditions, that liquid is in turn thickened. This is a matter of taste; you can serve a stir-fry with its thin, slightly reduced sauce, or you can thicken it. The easiest way to do this is to stir in a mixture of about one tablespoon cornstarch and two tablespoons cold water; this does the trick in an instant. One final word about stir-frying: It helps to lay in a good supply of basic Chinese seasonings: soy sauce, oyster sauce, dark sesame oil, gingerroot, and so on.

The Basics of Deep-Frying

The most challenging cooking method for home cooks, not because it is difficult—it's actually quite straightforward, given a few simple rules—but because it is invariably messy and usually smelly. As the bubbling oil cooks the food, small bits of it escape into the surrounding air. If the food you're cooking is benign, this isn't so bad; but almost all savory foods give off relatively strong odors that become unpleasant once they've attached themselves to your furniture. Only the most powerful of exhaust fans can whisk this oily smoke away before it travels through your house. If you don't mind any of this, follow any of the deep-frying recipes you'll find throughout the book; I love to deep-fry, but always remain aware of its difficulties.

The rules of deep-frying are simple: The oil (see The Basics of Oils, page 87) must reach a good temperature to brown the exterior of the food quickly, while cooking it. That temperature is almost always between 350° and 375°F—365°F is a good all-purpose compromise—and is most easily measured by using a frying thermometer. (If you have an electric deep fryer, of course, it will cycle off when it reaches the preset temperature.) You can use small amounts of oil in narrow pots to deep-fry—for example, it only takes a couple of cups of oil to gain a height of two or three inches in a small saucepan. But the disadvantage of this is that you can only cook small bits of food, and not very many of them at once.

That's because it's essential to avoid crowding when deep-frying (it's important to avoid crowding whenever you want to brown food). The food must be surrounded by bubbling oil, and you must keep the temperature from falling too much. If you add a relatively large amount of food to a relatively small amount of oil, the temperature will plummet and the food will wind up greasy and soggy—and this holds true whether you are deep frying in a saucepan or in an electric deep fryer. So the basic recommendations: Use plenty of oil (although, to prevent the oil from bubbling over, never fill the pot more than halfway); dry the food well with paper towels before adding it to the pot, in order to reduce spattering; and add the food in small increments to keep the temperature from falling too much.

The Basics of Cooking in Liquid: Braising, Stewing, Poaching, Steaming, and Parboiling

Cooking in liquid is useful and easy, and it can perform just about any cooking task you demand of it except browning. No other technique is as efficient at tenderizing as moist cooking. There are several different ways to use liquid in cooking:

Braising Braising begins like sautéing—you brown the food in a bit of fat. But it continues by adding liquid to the pan, covering it, and finishing the cooking over moist, low heat (you don't boil the food, you simmer it). It's the ideal way to cook larger cuts of meat, or big chunks, especially those that need tenderizing, such as certain lean cuts of beef or veal, or those that might dry out if cooked otherwise, such as chicken parts or whole fish.

Many liquids can be used to braise foods, and it is that choice, along with the choice of herbs and spices, that provides much of the seasoning. The covered and relatively long, slow cooking ensures that not only will intrinsic flavors be preserved but that those of all ingredients will mingle and intensify. This is the magic of stews, daubes, goulashes, ragouts, and so on. Note that in many of my braising recipes I make the browning step optional; yes, it adds flavor, and without question improves the dish. But it is also a step that adds time and hassle, and it is not one that makes the difference between success and failure.

You can also "reverse-braise"—cook the food in liquid until tender, then run it under the broiler to crisp it up a bit.

Stewing Braising, but usually with no initial browning (although this is not an iron-clad rule) and with more liquid.

Poaching/Simmering/Boiling Cooking food through in water (or lightly flavored water or even stock) to cover. Usually the temperature is moderated so that the water just bubbles during cooking; you want to start it at the boiling point, or a little below, but moderate it. It's very rare that you want to actually cook food at a rapid boil (pasta being one notable exception). Temperatures can be controlled not only by raising and lowering the heat of the burner but by partially covering the pot.

Steaming Steaming, of course, is cooking over—not in—liquid; the liquid is usually water, and is usually not used in the finished dish, but there are exceptions. You can use a bamboo steamer, or a collapsible steamer insert, or simply elevate the food above the simmering water by building a little platform for it, using chopsticks or a couple of upside-down cups. In any case, keep the water simmering, not rapidly boiling, and make sure it does not boil away—add boiling water to the pot if necessary. Steaming, is usually (but not exclusively) used for quickly cooked foods.

Parboiling/Blanching To parboil, or blanch, you partially cook food, usually vegetables, in boiling water to cover. This is an excellent technique for keeping vegetables bright and partially tenderizing them, detailed in "Vegetables" (pages 529–617).

Appetizers

Of the one-thousand-plus savory recipes in this book, more than half can be served as appetizers: Pasta, of course, is always served as a first course in Italy; salads are wonderful starters, and one of the truly American traditions when served that way; and soups are eaten before other foods more often than not.

In addition, many of the dishes found in other chapters can be passed as finger foods. This is especially true for all grilled meats or vegetables—especially those that have been skewered, but for others as well; for many other meat, chicken, and fish dishes; for pizza and like foods; and for many eggs dishes, especially quiches and frittate. Furthermore, there are many vegetable, bean, and even meat dishes that can serve as dips.

What remains to be covered in this chapter are those dishes specifically intended to be served as finger food, those foods that are not filling enough or "serious" enough to be served as a main course, or that are in fact too rich to eat a plateful, or that are traditional starters or snacks. These range from simply spiced nuts to the rather complex filled shells originally from other countries, such as egg rolls, empanadas, and samosas.

Most of these are thought of as dishes for entertaining, and rightfully so. With the exception of buffet-style dinners, few meals are ready the moment guests walk in the door. Even with a buffet, a certain amount of time passes between the arrival of the first and usually somewhat early guest to the arrival of the latecomers. During that time, it's essential to have a few things to nibble on while you open a bottle of wine or mix a few cocktails. At the minimum, you might make a bowl of nuts and marinated olives, both of which can be done well in advance. At the maximum, you can make the greeting food as impressive as the meal. The options for these kinds of dishes are literally endless.

A note about serving sizes   All serving sizes, for any recipe, depend on the appetite of the eaters and the amount and type of other foods being served. That goes double for these recipes: A hungry television watcher can eat two cups of nuts in thirty minutes with no problem; put those same nuts out at a party with five other finger foods and they'll be enough for ten people to nibble on. So use the serving sizes here as guidelines rather than literal truth.

Simple Finger Foods

These can serve as casual snacks for family and friends, or can be set out as part of an assortment of finger foods for a larger party. All can be made well in advance.

Roasted Buttered Nuts

Makes 4 to 6 servings

Time: 15 minutes

Simple as these are, they are a revelation, so far from canned mixed nuts that you may have trouble believing it. For one thing, canned mixed nuts are almost always heavy on peanuts and Brazil nuts, both of which are inexpensive. But the first are common, and the second become rancid very quickly after being shelled. For your own mix, I suggest relying heavily on pecans, almonds, and cashews, with a sprinkling of anything else you can lay your hands on, from hazelnuts (filberts) to pistachios to sunflower seeds.

2 cups (about 1 pound) unsalted mixed shelled nuts

1 tablespoon peanut oil or melted butter

Salt and freshly ground black pepper to taste

① Preheat the oven to 450°F.

② Toss the nuts in a bowl with the oil or butter, salt, and pepper. Place on a baking sheet and roast, shaking occasionally, until lightly browned, about 10 minutes. Cool before serving; they will crisp as they cool.

Sautéed Buttered Nuts: With more fat, even better-tasting. Place 4 tablespoons (¹/₂ stick) butter or peanut oil in a large skillet and turn the heat to medium-low. When the butter melts or the oil is hot, add the nuts and cook, stirring, until lightly browned, about 10 minutes. Be patient; high heat will burn the nuts. As they cook, season with salt and pepper. Cool before serving.

Spiced Buttered Nuts: Add 1 teaspoon to 1 tablespoon of any spice mixture, such as chili powder or All-Purpose Curry Powder (page 778), to the mix. When roasting, toss the spice with the nuts at the beginning. When sautéing, add it to the butter or oil as it heats.

Real Buttered Popcorn

Makes 4 to 6 servings

Time: About 10 minutes

Microwave popcorn is not bad, but it doesn't compare to the real thing, which doesn't take much longer. And with real popcorn, if you want butter flavor, you can add butter, rather than artificially butter-flavored oil. To make cheese popcorn, sprinkle the hot popcorn with finely grated Cheddar, Parmesan, or other hard cheese and toss. Or toss with any seasoning you like.

2 tablespoons canola or other neutral oil

¹/₂ cup popping corn

4 tablespoons (¹/₂ stick) butter (optional)

Salt to taste

1 Place the oil in the bottom of a large, deep saucepan (6 quarts or so) that can later be covered and turn the heat to medium. Add 3 kernels of corn and cover.

2 When the 3 kernels pop, remove the cover and add the remaining corn. Cover and shake the pot, holding the lid on as you do so. Cook, shaking the pot occasionally, until the popping sound stops, about 5 minutes. Meanwhile, melt the butter if you choose to use it.

3 Turn the popcorn into a large bowl, drizzle with the butter, and sprinkle with salt. Serve immediately if possible; popcorn is best when hot.

Fiery Pumpkin Seeds
Makes 2 cups

Time: About 45 minutes

Crisp-baked pumpkin seeds are fine with salt, but adding some fire turns them into a great pre-dinner tidbit, or a fine snack with beer. You can also make this with any spice mix, such as All-Purpose Curry Powder (page 778), Garam Masala (page 778), or chili powder.

2 cups (approximately) fresh pumpkin seeds
2 tablespoons light vegetable or olive oil
About 1 teaspoon salt
About 1 teaspoon cayenne, or more if you like
1/2 teaspoon cumin, optional

1 Separate the seeds from the pumpkin strings by rinsing them in a bowlful of water. Dry the seeds between paper towels.

2 Mix the oil with salt, cayenne, and cumin, and toss the seeds with this mixture until they are coated. (Then wash your hands well.)

3 Bake the seeds on a baking sheet in a 350°F oven for 30 to 45 minutes, tossing occasionally, until they are tan and crisp, or spread the seeds between 2 layers of paper towels and microwave on high for 10 to 15 minutes, stirring every 5 minutes, until seeds are tan and crisp. They will crisp up further as they cool.

Simplest Cheese Straws
Makes 5 to 10 servings

Time: 20 minutes

Easy, light, and quite irresistible. Consider adding fresh or dried herbs to the mix, and use any cheese you like, as long as it is hard enough to grate.

1 pound Cheddar or other hard, flavorful cheese
2 cups (about 9 ounces) all-purpose flour
Pinch cayenne
8 tablespoons (1 stick) chilled butter, plus a little more for greasing the baking sheet
Few drops ice water, if necessary
Coarse salt (optional)

1 Preheat the oven to 450°F.

2 Grate the cheese (you can use the food processor for this), then remove the cheese from the bowl. Add the flour and cayenne to the bowl and pulse. Cut the 8 tablespoons butter into pieces, then toss it in. Process until butter and flour are combined.

3 Remove the dough from the bowl and stir in the cheese. Knead by hand until it comes together, adding a few drops of ice water (no more than 1 tablespoon) if necessary. (You may prepare the recipe in advance up to this point; wrap well in plastic and refrigerate for up to 2 days before proceeding.)

4 Roll out into a rectangle about 1/4 inch thick, then cut into strips as long as you like and about 1/2 inch wide. Place on a lightly greased baking sheet and sprinkle with the optional salt. Bake until golden brown, 5 to 8 minutes. Serve hot, warm, or at room temperature.

My requirements for these: that they are small, or can be made into small pieces; that they can be picked up reasonably neatly with fingers or served on a toothpick; and that they are not difficult to produce in quantity.

1. Any bean puree can serve as a dip, pages 508–509
2. Roasted Chickpeas, page 518
3. Indian-Style Split Pea Fritters, page 522
4. Indian Potato-Stuffed Flat Breads (Aloo Paratha), page 238
5. Any frittata, cut into small pieces, pages 740–741
6. Salt Cod Cakes, page 320
7. Spicy Grilled or Broiled Shrimp, page 325
8. Crab Cakes, page 331
9. Grilled Scallops with Basil Stuffing, page 350
10. Hush Puppies, page 190
11. Any pizza, focaccia, calzone, or bruschetta, pages 255–266
12. West Indian Crispy Pork Bits, or its variations, pages 461–462
13. Pork Satay, page 462
14. Grilled or Broiled Lamb Ribs (with plenty of napkins), page 489
15. Beet Roesti with Rosemary, page 542
16. Boiled, Grilled, or Roasted Chestnuts, page 561
17. Garlic Bruschetta, page 575
18. Spicy Chicken Thigh Kebabs, or its variations, pages 397–398
19. Chicken Satay, page 399

Pastry Cheese Straws

Makes 5 to 10 servings

Time: 30 minutes

This is more complicated than the preceding recipe, but it makes a superior cheese straw, one that resembles puff pastry in its flakiness.

1 recipe Generous Pie Shell, page 686 (See Step 1)
1 1/2 cups freshly grated Parmesan cheese

1   Make the pastry, incorporating about 1/2 cup grated cheese into it. Roll it out until it is about 1/4 inch thick, then sprinkle it with another 1/2 cup cheese. Fold the dough in half and press the edges together. Sprinkle with half the remaining cheese, then repeat the rolling folding process; press the edges together again. Repeat, using the remaining cheese.

(You may prepare the recipe in advance up to this point; wrap well in plastic and refrigerate for up to 2 days before proceeding.)

2   Finally, roll out into a rectangle about 1/4 inch thick. Cut into strips as long as you like and about 1/2 inch wide. Place on a lightly buttered (or oiled) baking sheet and, if time allows, chill for 1 hour.

3   Preheat the oven to 450°F. Bake the straws until golden brown, 10 to 15 minutes. Serve warm (they cool off almost instantly), or at room temperature.

Marinated Olives

Makes 10 servings or more

Time: 5 minutes, plus marinating time

Olives are so much better when marinated than when eaten straight from the jar or barrel that most people assume there is some trick to them. But there is not, other than to start with good olives. I do not use red pepper flakes when I marinate olives, but many people like a little bit of heat here; the choice is yours.

Note that these keep, and improve in flavor, for several weeks in the refrigerator. Always bring to room temperature before serving.

1 pound green or black olives, or a mixture,
    preferably imported from Greece, Italy, or Spain
1 teaspoon wine vinegar, or to taste
1/4 cup extra-virgin olive oil
4 cloves garlic, crushed
Several sprigs fresh thyme, 1 teaspoon fresh thyme
    leaves, or 1/2 teaspoon dried thyme
2 bay leaves
1 teaspoon crushed red pepper flakes (optional)

1 Using the side of a broad knife, crush the olives lightly.

2 Mix together all other ingredients and pack into a jar or place in a serving bowl; taste and add more vinegar if necessary. You can serve these immediately, although they are better if they sit, covered and refrigerated, for a day or two. Bring to room temperature before serving.

Deviled (Stuffed) Eggs

Makes 4 servings

Time: 5 minutes with precooked eggs,
    20 with raw eggs

There are standard deviled eggs—the yolks mashed with mayonnaise and mustard—and there are dozens of possible variations. I give a couple of them here, but you can use almost any herb, spice, or other seasoning in the mix. Make lower-fat deviled eggs by replacing the mayonnaise with low-fat yogurt.

4 Hard-Boiled Eggs (page 733)
Salt to taste
2 tablespoons mayonnaise, preferably homemade
    (page 761)
1 teaspoon Dijon mustard, or to taste
1/4 teaspoon cayenne, or to taste
Paprika or minced fresh parsley leaves for garnish

1 Cool the eggs, peel them, cut them in half the long way, and carefully remove the yolks.

2 Mash the yolks with salt, mayonnaise, mustard, and cayenne. Taste and adjust seasoning. Spoon the filling back into the whites. (If you are making a lot of deviled eggs and want them to be especially attractive, use a pastry bag to pipe them back into the whites.)

3 Garnish and serve, or cover and chill, well wrapped, for up to a day before serving.

Anchovied Eggs: In Step 2, substitute 1 tablespoon olive oil for the mayonnaise; mash 2 or more minced anchovies with the yolks. Garnish with a piece of anchovy fillet and a couple of capers.

Herb-Stuffed Eggs: In Step 2, substitute 1 tablespoon olive oil for the mayonnaise. Add 1/4 teaspoon finely minced garlic, 2 tablespoons minced fresh parsley leaves, 1 tablespoon drained and chopped capers (optional), and 1 teaspoon minced fresh tarragon leaves or 1 tablespoon minced fresh basil leaves. Garnish with parsley sprigs or small basil leaves.

Eggs Stuffed with Spinach: This makes enough stuffing for at least 8 eggs; it is very, very good, and quite attractive as well. Steam or parboil 6 to 8 ounces of trimmed spinach; drain, squeeze dry, and chop finely. Mash it, as in Step 2, with the egg yolks, 1/2 cup freshly grated Parmesan cheese, 2 tablespoons butter, a tiny grating of nutmeg, salt, and pepper. Taste and adjust seasoning before stuffing the whites.

Spiced Melon Balls

Makes 10 to 15 servings

Time: 20 minutes

Melon balls are melon balls, until you do something to them. This converts them to an exotic Asian-style dish, easily eaten with toothpicks.

> 1 ripe cantaloupe or other orange-fleshed melon
> 1 ripe honeydew or other green-fleshed melon
> 1/2 teaspoon salt
> 1 teaspoon ground coriander
> 1/4 teaspoon cayenne, or to taste
> 1 tablespoon very finely minced cilantro leaves
> 2 tablespoons freshly squeezed lime juice
> Sugar to taste (optional)

1 Use a melon baller to remove all the flesh from the melons. Combine the balls in a bowl with the salt, coriander, cayenne, cilantro, and lime juice.

2 Taste and adjust seasoning; you may add more of anything. If the melon is not sufficiently sweet, add a bit of sugar. Cover and refrigerate until ready to serve, up to 2 hours.

The Basics of Dips and Spreads

Many of the sauces and salsas in "Sauces, Salsas, and Spice Mixtures," from mayonnaise to compound butters to salsas, can be used as dips or spreads. But here are a few recipes that will allow you to prepare dozens of others. Generally, dips are served in bowls, with cut-up vegetables, crackers, or toasted bread. Spreads, naturally, are spread on crackers or bread—when topped with a little garnish, they make canapés—or in the natural folds of celery or endive. But it's worth noting that almost any "spread" can be made into a "dip" by thinning it slightly with sour cream, yogurt, cream, milk, or mayonnaise. Conversely, nearly any "dip" can be converted to a "spread" by stiffening it a little; just increase the proportion of cream cheese, or replace some of the sour cream with butter or cream cheese. Refrigeration also stiffens most of these combinations.

Minced Vegetable Dip

Makes at least 10 servings

Time: 10 minutes

The most basic of dips, and one you can almost always make with ingredients you have on hand. Feel free to substitute other vegetables if you don't have this exact combination.

> 1 cucumber
> 1 red bell pepper
> 1 scallion
> 1 tablespoon freshly minced dill leaves or 1 teaspoon dried dill
> 1 cup sour cream or plain yogurt
> Salt and freshly ground black pepper to taste
> Freshly squeezed lemon juice to taste (optional)

1 Peel the cucumber, then cut it in half the long way and scoop out the seeds. Stem and seed the pepper (you can peel this, too, if you like). Trim the scallion.

2 Mince all the vegetables fine, or put them in the container of a food processor and pulse a few times; do not overprocess. You want to mince the vegetables, not puree them.

3 Mix the vegetables with the dill, sour cream, salt, and pepper; taste and adjust seasoning, adding a little lemon juice if necessary. Cover and refrigerate until ready to use. (You may prepare this recipe in

advance; refrigerate, well wrapped or in a covered container, for up to a day before serving.) Serve with vegetables or crackers.

Horseradish Dip: Omit the dill; omit or include the vegetables as you like. Add 1 tablespoon or more prepared horseradish. Add Dijon mustard to taste to give this dip even more kick.

Real Onion Dip: Omit the vegetables and dill. Add ¹/₂ cup very finely minced or pureed onion and ¹/₄ cup minced fresh parsley leaves.

Smoked Salmon or Trout Dip: Omit the dill; omit or include the vegetables as you like. Add ¹/₂ cup flaked smoked trout or minced smoked salmon and 2 tablespoons minced fresh parsley leaves and lemon juice.

Bean Dip for Tortilla Chips
Makes at least 10 servings

Time: 10 minutes with precooked beans

After you try this, you will only resort to the store-bought variety in extreme emergencies.

    1 recipe Twice-Cooked ("Refried") Beans with Cumin
        (page 511) or 3 cups other well-seasoned beans
    Bean cooking liquid, chicken stock (see "Soups" for
        stock recipes), sour cream, or plain yogurt as needed
    ¹/₂ cup stemmed, peeled if desired, seeded,
        and minced red bell pepper
    ¹/₂ cup minced onion
    ¹/₂ cup peeled, cored, seeded, drained, and diced
        tomato (optional)
    1 teaspoon red wine or other vinegar
    Chili powder to taste
    Salt and freshly ground black pepper to taste
    Cayenne or Tabasco or other hot sauce to taste

① Place all but 1 cup of the beans in the container of a food processor or blender. Add enough bean cooking liquid, chicken stock, sour cream, or yogurt to enable you to puree the mixture.

② Lightly mash the remaining beans by hand, using a fork or potato masher; combine with the puréed beans. Stir in the pepper, onion, tomato (if you are using it), vinegar, chili powder, salt, pepper, and hot sauce. Taste and adjust seasoning if necessary; thin with more liquid if necessary. (You may prepare this recipe in advance; refrigerate, well wrapped or in a covered container, for up to 2 days before serving.)

Feta Cheese Dip
Makes at least 6 servings

Time: 10 minutes

To convert this dip to a spread, use cream cheese in place of sour cream and add about one tablespoon of freshly squeezed lemon juice. If you like a very smooth dip, use a blender or food processor to combine the ingredients.

    About 1 cup crumbled feta cheese
    1 cup sour cream
    2 tablespoons minced scallion
    2 tablespoons minced fresh parsley, plus some more
    ¹/₂ teaspoon minced garlic (optional)
    1 teaspoon minced fresh marjoram or oregano leaves
        or ¹/₂ teaspoon dried
    ¹/₂ teaspoon minced fresh thyme leaves or
        ¹/₄ teaspoon dried thyme
    Lots of freshly ground black pepper
    Salt to taste (optional)
    Freshly squeezed lemon juice to taste (optional)

① Combine all ingredients except the salt and lemon juice and mash with a fork or potato masher. Taste and add salt and lemon juice if necessary.

2 Garnish with extra parsley and serve immediately, with bread, crackers, pita, or vegetables, or cover and refrigerate for up to a day.

Taramasalata
Greek Fish Roe Dip
Makes at least 6 servings

Time: 15 minutes

This creamy, mayonnaise-like dip is made from tarama, cod or mullet roe which is salted like caviar (which is sturgeon roe), but is much less expensive. Tarama is pink, and sold in seven- or eight-ounce jars in specialty stores and sometimes supermarkets. (Some stores also sell premade taramasalata; make sure you buy roe only.) Salmon roe may be substituted.

1 tablespoon chopped onion
1 teaspoon chopped garlic
1 (7- or 8-ounce) jar tarama
2 tablespoons freshly squeezed lemon juice,
   plus a little more for garnish
1 cup extra-virgin olive oil
8 ounces good white bread, preferably stale
1 tablespoon water, plus more if necessary (optional)
Minced fresh parsley leaves for garnish

1 Combine the onion, garlic, tarama, and lemon juice in the container of a food processor or blender. With the machine running, add olive oil through the feed tube or top, just as you would in making Basic Mayonnaise (page 761). When the mixture is thick and all the oil is added, turn off the machine.

2 Trim the crusts from the bread and soak it in cold water for about 1 minute, until soggy. Squeeze the water from the bread and, with the machine running, add the bread, a bit at time, to the olive oil mixture. When all the bread is added, the mixture should be creamy and fairly light; if it seems too stiff, add water, 1 tablespoon at a time.

3 Refrigerate for up to a day before serving. Garnish with lemon juice and parsley and serve with vegetables, pita, or crackers.

Guacamole
Makes 2 to 4 servings

Time: 10 minutes

Among the most delicious dips there is, and just about the simplest. Add one-half cup peeled, cored, seeded, and diced tomato only if the tomato is perfectly ripe.

1 large or 2 small avocado(s)
1 tablespoon minced onion or shallot
$1/4$ teaspoon minced garlic (optional)
1 teaspoon stemmed, seeded, and minced jalapeño
   or other fresh chile, or 1 teaspoon chili powder,
   or to taste
Salt and freshly ground black pepper to taste
1 tablespoon freshly squeezed lemon or lime juice,
   or to taste
Minced cilantro leaves for garnish

1 Cut the avocado(s) in half and reserve the pit(s) if you will not be serving the guacamole right away. Mash the pulp in a bowl with a fork or potato masher, along with the onion or shallot, garlic (if you are using it), chile or chili powder, a little salt and pepper, and 1 tablespoon of lemon or lime juice. Taste and adjust seasoning as necessary.

2 Garnish and serve, or tuck the pit(s) back into the mixture, cover with plastic wrap, and refrigerate for up to 4 hours (this will keep the guacamole from turning brown). Remove the pit(s) before garnishing and serving.

Hummus

Makes at least 8 servings

Time: 20 minutes with precooked chickpeas

Too often, hummus, which can be used as dip or spread, tastes like nothing but raw garlic; this is smoother and more complex in flavor. When making the chickpeas, let them cook a little longer than usual, so that they're nice and soft. (This is a good place to use canned chickpeas.)

2 cups drained well-cooked or canned chickpeas
$1/2$ cup tahini (sesame paste)
$1/4$ cup sesame oil from the top of the tahini
   or olive oil
1 small clove garlic, peeled, or to taste;
   or 1 tablespoon mashed Roasted Garlic
   (page 575), plus more as needed
Salt and freshly ground black pepper to taste
1 tablespoon ground cumin, or to taste, plus a
   sprinkling for garnish
Juice of 1 lemon, plus more as needed
About $1/3$ cup water, or as needed
1 teaspoon olive oil, approximately

1 Place everything except water and 1 teaspoon olive oil in the container of a food processor and begin to process; add water as needed to make a smooth puree.

2 Taste and add more garlic, salt, lemon juice, or cumin as needed. Serve, drizzled with a little olive oil and sprinkled with a bit of cumin. Serve with vegetables, crackers, or pita.

White Bean Dip: Lighter in texture, flavor, and color than hummus. Omit tahini, lemon juice, and water, and use white beans in place of the chickpeas. Combine the beans with olive oil, garlic, salt, pepper, 2 teaspoons ground cumin, $1/2$ teaspoon

ground cinnamon, $1/2$ teaspoon ground cardamom, and $1/2$ teaspoon ground or peeled and minced fresh ginger. Finish as above.

Roasted Eggplant Dip

Makes at least 6 servings with bread or crackers

Time: About 1 hour, plus time to preheat the grill

Roasting eggplant gives it such a wonderful smoky flavor that even people who claim not to like eggplant often eat this dip enthusiastically.

2 medium or 4 small eggplant, about 1 pound
$1/4$ cup freshly squeezed lemon juice
$1/4$ cup extra-virgin olive oil
$1/2$ teaspoon minced garlic, or to taste
$1/2$ cup freshly grated Parmesan cheese
Salt and freshly ground black pepper to taste
Minced fresh parsley leaves for garnish

1 Start a charcoal or wood fire, or preheat a gas grill, or turn the oven to 500°F. Pierce the eggplant in several places with a thin-bladed knife or skewer. Grill or roast, turning occasionally, until the eggplant collapses and the skin blackens, 15 to 30 minutes depending on size. Remove and cool.

2 When the eggplant is cool enough to handle, part the skin (if it hasn't split on its own), scoop out the flesh, and mince it finely. Mix it with the lemon juice, oil, garlic, cheese, salt, and pepper. Taste and adjust seasonings, then garnish and serve, with bread or crackers.

Baba Ghanoush: Like Hummus (opposite), this can serve as a dip or spread. Omit the oil and cheese. While the eggplant is grilling or roasting, toast $1/2$ cup pine nuts by heating them in a dry skillet over medium heat, shaking occasionally, just until they begin to brown. When the eggplant is cool, put it in the container of a food processor with the pine nuts, lemon juice, garlic, pepper, and $1/3$ cup tahini (sesame paste). Process until very smooth, adding a few teaspoons of water or olive oil if necessary. Taste and add salt and/or more lemon juice or garlic if necessary. Garnish with minced parsley and serve.

Cream Cheese Spread

Makes at least 8 servings

Time: 10 minutes

Here's a stiff cream cheese–based spread that can be thinned with sour cream, yogurt, mayonnaise, or cream to make a dip. For the blue cheese, substitute caviar, chopped olives or ham, any minced herb, or any combination that appeals to you.

> $1/2$ pound Roquefort, bleu d'Avergne, Stilton, Maytag blue, or other good blue cheese
> $1/2$ cup cream cheese
> Sour cream or plain yogurt as needed
> Cayenne or Tabasco or other hot sauce to taste

1 In a bowl, cream the blue and cream cheeses together with a fork.

2 Stir in enough sour cream or yogurt to thin the mixture to a spreading consistency, or use more to make a dip. Add cayenne or Tabasco to taste; refrigerate until ready to use.

Roasted Pepper and Garlic Spread: This is good with a little minced ginger, and some minced cooked bacon. Omit the blue cheese. Add 1 cup minced roasted red bell pepper (page 593; or use bottled pimentos) and about half a head of Roasted Garlic (page 575) to the cream cheese. Thin with extra-virgin olive oil in place of sour cream. Mash well and proceed as above. Add salt, pepper and freshly squeezed lemon juice in place of the cayenne.

Anchovy Spread: Omit the blue cheese. Add 4 mashed anchovy fillets, or more to taste, and $1/4$ teaspoon minced garlic to the cream cheese. Mash well and proceed as above. Add black pepper and lemon juice in place of the cayenne.

Crab or Shrimp Spread: Increase cream cheese to $3/4$ cup; omit blue cheese. Add about 1 cup shredded or minced cooked crabmeat or shrimp, 1 tablespoon mayonnaise, and a few dashes of Worcestershire or soy sauce to the cream cheese. Thin with lemon juice, if necessary, in place of sour cream. Mash well and proceed as above. Add salt and cayenne.

Herbed Goat Cheese

Makes at least 8 servings

Time: 10 minutes

Use this as a spread or a dip; its consistency is somewhere in between. Fresh goat cheese is just a little thicker than cottage cheese.

> 1 pound fresh goat cheese
> About 2 tablespoons cream, sour cream, plain yogurt, or milk
> $1/4$ teaspoon finely minced garlic, or to taste
> $1/2$ cup mixed chopped fresh mild herbs, such as basil, parsley, chervil, dill, and/or chives
> 1 teaspoon minced fresh tarragon or $1/4$ teaspoon dried tarragon
> Salt and freshly ground black pepper to taste
> 1 tablespoon extra-virgin olive oil

1 Thin the goat cheese with enough of the cream, sour cream, yogurt, or milk to give it a spreadable consistency; the amount will depend on the thickness of the cheese and whether you want a thick spread or a thinner dip.

2 Stir in the garlic and herbs. Taste and add salt if necessary (some goat cheese is quite salty) and pepper to taste. Drizzle with the olive oil and serve, or refrigerate for up to several hours, then add olive oil and save.

Goat Cheese–Stuffed Figs: This makes 4 to 8 servings. Take 8 ripe fresh figs and cut them in half. Use only $1/2$ pound of goat cheese. Thin the cheese as above, just until it is thin enough to spread, but omit the garlic and herbs; taste the mixture and add salt if necessary. Spread about 1 tablespoon of the cheese onto the top of each fig, pressing just enough so that it adheres. Drizzle with a little olive oil, sprinkle with some freshly ground black pepper, and serve, or refrigerate for up to an hour, before garnishing and serving.

Parmesan Toasts

Makes 4 to 8 servings

Time: 20 minutes

Real Parmesan cheese—with the words "Parmigiano-Reggiano" stenciled on the rind—makes all the difference here.

1 cup freshly grated Parmesan cheese
3 to 4 tablespoons cream or milk
Pinch cayenne, plus a little more if necessary
$1/4$ cup minced fresh parsley leaves
Salt to taste
8 thin slices Italian or French bread, lightly toasted and lightly buttered

1 Preheat the oven to 450°F.

2 Combine the Parmesan, cream or milk, cayenne, and parsley. Taste and add a little salt or more cayenne if necessary. Spread on the toasts.

3 Bake until hot and melted, 5 to 10 minutes. Cool for a couple of minutes, then serve; or serve at room temperature.

Mushroom Spread for Toast

Makes at least 6 servings

Time: 20 minutes

Seasoned mushrooms, bound with just enough egg to hold them together, make a wonderful topping for bread rounds or toast. Pass as finger food, make larger toasts to serve as formal appetizers, or serve it all as a main course for two.

4 tablespoons olive oil
About 1 pound fresh mushrooms, preferably a mixture, trimmed and roughly chopped
$1/4$ cup reconstituted, drained, and chopped dried mushrooms (optional)
Salt and freshly ground black pepper to taste
1 tablespoon minced shallot
1 teaspoon minced garlic
2 tablespoons cream (optional)
2 eggs, lightly beaten

1 Place the olive oil in a large, deep skillet and turn the heat to medium. A minute later, add the mushrooms. Season with salt and pepper. Cook, stirring, about 10 minutes, until they are quite soft but not yet brown.

2 Stir in the shallot, garlic, and cream (if using), and cook another 5 minutes. Stir in the eggs and cook, stirring, just until the mixture holds together, 3 to 5 minutes. Serve immediately, on toast.

Black Olive Paste

Tapenade

Makes at least 8 servings with bread or vegetables

Time: 20 minutes

This Provençal paste can be used not only as a spread for toasted bread but as a dip for raw vegetables, a sandwich spread, or as an ingredient in salad dressing. You can also spread it over meat or fish before roasting, grilling, or broiling. This is a lot of tapenade, but it keeps, refrigerated, for at least a month—halve the recipe if you have a use for the leftover anchovies.

1 pound good black olives, preferably oil-cured
    (the wrinkled kind)
3 tablespoons capers (see Step 2 below)
1 (2-ounce) tin anchovies, with their oil
1 or 2 cloves garlic, smashed
About ¹/₂ cup extra-virgin olive oil, plus more
    if desired

1 Pit the olives; the easiest way to do this is to flatten a few at a time by placing the broad side of a large knife (or the bottom of a pot) on top of them and pressing down. This will cause them to split and expose the pit. None of this will take as long as you fear.

2 If you are using salted capers, rinse them, then mix them with 1 tablespoon or so of good vinegar. if you are using brined capers, include some of their liquid in the measurement.

3 Add the olives, capers, anchovies, and garlic to the container of a food processor or blender, along with a bit of the olive oil. Pulse the machine once or twice, then turn it on and add the remaining olive oil rather quickly; you don't want to make this puree too uniform, but rather want to get the kind of rough texture you would if you had the energy to use a mortar

and pestle (of course you may use a mortar and pestle if you like).

4 Thin with more olive oil if you like, and use in any of the ways mentioned above.

Bagna Cauda

Warm Anchovy Dip

Makes 4 servings

Time: 10 minutes for the sauce, more to prepare
    the vegetables

The classic Piedmontese appetizer, a savory dip of anchovies, olive oil, butter, and garlic. You'll need a fondue-like setup to keep this warm at the table.

¹/₂ cup extra-virgin olive oil
4 tablespoons (¹/₂ stick) butter or another ¹/₄ cup
    extra-virgin olive oil
1 tablespoon minced garlic, or to taste
8 to 10 anchovy fillets, either canned or salted
    (and rinsed), minced
Freshly ground black pepper to taste
Salt if necessary
4 to 6 cups cut-up assorted raw or lightly cooked
    vegetables—red pepper, celery, Belgian endive,
    artichoke, broccoli, cauliflower, radishes, etc.—
    for dipping

1 Heat the olive oil and butter over medium heat in a small saucepan until the butter melts. Add the garlic and anchovies and continue to cook, stirring and mashing the anchovies, until they fall apart. Taste and add pepper and a little salt if necessary.

2 To serve, bring the pot to the table and keep it warm (improvise with a coffee warmer, or use a double boiler and bring the whole thing to the table; it will stay hot enough as long as you eat right away). Dip the vegetables in the sauce and eat.

Simple Fried Finger Foods

Frying is an undeniable hassle for you but a treat for your guests (and for you, to the extent you eat while you're cooking). Both Tortilla Chips and Plantain Chips (see below) are much easier than other foods to fry, because they require, literally, less than 2 minutes in the oil. This means that you can produce a significant amount in 10 or 15 minutes. Other foods, such as Tempura (page 28), are more difficult, but you should try them at least once, because the results are usually worth the effort.

Fried Tortilla Chips

Makes 50 large or 100 small, enough for 5 to 10 people

Time: 15 to 30 minutes

Fresh tortilla chips are special, no matter how good your store-bought chips are. They're easy, and—as you'll see—they do not absorb much oil (if you bake them—see the variation—the oil used is minimal anyway). Sprinkle them with any spice mixture or seasoned salt when they're done, or top them with grated cheese (and cooked beans, if you like) and bake until the cheese melts to make nachos.

Lard (traditional) or vegetable oil for deep-frying
12 corn tortillas, 6 or 8 inches in diameter
Salt to taste

1 Put enough oil to come to a depth of at least 1 inch in a large, deep skillet or saucepan. The broader the vessel, the more of these you can cook at once, but the more oil you will use. (They cook very quickly, so don't worry if your pan is narrow.) Turn the heat to medium-high; you want the temperature to be at about 350°F when you start cooking.

2 Stack the tortillas and cut them, pie-like, into 4 to 8 wedges. Fry as many at once as will fit without crowding, turning if necessary. Total cooking time will be about 2 minutes; the chips should not brown, but just begin to darken in color. Remove with a tongs or slotted spoon and drain on paper towels or paper bags. Sprinkle with salt and serve hot or at room temperature.

Baked Tortilla Chips: Preheat the oven to 400°F. Lightly brush each tortilla on both sides with peanut or canola or other neutral-flavored oil. Stack and cut as above. Bake on ungreased baking sheets, shaking once or twice, until just beginning to color, 6 to 10 minutes. Sprinkle with salt and serve hot or at room temperature.

Plantain Chips

Makes 2 to 4 servings

Time: 15 minutes

Easier to fry than potatoes, more flavorful, and crisper by far. Best, of course, served hot, but not at all bad a few hours later. Fry these in lard if you want to be authentic.

Lard (traditional) or vegetable oil for deep-frying
2 medium-ripe plantains (yellow-green, not green, yellow, or yellow-black), peeled (page 595)
Salt to taste
Lime wedges

1 Put enough oil to come to a depth of at least 1 inch in a large, deep skillet or saucepan. The broader the vessel, the more of these you can cook at once, but the more oil you will use. (They cook very quickly, so don't worry if your pan is narrow.) Turn the heat to medium-high; you want the temperature to be at about 350°F when you start cooking.

2 While the oil is heating, shave the plantains, using a sharp knife or a mandoline set to just about the thinnest setting. Traditionally, they're cut the long way, but you can make round chips if you find it easier.

3 Fry as many slices at once as will fit without crowding, turning if necessary. Total cooking time will be about 2 minutes; the chips should not brown, but turn a deeper yellow. Remove with a tongs or slotted spoon and drain on paper towels or paper bags. Sprinkle with salt and lime juice and serve as soon as you can; they will remain crisp and delicious for several hours, however.

Vegetable or Fish Tempura

Makes 4 servings

Time: About 40 minutes

Of all batter-fried foods, tempura is the lightest and easiest to make. Serve immediately; like many fried foods, it's best eaten standing up, around the stove. But it will hold in a low oven for a few minutes. You'll note from the variations that Japan is not the only country to serve batter-fried vegetables as a light dish.

Vegetable oil for deep-frying

$1/4$ cup soy sauce

$1/4$ cup water

1 tablespoon peeled and minced fresh ginger

1 teaspoon minced garlic

1 teaspoon rice or other vinegar

$1^1/2$ to 2 pounds assorted vegetables: broccoli, zucchini, eggplant, winter squash, mushrooms, bell pepper, string beans, etc.

1 egg yolk

$1^1/2$ cups ice water

2 cups all-purpose flour

$1/2$ pound shrimp, peeled and sliced in half the long way (optional)

1 Put enough oil to come to a depth of at least 3 to 4 inches in a large, deep saucepan. The broader the saucepan, the more of these you can cook at once, but the more oil you will use. Turn the heat to medium-high; you want the temperature to be at about 375°F when you start cooking. Combine the next five ingredients and set aside as dipping sauce.

2 Prepare the vegetables: Peel the broccoli and break it into florets; wash the zucchini and/or eggplant and slice it thin; peel and seed the winter squash and slice it thin; clean the mushrooms, then cut them into quarters if they're large; stem and seed the pepper and cut it into strips; trim and wash the string beans; and so on. Dry all vegetables well.

3 Combine the egg yolk and ice water in another bowl and beat well. Mix in 1 cup of the flour, just until blended. Don't worry about a few remaining lumps.

4 One piece at a time, dredge the vegetables and shrimp (if you are using) in the remaining flour, then dip in the batter. Fry each piece until golden, turning once if necessary, less than 5 minutes total. Drain on paper towels and serve immediately, with the dipping sauce.

Pakoras: The batter-fried vegetables of India, good served with any dipping sauce or wedges of lime. Make a thick batter by mixing together 2 cups flour, 1 teaspoon baking powder, 1 teaspoon salt, 1 egg, 1 tablespoon oil, and about 1 cup water (or milk). Season the batter with 1 tablespoon curry powder. Proceed to Step 4 and fry as above. Serve with the dipping sauce or lime wedges.

Fritto Misto: The batter-fried dish of Italy; usually vegetables but also bits of meat or fish. Make a batter using 1 cup flour, 1 teaspoon baking powder, 1 teaspoon salt, 1 egg, and $3/4$ cup white wine or beer. Proceed to Step 4 and fry as above. Serve with lemon wedges.

Gougères

Makes 30 to 40 gougères

Time: About 30 minutes

Take a cream puff–like pastry, add cheese, and fry or bake: The result is crisp, light, rich, and cheesy, an almost perfect finger food and the best fritters you can produce. Gougère dough can support any number of ingredients; so, for example, try substituting minced cooked shrimp or other shellfish or sautéed mushrooms for the cheese.

Vegetable oil for deep-frying (optional)
1 cup water
4 tablespoons (1/2 stick) butter
1/2 teaspoon salt
1 1/2 cups (about 7 ounces) all-purpose flour
3 eggs
1 cup freshly grated Emmenthal, Gruyère, Cantal,
   or Cheddar cheese
1 cup freshly grated Parmesan or other hard cheese

1 If you plan to fry the gougères, put enough oil in a large, deep saucepan to come to a depth of about 2 inches. The broader the saucepan, the more of these you can cook at once, but the more oil you will use. (They cook very quickly, so don't worry if your pan is narrow.) Turn the heat to medium-high; you want the temperature to be at about 350°F when you start cooking. If you plan to bake the gougères, lightly grease a baking sheet and preheat the oven to 425°F.

2 Combine the water, butter, and salt in a medium saucepan; turn the heat to medium-high and bring to a boil. Cook, stirring, until the butter melts, just a minute or two longer. Add the flour all at once and cook, stirring constantly, until the dough holds together in a ball, 5 minutes or less.

3 Add the eggs one at a time, beating hard after each addition (this is a little bit of work; feel free to use an electric mixer). Stop beating when the mixture is glossy. Stir in the cheeses.

4 To fry the gougères, drop teaspoonfuls into the hot oil and cook, turning once if necessary, until lightly brown, just 3 or 4 minutes. Don't crowd; you'll probably need to cook in batches. Drain on paper towels or paper bags and serve at once, or keep warm in a low oven for up to 30 minutes.

5 To bake the gougères, drop teaspoonfuls onto the baking sheet and bake until light brown, 10 to 15 minutes.

Classic First Courses Eaten as Finger Foods

Of course you can sit down to eat any of these (you can eat anything sitting down, if you like), but they are all easily adapted as finger foods as well.

Prosciutto and Melon

Makes 8 servings

Time: 10 minutes

Prosciutto di Parma—the real thing—is now sold throughout most of the country, so there is only one challenge here: finding a good melon. If you have ripe figs, or fresh dates, the results will be equally fine. The combination of sweet, juicy fruit and dry, salty ham is incomparable.

1 ripe cantaloupe or other melon
About 10 thin slices prosciutto, cut in pieces

1 Cut the melon into eighths, scrape out the seeds, and remove the rind. Cut the slices into chunks.

2 Use a toothpick to skewer a piece of ham and a chunk of melon, and repeat until all the ham and

melon are used up. Serve immediately, or refrigerate, covered, for up to 2 hours. Serve cool but not ice cold.

Carpaccio
Makes 4 to 8 servings

Time: About 1¹/₂ hours, largely unattended

The now-classic appetizer of the 1980s, which can be made with beef, tuna, or salmon. Needless to say, use only the highest-quality beef, from a completely trustworthy source.

¹/₂ pound beef filet ("filet mignon"), in 1 piece
1 tablespoon extra-virgin olive oil, or a little less
2 teaspoons freshly squeezed lemon juice
Coarse salt and freshly ground black pepper to taste
¹/₄ pound Parmesan cheese, in 1 chunk

① Cover the beef well with plastic wrap and freeze it for an hour or so, until it is very firm. Slice it as thin as possible (a slicing machine is ideal; alternatively, use a very sharp carving knife).

② Toss the beef with the oil, lemon juice, salt, and pepper. Break the Parmesan into chunks. Use a toothpick to skewer a piece of beef and a piece of cheese, and repeat until all the beef and cheese are used up. Serve immediately or refrigerate for up to an hour.

Quick Marinated Mushrooms
Makes 4 servings

Time: 5 minutes

Arguably, this is the best use for white button mushrooms, which have more flavor raw than they do cooked.

Twenty-Three Other Dishes You Can Serve as Sit-Down Appetizers

Obviously, you can make small portions of almost any savory dish and call it an appetizer; and virtually any pasta or soup qualifies as well. These are some of my personal favorites to serve before a meal.

1. Falafel, page 523
2. Grilled Squab, Vietnamese-Style, page 418
3. Basic Cheese Quiche, page 743
4. Gefilte Fish, page 292
5. Gravlax (Salt-and-Sugar-Cured Salmon), page 300
6. Salmon Croquettes, page 306
7. Creamed Salt Cod Mousse, page 320
8. Marinated Fresh Anchovies, page 321
9. "Grilled" Sardines, page 321
10. Shrimp Cocktail, page 324
11. Dungeness Crab Salad, page 332
12. Grilled Octopus, page 339
13. Baked Stuffed Clams, page 345
14. Basic Steamed Clams ("Steamers"), page 345
15. Basic Steamed Mussels (or almost any mussels dish), page 346
16. Fresh Snails with Garlic Butter, page 352
17. Any polenta, pages 187–190
18. Any risotto, pages 207–211
19. Slow-Grilled Ribs with Chris's Great Rub, or other rib dishes, pages 471–473
20. Any artichoke recipe, pages 533–536
21. Beet Roesti with Rosemary, page 542
22. Any leeks recipe, pages 579–581
23. Grilled Portobello Mushrooms, page 584

1/2 pound mushrooms, trimmed and cut into chunks

Juice of 1 lemon

About 1 tablespoon extra-virgin olive oil

Salt and freshly ground black pepper to taste

1/4 pound Parmesan cheese, in 1 chunk

1 Gently toss the mushrooms with the lemon juice, olive oil, salt, and pepper. Taste and adjust seasonings.

2 Break the Parmesan into small chunks. Use a toothpick to skewer a mushroom and a piece of cheese, and repeat until all the mushrooms and cheese are used up. Serve immediately or refrigerate for up to an hour.

Stuffed Mushrooms

Makes at least 6 servings

Time: 30 minutes

Another good use for button mushrooms, which have a fine shape for stuffing.

1 pound large button (white) mushrooms

1 egg

1/2 cup fresh bread crumbs

1/2 cup freshly grated Parmesan cheese

1/2 cup minced fresh parsley leaves

Salt and freshly ground black pepper to taste

1 teaspoon minced garlic

Extra-virgin olive oil as needed, plus some for
    greasing the baking sheet

1 Preheat the oven to 400°F. Clean the mushrooms, trim off their bottoms, and remove the stems, taking care to leave the caps intact. Chop the stems and combine them in a bowl with the egg, bread crumbs, cheese, parsley, salt, pepper, and garlic.

2 Stir enough olive oil into the mix to make it shine—a tablespoon or two. Use some more olive oil to lightly grease a baking sheet. Stuff the mushroom

caps with the stem mixture and bake, stuffed side up, until lightly browned on top, about 15 minutes. Serve hot or at room temperature.

Peppers and Anchovies

Makes 4 servings

Time: 30 minutes with raw peppers, 5 minutes if
    they're already roasted

Best with Marinated Roasted, Grilled, or Broiled Peppers, page 593, this is still good with canned or jarred red peppers ("pimentos").

4 roasted peppers, peeled, stemmed, and seeded

Salt and freshly ground black pepper to taste

8 anchovy fillets, rinsed if salted

Extra-virgin olive oil to taste

Several drops of freshly squeezed lemon juice
    or balsamic vinegar (optional)

About 1 teaspoon capers (optional)

1 Cut the peppers in half and sprinkle them with a little bit of salt and with pepper. Top each half with an anchovy fillet.

2 Drizzle with olive oil and the optional lemon juice or vinegar. Serve on rounds of bread or toast (sprinkle a few capers on top if you like), or skewer with toothpicks.

Marinated Mozzarella

Makes 8 servings

Time: 20 minutes, plus resting time

If you can find small "mozzarella balls," or "cherries," by all means use them. Otherwise, cut a chunk of mozzarella into bite-sized pieces. In either case, use fresh mozzarella—which has the best flavor— if at all possible.

> $^{1}/_{4}$ cup extra-virgin olive oil
> $^{1}/_{4}$ cup chopped fresh basil, parsley, or oregano
>   leaves, or any combination
> 1 pound mozzarella (drained if packed in water),
>   cut into bite-sized pieces if necessary
> Salt and freshly ground black pepper to taste
> Crushed red pepper flakes to taste

1 Combine the oil and the herb; toss in a bowl with the mozzarella.

2 Taste and add salt and the two peppers to taste. If possible, let stand for at least 30 minutes before serving.

First Courses and Finger Foods in Wrappers

With wonton wrappers and phyllo dough now available at nearly every supermarket, making wrapped foods is easier than ever. And once you begin to experiment, you'll realize that you can fill them with anything you like. Not all dumplings are fried: Phyllo and empanadas are baked, samosas can be baked, pot stickers are sautéed, and rice paper dumplings are raw (and incredibly simple).

Wrappers for Wontons or Egg Rolls
Makes about 50

Time: About 30 minutes

This will make a somewhat cruder wrapper than those bought at a supermarket, but it will taste a little better, too, and it will give you the additional satisfaction of

knowing you made everything. But mostly, I'd see this as a stopgap if you're committed to making dumplings but haven't bought wonton wrappers in the store.

> 2 cups (about 9 ounces) all-purpose flour, plus a little
>   more as needed
> $^{1}/_{2}$ teaspoon salt
> 1 egg (optional)
> $^{1}/_{2}$ cup water, more or less

1 Combine the 2 cups flour and salt in a bowl. Stir the egg and some of the water into the flour mixture. Continue to add water and stir, just until you can gather the dough into a ball; the dough should be quite dry. You can also do this in a food processor: Add the water gradually while the machine is running. Let the machine run for about 15 seconds, or knead for about 5 minutes by hand, using as much flour as is necessary to keep it from sticking.

2 Shape into a ball, dust with flour, and cover with plastic wrap or a damp towel. Let sit from 10 minutes to 2 hours.

3 Knead the dough for a minute, then cut it into 4 pieces. Roll each piece into a 1-inch log, then pinch off 1-inch pieces and roll them into rough 3- or 4-inch squares, rectangles, or circles (if you want to make larger egg rolls, make larger wrappers). Use immediately or dust well with flour, stack, cover with plastic wrap, and refrigerate or freeze.

Fried Wontons or Egg Rolls
Makes at least 36, enough for 8 to 12 people

Time: About 30 minutes

These are the simplest and most basic dumplings, and they take almost no time to cook. They're deep-fried, but they don't spatter (as long as the package is sealed well enough to contain the filling), and they're virtually foolproof. This same filling may be used to fill egg roll skins. Finally, if you prefer, switch the proportions of pork and cabbage, using one-half cup of the former and one cup of the latter. Or omit the meat entirely and use a combination of minced vegetables.

Vegetable oil for deep-frying
1 cup ground or minced pork or shrimp,
   or a combination
1/4 cup minced scallion
1/2 cup finely shredded cabbage, preferably Napa
1 teaspoon minced garlic
1 teaspoon peeled and minced or grated fresh ginger
1/4 cup stemmed, seeded, and minced red bell
   pepper
Salt and freshly ground black pepper to taste
1 teaspoon soy sauce
1 teaspoon dark sesame oil
1 egg
36 to 48 wonton skins, or at least 6 egg roll skins

1 Put enough oil in a large, deep saucepan to come to a depth of at least 2 inches. The broader the saucepan, the more of these you can cook at once, but the more oil you will use. (They cook very quickly, so don't worry if your pan is narrow.) Turn the heat to medium-high; you want the temperature to be at about 350°F when you start cooking.

2 Combine all remaining ingredients except the wonton skins. To fill the skins, place 1 or 2 rounded teaspoons of filling in the center of each skin (use more for egg rolls); fold over to make a triangle and seal carefully with a few drops of water. Let rest on waxed paper until you have finished filling all the skins.

3 Place the wontons in the oil 2 or more at a time, raising the heat to maintain temperature. Cook, turning once, until nicely browned, a total of just 3 or 4 minutes. Drain on paper towels and serve immediately, with Soy and Sesame Dipping Sauce or Marinade, page 776.

Lighter, Steamed Wontons: In Step 1, set up a steamer; to improvise, fit a plate or a rack above 1 inch or so of boiling water in a covered pot. In Step 2, use minced shrimp or boneless chicken breast instead of the pork or shrimp; the other ingredients remain the same. Fill and seal the wontons as above; keep them moist by covering them with a damp towel until you're ready to cook. Steam the wontons in one or two batches, for about 10 minutes per batch. Serve hot, with Soy and Sesame Dipping Sauce or Marinade, page 776.

SHAPING EGG ROLLS

(Step 1) Lay the wrapper with one point facing you and place a large spoonful of filling about one-third of the way up, leaving a one-inch border on either side. (Step 2) Fold up the bottom point. (Steps 3–4) Fold in the sides and roll it up. Seal with a few drops of water or beaten egg.

Rice Paper Spring Rolls

Makes 2 to 4 servings

Time: About 30 minutes

These no-cook Vietnamese-style spring rolls are made with wonderfully pliable rice paper; if you have leftover shrimp (or chicken, or pork), you can make them in no time flat, especially once you've practiced on a batch or two.

1 small fresh chile, minced, or $1/2$ teaspoon crushed red pepper flakes

1 tablespoon rice or other mild vinegar

1 tablespoon fish sauce (*nuoc mam* or *nam pla*, available at Asian markets) or soy sauce

1 teaspoon sugar

1 tablespoon freshly squeezed lime juice

1 teaspoon minced garlic

8 medium-to-large shrimp, cooked, peeled, and cut in half the long way (precooked shrimp are okay, as are leftovers of any type)

1 cup peeled and grated, shredded, or julienned carrots

1 cup bean sprouts

2 scallions, cut into slivers the long way

2 tablespoons roughly chopped fresh mint leaves

2 tablespoons roughly chopped cilantro leaves

2 tablespoons roughly chopped peanuts (salted are okay)

4 sheets rice paper, 8 to 10 inches in diameter

1 Combine the first six ingredients and set aside as dipping sauce.

2 Prepare the other ingredients and set them out on your work surface. Set out a bowl of hot water (110° to 120°F) and a clean kitchen towel.

3 Put a sheet of rice paper into the water for about 10 seconds, just until soft (don't let it become too soft; it will continue to soften as you work). Lay it on the towel.

4 In the middle of the rice paper, lay a few shrimp pieces and about a quarter each of the carrots, bean sprouts, scallions, mint, cilantro, and peanuts. Roll up the rice paper, keeping it fairly tight and folding in the ends to seal. Repeat this process until all the ingredients are used up. Serve with dipping sauce.

Pot Stickers or Steamed Dumplings

Makes at least 24 dumplings, enough for 4 to 8 people

Time: 30 to 45 minutes

Make these with round wonton wrappers, about three or four inches in diameter. They are just as easily cooked as pot stickers or steamed dumplings.

1 cup ground pork or other meat, or minced shrimp, or shredded crabmeat

$1/4$ cup minced scallion

$1/4$ cup minced bamboo shoots, water chestnuts, cabbage, or peeled and shredded carrots

1 teaspoon minced garlic

1 teaspoon peeled and minced or grated fresh ginger

Salt and freshly ground black pepper to taste

1 tablespoon soy sauce

$1/2$ teaspoon sugar

1 teaspoon dark sesame oil

24 or more round wonton wrappers

4 tablespoons peanut oil, if pan-cooking

$3/4$ cup water, plus a little more

1 Combine the first nine ingredients. Place 1 rounded teaspoon of filling on each wonton wrapper, then fold the wrapper over to form a semicircle (see illustrations on page 35). Seal with a few drops of water. Keep the finished dumplings under a moist towel while you work.

2 To make pot stickers, put the peanut oil in a large, deep skillet and turn the heat to medium-high. Place the dumplings, one at a time, into the skillet, seam side up. Do not crowd; cook in two batches if necessary. Cover the pot and cook for about 5 minutes. Uncover and add ³⁄₄ cup water to the pot; re-cover and cook another 2 minutes, then uncover and cook about 3 minutes more, or until water has evaporated. Remove the dumplings with a spatula and serve with Soy and Sesame Dipping Sauce or Marinade, page 776.

3 To steam the dumplings, set up a steamer; to improvise, fit a heatproof plate or a rack above 1 inch or so of boiling water in a covered pot. Steam the dumplings in one or two batches, for about 10 minutes per batch. Serve hot, with dipping sauce.

MAKING POT STICKERS

(Step 1) Place a teaspoon of filling on one half of the dough. (Step 2) Brush circumference of the circle with a little water or beaten egg. (Steps 3–4) Fold over and pinch tightly to seal.

Potato-Filled Samosas
Makes 20 to 30, enough for 5 to 10 people

Time: At least 1 hour

The dumpling of India, and one of the best, because the dough, which is made with butter and yogurt, is rich and tangy. Traditionally, it is made by cutting the cold butter into bits and rubbing it and the flour very quickly between your fingers: Pick it up, rub it, and drop it. (If the mixture begins to feel greasy, refrigerate it for a few minutes before proceeding.) The food processor may not be as charming, but it's much easier. Take your pick.

Samosas are usually deep-fried, but you can bake them: Just place them on a lightly greased baking sheet and bake at 350°F for twenty to thirty minutes, until golden brown. Don't think of this as a compromise, either: Baked samosas are terrific.

About 1¹⁄₄ pounds baking potatoes, such as Idaho
  or Russet
2 cups (about 9 ounces) all-purpose flour, plus a
  little more as needed
1 teaspoon salt
8 tablespoons (1 stick) butter
2 tablespoons plain yogurt, sour cream, or buttermilk
1 tablespoon ice water, plus more as necessary
1 cup chopped onion
1 fresh chile, minced, or cayenne to taste
1 tablespoon minced garlic
2 teaspoons peeled and minced or grated
  fresh ginger
1 tablespoon All-Purpose Curry Powder (page 778),
  or store-bought curry powder
Salt and freshly ground black pepper to taste
¹⁄₂ cup green peas (frozen are fine; defrost them
  in water to cover while you prepare the other
  ingredients)
Vegetable oil for deep-frying

1 Peel the potatoes and dice them into $1/2$-inch cubes; set them in a pot of water to cover; turn the heat to high. Boil them until soft, 5 to 10 minutes. Drain.

2 Meanwhile, make the dough: Place the flour and 1 teaspoon of salt in the container of a food processor; pulse for a couple of seconds to blend. Cut half the butter into bits, add it to the flour, and turn on the machine; let it run until the butter and flour are combined. Add the yogurt, sour cream, or buttermilk and pulse a few times. Then, with the machine running, add ice water 1 tablespoon at a time through the feed tube. The instant the dough forms a ball, stop adding water.

3 Knead the dough for 1 minute by hand, then cover with plastic wrap or a damp towel and set aside. Place the remaining butter in a large skillet, preferably non-stick, and turn the heat to medium. Add the onion and the chile or cayenne and cook, stirring, until the onion softens, about 5 minutes; add the garlic, ginger, and curry powder. Add salt and pepper and cook, stirring, for about 2 minutes. Add the potatoes and peas (drain them if they've been sitting in water), raise the heat a little, and cook, stirring frequently, until the potatoes begin to brown, about 10 minutes. Taste and adjust seasoning if necessary; the mixture should be spicy but not fiery. Cool while you roll out the dough.

4 Knead the dough for a few seconds, sprinkling it with a little flour if necessary. Break off a small piece of the dough (you'll want to make 20 to 30 samosas, so judge accordingly) and roll it out on a lightly floured surface until it is a circle at least 3 inches in diameter. Make 5 or 6 circles, then fill them: Place 1 tablespoon or so of filling in the center, then fold over and seal with a few drops of water. Keep covered with a damp towel. Repeat until all the dough and filling are used up.

5 When you're about halfway through making the samosas, put enough oil to come to a depth of at least 2 inches in a large, deep saucepan. The broader the saucepan, the more samosas you can cook at once, but the more oil you will use. Turn the heat to medium-high; you want the temperature to be at about 375°F when you start cooking.

6 Fry the samosas a few at a time, turning if necessary, until they are golden brown. Drain on paper towels or paper bags and serve immediately, or keep warm in a low oven, or serve at room temperature, within an hour or so.

Beef-Filled Samosas: The dough and frying remain the same. To make the filling, heat 2 tablespoons butter or oil in a large skillet over medium heat. Add onion, chile, garlic, ginger, and curry as above. Add $3/4$ pound ground beef or lamb and cook, stirring, until the meat loses its color, about 5 minutes. Remove from the skillet with a slotted spoon, leaving all fat and other liquid in the pan. Stir $1/4$ minced cilantro into the mixture and proceed to Step 4.

Lentil-Filled Samosas: The dough and frying remain the same. For the filling, use half of the recipe for Split Peas, Mung Beans, or Lentils with Curry (Dal), on page 524. Drain the peas, beans, or lentils very well before proceeding to Step 4.

Empanadas Filled with Beans and Mushrooms
Makes 12, enough for 4 to 12 people

Time: About 1 hour with precooked beans

You can stuff empanadas with almost anything, including a ground beef and vegetable mixture, hard-boiled eggs chopped with onions and olives, or cooked shrimp and vegetables. I like this savory bean and mushroom filling best.

2 cups (about 9 ounces) all-purpose flour, plus a
    little more
1¹/₂ teaspoons baking powder
1 teaspoon salt
¹/₂ cup plus 2 tablespoons lard (traditional)
    or vegetable oil
About ¹/₂ cup cold water, or as needed
¹/₂ cup chopped onion
1 cup trimmed and chopped shiitakes or other
    mushrooms
1 dried chipotle chile, soaked in hot water until
    soft; or about 1 tablespoon mashed chipotle chile
    in adobo; or 1 fresh jalapeño chile, stemmed,
    seeded, and minced
1 cup beans from any of the following recipes:
    Sautéed Beans and Tomatoes (page 511); Twice-
    Cooked ("Refried") Beans with Cumin (page 511);
    Traditional Refried Beans (page 512); Black Beans
    with Cumin or Chili (page 512); Red Beans with
    Meat (page 513); Vegetarian Red Beans (page 513)
1 teaspoon to 1 tablespoon ground cumin, depending
    on the seasoning of the beans
Salt and freshly ground black pepper to taste
¹/₂ cup milk

1 Mix the flour, baking powder, and salt together
in a food processor fitted with the steel blade; process
for about 5 seconds. With the machine running, add
the ¹/₂ cup of lard or oil, and process 10 seconds.
Then, with the machine running, add just enough
water for the dough to form a ball. Don't add more
water than necessary; the dough should be fairly dry.
Knead by hand until smooth, just 1 minute or so.
Wrap in plastic or cover with a damp towel and let
rest for at least 20 minutes. (You can refrigerate the
dough overnight; be sure to let it come to room temperature before proceeding.)

2 Knead the dough for 1 minute, then cut it
into 12 pieces. On a well-floured surface, roll each
piece into a 6-inch circle, adding additional flour as

necessary. Dust the circles with flour, stack, and wrap
in plastic until you finish preparing the filling.

3 Place the remaining lard or oil in a large skillet over
medium heat. A minute later, add the onion and cook,
stirring, for 2 minutes. Add the mushrooms and cook,
stirring occasionally, until softened, about 5 minutes.
Add the chile and cook another minute, then add the
beans. Cook until hot, then season with cumin, salt, and
pepper. Turn off the heat and let the mixture cool a bit.

4 Preheat the oven to 450°F. Place a couple of
tablespoons of the filling on each of the circles, then
fold each circle over; seal the seam with a few drops of
water and press to close. Place on an ungreased baking sheet and brush lightly with milk. Bake until the
dough is golden brown and hot, about 20 minutes.
Serve immediately or at room temperature.

Cheese Quesadillas
Makes 8 to 16 servings

Time: 15 minutes

You can assemble all four quesadillas at once, then
wrap and refrigerate them until you're ready to cook.
(The cooking itself takes almost no time at all.) If you
prefer, dry-sauté these with no oil at all, in a non-stick
or well-seasoned cast-iron skillet.

8 tablespoons vegetable oil (optional)
8 (8-inch) flour tortillas
1 cup grated Cheddar, Jack, or other cheese,
    or a combination
¹/₂ cup minced scallion
¹/₄ cup minced canned green chiles
¹/₄ cup any salsa (optional)

1 The easiest way to make these is to "build" them
in the skillet. So: Place 1 tablespoon of oil, if you're
using it, in a medium skillet and turn the heat to

medium. A minute later, place a tortilla in the skillet. Top with a quarter of the cheese, scallion, chiles, and salsa (if you are using it), then with another tortilla.

2 Cook about 2 minutes, or until the cheese begins to melt. Turn and cook another 2 to 3 minutes, until the cheese is melted and both sides are toasted. Drain if necessary, then cut into wedges and serve, or keep warm until the remaining quesadillas are done.

Stuffed Grape Leaves

Makes about 30, enough for 10 to 15 people

Time: At least 1¹/₂ hours

This is a project, but a memorable one, especially if you begin with a visit to a grape arbor, as I did the first time I made these nearly thirty years ago. Unless you can get fresh grape leaves (which are not that hard to find in most parts of the country), you might prefer making these with cabbage or chard leaves instead of bottled grape leaves, which have little flavor.

Around 40 large grape leaves (you need extra because some will be imperfect)
2 tablespoons extra-virgin olive oil, plus more for garnish
1 cup minced onion
¹/₄ cup pine nuts
1 cup long-grain rice
¹/₂ teaspoon ground allspice
1 teaspoon salt
1¹/₂ cups chicken, beef, or vegetable stock, or water (see "Soups" for stock recipes)
Freshly ground black pepper to taste
2 tablespoons minced fresh mint or dill leaves
4 tablespoons freshly squeezed lemon juice

1 Set a large pot of water to boil. Parboil the grape leaves, a few at a time, until they are tender and pliable, just a couple of minutes. Drain, then cut off the stems and remove any hard veins near the base of the leaves. Pat dry with paper towels.

2 Meanwhile, place the olive oil in a large, deep skillet and turn the heat to medium-high. A minute later, add the onion and cook, stirring, until it is tender, about 5 minutes. Add the pine nuts, rice, allspice, 1 teaspoon salt, and the stock or water. Cover, turn the heat to medium-low, and cook until the rice is somewhat tender but still quite al dente, about 10 to 12 minutes. Cool in a large bowl, check for salt, and add lots of pepper, the mint or dill, and half of the lemon juice.

3 One at a time, place the grape leaves, shiny side down, on a work surface and put 1 tablespoon or so of the rice mixture in the middle of the leaf. Fold over the stem end, then the sides, then roll toward the tip, making a neat little package. Don't roll too tightly, as the rice will continue to expand during subsequent cooking.

4 Place the packages side by side in a roasting pan or skillet (you can layer them if you like), add water (or, even better, more stock) to come about halfway up the rolls, and weight with a heatproof plate. Cover the pan or skillet and cook over low heat for 30 minutes or so, until most of the liquid is absorbed. Drain; serve at room temperature, sprinkled with remaining lemon juice and a bit of olive oil.

Spinach-Cheese Triangles

Makes about 40 pieces

Time: About 1 hour

Typically made with cheese, these can be made with spinach only or cheese only; see the variations. Working with phyllo dough (sold in supermarkets, usually in the freezer compartment) is not at all difficult. Make sure to defrost phyllo dough overnight in the refrigerator. If you change your mind, or use only half a box, don't worry: It will keep for weeks in the fridge (and for months in the freezer). Allow yourself plenty of room, and keep a damp towel handy to cover those sheets of phyllo that you aren't working on; it dries out quickly. Brush the layers lightly with butter or oil; don't glob it on.

1½ pounds fresh spinach, trimmed and well washed

2 tablespoons olive oil

1 cup minced onion

½ cup minced scallion

Salt and freshly ground black pepper to taste

⅛ teaspoon freshly grated nutmeg

3 eggs

½ pound feta cheese, crumbled

½ pound cottage cheese or ricotta, drained

¼ cup minced fresh dill leaves or 1 tablespoon dried dill

¼ cup minced fresh parsley leaves

½ pound phyllo dough (about 15 sheets)

½ cup (1 stick) melted butter or extra-virgin olive oil

1 cup fresh bread crumbs

1 Steam or parboil the spinach until it wilts (page 604). Drain, squeeze dry, and chop.

2 Place the olive oil in a medium skillet and turn the heat to medium. Add the onion and scallion and cook, stirring, until softened, about 5 minutes. Add the spinach, salt, pepper, and nutmeg, and stir.

3 Beat the eggs with the cheeses. Stir in the spinach mixture and the dill and parsley. Preheat the oven to 350°F.

4 Unroll the phyllo sheets and cut them into thirds the long way. Working with 1 piece at a time, brush lightly with butter or oil, then sprinkle lightly with bread crumbs. Place 1 heaping teaspoon of spinach filling in one corner of the dough and fold the corner over to make a triangle. Continue to fold the phyllo, making triangles—as you learned to do with a flag. As each piece is finished, brush its top with butter or oil and place on a baking sheet.

5 When all the triangles are done, bake for about 20 minutes, or until nicely browned. Let rest for 5 to 10 minutes before serving.

Phyllo Triangles with Greens: This is also good with about 1 cup mushrooms cooked with the onions. In Step 1, steam or parboil any mixture of about 3 pounds of greens—spinach, kale, dandelions, escarole, etc.—until very tender. Drain and chop as above. In Step 2, add ½ cup crumbled walnuts to the onions; season the greens and onions with 2 tablespoons freshly squeezed lemon juice. Let cool for a few minutes, then stir in 2 beaten eggs; omit cheese. Proceed as above.

Phyllo Triangles with Cheese: Omit spinach and everything in Step 2. In Step 3, add 1 cup grated Parmesan, Pecorino, or other hard cheese (hard Greek sheep's milk cheese would be ideal) to the mix along with nutmeg and black pepper to taste; omit dill and parsley and proceed as above.

Scallion Pancakes
Makes 2 pancakes, enough for 2 to 8 people

Time: 1½ hours, largely unattended

This tough, chewy little pancake is easily made, and quickly cut into wedges for a crowd.

2 cups (about 9 ounces) all-purpose flour, plus a little more

1 teaspoon salt

1 cup boiling water, plus a little more as needed

1 cup finely chopped scallions

2 tablespoons lard (traditional) or vegetable oil

Coarse salt

1 Place the flour and salt in the container of a food processor; turn on the machine; add the water, through the feed tube, until the dough forms a ball. Add a little more water if necessary.

2 Knead by hand for about 1 minute, until the dough is smooth. Place in a bowl, cover with plastic wrap, and let rest for about 1 hour (or longer, refrigerated).

3 On a lightly floured surface, divide the dough in two; keep 1 ball covered. Use a rolling pin to shape the dough into a large, 1/4-inch-thick circle, adding flour as necessary. When the circle is about 1/4 inch thick, press half the scallions into it. Repeat with the remaining dough.

4 Place half the lard or oil in a large, deep skillet and turn the heat to medium-low. When the lard has melted or the oil is hot, place one of the pancakes in the skillet. Cook until lightly browned, 3 to 5 minutes, then turn and brown the other side. Repeat with the other pancake.

5 Sprinkle with coarse salt and serve warm.

Plum Tomato Tart with Pesto

Makes 6 to 12 servings

Time: About 3 hours, largely unattended

For this savory tart, a flaky pie crust is rolled flat on a baking sheet, partially baked, and then topped. The result is halfway between a pizza and a quiche.

1/3 cup extra-virgin olive oil, plus a little for drizzling

12 ripe plum tomatoes, cored, peeled, halved lengthwise, and seeded

6 garlic cloves, lightly crushed (don't bother to peel)

1 recipe Flaky Pie Crust (page 685), made without sugar, rolled out flat to less than 1/4-inch thickness, and chilled

1/2 cup Basic Pesto (page 766)

Salt and freshly ground black pepper to taste

1 cup crumbled Parmesan, Pecorino Romano, or feta cheese

1 Preheat the oven to 275°F. Cover a baking sheet with foil and pour the olive oil onto it; place the tomatoes in the oil, cut side down. Scatter the garlic cloves around the tomatoes. Bake 2 hours or longer, until the tomatoes are very soft and shriveled. Remove and cool.

2 Turn the oven to 425°F. Lay the crust on a baking sheet, and prick it all over with a fork. Bake 12 minutes. Reduce the heat to 350°F and bake about 10 minutes more, or until golden but not browned. Cool the crust, still on the sheet, for a few minutes on a rack.

3 Coat the bottom of the crust with pesto; top with the tomatoes and some salt and pepper. Remove the garlic cloves from their peels and mince or mash; spread over the tomatoes. Top with cheese and drizzle with a little more oil; sprinkle with a little more salt and pepper and bake 10 to 15 minutes, until the cheese has melted. Serve hot or at room temperature.

Soups

Making soup is among the most satisfying of kitchen tasks. In many instances, it is also the least precise, which makes it the easiest and most fun. It's almost impossible to make "bad" soup: At its most basic, you start with water, add some means of making it taste better—usually meat, poultry, fish, or aromatic vegetables, along with seasonings—and finish with a few (or a slew of) vegetables and/or grains.

There are, of course, certain general rules and basic techniques that make soup better. But the point is that although soup-making may conjure up an image of huge pots containing hundreds of ingredients simmering all day long, that need not be the case. You can make a batch of soup in the same amount of time it takes to make many other dinner dishes; the process need not be elaborate or especially time-consuming.

The Basics of Stock

Having said that, it's time to say that almost all soups, with few exceptions, are best when they are made with stock. Stock, also called broth (I usually call the basic ingredient "stock" and the enhanced, nearly-ready-to-serve soup "broth"), is a liquid in which solids have been cooked and then strained out, with the goal of transferring the flavor from the solids to the liquid. The solids are then usually (not always) discarded, and the liquid is strained and defatted if necessary. Then it's used as the basis for soups, as well as for sauces.

Is stock essential for every soup? No. Will it improve almost any soup? Yes. Even the simplest vegetable stock—an onion, a carrot, a celery stalk, a few other scraps, simmered together for twenty minutes—will make a difference in most soups. And a grand,

41

full-flavored chicken, meat, or fish stock is good enough to serve on its own.

Stock Ingredients

Stock need not be expensive: You can start with scraps of vegetables that you've frozen and saved over the course of weeks; I do this routinely. Use the trimmings and ends from celery, carrots, and onions (onion peels, especially, add a good deal of color to stocks), and other vegetables, bearing in mind that trimmings from strong-tasting vegetables such as broccoli and asparagus will lend a distinct flavor to the stock, one that you might not always want.

Save, too, every scrap (except for fat, chicken skin, and fish gills and innards) from trimming chicken, meat, or fish. Stock-making gives you yet another incentive for buying whole chicken and cutting it up; the meaty raw bones of a single chicken, combined with a few vegetables, provide enough flavor for a quart or two of stock.

Of course, it's easier and arguably better—if somewhat more expensive—to begin with fresh, whole ingredients. Take a carrot, an onion, a celery stalk, a chicken, some seasoning, at a total cost of less than five dollars (far less, if the chicken was on sale), and you can make three quarts of stock, enough for two or three batches of soup, or a batch of soup and a fantastic risotto. Keep the simmering time short and you can even make the soup and still have a chicken with enough flour to be worth eating.

Almost anything can substitute for anything else in stock, although onion, carrot, and celery should find their way into most stockpots. But if you have turkey and no chicken, use it. Use cooked meat instead of raw. If you have small amounts of many ingredients, rather than the amounts specified here, substitute. Just leave out as much visible fat as possible.

Bones, of course, are an integral part of many stocks, and are highly desirable for the body they lend to long-simmering stocks. But a stock made only of bones tastes like bones rather than meat. Most raw bones are quite meaty, so that isn't so much of a problem. But if you are making a stock with leftovers, and are using bones that have been completely stripped of meat, buy a few chicken wings, backs, or necks, and add them along with the bones; you'll improve the flavor significantly.

There are two extremely flavorful stock ingredients you should choose to include or omit based on your own taste. These are garlic and dried mushrooms. I like the scent of garlic in many savory soups and dishes, and sometimes I put a whole head right into my simmering stock. But once it's in you can't take it out, so I only do that when I'm making a relatively small amount of stock and know that the garlic will be a welcome addition whenever I use that stock.

The distinctive flavor of mushrooms is almost always a fine addition, and I usually throw some directly into the stock as it's simmering. There's really no reason not to do this; if I'm feeling economical, and dried porcini are too expensive, I use dried shiitakes, sold as black mushrooms in Chinese markets and very, very cheap. The trimmings from fresh mushrooms, of course, are also good. But I don't include either of these ingredients in my basic stock recipes because, as I said, their inclusion is up to you.

Stock Techniques

Considering fat   There are two special "techniques" for stock that concern fat. The first is really more something to remember than to learn: Don't allow stocks (or, for that matter, soups) to boil vigorously. This is a generalization; there are times it will do no harm at all. But once fat is rendered by the heat of the liquid, rapid boiling can cause it to become so thoroughly dispersed in the liquid that it will be difficult to remove it. This not only makes for a fattier stock (obviously), but can also lead to a somewhat greasy-tasting one. To cook stock, bring it just about to a boil, skim any foam that rises to the top, and then turn the heat down to about medium-low. What you want is a gentle simmer, a few bubbles hitting the surface all the time, or less often, but never a rolling boil. On some stoves it helps to turn the heat down and partially cover the pan at the same time.

The second technique—defatting—is simple enough, assuming you make your stock a day or two in advance. To remove nearly all the fat from any stock, strain it and then refrigerate it. (If the weather is cold—say 40°F or lower—just set the strained stock outside, covered of course.) When the fat rises to the top and solidifies—as long as a day later, depending on the quantity of stock and the temperature of the storage place—just skim it off with a spoon and discard it (or save it for cooking, especially if it is from chicken).

Browning Sometimes, ingredients for stock are roasted before they are cooked. This is done for exactly the same reasons you would brown anything before proceeding with the cooking process: to increase flavor and darken color. Roasted meats and vegetables make a darker, more complex stock, but not necessarily a better one. Those stocks that do not begin with browning are sometimes brighter and cleaner in flavor. The choice is yours, and techniques for both methods are given in the following pages.

Straining When you strain a stock—usually through a sieve (a *chinois*, or china-cap, is best, but almost any large sieve will do)—you have two options. If you press on the vegetables and other ingredients you intensify flavors; if you do not your stock will be clearer. I almost always opt for flavor, because to make a soup perfectly clear takes extreme measures that I'm rarely willing to take.

Reducing The less water a stock contains, the more intense the flavor, and the less room it takes to store. You can easily reduce a stock to the point where you can store the equivalent of twelve cups of stock in an ice cube tray. To use, just pop out the "ice cube" (it's actually best to pop them all out, then freeze the cubes in a tightly sealed container or plastic bag) and thaw it in a cup of boiling water. Concentrated stock, undiluted, makes a wonderful and very low-fat flavor addition to stir-fries, sauces, and plain steamed vegetables.

Concentrating stock takes time, however. Before beginning, you should strain and defat the stock. At that point, you can boil it down, stirring now and then and keeping an eye on things to prevent burning—which can occur when the mixture becomes very thick. And be aware that reducing, for example, a gallon to a quart takes a while—up to an hour; if you begin with three or four gallons, the time you'll need is even longer, of course. To speed the process, use the broadest pot you have, or divide the stock among two or more pots, so more of the liquid is exposed to the air, where it will evaporate more quickly.

Canned Stock and Bouillon Cubes

Canned stock—usually chicken, but sometimes beef and even vegetable—is far, far better than nothing, and the right canned stock is far better than the wrong one. Unfortunately, every tasting of canned stocks I've attended has come up with different results. I don't know whether manufacturers change their recipe annually or whether their stocks are subject to inexplicable fluctuations in quality. But to find a good stock, you must taste several, and then lay in a supply of the one you find best. I will offer these pointers, however:

- Low-salt canned stock tends to have more flavor than the "regular" varieties.
- Stock containing MSG should be avoided at all costs.

- Brand names are no guarantee of quality. The best stock I purchased last year was an off-brand that cost twenty-five cents a can. (Which, incidentally, meant that a gallon cost about three dollars, still more expensive than making decent stock from scratch.)

As for bouillon cubes, forget it. You're better off with water and a few extra vegetables.

The Basics of Soup

As you'll see from the recipes that begin on page 51, soup can be made with or without stock. There are some additional issues to consider:

Preparing foods for soup If you are going to puree vegetables to thicken soup or to make a creamy soup, it doesn't matter much how you cut them. It does, however, help to cut them to about the same size so they all finish cooking at the same time. If, however, you're going to leave whole cubes of vegetables or meat in the soup, keep two things in mind: Uniform cutting will allow the foods to cook evenly, so that your potatoes and carrots are both tender, instead of one being mushy while the other is still hard. And uniform cutting into small pieces will allow you to eat the soup elegantly, without either cutting in the bowl or cramming too-large pieces of food into your mouth. See the illustrations in "Vegetables" (pages 529–617) for vegetable-cutting techniques.

Using leftovers in soup One of my first cooking teachers made cream-of-something-or-other almost every night with leftover vegetables. She combined the vegetables with stock and seasonings, pureed, and reheated, sometimes with cream, sometimes with milk or yogurt, sometimes with nothing. This is a great idea, but remember one thing: Rinse off unwanted seasonings with boiling water before

beginning. That leftover broccoli may be great, but do you really want chili-vinaigrette in your soup? You get the idea.

Almost any leftover whose flavor does not conflict with the basic seasonings of your soup is fair game: pasta, rice, even bread (see below); meat, fish, or poultry; vegetables, even those such as mashed potatoes, which can blend in nicely.

Thickening soup Although thickening is no longer considered essential, it adds a sense of luxury in many instances. There are four types of thickeners:

- **Eggs:** These lend superb creaminess and a nice richness to soup. Because they've largely fallen from favor, you'll find few recipes containing eggs in this chapter. But there are two ways to use them: If you just stir some beaten eggs into soup, you'll get what amounts to egg drop soup. The eggs coagulate, are readily identifiable, and add a certain meatiness to many soups; it's a nice method.

  The classic way to use eggs as a thickener is to beat a couple of yolks, then stir some of the hot soup into the yolks, then gradually add the yolks back into the soup. Treated this way, the eggs do a beautiful job of building up the body of the soup. But it's largely cosmetic. Given that you probably don't get to eat as many eggs as you would really like to anyway, I'd save them for breakfast.
- **Cream:** Thick cream, sour cream, crème fraîche (page 671), or yogurt all can be added to adjust the body of any soup, as long as you don't mind the added calories and like the flavor. Add a little at a time and proceed with care, tasting frequently, especially with yogurt, which can quickly overwhelm subtle flavors.
- **Flour and cornstarch:** You can thicken a soup by adding flour in the early stages (just sprinkle a

tablespoon or more on the vegetables during the initial cooking) or by adding cornstarch (mix one tablespoon of cornstarch with two tablespoons of water or stock) at the end. Either will thicken a soup. But I don't see the reason for it, since neither adds flavor. I imagine it came about during those times when more expensive thickeners, such as eggs, vegetables, or grains, were in short supply.

• **Rice, potatoes, and bread:** You need a thickener in pureed soups, if for no other reason than because thin purees are depressing and meager-looking. But all you need to do to ensure that your puree will be pleasantly thick is to add a potato to the mix, or about one-half cup of rice, or a slice or two of bread (the bread can be added just a few minutes before pureeing). Any of these will give soup the creamy richness you're looking for.

Pureeing soup The advent of the blender (including the handheld immersion blender) has made it possible to puree almost any vegetable soup, and many others as well. (As it happens, however, a hand-cranked food mill is usually just as easy.) Thicken purees as described above and, if you like, stir in some cream, milk, half-and-half, yogurt, sour cream, or crème fraîche—any liquid dairy product can be used to enrich and adjust the thickness of purees. If your puree is too thick, stir in some water or, better still, half-and-half, which will add flavor, enhance texture, and thin the soup out all at the same time. If your puree is too thin (maybe you should have added that potato after all), stir in some thick cream, such as heavy cream or sour cream; it will add flavor and make the soup a little thicker.

It's worth noting that, except for the guilt induced by its fat content, heavy cream is almost always preferable. It adds great flavor and texture, and you don't

need much—one-half cup, or even less, is usually enough to have a wonderful impact on six cups of soup (of course more has even more of an impact).

Heating stock for use in soup Most soups begin by cooking some meat or vegetables, then adding stock or water. If you heat the stock or water while you prepare the solid ingredients, you will cut your cooking time, usually by as much as ten or fifteen minutes. For that reason, when I list stock as an ingredient in soups, I write, "preferably warmed." You can add ice-cold stock, of course, if you would rather not dirty an extra pot.

Adding pasta to soup Most soups rely on starches such as rice, pasta, or bread for body. But pasta, especially, is sometimes better cooked in separate water. Large amounts of pasta absorb so much water and give off so much starch that cooking it directly in a soup may change the character entirely. (There is nothing wrong with this, of course, but you should be aware of it.) My sometime preference, then, is to precook large amounts of noodles before adding them to soup. When, however, you're adding a little small pasta to soup—such as a few tablespoons of orzo—just cook it directly in the simmering broth, stirring frequently.

Storing Many soups can be made in advance, or at least partly so; I've noted the best time to interrupt cooking, if there is one. Generally, I don't recommend refrigerating or freezing any soup once you've added starches such as rice and pasta. Since they continue to absorb water, even during storage, they break down, losing all of their texture and thickening the soup unnecessarily (of course if you like these qualities, go right ahead). Nor should you store soups with dairy products, which are likely to curdle when reheated. Other soups, however, freeze brilliantly for a month or more, and there's rarely a reason not to double or even quadruple a given recipe to reserve some for future eating.

Quickest Chicken Stock

Makes 3 quarts

Time: 40 minutes to 1 hour

This stock has three distinct advantages: One, it takes less than an hour to make. Two, it has clear, clean flavor—not especially complex, but very good. And three, it gives you a whole cooked—but not overcooked—chicken, for salad or any other use.

1 whole (3- to 4-pound) chicken, rinsed and patted dry with paper towels
1 cup roughly chopped onion (don't bother to peel it)
1 cup chopped carrot
1/2 cup roughly chopped celery
1 sprig fresh thyme or pinch dried thyme
1/2 bay leaf
Several sprigs fresh parsley
1 teaspoon salt, plus more if necessary
About 3 1/2 quarts (14 cups) water

1   Cut the chicken up if you like; it will speed cooking.

2   Combine all ingredients except the water in a stockpot; add the water.

3   Bring just about to a boil, then partially cover and adjust the heat so the mixture sends up a few bubbles at a time. Cook just until the chicken is done, 30 to 60 minutes.

4   Strain, pressing on the vegetables and meat to extract as much juice as possible. Taste and add salt if necessary.

5   Refrigerate, then skim any hardened fat from the surface. Refrigerate for 4 to 5 days (longer if you boil it every third day, which will prevent spoiling), or freeze.

Chicken Stock with Ginger: Use this combination of ingredients in any other stock that you plan to use for Chinese-style cooking, or for any stock in which you want some extra flavor: Add to the mix 10 1/8-inch-thick slices of unpeeled fresh ginger and 2 cloves of unpeeled garlic. Omit the thyme and bay leaf. Also good, but optional, are the additions of 2 tablespoons dry sherry and 1 star anise, and the substitution of scallions for the onion.

Full-Flavored Chicken Stock

Makes 3 quarts

Time: 3 hours or more, largely unattended

This is a much richer stock, the kind that will solidify when refrigerated. Don't use cooked, meatless chicken bones by themselves or the stock will lack a meaty flavor. But a combination of bones and meat, or raw, meaty bones alone, is fine. You can also include some precooked chicken in the mix.

3 to 4 pounds chicken parts and/or bones, rinsed and patted dry with paper towels
1 cup roughly chopped onion (don't bother to peel it)
1 cup roughly chopped carrot
1/2 cup roughly chopped celery
1 sprig fresh thyme or pinch dried thyme
1/2 bay leaf
Several sprigs fresh parsley
1 teaspoon salt, plus more if necessary
About 4 quarts water (16 cups)

1   Combine all ingredients in a stockpot.

2   Bring just about to a boil, then partially cover and adjust the heat so the mixture sends up a few bubbles at a time. Cook until the meat falls from the bones and the bones separate from one another, at least 2 hours.

3   Strain, pressing on the vegetables and meat to extract as much juice as possible. Taste and add salt if necessary.

4 Refrigerate, then skim any hardened fat from the surface. Refrigerate for 4 to 5 days (longer if you boil it every third day, which will keep it from spoiling), or freeze.

Darker, Richer Chicken Stock

Makes 3 quarts

Time: 3½ hours or more, largely unattended

Roasting the bones first darkens the color and adds another dimension of flavor. This is a great stock for pan reductions and for very hearty soups, but be aware that it can overwhelm mild ingredients in light soups.

1 pound veal bones (optional)
3 to 4 pounds chicken parts and/or bones, rinsed and patted dry with paper towels
1 large onion, quartered (don't bother to peel it)
2 or 3 carrots, peeled and cut in half
2 celery stalks, cut in half
½ pound mushrooms, trimmed (optional)
1 sprig fresh thyme or pinch dried thyme
½ bay leaf
Several sprigs fresh parsley
1 teaspoon salt, plus more if necessary
3 quarts water (12 cups), plus 4 cups water

1 Preheat the oven to 500°F. Place the veal bones, chicken parts and bones, onion, carrots, celery, and mushrooms in a large roasting pan and put the pan in the oven. Roast, shaking the pan occasionally and turning the ingredients once or twice, until everything is nicely browned. This will take at least 30 minutes; don't rush it.

2 Use a slotted spoon to scoop all the ingredients into a stockpot; add the remaining ingredients and 3 quarts of the water. Turn the heat to high.

3 Pour off most of the fat from the roasting pan. Place the roasting pan over a burner set to high and add 2 to 4 cups of water, depending on the depth of the pan. Bring it to a boil and cook, scraping off all the bits of food that have stuck to the bottom. Pour this mixture into the stockpot (along with 2 more cups of water if you only used 2 cups for the reduction).

4 Bring the contents of the stockpot just about to a boil, then partially cover and adjust the heat so the mixture sends up a few bubbles at a time. Cook until the meat falls from the bones and the bones separate from one another, at least 2 hours.

5 Strain, pressing on the vegetables and meat to extract as much juice as possible. Taste and add salt if necessary.

6 Refrigerate, then skim any hardened fat from the surface. Refrigerate for 4 to 5 days (longer if you boil it every third day, which will prevent it from spoiling), or freeze.

Vastly Improved Canned Chicken Broth

Makes about 3 cups

Time: 20 minutes

There are three big problems with many canned broths: One, they're too salty. Two, they contain MSG, a "flavor-enhancer" you don't need or want. And three, they're weak. The first two problems can be solved by good shopping: Buy "low-sodium" varieties and avoid those containing MSG (fortunately, the two sometimes go hand in hand). The third can only be fixed by adding flavor boosts. Ideally, you'd simmer a few chicken bones in the stock, but let's assume you don't have those. In that case, do what follows: When you're done, you'll have a stock that will make a perfectly suitable chicken-rice or chicken-noodle soup, or the base for any other soup using chicken stock, or a good stock for risotto.

About 4 cups low-sodium chicken broth
1 carrot, peeled and cut into thin slices
1 small-to-medium onion, roughly chopped
(don't bother to peel it)
1 clove garlic, unpeeled
3 peppercorns
Several sprigs fresh parsley, if you have them
Salt and freshly ground black pepper to taste

1 Combine all ingredients in a medium saucepan; bring just about to a boil. Turn the heat a little lower and simmer, uncovered, for about 15 minutes.

2 Strain, then taste and adjust seasonings as necessary.

Vastly Improved Chicken Broth, Chinese-Style: Start with 2 cans broth, as above, and combine them with 2 tablespoons soy sauce; 2 scallions, trimmed and cut into 1-inch lengths; and 1 or 2 thin slices of unpeeled fresh ginger or $1/2$ teaspoon ground ginger. Simmer for 10 minutes, then add 1 tablespoon dark sesame oil. Adjust seasonings as necessary.

Egg Drop Soup: Stir a beaten egg or two into Vastly Improved Chicken Broth, Chinese-Style, and garnish with watercress.

Basic Beef Stock

Makes 4 quarts

Time: At least 3 hours, largely unattended

If you like, roast the beef and vegetables first, as in the recipe for Darker, Richer Chicken Stock, above. The resulting stock will be very dark brown, perfect for

Onion Soup (page 53), Beef and Vegetable Soup (page 56), and the like.

3 to 4 pounds meaty beef bones, such as shank
or shin, tail, or short ribs
1 cup roughly chopped onion (don't bother to peel it)
1 cup roughly chopped carrot
1 cup roughly chopped celery
2 parsnips, peeled and chopped (optional)
2 sprigs fresh thyme or $1/4$ teaspoon dried thyme
1 bay leaf
At least 10 sprigs fresh parsley
1 teaspoon salt, plus more if necessary
3 or 4 cloves
10 peppercorns
About 4 quarts water (16 cups)

1 Combine all ingredients in a stockpot.

2 Bring just about to a boil, then partially cover and adjust the heat so the mixture sends up a few bubbles at a time. Cook until the meat falls from the bones and the bones separate from one another, 2 to 3 hours.

3 Strain, pressing on the vegetables and meat to extract as much juice as possible. Taste and add salt if necessary.

4 Refrigerate, then skim any hardened fat from the surface. Refrigerate for 4 to 5 days (longer if you boil it every third day, which will keep it from spoiling), or freeze.

The Basics of Fish Stock

There are differences between fish stock and other stocks. For one thing, not all fish is suitable for stock, at least not for general purposes; stick with the heads and bones of white, mild-flavored fish if you want an all-purpose stock. (If, on the other hand, you want a stock to complement a salmon dish, by all means make salmon stock.) For another, fish yields its flavor almost instantly; fifteen to thirty minutes is plenty of time to simmer fish for a stock. Finally, the gills and innards do not have desirable flavor; remove them before cooking. Fish stocks are best made with heads, "racks" (skeletons), and meaty bones.

Fast Fish Stock

Makes 4 cups

Time: 30 minutes

This is a light, all-purpose fish stock that you can make whenever you have just filleted a fish, or when a fishmonger is able to give you a couple of heads and some skeletons. For more flavor, add some mushrooms (stems are fine), parsley, leeks, and, just before using, a tablespoon or two of butter or olive oil.

1 medium-to-large onion, quartered (don't bother
   to peel it)
1 carrot, peeled and cut into chunks
1 clove garlic, lightly crushed
10 peppercorns
1 teaspoon salt, plus more if necessary
1/2 cup dry white wine (optional)
At least 1 pound fish heads (gills removed) and/or
   skeletons, taken from white-fleshed fish
About 1 quart water (4 cups)

1. Combine all ingredients in a stockpot.
2. Bring just about to a boil, then partially cover and adjust the heat so that the mixture sends up a few bubbles at a time. Cook at a slow simmer for 20 minutes.
3. Strain, pressing on the vegetables and fish to extract as much juice as possible. Taste and add salt if necessary. Cool to room temperature and refrigerate

for 2 to 3 days (longer if you boil it every second day, which will prevent spoiling), or freeze.

Flavorful Fish and Vegetable Stock

Makes about 4 quarts

Time: About 1 hour

This is a strong, fresh-tasting base for any fish soup.

4 to 5 pounds assorted fish heads (gills removed),
   skeletons, and scraps, taken from white-fleshed fish
3 or 4 tomatoes, roughly chopped (canned are fine;
   include their liquid)
3 carrots, peeled and cut into chunks
2 medium onions or 1 large onion, quartered
   (don't bother to peel them)
2 celery stalks, cut into chunks
3 cloves garlic, unpeeled
1 clove
10 peppercorns
2 bay leaves
2 or 3 sprigs fresh thyme or 1/2 teaspoon dried thyme
1/2 cup roughly chopped fresh parsley (some stems
   are fine)
2 tablespoons olive oil
1 cup dry white wine
Salt and freshly ground black pepper to taste
1/2 lemon, rind and all
About 4 quarts water (16 cups)

1. Combine all ingredients in a stockpot.
2. Bring just about to a boil, then partially cover and adjust the heat so the mixture sends up a few bubbles at a time. Cook at a slow simmer for 45 minutes.
3. Strain, then taste and add salt if necessary. Cool to room temperature and refrigerate for 2 to 3 days (longer if you boil it every second day), or freeze.

Shrimp Stock

Makes 4 cups

Time: 20 minutes

The absolute easiest, best-tasting, most useful stock you can possibly make from something you might otherwise throw away, terrific for risotto, pasta sauces, and as a substitute for fish and even light chicken stock. Make a small batch every time you peel shrimp, or freeze shrimp shells as you accumulate them and make a large batch at once.

Shells from 1 to 2 pounds shrimp, about 4 loosely
   packed cups
1 teaspoon salt, plus more if necessary
About 4 1/2 cups water

1 Combine the shrimp shells, salt, and water in a small-to-medium saucepan. Bring to a boil, then turn the heat to very low and cover.

2 Cook for 15 minutes. Cool a bit. Strain, pressing on the shells to extract as much juice as possible; taste and adjust seasoning. Use, refrigerate for 2 to 3 days (longer if you boil it every second day, which will prevent spoiling), or freeze.

Vegetable Stock

Makes 3 quarts

Time: About 1 1/2 hours, largely unattended

There is really only one rule I slavishly follow when making vegetable stock, and that is to roast the vegetables before simmering them. The browning adds body and flavor that you don't get otherwise. Aside from that, you can substitute freely among these vegetables. Only leeks or onions, carrots, and celery are truly essential.

2 well-washed leeks, cut in half, or 2 large onions,
   quartered (don't bother to peel them)
4 carrots, peeled and cut in half
2 celery stalks, cut in half
2 parsnips, peeled and cut in half (optional)
2 white turnips, peeled and quartered (optional)
2 potatoes, peeled or well washed and quartered
   (optional; use these if you don't use the parsnips
   or turnips)
6 cloves garlic or 3 shallots, unpeeled
1 cup mushrooms, trimmed, or mushroom stems,
   or 1/4 cup reconstituted dried mushrooms with
   their soaking liquid
4 tablespoons extra-virgin olive oil
10 sprigs fresh parsley
2 or 3 sprigs fresh thyme
10 peppercorns
1/2 cup white wine
Salt to taste
2 quarts water (8 cups), plus 4 cups water

1 Preheat the oven to 400°F. Place the leeks, carrots, celery, parsnips, turnips, potatoes, garlic, and fresh mushrooms (hold off on adding reconstituted dried mushrooms) in a large roasting pan and drizzle with the olive oil; put the pan in the oven.

2 Roast, shaking the pan occasionally and turning the ingredients once or twice, until everything is nicely browned. This will take about 45 minutes; don't rush it.

3 Use a slotted spoon to scoop all the ingredients into a stockpot; add the remaining ingredients and the 2 quarts of water. Turn the heat to high.

4 Place the roasting pan over a burner set to high and add 2 to 4 cups of water, depending on the depth of the pan. Bring it to a boil and cook, scraping off all the bits of food that have stuck to the bottom. Pour this mixture into the stockpot (along with 2 more cups of water if you only used 2 cups for deglazing).

If you want a stock with clean flavor, use the recipes above and keep things simple. If, however, you want stocks in which one or more flavors shine, add one or more of these ingredients, many of which you'll have on hand anyway:

1. A whole head of garlic, left intact, which will lend a distinctive but mellow flavor
2. Dried seaweed, especially kelp or arame (page 602), which will give a pleasant brininess
3. Cleaned trimmings of any vegetable, as long as you're aware that those such as broccoli, asparagus, and beets will change not only the flavor but the color

4. Stems of light, bright-flavored herbs such as parsley, dill, or chervil, or small amounts of other herbs, such as thyme or tarragon
5. Wine, usually about one cup per gallon
6. Vinegar, usually about one tablespoon per gallon
7. Whole spices, fresh or dried, such as ginger, galangal, juniper berries, allspice, cloves, and so on—keep the amounts very small (such as a single clove, or a small chunk of ginger) until you have had some experience with this.
8. Dried mushrooms, or the stems of fresh mushrooms

5 Bring the contents of the stockpot just about to a boil, then partially cover and adjust the heat so the mixture sends up a few bubbles at a time. Cook until the vegetables are very soft, 30 to 45 minutes.

6 Strain, pressing on the vegetables to extract as much juice as possible. Taste and add salt if necessary.

7 Refrigerate, then skim any hardened fat from the surface if you like. Refrigerate for 4 to 5 days (longer if you boil it every third day, which will prevent spoiling), or freeze.

Vegetable Soups

Vegetable soups can be made without meat stock, and there are two good reasons to do so: One is if you have none. The other is if there are vegetarians present. In most other instances, you'll use meat stock. But it's the rare soup that cannot be made with water when no heartier liquid is available (or, of course, Vegetable Stock, page 50). Few vegetable soups are not improved by the addition of croutons (page 82).

"Boiled Water"

Makes 4 servings

Time: 20 minutes

The simplest soup imaginable, and very good. If you have chicken stock handy, move on to the next recipe.

4 cups water
6 to 10 cloves garlic, lightly crushed
1 bay leaf
Salt and freshly ground black pepper to taste
$1/4$ cup extra-virgin olive oil
4 thick slices French or Italian bread (slightly stale bread is fine)
$1/2$ cup freshly grated Parmesan or Pecorino Romano cheese
Minced fresh parsley leaves for garnish

1 Combine the first four ingredients in a saucepan or stockpot and bring to a boil. Cover partially and turn the heat to very low. Simmer gently for 15 minutes.

2 While the soup is cooking, place the olive oil in a large skillet over medium heat. Brown the slices of bread in the oil, turning occasionally, for a total of about 5 minutes.

3 Put the bread in bowls and top with the grated cheese. Strain the soup into the bowls, garnish, and serve.

Roasted Garlic Soup

Makes 4 servings

Time: 30 minutes

This basic, simple garlic soup will warm any winter dinner. Good stock makes all the difference here.

    4 tablespoons olive oil
    8 cloves garlic, peeled
    1 tablespoon ground cumin or paprika or 1 teaspoon
        chili powder
    4 thick slices French or Italian bread (slightly stale
        bread is fine)
    4 cups chicken, beef, or vegetable stock, preferably
        warmed
    Salt and freshly ground black pepper to taste
    Minced fresh parsley leaves for garnish

1 Place the olive oil in a large, deep saucepan and turn the heat to medium. Add the garlic cloves and cook, stirring and turning occasionally, until they are golden brown. Stir in the spice and cook, stirring, for about a minute.

2 Remove the garlic cloves and set them aside; turn the heat to medium-low. Add the bread and brown on both sides, for a total of about 5 minutes. Remove it.

3 Pour the stock into the saucepan and bring it to a simmer. Add the salt and pepper and let the flavors mingle for a few minutes over low heat. Chop the garlic coarsely and return it to the pot.

4 Place 1 piece of bread in each of four bowls. Top with some of the soup, garnish, and serve.

Garlic Soup with Spinach and Tomatoes: After removing the bread in Step 2, add 5 to 6 plum tomatoes, cored, peeled, seeded, and chopped if fresh, or just chopped if canned (don't bother to drain them). Cook stirring, for a minute or two longer, until they begin to break up. Add the stock, bring to a boil, lower the heat, and simmer for about 5 minutes. Meanwhile, remove the thickest stems from 8 to 10 ounces of spinach; wash it well and chop it coarsely. Add the spinach to the pot and cook for 3 or 4 minutes. Finish as above and serve.

Garlic Soup with Rice or Orzo and Peas: After removing the garlic in Step 2, substitute $1/2$ cup orzo or long-grain rice for the bread. Cook, stirring, for 30 seconds, or just long enough to coat the orzo or rice with oil. Add the stock as in Step 3, and cook, stirring occasionally, until the rice or orzo is tender, 10 to 15 minutes. Add $1/2$ cup fresh or thawed frozen peas. Finish as above and serve.

Lime and Garlic Soup

Makes 4 servings

Time: 30 minutes

Two great flavors combine in this Mexican soup, which takes a variety of forms. Add a little heat, in the form of ground cayenne, if you like. You can also add diced boneless chicken during the last ten minutes of cooking.

    2 tablespoons peanut or other oil
    $1/4$ cup minced garlic
    6 cups chicken, beef, or vegetable stock
    2 cups cored, peeled, seeded, and diced tomatoes
        (canned are fine; drain them first)
    $1/4$ cup freshly squeezed lime juice
    Salt and freshly ground black pepper to taste
    Cayenne (optional)

1 Place the peanut oil in the bottom of a large, deep saucepan or Dutch oven and turn the heat to medium. Add the garlic and stir. Cook, stirring occasionally, just until the garlic becomes blond, about 5 minutes.

2 Add the stock and tomatoes and turn the heat to medium-high. Cook, stirring, until the mixture boils, then turn the heat down to a minimum. Stir in the lime juice and salt and pepper. Add more salt, pepper, and/or lime juice if necessary, as well as a pinch or two of cayenne if you like. Serve immediately.

Miso Soup
Makes 4 servings

Time: 15 minutes

Best made with flakes of dried bonito (a dark, full-flavored fish) and kelp (a strong-flavored sea vegetable, page 602), both of which are readily available at every Asian market, this is still quite delicious without them.

> 4 cups water or chicken stock
> 1 (3- or 4-inch) piece kelp (optional; or use chicken stock)
> 1/4 cup (approximately) dried bonito flakes (optional; or use chicken stock)
> 2 tablespoons miso, any variety
> 1/2 pound silken or soft tofu or cooked chicken, cut into small cubes (optional)
> 2 scallions, finely minced

1 Place the water and kelp in a small saucepan and bring to a boil; turn the heat to the lowest possible setting (the broth should stay hot but not boil from this point on). Put the bonito flakes in a tea ball or bag made of cheesecloth and place in the pan. Let sit for 5 minutes, then remove the kelp and bonito. If you are using chicken stock, omit the kelp, bonito flakes, and water, and begin by heating the chicken stock to the boiling point and then turning the heat to very low.

2 Put the miso in a small bowl; add 2 or 3 tablespoons of the broth and blend with a fork or small wire whisk until it is smooth.

3 Stir the miso mixture into the soup.

4 Add the tofu or chicken and scallions. Let sit for 1 minute before serving.

Miso Soup with Spinach and Mushrooms: A hearty version of Miso Soup. Remove the thickest stems from 8 to 10 ounces of spinach; wash it well and chop it coarsely. At the end of Step 1, add the spinach to the soup. At the same time, trim and slice 6 fresh shiitake mushrooms and sauté in 1 tablespoon peanut oil over medium-high heat until slightly crisp and wilted. Remove a bit of the soup and mix it with the miso as above; stir in the cooked mushrooms and return the mixture to pan with soup. Omit tofu, and garnish with several thin slivers of lemon peel in place of the scallions.

Onion Soup
Makes 4 servings

Time: About 1 hour

This onion soup has a thin coating of good cheese rather than the more common gobs of mozzarella or Cheddar. It's light but incredibly deep in flavor.

> 4 tablespoons (1/2 stick) butter
> 4 large onions, thinly sliced (about 6 cups)
> 5 cups beef or chicken stock, preferably warmed
> 2 or 3 sprigs fresh thyme or pinch dried thyme
> 2 or 3 sprigs fresh parsley
> Salt and freshly ground black pepper to taste
> 2 tablespoons cognac (optional)
> 4 croutons (page 82), made with bread slices and butter
> 1 cup freshly grated Parmesan cheese

1 Melt the butter in a large, deep saucepan or casserole over medium heat. Add the onions and cook, stirring occasionally, until very soft and beginning to brown, 30 to 45 minutes.

2 Add the stock, turn the heat to medium-high, and bring just about to a boil. Turn down the heat so that the mixture sends up a few bubbles at a time. Add the seasoning herbs, salt, pepper, and cognac and cook for 15 minutes. Preheat the oven to 400°F. Fish out the parsley and thyme sprigs, if any. (You may prepare the soup in advance up to this point; cover and refrigerate for up to 2 days, then reheat before proceeding.)

3 Place a crouton in each of four ovenproof bowls. Add a portion of soup and top with cheese. Place the bowls in a roasting pan or on a sturdy baking sheet and bake for 10 minutes, or until the cheese melts. Serve immediately.

Kale and Potato Soup

Makes 4 servings

Time: 30 minutes

Kale soup, a Portuguese specialty, is frequently spiced with sausage or thickened with cream. Here, however, its assertive flavor is complemented by marjoram, and pureed potato adds a pleasant texture without fat or meat.

1 large baking potato, cut into eighths
1 clove garlic, lightly smashed
5 cups chicken, beef, or vegetable stock, or water,
  preferably warmed
About 3 cups roughly chopped kale leaves (stripped
  from the stalks and well rinsed before chopping)
1 teaspoon fresh marjoram or oregano leaves
  or ½ teaspoon dried marjoram or oregano
1 bay leaf
Salt and freshly ground black pepper to taste

1 Combine the potato, garlic, and 2 cups of the stock or water in a medium saucepan and turn the heat to medium-high. Cook until the potato is soft, about 15 minutes; cool slightly. (You may prepare the soup in advance up to this point. Cover, refrigerate for up to 2 days, and reheat before proceeding.)

2 At the same time, cook the kale in the remaining stock or water with the marjoram and bay leaf until tender, about 10 minutes. Remove the bay leaf.

3 Puree the potato, garlic, and stock or water together; the mixture will be thick. Stir it into the simmering kale, season with salt and pepper, and heat through. Serve immediately.

Kale Soup with Soy and Lime

Makes 4 servings

Time: About 20 minutes

An Asian-spiced soup that is fast and really delicious. Use fish sauce (*nuoc mam* or *nam pla,* available at Asian markets) instead of soy sauce if you have some.

2 tablespoons peanut oil
1 cup minced onion
2 tablespoons minced garlic
4 cups chicken, beef, or vegetable stock,
  or water, preferably warmed
1 tablespoon soy sauce
Salt to taste
About 3 cups roughly chopped kale leaves
  (stripped from the stalks and well rinsed)
Minced cilantro leaves for garnish
1 fresh jalapeño chile, stemmed and minced
  (optional)
1 lime, cut into eighths

1 Place the oil in a large, deep saucepan and turn the heat to medium-high. Add the onion and cook, stirring occasionally, until it begins to brown, 5 to 8 minutes.

2 When the onion is tender and golden, add the garlic. Cook 1 minute, then add the stock or water. Bring to a boil, turn the heat to low, add the soy sauce, and taste for salt; add some if necessary.

3 Add the kale to the simmering broth and cook until it is nice and tender, about 10 minutes. (You may prepare the soup in advance up to this point. Cover, refrigerate for up to 2 days, and reheat before proceeding.) Correct the seasoning (you may prefer to add more soy sauce rather than more salt), garnish, and serve, passing the minced jalapeño and pieces of lime at the table.

Cabbage Soup, Three Ways

Makes 4 servings

Time: About 45 minutes

This North European staple can always be improved by using Savoy cabbage in place of tight green head cabbage. For a thicker, more substantial soup, see the second variation.

> 1 small head green, Savoy, or Napa cabbage, about 1¹/₂ pounds
> 4 tablespoons (¹/₂ stick) butter or 3 tablespoons extra-virgin olive oil
> 1 large onion, sliced
> Salt and freshly ground black pepper to taste
> 2 tablespoons brown sugar
> ¹/₄ teaspoon ground allspice
> 5 cups chicken, beef, or vegetable stock, or water, preferably warmed
> Freshly squeezed lemon juice or white wine or rice vinegar to taste

1 Core and shred the cabbage (see page 547 for illustrations). Place the butter or oil in a large, deep saucepan or casserole and turn the heat to medium. When the butter melts or the oil is hot, add the cabbage, onion, salt, and pepper. Cook, stirring, until both the onion and cabbage are tender but not brown—turn the heat down a little if necessary—at least 20 minutes.

2 Stir in the sugar and allspice and cook, stirring, for 1 minute. Add the stock or water and cook, stirring occasionally, for about 15 minutes. (You may prepare the soup in advance up to this point. Cover, refrigerate for up to 2 days, and reheat before proceeding.)

3 Add a tablespoon or two of lemon juice, then taste and adjust seasoning. Serve hot.

Cabbage Soup, Asian-Style: Use Napa cabbage if possible. Cook the cabbage and onion in peanut or other oil over medium-high heat; let the vegetables brown a bit as they become tender. In Step 2, add 1 tablespoon peeled and minced fresh ginger in place of the sugar and allspice. Add 2 tablespoons soy sauce with the stock or water. Finish as above, using a squeeze of freshly squeezed lime juice in place of lemon juice at the end.

Cabbage Soup with Potatoes and Tomatoes: In Step 1, add 2 medium-to-large waxy potatoes, peeled and cut into small cubes, along with the cabbage. Substitute scallions for the onion if possible; reserve some for garnish. Just before adding the stock or water in Step 2, stir in 2 or 3 ripe tomatoes, cored, peeled, seeded, and roughly chopped, or about 1¹/₂ cups canned plum tomatoes, with their liquid, along with 1 teaspoon fresh thyme leaves or ¹/₂ teaspoon dried thyme. Simmer, stirring occasionally, until the potatoes are tender and the tomatoes have fallen apart, about 30 minutes. Omit the sugar and allspice and adjust seasoning as above. Garnish with remaining scallion, and serve.

Minestrone

Makes 4 servings

Time: 45 minutes to 1 hour

Essentially, vegetable soup, best made with a little bit of prosciutto. Consider this recipe a series of suggestions, rather than something ironclad; you can make minestrone with any vegetables you have on hand.

 4 tablespoons extra-virgin olive oil
 1 medium onion, minced
 1 carrot, peeled and diced
 $^1/_2$ cup minced prosciutto or other ham (optional)
 4 cups assorted mixed vegetables, cut into small
   cubes if necessary: potatoes, carrots, corn, peas,
   string beans, cooked dried beans (cranberry beans,
   or *borlotti,* are traditional), celery, zucchini or
   summer squash, pumpkin or winter squash, leeks,
   parsnips, turnips, etc.
 Salt and freshly ground black pepper to taste
 5 cups chicken, beef, or vegetable stock, or water,
   preferably warmed
 10 sprigs fresh parsley, more or less
 1 cup cored, peeled, seeded, and chopped tomatoes
   (canned are fine; include their juice)
 Freshly grated Parmesan cheese

 1 Place 3 tablespoons of the oil in a large, deep saucepan or casserole and turn the heat to medium. A minute later, add the onion and carrot. Cook, stirring, until the onion softens, about 5 minutes. Add the ham if you're using it and cook, stirring, another 3 minutes.

 2 Add the remaining vegetables, season with salt and pepper (go easy on the salt if you've included ham), and cook, stirring, for 1 minute. Add the stock or water, parsley, and tomatoes and turn the heat to medium-low. Cook, stirring every now and then, until the vegetables are very soft, about 30 minutes. (You may prepare the soup in advance up to this point. Cover, refrigerate for up to 2 days, and reheat before proceeding.)

 3 Sprinkle with the remaining olive oil and serve, passing the cheese at the table.

Beef and Vegetable Soup: Replace the ham with $^1/_2$ pound minced beef (leftover beef stew is not only okay but preferable). Use beef stock if at all possible.

Mushroom Soup

Makes 4 servings

Time: 30 minutes

Make this with plain button mushrooms if you must, but be aware that it is immeasurably improved by the addition of reconstituted dried mushrooms or fresh "wild" mushrooms.

 2 ounces or more dried porcini mushrooms (optional;
   use if you have only button mushrooms for fresh)
 2 tablespoons butter or extra-virgin olive oil
 1 pound fresh mushrooms, preferably a combination,
   cleaned, trimmed, and sliced, the stems reserved
   for another use, a few slices reserved for garnish
 Salt and freshly ground black pepper to taste
 2 tablespoons minced shallots
 1 teaspoon minced garlic
 4 cups chicken, beef, or vegetable stock, preferably
   warmed
 Minced fresh parsley leaves for garnish

 1 If you are using dried mushrooms, soak them in hot water to cover for about 15 minutes while you prepare the other ingredients.

 2 Place the butter or oil in a large, deep saucepan or casserole and turn the heat to medium. When the butter melts or the oil is hot, add the fresh mushrooms and turn the heat to medium-high. Cook, stirring, for about 10 minutes, until they begin to brown. As they cook, drain the dried mushrooms if you're using them (strain and reserve their soaking liquid), and stir them into the mixture. Season the mushrooms with salt and pepper as they cook.

3 Add the shallots and garlic and cook, stirring, for 1 minute. Add the stock and reserved mushroom-soaking liquid and bring the mixture just about to a boil. (You may prepare the soup in advance up to this point. Cover, refrigerate for up to 2 days, and reheat before proceeding.) Turn off the heat, garnish, and serve.

Cream of Mushroom Soup: Couldn't be easier. Reduce the amount of stock by 1 cup. Add 1 tablespoon dry sherry (optional) along with the stock. Stir in 1 cup light or heavy cream or half-and-half just before serving, and heat through (do not boil). Garnish with snipped chives and sliced mushrooms.

Mushroom-Barley Soup

Makes at least 6 servings

Time: About 1 hour

This is a quick soup that is made without stock; with a loaf of bread, it makes a fine weeknight meal.

8 cups water
1 cup pearled barley
1 cup roughly chopped carrots
1 cup roughly chopped onion
1 cup roughly chopped parsnip
1/2 ounce dried porcini mushrooms
1 pound fresh mushrooms, any kind
Salt and freshly ground black pepper to taste
1/2 cup snipped fresh dill, minced chives, or minced parsley leaves

1 Put the water in a stockpot and bring to a boil. Add the barley, carrots, onion, and parsnip.

2 Turn the heat to low and partially cover; the mixture should be bubbling, but only a little. Soak the dried mushrooms in warm water to cover until tender (about 10 minutes), and clean, trim, and slice the fresh mushrooms.

3 Strain the soaked mushrooms; reserve their liquid. Add all the mushrooms to the simmering soup. Add the mushroom-soaking liquid to the soup. Simmer the soup for 30 to 45 minutes more, until the barley and vegetables are tender.

4 Taste and season with salt and pepper. Stir in half the dill, chives, or parsley, then top individual servings with the remaining herb.

Corn, Tomato, and Zucchini Soup with Basil

Makes 4 servings

Time: About 30 minutes

A fresh-tasting late-summer vegetable soup.

4 cups chicken or vegetable stock
4 ears fresh corn
2 tablespoons butter or olive oil
1 medium onion, minced
2 cups cored, peeled, seeded, and chopped tomatoes
2 small or 1 medium zucchini, about 1/2 pound, diced
1 tablespoon minced garlic
Salt and freshly ground black pepper to taste
1/2 cup minced fresh basil leaves
1 teaspoon balsamic or other flavorful vinegar, or to taste

1 Heat the stock in a large, deep saucepan. Strip the kernels from the corn (see illustration on page 564) and add the cobs to the stock (break them in half if necessary to fit them into the pot); let them simmer there while you prepare the other vegetables.

2 Place the butter or oil in a large, deep saucepan or casserole and turn the heat to medium. A minute later, add the onion and cook, stirring, until it begins to soften, about 5 minutes. Add the tomatoes, zucchini, garlic, salt, and pepper, and cook, stirring occasionally, for about 10 minutes.

3 Remove the corn cobs from the stock and add the stock to the vegetables. Cook until the zucchini is tender but not mushy, about 5 minutes. Stir in the corn kernels and most of the basil. Add the vinegar. Taste and adjust seasoning as necessary.

4 Serve, garnishing with remaining basil.

Tomato Soup, Three Ways

Makes 4 servings

Time: 30 minutes

Make this with fresh tomatoes in late summer. The rest of the year, use good canned tomatoes.

> 2 tablespoons extra-virgin olive oil or butter
> 1 large onion, sliced
> 1 carrot, peeled and diced
> Salt and freshly ground black pepper to taste
> 3 cups cored, peeled, seeded, and chopped tomatoes (canned are fine; include their juice)
> 1 teaspoon fresh thyme leaves or $1/2$ teaspoon dried thyme or 1 tablespoon minced fresh basil leaves
> 2 to 3 cups chicken, beef, or vegetable stock, preferably warmed
> Minced fresh parsley or basil leaves for garnish

1 Place the oil or butter in a large, deep saucepan or casserole and turn the heat to medium. A minute later, add the onion and carrot. Season with salt and pepper and cook, stirring, until the onion begins to soften, about 5 minutes.

2 Add the tomatoes and the herb and cook until the tomatoes break up, about 10 minutes. Add 2 cups

of stock. (You may prepare the soup in advance up to this point. Cover, refrigerate for up to 2 days, and reheat before proceeding.) Adjust seasoning; if the mixture is too thick, add a little stock or water. Garnish and serve.

Pureed Tomato Soup: Increase the tomatoes to 4 cups and reduce the stock to 1 cup. When the soup is done, puree it carefully in a blender or pass it through a food mill. Reheat, garnish, and serve, preferably with croutons (page 82).

Cream of Tomato Soup: In the above variation, substitute 1 cup cream or half-and-half for the stock, added just before pureeing.

Simple Potato Soup with Carrots

Makes 4 servings

Time: 30 minutes

The simplest of potato soups (well, not really—you could omit the carrots), still quite delicious. This is a soup you can build upon: Add cut-up turnips, diced tomatoes, or any other vegetables you like.

> 1 tablespoon butter or extra-virgin olive oil
> 3 medium potatoes, any type, peeled and cut into small cubes
> 3 carrots, peeled and cut into small cubes
> Salt and freshly ground black pepper to taste
> 4 cups chicken, beef, or vegetable stock, preferably warmed

1 Place the butter or oil in a large, deep saucepan or casserole and turn the heat to medium. When the butter melts or the oil is hot, add the vegetables. Season with salt and pepper and cook, stirring, for 2 or 3 minutes.

2 Add the stock and cook until the vegetables are very tender, about 20 minutes. (You may prepare the soup in advance up to this point. Cover, refrigerate for up to 2 days, and reheat before proceeding.) Adjust seasoning and serve.

Potato Soup with Leeks: Substitute 2 large leeks, well washed and chopped, for the carrots; or add the leeks in addition to the carrots. Proceed as above.

Pureed Potato Soup with Leeks: Make the above variation, with or without carrots. Add $^1/_2$ to 1 cup cream, milk, or half-and-half. Puree in a blender, then reheat. Adjust seasoning, garnish with minced chives, and serve.

Ten Simple Additions to Vegetable Soups

Not all vegetable soups are the same; I would not, for example, add croutons to Miso Soup (page 53). But here are some things to consider:

1. Any croutons (page 82)
2. Any grain, cooked in the soup or left over (rinse first to remove unwanted seasonings)
3. Any vegetable that will not greatly change the character of the soup
4. Small pieces of rind from Parmesan cheese, or grated cheese
5. Any leftover bits of meat
6. Freshly chopped herbs or quick-cooking greens
7. Any spice you like, from jalapeños or other chiles to lots of black pepper to curry powder or other spice mixtures (pages 777–779)
8. A drizzle of extra-virgin olive oil (or, for soups with Asian seasonings, dark sesame oil)
9. A swirl of pesto, especially in Italian soups
10. Leeks Braised in Butter or Oil (page 580)

Vichyssoise: Make above variation and chill thoroughly before garnishing with minced chives.

Potato Soup with Sorrel: Add 1 teaspoon garlic to the potatoes; omit the carrots. In Step 2, when the potatoes are quite soft, add 3 cups washed, trimmed, and roughly chopped sorrel leaves. Cook for 2 minutes, then serve, garnished with a little chopped sorrel. Or puree and serve hot or cold.

Creamy Soups

See Pureeing Soup, page 45. Creamy soups need not contain cream, but are almost always best when enriched by something other than flour. In the following recipes, soups are thickened with dairy products, rice, potatoes, bread, and eggs. All of these are rich and hearty, great cold-weather soups.

Creamy Watercress, Spinach, or Sorrel Soup

Makes 4 servings

Time: About 30 minutes

You need not puree this soup, or the variation, but doing so makes the texture wonderfully creamy.

    2 tablespoons butter
    4 cups coarsely chopped watercress, spinach,
        or sorrel, well washed and trimmed of thick stems
    2 cups chicken, beef, or vegetable stock, preferably
        warmed
    2 cups half-and-half or milk
    Salt and freshly ground black pepper to taste

1 Place the butter in a large, deep saucepan or casserole and turn the heat to medium. When the butter melts, add the cress or other green and cook, stirring, until it wilts, about 5 minutes.

2   Add the stock, bring almost to a boil, lower the heat, and cook briefly, until the green is tender.

3   Put through a sieve or food mill, or carefully puree in a blender. (You may prepare the soup in advance up to this point. Cover, refrigerate for up to 2 days, and reheat before proceeding.) Return to the heat and add the half-and-half or milk. Season to taste, reheat gently—do not boil—and serve.

Watercress Soup with Potatoes: This is a very thick soup; if you prefer a thinner consistency add more stock in place of the half-and-half or milk. In Step 1, before sautéing the greens, add 2 coarsely chopped potatoes and 1 coarsely chopped onion to the melted butter. Cover and cook over medium-low heat, stirring occasionally, until the onions and potatoes are nearly tender, about 15 minutes. Add the watercress and proceed as above.

Creamy Pumpkin or Winter Squash Soup, Version I

Makes 4 servings

Time: 45 minutes

This soup is what was once called meager: a few ingredients, one of which is water, and bread as a thickener. It's fast and delicious. The alternate version is far more luxurious (and, of course, higher in fat).

2 pounds pumpkin or winter squash, peeled, seeded, and cut into 1- to 2-inch cubes
6 cloves garlic, peeled
4 cups water
4 or 5 slices stale, crustless French or Italian bread
Salt and freshly ground black pepper to taste
Minced fresh parsley leaves for garnish

1   Combine the pumpkin and garlic in a large pot, along with the water (if you use stock the flavor will be better, but it is far from essential), and turn the heat to medium-high.

2   Bring to a boil, then turn the heat to medium-low and cook for about 30 minutes, until the pumpkin is very soft. (You may prepare the soup in advance up to this point. Cover, refrigerate for up to 2 days, and reheat before proceeding.)

3   Tear the bread into pieces and add them to the broth; cook 5 more minutes.

4   Puree the soup in a food mill or blender, reheat, and add salt and pepper. Garnish and serve.

Creamy Pumpkin or Winter Squash Soup, Version II

Makes 4 servings

Time: 45 minutes

A more complex and interesting version than that above, but no more difficult to prepare.

3 tablespoons butter
1 pound pumpkin or winter squash, peeled, seeded, and cut into 1- to 2-inch cubes
1 pound crisp tart apples, such as McIntosh or Granny Smith, peeled, cored, and roughly chopped
1 large onion, roughly chopped
Salt and freshly ground black pepper to taste
4 cups chicken, beef, or vegetable stock, or water, preferably warmed
1/2 cup dry white wine
1 teaspoon fresh tarragon leaves or 1/4 teaspoon dried tarragon
1 cup heavy or light cream
Minced fresh parsley leaves or snipped chives for garnish

1 Place the butter in a large, deep saucepan; turn the heat to medium. When it melts, add the pumpkin, apples, and onion. Cook, stirring, until the onion softens, 5 to 10 minutes. Season with salt and pepper.

2 Add the stock or water, wine, and tarragon; turn the heat to medium-high and bring to a boil. Turn the heat down to low, partially cover, and cook for about 30 minutes, until the pumpkin is very soft. Cool slightly, then puree the soup in a food mill or blender. (You may prepare the soup in advance up to this point. Cover, refrigerate for up to 2 days, and reheat before proceeding.)

3 Return it to the pan and cook gently over medium-low heat until heated through; do not boil. Stir in the cream and cook, stirring, until hot, about 1 minute (do not boil). Garnish and serve.

Spinach and Egg Soup

Makes 4 servings

Time: 20 minutes

Use watercress instead of spinach, peanut oil instead of butter, and a couple of tablespoons of soy sauce instead of nutmeg and Parmesan, and you've got egg drop soup. Who said Italy and China were far apart?

1 pound spinach, well washed and picked over
2 tablespoons butter
Salt and freshly ground black pepper to taste
Pinch freshly grated nutmeg
5 cups chicken, beef, or vegetable stock, or water, preferably warmed
2 eggs
At least $1/2$ cup freshly grated Parmesan cheese

1 Steam or simmer the spinach in a medium-to-large saucepan until it wilts (see recipe, page 604). Cool it under cold water, squeeze it dry, and chop it finely.

2 Place the butter in a large, deep saucepan and turn the heat to medium. When it melts, add the spinach, salt, pepper, and nutmeg. Add the stock or water and bring to a boil.

3 Turn the heat to medium so that the soup is bubbling but not furiously. Mix the eggs with about $1/2$ cup of cheese, then add them to the soup in a steady stream. You want the eggs to "scramble," not just to thicken the soup, but you don't want them to lump up, so stir constantly.

4 Cook, stirring occasionally, until the eggs are cooked and the soup is thick, 2 or 3 minutes. Serve with bread, passing more Parmesan at the table.

Egg and Herb Soup

Makes 4 servings

Time: 10 minutes

This is as fast as anything you can make.

4 cups chicken, beef, or vegetable stock, or water, preferably warmed
3 eggs
$1/2$ to 1 cup minced tender and mild but flavorful herbs: chervil, parsley, chives, basil, dill, and/or fennel leaves
2 tablespoons butter, softened
Salt and freshly ground black pepper to taste
Freshly grated Parmesan cheese

1 Put the stock or water in a large, deep saucepan and bring it to a boil over medium-high heat. Beat the eggs lightly in a bowl.

2 Turn the heat to medium so that the stock or water is bubbling but not furiously. Stir in the eggs, in a steady stream. You want the eggs to "scramble," not just to thicken the soup, but you don't want them to lump up, so stir constantly.

3 When the eggs are all added, stir in the herbs and the butter. As soon as the butter melts, adjust the seasoning and serve with the grated cheese.

Cream of Broccoli (or Any Vegetable) Soup

Makes 4 servings

Time: 30 minutes

There are thousands of recipes for true cream of vegetable soups, but the differences among them are subtle at best. Basically, you cook the vegetable you want with good flavorings until it's done. Then you puree it and reheat it with cream. (The addition of rice or potatoes makes the soup smooth and creamy without outrageous amounts of cream. One-quarter cup is enough to lighten the color and smooth the texture; one full cup lends an incomparable richness.)

The options:

• The original cooking liquid may be water or milk, but it's best if it is stock.
• The cream may be replaced by milk or yogurt— but again, it's best if it is cream.
• The seasonings can be varied infinitely: Use whatever fresh herbs appeal to you, and take advantage of spices as well—garlic, of course, but also chiles and Indian and Asian spices.

About 1 pound broccoli, trimmed and cut up
   (page 543), to yield about 4 loosely packed cups
   broccoli, or the equivalent amount of cauliflower,
   carrots, turnips, celery, or other vegetable
$1/2$ cup rice or 1 medium baking potato, peeled and
   cut into quarters
4 cups chicken, beef, or vegetable stock, or water
Salt and freshly ground black pepper to taste
$1/4$ to 1 cup heavy or light cream or half-and-half
Minced fresh parsley leaves or chives for garnish

Nineteen Soups You Can Easily Turn into a Meal

Some soups need very little to become a main course. Others might take a few more vegetables or some meat or fish. Very chunky soups become stews if you cook them long enough to reduce the ratio of liquid to solid. See Ten Simple Additions to Vegetable Soups, page 59, and Eight Simple Additions to Bean Soups, page 67, for many ideas about how to make soups heartier.

1. Kale and Potato Soup, page 54
2. Cabbage Soup with Potatoes and Tomatoes, page 55
3. Simple Potato Soup with Carrots, page 58
4. Potato Soup with Leeks, page 59
5. Mushroom-Barley Soup, page 57
6. Minestrone, page 56
7. Beef and Vegetable Soup, page 56
8. Lentil Soup, page 65
9. Simplest Split Pea Soup and its variations, page 65
10. White Bean Soup and its variations, pages 63–65
11. Pasta and Bean Soup (Pasta e Fagioli), page 66
12. Black Bean Soup, page 67
13. No-Holds-Barred Clam or Fish Chowder, page 69
14. Lightning-Quick Fish Soup, page 71
15. One-Hour Bouillabaisse, page 72
16. Cotriade, page 71
17. Hot-and-Sour Soup, page 76
18. Scotch Broth, page 77
19. Hanoi Noodle Soup, page 78

1 Combine the broccoli, rice or potato, and stock or water in a large, deep saucepan or casserole and turn the heat to medium-high. Bring to a boil, then lower the heat to medium and cook until the vegetables are very tender, about 15 minutes.

2 Cool slightly, then puree in a food mill or in a blender. (You may prepare the soup in advance up to this point. Cover, refrigerate for up to 2 days, and reheat before proceeding.)

3 Return to the pot and reheat over medium-low heat. Season with salt and pepper, then add the cream; heat through again, garnish, and serve.

Bean Soups

Bean soups can be made quickly as long as you have cooked beans, either in your freezer or in a can. But some care must be taken not to overcook precooked beans in soups. For more information about beans, see pages 499–505.

White Bean Soup

Makes 4 servings

Time: At least 1^1/$_2$ hours

Like Simplest Split Pea Soup, (page 65) this makes the transition from simple to complex quite readily.

1^1/$_2$ cups navy, pea, or other dried white beans, washed and picked over (see The Basics of Buying and Preparing Beans, page 500)
About 6 cups chicken, beef, or vegetable stock, or water, plus more if necessary
1 medium onion, quartered
2 tablespoons butter or extra-virgin olive oil (optional)
Salt and freshly ground black pepper to taste
Minced fresh parsley leaves for garnish

1 Place the beans, stock or water, and onion in a large, deep saucepan or casserole; turn the heat to medium-high. When it boils, turn the heat down to medium-low and cover partially. Cook, stirring occasionally, until the beans are very soft, at least 1 hour.

2 Put the mixture through a food mill or strainer, or puree it in a blender. (You may prepare the soup in advance up to this point. Cover, refrigerate for up to 2 days, and reheat before proceeding.) Reheat, adding more stock or water if necessary to achieve the consistency you like. Stir in the butter or oil, season with salt and pepper, garnish, and serve.

White Bean Soup with Vegetables

Makes 4 servings

Time: At least 1^1/$_2$ hours

Less pure than the preceding, but more flavorful. Vary the vegetables as you wish.

1 cup navy, pea, or other dried white beans, washed and picked over (see The Basics of Buying and Preparing Beans, page 500)
6 cups chicken, beef, or vegetable stock, or water, plus more if necessary
2 carrots, peeled and roughly chopped
1 medium turnip or parsnip, peeled and roughly chopped
1 potato, peeled and roughly chopped
1 celery stalk, roughly chopped
3 or 4 sprigs fresh parsley, plus minced fresh parsley leaves for garnish
^{1}/$_2$ teaspoon fresh rosemary or thyme leaves or ^{1}/$_4$ teaspoon dried
2 tablespoons butter or extra-virgin olive oil (optional)
Salt and freshly ground black pepper to taste

1 Place the beans and stock or water together in a large saucepan or casserole and turn the heat to medium-high; add the carrots, turnip, potato, celery, parsley, and herb. When it boils, turn the heat down to medium-low and cover partially. Cook, stirring occasionally, until the beans are very soft, at least 1 hour.

2 Put the mixture through a food mill or strainer, or puree it in a blender. (You may prepare the soup in advance up to this point. Cover, refrigerate for up to 2 days, and reheat before proceeding.) Reheat, adding more stock or water if necessary to achieve the consistency you like. Stir in the butter or oil, season with salt and pepper, garnish, and serve.

White Bean Soup with Ham

Makes 8 or more servings

Time: At least 1^1/$_2$ hours

Add a ham bone to White Bean Soup and proceed directly to heaven.

1 ham bone or 2 or 3 smoked ham hocks
3 cups navy, pea, or other dried white beans, washed and picked over (see The Basics of Buying and Preparing Beans, page 500)
12 cups chicken, beef, or vegetable stock, or water
2 medium onions, quartered
Salt and freshly ground black pepper to taste
Minced fresh parsley leaves for garnish

1 Place the ham bone, beans, and stock or water together in a large saucepan or casserole and turn the heat to medium-high; add the onions. When this boils, turn the heat down to medium-low and cover partially. Cook, stirring occasionally, until the beans are very soft and any meat is falling off the bone, at least 1 hour.

2 Turn off the heat; remove the bone from the pot and let cool slightly. Take all the meat off the bone,

chop it, and set it aside. Mash or puree the beans, then return them to the pot along with the ham.

3 Reheat, season to taste, garnish, and serve.

White Bean Soup with Greens and Rice

Makes 4 to 6 servings

Time: About 1^1/$_2$ hours

This is a hearty, vegetarian soup, but if you're interested in turning it into a big-time stew, see the variation below, which serves at least six.

^{1}/$_2$ pound dried white beans, washed and picked over (see The Basics of Buying and Preparing Beans, page 500)
1 teaspoon fresh thyme leaves or ^{1}/$_2$ teaspoon dried thyme
1 bay leaf
1 whole onion (don't bother to peel it)
^{1}/$_2$ pound kale, collard, or other dark greens
Salt and freshly ground black pepper to taste
5 cups chicken, beef, or vegetable stock, or water, warmed
1 cup rice
1 teaspoon minced garlic

1 Combine the beans, thyme, bay leaf, and onion in a large pot and cover with water. Bring to a boil and simmer until the beans are tender, adding water as necessary (use only enough water to cover the beans), about 1 hour. (You may prepare the soup in advance up to this point. Cover, refrigerate for up to 2 days, and reheat before proceeding.) While the beans are cooking, wash the greens well, then strip the leaves from the stem and reserve the stems. Roll the leaves up and slice them across the roll, then chop. Cut the stems into 1-inch or shorter lengths.

② Remove the onion and bay leaf. Season the beans well and add the stock or water; bring to a boil and add the greens stems. Cook 2 minutes, then add the leaves and the rice and cook, stirring occasionally, until the rice is tender, about 15 minutes. Add a bit more water if necessary.

③ Stir in the garlic. Cook 1 minute, adjust the seasoning if necessary, and serve.

White Bean Soup with Greens, Rice, and Beef: Cook the beans with 2 pounds short ribs or 1 to $1^1/_2$ pounds brisket. When the beans are done, cut the meat into pieces, discarding the bones and fat, if any. Add 2 waxy, "new" potatoes, peeled and diced, along with the greens. Proceed as above, adding more stock or water if necessary. This is good with a teaspoon or two of vinegar added along with the garlic.

Simplest Split Pea Soup

Makes 4 to 6 servings

Time: About $1^1/_2$ hours

To make pea soup, you need split peas, water (or stock, of course), and croutons. Everything else is a luxury. Some of those luxuries are detailed in the variations, but you can combine them as you like.

2 cups green split peas, washed and picked over
    (see The Basics of Buying and Preparing Beans,
    page 500)
6 cups chicken, beef, or vegetable stock, or water
Salt and freshly ground black pepper to taste
Croutons (page 82)

① Combine the peas and the stock or water in a large, deep saucepan or casserole and bring to a boil over medium-high heat. Turn the heat to low, cover partially, and cook, stirring occasionally, until the peas are very, very soft, about 45 minutes to 1 hour.

② Mash the mixture with a fork or potato masher, or put it through a food mill or strainer, or puree it carefully in a blender. (You may prepare the soup in advance up to this point. Cover, refrigerate for up to 2 days, and reheat before proceeding.) Reheat, adding more stock or water if necessary to achieve the consistency you like. Season to taste and serve with croutons.

Split Pea Soup with Onion and Rice or Potato: For extra creaminess, add $^1/_2$ cup rice or 1 medium potato, peeled and quartered, along with the split peas. Add 1 medium onion, minced, about halfway through the cooking. You will probably need to add more stock or water at the end.

Split Pea Soup with Ham or Bacon and Carrots: Begin by cooking $^1/_2$ cup minced ham (preferably prosciutto or other dry-cured ham) or minced bacon in 2 tablespoons olive oil until fairly crisp. Remove the meat and set aside. Cook 1 medium onion, minced, in the fat remaining in the pan until softened. Add the split peas and stock or water as above. When the mixture boils, turn the heat to low and add 3 or 4 carrots, peeled and cut into 1-inch sections. Cook as above. In Step 2, when you mash or puree the split peas, hold the carrots aside, then add them when you reheat the mixture. Garnish with ham or bacon and croutons.

Lentil Soup

Makes 4 servings

Time: About 45 minutes

You can also make a wonderful lentil soup by adding more stock or water to Warm Lentils with Bacon, page 517.

1 cup lentils, washed and picked over (see The Basics
    of Buying and Preparing Beans, page 500)

1 bay leaf

Several sprigs fresh thyme or few pinches
    dried thyme

1 carrot, peeled and cut into $1/2$-inch or smaller cubes

1 celery stalk, cut into $1/2$-inch or smaller cubes

About 6 cups water or chicken, beef, or vegetable
    stock, preferably warmed

2 tablespoons olive oil

1 onion, chopped

1 teaspoon minced garlic

Salt and freshly ground black pepper to taste

1 Place the lentils, bay leaf, thyme, carrot, and celery in a medium pot with 6 cups of the stock. Bring to a boil, then turn the heat to low and cook, stirring occasionally.

2 Meanwhile, place the olive oil in a small skillet and turn the heat to medium-low. Add the onion and cook, stirring, until it softens. Add the garlic and stir. Cook for 1 minute more.

3 When the lentils are tender—they usually take about 30 minutes—fish out the bay leaf and the thyme sprigs and pour the onion mixture into the soup. (You may prepare the soup in advance up to this point. Cover, refrigerate for up to 2 days, and reheat before proceeding.)

4 Add more stock if necessary; the mixture should be thick, but still quite soupy. Season with salt and pepper and serve.

Spicy Lentil Soup: Omit the bay leaf. In Step 2, cook the onion and garlic as above, then add 1 cup chopped tomatoes (canned are fine; add their liquid to the simmering lentils); $1/2$ cup minced fresh parsley or cilantro leaves; 1 tablespoon peeled and minced fresh ginger; $1/4$ teaspoon cayenne, or to taste; and $1/2$ teaspoon ground cumin. Stir, then proceed as above.

Pasta and Bean Soup

Pasta e Fagioli

Makes 6 servings

Time: 45 minutes to 1 hour with precooked beans

A warm, delicious classic that can be varied in many ways but always contains two essential comfort foods at its heart.

5 tablespoons extra-virgin olive oil

1 large onion, chopped

2 teaspoons minced garlic

2 sprigs fresh rosemary or 1 teaspoon dried rosemary

3 cups drained cooked kidney, cannellini, borlotti,
    or other beans or a mixture

2 cups cored, peeled, seeded, and diced tomatoes
    (canned are fine; include their juice)

6 to 8 cups chicken, beef, or vegetable stock,
    or water, warmed

Salt and freshly ground black pepper to taste

$1/2$ pound tubettini or other small pasta (or larger
    pasta broken into bits)

$1/2$ cup minced fresh parsley leaves

$1/2$ cup freshly grated Parmesan cheese

1 Place 4 tablespoons of the olive oil in a large, deep saucepan or casserole and turn the heat to medium. A minute later, add the onion and half the garlic; cook until the onion softens, stirring occasionally, about 5 minutes.

2 Add the rosemary, beans, and tomatoes, and cook, stirring and mashing the tomatoes with your spoon, until the mixture is warm and the tomatoes begin to break down, about 10 minutes.

3 Add 6 cups of stock or water and a good amount of salt and pepper. Raise the heat to medium-high and bring to a boil. Turn the heat to medium-low and cook simmer for 10 minutes, stirring occasionally. (You may prepare the soup in advance up to this point. Cover, refrigerate for up to 2 days, and reheat before proceeding.)

4   Add the pasta, along with additional stock or water if necessary. Simmer until the pasta is nearly tender, 10 minutes or so. Add half the parsley and the remaining garlic and cook another 5 minutes, until the pasta is well done but not mushy.

5   Sprinkle with the remaining parsley and drizzle with the remaining olive oil. Serve, passing the cheese at the table.

Black Bean Soup

Makes 4 to 6 servings

Time: 30 minutes with precooked beans

The best way to serve this soup is to puree about half of it, then pour it back into the pot. But you can also just mash the contents of the pot with a potato masher or large fork to get a similar smooth-chunky effect.

2 tablespoons canola or other neutral oil
2 medium onions, chopped
1 tablespoon minced garlic
1 tablespoon chili powder, or to taste
3 cups drained cooked black beans
4 cups chicken, beef, or vegetable stock, or water, preferably warmed
Salt and freshly ground black pepper to taste
2 teaspoons freshly squeezed lime juice, or to taste
Sour cream or plain yogurt for garnish
Minced cilantro leaves for garnish

1   Place the oil in a large, deep saucepan or casserole and turn the heat to medium. A minute later, add the onions and cook, stirring, until softened, about 5 minutes. Stir in the garlic and chili powder and cook, stirring, another minute.

2   Add the beans and stock or water and season with salt and pepper. Turn the heat to medium-high and bring the soup just about to a boil. Turn the heat to medium-low, and cook, stirring occasionally, for about 10 minutes. Turn off the heat.

3   Force half the contents of the pot through a food mill or carefully puree it in a food processor or blender; or just mash the contents with a potato masher or large fork. (You may prepare the soup in advance up to this point. Cover, refrigerate for up to 2 days, and reheat before proceeding.)

4   Add the lime juice and stir; taste and adjust seasonings as necessary. Serve, garnished with sour cream or yogurt and minced cilantro.

Eight Simple Additions to Bean Soups

Like vegetable soups, bean soups are receptive to a wide variety of additions. Try, for example:

1. Scraps of smoked meats, such as ham or bacon (or cook the beans with a ham bone)
2. Precooked vegetables of any type, as long as the flavor does not conflict with that of the soup. Onions, carrots, and celery are almost always appropriate.
3. Any croutons (page 82)
4. A teaspoon or more of minced garlic or scallions, added about two minutes before the end of the cooking time
5. Any spice you like, from jalapeños or other chiles to lots of black pepper to curry powder or other spice mixtures (pages 777–779)
6. Diced fresh tomatoes as a garnish
7. Bean cooking liquid used in place of some or all of the liquid in the soup for a stronger bean flavor
8. Freshly chopped herbs or quick-cooking greens

Fish Soups

Good fish stock is wonderful stuff—just add a couple of potatoes and some fish and you have chowder—but few people keep it on hand. (Bear in mind, however, that it is easy to make; see Fast Fish Stock, page 49.) Shrimp or lobster stock are wonderful substitutes in some instances, and Shrimp Stock (page 50) has the distinct advantage of being quickly prepared from nothing more than shrimp shells.

But it's important to be able to make fish soup without specialized stock. I've designed most of these recipes so that you can make them not only with fish stock, but with chicken stock or, if necessary, water.

If you make a practice of freezing scraps of fish as you prepare it as a main course—just trim off an uneven part of a steak or fillet and throw it in the freezer—you can make fish soup routinely, without really thinking about it. Or you can buy fish especially for the recipes below.

Shrimp Soup with Cumin

Makes 4 servings

Time: 45 minutes

If you use Shrimp Stock (page 50) for this dish, the shrimp flavor will be incomparably intense.

    1 to 1¼ pounds shrimp, shells on
    5 cups shrimp or chicken stock, or water
    ¼ cup extra-virgin olive oil
    4 cloves garlic, peeled
    4 thick slices French or Italian bread
    1 teaspoon ground cumin
    Salt and freshly ground black pepper to taste
    Minced fresh parsley leaves for garnish

1 Peel the shrimp and simmer the shells in a medium saucepan with the stock or water while you continue with the recipe.

2 Place the olive oil in a large, deep saucepan or casserole and turn the heat to medium. Add the garlic cloves and cook, stirring occasionally, until they are a very deep golden, almost brown, about 10 minutes. Remove them with a slotted spoon and set aside to cool.

3 Turn the heat to low and brown the bread in the oil on both sides, in batches if necessary; it will take about 5 minutes. Remove the slices and spread each with about ½ clove of the cooked garlic. Mince the remaining garlic.

4 Cut each of the shrimp into 3 or 4 pieces. Strain the warmed stock into the casserole, turn the heat to medium, and bring to a gentle boil. Add the shrimp, cumin, salt, and pepper, and cook over low heat for 3 or 4 minutes.

5 Place a piece of bread in each of four bowls, then ladle in a portion of soup with shrimp. Sprinkle with the minced garlic, garnish, and serve.

Lobster Bisque

Makes 4 servings

Time: 1 hour

This is a relatively simple and quick lobster bisque, one that retains two critical qualities: big-time lobster flavor and a luxurious creaminess. There are two good ways to obtain lobster bodies—one is to save them from a lobster feast. The other is to beg them from fish markets, which either give them away or charge only minimally.

4 tablespoons (½ stick) butter

1 medium onion, chopped

1 teaspoon minced garlic

1 medium carrot, peeled and chopped

1 bay leaf

3 sprigs fresh thyme or ½ teaspoon dried thyme

4 to 8 lobster bodies, cooked or uncooked, with as
    many other lobster shells as you can scavenge,
    plus coral, tomalley, and any stray bits of meat
    you might find

1 cup dry white wine

1 cup cored, peeled, seeded, and chopped tomatoes
    (canned are fine; don't bother to drain)

6 cups chicken or fish stock, or strained liquid
    reserved from boiling lobsters

1 cup heavy cream

Salt and freshly ground black pepper to taste

Minced fresh parsley leaves for garnish

1 Place 2 tablespoons of the butter in a large, deep saucepan or casserole over medium heat. When it melts, add the onion, garlic, carrot, bay leaf, and thyme and cook, stirring, until the onion softens, 5 to 10 minutes.

2 Add the lobster bodies and, if they are uncooked, cook, stirring, until they turn red, about 10 minutes (if they're already cooked, cook, stirring, about 5 minutes).

3 Add the wine and tomatoes and turn the heat to medium-high. Bring to a boil, then turn the heat to low, cover, and cook for 10 minutes.

4 Add the stock, turn the heat to high, and bring back to a boil. Once again, turn the heat to low and cover; cook 20 minutes. Remove the bay leaf and thyme sprigs. Remove the lobster shells, crack them if necessary, and pick off any meat you find. Return the bits of meat to the soup (reserve any large pieces of meat you have for the final addition, below).

5 Pass the soup through a food mill or puree it in a blender. (You may prepare the soup in advance up to this point. Cover, refrigerate for up to 2 days, and reheat before proceeding.) Return the soup to the pot and bring to a boil. Add the remaining butter, in bits, until it melts. Add the cream and any bits of lobster meat and heat through. Season with salt and pepper, garnish, and serve.

No-Holds-Barred Clam or Fish Chowder

Makes 4 servings

Time: 30 minutes

This becomes corn chowder simply by substituting one (or more) cups of fresh corn kernels for the clams or fish. Better still, just add some fresh corn along with the fish. I sometimes use flour in this recipe, simply because most people are used to very thick chowders; but it isn't necessary.

4 to 6 slices good bacon (about ¼ pound), minced

1 cup minced onion

2 cups peeled and roughly chopped baking potatoes

2 tablespoons flour (optional)

1 teaspoon fresh thyme leaves or ½ teaspoon
    dried thyme

2 cups any chicken or fish stock, augmented by
    as much juice as you can salvage when opening
    the clams

Salt and freshly ground black pepper to taste

1 cup milk

1 cup heavy cream or half-and-half or more milk

24 hard-shell clams, shucked; or about 1 pint shucked
    clams, cut up if very large, with their juice; or
    about 2 cups diced or chunked fresh delicate
    white fish, such as cod (see the list on page 285
    for substitutions)

1 tablespoon butter

Minced fresh parsley leaves for garnish

1 Fry the bacon in a large, deep saucepan or casserole over medium-high heat until crisp. Remove with a slotted spoon and cook the onion and potatoes in the bacon fat until the onion softens, 10 minutes. Sprinkle with the optional flour and the thyme and stir. Add the stock and cook until the potatoes are tender, about 10 minutes. (You may prepare the soup in advance up to this point. Cover, refrigerate for up to 2 days, and reheat before proceeding.)

2 Add salt and pepper, then the milk and cream; add the clams or fish and bring barely to a simmer over low heat. Float the butter on top of the chowder; by the time it melts, the clams or fish will be ready. Garnish and serve.

Lower-Fat Clam or Fish Chowder

Makes 4 servings

Time: 40 minutes

If you have accumulated chunks of assorted white-fleshed fish in your freezer, this is the place to use them.

1 tablespoon olive oil

1 large onion, chopped

3 medium baking potatoes, peeled and cut into
    $1/_2$-inch cubes

4 cups fish or chicken stock, preferably warmed

24 hard-shell clams, shucked and with their juice;
    or about 1 pint undrained shucked clams, cut up
    if very large; or about 2 cups diced or cut-up fresh
    delicate white fish, such as cod (see the list on
    page 285 for substitutions)

2 cups corn kernels, preferably fresh

1 cup low-fat milk

Salt and freshly ground black pepper to taste

Minced fresh parsley leaves for garnish

1 Place the oil in a large, deep saucepan or casserole and turn the heat to medium. A minute later, add the onion and potatoes. Cook, stirring occasionally, until the onion is soft and the potato lightly browned, about 10 minutes.

2 Add the stock to the potatoes and onion and cook over medium-low heat until the potatoes are just tender, about 10 minutes. (You may prepare the soup in advance up to this point. Cover, refrigerate for up to 2 days, and reheat before proceeding.)

3 Add the clams or fish chunks and corn and cook about 5 minutes. Add the milk, then salt and plenty of pepper. Garnish and serve.

Clam Soup with Roasted Garlic

Makes 4 servings

Time: $1^1/_2$ hours

If you have Roasted Garlic (made by either of the methods on page 575), you can make this delicious, delicate soup in about twenty minutes. And it's easy, because you don't shuck the clams; they're cooked in their shells in the soup.

1 whole head garlic, separated but not peeled

2 tablespoons olive oil

1 large onion, minced

4 cups fish or chicken stock, preferably warmed

24 littleneck or other hard-shell clams, well scrubbed

Zest of 1 orange

Juice of 2 limes

Salt and freshly ground black pepper to taste

Minced cilantro leaves for garnish

1 lime, cut into small wedges

1 small fresh chile, such as jalapeño, stemmed,
    seeded and minced (optional)

1 Preheat the oven to 350°F. Place the garlic cloves in a small, ovenproof bowl with 1 tablespoon of the oil. Cover with aluminum foil and roast until tender, about an hour. Cool.

2 Squeeze the garlic meat from its husks and reserve. Place the remaining oil in a large, deep saucepan and turn the heat to medium-high. A minute later, add the onion, and cook, stirring, until soft, about 5 minutes.

3 Add the stock and bring to a boil. Turn the heat to low. Add the clams, cover, and cook until they open, 5 to 10 minutes.

4 Add the roasted garlic, orange zest, lime juice, salt, and pepper. Stir and taste for seasoning. Garnish and serve immediately, passing the lime wedges and jalapeño at the table.

Lightning-Quick Fish Soup

Makes 4 servings

Time: 20 minutes

If you have fish stock and fish scraps in the freezer, combine them here. If not, use chicken stock or water and fresh fish.

5 cups fish, chicken, or shrimp stock, or water
1 large onion, chopped
1 tablespoon minced garlic
1 teaspoon paprika
Pinch saffron (optional)
1 tablespoon extra-virgin olive oil
1 cup cored, peeled, seeded, and chopped tomatoes
    (canned are fine; include their liquid)
Salt and freshly ground black pepper to taste
1 1/2 pounds any white-fleshed fish, cut into small
    chunks, or fish mixed with shelled seafood,
    such as clams, shrimp, or scallops
Minced fresh parsley leaves for garnish

1 Combine all the ingredients except for the fish and parsley in a large, deep saucepan or casserole and turn the heat to high. Bring to a boil, then turn the heat to medium and cook for 5 minutes, stirring occasionally.

2 Add the fish and cook, stirring, until it cooks through, about 5 minutes. Garnish and serve.

Cotriade

Makes 4 servings

Time: 1 hour

A traditional stew of northern France.

1/2 cup minced bacon
2 large onions, roughly chopped
About 1 pound baking potatoes, peeled and
    cut into small chunks
Salt and freshly ground black pepper to taste
1 teaspoon fresh thyme leaves or 1/2 teaspoon
    dried thyme
6 cups fish or chicken stock, preferably warmed
About 2 pounds fillets or steaks of white fish,
    cut into chunks
Juice of 1 lemon
Minced fresh parsley leaves for garnish

1 Place the bacon in a large, deep saucepan or casserole and turn the heat to medium-high. Cook, stirring, until it is crisp, about 10 minutes. Remove with a slotted spoon and set aside.

2 Turn the heat to medium and cook the onions in the bacon fat, stirring, until softened, about 5 minutes. Add the potatoes and cook, stirring occasionally, until they are well mixed with the onions and covered with fat. Season with salt, pepper, and thyme; stir, then add the stock.

3 Cook over medium heat until the potatoes are just tender, about 15 minutes.

4 Add the fish and cook another 5 to 10 minutes, until the fish is opaque and tender but not falling apart. Add the lemon juice, ladle into bowls, garnish, and serve.

One-Hour Bouillabaisse

Makes 6 to 8 servings

Time: About 1 hour

This is the most basic bouillabaisse: a mess of fish cooked in broth. There is little reason to make a bigger deal of this essentially simple stew than this. Serve, if you like, with aioli (page 761).

> 4 tablespoons extra-virgin olive oil
> 1 large onion, chopped
> 3 cored, peeled, seeded, and chopped tomatoes (canned are fine; include their liquid)
> 2 or 3 ribbons orange zest, removed from an orange with a vegetable peeler
> 1 teaspoon fennel seeds
> 1 teaspoon minced fresh tarragon leaves or ¼ teaspoon dried tarragon
> 5 sprigs fresh parsley
> 4 cups fish or chicken stock, or water, warmed
> 12 slices crusty French bread
> 1 clove garlic, split in half, plus 1 tablespoon minced garlic
> 24 small hard-shell clams or mussels, well washed
> 1½ pounds fillet or steak fish, preferably a combination of halibut, cod, snapper, sea bass (anything but dark-fleshed fish such as tuna, salmon, or bluefish), cut into chunks
> 1½ pounds shellfish, preferably a combination of scallops and shrimp
> ¼ cup minced fresh basil leaves, plus more for garnish
> 1 tablespoon Pernod or other anise liqueur (optional)
> Salt and freshly ground black pepper to taste

1 Place 3 tablespoons of the olive oil in a large, deep saucepan or casserole and turn the heat to medium-low. A minute later, add the onion and cook, stirring, until it softens, about 5 minutes. Add the tomatoes, orange zest, fennel seeds, tarragon, and parsley. Stir to blend. Preheat the oven to 350°F.

2 Add the stock or water and turn the heat to high. Bring to a boil, cover, and turn the heat to medium-low; cook for 10 minutes. While the broth simmers, toast the rounds of bread in the oven until dried (about 20 minutes). Rub the toasts with the split clove of garlic and put a piece of bread in as many soup bowls as there are diners. Reserve the remainder to pass at the table.

3 Add the clams to the broth and continue to cook, covered, for about 5 minutes. Add the fish fillets or steaks to the broth and cook another 5 minutes. When the first of the clams begins to open, add the shellfish to the broth along with the garlic, basil, Pernod, and the remaining tablespoon of olive oil.

4 Cover and cook for 3 to 5 minutes. Taste and adjust seasoning. Spoon some fish and broth into each bowl over the toasted French bread, garnish with a bit more basil, and serve.

Chicken Soup

Ironically, few chicken soups contain much chicken. And, if the stock is good enough, there's no reason for them to. But if you like to have something meaty to chew on, by all means add chicken to your chicken soup.

Twice-Cooked Chicken Stock

Makes about 3 quarts

Time: About 1 hour

This makes a delicious stock, and gives you perfectly cooked chicken to add to any of the following chicken soups. It is a luxury, obviously, but a simple and not very expensive one.

3 quarts any chicken stock (pages 46–48)
1 small chicken or 2 or 3 pounds chicken parts, skin and all visible fat removed, rinsed and patted dry with paper towels
1 carrot, peeled and cut into chunks
1 clove garlic, peeled (optional)
Several sprigs fresh parsley or dill
Salt and freshly ground black pepper to taste

① Combine all ingredients except salt and pepper in a large, deep saucepan or casserole and turn the heat to medium-high. Bring just about to a boil, then turn the heat to medium-low and partially cover; adjust the heat so the mixture sends up a few bubbles at a time.

② Chicken parts will be done in 30 to 40 minutes, whole chicken in 45 to 60 minutes. Strain the stock. Remove the meat from the bones and either return it to the stock or reserve for another use. Season the stock with salt and pepper and use immediately, refrigerate for 4 to 5 days (longer if you boil it every third day), or freeze.

Chicken Soup with Rice or Noodles

Makes 4 servings

Time: 30 minutes

This is a thin chicken soup—a warming but not super-filling first course—with the rice, meat, and vegetables acting as a garnish rather than a major player; see the variation if you want something more substantial. Use orzo or other tiny pasta, angel hair or other thin noodles, ribbons or other egg noodles, or other cooked grains in place of the rice.

5 to 6 cups chicken stock
$1/2$ cup long-grain rice or pasta
1 carrot, peeled and cut into thin slices
1 celery stalk, minced (optional)
1 cup raw or cooked chopped boneless skinless chicken, or more
Salt and freshly ground black pepper to taste
Minced fresh parsley or dill leaves for garnish

① Place the stock in a large, deep saucepan or casserole and turn the heat to medium-high. When it is just about boiling, turn the heat down to medium so that it bubbles but not too vigorously. Stir in the rice, carrot, and celery and cook, stirring occasionally, until they are all tender, about 20 minutes.

② Stir in the chicken. If it is raw, cook another 5 to 8 minutes, until it is cooked. If it is cooked, cook 2 or 3 minutes, until it is hot. Season with salt and pepper, garnish, and serve.

Thick Chicken Soup with Rice or Noodles: Increase the amount of rice or pasta to 1 cup; use 2 carrots and 2 celery stalks. Use as much chicken as you like. If you plan to store this soup, cook the rice separately and stir it in during the last stage of cooking or it will absorb too much liquid during storage.

Chicken Soup with Matzo Balls

Makes 6 servings

Time: At least 2 hours

Traditionally, matzo balls are served in a broth cooked only with carrots (thick-cut instead of sliced), but feel free to add other vegetables, rice or noodles (thin egg noodles are good), and chicken meat.

3 eggs

6 to 9 cups chicken stock

$1/4$ cup minced or grated onion (optional)

$1/4$ cup melted rendered chicken fat or canola
  or other neutral oil

$1/2$ teaspoon salt

$1/2$ teaspoon freshly ground black pepper

About 1 cup matzo meal

4 carrots, peeled and cut into chunks

1. Beat together the eggs and $1/2$ cup of the stock. (If you would prefer very light matzo balls, separate the eggs and beat the yolks with the stock. Beat the whites until stiff and fold them in after adding the matzo meal.)

2. Stir in the onion, fat, salt, and pepper. Add the matzo meal; the dough should be quite moist, barely stiff enough to make into balls. If it is too moist, add a little more meal.

3. Cover the mixture and refrigerate for an hour or overnight. When you're ready to cook, place a large pot of salted water to boil. (You can also cook the matzo balls directly in your stock, but use the larger quantity of stock.) Using wet hands, shape the mixture into small balls, about 1 inch in diameter. Meanwhile, cook the carrots in the $5^1/2$ cups stock.

4. Turn the heat under the boiling water to medium-low and cook the balls until expanded and set, about 30 minutes. Set them in soup bowls and ladle the stock and carrots over them.

Chicken Soup with Butter Dumplings

Makes 4 servings

Time: 20 minutes

You can make dumplings with almost anything, even flour and water. But I strongly believe they ought to taste like something, and these do. Serve in any chicken soup.

6 cups chicken stock

4 tablespoons ($1/2$ stick) butter, softened

2 eggs

$1/2$ cup flour

$1/4$ cup minced fresh parsley leaves

$1/4$ cup minced or grated onion

Salt and freshly ground black pepper to taste

1. Heat the stock in a large pot. Cream the butter in a bowl with the back of a fork, then beat in the eggs. Stir in the flour, parsley, onion, salt, and pepper, blending well. Add heated stock 1 tablespoon at a time, just until the batter is soft; do not make it too loose or the dumplings will fall apart.

2. Drop the batter by the scant teaspoonful into the simmering broth. Cook until set and cooked through, about 10 minutes, removing the dumplings as they are done. Serve immediately in the soup.

Chicken Soup with Passatelli

Makes 4 servings

Time: About 20 minutes

These Parmesan-flavored dumplings are my favorite garnish for simple chicken soup. There is a special utensil for making passatelli, but a food mill works perfectly.

6 cups chicken stock, plus 1 tablespoon if necessary

1 cup freshly grated Parmesan cheese

$1/2$ cup fresh bread crumbs

$1/4$ cup minced fresh parsley leaves

Salt and freshly ground black pepper to taste

$1/8$ teaspoon freshly grated nutmeg

2 eggs, lightly beaten

1 Bring the stock to a boil in a large pot. Combine the cheese in a bowl with the bread crumbs, parsley, salt, pepper, and nutmeg, then stir in the eggs. The mixture should be like a wet dough, barely holding together. If it seems too stiff, add 1 tablespoon of water or stock.

2 Adjust the heat so that the stock simmers. Put the dough in a food mill or ricer with big holes and hold the utensil directly over the soup. Crank the food mill so that the dough falls in strands directly into the soup. Cook for 2 or 3 minutes, then turn off the heat and let sit for 2 or 3 minutes more before serving.

Chicken Soup with Tortellini and Watercress

Makes 4 servings

Time: About 30 minutes

You can simmer almost any soft, filled pasta in chicken soup, from Lighter, Steamed Wontons (page 33) to ravioli (page 156). Tortellini, which can be bought in any supermarket, is my favorite. Use less pasta if you want a light soup, more if you want this as a main course.

5 to 6 cups chicken stock, the best you have
2 carrots, peeled and cut into thin slices
1 onion, diced
Salt and freshly ground black pepper to taste
About 3 cups chopped watercress or spinach
 (trimmed, washed, and chopped)
1/2 to 1 pound tortellini (see illustrations, page 162)
Freshly grated Parmesan cheese to taste

1 Place the stock in a large, deep saucepan or casserole and turn the heat to medium-high. When it is just about boiling, turn the heat to medium-low and add the carrots and the onion. Simmer until the carrots are just about tender, 10 to 20 minutes depending on the thickness of the slices. Taste and add salt and pepper. Meanwhile, bring a pot of water to boil for the pasta.

2 Add the watercress or spinach to the simmering broth. Meanwhile, cook the tortellini until nearly tender. Drain it and add it to the soup.

3 Check and correct seasoning if necessary, spoon into bowls, and pass the Parmesan at the table.

Egg-Lemon Soup
Avgolemono

Makes 4 servings

Time: About 30 minutes

A Greek standard that I like diner-style, meaning with plenty of rice and chicken—more of a stew than a soup.

6 cups chicken stock, the best you have
1/2 cup long-grain rice or orzo
1 carrot, peeled and cut into thin slices
1 celery stalk, minced
Salt and freshly ground black pepper to taste
2 cups shredded or chopped cooked boneless
 skinless chicken
2 eggs
3 tablespoons freshly squeezed lemon juice,
 plus more if desired
Minced fresh dill or parsley leaves for garnish

1 Place the stock in a large saucepan and turn the heat to medium-high. When it is just about boiling, turn the heat down to medium so that it just bubbles. Stir in the rice, carrot, and celery and cook, stirring occasionally, until they are all tender, about 20 minutes. Season with salt and pepper and add the chicken. Turn the heat to low.

2 Place the eggs in a blender and whir for 10 seconds; add the lemon juice and blend briefly. With the motor running, drizzle in about 2 cups of the hot soup. Pour this mixture back into the soup, stirring, and cook briefly, until the soup is slightly thickened, just a couple of minutes; do not boil. Taste and adjust seasoning (you may add more lemon juice if you like). Garnish and serve.

Chicken Soup with Cabbage and Thin Noodles

Makes 4 servings

Time: 30 minutes

Chicken noodle soup, Chinese-style.

6 cups chicken stock, the best you have
1 pound raw or cooked chopped boneless skinless chicken
1 pound bok choy or other cabbage, trimmed and washed
1 tablespoon peanut oil
1 teaspoon minced garlic
1 teaspoon peeled and minced fresh ginger
1 tablespoon soy sauce, plus more for serving
Salt to taste
8 ounces fresh (preferred) or dried thin Chinese egg noodles (see Noodle Dishes from China, page 170)

1 Place the stock in a large, deep saucepan or casserole and turn the heat to medium-high. When it is just about boiling, turn the heat down to medium so that it bubbles but not too vigorously. If you are using raw chicken, cook it in the stock for about 2 minutes. Remove and set aside. If you are using cooked chicken, proceed to the next step.

2 Bring a large pot of water to a boil and salt it. Heat a wok or large skillet over medium-high heat. Cut the bok choy into 1- to 2-inch pieces, smaller for the stems, larger for the leaves. Add the peanut oil to the wok and cook the garlic and ginger, stirring, for

15 seconds, then add the bok choy. Raise the heat to high and stir-fry until the bok choy is fairly tender, 5 to 10 minutes. Add the soy sauce, taste for salt, and turn off the heat.

3 Cook the noodles in the boiling water until not quite tender; drain them. Add the noodles, cabbage, and chicken to the stock and cook until everything is heated through. Serve immediately.

Hot-and-Sour Soup

Makes 4 servings

Time: About 40 minutes

As taught to me many years ago by my good friend Peter Cheng, who made this daily for thirty years. All of the dried ingredients can be found in any Asian market and many supermarkets.

1 whole chicken breast, bone-in, about 1 pound, skin and excess fat removed
6 cups chicken stock or water
5 dried lily buds, available at Asian markets
3 or 4 dried cloud ear or tree ear fungus, available at Asian markets
3 or 4 dried shiitake (sometimes labeled "black") mushrooms
1/2 pound soft or firm tofu, cut into 1/2-inch cubes
1 tablespoon soy sauce
2 tablespoons rice or white vinegar
1/2 teaspoon freshly ground black pepper, plus more to taste
Salt to taste
2 eggs, lightly beaten
1 tablespoon cornstarch mixed with 2 tablespoons water (optional)
1 tablespoon dark sesame oil
Minced scallions for garnish
Tabasco or other bottled hot sauce or hot sesame oil

Sometimes I think the phrase "everything but the kitchen sink" was invented to describe what can be added to chicken soups. In some ways, the better question is, "What can't you add?" to chicken soups.

1. Herbs, especially dill, parsley, or chervil, but almost anything else
2. Spices, especially ginger, chiles, garlic, or other strong spices
3. Any starch you like—croutons, rice, noodles, and more
4. Leftover chicken, grilled fresh chicken, small cubes of raw boneless chicken (which will cook in two minutes), or any other poultry
5. Small pieces of rind from Parmesan cheese, or grated cheese
6. Precooked vegetables of any type, as long as the flavor does not conflict with that of the soup. Onions, carrots, and celery are almost always appropriate.

① Place the chicken and the stock together in a large, deep saucepan or casserole and turn the heat to high. When the stock or water boils, reduce the heat to medium-low and partially cover. Cook for 20 minutes, or until the chicken is just cooked through. Meanwhile, soak the lily buds, fungus, and shiitakes in hot water to cover until soft, 10 to 15 minutes; if the water cools before the shiitakes soften, drain and add more hot water.

② Remove the chicken and, as soon as it is cool enough to handle, strip the meat from the bones and chop it. Trim and shred the lily buds, trim and mince the fungus and mushrooms, and add all of this to the simmering broth. Return the chicken meat to the broth, along with the tofu, soy sauce, vinegar, and plenty of pepper—at least $1/2$ teaspoon.

③ Taste and add more soy sauce, salt, pepper, and/or vinegar if necessary. Raise the heat a little bit and stir the eggs into the soup, followed, if you like, by the cornstarch, which will thicken the already fairly thick mixture even more. Float the sesame oil on top of the soup, garnish, and serve, passing hot sauce or hot oil at the table.

Meat Soups

Most meat soups are more like stews, and so are found in the meat chapter. But here are a couple that are traditionally more "soupy" than "stewy."

Scotch Broth

Makes 6 to 8 servings

Time: About 2 hours

Typically, Scotch broth is very thick, almost stewlike, and serves as a main course. But you can make it thinner by reducing the amount of meat and eliminating the split peas. You can also make lamb stock to use in this soup by simmering some lamb bones for a couple of hours with aromatic vegetables. Skim fat and proceed.

10 cups chicken, beef, or vegetable stock, or water, or a combination
$1/2$ cup pearled barley
$1/2$ cup yellow or green split peas, washed and picked over (see The Basics of Buying and Preparing Beans, page 500)
$1^1/2$ to 2 pounds boneless lamb, preferably from the shoulder or leg, trimmed of excess fat and cut into 1-inch cubes
1 large or 2 medium leeks, trimmed, well cleaned, and chopped
2 or 3 carrots, peeled and cut into 1-inch chunks
3 medium turnips, potatoes, or a combination, peeled and cut into 1-inch chunks
2 celery stalks, chopped
Salt and freshly ground black pepper to taste
Minced fresh parsley leaves for garnish

1 Combine the stock or water, barley, peas, lamb, and leeks in a large, deep saucepan or casserole and turn the heat to high. When it boils, turn the heat to low. Skim any foam that rises to the top and cook, stirring occasionally, until the lamb and barley are very tender, at least 45 minutes.

2 Add the remaining vegetables and cook, stirring occasionally, for 20 minutes. Taste and add salt and pepper. Cook until everything is very tender, another 10 to 20 minutes. Adjust seasoning, garnish, and serve.

Hanoi Noodle Soup

Makes 4 main-course servings

Time: About 1 hour

Usually made with beef, this anise- and cinnamon-scented soup is equally good with chicken, or with no meat at all. Rice noodles (discussed in detail on page 173), sold in Asian markets and many supermarkets, can be softened just by soaking in warm water.

8 cups beef (preferred), chicken, or vegetable stock

4 star anise

1 cinnamon stick

1 (1-inch) chunk peeled fresh ginger

1 onion, quartered (don't bother to peel)

4 cloves

1 pound rice vermicelli

$1/2$ pound boneless skinless chicken or beef
(preferably sirloin, tenderloin, or round), cut into
thin slices, rinsed and patted dry with paper towels

2 tablespoons fish sauce (*nam pla* or *nuoc mam*,
available at Asian markets) or soy sauce

Freshly ground black pepper to taste

Salt to taste

Minced cilantro leaves for garnish

Lime wedges

1 fresh jalapeño chile, stemmed, seeded, and minced

1 Combine the first six ingredients in a large, deep saucepan or casserole and turn the heat to high. When it boils, turn the heat to very low and cover. Let cook, undisturbed, for as little as 20 and as long as 60 minutes, depending on your time frame. Strain and return to the saucepan.

2 Soak the rice noodles in hot water to cover until soft, 15 to 30 minutes. Rinse under cold water for a minute or so; drain.

3 Turn the heat under the soup to medium; place the chicken or the beef in the pot and cook for 2 minutes, stirring occasionally. Divide the noodles among four large bowls. Add the fish or soy sauce and plenty of pepper to the soup. Taste and add salt or more seasoning if necessary.

4 Top the noodles with broth and meat, then garnish with cilantro. Serve, passing the lime wedges and minced chile at the table.

Quick Asian Noodle Soup with Pork: Season broth and soak noodles as above; cook the broth for only 20 minutes. Instead of the uncooked chicken or beef, add to the broth $1/2$ recipe Sweet Pork with Spicy Soy Sauce (page 470), along with some of its liquid. Omit the fish or soy sauce. Season to taste and proceed as above.

Cold Soups

Most cold soups—which may be savory, as in borscht or gazpacho, or sweet, as in fruit soups—are in fact not best when ice cold. Extreme cold appears to dull the perception of flavor, so if you're serving savory soups, you probably want to oversalt a bit; with sweet soups, it's best to add more sugar than you might believe is necessary. In either case, remove the soup from the refrigerator for at least fifteen minutes before serving, to take the edge from its iciness.

Cold Cucumber and Dill Soup

Makes 4 servings

Time: About 20 minutes, plus time to chill

Here's a fast way to make cucumber soup: Blend peeled cucumber, yogurt, and chicken stock in a blender. Season to taste. Perfectly decent. But this recipe, which requires a bit of cooking, is better-tasting.

> 2 medium or 4 small cucumbers, unpeeled
> 1 teaspoon salt
> 2 tablespoons butter
> 4 shallots or 1 small onion, minced
> 4 cups chicken stock
> 1 tablespoon snipped fresh dill or other herb, such as basil or tarragon (use only 1 teaspoon tarragon), plus dill for garnish (optional)
> Freshly ground black pepper to taste
> 1/2 cup heavy or sour cream or plain yogurt

❶ Cut a few thin slices of cucumber for garnish and set aside. Then cut the cucumbers in half lengthwise and scoop out the seeds with a spoon. Chop them coarsely and sprinkle with 1 teaspoon of salt. Set in a colander and let drain while you proceed with the recipe.

❷ Place the butter in a medium saucepan and turn the heat to medium. When it melts, add the shallots or onion, turn the heat to medium-low and cook, stirring occasionally, until soft, about 5 minutes. Add the stock and the dill.

❸ Rinse the cucumbers and add them to the soup. Cook over medium heat for 5 minutes. Cool slightly, then puree in a blender or force through a food mill. Taste and adjust seasoning, then chill.

❹ When you're ready to eat, adjust seasoning again, then stir in the cream or yogurt. Garnish with dill (if you're using it) and cucumber slices, and serve.

Basic Red Gazpacho

Makes 6 servings

Time: 20 minutes, plus time to chill

There is no "genuine" gazpacho; basically, the term can be applied to any cold vegetable soup that contains vinegar. This one, however, is not only conventional, but fast and fresh-tasting.

> About 3 pounds ripe tomatoes, cored, peeled, seeded, and roughly chopped
> 1 red or yellow bell pepper, stemmed, peeled if desired, seeded, and roughly chopped
> 2 pickling ("Kirby") cucumbers, peeled and roughly chopped
> 4 slices good stale white bread (about 4 ounces), crusts removed
> 6 cups cold water
> 1 large or 2 small cloves garlic, peeled
> 1/4 cup sherry or good wine vinegar, or to taste
> 1/2 cup extra-virgin olive oil
> Salt and freshly ground black pepper to taste
> Croutons (page 82) for garnish (optional)

❶ Mince a bit of the tomato, pepper, and cucumber for garnish and set aside. Soak the bread in 1 cup of the water for 5 minutes, then squeeze out the excess water.

❷ Place the bread in the container of a blender or food processor with the remaining tomato, pepper, cucumber, and water, as well as the garlic and vinegar; process until smooth, then add the olive oil slowly, with the machine running.

❸ Season with salt and pepper and refrigerate until ready to serve; the flavor will improve over a few hours. Before serving, check seasoning again. Garnish with reserved tomato, pepper, and cucumber and, if desired, croutons.

Roasted Gazpacho

Makes 6 servings

Time: 45 minutes, plus time to chill

My friend Ignacio Blanco makes this sensational gazpacho at his Connecticut restaurant, Meson Galicia.

4 ripe tomatoes
2 small or 1 medium eggplant, peeled and cut into
     large chunks
4 small or 2 medium zucchini, cut into large chunks
2 medium onions, cut into large chunks
About 10 cloves garlic, peeled
1/2 cup extra-virgin olive oil
1/4 cup sherry vinegar
Salt and freshly ground black pepper to taste
4 cups water
4 slices stale bread, crusts removed and torn up
Croutons (page 82) for garnish

1 Preheat the oven to 400°F. Combine the tomatoes, eggplant, zucchini, onions, garlic, and olive oil in a large roasting pan; roast until the eggplant is tender, stirring occasionally, about 30 minutes.

2 Turn the mixture into a bowl and add the vinegar, salt, pepper, water, and bread. Refrigerate and let sit several hours or overnight.

3 In a food processor or blender, blend the mixture until smooth. Put it through a food mill or strainer to remove any remaining bits of skin, seeds, and other solids. Check the seasoning, garnish, and serve.

Borscht

Makes 4 servings

Time: About 45 minutes, plus time to chill

Borscht—essentially beet soup—can be served hot, and was once most often made with a piece of stew meat, such as short ribs or flanken. But cold borscht, with sour cream, is the ideal.

3 pounds beets
1 large onion
6 cups water
Juice of 1 lemon
Salt and freshly ground black pepper to taste
2 eggs, lightly beaten
4 medium or 8 or 10 small baking potatoes
Minced fresh dill or chives for garnish
Sour cream

1 Peel and grate the beets and onion (the food processor does a nice job of this). Combine them in a large pot with the water and bring to a boil. Turn the heat to medium-low and simmer gently for about 30 minutes. Add the lemon juice, salt, and pepper and cook another 5 minutes. Taste and adjust seasoning.

2 Gradually add about 1 cup of the soup to the eggs, beating all the while. Then stir this mixture back into the soup. Refrigerate until very well chilled.

3 When you're just about ready to eat, boil the potatoes until soft; cool them until able to handle and peel.

4 Serve the hot potatoes in or alongside of the cold soup, garnished with dill or chives; pass the sour cream at the table.

Summer Fruit Soup

Makes 4 servings

Time: 30 minutes, plus time to chill

Less important than the types of fruit you use here is that they must all be completely and perfectly ripe; hard fruit will give you an unpleasant texture, and overripe fruit may give off-flavors. Serve, if you like, with whipped cream, sour cream, or yogurt.

2 cups pitted cherries or plums

2 cups pitted and chopped peaches or nectarines

2 cups cored and chopped pears or picked-over
    blueberries

5 cups water or 4 cups water and 1 cup fruity
    red wine

1/2 cup sugar, plus more to taste if desired

Pinch salt

1 cinnamon stick

1/2 teaspoon vanilla extract

1 tablespoon cornstarch

Fresh mint sprigs for garnish

1 Combine the first seven ingredients in a medium saucepan. Cover and cook over medium-low heat until the fruit is very soft, about 15 minutes. Remove the cinnamon stick, then add the vanilla extract. Taste and add more sugar if you like.

2 Puree in a blender or food processor or force through a food mill. Mix the cornstarch with a couple of tablespoons of the soup, then stir this mixture into the soup, heating gently until the soup thickens slightly. Chill.

3 Garnish and serve.

Sweet Blueberry Soup with Yogurt

Makes 4 servings

Time: 20 minutes, plus time to chill

A wonderful first course, dessert, or, best yet, snack. The most beautiful color of any soup.

1 pint blueberries, picked over and washed

2 cups water

1/2 cup sugar, plus more if needed

1 teaspoon ground cinnamon, plus more if needed

1 cup plain yogurt or sour cream, plus more for garnish

1 Combine the blueberries, water, sugar, and cinnamon in a medium saucepan and turn the heat to medium. Cook, stirring occasionally, until the blueberries fall apart, 10 to 15 minutes.

2 Cool the mixture a little, then puree in a blender, taking care not to burn yourself (or tarnish things with the blueberry juice, which will stain). Taste and add more sugar or cinnamon if necessary. Chill, then stir in yogurt or sour cream. Serve cold, garnished with more yogurt or sour cream.

Cherry Soup

Makes 4 servings

Time: 20 minutes, plus time to chill

Best made with fresh sour cherries, which you can get from a tree or a nearby orchard. If these are not available, use fresh sweet cherries and reduce the sugar to a tablespoon or two.

2 pounds fresh sour cherries

1 teaspoon cornstarch mixed with 2 teaspoons water

Pinch salt

1/4 teaspoon ground cinnamon

1/4 cup sugar, or to taste

1 teaspoon grated or minced lemon zest

4 dollops sour cream or plain yogurt (optional)

Sprigs fresh mint for garnish

1 Pit the cherries and combine them in a medium saucepan with water barely to cover, 2 cups or less. Add the cornstarch, salt, and cinnamon. Turn the heat to medium and cook, stirring occasionally, until the cherries are very soft, 10 to 15 minutes.

2 Add sugar to taste and the lemon zest. Puree the mixture, or not—your choice. Chill, then serve cold, with a dollop of sour cream or yogurt in each bowl and a few mint sprigs.

Croutons

Croutons are nothing more than crisped bits or whole slices of bread. They may be dried in the oven with no seasonings at all, or cooked in oil or butter, with or without garlic and/or herbs. Here are three basic recipes to get you started:

Low-Fat Baked Croutons

Makes about 2 cups cubes

Time: 20 to 40 minutes

If you like, rub the whole slices of bread with a cut clove of garlic before cooking.

4 to 6 slices any bread, preferably slightly stale

1 Preheat the oven to 300°F. Cut the bread into cubes of any size, or leave the slices whole. Place them on a baking sheet.

2 Bake, shaking the pan occasionally if you used cubes, or turning the slices every 10 minutes or so if you left the slices whole. The croutons are done when they are lightly browned and thoroughly dried. Store in a covered container at room temperature for up to a week.

Garlic Croutons

Makes about 2 cups cubes

Time: 10 to 15 minutes

A perfect use for stale bread, and one which will probably convince you never to resort to store-bought croutons again.

4 tablespoons extra-virgin olive oil, butter,
 or a combination
4 cloves garlic, peeled
4 to 6 thick slices any bread, cut into cubes if you like
Salt to taste

1 Place the olive oil in a large skillet and turn the heat to medium-low heat. Add the garlic and cook it in the oil, turning occasionally, until it is lightly browned. Remove the garlic and reserve it for another use or toss it in a salad or soup; it will be very mild.

2 Turn the heat to medium and cook the bread in the oil, turning occasionally, until brown all over. Remove and sprinkle lightly with salt. Store in a covered container at room temperature for up to a week.

Herb Croutons

Makes about 2 cups cubes

Time: 10 to 15 minutes

Another simple crouton, my favorite for salads.

4 tablespoons extra-virgin olive oil, butter,
 or a combination
4 to 6 thick slices any bread, cut into cubes if you like
2 teaspoons or more minced fresh herbs: parsley, dill,
 chervil, thyme, or marjoram alone, or any mixture
 of fresh herbs you like
Salt to taste

1 Place the olive oil or butter in a large skillet and turn the heat to medium. When the oil is hot or the butter melts, add the bread cubes and cook, stirring, until brown all over.

2 Add the herbs and continue to cook for 1 minute more. Remove and sprinkle lightly with salt. Store in a covered container at room temperature for up to a week.

Salads

Salads are among the quickest dishes to prepare, especially if you take advantage of three basic facts:

1. Because most salads are cold, many of the ingredients can be prepared in advance, and leftovers can readily be thrown into the mix.
2. Most salad dressings—especially vinaigrettes, which contain little more than oil and vinegar— keep for at least a few days, and often longer, as long as they're refrigerated.
3. Anything you want to call a salad *is* a salad, from canned tuna mixed with bottled mayonnaise to a variety of exotic greens tossed with oil and vinegar.

Of course there are differences among salads. And, in some ways, the simple green salad is more challenging than the more "complex" salads that contain grains, beans, meat, or seafood. Although quality ingredients are always important, the difference between an average green salad and a great one is determined by just three things: the greens, the oil, and the vinegar. Every household should have good-tasting extra-virgin olive oil, and some special vinegar—such as sherry vinegar, balsamic vinegar, or well-made wine vinegar—to be used for salads and other dressings. But drizzle these on some tasteless lettuce and all you have is tasteless lettuce with good dressing. These days, even average supermarkets have a good assortment of greens, and it always pays to combine at least two or three—preferably more— with varying flavors and textures.

In fact, there are literally hundreds of edible green, leafy vegetables, and although chances are that many of them look the same to you, each has its own personality. They range from mustard greens, which can be searingly hot—not surprising, since it's where mustard comes from—to chard, which is beet-sweet (it is, essentially, a beet grown for its leaves). In between is a spectrum of flavors as varied as that of the animal kingdom. (In addition, many greens are high in traditional nutrients, important trace elements, and some of the newly discovered micro-nutrients now believed to be potent disease fighters.)

Even in far-from-trendy suburban supermarkets, even in winter, you can find more than a dozen greens for sale, from the standards—iceberg, green leaf, red leaf, romaine, and Boston lettuces—to radicchio, dandelion, mustard, turnip, arugula, kale, chard (red and white), collards, bok choy, watercress, endive, chicory, escarole, frisée, mesclun, and a slew of pre-packed salad mixes.

Here's a brief primer for the salad greens you're most likely to encounter. Some other greens are detailed in "Vegetables" (pages 529–617).

The Simple Lettuces

Description   These are useful staples of four types: the all-too-familiar iceberg, little more than a light-green ball of crisp water; Cos or romaine lettuce, with long, narrow leaves, fleshy, crunchy ribs, and a slight tang; butterhead or Boston lettuce, which sports soft but fairly well-defined heads with lots of loose outer leaves; and the more distinctive, pleasantly bitter loose leaf, bunching, or cutting lettuce, like green and red leaf.

Availability and cost   Lettuces are almost always available and, except in the dead of winter, they are inexpensive. They can be grown with little trouble in greenhouses or mild climates (they don't like heat, but will tolerate cool weather), and are in high demand, so it's rare that they sell for more than a dollar a head, or a dollar a pound, and they're often on sale for much less.

Storage   Iceberg keeps brilliantly, romaine only slightly less so, because the outer leaves keep the inner ones moist. Loose leaf lettuces should be used quickly; they won't keep for more than a few days, even when stored in a plastic bag.

Uses   These are the basic salad greens, but remember this: They're always better in combination than they are singly; the bland tenderness of Boston-style lettuce mingles nicely with some bitter loose leaf and super-crisp romaine (the addition of iceberg is not necessarily positive, but it doesn't do much harm). In any case, Caesar salad notwithstanding, the days of the one-lettuce salad are over.

The Chicories and Endives: Radicchio, Belgian Endive, Curly Endive, Escarole, Frisée

Description   If you can tell the difference with your eyes closed between radicchio (seven dollars per pound) and escarole (fifty-nine cents a pound), you deserve a Julia Child award for Most Sophisticated Palate. These are all different forms of chicory (there are many others, but these are the ones you're most likely to encounter), sharp, crunchy greens that vary wildly in appearance but much less so in taste and texture: Tight-headed bright red radicchio; long, green leafy radicchio (also called endive); lettuce-looking escarole; and lacy, frilly frisée. All are quite crunchy and feature a stark bitterness that is readily tamed by cooking or smoothed by olive oil. In general, the flavor, texture, and versatility of this group of greens is unmatched.

Availability and cost   Pretty much year-round, because these are very cold-tolerant greens. Prices are all over the map. Escarole is usually fairly inexpensive, less than a dollar a pound. Frisée used to be cheap, too, but then it became a trendy garnish, and now it's almost as expensive as radicchio. Belgian endive, those delightfully bittersweet little ovals, fall somewhere in between.

Storage Keep in plastic, in the vegetable bin, and count on at least a few days before you see browning or wilting. But the sooner you eat them the better.

Uses Other than endive, these are almost too bitter to use alone in salads, but are great mixed with other greens. Endive can be served like celery, spread with cream cheese mixed with seasonings, or lightly braised with anchovies and lemon juice. And all of these are delicious braised (try, for example, escarole simmered with cooked white beans, olive oil, garlic, and a little broth), sautéed, even brushed with olive oil, sprinkled with garlic and salt, and grilled. See "Vegetables" (pages 529–617) for recipes.

The Potent Powerhouses: Dandelion, Arugula, and Watercress

Description Unrelated greens that are intensely flavorful. Dandelion has the distinction of being among the most vitamin-packed foods on the planet (if it were a processed food it might require FDA approval). When young, it is mild-flavored; when mature, it is the most bitter of greens. Arugula is the most strangely flavored of all the greens, possessing a distinctive hot muddiness that may be an acquired taste, but an easily acquired one. And super-peppery watercress is unjustly used more as a garnish than as a food.

Availability and cost These are spring, summer, and fall greens. Dandelion, which grows like a weed (some people think it is one), is rarely more than a dollar a pound. Arugula and watercress are usually

about a dollar a bunch, or more, and a bunch weighs a few ounces. Pricey, yes, but you don't need a lot for impact.

Storage As strong-tasting as these greens are, they're fairly fragile. Buy and use quickly or risk rotting. If you're desperate to store these for more than a couple of days, dunk their stems ends in a glass half-full of water and wrap the whole thing, glass and all, in a plastic bag. Store this cool tropical mini-environment in the refrigerator.

Uses Arugula can be cooked, but it's best as a salad green, alone for aficionados, in combination with other greens for novices. It is also great as a bed for grilled foods (especially when it wilts a little and absorbs some grilling juices), in a salad with tomatoes, or chopped on top of veal chops or other robust meats. Watercress makes a fine addition to salads, but is also good on sandwiches and in soups—cook with potatoes, in broth or water, and puree to make a vichyssoise-like soup. Dandelions can be eaten in salads when young, but quickly become too bitter to eat raw, and are then best when stir-fried, with soy sauce or garlic and lemon. For this and other recipes, see pages 529–617.

Mustards and Cabbages: Kale, Collards, Chinese Cabbages, and Others

Description Members of the cabbage family, related to broccoli, these are all quite flavorful. Some of them—mustard greens, turnip greens, and collards, for example—are the pot greens of the South, traditionally boiled to death with smoked meat. Others, like bok choy and Napa cabbage, are newcomers to the supermarket but omnipresent in Chinese cooking. Most are better cooked than raw when mature, although young specimens—available only to gardeners—work nicely in salads, and some, like red mustard, mizuna (also called spider mustard), and tah-tsoi (a kind of Chinese cabbage), are found in good mesclun. All are discussed in more detail in "Vegetables" (pages 529–617).

Availability and cost   Year-round and dirt-cheap, almost always under a dollar a pound and usually less than that.

Storage   These are mature, sturdy greens that can be stored for up to a couple of weeks; store wrapped in a plastic bag.

Uses   Only good for salads when very young. For other uses, see "Vegetables" (pages 529–617).

The King of Trendiness: Mesclun

Description   *Mesclun,* from the Niçoise dialect for "mixture," is a word used to describe a collection of a dozen or more wild and cultivated greens, herbs, and edible flowers. There is no single "mesclun"—it's any mixture that can be eaten raw as a salad. Unfortunately, supermarket mesclun contains no herbs or flowers and relatively few greens. Furthermore, it rarely contains the most flavorful ones. Unless you're a gardener, you have no choice about what is included in a mesclun mix, but a good one will contain greens of various textures and flavors—some sweet (young chard or beet greens, for example), some spicy (like red mustard), some bitter (chicories, endives, or young broccoli raab or kale), almost always arugula, and at least a smattering of herbs (especially dill, parsley, fennel, and chervil).

Availability and cost   Mesclun mix has become a year-round staple. Relatively speaking, it costs a fortune. Even in bulk, mesclun is a minimum of five dollars a pound, usually far more. But half a pound will serve four, and good mesclun is a treat. Steer clear, though, of the insipid mesclun-like concoctions sometimes sold in supermarkets with names such as "European Salad Mix," for three bucks for five ounces—about ten dollars a pound.

Storage   Young greens wilt quickly. Store mesclun in a plastic bag and use it within a couple of days.

Uses   Mesclun makes the best salad, but it's also good as a base for grilled food.

Convenience at a Price: Prepacked Salads

Description   Various mixtures of greens packed in a preweighed plastic bag, most with just two or three in a package, sometimes with a bit of shredded carrot or cabbage, and sometimes with an abominable dressing mix. Usually, the mix is of the most ordinary varieties, such as iceberg or romaine.

Availability and cost   Sold year-round, but at outrageous prices: Prepacked iceberg and romaine lettuces mixed with a little red cabbage go for three dollars for ten ounces. Mix it yourself and it would cost seventy-nine cents.

Storage   These keep very well. Most have sell-by dates, and—although not listed on the label—it may be that some preservative is added to the mix or the packaging.

Uses   If you're willing to pay someone the equivalent of a couple of bucks to wash and tear up your iceberg lettuce, go right ahead.

To Wash and Dry Greens

As long as you do this correctly, it's a fast and easy process. Simply place your greens, all together, into a salad spinner, or a colander inside a large pot. Fill the container with water and swirl the greens around. Now lift the colander or salad spinner insert out of the water. Pour out the water, and repeat as necessary until the water contains no traces of sand. Then spin the greens or pat them with towels to dry.

The Basics of Oils

Edible oils are made from nuts (such as walnut), seeds (such as sesame and cotton), vegetables (such as corn), legumes (such as soy), and fruits (such as olive). But—at least in my opinion—they all fall into just three categories: neutral, all-purpose, and highly flavorful.

Neutral Oils: For Cooking Only

Neutral oils add little or no flavor when used in salad dressings or cooking. But they are inexpensive (you can buy a gallon on sale for as little as four dollars) and they are useful. The best of these are canola and grapeseed, both of which are extremely low in saturated fats, have high burning points, and do not detract from the flavor of the foods with which they are combined. I don't usually recommend them for salads—all they add is a vague oiliness—but they're great for deep-frying and acceptable for sautéing. Other neutral oils (in my personal order of preference) include corn, sesame, sunflower, soy, cottonseed, and so on. It's worth noting that most neutral oils, especially those sold in bulk, are extracted by chemical processes and therefore are somewhat less desirable than "cold-pressed" oils.

Olive Oil: The All-Purpose Oil

You can buy cold-pressed neutral oils, but at that point you are spending as much money as you would on olive oil—which is really the only all-purpose oil. There are three kinds of olive oils, and only two worth considering buying. The best is extra-virgin oil; technically it's defined by the amount of acid it contains (which is low) and, in the Mediterranean (at least theoretically) can only be so labeled after being judged to have no negative qualities. In reality, you can think of extra-virgin oil as the first, cold pressing of olives. There are no chemicals used in this process and the result, more often than not, is oil of distinctively fine character. It can be very expensive—twenty-dollar liter bottles are not uncommon—but it can also be reasonably priced at about twenty dollars a gallon. Many people do not consider extra-virgin oil all-purpose because it is expensive and highly flavorful—too flavorful, some believe, for cooking. I don't buy this; if you can't afford extra-virgin oil for cooking, you should certainly turn to other oils. But if you can, try it; usually, its flavor is welcome. In any case, it is the one olive oil you must have in your pantry for salad-making.

"Pure" olive oils may be extra-virgin oils that don't quite make the grade or, more often, oils extracted (either mechanically or chemically) from the pulp left after making extra-virgin oils. It is not nearly as flavorful as extra-virgin oil, but it is very useful stuff. (The so-called "light" olive oil made by some large producers, essentially a neutral oil, is a pure olive oil.) Most pure oils have decent flavor, good enough to use in a salad, and excellent for sautéing and even deep frying. You should expect to spend about twelve dollars a gallon for pure olive oil.

Forget about olive oil labeled "pomace," which is made by extracting oil (usually chemically) from the pits and leftover pulp after the first two pressings. It is not inexpensive enough to bother with, and never has good flavor. If you cannot find or afford good olive oil, stick with neutral oil.

Flavorful Oils: Delicious, but Use with Care

For the most part, these are nut oils, but there are exceptions; most notably the dark sesame oil, which has delicious flavor. Other highly flavorful oils are made from hazelnuts and walnuts, both of which are wonderful and should (almost) never be used for cooking, but for salad dressings and drizzling over cooked foods. There is one flavorful oil which borders on all-purpose, and that is peanut; its flavor, though distinctive, is not overpowering, and it is a great oil for cooking (especially highly spiced foods, and Asian dishes in which olive oil is out of place) as well as for the occasional salad dressing.

On Storing Oils

Oil, like all fat, can go bad. Stored in a cool, dark place (or in an opaque container), most oil will keep well for about a year. If you plan to keep it longer than that, or you live in a warm climate, it's best to use the refrigerator. And always use the refrigerator for nut oils, which become rancid more quickly than other oils.

Some Personal Recommendations

You almost must keep extra-virgin olive oil in the house. And if you have nothing else, you won't suffer too badly. But I usually keep the following oils in stock, for these uses:

Extra-virgin olive oil: For salads and most cooking.

Canola oil: For deep-frying and the occasional sauce or dressing in which I want another flavor to dominate.

Peanut oil: For some sautéing and all stir-frying.

Walnut or hazelnut oil: For the occasional salad dressing.

Sesame oil (the dark kind): For drizzling on stir-fries and certain other Asian dishes.

The Basics of Vinegars

Like oil, there are several types of vinegars. There is chemically produced, distilled vinegar, the familiar, extremely inexpensive "white" vinegar. If you want nothing more than a clean, sour flavor, you could do worse than this. But acidity is only part of the reason to use vinegar (or lemon juice): good flavor is the other. I use white vinegar occasionally, but more often for cleaning windows than for cooking.

Wine, cider, rice, malt, and other vinegars may be made by the traditional "Orleans" method—that is, by aging in barrels. Some of these are exceptional, with depth of flavor nearly equaling good balsamic or sherry vinegars, but most vinegars—and almost all reasonably priced ones—are made by more efficient methods. Assuming, however, that they start with good ingredients (for example, wine vinegar should contain no more than wine; Champagne vinegar real Champagne), commercially made vinegar can be quite decent. Good raspberry, tarragon, or other flavored vinegars usually begin with high-quality wine vinegar.

Balsamic vinegar is probably the most misunderstood food product to have hit the market in the last twenty years. Until then, it was only made in open attics in central Italy, by an arcane method that begins with unfermented grape juice aged for at least fifteen years in a series of increasingly small wooden casks.

The natural evaporation over that period of time assures an intensely woody, near-unique product. (It's near-unique because some sherry vinegar, a recent addition to our markets, is made in a similar fashion.) It also assures a very, very expensive product: Truly traditional balsamic vinegar costs at least fifty dollars for a quarter-liter, and usually more. It may be worth it: A few drops can change a dish. But few people keep real balsamic vinegar in their homes, even in Italy.

What we call balsamic vinegar, then, did not exist until marketers realized the appeal of a sweet, oaky vinegar. They came up with a cheap product, usually selling for about four dollars per half-liter, that contains no more than cheap wine vinegar with sweetener and coloring added, and which can be made overnight. Nevertheless, it can be legally labeled "*aceto balsamico di Modena*" (balsamic vinegar of Modena), just like the expensive stuff. But it is not worth buying.

These days, there are some producers who are making what you might call a "halfway" balsamic vinegar, aging wine must in wooden barrels for up to three years and selling the product—which can be quite good—for about ten dollars a half-liter. This is not cheap, but if you find a brand that has good, "warm" flavor, stick with it and you will be satisfied.

The alternative is Spanish sherry vinegar, which is essentially a good wine vinegar with a strong flavor of wood. It's almost always a good substitute for balsamic vinegar.

A Word about Acidity

All vinegar contains acetic acid, which can make up from 4.5 to 9 percent of the total. This means that some vinegars are twice as acidic as others. As long as your vinegar contains at least five percent acid, it can act as a preservative in pickle-making. Other than that, acidity is a matter of taste, but obviously stronger vinegars will require a higher percentage of oil in making vinaigrettes. Vinegar of relatively low acidity, from 4.5 to six percent, will give you all the flavor you need without adding more sourness than you want. (Most rice vinegar is 4.5 percent; most wine and balsamic vinegar is about six percent.)

Freshly squeezed lemon juice and, to some extent, lime juice, can substitute for vinegar in every instance except for preserving. The flavor, of course, will be different.

Some Personal Recommendations

I buy good vinegar when I see it, or when someone recommends it. But here's what I keep in the house at all times:

Good balsamic vinegar: At ten dollars a bottle, I use it fairly sparingly.
Sherry vinegar: A flavor I love in salads, but also as a quick marinade for grilled or broiled dishes.
Rice vinegar: The vinegar of choice in Asian cooking, and not at all bad in salads.
Wine vinegar, both white (or Champagne) and red: My staple for salads; white is lighter-tasting and makes a nicer-looking vinaigrette—those made with red vinegar are on the pink side—but as long as they are of good quality they are more or less interchangeable.

The Basics of Making Vinegar

Commercial vinegar is made by a variety of processes, but home vinegar is made only one way: You take good wine and allow it to sit in a cask, crock, or jar with a "mother"—vinegar-making bacteria—until all the alcohol is converted to acetic acid, the basis of vinegar. Given this natural process, which you cannot assume is the case with commercial vinegars, and given decent wine to start with, the vinegar will be superior. It is not a difficult process, and it takes virtually no work or money (unless you decide to buy an oak barrel, which is costly), but it can be tricky; the bacteria are fickle, and I would be lying if I said that everyone succeeds with his or her vinegar-making. Still, almost everyone succeeds who is persistent, and—as the effort is minimal—I think it's worth a try, especially if you are a wine drinker, because there is no better use for leftover wine.

Homemade Vinegar

Makes about 1 gallon

Time: Several weeks, largely unattended

Please read the above paragraph. Once you get a vinegar culture going, you will have more than enough for yourself and your friends, unless you do some serious pickling. The wine for this may be accumulated over a period of days, even a couple of weeks; in fact that is preferable. But the wine should be high quality; bulk-processed wines may have so many sulfites that the vinegar-making bacteria will be inhibited. Use red wine to make red vinegar, white wine to make white.

About 2 quarts leftover wine, red or white
About 2 quarts distilled water
About 1 quart organic vinegar, vinegar from a friend's barrel, or vinegar "starter" or "mother," available at most wine- and beer-making shops

1   Pour the wine back and forth between two wide-mouthed containers several times to aerate it.

2   Combine the wine, water, and vinegar or "mother" in a glass or pottery jar or other non-metallic container; the container should be no more than two-thirds full. Cover very loosely with cheesecloth, paper towel, napkin, or rag. Let sit in a warm place, undisturbed.

3   Check the vinegar after 2 weeks. If it has a slimy coating on top and is beginning to smell more like vinegar than like wine, you're in good shape. Let it sit until it is completely converted, a total of 2 more weeks to 2 months. (If nothing happens during that time, try again, using different wine, different starter, and a different location.)

4   Once the vinegar is going, you can take vinegar out and use it or bottle it, and add more wine. Never fill the container more than two-thirds full, and never remove more than half the vinegar at once. Each time you add wine, allow the brew to sit long enough for it to be converted to vinegar, then draw some of it off before adding more wine.

The Basics of Vinaigrettes

The most common dressing for salad is vinaigrette. A vinaigrette is acid and oil, combined; every other addition is up for grabs. The acid may be freshly squeezed citrus juice, usually lemon or lime, or vinegar—the best you can find. The acidic ingredient is the most basic flavor of a vinaigrette, so it should be delicious.

The oil, most often olive, may be a nut oil or a neutral vegetable oil. Oil can add to a vinaigrette or it may be nothing more than a carrier of other flavors. Extra-virgin olive oil, walnut oil, and peanut oil are examples of strong, delicious flavors that can boost a vinaigrette. "Pure" olive oil, canola oil, and grapeseed oil are examples of neutral oils that add little besides body. Rancid oils, no matter what their origin, can ruin vinaigrette. Smell oil before adding it to avoid this; you'll know when its taste will be negative rather than positive.

Aside from added flavors, there are two major determinations to make whenever you make a vinaigrette, and they are both based on personal taste. First, you must decide the ratio of oil to vinegar; second you must decide whether to emulsify the dressing.

The first question cannot be answered routinely. Lemon juice measures three or four percent acid; strong vinegar measures twice that. If you use the same amounts one dressing will be twice as strong as the other. Similarly, some oils are much stronger-tasting than others, and seem better at balancing acidic flavors.

What you can do is determine your general personal preference and work from there. I recommend starting with a ratio of two parts oil to one part vinegar. You may end up with three or even four to one; you may end up at one to one, especially when you replace the vinegar with lemon juice. (You may even prefer more vinegar than olive oil; there's nothing wrong with that.) But try to get a sense of the ratio that you prefer, and use that as your starting point. Then taste, taste, taste.

As for emulsifying, it's purely a matter of choice. Traditionally, vinaigrettes are an emulsion of vinegar and oil, and emulsions are creamier, and marginally more pleasing texturally, than vinegar and oil separately. Having said that, it's worth noting that drizzling a salad with olive oil and vinegar or lemon juice is not only a good alternative tradition, but one that gives you a chance to adjust the ratio of oil and vinegar while you taste the dressing with the greens. Although it's always possible to make a good-tasting vinaigrette, you cannot always predict how it will taste when tossed with greens. But if you drizzle olive oil and vinegar over a bowl of greens and toss, it's easy to adjust the taste by adding more of one or the other.

Should you decide to emulsify, you have several choices. Both food processors and blenders—whether the more common stand-up type or the new immersion variety—make perfectly emulsified vinaigrettes. These emulsions are stable for hours and sometimes longer, so they're especially nice for buffets.

You can also simply whisk the oil into the vinegar and seasonings, or shake everything together in a jar. These emulsions are less stable, but fine for dinner or other occasions when longevity is unimportant. A spoonful of Dijon mustard (or of pureed Roasted Garlic, page 575) not only boosts the flavor of many vinaigrettes but makes emulsions even more stable.

Vinaigrette is best made fresh, but some versions store well enough for a few days in the refrigerator, covered tightly.

Basic Vinaigrette

Makes 1 cup

Time: 5 minutes

Emulsified vinaigrettes are only important if you care. Sometimes that extra creaminess is nice (and an immersion blender works brilliantly). But usually it doesn't matter much; I just toss everything in a bowl and whisk it for thirty seconds or so.

$^1/_4$ cup good vinegar, such as sherry, balsamic, or
    high-quality red or white wine, plus more to taste
$^1/_2$ teaspoon salt, plus more if needed
$^1/_2$ teaspoon Dijon mustard (optional)
$^3/_4$ cup extra-virgin olive oil, plus more if needed
2 teaspoons minced shallots (optional)
Freshly ground black pepper to taste

1 Briefly mix the vinegar, salt, and optional mustard with an immersion blender, food processor or blender, or with a fork or wire whisk.

2 Slowly add the oil in a stream (drop by drop if whisking) until an emulsion forms; or just whisk everything together briefly. Add the remaining oil faster, but still in a stream.

3 Taste to adjust salt and add more oil or vinegar if needed. Add the shallots and pepper. This is best made fresh but will keep, refrigerated, for a few days; bring back to room temperature before using.

To make a small amount of Basic Vinaigrette: Combine 1 to $1^1/_2$ tablespoons vinegar, $^1/_4$ teaspoon salt, $^1/_2$ teaspoon mustard, 3 to 4 tablespoons oil, and $^1/_2$ teaspoon minced shallots as above. Add pepper, then taste and add more vinegar, salt, or oil as necessary.

Walnut Oil Vinaigrette

Makes about ³/₄ cup

Time: 5 minutes

I find that the strong, wonderful flavor of walnut oil allows me to use less of it in a dressing. But remember—the ratio of oil to vinegar is as much a function of taste as of chemistry.

¹/₄ cup sherry, balsamic, or good red wine vinegar
¹/₂ teaspoon salt
1 teaspoon Dijon mustard (optional)
¹/₂ cup walnut oil, plus a little more if needed
2 teaspoons minced shallots (optional)
Freshly black ground pepper to taste

1 Briefly mix the vinegar, salt, and mustard with an immersion blender, food processor or blender, or fork or wire whisk. Slowly add the oil in a stream (drop by drop if whisking) until an emulsion forms.

2 Add the remaining oil faster, but still in a stream. Taste to adjust salt and add more oil if needed. Add the shallots and pepper. This is best made fresh but will keep, refrigerated, for a few days; bring back to room temperature before using.

Lemon or Lime Vinaigrette

Makes about ³/₄ cup

Time: 5 minutes

An all-purpose vinaigrette, especially wonderful for salads or warm dishes that contain fish. Lemon and lime juices are less acidic than vinegar, so you can use them in higher proportions. Do not make this dressing more than an hour or so in advance; lemon and lime juices lose their flavor much more quickly than vinegar.

1 teaspoon minced or grated lemon or lime zest
¹/₂ teaspoon salt
¹/₄ cup freshly squeezed lemon juice, plus a bit more if needed
¹/₂ cup extra-virgin olive oil, plus a little more if needed

1 Mix the zest, salt and juice briefly with an immersion blender, food processor or blender, or fork or wire whisk. Slowly add the oil in a stream (drop by drop if whisking) until an emulsion forms.

2 Add the remaining oil faster, but still in a stream. Taste to adjust salt and add more oil if needed. Let sit to develop flavor; if you are serving this immediately, you may want to add a bit more lemon juice to sharpen the flavor.

Lemon- or Lime-Thyme Vinaigrette: Add ¹/₂ teaspoon finely minced fresh thyme to the vinaigrette.

Lemon- or Lime-Dill Vinaigrette: Add 2 teaspoons finely minced dill; this should sit for about 15 minutes in order for the flavor to develop.

Lemon- or Lime-Tarragon Vinaigrette: Add ¹/₂ teaspoon minced fresh or crumbled dried tarragon, or to taste, to the vinaigrette; or, for a fuller flavor, add ¹/₂ teaspoon Dijon mustard to the vinegar and reduce the salt to ¹/₄ teaspoon; then add tarragon to the completed vinaigrette.

Lemon- or Lime-Onion Vinaigrette: Add 1 small onion, minced; again, this is best if it sits for 15 minutes or so before serving.

Orange Vinaigrette: Any of the above recipes can be made with orange as well, but some lemon juice or vinegar must be added or the flavor will not be sharp enough. Start with ¹/₄ cup orange juice plus 1 tablespoon freshly squeezed lemon juice and proceed from there.

Nutty Vinaigrette

Makes about 1 cup

Time: 10 minutes

You can use almost any nuts you like for this dressing; peeled ones are best.

> $^1/_2$ cup almonds, hazelnuts, pine nuts, pecans, or walnuts
> 1 small clove garlic, peeled
> $^1/_4$ cup sherry, balsamic, or good red wine vinegar, plus more if desired
> Salt and freshly ground black pepper to taste
> $^3/_4$ cup extra-virgin olive oil

1 Toast the nuts in a dry skillet over medium heat, shaking almost constantly, until fragrant. Place them in the container of a blender or small food processor along with the garlic and pulverize.

2 Place the ground nuts and garlic in a bowl and add the vinegar, salt, and pepper; stir. Add the oil a bit at a time. The mixture will become creamy and quite thick. Taste to make sure the acid balance pleases you and add more vinegar if you like; if the taste is good but the mixture is too thick, add warm water, a teaspoon at a time. This is best made fresh but will keep, refrigerated, for a day or so; bring back to room temperature before using.

Anchovy-Caper Vinaigrette

Makes about 1 cup

Time: 10 minutes

A pungent dressing, not for the faint of heart. Use on flavorful greens.

> 4 anchovy fillets, with a bit of their oil
> 1 teaspoon capers, with a bit of their brine
> About $^3/_4$ cup extra-virgin olive oil
> About $^1/_4$ cup sherry, balsamic, or good red wine vinegar
> 1 teaspoon Dijon mustard
> Salt and freshly ground black pepper to taste
> 1 tablespoon minced fresh parsley

1 Mince the anchovy fillets and mix them with their oil, the capers and their brine, and all the remaining ingredients except for the parsley.

2 Taste and correct seasoning if necessary. Add parsley just before serving. Do not make this dressing in advance.

Vinaigrette in the Style of Mayonnaise

Makes about 1 cup

Time: 10 minutes

This is something of a cross between vinaigrette and mayonnaise, more vinegary and much thinner than the latter but much creamier than most vinaigrettes. If the thought of raw eggs worries you, substitute an equivalent amount of a pasteurized egg substitute such as Egg Beaters.

> 1 egg
> 1 teaspoon Dijon mustard
> 1 teaspoon minced shallot
> $^1/_4$ cup sherry, balsamic, or good red wine vinegar
> $^3/_4$ cup extra-virgin olive, walnut, or hazelnut oil
> Salt and freshly ground black pepper to taste

1 Break the egg into a small bowl or the container of a blender or small food processor and beat with the mustard, shallot, and vinegar.

1. Any fresh or dried herb, in small proportions, usually less than one teaspoon (fresh) per cup
2. Minced fresh ginger, as much as one teaspoon per cup
3. Minced fresh garlic, usually one-eighth to one-fourth teaspoon per cup
4. Soy sauce, Worcestershire sauce, or other liquid seasonings, as much as one tablespoon per cup
5. Honey or other sweeteners, from one teaspoon to one tablespoon per cup
6. Whole grain mustards, one teaspoon to one tablespoon per cup. Or dry mustard, about one-half teaspoon per cup
7. Cayenne, crushed red pepper flakes, or minced fresh chiles, from a pinch to one-half teaspoon per cup
8. Crushed coriander seeds, about one teaspoon per cup; add minced cilantro at the same time
9. Freshly grated Parmesan or other hard cheese, or crumbled Roquefort or other blue cheese, at least one tablespoon per cup
10. Minced cucumber or fennel, about one-fourth cup per cup (increase liquids a bit)
11. Minced pickles, preferably cornichons, from one-fourth to one-eighth cup per cup
12. Sour cream, yogurt, or pureed soft tofu, about two tablespoons per cup
13. Prepared or freshly grated horseradish, at least one teaspoon per cup
14. Ground spices such as curry powder, five-spice powder, or nutmeg, in very small quantities
15. Minced tomatoes or ripe avocado

2. Drizzle in the oil, beating constantly with a fork/wire whisk, or with the machine running. When the mixture is as thick as heavy cream, add salt and pepper.

Creamy Vinaigrette

Makes about 1 cup

Time: 5 minutes

The "secret" ingredient here is cream. But the amount is small, and the addition makes a glorious dressing.

1 small shallot, minced
Salt and freshly ground black pepper to taste
1 teaspoon Dijon mustard, plus more as needed
$^1/_2$ cup extra-virgin olive oil
About $^1/_4$ cup top-quality white wine vinegar, plus more as needed
$^1/_4$ cup heavy cream

1. Mix together the shallot, salt, pepper, and mustard in a small bowl or a blender or food processor.

2. Add the olive oil and whisk well with a fork or keep the machine running; add most of the vinegar and cream and whisk again. Taste, and add salt, pepper, mustard, and/or vinegar as needed. Use immediately.

The Best and Simplest Green Salad

Makes 4 servings

Time: 10 minutes

Almost any combination of greens can make a salad, and you don't have to get fussy about dressings, either. Most are just dressed with freshly squeezed lemon juice or vinegar, olive oil, and salt and fresh pepper, all to taste. Substitute any vinaigrette (pages 91–94) or other dressing you like for the oil and vinegar.

4 to 6 cups torn assorted greens (trimmed, washed, and dried)

1/4 to 1/3 cup extra-virgin olive oil or walnut oil

1 or 2 tablespoons balsamic vinegar or sherry vinegar

Pinch salt, plus more to taste

Freshly ground black pepper to taste (optional)

Place the greens in a bowl and drizzle them with oil, vinegar, and a pinch of salt. Toss and taste. Correct seasoning, add pepper if desired, and serve immediately.

Simple Greek Salad: A bright-tasting salad. Toss together 4 to 6 cups torn mixed greens (at least some should be strong-tasting) with 1/4 cup cleaned and chopped radish; 1/4 cup minced fresh mint leaves or mint mixed with parsley; 1/4 cup chopped feta cheese, or more to taste; and 1/4 cup pitted and chopped black olives. Drizzle with olive oil and freshly squeezed lemon juice to taste.

Green Salad with Tomatoes: Use 4 to 6 cups torn mixed greens as in the original recipe. Core 2 or 3 perfectly ripe tomatoes, cut them in half, then squeeze and shake out the seeds. Chop and toss with the greens. Best with good balsamic vinegar.

Wild Greens Salad: Toss together 2 or 3 cups each of torn arugula and dandelion greens, or similar strong-tasting greens. Add 1 tablespoon minced shallot. Use lemon juice in place of vinegar, and toss with a Soft-Boiled Egg (page 733) if you like to take the edge off the bitter greens.

Arugula and Blue Cheese Salad: Top 4 to 6 cups torn arugula with a crumbling of blue cheese, preferably Roquefort, Gorgonzola, or Stilton. Add 1/2 cup pitted and roughly chopped black olives. Use olive oil and freshly squeezed lemon juice for dressing.

Watercress and Endive Salad: A strong, bitter salad. Toss together 2 to 3 cups watercress and 2 to 3 cups trimmed and shredded Belgian endive. Add 1/2 cup broken or roughly chopped walnuts or hazelnuts, toasted in a dry skillet over a medium flame until fragrant. Dress with walnut or hazelnut oil if you have it, and good vinegar.

Nine Simple Additions to Salads

1. Any nuts or seeds, crumbled or chopped if necessary
2. Fresh herbs, torn into pieces
3. Sliced pears, apples, or other fruit
4. Sectioned citrus fruit, such as grapefruit or orange
5. Sea vegetables (page 602), such as dulse, hijiki, or arame, soaked briefly in water, squeezed dry, and cut up
6. Thinly sliced celery or fennel
7. Very thinly sliced Parmesan (use a vegetable peeler to produce thin curls) or other hard cheese
8. Crumbled Hard-Boiled Egg (page 733)
9. Diced roasted red or yellow peppers (or canned pimentos), olives, capers, or anchovies

Cabbage and Carrot Salad

Makes 4 servings

Time: 15 minutes

A nice, Asian-style variation on the simple green salad.

1 pound Napa or Savoy cabbage, cored and shredded (page 547)

2 carrots, peeled and grated

2 or 3 scallions, minced

1/4 to 1/3 cup peanut (preferred) or canola oil

2 tablespoons freshly squeezed lime juice

1 teaspoon soy sauce

Salt and freshly ground black pepper to taste

Combine the vegetables. Whisk together the oil, lime juice, and soy; taste and add salt and pepper if necessary. Toss the dressing with the vegetables and serve.

Caesar Salad

Makes 4 servings

Time: 20 minutes

The essentials in a great Caesar salad are garlic, egg, lemon juice, anchovies, and real Parmesan. Compromise on any of these and you'll still have a good salad, but you won't have a great Caesar.

    1 clove garlic, cut in half
    2 eggs, or substitute $1/2$ cup pasteurized egg product
    2 tablespoons freshly squeezed lemon juice
    6 tablespoons extra-virgin olive oil
    2 tablespoons minced anchovies, or to taste
    Dash Worcestershire sauce
    Salt and freshly ground black pepper to taste
    1 large head romaine lettuce, trimmed, washed, dried, and torn into bits
    Garlic Croutons (page 82)
    $1/2$ to 1 cup freshly grated Parmesan cheese

  1 Rub the inside of your salad bowl with the garlic clove; discard it.

  2 Bring a small pot of water to a boil. Pierce a tiny hole in the broad end of each of the eggs with a pin or a needle and boil them for 60 to 90 seconds; they will just begin to firm up. Crack them into the salad bowl, making sure to scoop out the white that clings to the shell.

  3 Beat the eggs with a fork, gradually adding the lemon juice and then the olive oil, beating all the while.

  4 Stir in the anchovies and the Worcestershire. Taste and add salt if needed and plenty of pepper. Toss

well with the lettuce; top with the croutons and Parmesan, then bring to the table and toss again. Serve immediately.

Chicken Caesar Salad: Top the salad with slices of Basic Grilled or Broiled Chicken Cutlets, page 380.

Mesclun with Goat Cheese and Croutons

Makes 4 servings

Time: About 20 minutes

Make sure the goat cheese is at room temperature before serving (you may warm it gently in the oven if you like).

    5 to 6 cups torn mixed greens (trimmed, washed, and dried)
    Basic Vinaigrette (page 91)
    4 croutons (page 82), any style, made without cubing the bread
    4 ounces soft goat cheese, at room temperature, cut into quarters

  1 Toss the greens with the vinaigrette and divide among four plates.

  2 Spread the croutons with the goat cheese, and top each portion of greens with a crouton.

Dandelion Greens with Bacon

Makes 4 servings

Time: About 30 minutes

With good bacon, one of the great food combinations ever. Must be served warm.

2 tablespoons olive oil

About ½ pound best slab bacon you can find,
cut into ½-inch cubes

1 tablespoon chopped shallot

4 cups torn dandelion or other bitter greens, such as
arugula, cress, or frisée (trimmed, washed, and
dried)

About ¼ cup top-quality red wine vinegar

1 teaspoon Dijon mustard

Salt and freshly ground black pepper to taste

1 Place the olive oil in a skillet and turn the heat to medium. Add the bacon and cook slowly until it is crisp all over, 10 minutes or more. Add the shallot and cook a minute or two longer, until the shallot softens. Keep the bacon warm in the skillet.

2 Heat a salad bowl by filling it with hot water and letting it sit for a minute. Dry it and toss in the greens. Add the vinegar and mustard to the skillet, and bring just to a boil, stirring. Pour the liquid and the bacon over the greens, season to taste (it shouldn't need much salt), and serve immediately.

Cold Cooked Greens, Greek-Style

Makes 4 servings

Time: 20 minutes

This is a wonderful use for already-cooked greens (including leftovers), but it's so good that you may buy dark greens simply in order to cook and serve them this way.

1 to 2 pounds dark leafy greens, such as collards,
kale, or spinach

Several tablespoons extra-virgin olive oil

Freshly ground black pepper to taste

2 lemons, cut in half

1 Bring a large pot of water to a boil and salt it. Trim the greens of any stems thicker than ¼ inch; discard them. Wash the greens well.

2 Simmer the greens until tender, just a minute or two for spinach, up to 10 minutes or even longer for older, tougher greens. Drain them well and cool them quickly by running them under cold water.

3 Squeeze the greens dry and chop them. (You may prepare the salad in advance up to this point; cover and refrigerate for up to a day, then bring to room temperature before proceeding.) Sprinkle with olive oil, salt, and pepper, and serve with lemon halves.

Sorrel Salad with Hard-Cooked Eggs

Makes 4 servings

Time: 20 minutes

This is a rich, old-fashioned salad, full of flavor.

2 eggs

2 cups torn tender, mild lettuce, such as Boston
(trimmed, washed, and dried)

4 cups torn sorrel (trimmed, washed, and dried)

Creamy Vinaigrette (page 94)

1 Pierce a tiny hole in the broad end of each of the eggs with a pin or a needle. Place the eggs in a small pot of water and turn the heat to medium-high. Bring the water to a boil, lower the heat, and cook gently for 10 to 12 minutes. Leave the eggs in the pot and run them under cold water to chill.

2 Meanwhile, toss the lettuce and the sorrel together. Peel the eggs, chop them up coarsely, and toss them and the dressing with the greens. Serve immediately.

Endives, Scallions, and Mint with Yogurt Dressing

Makes 4 servings

Time: 15 minutes

This is everything a salad should be: bitter, sharp, sour, and refreshing.

4 Belgian endives, trimmed and separated into leaves
4 fresh scallions, trimmed and minced
2 cups plain yogurt
1 small clove garlic, minced
Salt and freshly ground black pepper to taste
¼ cup minced fresh mint leaves, plus several whole
    leaves for garnish

1 Lay the endive leaves out in a spoke pattern on a serving platter; sprinkle the scallions over them.

2 Mix together the yogurt, garlic, salt, pepper, and minced mint; dress the endive with this mixture, garnish, and serve.

Tender Greens with Peanuts and Tomatoes

Makes 4 servings

Time: 15 minutes

A spicy, crunchy salad, best with bitter greens—mild ones would be overwhelmed by the sauce.

Twenty-Two Salads You Can Eat as a Main Course

There are people who eat any salad as a main course but I (unfortunately, at times) am not among them. These are salads with some heft; I find them especially satisfying. See also Nine Simple Additions to Salads, page 95.

1. Simple Greek Salad, page 95
2. Caesar Salad, page 96
3. Mesclun with Goat Cheese and Croutons, page 96
4. Tomato, Mozzarella, and Basil Salad, page 101
5. Tabbouleh, page 112
6. Couscous Salad with Mint and Parsley, page 113
7. Cress and Barley Salad with Dill Vinaigrette, page 114
8. Arborio Rice Salad with Peas, page 114
9. Grilled Chicken Salad, page 114
10. Chicken Salad with Olive Oil and Chives, page 115
11. Curried Chicken Salad, page 116 (see also Twelve Poultry Dishes that Go Great on Greens, page 117)
12. Chicken Salad with Cabbage and Mint, page 115
13. Chicken or Duck Salad with Walnuts, page 116
14. Beef Salad with Mint, page 117 (see also "Fourteen Meat Dishes That Go Great on Greens," page 118)
15. Chef's Salad, page 118
16. Shrimp Salad, Mediterranean-Style, page 119 (see also "Thirteen Fish and Shellfish Dishes that Go Great on Greens," page 123)
17. Seafood Salad, Adriatic-Style, page 119
18. Grilled Shrimp and Tomato Salad, page 120
19. Mussel and Potato Salad, page 121
20. Fried Chili-Spiced Clam Salad, page 123
21. Salmon Salad with Beans, page 121
22. Salade Niçoise, page 122

4 cups coarsely chopped young, tender arugula, dandelion, mizuna, romaine lettuce, or other greens (trimmed, washed, and dried)

1 tablespoon peanut oil

1 teaspoon chili powder

1/2 cup roasted peanuts, with or without salt

Salt to taste

1 cup cored, peeled, seeded, and chopped ripe tomatoes (page 610)

Juice of 1 lime

1 Place the chopped greens in a bowl.

2 Place the peanut oil in a small saucepan and turn the heat to medium. Add the chili powder and cook, stirring, until the chili powder darkens, 30 to 60 seconds. Add the peanuts, toss, and cook, stirring constantly, for about a minute. Add salt if necessary.

3 Toss together the greens, peanuts, and tomatoes. Taste for salt and add more if necessary. Sprinkle the lime juice over all and serve.

Watercress and Sesame Salad

Makes 4 servings

Time: 10 minutes

The peppery cress makes a perfect foil for the mild sweetness of this dressing.

About 4 cups coarsely chopped watercress (trimmed, washed, and dried)

2 tablespoons rice or wine vinegar

2 tablespoons soy sauce

1/2 teaspoon sugar

1/4 teaspoon cayenne, or to taste

1 teaspoon dark sesame oil

Salt to taste

2 tablespoons Toasted Sesame Seeds (page 776)

1 Place the chopped watercress in a bowl. Mix together the vinegar, soy sauce, sugar, and cayenne, and dress the cress with this mixture.

2 Toss, add the sesame oil, and toss again. Taste for salt and add it if necessary. Garnish and serve.

Red and Green Salad

Makes 4 servings

Time: 30 minutes

This simple dish contains an astonishing variety of flavors and textures.

1 cup fresh or frozen green peas

2 heads radicchio, about 1/2 to 3/4 pound total

3 red apples, skins left on, cored and cut into 1/2-inch dice

1 red bell pepper, roasted (page 593), stemmed, peeled, seeded, and minced, or 1/2 cup minced canned pimento

1/2 cup low-fat or non-fat plain yogurt

1 heaping tablespoon prepared horseradish, or to taste

1 tablespoon cider, sherry, or white wine vinegar

Salt and freshly ground black pepper to taste

1 If the peas are frozen, defrost them in cold water to cover while you prepare the other ingredients.

2 Wash and dry the radicchio; tear leaves into small pieces. Toss in a bowl with the apples and red pepper. Boil the peas (whether thawed or fresh) in salted water for 1 minute. Drain and rinse in cold water.

3 Toss three quarters of the peas with the salad. Combine the yogurt, horseradish, vinegar, salt, and pepper in a blender or bowl and blend or whisk until smooth. Taste and correct seasoning, then dress the salad. Garnish with the reserved peas.

Vegetable Salads

We first think of salads as green, but other vegetables cooked in advance, lightly dressed and served cold or at room temperature, can be wonderful, easy, and even impressive. Somehow, for example, a bowl of steaming hot beets turns into something enchanting when the beets are thinly sliced and served at room temperature with a bit of green and a drizzling of olive oil. And it doesn't take much to turn the everyday carrot into a salad course that may become the star of the meal. Many of the simple recipes in "Vegetables" (pages 529–617), such as Basic Steamed Artichokes (page 535), Beets Baked in Foil (page 541), or Grilled Spanish Onions (page 587), can be served at room temperature or chilled and dressed with any vinaigrette.

Beet and Fennel Salad

Makes 4 to 6 servings

Time: 1 to 1½ hours

This is a dish of lovely contrasts and syntheses: red and white, with the slight licorice flavor of tarragon playing with the crunchy fennel and the smooth beets.

4 medium beets, a little more than 1 pound
1 fennel bulb
2 tablespoons extra-virgin olive oil
1 tablespoon freshly squeezed lemon juice
1 tablespoon minced fresh basil leaves, 1 teaspoon minced fresh tarragon leaves, or ½ teaspoon dried tarragon, plus additional chopped fresh herb for garnish (optional)
Salt and freshly ground black pepper to taste

1 Preheat the oven to 400°F. Wash the beets well. Wrap them individually in foil and place them on a baking sheet or roasting pan.

2 Cook, undisturbed, for 45 to 90 minutes, until a thin-bladed knife pierces one with little resistance (they may cook at different rates; remove each one when it is done). While they're cooking, trim the fennel and chop it into ½- to 1-inch dice.

3 Remove the beets and plunge them into ice water until cool. Peel them and cut them into pieces the same size as the fennel.

4 Toss the beets, fennel, and the remaining ingredients together and serve immediately. If you plan to let the salad sit, hold out the lemon juice until the last minute (and don't be surprised when the fennel turns red). Garnish, if you like, with a bit of chopped fresh herb.

Carrot Salad with Cumin

Makes 4 servings

Time: 15 minutes

Here's a simple salad in a typically North African style that features the sweetness of fresh oranges offset nicely by the tang of ground cumin. You can also combine carrot and celeriac, jicama, or sunchokes, using the same dressing.

1½ pounds carrots, peeled and grated
Juice of 2 oranges
Juice of 1 lemon
2 tablespoons extra-virgin olive oil
Salt and freshly ground black pepper to taste
1 teaspoon ground cumin, or more to taste

1 Use the julienne cutter of a food processor to cut the carrots into fine shreds, or cut into ⅛-inch-thick slices.

2 Blend the remaining ingredients and pour the sauce dressing over the carrots. Toss and serve.

Tomato, Mozzarella, and Basil Salad

Makes 4 servings

Time: 5 to 15 minutes

This is barely more than the three ingredients listed above, so all three must be of excellent quality. I like to salt the tomatoes a little bit before assembling the salad—it removes a little of their excess liquid—but it isn't strictly necessary.

4 medium perfectly ripe tomatoes
Salt to taste
8 (¹/₄-inch-thick) slices fresh mozzarella, plus more
   if desired
8 basil leaves, washed and dried
Freshly ground black pepper to taste
Extra-virgin olive oil for drizzling

1 Core and cut the tomatoes into about ¹/₄-inch-thick slices (page 610). If you like, lay them on a board and sprinkle them lightly with salt. Set the board at an angle so the liquid can drain into the sink (or a bowl; it makes a refreshing drink).

2 Layer tomatoes, mozzarella, and basil on a platter or four individual plates. Sprinkle with salt and pepper, drizzle with olive oil, and serve.

Jicama and Orange Salad

Makes 4 servings

Time: 15 minutes

Crunchy and sweet, fresh jicama slices need little more than a sprinkling of lime or lemon, but this recipe really showcases cilantro at its best. Use lime juice with cilantro, lemon juice with basil or chervil.

1 jicama, about 1 pound
3 small sweet oranges or tangerines
Salt to taste
1 tablespoon freshly squeezed lime or lemon juice
2 tablespoons minced cilantro, fresh basil, or chervil
   leaves

1 Peel the jicama and cut it into small cubes, ¹/₄ inch or so, or into julienne strips.

2 Squeeze the juice from one of the oranges, pour it over the jicama, add salt and lime juice, and let it sit while you prepare the other oranges (the jicama may marinate for several hours if you wish).

3 Peel the remaining oranges and cut into small pieces, removing any pits and tough, fibrous material. Add oranges and cilantro to jicama, toss, taste and correct seasoning, and serve.

Orange, Onion, and Rosemary Salad

Makes 4 servings

Time: 15 minutes

A simple, unusual first course. Add some Niçoise or Calamata olives to this if you like.

4 navel oranges
1 small red onion
1 teaspoon minced fresh rosemary or ¹/₂ teaspoon
   dried rosemary, plus sprigs fresh rosemary for
   garnish (optional)
Salt and freshly ground black pepper to taste
2 tablespoons extra-virgin olive oil

1 Peel the oranges and section them (see illustrations, page 638) or slice them thinly. Peel the onion and slice it thinly. Toss both with the minced fresh or dried rosemary, a small amount of salt and pepper, and the olive oil.

2 Serve immediately or refrigerate for up to 2 hours (bring to room temperature before serving). Garnish with rosemary sprigs, if you have them, before serving.

Eggplant Salad, Italian-Style

Makes 4 servings

Time: About 1 hour

You can call this caponata; the Italians do, and it would be hard to imagine it evolving anywhere but southern Italy. Make it in quantity if you like, because it keeps quite well for up to one week. Always bring to room temperature before serving, with bread or crackers.

About 2 pounds eggplant

Salt to taste

6 tablespoons extra-virgin olive oil

Freshly ground black pepper to taste

1 large onion, chopped

2 cloves garlic, minced

1 red bell pepper, stemmed, peeled if desired, seeded, and sliced

2 ripe tomatoes, cored and chopped (page 610), or about 1¹/₂ cups canned tomatoes, drained and crushed

3 tablespoons capers

1 tablespoon sugar

1 tablespoon red or white wine vinegar (or less; see Step 3)

Handful chopped fresh parsley leaves

1 Peel the eggplant if you like, then cut it into ¹/₂-inch cubes. Salt them liberally and place them in a colander for a half-hour or more. Rinse them thoroughly, then press between paper towels to remove as much moisture as possible.

2 Place the olive oil in a large non-stick skillet over medium heat. Add the eggplant, stirring and shaking almost constantly, until it absorbs all the oil and begins to brown and soften. Add the black pepper, onion, garlic, red pepper, and tomatoes, and continue to cook until all the vegetables soften and the mixture is thick, about 15 minutes; do not overcook—the vegetables should remain distinct.

3 Add the capers, sugar, and vinegar (a bit less if you used vinegar-packed capers), parsley, additional salt (probably not needed), and pepper; remove from heat. Serve at room temperature.

Caponata with Raisins and Pine Nuts: In Step 1, soak ¹/₂ cup raisins in some red wine; add them and their liquid along with the onion in Step 2. In Step 3, add ¹/₂ cup lightly toasted pine nuts with the capers. You can also add ¹/₂ cup pitted, chopped green or black olives (or both) along with the capers.

Eggplant Salad with Sesame Dressing

Makes 2 to 4 servings

Time: About 40 minutes, plus time to preheat the grill

Charred eggplant has so much flavor that a simple dressing is all you need to make it special.

1 eggplant, about 1 pound

2 tablespoons Toasted Sesame Seeds (page 776)

2 tablespoons soy sauce

1 tablespoon freshly squeezed lemon juice

¹/₂ teaspoon sugar

1. Start a charcoal or wood fire, or preheat a gas grill or broiler, set the rack about 4 inches from the heat source. Or preheat the oven to 450°F. Grill, broil, or roast the eggplant until it collapses, from 20 to 40 minutes, turning frequently so the skin darkens but does not burn.

2. Use a paring knife to remove the skin from the eggplant, then cut the eggplant into chunks, or just shred it. Toss it with all the remaining ingredients and serve within 30 minutes.

Potato Salad with Double Mustard Dressing

Makes 4 servings

Time: 30 minutes, plus cooling time

If you don't have both kinds of mustard in the house, use one or the other—the salad will still be delicious.

1 1/2 pounds waxy potatoes, such as red new potatoes
1/4 cup Dijon mustard
1/4 cup grainy mustard
1/2 cup olive oil
1 tablespoon balsamic, sherry, or other flavorful
    vinegar
3 tablespoons chopped fresh basil leaves
Salt and freshly ground black pepper to taste

1. Bring a medium pot of water to a boil; salt it. Peel the potatoes if you like (or wash and scrub them well), then cut them into bite-sized pieces; cook them in the water until tender but still firm and not at all mushy, 15 minutes or so. Drain.

2. Mix together the mustards, oil, vinegar, and basil, and toss with the potatoes. Season with salt and pepper. Serve warm or at room temperature. (This can be refrigerated for up to a day; bring back to room temperature before serving.)

Classic American Potato Salad

Makes 4 servings

Time: 30 minutes, plus cooling time

Especially good with homemade mayonnaise (page 761), which can be made in five minutes.

1 1/2 pounds waxy potatoes, such as red new potatoes
1/2 cup minced fresh parsley leaves
1/4 cup minced onion
Mayonnaise to taste (start with 1/2 cup)
Salt and freshly ground black pepper to taste

1. Bring a medium pot of water to a boil; salt it. Peel the potatoes if you like (or wash and scrub them well), then cut them into bite-size pieces; cook them in the water until tender but still firm and not at all mushy, 15 minutes or so. Drain, rinse in cold water for a minute, then drain again.

2. Toss the still-warm potatoes with the parsley and onion. Add mayonnaise until the mixture is as creamy as you like. Season with salt and pepper and refrigerate until ready to serve. (You may prepare the salad in advance up to this point; cover and refrigerate for up to a day, then bring to room temperature before serving.)

Twelve Simple Additions to Classic American Potato Salad

In addition to these quick additions, see Mussel and Potato Salad (page 121).

1. Minced red pepper, fresh or roasted (or used canned pimentos)
2. Chopped shallots, raw or lightly sautéed in olive oil
3. Minced fresh herbs to taste

4. Minced anchovies, capers, or olives
5. All-Purpose Curry Powder or other spice mixtures (page 778)
6. Cooked fresh peas
7. Crumbled bacon
8. Minced Hard-Boiled Egg (page 733)
9. Minced celery or fennel
10. Minced pickle, preferably sweet pickle
11. Mustard or use homemade mayonnaise (page 761), heavily spiked with mustard
12. Cayenne or minced fresh chiles

Spicy Coleslaw

Makes about 2 quarts

Time: 20 minutes

More interesting, more flavorful, and far less fat-laden than traditional coleslaw.

    2 tablespoons Dijon mustard
    2 tablespoons sherry or balsamic vinegar
    $1/2$ cup olive, peanut, or vegetable oil
    1 tablespoon sugar
    6 cups cored and shredded Napa, Savoy, green, and/or red cabbage (page 547)
    2 red bell peppers, stemmed, peeled if desired, seeded, and diced
    1 cup diced scallions
    Salt and freshly ground black pepper to taste
    $1/4$ cup minced fresh parsley leaves

① Whisk together the mustard and vinegar in a small bowl; add the oil a little at a time, whisking all the while.

② Add sugar and whisk to dissolve.

③ Combine the cabbage, peppers, and scallions, and toss with the dressing. Season with salt and pepper and refrigerate until ready to serve (it's best to let this

rest for an hour or so before serving to allow the flavors to mellow; you can let it sit longer, up to 24 hours, if you like). Just before serving, toss with parsley.

Waldorf Salad

Makes 4 servings

Time: 15 minutes

A quick, filling salad that can almost always be made in mid-winter with ingredients on hand. Don't overdo it with the mayonnaise. And please: Don't add marshmallows.

    3 or 4 medium or large apples
    2 celery stalks
    About $1/2$ cup mayonnaise, plus more if desired
    Salt and freshly ground black pepper to taste
    $1/2$ cup walnuts, roughly chopped
    Freshly squeezed lemon juice to taste (optional)

① Peel and core the apples; cut them into $1/2$-inch dice. Chop the celery into $1/2$-inch dice. Toss them together and add just enough mayonnaise to make the mixture slightly creamy.

② Add salt, pepper, and walnuts and toss. Taste and add more salt, pepper, or lemon juice if needed.

Pear and Gorgonzola Salad

Makes 4 servings

Time: 20 minutes

Something about this combination is magical: the smooth sweetness of the pears, the creamy saltiness of the cheese, the crunchiness of walnuts. . . . It's a great salad. Look for a creamy, nice blue, such as Gorgonzola, Roquefort, or Stilton.

1 cup walnut halves

4 to 6 cups torn mixed greens (trimmed, washed, and dried)

1/2 cup any vinaigrette (page 90)

2 pears, peeled, cored, and cut into slices

1/4 pound Gorgonzola, Roquefort, or other good creamy blue cheese

1 Place the walnuts in a dry skillet and turn the heat to medium. Toast, shaking the pan frequently, until they are aromatic and beginning to darken in color, 3 to 5 minutes. Set aside to cool while you prepare the other ingredients.

2 Toss the greens with most of the vinaigrette and divide among four plates. Decorate with pear slices and crumble the cheese over all. Crumble or coarsely chop the walnuts and scatter them over the salad.

3 Drizzle with the remaining vinaigrette and serve.

Seaweed and Cucumber Salad

Makes 4 servings

Time: 15 minutes

This is based on a traditional Japanese dish that remains popular today, and is used as a garnish by many Western chefs who've visited Japan. It's a wonderful use of sea vegetables, which take just minutes to prepare. (For more information about sea vegetables, see pages 602–603.)

1/2 cup wakame, hiziki, or arame (page 602)

1 medium cucumber, as fresh as possible, preferably not peeled

2 tablespoons rice vinegar

1/2 teaspoon sugar (optional)

1 teaspoon soy sauce

1 Bring a small pot of water to the boil while you soak the wakame in cool water for 10 minutes. Plunge the seaweed into the boiling water, remove immediately, then plunge it into cold water. Dry the seaweed, trim any tough parts, and chop.

2 Meanwhile, cut the cucumber in half lengthwise; if it has lots of seeds, scrape them out. Slice it as thinly as possible. Mix the cucumber and seaweed. Combine the remaining ingredients and pour over the vegetables. This can be chilled for up to 2 hours before serving.

Quick Pickled Vegetables

Vinegar-cured pickles are a venerable American tradition, but pickles can also be made with little or no cooking or vinegar, no intimidating canning, and no sugar. In much of the world, pickling is accomplished with salt and little else. And although salting does not necessarily yield vegetables that can sit unrefrigerated until next August, it does produce crisp, savory morsels that complement most meals or serve as small salads on their own.

Salt extracts liquid, which is why it is used in drying and preserving. The kind of salt you use doesn't matter much, but it is easier to sprinkle coarse kosher or sea salt than ordinary table salt. Most vegetables are eighty to ninety percent water, and much of that liquid is drawn out by salting, thus enhancing crispness and intensifying flavor. If the vegetable is sitting in flavoring as well as salt, some of those flavorings replace the departing liquid, thereby increasing the flavor.

All of the following recipes exploit this phenomenon, using variations on one simple theme: After cutting vegetables into small portions, you apply salt to the exposed areas. The swiftness with which the vegetable is pickled is determined by the thickness and density of the vegetable itself and the amount of salt used (take care not to use too much salt, or the resulting pickle may be unpalatable). If you start thin-sliced cucumbers at five-thirty, for example, you can have them on the table, in the form of cucumber salad, at six. On the other hand, whole cucumbers sitting in brine or slices of turnip buried in miso may take up to two days to pickle.

Treat these pickles as you would cooked food, keeping them in the refrigerator between uses and finishing them within a few days—which, if you are a pickle lover, will not present any problems.

Quick Pickled Beets

Makes at least six servings

Time: About an hour plus processing time

Real pickled beets, like these, are delicious, a nice counterpoint to rich meals or as a small salad.

    12 medium beets, about 2 pounds
    Salt
    2 cups white vinegar
    1 cup sugar
    2 tablespoons kosher, canning, or other
        non-iodized salt
    1 teaspoon allspice berries
    1/4 teaspoon cloves
    1/2 cinnamon stick, optional
    1 medium onion, peeled and sliced

1 Remove all but an inch of the beet greens (reserve the greens for another use). Wash and scrub beets, then simmer in boiling salted water to cover until tender, 30 to 60 minutes. Cool enough to peel off the skins. Slice the beets, not too thinly.

2 Bring the vinegar, sugar, salt, and spices to a boil. Add the beets and the onion and cook for about

a minute. Cool, then refrigerate, and eat within two weeks.

Quick Pickled Vegetables

Makes 4 servings

Time: 1 hour or less

You won't believe how much an hour of salting changes these vegetables.

    1 pound cucumber, zucchini, summer squash,
        or eggplant
    1 tablespoon salt
    1/2 teaspoon sugar
    1 tablespoon minced fresh dill or 1 teaspoon
        dried dill
    2 teaspoons any vinegar

1 Wash the vegetables, peel them if you like, and slice them as thinly as possible (a mandoline is perfect for this). Place them in a colander and salt them. Toss the slices with the salt, kneading the salt into them with your hands for a minute.

2 Let sit for 15 to 30 minutes (cucumbers take less time than eggplant), tossing and squeezing every few minutes. When little or no more liquid comes out of the vegetable, rinse well in cold water. Place in a bowl.

3 Toss with the sugar, dill, and vinegar; serve immediately; this does not keep well.

Quick Pickled Vegetables, Asian-Style: In Step 3, toss the vegetables with the sugar, 1/2 teaspoon dark sesame oil, 1 tablespoon soy sauce, and about 1 teaspoon rice vinegar.

Quick Pickled Cabbage

Makes 4 to 6 servings

Time: At least 45 minutes

This makes a very light pickle, quickly. It's a nice side dish for grilled food, in place of the usual coleslaw.

6 cups cored and shredded red or green cabbage, about one small head (page 547)

1 tablespoon salt

1 red onion

1 cucumber

1 teaspoon caraway seeds

2 tablespoons rice or wine vinegar

1 Toss the cabbage in a colander with the salt.

2 Peel and slice the red onion; separate it into rings and toss with the cabbage. Peel the cucumber if necessary and cut it in half lengthwise. If there are a lot of seeds, scoop them out with a spoon. Slice the cucumber thinly and mix the slices with the cabbage and onion.

3 Lay a plate over the vegetable mixture while it is still in the colander, and weight the plate with whatever is handy: a few cans, your teakettle filled with water, or a brick, for example. Let rest for about 30 minutes; 1 hour is fine.

4 Rinse the mixture, dress with the caraway seeds and vinegar, and serve. This will keep refrigerated quite nicely for a day or two.

Quick Pickled Ginger

Makes about 1 cup

Time: About 1 hour

There are three ways to make the pickled ginger served with sushi. One, which is traditional, takes about a week and is suitable only if you eat pickled ginger on a daily basis. One is a mysterious manufacturing process we probably don't want to know about. And one follows; it's easy and foolproof, and can be done while you make dinner.

1 big piece ginger, 2 to 4 ounces

1 teaspoon salt

1 tablespoon sugar

2 tablespoons rice vinegar

1 tablespoon water

1 Peel the ginger and slice it thinly on a mandoline or the slicing side of a grater. Sprinkle it with salt and let sit for about 30 minutes.

2 Rinse the ginger and dry it lightly. Toss it with the sugar, vinegar, and water. Let sit for 15 minutes. Taste and add more vinegar, sugar, or salt if necessary, then serve. This "pickled" ginger will not keep for more than 1 day.

Salted Cabbage with Szechwan Peppercorns

Makes 6 to 8 servings

Time: About 2 hours, largely unattended

A little slower than the above recipe, with a more pickled and very Asian flavor.

1 tablespoon salt

1 tablespoon Szechwan peppercorns, left whole

1 tablespoon mirin (sweet Japanese rice wine), sherry, or sake

1 tablespoon soy sauce

1 teaspoon dark sesame oil

6 cups cored and shredded green cabbage, about 1 small head (page 547)

1 Combine all ingredients except cabbage in a large glass or plastic container. Toss in the cabbage and mix very well.

2 Find a plate or pot cover that is just a bit smaller than the top of the container, and place it on top of the cabbage mixture. Weight it with rocks, a teakettle filled with water, a 5-pound bag of flour or sugar (wrapped in plastic to keep it from getting wet), whatever.

3 Let sit for 1 hour, then remove the weight and toss the mixture around. Let it sit for another hour, by which time it will be nice and juicy. Eat or refrigerate; this will keep well for a few days, and is good cold or at room temperature.

Fresh Napa Kimchi

Makes 12 to 20 small servings

Time: 2 to 3 hours

Kimchi is not for the faint of heart: It reeks of raw garlic and hot chiles. If that sounds good to you—or if you are already a convert—you'll be pleased by how easy it is to prepare.

    1 head Napa cabbage, about 2 pounds
    5 tablespoons coarse salt
    1 cup peeled and julienned daikon radish
    1 tablespoon or more ground Korean red chiles
        (available at Asian markets) or crushed red
        pepper flakes
    4 tablespoons fish sauce (*nuoc mam* or *nam pla,*
        available at Asian markets) or soy sauce
    2 tablespoons peeled and minced garlic
    1 tablespoon peeled and minced or grated
        fresh ginger
    2 tablespoons sugar
    3 tablespoons tiny salted shrimp (optional)
        (available at Asian markets)
    1/2 cup minced scallions, green part only

1 Place the cabbage in a colander and sprinkle it with the salt, making sure to get plenty of salt between the layers of leaves. Let sit, undisturbed, for about 2 hours.

2 When the cabbage is very wilted, rinse it well, again making sure to rinse between the layers of leaves. Shake it dry.

3 Mix together all remaining ingredients; the mixture will be bright red. (Take care to avoid touching your eyes or sensitive parts of your skin during this process; the chiles are very hot. You may want to wear disposable rubber gloves.)

4 Either cut the cabbage up and toss it with the spice mixture, or use your fingers to pack the whole cabbage, inside and out, with the spice mixture. Serve immediately, whole or cut up, or refrigerate. Keeps well for at least a week, becoming spicier every day.

Kosher Pickles, the Right Way

Makes about 30 pickle quarters or 15 halves

Time: 1 to 2 days

The best pickles—in my opinion at least—contain no vinegar. Of course they don't keep very long. But unless you have a bushel or two to put away, these won't last very long either—you'll eat them long before they begin to turn.

    1/3 cup kosher salt
    1 cup boiling water
    2 pounds small ("Kirby") cucumbers, washed
        (scrub if spiny) and cut lengthwise into halves
        or quarters
    At least 5 cloves garlic, smashed
    1 large bunch dill, preferably fresh and with flowers,
        or substitute 2 tablespoons dried dill and 1 teaspoon
        dill seeds or 1 tablespoon coriander seeds

1. Combine the salt and boiling water in a large bowl; stir to dissolve the salt. Add a handful of ice cubes to cool down the mixture, then add all the remaining ingredients.

2. Add cold water to cover. Use a plate slightly smaller than the diameter of the bowl and a small weight to hold the cucumbers under the water. Keep at room temperature.

3. Begin sampling the cucumbers after 4 hours if you've quartered them, 8 hours if you've cut them in half. In either case, it will probably take from 12 to 24 or even 48 hours for them to taste "pickle-y" enough to suit your taste.

4. When they are ready, refrigerate them, still in the brine. The pickles will continue to ferment as they sit, more quickly at room temperature, more slowly in the refrigerator. They will keep well for up to a week.

Miso-Cured Vegetables

Makes 4 servings

Time: 1 or 2 days

Simple, traditional, and appealing Japanese pickles.

> 2 or 3 turnips, carrots, eggplant, or zucchini, or a mixture
> At least 2 cups any type miso

1. Peel the vegetables and cut them into slices $1/4$ inch thick or thinner.

2. Spread the miso in a bowl, an inch or two deep, and bury the vegetable slices in the miso. Cover with plastic wrap and let stand at room temperature.

3. After 24 hours, fish out one of the slices, rinse it off, and sample it; depending on the vegetable and thickness of the slice, it may require another 24 hours.

4. To serve, rinse the slices and cut them into small pieces. Refrigerate the miso, which may be reused

several times to make pickles, or for any other recipe requiring it.

Bean Salads

Creamy and soft, beans make wonderful salads, whether they are served cold or at room temperature. But remember that beans are bland—far blander than greens or most vegetables—and must be seasoned accordingly.

Warm Split Pea Salad

Makes 4 servings

Time: 45 minutes

A traditional Greek salad that is also good with strong mint, or a combination of mint and thyme. Spread it on pita bread or crackers or serve it on a bed of greens dressed with lemon.

> 1 cup green or yellow split peas, washed and picked over (see The Basics of Buying and Preparing Beans, page 500)
> 2 cloves garlic, peeled, plus 1 teaspoon minced garlic
> 1 cup minced onion
> 1 cup cored and chopped tomatoes (page 610), approximately (canned are fine; drain them first)
> Salt and freshly ground black pepper to taste
> 2 teaspoons minced fresh thyme leaves or about 1 teaspoon dried thyme
> 1 tablespoon extra-virgin olive oil
> Minced fresh parsley leaves for garnish

1. Place the split peas in a medium saucepan with the whole garlic and add water to cover by about 1 inch. Bring to a boil, reduce heat, and simmer, covered, for about 15 minutes.

2 Uncover and add the onion, minced garlic, tomatoes, salt, pepper, and half the thyme. Re-cover and cook, stirring occasionally, until the mixture is smooth and the water is absorbed. (Add more water if the peas are not sufficiently cooked.)

3 Remove the whole garlic. (You may prepare the salad in advance up to this point; cover and refrigerate for up to a day, then bring to room temperature before proceeding.) Serve warm or at room temperature; just before serving, mix in the remaining thyme and sprinkle with olive oil and parsley.

Chickpeas with Lemon
Makes 6 to 8 servings

Time: About 2 hours

This chickpea salad is great to have around. Eat it warm, at room temperature, or cold—but add the lemon juice at the last minute for maximum flavor.

2 cups dried chickpeas, washed and picked over (see The Basics of Buying and Preparing Beans, page 500)
1 bay leaf
1 clove garlic, peeled
2 tablespoons minced shallot, onion, or scallion
3 tablespoons extra-virgin olive oil
Salt and freshly ground black pepper to taste
Freshly squeezed lemon juice to taste
Minced fresh parsley or cilantro leaves for garnish

1 Cook chickpeas, with the bay leaf and garlic, according to the recipe for Basic Beans (page 505) or Pressure-Cooked Beans (page 507), until they are quite tender.

2 Remove the bay leaf and garlic and drain. While the chickpeas are still warm, toss them with the shallot and olive oil and season with salt and pepper.

(You may prepare the salad in advance up to this point; cover and refrigerate for up to a day, then bring to room temperature before proceeding.) Serve warm or at room temperature; just before serving add plenty of lemon juice and garnish.

White Bean Salad
Makes 4 servings

Time: 15 minutes to 2 hours

For speed, make this salad with canned white beans.

1½ cups dried white beans, washed and picked over (see The Basics of Buying and Preparing Beans, page 500), or 3 cups cooked or canned white beans, drained
1 teaspoon fresh thyme, marjoram, or sage leaves or ½ teaspoon dried herb
3 shallots or scallions, minced
¼ cup minced red bell pepper
6 tablespoons olive oil, approximately
About 2 tablespoons balsamic, sherry, or wine vinegar
½ teaspoon Dijon mustard
Salt and freshly ground black pepper to taste

1 If you're using dried beans, cook them according to the recipe for Basic Beans (page 505) or Pressure-Cooked Beans (page 507), until they are quite tender. Drain them and place them (or the canned beans) in a medium saucepan with half of the thyme; turn the heat to medium and cook for 5 minutes, or until just heated through. Turn off the heat, add the shallots or scallions and red pepper, and cool.

2 Place the olive oil, vinegar, remaining thyme, and mustard in a jar with a lid and shake well; or use a small food processor, blender, or immersion blender. Taste for seasoning and add salt, pepper, and additional oil or vinegar as desired. Pour over the beans and, if you have time, let rest for an hour (or up to 24 hours, refrigerated) before serving.

Black Bean Salad

Makes 6 servings

Time: 15 minutes with precooked to 2 hours

When fresh corn is in season, add a cup or so of quickly sautéed kernels for more flavor and color.

1½ cups dried black beans, washed and picked over (see The Basics of Buying and Preparing Beans, page 500), or 3 cups cooked black beans, drained
Salt and freshly ground black pepper to taste
1 red bell pepper, stemmed, peeled if desired, seeded, and minced
1 medium red onion, minced
¼ cup minced cilantro or fresh parsley leaves, plus more as needed, plus a few sprigs for garnish
2 tablespoons red wine vinegar, plus more as needed

① If using dried beans, cook them according to the recipe for Basic Beans (page 505) or Pressure-Cooked Beans (page 507), until they are quite tender.

② Drain the beans. Season them with salt and pepper, then toss them with the remaining ingredients. (You may prepare the salad in advance up to this point; cover and refrigerate for up to a day, then bring to room temperature before proceeding.) Taste and add more salt, pepper, cilantro or parsley, or vinegar as needed. Garnish and serve at room temperature.

Grain Salads

Adding grains to a salad changes things completely, providing texture that you can't get from vegetables alone and making for a much more substantial dish. The great thing about cooked grains is that they usually keep well as leftovers, and are quickly revived by the addition of oil and vinegar: Even sticky rice separates, and stale bread becomes tender again.

A note about pasta salads   Cold pasta is a fact of life, and—if not overcooked to begin with and rinsed of excess starch and dressing—it can make a decent addition to any salad. To me, however, it makes no sense to intentionally cook pasta for salad. Grains such as rice, barley, and quinoa keep better, retain their structural integrity better (that is, they don't fall apart), taste better, and offer better texture—they are not at all gummy—than cold pasta. So if you have some leftover pasta you want to integrate into a salad, by all means go ahead. But don't set out to make "pasta salad."

Fattoush
Lebanese Bread Salad

Makes 4 servings

Time: 30 minutes

This traditional Lebanese dish is a great way to use stale pita or other bread. Serve this over lettuce if you like.

4 (6-inch) pita breads, or about 8 slices any other bread
½ cup minced fresh mint, parsley, or basil leaves
¼ cup minced fresh parsley leaves
1 small red onion, minced
1 large or 2 medium ripe tomatoes, cored, seeded if desired, and roughly chopped (page 610)
1 medium cucumber, peeled, seeded if desired, and roughly chopped
1 red bell pepper, stemmed, peeled if desired, seeded, and chopped
About ½ cup Basic Vinaigrette (page 91) or extra-virgin olive oil and freshly squeezed lemon juice

1 Preheat the oven to 350°F.

2 Place the pitas on a baking sheet and put them in the oven for about 15 minutes, turning once or twice, until they are dry, slightly crisp, and a little but far from completely browned. Tear them into bite-sized pieces.

3 Toss the pitas with all the remaining ingredients, adding vinaigrette or oil and lemon juice to taste. Serve immediately.

Panzanella
Italian Bread Salad
Makes 4 servings

Time: 30 minutes

One classic Italian way to use stale bread is to toast it for extra flavor, soften it with liquid, and use it as the backbone of a salad. If you like, add a couple of minced anchovies, capers, and/or minced roasted red pepper to the mix. Without those additions, this recipe is basic, but remains a delicious midsummer treat.

    4 medium perfectly ripe tomatoes, cored and peeled
        (page 610)
    About 1/2 teaspoon salt, plus more if needed
    1 clove garlic, peeled
    8 thick slices good bread, preferably a couple of
        days old
    1 teaspoon fresh oregano, marjoram, or thyme leaves
        or 1/4 cup minced fresh basil or parsley leaves
    1/3 cup extra-virgin olive oil
    1 tablespoon balsamic or other good vinegar,
        or to taste
    Freshly ground black pepper to taste

1 Use your fingers to remove the liquid center and seeds from the tomatoes; place in a strainer over a bowl and add the meat of the tomatoes. Sprinkle the tomatoes with about 1/2 teaspoon of salt and set aside while you prepare the bread.

2 Preheat the broiler. Cut the garlic clove in half and rub the bread all over with it. Toast the bread under the broiler, taking care not to burn it. When it is nicely browned and crisp throughout, cool it for a minute, then tear it into bite-sized pieces. Place it in a bowl with the juices extracted from the tomatoes.

3 Discard the tomato seeds and chop the meat into smaller pieces. When the bread has softened a bit, add the tomatoes, herb, oil, vinegar, and some black pepper. Taste and adjust seasoning as necessary; serve immediately.

Tabbouleh
Makes 4 to 6 servings

Time: About 40 minutes

The Americanized version of this dish focuses on cracked wheat and tomato, but this more authentic Middle Eastern dish is little more than loads of herbs given substance. It's delicious.

    1/2 cup fine-grind (Number One) or medium-grind
        (Number Two) bulgur
    2 cups minced fresh parsley leaves
    1 cup minced fresh mint leaves
    2 cups cored, seeded, and chopped tomatoes
        (page 610)
    1 small red or white onion, finely chopped
    1/2 cup extra-virgin olive oil
    4 tablespoons freshly squeezed lemon juice,
        or to taste
    Salt and freshly ground black pepper to taste

1 Soak the bulgur in water to cover until tender, 15 to 30 minutes. Drain well, squeezing out as much of the water as possible.

2 Combine the bulgur with the parsley, mint, tomatoes, and onion; whisk together the olive oil and lemon juice and toss with the salad. Season with salt and pepper and taste; adjust seasoning if necessary. You can refrigerate this for a few hours if you like, but let it warm up a bit before serving.

Couscous Salad with Mint and Parsley

Makes 4 servings

Time: About 30 minutes

This salad is not unlike Tabbouleh (page 112), in that it is dominated by the flavors of mint and parsley. But it is much more "grainy," in that it contains plenty of couscous.

About 3 cups Basic Couscous (page 191), made with olive oil instead of butter

1½ cups minced fresh parsley leaves

1 tomato, cored, peeled, seeded, and chopped (page 610)

½ cup minced scallions

1 cup minced fresh mint leaves

⅓ cup freshly squeezed lemon juice, or to taste

⅓ cup olive oil

Salt and freshly ground black pepper to taste

1 Mix together all ingredients, reserving 2 tablespoons of the lemon juice. Set aside until ready to serve (at room temperature for up to an hour; refrigerated for up to 2 hours, but bring back to room temperature before serving).

2 Drizzle with remaining lemon juice and adjust seasoning just before serving.

Twenty-Four Great Salads for a Picnic

Delicate greens cannot be tossed with dressing before traveling, although you can, of course, take them and dressing separately and toss on the spot. But the salads below can be finished and packed to travel—carefully, of course—then served with little or no loss of quality. Some of these have greens as a base; pack the greens separately and assemble at the last minute.

Cress and Barley Salad with Dill Vinaigrette

Makes 4 servings

Time: 30 minutes

Make sure the barley is nice and tender before proceeding.

¹/₂ cup pearled barley
1 medium cucumber, peeled if desired
3 cups coarsely chopped watercress, trimmed, washed, and dried
About ¹/₂ cup Lemon-Dill Vinaigrette (page 92)

① Cook the barley according to The Basics of Cooking Grains, page 181. Drain, rinse briefly in cool water, and set aside. Meanwhile, cut the cucumber in half lengthwise, scoop out the seeds if there are a lot of them, then dice the flesh.

② Toss the chopped cress with the barley. Top with the chopped cucumber, drizzle with the vinaigrette, and serve.

Arborio Rice Salad with Peas

Makes 4 to 6 servings

Time: About 30 minutes

You can use any short- or medium-grained rice for this dish, but using Arborio makes it special. Add some pieces of cubed ham if you like.

¹/₂ cup fresh or frozen peas
1 cup Arborio rice
¹/₄ cup minced shallot
About ¹/₄ cup freshly squeezed lemon juice
¹/₃ cup extra-virgin olive oil, plus more as needed
¹/₄ cup minced fresh parsley leaves
Salt and freshly ground black pepper to taste

① Bring a small pot of water to a boil; salt it. Bring a large pot of water to a boil; salt it. Cook the peas in the small pot for about 2 minutes, or until they lose their raw flavor. Drain and rinse in cold water to stop the cooking. Drain and set aside.

② When the large pot of water comes to a boil, add the rice and cook, stirring, until it is completely tender, about 15 minutes. Drain the rice and rinse it quickly under cold water to stop the cooking, but don't chill it entirely.

③ Stir the shallot into the rice and mix well. Add the lemon juice and olive oil and mix well again. Add the parsley, peas, salt, and pepper, and mix. Taste and add more olive oil, lemon juice, salt, or pepper as needed. (You may prepare the salad in advance up to this point; cover and refrigerate for up to a day, then bring to room temperature before proceeding.) Serve immediately.

Salads with Chicken, Meat, or Fish

When you add animal protein to a salad you bring it to another level; there is no longer any way the salad is a side dish. It may be lunch, it may be a hearty or elegant first course, or it may be a meal in itself.

Salads are the ideal use for leftover meats, or for the scraps of meat or fish that remain after you've made stock.

Grilled Chicken Salad

Makes 4 servings

Time: About 1 hour, including marinating time, plus time to preheat the grill

This is a great summer salad, when greens are abundant and you've got the grill going full time.

1 pound boneless skinless chicken breast, about 4 pieces, rinsed and patted dry with paper towels
1/4 cup soy sauce
6 to 8 cups torn assorted salad greens (trimmed, washed, and dried)
Juice of 1 large lemon, plus more to taste
1/3 cup extra-virgin olive oil, approximately
1 teaspoon dark sesame oil

1 Start a charcoal or wood fire or preheat a gas grill or broiler; the fire should be quite hot and the rack about 2 inches from the heat source.

2 Pound the chicken lightly between 2 pieces of waxed paper so that it is of uniform thickness, less than $^1/_2$ inch thick. Marinate the pieces in the soy sauce while the grill preheats.

3 Grill the chicken very quickly, on the hottest part of the grill; it should take no more than 2 minutes per side to become lightly browned.

4 Dress the greens with the lemon juice and olive oil, then cut up the chicken and scatter it over the salad. Sprinkle with the sesame oil. Taste and add more lemon juice if necessary, and serve.

Chicken Salad with Olive Oil and Chives

Makes 4 servings

Time: About 1 hour

If you don't have chicken stock, it's worth it here to buy your chicken breasts on the bone, take the meat off, and simmer the bones for one-half hour, with an onion and a carrot, to make a quick, light stock in which to cook the meat.

4 cups chicken or vegetable stock (see "Soups" for stock recipes), or water
1 pound boneless skinless chicken breast (leftover chicken is fine; don't recook it), rinsed and patted dry with paper towels
1/3 cup extra-virgin olive oil, plus more to taste
Salt and freshly ground black pepper to taste
2 tablespoons freshly squeezed lemon juice, plus more to taste
1/2 cup minced fresh chives, parsley, chervil, dill, or basil
4 to 6 cups torn assorted greens (trimmed, washed, and dried)

1 Place the stock in a medium saucepan and bring it to a boil over medium-high heat. Turn the heat to medium-low and add the chicken breasts. Cook for about 10 minutes, or until the chicken breast is cooked through. Remove the meat; strain and reserve the stock for another use.

2 Cool the chicken, cut it into small pieces, and mix it with the olive oil, salt, pepper, lemon juice (at least 2 tablespoons), and all but about 1 teaspoon of herb.

3 At this point you can serve the chicken salad or let it marinate, refrigerated and covered, for about a day, stirring occasionally. When you're ready, taste for seasoning and serve over the greens, drizzled with additional oil and lemon juice. Garnish the salad with the remaining herb.

Chicken Salad with Cabbage and Mint

Makes 4 servings

Time: 30 minutes or less

A variation on a Vietnamese standard.

4 cups chicken or vegetable stock (see "Soups" for stock recipes), or water

1 pound boneless skinless chicken breast (leftover chicken is fine; don't recook it), rinsed and patted dry with paper towels

2 tablespoons fish sauce (*nuoc mam* or *nam pla*, available at Asian markets)

1 small head Napa, Savoy, or green cabbage, cored and shredded (page 547)

2 carrots, peeled and shredded

$3/4$ cup roughly chopped fresh mint, basil, cilantro, or dill leaves

Salt and freshly ground black pepper to taste

$1/2$ teaspoon cayenne, or to taste

4 tablespoons freshly squeezed lime juice

1 Place the stock into a medium saucepan and bring it to a boil over medium-high heat. Turn the heat to medium-low and add the chicken breast. Cook for about 10 minutes, or until the chicken breast is cooked through. Remove the meat; strain and reserve the stock for another use.

2 Cool the chicken; cut it into small pieces. Combine it with all but 1 teaspoon of the fish sauce, along with the cabbage, carrots, and $1/2$ cup mint. Season with the salt, pepper, and cayenne.

3 Dress the salad with the remaining fish sauce and the lime juice; mince the remaining mint and use it as a garnish.

Chicken or Duck Salad with Walnuts

Makes 4 servings

Time: Less than 30 minutes

You can make this rich dish with the meat of any bird, from turkey to partridge; the stronger the flavor, the better the dish.

1 tablespoon canola or other neutral oil

2 cups chopped raw boneless skinless chicken, duck, or other meat, preferably from the leg (chop the meat into $1/2$-inch cubes), rinsed and patted dry with paper towels

2 tablespoons butter or olive oil

1 clove garlic, minced

$1/2$ cup walnuts or pecans, coarsely crumbled (do not chop)

$1/2$ cup port, cassis, or sweet sherry or wine

4 to 6 cups torn assorted salad greens (trimmed, washed, and dried)

About $1/2$ cup any vinaigrette (page 90)

A small handful minced fresh herb leaves, such as parsley or chervil, for garnish

1 Place the tablespoon of oil in a medium skillet and turn the heat to medium-high. A minute later, cook the meat in the oil, stirring, for about 2 minutes. Remove and set aside.

2 Wipe out the skillet and add the butter, still over medium-high heat; when the foam subsides, add the garlic and cook for 1 minute.

3 Add the walnuts and stir for 30 seconds. Add the wine and let it bubble out until the mixture is syrupy, stirring occasionally. Turn off the heat and return the meat to the pan to warm it up.

4 Dress the greens with the vinaigrette and toss; add more vinaigrette if necessary. Scatter the meat and nut mixture on top of the greens, garnish, and serve.

Curried Chicken Salad

Makes 4 servings

Time: About 30 minutes

Some freshly made chutney (page 784) stirred into this salad is wonderful.

Almost any leftover (or even just-cooked) poultry, without sauce, turns a salad into a meal. If you place the poultry on the greens while it is hot, the greens will wilt and mingle with the juices, a nice touch.

1. Simple Roast Chicken (page 358)
2. Chicken Under a Brick (page 365)
3. Grilled or Broiled Split Chicken (page 366)
4. Roast Chicken Parts with Herbs and Olive Oil (page 374)
5. Basic Grilled or Broiled Chicken Cutlets (page 380)
6. Herb-Roasted Chicken Cutlets (page 393)
7. Chicken Satay (page 399)
8. Simple Roast Capon (page 410)
9. Basic Roast Duck (page 413)
10. Steamed and Roasted Duck (page 414)
11. Tea-Smoked Duck (page 415)
12. Grilled Squab, Vietnamese-Style (page 418)

4 cups chicken or vegetable stock (see "Soups" for stock recipes), or water
1 pound boneless skinless chicken breast (leftover chicken is fine; don't recook it), rinsed and patted dry with paper towels
1 tablespoon mayonnaise
1 tablespoon plain yogurt (or use more mayonnaise)
Salt and freshly ground black pepper to taste
1 tablespoon All-Purpose Curry Powder (page 778) or Garam Masala (page 778) or store-bought curry powder, or to taste
1/2 cup peeled and diced apple or 1/2 cup lightly toasted blanched slivered almonds

1 Place the stock in a medium saucepan and bring it to a boil over medium-high heat. Turn the heat to medium-low and add the chicken breast. Cook for about 10 minutes, or until the chicken breast is cooked through. Remove the meat; strain and reserve the stock for another use.

2 Cool the chicken, cut it into small pieces, and toss it with the remaining ingredients. Taste, correct seasoning, and serve.

Beef Salad with Mint

Makes 3 to 4 light servings

Time: 25 minutes, plus time to preheat the grill

This is a meaty salad, a nice compromise between eating a huge cut of steak and none at all.

1 (8- to 10-ounce) piece beef tenderloin (such as filet mignon) or sirloin
4 cups torn Boston or romaine lettuce, mesclun, or any salad greens mixture (trimmed, washed, and dried)
1/4 cup minced fresh mint, parsley, basil, or cilantro leaves
1 small red onion, sliced into thin rings
1 small cucumber, preferably unwaxed and unpeeled, thinly sliced
4 tablespoons freshly squeezed lime juice
1 tablespoon fish sauce (*nuoc mam* or *nam pla*, available at Asian markets) or soy sauce
1/8 teaspoon cayenne, or to taste
1/2 teaspoon sugar

1 If you are starting with raw meat, start a charcoal or wood fire or preheat a gas grill or broiler; the rack should be about 4 inches from the heat source. Grill or broil the beef until medium-rare, about 10 to 12 minutes; set it aside to cool.

2 Toss the lettuce with the mint, onion, and cucumber. Combine all remaining ingredients, and toss the greens with this mixture, reserving about 1 tablespoon of the dressing.

3 Slice the beef thinly, reserving its juice; lay the slices over the salad. Mix the juice and reserved dressing, drizzle over the beef, and serve.

Chef's Salad

Makes 4 to 6 servings

Time: About 45 minutes

An American-style Salade Niçoise (page 122), served with meat instead of fish. If you like, substitute Russian Dressing (page 763) for vinaigrette.

1 cucumber, peeled if desired

8 cups torn assorted lettuces and other salad greens (trimmed, washed, and dried)

1 celery stalk, chopped

2 carrots, peeled and shredded or cut into julienne strips

About 1 cup thinly sliced and cut-up meat, such as ham, roast beef, or turkey (cut into strips)

2 Hard-Boiled Eggs (page 733), peeled and cut into slices

1 bell pepper (any color but green), stemmed, peeled if desired, and cut into rings

Several very thin slices Parmesan or Pecorino Romano cheese (use a vegetable peeler to make the slices)

2 scallions, minced

2 tomatoes, cored, seeded, and cut into chunks (page 610)

Any croutons (page 82)

Creamy Vinaigrette (page 94), or any other vinaigrette

Fourteen Meat Dishes That Go Great on Greens

As with poultry, you can use many unsauced meat dishes—either hot or cold—on a bed of greens.

1. Grilled Steak, American-Style, or its variations (page 425)
2. Grilled Marinated Flank Steak (page 427)
3. Boneless Prime Rib (leftovers only) (page 431)
4. Grilled or Broiled Beef and Vegetable Kebabs or its variation (page 442)
5. Spice-Rubbed Beef Kebabs (page 442)
6. Broiled or Grilled Veal Heart (page 453)
7. Grilled Pork Chops (page 458)
8. West Indian Crispy Pork Bits, or its variations (page 461)
9. Grilled Pork Tenderloin with Mustard Curry (page 463)
10. Baked Country Ham or Baked Wet-Cured Ham (leftovers only) (pages 475–6)
11. Basic Roast Leg of Lamb, or its variations (leftovers only) (page 479)
12. Grilled Leg of Lamb (leftovers only) (page 480)
13. Basic Grilled or Broiled Butterflied Leg of Lamb (page 482)
14. Grilled Skewered Lamb Chunks (Shish Kebab) (page 483)

1 Cut the cucumber in half lengthwise; scoop out the seeds if necessary. Slice and toss with the lettuces, celery, and carrots.

2 Decorate the top of the salad with all the remaining ingredients, except the salad dressing, then drizzle with the vinaigrette. Toss and serve.

Shrimp Salad, Mediterranean-Style

Makes 4 servings

Time: 30 minutes

This is worlds away from the typical mayonnaise-laden shrimp salad.

4 cups Fast Fish Stock (page 49), Shrimp Stock
   (page 50), or canned chicken stock
2 pounds medium-to-large shrimp, peeled
$^1/_2$ cup minced parsley
2 tablespoons capers
1 small clove garlic, finely minced
$^1/_3$ to $^1/_2$ cup extra-virgin olive oil
Salt and freshly ground black pepper to taste
Freshly squeezed lemon juice to taste
Lemon wedges

1 Place the stock in a large saucepan or deep skillet and bring to a boil over medium-high heat. Turn the heat to medium-low and add the shrimp. Cover and simmer for 2 minutes, then turn off the heat, uncover, and let the shrimp cool in the liquid for about 10 minutes. Drain the shrimp, reserving the stock for another use.

2 Toss the shrimp with the parsley, capers, garlic, $^1/_3$ cup of the olive oil, salt, pepper, and lemon juice. Taste and add additional olive oil or lemon juice if necessary. Serve with lemon wedges.

Seafood Salad, Adriatic-Style

Makes 10 to 15 servings

Time: 2 hours, plus marinating time

I had this more elaborate version of the above salad in the not-especially charming town of Rimini, on the Adriatic coast of Emilia-Romagna, a place where fish is treated as it should be: simply and respectfully. It's best as part of a feast; you can vary the ingredients as you like, including more raw vegetables, and a larger or smaller variety of fish, depending on what is available. The preparation of this dish takes some time, but there is nothing complicated about it.

8 cups Flavorful Fish and Vegetable Stock (page 49)
   or 8 cups water
Salt and freshly ground black pepper to taste
1 onion, cut in half but unpeeled, if using water
3 cloves garlic, lightly crushed, if using water
1 carrot, peeled and cut into chunks, if using water
$^1/_2$ bunch fresh parsley, if using water
2 bay leaves, if using water
1 tablespoon vinegar, if using water
$^1/_2$ cup dry white wine, if using water
About 3 pounds octopus, cleaned
3 pounds salmon fillet
3 pounds squid, cleaned (page 338)
3 pounds medium-to-large shrimp
1 to 2 pounds Marinated Fresh Anchovies or
   "Grilled" Sardines (page 321)
4 cups cooked or canned white beans (page 501),
   drained
An assortment of vegetables: raw fennel, roasted red
   pepper (page 593), steamed carrots and/or new
   potatoes, and a mixture of washed and dried greens
Extra-virgin olive oil to taste
Lemon wedges

1 Bring the stock to a boil in a large pot, or simmer together 8 cups of water and the salt, pepper, onion, garlic, carrot, parsley, bay leaves, vinegar, and white wine for about 10 minutes; strain and discard solids.

2 Add the octopus and simmer until tender (see page 337), about 1 hour. Add the salmon and turn the heat to an absolute minimum; cook 3 minutes. Add the squid and the shrimp and cook until the shrimp begin to turn pink, 2 or 3 minutes. Turn off the heat and let the seafood cool in the water for 10 minutes.

3 Strain. Reserve the stock for another use (or use to poach vegetables for the salad). Shell the shrimp; cut the octopus, squid, and shrimp into bite-sized pieces.

4 Arrange the shellfish in small piles on a platter, along with the marinated anchovies or sardines, poached salmon, beans, and vegetables. Sprinkle all with salt and pepper. (You can cover and refrigerate at this point for a couple of hours, but let the salad return to room temperature before serving.)

5 To serve, drizzle everything with olive oil and pass the platter, along with more olive oil and lemon wedges.

Warm Salad of Scallops and Tender Greens

Makes 4 servings

Time: About 15 minutes

You can make this with shrimp as well; slice them in half the long way and cook just one minute per side.

2 tablespoons freshly squeezed lemon juice
3 tablespoons peanut or other oil
1 tablespoon minced shallot
1 tablespoon water
Salt and freshly ground black pepper to taste
1 pound sea scallops, cut in half horizontally
6 cups torn tender greens, such as Boston lettuce or mâche, or a mixture (trimmed, washed, and dried)

1 Whisk together the lemon juice, $1^1/_2$ table-spoons of the oil, the shallot, and the 1 tablespoon of water in a small bowl. Season with salt and pepper.

2 Heat the remaining oil in a large non-stick skillet over high heat. Add the scallops and sear until golden, 2 to 3 minutes per side.

3 Toss the greens with half of the dressing in a large bowl. Divide the salad among four plates, arrange the scallops over the salad, and drizzle the remaining dressing over them. Serve immediately.

Grilled Shrimp and Tomato Salad

Makes 4 servings

Time: 45 minutes, plus time to preheat the grill

This dish needs delicious tomatoes to make it work.

1 pound large-to-extra-large shrimp (about 20), peeled
About $^1/_2$ cup extra-virgin olive oil
Salt and freshly ground black pepper to taste
2 to 3 tablespoons balsamic or sherry vinegar
1 shallot, minced
1 teaspoon Dijon mustard
4 large ripe tomatoes, cored, seeded, and cut into chunks (page 610)
20 fresh basil leaves, roughly chopped

1 Start a charcoal or wood fire or preheat a gas grill or broiler; the fire should be quite hot, and the rack as close to the heat source as possible.

2 Brush the shrimp with a bit of the olive oil; sprinkle them with salt and pepper.

3 Mix together the remaining olive oil, 2 table-spoons of the vinegar, the shallot, and mustard, and season with additional salt and pepper. Taste and add more vinegar if needed.

4 Set the tomatoes in a large bowl to marinate with the vinaigrette and basil. Grill the shrimp over high heat until they turn pink, about 2 or 3 minutes per side. Top the tomatoes with the shrimp and serve.

Salmon Salad with Beans

Makes 4 servings

Time: About 1$\frac{1}{2}$ hours, plus time to preheat the grill

This is a great salad to make when you have leftover grilled salmon.

$\frac{1}{2}$ pound salmon steak (leftover grilled salmon is fine)

$\frac{1}{3}$ cup extra-virgin olive oil, plus 2 tablespoons if using raw fish, plus more to taste if necessary

Several sprigs fresh thyme or $\frac{1}{2}$ teaspoon dried thyme, if using raw fish

1 red or yellow bell pepper

Juice of 1 large lemon, plus more to taste if necessary

3 cups cooked or canned white beans (page 501), drained

10 cherry tomatoes, halved

$\frac{1}{4}$ cup diced shallots

12 to 15 good black or green olives, pitted and coarsely chopped

$\frac{1}{4}$ cup minced fresh basil leaves

$\frac{1}{4}$ cup minced fresh parsley leaves

Salt and freshly ground black pepper to taste

4 cups torn assorted salad greens (trimmed, washed, and dried)

1 If you are starting with raw salmon, start a charcoal or wood fire or preheat a gas grill or broiler; the rack should be about 4 inches from the heat source. Marinate the fish in the 2 tablespoons of olive oil and the thyme.

2 When the fire is ready—it should be quite hot—grill the fish for 3 to 4 minutes per side. At the same time, grill the red pepper (detailed instructions for grilling red peppers appear on page 593). Cool, peel, and seed it, then cut into strips.

3 Cool the fish, then cut it into small cubes and toss it with the lemon juice, beans, and remaining olive oil while you prepare the other ingredients. Add the tomatoes, shallots, olives, and herbs to the salmon. Taste for salt and pepper and correct the balance between olive oil and lemon juice if necessary. Serve on a bed of greens, topped with the strips of grilled red pepper.

Mussel and Potato Salad

Makes 4 servings

Time: 1 hour

You can easily make this with leftover mussels, should you have any, but it's worth starting it from scratch. If you don't have grainy mustard in the house, use Dijon—the salad will still be delicious.

3 or 4 pounds mussels, prepared according to the recipe for Basic Steamed Mussels (page 346)

1$\frac{1}{2}$ pounds waxy red or white potatoes

$\frac{1}{4}$ cup grainy or Dijon mustard, or to taste

$\frac{1}{3}$ cup extra-virgin olive oil

1 tablespoon balsamic or sherry wine vinegar, or to taste

3 tablespoons chopped fresh basil leaves

Salt and freshly ground black pepper to taste

1 Shell the mussels; strain the broth, then place it in a large covered saucepan over high heat.

2 Peel the potatoes or scrub them well, then cut them into bite-sized pieces. Place them in the mussel broth—don't worry if it doesn't completely cover the potatoes—cover, turn the heat to medium-low, and cook until the potatoes are tender but not mushy, about 15 minutes. Drain. (Reserve the broth for another use.)

3 Mix together the mustard, oil, vinegar, and basil, and toss with the mussels and potatoes, while the potatoes are still warm. Season with salt and pepper, then taste and adjust seasoning as necessary.

Salade Niçoise

Makes 4 to 6 servings

> **Time:** About 45 minutes, far less if you prepare some ingredients in advance

Certain basics are essential in salade Niçoise—tuna, tomatoes, anchovies, and, of course, greens. Hard-boiled eggs are also traditional, as are capers, olives, and onions, but the omission of one or another is hardly cause for concern. Feel free to improvise—if you have fresh tuna, for example, grill it and use it.

$1/2$ pound green beans, trimmed

4 to 6 cups torn assorted lettuces and other salad greens (trimmed, washed, and dried)

2 cans Italian-style tuna in olive oil (preferred) or other tuna

2 Hard-Boiled Eggs (page 733), peeled and cut into slices

1 cup good black olives (oil-cured are good for this)

3 ripe tomatoes, cored, seeded, and cut into quarters or eighths (page 610)

1 bell pepper (any color but green), stemmed, peeled if desired, and cut into rings

6 anchovies (optional)

1 teaspoon capers (optional)

$1/8$ cup red wine vinegar, plus a little more if needed

About $1/2$ cup extra-virgin olive oil

Salt and freshly ground black pepper to taste

1 small shallot, minced

1 teaspoon Dijon mustard

1 Steam or parboil (page 14) the green beans for 4 minutes. Drain, then dunk into ice water. Drain again.

2 Arrange all the salad ingredients nicely on a platter—greens on the bottom, topped with tuna, egg slices, green beans, olives, tomatoes, and pepper, with the anchovies and capers sprinkled over all if you like. Or—less attractive but easier to serve—toss all the ingredients together.

3 Make the vinaigrette by adding the vinegar to the oil, along with the salt and pepper, shallot, and mustard. Stir and taste. Add more vinegar if necessary and adjust seasoning. Stir or shake vigorously, pour over the salad, and serve.

Fried Chili-Spiced Clam Salad

Makes 4 servings

> **Time:** 30 minutes

This combination contains the elements that almost everyone loves: It's spicy, it's crunchy, it's cool, and it's moist. A winner, which can also be made with oysters or chunks of boneless chicken.

6 tablespoons olive oil

2 tablespoons balsamic vinegar

2 teaspoons Dijon mustard

$1/2$ cup cornmeal

2 tablespoons chili powder

Salt and freshly ground black pepper to taste

3 tablespoons peanut, olive, or vegetable oil

20 to 25 fresh littleneck or other hard-shell clams, shucked

6 cups torn assorted salad greens (trimmed, washed, and dried)

① Mix together the olive oil, balsamic vinegar, and mustard.

② Season the cornmeal with chili powder, salt, and pepper. Heat a large non-stick skillet over medium-high heat for about 2 minutes. Add the peanut oil. When the oil is hot—a pinch of cornmeal will sizzle—dredge the clams and add them, a couple at a time, to the skillet. Raise heat to high and cook until golden, turning once, about 2 minutes total.

③ Drain the clams on paper towels and toss the greens with the dressing. Divide the greens among four plates and top each with a portion of clams. Serve immediately.

Pasta

It doesn't much matter who "invented" pasta—some have it the Chinese, others the Etruscans, who were among the earliest inhabitants of Italy. Whatever the origin, we associate pasta primarily with Italy, although noodles are equally important in parts of Asia.

More to the point, noodles have become the new American staple carbohydrate, steadily gaining on bread as the staff of life. And the internationalization of pasta—the United States isn't the only non-Italian country in which pasta has become common—is probably the biggest culinary change of the late twentieth century. Which makes sense; pasta is the perfect food for people who are trying to cut down on heavy doses of meat and who don't have a lot of time to cook.

Although there are classic, centuries-old recipes, pasta is perfect for improvisational sauces. This has its problems, not the least of which is restaurants that offer "Penne with Artichoke Hearts, Shrimp, Goat Cheese, Pine Nuts, Sun-Dried Tomatoes, Basil, Cream, and Parmesan." Any two or three of these ingredients might make a pleasant pasta sauce—together they make a mess.

Fortunately, this doesn't happen so much at home, where your goal is not to impress anyone with the length of your recipe titles but to put together a decent meal. So a good sauce might contain nothing more than olive oil, garlic, and parsley (and you can live without the parsley if you need to); butter, sage, and Parmesan; olive oil, fresh tomatoes, and basil; or chicken stock, soy sauce, garlic, and ginger. All of these are traditional, legitimate, and unsurpassable, for both simplicity and flavor.

But, within reason, there is nothing wrong with "new" pasta combinations, which allow you to vary ingredients according to season and, probably more important, what's in the house. As you get the feel of making sauces for pasta, you'll discover both its freedoms and its limitations. What I offer here is a majority of simple, traditional recipes, a few of my own creations, and plenty of ideas for you to build on. Most pasta-eating countries make both fresh and dried noodles and, although I concentrate on the more convenient dried variety, I cover both in these pages.

The Basics of Pasta-Making

There are rules for pasta-making. These apply to all wheat noodles, whether they are Italian in style, or European, or American, or Chinese, Japanese, or other. (Rice noodles and other less common noodles are prepared differently, as you'll see.) In some areas, such as the use of cheese, amount of sauce, or selection of shape, you can be flexible. After all, tradition may dictate one thing (some chefs and writers act as though the pasta police are right around the corner, making sure you do things according to some canon), and your personal taste (or the harsh realities of your day!) another.

Nevertheless, there are certain rules worth heeding, in order to ensure the best possible results:

Buy good pasta The best pasta is one hundred percent durum wheat. It may come from the United States, or from Italy—the difference in price can determine your preference, although Italian pasta is not expensive. Most experienced cooks choose Italian pasta, which is now widely available. The best pastas are easier to keep from overcooking and have a deeper, more appealing color and a texture that "grabs" the sauce better.

Use enough water A gallon or, better still, five quarts per pound is about right; more than that is fine, but will take longer to come to a boil. If you're cooking pasta for two, one-half pound or so, you can get

away with three quarts (twelve cups) of water, and probably a smaller pot. If you have problems with pasta sticking, it's either because you don't use enough water or you don't stir. No matter what you learned in college, adding oil to the water will not cure the problem.

If your pot is not deep enough for spaghetti or other long pasta, you have two choices (three, really—you can always get a bigger pot): One, break the pasta in half. The pasta police frown on this, but I don't see anything wrong with it, although it could be argued that it deprives you of some of the pleasure of twirling. If that concerns you, go to option two: Hold the noodles by one end and dunk the other. As the bunch softens, swirl the strands around until they bend enough for you to submerge the whole thing. Easy enough.

Salt the water Unless you have hypertension or some other problem that prevents you from using salt, don't skip this step. Salting the water immeasurably improves the flavor of the pasta and indeed the final dish. How much salt? I use a good handful per pound, which measures a very heaping tablespoon. Try that amount and make adjustments as you see necessary. This may seem like a lot, but most of salt goes back down the drain with the cooking water.

People argue about the correct moment to salt the water. I add salt just before adding the pasta, because salted water takes a little longer to come to a boil than unsalted. Some people contend that salting earlier gives the water a bad flavor, but I have not found that to be true. In any case, salting the water itself is far more important than the timing of the act.

Boil the water, and keep it boiling It's okay to cover the pot after you add the pasta to bring the water back to a boil quickly. Just make sure to keep an eye on the pot and remove the cover before the water boils over onto the stove. Lower the heat if the water is boiling too furiously, but keep those bubbles rising.

Stir the pasta It will stick if you don't. Add the pasta, stir, cover the pot if necessary, then uncover it no more than a minute later and stir again. If the water has not come back to a boil, re-cover, but make sure to stir at least every minute. When the water begins boiling again, remove the cover, and stir whenever you think of it, at least every minute or two. Generally, stir more frequently during the early part of the cooking than later on. If the water in the pot threatens to boil over, lower the heat a bit but maintain a steady boil. Use a larger pot next time.

Don't undercook or overcook This is not a big deal, but you'd think it was. For years, most Americans cooked pasta until it was mushy—the joke was to cook it until a piece thrown at the refrigerator stuck to it. This wasn't completely our fault; American pasta makers often included inferior flours, so that the pasta became mushy about a tenth of second after it became tender; this is why so many cooks prefer imported pasta. Then we learned the magic words: *al dente,* the term for cooking pasta until it is firm to the bite. Now, undercooked pasta is as common as overcooked pasta, even in Italy.

There's an easy way to cook pasta correctly: Taste it. When it's just about done, when it retains a little bite but is no longer chalky, start draining. It will cook a little more between pot and table—perfect. It doesn't take much practice to get this right.

By the way, don't trust anyone's pasta cooking times. It varies from box to box and even day to day. Cook by taste and you'll never go wrong. This holds true for every noodle you make, from fresh egg pasta made in your own kitchen to dried rice noodles from Thailand.

Have a hot bowl ready Pasta cools quickly; you want to eat it hot. A bowl from your 50°F pantry is going to put quite a dent in the heat level of your pasta. Warm a heatproof bowl with hot water (often, you can put it under the colander so that the draining cooking water heats it) or put it in a warm oven while you're cooking.

Don't overdrain, don't oversauce Throw the pasta in a colander, then put it in the bowl. Some water should cling to the noodles and thin the sauce slightly.

It's said that Americans oversauce. "You should be eating pasta, not sauce," say the strict traditionalists, whose genetic memory reminds them that pasta is cheap and sauce is expensive. You're certainly entitled to put as much sauce on your pasta as you like, but the real problem is that we make our sauces too thick, with too little liquid, and therefore overcompensate by drowning the pasta in sauce in an attempt to moisten it. If you have a thick sauce, one that is clumping up on the pasta instead of nicely coating it, thin it out before serving—use a little of the pasta cooking water (a technique employed by every Italian home cook), water you used for cooking vegetables, some fresh or canned stock, tomato juice . . . in short, whatever you have that makes sense. Your pasta will be more evenly sauced and your sauces will go further. (If you want to see what the ideal thickness of a sauce is, make the Meat Sauce, Bolognese-Style [Ragu] on page 150, following the recipe carefully. It's a medium-bodied sauce that coats pasta beautifully.)

Pasta and Cheese

I am not wild about cheese in cooking, but Parmesan and pasta are another story entirely, one of those great culinary marriages. When to use grated cheese is of course a matter of personal taste. I don't use cheese with any fish-based sauce, and I usually use it sparingly or not at all with sauces that contain meat or lots of olive oil. I like to use cheese when I can feature it: in dairy-based sauces, or with herbs that complement it. But, again, it's a matter of taste.

I do feel more strongly about the kind of cheese. Nothing can compare with freshly grated cheese. Real Parmesan, from the area around Parma, is now sold everywhere. It's expensive—about ten dollars a pound—but it lasts a long time (unless you start

Unless you have a restaurant stove, it takes at least ten minutes to boil a gallon of water. It also takes at least ten minutes to cook most dried pasta. Here is a list of recipes in which the sauces are prepared in ten to thirty minutes:

1. Basic Tomato Sauce (page 130)
2. Buttery Tomato Sauce (page 130)
3. Aromatic Tomato Sauce (page 130)
4. Tomato Sauce with Wine (page 130)
5. Thickened Tomato Sauce (page 130)
6. Tomato Sauce with Bay Leaves (page 130)
7. Tomato Sauce with Herbs (page 131)
8. Pureed Tomato Sauce (page 131)
9. Pink Tomato Sauce (page 131)
10. Mozzarella Tomato Sauce (page 131)
11. Puttanesca Sauce (page 131)
12. Tuna Sauce (page 131)
13. Fiery Tomato Sauce (page 131)
14. Mushroom Sauce (page 131)
15. Linguine with Fresh Tomato Sauce and Parmesan (page 131)
16. Garlicky Fresh Tomato Sauce (page 132)
17. Fresh Tomato Sauce with Olive Oil (page 132)
18. Lower-Fat Fresh Tomato Sauce (page 132)
19. Fresh Tomato Sauce with Pesto (page 132), assuming you have Basic Pesto (page 766) on hand
20. Penne Arrabbiata (page 132)
21. Pasta with Raw Tomato Sauce (page 133)
22. Pasta Primavera (page 139)
23. Pasta with Butter, Sage, and Parmesan (page 140)
24. Spaghetti alla Carbonara (page 141)
25. Ziti with Creamy Gorgonzola Sauce (page 142)
26. Fettuccine with Spinach, Butter, and Cream (page 143)
27. Penne with Ricotta, Parmesan, and Peas (page 144)
28. Linguine with Garlic and Oil (page 144)
29. Spaghetti with Pesto (page 146), assuming you have Basic Pesto (page 766) on hand
30. Linguine with Clams (page 146)
31. Linguine with Scallops (page 148)

nibbling on it, which is understandable). Look for the brown rind with "Parmigiano-Reggiano" stenciled on it. Everything else called "Parmesan" is an imitation, although some of the imitations are decent.

There are two other kinds of cheese worth considering for Italian pasta dishes. Grana Padano, a Parmesan-like cheese from the far north of Italy, is an acceptable substitute for grating. However, its flavor is usually not quite as complex as that of Parmesan, and it's just as expensive.

Hard cheeses made from sheep's milk, such as Pecorino Romano, are wonderful for grating on very strong dishes, where the flavor of Parmesan might be overwhelmed. And good pecorino cheese is delicious for nibbling. I keep both pecorino and Parmesan in the refrigerator at all times; well wrapped in plastic or foil, they last for weeks and even months.

Pairing Pasta with Sauce

Dried Italian pasta (even when it is made elsewhere, the shapes are still typically Italian with Italian names) comes in more than one hundred shapes; see page 156 for an illustration of twists. Almost all of them have more than one name. There are times when shape matters and times when it does not. Tiny shapes, for example, such as orzo, stellini, and ditalini, are best in soups, since they fit on a spoon. It's also true that long pastas, like spaghetti and linguine, are best with sauces that don't have large chunks in them. Sauces with chunks should be served with bigger, tube-shaped pasta, such as penne, rigatoni, or ziti, or with shells and elbows, all of which gather in the chunks.

But it's rare that you should change the type of sauce you're making because you don't have the "correct" pasta shape. If you make spaghetti with a chunky sauce, some of the sauce will stay at the bottom of the bowl. This is less than ideal, of course, but you can eat that sauce with a spoon, or some bread, and next time you shop you might remember to stock up on penne.

How Much Pasta to Cook?

There is no rule about how much pasta to cook. In Italy, where pasta is served as a small first course, a pound will easily feed six to eight people. In my house, and many others, where pasta, bread, and a vegetable is often called dinner, a pound usually serves four, including two adults, one ravenous teenager, and one often finicky twelve-year-old. (I might add that when I was in high school, a friend of mine—whose mother made memorable meat sauce—used to prepare a pound for the two of us, and we usually finished it.) The kind of sauce and the shape of the pasta also affect how much you will eat; spaghetti with garlic and oil or a simple tomato sauce goes much faster than rigatoni with eggplant and mozzarella. Generally, I believe the recipes here serve three to four people, but you may find that they can be stretched to feed five, even as a main course.

If there are leftovers, by all means refrigerate them. You can reheat pasta in a microwave, oven, or non-stick skillet, without additional fat (you can eat it cold, too). All of these methods are frowned on by the pasta police, but I'd wager that even three out of four of them are closet eaters of leftover pasta. Yes, it will become overcooked and somewhat mushy, but you're hungry, right? It's fine; enjoy it. The pasta police are busy elsewhere, hassling people for using spaghetti where tradition calls for capellini.

The Basics of Tomatoes and Tomato-Based Sauces

The best tomatoes for sauce are meaty and very ripe. They're also peeled, cored, and seeded. What does this mean to you when you're buying tomatoes? First, it means that plum tomatoes are the best tomatoes for sauce, because they have a higher proportion of meat to liquid than round tomatoes. Whether you're buying fresh tomatoes or canned tomatoes, buy plum tomatoes if you can.

Fresh tomatoes can be treated in two ways: You can core them (page 610), roughly chop them, and use them as is. You might fish out the skins when they float to the top of the sauce, or you might ignore them entirely. This will be imperfect sauce, with a trace of bitterness from skins and seeds, but if the tomatoes tasted good to begin with, it will be just fine.

To make a sauce more refined, start by coring and peeling (page 610) the tomatoes, which will take you about five extra minutes of work. Then cut the tomatoes in half and squeeze out the seeds and liquid (page 610) into a strainer set over a bowl; discard the seeds. Chop the flesh and combine it with the reserved liquid. Those are your tomatoes for sauce.

Canned tomatoes are usually peeled. You can strain out the seeds as above, or ignore them (most people, in my experience, choose the latter course, although straining out the seeds takes just a moment). Canned tomatoes are usually sold swimming in liquid, most of which is practically useless; the tomatoes themselves contain enough liquid for your sauce. Drain the liquid and reserve it; in the unlikely event that your sauce is too dry, add a little of it back to the tomatoes.

What kind of canned tomatoes are best? The easy answer is whole, peeled, plum tomatoes from San Marzano, in Italy. But San Marzano tomatoes are not always available, and they are sometimes two or three times the cost of domestic or other imported tomatoes. They're better, but not two dollars a pound better (unless, of course, money is no object). So let's say this: Try to buy peeled plum tomatoes packed in tomato juice or puree. Generally speaking, these are better than buying crushed tomatoes or tomato puree, which I suspect serve as a reservoir for inferior tomatoes and give you no control over the texture of your sauce.

Basic Tomato Sauce

*Makes enough for at least 1 pound of pasta,
about 4 servings*

Time: 20 minutes

If you keep canned tomatoes on hand, you'll always be able to make fresh, delicious sauce in about the time it takes to bring water to a boil and cook the pasta. You can pass freshly grated Parmesan (or Pecorino Romano) cheese with this, but it is not essential.

3 tablespoons olive oil
3 cloves garlic, lightly smashed, or 1 small onion, minced
1 (28-ounce) can whole plum tomatoes
Salt and freshly ground black pepper to taste

1 Warm 2 tablespoons of the oil with the garlic or onion in a medium skillet over medium-low heat.

Cook, stirring occasionally, until the garlic is lightly golden or the onion is translucent.

2 Drain the tomatoes and remove their seeds if you choose to do so. Crush them with a fork or your hands and add them to the skillet, along with salt and pepper. Raise the heat to medium-high and cook, stirring occasionally, until the tomatoes break down and the mixture becomes "saucy," about ten minutes. Remove the garlic if you like. Stir in the remaining tablespoon of oil, taste for salt, and add more if necessary. (This sauce may be covered and refrigerated for a day or two, or put in a closed container and frozen for several weeks.) Serve over any long pasta.

Thirteen Ways to Quickly Vary Basic Tomato Sauce

Here are some of the myriad of options you have if you want to make this simple tomato sauce somewhat more complex. You can pick and choose among these options, or combine them, almost at will. Each takes a little more work, requires another ingredient or two, and adds refinement.

1. **Buttery Tomato Sauce:** Substitute butter for the oil.
2. **Aromatic Tomato Sauce:** Omit the garlic if you like. Add one-half cup each peeled, minced carrot, minced celery, and minced onion and cook until tender, about ten minutes, before adding the tomatoes. Especially good pureed (see below).
3. **Tomato Sauce with Wine:** Add one-half cup dry white or red wine before adding the tomatoes; let about half of it bubble away before proceeding.
4. **Thickened Tomato Sauce:** Stir in two tablespoons of tomato paste before adding the tomatoes.
5. **Tomato Sauce with Bay Leaves:** Add five to ten bay leaves and a good pinch (about one-eighth

teaspoon) of ground cinnamon before adding the tomatoes. Remove and discard the bay leaves before serving.

6. **Tomato Sauce with Herbs:** Stir in two or three tablespoons of minced fresh basil leaves, or one teaspoon minced fresh oregano or marjoram leaves (or one-half teaspoon dried), while the tomatoes are cooking. If you're using basil, add more as a garnish. Or simply garnish with plenty of fresh minced parsley, basil, or mint leaves.

7. **Pureed Tomato Sauce:** Puree the finished sauce by passing it through a food mill or whizzing it in a blender or food processor. Reheat it briefly before saucing the pasta.

8. **Pink Tomato Sauce:** Thin about one cup of ricotta cheese with about two tablespoons of the pasta cooking water and stir into the sauce just before serving. Kids love this pink sauce.

9. **Mozzarella Tomato Sauce:** Another kid-pleaser: Stir about one cup minced or grated mozzarella into the pasta with the sauce; this gives the pasta a pizza-like quality.

10. **Puttanesca Sauce:** Stir two tablespoons of capers (drained), some crushed red pepper flakes if you like, and/or one-half cup pitted black olives (the wrinkled, oil-cured type are best here) into the sauce after adding the tomatoes.

11. **Tuna Sauce:** Add one (six-ounce) can tuna, preferably the Italian kind packed in olive oil, to the sauce after adding tomatoes. This is especially good with the additions given for Puttanesca, above.

12. **Fiery Tomato Sauce:** Add a sprinkling of crushed red pepper flakes with the garlic or onion; add some more when the sauce is done, to taste.

13. **Mushroom Sauce:** Add about one cup of reconstituted dried porcini, or two cups of fresh mushrooms, trimmed and chopped, or a combination to the oil, about two minutes after the garlic or onion. Cook for about five minutes, stirring, before adding the tomatoes.

Linguine with Fresh Tomato Sauce and Parmesan

Makes about 4 servings

Time: 20 minutes

A seasonal dish, barely worth making unless the tomatoes are so good you'd eat them like apples. (The Parmesan must be high quality too.) This is my down-and-dirty, high-fat version; it takes no time at all and is almost perfect, as long as you don't mind tomato skins. One variation is more elegant; another is lower in saturated fat. All of the variations may be incorporated singly or in combination. The basil is optional; the sauce will be successful without it. But when you have fresh tomatoes, you can usually find fresh basil without trouble.

5 tablespoons butter

3 or 4 medium-to-large tomatoes, about 1 pound total, cored and roughly chopped

1/2 cup shredded fresh basil leaves

1 pound linguine

Salt and freshly ground black pepper to taste

Lots of freshly grated Parmesan cheese

1 Bring a large pot of water to a boil.

2 Melt 4 tablespoons of the butter in a medium-to-large skillet over medium heat. When the foam subsides, add the tomatoes.

3 Cook, stirring occasionally, until the tomatoes break up, about 10 minutes; fish the tomato skins from the sauce as they separate from the pulp (or leave them in if you're not after elegance). Add most of the basil, reserving some for garnish.

4 Meanwhile, salt the boiling water and cook the pasta until it is tender but firm. Season the sauce with salt and pepper; if it is thick—which it may be if you used meaty plum tomatoes or cooked out some of the liquid—thin it with some of the pasta cooking water. Drain the pasta and toss it with the sauce and

remaining 1 tablespoon butter. Garnish with the reserved basil and serve with the Parmesan.

Elegant Fresh Tomato Sauce: Peel and seed the tomatoes (page 610) before beginning. (You can also puree the sauce when it's done, using a food mill or food processor, but I prefer a chunky texture.)

Garlicky Fresh Tomato Sauce: In Step 2, cook 1 tablespoon or more minced garlic in the butter as it is heating over medium-low heat. When it just begins to color, raise the heat to medium and add the tomatoes. For even more garlic flavor, add another teaspoon of minced garlic no more than 1 or 2 minutes before the sauce is done.

Fresh Tomato Sauce with Olive Oil: Substitute top-quality extra-virgin olive oil for the butter. I almost always make this variation with garlic, and omit the Parmesan. Use plenty of basil if you have it.

Lower-Fat Fresh Tomato Sauce: Replace the butter with just enough olive oil to film the bottom of the pan, 1 tablespoon or less. Use an extra tomato and finish with oil instead of butter.

Fresh Tomato Sauce with Pesto: Toss pasta with Fresh Tomato Sauce and 1/2 cup Basic Pesto (page 766), or to taste. Serve with Parmesan.

Penne Arrabbiata

Makes about 4 servings

Time: 30 minutes

This simple, "angry" pasta is a classic. But it is definitely a grown-up treat; most kids hate it. Best served with grated Pecorino Romano cheese—Parmesan is too mild for this.

1/4 cup olive oil

3 cloves garlic, cut into chunks or slices

3 or 4 small dried hot red chiles (or about 1 teaspoon crushed red pepper flakes)

1 (28-ounce) can whole plum tomatoes

Salt and freshly ground black pepper to taste

1 pound penne, ziti, or other cut pasta

1/4 cup minced fresh parsley leaves

Grated Pecorino Romano (optional)

1. Bring a large pot of water to a boil.

2. Heat the olive oil, garlic, and chiles in a large skillet over medium-high heat. Cook, stirring occasionally, until the garlic becomes quite brown—but not black—7 or 8 minutes. Turn off the heat for 1 minute (this will reduce the spattering when you add the tomatoes).

3. Meanwhile, drain the tomatoes and remove their seeds if you choose to do so (see above). Crush them with a fork or your hands and add them to the skillet, along with salt and pepper; turn the heat to medium. Cook, stirring occasionally, until the mixture becomes saucy, 10 to 15 minutes. Season with salt and pepper. (This sauce may be covered and refrigerated for a day or two, or put in a closed container and frozen for several weeks.)

4. Meanwhile, salt the boiling water and cook the pasta until it is tender but firm. When it is done, drain it and sauce it. Top with parsley and serve, with grated cheese if desired.

Pasta with Onion and Bacon

Linguine all'Amatriciana

Makes about 4 servings

Time: 30 minutes

This is one of the greatest of all pasta dishes, sweet from onion, salty and meaty from bacon, acidic from tomatoes. The balance is incredible.

2 tablespoons olive oil

$1/4$ to $1/3$ cup minced good bacon or pancetta

1 small onion, minced

1 (28-ounce) can whole plum tomatoes, drained

1 pound linguine, spaghetti, fettuccine, or other long pasta

Salt and freshly ground black pepper to taste

Freshly grated Parmesan or Pecorino Romano cheese

Minced fresh parsley leaves

1. Bring a large pot of water to a boil.

2. Place the oil and bacon or pancetta in a medium skillet over medium heat. Cook, stirring, until the meat becomes crisp, about 10 minutes.

3. When the meat is done, remove it with a slotted spoon, leaving the fat in the pan. Add the onion and cook, stirring, until it browns. Turn off the heat for a minute (this will reduce the spattering when you add the tomatoes).

4. Crush the tomatoes with a fork or your hands and add them to the pan. Turn the heat to medium-high. Cook, stirring occasionally, until the tomatoes break down and the mixture becomes saucy, about 10 to 15 minutes.

5. Meanwhile, salt the boiling water and cook the pasta until it is tender but firm. Drain it, toss it with the sauce, and top with the reserved bacon, the Parmesan, and the parsley. Serve, passing additional Parmesan at the table.

Pasta with Whole Cloves of Garlic

Maccheroni alla San Giovanniello

Makes about 4 servings

Time: About 30 minutes

A rougher, heartier version of the above. Not for the timid, but beloved by many, myself included.

$1/3$ cup olive oil or butter

10 cloves garlic, lightly crushed

$1/2$ cup prosciutto or other salted ham or slab bacon, cut into cubes or strips

6 plum tomatoes or $1 1/2$ cups drained canned tomatoes

Salt and freshly ground black pepper to taste

1 pound cut pasta, such as ziti or penne

1 cup roughly chopped fresh basil leaves

1 cup freshly grated Pecorino Romano or Parmesan cheese, or a combination

1. Bring a large pot of water to a boil.

2. Combine the oil, garlic, and ham in a medium to large skillet over medium-low heat. Cook slowly, stirring occasionally, until the garlic becomes deep golden, nearly brown, all over, 10 to 15 minutes.

3. Core and chop the plum tomatoes (or crush the canned tomatoes) and add them, along with salt and pepper, to the skillet. Stir and simmer while you salt the boiling water and cook the pasta.

4. Drain the pasta when it is tender but firm, reserving a little of the cooking water and adding it to the sauce if it appears dry (quite likely if you used fresh tomatoes). Toss the pasta with the sauce and most of the basil, along with the cheese. Mince the remaining basil, garnish the pasta with it, and serve.

Pasta with Raw Tomato Sauce

Linguine con Salsa Cruda

Makes about 4 servings

Time: About 30 minutes

You can make this sauce in less than the time it takes for the water to boil, a definite advantage if you're hungry. It's a wonderful all-purpose topping that also can be used as a dipping sauce for fried foods (or chips, for that matter), or on top of soft polenta (see Basic Polenta, Version II, page 188).

A couple of guidelines: You can use good-quality canned plum tomatoes, as long as you drain them thoroughly first—the results will not be bad at all. But do not use dried basil. And don't smash the garlic too roughly or you'll have trouble removing it before serving.

2 cups cored and roughly chopped ripe tomatoes
2 tablespoons extra-virgin olive oil
Salt and freshly ground black pepper to taste
2 cloves garlic, smashed
$^{1}/_{4}$ to $^{1}/_{2}$ cup roughly minced fresh basil leaves
1 pound linguine or other long pasta
Freshly grated Parmesan cheese

1 Bring a large pot of water to a boil.

2 Place the tomatoes, oil, salt, pepper, garlic, and half the basil in a broad-bottomed bowl. Mash together well, using a fork or potato masher, but do not puree. (You can make the sauce an hour or two before you're ready to eat and let it rest, at room temperature.)

3 Salt the boiling water and cook the pasta until it is tender but firm. Ladle some of the cooking water into the sauce to thin it out a bit and warm it up. Remove the garlic. Toss the pasta with the sauce and top with the remaining basil; pass the grated Parmesan at the table.

The Basics of Vegetable-Based Pasta Sauces

There are some very real advantages to making pasta sauces that use other vegetables in addition to or instead of tomatoes. It's an easy way not only to vary flavor but to make a more filling sauce, and therefore a pasta that more easily serves as a main course. In addition, it's a good way to use leftover vegetables, as long as they have not been overcooked (or over-sauced) in the first place; if necessary, rinse them briefly with hot water to remove seasonings from their first cooking.

A couple of rules for vegetable sauces: You will usually want to cut the vegetables into bite-sized pieces, or even a small dice, before cooking them, or crush them with a fork or a spoon as they soften during cooking; generally, you don't want to use a knife to eat pasta. And add or substitute freely: Peas are almost always welcome; broccoli and cauliflower can substitute for one another; and so on. View the following as a collection of techniques rather than as a series of ironclad recipes and you will rapidly expand your repertoire.

Pasta with Cauliflower or Broccoli
Makes about 4 servings

Time: About 40 minutes

You can take this preparation in a variety of directions (see the variations) but in any case it's a big, flavorful, filling dish which needs only bread to become a meal. Substitute broccoli (or broccoflower) if you like, in either the main recipe or the variations.

1 head cauliflower, 1 pound or more
$^{1}/_{4}$ cup olive oil
1 tablespoon minced garlic
1 pound penne, ziti, or other cut pasta
Salt and freshly ground black pepper to taste
Minced fresh parsley leaves for garnish

1 Bring a large pot of water to a boil; salt it.

2 Trim the cauliflower and divide it into florets. Salt the water and cook the cauliflower in it until it is tender but not soft when pierced by a knife (the cauliflower will cook further in the sauce, so be careful not to overcook it). Remove the cauliflower and set it aside.

3 Meanwhile, cook the oil and garlic together in a large, deep skillet over medium-low heat, stirring occasionally. When the garlic is golden, turn off the heat if you're not ready to proceed.

4 Add the cauliflower to the skillet and turn the heat to medium. Cook, stirring and mashing the cauliflower, until it is hot and quite soft.

5 Meanwhile, cook the pasta. When the pasta is just about done, drain it, reserving about a cup of the cooking liquid. Add the pasta to the skillet with the cauliflower and toss with a large spoon until well combined. Add salt and pepper, along with some of the pasta water to keep the mixture from drying out. Garnish and serve.

Pasta with Cauliflower, Anchovies, and Hot Red Pepper: In Step 3, add 4 to 6 anchovy fillets (with their oil, if any; rinsed and picked over if salted), and 3 small dried hot red chiles, or to taste (or use crushed red pepper flakes) along with the garlic. Mash the anchovies as they cook and proceed as above.

Garlicky Pasta with Broccoli Raab: In Step 2, substitute 1 pound broccoli raab (page 543), roughly chopped into 1-inch pieces, for the cauliflower. Again, take care not to overcook it. Follow either the master recipe or the above variation. Mince an additional teaspoon or so of garlic and, in Step 5, add it to the vegetable mixture along with the pasta. This is also good with a teaspoon or two of balsamic vinegar stirred into the mixture about a minute before serving.

Pasta with Cauliflower and Sausage: Cut 2 or 3 (about $1/2$ pound) hot or sweet Italian sausages into thin slices and, in Step 3, cook them along with the garlic (and hot pepper to taste, if you like) until nicely browned. Proceed as in master recipe.

Pasta with Saffron-Cauliflower Sauce

Makes about 4 servings

Time: About 40 minutes

This is a Sicilian masterpiece, taught to me by my friend Michael Lomonaco, chef at New York's Windows on the World.

1 head cauliflower, 1 pound or more
Several threads saffron
$1/4$ cup olive oil
1 medium onion, finely chopped
4 to 5 anchovy fillets (with their oil, if any; rinsed and picked over if salted), roughly chopped
1 tablespoon tomato paste
$1/3$ cup dried currants or raisins
$1/4$ cup pine nuts
Salt and freshly ground black pepper to taste
1 pound bucatini, perciatelli, or linguine

1 Bring a large pot of water to a boil.

2 Trim the cauliflower and divide it into florets. Salt the water and cook the cauliflower in it until it is tender but not soft when pierced by a knife (the cauliflower will cook further in the sauce, so be careful not to overcook it). Remove the cauliflower and set it aside. Remove $1/4$ cup of the water and soak the saffron threads in it. Keep the water in the pot for the pasta and return to a boil.

3 Warm the olive oil for a minute in a large, deep skillet over medium heat. Add the onion and cook for 7 to 10 minutes, stirring, until translucent. Add the anchovies and stir to combine. Add the cauliflower

florets, stir, and cook for 5 minutes. Add the saffron water, $1/2$ cup of the cauliflower cooking water, and the tomato paste. Bring to a boil and reduce the heat to low.

4 Cook the pasta in the pot of boiling water. Add the currants and pine nuts to the sauce and season with salt and pepper.

5 When the pasta is done, drain and place in a large, warm serving bowl. Add half the cauliflower sauce and toss. Serve each portion with additional sauce on top.

Pasta with Radicchio, Pine Nuts, and Raisins: Substitute 2 or 3 heads of radicchio, about $3/4$ to 1 pound total, trimmed and shredded, for the cauliflower. Omit the saffron. Do not parboil the radicchio, but, in Step 3, add it along with the anchovies; turn up the heat a bit, and cook until the radicchio becomes tender, about 5 minutes. Proceed as above; reserve 1 cup or so of the pasta cooking water, and after you've tossed together the radicchio mixture and pasta, add it as necessary to keep the dish moist and saucy.

Spaghetti with Eggplant

Makes 4 servings

Time: $1 1/2$ hours, less if you choose not to salt the eggplant

There are many ways to combine eggplant and pasta; my favorite begins with salting and sautéing, admittedly a chore. (The salting step can always be omitted, with a minor sacrifice in quality.) But well-sautéed eggplant (see page 569 for tips) is a creamy, savory treat, one that graces pasta beautifully. Still, there are less time-consuming alternatives; see the variations for a few.

2 small or 1 medium-to-large eggplant,
    about 1 pound total
Salt to taste
$1/2$ to $3/4$ cup olive oil
1 tablespoon minced garlic
$1/2$ teaspoon crushed red pepper flakes, or to taste
2 cups fresh or canned (drained) plum tomatoes,
    roughly chopped
1 pound spaghetti, linguine, or other long pasta
Minced fresh parsley leaves for garnish

1 Peel the eggplant if you like; cut it into $1/2$-inch-thick or thinner slices, and salt and squeeze according to the directions on page 568.

2 Bring a large pot of water to a boil.

3 Place $1/4$ cup of oil in a large skillet and turn the heat to medium. When the oil shimmers, cook the eggplant slices in batches, without crowding, until nicely browned and tender, about 3 to 5 minutes per side. Regulate the heat so that the eggplant does not burn, and add additional oil as necessary. As the slices are cooked, set them on paper towels to remove excess oil.

4 When the eggplant is done, drain all but a film of oil from the skillet, and, with the heat still on medium, add the garlic and red pepper. Cook and stir for about 30 seconds, then add the tomatoes and salt. Cook, stirring occasionally, until the tomatoes break up and the mixture becomes saucy, 10 to 15 minutes. Meanwhile, salt the boiling water and cook the pasta. Cut the eggplant into strips.

5 When the sauce is done, taste it and adjust the seasoning, then stir half the eggplant into it. Drain the pasta when it is tender but firm and combine it with the sauce in a warm bowl. Top with the remaining eggplant, garnish, and serve.

Pasta with Eggplant, Anchovies, Olives, and Capers: In Step 4, add 4 to 6 anchovy fillets (with their oil, if any; rinsed and picked over if salted) to the skillet along with the garlic. Add $1/2$ cup pitted black olives (the wrinkled, oil-cured kind are best here) and 1 tablespoon of drained capers to the skillet along with the tomatoes. Go easy on the salt. Proceed as above.

Pasta with Eggplant, Onion, and Two Cheeses: In Step 1, cube the eggplant instead of slicing it (page 568); salt and squeeze it if you have time. In Step 3, cook the eggplant in $1/3$ cup olive oil with 1 cup of peeled, diced onion until both eggplant and onion are tender, 10 to 15 minutes. In Step 4, omit the garlic, red pepper, and tomatoes. In Step 5, thin $1/2$ cup ricotta with a bit of the pasta cooking water and toss it together with the pasta, eggplant and onion mixture, and plenty of freshly grated Parmesan. Garnish with parsley or freshly shredded basil leaves.

Lower-Fat Pasta with Eggplant and Basil: In Step 1, preheat the oven to 450°F. Cube the eggplant instead of slicing it (page 568); salt and squeeze it if you have time. Toss it in a roasting pan or large ovenproof skillet with 1 tablespoon of oil, then roast it, shaking the pan occasionally, until tender, about 20 minutes. Meanwhile, heat 1 tablespoon of oil with 1 tablespoon of minced garlic in a large, deep skillet; add the tomatoes and cook as in Step 4, above. When the sauce is done, stir in the eggplant and $1/4$ cup shredded fresh basil leaves. Toss with the pasta and garnish with more basil.

Linguine with Slow-Cooked Onions

Makes about 4 servings

Time: About 1 hour

Cooked slowly and leisurely, onions turn so sweet that they need plenty of salt, pepper, and Parmesan, or this preparation is one-dimensional. But properly balanced, it's a revelation. If you like, try adding anchovies, capers, olives, or a little vinegar near the end of cooking. All make this dish more complex.

5 or 6 medium-to-large onions, about 2 pounds
$1/3$ cup plus 2 tablespoons extra-virgin olive oil
Salt and freshly ground black pepper to taste
1 pound linguine, spaghetti, capellini (angel hair), fettuccine, or other long pasta
Freshly grated Parmesan cheese

1 Slice the onions thinly; this is a good job for the food processor's slicing disk. Place them in a large dry skillet. Cover the pan and turn the heat to medium-low. Check and stir every 5 minutes. The onions will first give up lots of liquid, then dry out; after about 20 to 30 minutes, when they begin to brown and stick to the pan, remove the cover. Add the $1/3$ cup of olive oil, along with a healthy sprinkling of salt and pepper. Turn the heat to medium.

2 Bring a large pot of water to a boil.

3 Continue to cook the onions until they are uniformly brown and soft, almost pasty, 10 to 20 minutes more. Salt the boiling water and cook the pasta until it is tender but firm.

4 Taste the onions and adjust the seasoning as necessary; add the remaining 2 tablespoons olive oil and a little of the pasta cooking water. Drain the pasta and toss it in a warm bowl with the onions and some Parmesan. Serve, passing additional Parmesan at the table.

Pasta with Lentils

Makes 6 to 8 servings

Time: About 1 hour

A dish similar to this one is made in the Middle East, substituting ground coriander for the oregano. You can also make it with cooked beans such as kidney, pinto, or any beans you like; start with about one cup of dried beans, because beans swell more than lentils; and remember they'll take longer to become tender.

1 1/2 cups lentils, washed and picked over (see The
  Basics of Buying and Preparing Beans, page 500)

2 carrots, peeled and minced

1 medium onion, minced, plus 1 medium onion,
  sliced

1 cup cored and chopped tomato (canned is fine;
  drain first)

Salt and freshly ground black pepper to taste

1 tablespoon minced fresh oregano or marjoram
  leaves or 1 teaspoon dried

2 tablespoons olive oil

1 pound elbows, shells, or similarly shaped pasta

1 teaspoon minced garlic

1 Combine the lentils, carrots, minced onion, and water to cover in a large pot over medium heat. Simmer until the lentils are tender but not at all mushy, 20 to 30 minutes (some lentils may take even longer, but check frequently to avoid overcooking). Add the tomato, salt, pepper, and half the oregano, stir, and keep warm over low heat. (This sauce may be made up to this point and covered and refrigerated for a day or two ahead, or put in a closed container and frozen for several weeks.)

2 Meanwhile, heat the olive oil in a medium skillet over medium-high heat for 1 minute. Add the sliced onion and cook, stirring, until it begins to brown and become crisp, about 10 minutes.

3 Bring a large pot of water to a boil.

4 When the lentils are done, salt the boiling water and cook the pasta until it is still quite firm and a bit chalky in the center. Drain it, reserving a cup or so of

Twenty-Three Pasta Sauces You Can Make in Advance

Even though some of these are delicate, fresh sauces, they can be made several hours or even a day in advance as long as they are not overcooked and are reheated gently. Most can be successfully frozen as well. If possible, add some fresh herbs during reheating; a drizzling of olive oil, if used in the basic sauce, is another good last minute addition.

the cooking liquid. Stir the pasta into the lentils along with the garlic, the cooked onion, and the remaining oregano. Add enough of the pasta water to moisten the mixture. Cook for 2 or 3 minutes, or until the pasta is tender. Taste, adjust seasoning if necessary, and serve in a warm bowl.

Pasta Primavera

Makes about 4 servings

Time: About 30 minutes

Primavera means "spring," but you can use any combination of vegetables you like for this simple dish. Think of the ingredient list below as a "for instance."

1¹/₂ cups chicken, meat, or vegetable stock
    (see "Soups" for stock recipes)
2 sprigs fresh thyme
Salt
¹/₂ cup peeled and diced carrot
1 cup asparagus tips, each about 1 inch long
¹/₂ cup diced zucchini or summer squash
¹/₂ cup shelled fresh or frozen peas, or snow peas
1 pound penne or other cut pasta
2 tablespoons extra-virgin olive oil or butter
Freshly ground black pepper to taste
1¹/₂ cups freshly grated Parmesan cheese

① Bring a large pot of water to a boil.

② Bring 1 cup of the stock to a boil in a medium skillet; add the thyme, and salt if necessary. Add the carrot and cook for 3 minutes. Add the asparagus tips and cook for 2 minutes. Add the zucchini and cook for 2 minutes. Add the peas and cook until all the vegetables are just tender, and the stock has just about evaporated. Turn off the heat.

③ Salt the boiling water and cook the pasta until it is tender but firm.

④ When the pasta is just about done, turn the heat under the vegetables to medium and stir in the olive oil or butter. Cook for about a minute, then add the remaining stock. Cook until the vegetables are very tender but not mushy.

⑤ Drain the pasta and toss it with the cooked vegetables and their broth; add salt and pepper to taste. Top with about a cup of Parmesan, or enough to thicken the sauce and serve, passing additional Parmesan at the table.

Pasta with Potatoes

Makes 8 servings

Time: At least 1 hour

I learned this classic Neapolitan dish from my friend Andrea Graziosi, a dedicated collector of pasta recipes. This is one of the traditional ways of using those bits of pasta that sit in your cupboard, and one of the few pasta dishes in which overcooking is mandatory. Keep it thin and serve it as a kind of soup, or allow it to thicken and serve it as a pasta dish or main course. It's great for (very) informal entertaining in the dead of winter.

2 tablespoons olive oil
About 4 ounces bacon, preferably good slab bacon,
    minced
1 teaspoon crushed red pepper flakes, or to taste
1 tablespoon chopped garlic
4 or 5 medium waxy potatoes, peeled and cut into
    bite-sized chunks
1 (28-ounce) can whole plum tomatoes, not drained
About 1¹/₂ pounds assorted leftover pasta, broken up
Salt and freshly ground black pepper to taste

① Combine the olive oil, bacon, and red pepper in a large soup kettle over medium heat. Cook, stirring occasionally, until the bacon has given up its fat and become crisp, about 10 minutes. Add the garlic, cook 1 minute more, then add the potatoes. Raise the heat to medium-high, and cook, stirring occasionally, until the potatoes brown a bit, about 10 minutes.

2 Add the tomatoes and their juice along with 1 cup of hot water. Add the pasta, salt, and pepper. Simmer over low heat, uncovered, stirring occasionally to prevent sticking and adding hot water as necessary— the texture should remain thick and stewy, never dry.

3 About 30 minutes later, when the potatoes are tender and the pasta is mushy, it's done. (This dish may be covered and refrigerated for a day or two, or put in a closed container and frozen for several weeks; it's likely that you will need to add more liquid when you reheat.) Check the seasoning and add more crushed red pepper flakes, black pepper, and/or salt if needed.

The Basics of Dairy-Based Sauces for Pasta

One of the best and simplest combinations for pasta sauces is butter and Parmesan—the first offers creamy richness, the second intense flavor. Many other possible combinations stem from this one.

But Parmesan is far from the only cheese that takes well to pasta. Gorgonzola (or another creamy blue cheese) makes a brilliant, strong-flavored pasta sauce; ricotta—especially creamy fresh ricotta (sold in Italian and specialty food stores), which is moister and more flavorful than the overly processed ricotta sold in supermarkets—makes a sweet, creamy sauce, whether blended with tomato sauce or simply thinned with pasta-cooking water); and other strong-tasting cheeses, such as fontina and taleggio, combine beautifully with butter, milk, cream or, again, pasta-cooking water to make a simple sauce.

Don't make the mistake of thinking that you need a ton of dairy to make a good pasta sauce. Many dairy ingredients have good, strong flavor, and it doesn't take much to transfer that flavor to the pasta. In order to make the thicker dairy products into a sauce, you simply need to add enough pasta cooking water to thin them. When the pasta is nearly done cooking, scoop out a cup or so of the water. After you drain the pasta and add the sauce ingredients, stir in the water a little at a time. Stop adding water when the sauce has reached the right consistency.

Pasta with Butter, Sage, and Parmesan
Makes about 4 servings

Time: 30 minutes

If you eliminate the sage, this becomes kid food (there are homes in Italy where pasta with butter and Parmesan is the equivalent of pabulum). But most grown-ups prefer the sharper edge that sage provides. Like many others, this sauce can be prepared in the time it takes water to boil. Note that Fettuccine Alfredo is a variation on this basic theme.

6 tablespoons ($^3/_4$ stick) butter
20 or 30 fresh sage leaves or about 1 tablespoon
    dried whole sage leaves
Salt and freshly ground black pepper to taste
1 pound cut pasta, such as ziti or penne, or
    long pasta, such as linguine or spaghetti
1 cup freshly grated Parmesan cheese

1 Bring a large pot of water to a boil.
2 Melt the butter in a small saucepan over low heat. Add the sage, salt, and pepper. Cook until the butter turns light brown, about 10 minutes.

3 Salt the boiling water and cook the pasta until it is tender but firm. Spoon 2 or 3 tablespoons of the pasta cooking water into a warm serving bowl. Drain the pasta and toss in the serving bowl with the butter, more pepper, and half the Parmesan. Pass the remaining Parmesan at the table.

Pasta with Olive Oil and Sage: Substitute olive oil for all or part of the butter. A peeled, crushed garlic clove does nicely here, added along with the sage and removed before it becomes too brown. The cheese is optional.

Fettuccine Alfredo (Pasta with Butter, Eggs, Cream, and Parmesan): Reduce the butter to 2 tablespoons and melt it gently (if you have a few threads of saffron, add them for a lovely color and aroma); eliminate the sage. In Step 3, while the pasta cooks, warm a large bowl in the oven or by filling it with hot water; when it's warm, add 2 eggs, $1/2$ cup heavy cream, and 1 cup of grated Parmesan; beat briefly. Season with pepper. When the pasta is cooked, toss it with the cheese-egg-cream mixture, adding a little of the cooking water if necessary to keep the mixture moist. Drizzle with the butter, toss well, and serve immediately.

Six Simple Additions to Pasta with Butter and Parmesan

Remove the sage from this basic dish and add, as you like:

1. Any minced herb of your choice, or a mixture of minced herbs
2. Crisp-cooked and crumbled bacon
3. Minced ham
4. Cooked sweet peas
5. Cooked, drained, and minced spinach
6. Sautéed onions or shallots

Spaghetti alla Carbonara
Makes about 4 servings

Time: 30 minutes

In the seventies, when most Americans first realized that there was pasta beyond tomato sauce, spaghetti alla carbonara was a revelation. Since that time, it has become a joke: Who wants pasta—the epitome of moderate eating—with bacon, eggs, and cheese? But the fact is, pasta, carbonara-style (named after the charcoal producers, who remained in the woods for weeks at a time and had access only to long-keeping foods such as pasta, eggs, bacon, and hard cheese), is delicious—sinfully so, like an egg-butter-sugar dessert. If guilt overwhelms you, try the somewhat more moderate variation with zucchini.

1 tablespoon olive oil
4 ounces minced bacon, preferably slab bacon, or pancetta
2 eggs
1 cup freshly grated Parmesan cheese, plus more
1 pound spaghetti, linguine, or other long pasta
Salt and freshly ground black pepper to taste

1 Combine the olive oil and bacon in an medium skillet over medium heat. Cook, stirring occasionally, until the bacon is crisp.

2 Meanwhile, bring a large pot of water to a boil. Warm a large bowl in the oven, or by filling it with very hot water.

3 Beat the eggs and Parmesan together in the bowl. Salt the boiling water and cook the pasta until it is tender but firm. When it is done, drain it and toss it immediately with the egg-cheese mixture; add the bacon and any fat remaining in the skillet. Add lots of pepper; taste and add salt and more pepper if necessary. Serve immediately, passing more grated Parmesan at the table.

Spaghetti with Zucchini and Eggs: In Step 1, rinse and thinly slice 2 or 3 medium zucchini; dice a small onion. Substitute these for the bacon, increasing the olive oil to 3 tablespoons. Cook, stirring frequently, until the zucchini browns, about 10 minutes. In Step 3, add $1/4$ cup minced fresh mint, basil, or parsley leaves to the egg-cheese mixture. Proceed as above, garnishing with more minced mint, basil, or parsley.

Orzo "Risotto"

Makes 4 to 6 servings

Time: 20 minutes

Like "real" risotto, this is best as a first course or side dish than as the centerpiece of a meal. Having said that, it should be mentioned that everyone loves this dish, which has an indisputably warm, cozy feel to it. You can make this with canned stock, but its flavor is exceptional when you use strong homemade stock, such as one of those on pages 46–51.

2 tablespoons butter (preferred) or olive oil
1 small onion, minced
3 cups chicken, beef, or vegetable stock, plus $1/2$ cup more if needed (see "Soups" for stock recipes)
$1^1/2$ cups orzo (rice-shaped pasta)
Salt and freshly ground black pepper to taste
1 cup freshly grated Parmesan cheese
$1/2$ cup minced fresh parsley leaves

1 Place the butter in a 3- or 4-quart saucepan and turn the heat to medium; when the foam subsides, add the onion and cook, stirring, until it becomes translucent. Meanwhile, heat the stock in a separate pan.

2 Add the orzo to the onion and stir once or twice; season with salt and pepper and add the stock, all at once. Cover and reduce heat to medium-low.

3 Cook, stirring every few minutes to prevent sticking, until the liquid is absorbed and the pasta is tender, about 15 minutes. Taste and adjust seasoning if necessary. In the unlikely event that the pasta is underdone, add $1/2$ cup more hot water or stock and cook another 5 minutes or so, until it is absorbed and the pasta is done. Stir in half the Parmesan and parsley. Garnish with the remaining parsley and serve, passing the remaining Parmesan at the table.

Ziti with Creamy Gorgonzola Sauce

Makes about 4 servings

Time: 30 minutes

The best Gorgonzola (which, not surprisingly, is imported from Italy), is soft and creamy to begin with. Combine it with butter and cream and you have luxury combined with intense flavor.

2 tablespoons butter
$1/2$ cup crumbled Gorgonzola cheese
$1/2$ cup milk, half-and-half, or cream
1 pound ziti, penne, or other cut pasta
$1/2$ cup freshly grated Parmesan cheese, plus more if desired
Salt to taste

1 Bring a large pot of water to a boil.
2 Melt the butter in a 1- or 2-quart saucepan over low heat. While it is melting, put the Gorgonzola in a small bowl and mash it with a fork or potato masher, gradually adding the milk. Don't worry about making it smooth, just make sure it is well combined. When the butter is melted, add the cheese-milk mixture and continue to cook, stirring and mashing occasionally.
3 Meanwhile, salt the boiling water and cook the pasta until it is tender but firm. When it is done,

drain it and mix with the sauce in a large, warm bowl; stir in the Parmesan, then taste for salt and add some if necessary. Serve, passing additional Parmesan at the table if you like.

Baked Ziti with Radicchio and Gorgonzola

Makes 4 servings

Time: About 1 hour

Another dish showcasing the super flavor of Gorgonzola. Be careful not to cook the pasta to complete doneness; you should remove it from the cooking water when it is still so firm that you wouldn't want to eat it.

1 pound ziti, penne, or other cut pasta
2 small heads radicchio, about ½ pound, shredded
4 scallions, trimmed and very thinly sliced
2 cups milk, half-and-half, or cream
1 cup Gorgonzola, crumbled
1 cup freshly grated Parmesan cheese
Salt and freshly ground black pepper to taste
Butter for greasing the baking pan
½ cup plain bread crumbs, preferably fresh

1 Bring a large pot of water to a boil. Preheat the oven to 375°F.

2 Salt the boiling water and cook the pasta until it is barely tender, with a fairly chalky interior. Drain it well.

3 Mix the pasta with the radicchio, scallions, milk, Gorgonzola, and half the Parmesan. Taste for salt (it may not need any) and add pepper to taste.

4 Grease a 9 × 13-inch baking pan with butter and pour in the pasta mixture. Mix together the bread crumbs and remaining Parmesan and spread this on top of the pasta. Bake for about 30 minutes, until the

mixture is hot and bubbly, then raise the heat to 450°F and continue to bake until the bread crumb mixture browns nicely, another 10 minutes or so. You can let this rest for 10 or 15 minutes before serving if you like.

Fettuccine with Spinach, Butter, and Cream

Makes about 4 servings

Time: 30 minutes

The combination of spinach and cream is old-fashioned but great. This sauce is also good with a liberal grating of nutmeg added to it.

10 ounces fresh spinach, trimmed, washed, and dried (page 604)
4 tablespoons (½ stick) butter
Salt and freshly ground black pepper to taste
1 cup heavy cream, light cream, or half-and-half
1 pound spaghetti, linguine, or fettuccine
1 cup freshly grated Parmesan cheese

1 Bring a large pot of water to a boil.

2 Chop the spinach coarsely. Over medium heat melt 2 tablespoons of the butter in a large skillet that can later be covered. Add the spinach, along with some salt and pepper. Cover, reduce the heat, and cook, stirring occasionally, until the spinach is very tender, about 10 minutes. Uncover, add half the cream, and cook gently for about 5 minutes.

3 Meanwhile, salt the boiling water and cook the pasta until it is tender but firm. When it is just about done, put the remaining butter in a large, warm bowl and add a couple of tablespoons of the cooking water. Drain the pasta and toss it with the butter and half the Parmesan. Add the spinach sauce and serve, passing the remaining Parmesan at the table.

Penne with Ricotta, Parmesan, and Peas

Makes about 4 servings

Time: 30 minutes

The butter is optional here, but it lends richness. Add a bit of minced sautéed ham or mushrooms if you like, or use Basic Tomato Sauce (page 130) to thin the ricotta in place of the pasta cooking water.

1 cup freshly shelled or frozen peas

1 pound penne, ziti, or other cut pasta

About 1 cup fresh ricotta, available in Italian and specialty food markets

1 tablespoon softened butter (optional)

1 cup freshly grated Parmesan cheese

Salt and freshly ground black pepper to taste

1   Bring a large pot of water to a boil.

2   Cook the peas in boiling salted water to cover, just until tender, about 3 minutes. Drain and rinse in cold water to stop the cooking; drain and set aside.

3   Salt the boiling water and cook the pasta. While it is cooking, mix together the ricotta, butter, and half of the Parmesan in the bottom of a warm bowl. When the pasta is just about done, remove about a cup of the pasta cooking water and use as much of it as you need to smooth the ricotta mixture into a sauce.

4   Toss the pasta with the ricotta mixture, add additional pasta cooking water if necessary, and serve, passing the remaining Parmesan at the table.

The Basics of Oil-Based Sauces for Pasta

The increasing and justified popularity of olive oil has made oil-based sauces more popular than ever. Of course most pasta sauces—even those from outside of Italy—are oil-based. But the following few use oil as one of their primary flavors. For this reason, you should always use the best extra-virgin oil you have to make them.

There are times when an oil-based sauce is not thin enough to adequately coat your pasta. In this case you have two options: Add more extra-virgin olive oil, or add a bit of pasta cooking water, which adds fewer calories but less flavor. Either option is perfectly fine.

Linguine with Garlic and Oil

Makes about 4 servings

Time: 20 minutes

Not only is this Roman standard one of the world's quickest and simplest pasta dishes, it is among the most delicious. For variety, add a dried hot chile or two to the oil at the beginning, or add a handful of chopped parsley to the oil just before pouring it over the pasta. Gardeners should be sure to try the mixed herb variation.

2 tablespoons minced garlic

$1/2$ cup extra-virgin olive oil

Salt to taste

1 pound linguine, spaghetti, or other long, thin pasta

Minced fresh parsley leaves (optional)

1   Bring a large pot of water to a boil.

2   In a small skillet or saucepan over medium-low heat, combine the garlic, oil, and salt. Allow the garlic to simmer, shaking the pan occasionally, until it turns golden; do not allow it to become dark brown or it will be bitter rather than sweet.

3   Salt the boiling water and cook the pasta until it is tender but firm. When it is done, drain it, reserving a bit of the cooking water. Reheat the garlic and oil

mixture briefly if necessary. Dress the pasta with the sauce, adding a little more oil or some of the cooking water if it seems dry. Garnish with parsley if you like.

Linguine with Chickpeas: In Step 2 add 1 or 2 small dried hot red chiles to the oil if you like. In Step 3, substitute cut pasta such as ziti, penne, or shells for the linguine. Toss the cooked pasta with 1 cup warm cooked chickpeas (canned are fine).

Linguine with Garlic, Oil, and Anchovies: In Step 2, add 4 to 6 anchovy fillets (with their oil, if any; rinsed and picked over if salted) to the oil along with the garlic. Cook as above, mashing the anchovies until they break up and virtually dissolve into the oil.

Linguine with Anchovies and Walnuts: Toast $^1/_2$ cup chopped walnut pieces in a 350°F oven, shaking occasionally, for about 10 minutes, or until they are aromatic. In Step 2, proceed as in Linguine with Garlic, Oil, and Anchovies. In Step 3, after cooking the pasta, dilute the garlic-anchovy sauce with $^1/_4$ to $^1/_2$ cup of the pasta water. Toss the sauce, pasta, and walnuts together.

Linguine with Fresh Herbs: In Step 2, when the garlic is done, toss in a mixture of 1 cup or more fresh herbs, whatever you have on hand; try, for example, $^1/_4$ cup minced parsley leaves, $^1/_4$ cup minced basil or chervil leaves, 1 sprig tarragon, minced, several sprigs of dill, minced, a sprig or two of thyme, leaves stripped from the stem and minced, and 1 tablespoon or more of minced chives (this is merely a suggestion; substitute freely). The mixture will absorb all the oil so, in Step 3, when you toss it with the pasta, be sure to add more oil or some of the pasta cooking water. Garnish with more fresh herbs, finely minced.

Pasta with Porcini

Makes about 4 servings

Time: 30 minutes

If you're lucky enough to come across a pound of fresh porcini, here's what to do. If not, try the variation, which combines dried porcini with fresh mushrooms for nearly comparable flavor.

1 pound porcini (cèpes) or other fresh wild
   mushrooms
$^1/_3$ cup olive oil, plus 1 tablespoon
Salt and freshly ground pepper to taste
2 tablespoons minced shallots or 1 tablespoon
   minced garlic
1 pound any long or cut pasta
$^1/_2$ cup chicken, beef, or vegetable stock, or pasta
   cooking water (see "Soups" for stock recipes)
About $^1/_2$ cup minced fresh parsley leaves,
   plus more for garnish

1 Bring a large pot of water to a boil.
2 Wipe the mushrooms clean, or rinse them quickly if they are very dirty. Trim them of any hard, tough spots and cut them into small chunks or slices.
3 Heat the $^1/_3$ cup of oil in a medium-to-large skillet over medium heat for 1 minute. Add the mushrooms and season with salt and pepper. Raise the heat to medium-high and cook, stirring occasionally, until the mushrooms begin to brown, at least 10 minutes. Add the shallots or garlic, stir, and cook for another minute or two until the mushrooms are tender. Turn off the heat.
4 Salt the boiling water and cook the pasta until it is tender but firm. When it is almost done, add $^1/_2$ cup of stock or cooking water to the mushrooms, turn the heat to low, and reheat gently. Drain the pasta, reserving a little more of the cooking water if you have no stock. Toss the pasta and the mushrooms together

with the remaining tablespoon of olive oil; add a little more liquid if the dish seems dry. Stir in about $^1/_2$ cup of parsley, and serve garnished with more parsley.

Linguine with Dried Porcini: In Step 2, prepare a pound of fresh domesticated mushrooms—button, cremini, shiitake, oyster, or a combination—as above. Soak at least $^1/_4$ cup of dried porcini in hot water to cover for about 10 minutes, or until softened. Drain the porcini and squeeze out excess moisture, reserving the soaking liquid. Cut the porcini into bits and cook them with the fresh mushrooms and shallots or garlic, as in the master recipe. Follow the steps above, using the mushroom soaking liquid to augment or replace stock or pasta cooking water.

Spaghetti with Pesto

Makes about 4 servings

Time: 20 minutes

One of the fastest and easiest pasta sauces, assuming you have ready-made Basic Pesto (page 766) on hand.

    1 pound spaghetti or other long pasta
    2 tablespoons extra-virgin olive oil
    1 cup Basic Pesto (page 766)
    Freshly grated Parmesan cheese

1 Bring a large pot of water to a boil; salt it. Cook the pasta until it is tender but firm.

2 Meanwhile, stir the olive oil into the pesto to thin it a little. When the pasta is almost done, thin the pesto further with pasta cooking water, until it has the consistency of heavy cream.

3 Toss the pasta with the pesto, top with grated cheese, and serve, passing additional grated cheese at the table.

The Basics of Seafood-Based Sauces for Pasta

There are a couple of generalizations that can be made about fish sauces for pasta. Usually, the fish should be cooked at the last minute, often after you begin cooking the noodles. No fish benefits from overcooking, and many toughen or fall apart if cooked longer than a couple of minutes.

Also, few—if any—pasta sauces with fish need added cheese. This is a matter of personal preference, of course, but both minced parsley or lightly toasted bread crumbs—or a combination—are better suited than grated cheese as garnishes for fish sauces.

Linguine with Clams

Makes about 4 servings

Time: 30 minutes

Clam sauce made with canned clams is acceptable, but it can't hold a candle to this, which leaves you with a few delicious clams to eat before you get down to the business of the pasta. Quick and authentic. To read more about clams, see page 342.

    At least 40 littleneck clams, the smaller the better,
        or at least 3 pounds of cockles
    $^1/_2$ cup dry white wine, plus little more if necessary
    Pinch of cayenne
    $^1/_4$ cup extra-virgin olive oil
    1 tablespoon minced garlic
    1 large or 2 small plum tomatoes, peeled, seeded,
        and minced (optional)
    1 pound long pasta, such as linguine or spaghetti
    $^1/_2$ teaspoon minced fresh tarragon, or 1 tablespoon
        minced fresh basil or chervil
    $^3/_4$ cup roughly chopped parsley

1. Bring a large pot of water to a boil.

2. Wash the clams well, scrubbing them with a soft brush if necessary. Place them in a broad saucepan or skillet with a cover, along with the wine and cayenne. Cover and turn the heat to high. Cook, shaking the pan occasionally. After 3 minutes, check the clams to see if any have opened. As soon as the majority of littlenecks or cockles are open, remove them; don't worry if many are still closed. Transfer the clams to a bowl. Pass the juice through a sieve lined with cheesecloth to remove all traces of sand.

3. Combine the olive oil and minced garlic in a broad, deep skillet and turn the heat to medium. When the garlic starts to sizzle, salt the water and begin cooking the pasta; you will want it to be quite firm when it's done. Turn the heat under the garlic to low and cook, shaking the pan occasionally, just until the garlic begins to color, about 5 minutes.

4. Measure the clam juice; if it is less than a cup, add the tomatoes, or as much wine as you would need to make a cup of juice to the garlic in the skillet (do not add the clam juice yet). You can add the tomatoes if you like in any case, but do not add additional wine if you have a cup of clam juice. Raise the heat to high and let the mixture bubble for about 2 minutes; stir in the tarragon.

5. Stir in the clams and cover; cook over high heat until almost all of the clams open, another minute or two. (Don't worry if some of the clams never open, as often happens with littlenecks; just open them with a paring or similar knife.) Drain the pasta and toss it into the skillet with the garlic; add the reserved clam juice and cook for 30 seconds, or until the pasta is tender but still firm and the sauce is a pleasing consistency Stir in the parsley and serve.

Clams with Pesto and Pasta: Prepare the clams as instructed above. In Step 5, when the clams begin to open, uncover and stir in 1 cup Basic Pesto (page 766). Continue as above.

Penne with Tomato-Shrimp Sauce
Makes at least 4 servings

Time: 40 minutes

This is an all-purpose recipe, useful for almost any fin-fish or shellfish you have in the house; see the variations for a couple of suggestions.

3 tablespoons olive oil
1 small dried hot red chile or crushed red pepper flakes to taste
2 cloves garlic, lightly crushed
2 cups cored and chopped tomatoes, seeded if fresh, drained if canned
1 teaspoon minced fresh rosemary or $1/2$ teaspoon dried rosemary
Salt and freshly ground black pepper to taste
1 pound penne or other cut pasta
$3/4$ to 1 pound medium-to-large shrimp, peeled, cut up if very large
$1/2$ cup minced fresh parsley leaves

1. Bring a large pot of water to a boil.

2. Heat the oil in a large skillet over medium-high heat for a minute. Add the chile and garlic and cook, stirring, until the garlic becomes brown (this is a somewhat strong-tasting sauce). Remove and discard the pepper and garlic and add the tomatoes. Cook, stirring, until the tomatoes begin to liquefy, about 5 minutes; add the rosemary, salt, and pepper. Cook another 5 minutes. (This sauce may be covered and refrigerated for a day or two, or put in a closed container and frozen for several weeks. Reheat before adding shrimp.)

3. Salt the boiling water and cook the pasta; when it begins to soften, stir the shrimp into the sauce—they need only cook for 3 or 4 minutes—along with most of the parsley. Drain the pasta when it is tender

but still firm, then dress with the sauce and remaining parsley.

Pasta Sauce with Squid: Substitute squid for shrimp. Clean and rinse the squid, then cut it up (see illustrations on page 338). Proceed as above, adding the squid only when the sauce is done, in Step 3. Cook for 2 minutes, then taste for doneness. Be careful not to overcook.

Pasta Sauce with Scungilli (Conch): Substitute conch for shrimp. Most conch is sold precooked, but still takes some time to become tender. Cut it into small pieces and add it to the saucepan along with the tomatoes in Step 2. Proceed as above.

Pasta Sauce with Seafood: Following the general guidelines in "Fish" for the specific fish you choose, add any variety of seafood, always ending with those that will cook the most quickly. If you choose to add clams and/or mussels near the end of cooking, cover the skillet until they open. Remember, too, that as you add more seafood you will be adding more liquid indirectly (most fish give up water as they cook) and, of course, more solids, so you will be able to sauce more pasta and serve more people.

Mussels, Portuguese-Style, over Pasta

Makes 6 servings

Time: 45 minutes

You can serve any of the steamed mussel preparations on pages 346–347 over pasta, but to me these mussels beg for noodles. Use good fresh tomatoes if you have them, and be sure to serve this with plenty of crusty bread.

$1/2$ to 1 pound linguiça, chorizo, kielbasa, or other hard sausage
1 tablespoon olive oil
2 cloves garlic, chopped
4 or 5 plum tomatoes, cored and roughly chopped (canned are fine; don't bother to drain)
$1/4$ cup shredded fresh basil or minced parsley leaves, plus some for garnish
$1/2$ cup water, more or less (you won't need this if you use canned tomatoes)
About 3 pounds mussels, cleaned as described on page 346
$1 1/2$ pounds linguine, spaghetti, or other long pasta

1 Bring a large pot of water to a boil.

2 Remove the skin from the sausage and chop into $1/4$- to $1/2$-inch pieces. Combine the olive oil and sausage in a large, deep pot over medium heat and cook, stirring, for about 5 minutes. When the sausage begins to brown, add the garlic. Cook 1 or 2 minutes longer, stirring occasionally, then add the tomatoes and $1/4$ cup basil. Cook a minute or two, stirring, until the tomatoes soften, a few minutes. Add the water if you are not using canned tomatoes, stir, add the mussels, cover, and raise the heat to high.

3 Salt the boiling water and cook the pasta until it is tender but firm. Continue to cook the mussels, shaking the pot occasionally, until all of them are open, about 10 minutes. Drain the pasta, place it in a very large serving bowl, and pour the mussels and sauce over it. Garnish and serve.

Linguine with Scallops

Makes about 4 servings

Time: 30 minutes

You can use this recipe for sea, bay, or calico scallops. Take care to keep the cooking time brief, not only to avoid overcooking but to preserve the liquid given up by the scallops.

3/4 pound sea, bay, or calico scallops
1/4 cup olive oil, plus 1 tablespoon
4 tablespoons (1/2 stick) butter (optional)
1 tablespoon minced garlic
Salt and freshly ground black pepper to taste
1/4 cup toasted plain bread crumbs (page 239)
1/2 cup minced fresh parsley leaves
1 pound linguine or spaghetti

1 Bring a large pot of water to a boil. If you're using sea scallops, cut them into 1/4- to 1/2-inch chunks; cut bay scallops in half; leave calicos whole.

2 Combine the 1/4 cup olive oil with the butter, if you are using it, and the garlic in a small saucepan over low heat. Cook until the garlic turns pale tan, stirring occasionally. Raise the heat to medium-high, add the scallops, salt, and pepper, and cook just until the surface of the scallops turns opaque, about 2 minutes. Add the bread crumbs and half the parsley and turn off the heat.

3 Salt the boiling water and cook the pasta until it is tender but firm. When it is just about done, reheat the scallops over medium heat. Drain the pasta, reserving some of the cooking liquid if you omitted the butter. Toss the pasta with the sauce and the remaining olive oil, add a little pasta-cooking water if necessary, and top with the remaining parsley.

Pasta with Provençal Seafood Sauce

Makes at least 4 servings

Time: About 1 hour

As with the preceding recipe, you can use this basil-scented sauce as a base for almost any seafood you like, from squid and/or clams to conch and/or cod. Just be careful not to overcook the fish.

1 tablespoon olive oil
1/2 cup diced onion
1 teaspoon minced garlic
1/2 teaspoon crushed red pepper flakes, or to taste
1/2 cup dry white wine
2 cups canned crushed tomatoes, not drained
1 pound linguine or other pasta
1/4 cup minced fresh parsley leaves
1/2 cup shredded fresh basil leaves
1 teaspoon fennel seeds
1 tablespoon minced lemon or orange zest
Salt and freshly ground black pepper to taste
1/2 pound medium-to-large shrimp, peeled,
    cut up if very large
1/2 pound sea scallops, cut in half if very large

1 Bring a large pot of water to a boil.

2 Put the oil in another large, deep pot over medium heat. One minute later, add the onion and cook, stirring, for 2 to 3 minutes. Add the garlic and cook for 1 minute. Add the red pepper flakes, wine, and tomatoes, bring to a boil, reduce the heat to medium-low, and let cook for about 15 minutes. (This sauce may be covered and refrigerated for a day or two, or put in a closed container and frozen for several weeks. Reheat before adding the seafood.)

3 Salt the boiling water and cook the pasta until it is tender but firm. When the pasta is almost done, add the parsley, half the basil, and all remaining ingredients to the sauce; simmer until the seafood is cooked through, about 4 to 5 minutes.

4 Drain the pasta and serve with the sauce, garnished with the remaining basil.

The Basics of Meat-Based Sauces for Pasta

Without exception, these are big, heavy sauces, with enough meat so that you will almost definitely not want a second course—unless, of course, you serve very small amounts, which is not a bad idea.

For the most part, too, they are long-cooking sauces, not the kind of dishes you whip up while the water is coming to a boil. They need slow simmering to tenderize meat and transfer its flavor to the sauce. But few meat-based pasta sauces use expensive cuts of meat, and few of them use a great deal of meat per serving, so they are good alternatives to the typical twentieth-century American style of meat-eating.

Meat Sauce, Bolognese-Style

Ragu

Makes a little more than 1 quart, enough for about 3 pounds of pasta

Time: Several hours, largely unattended

Ragu is the perfect sauce for fresh pasta, cheese-filled ravioli, or lasagne. Although the sauce doesn't require much in the way of work, it does require some attention over the course of a morning or afternoon. Double or triple the recipe if you like and freeze it in one-half pint or pint containers. Feel free to halve the amount of meat if you're so inclined. Even if you do, this is a meaty sauce, and it should be a meaty-tasting one; the quality of the stock makes a difference.

2 tablespoons olive oil
1 small onion, minced
1 carrot, peeled and minced
1 celery stalk, minced
¼ cup minced bacon or pancetta
½ pound lean ground pork (or use all beef)
½ pound lean ground beef
¾ cup dry white wine (or juice from the tomatoes)
1 (28- or 35-ounce) can whole plum tomatoes, drained (reserve juice, if needed instead of wine)
1 cup beef or chicken stock, preferably homemade (see "Soups" for stock recipes)
Salt and freshly ground black pepper to taste
1 cup cream, half-and-half, or milk
Freshly grated Parmesan cheese (optional)

1 Put the olive oil in a large, deep skillet or saucepan. Turn the heat to medium-low and, a minute later, add the onion, carrot, celery, and bacon or pancetta. Cook, stirring occasionally, until the vegetables are tender, about 10 minutes.

2 Add the ground meat and cook, stirring and breaking up any clumps, until all traces of red are gone, about 5 minutes. Add the wine or tomato juice, raise the heat a bit, and cook, stirring occasionally, until most of the liquid is evaporated, about 5 minutes.

3 Crush the tomatoes with a fork or your hands and add them to the pot; stir, then add the stock. Turn the heat to low and cook at a slow simmer, stirring occasionally and breaking up the tomatoes and any clumps of meat that remain. After an hour or so, add salt and pepper. Cook for at least another hour, until much of the liquid has evaporated and the sauce is very thick. (This sauce may be covered and refrigerated for a day or two, or put in a closed container and frozen for several weeks. Reheat before completing.)

4 Add the cream, half-and-half, or milk and cook for another 15 to 30 minutes, stirring occasionally; taste and add more salt and/or pepper as needed. Serve immediately with any dried or fresh pasta, passing grated Parmesan, if you like, at the table.

Pasta Sauce with Beef Ribs and Cinnamon

Makes about 6 to 8 cups, enough for at least 3 pounds of pasta

Time: 2 hours

This is a dark, rich, slow-cooked pasta sauce, with great depth of flavor. Since this sauce takes so long to cook, I usually make a large batch and freeze half for later use.

2 tablespoons olive oil
2 to 3 pounds meaty short ribs of beef
Salt and freshly ground black pepper to taste
2 (28-ounce) cans whole plum tomatoes, with their juice
Several cloves garlic, roughly chopped
1 teaspoon ground cinnamon
$1/4$ teaspoon ground cloves
1 pound ziti, rigatoni, or other large cut pasta

1 Heat the olive oil in a heavy Dutch oven or casserole over medium-high heat; a minute later, brown the meat on all sides, seasoning with salt and lots of pepper as it cooks. Add the tomatoes, garlic, cinnamon, and cloves, reduce the heat to low, and cover, with the lid slightly ajar.

2 Simmer gently, stirring occasionally, for at least $1^1/_2$ hours, until the meat falls from the bone; if the sauce begins to get too thick, add a little water and continue to cook.

3 When the meat is tender and fallen from the bone, remove the bones from the sauce and break the meat up with a spoon. Taste and adjust seasoning. (This sauce may be covered and refrigerated for a day or two, or put in a closed container and frozen for several weeks.)

4 To prepare pasta, follow Step 3 in Andrea's Pasta with Ribs (the next recipe).

Andrea's Pasta with Ribs

Makes 4 servings

Time: $1^1/_2$ hours

One of my favorite pasta recipes, a Neapolitan specialty that can make just a few ribs go a long way.

2 tablespoons olive oil
2 small dried hot red chiles (optional)
3 cloves garlic, chopped
6 to 8 meaty spare ribs, separated
Salt and freshly ground black pepper to taste
1 (28-ounce) can whole plum tomatoes, with their juice
1 pound ziti, penne, or other cut pasta
Freshly grated Pecorino Romano cheese (optional)

1 Warm the olive oil in a deep, broad saucepan over medium heat. After a minute, add the chiles, if you are using them, and garlic and cook, stirring, for about 30 seconds. Add the ribs and raise the heat to medium-high; cook, stirring occasionally, until the ribs have browned and given off some of their fat, about 10 to 15 minutes. Sprinkle with salt and pepper, crush the tomatoes with a fork or your hands, and add them to the pot with their juice.

2 Turn the heat to medium or medium-low— enough to maintain a nice steady bubbling, but nothing violent. Cook, stirring occasionally, until the ribs are very tender, nearly falling off the bone, about 1 hour. Remove the chiles from the sauce, if you have used them.

3 Bring a large pot of water to a boil. Salt the boiling water and cook the pasta until it is tender but firm. Drain it and sauce it; serve a rib or two to each diner along with the pasta. Pass the grated cheese at the table if you like.

Spaghetti and Meatballs

Makes at least 4 servings

Time: About 1 hour

This is the one pasta dish that all non-Italians knew how to make when I was growing up in the fifties. Most, of course, made it pretty badly (sorry, Mom). But it has its good points, not the least of which is that it is as filling a pasta dish as exists. And kids love it.

³/₄ to 1 pound ground meat—beef, pork, veal, or a combination
1 egg
1 cup freshly grated Parmesan cheese
¼ cup minced fresh parsley leaves
1 teaspoon minced garlic
½ cup plain bread crumbs, preferably fresh
Salt to taste
2 tablespoons olive oil
1 medium onion, minced
1 (28- or 35-ounce) can whole plum tomatoes, with their juice
1 pound spaghetti, or more

1 Lightly combine the meat, egg, half the Parmesan, parsley, garlic, bread crumbs, and salt in a bowl. Form into small or large balls, as you like (I prefer walnut-sized meatballs).

2 Heat the olive oil for about 3 minutes in a broad, deep skillet over medium heat. Add the meatballs (do not crowd—cook in batches if necessary) and cook, shaking the pan every minute or so to prevent sticking, and turn the meatballs. When the meatballs are nicely browned all over—this will take about 15 minutes—remove them to a plate and turn off the heat.

3 Pour off all but a film of the fat that has accumulated in the pan. Turn the heat back to medium and cook the onion in the fat, stirring, until it begins to brown. Crush the tomatoes with a fork or your hands and add them, along with their juice, to the pan. Cook, stirring occasionally, until the tomatoes begin to break up, 5 to 10 minutes.

4 Bring a large pot of water to a boil. Meanwhile, add the meatballs and salt to taste to the sauce and cook about 15 minutes more, until the meatballs are cooked through.

5 Salt the boiling water and cook the pasta until it is tender but firm. Put it in a large, warm bowl and toss it with some of the sauce (you may not need it all, depending on how much pasta you've cooked). Top with meatballs and serve, passing the remaining Parmesan at the table.

Spaghetti with Sausage: Easier, faster, and just as good: Omit Step 1. Instead, cut 1 pound of sweet or hot Italian sausage (or a combination) into 1-inch chunks. In Step 2, omit the olive oil; heat a large skillet over medium heat for 3 or 4 minutes, then add the sausage. Cook, stirring occasionally, until nicely browned and crisp all over. Pour off the excess fat (leave the sausage in the pan), turn the heat to medium-low, and add the onion, as in Step 3. Cook until the onion softens, then proceed as above. Serve the pasta with the sauce and the sausage, garnishing with minced parsley and passing Parmesan if desired.

Miscellaneous European and American Pasta Dishes

This is an eclectic little collection of non-Italian, non-Asian noodle dishes, most of which are dairy-based. But with the exception of Baked Macaroni and Cheese (page 153), which is far superior to the boxed kind, it's unlikely that you're familiar with all of these, and they're all worth trying.

Baked Macaroni and Cheese

Makes 4 to 6 servings

Time: About 45 minutes

This is macaroni and cheese for grown-ups; not that kids won't like it, but it's far from sweet and gooey. Rather, it is fragrant and almost sharp, thanks to the bay leaves and Parmesan.

> 2¹/₂ cups milk (low-fat is fine)
>
> 2 bay leaves
>
> 1 pound elbow, shell, ziti, or other cut pasta
>
> 4 tablespoons (¹/₂ stick) butter
>
> 3 tablespoons flour
>
> 1¹/₂ cups grated cheese, such as sharp Cheddar
>   or Emmenthal
>
> ¹/₂ cup freshly grated Parmesan cheese
>
> Salt and freshly ground black pepper to taste
>
> ¹/₂ cup or more plain bread crumbs, preferably fresh

1 Preheat the oven to 400°F. Bring a large pot of water to a boil.

2 Cook the milk with the bay leaves in a small saucepan over medium-low heat. When small bubbles appear along the sides, about 5 minutes later, turn off the heat and let stand. Salt the boiling water and cook the pasta to the point where it still needs another minute or two to become tender. Drain it, rinse it quickly to stop cooking, and place it in a large bowl.

3 In a small saucepan over medium-low heat, melt 3 tablespoons of the butter; when it is foamy, add the flour and cook, stirring, until the mixture browns, about 5 minutes. Remove the bay leaves from the milk and add about ¹/₄ cup of the milk to the hot flour mixture, stirring with a wire whisk all the while. As soon as the mixture becomes smooth, add a little more milk, and continue to do so until all the milk is used up and the mixture is thick and smooth. Add the Cheddar or Emmenthal and stir.

4 Pour the sauce over the noodles, toss in the Parmesan, and season with salt and pepper. Use the remaining butter to grease a 9 × 13-inch or like-sized baking pan and turn the noodle mixture into it. Top liberally with bread crumbs and bake until the crumbs turn brown, about 15 minutes. Serve hot.

Pastitsio

Makes 6 to 12 servings

Time: About 1¹/₄ hours

Often referred to as Greek lasagne, pastitsio is, generally speaking, easier to make and equally delicious. Like lasagne (pages 163–165), it can be made in a variety of ways; this is the classic version. Use a meatless tomato sauce if you prefer.

> 8 tablespoons (1 stick) butter
>
> 1 pound ziti, penne, elbows, or other cut pasta
>
> 4 tablespoons plain bread crumbs, preferably fresh
>
> 3 cups milk
>
> ¹/₄ cup flour
>
> ¹/₈ teaspoon freshly grated nutmeg, plus a little more
>   if desired
>
> Salt and freshly ground black pepper to taste
>
> 4 eggs, beaten
>
> 2 cups freshly grated Parmesan or hard feta cheese
>
> 4 cups Meat Sauce, Bolognese-Style (Ragu)
>   (page 150) or other tomato sauce

1 Bring a large pot of water to a boil. Preheat the oven to 350°F.

2 Melt the butter in a 2-quart saucepan over low heat. Salt the boiling water and cook the pasta until it is barely tender, not quite done enough to eat. Drain the pasta. Place pasta in a large bowl and toss with 2 tablespoons of the melted butter and 2 tablespoons of the bread crumbs. Set aside. Use 1 tablespoon of the melted butter to grease a large baking pan or casserole.

3 In a small saucepan or microwave, heat the milk until small bubbles appear. Reheat the remaining butter over medium-low heat in its saucepan. Add the flour to the melted butter and stir almost constantly with a wire whisk until the mixture turns golden, about 5 minutes. Slowly add the milk, whisking all the while; cook, whisking, until the mixture thickens, about 3 to 5 minutes. Add the nutmeg, salt, and pepper.

4 Stir a couple of tablespoons of the hot sauce into the beaten eggs, then a little more. Pour this mixture back into the sauce and stir. Add most of the Parmesan—reserve some for sprinkling—and stir again.

5 Put half the pasta in the baking dish; cover with half the tomato sauce. Cover with the remaining pasta, then the remaining tomato sauce and all the cheese sauce. Sprinkle with the remaining Parmesan or feta and the remaining bread crumbs (another little grating of nutmeg here won't hurt, either). Bake about 45 minutes, or until the top turns golden brown. Let rest for a few minutes before cutting and serving.

Pastitsio with Eggplant or Potatoes: Either of these vegetables can add a surprisingly solid texture to the middle of the dish; you can also use them together. Make broiled eggplant slices (see Grilled or Broiled Eggplant Slices, page 568) with about 1 pound of eggplant, or peel and parboil 1 pound potatoes (page 596); slice them thinly. Place the slices between the layers of noodles and proceed as above.

Kasha Varnishkes

Makes about 4 servings

Time: 40 minutes or less

Onions lend sweetness here, and kasha its distinctive nuttiness. The result is a classic East European pasta dish that deserves more attention. Traditionally made with rendered chicken fat (page 358), it is equally good with olive oil.

2 cups chopped onions, or more
$^{1}/_{3}$ cup rendered chicken fat or olive oil
$1^{1}/_{2}$ cups water
$^{3}/_{4}$ cup kasha (see page 194)
Salt and freshly ground black pepper to taste
1 pound bow-tie, shell, or broad egg noodles

1 Place the onions in a large skillet and turn the heat to medium. Cover the skillet and cook, for about 10 minutes, until the onions are dry and almost sticking to the pan. Add the fat, raise the heat to medium-high, and cook, stirring, until the onions are nicely browned, another 10 minutes or so. Bring a large pot of water to a boil.

2 Meanwhile, bring $1^{1}/_{2}$ cups water to a boil in a medium saucepan and stir in the kasha and about 1 teaspoon of salt. Cover and simmer until kasha is soft and fluffy, about 15 minutes. Let stand, covered, while you finish the rest of the preparation.

3 At the same time, salt the boiling water and cook the noodles until tender but still firm. Drain and combine with the onions and kasha, adding more fat or oil if you like. Season with salt and pepper and serve immediately.

The Basics of Fresh Pasta

It is generally agreed—at least among those who do not have an ancestral stake in one of the other pasta doughs—that egg-based pasta dough makes the best pasta. If you have never made this dough, but have eaten in a fine Italian restaurant and wondered why the pasta—not the sauce, the pasta—was so wonderfully delicious, it was probably because it was freshly made egg pasta.

So-called "fresh" pasta sold in packages in supermarkets is not the same thing (in fact, normal dried pasta is almost always preferable to this hybrid). What is good, and can be readily obtained by that percentage of people who live in or near a real Italian bakery, is pasta that is made fresh daily and sold over the counter. But even this cannot compare with homemade pasta, which, even on your first try, is likely to strike you as nothing short of miraculous.

Homemade pasta, at its simplest, contains three ingredients: flour (use all-purpose), eggs, and salt. You'll sometimes need a teaspoon or two of water, especially if the eggs were on the small side. You can add oil or butter, use whole-wheat flour or semolina, and add flavorings, but the basic pasta is made of this basic trinity. Topped with simple sauces such as butter and Parmesan or a quick tomato sauce, or with rich sauces such as Meat Sauce, Bolognese-Style (Ragu) (page 150), it is irresistible.

Traditionally, fresh pasta is made on a board or counter, without the use of so much as a bowl. The flour and salt are combined in a pile, the eggs beaten into a well in the middle, the dough kneaded (it's an easy dough to work), rolled out thin with a rolling pin, cut and shaped with a knife, or with a variety of odd tools that developed over the course of centuries.

On the other end of the pasta-producing spectrum are electric pasta machines, essentially food processors with built-in extrusion devices. You put all the ingredients in a hopper and, bingo, out comes pasta. Unfortunately, these machines just don't work that well. If you already own one, fine. If not, I strongly suggest making pasta entirely by hand at least once—just to put you in touch with the roots of one of cooking's great traditions—and then making it with a combination of the food processor and, if you like, one of the sturdy metal manual pasta-rolling machines sold in Italian and other food stores.

What to Do with Fresh Pasta Dough

Once you have made pasta dough, you can do a number of things with it. (One of them is to freeze it, but there's little reason for that, because mixing the dough, especially in the food processor, takes less than five minutes.) You can cut it by hand or machine into noodles, such as fettuccine or tagliatelle (the manual machines have cutters for this). You can cut it into odd shapes to sauce or serve in soup (frequently, scraps are reserved for this purpose). You can cut it into long, broad strips to make lasagne. You can also make it into elaborate shapes, such as penne (quills), although this is something for which few home cooks have the time. And finally, you can cut it into squares or circles for stuffing, to make ravioli (page 160) or other filled pastas; and this is something that you should try, because the results are usually very satisfying.

How to Use a Manual Pasta-Rolling Machine

A manual machine is easy to use. You clamp it to the counter and pass the dough through a pair of rollers, making them successively narrower with each pass. The first few passes finish working the dough for you, making it perfectly smooth and elastic. The last few make the pasta thinner and thinner, until the sheets are all but translucent. Here are step-by-step guidelines.

1. Make the pasta dough by hand or in a food processor; it should be slightly sticky but smooth. If time allows, wrap in plastic and refrigerate for one to twenty-four hours.
2. Clamp the machine to a counter, and sprinkle a nearby surface lightly with flour. Have more flour ready.
3. Cut off about one sixth of the dough; wrap the rest in plastic while you work.
4. Roll the dough lightly in the flour, and flatten it a bit with your hands.

5. Set the machine to "1" and crank the dough through. If it sticks, dust it with a little more flour.
6. Set the machine to "2" and pass the flattened dough through again. Repeat, setting the machine to a higher number with each successive pass. If at any point the dough sticks or tears, bunch it together and start again. You will quickly get the hang of it. Use as much flour as you need to, but no more than necessary or the dough will become too dry.
7. When you pass the dough through setting number "6," set it aside on a lightly floured towel. Repeat the process with the remaining dough.
8. To make lasagne (page 163–165), cannelloni, ravioli (page 160), or any other stuffed pasta, leave the sheets whole. To make fettuccine or tagliatelle, cut each ribbon in half, then pass each through the appropriate cutting blades. Separate the strands, then hang on a series of dowels or hangers, or spread on a large tablecloth, until ready to cook.

Any of these recipes can be used in electric pasta machines. And, note that although there are minor differences, fresh pasta can be used in Asian pasta dishes (pages 167–177) as well as Italian ones.

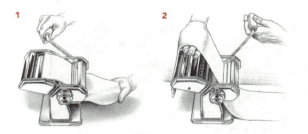

(Step 1) Begin by putting a piece of dough through the widest setting, usually #1. (Step 2) Decrease the distance between the two rollers, making the strip of dough progressively thinner. Note that as the dough becomes longer, it will become more fragile. Dust with flour between rollings if necessary.

You can make fresh pasta into any shape you like (there's even a kind called "badly cut," in which the sheet of dough is cut into random shapes), but one of the easiest and most fun is corkscrews.

(Step 1) Roll out a sheet of pasta, as long as you like and about five inches wide. Cut into half-inch strips. (Step 2) Twist each piece into a corkscrew shape. Dust very lightly with flour or cornmeal and let dry a little before cooking.

Traditional Egg Pasta Dough

Makes about 1 pound, enough for 3 to 4 main-course servings or 4 to 6 first-course servings, or 25 to 30 raviolis

Time: 20 minutes to 1 hour, depending on the method

This is classic pasta dough, delicious in flavor, fantastic in texture. If you prefer, you can make it with two eggs and more water. Cook the finished pasta as soon as it's done, or allow it to dry for a few hours (or even a few days) and cook it later. See page 155 for more information on handling pasta dough.

2 cups (10 ounces) all-purpose flour, plus more as needed

1 teaspoon salt

3 eggs

A few drops water, if needed

1 To make the dough by hand, mound the flour on a smooth countertop, or place it in a bowl. Make a well in the center and add the salt. Then break in an egg, beating with a fork and incorporating a little of the flour. Beat in another egg and repeat, until all the flour is mixed with the eggs. Gather the mixture in a ball.

To make the dough in a food processor, combine the flour and salt in the container and pulse once or twice. Add the eggs all at once and turn the machine on. Process just until a ball begins to form, about 30 seconds. Add a few drops of water if the dough is dry and grainy; add a tablespoon of flour if dough sticks to the side of the bowl.

2 Turn the dough out onto a dry, lightly floured work surface and knead until it is smooth, just a minute or two. Add water by the half-teaspoonful if the mixture is dry; add flour if it is sticky. This should be an easy dough to work. Cut the dough into 6 pieces; wrap 5 pieces in plastic.

3 Roll the dough out with a pin until it is as thin as you can make it, then proceed to make one of the shapes illustrated on pages 160 and 162. Or see How to Use a Manual Pasta-Rolling Machine (page 155).

Hot Water Dough

Makes about 1 pound, enough for 3 to 4 main-course servings or 4 to 6 first-course servings

Time: 20 minutes to 1 hour, depending on the method

Although egg-based dough is easy to handle, this is even easier, and contains no eggs. It is not quite as flavorful, but the olive oil or butter does give it character.

2 cups (10 ounces) all-purpose flour, plus more as needed.

1 teaspoon salt

2 tablespoons butter or extra-virgin olive oil

1 To make the dough by hand, place the flour in a bowl and stir in the salt. Cut the butter into small bits and cut it in, or stir in the olive oil. Pour in enough hot water to make a stiff, easily worked dough. Shape into a ball. To make the dough in a food processor, combine the flour and salt in the container and pulse once or twice. Add the butter or oil and pulse a few times. Add $1/2$ cup very hot water and turn the machine on, then drizzle more water through the feed tube until a ball begins to form. Shape into a ball.

2 Turn the dough out onto a dry, lightly floured work surface and knead until it is smooth, just a minute or two. Add water by the half-teaspoonful if the mixture is dry; add flour if it is sticky. This should be an easy dough to work. Cut the dough into 6 pieces; wrap 5 pieces in plastic.

3 To continue by hand, roll the dough out with a pin until it is as thin as you can make it. Proceed to make one of the shapes illustrated on pages 160 and 162. Or see How to Use a Manual Pasta-Rolling Machine (page 155).

Semolina Dough: Somewhat more flavorful and a bit grainy. Use half semolina flour in place of the all-purpose flour. This dough may be made with eggs, as in Traditional Egg Pasta Dough (page 156), or without, as in Hot Water Dough (page 157).

Whole Wheat Dough: More flavorful and more fragile. Use half whole wheat flour in place of the all-purpose flour. This dough may be made with eggs, as in Traditional Egg Pasta Dough (page 156), or without, as in Hot Water Dough (page 157).

About Flavored Pasta

Like bread, pasta can be flavored with almost anything. There is some controversy about flavoring pastas, but this results mostly from the excesses of overenthusiastic pasta makers who have used flavorings such as chocolate and chipotle chiles. Nothing wrong with that, in theory at least, but it cannot be argued that these are traditional Italian ingredients.

Two pasta seasonings that are inarguably traditional are spinach, which produces a green-flecked pasta, and tomato paste (or, sometimes, beets), which produces reddish-pink pasta. Both are good-tasting as well as attractive, and not much more work than basic pasta.

I also like flavoring pasta dough with herbs and spices, and each of these variations has its regional base and traditions. Saffron produces beautiful, golden pasta, and black or red pepper gives the pasta itself a kick, which is kind of fun. But my favorite flavored pasta is made with fresh herbs, which can be varied on a daily basis; as long as the technique is not overdone, this provides a flavor base that can be brilliant used in combination with the right sauce.

Note: All of these pastas can be made with Hot Water Dough if you prefer.

Spinach Pasta

Makes just over 1 pound, enough for 3 to 4 main-course servings or 4 to 6 first-course servings

Time: 20 minutes to 1 hour, depending on the method

Don't expect this to have the uniform color of commercial "spinach" pasta, which may in fact be tinted with food coloring rather than spinach.

$1/2$ pound fresh spinach or $1/4$ pound frozen chopped spinach
About $2^{1}/2$ cups (12 ounces) all-purpose flour, plus more as needed
1 teaspoon salt
3 eggs

1 Stem and clean the spinach if necessary. Cook it (page 604), then drain it thoroughly, squeezing out every drop of water you can. Chop it finely.

2 To make the dough by hand, place the flour in a bowl; stir in the salt. Then break in the eggs, one at a time, alternating with the spinach and incorporating a little of the flour at a time. Gather the mixture in a ball. To make the dough in a food processor, combine the flour and salt in the container and pulse once or twice. Add the eggs and spinach and turn the machine on. Process just until a ball begins to form, about 30 seconds; add a few drops of water if the dough is dry and grainy or—more likely in this instance—a little more flour if it is gummy and sticky.

3 Proceed as for Traditional Egg Pasta Dough (page 156).

Red Pasta: You can also substitute about $1/2$ cup well-drained pureed beets or pureed, peeled, stemmed, and seeded red bell pepper for the tomato paste if you like but this is easiest: Follow the directions for Traditional Egg Pasta Dough (page 156), adding 3 tablespoons tomato paste along with the eggs.

Peppery Pasta: Great with the sauce from Penne Arrabbiata (page 132) or other spicy sauces, or simply dressed with olive oil and minced parsley, with just a touch of garlic. Follow the directions for Traditional Egg Pasta Dough (page 156), adding 1 tablespoon freshly ground black pepper or 1 teaspoon crushed red pepper flakes along with the salt.

Saffron Pasta: Best with rich meat and/or tomato sauces. Crumble $1/4$ teaspoon or more saffron threads with your fingers and combine it with the flour and salt. Follow the directions for Traditional Egg Pasta Dough (page 156).

Herb Pasta

Makes about 1 pound, enough for 3 to 4 main-course servings or 4 to 6 first-course servings

Time: 20 minutes to 1 hour, depending on the method

Some might prefer far more herb flavor than this; I like to keep it on the subtle side, but make adjustments as you see fit. In any case, don't bother to make this if you don't have fresh herbs. Serve this pasta with butter or oil and freshly grated Parmesan cheese, or with light tomato sauces.

> 1 tablespoon fresh sage leaves, 1 teaspoon fresh rosemary or thyme leaves, or 1/4 cup fresh basil, chervil, or parsley leaves
> 2 cups (10 ounces) all-purpose flour, plus more as needed (see below)
> 1 teaspoon salt
> 3 eggs
> A few drops water, if needed

1 Mince the herb and combine it with the flour and salt. Adjust the amount of flour based on the amount of herb you use and its moisture content; 1/4 cup of parsley, for example, will take considerably more flour than 1 teaspoon of rosemary.

2 Follow the directions for Traditional Egg Pasta Dough (page 156).

The Basics of Filled Pastas

The essential blandness of pasta not only makes it receptive to a myriad of sauces, but to an equally large number of fillings, such as meat, cheese, vegetables, or herbs, even fish, or a combination. The trick, however, lies in combining filling and sauce. In my experience, both in my travels in Italy and in my own kitchen,

filled pasta is best topped with simple sauces. It's delicious in a good broth, where the only other flavor might be that of a handful of grated Parmesan; or it may be served as you would dried or unstuffed fresh pasta, with little more than butter and cheese, or a fresh tomato sauce. What doesn't work—for me at least—is to serve a complicated filling with a complicated sauce.

Meat Filling for Fresh Pasta

Makes enough to fill 50 to 60 ravioli, or the equivalent number of other shapes

Time: About 1 hour

You can use almost any boneless meat or poultry stew to stuff ravioli (try, for example, Sweet Beef Brisket with Garlic, page 438). Just be sure to cook it for so long that the meat is really, really tender, and also make sure that the seasoning is quite strong; you will not be using much of it in each individual piece of pasta. This recipe, which uses ground meat, is faster (believe it or not) than most traditional ones, which rely on very long, slow cooking. The variation is even quicker.

> 2 tablespoons olive oil
> 1 pound ground meat, preferably a meat loaf–like mixture of beef, veal, and pork or pork sausage
> 1 cup red wine or good meat or chicken stock, or as needed (see "Soups" for stock recipes)
> Salt and freshly ground black pepper to taste
> 1 teaspoon minced garlic
> 1/4 cup minced prosciutto or other ham (optional)
> 1/2 cup minced fresh parsley leaves
> 1/2 cup freshly grated Parmesan cheese
> 1 egg
> Plain bread crumbs, if needed

1 Place olive oil in a large, deep skillet; turn the heat to medium. Add the meat and cook, stirring and breaking up any lumps, until it loses its color.

2 Add the wine or stock and salt and pepper, then turn the heat to very low. Cook, stirring occasionally and adding more liquid if necessary, until the meat is tender and the sauce thickened, about 45 minutes.

3 Add the garlic and ham and cook another 5 minutes. Cool slightly, then stir in the parsley, Parmesan, and egg. If the mixture is still liquidy, stir in some bread crumbs. Use to fill the pasta immediately, or refrigerate for up to a day before using.

Lighter, Quicker Meat Filling for Fresh Pasta: Good with $^{1}/_{2}$ teaspoon of freshly grated nutmeg added along with the egg. Use 1 tablespoon olive oil and $^{3}/_{4}$ pound meat, preferably pork. In Step 2, use $^{1}/_{2}$ cup dry white wine in place of red wine or stock. In Step 3, increase garlic (or use shallots) to 2 teaspoons and omit the ham. Cook for a few minutes, then cool slightly; stir in the parsley, Parmesan, egg, bread crumbs (if needed), and salt and pepper to taste.

Five Best Sauces for Meat-Filled Pasta

1. Basic Tomato Sauce (page 130)
2. Aromatic Tomato Sauce (page 130)
3. Tomato Sauce with Herbs (page 131)
4. Tomato Sauce with Bay Leaves (page 130)
5. Pureed Tomato Sauce (page 131)

MAKING RAVIOLI

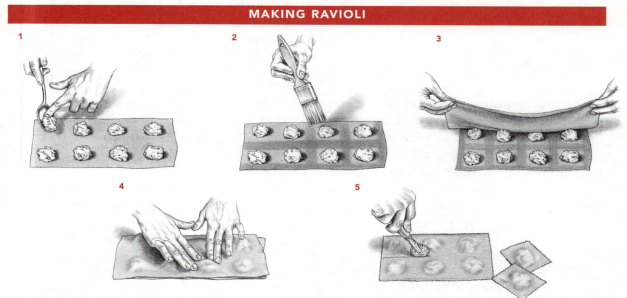

(Step 1) On a counter lightly dusted with flour, cut any length of fresh pasta dough (page 156) so that it is four or five inches wide. Place small spoonfuls of filling evenly on the dough, about 1 inch apart. *(Step 2)* Brush some water between the filling so that the dough will stick together. *(Step 3)* Cover with another piece of dough of equal size. (Alternatively, make only one row of filling and fold one half of the dough over onto the other.) *(Step 4)* Press down to seal between the ravioli. *(Step 5)* Cut with a pastry wheel or sharp paring knife. Keep the ravioli separate until you are ready to cook.

Cheese Filling for Fresh Pasta

Makes enough to fill 50 to 60 ravioli, or the equivalent number of other shapes

Time: About 10 minutes

This can be made mild and creamy, as in the basic recipe, or stronger-tasting, as in the variation. It can also be made without eggs. To drain fresh ricotta, which, like fresh mozzarella, is sold in many Italian markets, simply put it in a fine strainer for a few minutes.

2 eggs
2 cups ricotta, preferably fresh, drained briefly
4 ounces mozzarella, preferably fresh, cut into small dice
1 cup minced fresh parsley leaves
Salt and freshly ground black pepper to taste
$1/2$ teaspoon freshly grated nutmeg

Combine all ingredients; taste and adjust seasonings if necessary, then refrigerate until ready to use, up to a day.

Stronger Cheese Filling: Omit the mozzarella and the eggs, and substitute $1/2$ cup freshly grated Parmesan or other hard cheese (strong sheep cheese is great here). Reduce the nutmeg to a pinch.

Eggless Cheese Filling: Omit the mozzarella; reduce the parsley to $1/2$ cup. Add 1 cup freshly grated Parmesan. Reduce the nutmeg to a pinch.

Ricotta-and-Spinach Filling for Fresh Pasta

Makes enough to fill about 50 to 60 ravioli, or the equivalent number of other shapes

Time: About 20 minutes

This is a traditional and near-perfect filling for ravioli (page 160).

10 ounces spinach, cleaned and trimmed (page 604)
1 egg
1 cup ricotta, preferably fresh, drained for a few minutes in a fine strainer
1 cup freshly grated Parmesan cheese
Salt and freshly ground black pepper to taste
$1/2$ teaspoon freshly grated nutmeg

1 Plunge the spinach into boiling salted water; remove it 30 seconds later. Drain, cool, and chop finely.

2 Combine the spinach with the remaining ingredients; taste and adjust seasonings if necessary. Use to fill the pasta immediately, or refrigerate for up to a day before using.

Spinach Filling for Fresh Pasta: This is also good made with chard. Omit the ricotta. After cooking and chopping the spinach, heat 2 tablespoons butter or olive oil in a large skillet with 1 teaspoon

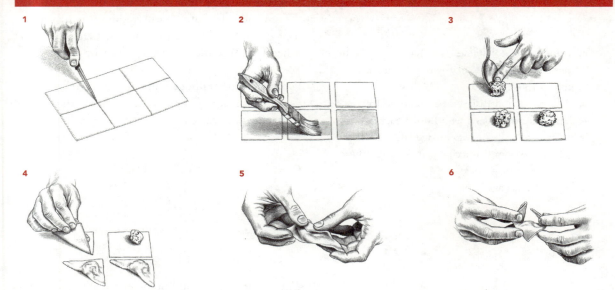

(Step 1) On a counter lightly dusted with flour, cut any length of fresh pasta dough (page 155) so that it is four or five inches wide. Cut into two- to 2¹/₂-inch squares. *(Step 2)* Brush the dough very lightly with water so it will stick together when you go to shape the tortelllini. *(Step 3)* Place a small mound of filling on each square. *(Step 4)* Fold into a triangle, pressing tightly to seal the edges. *(Step 5)* Fold the widest point toward the filling. *(Step 6)* Pick up the triangle and press the two bottom points together. Place your finger inside the newly formed ring and fold over the top of the dough inside the circle. Press to seal. Keep the tortellini separate until you are ready to cook.

minced garlic. When the garlic softens, stir in the spinach. Season with salt and pepper, then cool and stir in the egg, Parmesan, and nutmeg. A couple of tablespoons of minced prosciutto or pancetta cooked along with the garlic is great in this.

Spinach-and-Fish or Shrimp Filling for Fresh Pasta

Makes enough to fill 50 to 60 ravioli, or the equivalent number of other shapes

Time: About 40 minutes

A fine way to use leftover fish if you have it.

¹/₂ pound filleted white fish, such as flounder or cod, or peeled shrimp

10 ounces spinach, cleaned and trimmed (page 604)

2 tablespoons butter or olive oil

¹/₂ cup minced onion

Salt and freshly ground black pepper to taste

1 egg

Pinch cayenne

1 Plunge the fish into boiling salted water; cook until it is barely done, 2 or 3 minutes for thin fillets, 5 or 6 for thicker ones. Remove with a slotted spoon, drain, and dry; chop.

2 Plunge the spinach into boiling salted water; remove it 30 seconds later. Drain, cool, and chop finely.

3 Place the butter or oil in a medium skillet and turn the heat to medium. When the butter melts or the oil is hot, add the onion and cook, stirring occasionally, just until it softens, about 5 minutes. Stir in the spinach and fish and turn the heat to low. Cook, stirring, for about 5 minutes.

4 Spoon the mixture into a bowl and season it with salt and pepper; stir in the egg and cayenne. Taste and adjust seasonings. Use to fill the pasta immediately, or refrigerate for up to a day before using.

Six Best Sauces for Spinach-and-Fish or Shrimp Filling for Fresh Pasta

1. Basic Tomato Sauce (page 130)
2. Aromatic Tomato Sauce (page 130)
3. Tomato Sauce with Herbs (page 131)
4. Pureed Tomato Sauce (page 131)
5. The sauce from Pasta Primavera (page 139)
6. The sauce from Penne with Tomato-Shrimp Sauce (page 147), made with $1/4$ pound of shrimp, cut into bits

---

Sweet Potato or Squash Filling for Fresh Pasta

Makes enough to fill 50 to 60 ravioli, or the equivalent number of other shapes

Time: About 1 hour

Zucca is a pumpkin-like squash that is popular with pasta in northern Italy throughout the fall. Our pumpkin is too watery to use for this purpose, but butternut squash or sweet potato have similar texture and flavor. This filling is deliciously sweet and creamy.

2 cups cooked (preferably baked) butternut squash or sweet potato, seeds, strings, and peels removed
2 eggs
$1/2$ teaspoon freshly grated nutmeg
Salt and freshly ground black pepper to taste
1 teaspoon sugar, or to taste
$1/2$ cup freshly grated Parmesan cheese

1 Puree the squash or potato, preferably by passing it through a food mill or ricer. Combine it in a bowl with the eggs, nutmeg, salt, and pepper.

2 Taste; if the mixture is not sweet, add a little sugar. Stir in the Parmesan and taste again; add more of any seasoning you like. Use to fill the pasta immediately, or refrigerate for up to a day before using.

Three Best Sauces for Sweet Potato or Squash Filling for Fresh Pasta

1. The sauce from Pasta with Butter, Sage, and Parmesan (page 140), or its variation
2. The sauce from Fettucine with Spinach, Butter, and Cream (page 143)
3. The sauce from Linguine with Garlic and Oil (page 144), without the hot pepper

---

The Basics of Lasagne

Take some thick sheets of noodles, layer them with sauce and flavorings, bake, and you have lasagne. With such a simple, broad definition (the "noodles" can even be made of polenta if you like), it's no wonder there are dozens of types of lasagne. The great thing is that most of them can be improvised.

Three suggestions, good for any lasagne you choose to make: First, lasagne is incomparably better with fresh noodles than dried (it is great with dried; it is heavenly with fresh). But no matter which noodles you choose, undercook them quite a bit; you should not find them ready to eat when you remove them from the pot. They will continue to cook in the oven.

Finally, keep the sauce in the correct proportion to the noodles. The noodles will absorb lots of liquid, so you need plenty of sauce or the lasagne will be dry. On the other hand, you don't want so much sauce that the noodles are swimming in it when you remove the lasagne from the oven. Generally, you want about equal weights of pasta and sauce (including solids), which translates to one pound of raw pasta to about a quart of sauce.

Classic Lasagne, Bolognese-Style

Makes about 6 servings

Time: 45 minutes (with premade sauce)

Spinach pasta is traditional, but you can use any pasta you like here. If you are making fresh pasta, use a little more flour than called for in the recipe on page 156; about three cups. This makes a slightly stiffer dough that is a little easier to handle.

> At least 5 quarts water
> 1 recipe Spinach Pasta (page 158) or other fresh
>   pasta or 12 dried lasagne noodles
> 1 recipe Béchamel Sauce (page 787), about 1¹/₂ cups
> 3 cups, more or less, Meat Sauce, Bolognese-Style
>   (Ragu) (page 150)
> 2 tablespoons softened butter (preferred) or
>   extra-virgin olive oil
> 1¹/₂ cups freshly grated Parmesan cheese
> Freshly ground black pepper to taste
> Salt, if needed

1 Set at least 5 quarts of water in a large pot over high heat. When it comes to a boil, salt it.

2 Meanwhile, if you are using fresh pasta, roll it out. Assuming your baking pan is 9 inches across and 13 inches long, make your pasta ribbons 26 inches long, then cut them in half. You will still need to cut the noodles so that they fit reasonably snugly into your pan.

3 Cook the noodles a few at a time; keep them underdone (if they are fresh, this means little more than a minute of cooking time). Drain carefully in a colander, then allow to rest on towels while you prepare the béchamel sauce. Preheat the oven to 400°F.

4 Smear the bottom of your baking pan with the butter or oil, then place a layer of noodles, touching but not overlapping. Trim any overhanging edges. Cover the noodles with about one-quarter each of the béchamel, meat sauce, and Parmesan, then with a light sprinkling of black pepper (between the meat sauce and the Parmesan, there should be enough salt, but if you feel it is underseasoned, add a little salt to each layer also). Make four layers, ending with a sprinkling of Parmesan. (The dish can be prepared in advance up to this point, then well wrapped and refrigerated for a day or frozen for a month; defrost in the refrigerator for a day before cooking if possible.)

5 Bake for about 20 to 30 minutes, until the lasagne is bubbly. Remove from the oven and let rest for 5 minutes before cutting and serving. Or let cool completely, cover well, and refrigerate for up to 2 days, or freeze for up to a month.

Vegetarian Lasagne: Substitute Mushroom Sauce (page 131), or any vegetarian tomato sauce, for the Meat Sauce, Bolognese-Style (Ragu).

Classic Lasagne, Italian-American-Style: Omit the béchamel. On each layer of the first three layers of noodles, spread about 1 cup of ricotta (thinned, if necessary, with some of the sauce). Top the ricotta with meat sauce, the meat sauce with about a cup of grated mozzarella, the mozzarella with a sprinkling of Parmesan. On the top layer, omit the ricotta.

Seven Simple Ideas for Lasagne

You can employ these ideas singly or in combination.

1. Add a layer or two of small, cooked Basic Meatballs (page 494), slices of Italian sausage, or stewed meat such as Veal Stew with Tomatoes (page 446).
2. Omit the tomato sauce entirely, double the amount of béchamel. Especially good with some ham and sautéed mushrooms and/or spinach nestled among the layers.
3. Add a layer or two of sliced, sautéed vegetables such as mushrooms, eggplant, or cauliflower.
4. Add a layer of roasted red bell peppers (see Marinated Roasted, Grilled, or Broiled Peppers, page 593).
5. Add a layer of strong cheese, such as Gorgonzola.
6. Add fresh herbs, especially basil (whole leaves are nice) or chopped parsley.
7. Substitute the sauce from Penne with Tomato-Shrimp Sauce (page 147), or other non-meat sauces for the Meat Sauce, Bolognese-Style (Ragu) (page 150).

Gnocchi

Makes 4 first-course servings or 2 main-course servings

Time: 1 hour, or a little more

Gnocchi are essentially dumplings served as pasta. They're made fresh and are best that way. If you've only had frozen gnocchi, or those served in restaurants (sadly, rarely the genuine article), you will quickly become a convert. When referred to generically, gnocchi are made from potatoes, and, with a little practice, become the easiest fresh pasta to prepare. But gnocchi can also be made with spinach, ricotta, or other ingredients. You must use baking ("Russet" or "Idaho") potatoes here; waxy potatoes will not work.

1 pound baking potatoes, whole and unpeeled
Salt and freshly ground black pepper to taste
About 1 cup flour

1 Wash the potatoes and put them in a pot with salted water to cover. Cook until they are very tender, 30 to 45 minutes.

2 Drain the potatoes and peel them while they are hot (use a pot holder to hold them). Put them through a ricer, or mash them with a fork or potato masher; do not use a food mill or food processor. Place the riced potatoes in a bowl and season with salt and pepper. Bring a large pot of water to a boil and salt it.

3 Stir about $1/2$ cup of flour into the bowl with the potatoes, and keep adding flour until the mixture forms an easy-to-handle dough. The amount of flour you add will depend on the potatoes. Not enough flour will make gnocchi that fall apart; more will make them firm and light; too much will rob them of flavor. Knead for a minute or so on a lightly floured surface. If this is the first time you have made gnocchi, pinch off a piece of the dough and boil it to make sure it will hold its shape; if it does not, knead in a bit more flour.

4 Break off a piece of the dough and roll into a rope about $1/2$ inch thick. Cut the snake into $3/4$- to 1-inch lengths; if you like, spin each of the sections off the tines of a fork (see illustrations, page 166) to score and curve it slightly. As you finish, place the gnocchi on a piece of waxed paper or a lightly floured baking sheet or similar surface, in one layer.

5 Gently transfer the gnocchi to the boiling water, a few at a time. Stir gently. The gnocchi are done about a minute after they rise to the surface, which will happen very quickly; remove them with a slotted spoon as they finish cooking. Serve with any tomato sauce (pages 130–134), with butter and Parmesan, or with olive oil and garlic (see Linguine with Garlic and Oil, page 144).

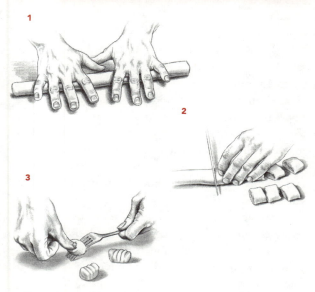

(Step 1) Start by rolling a piece of the dough into a log. Use flour as necessary, but try to keep it to a minimum. (Step 2) Cut the dough into approximately 1-inch lengths. (Step 3) Roll each of the sections off the back of the fork to give it the characteristic ridges.

Spinach Gnocchi

Makes 4 first-course servings
or 2 main-course servings

Time: 1 hour, or a little more

More flavorful than potato gnocchi, and not much more time-consuming.

10 ounces spinach, cleaned and trimmed (page 604)
1 pound baking potatoes, whole and unpeeled
Salt and freshly ground black pepper to taste
Pinch freshly grated nutmeg
About 1 cup flour

1 Bring a pot of water to boil and add salt. When the water boils, cook the spinach until it wilts and the stems become tender, 30 seconds to 2 minutes. Remove it with a strainer or slotted spoon and immediately plunge it into a bowl of ice water; when it has cooled off, squeeze the excess water from it and chop it very fine.

2 Wash the potatoes and cook them in the same water until they are very tender, 30 to 45 minutes. Drain the potatoes and peel them while they are hot (use a pot holder to hold them). Put them through a ricer, or mash them with a fork or potato masher; do not use a food mill or food processor. Bring a large pot of water to a boil and salt it.

3 Combine the potatoes with the spinach, salt, pepper, and nutmeg. Add the flour a bit at a time, kneading with your hands, until the mixture is no longer extremely sticky. The amount of flour you add will depend on the potatoes. Not enough flour will make gnocchi that fall apart; more will make them firm and light; too much will rob them of flavor. Knead for a minute or so on a lightly floured surface. Pinch off a piece of the dough and boil it to make sure it will hold its shape; if it does not, knead in a bit more flour.

4 Break off a piece of the dough and roll into a rope about ¹/₂ inch thick. Cut the snake into ³/₄- to 1-inch lengths; if you like, spin each of the sections off the tines of a fork (see illustrations, opposite) to score and curve it slightly. As you finish, place the gnocchi on a piece of waxed paper or a lightly floured cookie sheet or similar surface, in one layer.

5 Gently transfer the gnocchi to the boiling water, a few at a time. Stir gently. The gnocchi are done about a minute after they rise to the surface, which will happen very quickly; remove them with a slotted spoon as they finish cooking. Serve with any tomato sauce (pages 130–134), with butter and Parmesan, or with olive oil and garlic (see Linguine with Garlic and Oil, page 144).

The Basics of Asian Noodles

The main difference between Asian and Italian noodles is that noodles in Japan, China, and Southeast Asia are more frequently made from ingredients other than wheat. (I say "more frequently" because the Italians sometimes make pasta from other grains as well.) The two most unusual noodles from Asia are the Japanese soba, which is made from buckwheat, and the nearly ubiquitous bean thread, or cellophane noodle, made from ground mung beans and most often added to soups. But rice noodles, which are very common, especially in Southeast Asia, are also a novelty for many Americans. Rice noodles may be soaked rather than boiled before combining with other foods, but are best when soaked, then boiled for a minute or two, as on page 173.

Still, most Asian noodles are made from wheat, or wheat and eggs, and are not that much different from the European noodles to which most Americans are accustomed. In fact, you might say that "noodles are noodles" and that the nature of any dried pasta dish is determined more by its sauce than by its composition. And, with wheat noodles, you'd be roughly correct: You can substitute similar shapes of Italian dried pasta for Japanese or Chinese noodles without missing much.

But part of the fun of cooking is shopping for authentic ingredients, and almost all Asian noodles—fresh and dried—can now be found in many supermarkets. And they're certainly easy enough to find in Asian markets, which exist in virtually every city with a population of more than fifty thousand. Here, then, is a quick tour of Asian noodle traditions and ingredients, followed by a smattering of representative recipes.

Noodle Dishes from Japan

Not long ago, it was routinely said that noodles were the Japanese equivalent of fast food. Now that McDonald's, Kentucky Fried Chicken, and other American fast-food chains have invaded the islands, this is no longer quite the case. Still, noodles remain a staple of the Japanese diet.

Generally speaking, Japanese noodle dishes are simpler than those of other countries. Many, in fact, are served plain, with a dipping sauce—cold in summer and warm in winter—or in soups. (Although so many Japanese noodle dishes are "soupy," I've included them here rather than in "Soups," because they are essentially noodle dishes.)

There are three important types of Japanese noodles that you can find easily. There are others, but these are the most important:

- **Soba:** Buckwheat noodles, thin, brownish-gray, and coarse, with squared edges. Like most foods made with buckwheat (kasha, for example), they're most popular in the colder North, where buckwheat grows better than wheat. Soba is typically served hot in stock (with peppery *schichimi* powder), or chilled, topped with toasted nori and a seasoned soy sauce mixture.

- **Udon:** Thick and cream-colored, these wheat noodles are more like the pasta known by most Americans. In Japan, these are the noodles of the South, and are also mostly found in seasoned stocks, with a few other ingredients.

- **Somen:** The thinnest wheat noodles you've ever seen (these make angel hair pasta look thick). Usually served cold, but I prefer them hot in soups; they cook in no time flat.

When you're buying these, you may occasionally see fresh (*nama*) noodles; treat them as you would fresh Chinese (or, for that matter, Italian) noodles. You may also see them labeled "alimentary paste." Don't let that bother you: translate "alimentary" as "edible," and "paste" as "pasta" and you'll be fine.

The Japanese cook their noodles by what they call the *sashimizu* ("add water") technique, slowing the cooking by adding cold water whenever the water in the pot comes to a rolling boil. This works well, but I've had no problem cooking Japanese noodles by the usual method. Somen cooks in about three minutes, soba in six to eight minutes, udon in ten to twelve minutes. As with any pasta, time is not nearly as important as taste: Cook according to the directions given at the beginning of this chapter. And if you're going to use the noodles in soup, undercook them slightly. The Japanese rinse their noodles after cooking, but this isn't necessary.

Dashi

Makes 1 quart

Time: 15 minutes

Dashi is among the simplest stocks you can make; unfortunately its two main ingredients are rarely found in the pantries of Westerners. But these staples—kombu, or kelp (page 602), and dried bonito flakes—are easily found in Asian markets or natural foods stores, and keep, unrefrigerated, for years. Dashi is the basis of Japanese noodle stock, but chicken, shrimp, or vegetable stocks (see "Soups" for stock recipes) are all different but wonderful substitutes.

1 quart cold water
1 (6- to 8-inch) piece kombu (kelp)
$^{1}/_{2}$ to $^{3}/_{4}$ cup dried bonito flakes

1 Combine the water and kombu in a 2- to 3- quart saucepan over medium-low heat. Allow to come almost to a boil; if the kombu is tender, remove it. If not, add a little cold water and cook for a few more minutes. Do not let the mixture boil. Remove the kombu (you can use it in stir-fries or soups) and turn off the heat.

2 Add the bonito flakes to the mixture and let it sit for a minute or two longer. Strain the stock, pressing the flakes to extract as much liquid as possible. Use the stock immediately, or refrigerate for a day or two.

"Secondary" Dashi: Reheat the used kombu and bonito flakes together with fresh water for 15 to 20 minutes, never letting the water rise above a gentle simmer. Add $^{1}/_{2}$ cup fresh bonito flakes and proceed as above. This makes a stronger stock, well suited for noodles.

Japanese Noodles with Stock

Makes about 4 servings

Time: 20 minutes

Udon noodles have a slightly different texture than the wheat noodles of other countries, but you can substitute Chinese wheat noodles or Italian pasta—spaghetti, capellini, linguine, or fettuccine are the best shapes. Somen noodles are also good in this stock, but be especially careful not to overcook them.

This is a dish that can take many, many different directions. If you try the variations you will see that the possibilities are endless.

1 pound udon (Japanese wheat) or soba (buckwheat) noodles
4 cups Dashi (see opposite), or not overly strong chicken, shrimp, or vegetable stock (see "Soups" for stock recipes)
$^{1}/_{3}$ cup mild soy sauce
$^{1}/_{3}$ cup mirin (Japanese sweet rice wine)
1 tablespoon sugar
Salt, if needed
$^{1}/_{2}$ cup finely minced scallions
1 tablespoon peeled and grated fresh ginger (optional)

1 Bring a large pot of water to a boil. Salt the water and cook the noodles until they are just tender—a little bit underdone. Drain and rinse them with cold water.

2 While the noodles are cooking, heat the stock and add to it the soy sauce, mirin, and sugar; stir to combine. Taste and add salt if necessary. Keep the stock hot but do not let it boil. When the noodles are done, reheat them gently in the stock, then ladle portions of noodles and soup into individual bowls. Garnish with the scallions and ginger if you like, and serve immediately.

Japanese Noodles with Shiitakes and Sesame: Step 1 remains the same. Soak 2 or 3 dried shiitake (also called black) mushrooms in hot water for 10 minutes. Add the soaking liquid to the stock in Step 2, trim the mushrooms of any hard spots, then cut them into thin slices. Add them to the stock and proceed as above. When the noodles and stock are combined, drizzle with 1 tablespoon dark sesame oil. Substitute $^1/_3$ cup lightly Toasted Sesame Seeds (page 776) for the scallions; the ginger remains optional.

Japanese Noodles with Miso: Step 1 remains the same. While the noodles are cooking, stir $^1/_4$ cup of the stock with 2 tablespoons miso until smooth; return the mixture to the stock, along with 1 tablespoon of rice vinegar or other mild vinegar, and keep warm. Proceed as in original recipe. Garnish with scallions and, if you like, ginger, *schichimi*, or crushed red pepper flakes.

Japanese Noodles with Egg: These are known as "moon-viewing noodles" in Japan, for obvious reasons. Begin with either the original recipe or one of the variations. Place a raw egg into each of the soup bowls. Ladle the soup and noodles over the egg and let rest a minute before serving (if you like, cover the bowls to retain heat). The heat of the stock will poach the egg.

Japanese Noodles with Chicken, Vegetables, Fish, or Meat: These noodles can be augmented by an infinite variety of other ingredients. For example: Poach a boneless chicken breast (or a few shrimp or scallops) in the stock while you are cooking the noodles, then shred it and add it to the finished dish. Similarly, simmer a couple of chopped carrots or broccoli florets in the stock; leave them in there when you add the noodles. Or, brush a small fillet of fish or a piece of pork or beef with a bit of soy sauce sweetened with a teaspoon of mirin or honey; broil until done, then cut into slices and combine with the noodles.

Cold Soba Noodles with Mushrooms

Makes 4 servings

Time: 30 minutes

This dish works well as an appetizer, small main course, or side dish. It also complements grilled poultry very nicely.

12 to 16 ounces soba (buckwheat) noodles (you can substitute wheat noodles, such as capellini)

4 dried shiitake ("black") mushrooms, reconstituted by soaking in hot water for 20 minutes (4 large or 8 small fresh white mushrooms may be substituted; parboil for 2 minutes, then drain)

3 scallions, minced

1 tablespoon peeled and minced or grated fresh ginger

$^1/_2$ cup chicken stock, or cooking water from the noodles (see "Soups" for stock recipes)

3 tablespoons soy sauce

1 teaspoon dark sesame oil

1 tablespoon honey or mirin (Japanese sweet rice wine)

1 tablespoon Toasted Sesame Seeds (page 776)

1 Bring a large pot of water to a boil. Salt the boiling water and cook the noodles until they are just tender (start tasting after 3 minutes). Drain them and immediately plunge them into a bowl of ice water. Rinse and drain again.

2 Cut the mushrooms into slivers, and toss them, along with the scallions and the ginger, with the noodles. Mix together the stock or water, soy sauce, sesame oil, and honey or mirin. Pour this dressing over the noodles and toss. Taste and correct seasoning (you may add more soy sauce, sesame oil, or salt). Top with sesame seeds just before serving.

Noodle Dishes from China

The Chinese, like the Italians, have been eating noodles for at least two thousand years, long enough to develop some great recipes. Like the Italians, the Chinese rely primarily on two kinds of noodles: white wheat noodles, made with flour and water, and yellow egg noodles. You can find both varieties fresh in supermarkets and, of course, Asian food stores. Look out for preservatives, which are especially common in egg noodles. Use fresh noodles without preservatives within two or three days of buying them, or freeze them (defrost them in the refrigerator before cooking if possible). The Chinese also cook rice noodles (see the Southeast Asia section below) and bean thread noodles.

There are four main ways in which Chinese noodles are traditionally used after the initial cooking: They may be combined with other ingredients in a stir-fry; drained until dry and cooked in oil until crisp and then used as a bed for a stir-fry (Crisp Pan-Fried Noodle Cake, page 172); added to soups (see Chicken Soup with Cabbage and Thin Noodles, page 76); or topped with sauce.

Regardless of their ultimate use, the noodles are best cooked in water, like pasta, before draining and cooking further (it's possible to stir-fry fresh egg noodles without parboiling, but they have a doughy, raw quality that is not terrific). Fresh Chinese noodles take a little longer to cook than you might think, and traditionally are not served al dente. Cook dried Chinese wheat noodles exactly as you would Italian pasta. If you like, you can cook noodles for Chinese dishes until they're just about done, then drain and rinse them, then toss them with a tablespoon or two of oil per pound of noodles (at this point you may continue cooking or store the noodles, covered, in the refrigerator for a few hours). Dark sesame oil is great for this, adding a flavor that will work just fine in whatever comes next.

Note that the recipes here that use fresh noodles call for twelve ounces, because that is the size most commonly found in supermarkets. If you find one-pound packages (or are lucky enough to buy fresh Chinese noodles in bulk), use that amount, increasing the amount of sauce if necessary.

Chinese Egg Noodles in Stock

Makes 4 servings

Time: 20 minutes

These are slightly different from the Japanese soup-and-noodle dishes above. For one thing they're best made with fresh Chinese egg noodles, available not only in Asian markets but in many supermarkets; look for a brand that contains no more than wheat, egg, salt, and water. (You may also use fresh spaghetti or other Italian egg noodles.) For another, the flavor of the stock is stronger.

Like Japanese noodles, however, they take well to a variety of additions: You can top these with almost any stir-fry mixture; with some quickly cooked diced vegetables or diced or ground meat; or with shredded, quickly steamed greens, such as spinach, collards, or watercress. This dish is also wonderful topped with Pork Bits with Asian Flavors (page 462) or pieces of Tea-Smoked Duck (page 415).

6 cups Full-Flavored Chicken Stock (page 46)

2 cloves garlic, lightly smashed

2 tablespoons soy sauce

Salt and freshly ground white (or black) pepper
  to taste

12 ounces fresh egg noodles

1/2 cup minced scallion (optional)

1 tablespoon dark sesame oil (optional)

1 Bring a large pot of water to a boil. At the same time, in a large saucepan over medium heat, bring the stock almost to a boil. Add the garlic to the stock and raise the heat. When the stock boils, reduce the heat to a minimum and add the soy sauce. Taste and add salt and pepper if necessary.

2 Salt the boiling water and cook the noodles for 3 or 4 minutes, no longer; they will be tender by then. Drain them, rinse quickly, and immediately add them to the simmering stock. Cook for 1 to 2 minutes longer, until the noodles are hot but not too soft. Remove the garlic cloves if you like. Serve immediately, garnishing each serving with some of the scallion and some of the sesame oil.

Stir-Fried Chinese Noodles with Vegetables

Makes about 4 servings

Time: 20 to 30 minutes

You can make Chinese-style stir-fried noodles with dried wheat or rice noodles, or with fresh egg noodles. And this recipe can be made with virtually any green vegetable. For example, I've used asparagus; substitute at will, making sure the vegetable is cut into bite-sized

pieces and cooked until tender before proceeding. If you'd like to use sautéed rather than parboiled vegetables, see the second variation, below. You can also combine these noodles with almost any stir-fried dish.

1 pound asparagus, more or less, no thicker than
  a pencil

1 pound Chinese wheat noodles, of spaghetti-like
  thickness

3 tablespoons peanut (preferred) or other oil

1 tablespoon minced garlic

1 tablespoon peeled and minced fresh ginger

1/2 cup chicken or vegetable stock or reserved
  cooking water (see "Soups" for stock recipes)

1 tablespoon soy sauce

1/4 cup minced scallion or chives

1 tablespoon dark sesame oil (optional)

1 Bring a large pot of water to a boil; salt it. Meanwhile, break the bottoms of the asparagus (they usually snap right at the point there the stalk is tender enough to eat); cut them into 1- to 2-inch lengths. When the pot of water is boiling, blanch the asparagus just until they begin to become tender, 1 to 3 minutes depending on their thickness. Remove them from the water with a slotted spoon and quickly plunge into ice water to stop the cooking.

2 Using the same water, cook the noodles, stirring occasionally and beginning to taste after 4 or 5 minutes (less time if you're using fresh noodles). When they are just tender, drain thoroughly, reserving 1/2 cup cooking liquid if you do not have any stock. Toss with a tablespoon of the oil (a little more if you are not proceeding with the recipe right away), and set aside.

3 Just before you are ready to eat, heat a large skillet or wok (preferably non-stick) over medium-high heat for 3 or 4 minutes. Add the remaining oil, then the garlic and ginger; let sizzle for about 15 seconds, then toss in the noodles. Raise the heat to high and let the noodles sit for about a minute, until they begin to brown on the bottom. Toss once or twice and allow to sit again. Add the stock or cooking water and stir, scraping to loosen any bits that may have stuck to the bottom. Add the (drained) asparagus and stir a few times; add the soy sauce and scallion or chives and the sesame oil if you are using it. Stir and serve.

Stir-Fried Noodles with Meat or Shrimp: Omit asparagus. Mince 2 or 3 shiitake mushrooms (or substitute dried; soak them in hot water for 10 minutes, then drain and mince), 1 small onion, and 2 or 3 scallions. Cook this mixture, stirring, over medium-high heat in 1 tablespoon peanut oil until the onion is translucent; add $1/2$ pound ground, minced, diced, or sliced turkey, chicken, pork, or beef (leftovers are okay too), or $1/2$ pound peeled shrimp, cut into pieces if they are large. Raise the heat to high and cook, stirring almost constantly, until browned. Add 2 tablespoons soy sauce and $1/2$ cup stock or water; taste and add salt as necessary. Cook the noodles and toss with the oil as in Step 2, then substitute this mixture for the asparagus in Step 3. Finish as in above recipe.

Stir-Fried Noodles with Stir-Fried Vegetables: Omit asparagus. Use about 1 pound of tender vegetables, such as spring onions, leeks, broccoli raab, celery, bean sprouts, Napa cabbage, bok choy, snow peas, or a combination. Trim and chop into small pieces if necessary; cook them in a large non-stick skillet or wok over high heat with 2 or 3 tablespoons of peanut oil. Stir every 10 seconds or so until vegetables are brown and tender. Cook the noodles as in Step 2, then substitute this mixture for the asparagus in Step 3.

Crisp Pan-Fried Noodle Cake

Makes 4 to 6 servings

Time: 30 minutes

A great side dish for almost any meal that has some spice, Chinese or not, this noodle cake is most appro-

---

Simple Additions to Stir-Fried Noodles

Chinese noodles, like Italian pasta, are a catch-all for anything that seems appropriate. Here are four ideas:

1. Any cooked or raw vegetable (rinsed of seasonings with boiling water if necessary), cut into bite-sized pieces
2. Any raw meat, diced or ground
3. Incorporate all or leftover parts of the following recipes, stripped from the bone and chopped:
   Anise-Scented Short Ribs, (page 434)
   Sweet Simmered Pork Chops (page 459)
   Sweet Pork with Spicy Soy Sauce (page 470)
   Chinese Grilled Ribs (page 473)
   Any stir-fried chicken (page 383)

Broiled or Grilled Chicken with Soy and
   Ginger (page 376)
Sautéed Chicken Thighs with Soy Glaze,
   or its variations (page 397)
Steamed and Roasted Duck (page 414)
Tea-Smoked Duck (page 415)
Curried Shrimp (page 326)

4. Vary the spicing, by adding:
   toasted, ground Szechwan peppercorns
   a tablespoon or two of hoisin, oyster, plum,
      or ground bean sauce
   curry or five-spice powder to taste
   hot sauce to taste

priately used in place of rice as a bed for any moist stir-fry. Great hot or at room temperature as a snack, too.

12 ounces fresh egg noodles

1/4 cup minced scallion

1 tablespoon soy sauce

4 tablespoons peanut (preferred) or other oil, plus more if needed

1 Cook the noodles in boiling salted water until tender but not mushy. Drain, then rinse in cold water for a minute or two. Toss with the scallion, soy sauce, and 1 tablespoon of the oil.

2 Place the remaining oil on the bottom of a heavy medium to large skillet, preferably non-stick; turn the heat to medium-high. When the oil is hot, add the noodle mix, spreading it out evenly and pressing it down.

3 Cook 2 minutes, then turn the heat to medium-low. Continue to cook until the cake is holding together and is nicely browned on the bottom. Turn carefully (the easiest way to do this is to slide the cake out onto a plate, cover it with another plate, invert the plates, and slide the cake back into the skillet, browned side up), adding a little more oil if necessary.

4 Cook on the other side until brown and serve.

Cold Noodles with Sesame or Peanut Sauce

Makes 4 to 6 servings

Time: About 30 minutes

A wonderful starter or side dish; the noodles and sauce each can be made in advance and combined at the last minute. Add cooked shredded chicken and or diced seeded cucumber to this to add substance and crunch.

12 ounces fresh egg noodles, or any dried noodles, such as spaghetti

2 tablespoons dark sesame oil

1/2 cup sesame paste (tahini) or natural peanut butter

1 tablespoon sugar

1/4 cup soy sauce

1 tablespoon rice or wine vinegar

Hot sesame oil, chili-garlic sauce, Tabasco, or other hot sauce to taste

Salt and freshly ground black pepper to taste

At least 1/2 cup minced scallions for garnish

1 Cook the noodles in boiling salted water until tender but not mushy. Drain, then rinse in cold water for a minute or two. Toss with half the sesame oil and refrigerate up to 2 hours, or proceed with the recipe.

2 Beat together the tahini or peanut butter, sugar, soy sauce, and vinegar. Add a little hot sauce and salt and pepper; taste and adjust seasoning as necessary. Thin the sauce with hot water, so that it is about the consistency of heavy cream.

3 Toss together the noodles and the sauce, and add more of any seasoning if necessary. Drizzle with the remaining sesame oil, garnish, and serve.

Noodle Dishes from Southeast Asia

Rice noodles are more important in Southeast Asia than elsewhere. For the most part, we see only dried rice noodles (fresh ones exist, but are not widely available), sold in cellophane packages of varying sizes. Three widths are common: thin and wiry rice "sticks," spaghetti-width rice "vermicelli," and broad, flat, fettuccine-like noodles. All should be soaked in very hot water for at least fifteen minutes before further cooking and, ideally, should be boiled for a minute or two after that to remove their raw flavor. After cooking, use rice noodles as you would wheat noodles; they are excellent in stir-fries, and I've included some recipes for them here.

Curried Rice Noodles with Vegetables

Makes about 4 servings

Time: About 45 minutes, including time to soak the noodles

Dried rice noodles can be soaked until soft and then stir-fried without further cooking, but a quick boil after soaking is ideal; skip this step if you're rushed. This group of recipes combines stir-fried noodles with vegetables, meat, and/or fish and curry powder, long associated with India but widely in use throughout Southeast Asia. If you like your stir-fries spicy, stir in a little Vietnamese or Indonesian chile paste (available at all Asian markets) just before serving.

12 ounces thin or thick rice noodles

4 tablespoons peanut (preferred) or other oil

1 tablespoon minced garlic

2 teaspoons peeled and minced fresh ginger

1 cup roughly chopped onion

$^1/_2$ cup stemmed, peeled if desired, seeded, and roughly chopped red or yellow bell pepper

$^1/_2$ cup trimmed snow peas (or substitute green peas, thawed if previously frozen)

2 tablespoons All-Purpose Curry Powder or Garam Masala, preferably homemade (page 778)

1 teaspoon sugar

$^1/_2$ cup chicken, beef, or vegetable stock (see "Soups" for stock recipes)

2 tablespoons soy sauce or fish sauce (*nuoc mam* or *nam pla*), or more to taste

Salt, if necessary

Minced cilantro leaves for garnish

1 Soak the noodles for about 15 to 30 minutes in very hot water to cover; meanwhile, bring a large pot of water to a boil. When the noodles are soft, cook them in the boiling water for about 1 minute, just until they lose their raw taste. Drain thoroughly while you prepare the other ingredients.

2 Heat half the oil in a wok or large, deep non-stick skillet, over medium-high heat. A minute or so later, when the first wisp of smoke appears, add the garlic and ginger and stir for 10 seconds; add the onion and cook over high heat, stirring, until it begins to soften, 2 or 3 minutes. Add the red pepper and cook, stirring, for another 2 minutes. Add the snow peas and cook 1 minute, stirring.

3 Turn the heat to medium and sprinkle the vegetables with the curry powder; stir until well blended, then add the sugar and stir. Remove the vegetables with a slotted spoon and set aside.

4 Using the same skillet, heat the remaining oil over high heat for about a minute; add the noodles and cook, stirring and separating almost constantly, until heated through and beginning to brown, about 5 minutes. Add the vegetables and the stock and cook, stirring, until well combined. Add the soy or fish sauce, stir and cook for 30 seconds more, and turn off the heat. Taste and add more soy or fish sauce or some salt if necessary, garnish, and serve.

Curried Rice Noodles with Ground Meat: In Step 2, reduce the amount of onion, pepper, and peas by about half, or use onion only. After adding the peas, add $^1/_2$ pound ground beef, pork, turkey, or chicken. Cook until the meat loses all traces of red or pink, then proceed with recipe.

Curried Rice Noodles with Fresh Shrimp: Shell $^1/_2$ pound of shrimp (devein if you like; page 323). Steam the shells in a covered pot with 1 cup of water for 10 to 15 minutes; strain and use the liquid to replace the stock. In Step 2, reduce the amount of onion, pepper, and peas by about half, or use onion only. In Step 3, after you remove the vegetables, stir-fry the shrimp with an additional teaspoon of minced garlic, just until pink. Stir in 1 tablespoon soy sauce and remove; combine with the vegetables and continue with recipe.

Curried Rice Noodles with Cabbage and Mushrooms: In Step 1, while you soak the noodles, soak 3 or 4 dried black (shiitake) mushrooms in hot water to cover until soft, 10 minutes or so. Drain, squeeze dry, trim, and mince. In Step 2, use onion only; stir-fry them with 2 cups of shredded Napa cabbage. Cook until the cabbage wilts, then stir in the mushrooms. Cook for an additional minute, and proceed to Step 3.

Pad Thai

Fried Noodles, Thai-Style

Makes 4 servings

Time: About 45 minutes, including time to soak the noodles

Pad Thai is packed with strong flavors: It's sweet, sour, spicy, even a little hot. Once you've soaked the rice noodles and assembled the ingredients, this will take you less than ten minutes to cook.

12 ounces rice noodles, preferably vermicelli

3 tablespoons peanut (preferred) or other oil

2 tablespoons minced garlic

1 cup peeled large shrimp, roughly chopped (or use small shrimp and leave whole)

2 eggs, lightly beaten

2 tablespoons fish sauce (*nuoc mam* or *nam pla*, available at Asian markets)

1 tablespoon sugar

Salt, if needed

$1^1/_2$ cups mung bean sprouts

$^1/_4$ cup roasted salted peanuts, chopped

$^1/_2$ teaspoon crushed red pepper flakes, or to taste

Minced cilantro leaves

2 limes or lemons, quartered

① Soak the noodles in warm water to cover until soft; this will take from 15 to 30 minutes. You can change the water once or twice to hasten the process slightly. Drain thoroughly, then toss with half the oil.

② Heat the remaining oil over medium-high heat in a wok or large, deep non-stick skillet, for a minute or so, until the first wisp of smoke appears. Add the garlic and cook, stirring, for 30 seconds. Add the shrimp and cook, stirring, for another 30 seconds; don't worry about fully cooking the shrimp.

③ Add the eggs and let sit for 15 seconds or so, until they begin to set. Then scramble with the shrimp and garlic, breaking up any large clumps. Add the fish sauce and sugar and cook, stirring, for 15 seconds. Add the noodles and toss and cook until heated through. Taste and add salt as needed. Add 1 cup of bean sprouts and toss to distribute through the noodles.

④ Turn the noodles out onto a platter and garnish with the remaining bean sprouts, the peanuts, a sprinkling of crushed red pepper flakes, and some cilantro. Squeeze some lemon or lime juice over all and serve, passing more lemon or lime separately.

Vegetarian Pad Thai: In Step 2, omit the shrimp. Substitute 3 or 4 dried shiitake ("black") mushrooms, soaked in hot water for about 10 minutes then squeezed dry, trimmed, and chopped; $^1/_2$ cup scallions, trimmed and cut into 1-inch sections; and $^1/_4$ cup roasted salted peanuts (unchopped). Cook for about 2 minutes before adding the eggs and proceeding as in Step 3, above. Just before stirring in the bean sprouts, you may also add $^1/_2$ cup diced pressed tofu (see The Basics of Tofu, page 525), but this is far from essential.

Quick Rice Noodles with Charred Onions and Cilantro

Makes 4 servings

Time: About 30 minutes

This is a little speedier than other rice noodle dishes because the noodles are boiled rather than soaked (although you can soak the noodles as in the previous recipes if you prefer). If you don't like the strong taste of cilantro, try the following recipe, which features basil.

4 tablespoons peanut (preferred) or other oil

2 or 3 medium onions, thinly sliced

Salt to taste

1 clove garlic, crushed

1/2 cup loosely packed cilantro leaves

1/2 teaspoon freshly ground black pepper

2 limes

1 pound broad rice noodles (fettuccine-sized)

1 Bring a large pot of water to a boil. Heat a wok or large, deep skillet, preferably non-stick, over medium-high heat for 3 or 4 minutes, then add 3 tablespoons of the oil. Wait another 30 seconds—you want the oil to be really hot—then add the sliced onions. Raise the heat to high and cook them, not stirring too often, until they are dark brown, with some crisp edges, about 10 minutes. Reduce the heat and keep them warm.

2 While the onions are cooking, process some salt, the garlic, cilantro, pepper, the juice of one of the limes, and the remaining tablespoon of oil in a small food processor or blender. Use a rubber spatula if necessary to scrape down the sides of the container, and process until you have a loose paste.

3 Salt the boiling water and cook the pasta, beginning to taste after 5 minutes to see if it is done; do not overcook. When the pasta is tender, drain and toss with the onions and cilantro paste. Add salt to taste. Quarter the remaining lime and serve with the pasta.

Broad Rice Noodles with Chiles, Pork, and Basil

Makes about 4 servings

Time: About 45 minutes, including time to soak the noodles

This is an almost assaultive noodle dish, one which heat—accented by vinegar and only slightly moderated by sugar and basil—should dominate. I like to make it mildly hot, then pass crushed red chiles at the table for those with cast-iron palates.

12 ounces rice noodles (fettuccine-width)

2 tablespoons peanut (preferred) or other oil

1 tablespoon minced garlic

5 small dried hot red chiles, or to taste

1/3 to 1/2 pound ground pork (preferred) or other ground meat, such as beef or turkey

1 tablespoon soy sauce and 2 tablespoons fish sauce (*nuoc mam* or *nam pla*, available at Asian markets), or a combination of either

1 tablespoon sugar

2 tablespoons rice (preferred) or other vinegar

1 cup shredded fresh basil leaves

Salt, if necessary

Crushed red pepper flakes (optional)

1 Soak the noodles in warm water to cover until soft; this will take from 15 to 30 minutes. You can change the water once or twice to hasten the process slightly, or you can simply cook the noodles as you would any other, taking care not to overcook. Drain thoroughly, then toss with half the oil.

2 Heat the remaining oil over medium-high heat in a wok or large, deep non-stick skillet for a minute or so, until the first wisp of smoke appears. Add the garlic and chiles and cook, stirring, for a minute. Add the meat and turn the heat to medium. Cook, stirring and mashing with a wooden spoon to break up clumps.

3 When almost all traces of red or pink disappear, add the soy and/or fish sauces and the sugar; stir to mix. Add the drained noodles and toss and stir to combine. Add the vinegar and most of the basil. Stir and taste; add salt if necessary. Serve, garnished with the remaining basil and passing the crushed pepper on the side.

Rice Noodles with Coconut Milk: In Step 2, add $1/2$ cup sliced onion and $1/2$ cup roughly chopped red bell pepper after the initial cooking of the garlic and chiles. Increase the sugar to 2 tablespoons. In Step 3, use 1 cup canned or Fresh Coconut Milk (page 291) in place of the vinegar.

Rice Noodles, Vegetarian-Style: In Step 2, add 1 teaspoon peeled and minced fresh ginger along with the garlic and chiles. Cook $1/2$ cup trimmed scallions, cut into 1-inch lengths, and $1/2$ cup roughly chopped red bell pepper after the initial cooking of the garlic and chiles. Substitute 1 cup pressed or frozen tofu, diced (page 526), or 1 cup chopped seitan (processed wheat gluten, available at Asian markets) for the meat. You can also successfully combine this variation with the coconut milk variation, above.

Grains

Most people don't need to be sold on grains. In the past twenty years, our consumption of rice has tripled, and our consumption of pasta (another form of grain, after all) has multiplied by a factor of more than ten. But many grains remain esoteric. Among them are some that are less common forms of familiar grains—whole wheat berries, for example—or those that are staples elsewhere in the world but are simply not appealing enough to become a staple in our richer society.

Some exotic grains are among the oldest foods eaten by our species—in some cases even before they were cultivated—and they still deserve a place on today's tables. Quinoa, the ancient sacred grain of the Andes, so important that the conquistadores destroyed it to demoralize and physically weaken the indigenous population, has a fine taste and texture. Kasha, or toasted buckwheat, has been a staple of central and eastern Europe since the beginning of recorded history; its flavor demands recognition. Bulgur, kernels of soft wheat that have been steamed, dried, and cracked, has been found in the tombs of the pharaohs; it is an original and sensational convenience food.

In fact, most of these grains are versatile and easy to prepare. Tiny quinoa cooks in just fifteen or twenty minutes; kasha and bulgur, which are precooked before sale, are also fast. But each requires slightly different treatment and can give a range of textures depending on what you do; I give details under the heading of each grain.

The Basics of Grains and Health

Like any complex carbohydrates, whole grains benefit the body because they are extremely low in fat, containing virtually no saturated fat; eating them in place of high-fat foods is a step that would be to the advantage of almost every American. But whole grains offer even more benefits than processed foods such as pasta and white rice. Quinoa, for example, comes from a leafy green, and as a result is not only high in protein and calcium, but in certain phytochemicals, the benefits of which are only now being discovered. Kasha, like oats, appears to moderate blood pressure and lower cholesterol; it may also be a factor in preventing diabetes. And all whole grains are being studied for a variety of other health benefits.

The Basics of Buying, Storing, and Preparing Grains

Sadly, the supermarket is rarely the best place to buy any grain except perhaps white rice. Most grains, even when processed to remove their hulls, or lightly precooked in the traditional style (as are bulgur and kasha), retain most of their natural oils, so buying them as fresh as possible is key to avoiding rancidity. Buy them in bulk, from a place with fast turnover. That means either a specialty store (for instance, you can get great bulgur in a Middle Eastern store) or a natural foods store.

Once grains are in your home, you can store them in the refrigerator, but if there is room in the freezer, that's even better; there's no need to defrost before cooking.

Most grains need no preparation before cooking, although tough whole grains, such as wheat and rye, are easier to cook if you toast and soak them first. But most (bulgur and kasha are the exceptions) should be rinsed. Some, such as quinoa, should be washed until the water runs clear; that's the traditional way to prepare rice, too, although it isn't necessary. Others can just be rinsed to remove surface dust and residues of pesticides.

This chapter deals with whole or minimally processed grains. Grains that are shredded or flaked are usually destined to become breakfast cereals, and you'll find recipes for them in "Eggs, Breakfast, and Brunch Dishes." Grains that are milled into flour, of course, are discussed in "Breads" (pages 217–253).

Finally, there are some grains whose popularity and availability are so minimal that I will just tell you to which more common grains they are closely linked. That way, should you develop a burning desire to cook them, you can substitute them in a recipe.

Amaranth: Tiny seeds that are often ground into flour. Cook as for millet, or toast and use as you would sesame seeds (page 776).

Kamut and Spelt: Close relatives of wheat; especially useful as substitutes for those with wheat allergies; most often ground into flour, but whole grains can be treated exactly as you would wheat berries.

Teff: The tiniest edible seed. Always ground into flour to make bread in Ethiopia, where it is a staple. Can also be made into a strong-flavored, somewhat nutty cereal; cook it as you would cornmeal or oatmeal, in proportions of two parts water to one part teff.

About Grains and Liquid

Without exception, grains are cooked with liquid. And although grains have good flavor of their own, cooking them with chicken, beef, or vegetable stock is almost always an improvement; there are times when fish stock is an asset as well. But, with few exceptions, you can use water in grain recipes calling for stock. The resulting dish will be somewhat less intensely flavored, of course, but will not suffer otherwise.

The Basics of Cooking Grains

Because grains are all dried foods, they must be rehydrated and cooked at the same time. The time this takes depends on five factors: the nature of the grain; how dry the grain is (older grains are drier than newer ones); how much of its outer coating it retains (brown rice has a hull; white rice does not); whether it has been milled ("rolling" or "cutting" oats exposes more surface area); and whether it has been precooked.

Aside from timing, however, you can cook many grains by the following method, which does not require either precise timing or guesswork about the quantity of water that must be added. Rather, it enables you to cook the grain as you would pasta, by tasting it until it is done. Once the grain is tender and you have drained it, you may serve it immediately, set it aside and reheat it later, or drain it and store it in the refrigerator to be reheated in a day or two.

These are the grains that cook well using this method:

Long-grain white rice
Brown rice
Pearled barley
Whole wheat (wheat berries), preferably after dry-toasting in a skillet (see Basic Kasha, page 194) followed by an overnight soaking in water to cover
Whole rye (rye berries), preferably after dry-toasting in a skillet (see Basic Kasha, page 194) followed by an overnight soaking in water to cover

Hominy (pozole)
Wild rice

Simple Precooked Grains
Makes 4 servings

Time: 10 minutes to more than 1 hour, depending on the grain

See above for a full description of this method, and a list of the grains for which it works best.

At least 6 cups water
1¹/₂ cups any grain listed above, rinsed

1 Bring at least 6 cups water to a boil in a medium-to-large pot; salt it. Stir in the grain and adjust the heat so that the water boils, but not furiously.

2 Cook, stirring occasionally, until the grain is tender. This will take about 7 or 8 minutes with some white rice, and as long as 1 hour or more for some brown rice, unpearled barley, wheat berries, and other unhulled grains. Add additional boiling water if necessary to keep grains covered.

3 Pour the grain into a strainer; plunge the strainer into ice-cold water to stop the cooking. Drain again. Reheat within 1 hour (see next page) or refrigerate for later use.

Pressure-Cooked Tough Grains
Makes 4 to 6 servings

Time: About 45 minutes, or longer

Some grains—whole barley, wheat, rye, and oats—may take two hours, and sometimes longer, to cook by the above method. (In fact, they never become what you'd call tender, no matter how long you cook them, because bran doesn't soften.) But you can cook most of them in a pressure cooker in about thirty minutes; see The Basics of Pressure Cookers, page 506.

1 cup any whole (unhulled) grain: wheat, rye, barley, oats, brown rice, or a mixture, rinsed
4 cups water (4^1/$_2$ for barley)
1 tablespoon oil
1 teaspoon salt

1 Combine all ingredients in a pressure cooker and lock on the lid. Turn the heat to high.

2 Bring to high pressure, then adjust the heat so that it is just high enough to maintain pressure. Cook 30 minutes (40 for barley).

3 Cool the pressure cooker by running cold water over the top. When the pressure is down, carefully remove the top and taste a grain. If it is done, serve or store, then follow any recipe for precooked grains. If water remains and the grain is tender, cook over medium heat, stirring, until no liquid remains; or simply drain. If it is almost done, add more water if necessary, and cook without the lid for a few minutes. If it is still quite chewy, add more water and repeat Steps 1 and 2, cooking for 5 to 10 minutes at a time.

Precooked Grains with Butter or Oil

Makes 4 servings

Time: 10 minutes or more

Once you've cooked grains with either of the methods above, reheating them is a snap. At the same time, you can add a variety of different flavorings to them, as you'll see in the following recipes.

3 tablespoons olive oil, butter, or a combination
3 to 4 cups precooked grains (page 181) or pressure-cooked grains (page 181)
Salt and freshly ground black pepper to taste
Minced fresh parsley leaves for garnish

1 Place the oil and/or butter in a large skillet, preferably non-stick, and turn the heat to medium. When the oil is hot or the butter melted, add the grains. Cook, stirring occasionally, until heated through, about 10 minutes.

2 Season with salt and pepper, garnish, and serve.

Precooked Grains with Garlic or Onions

Makes 4 servings

Time: 15 to 20 minutes

You can change the flavor of this dish by substituting minced shallots (about one-quarter cup) or chopped leeks (about one-half cup) for the garlic or onion.

3 tablespoons olive oil, butter, or a combination
1 tablespoon minced garlic, or to taste, or ^{1}/$_2$ cup chopped onion
3 to 4 cups precooked grains (page 181) or pressure-cooked grains (page 181)
Salt and freshly ground black pepper to taste
Minced fresh parsley leaves for garnish

1 Combine the oil and/or butter and the garlic or onion in a large skillet, preferably non-stick, and turn the heat to medium-low. Cook, stirring occasionally, just until the garlic or onion softens and begins to brown, 5 to 10 minutes.

2 Add the grains and cook, stirring occasionally, until heated through, about 10 minutes.

3 Season with salt and pepper, garnish, and serve.

Precooked Grains with Mushrooms: In Step 1, add 1 cup trimmed and chopped mushrooms (a tablespoon or two of reconstituted dried mushrooms [page 583] is a nice addition), along with the garlic or onion. Cook, stirring occasionally, until the mushrooms are softened and begin to brown, 5 to 10 minutes. Add the grains and finish as above.

Precooked Grains with Toasted Spice: In Step 1, add 1 tablespoon of any spice mixture from page 778, or 1 tablespoon All-Purpose Curry Powder (page 778) or store-bought curry powder, or to taste, along with the garlic or onion. Cook, stirring frequently, until the garlic or onion softens. Add the grains and finish as above.

Precooked Grains with Toasted Nuts or Seeds: In Step 1, add ¹/₂ cup roughly chopped (but not minced) cashews, walnuts, unsalted (preferably raw) peanuts, blanched almonds, sunflower seeds, or toasted, shelled pumpkin seeds (pepitas) after the garlic or onions soften. Cook, stirring frequently, until they begin to brown, about 3 minutes. Add the grains and finish as above.

Precooked Grains with Pesto: Follow the original recipe to the end, then stir ¹/₂ cup Basic Pesto (page 766), or to taste, into the grains. Garnish, if possible, with chopped fresh basil.

Seven Ideas for Precooked Grains

1. Stir in any minced herb or cooked vegetable during the last minute of cooking.
2. Add dried fruit such as raisins or minced apricots along with the grains.
3. Use in any green salad, or make into a salad (see pages 111–114 for grain salads).
4. Add to bread dough, pancake batters, or muffins.
5. Make into fritters, as you would beans (page 520).
6. Combine with vegetables and seasonings to make stuffing (see Quinoa Stuffing with Bacon and Nuts, page 196).
7. Add to soups at the last minute.

The Basics of Barley

More barley is used in making alcoholic beverages (especially beer) than in cooking, but this grain, which was among the first humans cultivated, should be in every pantry. It makes a wonderful substitute for rice in side dishes and is probably the best grain for soup-making (it also makes good flour, which can be added to any of the French or sourdough breads on pages 224–227).

You can buy whole barley, which is the equivalent of brown rice. But it never becomes what you'd call tender, no matter how long you cook it. Thus most barley has its hull and bran removed. This "pearled" barley cooks relatively quickly (usually in less than half an hour) and retains a pleasant chewiness in addition to its great flavor.

Job's tears is another form of barley; it's larger and takes a little longer to cook.

Basic Barley
Makes 4 servings

Time: About 40 minutes

This method is a little quicker than cooking barley by Simple Precooked Grains (page 181). Remember that barley absorbs more water than most other grains, tripling its original volume.

1 cup pearled barley, rinsed
3 cups chicken, beef, or vegetable stock, or water, plus
    a little more if needed (see "Soups" for stock recipes)
Salt and freshly ground black pepper to taste
1 or 2 tablespoons butter (optional)

1 Combine all ingredients in a medium saucepan and bring to a boil over medium-high heat.

2 Cover, turn the heat to low, and cook, undisturbed, for 30 minutes. Check the barley's progress: It is done when quite tender and all the liquid is absorbed. Continue to cook if necessary, adding a tablespoon or two more liquid if all the liquid has been absorbed and the barley is not quite done. Or, if the barley is tender but a little liquid remains, simply cover and turn off the heat; the barley will absorb the liquid within 10 minutes. If $1/4$ cup or more of water remains (unlikely), uncover and raise the heat a bit; cook, stirring, until the barley is fluffy and the liquid evaporated.

3 Serve, with butter if you like.

Barley, Pilaf-Style

Makes 4 servings

Time: 45 minutes

You can make barley using the variations for Rice Pilaf (pages 202–204), following this basic recipe.

2 tablespoons butter or extra-virgin olive oil
$1/2$ cup chopped scallions or 1 medium onion, chopped
1 cup pearled barley, rinsed
1 teaspoon chopped fresh tarragon, chervil, or mint leaves or $1/2$ teaspoon dried tarragon or chervil
3 cups chicken, beef, or vegetable stock, or water, warmed, plus a little more if needed (see "Soups" for stock recipes)
Salt and freshly ground black pepper to taste
Minced fresh parsley or mint leaves for garnish

1 Place the butter or oil in a medium-to-large skillet over medium heat; when the butter melts or the oil is hot, add the scallions or onion and cook, stirring, until softened, about 5 minutes.

2 Add the barley and cook, stirring, for 1 minute; add the herb, liquid, and salt and pepper. Bring to a boil.

3 Turn the heat to low, cover, and cook for 30 minutes. Check the barley's progress: It is done when it's quite tender and all the liquid is absorbed. Continue to cook if necessary, adding a tablespoon or two more liquid if all the liquid has been absorbed and the barley is not quite done. Or, if the barley is tender but a little liquid remains, simply cover and turn off the heat; the barley will absorb the liquid within 10 minutes. If $1/4$ cup or more of water remains (unlikely), uncover and raise the heat a bit; cook, stirring, until the barley is fluffy and the liquid evaporated. Garnish and serve.

Barley "Risotto" with Mushrooms

Makes 4 servings

Time: About 1 hour

When given more liquid than usual, barley becomes almost creamy; this technique is a little labor-intensive but very reliable. You can use the flavor ingredients of any risotto (pages 208–211) in this recipe.

1 ounce dried porcini mushrooms
4 to 6 cups chicken, beef, or vegetable stock, heated to the boiling point (see "Soups" for stock recipes)
3 tablespoons butter or extra-virgin olive oil, plus 1 tablespoon butter, softened (optional)
2 tablespoons minced shallot, scallion, or onion
1 cup trimmed and chopped fresh mushrooms, any variety
1 cup pearled barley, rinsed
1 teaspoon minced fresh oregano, marjoram, or thyme leaves or $1/2$ teaspoon dried
Salt and freshly ground black pepper to taste
$1/2$ cup dry white wine
Minced fresh parsley leaves for garnish

1 Soak the porcini in 1 cup of the hot stock. While they are soaking, place the butter or oil in a medium-to-large, deep skillet or casserole over medium heat; when the butter melts or the oil is hot, add the shallot, scallion, or onion and cook, stirring, until softened, about 5 minutes.

2 When the porcini are softened—it will take 10 to 20 minutes—drain them; reserve and strain the soaking stock. Trim them of any hard spots, chop, and add to the skillet, along with the fresh mushrooms. Cook, stirring occasionally, until the mushrooms are tender, 5 to 8 minutes.

3 Add the barley and cook, stirring, until it is glossy, about 1 minute. Add the herb, salt, pepper, and white wine; turn the heat to medium-high and let the wine bubble away while you stir. Add the mushroom-soaking liquid and cook, stirring, until it just about evaporates.

4 Return the heat to medium and begin to add the remaining stock, $1/2$ cup or so at a time, stirring after each addition and every minute or so. When the stock is just about evaporated, add more. The mixture should be neither soupy nor dry; stir frequently.

5 Keep adding liquid until the barley is tender, at least 30 minutes. Stir in the optional softened butter, garnish, and serve.

The Basics of Bulgur

Bulgur (or bulghur), a traditional grain of the Middle East, is not just cracked wheat; it is wheat which is first steamed, then hulled, then dried, and then cracked. The result is a quick-cooking grain (in fact, you don't even cook some bulgur, you just soak it) that filled the historical need of conserving fuel and today provides convenience and great flavor.

The best-known use for bulgur is in Tabbouleh (page 112), in which it plays a major role, along with parsley and/or mint. But bulgur makes wonderful pilaf-style dishes, especially when combined with vegetables or noodles.

Bulgur comes in four grinds, numbered one through four. Number One is so fine that it is almost always just soaked (see Basic Bulgur, below) rather than cooked. Number Two, considered medium, can be soaked or cooked. Number Three (coarse) must be cooked. Number Four is very coarse; you won't see it often. Most supermarkets stock Number Two, which you can consider all-purpose if you like; Number One and Number Three can be found in many natural foods stores, specialty food markets, and, of course, Middle Eastern stores.

Basic Bulgur
Makes 4 servings

Time: Less than 30 minutes

Bulgur, which has wonderful flavor, cooks up so nice and fluffy that it is actually a bit dry. Thus it really benefits from the addition of butter or some kind of sauce (pasta sauces, pesto, or the pan juices from meat are all delicious). This is also the way to make bulgur for inclusion in other dishes, such as Tabbouleh (page 112).

1 cup medium-grind (Number Two) or fine-grind (Number One) bulgur
$2^1/2$ cups boiling water

1 Place the bulgur in a bowl and pour the water over it. Stir once and let sit.

2 Fine bulgur will be tender in 15 to 20 minutes (sample some); medium in 20 to 25 minutes. If any water remains when the bulgur is done, squeeze the bulgur in a cloth or place it in a fine sieve and press down on it.

3 Serve immediately.

Bulgur with Spinach

Makes 4 servings

Time: 45 minutes

A good use for leftover spinach if you have it.

1 pound spinach, washed and trimmed (page 604)
2 tablespoons butter or olive oil
1 small onion, minced
Pinch ground cloves
1 cup medium-grind (Number Two) or coarse-grind
    (Number Three) bulgur
Salt and freshly ground black pepper to taste
1³/₄ cups chicken, beef, or vegetable stock, or water,
    heated (see "Soups" for stock recipes)

1 Steam or simmer the spinach (page 604) just until wilted, 1 to 3 minutes; plunge into ice water to stop the cooking. Drain, squeeze dry, and chop coarsely.

2 Place the butter or oil in a large saucepan or skillet, preferably non-stick, and turn the heat to medium. When the butter melts or the oil is hot, add the onion and cook, stirring, until it softens, about 5 minutes. Stir in the cloves.

3 Add the bulgur and stir until it is coated with butter or oil. Add the spinach and a little salt and pepper; stir until all ingredients are blended, then add the liquid, all at once. Turn the heat as low as possible, stir, and cover. Cook for 10 minutes, then turn off the heat and let sit for 15 minutes more. Adjust the seasoning and serve.

Curried Bulgur with Nuts, Carrots, and Raisins

Makes 4 servings

Time: About 30 minutes

An attractive, pleasantly sweet dish.

2 tablespoons canola or other neutral oil
1 medium onion, chopped
2 tablespoons All-Purpose Curry Powder (page 778)
    or store-bought curry powder
1 cup medium-grind (Number Two) or coarse-grind
    (Number Three) bulgur
2 large carrots, peeled and grated or finely chopped
1³/₄ cups chicken, beef, or vegetable stock, or water,
    heated to the boiling point (see "Soups" for stock
    recipes)
¹/₄ cup blanched slivered almonds
¹/₄ cup raisins
Salt and freshly ground black pepper to taste

1 Place the oil in a medium skillet or saucepan that can later be covered and turn the heat to medium. Add the onion and cook, stirring, until it is soft, about 5 minutes.

2 Add the curry powder and continue to cook for another minute. Add the bulgur and stir to coat with the oil. Add the carrots and stir once or twice.

3 Add the liquid, almonds, and raisins, cover, and cook over very low heat for 10 minutes. Turn off the heat and let sit for 15 minutes more. Season with salt and pepper and serve.

Bulgur Pilaf with Vermicelli

Makes 4 servings

Time: 30 minutes

Heavenly with butter, wonderful with oil, this is among the best side dishes there is, and a good way to use up odd bits of noodles. If you don't have vermicelli, use any long pasta. If you only have cut pasta, such as ziti or shells, put it in a plastic bag and smack it a few times with a rolling pin or skillet to break it into smaller pieces.

4 tablespoons (1/2 stick) butter or extra-virgin olive oil

2 medium onions or 1 large onion, chopped

1/2 cup vermicelli, broken into 2-inch-long or shorter lengths, or other pasta

1 cup medium-grind (Number Two) or coarse-grind (Number Three) bulgur

Salt and freshly ground black pepper to taste

1 tablespoon tomato paste (optional)

2 1/4 cups chicken, beef, or vegetable stock, or water, heated to the boiling point (see "Soups" for stock recipes)

1 Place the butter or oil in a medium skillet or saucepan that can later be covered and turn the heat to medium. Add the onion and cook, stirring, until it is soft, about 5 minutes.

2 Add the vermicelli and the bulgur and cook, stirring, until coated with butter or oil. Add all the remaining ingredients, turn the heat to low, and cover. Cook for 10 minutes, then turn off the heat and let sit for 15 minutes more. Adjust the seasoning and serve.

The Basics of Cornmeal

Unless you are a southerner and grew up on grits or hush puppies (or are of Romanian descent and grew up eating mamaliga, the East European version of polenta), you thought cornmeal was for corn bread (and it is; see page 243). But polenta has changed that. This cornmeal mush—that's all it is—has been fussed over more than any other food in the last ten years or so. But basically it's a fluffy combination of cornmeal and water, with flavorings stirred into it and sauces poured onto it. Polenta, like rice, is a fairly neutral base. If you make it with lots of butter and cheese, it can stand on its own. If you make it with just enough butter or oil to keep it moist, you'll want to serve it with something else—try any tomato sauce;

virtually any braised or stewed meat or poultry; or roasted, broiled, or grilled meat or poultry, with its juices.

Making good polenta is fairly easy; see Basic Polenta, below. Making exceptional polenta takes more time, patience, and stirring, but it isn't difficult either; food writer Sarah Fritschner developed a foolproof technique for doing so in a double boiler, and I've included that as a variation.

Buying good cornmeal can sometimes be a challenge. Many Italian stores and supermarkets sell instant polenta, which is incredibly easy to make—and not bad if you're going to produce Polenta "Pizza" (page 189) or a similar dish afterward—but has no flavor. Short on taste, too, are the mass-produced commercial cornmeals sold in supermarkets, although "stone-ground" cornmeal sold in the baking aisles can be good. I recommend you go out of your way to buy fresh stone-ground cornmeal from a natural foods store, and store it in the freezer. Medium-grind cornmeal is best for both flavor and texture; although it takes a little longer to cook, it's worth the time.

Basic Polenta, Version I
Makes 4 servings

Time: About 30 minutes

As detailed above, you can spend more time making polenta if you like. But as long as you use enough water, fifteen minutes of stirring is usually sufficient, although cooking time is to some extent dependent on the consistency you are trying to achieve, which in turn determines the amount of water you use. Of course, adding plenty of butter and cheese at the end of cooking helps matters along. (See also Ten Dishes to Serve with Soft Polenta, page 189.)

4 cups water (5 if you would like very soft polenta; 3½ if you plan to spread and cut the polenta)

1 teaspoon salt, plus more if necessary

1 cup medium-grind cornmeal (see above)

Freshly ground black pepper to taste

2 tablespoons butter (optional)

¼ cup or more freshly grated Parmesan or crumbled Gorgonzola cheese (optional)

Snipped fresh chives or dill or minced fresh parsley leaves for garnish

1 Bring the water to a boil in a heavy medium pot, preferably non-stick; salt it and turn the heat to medium. Add the cornmeal a little bit at a time, whisking constantly with a wire whisk. Once you've whisked in all the cornmeal, turn the heat to low.

2 Cook, whisking every minute for the first 5 minutes, then switching to a flat-bottomed wooden spoon. Stir frequently, almost constantly, until all the water is absorbed. Soft polenta should be creamy; firmer polenta, such as that needed for slicing and grilling, or for the next recipe, should begin to pull away from the sides of the pot. This will take about 15 minutes with the minimum amount of water and 30 to 40 with the maximum. Turn off the heat; taste and add more salt if necessary, along with some pepper.

3 Stir in the optional butter and cheese and stir until they dissolve. Garnish and serve immediately, passing more cheese at the table, if you like.

Basic Polenta, Version II

Makes 4 servings

Time: About 1½ hours

This technique, developed by Louisville food writer Sarah Fritschner, makes exceptionally fluffy polenta. It takes a while, but requires very little work. (See also Ten Dishes to Serve with Soft Polenta, page 189.)

4 cups water (5 if you would like very soft polenta)

1 teaspoon salt

1 cup medium-grind cornmeal (see above)

Freshly ground black pepper to taste

2 tablespoons butter (optional)

¼ cup or more freshly grated Parmesan or crumbled Gorgonzola cheese (optional)

Snipped fresh chives or dill or minced fresh parsley leaves for garnish

1 In the top portion of a double boiler over simmering water, combine the water and salt. Add the cornmeal a little bit at a time, whisking constantly.

2 Cover, then cook for about 1½ hours, stirring every 5 to 10 minutes, until all the water is absorbed and the polenta is creamy. Turn off the heat; taste and add more salt if necessary, along with some pepper.

3 Stir in the optional butter and cheese and stir until it dissolves. Garnish and serve immediately.

Basic Polenta, Version III

Makes 4 servings

Time: About 30 minutes

This requires much less stirring. Although it takes much longer than instant polenta, it is really no work at all and gives good results. (See also Ten Dishes to Serve with Soft Polenta, page 189.)

4 cups water

1 teaspoon salt

1 cup medium-grind cornmeal (see above)

Freshly ground black pepper to taste

2 tablespoons butter (optional)

¼ cup or more freshly grated Parmesan or crumbled Gorgonzola cheese (optional)

Snipped fresh chives or dill or minced fresh parsley leaves for garnish

1 Bring the water to a boil in a heavy medium pot, preferably non-stick; salt it and turn the heat to medium. Add the cornmeal a little bit at a time, whisking constantly with a wire whisk. Once you've whisked in all the cornmeal, turn the heat to very low and cover; the mixture should be just bubbling.

2 Uncover and stir with a flat-bottomed wooden spoon for about 1 minute out of every 10. When the polenta is nearly done, after 35 to 40 minutes, uncover and stir frequently for about 5 minutes.

3 Stir in the pepper, optional butter, and cheese and stir until it dissolves. Garnish and serve immediately, passing more cheese at the table, if you like.

Polenta with Fresh Corn: A rich and very American "polenta," best with butter and Gorgonzola or other strong cheese added. You can make this with any of the three preceding techniques: Use 2 cups water and 2 cups milk and proceed as above. When the polenta is almost ready, stir in the kernels stripped from 2 ears of corn and cook 1 minute more.

Ten Dishes to Serve with Soft Polenta

You can top soft polenta with almost any savory, liquid dish, just as you would rice. Here are some ideas:

1. Chicken, Provençal-Style (page 368)
2. Cod or Other Thick White Fillets Poached in Tomato Sauce (page 289) or Cod or Other Thick White Fillets with Winter Vegetables (page 290)
3. Classic Beef Stew (page 435) or its variations, or Garlicky Beef Daube (page 436)
4. Veal Stew with Tomatoes (page 446) or its variations
5. Sautéed "Italian" Sausage with Peppers and Onions (page 474)
6. Lamb Shanks with Tomatoes and Olives (page 488)
7. Any tomato-based pasta sauce, with or without meat (pages 130–134)
8. Cauliflower with Garlic and Anchovies (page 554)
9. Collards or Kale with Double Garlic (page 562)
10. Chard with Garlic, Pine Nuts, and Currants (page 558)

Polenta "Pizza"

Makes 4 servings

Time: About 40 minutes

Use any pizza toppings (page 260) you like on this polenta crust.

1 tablespoon extra-virgin olive oil, plus more
   as needed
1 recipe Basic Polenta I or III, made with 3 1/2 cups
   water and without butter or cheese
1 1/2 to 2 cups Basic Tomato Sauce (page 130)
1 to 2 cups freshly grated mozzarella, Parmesan,
   Gorgonzola, fontina, or a combination
Salt and freshly ground black pepper to taste
Fresh minced herbs, such as basil, parsley, and/or
   oregano or marjoram

1 Preheat the oven to 400°F. Brush a little olive oil on a pizza pan or baking sheet. Stir 1 tablespoon oil into the cooked polenta and spoon onto the prepared pan. Work quickly, so the polenta doesn't stiffen.

2 When the polenta is cool enough to handle, cover it with a sheet of plastic wrap or waxed paper. Use your hands to flatten it to a thickness of about 1/2 inch all over. Cover the crust with tomato sauce, then sprinkle with cheese, salt, pepper, and the herbs. Drizzle with a little more olive oil and place in the oven.

3 Bake until the cheese is melted and the pizza is hot, 12 to 15 minutes. Cut into slices and serve hot or at room temperature.

Broiled Polenta with Parmesan

Polenta Crostini

Makes 4 servings

Time: At least 2 hours, largely unattended

This recipe and its variation are great ways to enjoy polenta that has been cooked in advance.

1 teaspoon butter
1 recipe Basic Polenta I or III, made with 3¹/₂ cups
    water and butter, Parmesan cheese, and herb
About ¹/₄ cup freshly grated Parmesan cheese

1 Smear the teaspoon of butter in a thin layer on a baking sheet or on an 11 × 17-inch jelly-roll pan. Pour and spoon the cooked polenta onto the sheet. Work quickly, so the polenta doesn't stiffen.

2 When the polenta is cool enough to handle, cover it with a sheet of plastic wrap or waxed paper. Use your hands to flatten it to a thickness of about ¹/₂ inch all over. Refrigerate it until it is thoroughly cooled, at least 1 hour or overnight.

3 When you're ready to cook, preheat the broiler. Cut the polenta into serving-sized pieces, right on the baking sheet. Sprinkle with Parmesan and run under the broiler until heated through and lightly browned, 5 to 10 minutes. Serve immediately.

Pan-Fried Polenta: In Step 3, when you're ready to cook, cut the polenta into serving-sized pieces. Place 3 tablespoons butter in a large skillet over medium heat. Beat 2 eggs in a bowl; grate about 2 cups Parmesan onto a plate (or use bread crumbs). When the butter melts, dip each piece of polenta into the eggs, then into the Parmesan or bread crumbs. Cook in the butter until lightly browned on both sides and serve with tomato sauce.

Five Ideas for Broiled Polenta

1. Broil with any good melting cheese, from mozzarella to fontina to Cheddar, singly or in combination with Parmesan.
2. Spread with Garlic Oil (page 775) before broiling.
3. Dot with room-temperature Black Olive Paste (Tapenade) (page 26) just after broiling.
4. Spread with warm Duxelles (page 583) just after broiling.
5. Spoon over a bit of any tomato sauce (pages 130–134) and return to the broiler for thirty seconds to one minute.

Hush Puppies

Makes 4 to 6 servings

Time: 30 minutes

In the South, this is the traditional accompaniment to fried fish. These will stay crisp in a low oven.

1¹/₂ cups medium-grind cornmeal
¹/₂ cup all-purpose flour
1 tablespoon baking powder
1 teaspoon freshly ground black pepper or
    ¹/₂ teaspoon cayenne, or to taste (optional)
1 teaspoon salt
1 teaspoon minced fresh sage leaves or ¹/₂ teaspoon
    dried sage
1 cup milk
3 scallions, trimmed and minced
1 egg, beaten
Canola oil or other neutral oil for deep frying

1 Mix the dry ingredients together in a bowl. Stir the milk and scallions into the egg and combine with the dry ingredients, stirring well to moisten but not beating. Refrigerate for an hour or two if you like.

Preceded by soup, or served with a salad and/or bread, many grain dishes are attractive, filling, and satisfying enough to occupy the center of the plate. Here are a few of my favorites:

1. Barley "Risotto" with Mushrooms, page 184
2. Bulgur with Spinach, page 186
3. Curried Bulgur with Nuts, Carrots, and Raisins, page 186
4. Flash-Cooked Hominy with Kale or Collards, page 193
5. Kasha with Golden Brown Onions, page 195
6. Persian Rice with Potatoes, page 201
7. Pilaf with Onions, Raisins, and Pine Nuts, page 202
8. Rice with Onions (Soubise), page 204
9. Coconut Rice with Beans, page 204
10. Cumin-Scented Rice with Shrimp, page 206
11. Any risotto, pages 208–211
12. Shrimp Jambalaya, page 211
13. Fried Rice with Egg, page 212
14. Shrimp or Pork Fried Rice with Peas, page 212
15. Fried Rice with Greens, page 212
16. Brown Rice with Cashews and Herbs, page 213
17. Stir-Fried Brown Rice with Vegetables and Soy, page 214
18. Brown Rice with Lentils and Apricots, page 214

2 Preheat the oven to 200°F. Place at least 2 inches of oil in a large, deep saucepan; turn the heat to medium-high. When the oil reaches 375°F, drop the batter into the pan by the tablespoonful; do not crowd.

3 Fry about 1 minute on each side, or until dark and crisp. Drain on paper towels and keep warm in the oven until ready (they keep fairly well for 30 minutes or so).

The Basics of Couscous

Couscous is not a grain—it's actually pasta of North African origin—but we treat it as one. There's a traditional method of preparing it, which involves moistening the couscous, then resting it, then steaming it, then moistening it again, then salting it, then cooling it, then steaming it once more, and finally serving it with a stew. Most highly dedicated cooks try that method at least once, but it is a big production. If you want to give it a shot, I refer you to the revised version of Paula Wolfert's classic *Mediterranean Cooking* (HarperCollins, 1994).

In fact, there is a simple way to prepare couscous. It may not be ideal, but it's good. Serve couscous with any moist stew or other dish with plenty of gravy; it does not have a lot of flavor of its own.

Basic Couscous

Makes 4 servings

Time: About 15 minutes

All couscous, even that which is not labeled "instant," is precooked, so preparation time is minimal. For best results, use this technique even if you buy a box of couscous that gives different directions.

3 tablespoons butter

1½ cups couscous

2¼ cups chicken, beef, or vegetable stock, warmed (see "Soups" for stock recipes)

½ teaspoon salt, plus more if necessary

Freshly ground black pepper to taste

Minced fresh parsley leaves for garnish

1 Place 2 tablespoons butter in a medium saucepan and turn the heat to medium-low. When it melts, add the couscous and cook, stirring, until it is coated with butter, about 1 minute.

2 Add the stock all at once, along with $^1/_2$ teaspoon salt. Bring to a boil, then turn the heat down to its minimum. Cover and cook until all the liquid is absorbed, 5 to 8 minutes.

3 Pour the couscous into a large serving bowl and stir in the remaining tablespoon butter with a fork, fluffing the couscous and breaking up any lumps. Add pepper and more salt if necessary, garnish, and serve.

Couscous with Raisins and Pine Nuts

Makes 4 servings

Time: About 15 minutes

A basic couscous recipe in which you can feel free to vary seasonings to your taste.

2$^1/_4$ cups chicken, beef, or vegetable stock, or water
(see "Soups" for stock recipes)
1 cinnamon stick
5 cardamom pods
Salt and freshly ground black pepper to taste
$^1/_3$ cup raisins or other minced dried fruit such as
apricots or figs, or a combination
$^1/_3$ cup hot water or stock
4 tablespoons ($^1/_2$ stick) butter
$^1/_2$ cup pine nuts
1$^1/_2$ cups couscous
Minced fresh parsley or cilantro leaves for garnish

1 In a small saucepan, warm the 2$^1/_4$ cups stock with the cinnamon, cardamom, salt, and pepper while you prepare the other ingredients. Soak the raisins in the $^1/_2$ cup hot water or stock.

2 Place 1 tablespoon butter in a small skillet and turn the heat to medium. When it melts, add the pine nuts and cook, stirring occasionally, until they brown lightly, about 5 minutes. Set aside.

3 Place 2 tablespoons butter in a medium saucepan and turn the heat to medium-low. When it melts, add the couscous and cook, stirring, until it is coated with butter, about 1 minute. Strain the stock or water and add it all at once. Bring to a boil, then turn the heat down to its minimum. Cover and cook until all the liquid is absorbed, 5 to 8 minutes. Drain the raisins and gently stir them in, along with the pine nuts and remaining butter. Fluff with a fork to break up any lumps. Garnish and serve.

Eight Dishes to Serve with Couscous

Like polenta, couscous is best served with savory stews, whether meat or vegetable. Some ideas:

1. Braised Cauliflower with Curry and Tomatoes (page 555)
2. Indian-Spiced Duck with Lentils (page 416)
3. Chicken, Provençal-Style (page 368)
4. Beef Stew, Greek-Style (page 436)
5. Sweet Beef Brisket with Garlic (Tsimmes) (page 438)
6. Veal Stew, Central Asian–Style (page 447)
7. Braised Pork with Vinegar and Bay (page 468)
8. Stewed Chickpeas with Chicken, or its variation, Stewed Chickpeas with Vegetables (page 519)

The Basics of Hominy, or Pozole

This traditional food of Native Americans is made from dried corn that has been treated with slaked limestone or wood ash, which expands the kernels. (Ground, hominy becomes masa harina, the meal used to make tortillas.) Usually sold canned and ready to eat, hominy is increasingly found dried, in natural foods and specialty stores. It's better that way, although cooking it takes some time. (You can save some of that time by using a pressure cooker; see Pressure-Cooked Tough Grains, page 181.)

Basic Hominy
Makes 4 servings

Time: At least 2 hours, largely unattended

Canned hominy, like canned beans, is convenient. But it lacks the intense flavor of corn you get from reconstituting and cooking dried hominy, or pozole. The method is the same as that for dried beans; soaking overnight speeds cooking but is not essential.

> 1 cup whole dried hominy (pozole)
> Salt

1 Rinse the hominy once, then soak it in water to cover overnight, if time allows.

2 Drain and place in a medium saucepan with water to cover by at least 2 inches. Bring the water to a boil, turn the heat to medium-low, and simmer, stirring occasionally, until the hominy is tender, at least 1 hour (and quite often twice that long). Season with salt and drain. Or drain partially and refrigerate, covered with some of the cooking water, for 2 or 3 days.

Creamed Hominy
Makes 4 servings

Time: About 20 minutes

This is good, old-fashioned creamed corn.

> 1 recipe Basic Hominy, well drained
> 1 cup cream, half-and-half, or whole milk
> 2 tablespoons butter
> Salt and freshly ground black pepper to taste

1 Roughly chop about half the kernels of hominy. Combine the chopped and whole kernels in a medium saucepan with the cream and turn the heat to medium-high.

2 Bring to a boil, stirring occasionally, then turn the heat to medium-low. Simmer, stirring occasionally, until most of the cream is absorbed, 5 to 10 minutes.

3 Stir in the butter and season with salt and pepper.

Flash-Cooked Hominy with Kale or Collards
Makes 4 servings

Time: About 20 minutes

This is a strong-tasting side dish, one to serve with spicy grilled meats or poultry.

> About 1 pound young kale or collards, or other dark green, washed (see The Basics of Buying Vegetables, page 530) and very well dried
> 3 tablespoons peanut (preferred) or canola or other oil
> 1 tablespoon seeded and chopped jalapeño or other hot chile, or to taste; or use 4 or 5 dried red chiles, or to taste
> 1 clove garlic, smashed and peeled, plus 1 tablespoon minced garlic
> 1½ cups cooked or canned hominy, very well drained
> Salt and freshly ground black pepper to taste
> Freshly squeezed juice of 2 limes, plus more if needed

1 Chop the greens into fairly small pieces; no dimension should be more than 2 inches.

2 Put the oil in a wok or large skillet and turn the heat to high. A minute later, add the chile and the crushed garlic. Cook, stirring, until the garlic turns brown, 3 to 5 minutes. Turn off the heat and scoop out and discard the solids.

3 Return the heat to high and add the hominy. Cook, stirring occasionally but not constantly, until the kernels begin to brown, about 5 minutes.

4 Add the chopped greens and minced garlic. Cook, still over high heat, stirring almost constantly, until the greens wilt and begin to char at the edges, 5 to 8 minutes.

5 Season with salt and pepper and add the lime juice. Taste, adjust seasoning—add more lime juice if necessary—and serve immediately.

The Basics of Kasha

Buckwheat is the hardiest of grains, because it isn't a grain at all but a grass related to rhubarb. It grows where true grains do not, in the poor soil and bad weather of northern Europe and central Asia. It's healthy, it's cheap, it's easy to cook, and it has flavor. But it isn't popular, because its flavor is distinctive. Some might say that buckwheat is an acquired taste, but it sometimes seems you either love it or hate it, and that's that. (If, however, a taste for buckwheat could be acquired, it would be through eating Kasha Varnishkes, the noodle dish on page 154.) It is certainly among the strongest-tasting grains, with a flavor unlike that of anything else: bold, toasty, and earthy.

You can find plain buckwheat, but it is difficult. Most of it is roasted, which turns it into kasha. (Some buckwheat is milled into flour, to be made into pancakes, soba noodles, and pizzoccheri, the buckwheat noodles of northern Italy.) Kasha—also called

buckwheat groats—is sold in every supermarket; you want the whole variety, not the cracked, which is best used as a porridge.

Basic Kasha
Makes 4 servings

Time: About 20 minutes

Traditionally, kasha is combined with egg before roasting in a skillet. A brief toss in a little oil achieves much the same effect.

1 egg, 2 tablespoons canola or other neutral oil,
    or 2 tablespoons rendered chicken fat (page 358)
1 cup whole kasha
Salt and freshly ground black pepper to taste
2 cups chicken, beef, or vegetable stock, or water,
    warmed (see "Soups" for stock recipes)
1 to 2 tablespoons butter or rendered chicken fat
    (optional)

1 If you're using the egg, beat it, then toss it in a bowl with the kasha. Place the mixture in a heavy, deep large skillet along with some salt and pepper, and turn the heat to medium-high. Cook, stirring, until the mixture smells toasty, about 3 minutes.

2 If you're using the oil or chicken fat, place it in a heavy, deep skillet and turn the heat to medium-high. A minute later, add the kasha, along with some salt and pepper, and cook, stirring, until the mixture smells toasty, about 3 minutes.

3 Turn the heat to a minimum and carefully add the liquid. Cover and cook until the liquid is absorbed, about 15 minutes. Turn off the heat. Serve immediately or let the kasha sit for up to 30 minutes before serving.

4 When you're ready to serve, fluff with a fork, adding the optional butter at the same time.

Kasha with Golden Brown Onions: Place 3 cups chopped onions in a large skillet and turn the heat to medium. Cover the skillet and cook, for about 10 minutes, until the onions are dry and almost sticking to the pan. Add ⅓ cup rendered chicken fat, butter, or canola or other neutral oil, raise the heat to medium-high, and cook, stirring, until the onions are nicely browned, another 10 minutes or so. Stir into the cooked kasha just before serving.

The Basics of Millet

A small, high-protein grain that looks like couscous and is a staple throughout Africa and in much of Asia, millet is fast-cooking and can be made using any white rice recipe. It can also fill in for couscous, or even polenta, because it has a somewhat gummy texture when cooked. All millet is hulled before sale; the outer layer is inedible.

Basic Millet

Makes 4 servings

Time: About 20 minutes

If you prefer, you can "dry-toast" the millet with no fat; just cook it over medium heat, stirring, for about 3 minutes, before adding the liquid.

  2 tablespoons extra-virgin olive oil or butter
  1 cup millet, rinsed
  Salt and freshly ground black pepper to taste
  2 cups chicken, beef, or vegetable stock, or water, warmed (see "Soups" for stock recipes)
  Minced fresh parsley leaves for garnish

1 Place the oil or butter in a medium saucepan or medium-to-large skillet and turn the heat to medium.

When the oil is hot or the butter melts, add the millet, salt, and pepper, and stir. Cook, stirring, until the millet is glossy, just a minute or two.

2 Add the liquid, cover, and turn the heat to low. Cook about 20 minutes, or until the liquid is absorbed and the millet is tender. Turn off the heat, garnish, and serve immediately, or let the millet sit for up to 30 minutes before serving.

The Basics of Quinoa

Like millet, quinoa is a tiny grain that is known by few Americans. But it has much more going for it: Handled correctly, it cooks up light and fluffy, and has a light, grassy, easy-to-like flavor. There are literally thousands of varieties of quinoa, and they vary in intensity of flavor and in color, from pale beige to nearly black. All have this in common: The tiny grains are coated with saponin, a natural insect repellent that must be removed before cooking. Although most quinoa is washed before you buy it, it's worth rinsing a couple of times before proceeding with any recipe.

Basic Quinoa

Makes 4 servings

Time: 20 minutes

As with any other grain, a pat of butter at the end of cooking does no harm. But quinoa is flavorful and light without it. Quinoa is also great with a spoonful or two of Basic Pesto or any of its variations (page 766) stirred into it.

  1 cup quinoa, rinsed in several changes of water
  2 cups water, plus ¼ cup if needed
  Salt and freshly ground black pepper to taste

1 Combine the quinoa, water, salt, and pepper in a medium saucepan and turn the heat to high. Bring to a boil, cover, lower the heat, and simmer gently for about 15 minutes.

2 If all the water has been absorbed but the quinoa is not tender, add ¹/₄ cup water and continue to cook until tender. If any water remains, remove the lid and raise the heat a bit. Cook, stirring, until the water evaporates.

Quinoa "Pilaf"

Makes 4 servings

Time: About 30 minutes

You can simply dry-roast quinoa in the skillet before adding stock or water, but this method is even better.

2 tablespoons peanut or olive oil
¹/₂ cup chopped onion or leek
1 cup quinoa, rinsed in several changes of water
Salt and freshly ground black pepper to taste
1³/₄ cups chicken, beef, or vegetable stock, or water, warmed (see "Soups" for stock recipes)

1 Place the oil in a medium-to-large, deep skillet and turn the heat to medium. A minute later, add the onion and cook, stirring occasionally, until the onion softens, about 5 minutes.

2 Add the quinoa and cook, stirring, for a good 5 minutes. Season with salt and pepper, then add the liquid all at once.

3 Cover and cook until the quinoa is tender, about 15 minutes. If all the liquid has been absorbed but the quinoa is not tender, add ¹/₄ cup water and continue to cook until tender. If any liquid remains, remove the lid and raise the heat a bit; cook, stirring, until the liquid evaporates.

Quinoa Stuffing with Bacon and Nuts

Makes enough to stuff a 6- to 8-pound bird

Time: 30 minutes

Use this stuffing with any poultry; capons, increasingly hard to find, are especially terrific. Double or triple the quantities here for turkey, depending on size.

¹/₂ pound good bacon
2 cups chopped onions
1 teaspoon minced garlic
1 recipe Basic Quinoa (page 195), about 2 cups
¹/₂ cup pine nuts or walnuts
¹/₂ cup dry white wine (preferred), chicken, beef, or vegetable stock, or water (see "Soups" for stock recipes)
1¹/₂ teaspoons fresh thyme leaves or about
    ³/₄ teaspoon dried thyme, or 1 teaspoon fresh or dried rosemary or winter savory
1 bay leaf
Salt and freshly ground black pepper to taste

1 If using slab bacon, cut it into ¹/₂-inch cubes. Cook the bacon cubes or strips in a large skillet over medium heat, stirring or turning, until crisp but not burned. Remove the bacon with a slotted spoon and drain all but 3 tablespoons of the fat from the skillet.

2 Still over medium heat, add the onions and cook, stirring, until softened, about 5 minutes; add the garlic, quinoa, nuts, liquid, thyme, bay leaf, and bacon (crumble if using strips).

3 Cook for 2 minutes, stirring. Season to taste with salt—you may not need any—and pepper, and remove from the heat. Cool to room temperature, remove and discard the bay leaf, then stuff the bird and roast it.

The Basics of Rice

There are essentially two kinds of rice: long and short grain. (Technically, almost all rice is *Oryza sativa* and, within that species, there are *O. sativa indica*, long grain, and *O. sativa japonica*, short grain.) But within each of those categories are many, many varieties (probably forty thousand or more in all), and many different ways in which the basic grain is treated.

By far the majority of rice eaten in this country is long grain, although Asian immigrants and our new-found love for risotto are changing that. Long-grain rice, handled correctly, cooks in separate, firm, dry kernels, a tendency that can be enhanced by cooking the rice in butter or oil before adding liquid. Basmati and most other aromatic rices are long grain.

Short-grain (and so-called medium-grain) rice cooks up soft, moist, and a little sticky, because its outer layer softens readily and absorbs more liquid—and also more flavor—than long-grain rice (or, in fact, any other commonly cooked starchy food). This tendency can be mitigated by cooking the rice gently, or taken advantage of by stirring the rice during cooking—as in risotto—which allows more of the starch to leach out, making for a rice dish that is downright creamy.

The other major distinction in rice is how it is milled. Like many other grains, all rice grows with a husk. Inside the husk, which is always removed, is a layer of bran. Brown rice is rice with an intact bran layer. It takes longer to cook, largely because it takes longer for the water to penetrate the bran layer and soften the starch, and it never becomes soft—bran is largely unaffected by cooking. It is more nutritious than white rice (even "enriched" white rice), especially in its thiamine content. But since most Americans don't eat rice for its nutrients, this isn't necessarily important.

Brown rice also contains far more fiber, a distinct advantage. But the culinary history of grains is the history of refinement: People generally prefer white rice, pearled barley, and white flour; it's not a choice that people make based on nutrients. For those who want to compromise, there is rice that is milled so that it falls halfway between brown and white rice, and has some of the qualities of each—faster cooking than brown rice, it's a little crunchier than white, with a higher fiber content.

So most rice is "white": The bran is completely removed, and the kernel fully milled, or polished. Some white rice is parboiled or "converted" (such as Uncle Ben's), which means it is steamed before milling. This process forces some of the nutrients back into the kernel, making the rice somewhat more nutritious than other white rice (but still less so than brown rice). But converted rice is relatively expensive, and does not have the flavor of "ordinary" white rice. Instant ("minute") rice is precooked; you just reconstitute it at home. But it is expensive, and its flavor is closer to that of cardboard than to most other rices; since rice cooking is easy anyway, you don't need it.

I recommend buying standard white rice, whether long- or short-grain, in five- or ten-pound bags. I recommend that you buy domestic product, for two reasons: The United States is a minor but significant producer and exporter of rice, and our production is high quality; and some imported rice is coated with talc, and requires a thorough washing before use. Just look for a good price, and for unbroken kernels. Note that much American rice is called Carolina rice (and, of course, Carolina is also a brand name), but little rice is actually grown in the Carolinas anymore.

As for the more subtle distinctions among specialty rices:

- Basmati is the most important long-grain specialty rice. It is extra-long-grain, thin, cream-colored, and intensely aromatic, filling the kitchen with an alluring aroma from the moment it begins to cook. Most basmati is imported, making it relatively expensive, but it is incomparable stuff. There are other aromatic rices—Texmati, Wild Pecan, Popcorn (all brand names)—and they are good. But they are usually no less expensive than imported basmati.

- Wehani is another domestic aromatic long grain, but it's sold brown—that is, unpolished. It has a deep bronze-brown color and a very sweet flavor—nice stuff. It can be cooked and used like regular brown rice.
- Jasmine rice is also long grain, and also aromatic. But it cooks as if it were short grain; that is, moist and somewhat sticky. It has a wonderful aroma and flavor, and is associated with Thai food.
- Short-grain rice seems exotic to many Americans, but it is a standard product throughout most of the rest of the world, where it is preferred to long-grain varieties.

    To us, the most important specialty short-grain rices are Arborio and its cousins (Vialone Nano, Roma, Carnaroli, and so on), all of which are grown in northern Italy (or eastern Spain), and which are used almost exclusively to make risotto (or paella). You will most easily find Superfino Arborio, and that's what you want. Note (as I do in the recipes for risotti, pages 208–211), that any short- or medium-grain rice will make acceptable risotto. Arborio gives the best results, but if you must resort to other short-grain rice for reasons of economy (Arborio costs five times as much as standard rice) or convenience (not every supermarket stocks Arborio), don't worry about it.
- Other short-grain rices worth noting are red rice, a brown short-grain not unlike Wehani; black rice, a semipolished rice that is nice to cook with white rice (and will stain it purple); sticky (or glutinous) rice, a very-short-grain Asian rice that is, as you've already guessed, very sticky, and is great for desserts.
- Wild rice, by the way, is not a rice but a grass; nevertheless, it belongs in this chapter, and you'll find it on page 215.

Cooking rice is easy, or should be. In fact, it's so easy that there's hardly a method that won't work for it (you can cook rice in a pressure cooker or microwave but—with the exception of brown rice—it won't save you any time, and it certainly isn't more convenient). Basically, you cook it like pasta (see Simple Precooked Grains, page 181), or you combine it with one and a half to two times as much water and cook until the water is absorbed. If you cook rice every day, you might want to investigate an electric rice cooker, which works automatically and quite well.

But there are many subtleties involved in cooking rice. These are explained in the recipes that follow.

Basic Long-Grain Rice
Makes 4 servings

Time: About 20 minutes

As discussed above, cooking rice is easy. Just be sure to use gentle heat once the water comes to a boil. If the pot dries out before the rice is tender, add a couple of tablespoons of hot or boiling water and re-cover.

1 1/2 cups long-grain rice
2 1/4 cups any stock or water (see "Soups" for stock recipes)
1 teaspoon salt, or to taste

① Combine the rice, liquid, and salt in a medium saucepan and turn the heat to medium-high. Bring to a boil.

2 Turn the heat to medium-low and cover. Cook for 15 minutes, or until the water is absorbed and the rice is tender. At this point:

• If the water is not absorbed but the rice is tender, uncover and raise the heat a bit. Cook, stirring (you can add a little butter or oil if you like to prevent sticking), until the liquid evaporates.

• If the water is not absorbed and the rice is not yet tender, re-cover and check in 3 minutes.

• If the water is absorbed and the rice is not yet tender, add a few tablespoons of hot or boiling liquid, re-cover, and check in 3 minutes.

Basic Short- or Medium-Grain Rice, Version I: Short-grained rice absorbs less water before it is done. Wash the rice very well, in several changes of water, until the water runs clear. Then follow the identical procedure as above, using 2 cups water to 1¹/₂ cups rice.

Basic Short- or Medium-Grain Rice, Version II

Makes 4 servings

Time: About 45 minutes

This method takes more time, but is very easy and reliable, and produces rice that keeps well in the pot. It produces sticky, clumpy rice that is easy to eat with chopsticks and nice and chewy.

1¹/₂ cups short- or medium-grain rice, well rinsed
    and drained
2¹/₂ cups water
1 teaspoon salt, or to taste

1 Combine all ingredients in a medium saucepan and let sit for about 30 minutes. The rice will absorb much of the water.

2 Cover the pan, place it over high heat, and bring to a boil. Turn the heat to medium-low and cook, undisturbed, for 15 minutes.

3 Turn off the heat. The rice will be done in 10 minutes, or will hold for up to 1 hour.

Fast-Cooked Short- or Medium-Grain Rice: This is considerably faster because you don't need to soak the rice first: Combine all ingredients in a small saucepan and turn the heat to high. When the water starts boiling, turn the heat down to medium-high. In 8 to 12 minutes small craters will appear on the surface of the rice, indicating that the water is almost all absorbed. Cover the pot, turn the heat to low, and cook until tender, about 5 more minutes. Serve immediately or let the rice sit for up to an hour before serving.

Sushi Rice

Makes 6 or more servings

Time: About 40 minutes

Sushi rice is short-grain rice cooked by either of the above two methods (Version II or Fast-Cooked Short- or Medium-Grain Rice), stirred with a sweet-sour-salt mixture as it cools. You can roll it in nori seaweed (instructions are below), either alone or with cooked or raw fish or vegetables.

1 recipe Basic Short- or Medium-Grain Rice, Version II
    or Fast-Cooked Short- or Medium-Grain Rice
¹/₃ cup rice or other mild vinegar
¹/₄ cup sugar
1 tablespoon salt

1 While the rice is cooking, combine the vinegar, sugar, and salt in a small saucepan. Turn the heat to medium and cook, stirring, until the sugar dissolves, less than 5 minutes. Place the vinegar mixture in a bowl, set inside another bowl filled with ice and stir it to cool.

2 When the rice is done, place it in a bowl more than twice the size needed to hold the rice—probably the largest bowl you have. Begin to toss the hot rice with a flat wooden paddle or spoon or rubber spatula—as if you were folding egg whites into a batter, but much faster and not quite as gently. While you're tossing, sprinkle the rice with the vinegar mixture (if the paddle becomes encrusted with rice, dip it in some water, then shake the water off and proceed). The idea is to cool the rice quickly as it absorbs the vinegar.

3 Sushi rice will not keep for long, but if you cover it with a damp cloth you can wait a couple of hours to proceed. Or eat it right away: Place it in bowls topped with raw or cooked vegetables or fish, or bits of cooked meat; drizzle with soy sauce and serve with Wasabi (page 764) and Quick Pickled Ginger (page 107).

Sushi Rolls

Makes 6 rolls

Nori is easy to roll; by the end of your first session, you'll be confident. Use any filling you like for the rolls, but keep the quantity of the filling down. Sushi rolls should be mostly rice, sparked by simple flavorings. You'll need a bamboo mat made for rolling sushi (they're cheap, and available at any Asian market).

6 or more sheets of nori seaweed, about 1 package
  (also called laver; see page 602)
1 cup water
2 tablespoons rice or other mild vinegar
1 recipe Sushi Rice (above)
Wasabi (page 764)
Thin strips peeled cucumber
Toasted Sesame Seeds (page 776)
Quick Pickled Ginger (page 107)
Soy sauce

1 Begin by toasting 6 squares of nori: Use tongs to hold them, one at a time, over a medium-high flame for a few seconds, until they change color. If you have an electric stove, run them under the broiler for 15 seconds to a minute on each side. Mix 1 cup water with the vinegar (this is called "hand water").

2 Place a square of nori, shiny side down, on the bamboo mat. Spread it evenly with $1/2$-inch layer of sushi rice, leaving a 1-inch border on all sides; rinse your hands in the hand water as needed. (Although rolling is easy, you won't do it perfectly at first, so you might start with a slightly thinner layer of rice.) Smear the rice with a fingerful of wasabi (careful; it's hot), then top with some cucumber and a few sesame seeds.

3 Use the mat to tightly roll the nori around the rice, forming it into a log; you can unroll the mat at any time and check to see how things are going. This takes a little bit of practice, but is not at all difficult; you'll quickly get the hang of it. Slice the rolls into 1-inch sections and serve with pickled ginger and soy sauce.

Eight Simple Ideas for Sushi Rice

You need not roll sushi rice with bits of food to serve sushi; in fact, *charashi-sushi* is nothing more than sushi rice with garnish on top. Whether you roll or not, here are some frequently seen additions. Use them singly or in combination, but sparingly; sushi is a rice dish. Use Wasabi (page 764) and/or soy sauce for condiments.

1. Thin slices of spanking-fresh raw fish, such as tuna or sea scallops
2. Sliced or chopped simply cooked fish, such as lightly poached and chilled shrimp or cooked crabmeat
3. Bits of smoked or pickled fish, such as smoked salmon or pickled mackerel
4. Chopped umeboshi plums or pickled burdock (available at Asian markets)

5. Thinly sliced cucumber, scallions, shiitake ("black") mushrooms, and/or other fresh vegetables

6. Pieces of avocado

7. Pickled ginger (available at Asian markets), or freshly grated ginger

8. Crumbled toasted nori (see above recipe) or chopped fresh shiso, available at Asian markets and stores selling many fresh herbs

Lemon Rice

Makes 4 servings

Time: 15 minutes with precooked rice

With great thanks to Judy Lieberman, one of my oldest friends and informal teachers. You can use almost any precooked grains in this recipe.

4 tablespoons (¹/₂ stick) butter (preferred) or extra-virgin olive oil
3 to 4 cups cooked rice, made by any method
Salt and lots of freshly ground black pepper
1 teaspoon minced garlic
Juice of 2 lemons, plus more if needed
1 lemon, quartered

① Heat half the butter or oil over medium-high heat in a large non-stick skillet; when the butter foam subsides or the oil is hot, spoon in the cooked rice, tossing and stirring.

② Season with salt to taste, lots of pepper, the garlic, and most of the lemon juice. Cook, stirring frequently, for about 5 minutes, or until hot. Stir in the remaining butter or oil and cook for 1 minute.

③ Remove the rice from the pan to a platter, add the remaining lemon juice and serve, with lemon quarters.

Persian Rice with Potatoes

Makes 4 servings

Time: At least 1 hour with precooked rice

You must use precooked rice for this dish, and it's best to use rice that has been cooked by the pasta-like method described on page 198 (see The Basics of Cooking Grains). Other than that, the only "secret" is to use a pot with a very tight-fitting lid.

8 tablespoons (1 stick) butter, plus 1 tablespoon
2 large potatoes, peeled and thinly sliced
1 medium onion, thinly sliced
2 cups cooked rice, slightly undercooked, rinsed, and drained
Salt and freshly ground black pepper to taste
¹/₂ cup blanched slivered almonds

① Melt all but the tablespoon of butter in a small saucepan. Use a little of it to film the bottom of a medium saucepan or casserole with a heavy, tight-fitting lid. Arrange the potato slices to completely cover the bottom of the casserole. Top with the onion and a thin layer of rice. Drizzle about half the melted butter over this and season with salt and pepper.

② Pile on the rest of the rice and drizzle on the remaining melted butter. Season with salt and pepper. Put the top on the casserole and place over low heat. Cook, undisturbed, for about an hour.

③ Ten minutes before the dish is finished, melt the remaining butter in a small skillet over medium heat. Add the almonds and cook, stirring, until very lightly browned, about 5 minutes.

④ Stir the almonds into the rice without disturbing the bottom layer. To serve, scoop up some of the rice, then dig to the bottom of the casserole and scrape out some of the potatoes, which should be nicely browned.

Rice Pilaf

Makes 4 servings

Time: About 30 minutes

There are many definitions of pilaf, but two are common to all: The rice must be briefly cooked in oil or butter before adding liquid, and the liquid must be flavorful. The oil or butter may be flavored with vegetables, herbs, or spices; the liquid may be anything from lobster stock to yogurt; and other foods may be added to the pot.

> 2 tablespoons butter or oil
> 1 cup chopped onion
> 1 1/2 cups long-grain rice
> Salt and freshly ground black pepper
> 2 1/2 cups chicken, beef, vegetable stock, or water, heated to the boiling point (see "Soups" for stock recipes)
> Minced fresh parsley leaves for garnish

1 Place the butter or oil in a large, deep skillet which can later be covered and turn the heat to medium-high. When the butter melts or the oil is hot, add the onion. Cook, stirring, until the onion softens but does not begin to brown, 5 to 8 minutes.

2 Add the rice all at once, turn the heat to medium, and stir until the rice is glossy and completely coated with oil or butter, 2 or 3 minutes. Season well, then turn the heat down to low and add the liquid, all at once. Cover the pan.

3 Cook for 15 minutes, then check the rice. When the rice is tender and the liquid is absorbed, it's done. If not, cook for 2 or 3 minutes and check again. Check the seasoning, garnish, and serve immediately.

Pilaf with Onions, Raisins, and Pine Nuts: In Step 2, stir in 1/2 cup raisins or dried currants and 1/4 cup pine nuts along with the rice. Finish as above.

Four Ways to Make Yellow Rice

Each of these has a different flavor; all are bright yellow.

1. Cook the onion in two tablespoons Achiote Oil (page 775).
2. Sprinkle the onion with one teaspoon ground turmeric.
3. Add a pinch of saffron to the stock while warming it.
4. Sprinkle the onion with two teaspoons curry powder, or with one-half teaspoon each ground cumin, turmeric, and ginger.

Pilaf with Indian Spices

Biryani

Makes 4 servings

Time: About 30 minutes

To make this a whole-meal dish, add small pieces of boneless chicken along with the stock, and increase the spices by half.

> A few threads of saffron or 1 teaspoon ground turmeric
> 2 1/2 cups chicken, beef, or vegetable stock, or water, heated to the boiling point (see "Soups" for stock recipes)
> 2 tablespoons butter or oil
> 6 cardamom pods or 2 teaspoons ground cardamom
> Pinch ground cloves
> 1/2 cinnamon stick or 1/2 teaspoon ground cinnamon
> 1 bay leaf
> 1 cup chopped onion
> 1 tablespoon peeled and minced or grated fresh ginger or 1 teaspoon ground ginger
> 1 1/2 cups long-grain rice, preferably basmati
> Salt and freshly ground black pepper
> Minced cilantro leaves for garnish

1 If you're using saffron, put it in the stock.

2 Place the butter or oil in a large, deep skillet which can later be covered and turn the heat to medium-high. When the butter melts or the oil is hot, turn the heat down to medium and add the cardamom, cloves, cinnamon, bay leaf, and turmeric if you are using it. Cook, stirring very frequently, until the spices are fragrant, about 2 minutes.

3 Add the onion and ginger and cook, stirring, until the onion softens, about 5 minutes. Add the rice all at once, turn the heat to medium, and stir until the rice is glossy and coated with oil or butter, 2 or 3 minutes. Season well, turn the heat down to low, and add the liquid, all at once. Cover.

4 Cook for 15 minutes, then check the rice. When it is tender and the liquid absorbed, it's done. If not, cook for 2 or 3 minutes and check again. Remove the cinnamon stick and the bay leaf, garnish, and serve.

Pilaf with Wine and Tomatoes

Makes 4 servings

Time: 30 minutes

A full-flavored rice dish that's easier than risotto.

- 2 tablespoons olive oil
- 1 cup chopped onion
- 1½ cups long-grain rice
- Salt and freshly ground black pepper
- 1 cup dry white wine (red will also do fine)
- 2 cups chicken, beef, or vegetable stock, or water, heated to the boiling point (see "Soups" for stock recipes)
- About 1 cup chopped tomatoes (canned are fine; don't bother to drain)
- Freshly grated Parmesan cheese (optional)

1 Place the oil in a large, deep skillet which can later be covered and turn the heat to medium-high. When the oil is hot, add the onion. Cook, stirring, until the onion softens but does not begin to brown, 5 to 8 minutes.

2 Add the rice all at once, turn the heat to medium, and stir until the rice is glossy and completely coated with oil, 2 or 3 minutes. Season well, then add the wine and cook, stirring, until some of it has bubbled away, about 2 minutes. Turn the heat to medium-high and add the liquid and the tomatoes.

3 Bring to a boil, then turn the heat to low and cover the pan. Cook for 20 minutes, then check the rice. When the rice is tender and the liquid is absorbed, it's done. If not, cook for 2 or 3 minutes and check again. Serve, topped with grated Parmesan.

Pilaf with Spinach: In Step 1, add 2 cups trimmed, carefully washed, and chopped spinach along with the onion. In Step 2, use white wine and substitute 1 teaspoon minced garlic for the tomatoes.

Rice, Mexican-Style

Arroz Blanco

Makes 4 servings

Time: About 40 minutes

An unusual pilaf in which the rice is cooked for quite a while before adding the seasonings.

- 3 tablespoons canola or other neutral oil
- 1½ cups long-grain rice
- 1 medium onion, minced
- 1 tablespoon minced garlic
- Salt and freshly ground black pepper
- 3 cups chicken, beef, or vegetable stock, or water, warmed (see "Soups" for stock recipes)

① Place the oil in a large, deep skillet which can later be covered and turn the heat to medium. A minute later, add the rice and cook, stirring almost constantly, for 5 to 10 minutes, until it begins to change color but not to brown.

② Add the minced onion and garlic and stir for 30 seconds. Season well.

③ Add the liquid, stir, cover, and turn the heat to low. Cook for 20 minutes, then check the rice. When the rice is tender and the liquid is almost entirely absorbed, turn off the heat and let rest for 10 to 30 minutes before serving.

Rice with Onions

Soubise

Makes 4 to 6 servings

Time: At least 1 hour

This is a kind of pilaf, but probably unlike any other you've had. Its base is slow-cooked onions, which become creamy and almost dissolve when cooked with the rice. The flavor is sweet and delicious.

3 to 4 cups sliced onions
4 tablespoons (¹/₂ stick) butter (preferred) or
    extra-virgin olive oil
1¹/₂ cups long-grain rice
Salt and freshly ground black pepper to taste
1 teaspoon fresh thyme leaves, 2 or 3 sprigs fresh
    thyme, or ¹/₂ teaspoon dried thyme
3 cups chicken, beef, or vegetable stock, or water,
    warmed (see "Soups" for stock recipes)
Minced fresh parsley leaves for garnish

① Place the onions in a large, deep skillet or casserole over medium-low heat. Cover the skillet. Cook, stirring once or twice, until the onions have given up

most of their liquid and are fairly dry but not at all brown, about 10 minutes.

② Remove the cover and turn the heat to medium. Add the butter to the onions. Cook, stirring, until the butter melts and the onions are coated with it. Add the rice, salt, pepper, and thyme.

③ Stir in the liquid, cover, and turn the heat to low. Cook for 30 to 45 minutes, stirring every 10 minutes or so, or until the rice is tender and the liquid absorbed. Garnish and serve.

Coconut Rice

Makes 3 to 4 servings

Time: 20 minutes

A simple and wonderful side dish, essential in the cuisines of the Caribbean. It's so much more delicious than plain rice—and not much more difficult to make—that you may make it your basic rice dish.

1 tablespoon peanut (preferred) or vegetable oil
1 cup long-grain white rice
Salt and freshly ground black pepper to taste
2 cups canned or Fresh Coconut Milk (page 291),
    warmed

① Place the oil in a medium saucepan over medium heat. Stir in the rice and cook, stirring, until it becomes translucent, about 2 minutes. Season with salt and pepper and stir in the coconut milk.

② Bring to a boil, turn the heat to low, cover, and cook for about 15 minutes, or until all the liquid is absorbed. The rice can rest, covered, for 10 to 15 minutes before serving.

Coconut Rice with Beans: Stir in ¹/₂ to 1 cup cooked pinto, kidney, or other red beans along with the coconut milk. Add a pinch of allspice, ¹/₂ teaspoon

Some grain dishes must be eaten the minute they're done. Others are not bad eaten standing in front of the refrigerator the next day. Still others reheat well. Here's a list of those that retain much of their quality for a day or two. To serve as a cold salad, moisten with a little oil, vinegar, stock, or whatever seems appropriate. To reheat, cook gently in a little oil or butter. I include risotto in this list even though it is heresy to do so; but, like pasta, risotto is frequently eaten cold although few people admit to it.

1. Barley "Risotto" with Mushrooms, page 184
2. Bulgur Pilaf with Vermicelli, page 186
3. Couscous with Raisins and Pine Nuts, page 192
4. Creamed Hominy, page 193
5. Flash-Cooked Hominy with Kale or Collards, page 193
6. Quinoa "Pilaf," page 196
7. Lemon Rice, page 201
8. Rice Pilaf, page 202
9. Pilaf with Onions, Raisins, and Pine Nuts, page 202
10. Pilaf with Indian Spices (Biryani), page 202
11. Any risotto, pages 208–211
12. Fried Rice with Egg, page 212
13. Shrimp or Pork Fried Rice with Peas, page 212
14. Fried Rice with Greens, page 212
15. Stir-Fried Brown Rice with Vegetables and Soy, page 214
16. Brown Rice with Lentils and Apricots, page 214
17. Wild Rice with Curried Nuts, page 215
18. Wild Rice with Vegetables and Dried Mushrooms, page 216

ground cinnamon, or 1 teaspoon minced fresh oregano or marjoram or $1/2$ teaspoon dried.

Coconut Rice with Chipotles: Soak 2 dried chipotle chiles (or to taste) in 1 cup very hot water. Stem, seed, and mince them when they are softened. Add them to the pot along with the rice in Step 1. Proceed as above.

Spice-Scented or Herbed Rice

There are two easy ways to infuse the flavors of herbs and spices into rice as it cooks. The first—which is most useful for spices whose flavors benefit from long cooking—is to stir them into a bit of oil at the beginning. The second, best for more fragile herbs, is to reserve at least a portion of them to stir in at the end. Here are a couple of examples of each.

Cumin-Scented Rice

Makes 4 servings

Time: 20 to 30 minutes

Make this with cumin, anise, caraway, or other spices, or with curry or chili powder (page 777), or any other spice mixture you like. Generally, a teaspoon to a tablespoon of spice is about the right amount; use your judgment based on your own palate.

2 tablespoons peanut or olive oil
1 small onion, minced
1 tablespoon cumin seeds
$1^1/2$ cups long-grain rice
Salt and freshly ground black pepper to taste
$2^1/2$ cups chicken, beef, or vegetable stock, or water, heated to the boiling point (see "Soups" for stock recipes)
Minced cilantro leaves for garnish

1 Place the oil in a medium saucepan or skillet over medium heat. A minute later, add the onion and cook, stirring, until it wilts, 3 to 5 minutes.

2 Add the cumin seeds and stir to coat with oil; cook, stirring frequently, for 1 minute. Add the rice and cook, stirring, for about 1 minute; add salt and pepper.

3 Turn the heat to low and add the liquid. Cover and cook 15 minutes, or until the liquid is absorbed. Garnish and serve.

Cumin-Scented Rice with Shrimp

Makes 4 servings

Time: 30 to 45 minutes

You can follow this same basic recipe to make spice-scented rice with chicken or meat; just be sure to add the chunks with enough time to cook through before the rice finishes. Generally, however, if the pieces are small and the meat tender, just a few minutes will suffice.

> 24 medium-to-large shrimp, with shells
> 2$\frac{1}{2}$ cups water (optional) (if you need to make stock; see Step 1 below)
> 2 tablespoons olive oil
> 1 small onion, minced
> 1 tablespoon cumin seeds
> 1$\frac{1}{2}$ cups long-grain rice
> Salt and freshly ground black pepper to taste
> 2$\frac{1}{2}$ cups chicken or fish stock, heated to the boiling point (see "Soups" for stock recipes), or make stock with water and shrimp shells as described below
> Minced fresh parsley or cilantro leaves for garnish

1 Peel the shrimp; if you need to make stock, gently heat 2$\frac{1}{2}$ cups water with the shells in a medium

saucepan as you prepare the other ingredients. Cut the shrimp in half.

2 Place the oil in a medium saucepan or skillet over medium heat. A minute later, add the onion and cook, stirring, until it wilts, 3 to 5 minutes.

3 Add the cumin seeds and stir to coat with oil; cook, stirring frequently, for 1 minute. Add the rice and cook, stirring, for about 1 minute; add salt and pepper.

4 Turn the heat to low. Strain the shrimp stock if necessary; add it or other stock to the rice. Cover and cook 15 minutes, until almost all the liquid is absorbed. Stir in the shrimp, re-cover, and cook an additional 2 to 3 minutes, or until the shrimp is pink. Garnish and serve immediately.

Rice with Fresh Herbs

Makes 4 servings

Time: About 30 minutes

This is especially wonderful with butter and basmati or other aromatic rice.

> 2 tablespoons butter or oil
> $\frac{1}{2}$ cup minced fresh chervil, basil, shiso, mint, parsley, cilantro, or other leafy herb, or a mixture
> 1$\frac{1}{2}$ cups basmati or other long-grain rice
> 2$\frac{1}{4}$ cups water
> Salt and freshly ground black pepper to taste

1 Melt the butter over medium heat in a medium saucepan. Cook half the herb in the butter for 30 seconds. Add the rice and cook, stirring, until the rice is coated with butter.

2 Add the water and some salt and pepper. Turn the heat up a bit and bring the mixture to a boil. Cover and turn the heat to medium-low.

3 After 15 minutes, turn off the heat but leave the cover on the rice. Wait 10 minutes, then stir in the remaining herb. Check the seasoning and serve immediately.

Rice with Pesto or Herb Oil
Makes 4 servings

Time: About 30 minutes

Use a mild-flavored oil here so that the dominant flavors are those of rice and herb.

1 tablespoon canola or other neutral oil
1¹/₂ cups basmati or other long-grain rice
2¹/₄ cups water
Salt and freshly ground black pepper to taste
¹/₂ cup Basic Pesto (page 766) or 1 cup fresh herb
   of your choice: chives, parsley, chervil, or cilantro,
   ¹/₄ cup canola or other neutral oil,
   and 1 to 2 tablespoons water if needed

① Heat the tablespoon of oil in a medium saucepan over medium heat. Add the rice and cook, stirring, until the rice is coated with oil.

② Add the water and season with salt and pepper. Turn the heat up a bit and bring the mixture to a boil. Cover and turn the heat to medium-low.

③ If you do not have pesto: While the rice is cooking, rinse the herb and place it in the container of a blender or small food processor. Turn the machine on and gradually add the ¹/₄ cup oil. Blend or process until smooth, stopping the machine now and then to stir down the mixture. If necessary, add a tablespoon or two of water to the mixture; it should be the texture of heavy cream.

④ After 15 minutes, turn off the heat under the rice, but leave the cover on. Wait 10 minutes, then stir in the pesto or herb oil. Check the seasoning and serve immediately.

Short-Grain Rice with Chives
Makes 4 servings

Time: 45 minutes

This is what you might call "faux" risotto—it takes less work but still makes a fairly creamy dish.

4 tablespoons (¹/₂ stick) butter or olive oil
1 small onion, minced
¹/₂ cup peeled and minced carrot
1 cup Arborio or other short-grain rice
3¹/₂ cups chicken, beef, or vegetable stock, or water
   (see "Soups" for stock recipes)
Salt and freshly ground black pepper
¹/₂ cup minced fresh chives, plus 1 tablespoon
   for garnish

① Place 2 tablespoons of butter in a medium saucepan over medium heat; when it melts, add the onion and carrot. Turn the heat to medium-low and cook, stirring, until soft, about 10 minutes.

② Add the rice and stir to coat with butter. Add the liquid, all at once, season with salt and pepper, and simmer, uncovered, over medium heat, stirring occasionally.

③ When all the liquid has been absorbed, 15 to 20 minutes, stir in ¹/₂ cup chives and the remaining butter. Cook over low heat, stirring, for 3 minutes, and serve immediately, garnished with remaining chives.

The Basics of Risotto

Much fuss has been made about risotto, the creamy rice dish of Italy, in the last ten years or so. Although this unique rice dish has its own set of rules, they are quite simple. Thus there is no reason you cannot make wonderful risotto on your first try. Just remember:

- Arborio rice is preferable but not essential. You can use other short-grained rice imported from Italy or Spain (Valencia rice, the kind used for paella, works well), and get excellent results. Ordinary short- or medium-grain rice is also satisfactory, although the risotto will not be as creamy.
- Liquid must be added a bit at a time, and the heat must be kept fairly high. You must pay attention while making risotto. It doesn't require constant stirring, as some would have you believe, but neither should you leave the stove for more than a minute or so once you start the process.
- You must stir frequently—not constantly, but often. With high heat and a delicate balance between rice and liquid, the danger of scorching is ever present. Non-stick skillets are helpful.
- Do not overcook. As with pasta, you should stop the cooking when there is still a tiny bit of crunch in the center of the rice kernels.
- Experiment. You can add almost anything you like to a risotto: Different combinations of herbs and spices, cooked vegetables, meats, or fish, quick-cooking raw vegetables, meats, or fish, even leftovers. Use the following recipes as springboards to learn how to incorporate different flavors.
- Some risotti (such as classic Risotto alla Milanese) are not compatible with low-fat diets. Yes, you can substitute olive oil for butter. Yes, you can cut it back to the minimum. The dish will be eminently acceptable, but it will not be creamy, rich, breathtaking risotto.

Risotto alla Milanese

Makes 4 to 6 servings

Time: 45 minutes

True risotto alla Milanese contains bone marrow, which—unfortunately—is not that easy to come by.

If you have some, by all means add it at the beginning. It also contains saffron, which is a very wonderful but not absolutely essential addition. This is the traditional dish to precede Classic Osso Buco (page 450).

4 to 6 cups chicken, beef, or vegetable stock,
    or water (see "Soups" for stock recipes)
$^{1}/_{2}$ teaspoon saffron threads (optional)
2 tablespoons butter or extra-virgin olive oil,
    plus 2 tablespoons butter, softened (optional)
1 medium onion, minced
$1^{1}/_{2}$ cups Arborio or other short- or medium-grain rice
Salt and freshly ground black pepper to taste
$^{1}/_{2}$ cup dry white wine
$^{1}/_{2}$ cup freshly grated Parmesan cheese, or to taste

1. Warm the liquid in a medium saucepan over medium heat, crumble the saffron into it, and leave the heat on.

2. Place the butter or oil in a large saucepan or skillet, preferably non-stick, and turn the heat to medium. When it's hot, add the onion and cook, stirring occasionally, until it softens, 3 to 5 minutes.

3. Add the rice and stir until it is coated with butter. Add a little salt and pepper, then the white wine. Stir and let the liquid bubble away.

4. Begin to add the warmed stock, $^{1}/_{2}$ cup or so at a time, stirring after each addition and every minute or so. When the stock is just about evaporated, add more. The mixture should be neither soupy nor dry. Keep the heat medium to medium-high, and stir frequently (constant stirring is not necessary).

5. Begin tasting the rice 20 minutes after you add it; you want it to be tender but with still a tiny bit of crunch. It could take as long as 30 minutes to reach this stage. When it does, add the softened butter and Parmesan. Check the seasoning, adjust if necessary, and serve immediately.

Risotto with Spinach: You can use almost any cooked or raw greens in this variation. In Step 1, omit the saffron. Boil or steam 10 to 16 ounces well-washed spinach (page 604) just until tender. Drain, drop into ice-cold water, drain again, then squeeze dry and chop. Add the spinach to the risotto in Step 3, just after adding the rice.

Risotto with Dried Mushrooms

Makes 4 to 6 servings

Time: 45 minutes

Of course you can use fresh wild mushrooms in this dish; see the first variation. But one great thing about it is that it can be made entirely from staples that you will (or should) always have on hand.

1 to 2 ounces dried porcini mushrooms

About 1½ cups hot water

3 to 5 cups chicken, beef, or vegetable stock, or water (see "Soups" for stock recipes)

2 tablespoons butter or extra-virgin olive oil, plus 2 tablespoons butter, softened (optional)

2 shallots or 1 medium onion, minced

1½ cups Arborio or other short-grain rice

Salt and freshly ground black pepper to taste

½ cup dry white wine

Freshly grated Parmesan cheese (optional)

① Soak the mushrooms in about 1½ cups hot water. Warm the stock over medium heat and leave the heat on.

② When the mushrooms soften, place the butter or oil in a large saucepan or skillet, preferably nonstick, and turn the heat to medium. When it's hot, add the shallots or onion and cook, stirring occasionally, for 1 minute. Drain the mushrooms, reserving the soaking liquid. Squeeze them dry, trim them of any hard spots, chop them, and add them to the cooking shallots or onion. Cook, stirring occasionally, for about 3 minutes; do not let the mushrooms brown.

③ Add the rice and stir until it is coated with butter. Add a little salt and pepper, then the white wine. Stir and let the liquid bubble away.

④ Strain the mushroom-soaking liquid and add it to the rice; stir and let the liquid bubble away. Begin to add the stock, ½ cup or so at a time, stirring after each addition and every minute or so. When the stock is just about evaporated, add more. The mixture should be neither soupy nor dry. Keep the heat medium to medium-high, and stir frequently (constant stirring is not necessary).

⑤ Begin tasting the rice 20 minutes after you add it; you want it to be tender but with still a tiny bit of crunch. It could take as long as 30 minutes to reach this stage. When it does, add the softened butter and Parmesan. Check the seasoning, adjust if necessary, and serve immediately.

Risotto with Fresh Mushrooms: This requires a few more minutes of cooking time. Omit dried mushrooms and Step 1. In Step 2, add 1 to 1½ cups trimmed and chopped fresh mushrooms (whatever variety is available, or a combination) to the cooking shallots and cook, stirring frequently, until they are tender, about 10 minutes. Then proceed with the recipe, adding an additional cup of stock to compensate for the lack of mushroom-soaking liquid.

Risotto with Mushrooms, Garlic, and Anchovies: Use olive oil. In Step 2, use 1 teaspoon minced garlic in place of the shallots or onion, and add it along with the prepared dried mushrooms and 2 minced anchovy fillets; cook, stirring, until the garlic begins to color and the anchovies disintegrate, 2 to 4 minutes. Proceed with the recipe, omitting the finishing butter and Parmesan.

Risotto with Parsley and Basil

Makes 4 to 6 servings

Time: 45 minutes

This is a lower-fat risotto. You can use any fresh herbs you like (chervil is especially good), but do not substitute dried ones.

4 to 6 cups chicken, beef, or vegetable stock,
   or water (see "Soups" for stock recipes)
2 tablespoons extra-virgin olive oil
1 medium onion, minced
1 1/2 cups Arborio or other short- or medium-grain rice
Salt and freshly ground black pepper to taste
1/2 cup dry white wine
1/2 cup chopped fresh parsley leaves
1/2 cup chopped fresh basil leaves
2 tablespoons softened butter (optional)
1/2 cup freshly grated Parmesan cheese, or to taste

1 Warm the stock in a medium saucepan over medium heat and leave the heat on.

2 Place the oil in a large saucepan or skillet, preferably non-stick, and turn the heat to medium. When it's hot, add the onion and cook, stirring occasionally, until it softens, 3 to 5 minutes.

3 Add the rice and stir until it is coated with oil. Add a little salt and pepper, then the white wine. Stir and let the liquid bubble away.

4 Begin to add the warm stock, 1/2 cup or so at a time, stirring after each addition and every minute or so. When the stock is just about evaporated, add more. The mixture should be neither soupy nor dry. Keep the heat medium to medium-high, and stir frequently (constant stirring is not necessary).

5 Begin tasting the rice 20 minutes after you add it; you want it to be tender but with still a tiny bit of crunch. It could take as long as 30 minutes to reach this

stage. When it does, add the butter, herbs, and Parmesan. Adjust the seasoning and serve immediately.

Risotto with Tomatoes: In Step 2, add 1 1/2 cups peeled, seeded, and chopped tomatoes (canned are fine; don't bother to drain) after the onion softens. Proceed with the recipe, decreasing the amount of stock slightly.

Risotto with Pesto: Use 1/2 cup Basic Pesto (page 766), or to taste, in place of the herbs in Step 5.

Risotto with Vegetables

Makes 4 to 6 servings

Time: 45 minutes

Another risotto you can usually make when it seems you have nothing in the house. Of course, if you have more vegetables, use them; just make sure to barely cook them before adding the rice and liquid.

4 to 6 cups chicken, beef, or vegetable stock,
   or water (see "Soups" for stock recipes)
2 tablespoons butter or extra-virgin olive oil,
   plus 2 tablespoons butter, softened (optional)
1 medium onion, minced
1 celery stalk, minced
1 medium carrot, peeled and minced
1 1/2 cups Arborio or other short-grain rice
Salt and freshly ground black pepper to taste
1/2 cup dry white wine
1/2 cup fresh or frozen and thawed peas
Freshly grated Parmesan cheese

1 Warm the stock over medium heat.

2 Place the butter or oil in a large saucepan or skillet, preferably non-stick, and turn the heat to medium. When it's hot, add the onion, celery, and carrot and cook, stirring occasionally, until the onion softens, 3 to 5 minutes.

3 Add the rice and stir until it is coated with butter. Add a little salt and pepper, then the white wine. Stir and let the liquid bubble away.

4 Begin to add the stock, $1/2$ cup or so at a time, stirring after each addition and every minute or so. When the stock is just about evaporated, add more. The mixture should be neither soupy nor dry. Keep the heat medium to medium-high, and stir frequently (constant stirring is not necessary).

5 Begin tasting the rice 20 minutes after you add it; you want it to be tender but with still a tiny bit of crunch. It could take as long as 30 minutes to reach this stage. When it does, add the peas, followed 1 minute later by the softened butter and Parmesan. Check the seasoning, adjust if necessary, and serve immediately.

Risotto with Meat: Use olive oil instead of butter. In Step 2, add 2 to 4 ounces of any of the following: ground meat (beef, pork, veal, or poultry); sausage, removed from its casing; prosciutto, country ham, or pancetta, cut into bits. You may substitute the meat for the vegetables, or add it along with them. Cook 3 to 5 minutes, stirring and breaking up any lumps that form. Proceed with the recipe, omitting the finishing butter (the Parmesan is still nice).

Shrimp Jambalaya

Makes 8 servings

Time: About 1 hour

Some old-fashioned jambalaya recipes start with a pound each of pork, ham, and sausage, and finish with shrimp. If you want to add good ham and sausage, do so at the beginning, along with the onions—I suggest a total of a pound or so.

3 tablespoons extra-virgin olive oil
2 cups sliced onions
2 cups diced bell pepper, preferably red or yellow
Salt and freshly ground black pepper to taste
4 cups chicken, beef, vegetable, or shrimp stock or water (see "Soups" for stock recipes)
2 tablespoons minced garlic
$1/2$ teaspoon cayenne, or to taste
2 teaspoons fresh thyme leaves, several sprigs fresh thyme, or 1 teaspoon dried thyme
2 cups peeled, seeded, and chopped tomatoes (canned are fine; drain first)
2 cups long-grain rice
2 pounds shrimp, peeled (and deveined, if you like) and cut into pieces if very large
Minced fresh parsley or cilantro leaves for garnish

1 Place the olive oil in a medium-to-large casserole and turn the heat to medium-high. Add the onions and bell pepper, sprinkle with salt and pepper, and cook, stirring occasionally, until the onion softens and just begins to brown, about 10 minutes. Warm the stock in a small saucepan over medium heat.

2 Stir in the garlic, cayenne, and thyme, and stir for about 30 seconds. Add the tomatoes and turn the heat to medium-high. Cook, stirring, for 5 minutes, or until the tomatoes begin to break up.

3 Stir in the rice, then the stock. Bring to a boil, turn the heat to medium, and cook, uncovered, stirring occasionally, until the rice is tender and the liquid just about absorbed, 20 to 30 minutes.

4 Add the shrimp and stir. Cook 2 or 3 minutes, then raise the heat if necessary to cook off the remaining liquid. Garnish and serve.

Fried Rice with Egg

Makes 4 servings

Time: 20 minutes or less with precooked rice

Leftover rice is ideal for fried rice.

3 tablespoons peanut (preferred) or canola or other oil
1 teaspoon minced garlic
1 teaspoon peeled and minced fresh ginger
2 tablespoons chopped scallion, plus minced scallion
   for garnish
3 to 4 cups leftover or cooked rice (any method is
   fine), cooled
2 eggs, lightly beaten
2 tablespoons soy sauce
Salt and freshly ground black pepper to taste

1 Place the oil in a wok or large skillet, preferably non-stick, and turn the heat to high. A minute later, add the garlic, ginger, and chopped scallion and cook, stirring almost constantly, for 1 minute.

2 Turn the heat down a little bit and add the rice, a little bit at a time, crumbling it with your fingers to eliminate lumps if necessary. Stir frequently for about 3 minutes.

3 Make a little hole in the center of the rice and pour in the eggs. Scramble, incorporating them gradually with the rice as you bring bits of the rice back to the center.

4 Add the soy sauce and stir. Add salt and pepper if necessary. Garnish and serve.

Shrimp or Pork Fried Rice with Peas: In Step 2, after adding the rice, stir in about 1 cup chopped Pork Bits with Asian Flavors (page 462), or any leftover roast pork; or shelled (and deveined, if you like) shrimp and $^1/_2$ cup briefly cooked peas (fresh or frozen). Proceed as above; the eggs are optional.

Fried Rice with Greens

Makes 4 servings

Time: 20 minutes or less with precooked rice

This is best with strong-flavored greens such as dandelion, mustard, or turnip. Be sure to wash and dry them very thoroughly.

2 cups bitter greens, well washed and dried,
   all stems removed
3 tablespoons peanut (preferred) or canola or other oil
1 teaspoon minced garlic
1 teaspoon peeled and minced fresh ginger
2 tablespoons chopped scallion, plus minced scallion
   for garnish
$^1/_4$ teaspoon crushed red pepper flakes (optional)
3 to 4 cups leftover or cooked rice (any method is
   fine), cooled
2 tablespoons soy sauce
1 tablespoon oyster or hoisin sauce, or more
   soy sauce
Salt and freshly ground black pepper to taste
Toasted Sesame Seeds (page 776) for garnish

1 Chop the greens roughly into fairly small pieces, with no dimensions larger than 2 inches. Place the oil in a wok or large skillet (preferably non-stick) and turn the heat to high. A minute later, add the garlic, ginger, chopped scallion, and red pepper and cook, stirring almost constantly, for 1 minute.

2 Turn the heat down a little bit and add the rice, a little bit at a time, crumbling it with your fingers to eliminate lumps if necessary. Stir frequently for about 1 minute, then add the greens. Cook, stirring frequently, until the greens become tender, about 3 minutes.

3 Add the soy sauce and oyster sauce and stir. Add salt and pepper if necessary. Garnish and serve.

The Basics of Brown Rice

See The Basics of Rice, page 197. Any rice can be brown: You can even find brown basmati (which is delicious). Although brown rice does not have the versatility of its more highly processed descendant, it does have good flavor.

Basic Brown Rice

Makes 4 servings

Time: About 45 minutes

Long-grain brown rice is easier to cook by the method on page 181 (Simple Precooked Grains), although this technique works fine. I do prefer this method for short- or medium-grained brown rice, which you want a little on the sticky side.

1 cup any brown rice, rinsed
2¹/₂ cups chicken, beef, or vegetable stock, or water, plus more if needed (see "Soups" for stock recipes)
Salt and freshly ground black pepper to taste
1 tablespoon butter, or more to taste (optional)

1 Combine all ingredients in a medium saucepan and bring to a boil over medium-high heat.

2 Cover, turn the heat to low, and cook, undisturbed, for 40 minutes. Check the rice: It is done when it is quite tender and all the liquid has been absorbed. If the rice is not quite done, continue to cook, adding a tablespoon or two more liquid if all the liquid has been absorbed. Or, if the rice is tender but a little liquid remains, simply cover and turn off the heat; the rice will absorb the liquid within 10 minutes. If ¹/₄ cup or more of water remains (unlikely), uncover and raise the heat a bit; cook, stirring, until the rice is fluffy and the liquid evaporated.

3 Serve, with butter if you like.

Brown Rice with Cashews and Herbs

Makes 4 servings

Time: About 45 minutes

A pleasantly chewy side dish; substitute other nuts for the cashews if you like.

2 tablespoons olive or other oil or butter
1 medium onion, chopped
1 teaspoon minced garlic
1 cup any brown rice, rinsed
¹/₂ cup cashew pieces
1 bay leaf
¹/₂ teaspoon fresh thyme leaves or ¹/₄ teaspoon dried thyme
Salt and freshly ground black pepper
2 cups chicken, beef, or vegetable stock, or water (see "Soups" for stock recipes)
Minced fresh parsley leaves for garnish

1 Place the oil or butter in a medium-to-large skillet over medium heat; when the oil is hot or the butter melts, add the onion and garlic and cook, stirring, until softened, about 5 minutes.

2 Add the brown rice and nuts and cook, stirring, for 1 minute; add the herbs, salt, pepper, and liquid. Bring to a boil.

3 Turn the heat to low, cover, and cook for 30 minutes. Check the rice's progress: It is done when tender but still a little chewy. Continue to cook if necessary, adding a tablespoon or two more liquid if all the liquid has been absorbed and the rice is not quite done. Or, if the rice is tender but a little liquid remains, simply cover and turn off the heat; the rice will absorb the liquid within 10 minutes. If ¹/₄ cup or more of water remains (unlikely), uncover and raise the heat a bit; cook, stirring, until the rice is tender and the liquid is evaporated. Remove the bay leaf. Garnish and serve.

Stir-Fried Brown Rice with Vegetables and Soy

Makes 4 servings

Time: About 1 hour

If you start with precooked (or leftover) brown rice, this recipe will take no longer than any other stir-fry—about fifteen minutes from start to finish.

> 2 cups bite-sized broccoli florets
> 2 tablespoons peanut (preferred) or canola or other oil
> 1 medium-large onion, sliced
> 1 teaspoon minced garlic
> 1 teaspoon peeled and minced fresh ginger
> 3 to 4 cups cooked and cooled brown rice (see Basic Brown Rice, above, or Simple Precooked Grains, page 181)
> 1 cup chicken, beef, or vegetable stock, or water (see "Soups" for stock recipes)
> 2 tablespoons soy sauce
> Salt and freshly ground black pepper to taste
> 1 teaspoon dark sesame oil (optional)

1 Steam or simmer the broccoli (page 544) just until bright green, 2 to 4 minutes; plunge into ice water to stop the cooking.

2 Place the oil in a wok or large skillet, preferably non-stick, and turn the heat to high. A minute later, add the onion and cook, stirring almost constantly, for 1 minute or so, until the onion softens. Add the garlic and ginger and cook, stirring, for another minute.

3 Add the broccoli and cook, stirring, for 1 minute. Turn the heat down a little bit and add the rice, a little bit at a time, squeezing it with your hands to eliminate lumps if necessary. Add the liquid and cook, stirring frequently, until almost all of the liquid has evaporated, about 3 minutes.

4 Add the soy sauce and stir. Add salt and pepper if necessary. Drizzle with the sesame oil and serve.

Brown Rice with Lentils and Apricots

Makes 4 servings

Time: About 1 hour

Because brown rice and lentils take about the same amount of time to cook, you can simmer them together from the start.

> 1/2 cup lentils, washed and picked over (see The Basics of Buying and Preparing Beans, page 500)
> 1 cup any brown rice, rinsed
> About 3 1/4 cups beef, chicken, or vegetable stock, or water, plus more as needed (see "Soups" for stock recipes)
> 1 bay leaf
> About 1 teaspoon salt
> Freshly ground black pepper to taste
> 1 teaspoon wine vinegar
> 3 tablespoons butter or extra-virgin olive oil
> 1 medium onion, chopped
> 1/2 cup diced dried apricots or other dried fruit (raisins are fine)
> Minced fresh parsley leaves for garnish

1 Combine the lentils and rice in a medium saucepan; add enough liquid to cover by at least 2 inches, about 3 cups. Turn the heat to high and add the bay leaf, about 1 teaspoon salt, some pepper, and the vinegar. When the mixture boils, turn the heat to medium, skim off any foam that has formed on top, and cook, stirring infrequently. If you need to add more liquid to keep the mixture wet do so, a little at a time.

2 When the lentils and rice are both tender—it will take between 30 and 45 minutes—drain them; do not rinse. Remove the bay leaf.

3 Meanwhile, place 1 tablespoon butter or olive oil in a small saucepan over medium heat. Add the onion and cook, stirring, until it softens, about 5 minutes. Add the apricots and the remaining $1/4$ cup of the liquid. When the liquid simmers, turn off the heat.

4 When the lentil/rice mixture is ready, place the remaining butter or oil in a large skillet, preferably non-stick, and turn the heat to medium. When the butter has melted or the oil is hot, add the lentils and rice and cook, stirring, until heated through, 3 to 5 minutes. Add the onions and apricots and cook, stirring, for another minute. Garnish and serve.

The Basics of Wild Rice

Wild rice, which is indigenous to North America, is not a grain but a grass. It is, of course, treated as a grain and therefore included here. There is cultivated wild rice (mostly from California) and wild wild rice (mostly from Minnesota). Either can be quite good, and either can taste like pine needles; but a good batch of hand-harvested wild rice can be a revelation. (The best I've ever had was from Coteau Connoisseur; see Mail-Order Sources, page 886.) It is expensive—upward of six dollars a pound—and so it is often combined with white rice. But don't buy the little boxes you find in the supermarket; the price is outrageous, and the quality suspect.

Basic Wild Rice

Makes 4 servings

Time: About 40 minutes

It's best to cook wild rice using Simple Precooked Grains (page 181). But you can also cook it this way.

1 cup wild rice, well rinsed
2 cups chicken, beef, or vegetable stock, or water
   (see "Soups" for stock recipes)
1 bay leaf
Salt and freshly ground black pepper to taste
1 tablespoon butter (optional)
Minced fresh parsley leaves for garnish

1 Combine all ingredients except the butter and parsley in a medium saucepan and bring to a boil over medium-high heat.

2 Cover, turn the heat to low, and cook, undisturbed, for 30 minutes. Check the progress: The rice is done when the grains have puffed up and are quite tender, regardless of whether the liquid has been absorbed. If the rice is not done, continue to cook, adding more liquid if necessary. If it is done, drain if necessary.

3 Stir in the optional butter, garnish, and serve.

Wild Rice with Curried Nuts: While the rice is cooking in the above recipe, melt 2 tablespoons butter in a large skillet. Add 1 tablespoon curry powder (or any other spice mixture from pages 777–778) and cook, stirring, for 1 minute. Stir in $1/2$ to 1 cup broken-up cashews, almonds, pecans, or walnuts (broken into bits, not finely chopped). Cook, stirring, until they begin to brown. Turn off the heat until the rice is done, then drain the rice if necessary and add it to the nut-butter mixture. Cook over medium-low heat, stirring, until hot.

Wild Rice with White Rice: Start with equal parts of cooked wild and white rice. Cook as for Precooked Grains with Garlic or Onions (page 182), or use any of the variations.

Wild Rice with Vegetables and Dried Mushrooms

Makes 4 servings

Time: About 1 hour

Precooking the wild rice briefly shortens the overall cooking time and allows it to finish cooking before the vegetables become soggy.

2 ounces dried porcini mushrooms

About 6 to 8 cups water

1 cup wild rice, well rinsed

2 tablespoons butter or extra-virgin olive oil,
   plus 1 tablespoon butter (optional)

1 cup chopped carrots

$1/2$ cup chopped celery

1 cup chopped onion

$1/4$ cup chopped garlic (mincing is not necessary)

1 bay leaf

Freshly ground black pepper to taste

1 teaspoon fresh thyme leaves or $1/2$ teaspoon
   dried thyme

3 cups chicken, beef, or vegetable stock, or water,
   warmed, plus more if necessary (see "Soups"
   for stock recipes)

1 Soak the dried mushrooms in hot water to cover. Bring about 6 to 8 cups water to a boil in a medium-to-large pot; salt it. Stir in the wild rice and adjust the heat so that the water boils, but not furiously.

2 Cook, stirring occasionally, for 10 minutes; the rice will just begin to soften. Drain it. Drain the mushrooms, reserving the soaking liquid; trim them of any hard spots and chop.

3 Meanwhile, place the butter or oil in a large, deep skillet which can later be covered and turn the heat to medium-high. When the butter melts or the oil is hot, add the mushrooms, carrots, celery, onion, garlic, bay leaf, pepper, and thyme. Cook, stirring, until the onion begins to soften, about 5 minutes.

4 Strain the reserved soaking liquid and stir it into the vegetables. A minute later, add the stock or water all at once and bring to a boil. Add the rice. Turn the heat to low, cover, and cook for about 30 minutes. Uncover and taste the rice. If it is done, raise the heat and cook off the remaining liquid, stirring. If it is not done, re-cover and cook an additional 10 minutes. (In the unlikely event that more liquid is needed, add it, about $1/4$ cup at a time.)

5 Remove the bay leaf. Stir in the optional butter and serve.

Breads

There have always been great reasons for baking bread at home: You know exactly what it contains, the process is pleasant, and the wonderful-tasting results can be enjoyed at almost any meal. People who make bread regularly—I count myself among them—eat it several times a day, as toast for breakfast, in sandwiches for lunch, as a ready-made carb at dinner.

All of these reasons have made bread-making more common among home cooks. And since bread—especially the home-baked variety—is not only a healthy part of a good diet, it's an essential part (look at what's on the bottom of the USDA's new food pyramid), this isn't surprising. In addition, mixers, food processors, and bread machines have made it easier than ever to produce bread at home.

Although you can make bread with just flour and water (the ingredients in unleavened bread and the simplest crackers), the best breads contain at least four elements: flour, leavener, water, and salt. In yeast breads, the leavener is yeast, or sometimes a combination of sourdough starter and yeast. In quick breads—so named because there is no rising time involved—the leavener is usually baking powder. Whether quick or yeast, breads can contain a variety of other ingredients too, of course, from butter, eggs, and milk to fruits, nuts, sweeteners, and whole grains.

There are two important non-food ingredients that go into bread as well: energy (this need not be yours, or much of it), and time. Quick breads, biscuits, muffins, and other baked goods leavened with baking powder or soda don't take long; you can make almost any one in an hour or so. There are even yeast breads you can make in just over an hour (see Fastest Yeast Bread, page 228), but the best yeast bread takes the better part of a day to make. Fortunately, most of that time is completely unattended.

The Basics of Ingredients for Bread

Flour is the most important ingredient in bread, and is discussed separately below. But other ingredients are important too. Today's leaveners—whether yeast or baking powder—store well, and are convenient and reliable. You can buy little packages of yeast sold in supermarkets, but buying bulk yeast from the natural foods store is far cheaper. And, because dried yeast is dormant, it keeps a long, long time in the refrigerator. (I buy a pound every year or so, I ignore the expiration dates, and I've never had a problem.) Cake yeast, which works well, takes a bit more work, without any real benefit. I favor the new "instant" yeasts, not so much because they rise bread faster (they do not) but because they require no dissolving in water; you just mix them with the dry ingredients and proceed. As you'll see, this means that you can make bread dough in a food processor without much more effort than it takes to make it in a bread machine.

Baking powder, contrary to popular opinion, is not all the same, nor does it last forever. Try to buy a brand that contains no more than bicarbonate of soda (baking soda) and calcium acid phosphate or tartaric acid (some cornstarch in the mix is also okay). You do not need aluminum in your baking powder. If you don't use baking powder often, replace it once a year. Even if you do, store it in a dry place; moisture robs it of its potency. To make baking powder at home, see page 708.

You can use any water you want to make bread, although obviously the purer the better. At one time, water temperature mattered greatly; you needed warm water to proof the yeast. But instant yeast, which can be mixed in with the dough, responds to water at any temperature. (Of course, if your water is ice cold, your dough will be cold and take longer to rise.) So I recommend using cold water from the tap, with two exceptions: In the dead of winter, when water from the tap may be forty degrees, use lukewarm water, about sixty or seventy degrees. And if you're in a hurry and want the dough to rise more quickly, use very warm water, hot to the touch, about one hundred and five degrees (this is unnecessary if you use a food processor, which raises the temperature of the dough to a good level for rising regardless of the temperature of the water).

You can also use any type of salt: table salt, sea salt, or kosher salt. I cook with coarse kosher or sea salt, and these recipes reflect that; cut back on the salt a bit if you're using table salt, which contains more "saltiness" per equal measure. In any case, don't omit the salt unless you're on a restricted diet for health reasons; salt-free bread is extremely dull—taste a piece of unsalted dough and you'll see what I mean.

Fat, in the form of milk, oil, butter, or eggs, adds flavor, richness, and tenderness, and helps finished loaves retain freshness. But it is not needed in breadmaking. That's one of the beauties of basic yeast bread; it's as lean as oatmeal or pasta, but more variable and useful than either.

In sandwich breads, muffins, most quick breads, biscuits, and other baked goods in which you want tenderness rather than a crisp crust and tough interior, fat is a must. It may be no more than substituting milk for water, and adding a little oil—in the case of relatively low-fat muffins—or as much as eggs, milk, and butter, in the case of a cake-like quick bread.

Finally, there is sweetener. Basic bread and biscuits need none, but muffins and quick breads are usually quite reliant on sweetener for flavor. Some rich yeast breads are also better with a touch of sweetening. In many cases, honey, malt, or maple syrup are preferable to sugar, because they add rather than detract from the moistness of the bread.

In addition to the basic ingredients, you can mix almost anything into almost any type of bread while you're making it: seeds, whole or sprouted grains, chopped fruits or nuts, other flours, herbs and spices, even leftovers such as mashed potatoes or other vegetables. It's all possible once you master the basics and get a sense of what a good dough looks and feels like.

The Basics of White Flour

There are many types of flour, each with a different purpose. The most important flour for most bakers is white wheat flour, which falls roughly into three different types. There is another distinction, and that is between bleached and unbleached flour. But bleaching uses chemical ingredients and robs the flour of nutrients, flavor, and color, all for the questionable end of making it whiter than white. There is absolutely no reason to buy bleached flour; it's even illegal in some European countries.

Most flour is made from a blend of wheats. Each wheat has a name, such as "hard spring" and "soft winter," and each has different characteristics. Generally speaking, you won't know which wheat you're buying; the type of wheat is rarely printed on the sack of flour, and most flours are made up of a blend of wheats. What you will know is the protein content of the flour. (Regardless of labeling, you can simply read the nutritional information on the side of the sack to determine the protein level of a given flour.) Different wheats contain different amounts of protein, and that protein gives the resulting baked goods different characteristics. Flour can be described as "hard," "soft," or "all-purpose."

Hard flour, also called bread flour, has the most protein, usually around fourteen percent (the percentage is nothing more than the number of grams of protein per hundred grams of flour). Hard flour is the best flour for making crusty, coarse-textured bread.

You can make good bread with all-purpose flour, and there are breads for which all-purpose flour is preferable, but for the kind of bread that's a challenge to cut and chew, use bread flour.

Soft flour, also called cake flour, is described in more detail on page 682. It has the lowest percentage of protein, usually about seven percent or less, and makes delicate breads (or, more often, cakes) with a fine crumb. You can use some cake flour in some quick breads or muffins if you like, but as long as you don't overwork the dough they will be perfectly tender when made with all-purpose flour.

All-purpose flour is the standard, and the kind you see most often. All brands of all-purpose flour are not the same, because some have more protein than others; ten percent is average, but check the label and you'll see. You can make great quick breads, muffins, pancakes, waffles, and other baked goods with all-purpose flour, and you can make very good yeast breads and cakes as well; if you venture into baking on a regular basis, you'll want to stock your pantry with all three flours. If you are an occasional baker, keeping all-purpose flour on hand will suit your needs.

"Flour," of course, is shorthand for almost any finely ground grain, or even seeds or legumes. Chickpea flour and rice flour, for example, are common in Asia, and can be added to breads. In fact, as long as you keep the amounts within reason—say, about five percent of total weight of the dough—you can add almost anything else you want to bread, and the dough will support it: That's why you can make nut bread, prosciutto bread, olive bread, and so on.

The Basics of Non-White Flour

There are, of course, alternatives to white flour, and each has its own characteristics. But it's safe to say that they all have more flavor than white flour, they will not rise as much as white flour, and they have a more beneficial nutritional profile than white flour.

If you want crusty yeast bread, your dough should contain at least eighty percent all-purpose or bread flour. But plain white bread eventually becomes boring, even when it has a crackling-crisp crust. So many bread makers vary the flours in their breads, adding whole grain flours for fiber, nutritional content, and variety of flavor and color. Flours and grains can be mixed in almost any way you like, although a certain amount of white flour is always nice, not only for the crust but for lightness of flavor and texture; one hundred percent whole grain breads tend to be dense, heavy, and so distinctive that they can be difficult to pair with food. Here is a rundown of the kinds of additions you can make to breads:

- **Whole wheat flour:** White flour has had the germ and the bran removed; whole wheat flour contains both. It is nutritionally superior and has a stronger flavor that not everyone likes. Whole Wheat Sandwich Bread (page 229) is flavorful and tender, and contains about fifty percent whole wheat flour; more than that and the taste becomes muddy and the texture quite dense. I like to add ten percent whole wheat flour (or a mixture of whole wheat and rye), to my basic French-style bread (Easiest and Best French Bread, page 224), or my Sourdough Bread (page 226). See below for storage information.
- **Rye flour:** Whole rye flour has the most flavor. It's a necessity for rye bread, of course (which is to some extent misnamed, because except in Scandinavian-style rye bread it almost never contains more than fifty percent of rye flour) but also good added in small amounts (five or ten percent) to Easiest and Best French Bread, page 224, or Sourdough Bread (page 226). See below for storage information.

- **Cornmeal:** Adds good flavor, lovely color, and, if you use coarse stone-ground cornmeal, some crunch. In yeast breads, use up to ten percent. In corn breads, use fifty to one hundred percent. Try to use fresh, stone-ground cornmeal whenever possible. See below for storage information.
- **Barley flour:** An excellent addition to Easiest and Best French Bread, page 224, or Sourdough Bread, page 226. Barley has good flavor and a great deal of protein; on its own, however, it is somewhat bitter and will not produce a crusty bread. See below for storage information.

Storing Flour

All-purpose, bread, and cake flours have had the germ and bran removed, and are more or less incapable of spoiling. This does not mean, however, that they will last forever: Flour picks up ambient flavors no matter where it is stored, and I don't recommend keeping any flour for more than six months.

Whole grain flours should be bought as fresh as possible and stored, if you have the room, in the freezer; you need not defrost them before using. The ground germ of these flours contains oil, which can grow rancid and give a bitter taste to the flour. Stored in the freezer, they keep well for months but, like all-purpose flour, they will eventually pick up the flavors of other foods stored nearby. Therefore, I recommend that you buy only as much as you plan to use in the following month or so.

The Basics of Bread-Making Equipment

Dedicated bakers tend to be fanatics about equipment. But you can make bread with nothing more than your hands, a countertop, and a baking sheet or loaf pan. Nearly everything else is a matter of convenience. Assuming you have the basic kitchen utensils—measuring cups and spoons, bowls, oven thermometer, etc.—you're probably all set for bread-baking. But there are some other items that you should consider:

- **Food processor:** If you want to make yeast bread and don't enjoy kneading by hand, you will want one. And, fortunately, it has many other uses beyond producing near-perfect bread dough in less than a minute. Buy a machine that can handle at least five cups of dough.
- **Scale:** Some people find it more convenient to measure flour by weight than by volume and, indeed, it is more accurate. (When you have some experience baking you'll learn that it's all about proportions—no matter how much flour you begin with, you will know how much liquid to add to produce a dough of the correct consistency.) But if you don't have a scale, it's fairly safe to assume that one pound of flour equals five hundred grams (one-half kilogram) or $3^1/_2$ cups.
- **Standing mixer:** You can use a wooden spoon to mix quick breads, muffins, and the like, and it's easy enough. But a standing mixer is easier. (You can also use a food processor if you're careful, but it's very easy to overwork the dough.) If you make a lot of delicate baked goods, such as cakes and cookies, you will want one anyway.
- **Muffin tins, loaf pans, etc.:** Non-stick muffin tins are a revelation, although good cast iron works almost as well and is more attractive. Loaf pans for sandwich breads may be of any material; bread dough doesn't stick to well-oiled surfaces, and even cheap aluminum can produce an attractive loaf. Special "baguette" pans, designed to produce long French-style loaves, are not necessary, as you'll see in the Easiest and Best French Bread recipe on page 224.

- **Spray bottle:** The crust of yeast breads can be made even crisper by spraying the oven with water before baking and during its initial stages. You can use the one you bought for your house plants (make sure there's no fertilizer in it!).
- **Peel:** A wooden (or metal) pizza peel is the ideal tool for sliding large breads (such as "boules," or ball-shaped loaves) that are baked without a pan into the oven. For baguettes, a 4×15-inch plank of wood is even better.
- **Baking stone:** You can bake any bread that isn't placed in a pan on a baking sheet, but the crust will cook more evenly and become crisper if you put a baking stone in the oven first. Just leave it there, on the bottom rack; you can cook anything on it, and won't have to replace it for at least a couple of years.
- **Razor blade:** For slashing the tops of bread loaves. A good sharp knife will work nearly as well.

The Basics of Bread Machines

Bread machines—which cost from one hundred to four hundred dollars—are miraculous. You throw in the ingredients, turn on the machine, and walk away. In four hours (sometimes even less), you have bread. The appeal, obviously, is enormous.

But is it worth it? In addition to their price, bread machines have two major disadvantages: They take up a lot of counter or cabinet space (do you really want another major appliance, and one that performs a single task?) and, although most of them make decent bread, none of them is capable of making great bread; the crust is always disappointing, the crumb usually too fine. Not bad for sandwich bread, but a far cry from even the simplest bread made by more traditional methods.

Nor are bread machines completely foolproof; some of the manufacturers' recipes don't work in their machines (!), requiring you to fool about a bit with the recipe before you're satisfied with the results.

Try making your own bread before investing in a machine. You can do it; it's easy, it doesn't take that much of your time, and, by your third try (at worst), your own bread will be far superior to that made in a bread machine. If, however, you want to make bread but minimizing the work is a priority, you might want to consider a bread machine—as long as you don't mind a tender crust. Models change constantly, but machines made by Panasonic, Zojirushi, and Hitachi have been pretty consistent over the years. All of the ideas behind the recipes in this chapter will work in a bread machine, although some modifications in proportions are likely.

The Basics of Making Yeast Bread

Yeast bread is all about dough-making. Although there are fine points of baking, starting with the wrong dough will guarantee an unsatisfactory bread no matter how perfect your baking. Starting with the right dough, however, will usually give you a good bread, even if your oven is inaccurate, you turn down the heat too late, you forget to spray the oven, you don't have a baking stone, and so on.

Making the Dough

Though tactile sensation is important in bread-making, this does not mean that you must knead the dough by hand, a process that can be quite time-consuming and nearly aerobic, especially if you like to add whole grain flour to your breads. Kneading allows the flour-and-water mixture to develop gluten, the protein that gives the bread structure and chewiness. It can be accomplished by hand, but with more ease in a powerful standing mixer, and best of all in a food processor. The food processor is ideal because it allows you to maximize the water-to-flour ratio, and good yeast dough is wet, usually too wet to handle comfortably. The food processor doesn't care how sticky the dough is, and if you flour your hands and the work surface lightly after making the dough, you'll have no trouble handling the dough from then on.

Hand kneading—repeatedly folding, pressing, pushing, and beating the dough, adding a little more flour at a time—is much more work. And the tendency is to add more flour than is good for the bread, because it makes the dough easier to handle. In older bread recipes, you often read that dough should be kneaded "until smooth, elastic, and no longer sticky." But such dough is overkneaded and contains too much flour; it will have a smooth, cakey crumb, fine for sandwich bread, but not for crusty, country-style bread.

Rising the Dough

Most recipes call for letting the bread rise in a warm place, but I've found—as have many bread makers throughout history—that longer rises give more flavor. You can rush the rising of bread by doubling the amount of yeast, or by letting it rise in a warm (no more than 150°F) oven, but if you have the time, you might consider a schedule like this: Mix the dough in the morning, let it rise at room temperature until noon or early afternoon, then shape it (or deflate the dough and allow it to rise again) and let it rest for another hour or more before baking. Contrary to older recipe directions, there are no precise rising times; dough is really quite flexible.

The fact is that bread-making can be suited to your schedule. You can mix dough at night and refrigerate it, allowing it to rise slowly for a day or even more; you can hurry the rise, starting the dough two hours or so before baking it and letting it rise in a warm place; and, in a pinch, you can even skip rising: Make the dough, shape it, let it rest while you preheat the oven, and bake it. This won't be the tastiest bread you've ever had, but it'll still beat any loaf you buy in the supermarket.

I have two different schedules. When I have it together, I make Sourdough Bread (page 226, which is a very mild sourdough), letting the dough rise overnight on the counter, shaping it in the morning, letting it rise part or even most of the day in a cool place, and baking it in the afternoon. On other days, I whip up a double batch of regular dough, enough to make six dough balls. I let the dough rise all day or overnight, then divide it, wrap the balls in plastic, and toss them in the freezer. Then, when I know I'll want bread for dinner but haven't had the time or foresight to make sourdough (which happens to be most mornings), I remove a dough ball from the freezer when I wake up (if company is coming, I'll use two). This sits on the counter if I'm going to be around during the day, in the fridge if I'm away. Late in the afternoon, I shape the dough; while I'm making dinner, I bake it. Dough balls keep well in the freezer for a couple of weeks; after that the yeast begins to lose power.

There are many more ways in which bread-making schedules can be concocted; after a time, you'll find the ones that suit you best.

Shaping the Dough

Shaping bread dough is a matter of taste. You can pat the dough into a rectangle, then roll it up and place it in a loaf pan. Or you can shape it into a round or oval loaf, to bake on a baking sheet. You can also roll it—just like the play-dough snakes you made as a kid—and let it rise in a heavy cloth, specially shaped baguette pan, or on a baking sheet. Really, you can make any shape you like with basic bread dough, including rolls and pizza. Most surfaces should be lightly oiled or dusted with flour or cornmeal before putting the dough on them. You'll find illustrations for making the most popular shapes on pages 226–234.

Baking the Dough

If you like crusty bread, baking technique is important. Start with a hot oven and spray the oven walls with water just before inserting the bread and once or twice more during the first fifteen to twenty minutes of baking. I usually turn the oven heat down about halfway through the baking, but it isn't necessary as long as you keep an eye on the bread. Most bread is done when it makes a hollow sound when you thump it, or when an instant-read thermometer inserted into the center of the loaf reads 210°F. If you're going to reheat it, which is often the case, underbaking is no big deal, and you can consider anything above 190°F "done."

Storing Bread

As I've already noted, you can store unbaked dough, well wrapped in aluminum foil or plastic, in the freezer for a couple of weeks. You can also store baked bread, wrapped in waxed paper—plastic makes the crust soggy—on the counter for up to four or five days; large loaves containing some whole grain flour keep better than small ones baked with just white flour. And baked bread can also be frozen; in this instance aluminum foil or heavy plastic bags are fine, because you'll need to recrisp the bread anyway. Unwrap, then place thawed or unthawed bread in a preheated 350°F oven for five to fifteen minutes, until thawed and crisp.

All of this may sound like a lot, but making bread—unlike making cakes, for example, or even brownies—offers loads of latitude. The schedule can be molded to meet your own and, as long as your yeast is alive, the chances are good you'll be far more successful than you imagine.

Simple Yeast Breads

These are the basic "French" or "Italian" breads, traditional breads that contain nothing but flour, water, yeast, and salt. They have great flavor and texture, the best crust, and can be made in any shape, including rolls. They are not fancy, nor do they have the best keeping power; you need fat for that.

Easiest and Best French Bread

Makes 3 or 4 baguettes, 1 boule, or 12 to 16 rolls

Time: At least 3 hours, largely unattended

This bread can be made by hand or with an electric mixer (see the variations), but I much prefer the food processor, for the reasons described above. The technique was introduced along with the first food processors, but it has been refined continually, especially by my friend Charlie Van Over, whose book *The Best Bread Ever* (Broadway Books, 1997) is a must for anyone who wants to pursue simple bread-making. I have made my own adjustments to Charlie's methods, but I am forever indebted to him. This process, as well as that for making other shapes, is illustrated on pages 226 and 227.

3¹/₂ cups (about 1 pound) bread or all-purpose flour, plus more as needed

2 teaspoons salt

1 teaspoon instant or rapid-rise yeast

Scant 1¹/₂ cups water

1   Place the flour in the container of a food processor fitted with the steel blade. Add the salt and yeast and process for 5 seconds. With the machine running, pour most of the water through the feed tube. Process about 30 seconds. The dough should be in a defined but shaggy ball, still sticky; you would not want to knead it by hand. If the dough is too dry, add water 1 tablespoon at a time and process for 5 or 10 seconds after each addition. (If it is too wet, which is unlikely, add another tablespoon of flour and process briefly.)

2   Dump the lump of dough into a large bowl. Cover loosely with a plastic bag, plastic wrap, or towel. Let sit for 2 to 3 hours, at room temperature. If you would like to let the dough rise for a longer period of time, which will help it develop flavor, refrigerate for up to 12 hours; bring it back to room temperature before proceeding.

3   Sprinkle a very small amount of flour onto a counter or tabletop, cut the dough into 3 or 4 equal pieces (about 10 to 13 ounces each) and shape each into a ball, sprinkling with a little more flour if necessary. (If you would like to make 1 large loaf, leave the dough in 1 piece and follow the directions for Sourdough Bread, page 226. If you would like to make rolls, cut into 12 to 16 equal pieces and follow the directions for Dinner Rolls, page 233.) Cover with a towel and let rest for 20 to 30 minutes (you can cut this to 10 minutes if you are pressed for time).

4   Spread a large, heavy piece of canvas or cotton (you can use a large tablecloth, folded into quarters to give it extra stiffness) on a table or countertop and sprinkle it very lightly with flour. Or use baguette pans, sifting a little bit of flour into them.

5   Press each dough ball flat, then fold it over onto itself twice; seal the resulting seam and, using your hands, roll the dough into a long snake (as you did with clay when you were a child). Do not use too much flour or the dough will slide all over the countertop and you will not be able to roll it. Place the loaf, seam side up, in a fold of the cloth (this is called a couche, or

bed), or seam side down in the baguette pan. When all the loaves are formed, cover with a cloth and let rise for 1 to 2 hours at room temperature; the loaves will be about 1¹/₂ times their original size.

6 About 30 minutes before you're ready to bake, preheat the oven to 450°F. When you are ready to bake, sprinkle each loaf very lightly with flour and slash the top several times with a razor blade. If the dough has risen on a cloth, slide it onto floured baking sheets or gently move it onto a plank of wood measuring about 4 × 15 inches, then slide the bread off the plank directly onto a baking stone. If the dough has risen in baguette pans, place them in the oven. Spray the inside of the oven to create steam, then put the loaves in the oven.

7 After 5 minutes, spray again. Bake 25 to 35 minutes, or until the crust is golden brown and the internal temperature of the bread is at least 210°F. Remove, spray with a bit of water if you would like a shinier crust, and cool on a wire rack.

To make this bread by hand: Combine half the flour with the salt and yeast and stir to blend. Add all of the water and stir with a wooden spoon until smooth. Add remaining flour a bit at a time; when the mixture becomes too stiff to stir with a spoon, begin kneading, adding as little flour as possible— just enough to keep the dough from being a sticky mess. Knead until smooth but still quite moist, about 10 minutes. Proceed as above.

(Step 1) Using as little flour as possible, press the lump of dough down with your hands. (Step 2) Repeatedly fold and press until the dough becomes far less sticky (it should never be completely smooth) and much more elastic.

To make this bread with a standing mixer: The machine must be a fairly powerful one or it will stall. Combine half the flour with the salt, yeast, and all of the water; blend with the machine's paddle. With the machine on slow speed, add flour a little at a time, until the mixture has become a sticky ball that pulls away from the sides of the bowl (switch to the dough hook if necessary). Knead for 1 minute by hand, adding as little flour as possible, then proceed as above.

Whole Grain Bread: You can add color and flavor to this bread by adding whole wheat, rye, or barley flours, or cornmeal, alone or in combination. Simply substitute the whole grain flour for some of the all-purpose flour. If you keep the addition to ¹/₂ cup or less, you will retain the great texture of this bread. You may add much more—up to ¹/₃ the total amount of flour, or just over 1 cup—and still have a very good bread with a crisp crust. Adding more than that produce the soft crust and doughy crumb typical of breads high in whole grain; better, at that point, to make Whole Wheat Sandwich Bread (page 229), Onion-Rye Bread (page 233), or one of the other breads designed specifically for whole grain.

Herb and Onion Bread: Vary this as you like. In Step 3, make only 2 dough balls. After Step 3, mix together 1 clove garlic, minced; 2 tablespoons finely chopped onion; 2 tablespoons minced fresh parsley leaves; 1 teaspoon fresh or dried thyme leaves (other possibilities: ¹/₂ teaspoon fresh or dried rosemary; ¹/₂ teaspoon minced fresh or dried oregano leaves; 1 teaspoon minced fresh chervil leaves; 1 teaspoon minced fresh chives); and ¹/₂ teaspoon freshly ground black pepper. Press out the dough as above, then before folding it onto itself, spread it with this mixture. Proceed as above.

(Step 1) Press the dough into a rectangle; it may be any length that will fit into your oven. (Step 2) Fold each long side of the rectangle up into the middle. (Step 3) Roll into a log and use your fingers to press the resulting seam together tightly. (Step 4) Slash the dough in several places with a sharp knife or razor blade just before baking.

If you'd like, you can start by making a baguette (Steps 1 through 3, above), and shape the loaf into a ring, or crown.

SHAPING A CROWN

(Step 1) Roll the dough into a long log. (Step 2) Bend the ends of the loaf toward one another. (Step 3) Use your fingers to tightly press together the ends to make a seam.

Seven Additions for Any Bread

With the exception of the bulgur (#7), all of these are best added by hand after the dough ball is formed.

1. Chopped nuts or seeds, toasted if you like, up to one cup per recipe
2. Chopped dried fruit or raisins (especially good with walnuts), up to one-half cup per recipe
3. Bean or seed sprouts, up to one cup per recipe
4. Chopped pitted olives, up to one-half cup per recipe (excellent with two teaspoons minced fresh rosemary added at the same time)
5. Minced cooked bacon or ham, up to one-half cup per recipe
6. Grated hard cheese, such as Parmesan, up to one cup per recipe
7. One-half cup fine or medium-grain bulgur soaked for fifteen minutes in one cup hot water, added to the flour-yeast mixture before the water (reduce the amount of water by about half)

Sourdough Bread

Makes 3 or 4 baguettes, 1 boule, or 12 to 16 rolls

Time: At least 48 hours the first time, roughly 24 hours thereafter, largely unattended

Much has been made of the challenges of sourdough bread, but although making a good sourdough takes a little time, the process can become simple and routine with only a little practice. To begin, you make a starter, and a couple of days later you begin the bread. From then on, you can use the starter to make bread in less than twenty-four hours; always bring it to room temperature first.

> 1½ cups (about 7 ounces) bread or all-purpose flour, plus 3½ cups (about 1 pound), plus more as needed
> ⅛ teaspoon instant yeast, plus ¼ teaspoon
> 1 cup warm water, plus scant 1⅓ cups water, plus more as needed
> 2 teaspoons salt

1 At least 2 days before you plan to bake, mix together the 1½ cups flour, ⅛ teaspoon yeast, and 1 cup warm water. Stir, cover loosely, and place on top of your refrigerator or another out-of-the-way place. Stir every 8 to 12 hours; the mixture will become bubbly, and eventually develop a sour smell. If your kitchen is warm, this may happen in 24 hours; usually it takes a couple of days.

2 The night before you're ready to bake, place half of the starter in the container of a food processor fitted with the steel blade. (To maintain the starter, add about ¾ cup of flour and ½ cup of water to the remainder and stir well. Cover and refrigerate. Use within a week, or add a little more flour and water to the starter to keep it going. If you always take half the starter and rejuvenate it this way, it will last forever.) Add the remaining flour, salt, and yeast, and process for 5 seconds. With the machine running, pour (don't drizzle) most of the remaining water through the feed tube. Process about 30 seconds, then remove the cover. The dough should be in a defined but shaggy ball, still quite sticky; you would not want to knead it by hand. If the dough is too dry, add water, 1 tablespoon at a time, and process for 5 or 10 seconds after each addition. (If it is too wet, which is unlikely, add another tablespoon or two of flour and process briefly.)

3 Dump the lump of dough into a large bowl. Cover loosely with a plastic bag, plastic wrap, or towel. Let sit for several hours or overnight at cool room temperature or in the refrigerator if the weather is warm (bring it back to room temperature before proceeding).

4 Sift a very small amount of flour onto a counter or tabletop, and shape the dough into a ball, sprinkling with a little more flour if necessary. Pinch together the seam that forms at the bottom of the ball.

5 Place a clean kitchen towel in a colander or round basket about the size of a standard colander. Sprinkle it very well with flour. Place the dough ball, seam up, in the towel and sprinkle it generously with more flour. Fold the towel over the dough and let rise from 2 to 6 hours.

6 About 30 minutes before you're ready to bake, preheat the oven to 450°F. When you are ready to bake, gently turn the dough ball onto a baking sheet or pizza peel; slash the top of the ball several times with a razor blade. Spray the inside of the oven to create steam, then either put the baking sheet in the oven or slide the loaf from the peel onto a baking stone.

7 Spray two or three times during the first 10 minutes of baking. After 20 minutes, lower the heat to 350°F. Bake a total of about 45 minutes, or until the crust is golden brown (the internal temperature of the bread will be about 210°F). Remove, spray with a bit of water if you would like a shinier crust, and cool on a wire rack.

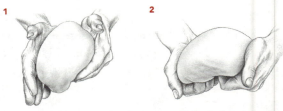

(Step 1) To make a "boule," or round loaf, shape the dough into a ball. (Step 2) Working around the ball, continually tuck the dough toward the center of the bottom, stretching the top slightly and creating surface tension. Pinch together the seam created at the bottom of the dough.

Fastest Yeast Bread

Makes 1 loaf

Time: 1½ hours, largely unattended

This does not have the great crust, crumb, and flavor of the breads above, but you can start it at five-thirty and be eating it warm at seven. Add one tablespoon or so of minced fresh herbs—such as parsley, dill, or sage—for variety. If you have two ovens, allow the bread to rise in one that has been turned on for just two minutes, then turned off again, while you preheat the other.

3 cups (about 14 ounces) bread or all-purpose flour, plus more as needed

2 teaspoons instant yeast

1 teaspoon salt

1 cup warm water (1¼ cups if you omit the olive oil), plus more if necessary

¼ cup olive oil (optional)

Coarse salt to taste (optional)

1 Combine the flour, yeast, and salt in a bowl or food processor. Add the water all at once, stirring with a wooden spoon or with the machine on; add the olive oil and continue to mix, for a minute or two longer by hand, about 30 seconds total with the food processor. Add water by the tablespoon if necessary, until a ball forms.

2 Shape the dough into a flat round or long loaf, adding only enough flour to allow you to handle the dough (see illustrations on pages 226 and 227). Place dough on baking sheet or pizza peel. Let rise in the warmest place in your kitchen, covered, while you preheat the oven to 425°F.

3 Brush the loaf with water, sprinkle it with coarse salt if you like, and bake on a sheet or slide onto a stone for 15 minutes. Lower the heat to 350°F and continue baking until done—the crust will be golden and crisp—about 30 to 45 minutes more.

Rich Yeast Breads

Adding fat to dough makes it more tender and flavorful, and usually improves its keeping qualities. These breads, which have a more cake-like crumb, now share the stage with the four-ingredient breads in the preceding pages.

Sandwich Bread

Makes 1 large loaf

Time: At least 3 hours, largely unattended

This typical "white" bread is richer and therefore much more tender than the European-style breads above. It's also typically baked in a loaf pan, which helps to keeps the crust tender. Generally, breads like this are good candidates for the bread machine but are also made quickly and easily in a food processor. To make this bread by hand or with a standing mixer, follow the guidelines under Easiest and Best French Bread (page 224).

3½ cups (about 1 pound) all-purpose flour, plus more as needed

2 teaspoons salt

1½ teaspoons instant yeast

1 tablespoon sugar or honey, or more to taste

2 tablespoons butter, at room temperature if you're working by hand, plus more for greasing the bowl and the pan

Scant 1⅓ cups cool milk, preferably whole or 2 percent (warm the milk to at least 70°F if you are working by hand)

1 Place the flour in the container of a food processor fitted with the steel blade. Add the salt and yeast and process for 5 seconds. With the machine running, add the sweetener, softened butter, and most of the milk through the feed tube (you will need a little less milk if you are using a liquid sweetener). Process about 30 seconds, then remove the cover. The dough should be in a well-defined, barely sticky, easy-to-handle ball. If it is too dry, add milk 1 tablespoon at a time and process for 5 or 10 seconds after each addition. If it is too wet, which is unlikely, add a tablespoon or two of flour and process briefly. Knead for a minute or so by hand.

2 Use half the oil or melted butter to grease a large bowl. Shape the dough into a rough ball, place it in the bowl, and cover with plastic wrap or a damp towel. Let rise for at least 2 hours, until nearly doubled in bulk. Deflate the ball and shape it once again into a ball; let rest on a lightly floured surface for about 15 minutes, covered.

3 Using only enough flour to keep the dough from sticking to your hands or the work surface, flatten it into a rectangle, then shape it into a loaf (see below for illustrations). Use the remaining oil or butter to grease a 9 × 5-inch loaf pan. Place the loaf in the pan, flattening the top of it with the back of your

hand as shown in Step 5, below. Cover and let rest for 1 hour, or until the top of the dough is nearly level with the top of the pan.

4 Preheat the oven to 350°F. Brush the top of the loaf lightly with water, then place in the oven. Bake about 45 minutes, or until the bottom of the loaf sounds hollow when you tap it (it will fall easily from the loaf pan) or the internal temperature reads about 200°F. Remove loaf from pan and cool on a wire rack before slicing.

Herbed Sandwich Bread: Experiment with different combinations of herbs to find those you like best. Add about $1/2$ cup minced onion (you can mince it simply by adding chunks to the food processor along with the flour), 2 tablespoons fresh dill or parsley leaves, and 1 teaspoon fresh rosemary or $1/2$ teaspoon dried rosemary, to the flour. Proceed as above.

Whole Wheat Sandwich Bread: Substitute half whole wheat flour for half of the white flour. Use honey

SHAPING A SANDWICH LOAF

(Step 1) If the dough has risen in an oiled bowl, you need no flour; otherwise, work on a very lightly floured surface. Use the heel of your hand to form the dough into a rectangle. (Step 2) Fold over the long sides of the rectangle to the middle. (Step 3) Pinch the seam closed, pressing tightly with your fingers. (Step 4) Fold under the ends of the loaf. (Step 5) Use the back of your hand to press the loaf firmly into the pan.

for sweetener, adding 2 tablespoons or more. Proceed as above, increasing the rising times to at least 2 hours in Step 2 and the resting time to 45 minutes to 1 hour in Step 3.

Bran and Oat Sandwich Bread: Decrease the flour to 2 cups. Add $^1/_2$ cup wheat or oat bran and $^3/_4$ cup whole wheat flour. Use about $^1/_4$ cup honey or maple syrup for sweetener and decrease milk to about 1 cup. Knead in $^3/_4$ cup rolled oats by hand. (If you wet your hands, it will be easier to handle.) Proceed as above.

Anadama Bread: Substitute $^1/_2$ cup cornmeal for $^1/_2$ cup flour. (You may also substitute 1 cup whole wheat flour for 1 cup white flour at the same time.) Replace the sugar or honey with $^1/_2$ cup molasses and use a little less milk. Proceed as above.

English Muffins: Much easier than you think, in some ways easier than bread. Steps 1 and 2 remain the same. In Step 3, cut the dough into 12 roughly equal pieces (if you want perfectly sized muffins, use a scale). Using just enough flour to enable you to handle the dough, shape each into a 3- to 4-inch disk. Dust with flour and let rise for 30 to 45 minutes, or until puffy. Preheat a griddle or large skillet over low heat for about 10 minutes; do not oil it. Sprinkle it with cornmeal, then bake the muffins, a few at a time, on both sides, turning occasionally, until lightly browned; a total of about 15 minutes. Cool on a rack and split with a fork before toasting.

Breadsticks

Makes about 30 breadsticks

Time: About 3 hours, largely unattended

The specialty of northwestern Italy, where breadsticks are ubiquitous and fabulous. Carefully homemade ones are great, too, and not at all difficult. To make these by hand or with a standing mixer, follow the guidelines under Easiest and Best French Bread (page 224). For best flavor, use lard or extra-virgin olive oil.

> $3^1/_2$ cups (about 1 pound) all-purpose or bread flour, plus more as needed
> 2 teaspoons salt
> 1 teaspoon instant yeast
> 1 tablespoon honey or malt syrup
> 2 tablespoons lard, olive oil, or butter, plus a little olive oil for greasing the bowl
> $1^1/_3$ cups water

1 Place the flour in the container of a food processor fitted with the steel blade. Add the salt and yeast and process for 5 seconds. With the machine running, add the sweetener, fat, and most of the water through the feed tube. Process about 30 seconds, then remove the cover. The dough should be in a well-defined, barely sticky, easy-to-handle ball. If it is too dry, add water 1 tablespoon at a time and process for 5 or 10 seconds after each addition. If it is too wet, which is unlikely, add another tablespoon or two of flour and process briefly. Knead for a minute or so by hand.

2 Shape the dough into a rough ball, place it in a lightly oiled large bowl, and cover with plastic wrap or a damp towel. Let rise for at least $1^1/_2$ hours, until nearly doubled in bulk. Deflate the ball and shape it once again into a flat rectangle; let rest on a lightly floured surface for about 15 minutes, covered.

3 Work along the long side of the rectangle and cut thin strips. Pull or roll them into long, round sticks, then place on lightly floured (you can also use cornmeal or semolina flour) baking sheets or a pizza peel. Let rest, covered, while you preheat the oven to 450°F. You will find them easier to roll if you keep flour to a minimum. Don't strive for perfection—irregular breadsticks are just fine.

4 Bake on the baking sheets (or slide them directly onto baking stones) for about 15 minutes, or until lightly browned. Cool on racks before serving. These keep fairly well wrapped in waxed paper or stored in a tin, but they are best the day you make them.

Challah

Makes 1 large loaf

Time: At least 3 hours, largely unattended

The traditional Sabbath bread of European Jews is rich, eggy, and very, very tender. It is easy to make, and fun to shape. However, unless you have a large food processor (one with at least an eleven-cup workbowl), you will have to make this by hand or with a standing mixer. In that case, follow the guidelines under Easiest and Best French Bread (page 224). Leftover Challah makes excellent French Toast (page 754).

5 cups (scant 1½ pounds) all-purpose flour, plus more as needed

2 teaspoons salt

2 teaspoons instant yeast

A few threads saffron (optional)

1 tablespoon honey or sugar

3 eggs plus 1 yolk

1⅓ cups water or milk, warmed to about 70°F if you are working by hand, plus 1 teaspoon water

1 teaspoon canola or other neutral oil, or room-temperature butter, for greasing the bowl, plus some for greasing the baking sheet

1 tablespoon poppy seeds

Coarse salt to taste (optional)

1 Place the flour in the container of a food processor fitted with the steel blade. Add the salt, yeast, and optional saffron and process for 5 seconds. With the machine running, add the sweetener, whole eggs, and most of the water or milk through the feed tube.

MAKING CHALLAH

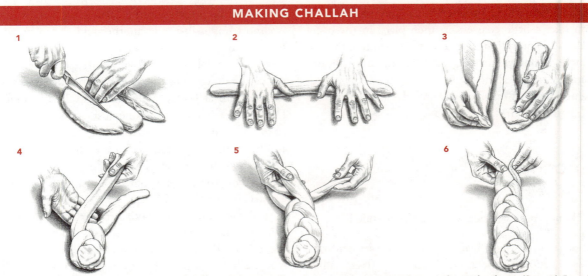

(Step 1) Cut the dough into three equal pieces. (Step 2) Roll each piece into a strip at least twelve inches long. (Step 3) Lay the strips next to each other and press their ends together. (Step 4) Braid, just as you would hair. (Steps 5–6) Finish braiding and use your fingers to tightly press the ends together.

Process about 30 seconds, then remove the cover. The dough should be in a well-defined, barely sticky, easy-to-handle ball. If it is too dry, add water or milk 1 tablespoon at a time and process for 5 or 10 seconds after each addition. If it is too wet, which is unlikely, add another tablespoon or two of flour and process briefly. Knead for a minute or so by hand.

2 Use the oil or butter to grease a large bowl. Shape the dough into a rough ball, place it in the bowl, and cover with plastic wrap or a damp towel. Let rise for at least 1½ hours, until nearly doubled in bulk. Deflate the ball and cut it into 3 equal pieces; shape them into balls and let them rest on a lightly floured surface for about 15 minutes, covered.

3 Roll each of the balls into ropes about 14 inches long and 1 inch thick. Braid them on a lightly greased baking sheet, as illustrated on page 231. Cover and let rest for 30 minutes while you preheat the oven.

4 Preheat the oven to 375°F. Beat the egg yolk with 1 teaspoon of water and brush the top of the loaf with this mixture; sprinkle with poppy seeds and, if you like, a little coarse salt, then place in the oven. Bake 40 to 50 minutes, or until the bottom of the loaf sounds hollow when you tap it or the internal temperature reads about 200°F. Cool on a wire rack before slicing. Best eaten within a day (store in waxed paper if necessary).

Brioche

Makes 2 loaves

Time: At least 3 hours, largely unattended

Brioche, a rich, eggy loaf, can be baked as a sandwich bread (a superb use), as a decorative loaf (like challah, to which is it similar), or as rolls. Leftover brioche makes superb French Toast (page 754).

4 cups (about 18 ounces) all-purpose flour, plus more as needed
1 teaspoon salt
¼ cup sugar
1½ teaspoons instant yeast
8 tablespoons (1 stick) cold butter, cut into chunks, plus softened butter as needed for greasing the bowl, plus some for greasing the pans
3 eggs, plus 1 egg yolk
½ cup milk, plus 2 tablespoons
⅓ cup water, plus more if necessary

1 Combine the flour, salt, sugar, and yeast in the container of a food processor fitted with the steel blade and process for 5 seconds. Add the cold butter and the whole eggs and process for 10 seconds. With the machine running, pour (don't drizzle) ½ cup milk and ⅓ cup water through the feed tube. Process about 30 seconds, then remove the cover. The dough should be very sticky, almost like batter. If it is too dry, add water 1 tablespoon at a time and process for 5 or 10 seconds after each addition. If it is too wet, which is almost impossible, add another tablespoon or two of flour and process briefly.

2 Grease a large bowl with softened butter and scrape the dough into it. Cover with plastic wrap and let rise until at least doubled in bulk, 2 to 3 hours. Deflate the dough and, using just enough flour to enable you to handle it, shape it into 2 loaves, as in Sandwich Bread, page 228. Place each loaf in a buttered 8 × 4-inch or 9 × 5-inch loaf pan. Or shape the dough into rolls, as illustrated on page 234. Cover and let rise for about 1 hour.

3 Preheat the oven to 400°F. Mix the reserved egg yolk with the remaining 2 tablespoons milk and brush the top of the loaves with this mixture. Bake the brioche for about 30 minutes, or until nicely browned. When done, the bottom will sound hollow when you tap it (it will fall easily from the loaf pan) and the interior temperature will be at least 190°F.

Onion-Rye Bread

Makes 1 large round or oval loaf

Time: About 4 hours, largely unattended

This is a rather easy rye bread, especially if you use a food processor, which you should. You can complete it, with little effort, in just a few hours.

> 1¹/₂ cups (7 ounces) all-purpose or bread flour, plus more as needed
>
> 1 cup (about 4¹/₂ ounces) rye flour, preferably stone-ground
>
> ¹/₂ cup cornmeal, plus some for dusting the baking sheets
>
> 2 teaspoons instant yeast
>
> 1 tablespoon sugar, honey, or molasses
>
> 2 teaspoons salt
>
> ²/₃ cup milk
>
> ¹/₃ cup water
>
> ¹/₂ cup finely chopped onion
>
> 1 tablespoon caraway seeds, plus 1 teaspoon
>
> 2 teaspoons canola or other neutral oil for greasing the bowl

1 Combine the flours, ¹/₂ cup cornmeal, yeast, sweetener, and salt in the container of a food processor fitted with the steel blade and process for 5 seconds. With the machine running, pour (don't drizzle) the milk and most of the water through the feed tube. Process about 30 seconds, then remove the cover. The dough should be in a defined but shaggy ball, still quite sticky; you would not want to knead it by hand. If the dough is too dry, add water 1 tablespoon at a time and process for 5 or 10 seconds after each addition. (If it is too wet, which is unlikely, add another tablespoon or two of flour and process briefly.) Turn dough out onto a lightly floured counter and knead in onion and 1 tablespoon of caraway seeds by hand.

2 Place the oil in a large bowl and turn the dough into it. Turn it all around so that it has a light covering of oil and cover with plastic wrap. Allow to double in size, at least 2 hours (you can retard this by refrigerating, or hasten it by putting it in a warm place).

3 Using only enough flour to keep the dough from sticking to your hands or the work surface, flatten it into a rectangle, then shape it into a long oval by rolling it up, pinching all the seams closed. (The process is essentially the same as shaping a sandwich loaf, but without the pan; see page 229.) Sprinkle a baking sheet or pizza peel with cornmeal and lay the loaf on top. Cover again and let rise for about an hour.

4 Preheat the oven to 450°F; slash the top of the loaf with a sharp knife or razor blade in 4 or 5 places; brush with water, then sprinkle with remaining caraway seeds. Place the baking sheet in the oven or slide the dough directly onto a baking stone; bake for 15 to 20 minutes.

5 Lower the heat to 350°F and bake until the loaf is nicely browned and its bottom sounds hollow when you tap it, another 30 to 45 minutes; the internal temperature will be 210°F. Cool on a rack before slicing and store wrapped in waxed paper after you cut it.

Dinner Rolls

Makes about 20 rolls

Time: At least 2¹/₂ hours, largely unattended

The same basic dough—a rich, buttery dough that is essentially an update of the dough used in the now-standard Parker House rolls—can make a number of different kinds of dinner rolls. If you want crisp rolls made without added fat, simply use the recipe for Easiest and Best French Bread (page 224), and shape and bake the rolls according to the directions here.

3¹/₂ cups (about 1 pound) all-purpose flour, plus more as needed

1 tablespoon salt

1 tablespoon sugar

2 teaspoons instant yeast

3 tablespoons cold butter, plus a little soft butter for greasing the bowl

1 egg, plus second egg for brushing on rolls if desired

1 cup milk, plus more as needed

1 Combine the flour, salt, sugar, and yeast in the container of a food processor fitted with the steel blade and process for 5 seconds. Add the cold butter and 1 egg and process for 10 seconds. With the machine running, pour (don't drizzle) the milk through the feed tube. Process about 30 seconds, then remove the cover. The dough should be in a well-defined, barely sticky, easy-to-handle ball. If it is too dry, add milk 1 tablespoon at a time and process for 5 or 10 seconds after each addition. If it is too wet, which is unlikely, add another tablespoon or two of flour and process briefly. Knead for 1 minute or so by hand. It should be smooth, silky, and very elastic, and not too stiff.

2 Grease a large bowl, shape the dough into a rough ball, place it in the bowl, and cover with plastic wrap or a damp towel. Let rise for 1 to 1¹/₂ hours, until nearly doubled in bulk. Deflate the ball and shape it once again into a ball; let rest on a lightly floured surface for about 15 minutes, covered.

3 Roll the dough out until it is about ¹/₂ inch thick, using no more flour than necessary to keep the dough from sticking to the work surface or rolling pin. Use a 2-inch cookie cutter or other utensil to cut out circles, or simply pinch off bits of flour and shape them into round balls (see illustrations, right).

4 Preheat the oven to 375°F. If you want the rolls to have a glossy top, brush them lightly with an egg beaten with a little milk. Bake about 20 minutes, or until the rolls are lightly browned and their bottoms

sound hollow when tapped. Cool on a rack, or serve straight from the oven.

Parker House Rolls: Steps 1 through 3 remain the same. Before baking, brush the tops of the rolls liberally with melted butter, crease them with a chopstick, fold in them half, and brush with butter again. As you finish with each roll, place it on a lightly greased baking sheet. Cover and let rise while you preheat the oven. Don't worry if the rolls rise so much that their sides touch.

(Step 1) To make dinner rolls, first roll a small lump of dough on a lightly floured surface until the seam is closed and smooth. (Step 2) Slash it with a razor or sharp knife before cooking.

To make a fancier dinner roll (knots):

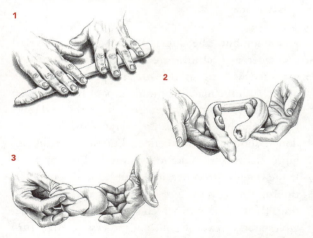

(Step 1) Roll out a snake, using light pressure. (Step 2) Bring the ends of the roll together. (Step 3) Tie them in a simple knot. Press the ends to seal any seams.

Bagels

Makes 8 to 12 bagels

Time: 3 to 4 hours, largely unattended

These are real bagels—crisp bagels—not the puffy kind sold so often nowadays. Cooking a real bagel is a two-step process: first you boil, then you bake. (I like to make them in small quantities because the boiling step is a bit of work.) Other than that, they are as simple as any other bread.

> 3¹/₂ cups (about 1 pound) bread or all-purpose flour, plus more as needed
>
> 2 teaspoons salt
>
> 1 teaspoon instant yeast
>
> 2 tablespoons malt syrup, maple syrup, molasses, or sugar
>
> 1¹/₄ cups water, plus more as needed
>
> Canola or other neutral oil, as needed, plus some for greasing the baking sheet (optional)

1 Place the flour in the container of a food processor fitted with the steel blade. Add the salt, yeast, and sweetener and process for 5 seconds. With the machine running, pour (don't drizzle) all of the water through the feed tube. Process about 30 seconds, then remove the cover. The dough should be in a well-defined ball, only slightly sticky and very easy to handle. If the dough is too dry, add water 1 tablespoon at a time and process for 5 or 10 seconds after each addition. If it is too wet, add a tablespoon or two of flour and process briefly. Turn the dough out onto a lightly floured counter or tabletop and knead for a minute or two longer by hand, adding as much flour as necessary to make a smooth, tough, very elastic dough.

2 Dump the lump of dough into a large bowl. Cover loosely with a plastic bag, plastic wrap, or towel. Let rise for about 2 hours, at room temperature, or until the dough has about doubled in bulk.

If you would like to let the dough rise for a longer period of time, which will help it develop flavor, refrigerate; bring it back to room temperature before proceeding.

3 Deflate the dough ball and let it rest on a lightly floured surface, covered, for about 10 minutes. Cut it into 8 or 12 equal pieces, depending on whether you want large or small bagels. Roll each ball into a 6- to 8-inch-long rope and then shape into a circle, or simply poke a hole in the middle of each ball and pull into a bagel shape. Keep all the balls covered as you work, and lightly flour and cover the shaped bagels as well. When they're all done, cover and let rise for about 30 minutes.

4 Bring a large pot of water to a boil; preheat the oven to 400°F. Drop the bagels, one at a time, into the boiling water; don't crowd. The bagels will sink, then rise to the surface. Boil 1 minute on each side, then remove them with a slotted spoon and place on a lightly greased rack to drain.

5 Lightly grease a baking sheet (or use a non-stick baking sheet). Alternatively, place the bagels on a floured pizza peel and bake them directly on baking stones. Spray the inside of the oven to create steam, then put the bagels in the oven. After 5 minutes, spray again. Bake 20 to 25 minutes, or until the bagels are nicely browned. Remove, spray with a bit of water if you would like a shinier crust, and cool on a wire rack.

Onion Bagels: The best, in my opinion. Two methods: The first, which is simple, is to add about ¹/₂ cup roughly chopped onion to the food processor along with the flour. The second, a little more flavorful, is to sauté ¹/₂ cup minced onion in 1 tablespoon butter or oil until very soft, stirring, about 10 minutes. Knead these into the dough by hand after removing it from the food processor. In either case, when you're ready to bake the bagels, brush them with a little water and sprinkle each with about a teaspoon of very finely minced onion.

Raisin Bagels: Knead about $1/2$ cup raisins into the dough by hand after removing it from the food processor. About $1/2$ teaspoon of ground cinnamon is good here as well.

Bagels Topped with Sesame Seeds, Poppy Seeds, Coarse Salt, etc.: There are two ways to do this. As you remove the bagels from the boiling water, drain briefly, dip the top of each into a plate containing whatever topping you like. Alternatively, just before baking, brush the bagels lightly with water and sprinkle with whatever topping you like. The first method gives you a thicker topping, the second gives you more control.

The Basics of Flatbreads

Pizza (pages 255–265) is a type of flatbread and, arguably, so are Crackers (page 239). But the term *flatbread* has come to mean breads—with or without leavening—that are rolled or pressed out, allowed to rise only minimally, and baked not until crisp and crusty but until soft and pliable. Pita bread is a typical, representative flatbread, but there are others, some quite simple and some—like the magnificent aloo paratha of India—rather complex.

Pita Bread

Makes 6 to 12 pitas

Time: About 3 hours, largely unattended

Pita (sometimes called pocket) bread is the ideal sandwich bread, but is also a good all-around bread, wonderful toasted, good for scooping up sauces and stews. Use half whole wheat flour if you like.

$3^1/2$ cups (about 1 pound) bread or all-purpose flour, or a combination of either of these and whole wheat flour, plus more as needed

2 teaspoons salt

$1^1/2$ teaspoons instant yeast

1 tablespoon olive oil, plus some for greasing the bowl

1 cup water, plus more as needed

1 Place the flour in the container of a food processor fitted with the steel blade. Add the salt and yeast and process for 5 seconds. With the machine running, add the tablespoon of olive oil and water through the feed tube. Process about 30 seconds, then remove the cover. The dough should be in a well-defined, barely sticky, easy-to-handle ball. If it is too dry, add water 1 tablespoon at a time and process for 5 or 10 seconds after each addition. If it is too wet, add another tablespoon or two of flour and process briefly. Turn the dough out onto a floured counter or tabletop and knead for 1 minute or so by hand.

2 Lightly oil a large bowl and put the round of dough in it. Cover and let rise until it has about doubled in bulk, about 2 hours. Deflate the dough ball and divide it into 6 to 12 pieces. Keep all pieces lightly floured and covered. Preheat the oven to 500°F. If you have baking stones, use them; if you do not, place a baking sheet on each oven rack.

3 On a lightly floured surface, flatten each piece into a disk, then roll it out to a 6- to 8-inch circle. Lightly flour each circle as you finish it, and cover it; do not stack.

4 When the oven is preheated, place as many of the pita rounds as will comfortably fit on your stones or baking sheets (start with the rounds you rolled out first). In 2 to 3 minutes, the dough will puff up; remove it from the oven and repeat the process. If the breads do not puff up, they will still be fine, but next time try to make sure that there are no creases or seams in the dough after rolling it out.

Many breads freeze well. With crusty breads, just toss them in a plastic bag in the freezer. Use them as soon as possible, either by defrosting and then crisping up in a 350°F oven for 10 minutes or so, or by reheating them while still frozen, in a 400°F oven for about 20 minutes.

Softer, moister breads—such as most quick breads—should be wrapped in a double layer of foil before freezing. Thaw them before eating, and reheat gently if at all.

Whole Grain Flatbread

Makes 8 to 10 pita-sized breads

Time: About 3 hours, largely unattended

Whole grains are ideal for flatbread, because you are looking for neither bulk nor tough crust. I like flatbread with anise flavors, but you can leave out the spice altogether, or use any seasonings you like, such as rosemary or curry powder; the recipe below will get you started.

2 cups (about 9 ounces) whole wheat flour

1 cup (about 4¹/₂ ounces) rye flour

2¹/₂ cups (about 12 ounces) all-purpose flour, plus more as needed

1 tablespoon sugar

2 teaspoons instant yeast

¹/₂ tablespoon anise seed

1 teaspoon fennel seed

³/₄ tablespoon salt

2 cups water, plus more as needed

1 teaspoon oil

1 Mix all the dry ingredients together in a food processor fitted with the steel blade; process for about 5 seconds. With the machine running, add 2 cups of the water and process until the dough forms a ball, adding additional water a little bit at a time if necessary; don't process for more than 45 seconds or so.

2 Use the oil to grease a bowl; add the dough. Cover and let it rise until doubled in bulk, about 2 hours.

3 Divide into 8 to 10 balls; roll each ball into an 8-inch flat disk on a lightly floured surface. Let rise, lightly covered, until they puff up a little, about 30 minutes. Meanwhile, preheat the oven to 350°F.

4 Bake the flatbreads on baking sheets or directly on baking stones until lightly browned, 12 to 15 minutes. Cool on a rack and serve warm, at room temperature, or reheat on a grill before serving.

Whole Grain Flatbread with Onion and Cumin: Omit the sugar. In Step 3, add 1 tablespoon minced onion and ¹/₂ teaspoon ground cumin or cumin seeds to each of the balls as you are forming them; knead in the onion and cumin as you shape the balls into disks. Proceed as above.

Indian Potato-Stuffed Flatbreads

Aloo Paratha

Makes 12 breads, enough for 6 to 12 servings

Time: About $1^1/_2$ hours

I was taught to make these many years ago by the great Indian cook Julie Sahni, and have changed them very little. Although thyme (or, actually, ajwain, a thyme-like spice) is the traditional seasoning, I prefer cumin.

    4 medium baking potatoes, such as Idahos
       or Russets, about $1^1/_2$ pounds
    $1^1/_2$ cups (about 7 ounces) whole wheat flour
    $1^1/_2$ cups (about 7 ounces) all-purpose flour,
       plus more as needed
    2 teaspoons ground cumin
    1 teaspoon salt
    3 tablespoons peanut or other oil, plus a little more
       for cooking
    1 cup water, plus more as needed
    Cayenne to taste
    Salt and freshly ground black pepper to taste
    1 tablespoon freshly squeezed lemon juice

① Boil the potatoes in salted water to cover.

② While they're cooking, mix the flours, cumin, and 1 teaspoon of salt in a food processor fitted with the steel blade. Process for 5 seconds. With the machine running, pour (don't drizzle) 2 tablespoons of oil, then the water, through the feed tube. Process about 30 seconds, then remove the cover. The dough should be in a well-defined but somewhat sticky ball. If the dough is too dry, add water 1 tablespoon at a time and process for 5 or 10 seconds after each addition. If it is too wet, add a tablespoon or two of flour and process briefly. Knead by hand on a lightly floured surface until quite smooth, another 3 or 4 minutes. Cover the dough with plastic wrap and set aside while you prepare the potatoes.

③ When the potatoes are tender, drain, peel, and mash them with the cayenne, salt, pepper, lemon juice, and 1 tablespoon of oil. Taste and adjust seasoning. Cover and refrigerate if you're not proceeding right away.

④ On a lightly floured surface, roll the dough into a 12-inch-long snake; cut it into 12 pieces. Keeping the pieces covered while you're not working on them, use a rolling pin to shape each into a 4- to 5-inch round. Spoon about 2 tablespoons of the potatoes into the center of each round, then bring the edges of the dough over the filling to enclose it completely. Pinch the dough closed and press down on the top to spread the filling evenly within. Carefully roll each round a little wider.

⑤ Place a large cast-iron or non-stick skillet over medium-high heat for 2 or 3 minutes. Add another tablespoon or two of oil to the skillet, then pour it right out; you just want a film of oil on the bottom. Cook each of the breads for 3 or 4 minutes per side, just until brown spots appear; repeat until all are cooked. Serve hot or at room temperature. These can be stored, well-wrapped and refrigerated, and reheated gently in oven or microwave before eating.

Wheat Flour Tortillas

Makes 6 tortillas

Time: 1 hour, or longer if you have time, largely unattended

These are a lot easier than you might think, and more flavorful than the ones you buy in the supermarket. Lard is the traditional fat here, but you can use butter or oil if you prefer.

1½ cups (about 7 ounces) all-purpose flour,
  plus more as needed
¼ teaspoon salt
2 tablespoons lard, butter, or canola or other
  neutral oil
About ½ cup warm water, plus more as needed

1 Combine the flour and salt in the container of a food processor or a bowl. Pulse in the fat, or cut it in with two knives.

2 If you're using a food processor, add water slowly, with the machine running, just until the dough forms a ball. By hand, mix in water a tablespoon or two at a time, until the dough holds together. Either way, knead on a lightly floured surface, adding flour as necessary to keep the dough from sticking, until the dough is quite smooth and elastic, about 1 minute if you used a food processor, 4 or 5 minutes if you're working by hand.

3 If you have the time, wrap the dough in plastic and let it sit, at room temperature (or refrigerated if the room is very warm), for several hours. If not, proceed to the next step.

4 Bring the dough to room temperature if it was refrigerated and divide it into 6 pieces. On a lightly floured surface, press each piece into a disk and then roll it out as thin as possible, to a circle 8 inches or more in diameter.

5 Heat a large skillet, preferably cast iron, over medium heat for 4 or 5 minutes. One at a time, cook the tortillas on the griddle until brown spots begin to appear; turn and cook the other side. Total cooking time will be 4 or 5 minutes per tortilla.

6 Serve warm or cool and wrap in a plastic bag. Use as you would store-bought tortillas.

Crackers

Makes about 4 servings

Time: About 15 minutes

Crackers are ridiculously easy to make, and once you produce your first batch you'll have little trouble figuring out how to create your favorites. Sprinkle them with salt, sesame seeds, or poppy seeds; work a tiny bit

---

Three Uses for Stale Bread: Melba Toast, Zwieback, or Bread Crumbs

Time: About 30 minutes

Stale bread can be used in salads (page 83), as croutons (page 82), or in any of these ways:

1. To make melba toast, slice stale (but not completely dry) bread as thinly as possible—one-eighth inch thick is best (use a slicing machine if you have one). Bake on a baking sheet in a 250°F oven for about thirty minutes, turning once, or until thoroughly dry. Cool on a rack and store in a tin.

2. To make zwieback, slice stale (but not completely dry) bread into one-half-inch-thick slices. Bake in a 250°F oven for about one hour, turning once,

or until thoroughly dry. Cool on a rack and store in a tin.

3. To make bread crumbs, break fairly fresh or quite stale bread into chunks, and grind in a food processor or blender, a few chunks at a time. Toast crumbs on a baking sheet for ten minutes in a 350°F oven if you like, or store untoasted and toast, if you like, before using. Store bread crumbs in a sealed plastic bag in the freezer; they will keep forever.

of garlic or herbs into the dough; or substitute whole wheat or rye flour for some or all of the white flour.

1 cup (about 4$^1/_2$ ounces) all-purpose flour, plus more
    as needed
$^1/_2$ teaspoon salt
2 tablespoons butter
About $^1/_4$ cup water, plus more as needed

1 Preheat the oven to 400°F.

2 Place the flour, salt, and butter together in a large bowl or in the container of a food processor fitted with the steel blade. Blend with a fork or pulse, until the flour and butter are combined. Add about $^1/_4$ cup of water and blend, then continue to add water until the mixture holds together but is not sticky.

3 Roll out on a lightly floured surface until $^1/_4$ inch thick, or even less. Don't worry about overhandling— add flour as needed, and keep rolling. Score lightly with a sharp knife or razor if you want to break these into nice squares or rectangles later on. Bake on a lightly floured baking sheet, or directly on baking stones, until lightly browned, about 10 minutes. Cool on a rack; serve warm or at room temperature, or store in a tin.

Cream Crackers: These are quite rich and yummy; you'll have no trouble eating them with no toppings at all. Increase the butter to 4 tablespoons ($^1/_2$ stick). Substitute milk or cream for the water. Proceed as above.

The Basics of Sweet Yeast Buns and Coffee Cakes

Yeast breads are typically savory, but there is a place for yeast in baking sweets as well. Baking powder coffee cakes are fine, but nothing compares to the light, airy texture of a yeast-risen dough. As with yeast breads, yeasted rolls and cakes can be adapted to your schedule; if you are pressed for time, accelerate the rising by moving the dough to a warm place. If you must leave the house, put the dough in the refrigerator, where it will rise very slowly.

Traditionally, most yeasted "sweet" rolls are not all that sweet, but you can add more sugar if you like.

Basic Sweet Rolls
Makes about 24

Time: About 3$^1/_2$ hours, largely unattended

This rich, sweet variation of bread dough is not at all bad by itself, but is even better when made with one of the variations.

2$^1/_2$ cups (about 9 ounces) all-purpose flour,
    plus more as needed
1$^1/_2$ teaspoons instant yeast
$^1/_2$ teaspoon salt
$^1/_3$ cup sugar, plus more for sprinkling on rolls if
    desired
2 tablespoons butter, plus more for greasing the bowl
    and pan and for glazing
1 egg
$^1/_2$ cup milk, plus more as needed

1 Combine the flour, yeast, salt, and sugar in the container of a food processor fitted with the steel blade and process for 5 seconds. Add the 2 tablespoons butter and the egg and pulse a few times, until well combined. With the machine running, drizzle most of the milk through the feed tube. Process just until a dough ball forms; add more milk, 1 teaspoon at a time, if necessary. Knead by hand on a lightly floured surface for a minute or two longer, adding a little more flour or milk if necessary, until the dough is silky smooth and quite elastic.

2 Butter a bowl; place the dough in it. Cover and let rise until doubled in bulk, at least 2 hours. (You can hasten the process by placing it in a warm place.) Divide and shape as for dinner rolls (see illustrations on page 234); place on a greased baking sheet or in a buttered 12-compartment muffin tin. Cover and let rise until puffy, about 1 hour.

3 Preheat the oven to 400°F. Brush the tops of the rolls lightly with melted butter (you can also sprinkle them with a little sugar if you like) and bake until nicely browned, 20 to 30 minutes.

Cinnamon Rolls: After the first rise, roll out the dough into a $^1/_2$-inch-thick rectangle. Brush liberally with melted butter, then spread with a mixture of $^1/_2$ cup sugar and 2 teaspoons ground cinnamon. If you like, dot it with about $^3/_4$ cup currants, raisins, chopped nuts, or a mixture. Roll it up, lengthwise, then cut into 1- to 1$^1/_2$-inch-thick slices. Place in a buttered 12-compartment muffin tin and let rise and bake as above. Brush with additional butter and sprinkle with sugar just before baking.

Caramel Rolls: After the first rise, roll out the dough into a $^1/_2$-inch-thick rectangle. Brush liberally with melted butter, then sprinkle with $^1/_2$ cup brown sugar. If you like, dot it with about $^3/_4$ cup currants, raisins, chopped nuts, or a mixture. Roll it up, lengthwise, then cut into 1- to 1$^1/_2$-inch-thick slices. Place in a buttered 12-compartment muffin tin and let rise and bake as above. Brush with additional butter and sprinkle with sugar just before baking.

Orange-Date Rolls: After the first rise, roll out the dough into a $^1/_2$-inch-thick rectangle. Brush liberally with melted butter, then sprinkle with $^1/_2$ cup brown sugar, 2 tablespoons minced orange zest, and $^1/_2$ cup minced dates; add $^1/_2$ cup chopped nuts if you like. Roll it up, lengthwise, then cut into 1- to 1$^1/_2$-inch-thick slices. Place in a buttered 12-compartment

muffin tin and let rise and bake as above. Brush with additional butter and sprinkle with sugar just before baking. While rising, boil together $^1/_2$ cup sugar and $^1/_2$ cup orange juice until thickened. Brush the slices liberally with this mixture before baking as above.

Yeasted Coffee Cake

Makes 2 loaves

Time: 4 hours or more, largely unattended

This is slightly sweet, with a crunchy top. I bake it in loaf pans, because it's best sliced and toasted.

> 3 cups (about 13 ounces) all-purpose flour, plus more as needed
> 1$^1/_2$ teaspoons instant yeast
> $^1/_2$ teaspoon salt
> 1 cup sugar
> Pinch ground cloves
> 2 teaspoons ground cinnamon
> 6 tablespoons ($^3/_4$ stick) butter, plus more for greasing the bowl and pans
> 1 egg
> 1 teaspoon almond extract
> $^1/_2$ cup milk
> $^1/_2$ cup raisins (optional)
> $^1/_2$ cup chopped almonds, pecans, or walnuts

1 Combine 3 cups flour, yeast, salt, $^3/_4$ cup sugar, cloves, and $^1/_2$ teaspoon cinnamon in the container of a food processor fitted with the steel blade and process for 5 seconds. Add 2 tablespoons of the butter, the egg, and the almond extract and pulse a few times, until well combined.

2 With the machine running, drizzle most of the milk through the feed tube. Process just until a dough ball forms, adding milk 1 teaspoon at a time if necessary. Add the raisins if you like, and knead by hand on a lightly floured surface for a minute or two longer, adding a little more flour or milk if necessary, until the dough is silky smooth and quite elastic.

3 Butter a large bowl and turn the dough ball in it. Cover and let rise until about doubled in bulk, at least 2 hours. Grease two 9 × 5-inch loaf pans. Cut the dough in half and shape into rectangular loaves (see illustrations, page 229); press the loaves into the prepared pans. Cover with plastic wrap and let rise until light and puffy, about 1 hour. Preheat the oven to 375°F.

4 Use a wooden spoon to beat the remaining butter, sugar, flour, and cinnamon, along with the nuts and optional raisins. Sprinkle the cakes with this mixture and bake for 25 to 30 minutes, or until a toothpick inserted in the center comes out clean. Cool on a wire rack in the pans, then remove and slice.

Hot Cross Buns

Makes 12

Time: About 3 hours, largely unattended

These are delicate, tender buns, scented with cloves, enriched with currants, and topped with a simple icing.

3 to 3½ cups (about 14 to 16 ounces) all-purpose
   flour, plus more as needed
1½ teaspoons instant yeast
¾ cup sugar
1 tablespoon brown sugar
⅛ teaspoon freshly grated nutmeg
¼ teaspoon ground cinnamon
½ teaspoon ground cloves
½ teaspoon salt
6 tablespoons (½ stick) butter, plus some for
   greasing the baking sheet
2 eggs
¾ cup milk
½ cup currants (optional)

1 Combine the flour, yeast, sugars, spices, and salt in the container of a food processor fitted with the steel blade and process for 5 seconds. Add 4 tablespoons of the butter and the 2 eggs and pulse a few times, until well combined. With the machine running, drizzle most of the milk through the feed tube. Process just until a dough ball forms; add more milk, a teaspoon at a time, if necessary. Knead by hand on a lightly floured surface for a minute or two, adding more flour or milk if necessary, until the dough is silky smooth and quite elastic. Knead in the currants.

2 Put the dough in a bowl, cover the bowl with plastic wrap, and let the dough sit until it is double in bulk, at least 2 hours. Punch it down, roll into a foot-long snake, and cut it into 12 sections. Shape each section into a ball; place the balls close together—just about touching—on a buttered baking sheet and let rise again, this time for about 30 minutes.

3 Heat the oven to 375°F. Melt the remaining butter and brush the tops of the rolls with it. Use a razor blade to slash a deep "x" in the top of each bun, and bake them for about 20 minutes, until nicely browned. While they're baking, boil the remaining ¼ cup milk and ¼ cup sugar until just thick, but not at all brown, about 10 minutes (if you see it changing color, remove it from the heat immediately); when the buns come out of the oven, trickle a bit of this mixture into the "x" on each roll, using just over half of it. Five minutes later, spoon the remaining mixture over the buns. Cool on a rack, then serve warm or at room temperature.

The Basics of Quick Breads

Quick breads are leavened with baking powder (and sometimes baking soda as well), so they rise instantly. Generally, the goal in quick breads (and muffins, too, a form of quick bread) is a delicate, cake-like crumb, moist interior, and nicely browned but still tender crust. Thus they usually contain some fat, which contributes to flavor and tenderness.

Making quick breads is easy: You combine the dry ingredients, then combine the wet ingredients, then combine the two, and then bake. There are no special techniques or equipment needed; you don't even really need a bread pan—if you like, bake quick breads in a square baking tin or even an ovenproof skillet.

There is, however, one thing to remember: Overhandling of the batter can make quick breads tough. While in most yeast breads you want to develop gluten in order to get a tough crust and chewy crumb, in quick breads you want to retard its development to keep the bread nice and light. So heed this warning: Combine dry and wet ingredients as quickly as you can, and don't beat or even stir any more than is necessary. When you see no more dry bits of flour, the job is done; don't worry about remaining lumps.

Corn Bread

Makes about 6 servings

Time: About 45 minutes

This is one of the most important recipes I know. With the possible exception of brownies, there is no other baked good that packs so much flavor, and can be used in so many situations, with so little work. When you memorize this recipe—and make the inevitable changes in it that personalize it—you will have the batter made before the oven is preheated, and produce it without thinking. This batter can also be made into muffins or, if you have a mold, corn sticks. You can make corn bread with sweet milk or buttermilk, yogurt, or soured milk; the major difference is taste, although buttermilk (or soured milk) makes a somewhat lighter bread.

1¼ cups buttermilk, milk, or yogurt (or 1¼ cups milk and 1 tablespoon white vinegar—see Step 2 below), plus more as needed

2 tablespoons butter, olive oil, lard, or bacon drippings

1½ cups (about 7 ounces) medium-grind cornmeal

½ cup all-purpose flour

1½ teaspoons baking powder

1 teaspoon salt

1 tablespoon sugar, plus more if you like sweet corn bread

1 egg

1 Preheat the oven to 375°F.

2 If you are using buttermilk, milk, or yogurt, ignore this step. If you want to use soured milk (a good substitute for buttermilk), warm the milk gently—1 minute in the microwave is sufficient, just enough to take the chill off—and add the vinegar. Let it rest while you prepare the other ingredients.

3 Place the fat in a medium ovenproof skillet or in an 8-inch square baking pan over medium heat; heat until good and hot, about 2 minutes, then turn off the heat. Meanwhile, combine the dry ingredients in a bowl. Mix the egg into the buttermilk, milk, yogurt, or soured milk. Stir the liquid mixture into the dry ingredients, combining well; if it seems too dry, add another tablespoon or two of milk. Pour the batter into the preheated fat, smooth out the top if necessary, and place in the oven.

4 Bake about 30 minutes, until the top is lightly browned and the sides have pulled away from the pan; a toothpick inserted into the center will come out clean. Serve hot or warm.

Lighter, Richer Corn Bread: Use 4 tablespoons of butter (do not use other fat). Increase sugar to ¼ cup. Use 2 eggs; stir their yolks into the milk, as above, and beat the whites until stiff but not dry, then gently stir them into the prepared batter after yolks and milk have been incorporated. Bake as above.

Bacon Corn Bread: Before beginning, sauté $^1/_2$ cup minced bacon in 1 tablespoon canola or other neutral oil, bacon fat, or lard until crisp. Remove the bacon with a slotted spoon, leaving the fat behind. Keep the fat hot, and prepare the batter as above. Stir the bacon into the prepared batter and cook as above.

Corn and Bean Bread: Surprisingly wonderful. Use 2 eggs and 1 cup buttermilk or soured milk; omit the white flour. Stir $1^1/_2$ cups well-cooked white beans (canned are fine), pureed and strained, into the milk-egg mixture before adding to the dry ingredients. Proceed as above.

Seven Quick Additions to Corn Bread

Use these singly or in combination.

1. Chili powder or cumin, about one tablespoon
2. Fresh or creamed corn, about one cup
3. Minced or pickled jalapeños to taste
4. Grated cheese, typically Cheddar, about one cup
5. Molasses or honey, in place of the sugar, about one-quarter cup
6. Minced herbs, especially cilantro or fresh parsley, about two tablespoons
7. Sautéed onions, shallots, or leeks, about one-half cup (especially good with bacon)

Boston Brown Bread

Makes 2 small loaves

Time: About $1^1/_2$ hours

This soft-crusted bread, traditionally eaten with baked beans, is best with a mixture of flours.

Although it can be baked or steamed, I prefer baking. Steaming, however, is a nice traditional technique, and is described in the variation. Stir up to one cup raisins into the prepared batter if you like.

Butter or oil for greasing the pans
2 cups buttermilk or plain yogurt, or 2 cups less
   2 tablespoons milk and 2 tablespoons white
   vinegar (see Step 2 below)
3 cups assorted flour (about 14 ounces total), such as
   1 cup each of rye, corn meal, and whole wheat or
   all-purpose
$1^1/_2$ teaspoons salt
$1^1/_4$ teaspoons baking soda
$^3/_4$ cup molasses or maple syrup

1 Preheat the oven to 300°F. Liberally grease two 8 × 4-inch loaf pans.

2 If you are using buttermilk or yogurt, ignore this step. If not, warm the milk gently—1 minute in the microwave is sufficient, just enough to take the chill off—and add the vinegar. Let it rest while you prepare the other ingredients.

3 Mix the dry ingredients, then add the sweetener and the milk or yogurt. Stir just until mixed; this is a loose batter, not a dough. Pour or spoon into the loaf pans and bake for about an hour, or a little longer, or until a toothpick inserted into the center of the loaf comes out clean. Let cool on a rack for 10 minutes before removing from the pans; eat warm.

Onion Pan Bread

Makes about 6 servings

Time: 1 hour

Precooking the onions makes them tender and sweet; this is a wonderful quick bread to serve with moist, full-flavored meat dishes.

3 tablespoons butter

2 large onions, sliced about $1/4$ inch thick

2 tablespoons brown sugar

2 cups (about 9 ounces) all-purpose flour

1 tablespoon baking powder

1 teaspoon salt

1 teaspoon sugar

1 egg

1 cup milk

$1/4$ cup canola or other neutral oil

1. Preheat the oven to 350°F.

2. Place 2 tablespoons of the butter in a medium-to-large skillet and turn the heat to medium; sauté the onions, stirring occasionally, until softened, about 10 minutes.

3. Use the remaining butter to grease a 9-inch round baking dish, pie plate, or ovenproof skillet. Sprinkle with brown sugar and spread the onions around the bottom.

4. Combine the flour, baking powder, salt, and sugar. Beat together the egg, milk, and oil, add to the dry ingredients, and stir together quickly.

5. Spread the batter over the onions and bake about 35 to 40 minutes, or until a toothpick inserted into the middle comes out dry. Let stand 5 minutes before cutting into wedges and serving warm.

Irish Soda Bread

Makes 1 round loaf

Time: About 45 minutes

Although you bake soda bread in a round loaf, its texture is unlike that of the yeast breads it resembles. Instead, it has a very fine crumb, one which takes very well to toasting. Slice it thin.

About $1^1/2$ cups buttermilk or plain yogurt, or $1^1/2$ cups milk and $1^1/2$ tablespoons white vinegar (see Step 2 below)

4 cups (about 18 ounces) all-purpose flour or 2 cups all-purpose flour and 2 cups whole wheat flour

2 teaspoons salt

$3/4$ teaspoon baking soda

$3/4$ teaspoon baking powder

Butter or canola or other neutral oil for greasing the baking pan

1. Preheat the oven to 375°F.

2. If you are using buttermilk or yogurt, ignore this step. If you are not, warm the milk gently—1 minute in the microwave is sufficient, just enough to take the chill off—and add the vinegar. Let it rest while you prepare the other ingredients.

3. This is an easy enough dough to handle by hand, but it's even easier in a food processor: Combine all the dry ingredients and process (or stir) to combine. Add enough milk or yogurt to make a soft but not-too-sticky dough. Process for 30 seconds in the food processor or knead about 3 minutes by hand; the dough will be smooth and elastic. Let the dough rest for a few minutes.

4. Butter a baking sheet or baking pan and shape the dough into a round loaf. Slash the top with a razor blade (see illustrations on page 226). Bake for at least 45 minutes, or until the loaf is golden brown and sounds hollow when you thump the bottom (its internal temperature will be about 200°F). Let cool thoroughly. This bread does not keep well; plan to eat it within a day of making it. Store wrapped in waxed paper.

Banana Bread

Makes 1 loaf

Time: About 1 hour

I love all banana bread (especially toasted, the next day, with peanut butter), but I have been making them for thirty years and I do think this one is the ultimate—the coconut is what does it, although the butter helps too.

8 tablespoons (1 stick) butter, plus some for greasing the pan
1½ cups (about 7 ounces) all-purpose flour
½ cup whole wheat flour
1 teaspoon salt
1½ teaspoons baking powder
¾ cup sugar
2 eggs
3 very ripe bananas, mashed with a fork until smooth
1 teaspoon vanilla extract
½ cup chopped walnuts or pecans
½ cup grated dried unsweetened coconut

1   Preheat the oven to 350°F. Grease a 9 × 5-inch loaf pan.

2   Mix together the dry ingredients. Cream the butter and beat in the eggs and bananas. Stir this mixture into the dry ingredients; do not mix more than necessary. Gently stir in the vanilla, nuts, and coconut.

3   Pour the batter into the loaf pan and bake for 45 to 60 minutes, until nicely browned. A toothpick inserted into the center of the bread will come out fairly clean when it is done, but because of the bananas this bread will remain moister than most. Do not overcook. Cool on a rack for 15 minutes before removing from the pan. To store, wrap in waxed paper.

Cranberry Nut Bread

Makes 1 loaf

Time: About 1¼ hours

Sweet, tart, and rich, this is not only the model bread for Thanksgiving or Christmas, it's the perfect quick bread for afternoon tea. The added orange is a great flavor boost.

4 tablespoons (½ stick) cold butter, plus some for greasing the pan
2 cups (about 9 ounces) all-purpose flour
1 cup sugar
1½ teaspoons baking powder
½ teaspoon baking soda
1 teaspoon salt
¾ cup orange juice
1 tablespoon minced or grated orange zest
1 egg
1 cup cranberries, washed, dried, and coarsely chopped
½ cup chopped walnuts or pecans

1   Preheat the oven to 350°F. Grease a 9 × 5-inch bread pan.

2   Stir together the dry ingredients. Cut the butter into bits, then use a fork or two knives to cut it into the dry ingredients, until there are no pieces bigger than a small pea. (You can use a food processor for this step, which makes it quite easy, but you should not use a food processor for the remaining steps or the bread will be tough.)

3   Beat together the orange juice, zest, and egg. Pour into the dry ingredients, mixing just enough to moisten; do not beat, and do not mix until the batter is smooth.

4   Fold in the cranberries and the nuts, then pour and spoon the batter into the loaf pan. Bake about an hour, or until the bread is golden brown and a

toothpick inserted into its center comes out clean. Cool on a rack for 15 minutes before removing from the pan.

Quick Whole Wheat and Molasses Bread

Makes 1 loaf

Time: About 1¹/₄ hours

This is a quick, simple, and hearty bread, rich despite the fact that it contains no eggs or butter. Although it can be used as a sandwich bread, it's best served warm, with a hearty meal.

> Butter or oil for greasing the pan
> 1²/₃ cups buttermilk or plain yogurt, or 1¹/₂ cups milk and 2 tablespoons white vinegar (see Step 2 below)
> 2¹/₂ cups (about 12 ounces) whole wheat flour
> ¹/₂ cup cornmeal
> 1 teaspoon salt
> 1 teaspoon baking soda
> ¹/₂ cup molasses

① Preheat the oven to 325°F. Grease an 8 × 4-inch or 9 × 5-inch loaf pan.

② If you are using buttermilk or yogurt, ignore this step. If you are not, warm the milk gently—1 minute in the microwave is sufficient, just enough to take the chill off—and add the vinegar. Let it rest while you prepare the other ingredients.

③ Mix together the dry ingredients. Stir the molasses into the buttermilk or yogurt or into the soured milk. Whisk the liquid into the dry ingredients, then pour into the loaf pan. Bake until firm and a toothpick inserted into the center comes out clean, about an hour. Cool on a rack for 15 minutes before removing from the pan.

Lighter Whole Wheat Bread: Use 1¹/₂ cups whole wheat and 1¹/₂ cups all-purpose flour; omit the cornmeal. Substitute honey for the molasses for lighter flavor and color. Beat 1 egg into the wet ingredients.

Whole Wheat Bread with Sweet Milk: Use sweet milk and substitute 2 tablespoons baking powder for the baking soda. Beat 1 egg into the wet ingredients.

Nut Bread

Makes 1 loaf

Time: About 1¹/₄ hours

A lighter bread than Quick Whole Wheat and Molasses Bread (opposite), and one that has more possibilities (although you may use these variations with that recipe as well). Substitute two tablespoons canola or other neutral oil for the butter if you would like a bread lower in saturated fat.

> ¹/₄ cup melted butter, plus butter for greasing the pan
> 3 cups (about 14 ounces) all-purpose flour (or use 1¹/₂ cups all-purpose and 1¹/₂ cups whole wheat)
> 4 teaspoons baking powder
> 1 teaspoon salt
> ¹/₂ teaspoon ground cinnamon
> ²/₃ cup sugar
> 1¹/₂ cups milk
> 1 egg
> 1 cup roughly chopped walnuts or pecans

① Preheat the oven to 350°F. Butter a 9 × 5-inch loaf pan.

② Mix together the flour, baking powder, salt, cinnamon, and sugar. Beat together the milk, melted butter, and egg. Make a well in the center of the dry ingredients and pour the wet ingredients into it. Using a large spoon or rubber spatula, combine the ingredients swiftly, stirring and folding rather than beating, and stopping as soon as all the dry ingredients are moistened. The batter should be lumpy, not smooth.

3 Gently stir in the walnuts, and pour and scrape the batter into the buttered pan. Bake for about 45 minutes to 1 hour, or until a toothpick inserted into the center comes out clean. Cool on a rack for at least 10 minutes before removing from the pan.

Raisin or Nut-and-Raisin Bread: Substitute raisins for the nuts, or add raisins in addition to the nuts; the total of nuts and raisins should be no more than $1^1/_2$ cups. Increase cinnamon to 1 teaspoon and add a pinch of ground cloves.

Date-Nut Bread: Reduce the nuts to $^1/_2$ cup and add 1 cup chopped dates (or prunes, figs, or apricots) to the mix. Use brown sugar in place of regular sugar. Add 1 teaspoon vanilla extract to the wet ingredients.

Orange-Nut Bread: Substitute orange juice (preferably freshly squeezed) for the milk. Add 1 tablespoon minced orange zest to the dry ingredients. Use 1 teaspoon baking powder and 1 teaspoon baking soda. Increase sugar to 1 cup.

Apple Bread

Makes 1 loaf

Time: About $1^1/_4$ hours

Carrots, apples, zucchini, pumpkin . . . you can add almost any grated fruit or vegetable to a basic quick-bread batter and gain moisture, flavor, fat-free nutrients and—usually—sweetness. I like this kind of bread with some whole wheat flour and cornmeal, but you can use all white flour if you like.

    2 cups (about 9 ounces) all-purpose flour
    $^1/_2$ cup whole wheat flour
    $^1/_2$ cup cornmeal
    $^1/_2$ teaspoon salt
    1 tablespoon baking powder
    $^3/_4$ cup sugar, plus more to taste
    1 egg
    $^1/_4$ cup ($^1/_2$ stick) melted butter, plus more for
        greasing the pan
    $1^1/_4$ cups milk
    1 cup peeled and grated apple (drain if it is very
        watery)

1 Preheat the oven to 350°F. Butter a 9 × 5-inch loaf pan.

2 Combine all the dry ingredients. Beat the egg with the butter and milk. Make a well in the center of the dry ingredients and pour the wet ingredients into it, along with the apple. Using a large spoon or rubber spatula, combine the ingredients swiftly, stirring and folding rather than beating, and stopping as soon as all the dry ingredients are moistened. The batter should be lumpy, not smooth.

3 Pour into the prepared loaf pan and bake about an hour, or until a toothpick inserted in the center of the loaf comes out dry. Cool on a rack for at least 10 minutes before removing from the pan.

Apple-Nut Bread: Add 1 teaspoon ground cinnamon to the dry ingredients. Add 1 teaspoon vanilla extract to the wet ingredients, and use 2 eggs. Stir 1 cup chopped walnuts or pecans into the batter along with the apples.

Carrot Bread: Add $^1/_2$ teaspoon ground cinnamon to the dry ingredients, and increase the sugar to 1 cup.

Add 1 teaspoon vanilla extract to the wet ingredients, and use 2 eggs. Substitute carrots for the apples.

Zucchini or Pumpkin Bread: Thoroughly drain 1 cup shredded zucchini or pureed cooked or canned pumpkin. Add 1 teaspoon ground cinnamon, $1/2$ teaspoon ground ginger, and 1 pinch each of ground cloves and freshly grated nutmeg to the dry ingredients, and increase the sugar to 1 cup. Use 2 eggs. Add $1/2$ cup chopped walnuts or pecans if you like.

Basic Muffins

Makes 8 large or 12 medium muffins

Time: About 40 minutes

Fast, easy, and almost infinitely variable (there isn't a single quick-bread batter that cannot be baked as muffins, or vice versa), muffins have somehow become the domain of doughnut shops. But baking at home gives you control over fat content and quality of ingredients, and introduces you to one of life's great luxuries: the fresh-from-the-oven muffin.

I do not like very sweet muffins, so I have kept the sugar to a minimum. See the following recipe, Sweet and Rich Muffins (page 250), if you like your muffins sweeter.

3 tablespoons melted butter or canola or other
   neutral oil, plus some for greasing the muffin tin
2 cups (about 9 ounces) all-purpose flour
$1/4$ cup sugar, or to taste
$1/2$ teaspoon salt
3 teaspoons baking powder
1 egg
1 cup milk, plus more if needed

1 Preheat the oven to 400°F. Grease a standard 12-compartment muffin tin.

2 Mix together the dry ingredients in a bowl. Beat together the egg, milk, and butter or oil. Make a well in the center of the dry ingredients and pour the wet ingredients into it. Using a large spoon or rubber spatula, combine the ingredients swiftly, stirring and folding rather than beating, and stopping as soon as all the dry ingredients are moistened. The batter should be lumpy, not smooth, and thick but quite moist; add a little more milk or other liquid if necessary.

3 Spoon the batter into the muffin tins, filling them about two-thirds full and handling the batter as little as possible. (If you prefer bigger muffins, fill the cups almost to the top. Pour $1/4$ cup water into those cups left empty.) Bake 20 to 30 minutes, or until the muffins are nicely browned and a toothpick inserted into the center of one of them comes out clean. Remove from the oven and let rest for 5 minutes before taking them out of the tin. Serve warm.

Banana-Nut Muffins: This is good with half bran or whole wheat flour. Add $1/2$ cup roughly chopped walnuts, pecans, or cashews to the dry ingredients. Substitute 1 cup mashed very ripe banana for $3/4$ cup of the milk. Use honey or maple syrup in place of sugar if possible.

Bran Muffins: Substitute 1 cup oat or wheat bran for 1 cup of the all-purpose flour (you can use whole wheat flour for the remainder if you like). Use 2 eggs and honey, molasses, or maple syrup for sweetener. Add $1/2$ cup raisins to the prepared batter if you like.

Blueberry or Cranberry Muffins: Add 1 teaspoon ground cinnamon to the dry ingredients; increase sugar to $1/2$ cup. Stir 1 cup fresh blueberries or cranberries into the batter at the last minute. You can also use frozen blueberries or cranberries here; do not defrost them first. Blueberry muffins are good with $1/2$ teaspoon lemon zest added to the batter along with the wet ingredients. Cranberry muffins are excellent with $^1/_2$ cup chopped nuts and/or 1 tablespoon minced orange zest added to the prepared batter.

Spice Muffins: Add 1 teaspoon ground cinnamon, $^1/_2$ teaspoon each ground allspice and ground ginger, and 1 pinch ground cloves and mace or nutmeg to the dry ingredients; use 1 cup whole wheat flour in place of 1 cup all-purpose flour. Add $^1/_2$ cup raisins or currants to the prepared batter if you like.

Sour Cream or Yogurt Muffins: These are very rich and tender. Reduce baking powder to 1 teaspoon, and add $^1/_2$ teaspoon baking soda to dry ingredients. Substitute $1^1/_4$ cups sour cream or yogurt for the milk and cut the butter or oil back to 1 tablespoon.

Coffee Cake Muffins: Mix together $^1/_2$ cup packed brown sugar; 1 teaspoon ground cinnamon; 1 cup finely chopped walnuts, pecans, or cashews; and 2 extra tablespoons melted butter. Stir half of this mixture into the original batter with the wet ingredients, and sprinkle the rest on top before baking.

Savory Muffins: Cut sugar back to 1 tablespoon. Add up to 1 cup of minced cooked bacon, minced ham, or shredded cheese—alone or in combination—to the batter just before baking.

Sweet and Rich Muffins

Makes 8 large or 12 medium muffins

Time: About 40 minutes

You can do anything to this muffin batter that you can do to the less sweet, less rich batter above.

Nine Easy Changes to Basic or Sweet and Rich Muffins

These changes can be made alone or in combination.

1. Substitute whole wheat flour for half the all-purpose flour.
2. Add one-half cup chopped raisins, currants, dates, figs, prunes, or apricots to the batter.
3. Add one-half cup or more chopped walnuts, pecans, or cashews to the batter.
4. Use two eggs, and separate them. Add the yolks as usual; beat the whites until stiff but not dry and fold in very gently at the last moment. This produces lighter muffins.
5. Add ground cinnamon, nutmeg, mace, ginger, and/or allspice to taste.
6. Add one-half to one teaspoon grated citrus zest.
7. Add up to one-half cup chocolate chips to the batter.
8. Add other fresh fruits, such as raspberries or grated apple or pear to the batter, as in Blueberry or Cranberry Muffins, above.
9. Sprinkle the tops of unbaked muffins with some sugar, or a mixture of cinnamon and sugar.

---

6 tablespoons ($^3/_4$ stick) butter, at room temperature, plus some for greasing the muffin tin

$^3/_4$ cup sugar

$^1/_2$ teaspoon salt

3 teaspoons baking powder

2 cups (about 9 ounces) all-purpose flour

2 eggs

$^1/_2$ cup milk, plus more as needed

1 Preheat the oven to 400°F. Grease a standard 12-compartment muffin tin (grease it very well if the tin does not have a non-stick surface; even better, grease the tin and place a paper muffin liner in each compartment).

2 Use a wooden spoon or standing mixer to cream together the 6 tablespoons butter and the sugar.

3 Mix together the salt, baking powder, and flour; beat the eggs with the milk.

4 Add about a third of the dry ingredients to the butter-sugar mixture, then moisten with a little of the milk. Repeat until all the ingredients are used up. The batter should be lumpy, not smooth, and thick but moist; add a little more milk or other liquid if necessary.

5 Spoon the batter into the muffin tins, filling them about two-thirds full and handling the batter as little as possible. (If you prefer bigger muffins, fill the cups almost to the top. Pour $1/4$ cup water into those cups left empty.) Bake 20 to 30 minutes, or until the muffins are nicely browned and a toothpick inserted into the center of one of them comes out clean. Remove from the oven and let rest for 5 minutes before taking them out of the tin. Serve warm.

The Basics of Popovers, Biscuits, and Scones

These are last-minute rolls, made either for dinner or—in the case of scones—for an afternoon snack. They are light and easy. Biscuits, especially, can be made as part of a one-hour dinner without much effort, especially after a little practice. Like quick breads, they should all be handled as little as possible to keep them light and tender.

Yogurt or Buttermilk Biscuits

Makes 10 or more biscuits

Time: 20 to 30 minutes

These are the best, especially (I think) when made with yogurt. When made correctly—and you can do

it the first time, I swear—they're sweet, slightly sour, crisp, and tender. Oh, and very, very fast. Don't substitute soured milk here; just move on to the Baking Powder Biscuit variation.

2 cups (about 9 ounces) all-purpose or cake flour,
  plus more as needed
1 scant teaspoon salt
3 teaspoons baking powder
1 teaspoon baking soda
2 to 5 tablespoons cold butter (more is better)
$7/8$ cup plain yogurt or buttermilk

1 Preheat the oven to 450°F.

2 Mix the dry ingredients together in a bowl or food processor. Cut the butter into bits and either pulse it in the food processor (the easiest) or pick up a bit of the dry ingredients, rub them with the butter between your fingers, and drop them again. All the butter should be thoroughly blended before proceeding.

3 Use a large spoon to stir in the yogurt or buttermilk, just until the mixture forms a ball. Turn the dough out onto a lightly floured surface and knead it ten times; no more. If it is very sticky, add a little flour, but very little; don't worry if it sticks a bit to your hands.

4 Press into a $3/4$-inch-thick rectangle and cut into 2-inch rounds with a biscuit cutter or glass. Place the rounds on an ungreased baking sheet. Gently reshape the leftover dough and cut again; this recipe will produce 10 to 14 biscuits.

5 Bake 7 to 9 minutes, or until the biscuits are a beautiful golden brown. Serve within 15 minutes for them to be at their best.

Baking Powder Biscuits: Use 4 teaspoons baking powder and sweet milk in place of yogurt or buttermilk. Proceed as above.

Cheese Biscuits: Stir in $1/2$ cup grated Cheddar, Gruyère, Fontina, blue, or Parmesan cheese and $1/4$ teaspoon cayenne (optional) along with the yogurt or milk. Lightly grease the baking sheet and proceed as above. This will make 14 to 16 biscuits.

Drop ("Emergency") Biscuits: These cut 5 minutes off the prep time. Increase the yogurt or milk to 1 cup and drop tablespoons of the dough onto a greased baking sheet. Bake as above.

Sweet Potato Biscuits: A classic. Stir 1 cup cooked, drained, and pureed sweet potatoes or winter squash into the butter-flour mixture. Add only enough yogurt or buttermilk to form the dough into a ball, usually between $1/2$ and $3/4$ cup (if your potatoes are very dry, you may need the whole $7/8$ cup). Roll a little thinner—about $1/2$ inch. Cut as above, into about 24 biscuits, and bake on a greased baking sheet at 450°F for 12 to 15 minutes.

Cream Scones

Makes 10 or more scones

Time: 20 minutes

Scones are no more than ultra-rich biscuits. You can make them with milk, but that's missing the point.

2 cups (about 9 ounces) all-purpose or cake flour,
    plus more as needed
1 scant teaspoon salt
4 teaspoons baking powder
2 tablespoons sugar
5 tablespoons cold butter
3 eggs
$3/4$ cup heavy cream
$1/3$ cup dried currants or raisins
1 tablespoon water

1. Stir one-half cup or more chopped nuts into the prepared batter.
2. Use up to fifty percent whole wheat flour.
3. Substitute chopped fresh fruit (apples, pears, peaches), whole berries (blueberries, cranberries), or minced dried fruit (figs, apricots) for the currants.
4. Add one teaspoon or more of ground cinnamon or ginger, or a pinch of ground nutmeg or allspice, to the dry ingredients.
5. Add one-half cup grated cheese along with the eggs and cream; reduce the sugar to one teaspoon.
6. Add minced fresh herbs to taste—dill, parsley, and chervil are especially good; reduce the sugar to one teaspoon.
7. Add one-half cup or more of minced cooked meat along with the eggs and cream; reduce the sugar to one teaspoon.

1 Preheat the oven to 450°F.

2 Mix the dry ingredients together in a bowl or food processor, reserving 1 tablespoon of the sugar. Cut the butter into bits and either pulse it in the food processor (the easiest) or pick up a bit of the dry ingredients, rub them with the butter between your fingers, and drop them again. All the butter should be thoroughly blended before proceeding.

3 Beat 2 of the eggs with the cream; with a few swift strokes, combine them with the dry ingredients. Use only a few strokes more to stir in the currants. Turn the dough out onto a lightly floured surface and knead it ten times; no more. If it is very sticky, add a little flour, but very little; don't worry if it sticks a bit to your hands.

4 Press the dough into a $3/4$-inch-thick rectangle and cut into 2-inch rounds with a biscuit cutter or

glass. Place the rounds on an ungreased baking sheet. Gently reshape the leftover dough and cut again; this recipe will produce 10 to 14 biscuits. Beat the remaining egg with 1 tablespoon of water, and brush the top of each scone; sprinkle each with a little of the remaining sugar.

5 Bake 7 to 9 minutes, or until the scones are a beautiful golden brown. These keep better than biscuits, but should still be eaten the same day you make them.

Popovers

Makes 12 popovers

Time: About 45 minutes

Popovers are best made at the last minute, but they're good leftover as well. I think they go incredibly well with scrambled eggs.

1 tablespoon melted butter or canola or other neutral oil, plus some for greasing the muffin tin

2 eggs

1 cup milk

1 teaspoon sugar

$1/2$ teaspoon salt

1 cup (about $4^1/2$ ounces) all-purpose flour

1 Preheat the oven to 425°F. Grease a standard 12-compartment muffin tin and place it in the oven while you make the batter.

2 Beat together the eggs, milk, butter or oil, sugar, and salt. Beat in the flour a little bit at a time; the mixture should be smooth. Fill the muffin tins at least halfway (if your tin is large, this might make fewer than 12 popovers). Place in the oven and bake for 15 minutes, then reduce the heat to 350°F and continue baking for 15 minutes more, or until the popovers are puffed and browned (do not check the popovers until they have baked for a total of 30 minutes). Serve hot.

Pizza, Bruschetta, Sandwiches, Pitas, and Burritos

Once, most Americans thought only of sandwiches when making bread-based meals. Now, thanks in large part to Italy, but also to breads and fillings from Mexico, the Middle East, and elsewhere, we have many more options.

Pizza is no longer the domain of the pizza parlor; anyone can make pizza quickly and easily at home, whether by making dough, or simply by buying fresh pizza dough from a local pizza maker, or frozen dough at the supermarket. Similarly, pita bread and flour tortillas are sold almost everywhere, and they take well to a variety of fillings.

The Basics of Pizza

Pizza-making requires practice, but it doesn't take anything approaching a magic touch. Toppings are simple: You can put nearly anything you want on a pizza, as long as it isn't too wet or too dry; wet toppings make for a soggy crust, dry ones usually fall off. Not long ago, almost all American pizza makers believed that you had to have cheese on top of every pizza in order to bind all the other ingredients together. But that time has passed, and cooks now know that as long as there are some moist ingredients on top of a pizza—from olive oil to tomatoes to pesto to, of course, cheese—the pie will hold together.

Shaping the Dough

Making pizza dough is easy; it's essentially the same as bread dough, sometimes with a little olive oil added for better texture. Like bread dough, the best texture is achieved with a fairly moist dough that isn't quite as easy to handle as firmer, drier dough. But this is a quickly overcome hurdle; use flour judiciously and you won't have problems. And, like bread dough, pizza dough is best made in a food processor, although it certainly can be made by hand or in a standing mixer.

The only tricky part of handling pizza dough comes in the final shaping. As with any kneaded, yeast-risen bread dough, pizza dough is elastic, and this elasticity sometimes causes difficulties in stretching the dough to the dimensions you like. Even if you want a real thick-crust pizza (or focaccia), this can be a problem, and if you want a thin crust, you may find holes appearing long before the dough is stretched as thin as you like it.

The solution to this is patience: Rising time is not critical in making pizza dough, nor is the size to which the dough rises. But patience in waiting for the risen dough to relax before stretching is essential. In order to get the dough to the size you want it, it often takes a few tries spread over a brief period of time, with intervals to allow the dough to relax.

Experienced pizza makers gently stretch dough over the backs of loosely held fists, and this gentle handling keeps the dough light and airy. But most of us press the dough with our fingers or roll it with pins; either of these is easy (the first, being somewhat gentler, is preferable), and both work well.

In any case, start by patting the dough out into a round disk, then roll, pat, or stretch it a bit more. As soon as you see that the dough is resistant—it returns to its former shape and size despite your best efforts—walk away. Come back a few minutes later and roll, pat, or stretch it some more. This process may take as long as twenty or even thirty minutes, with a few minutes of rest between each attempt. Take it slow and it will work out fine. See the illustrations below.

Pizza Ingredients and Equipment

The ingredients needed for making pizza are identical to those for making bread (page 218). Use all-purpose or bread flour (the latter gives a tougher, chewier crust, which you may or may not prefer); instant yeast; and coarse (kosher) salt, especially for sprinkling. When you use olive oil in a dough, it need not be extra-virgin olive oil.

Pizza cooks best in an oven equipped with a pizza stone, but it is also just fine baked on a flat baking sheet, or even one with a small lip. (Pizza also bakes well directly on a grill.) If you have a pizza stone, use it. If you want to buy one, look for a rectangular stone that is large enough to accommodate an entire pizza. A pizza stone makes a peel—a broad sheet of wood or metal with a handle—almost essential. And a peel

SHAPING PIZZA

(Step 1) Begin by patting the dough into a round disk (or a rectangle as you prefer). Let the dough relax for a few minutes before continuing. *(Step 2)* Stretch the dough by pulling and patting it, adding flour (or use olive oil) as necessary. If you allow the dough to rest every now and then the gluten will relax and the dough will be less resistant to stretching. *(Step 3)* When you have stretched the dough out to the edges of the pan, it is ready.

simplifies the whole process: If you sprinkle flour or cornmeal on it you can roll the dough out on it directly, then slide the dough right onto the stone. You can also use the peel for removing the pie from the oven, and even for serving if you like. Wooden peels are more attractive, but are difficult to wash (since they only come in contact with flour or cornmeal, the need to wash them is minimal); metal peels can be kept spotless.

There's another difference between using a peel and using a baking sheet: You will sprinkle a peel with flour or cornmeal to keep the pizza from sticking, in order to slide it onto a stone. But with a baking sheet, it's best to use a light drizzle of olive oil; you can then press the dough out onto the sheet and bake it without reoiling. This is the easiest way to make pizza.

Size and Thickness of Pizza

The Basic Pizza Dough recipe on page 258 makes one fairly large or two or more smaller pizzas. Choose the number of pizzas based on your preference for size and thickness. If you're grilling, start with smaller pies, which are much easier to handle; thicker crusts are also more forgiving than thin ones. To make more than one pizza at a time, divide the dough in half and make the first pizza. When it's in the oven, start work on a second one (on which, of course, you may use different toppings). By the time the first one is done, you'll be ready to slide the second into the oven. By the time you've finished eating the first, the second will be ready.

Toppings for Pizza

As with pasta, I like my pizza to have distinct, clean flavors: tomatoes, basil, and Parmesan; tomato sauce and mozzarella; roasted peppers and anchovies; and so on. When you start mixing too many ingredients, as in the typical "House Special" served in many pizza parlors, you muddy all of them and wind up tasting none. So I encourage you when you begin making your own pizza to keep it simple. White Pizza (Pizza Bianca) (page 259)—white pizza seasoned with salt, olive oil, and perhaps some rosemary—is among the best.

The Basics of Grilling Pizza

I have had some fairly intense arguments with people who believe that it is impossible to grill pizza unless you do so over wood. I have had great success, however, grilling pizza not only over wood but over briquettes and even on a gas grill. Grilling over wood is ideal, but only if you have a minimum of toppings, and only if you don't mind that those toppings are not piping hot. Without special equipment, it's difficult, for example, to melt cheese on a pizza grilled over a wood fire.

Regardless of the fuel, however, a covered grill makes the process incredibly simple. First of all, you want a grill with as broad a surface area as possible (if you are using a gas grill with two levels, remove the top level). Second, you want a fire that is hot enough to brown the dough, but not so hot that it scorches it before the interior cooks; the ideal fire is one you can hold your hand a few inches above for at least three or four seconds. If you are making smaller pizzas, you can turn them with tongs as soon as they firm up a bit; if the pizza is larger, you may need a peel or two spatulas to turn it.

The procedure is straightforward: Grill one side of the pizza, just enough to firm it up and brown it a bit, then flip it and add toppings. If you want the toppings to become very hot, you just cover the grill. If you don't care whether they actually cook, but just warm up a bit, you can leave the grill open. That's about it.

Basic Pizza Dough

Makes 1 large or 2 or more small pizzas

Time: At least 1 hour, largely unattended

You can knead this dough with a mixer (use the dough hook), or by hand, but I like the food processor best. The pizzas can be grilled or baked in an oven—the hotter the better (commercial pizza ovens are usually about 700°F). This is the simplest, most basic pizza (and bread) dough you can make. Olive oil makes a smoother, more flavorful dough and a slightly cracklier crust—but you can omit it if you like—just add a little more water to the dough if you do.

1 teaspoon instant or rapid-rise yeast

3 cups (about 14 ounces) all-purpose or bread flour, plus more as needed

2 teaspoons coarse kosher or sea salt, plus extra for sprinkling

1 to 1¼ cups water

2 tablespoons plus 1 teaspoon olive oil

1 Combine the yeast, flour, and 2 teaspoons salt in the container of a food processor. Turn the machine on and add 1 cup water and the 2 tablespoons of oil through the feed tube.

2 Process for about 30 seconds, adding more water, a little at a time, until the mixture forms a ball and is slightly sticky to the touch. If it is dry, add another tablespoon or two of water and process for another 10 seconds. (In the unlikely event that the mixture is too sticky, add flour, a tablespoon at a time.)

3 Turn the dough onto a floured work surface and knead by hand a few seconds to form a smooth, round dough ball. Grease a bowl with the remaining olive oil, and place the dough in it. Cover with plastic wrap or a damp cloth and let rise in warm, draft-free area until the dough doubles in size, 1 to 2 hours. You can cut this rising time short if you are in a hurry, or you can let the dough rise more slowly, in the refrigerator, for up to 6 or 8 hours.

4 Proceed with any recipe below, or wrap the dough tightly in plastic wrap and freeze for up to a month. Defrost in a covered bowl in the refrigerator or at room temperature.

To make this dough by hand: Combine half the flour with the salt and yeast and stir to blend. Add 1 cup water and the 2 tablespoons olive oil; stir with a wooden spoon until smooth. Add remaining flour a bit at a time; when the mixture becomes too stiff to stir with a spoon, begin kneading, adding as little flour as possible—just enough to keep the dough from being a sticky mess. Knead until smooth but still quite moist, about 10 minutes. Proceed as above.

Six Quick Ideas for More Flavorful Pizza Dough

The options are infinite, but be careful; you want the dough to cook up crisp, and too many additions will make it soggy. You also want it to act as a flavor carrier, not as the dominant flavor. But before adding the water to the dough, try the following, alone or in combination:

1. Add one-half to one teaspoon freshly cracked black pepper.
2. Add one tablespoon pureed cooked garlic (roasted is best) or one-half teaspoon minced raw garlic, or to taste.
3. Add one teaspoon to one tablespoon fresh herbs.
4. Substitute one-half cup to one cup whole wheat or semolina flour for the white flour.
5. Add one-fourth to one-half cup minced prosciutto, ham, or cooked bacon.
6. Use flavored olive oil, such as garlic or rosemary oil, in place of regular olive oil.

To make this dough with a standing mixer: The machine must be fairly powerful or it will stall. Combine half the flour with the salt, yeast, 2 tablespoons olive oil, and 1 cup water; blend with the machine's paddle. With the machine on slow speed, add flour a little at a time, until the mixture has become a sticky ball that pulls away from the sides of the bowl (switch to the dough hook if necessary). Knead for a minute by hand, adding as little flour as possible, then proceed as above.

Crunchier Pizza Dough: This dough may be a little more difficult to handle, but it has superior flavor and a pleasant crunch: Substitute $1/2$ cup cornmeal for $1/2$ cup of the flour.

White Pizza

Pizza Bianca

Makes 1 large or 2 or more small pizzas

Time: About 3 hours, largely unattended, plus time to preheat the grill

The most basic of pizzas, and among the best, this can be made on a grill or in the oven; directions for both follow.

1 recipe Basic Pizza Dough (page 258)
Extra-virgin olive oil as needed
Coarse kosher or sea salt to taste
1 tablespoon or more roughly chopped fresh rosemary leaves
Several fresh rosemary sprigs (optional)

① When the dough is ready, knead it lightly, form it into a ball, and divide it into as many equal pieces as you like; roll each piece into a round ball. Place each ball on lightly floured surface, sprinkle with a little more flour, and cover with plastic wrap

or a towel. Let rest until they puff slightly, about 20 minutes.

② For grilled pizza, start a medium-hot charcoal or wood fire, or preheat a gas grill to the maximum. Roll or lightly press each dough ball into a flat round, lightly flouring the work surface and the dough as necessary (do not use more flour than you need to). Let the rounds sit for a few minutes; this will relax the dough and make it easier to roll out. Then roll or pat out the dough, as thinly as you like, turning occasionally and sprinkling the top with flour as necessary.

For baked pizza, preheat the oven to the maximum. Oil one or more baking sheets, then press each dough ball into a flat round directly on the oiled sheet(s). In either case, let the rounds sit for a few minutes; this will relax the dough and make it easier to roll out. Then pat out the dough, as thinly as you like, oiling your hands if necessary.

Alternatively, preheat the oven (with a baking stone) to the maximum, and roll or pat out the dough as for grilled pizza, above.

③ To grill the pizza, either slide it directly onto the grill or brush the top with oil and flip it onto the grill, oiled side down. In either case, brush the top side with oil. The pizza will be soft at first, but will quickly firm up. Move it around the grill as necessary to avoid burning the bottom, and cook until brown grill marks appear, from 1 to 6 minutes depending on your grill heat. Turn with a spatula or tongs, then brush again with oil. Sprinkle with salt and rosemary leaves and garnish, if desired, with a sprig of rosemary. Grill until the bottom is crisp and brown, 1 to 6 minutes depending on grill heat.

To bake the pizza, top with salt and rosemary, slide the baking sheet into the oven (or the pizza itself onto the stone), and bake from 6 to 12 minutes, depending on the oven heat, until nicely browned.

④ Serve the pizzas immediately or at room temperature; these will keep for a few hours.

White Pizza with Prosciutto and Parmesan: Omit the salt and rosemary. Top each pizza with a few very thin slices of prosciutto, a drizzling of olive oil, and a grating of Parmesan cheese. Add the toppings after you turn the pizza (if you're grilling) or about halfway through the baking time (if you're baking).

White Pizza with Clams: Also good with diced, lightly cooked, peeled shrimp or lightly steamed and shelled mussels. Omit the rosemary. Top each pizza with a few freshly shucked littleneck clams (and some of their juice, if you have it), a few very thin slivers of garlic, a little coarse salt, and some minced fresh parsley leaves. If you're grilling, add the toppings after turning, then cover the grill if possible. If you're baking, add the toppings at the beginning.

White Pizza with Mushrooms: Omit the rosemary. Top each pizza with some Sautéed Mushrooms with Garlic (page 584). Use plenty of minced fresh parsley leaves; sage is also good. If you're grilling, add the toppings after turning, then cover the grill if possible. If you're baking, add the toppings about halfway through cooking.

Fifteen Quick Ideas for Pizza Toppings

Use these alone or in combination, but bear in mind the following guidelines:

- When you add moist ingredients such as cheese or tomatoes, cover the grill if possible or they may not cook through.
- Don't overload grilled pizzas: you risk losing part of the topping. Switch to the oven instead.
- Think before topping oven-baked pizzas; delicate ingredients may overcook if left in the oven for the full baking time. Instead, add them about halfway through the cooking.

1. Lightly cooked sausage, bacon, or salami (no need to cook first), or other meat
2. Thin-sliced tomatoes and basil, with olive oil and/or grated Parmesan; or peeled, seeded, and chopped tomatoes tossed with basil
3. Well-washed and dried tender greens, especially spicy ones such as arugula and cress. If you're using the oven, add greens when pizzas are finished baking and let the heat from the crust wilt them (it takes about one minute).
4. Small amounts of Gorgonzola or other blue cheese or fontina or other semisoft cheese. Gratings of Parmesan are almost always welcome.
5. Pitted black olives, especially the oil-cured kind (good in combination with Caramelized Onions and Vinegar, above). Green olives are good, too.
6. Marinated Roasted, Grilled, or Broiled Peppers (page 593)
7. Grilled or Broiled Eggplant Slices (page 568) or the pan-cooked eggplant slices from Eggplant Parmesan (page 571)
8. Slices of grilled zucchini (see Grilled Mixed Vegetables, page 617)
9. Canned anchovy fillets, with some of their oil
10. Minced raw or mashed roasted garlic
11. Shredded mozzarella
12. Basic Pesto (page 766)
13. Shredded canned tuna, canned clams, or any lightly cooked seafood
14. Soft goat cheese or ricotta
15. Reconstituted sun-dried tomatoes (or Oven-Dried Tomatoes, page 611)

White Pizza with Caramelized Onions and Vinegar: This takes some work in advance: Place about 4 cups of thinly sliced onion in a large skillet, turn the heat to medium, and cover. Cook, stirring every 5 minutes, until the onions are dry and almost sticking to the pan, about 20 minutes. Uncover and add 4 tablespoons extra-virgin olive oil; continue to cook, stirring, until the onions are nicely browned, another 20 minutes or so. Season to taste with salt and pepper, then stir in about 1 tablespoon of balsamic vinegar, or to taste. Omit the rosemary. Top each pizza with a portion of these onions and some minced fresh basil, thyme, or sage leaves. A sprinkling of plain bread crumbs is also good. If you're grilling, add the toppings after turning, then cover the grill if possible. If you're baking, add the toppings about halfway through cooking.

Baked Pizza with Tomato Sauce and Mozzarella

Makes 1 large or 2 or more small pizzas

Time: About 3 hours, largely unattended

The oven is best for pizzas with many toppings, or for those with wet or gooey ingredients. It's also best, of course, if the weather forbids grilling. If you can get fresh mozzarella (which is packed in water), use less, and don't expect pizza-parlor-like results, for which you need the firmer, plastic-wrapped cheese. For variations, see Fifteen Quick Ideas for Pizza Toppings, page 260.

1 recipe Basic Pizza Dough (page 258)
2 tablespoons extra-virgin olive oil, approximately
2 cups Basic Tomato Sauce (page 130), or any other tomato sauce
2 cups freshly grated mozzarella cheese
Salt and freshly ground black pepper to taste

1 Preheat the oven to 500°F; make sure the oven is thoroughly preheated.

2 Knead the dough ball lightly, form it into a ball, and divide it into as many equal pieces as you like; roll each piece into a ball. Place each ball on lightly floured surface, sprinkle with a little more flour, and cover with plastic wrap or a towel. Let rest until they puff slightly, about 20 minutes.

3 Roll or lightly press each dough ball into a flat round, lightly flouring the work surface and the dough as necessary (do not use more flour than you need to). Let the rounds sit for a few minutes; this will relax the dough and make it easier to roll out. Roll or pat out the dough on a lightly oiled baking sheet or floured pizza peel. Roll the dough as thinly as you like.

4 Drizzle the rounds with the olive oil, then top them with the sauce and cheese; sprinkle with salt and pepper. Place the baking sheet in the oven or slide the pizza directly onto the stones and bake until the crust is crisp and the cheese melted, usually 8 to 12 minutes.

Baked White Pizza with Potatoes

Makes 1 large or 2 or more small pizzas

Time: About 3 hours, largely unattended

This Roman classic takes a little more work, but is sheer delight for potato lovers. Best baked on a sheet in the oven.

2 or 3 medium waxy red or white potatoes, about 1 pound, peeled and sliced
Salt
1 recipe Basic Pizza Dough (page 258)
4 tablespoons extra-virgin olive oil, plus more for greasing the baking sheet (and your hands if necessary)
1 tablespoon or more minced fresh rosemary

1 Preheat the oven to 500°F; make sure the oven is thoroughly preheated.

2 Cook the potato slices in boiling salted water to cover for 3 to 5 minutes, until they are just beginning to become tender. Drain well.

3 Oil one or more baking sheets, then press each dough ball into a flat round directly on the oiled sheet(s). Let the rounds sit for a few minutes; this will relax the dough and make it easier to roll out. Then pat out the dough, as thinly as you like, oiling your hands if necessary.

4 Top the pizzas with the potatoes, 4 tablespoons olive oil, and plenty of rosemary. Slide the baking sheet into the oven and bake from 6 to 12 minutes, depending on the oven heat, until the potatoes begin to brown and the olive oil sizzles.

Pissaladière

Makes 1 thick-crust pizza, enough for a main course for 4 or an appetizer for 8

Time: About 3 hours, largely unattended

Pissaladière, the Niçoise version of pizza, is sold almost everywhere in Nice, often at room temperature. Although it never contains cheese, other ingredients vary. One, however, is essential: a large quantity of onions (use a food processor to chop them if you have one), simmered slowly until soft and sweet.

Cooking time can be accelerated somewhat by cooking the onions more quickly, uncovered, but some of their subtle flavors will be lost. In any case, do not let the onions brown.

1 recipe Basic Pizza Dough (page 258)
4 tablespoons olive oil
3 pounds onions (about 8 or 10 medium), chopped
1 bay leaf
4 sprigs fresh thyme or 1 teaspoon dried thyme
Salt and freshly ground black pepper to taste
2 or 3 tomatoes, cored and thinly sliced
1 (2-ounce) can flat oil-packed anchovy fillets,
    drained and coarsely chopped
30 tiny Niçoise olives or 10 or 15 larger Calamata
    or oil-cured olives, pitted

1 While the dough is rising, heat 3 tablespoons of the olive oil in a large, heavy skillet or casserole over low heat. Add the onions, bay leaf, and thyme. Cover and cook very slowly, stirring occasionally, until the onions have given up their liquid and turned golden, at least 1 hour. Remove the bay leaf and thyme sprigs if using and add salt and pepper. Turn the heat to high for a couple of minutes to cook off most of the liquid.

2 Meanwhile, knead the dough ball lightly, form it into a ball, and place it on a lightly floured surface. Sprinkle with a little more flour and cover with plastic wrap or a towel. Let rest while the oven preheats. Preheat the oven to 400°F.

Five Pizzas You Can Serve at Room Temperature

Pizza is often served at room temperature in Italy, a practice that makes it even more convenient. These are the best pizzas to hold for a few hours at room temperature.

1. White Pizza (Pizza Bianca), page 259
2. White Pizza with Prosciutto and Parmesan, page 260
3. Baked White Pizza with Potatoes, page 261
4. Pissaladière, page 262
5. Sicilian Onion Pizza, page 263

---

3 Roll or lightly press the dough ball into a flat round, lightly flouring the work surface and the dough as necessary (do not use more flour than you need to). Let the round sit for a few minutes; this will relax the dough and make it easier to roll out.

4 Use the remaining tablespoon of olive oil to grease an 11 × 17-inch jelly-roll pan. Press the dough into a small rectangle and place it in the pan. Let it relax in the pan for a few minutes. Press the dough to the edges of the pan. If it resists stretching, stretch it gently, then let it rest for a few minutes. Sometimes this takes a while, because the dough is so elastic. Don't fight it; just stretch, let it rest for 5 minutes, then stretch again. Try not to tear the dough. When you're done, the dough should be no more than $^{1}/_{4}$ inch thick except at the extreme edges. Cover the dough with the cooked onions, spreading them evenly.

5 Decorate the onions with the tomatoes, anchovies, and olives. Lower the oven temperature to 350°F and bake for 30 to 40 minutes, or until the crust is golden brown. Pissaladière reheats well, so you can undercook it slightly at first, remove it from the oven, and finish the cooking later in the day. It is also excellent served at room temperature.

Sicilian Onion Pizza: Omit the tomatoes and olives. In Step 1, stir the anchovies into the cooked onions and cook for 5 minutes. Stir a 6-ounce can of tomato paste into the onions and cook for a few more minutes, always over low heat. Season to taste. Drizzle the rolled-out dough with 2 tablespoons olive oil and bake for 10 to 12 minutes, or until the bottom begins to turn pale golden. Spread the partially baked dough with 1 cup plain bread crumbs, preferably fresh, then spread with the onion mixture. Return to the oven and bake for 15 to 20 minutes more, until the bottom is dark golden but not burned, and the top is a richly colored caramel. Remove and allow to cool for a few minutes before cutting; best served hot or warm.

Focaccia
Makes 1 focaccia

Time: About 3 hours, largely unattended

If you make a thick-crust pizza, dimple its surface with your fingertips, sprinkle it with olive oil and salt, and cool it until just warm or at room temperature, you have focaccia. Of course you can make more complex focaccia than that, just as you can make more complex pizza.

1 recipe Basic Pizza Dough (page 258), made with
    an extra tablespoon olive oil
3 tablespoons olive oil
Coarse salt

1 When the dough is ready, knead it lightly, form it into a ball, and place it on a lightly floured surface. Sprinkle with a little more flour and cover with plastic wrap or a towel; let it rest for 20 minutes.

2 Use 1 tablespoon of the oil to grease an 11× 17-inch jelly-roll pan. Press the dough into a small rectangle and place it in the pan. Let it relax in the pan for a few minutes. Press the dough to the edges of the pan. If it resists stretching, stretch it gently, then let it rest for a few minutes. Sometimes this takes a while, because the dough is so elastic. Don't fight it; just stretch, let it rest for 5 minutes, then stretch again. Try not to tear the dough.

3 Cover the dough and let it rise for at least 30 minutes or until somewhat puffy. Meanwhile, preheat the oven to 425°F. Uncover the dough and dimple the surface all over with your fingertips. Drizzle with the remaining olive oil and sprinkle with coarse salt.

4 Place in the oven, lower the temperature to 375°F, and bake for about 30 minutes, or until the focaccia is golden. Remove and cool on a rack before serving. Cut focaccia into squares and serve with meals or as a snack. Or cut squares in half horizontally and use to make sandwiches. Focaccia, well wrapped (first in plastic, then in foil), freezes fairly well for 2 weeks or so. Reheat, straight from the freezer (unwrap, remove plastic, and then rewrap in foil), in a 350°F oven for 10 to 15 minutes.

Eight Simple Ideas for Focaccia

Focaccia is *like* pizza, but it is *not* pizza. It is meant to be a snack or a meal accompaniment, not a meal, so keep the toppings simple. That said, you can make focaccia into a thick-crust pizza by adding any of the Fifteen Quick Ideas for Pizza Toppings, page 260. But to keep focaccia focaccia, add any of the following, singly or in limited combinations:

1. Any minced fresh herb, especially rosemary, sage, or basil (fragile herbs such as sage and basil should be added toward the end of cooking)
2. Thinly sliced tomato or reconstituted sun-dried tomatoes, or Oven-Dried Tomatoes (page 611)
3. Caramelized onions (see White Pizza with Caramelized Onions and Vinegar, page 261)
4. Pitted black or green olives, or Black Olive Paste (Tapenade) (page 26)
5. Freshly grated Parmesan cheese
6. Thinly sliced mushrooms
7. Strips of Marinated Roasted, Grilled, or Broiled Peppers (page 593)
8. Thin slices of prosciutto (added toward the end of cooking to prevent them from drying out)

Calzone

Makes 2 calzones, enough for 4 main-course servings

Time: About 3 hours, largely unattended

Here's how I "discovered" calzone: One day, I messed up on sliding a pizza into the oven; it folded onto itself in a heap on the stone. I couldn't take it back out, and I couldn't bake it the way it was. So I quickly folded it over neatly, encasing the filling entirely in the dough. It was what you call making the best of a bad situation.

Intentionally made calzone is better than that. While you can make calzone using any pizza topping as a filling (see page 260 for suggestions), it's best with cheese, vegetables, and/or meat. While the filling should be substantial, it should also be fairly dry; very liquidy fillings will leak or make the dough soggy; that's why drained ricotta, which is moist but not wet, is the ideal base.

Calzones can also be topped with Basic Tomato Sauce, page 130, or any other tomato sauce.

1 recipe Basic Pizza Dough (page 258)
2 cups ricotta cheese
1 cup finely chopped prosciutto or other ham
   or 1 cup well-washed, dried, and finely chopped
   cooked spinach or other greens, such as chard
   or broccoli raab (page 604)
1 cup chopped or grated mozzarella cheese
1 cup freshly grated Parmesan cheese
Salt and freshly ground black pepper to taste

1 When the dough is ready, knead it lightly, and cut it in two. Form 2 balls, and place them on a lightly floured surface. Sprinkle with a little more flour and cover with plastic wrap or a towel; let them rest for 20 minutes. If the ricotta is very moist, drain it in a fine sieve for 10 minutes or so to remove excess moisture.

2 Combine the ricotta, ham or spinach, mozzarella, and Parmesan. Taste and add salt, if necessary, and pepper. Preheat the oven to 350°F.

3 Roll or lightly press each dough ball into a flat round, lightly flouring the work surface and the dough as necessary (do not use more flour than you need to). Let the rounds sit for a few minutes; this will relax the dough and make it easier to roll out. Roll or

pat out the dough into an 8- to 10-inch round, not too thin, on a floured pizza peel or lightly oiled baking sheet.

4 Place half the filling into the middle of each dough round. Moisten the edges with a little water. Fold one end over onto the other and press closed with your fingertips.

5 Bake the calzones on a baking sheet or directly on a baking stone for 30 to 40 minutes, or until nicely browned. Serve hot or warm.

Bruschetta

Makes 4 appetizer servings

Time: 20 minutes, plus time to preheat the grill

Bruschetta is grilled (or broiled, or even toasted) bread, rubbed with garlic and drizzled with olive oil. There are two requirements: Good coarse, crusty bread (like Easiest and Best French Bread, page 224, shaped into a boule, page 227) and good olive oil. Once you make basic bruschetta, you'll probably want to try variations; I give some, but the possibilities—as with any sandwich—are endless.

4 slices good bread, preferably cut from a large
    round loaf
Extra-virgin olive oil
1 clove garlic, halved
Salt to taste

1 Preheat the broiler or grill and adjust the rack so that it is at least 4 inches from the heat source. Brush the bread on one or both sides with a little olive oil and rub one or both sides of each slice with the garlic. (The energy you put into this will determine the intensity of the flavor of the finished product: Rub hard, letting the garlic disintegrate into the bread, and the flavor will be more pronounced; give it a cursory run-through, and the flavor will be mild.) Sprinkle with a little salt.

2 Broil or grill the bread until lightly browned on both sides, taking care not to burn it or toast it all the way through. If you like, drizzle with a little more olive oil and rub with more garlic. Serve immediately.

Bruschetta with Roasted or Simmered Garlic: Prepare the bread with olive oil as above and broil or grill one side. Turn it over and broil or grill it for a minute or two longer on the other side. Spread the top with a tablespoon or so of mashed garlic puree (see Garlic Bruschetta, page 575); sprinkle with additional olive oil and salt if you like. Broil or grill until hot and lightly browned on top (broiler) or bottom (grill), taking care not to burn.

Bruschetta with Tomatoes and Basil: Take care not to use overly juicy tomatoes or the bread will become soggy. (For this reason plum tomatoes are best.) Peel, core, seed, and dice 1 small-to-medium tomato per slice of bread. Drain in a strainer for a few minutes, while you preheat the grill or broiler. Prepare the bread with olive oil and garlic as above and broil or grill one side. Turn it over and broil or grill it for 1 minute on the other side, until hot and lightly brown, taking care not to burn. Spread the top with the tomato, then drizzle with olive oil. Garnish with torn or whole basil leaves (or other fresh herb), then drizzle with a little more olive oil and salt if you like.

Sixteen Simple Ideas for Topping Bruschetta

Generally, it's best to add toppings when the bruschetta is done to retain its freshness; you don't really want to cook any of these additions.

1. Prosciutto or other ham
2. Minced fresh or dried hot chiles, especially with tomatoes

3. Chopped fresh herbs
4. Chopped tender greens such as arugula or watercress
5. Basic Pesto (page 766), especially mixed with tomatoes as in Bruschetta with Tomatoes and Basil (above)
6. Black Olive Paste (Tapenade) (page 26)
7. Small amounts of freshly grated Parmesan, mozzarella, or other cheese
8. Marinated Roasted, Grilled, or Broiled Peppers (page 593), or canned pimentos
9. Anchovy fillets, with a little of their oil
10. Chopped cooked seafood, especially shrimp
11. Grilled or sautéed mushrooms (grilled fresh porcini or portobellos are especially nice)
12. Capers, especially with tomatoes
13. Mashed white beans (White Beans, Tuscan-Style, page 509, are especially good)
14. Caramelized Small Onions or Shallots (page 588), or sautéed or grilled onions
15. Cooked spinach or other greens, well drained; or Collards or Kale with Double Garlic (page 562)
16. Grilled eggplant or zucchini (see Grilled Mixed Vegetables, page 617)

The Basics of Sandwiches

Ever since the Earl of Sandwich slapped two pieces of bread around a hunk of meat, the sandwich has been associated with simplicity, speed . . . and fat. Just look at the American classics: the hamburger, certainly the paradigm of the twentieth-century sandwich; the BLT, in which vegetables play a subsidiary role; the deli sandwiches of corned beef, roast beef, pastrami, or what-have-you, in which vegetables play no role; and the "sub," containing more of the same but usually with different condiments. Even the traditional "light" sandwiches—tuna salad or breast of turkey—

are, more often than not, slathered with enough mayonnaise to make a dietitian cringe.

It need not be that way. The plethora of new ingredients available to us in supermarkets, the knowledge we have gained in exploring the cuisines of the world, and the widespread availability of good bread of all types have combined to make it possible to create new sandwiches and remodel old ones, often with a superior nutritional profile. Best of all, the sandwich remains simple food. (Of course you can still slap two pieces of bread around a hunk of meat, but you don't need a recipe for that.)

There are some basic challenges involved in sandwich-making: keeping moist ingredients from soaking into the bread and making it soggy, keeping green leaves from wilting, tomatoes from falling apart, interiors from leaking out. In short, keeping the sandwich intact. One solution to this problem is to make sandwiches when you are about to eat them. At home, this is not a problem, nor should it be on picnics, when it's just as easy to pack up ingredients individually and assemble sandwiches at the last minute as to make everything in advance.

When you need to carry a sandwich, however—to work, school, a ball game, in the car—the job becomes a little trickier. When every slice of bread was heavily buttered, that butter offered the bread some protection against the invasion of moisture from the sandwich ingredients. Now, the use of butter seems not only ill-advised but also superfluous, since its subtle flavor would be lost among the stronger flavors of today's sandwich ingredients.

There are, however, some guidelines for making sandwiches that taste great and travel well:

The Greens Lettuce offers little in the way of taste and wilts quickly. If you want greens, go with something sturdy that will last a few hours: arugula, kale, or watercress, for example. You'll gain both flavor and texture.

The Tomatoes Tomatoes are great on a sandwich you'll eat on the spot, but pass on them if you are packing a sandwich to go; there's no surer guarantee of sogginess. If you want some nice red juicy thing, substitute a couple of slices of roasted red pepper, available in cans or jars at any supermarket. Pat them lightly with a paper towel to remove excess moisture before making the sandwich.

The Bread Again, for a sandwich made and eaten within minutes, use any bread you want. But for a sandwich to go, start with thick, hard, crusty bread, bread that is almost too hard to eat fresh; after a few hours of being wrapped, it will become softer, but not mushy. These days, sandwiches are no longer necessarily based on bread or rolls (and, thankfully, the days of white-bread-or-nothing are long gone). Both pita breads (page 236) and soft flour tortillas (see Wheat Flour Tortillas, page 238) are sold at most supermarkets, and both are at least as good as bread or standard rolls for sandwiches. Pitas have the distinct advantage of being closed on all but the filling end, so they are excellent for moist fillings. And because of their virtually nonexistent crumb, tortillas are more moisture-resistant than other breads. If you don't overfill them, and roll them tightly, you can fill them with almost anything, even stew or cooked beans. Focaccia (recipe, page 263), too, makes a good basic sandwich. Let it cool, slice it horizontally, and use as you would bread.

The Condiments There are the obvious choices—mustard, mayonnaise, ketchup, and so on—and then there are the not-quite-so-obvious ones. Try Tahini Dressing (page 770), or any other fairly thick salad dressing; lemon juice; Worcestershire or other prepared sauces; miso; hoisin sauce; horseradish; any pesto (page 765–767); yogurt, seasoned with curry powder or chiles; or any salsa (page 772–773). If at all possible, carry your condiments separately and add them to the sandwich before eating; this not only gives everyone a choice of toppings but helps mightily to avoid sogginess.

The Extras These are the additions that can really make a sandwich special: torn-up herbs, Sprouts (page 524), grated vegetables, Quick Pickled Vegetables (page 106), grapes, Caramelized Small Onions or Shallots (page 588), minced nuts, crumbled feta cheese, grated Parmesan, minced scallions, mashed Roasted Garlic (page 575), anchovies, capers, Black Olive Paste (Tapenade) (page 26), Caponata with Raisins and Pine Nuts (page 102), or Oven-Dried Tomatoes (page 611) (or reconstituted sun-dried tomatoes).

The Filling Even aside from the obvious—grilled, roasted, or fried meat or chicken leap to many minds, understandably so—the list is almost infinite:

Roasted vegetables of all types (see "Vegetables," pages 529–617)
Sautéed vegetables—especially greens—with olive oil (see "Vegetables," pages 529–617)
Oven-Baked Ratatouille (page 616)
Goat cheese
Avocado (page 540) or Guacamole (page 22)
Mozzarella or smoked mozzarella
Grilled Portobello Mushrooms (page 584)
Weekday Morning Scrambled Eggs (page 735), or any variation
Any frittata (pages 740–741)
Falafel (page 523)
Simple Bean Croquettes (page 521)
Deep-Fried Catfish or Other Fillets (page 283)
Sautéed Soft-Shell Crabs, Version I (page 332)
Spicy Grilled or Broiled Shrimp (page 325)
Shrimp Salad, Mediterranean-Style (page 119)

That's the general idea. Following are some step-by-step examples to get you started.

Grilled Cheese, Simple and Complex

Makes 1 sandwich

Time: 10 minutes

From the simple and time-honored technique of melting cheese on bread come the now-classic Tuna Melt, Reuben, and, best of all, the Cuban Sandwich (see variations below). Grilled cheese is vastly improved by the addition of your favorite dressing, from spicy mustard to Russian Dressing (page 763), to any salsa (pages 772–773). Or you can add ham, bacon, or other cooked meat, or tomatoes, pickles, or other sliced vegetables.

    1 tablespoon butter or oil
    2 slices any bread
    2 or 3 ounces (several slices) good melting cheese:
        Emmenthal, Gruyère, Jarlsberg, Cheddar, etc.

1 Place a small skillet over medium heat and add the butter or oil. Make a sandwich of the bread and cheese.

2 When the butter melts or the oil is hot, place the sandwich in the skillet. Cover it with a plate and weight the plate with whatever is at hand—a couple of cans of soup or a small but heavy pot cover, for example.

3 Cook until the bottom of the bread is lightly browned, about 2 or 3 minutes. Turn and repeat. Eat immediately.

Tuna Melt: Add $1/4$ to $1/2$ cup tuna salad to the sandwich. Follow the procedure above.

Reuben: Use rye bread if possible. Make a sandwich of cheese, Russian Dressing (page 763) or mustard, 2 or 3 ounces of pastrami or corned beef, and $1/4$ cup of drained sauerkraut. Follow the procedure above.

Cuban Sandwich: Use a 6- to 10-inch section of a long French loaf (or baguette, page 224). Make a sandwich of cheese, roast pork, ham, and mortadella (optional), and dill pickle (or cucumber from Quick Pickled Vegetables, page 106); add yellow mustard. Follow the procedure above.

Pan Bagna with Chicken Breast

Makes 4 servings

Time: 1 hour, plus unattended overnight resting time and time to preheat the grill

Pan bagna—which translates as "bathed bread"—is not only one of the most beautiful sandwiches you've ever seen, it is ideal for picnics: The longer it sits (within reason), the better it gets. View this recipe as a general set of guidelines rather than as a firm formula; you can make it with whatever you have on hand, including leftover grilled fish or meat and leftover vegetables. Just make sure to weight it for a while to allow the flavors to mingle and the bread to soften. Serve it with plain raw vegetables; the sandwich is plenty savory.

    1 medium zucchini, summer squash, or eggplant
    $1/2$ pound boneless, skinless chicken breast, rinsed
        and patted dry with paper towels
    Salt and freshly ground black pepper to taste
    1 or 2 red bell peppers (or use canned "pimentos")
    1 (8- to 10-inch) round crusty loaf of bread
    1 teaspoon drained capers, plus more if desired
    6 or 8 good olives, black or green, pitted
    4 to 6 anchovy fillets, plsu more if desired
    4 marinated artichoke hearts, quartered
    2 or 3 slices ripe tomato
    Minced fresh parsley or basil leaves
    2 or 3 tablespoons extra-virgin olive oil
    Juice of $1/2$ lemon

① Rinse the zucchini, squash, or eggplant and cut it lengthwise into $1/4$-inch slices; if time allows, place it in a colander and salt liberally. Let sit for 30 to 45 minutes; rinse and dry thoroughly, pressing to extract excess moisture. Meanwhile, preheat a gas grill or start a charcoal fire; heat should be moderate.

② Sprinkle the chicken breast with salt and pepper and grill for 2 to 4 minutes per side, depending on thickness. At the same time, grill the zucchini, squash, or eggplant until lightly browned on both sides. Grill the red peppers until the skin blackens and blisters all around. When the peppers are cool enough to handle, peel, core, and seed them; cut into strips.

③ Cut the bread in half, horizontally. Remove some of the white crumbs from each half to make the bread somewhat hollow. Then build the sandwich, placing the chicken, pepper, zucchini, squash, or eggplant, capers, olives, anchovies, artichoke hearts, tomato, herbs, salt, and pepper. Drizzle with the olive oil and sprinkle with lemon juice.

④ Close the sandwich; wrap well in aluminum foil. Place it on a plate, with another plate on top, and weight the second plate with rocks, bricks, a gallon jug of water, whatever is handy. Use a lot of weight—5 pounds or more. Let the sandwich sit overnight. To serve, unwrap and cut into wedges.

Roasted Eggplant Sandwich with Tomato-Garlic Sauce

Makes 6 sandwiches

Time: 40 minutes

Ideal on French or Italian bread, this sandwich is also good on a hard roll or any other firm, crusty loaf.

> 1 large or 2 medium firm unblemished eggplant, about $1\frac{1}{2}$ pounds total, peeled if you prefer
> 3 tablespoons olive oil

> 1 small onion, minced
> Salt and freshly ground black pepper to taste
> 2 cloves garlic
> 2 cups drained and chopped canned tomatoes (do not use tomatoes packed in puree)
> 2 tablespoons minced fresh basil leaves
> 6 thin slices mozzarella
> 6 rolls or 2 or 3 loaves of French or Italian bread

① Preheat the oven to 400°F. Slice the eggplant crosswise into 12 slices, each about $1/2$ inch thick. Brush a baking sheet lightly with 1 tablespoon of olive oil, and place the eggplant slices, in one layer, on the baking sheet. Brush tops of slices with another tablespoon of olive oil. Bake until the eggplant is lightly browned, turn, sprinkle with onion, salt, and pepper, and bake until tender, a total of 20 to 30 minutes.

② While the eggplant is baking, peel and crush 1 clove of garlic. Place it in a medium skillet with the remaining olive oil and turn the heat to medium. Add the tomatoes and cook briskly over medium heat, stirring frequently, until tomatoes are thick and not at all runny, about 15 minutes. Peel and mince the remaining garlic clove and add it, along with the basil, salt, and pepper, to the tomatoes. Cook an additional 2 minutes over low heat.

③ Use 2 slices of eggplant with a piece of cheese and a dollop of sauce for each sandwich. Serve hot or warm.

Gert's Pepper and Onion Sandwich

Makes 2 big or 4 small sandwiches

Time: 30 minutes

My mother's favorite, best with red or yellow peppers, but not bad with green either. This sandwich can be made far more substantial by adding grilled or sautéed sausage.

2 tablespoons butter or olive oil, plus more for the
     rolls if desired
2 bell peppers, preferably red or yellow, stemmed,
     peeled if desired, seeded, and cut into strips
2 medium-to-large onions, cut in half and thinly
     sliced
Salt and freshly ground black pepper to taste
2 to 4 hard rolls

1 Place the butter or oil in a large, deep skillet over medium heat. When the butter melts or the oil becomes hot, add the peppers and onions. Season with salt and pepper and cook, stirring occasionally, until very tender, about 20 minutes.

2 Butter the rolls if you like. Check the seasoning and pile the pepper-and-onion mixture into the rolls. Serve hot.

Mixed Veggie Sandwich with Tahini Dressing

Makes 4 sandwiches

Time: 20 minutes

Basic guidelines for turning a salad into a sandwich.

2 carrots, peeled and grated
1 cup alfalfa or other sprouts (page 524)
1/4 head red or other cabbage, shredded
1 cup (about 1 small can) sliced beets, drained and
     cut into strips
1/4 cup raisins
1/4 cup roughly chopped pecans or walnuts
1 cup tahini (sesame paste)
1 clove garlic, peeled
1/4 cup freshly squeezed lemon juice
1/4 cup water, more or less
Salt and freshly ground black pepper to taste

8 slices bread, 4 rolls, or 4 pita breads, cut in half
2 ripe tomatoes, cored and cut into 8 wedges
4 leaves romaine lettuce, washed and dried

1 Mix together the carrots, sprouts, cabbage, beets, raisins, and pecans.

2 Put the tahini in a blender or food processor with the garlic and lemon juice and process until smooth; add water gradually, processing until creamy, then add salt and pepper to taste. Thin with a little more water if necessary.

3 Toss the vegetable mixture with the tomato, and dressing, then make sandwiches with the lettuce. Serve immediately.

Tuna without Mayo

Makes 4 sandwiches

Time: 10 minutes

This low-fat alternative to the traditional tuna sandwich has lots more going for it: a soft flour tortilla and the sparkling flavors of lime and cilantro.

2 (6-ounce) cans tuna packed in water
Juice of 2 limes
3 scallions, minced
1/2 cup minced cilantro leaves
Salt and freshly ground black pepper to taste
Hot pepper sauce to taste
4 leaves romaine lettuce, washed and dried
2 ripe tomatoes, cored and sliced
4 soft whole wheat flour tortillas, pita breads, rolls,
     or 8 slices bread

1 Drain the tuna and mash it with the lime juice, scallions, cilantro, salt, pepper, and hot pepper sauce.

2 With the tuna mixture, lettuce, and tomatoes, make sandwiches. Serve immediately.

Chicken Breast Sandwich with Spinach

Makes 4 sandwiches

Time: 30 minutes

Garlicky greens make a great sandwich with or without chicken; grilled swordfish (page 294) is also good here.

    10 ounces spinach, trimmed and well washed
       (page 604)
    3 tablespoons olive or peanut oil
    1 pound boneless, skinless chicken breast, rinsed and
       patted dry with paper towels and cut into 4 pieces
    Flour or cornmeal for dredging
    1 teaspoon minced garlic
    2 tablespoons freshly squeezed lemon juice
    Salt and freshly ground black pepper to taste
    4 rolls or 8 slices bread

1 Cook the spinach according to the directions for Basic Boiled, Steamed, or Microwaved Spinach (page 604). Drain, rinse under cold water, and squeeze out excess moisture. Chop.

2 Place 2 tablespoons of the oil in a large, deep skillet over medium-high heat. A minute later, dredge each of the chicken pieces in flour or cornmeal and add them to the skillet. Cook about 3 minutes per side, until golden and just cooked through. Remove and set aside.

3 Turn the heat to medium and add the remaining oil to the pan. Add the garlic, followed almost immediately by the spinach. Cook, stirring frequently, until the spinach is hot and tossed with the oil, about 2 minutes. Stir in the lemon juice.

4 Make sandwiches with the spinach and chicken, then season to taste with salt and pepper. Serve hot or at room temperature.

Salmon Sandwich with Cress and Juniper

Makes 4 sandwiches

Time: 30 minutes

You can make this same sandwich with canned salmon if you wish. Juniper berries are sold in the spice section of any decent supermarket.

    1 (1-pound) salmon fillet, or about 16 ounces canned
       salmon
    ¼ cup olive oil
    20 juniper berries, lightly crushed with the broad side
       of a knife
    2 cups watercress or arugula, trimmed, washed,
       and dried
    8 slices any good bread
    Salt and freshly ground black pepper to taste

1 Place the salmon in a medium saucepan with water to cover and turn the heat to high. When the water boils, cover the pan and turn off the heat. Let the salmon rest until it is done, about 10 minutes, depending on the thickness of the fish.

2 Remove the salmon from the water and allow it to cool on a rack or several layers of paper towels. Slice or break it into several pieces. If you're using canned salmon, drain it of the canning liquid.

3 Meanwhile, warm the oil in a very small saucepan over low heat. Add the juniper berries and cook for about 5 minutes, until the oil is very fragrant. Strain and reserve the oil.

4 To make sandwiches, place some pieces of salmon on a slice of bread, top with cress, and drizzle lightly with a bit of the reserved oil. Add salt and pepper to taste, then top with another slice of bread. Serve immediately.

Curried Pork Tenderloin Sandwich with Chutney and Arugula

Makes 6 sandwiches

Time: 40 minutes, plus time to preheat the grill

This sandwich is best if you allow the meat to sit, refrigerated, for a day or so before slicing it.

    2 tablespoons Dijon mustard
    1 tablespoon All-Purpose Curry Powder or
       store-bought curry powder (page 778)
    1¹/₄ pounds pork tenderloin, in 1 piece
    1 cup mango or other chutney (page 784)
    2 cups arugula, trimmed, washed, and dried
    6 pita breads, flour tortillas, or hard rolls

1 Start a charcoal or wood fire or preheat a gas grill or broiler; the fire should be quite hot.

2 Blend the mustard and curry powder in a small bowl, then rub the meat all over with this mixture.

3 Grill or broil the meat, turning frequently, until done, 10 to 15 minutes. Allow it to cool at least 10 minutes (or, better still, refrigerated overnight) before slicing.

4 Slice as thinly as possible, then toss with the chutney and arugula before piling into pitas, rolling in tortillas, or spooning onto rolls. Serve immediately.

Pita with Ground Lamb and Zucchini

Makes 4 servings

Time: 20 minutes

Pita is great bread for moist fillings, especially if you handle it carefully and eat the sandwich right away.

    1 pound lean ground lamb
    1 large onion, chopped
    1 teaspoon minced garlic
    1 medium zucchini, chopped
    ¹/₄ cup chopped walnuts or pine nuts
    4 canned plum tomatoes, with their juice
    ¹/₂ teaspoon ground cinnamon
    Salt and freshly ground black pepper to taste
    6 to 8 medium pita breads
    Grated carrot or minced parsley for garnish

1 Place a large non-stick skillet over medium-high heat and add the lamb. Cook, stirring, until it begins to turn brown, about 5 minutes.

2 Add the onion, garlic, and zucchini, stir, and continue to cook until the vegetables are softened, about 5 minutes.

3 Add the walnuts, chopped tomatoes, cinnamon, salt, and pepper, and simmer for 10 minutes or so, until mixture is thick but still moist.

4 Meanwhile, warm the pitas in a 300°F oven for 3 to 5 minutes; or, wrap in a towel or napkin and microwave for 1 minute or so, until warm. Cut them in half.

5 Fill pitas with the lamb mixture, garnish, and serve.

Six Other Ideas for Filling Pitas

Not quite as moisture-resistant as burritos, but better at containing ingredients than bread, pitas can handle bulky ingredients best of all. Some ideas:

1. Almost any salad, lightly dressed (see "Salads")
2. Indian-Style Split Pea Fritters (page 522)
3. Falafel (page 523)
4. Pork Satay (page 462)
5. Grilled, broiled, or sautéed chicken cutlets (pages 380–391)
6. Extra-crisp or oven-fried fish fillets (pages 280–282)

Bean Burritos

Makes 4 servings

Time: 10 minutes with precooked beans

With cooked beans as the base, you can make great burritos in a flash.

About 2 cups Twice-Cooked ("Refried") Beans with
    Cumin (page 511) or Black Beans with Cumin or
    Chili (page 512)
4 large flour tortillas
1¹/₂ to 2 cups grated Cheddar or jack cheese
2 cups washed, trimmed, dried, and chopped lettuce
    or other greens
Any spicy sauce or salsa, such as Tomato-Onion Salsa
    (page 772); Cucumber-Yogurt Dip with Mint
    (page 771); Green Tomato Salsa (page 773);
    or Homemade Mild Chile Paste (page 774)
Minced cilantro leaves

1 Warm the beans in a small saucepan. To warm the tortillas, wrap them in foil and place in a 300°F oven for about 10 minutes, or stack them between two damp paper towels and microwave for 30 to 60 seconds.

2 Spread a portion of cheese onto each tortilla and top with a portion of beans, greens, sauce, and cilantro. Roll up and serve.

Bean Burritos with Meat

Makes 6 servings

Time: 30 minutes with precooked beans

If you have Pork Bits with Mexican Flavors (page 462), just add them to the beans in the above recipe (and use six tortillas). Or follow this recipe.

³/₄ to 1 pound ground meat or poultry, such as beef,
    turkey, or chicken, or a combination
¹/₂ cup chopped onion
1 tablespoon minced garlic
1 tablespoon chili powder, or to taste
About 2 cups Twice-Cooked ("Refried") Beans with
    Cumin (page 511) or Black Beans with Cumin or
    Chili (page 512)
Salt and freshly ground black pepper to taste
6 large flour tortillas
1¹/₂ to 2 cups grated Cheddar or jack cheese
2 cups washed, trimmed, dried, and chopped lettuce
    or other greens
Any spicy sauce or salsa, such as Tomato-Onion
    Salsa (page 772); Cucumber-Yogurt Dip with Mint
    (page 771); Green Tomato Salsa (page 773);
    or Homemade Mild Chile Paste (page 774)
Minced cilantro leaves

1 Place the meat in a large skillet and turn the heat to medium. Cook, stirring frequently, until the meat begins to lose its color. Stir in the onion and continue to cook, stirring, until the meat has lost all traces of pinkness and the lumps are broken up. Stir in the garlic and chili powder and cook for 1 minute longer.

2 Add the beans and cook, stirring, until they are warmed. Taste and add salt, pepper, and more chili powder if needed.

3 To warm the tortillas, wrap them in foil and place in a 300°F oven for about 10 minutes, or stack them between two damp paper towels and microwave for 30 to 60 seconds.

4 Spread a portion of cheese onto each tortilla and top with a portion of the bean-meat mixture, lettuce, sauce, and cilantro. Roll up and serve.

Fajitas

Makes 4 to 6 servings

Time: 30 minutes or more

There was a time when a fajita was a grilled marinated steak served with warm flour tortillas and lots of cooked vegetables, but it has come to mean any do-it-yourself assortment of meat, chicken, or even fish (usually shrimp) and grilled vegetables. Here's the basic formula:

> 1 pound Basic Grilled or Broiled Chicken Cutlets (page 380), or any variation or 1 pound Grilled Marinated Flank Steak (page 427), or 1 pound spicy grilled shrimp (page 325)
> 1 pound Grilled Mixed Vegetables (page 617)
> 1 cup sour cream
> 1 cup Guacamole (page 22)
> 1 cup Tomato-Onion Salsa (page 772), Green Tomato Salsa (page 773), or other salsa
> 2 cups washed, trimmed, dried, and shredded lettuce
> 2 cups cored, seeded, and diced tomato
> 8 to 12 flour tortillas

1 Cook the chicken, meat, or shrimp and vegetables and keep them warm. Meanwhile, place the sour cream, guacamole, salsa, lettuce, and tomatoes in serving bowls.

2 Heat the tortillas on a grill, for about 15 seconds per side; in a medium dry skillet over medium-high heat, for about 15 seconds per side; or all together in a 250°F oven, wrapped in a towel, just until warm. Serve the tortillas with all the fixings.

Nine Other Ideas for Filling Burritos

You can use any sandwich filling (see page 267) for burritos, but because they are more moisture resistant than bread, burritos lend themselves to wetter fillings. Try any of these.

1. Beans and Greens (page 510)
2. Sautéed Beans and Tomatoes (page 511)
3. Red Beans with Meat (page 513)
4. Chili non Carne (page 519)
5. Spicy Tofu with Ground Pork (page 526)
6. West Indian Crispy Pork Bits (page 461)
7. Spicy Chicken Thigh Kebabs (page 397)
8. Shrimp and Beans (page 328)
9. Broccoli Raab with Sausage and Grapes (page 545)

Fish

Fish is different from other animals we eat for one main reason: sixty or more kinds, on a rotating basis, make common appearances in the supermarket. This makes fish more confusing than it might be otherwise. People frequently ask me, for example, "How is scrod different from cod?" (Answer: It isn't: Scrod is a market term for cod, not another fish.)

But there is a feature of fish that makes the cooking much easier than it would be otherwise: Many fish are so similar that they can be readily substituted for one another. This also makes buying, the really challenging part, simpler, because there's almost always some fish, in good shape, in any market, that will meet your current need.

Most Americans are intimidated by the bewildering array of fish sold in fish markets today. Twenty years ago—even ten—you bought the same fish, usually local, that your parents did, and probably even your grandparents. Some seafood traveled exceptionally well (shrimp has been shipped frozen since around 1930), but for the most part, you ate local fish because it was available, it wasn't terribly expensive, and you knew how to cook it.

Today, fish from anywhere can turn up anywhere else. Supermarkets in Kansas sell seafood that was caught in the South Pacific, the Indian Ocean, and the Arctic and North seas. Even so, sales of fish in the United States have remained virtually unchanged over the past decade—we eat only about fifteen pounds each per year (the Spaniards eat four times that amount)—but the proportion of fish consumed in restaurants has climbed steadily. We currently eat twice as much fish in restaurants as at home, a statistic which becomes even more impressive when you consider that it includes the fish most commonly prepared by home cooks: canned tuna.

This confirms that many Americans are reluctant to buy and cook fish for themselves. To know the difference between wild pink salmon and farm-raised Atlantic salmon, between black tiger shrimp from Thailand and Pacific white shrimp from Ecuador, takes either experience, a guidebook, or a guide.

An honest, experienced fishmonger is such a guide. Which is great for those who live in Seattle, or New York, or New Orleans, or any of the dozen or so U.S. cities with thriving, not-to-be-believed fish markets. But what should you do if the nearest reputable fishmonger is an hour or more away, as it is for me?

The good news is that the revolutionizing of the seafood industry has afforded the opportunity for many supermarkets to step up their fresh seafood offerings, even in the most landlocked areas. And while they haven't evolved to the point of being able to offer the diversity of a great fish store (partly because we haven't created the demand), you can still make a good solid go of fish-eating by shopping at supermarkets. I do it all the time.

The Basics of Buying Fish

Here's the quick, no-nonsense course in supermarket fish-shopping; there are more details in the discussions of individual fish:

Avoid fish counters that smell or look dirty. I'd like to think that at this stage of the game, you wouldn't encounter such a disgrace, but if you do, run, don't walk. (It might not be a bad idea to stop long enough to complain to the management; it will encourage them to clean up their act, and let them know someone cares.)

Generally, steer clear of prewrapped fish. It might be good, and there's nothing intrinsically wrong with it, but it's difficult to evaluate. If you've had good experience with it in a given market, you're lucky; keep at it until your experience changes.

Purchasing shellfish is usually pretty straightforward: Lobster, crab, whole clams, oysters, mussels, crabs, and certain other mollusks must be alive when sold. Lobsters and crabs should be quite lively; if they seem tired, move on. The muscles of live mollusks make it difficult to pry their shells apart, and this is a good test. If, however, mollusks are shucked and separated from their guts, as scallops routinely are (and oysters frequently are), the shelf life is extended considerably. In this case, smell them if possible.

Shrimp are almost always shipped frozen and defrosted before sale. It's better, though, to buy them still frozen; you may get a more favorable price, and you can control how and when they are defrosted. The best way to defrost shrimp is in the refrigerator (which takes a while) or under cold running water (which is quite rapid).

Most fillets and steaks are cut before they even reach a supermarket fish counter. The surface should be bright, clear, reflective—almost translucent. The color should be consistent with the type of fish. For example, pearly white fish—and there are lots of these—should not have spots of pink, which are usually bruises, or brown, which indicate spoilage. Creamy or ivory-colored fish should have no areas of deep red or brown. Get to know the ideal appearance of your favorite fish, and reject any that doesn't meet your standard.

Whole fish gives you more signals than fillets or steaks (if your market doesn't carry whole fish, perhaps you should petition for change). Look for red gills, bright reflective skin, firm flesh, an undamaged layer of scales, and no browning anywhere. Again, the smell—even in the body cavity—should be sweet. The best whole fish look alive, as if they just came out of the water.

Trust your instincts. Good fish looks good, has firm, unmarred flesh, and smells like fresh seawater. If your supermarket fishmonger won't let you smell the fish, and it passes the appearance tests, try buying it, opening the package right on the spot, and, if the smell is at all off, handing it right back. If you're reluctant to do that, remember that if any fish doesn't meet your expectations when you cook it, bring it back to the supermarket for an exchange or a refund. Demand quality.

The Basics of Thin White Fish Fillets

The fillets of these fish have much in common. They are all stark-white, or nearly so. They are all well under an inch thick, ranging from flounder and the other flatfish, which are often a quarter-inch thick or so, to red snapper, whose fillets can reach an inch in thickness. They are all tender, some more than others. All of the sturdier ones (marked below with a ♦) can be substituted in the recipes that work for the more tender ones. (The converse is not true, however, but you can substitute one sturdy fish for another.) All of these fish, regardless of their texture, are mild-flavored.

- ♦ Catfish
- ♦ Dogfish, also known as Cape Shark
  Flatfish of any type: Flounder, Fluke, Sole, Dab, Plaice
  Haddock (likely to have skin on, but skin is edible)
  Large- or Small-Mouthed Bass (freshwater)
  Pickerel (freshwater)
  Pike (freshwater)
  Ocean Perch
- ♦ Red Snapper, or other Snappers
- ♦ Rockfish of any type
- ♦ Sea Bass
  Weakfish, also known as Sea Trout
- ♦ Wolffish, also known as Ocean Catfish
  Whiting, also known as Hake

These fish cook very, very quickly and overcook almost as fast. A quarter-inch-thick flounder fillet can, under the right circumstances, cook through in two minutes. Even a relatively thick piece of red snapper will be done in less than ten minutes in almost every instance. How do you know when they're done? Several ways:

1. By the time the outside of the thinner fillets is opaque, the inside is very nearly done. This is absolutely true if you turn the fish over, as you do in a pan. But even in a broiler or oven, external opacity is a sign of internal doneness.
2. With thinner fillets, when the thinnest part flakes, the thicker part is done. When the thicker part flakes, it's overcooked.
3. With thicker fillets, those up to one inch or so, you can roughly estimate doneness by timing: about eight minutes is the longest you want to cook any fillet under one inch thick. In addition, take a peek between the flakes of the fish; if most of the translucence is gone, and the fish is tender, it's done.

Remember, all food continues to cook between stove or oven and table, and fish is so delicate that fish that is fully cooked in the kitchen will likely be slightly overcooked in the dining room.

If you'd like to learn how to fillet fish (see the next page), practice on those like red snapper, mackerel, or striped bass, all of which have plenty of meat and a very simple bone structure. When you get the hang of it you'll be able to fillet almost anything. Remove the innards from the fish (see illustrations on page 312) before filleting. Use a meat boning knife or a flexible filleting knife to speed your work, and be sure to save the bones for stock.

(**Step 1**) *Lay the fish on its side and cut all the way down its back, just to one side of the top fin.* (**Step 2**) *Make a deep vertical incision just below the gills, from the top of the fish to the bottom.* (**Step 3**) *Cut over the backbone and the ribs, right down through the belly flap, to release the fillet. Repeat on the other side of the fish.*

Broiled Flatfish or Other White Fillets

Makes 4 servings

Time: 15 minutes

Simpler and faster than a steak. All-important: The fish must smell of seawater, no more.

About 1½ pounds fillets of flounder, sole, or any
   of the other fish listed on page 277, cut about
   ¼ inch thick, scaled or skinned
1 tablespoon olive oil or melted butter, plus a little
   more for the pan
Salt and freshly ground black pepper to taste
Lemon quarters or a sprinkling of vinegar

1 Preheat the broiler. It should be very hot, and the rack should be as close to the heat source as you can get it—even 2 inches is not too close. (You can also bake the fish at 450°F; it will take a minute or two longer.)

2 Lightly grease a baking sheet or broiling pan. Lay the fillets on it, then brush with the tablespoon of oil or butter. Sprinkle with salt and pepper.

3 Broil the fish for 2 to 4 minutes (without turning), depending on the heat of your oven and the distance from the heat source. (If the fish is thicker than ¼ inch, adjust cooking time accordingly, but few of these fillets will take more than 5 minutes in most ovens.) When the fish is done, it should be firm and barely cooked through; the edges will flake, but the center should still show a little resistance. If there is a little translucence in the very middle, it will disappear by the time you get the fish onto a plate.

4 Remove the fish with a spatula and serve immediately, squeezing lemon juice or drizzling vinegar over the fillets at the table. Serve immediately.

Broiled Flatfish or Other White Fillets with Mustard and Herbs: Steps 1 and 2 remain the same. Combine ⅓ cup Dijon mustard, 1 tablespoon sugar, 1 teaspoon minced fresh thyme leaves or ½ teaspoon dried thyme (or substitute rosemary or savory; or parsley, chervil, or basil in larger quantities) and 1 tablespoon freshly squeezed lemon juice. Spread this mixture over the fish. Proceed with Steps 3 and 4 as above; serve with lemon wedges.

Broiled Flatfish or Other White Fillets with Garlic-Parsley Sauce: Steps 1 and 2 remain the same; use olive oil. Combine 1 teaspoon minced garlic, ⅓ cup extra-virgin olive oil, ¼ cup freshly squeezed lemon juice, ½ cup minced fresh parsley leaves, and a little salt and pepper. Spoon some of this mixture over the fish. Proceed with Steps 3 and 4 as above; pass the rest of the sauce at the table.

Broiled Flatfish or Other White Fillets with Tomato Salsa: Steps 1 and 2 remain the same; use olive or peanut oil. Combine 2 cups cored and chopped tomatoes (drained if canned) with $1/2$ teaspoon cayenne (or to taste), $1/4$ cup freshly squeezed lime juice, $1/4$ cup minced cilantro leaves, and salt to taste. Spoon some of this mixture over the fish. Proceed with Steps 3 and 4 as above. Pass the rest of the sauce at the table.

Broiled Flatfish or Other White Fillets with Dill Butter: Dill is traditional (and wonderful), but use any fresh herb you have here. Steps 1 and 2 remain the same. Put 4 tablespoons ($1/2$ stick) butter in a blender, food processor, or small bowl with $1/2$ teaspoon minced garlic, $1/4$ cup minced fresh dill, and some salt and pepper. Blend until smooth. Dot the fillets with about two-thirds of the dill butter. Proceed with Steps 3 and 4 as above; spread the fillets with the remaining butter, and serve immediately, with lemon wedges.

Broiled Flatfish or Other White Fillets with Sweet Soy: First, mix together 1 teaspoon dark sesame oil; $1/4$ cup soy sauce; 1 tablespoon peeled and finely minced or grated fresh ginger; $1/4$ cup minced scallion; 1 teaspoon minced garlic; 1 tablespoon dry sherry, white wine, or water; and 1 tablespoon honey or sugar. Marinate the fillets in this for 5 minutes or more. Proceed with Steps 1 and 2, using peanut or vegetable oil to grease the pan but omitting the oil on top of the fish. Pour the remaining marinade over the fish and broil as in Step 3. Garnish with more minced scallions and some Toasted Sesame Seeds (page 776) if you like.

<table>
<tr><td colspan="2">**Four Simple Ideas for Broiled Fillets**</td></tr>
<tr><td>**1.**</td><td>Brush lightly, before and after cooking, with any compound butter (page 768), flavored oil (page 775), or vinaigrette (page 91).</td></tr>
<tr><td>**2.**</td><td>Broil plain, as in the master recipe, and serve with any salsa, pages 772–773.</td></tr>
<tr><td>**3.**</td><td>Serve over a bed of lightly dressed greens.</td></tr>
<tr><td>**4.**</td><td>Use cold or hot in sandwiches, with any mayonnaise (page 761) or other dressing.</td></tr>
</table>

Sautéed Flatfish or Other White Fillets

Makes 2 servings

Time: 20 minutes

This classic preparation for fillets of flatfish ("sole meunière") works equally well for any thin fillets. Note that this is for two people; if there is a disadvantage to this recipe, it is that the thinness of the fillets makes pan-cooking difficult—they simply take up too much room. Cook in batches if you're going to double the recipe. And serve the fish hot, hot, hot.

About $1/2$ to $3/4$ pound fillets of flounder, sole, or any of the other fish listed on page 277, cut about $1/4$ inch thick, scaled or skinned

Salt and freshly ground black pepper to taste

1 tablespoon extra-virgin olive oil

4 tablespoons ($1/2$ stick) butter

Flour for dredging

2 tablespoons freshly squeezed lemon juice

Minced fresh parsley leaves for garnish

Lemon wedges

1 Heat two dinner plates in a 200°F. oven. Season the fillets with salt and pepper.

2 Heat a large skillet, preferably non-stick, over medium-high heat for 2 or 3 minutes. Add the oil and half the butter. When the butter foam subsides, dredge the fillets, one by one, in the flour, shaking off any excess, and add them to the pan. Raise the heat to high and cook the fillets until golden on each side, 4 to 5 minutes total. Remove to the warm serving plates.

3 Turn the heat to medium and add the remaining butter to the pan. Cook until the butter foams, a minute or two. Add the lemon juice, and cook, stirring and scraping the bottom of the pan, for about 15 seconds. Pour the sauce over the fillets.

4 Garnish and serve immediately with the lemon wedges.

Sautéed Flatfish or Other White Fillets with Capers: Steps 1 and 2 remain the same. In Step 3, add 1 tablespoon capers to the skillet along with the lemon juice (you can also add a couple of minced anchovies if you like). Cook, stirring, for 30 seconds, then pour over the fillets.

Sautéed Flatfish or Other White Fillets with Curry and Lime: Same technique, markedly different results; serve, if you like, with the Green Tomato Salsa on page 773. First, rub the fish with 1 tablespoon freshly squeezed lime juice. Mix together 1 teaspoon salt, $1/2$ teaspoon ground black pepper, and 1 tablespoon All-Purpose Curry Powder or store-bought curry powder or similar spice mixture (page 778). Rub this into the fish. Proceed with Steps 1 and 2, using no butter and just enough peanut or vegetable oil to cook the fish. Use 3 tablespoons of lime juice in Step 3, minced cilantro and lime wedges in Step 4.

Sautéed Flatfish or Other White Fillets with Soy Sauce: Steps 1 and 2 remain the same; use peanut or vegetable oil in place of the butter. In Step 3, add an additional tablespoon of oil to the pan and, over medium heat, add 1 teaspoon minced garlic, 1 tablespoon peeled and minced or grated fresh ginger, 2 minced scallions; cook, stirring, about 30 seconds. Add $1/2$ cup any broth, white wine, or water, and let it bubble away for 30 seconds or so. Add 2 tablespoons soy sauce and the juice of 1 lime. Pour this sauce over the fish. Serve with lime wedges.

Sautéed Flatfish or Other White Fillets with Sesame Crust: Very crisp and tasty. First, rub the fish with 1 tablespoon dark sesame oil. Proceed with Step 1. In Step 2, dredge the fillets in 1 cup Toasted Sesame Seeds (page 776) instead of flour, patting to make the seeds adhere; use peanut or vegetable oil in place of the butter. Cook as in Step 3; no additional liquid is needed in cooking. Serve with a dipping sauce of 3 tablespoons soy sauce, 1 tablespoon white or rice vinegar, 1 teaspoon dark sesame oil, and a dash of cayenne (optional).

Extra-Crisp Red Snapper or Other Fillets with Butter-Toasted Pecans

Makes 4 servings

Time: 30 minutes or less

Because this recipe requires a bit more handling, and because longer cooking time means a crisper coating, it is best with fillets of red snapper or any of the sturdier fish marked with a ♦ on page 277. The technique will work with delicate fillets, but you may find them falling apart during cooking, and their extreme thinness means you must work in batches.

1/2 cup flour

1/4 teaspoon cayenne, or to taste

1/4 teaspoon dried thyme

1 tablespoon paprika

Salt to taste

1/4 cup peanut or vegetable oil

1/2 cup milk

4 red snapper or other fillets marked with a ◆ on
    page 277, about 6 ounces each, scaled or skinned

4 tablespoons (1/2 stick) butter

2/3 cup pecan pieces, plus some more for garnish

Freshly ground black pepper to taste

2 tablespoons freshly squeezed lemon juice

2 tablespoons minced fresh parsley leaves

1 Mix together the flour, half the cayenne, and the thyme, paprika, and salt in a bowl. Heat the oil in a large skillet, preferably non-stick, over medium-high heat until it is good and hot (a pinch of flour will sizzle).

2 Put the milk in a bowl. Dip the fillets, one by one, in the milk; dredge them in the seasoned flour, then put them in the pan. Cook over high heat, turning once, until nicely browned on both sides; total cooking time for fillets 1/2 to 3/4 inch thick will be 5 to 6 minutes. (The fillets will be white, opaque, and tender when done.)

3 Remove the fish to a platter and keep warm; wipe out the pan and immediately melt the butter in it over medium heat. Add the pecans, the remaining cayenne, salt, and pepper, and cook, stirring frequently, until the pecans are lightly browned and fragrant, 3 to 5 minutes.

4 Add the lemon juice and parsley. Spoon a portion of nuts over each fillet and serve immediately.

Extra-Crisp Red Snapper or Other Fillets with Apples

Makes 4 servings

Time: 30 minutes

This is a lovely combination, typical of the simple fish dishes of northern France. Again, best with red snapper or other sturdy fillets marked with a ◆ on page 277. Calvados, the apple brandy of northern France, is perfect here, but any good brandy will do.

4 crisp not-too-sweet apples, such as Granny Smiths

6 tablespoons (3/4 stick) butter

Flour for dredging

Salt and freshly ground black pepper to taste

1 egg

4 red snapper or other fillets marked with a ◆ on
    page 277, about 6 ounces each, scaled or skinned

Plain bread crumbs for dredging

2 tablespoons freshly squeezed lemon juice

1 tablespoon Calvados or brandy (optional)

1 Peel and core the apples, then cut them into rings or thin wedges. Melt half the butter in a medium skillet over medium heat. Add the apples, raise the heat to medium-high, and cook, tossing and stirring occasionally, until nicely browned on all sides, about 7 minutes. Keep warm in a 200°F oven while you proceed with the recipe.

2 Once you've started cooking the apples, preheat a large non-stick skillet over medium-high heat. Season the flour with salt and pepper and beat the egg in a bowl. Add the remaining butter to the skillet and, when the foam subsides, dredge each fillet in the flour, then dip it in the egg, dredge it in the bread crumbs, and place it in the pan.

3 Cook until the fillets are nicely browned on both sides, about 6 to 8 minutes total. The fillets will

be white, opaque, and tender when done. Remove the fish to a platter. Drizzle the apples with the lemon juice and Calvados and spoon a portion onto each fillet. Serve immediately.

"Oven-Fried" Catfish or Other Fillets

Makes 4 servings

Time: 25 minutes

This is a 1950s-style recipe that takes almost no effort. If you want to cut back on the fat, it will still work fine. Use it with any of the fillets listed on page 277; reduce the cooking time to four to five minutes for those under one-half inch thick.

About 1½ pounds catfish or other fillets (any of the
   fish listed on page 277), scaled or skinned
1½ cups milk
Plain bread crumbs for dredging
Salt and freshly ground black pepper to taste
3 tablespoons melted butter or olive oil
Lemon wedges

1 Soak the fillets in the milk while you preheat the oven to 500°F. Season the bread crumbs with salt and pepper.

2 When the oven is hot, dredge the still-wet fish in the bread crumbs, patting them to make sure they adhere. Drizzle a little of the butter over the bottom of a 9 × 13-inch baking pan, preferably non-stick, then lay the fillets in the pan. Drizzle with the remaining butter.

3 Bake near the top of the oven for about 8 minutes; the fish will be tender and opaque when done. Serve immediately, with lemon wedges.

Crisp Rockfish or Other Fillets on Mashed Potatoes

Makes 4 servings

Time: 45 minutes

This is a super dish, crisp, creamy, and—thanks to the quick sauce—very moist. The special one-sided cooking technique can be used only with sturdier fillets, those marked with a ◆ on page 277.

2 pounds baking potatoes, such as Idaho or russet,
   peeled
6 tablespoons (¾ stick) butter
1 cup milk
Salt and freshly ground black pepper to taste
1 cup flour
2 tablespoons olive oil
4 rockfish or other fillets marked with a ◆ on page
   277, about 6 ounces each, scaled, skin on
2 tablespoons minced shallot
1 cup dry white wine, or chicken, beef, or vegetable
   stock, or water (see "Soups" for stock recipes)
1 teaspoon Dijon or other good mustard
3 tablespoons minced fresh parsley leaves

1 Put the potatoes in a large pot and cover with cold water; bring to a boil, lower the heat to medium, and simmer until tender, 20 to 40 minutes. Drain and mash with 3 tablespoons of the butter, ¼ cup of the milk, salt, and pepper. Cover and keep warm in a low oven (or set aside and microwave before serving). Meanwhile, season the flour with salt and pepper. Preheat the oven to 200°F.

2 Heat 2 tablespoons of the butter and the oil over medium heat in a large non-stick skillet that can later be covered. When the butter melts, dip each fillet in the remaining milk, then dredge the skin side in the flour (the top should not be floured). When the butter foam subsides, place the fillets, skin side down, in the skillet. Cover and cook for about 5 minutes, undisturbed. At this point, the fillets should be white on top and crisp on the bottom; if not, cook another 2 minutes. Transfer the fillets to a platter and keep warm in the oven.

3. Raise the heat to high and cook the shallot, stirring, in the fat remaining in the pan until softened, a minute or so. Add the wine or stock and cook, stirring and scraping the bottom of the pan, for a minute or so. Stir in the mustard and parsley and cook for 30 seconds. Add the remaining tablespoon of butter and stir until the sauce is smooth. Reheat the mashed potatoes if necessary.

4. To serve, spoon some mashed potatoes onto a plate, top with a fillet, skin side up, and spoon some of the sauce over all.

Deep-Fried Catfish or Other Fillets

Makes 2 to 4 servings

Time: 30 minutes

Very thin fillets are too delicate for this operation, but those of catfish, red snapper, rockfish, or dogfish (which is the fish most frequently used in fish and chips in England) are perfect. Use a frying thermometer to make sure your oil is hot enough, and see The Basics of Deep Frying (page 13) for details. This is great with Red Pepper Relish (page 774) or Pico de Gallo (page 773).

1 cup milk
4 catfish or other fillets marked with a ♦ on
    page 277, about 6 ounces each, skinned
Vegetable, peanut, or corn oil for deep-frying
1 1/2 cups cornmeal
Salt and freshly ground black pepper to taste
Lemon wedges

1. Pour the milk into a bowl and let the fillets soak in it while you heat at least 2 inches of oil in a large, deep saucepan to 375°F.

2. Mix the cornmeal in a plastic bag with the salt and pepper. Drain the fillets, then shake them in the cornmeal in the bag; shake off any excess coating and fry them until golden on both sides, about 8 minutes. Do this in batches if necessary.

3. Drain on brown paper bags or paper towels and serve immediately, with lemon wedges.

Spicy Deep-Fried Catfish: Spike the cornmeal with 2 tablespoons or more of black pepper, mixed with cayenne if you like; curry, chili, or five-spice powder; or ground cumin or cinnamon. Or add 1 tablespoon, more or less, of dried or minced fresh thyme or sage, or with any other herb or spice that you fancy.

Poached Catfish or Other Fillets in Ginger Sauce

Makes 4 servings

Time: 30 minutes

Fresh ginger is essential here, but don't hesitate to substitute water for stock; there will be plenty of flavor.

2 tablespoons peanut or vegetable oil
1 clove garlic, minced
5 tablespoons peeled and very finely minced or
    grated fresh ginger
1/2 cup chicken, beef, or vegetable stock, or water
    (see "Soups" for stock recipes)
1/4 cup soy sauce
1/4 cup dry white wine, or more stock or water
Salt and freshly ground black pepper to taste
1 to 1 1/2 pounds catfish or other fillets marked with
    a ♦ on page 277, skinned

1 Warm the oil in a large, deep skillet over medium heat, then add the garlic and all but 1 tablespoon of the ginger; stir once. When the garlic begins to color, add the stock or water and the other liquids; raise the heat to high and reduce by about half; this will take just a few minutes. Season with salt and pepper.

2 Lay the fillets in the liquid, cover, turn the heat to medium, and poach until the fillets are white and opaque throughout, about 5 minutes. Garnish with the 1 tablespoon reserved ginger and serve immediately, over white rice.

Red Snapper or Other Fillets in Packages

Makes 6 servings

Time: 1 hour

Cooking "en papillote" is fun and virtually foolproof. Since all of the fish's essences are locked within the package, moistness is guaranteed. But because you can't peek into the packages to judge doneness, I wouldn't make this with very thin fillets, which are likely to overcook. On the other hand, it's a fine recipe for some of the thicker fillets marked with a ◆ on page 277; simply increase the cooking time by four or five minutes per one-half inch of thickness.

> About 1 pound waxy red or white potatoes, peeled and sliced as thinly as possible (you want 24 to 36 slices)
> 6 red snapper fillets or other fillets marked with a ◆ on page 277, 4 to 6 ounces each, scaled or skinned, cut in half
> 2 or 3 large tomatoes, cored and cut through the equator into 1/4-inch-thick slices (you want 12 slices)
> Salt and freshly ground black pepper to taste
> 24 fresh basil leaves
> About 2 tablespoons olive oil

1 Preheat the oven to 450°F. Cut twelve 1-foot-squares of aluminum foil or parchment paper. On each, place a thin layer of 2 or 3 potato slices, roughly the same size as the fillet, on the foil; top with a piece of fish, a slice of tomato, salt, pepper, 2 basil leaves, and a drizzle of oil. Fold over the foil to seal the packages and place them in a single layer in a large baking dish.

2 Bake for about 20 minutes, turning the pan in the oven after 10 minutes to ensure even cooking. Check the fish in one package; the snapper will be white, opaque, and tender when done, the tomato will have liquefied, and the potato will be cooked. Serve the packages closed, allowing each diner to open his or her own at the table.

Red Snapper or Other Fillets in Packages with Spinach: In Step 1, replace the potatoes with a bed of about 1 cup well-washed spinach (tough stems removed) in each package; top with about a tablespoon of chopped, sun-dried tomatoes rather than fresh; use tarragon (sparingly) in place of basil. Step 2 remains the same.

Red Snapper or Other Fillets in Packages with Tomato and Herbs: A very low-fat version. In Step 1, replace the potatoes with a bed of chopped fresh tomato (about 1/2 cup); top with a variety of minced fresh herbs; sprinkle with a few drops of dry white wine instead of the olive oil. Step 2 remains the same.

Red Snapper or Other Fillets in Packages with Carrots and Zucchini: In Step 1, replace the potatoes with a bed of about 1/2 cup mixed julienned carrots and zucchini, sprinkled with a few drops of balsamic vinegar; top with a drizzle of olive oil, chopped fresh tarragon, and a thin slice of lemon. Step 2 remains the same.

The Basics of Thick White Fish Fillets

Some of these are from the same fish as the preceding section (they're simply cut from larger fish), and some from fish that only produce thick fillets. In any case, they're all white, tender, and mild-flavored, at least a inch thick (and usually considerably thicker than that—one and a half inches is common, and two inches not unheard of).

With thin fillets the challenge is in preventing overcooking, but here you must take care to cook the fish thoroughly. This has a couple of advantages: It means that in broiling, and even roasting, you're likely to use cooking times that are long enough to assure browning. With the firmest fillets (those marked by a ♦ in the following list), it also means that they'll have plenty of time to crisp up in a skillet, yet remain sturdy enough to turn without breaking.

Atlantic Pollock, also known as Boston Bluefish
♦ Blackfish
Carp
Cod
♦ Grouper
♦ Monkfish (usually but not always suitable in recipes for other members of this group)
Orange Roughy
Pacific Pollock, also known as Alaskan Pollock
Red Snapper, or other Snappers
Sablefish, also known as Black Cod (usually but not always suitable in recipes for other members of this group)
♦ Striped Bass
Tilefish
Turbot
Weakfish, also known as Sea Trout
Whiting, also known as Hake

These fish all cook quickly, at a rate of eight to ten minutes per inch of thickness with most cooking methods. There is, of course, some variation based on the nature of the individual fish (striped bass, for example, needs slightly longer cooking to become tender; cod somewhat less to avoid dryness), its initial temperature, and the actual heat of your stove or oven. How do you know when they're done?

1. Begin checking the fish after about seven minutes of cooking time per inch of thickness. First, insert a very thin-bladed knife or skewer into the thickest part. If it penetrates with little or no resistance, the fish is done, or nearly so.

2. Use the same blade to gently pry open the fish at its thickest part and peek in there (a flashlight can be helpful here if your kitchen light is not direct). Once it is opaque throughout, the fish is completely done. You can stop cooking just before this point—when a bit of translucence remains—and the fish will finish cooking on the way to the table. This judgment will come easily with practice.

Note that some of these fish—striped bass, for example, or grouper—are large enough so that you can ask for a "center cut" of the fillet. Such a fillet will be of fairly even thickness from one end to the other, minimizing the differences in doneness between portions of the fish. A portion of a cod fillet can also be cut to more or less uniform thickness.

Finally, most of these fish will be sold with their skin removed, as they should be. But if you are roasting or pan-cooking the fish, and you'd like some crisp skin, choose red snapper, striped bass, or tilefish—even cod if you are lucky enough to see it with its skin.

Broiled Cod or Other Thick White Fillets

Makes 4 servings

Time: 20 minutes, plus time to preheat the broiler

As long as your fish is good and fresh, you need do no more than this; it will be delicious. There are, however, an infinite number of variations. I give some of them here; for others, see Four Simple Ideas for Broiled Fillets, page 279.

1 or 2 cod fillets, or any of the fish listed on page 285, at least 1 inch thick, weighing about 1 1/2 pounds total
1 tablespoon olive oil or butter, plus a little more for the pan
Salt and freshly ground black pepper to taste
1 lemon, quartered

1 Preheat the broiler. It should be very hot, with the rack about 4 inches from the heat source. (You can also bake the fish at 450°F; it will take a minute or two longer.)

2 Lightly grease a baking sheet or broiling pan. Lay the fillets on it, then brush with the tablespoon of oil or butter. Sprinkle with salt and pepper.

3 Place the pan in the broiler. Change its position every 2 minutes or so in order to brown the fish evenly, and baste once or twice with the melted fat from the bottom of the pan.

4 Generally, when the top of the fish is nicely browned, the fish is cooked through, or nearly so; as a general rule, figure about 8 to 10 minutes per inch of thickness, measured at the thickest point. If the fish is browning too quickly, turn off the broiler and finish the cooking with the oven set at 500°F. Most fillets are done when they offer no resistance to a thin-bladed knife and are opaque, or nearly so, throughout; avoid overcooking. Serve with lemon quarters.

Broiled Cod or Other Thick White Fillet with Flavored Bread Crumbs: Steps 1, 2, and 3 remain the same. While the fish is cooking (or before), heat 2 to 4 tablespoons of butter or oil in a medium skillet over medium heat; when hot, toss in 1/2 to 1 cup plain bread crumbs, with or without 1 teaspoon of minced garlic and 1/4 cup minced fresh parsley leaves. Spread the bread crumbs on top of the fish about 2 minutes before it finishes cooking in Step 4.

Broiled Cod or Other Thick White Fillet with White Wine and Herbs: A low-fat variation. Steps 1 and 2 remain the same; omit the butter or oil if you like. In Step 3, douse the fish with 1/4 cup dry white wine and a sprinkling of minced fresh herbs—tarragon, rosemary, parsley, chives, basil, chervil, savory, etc.—about halfway through the cooking. A teaspoon or so of minced garlic may be added at the same time. Step 4 remains the same; serve with the liquid and good crusty bread.

Broiled Cod or Other Thick White Fillet with Tomatoes and Olives: Steps 1 and 2 remain the same; use olive oil. Halfway through cooking in Step 3, top the fish with a mixture of 1/2 cup cored and chopped tomato, 1/4 cup pitted and chopped Calamata or other good black olives, 1 tablespoon chopped fresh parsley or basil leaves, 1 teaspoon minced garlic, 1 tablespoon olive oil, and 1 teaspoon balsamic vinegar. Finish as above.

Broiled Cod or Other Thick White Fillet with Pesto: Steps 1, 2, and 3 remain the same. About 2 minutes before the fish finishes cooking in Step 4, spread a few tablespoons of Basic Pesto (page 766) on top.

Broiled Cod or Other Thick White Fillet with Pureed Parsley: First, combine 2 cups loosely packed parsley leaves, 1 large clove garlic, peeled, the zest and juice of 1 lemon, 1/2 cup olive oil, and some salt and pepper in the container of a blender or food processor. Steps 1, 2, and 3 remain the same; use olive oil. About 2 minutes before the fish finishes cooking in Step 4, spread this parsley mixture on top of the fish. Serve with lemon wedges.

Grilled Striped Bass or Other Fillets

Makes 4 servings

Time: 40 minutes, plus time to preheat the grill

Most fillets are too delicate to grill. But there are some exceptions, most notably striped bass, blackfish, grouper, and monkfish. If the fish still has its skin, leave it on; it will give the fish even more stability on the grill.

1½ pounds center-cut striped bass fillet, or any of
    the fish marked with a ♦ on page 285, of fairly
    uniform thickness—1 inch or a little more
2 tablespoons olive oil
1 teaspoon minced garlic (optional)
Salt and freshly ground black pepper to taste
Lemon wedges

1 Start a charcoal or wood fire or preheat a gas grill or broiler; the fire should be quite hot, the rack 3 or 4 inches from the heat source. Drizzle the flesh of the fish with olive oil, and sprinkle it with salt and pepper. Rub the flesh with the garlic if you like.

2 When the fire is ready, grill the fish, flesh side down, about 5 minutes, inserting a metal spatula between the fish and the grill every 2 minutes or so to minimize sticking. Turn the fish and grill another 5 minutes, again making sure the fish doesn't stick. Check for doneness—the fish will still be firm and juicy, but will have lost its translucence, and a thin-bladed knife will pass through it fairly easily—and serve immediately (skin side down) with lemon.

Six Simple Ideas for Grilled Fish

1. Serve with any vinaigrette (page 91), salsa (page 772), mayonnaise (page 761), or compound butter (page 768).
2. Serve hot on a lightly dressed salad.
3. Dice and stir into Basic Tomato Sauce (page 130) or other tomato sauces; serve over pasta.
4. Use, hot or cold, in a sandwich, with freshly squeezed lemon juice, or other dressing.
5. Rub with olive oil and coarsely chopped fresh herbs before grilling.
6. Brush lightly with vinegar and rub lightly with spices such as All-Purpose Curry Powder (page 778) before grilling.

Roast Cod or Other Thick White Fillets with Potatoes

Makes 4 servings

Time: 1 hour

This is one of my favorite recipes in this category, largely because of its simplicity. Increase the cooking time slightly if you use one of the sturdier fillets marked with a ♦ on the list on page 285.

6 tablespoons (¾ stick) butter
2 to 3 pounds waxy red or white potatoes
Salt and freshly ground black pepper to taste
1 or 2 cod fillets, or any of the fish listed on
    page 285, about 1½ pounds

1 Preheat the oven to 425°F. Place 4 tablespoons of the butter in a large baking dish. Place the dish in the oven while it preheats to melt the butter.

2 Peel the potatoes and slice them about ⅛ to ¼ inch thick (I use a food processor or a mandoline for this). Remove the pan from the oven when the butter is melted. When the oven is hot, stir the potatoes into the butter and sprinkle them liberally with salt and pepper. Return the dish to the oven and set a timer for 10 minutes.

3 Every 10 minutes, turn the potatoes gently with a spatula. When they are browned all over—30 to 40 minutes—place the cod on top of them, dotting the fish with the remaining butter. Roast the cod for 8 to 12 minutes, depending upon the thickness of the fillets (cod is done when it is opaque throughout and offers no resistance to a thin-bladed knife; avoid overcooking). Serve.

Roast Cod or Other Thick White Fillet with Potatoes, Onions, and Olive Oil: In Step 1, gently heat 4 tablespoons of olive oil instead of butter. In Step 2, add 2 cups of sliced onions to the potatoes. In Step 3, drizzle the cod with 1 tablespoon additional olive oil. Finish as above.

Roast Cod or Other Thick White Fillet with Herbs: Use either the master recipe or the above variation. Step 1 remains the same. In Step 2, toss the potatoes with 1 or 2 tablespoons minced fresh herbs. In Step 3, top the fish with another $1/2$ to 1 teaspoon of minced herbs. Good herbs for this dish are parsley, chervil, summer savory, and dill, in the larger amounts; rosemary, marjoram, oregano, or tarragon in the smaller amounts. Finish as above.

Sautéed Cod or Other Thick White Fillets

Makes 4 servings

Time: 20 minutes

Take a fresh white fillet and cook it so that it's crisp on the outside and still tender and moist on the inside. Douse it with freshly squeezed lemon juice and you have one of eating's great pleasures. Plus, the possibilities for variations are endless.

$1/4$ cup olive, peanut, or vegetable oil
Salt and freshly ground black pepper to taste
2 cod fillets, or any of the fish listed on page 285, about $1^{1}/_2$ pounds (or 1 fillet cut into 2 or 4 pieces)
Flour for dredging
Minced fresh parsley leaves for garnish (optional)
Lemon wedges

1 Heat a large skillet, preferably non-stick, over medium-high heat for 2 or 3 minutes. Add the oil to the skillet and, when it is hot (a pinch of flour will sizzle), season the fillets well, then dredge them in the flour, shaking off any excess. Add them to the pan.

2 Raise the heat to high and cook until browned on each side, turning once. Total cooking time will be about 10 minutes. Any thick fillet, when done, will still be firm and juicy, but will have lost its translucence, and a thin-bladed knife will pass through it fairly easily. The sturdier fillets (those marked with a ◆ on page 285) will take a minute or two longer than cod and other relatively delicate fish.

3 Garnish and serve with lemon wedges.

Extra-Crisp Sautéed Cod or Other Thick White Fillets: In Step 1, dip the fillet in the flour, shake off the excess, then dip in a bowl containing 2 beaten eggs. Dip in flour again, or in plain bread crumbs. Steps 2 and 3 remain the same.

Sautéed Cod or Other Thick White Fillets with Spicy Garlic Sauce: Steps 1 and 2 remain the same; use peanut oil if possible. When the fish is done, remove it to a warm plate. Pour off any remaining oil in the pan, then wipe it out (carefully—it's still hot). Add 1 tablespoon of fresh oil, turn the heat to high. Add 2 tablespoons minced garlic and 1 tablespoon peeled and minced or grated fresh ginger;

cook for 15 seconds. Add 1 tablespoon dry white wine or sherry, followed almost immediately by $^1/_2$ cup chicken, beef, or vegetable stock, or water. Cook for 30 seconds, then add 1 tablespoon soy sauce and $^1/_2$ teaspoon crushed red pepper flakes, chile-garlic paste (available at Asian markets) or hot sauce, or to taste. Pour this sauce over the fish and serve immediately. Garnish with minced cilantro leaves and serve with lime wedges instead of lemon.

Sautéed Cod or Other Thick White Fillets with Raisins and Pine Nuts: First, soak $^1/_4$ cup dried currants or raisins in $^1/_2$ cup dry or sweet sherry, white wine, or port. Proceed with Steps 1 and 2, as above, using olive oil if possible and undercooking fish slightly (just until lightly browned on each side is fine). Turn the heat to medium and remove the fish to a plate. Cook 1 cup minced onion in the oil remaining in the pan for 5 minutes, or until softened, stirring occasionally. Add $^1/_2$ cup pine nuts, 1 teaspoon fresh thyme leaves or $^1/_2$ teaspoon dried thyme, and the currants or raisins and their liquid. Return the fish to the pan and cook over medium-high heat, turning once, until it has heated through, about 3 minutes. Serve immediately, with the onion mixture spooned over. Omit the lemon wedges.

Cod or Other Thick White Fillets Poached in Tomato Sauce

Makes 4 servings

Time: 40 minutes

When you're poaching fish and serving it in the poaching liquid, as you are here, it's best to remove the skin first. If it wasn't done in the store, see page

302 for directions. If you like your dishes spicy-hot, add one-half teaspoon or more of cayenne to the paprika before rubbing it into the fillets.

$^1/_4$ cup olive oil
1 onion, roughly chopped
$^1/_2$ cup dry white, any stock, or water (see "Soups" for stock recipes)
2 cups cored and chopped tomatoes (drained if canned)
Salt and freshly ground black pepper to taste
$^1/_2$ cup minced fresh parsley leaves
1 teaspoon paprika
$^1/_2$ teaspoon cayenne, or more (optional)
1 or 2 cod fillets, or any of the fish listed on page 285, about $1^1/_2$ pounds

1 Heat the olive oil over medium heat in a large skillet for 2 or 3 minutes. Cook the onion in it until it softens, 6 or 7 minutes.

2 Add the liquid and let it bubble away for 1 minute or so. Add the tomatoes, stir, and cook for about 10 minutes, stirring occasionally, until the tomatoes break down. Season with salt and pepper and add half the parsley.

3 Mix the paprika with some salt and pepper (and a little cayenne, if you like) and rub this mixture into the fillet. Lay the fish in the sauce and spoon some of the sauce over it. Cook just until a thin-bladed knife passes through the fillet with little resistance. Serve each piece of fish with some sauce on it, sprinkled with the remaining parsley.

Cod or Other Thick White Fillets in Neapolitan Tomato Sauce: In Step 1, substitute 2 lightly smashed garlic cloves and 2 small dried hot red chiles for the onion and cook, stirring, until the garlic browns. Discard the garlic and chiles and let the oil cool for a minute or two. In Step 2, omit the liquid; add the tomatoes, along with 1 tablespoon drained and rinsed capers, $^1/_2$ cup pitted and roughly chopped good black olives, and the salt, pepper, and parsley. Step 3 remains the same.

Cod or Other Thick White Fillets with Winter Vegetables
Makes 4 to 6 servings

Time: 1 hour, largely unattended

A wonderful one-pot casserole not unlike Chicken in a Pot (page 363), but considerably faster. Use Flavorful Fish and Vegetable Stock (page 49) if you have it.

3 tablespoons butter, softened, or extra-virgin
   olive oil
1 tablespoon minced garlic
$^1/_2$ pound carrots, peeled and cut into rounds,
   or use $^1/_2$ carrots and $^1/_2$ parsnips
$^1/_2$ pound celery, cut into $^1/_2$-inch dice
$^1/_2$ pound waxy red or white potatoes, peeled and
   cut into $^1/_2$-inch dice, or use $^1/_2$ potatoes and
   $^1/_2$ turnips
1 large onion, sliced into rings
1 or 2 cod fillets, or any of the fish listed on page
   285, about $1^1/_2$ pounds, cut into 10 or 12 pieces
Salt and freshly ground black pepper to taste
2 cups fish, chicken, or vegetable stock, a mixture of
   wine and water, or water (see "Soups" for stock
   recipes)

1 Preheat the oven to 375°F. Spread about one-third of the butter or oil on the bottom of a roughly 8 × 12-inch baking dish or casserole. Sprinkle the minced garlic on it, then top with about half each of the carrots, celery, potatoes, onion, and fish. Season

with salt and pepper, spread with a little more of the butter, and make another layer of vegetables and fish. Sprinkle with a little more salt and pepper, pour the stock over all, and dot with the remaining butter.

2 Cover and bake until the potatoes are cooked through, 45 minutes or so.

Red Snapper or Other Thick White Fillets, Provençal-Style
Makes 4 servings

Time: 30 minutes

I prefer to make this dish with the sturdier fish, those marked with a ◆ on the list on page 285. But you can use cod and other more delicate fish as long as you are extremely careful to remove the fillet before it starts to fall apart, which can happen quite suddenly once the fish is cooked.

2 tablespoons olive oil
2 medium onions, chopped
1 teaspoon minced garlic
2 cups cored and chopped tomatoes, fresh or canned
   (undrained)
$^1/_2$ cup dry white wine or water
1 cup tiny Niçoise or other good black olives, pitted
$^1/_2$ cup chopped fresh basil leaves
1 sprig fresh rosemary or $^1/_2$ teaspoon dried rosemary
1 sprig fresh thyme or $^1/_2$ teaspoon dried thyme
Salt and freshly ground black pepper to taste
About $1^1/_2$ pounds red snapper fillets, or any of
   the fish marked with a ◆ on page 285, cut into
   serving pieces

1 Heat the olive oil for 2 minutes in a large, deep skillet or casserole over medium heat. Add the onions and cook, stirring, until they have softened, about 5 minutes.

2 Add the garlic and tomatoes, raise the heat slightly, and cook, stirring occasionally, until some of the tomato juice bubbles away. Add the wine, stir, and cook another 5 minutes.

3 Add the olives, half the chopped basil, the rosemary and thyme, and some salt (remember that the olives are salty) and pepper. Cook 1 minute; submerge the fish in the sauce and cook over medium heat until the fillets are tender and white, about 8 minutes. Garnish with the remaining basil and serve with crusty bread.

Grouper or Other Thick White Fillets in Yellow Curry

Makes 4 servings

Time: 45 minutes

Here, you must use one of the sturdier fish marked with a ◆ on page 285; anything delicate is guaranteed to fall apart. Alternatively, you can make this with one or two whole fish—such as red snapper or porgy—cut into pieces, bones and all.

3 tablespoons peanut or vegetable oil
1 to 1½ pounds grouper fillets, or any of the fish
    marked with a ◆ on page 285, cut into chunks
Flour for dredging
2 cups sliced onions
1 teaspoon ground turmeric
¼ teaspoon cayenne, or to taste
½ teaspoon ground coriander
¼ teaspoon freshly ground black pepper
Salt to taste
2 cups canned or Fresh Coconut Milk (opposite)
2 tablespoons freshly squeezed lemon juice
Minced cilantro leaves for garnish

1 Put 2 tablespoons of the oil in a large skillet over medium-high heat until it is hot (a pinch of flour will sizzle). Dredge the grouper chunks lightly in the flour, shaking off the excess. Cook them in the oil, raising the heat to high, until lightly browned, 3 to 4 minutes. Remove the fish with a slotted spoon and set aside.

2 Pour out the oil and lower the heat to medium. Wipe out the skillet if there are black bits in it (carefully—it's hot). Add the remaining tablespoon of oil and the onions and cook, stirring, until they are very soft and beginning to turn brown, about 10 minutes. Stir in the turmeric, cayenne, coriander, pepper, and salt. Cook for about 2 minutes.

3 Strain the coconut milk if necessary and add the liquid to the onion mixture; bring to a boil over medium-high heat and reduce by about one third. Add the fish, reduce the heat to medium, and cook for about 5 minutes, or until the fish is tender. Add the lemon juice, taste and adjust the seasonings if necessary, garnish, and serve.

Fresh Coconut Milk

Makes about 2 cups

Time: 20 minutes

You can buy coconut milk in cans, but it's relatively expensive and, for me at least, more trouble than it's worth. On the other hand, a pound of dried coconut costs about two dollars at the natural foods store and will make gallons of coconut milk, thick or thin, with little effort. Be careful when blending this—it's hot.

2 cups water, plus 1 to 2 cups more if needed
2 cups dried unsweetened shredded or grated
    coconut

1 Bring 2 cups of water to a boil. Put the coconut in the container of a blender.

2 Pour 2 cups of water into the blender. Use a towel to hold the lid on tight and turn the switch on and off a few times quickly to get the mixture going. Then blend for about 30 seconds. Let rest for 10 minutes.

3 Pour the milk through a strainer. This will be fairly thick. If you need more milk, just pour additional water through the coconut, up to another cup or two. Press the coconut to extract as much liquid as possible. Use immediately or freeze indefinitely.

Gefilte Fish

Makes 8 to 12 servings

Time: About 2¹/₂ hours, largely unattended, plus time to chill

This is my grandmother's recipe, although she never used a food processor. It produces very light, flavorful fish balls in a delicious jelly. If you serve it on toothpicks, leave the jelly behind, but use prepared horseradish—or Homemade Horseradish, page 772—as a dipping sauce.

2 to 3 pounds fish scraps—bones, heads (gills removed), skin—from carp and other white-fleshed fish

3 cups sliced onions

3 pounds carp fillets and/or other freshwater fish, such as pike and whitefish, or white-fleshed saltwater fish such as red snapper, skinned and trimmed of dark meat

3 eggs, lightly beaten

2 tablespoons matzo or cracker meal

About 1 cup water

Salt and freshly ground white (traditional) or black pepper to taste

About 3 cups peeled carrot chunks

Prepared horseradish

1 Place the fish scraps in a large pot with about one third of the onions. Cover with plenty of water (top the scraps by 3 or 4 inches), bring to a boil, then reduce the heat to low.

2 Place the remaining onions and the fish fillets in the container of a food processor and pulse until coarsely chopped; do not overprocess. Add the eggs, one at a time, pulsing after each addition. Add the matzo meal and about ¹/₂ cup of water and process for a few seconds; the mixture should be light, smooth, and almost fluffy. Add a little more water if it seems too dry. Season with salt and pepper; the mixture should be well seasoned and delicious.

3 Drop the carrots into the simmering stock. With wet hands, shape the fish mixture into small ovals, about the size of eggs. Lower each one of them into the simmering stock; don't worry about crowding. Simmer for 1¹/₂ hours, covered. Turn off the heat and allow the fish to cool in the liquid.

4 With a slotted spoon, remove the fish balls and the carrots to a platter. Reduce the stock, if necessary, to about 2 cups. Strain it over the fish balls, cover the platter, and refrigerate. Remove the fish from the refrigerator about 30 minutes before serving it with a bit of the jelly, a few carrot pieces, and plenty of horseradish.

The Basics of Fish Steaks

Occasionally, a large specimen of a fairly mild-flavored fish such as cod, whiting, or tilefish is cut into steaks. But the days when these fish were allowed to grow old enough to become so large are in the past, and the world of steak fish is now dominated by a few of the giants of the sea, especially swordfish and tuna. (Salmon steaks, the most popular of all, are treated in a separate section, because salmon's taste, texture, and color put it in a class by itself.)

There are other steaks as well, as you'll see from the list below. Some are boneless (marked with a ★)

and some have a more delicate texture (marked with a 🦐). All can be grilled, although the more delicate fish such as halibut and cod need care, not only to prevent them from falling apart (the bane of most fish grillers) but because they overcook and dry out quite easily. In fact, until you gain some experience in grilling fish, I recommend you stick to the sturdy, flavorful, nearly foolproof steaks of tuna, sword, and shark.

Steaks can also be cooked by any other method; broiling, roasting, and pan-cooking are the easiest and the best. Since many of these fish are highly flavorful, complex flavor additions and procedures are neither necessary nor especially desirable. Furthermore, steaks are the most forgiving of all cuts of fish: Almost any recipe here can be adapted to any other cooking technique; I have made Grilled Mesclun-Stuffed Tuna or Swordfish Steaks (page 295), for example, on a grill, in the broiler, in the oven, and in a skillet. My preferred method is the one in each recipe, but feel free to change the process if the situation demands. Generally, they all take about the same length of time; when roasting, I usually plan for two or three minutes extra.

- 🦐 Bluefish (delicate but strong-flavored)
- 🦐 Cod
  Grouper
- 🦐 Halibut
- 🦐 Mackerel (delicate but strong-flavored)
  Mahi-mahi
- ★ Mako
- ★ Monkfish (not a true steak, but works well in steak recipes)
- ★ Sturgeon (may have some cartilage)
- ★ Swordfish (may have skin; it's inedible)
- 🦐 Tilefish
- ★ Tuna (may have skin; it's inedible)

(Step 1) To cut steaks mark the fish by scoring it lightly with a knife to ensure you'll make them even. (Step 2) With most fish, the backbone is so thick that you'll need a little help to get the knife through; use a meat mallet or an ordinary rubber or wooden mallet.

Because they are of uniform thickness, or nearly so, steaks cook evenly and at a fairly uniform rate. The problem with steaks is that some of these fish—most notably swordfish and tuna—are better when they're cooked to a medium, and even a medium-rare stage, than when they are cooked to well done. Others, such as halibut and cod, become quite dry if they're overcooked. And sturgeon and mako are on the tough side if they're either under- or overcooked. All of which leads me to believe that the best way to check doneness on steaks is by the following:

1. As with most other fish, begin checking the fish after about seven minutes of cooking time per inch of thickness. Cod, halibut, and tilefish are done when a thin-bladed knife passes easily through the center. If you're in doubt, take a very thin-bladed knife, a boning knife or something even thinner, and make a small cut near the center of one of the steaks. Pry the flesh apart and peek in there to judge the level of doneness; all traces of translucence should be gone.

2. For bluefish, mackerel, and mahi-mahi, start with the cut-and-peek technique described above. When they are white throughout, or very nearly so, remove them from the heat.

3. For mako, monkfish, and sturgeon, judge doneness not only by appearance but by tenderness; sometimes they are tender just before the translucence disappears, other times just after. It will just be a matter of a minute or two.

4. Swordfish is at its most moist if you stop cooking when just a little translucence remains in the center; cook it to the well-done stage if you prefer, but get it off the heat quickly or it will be dry.

5. Tuna is best when still red to pink in the center. Fully cooked tuna is inevitably dry.

Basic Grilled Swordfish, Tuna, or Other Steaks

Makes 4 servings

Time: 45 minutes, plus time to preheat the grill

Nothing simpler, few things better. The marinade just gives a bit of tang to the browning crust; you could eliminate it, and brush the grilling fish with a bit of olive oil or soy sauce if you prefer. Or, skip it entirely. Note the variations, and see Six Simple Ideas for Grilled Fish, page 287.

2 (1-inch-thick) swordfish or tuna steaks, or any of
    the steaks listed on page 293 marked with a ★,
    a total of 1¹/₂ to 2 pounds
Juice of 1 lime
2 tablespoons soy sauce
Lime or lemon wedges

1 Start a charcoal or wood fire or preheat a gas grill or broiler; the fire should be quite hot and the rack should be fairly close to the heat, 3 or 4 inches at most.

2 Soak the steak in a mixture of the lime juice and soy sauce for 15 to 30 minutes, if desired.

3 Grill the fish, brushing once or twice with the soy-lime mixture. After 4 minutes, the fish should be nicely browned; turn it. Three minutes later, check the fish for doneness by peeking between the layers of flesh with a thin-bladed knife—when the knife meets little resistance and just a touch of translucence remains, the swordfish is done. Serve immediately, with lime or lemon wedges.

Grilled Swordfish, Tuna, or Other Steaks with Mustard Sauce: This dish is great with boiled potatoes. Step 1 remains the same. In Step 2, omit the marinade. Instead, brush the fish with 1 tablespoon of olive or other oil, then sprinkle it with salt and pepper. Grill as in Step 3. Combine ¹/₄ cup olive oil, 3 tablespoons Dijon mustard, ¹/₄ cup minced shallots, 2 tablespoons minced fresh parsley leaves, 2 tablespoons freshly squeezed lemon juice, and salt and pepper to taste. Drizzle the steak with a bit of this, then pass the rest at the table. Omit the lemon or lime wedges.

Grilled Swordfish, Tuna, or Other Steaks with Corn and Tomato Relish: Don't bother to make this unless corn and tomatoes are fresh. Step 1 remains the same. In Step 2, omit the marinade. Instead, brush the fish with 1 tablespoon of olive or other oil, then sprinkle it with salt and pepper. Before grilling, heat a large skillet, preferably non-stick, over medium-high heat for 2 or 3 minutes. Add 2 tablespoons extra-virgin olive oil, then the kernels stripped from 4 ears of corn (see page 563). Cook, stirring, over high heat until lightly browned, a minute or two. Add 2 large cored and roughly chopped fresh tomatoes and ¹/₂ cup minced fresh basil leaves. Cook 30 seconds more, then turn off the heat. Season with salt and pepper. Grill the fish as in Step 3, then serve with the relish. Omit the lemon and lime wedges.

Herb-Rubbed Grilled Swordfish, Tuna, or Other Steaks: Step 1 remains the same. In Step 2, omit the marinade and, before grilling, rub the fish with a mixture of 1 tablespoon grated or minced lemon peel, 1 teaspoon coarse salt, 1 large minced clove garlic, and 2 tablespoons minced mixed fresh herbs, such as parsley, chives, basil, sage, thyme, and/or rosemary. Grill as in Step 3 and serve with lemon wedges.

Grilled Mesclun-Stuffed Tuna or Swordfish Steaks

Makes 4 servings

Time: 20 minutes, plus time to preheat the grill

Do not be intimidated by the creation of the pocket; it is easy, and takes just a minute.

Juice of 2 limes

$1/4$ cup soy sauce

1 medium clove garlic, minced

1 teaspoon strong mustard

2 teaspoons peeled and finely minced fresh ginger or 1 teaspoon ground ginger

$1/2$ teaspoon dark sesame oil

$1/2$ teaspoon coarsely ground black pepper

$1/4$ cup dry white wine or water

1 tuna or swordfish steak, no less than $1^{1}/4$ inches thick, about $1^{1}/2$ pounds

About $1^{1}/2$ cups mesclun or other assorted greens (trimmed, washed, dried, and torn)

1 Start a charcoal or wood fire or preheat a gas grill or broiler; the rack should be 3 to 4 inches from the heat source. Mix together all the ingredients except the tuna and the greens.

2 Using a sharp, thin-bladed knife (a boning knife, for example), make a small incision halfway down any edge of the tuna steak. Insert the knife almost to the opposite edge of the steak, then move it back and forth, flipping it over and creating a large pocket. Be careful not to cut through the top, bottom, or opposite edge of the tuna. Put the tuna in the soy mixture; you can leave it there for a few minutes or continue with the recipe right away.

3 Remove the tuna from the liquid and dry it with paper towels. Toss the mesclun with the marinade. Stuff the pocket with the mesclun, still drenched in the liquid. Seal the pocket opening with a couple of toothpicks.

4 Grill the tuna, turning once, about 5 minutes per inch of thickness (if your steak is $1^{1}/2$ inches thick, for example, turn it after about 4 minutes and cook 3 or 4 minutes more. It will be quite rare; if you want to cook it more, go right ahead. Serve cut into quarters or $1/2$-inch-thick slices.

Skewers of Swordfish, Tuna, or Other Steaks

Makes 4 to 6 servings

Time: 1 hour, plus time to preheat the grill

Skewered fish, a recent addition to the grilling repertoire, is becoming more popular, and rightfully so: It's flavorful, fast-cooking, and always tender.

1 to $1^{1}/2$ pounds swordfish steaks, or any of the steaks listed on page 293 marked with a ★, cut into 1- to $1^{1}/2$-inch chunks

3 medium onions, quartered

6 medium-to-large button or 2 portobello mushrooms, trimmed and quartered

6 bay leaves

6 slices bacon, cut into 3 or 4 pieces each (optional)

Salt and freshly ground black pepper to taste

1 teaspoon dried thyme, marjoram, oregano, mint, or fennel seeds

$1/4$ cup olive oil

Juice of 1 lemon

1 Thread the swordfish onto 6 skewers, alternating with pieces of onion, mushroom, bay leaf, and bacon. Lay the skewers on a platter and sprinkle with salt, pepper, and the herb of your choice. Drizzle with the olive oil and lemon juice and let sit for about 30 minutes (refrigerated if your kitchen is warm), turning occasionally.

2 Start a charcoal or wood fire or preheat a gas grill or broiler; the heat should be high, but the rack a good 6 inches or more from the heat source.

3 Grill the skewers for 12 minutes or a little more, turning occasionally. When they're done, the bacon should be cooked but not crisp, the swordfish browned but still moist (try a piece).

Skewers of Swordfish, Tuna, or Other Steaks with Rosemary: If you have a large rosemary bush, use long branches to skewer swordfish chunks before grilling, brushing with olive oil and lemon. If not, follow this recipe: Thread swordfish onto skewers as in Step 1, with or without vegetables. Make a marinade of 1 small onion, minced; the minced zest and juice of 1 lemon; $^1/_3$ cup olive oil; salt and pepper; and 1 tablespoon minced fresh rosemary or 1 teaspoon dried rosemary. Step 2 remains the same. In Step 3, toss a handful of fresh rosemary or a few rosemary branches directly onto the coals before grilling. Proceed as above.

Monkfish or Other Steaks Roasted with Herbs

Makes 4 servings

Time: 45 minutes

Roasting takes a bit longer than other methods, but it has a distinct advantage, especially if you begin with a little liquid in the pan: These, plus the juice from the fish combine to make a sauce with no effort on

your part. And the slightly moist environment and longer cooking time leave you a bit more margin for error.

$1^1/_2$ to 2 pounds monkfish fillets, or any of the steaks listed on page 293, about 1 inch thick

$^1/_2$ to 1 cup chopped mixed fresh herbs: parsley, basil, chervil, tarragon, rosemary, chives, marjoram, sage, or whatever you have on hand (use the lower amount if you're using stronger herbs)

1 cup flour

Salt and freshly ground black pepper to taste

2 tablespoons olive oil

1 cup chicken, fish, or vegetable stock, or water (see "Soups" for stock recipes)

1 Preheat the oven to 450°F. Rinse and dry the fish. Mix together the herbs, flour, salt, and pepper.

2 Heat a large ovenproof skillet over medium-high heat for about 2 minutes; add the olive oil. When it's good and hot (a pinch of flour will sizzle), dredge the monkfish in the flour and herb mixture. Shake off the excess flour and brown for a couple of minutes on all sides. Add the liquid to the pan and place it, uncovered, in the oven.

3 Roast until the monkfish is tender, 20 to 30 minutes, turning once or twice (1-inch-thick steaks of most other fish will take 5 or 10 minutes less).

Monkfish fillets (which are actually tails) have a thin gray membrane covering them. Remove as much of it as you can with your fingers and a sharp knife.

4 Remove the fish to a warm platter. If the pan juices are a little thin, reduce a bit; if they're too thick, add a little more stock or water and cook over medium heat for a minute or two. Serve with the fish, over rice or with bread, with the sauce spooned over.

Monkfish or Other Steaks Roasted with Fennel: In Step 1, substitute 2 tablespoons fennel seeds for the herbs. In Step 2, top the fish with several branches of the herb fennel (page 572) or several slices of bulb fennel, then add the broth. Steps 3 and 4 remain the same.

Sautéed Cod or Other Fish Steaks

Makes 4 servings

Time: 20 minutes

This recipe and its variations are wonderful served with Caramelized Small Onions or Shallots, page 588.

About 1 cup flour
Salt and freshly ground black pepper to taste
$^1/_2$ teaspoon cayenne, or to taste (optional)
2 tablespoons olive oil
2 tablespoons butter (or use more oil)
4 small cod steaks, or any of the fish listed on page 293, 4 to 6 ounces each, about $^3/_4$ to 1 inch thick
Minced fresh parsley leaves for garnish
Lemon wedges

1 Heat a large skillet over medium heat for 2 or 3 minutes.
2 Season the flour with the salt, lots of black pepper, and the cayenne if you like.
3 Add the olive oil to the pan; when it's hot, add the butter. When the butter foam subsides, dredge each steak in the flour. Place them in the skillet.

4 Cook over medium-high heat, rotating the steaks so they brown evenly, and turning after about 4 minutes. They will be done, or nearly so, after about 7 or 8 minutes of cooking. Check the fish for doneness by peeking between the layers of flesh with a thin-bladed knife—when the knife meets little resistance and little or no translucence remains in the center, the fish is done. Cook it a minute or two longer if necessary, garnish, and serve with lemon wedges.

Sautéed Cod or Other Fish Steaks in Green Sauce: Steps 1 and 2 remain the same. In Step 3, use $^1/_2$ cup olive oil, extra-virgin if you have it (no butter), and add 2 tablespoons minced garlic with it. As soon as the garlic begins to color, dredge the fish and add it to the pan. In Step 4, add 1 cup roughly chopped flat-leaf (Italian) parsley when you turn the fish. Finish cooking as above.

Sautéed Cod or Other Fish Steaks with Dill and Scallions: Step 1 remains the same. In Step 2, use cornmeal in place of flour. In Step 3, use all olive oil. Step 4 remains the same; remove the fish and keep it warm (do not garnish). Add 3 tablespoons minced fresh dill and 3 tablespoons minced scallions to the pan. Cook, stirring, over medium heat, for about 1 minute. Add $^3/_4$ cup wine, fish, vegetable, or chicken stock, or water, and stir while you let most of it bubble away. Pour the sauce over the fish and serve immediately, with lemon wedges.

Poached Halibut or Other Steaks with Vegetables

Makes 4 servings

Time: 30 minutes

You can use this recipe and its variations for any fish steak (or sturdy fillet, for that matter), but I think it's best with mild-flavored ones—not only halibut, but cod, grouper, monkfish, and tilefish.

> About 2 cups any fish, chicken, or mild vegetable stock (see "Soups" for stock recipes)
> 3 tablespoons butter
> 2 medium carrots, peeled and diced
> 2 medium onions, diced
> 2 stalks celery, diced
> 1 clove garlic, minced
> Salt and freshly ground black pepper to taste
> 2 halibut steaks (or see headnote), ³/₄ to 1 pound each

1 In a small saucepan, bring the stock to a boil. Lower the heat, and keep it warm.

2 In the smallest skillet or casserole that will later hold the fish steaks, melt the butter over medium heat. Add all ingredients except fish and stock and cook, stirring, until the vegetables wilt, 5 to 10 minutes.

3 Place the steaks on top of the vegetables and add the stock. Simmer over medium-low heat until the halibut is done, about 10 minutes (a thin-bladed knife inserted between bone and flesh should reveal little or no translucence). Remove the steaks and serve, topped with vegetables and a little of the broth.

Poached Halibut or Other Steaks with Vegetables and Mustard Sauce: Steps 1 through 3 remain the same, but undercook the fish slightly, remove it and the vegetables from the pan, and keep them all warm in a warm oven. Melt 1 tablespoon butter in a small saucepan over medium-low heat. Add 1 tablespoon flour and cook, stirring, until the mixture turns nut-brown, about 3 or 4 minutes. Strain 1 cup of the fish-cooking liquid and whisk it gradually into the butter-flour mixture, stirring constantly to eliminate lumps. Cook until slightly thickened, 4 or 5 minutes. Season with salt and pepper and add 1 to 2 tablespoons Dijon mustard,

or to taste. Serve the halibut and vegetables topped with the sauce and minced fresh parsley leaves.

Halibut or Other Steaks Simmered in Soy Broth

Makes 4 servings

Time: 20 minutes

This recipe is best with mild-flavored steaks: cod, grouper, halibut, monkfish, and tilefish.

> 1 tablespoon peanut or vegetable oil
> 1 or 2 halibut steaks (or see headnote), a total of about 1¹/₂ pounds
> 1 tablespoon minced garlic
> 1 tablespoon peeled and minced or grated fresh ginger
> 1 teaspoon dark sesame oil
> 2 tablespoons soy sauce
> ¹/₂ cup chicken, beef, or vegetable stock, or water (see "Soups" for stock recipes)
> ¹/₄ cup minced scallions

1 Heat a large non-stick skillet over medium-high heat for 2 or 3 minutes. Add the oil and raise the heat to high; cook the fish for 60 to 90 seconds on each side, just until it begins to brown.

2 Turn the heat to medium-low. Sprinkle the garlic and ginger around the fish, then drizzle the sesame oil over it. Add the soy sauce and stock or water to the skillet, raise the heat to medium, and bring to a boil. Turn the heat to low and cover.

3 Cook for 5 minutes. Remove the cover and, with the fish still in the liquid, raise the heat to high and reduce the liquid by about half (this should only take one minute or two).

4 Serve the fish over rice, with some of the sauce spooned over and garnished with the scallions.

The Basics of Salmon and Trout

Salmon and trout—close cousins—don't differ so much from other finfish in their appearance or bone structure, but in their flavor. They are distinctively rich, oily, and sometimes downright fatty, full of flavor but almost never "fishy."

Some Native Americans literally worshiped salmon, which clogged coastal rivers each spring, but by mid-twentieth century Atlantic salmon was almost extinct and most Pacific salmon—the best of which is leaner and darker in color—was smoked or canned. Fresh salmon was the near-exclusive domain of a few white-tablecloth restaurants in big cities.

The Norwegians changed all that. In the 1970s, they developed a profitable method for farming and shipping Atlantic salmon. Ten years later, salmon was a year-round product, and the Alaskans, who supply nearly all of our Pacific salmon, were forced to improve their handling and transportation techniques. Now, just about anywhere in the United States, you can find an Atlantic salmon that's been out of the water for seventy-two hours or less, occasionally feast on Pacific salmon flown from Alaska to your local airport, and pay less for those fish than you would have ten and twenty years ago. It's not surprising that salmon now ranks among the five favorite fish in the United States.

Gorgeous to look at when whole, salmon skins, steaks, and fillets beautifully (there are some large "pin bones" that run down the center of imperfect fillets, but you can remove these in the kitchen, page 302, or even at the table). You can use any cooking technique you like to prepare it, as long as you don't overcook it. And there's more: Salmon's ease of cooking and good flavor are largely thanks to its high fat content, something for which we can be grateful, since this particular fat seems to be associated with combating rather than encouraging disease.

The challenges associated with salmon are mostly in the buying: Although many markets and restaurants sell "Norwegian" salmon as if it were a distinct species, that is not the case. Salmon from Norway, like most farm-raised salmon, is Atlantic salmon. (Endangered in the wild, this fish is sold only when farm-raised, at least in this country.) But Atlantic salmon is now raised almost any place there is cold, protected seawater, such as Maine and the Maritime Provinces of Canada, the Pacific Northwest, northern Europe, and southern Chile, and almost all farm-raised salmon is quite good, so rich and fatty it looks "marbled."

What confuses the issue is that there are also five species of wild Pacific salmon. Two of these—king (or chinook) and sockeye (red, or blueback)—are leaner than Atlantic salmon, but almost as rich and arguably more flavorful. Of the three other Pacific species, coho (silver) is the best, and is occasionally farm-raised. Chum (keta) is not bad and sometimes sells for less than three dollars a pound in the supermarket, which makes it a good buy. Pink should be canned, and most of it is.

Unless you live in the Northwest, buying Alaskan salmon is difficult; deceptive or well-intentioned but ignorant purveyors will often tell you that their Alaskan salmon is "king." But king salmon accounts for a mere one percent of the total catch, and most sockeye salmon (like so many of our good fish) is, alas, shipped to Japan. What this means is that in a supermarket, you'll rarely be offered anything but chum (which causes prices to plummet each fall) and farm-raised Atlantic salmon. Top-quality fish markets offer real king and sockeye, and label it so, but usually only for a few weeks each summer. Frozen king, sockeye, and coho can be fantastic, but unfortunately the distribution of this fish is poor.

The chances are good, then, that you'll wind up with farm-raised fillets or steaks. Full-service fish markets scale their fish before cutting it up; since salmon skin is delicious, especially when it's crisp, this is a bonus. But, unfortunately, few supermarkets bother with this nicety, leaving you with three choices: Scale the fish yourself (page 311) which, for whole fish or fillets, is not difficult (it's nearly impossible to scale steaks once they've been cut); skin the fish, also quite easy to do; or, easiest of all, cook the fish with the scales on and discard the skin. This is a nice solution, because the scales give added protection against overcooking, and the skin peels right off afterward, taking the scales with it.

As for cooking techniques, with salmon you can use them all. I grill skin-on fillets without turning them at all, and cover the grill for the last two minutes of cooking to finish the top. Broiling is similar; I turn steaks once, fillets not at all. Roasting is good for whole fish, but I stick with the broiler for steaks and fillets.

For pan-cooking, try the technique I give here, cooking skin-on fillets with no added fat and finishing them in the broiler. It works great; peel the skin off after cooking.

Finally, there's poaching or steaming: You don't need fancy stocks to poach salmon; it has enough flavor already. Just be careful not to overcook. Again, don't bother to skin the fish first; peel it off after poaching.

The cooking time for salmon varies according to your taste. I prefer my salmon cooked to what might be called medium-rare to medium, with a well-cooked exterior and a fairly red center. Given that, I always look at the center of a piece of salmon to judge its doneness. Once again, remember that fish retains enough heat to continue cooking after it has been removed from the heat source, so stop cooking just before the salmon reaches the point you'd consider it done.

There are two reasons I have linked salmon and trout. The first is that, indeed, they're related. The second is that much trout is also farm-raised; unless you're a fisherman, or know one, you may never eat wild trout. Until recently, most farm-raised trout was almost tasteless, overrated compared to either salmon or its wild relatives. But there are now several farm-raised fish—steelheads, Arctic char, and orange-fleshed rainbow trout—that are sold as trout and look and taste like salmon. These are best treated as salmon, and can be used in any salmon recipe. The few trout recipes I offer here are designed for wild trout or store-bought—that is, farm-raised—trout.

Gravlax
Salt-and-Sugar-Cured Salmon
Makes 12 or more appetizer servings

Time: 20 minutes, plus at least 2 days to cure

Lovely, impressive, and incomparably delicious, gravlax is also among the simplest cured dishes. Use king or sockeye salmon when they're in season, Atlantic farm-raised salmon from a good source otherwise. In either case, the fish must be spanking fresh. Gravlax keeps for one week after curing; and, although it's not an ideal solution, you can successfully freeze gravlax for a few weeks.

1 (3- to 4-pound) salmon, weighed after cleaning
    and beheading, skin on
1 cup salt
2 cups brown sugar
1 tablespoon freshly ground black pepper
1/4 cup spirits: brandy, gin, aquavit, lemon vodka, etc.
2 good-sized bunches dill, roughly chopped,
    stems and all

1 Fillet the salmon (page 278) or have the fishmonger fillet it for you; the fish need not be scaled. Lay both halves, skin side down, on a plate.

2 Toss together the salt, sugar, and pepper, and rub the salmon all over (skin, too) with this mixture; splash on the spirits. Put most of the dill on the flesh side of one of the fillets, sandwich them together, tail to tail, and rub any remaining salt-sugar mixture on the outside; cover with any remaining dill, then wrap tightly in plastic wrap. Cover the sandwich with another plate and something that weighs a couple of pounds—some unopened cans, for example. Refrigerate.

3 Open the package every 12 to 24 hours and baste, inside and out, with the accumulated juices. When the flesh is opaque, on the second or third day (you will see it changing when you baste it), slice thinly as you would smoked salmon—on the bias and without the skin—and serve with rye bread or pumpernickel, lemon wedges, and, if you like, Cold Mustard Sauce (page 763).

Basic Grilled or Broiled Salmon Steaks

Makes 4 servings

Time: About 30 minutes, plus time to preheat the grill

Salmon needs nothing but heat to be delicious; be sure not to overcook and these will be wonderful. But a squeeze of lemon can add a lot. For other simple flavor additions, see below.

4 salmon steaks, ¼ to ⅓ pound each
1 tablespoon peanut or olive oil
Salt and freshly ground black pepper to taste
Lemon wedges

1 Start a charcoal or wood fire or preheat a gas grill or broiler; the fire should be quite hot and the rack about 4 inches from the heat source. Rub the salmon steaks with the oil and sprinkle with salt and pepper.

2 Grill or broil the salmon steaks from 3 to 5 minutes per side, turning once. Use a thin-bladed knife to peek at the flesh near the bone, and remove the steaks from the heat just before they are cooked to the degree of doneness you like.

3 When the fish is done, serve it with lemon wedges.

Seven Simple Ideas for Grilled or Broiled Salmon

1. Dress with a fancy butter sauce, such as Hollandaise Sauce (page 790).
2. Serve with any vinaigrette (page 91), compound butter (page 768), or salsa (page 772).
3. Serve hot on a lightly dressed bed of greens.
4. Chill and serve with mayonnaise (page 761) or other dressing.
5. Chill and use in a sandwich.
6. Drizzle with soy sauce or dark sesame oil.
7. Serve with a dollop of Cucumber-Yogurt Dip with Mint (page 771).

Crispy Skin Salmon with Gingery Greens

Makes 4 servings

Time: 40 minutes to 1 hour, plus time to preheat the grill

One of my all-time favorites, this features the rich flavor of salmon cut by sharp greens sparked with ginger. Steam the greens in advance if it's more convenient for you.

1 (2-pound) salmon fillet, skin on (but scaled),
  pin bones removed (below)
1 pound kale, collards, or other greens
About 5 tablespoons olive oil
1 teaspoon minced garlic
2 teaspoons peeled and minced or grated fresh
  ginger or 1 teaspoon ground ginger
1 tablespoon soy sauce
1 teaspoon dark sesame oil

1 Rinse the fish well and let it rest between paper towels, refrigerated, while you prepare the greens.

2 Wash the greens in several changes of water, and remove any pieces of stem thicker than $1/4$ inch in diameter. Steam or boil them (page 562) in a medium covered saucepan over 1 inch of water until good and soft, 10 minutes or more, depending on the green (older collards will require 30 minutes). Drain them, rinse in cool water, squeeze dry, and chop.

3 Preheat a covered gas grill or start a charcoal fire in a grill that can be covered. Heat 2 tablespoons of the olive oil in a large non-stick sauté pan. Add the garlic and cook 1 minute; do not brown. Add the greens and cook, stirring occasionally, for about 3 minutes; add the ginger and cook another minute, then add the soy sauce and sesame oil and turn off the heat. Remove to a platter and keep warm.

SKINNING A FILLET

Skinning a fillet is much easier than it looks; use any sharp knife.
(Step 1) Cut a small piece from the tail end, at an angle, so as to expose the skin. *(Step 2)* Grasp the exposed piece of skin (use a towel to get a grip if necessary), and insert the knife between skin and flesh, angled slightly toward the skin. *(Step 3)* Run the knife up the entire length of the fillet.

REMOVING PIN BONES

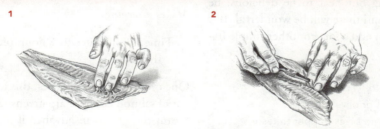

(Step 1) Fillets of many fish, no matter how skillfully removed, may contain long bones along their center which must be removed by hand. Feel with your fingers to see if your fillet contains pin bones. *(Step 2)* Remove them with a needle-nose pliers or similar tool.

4 With a sharp knife, score the skin of the salmon in a cross-hatch pattern. Oil the fish well with the remaining olive oil. Put the fillet on the preheated grill, skin side down, and cover; alternatively, broil the salmon 4 inches from the heat source, skin side up. In either case, cook undisturbed for 5 to 10 minutes, or until done.

5 Remove the fish carefully with a large spatula, and place it on top of the greens. Serve immediately, making sure everyone gets a piece of skin.

Grilled or Broiled Salmon Kebabs

Makes 4 to 6 servings

Time: 1½ hours, plus time to preheat the grill

This is best if the fish retains its skin (make sure it is scaled), which not only protects the fish but helps it to retain its shape and integrity. Since some vegetables, especially raw onions, take a little longer to cook than the fish, I usually cook them first and serve them at room temperature. Then I only have to worry about the salmon at the last minute.

⅓ cup soy sauce
1 teaspoon grated lemon zest
¼ cup freshly squeezed lemon juice
2 tablespoons olive oil
2 cloves garlic, minced
2 teaspoons Dijon mustard
2 teaspoons dark sesame oil
1 tablespoon minced fresh herbs, such as parsley, basil, rosemary, or thyme
2 pounds salmon fillets, preferably from the middle of the fish, skin on (but scaled), pin bones removed (see opposite)
Assorted vegetables for grilling, such as red bell pepper, red onion, zucchini or summer squash, and/or mushrooms

1 Whisk together all the ingredients except the fish and vegetables.

2 Cut the salmon into 1½- to 2-inch cubes or large rectangles; if the pieces are too small, the salmon will dry out during cooking. Skewer the fish, then spoon the marinade over it. Let sit, refrigerated if your kitchen is warm, for about 1 hour. Cut up the vegetables and skewer them if desired; marinate with the fish.

3 Start a charcoal or wood fire or preheat a gas grill or broiler; the rack should be about 4 inches from the heat source. The fish and vegetables can be grilled on skewers, in a basket, or—the most convenient method—on skewers in a basket. The salmon will take about 8 to 10 minutes to cook over high heat (its center should remain rare). Grill the vegetables for about the same amount of time, or until tender.

Pan-Grilled Salmon Fillets with Lemon

Makes 4 servings

Time: 20 minutes

This is an easy recipe which sacrifices the skin in order to leave the flesh moist. It will, however, create a fair amount of smoke, so turn on the exhaust fan if you have one.

1 to 1¼ pounds salmon fillet, preferably in 2 pieces of equal thickness, skin on (scaling is not necessary), pin bones removed (see opposite)
Salt and freshly ground black pepper to taste
Minced fresh parsley leaves for garnish
Lemon wedges

1 Preheat a large ovenproof skillet (cast iron is fine) for 3 or 4 minutes over medium-high heat.

Preheat the broiler as well, positioning the rack about 4 inches beneath the heat source.

2 Place the salmon fillets in the skillet, skin side down. Leave the heat on medium-high. Sprinkle with salt and pepper and cook, undisturbed, for about 6 minutes, or until the salmon flesh turns opaque about halfway up the fish.

3 Move the fish to the broiler and leave it there for 2 or 3 minutes, just until the top browns. The fish should still be moist and slightly undercooked in the middle.

4 Remove the fish, garnish, and serve with lemon wedges.

Pan-Grilled Salmon Fillets with Sesame Oil Drizzle: Steps 1, 2, and 3 remain the same; omit the salt, or at least go easy on it. While the fish is cooking, warm 2 teaspoons dark sesame oil and 1 teaspoon vegetable oil in a small saucepan over low heat. When they're hot, add 2 teaspoons soy sauce. When the fish is done, drizzle this sauce over it. Garnish with minced parsley, minced cilantro, or minced lemon zest; serve with wedges of lemon or lime.

Pan-Grilled Salmon Fillets with Lentils

Makes 4 servings

Time: About an hour

If you ever doubted the value of non-stick pans, try this recipe. The salmon cooks perfectly without the benefit of any fat (if you're on a strict low-fat diet, eliminate the olive oil from the lentils).

2 to 3 cups green lentils, washed and picked over (see The Basics of Buying and Preparing Beans, page 500)
2 medium carrots, peeled and cut into $1/4$-inch cubes
1 small potato, peeled and cut into $1/4$-inch cubes
1 medium onion, chopped
2 cloves garlic, minced
A few sprigs each fresh parsley, thyme, bay leaf, and chives, wrapped in cheesecloth for easy removal; or substitute about $1^1/2$ teaspoons mixed dry herbs
Salt and freshly ground black pepper to taste
2 tablespoons extra-virgin olive oil
Coarse salt
4 center-cut salmon fillets, 6 to 8 ounces each, skin on (but scaled) or off, pin bones removed (page 302)
Minced fresh parsley leaves or chives for garnish

1 Place the lentils in a large, deep saucepan with water to cover. Cook over medium heat, stirring occasionally, until they begin to soften, 15 to 20 minutes, then add the carrots, potato, onion, garlic, and herbs.

2 Continue to cook, adding water if necessary (keep this to a minimum), until the lentils and vegetables are tender, 45 to 60 minutes total. Remove the herbs, season with salt and pepper, add the olive oil, and keep warm.

3 Heat a large non-stick skillet over high heat for about 5 minutes. Sprinkle the bottom of the skillet with coarse salt, then add the salmon, skin side down. Cook over high heat until well browned on the bottom, about 5 minutes. Flip the salmon and cook 1 additional minute (more if you like your salmon well done). Place about 1 cup of lentils in the center of each of four serving plates and top with a salmon fillet. Garnish and serve.

Salmon Roasted in Butter

Makes 4 to 8 servings

Time: 15 minutes

If you make this with the most flavorful, beautiful fillet you can find—such as Alaskan sockeye in season, or a lovely side of farm-raised salmon—you will be amazed by the richness of flavor.

> 4 tablespoons (1/2 stick) butter
> 1 (2- to 3-pound) salmon fillet, skin on (but scaled) or off, pin bones removed (page 302)
> Salt and freshly ground black pepper to taste
> Minced fresh parsley leaves for garnish

1 Preheat the oven to 475°F. Melt the butter in a medium roasting pan—either on top of the stove or in the oven as it preheats—until the foam subsides.

2 Place the salmon in the butter, flesh side down, and put the pan in the oven. Roast about 5 minutes, then turn and roast 3 to 6 minutes longer, until the salmon is done (peek between the flakes with a thin-bladed knife). Sprinkle with salt and pepper, garnish, and serve immediately.

Salmon Roasted with Herbs: This lower-fat version is equally flavorful. In Step 1, use 2 tablespoons olive oil, or half oil and half butter. In Step 2, add a handful (2 to 4 tablespoons depending on their strength) of chopped fresh herbs: tarragon, parsley, chervil, basil, dill, thyme or a combination, and 2 tablespoons minced shallots, then roast as above.

Salmon Roasted with Buttered Almonds: In Step 1, use only 1 tablespoon of oil or butter. Before cooking the fish, melt 3 tablespoons of butter in a small saucepan over medium-low heat. When the butter foam subsides, add 1 cup blanched slivered almonds and cook, stirring, just until they begin to brown. Place the fish in the pan, season with salt and pepper, and spoon the browned almonds on top. Roast as in Step 2, but without turning.

Salmon Fillets in Red Wine

Makes 4 servings

Time: 30 minutes

A great recipe in which to use less expensive chum salmon, since it allows the fish to retain its moisture. Serve it with crusty bread or crisp potatoes.

> 2 tablespoons butter
> 1 tablespoon olive or vegetable oil
> 4 salmon fillets, about 6 ounces each, skinned, pin bones removed (page 302)
> Flour for dredging
> Salt and freshly ground black pepper to taste
> 1 medium onion, diced
> 1 teaspoon minced garlic
> 1 medium carrot, peeled and roughly chopped
> 1/2 cup minced fresh parsley leaves
> 1/4 cup fish, chicken, or vegetable stock, or water (see "Soups" for stock recipes)
> 1 cup dry, full-bodied red wine

1 Heat a large skillet, preferably non-stick, over medium-high heat for 2 or 3 minutes. Add the butter and oil, turn the heat to high, and wait for the butter foam to subside. Dredge each of the fillets in the flour and shake off the excess. Place them, flesh side down, in the skillet. Season with salt and pepper and brown them quickly, on one side only. Remove them (browned side up) from the pan to a plate, and keep warm.

2 With the heat on medium, add the onion, garlic, and carrot to the pan and cook, stirring, until the onion softens slightly, about 5 minutes. Add half the parsley and some salt and pepper and stir. Add the broth, raise the heat to high, and reduce until it is almost evaporated.

3 Add the wine and reduce by about half. Return the fillets to the pan, skin side down, and cook over medium heat until the fillets reach the desired degree of doneness (peek inside with a thin-bladed knife), about 3 to 5 minutes. Sprinkle with the remaining parsley and serve immediately.

Cold Poached Salmon with Lime-Ginger Sauce

Makes 4 to 6 servings

Time: 30 minutes, plus time to cool

This poaching method is easy and consistently results in a moist piece of fish without a lot of fuss.

> 1 whole salmon, 3 pounds or larger, gutted, gilled, and scaled, or 1 (3-pound) cross-cut section from a larger salmon, or 1 large (3-pound) fillet, skin on (but scaled), pin bones removed (page 302)
>
> 2 heaping tablespoons salt
>
> 1 tablespoon peeled and minced or grated fresh ginger
>
> 2 tablespoons peanut or vegetable oil
>
> 2 tablespoons soy sauce
>
> 6 tablespoons freshly squeezed lime juice
>
> 3 tablespoons minced fresh basil or chervil leaves, plus more for garnish, if desired

1 Place the salmon in a pot large enough to hold it (a deep roasting pan is not inappropriate). Cover the salmon with cold water and aluminum foil to make a lid for the pan. Add the salt and bring to a boil. Turn off the heat immediately and let the salmon sit in the hot water for 10 minutes for a fillet, up to 30 minutes for a large, whole fish. Check for doneness

by peeking near the center bone, using a thin-bladed knife; do not overcook. Remove the fish from the water, drain, and chill.

2 Meanwhile, whisk together the ginger, oil, soy sauce, lime juice, and the 3 tablespoons minced basil or chervil. Drizzle some of this over the fish. To serve the salmon, insert the tine of a fork under the skin at the mid-line of each side of the fish, then run it lengthwise, splitting the skin. The skin will peel off easily. Take the salmon off the bone in the kitchen or at the table, using a spoon and following the natural contours of the fish.

Eight Sauces for Cold Poached Salmon

1. Mix sour cream or yogurt with fresh dill, salt, pepper, and freshly squeezed lemon juice to taste; thin with cream or milk if necessary.
2. Mayonnaise (page 761) or any of its variations; again, thin if you like.
3. Any vinaigrette (page 91)
4. Yogurt-Avocado Dressing (page 771)
5. Cold Mustard Sauce (page 763)
6. Basic Pesto (page 766) or any of its variations
7. Cucumber-Yogurt Dip with Mint (page 771)
8. Spicy Yogurt Sauce (page 772)

Salmon Croquettes

Makes 4 servings

Time: 20 minutes

Whole salmon are large, which often means leftovers; this is the ideal use for them. If you don't want to pan-fry these croquettes, you can broil or even grill them. Keep them six to eight inches away from the heat source to avoid burning.

1 to 2 cups leftover salmon meat

1 to 2 cups leftover Mashed Potatoes (page 596)

1/2 to 1 cup minced onion or scallion

1/4 cup minced fresh parsley leaves

1 teaspoon peeled and minced or grated fresh ginger or garlic (optional)

1 egg

1 teaspoon Dijon mustard

Salt and freshly ground black pepper to taste

Plain bread crumbs as needed

1/4 to 1/2 cup olive oil

Lemon wedges

1 Combine the first eight ingredients; add just enough bread crumbs to stiffen the mixture, but don't make it too dry.

2 Shape into small cakes; dredge in bread crumbs, then dry on a rack, refrigerated, for 15 to 30 minutes. Heat a large, deep skillet over medium heat for 2 or 3 minutes. Add a film of the olive oil and cook the croquettes until they are browned on both sides, about 10 minutes total. If you must cook in batches, add more olive oil. Serve with lemon wedges.

Sautéed Trout

Makes 2 servings

Time: 30 minutes

There are countless ways to pan-fry trout, from the simple to the complex. If you catch your own fish, the simplest is best.

2 whole trout, about 3/4 pound each, gutted and split or filleted

4 tablespoons (1/2 stick) butter or olive oil

1 cup cornmeal

Salt and freshly ground black pepper to taste

Minced fresh parsley leaves for garnish

1 Rinse and dry the fish. Melt the butter over medium-high heat in a large non-stick skillet. When the foam subsides, dredge the fish in the cornmeal, place in the pan, and raise the heat to high.

2 Season with salt and pepper and cook on both sides until nicely browned and the interior turns white, 8 to 12 minutes total. Garnish and serve.

Sautéed Trout with Bacon: Step 1 remains the same. In Step 2, omit butter or oil. Cook 4 slices of good bacon in a skillet. When the bacon is nice and crisp, remove it to a warm oven. Proceed as above, cooking the trout in the bacon fat. Garnish with the bacon slices and parsley.

Sautéed Trout with Almonds (Trout Amandine): Step 1 remains the same. Before proceeding to Step 2, melt 1 tablespoon of butter in a small skillet over medium heat; when the foam subsides, cook 1/2 cup blanched slivered almonds, stirring frequently, until they start to brown, 2 or 3 minutes. Remove from the heat. Proceed with Steps 2 and 3. When the fish is done, garnish with the cooked almonds and the parsley, drizzle with a little freshly squeezed lemon juice, and serve.

The Basics of Fillets of Bluefish, Mackerel, and Like Fish

These are a special case, because their dark flesh is especially flavorful. Some people are prejudiced against these fish, usually not because they dislike the flavor but because they have had poor specimens, or those which were badly cooked. Because of their high oil content (like salmon, much of this is beneficial oil, high in Omega-3 fatty acids), dark fish spoil quickly.

In my years of cooking for people, I've found that these dishes draw the best crowd sounds from those who have fear of fish:

Properly handled and cooked, however, mackerel and its relatives are among the best. Most recipes for these fish contain vinegar or other acid, because sharp flavors are needed to balance their richness. Other fish that fall into this category and can be used in these recipes are bonito, mullet, king or Spanish mackerel, and pompano. To some extent, mahi-mahi and tuna are also similar.

Broiled Bluefish or Mackerel Fillets with Lime Mustard

Makes 4 servings

Time: 20 minutes

Absurdly simple, and very good.

1/2 cup Dijon or grainy mustard
Grated zest and juice of 1 lime
Salt and freshly ground black pepper to taste
1 tablespoon olive or vegetable oil
About 1 1/2 pounds bluefish or mackerel fillets, skin on (but scaled) or off
1 medium tomato, peeled if you have time, cored, seeded, and coarsely chopped
Lime wedges

1 Preheat the broiler; set the rack 4 to 6 inches from the heat source. Mix together the mustard, lime zest and juice, salt, and pepper. Brush a baking sheet or broiler pan with the oil, and lay the bluefish, skin side down, on it. Brush the fish with the mustard-lime mixture.

2 Broil the fish for 6 to 10 minutes, depending on its thickness (bluefish and mackerel turn white

throughout when done; peek between the layers of flesh with a thin-bladed knife). Sprinkle with the tomato and return to the broiler for 1 minute. Serve immediately, with lime wedges.

Broiled Bluefish or Mackerel Fillets with Vinegar and Mint: In Step 1, omit the mustard mixture. Instead, warm $1/4$ cup olive oil in a very small saucepan over low heat with $1/4$ cup balsamic vinegar and 1 teaspoon minced garlic. Spoon a little of this mixture over the fish and sprinkle with about $1/4$ cup minced fresh mint (or dill) leaves and some salt and pepper (omit the tomatoes). Broil as in Step 2, basting once with a bit of the oil and vinegar mixture. When it's done, garnish with a little mint and serve with the remaining sauce. Omit the lime.

Broiled Bluefish or Mackerel Fillets with Herbs: In Step 1, omit the mustard mixture. Instead, combine 3 tablespoons olive oil with the grated zest and juice of 1 lemon and 3 tablespoons chopped fresh herbs: parsley, thyme, rosemary, tarragon, chives, chervil, etc. Spoon a little of this mixture over the fish, along with some salt and pepper. Broil as in Step 2, basting once with a little of the herb mixture and adding the tomatoes or not, as you prefer. Serve with the remaining sauce, garnished with a little minced fresh herb. Serve with lemon wedges.

Broiled Bluefish or Mackerel Fillets with Tomato, Ginger, and Garlic: In Step 1, omit the mustard mixture. Instead, combine 1 cup cored and chopped tomatoes, 1 tablespoon peeled and minced or grated fresh ginger, 1 tablespoon minced garlic, and $1/4$ teaspoon cayenne, or to taste. Brush the fillets with this mixture and broil as in Step 2. Garnish with minced cilantro or parsley leaves.

Simmered Bluefish or Mackerel Fillets
Makes 4 servings

Time: 20 minutes

Fatty fish like mackerel are highly prized in Japan, and the flavors of Japanese cooking complement them brilliantly. Although I like to sear these fillets first, it isn't necessary; you can just combine all the ingredients except the fish, bring to a boil, place the fish in them, cover, and simmer.

About $1^1/_2$ pounds bluefish or mackerel fillets, skin on (but scaled) or off
2 tablespoons peanut or vegetable oil
1 tablespoon minced garlic
5 or 6 thin slices fresh ginger
2 tablespoons mirin (sweet cooking wine) or 1 tablespoon honey thinned with water
$1/4$ teaspoon cayenne, or to taste
2 tablespoons soy sauce
1 teaspoon sugar
$1/2$ cup water

1 Heat a large non-stick skillet over medium-high heat for 3 or 4 minutes. If you have 1 large fillet, cut it into 2 or 4 pieces. Add the oil to the skillet, wait 1 minute, and add the garlic. Stir once or twice and add the fillets. Raise the heat to high and sear about a minute on each side.

2 Add the remaining ingredients and stir. Turn the fish once or twice in the liquid, cover, and reduce the heat to low. Cook until done (the fish will be opaque throughout), about 6 minutes.

3 Remove the fish to a bowl and strain the broth over it. Serve immediately, with white rice.

Bluefish or Mackerel with Roasted Summer Vegetables

Makes 4 servings

Time: 40 minutes

This recipe will appeal especially to gardeners (who will also know that the vegetable list can be varied according to their garden's production). The vegetables help keep the fish moist; the high heat keeps the cooking time relatively short.

2 cups peeled and diced eggplant, salted if desired (page 567)

2 cups diced zucchini

2 cups cored and diced tomatoes

1 cup chopped onion

1 cup cut-up green beans (trimmed and cut in half)

1 tablespoon minced garlic

Salt and freshly ground black pepper to taste

1 tablespoon minced fresh rosemary leaves or 1 teaspoon dried rosemary

1/3 cup minced fresh parsley leaves, plus more for garnish

1/4 cup olive oil

About 1 1/2 pounds bluefish or mackerel fillets, skin on (but scaled) or off

1 teaspoon freshly squeezed lemon juice

1 Preheat the oven to 500°F. Mix the vegetables together with the garlic, salt, pepper, rosemary, parsley, and olive oil in a baking dish that can later accommodate the fish. Roast about 20 minutes, stirring once or twice, until the tomatoes have dissolved, the sauce is bubbling, and the zucchini and eggplant are fairly tender.

2 Lay the fish on top of the vegetables, spoon some of the vegetables over it, lower the heat to 450°F, and return the pan to the oven. Roast another 8 to 15 minutes, depending on the thickness of the fillets (the fish will become white and opaque when it's done), basting with pan juices once or twice. Drizzle with the lemon juice, garnish, and serve.

The Basics of Whole Fish

Regrettably not as popular as it once was, whole fish remains a special treat for those who have come to love it. And, really, there is little reason not to join its admirers: Any fishmonger can clean a whole fish for you and if you catch it by yourself, the process is easy enough (see pages 311–312).

The pleasures of whole fish are indisputable: crisp skin, flesh ranging from flaky and a little dry to moist and tender near the bone, and all the flavor that the fish has to offer.

There are, however, undeniable challenges in cooking whole fish. Grilling is difficult at best; you almost always lose the skin, and all too often some of the meat as well. The fish basket, sold in all kitchen supply stores, can make things a bit easier. This device, a long-handled grilling basket shaped like a fish, is best if it has a non-stick surface.

More often than not, however, broiling and roasting are better choices. Roasting, in fact, is a better choice for whole fish than for other cuts, because the cooking times are long enough to crisp up the outside before the inside overcooks. Braising, simmering, pan-cooking, and even steaming, are all good techniques for whole fish, as long as your cooking vessel can handle the amount you need. With these techniques, that is not often the case—few of us have skillets that can handle a whole fish much over a couple of pounds—so it's usually best to reserve these techniques for those occasions when only two people are eating.

SCALING FISH

Use a spoon or dull knife to scrape the scales from the fish, and always work from the tail up.

REMOVING GILLS

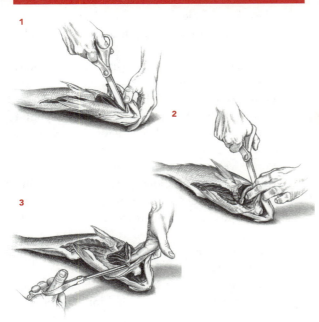

Use a scissors to remove gills, and be careful not to cut yourself; gills are sharp. Cut the gills on both sides from where they attach to the body. Remove and discard—gills are too bitter to use for stock.

BEHEADING FISH

Like the tail, the head is best left on unless your pot won't hold the fish without removing it (the "cheeks" are good to eat).

(**Step 1**) To remove it, make a cut right behind the gill covers to guide the knife. (**Step 2**) Use a mallet to pound the knife through the backbone if necessary.

REMOVING TAILS

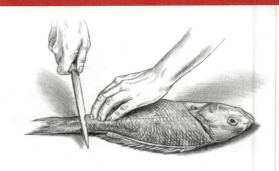

I do not recommend removing the tail unless your cooking method requires it or unless your utensil is too short to fit the whole fish in it. If you must, however, simply use a sharp, heavy knife to cut right through the tail.

Like the gills, fins are best tackled with a scissors. Note that they are only removed for appearances, and may be left on whole fish during cooking if you prefer.

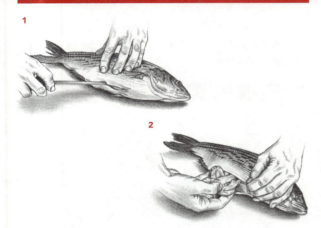

This may be "icky" but there are few culinary tasks that are easier. Use water to rinse out any remaining bits.

(Step 1) Cut a long slip from the end of the fish's "throat" to the rear vent. (Step 2) Reach in and pull out the guts. Discard; these are not good in stock.

Buying Fish

Many, many fish are sold whole in one place or another. My list concentrates on the most popular. Although flavor, density of flesh, and texture vary from one to another, the most important limitation is size. Within size groups, these can pretty much be substituted for one another.

- small to medium; from under one pound up to three pounds
- medium to large; never less than one pound, often over three pounds
- **Butterfish** (the smallest; often one-quarter pound each, rarely over one-half pound): Sweet, tiny, easy to eat, with scales that can be ignored. Allow three or four per person.
- **Croaker:** On the bony side, but sweet.
- **Flatfish:** Whole flounder and its relatives are easier to eat than you might believe, and usually delicious.
- **Grouper:** Very easy to eat, with flesh that pulls off the bones easily.
- **Pompano** (sometimes these run a bit larger, but they are usually in the one- to two-pound range): Flat, with darker flesh than most of these. Easy to eat, exceptional flavor.
- **Porgy:** Very sweet, quite bony.
- **Red snapper** (occasionally you can find tiny specimens): One of the best, with delicious flesh and simple bone structure that makes eating easy.
- **Rockfish:** A name that applies to a number of species, many similar to red snapper.
- **Sea bass:** Delicious fish with simple bone structure. Small size makes it ideal for pan-cooking and steaming.
- **Spot:** Sweet but bony.
- **Tilefish:** Similar to red snapper.
- **Whiting:** Very mild-tasting, moist fish with an unusual bone structure. Easy to eat because

properly cooked flesh separates readily from bones.

- **Wolffish:** Increasingly popular fish with dense flesh that comes off the bone with no trouble.

Whole fish must be cleaned, obviously, but there are several details worth mentioning:

The skin: It must be scaled. Get the fishmonger to do it if you can or see page 311.

The gills: These must be removed. You can do it yourself (page 311), but most fishmongers will do it for you. Discard the gills; they're too bitter for stock.

The head: Have the fishmonger leave it on; it has good meat in it. You can always cut it off at home (page 311) if the fish is too big for your pan. Always save it for stock.

The tail and fins: I like the tail on for presentation purposes, but it can be removed to help fit the fish in a pan. Use it for stock. Fins should always be removed; use a sturdy pair of scissors.

The innards: Remove and discard (page 312). Most roe sacks and livers are edible but few Americans pay attention to them.

When Is Whole Fish Done?

Perhaps the biggest challenge in cooking whole fish is in judging doneness. It's difficult to see the interior of the fish, and uneven thickness is a given, making cooking by time almost impossible.

But as long as you are willing to learn the situation is far from grim. As always, I prefer to make mistakes in undercooking rather than overcooking, because I'd rather embarrass myself by making my guests or family wait an extra five minutes than by serving them something so dry they have to choke it down. I start cooking by time, but almost always end up judging doneness with a knife. Here's my procedure:

1. Begin checking the fish after about eight minutes of cooking time per inch of thickness (ten for roasting), measured at the thickest point. Before going any further, press on the fish. Does it still feel a little mushy and raw? Give it a couple of more minutes before proceeding.

2. Pierce the fish at its thickest point with a not-too-thin knife (a chopstick is also a good tool for this). When you can poke right down to the bone without a lot of trouble, move to the next step.

3. Whole fish have blood and translucent or pinkish bones. All of this must be white and opaque, or very nearly so, for the fish to be cooked through. Use a boning or similar thin-bladed knife, and make a small cut at the thickest part of the fish. Pry the flesh apart and peek in there to judge the level of doneness; all traces of translucence should be gone, right down to the bone.

Remember, food continues to cook after you remove it from the heat source and—because of its mass—whole fish more so than other fish. So you can stop cooking when the fish is just short of complete doneness and it will be perfect. This takes some practice, of course, but it's an ideal to shoot for.

Grilled or Broiled Red Snapper or Other Large Whole Fish

Makes 2 to 4 servings

Time: 30 minutes, plus time to preheat the grill

Whole fish, as noted earlier, is not that easy to grill. But if you're going to try, begin with red snapper (or a large pompano, if you can find it), which has very firm flesh that is likely to remain on the bone as it cooks. Losing the skin, however, is inevitable if you choose to grill rather than broil.

Juice of 1 lemon

$1/4$ cup dry sherry or white wine

2 tablespoons olive oil

Salt and freshly ground black pepper to taste

1 red snapper, or any of the larger fish marked with ● on page 312, at least 2 pounds, gilled, gutted, and scaled

Several sprigs fresh rosemary or 1 tablespoon dried rosemary, plus more sprigs for garnish

Lemon wedges

1 Mix together the lemon juice, sherry, olive oil, salt, and pepper, and marinate the fish in this while you start a charcoal or gas grill or broiler; the fire should be medium-hot, and the grill rack should be about 4 inches from the heat source.

Six Simple Ideas for Grilled Whole Fish

You can make grilled whole fish simpler or more complex than the recipe above; here are some ideas.

1. Do not marinate; simply grill with salt and pepper and serve with lemon.
2. Serve with any vinaigrette (page 91), salsa (page 772), or pesto (page 766).
3. Dress lightly with Basic Tomato Sauce (page 130), or other tomato sauce.
4. Remove the meat from the fish and serve on a bed of lightly dressed greens, or toss with the greens.
5. Serve with Soy and Sesame Dipping Sauce or Marinade or its variations (page 776).
6. Serve with mayonnaise or its variations (page 761).

2 If you have plenty of rosemary, throw some directly on the coals; in any case, sprinkle some on the fish, then place it directly on the rack, or use a fish grilling basket. If you're broiling, oil the broiling pan lightly before putting the fish on it.

3 Grill or broil about 5 minutes per side, basting occasionally with the marinade, then check for doneness (peer along the central bone with a thin-bladed knife; the fish should be white and flaky). Garnish with rosemary sprigs and serve with lemon wedges.

Roasted Red Snapper or Other Large Whole Fish

Makes 4 servings

Time: 1 hour

Try to use fresh oregano or marjoram (or another fresh herb, such as rosemary or sage) in this Greek-style dish; it really makes a tremendous difference. You can also roast whole fish simply, and serve it with any of the Six Simple Ideas for Grilled Whole Fish.

1 (3- to 5- pound) red snapper, or any of the fish marked with ● on page 312, gilled, gutted, and scaled, with head left on or removed

1 teaspoon salt

2 cloves garlic, cut into very thin slivers

$1/4$ cup extra-virgin olive oil

1 lemon, thinly sliced

20 sprigs fresh oregano or marjoram or 1 teaspoon dried oregano or marjoram (or see headnote)

8 to 12 small waxy red or white potatoes, washed well and cut in half

8 small onions, cut in half

1 cup dry white wine or fish, chicken, or vegetable stock, or water, plus a little more if needed (see "Soups" for stock recipes)

Freshly ground black pepper to taste

1 Rinse the fish well. Cut three or four gashes on each side of the fish, from top to bottom. Salt the gashes and fish's cavity. Let it sit while you prepare the other ingredients. Preheat the oven to 450°F.

2 Push half of the garlic slivers into the gashes. Rub the fish with a little of the olive oil, and pour the rest on the bottom of a large baking pan. Spread the lemon slices over the bottom of the pan and top it with most of the oregano. Lay the fish over all, then spread the potatoes, onions, and remaining garlic around the fish. Pour the wine or other liquid over all, and sprinkle with salt and pepper. Top with the remaining oregano.

3 Cover with aluminum foil and bake, undisturbed, until the vegetables are nearly tender, 20 to 30 minutes. Uncover and continue to bake, shaking the pan occasionally, until the potatoes are nice and soft and the fish is cooked through, another 5 to 10 minutes (look at one of the gashes in the thickest part of the fish; the meat will appear opaque clear down to the central bone). If the pan is drying out, add a little more liquid.

4 To serve, scoop the flesh from the fish with a spoon, and top with some vegetables and sauce.

Roasted Red Snapper or Other Large Whole Fish with Tomatoes and Bread Crumbs: Step 1 remains the same. In Step 2, add 2 cups chopped tomatoes (canned are fine; don't bother to drain them) to the baking pan; reduce the wine to $1/2$ cup. After removing the aluminum foil in Step 3, mix together 1 cup minced fresh parsley and $1/2$ cup plain bread crumbs. Spread this mixture over the fish and continue baking until it browns lightly, another 5 to 10 minutes.

Roasted Red Snapper or Other Large Whole Fish with Fennel and Mushrooms: Step 1 remains the same. In Step 2, substitute 1 pound of fresh fennel, cut up (reserve the feathery tops), for the oregano, potatoes, and onions. Add about 1 pound of mushrooms

(fresh "wild" mushrooms, if possible, or a mixture of chopped wild and domestic mushrooms, or domestic mushrooms with some reconstituted dried porcini mixed in), 1 cup chopped tomatoes (canned are fine; don't bother to drain them), and the wine, salt, and pepper. Cover with aluminum foil and begin baking for 20 to 30 minutes. Uncover the fish and top it with the reserved fennel tops and a sprinkling of chopped scallions. Continue baking until the fish is done, another 5 to 10 minutes.

Whiting or Other Small Whole Fish Baked in White Wine

Makes 4 servings

Time: 20 minutes

A very basic, lightning-quick recipe you can use for any small whole fish.

4 whiting, or any of the fish marked with ◐ on
    page 312, about 1 pound each, gilled, gutted,
    and scaled, with heads on
1 cup dry white wine
1 tablespoon minced garlic
$1/4$ cup extra-virgin olive oil
2 tablespoons drained capers (optional)
$1/2$ cup chopped fresh parsley leaves
Salt and freshly ground black pepper to taste

1 Preheat the oven to 500°F.

2 Place the fish in a baking dish just large enough to hold them, then sprinkle all the remaining ingredients over them, putting some in the fish cavities. Bake until the fish flakes when probed with a fork, about 10 minutes; don't overcook. Serve at once, pouring the pan juices over the fish.

Whiting or Other Small Whole Fish Baked with Shallots and Herbs: Step 1 remains the same. In Step 2, substitute $^1/_4$ cup minced mixed fresh tarragon, parsley, dill, thyme, and/or chervil leaves for the parsley; $^1/_4$ cup minced shallots for the garlic; and, if you like, butter for the olive oil. Proceed as above, garnishing with minced parsley.

Braised Whole Grouper or Other Large Whole Fish with Hot-and-Sour Sauce

Makes 2 to 6 servings

Time: 30 minutes

Grouper, red snapper, and carp are the ideal fish for this dish, which is not at all difficult to make. Serve this with plenty of white rice.

1 (3- to 5-pound) grouper or other fish marked with ● on page 312, gilled, gutted, and scaled, preferably with head on

1 cup fish, chicken, or vegetable stock, or water (see "Soups" for stock recipes)

2 dried shiitake ("black") mushrooms

1/3 cup peanut (preferred) or vegetable oil

Flour for dredging

1 large onion, sliced

Salt to taste

2 teaspoons minced garlic

1 tablespoon peeled and minced or grated fresh ginger or 1 teaspoon ground ginger

$^1/_2$ teaspoon cayenne, or to taste

2 tablespoons sherry or white wine

2 tablespoons soy sauce

$^1/_4$ cup rice or white wine vinegar

1 teaspoon dark sesame oil

Minced scallions for garnish

1 Check to make sure that the fish will fit in your largest skillet. If not, cut off its head and tail (page 311) (or use a large, heavy baking pan). Make three shallow cuts, from top to bottom, on each side of the fish. Heat the stock or water and soak the mushrooms in it.

2 Preheat the skillet over medium-high heat for 3 or 4 minutes. Add the peanut oil; when a pinch of flour sizzles in it, dredge the fish in the flour. Shake off the excess flour and gently place the fish in the oil. Raise the heat to high until the oil sizzles loudly, then back off on the heat a little bit to avoid burning the oil or flour. Cook until golden brown, 3 to 5 minutes, then turn the fish carefully and brown the other side. Remove the fish to a plate.

3 Remove the mushrooms from the stock, rinse them, and slice them thinly. Pour the stock through a strainer lined with paper towels to remove any sand.

4 Pour off most of the oil from the pan you cooked the fish in, return the pan to the stove over high heat, and add the onion. Sprinkle with salt and cook, stirring, for 2 or 3 minutes. Add the garlic, ginger, and cayenne; cook another couple of minutes, until the onion is soft and brown. Add the mushrooms to the pan, then the sherry. Stir, then add the soy sauce, vinegar, and strained stock. Bring to a boil, cook 1 minute, then lower the heat and return the fish to the pan. Cover and cook gently until the fish is cooked through (peek in one of the slashes; the meat should be opaque clear to the bone), about 15 to 20 minutes.

5 Remove the fish to a platter, then raise the heat to high and reduce the braising liquid if it looks too thin. Add the sesame oil, and spoon the sauce and the onion over and around the fish. Garnish with the scallions. To serve, spoon the meat from the bone.

Pan-Fried Croaker or Other Small Whole Fish

Makes 2 servings

Time: 30 minutes

Many of these fish are so sweet that they are traditionally served with vinegar. I prefer freshly squeezed lemon juice, but you might also try any acidic sauce, such as vinaigrette (pages 91–94).

4 to 12 small croaker, or any of the smaller fish
   marked with ◖ on page 312, about 4 pounds
   total, skin on, gilled, gutted, and scaled
Salt and freshly ground black pepper to taste
Vegetable oil as needed
Flour for dredging
Lemon wedges or cider or malt vinegar

1 Rinse and dry the fish. Heat a large non-stick skillet over medium-high heat for 3 or 4 minutes. Sprinkle the fish with salt and pepper.

2 Add the vegetable oil to a depth of one-eighth of an inch, more or less. When the oil shimmers, dredge the fish in the flour, one at a time. Shake to remove excess flour, then place them gently in the pan.

3 Cook until nicely browned, about 3 to 5 minutes per side. Cook in batches if necessary, and add more oil to the pan as you need it. The fish are done when their flesh offers little or no resistance to a knife or even a chopstick; if you're in doubt, peek next to the bone—the flesh should be opaque.

4 Remove from the pan and drain quickly on brown paper bags or paper towels. Serve immediately, with lemon wedges or vinegar, or any acidic sauce.

Crispy Sea Bass or Other Small Whole Fish with Garlic-Ginger Sauce

Makes 2 servings

Time: 30 minutes

Although it does take one or two more ingredients, this relatively sophisticated method of pan-frying small fish is no more difficult than the traditional American method in the recipe above.

Vegetable oil as needed
2 black sea bass, or any of the fish marked with ◖
   on page 312, each about 1 pound, gilled, gutted,
   and scaled, with heads on
2 tablespoons peanut oil
1 tablespoon minced garlic
1 teaspoon peeled and minced or grated fresh ginger
1 tablespoon soy sauce
1 teaspoon dark sesame oil
Minced cilantro leaves for garnish

1 Heat a large non-stick skillet over medium-high heat for 3 or 4 minutes. Add the vegetable oil to a depth of one-eighth of an inch, more or less. When the oil shimmers, put the fish in it. Cook, undisturbed, for about 8 minutes on the first side. Turn carefully.

2 As the fish is cooking, heat the peanut oil over medium heat in a small saucepan. Add the garlic and ginger and cook, stirring, until the garlic begins to color. Add the soy sauce and sesame oil and keep warm.

3 Cook the fish 8 to 10 minutes on the second side. They're done when their flesh offers little or no resistance to a knife or even a chopstick; if you're in doubt, peek next to the bone—the flesh should be opaque.

4 Remove the fish to two plates, drizzle with the sauce, and garnish. Serve immediately.

Simmered Flounder or Other Flatfish

Makes 2 servings

Time: 15 minutes

A great way to prepare any whole flatfish that will fit in your skillet. The best way to eat it is to simply pick at the fish with a pair of chopsticks or your fingers. If you are making rice, make that first; this dish takes only twelve minutes or so.

1 clove garlic, crushed
2 thin peeled slices fresh ginger or $1/2$ teaspoon ground ginger
$1/4$ cup soy sauce
1 teaspoon dark sesame oil
1 teaspoon rice or other mild vinegar
1 whole (1- to $1^1/2$-pound) flatfish such as flounder or sole, gilled, gutted, and scaled

1 Place all the ingredients except the fish in a large skillet, preferably non-stick (one for which you have a cover), and bring to a boil over high heat.

2 Turn the heat to low, add the fish, and cover. Cook until the fish is done (it will just barely flake when prodded with a knife or fork), about 10 minutes. Serve, with the sauce, immediately.

Steamed Black Sea Bass or Other Small Whole Fish with Black Beans

Makes 2 servings

Time: 20 minutes

The rendered fish juices turn this simple spice paste into a delicious sauce during the steaming process.

Fermented black beans, which keep nearly forever without refrigeration, are a wonderfully flavorful ingredient used in much traditional Chinese cooking.

2 small sea bass, about 1 pound each, gilled, gutted, and scaled, with heads on or off, or any of the small fish marked with **●** on page 312
1 clove garlic, peeled
$1^1/4$-inch piece of peeled fresh ginger
1 small onion, peeled
2 tablespoons fermented black beans (sold in Asian markets)
1 tablespoon dry sherry or white wine
1 tablespoon soy sauce
2 scallions, thinly sliced

1 Score each side of the fish two or three times, from top to bottom, right down to the bone. Place all the remaining ingredients except for the scallions into a blender or small food processor and puree. Rub this paste into the fish; place the fish on a heatproof plate, cover, and refrigerate fish until ready to cook, from 5 minutes to 4 hours.

2 Place the fish, still on a plate, in a bamboo or other steamer and cover the steamer. Steam over boiling water, undisturbed, for 10 minutes. Check for doneness (since you scored the fish, you will be able to see clear to the bone and can easily tell if the fish is cooked through); cook an additional 3 or 4 minutes if necessary. Garnish with the scallions and serve immediately.

The Basics of Miscellaneous Fish

There are a number of fish that don't readily fit into any of the above categories. It's difficult to make generalizations about them, but the ones I've chosen here are some of the least obscure, even though they are far from making everyday appearances in the supermarket. When buying unusual fish, be extra careful to make certain of freshness; because there is less demand for these, there is a strong chance that they may sit around in the store for a while.

Shad Roe
Makes 2 servings

Time: 10 minutes

The roe of many fish are enjoyed around the world, but Americans have focused on that of shad, an indigenous fish that spawns in eastern rivers every spring. As with any fish, there are two keys to a great dish: Buy it fresh and don't overcook it. If you can witness the fishmonger take the roe from a nice-looking fish, so much the better. And keep the roe on the medium-to-rare side; overcooked roe is gritty. This can be served as an appetizer, or as a part of a larger meal; it is wonderful on a bed of lightly dressed greens.

4 tablespoons (1/2 stick) butter (you can use half this
    amount if you want to), cut into chunks
1 pair shad roe, about 6 ounces total
Salt and freshly ground black pepper to taste
Lemon wedges

1 Preheat a medium-to-large skillet over medium heat for 3 or 4 minutes.

2 Add the butter and let it melt. When the foam subsides, turn the heat to medium-high, add the roe, and cook until lightly browned, 3 to 4 minutes. Turn and brown the other side. Do not overcook; the roe should remain quite tender, not firm and springy. Sprinkle with salt and pepper and serve immediately, with lemon wedges.

Skate with Brown Butter
Makes 2 servings

Time: 20 minutes

Skate—which, along with ray, appears in every fictional depiction of the deep sea—actually lives fairly close to the shore. It's an unusually structured fish, but easy to eat: Just lift the meat off the central cartilage and you have a perfect fillet. Usually this is done after cooking, as it is here. One warning: Never buy skate that has not been skinned; the skin is virtually impossible to remove at home.

1 skate wing, 1 1/2 to 2 pounds, skinned
About 4 cups Fast Fish Stock (page 49) or a mixture
    of 4 cups water and 1/2 cup white or white wine
    vinegar
Salt to taste (optional)
1 onion, cut in half (optional)
1 bay leaf
1 tablespoon drained capers, lightly crushed
2 tablespoons minced fresh parsley leaves
4 tablespoons (1/2 stick) butter
1 tablespoon wine vinegar, red or white

1 Place the skate in a deep, wide saucepan or skillet and add enough liquid to cover. Salt the liquid if necessary and add the onion if desired and the bay leaf. Bring to a boil, skim off any foam, turn the heat to medium-low, and poach the skate until you can easily lift the meat off the cartilage at the wing's thickest point, about 10 minutes.

2 Remove the skate, drain it, and place it on a hot platter. If you like, you can lift the top half of the meat with a broad spatula, remove the cartilage, and replace the meat (it's not as difficult as it sounds). Top the fish with the capers and parsley.

3 During the last 5 minutes of the poaching, prepare the black butter: Heat the butter over medium heat.

After it foams it will turn golden and then darken; just when it becomes dark brown, take it off the heat and drizzle it over the skate. Rinse the saucepan with the vinegar and pour that over everything. Serve instantly.

Salt Cod Cakes

Makes 4 servings

Time: About 24 hours, largely unattended

Salt cod, once the most common form of the fish, has become rare. Still, it's available, and makes the best fish cakes. (If you choose not to use salt cod for these cakes, just substitute cod or another of the fish from the list on page 285; leftovers are fine). Vary these by adding one tablespoon of curry powder or minced fresh dill to the mixture.

About ¹/₂ pound salt cod

About 2 cups Mashed Potatoes (page 596)

¹/₂ cup grated onion

2 eggs

Salt and freshly ground black pepper to taste

Plain bread crumbs as needed

Olive oil, bacon drippings, butter, or a combination
    for pan-cooking

Flour or plain bread crumbs for dredging

Lemon wedges (optional)

1 To prepare the salt cod, cut it into a few large pieces. Soak them overnight (or up to 24 hours), changing the water at least four times. Simmer the fish in water to cover for 15 minutes, then drain and pick out any stray bones or pieces of skin. Measure the fish; there should be about 2 cups.

2 Mix together the fish, potatoes, onion, eggs, salt, and pepper. Add enough bread crumbs to make the mixture manageable, just a tablespoon or two. If you have time, shape the mixture into cakes and refrigerate on a rack; this will firm them up. If you don't have time, proceed.

3 Cover the bottom of a large skillet with fat to a depth of at least ¹/₈ inch. Heat over medium-high heat for 3 or 4 minutes; a pinch of flour will sizzle when it's hot enough. Shape the salt cod mixture into cakes or small balls; dredge them in the flour, then place them in the skillet. Adjust the heat so the cakes brown but do not burn, and move them around in the pan so they brown evenly. Turn after about 5 minutes and cook the other side. They're done when they are a beautiful brown all over. Serve with lemon wedges.

Creamed Salt Cod Mousse

Brandade de Morue

Makes 6 to 8 appetizer servings

Time: 45 minutes using soaked salt cod

One of the great Provençal creations, this rich, filling dish is truly special, and easily made in a food processor (use a mortar and pestle if you want to be traditional).

1 pound boneless salt cod, soaked overnight in
    several changes of cold water

2 cloves garlic, peeled

²/₃ cup extra-virgin olive oil

²/₃ cup heavy cream or milk

Freshly ground black pepper to taste

Juice of 1 lemon, or to taste

¹/₈ teaspoon freshly grated nutmeg

Salt (optional)

1 Place salt cod in one layer in a skillet or saucepan with water to cover; bring the water to a boil, turn off the heat, and let cool for 15 or 20 minutes. Drain and pick out any stray bones or pieces of skin.

2 Place the cod in the container of a food processor with the garlic and a couple of tablespoons of the olive oil. Start processing and, through the feed tube, add small amounts of olive oil alternating with small amounts of cream. Continue until the mixture becomes smooth, creamy, and light. (You may not need all of the oil and cream.) Add pepper, some of the lemon juice, and the nutmeg. Blend and taste; the mixture may need a bit of salt and more lemon juice.

3 To serve, reheat the brandade in a double boiler or in a 300°F oven, covered. Serve with crusty bread or, even better, Low-Fat Baked Croutons (page 82).

Marinated Fresh Anchovies

Makes 4 to 6 appetizer servings

Time: 30 minutes, plus at least 2 hours for marinating

Anchovies, sardines, and smelts are confusing little fish that, in most cases, can be substituted for one another. This recipe, however, requires spanking fresh anchovies, which are frequently found in Italian, Spanish, and Portuguese fish stores.

> About 1 pound (20 to 30) fresh anchovies
> 1/4 cup extra-virgin olive oil
> 1/4 cup freshly squeezed lemon juice
> 1 tablespoon minced garlic
> 1/4 cup minced fresh parsley leaves
> 1 teaspoon salt

1 To bone the anchovies, snap off the heads by grasping the body just behind the head and pulling down on the head. Most of the innards will come out with the head. Run your thumb along the belly flap, tearing the fish open all the way to the tail and removing any remaining innards. Then grab the backbone between your thumb and forefinger and pull it out, gently. Remove any spiny fin material and drop each boned fillet into a bowl of ice water.

2 Rinse the fish and dry them with paper towels. Place them in a shallow bowl. Mix together the olive oil, lemon juice, garlic, half the parsley, and salt. Refrigerate the anchovies in this mixture and marinate them, turning gently from time to time, until they turn white, 2 to 3 hours. (You can keep them, refrigerated, for a day or two.) Garnish with the remaining parsley and serve.

"Grilled" Sardines

Makes 2 servings

Time: 15 minutes, plus time to preheat the broiler

Not grilled but broiled, as they are throughout Europe, where they are a popular appetizer. If you have a grilling basket, you can cook these over hot coals, but the broiler does a wonderful job. You can follow these directions for smelts, too. Serve as directed below with lemon wedges, or with Mustard Butter (page 768).

> 6 to 12 large sardines, a total of about 1 pound, gutted, with heads on
> Melted butter or olive oil
> Salt and freshly ground black pepper to taste
> Minced fresh parsley leaves for garnish
> Lemon wedges

1 In this country, sardines are usually sold gutted, with their heads on. If they are whole, follow the instructions on page 312 to gut them. Rinse and dry well.

2 Preheat the broiler. Brush the fish inside and out with butter or oil; sprinkle with salt and pepper. Lay them in a baking dish that can hold them, side by side, without crowding. Broil, turning once, about 4 inches from the heat source, until browned on both sides, about 6 minutes total. (Sometimes these fish are too delicate to turn; just finish the cooking on the top

side, moving them a little farther from the heat if necessary to prevent burning.) Garnish and serve with lemon wedges.

Sautéed Smelts with Herb Butter

Makes 4 servings

Time: 30 minutes

Smelts are usually sold without their heads or innards, making them an easy "whole" fish. Some people eat their bones, but it's also a simple task to remove them while you're eating or as you would those of sardines.

1¹/₂ pounds not-too-large smelts, gutted and heads off
2 tablespoons Parsley Butter or dill butter (see Broiled Fillets with Dill Butter, page 279)
2 tablespoons butter or olive oil
Flour for dredging
2 eggs, beaten
Plain bread crumbs for dredging, seasoned with ¹/₄ cup of the minced herb you've chosen for the butter
Salt and freshly ground black pepper to taste
Lemon wedges

1 Drain the fish and dry them. Put a little dab of herb butter in the center of each fish and close it up, or spread 1 fillet with a bit of the butter and lay another on top of it.

2 Heat a large non-stick skillet over medium-high heat for 2 or 3 minutes. Add the plain butter and, when its foam subsides, begin to roll the smelts in the flour, shaking off any excess. Dip in the eggs, roll in the bread crumbs, and add to the pan. You'll need to do this in at least two batches.

3 Season the smelts as they cook and adjust the heat so they sizzle but don't burn (some of the herb butter will run out of the fish, but don't let it bother

you). Turn once, after 3 or 4 minutes. The smelts are done when nicely browned on both sides. Serve with some of the pan juices spooned over, and lemon wedges on the side.

The Basics of Shrimp

Shrimp, the most popular non-canned seafood in America, can be domestic or imported, wild or farm-raised. I prefer white shrimp from the Pacific or the Gulf of Mexico; unless, of course, I can get fresh, fairly local shrimp. That's rare, however, since almost all shrimp is frozen before sale.

For that reason, I recommend buying frozen shrimp rather than those that have been thawed. Since the shelf life of previously frozen shrimp is not much more than a couple of days, buying thawed shrimp gives you neither the flavor of fresh nor the flexibility of frozen. Stored in the home freezer, shrimp retain their quality for a month or more.

Most frozen shrimp are sold in blocks of five pounds (or two kilos, slightly less than that), and should be defrosted in the refrigerator or in cold water. Partial defrosting to cut a block in half in order to refreeze some for later use, while not ideal, is still preferable to buying thawed shrimp.

Despite the popularity of shrimp, there are few rules governing its sale. Small, medium, large, extra-large, jumbo, and other size classifications are subjective. Small shrimp of fifty to the pound are frequently labeled "medium," as are those twice that size. It helps to learn to judge shrimp size by the number it takes to make a pound, as retailers do. Shrimp labeled "16/20," for example, require sixteen to twenty individual specimens to make a pound. Those labeled "U-20" require fewer (under twenty) to make a pound. Shrimp of from fifteen or twenty to about thirty per pound usually give the best combination of flavor, ease (peeling tiny shrimp is a nuisance), and value.

Shrimp should have no black spots, or melanosis, on their shell, which indicate that a breakdown of the meat has begun. Be equally suspicious of shrimp with yellowing shells, or those that feel gritty, either of which may indicate the use of sodium bisulfite, a bleaching agent sometimes used to remove melanosis. Like most seafood, shrimp should smell of salt water and little else.

Avoid prepeeled and deveined shrimp; cleaning before freezing may deprive shrimp of some of their flavor and texture. Processors may compensate for this by using tripolyphosphate, an additive that aids in water retention.

If your palate is sensitive to iodine—not everyone's is—you might also want to steer clear of brown shrimp, especially large ones, which are most likely to taste of this naturally occurring mineral. The iodine is found in a type of plankton which makes up a large part of the diet of brown shrimp; traditionally, this distinctive flavor is preferred in certain parts of the country.

There are three hundred species of shrimp worldwide, but six are most commonly found in our markets. In my order of preference, they are:

Gulf White (*Panaeus setiferus*): Certainly the most expensive shrimp, and frequently the best.
Ecuadorean or Mexican White (*P. vannamei*): Similar to Gulf Whites, these may be wild or farm-raised.
Gulf Pink (*P. duorarum*): Another high-quality shrimp, wild or farm-raised. Shell is reddish or light brown.
Gulf Brown (*P. aztecus*): The wild shrimp most likely to taste of iodine, these tend to be reddish-brown; they are easily confused with Whites or Pinks.
Black Tiger (*P. monodon*): Common farmed shrimp from Asia. Dark gray with black stripes and red feelers or bluish with yellow feelers; pink when cooked. Inconsistent but frequently flavorful and firm.

Chinese White (*P. chinensis*): Asian farm-raised shrimp with grayish-white color, soft, sometimes watery texture, and mild flavor. Usually relatively inexpensive.

As for peeling: Shrimp should be peeled if it will be cooked in a sauce that will make it difficult to peel them at the table. They might also be peeled if you're feeling generous or energetic. The shells, by the way, make a super broth (see the recipes for Shrimp Stock, page 50, and for Stir-Fried Shrimp with Black Beans, page 326). For simple grilling or pan-cooking, however, it's arguable that shrimp with their peels on lose less liquid and flavor. In my experience, it's not a big deal either way.

And deveining? Some people won't eat shrimp that isn't deveined. Others believe that the "vein"—actually the animal's intestinal tract—contributes to flavor. It's a matter of personal taste; devein only if you choose to.

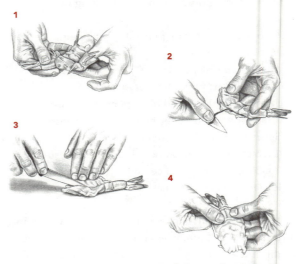

(Step 1) To peel shrimp, grasp the feelers on the underside and pull the peel away from the meat. *(Step 2)* Should you choose to devein, make a shallow cut on the back side of each shrimp, then pull out the long, black, threadlike vein. *(Steps 3–4)* To butterfly shrimp, cut most of the way through the back of the shrimp and open it up.

A couple of final words: I include crayfish (or crawfish) in this section. Although many devotees of that shellfish believe them to be not only different from shrimp but superior to them, I find them to be generally interchangeable.

Shrimp is among the easiest shellfish to cook. It isn't always done when it turns pink—some larger shrimp take a little longer to cook through—but it usually is. Cut one open to be sure.

Shrimp Cocktail
Makes 4 servings

Time: 20 minutes

Almost any shrimp recipe can be made into an appetizer, but this classic—among the best reasons to keep ketchup in the house—is never anything but.

    1 pound large shrimp, preferably with their peels on
    1/2 cup ketchup
    1 teaspoon chili powder
    3 tablespoons freshly squeezed lemon juice
    Salt and freshly ground black pepper to taste
    1 tablespoon Worcestershire sauce, or to taste
    Several drops Tabasco or other hot sauce
    1 tablespoon prepared horseradish, or to taste
    1 tablespoon finely minced onion (optional)
    Iceberg lettuce (optional)

1 Place the shrimp in salted water to cover and turn the heat to high; when it boils, reduce the heat to medium-low and cook just until the shrimp are pink all over, 3 to 5 minutes. Turn off the heat and rinse immediately in cold water. Peel and devein the shrimp (see page 323).

2 Combine all the other ingredients (except the lettuce); taste and adjust seasoning. If time allows, chill both shrimp and sauce.

3 Serve individual portions of shrimp, on a bed of lettuce if you like, with a small bowl of sauce.

Shrimp, My Way
Makes 4 servings

Time: About 30 minutes

This recipe is so good it makes people go nuts; if you like scampi, try this (or the scampi variation). It pays to look for good, fresh paprika for this recipe.

    1/2 cup extra-virgin olive oil
    3 or 4 big cloves garlic, cut into slivers
    1 1/2 to 2 pounds shrimp, in the 20 to 30 per pound
        range, peeled, rinsed, and dried
    Salt and freshly ground black pepper to taste
    1 teaspoon ground cumin
    1 1/2 teaspoons fresh spicy paprika
    Minced fresh parsley leaves for garnish

1 Preheat the broiler and adjust the rack so that it is as close to the heat source as possible.

2 Very gently, in a large, broad ovenproof skillet or baking pan, warm the olive oil over low heat. There should be enough olive oil to cover the bottom of the pan; don't skimp. Put the garlic in the oil and cook for a few minutes, still over low heat, until it turns golden.

3 Raise the heat to medium-high and add the shrimp, salt, pepper, cumin, and paprika. Stir to blend and immediately place under the broiler. Cook, shaking the pan once or twice and stirring if necessary, but generally leaving the shrimp undisturbed, until they are pink all over and the mixture is bubbly. This will take from 5 to 10 minutes, depending on the heat of your broiler. Garnish and serve immediately.

Shrimp "Scampi": Don't preheat the broiler; use a large, deep skillet instead. Step 2 remains the same.

In Step 3, omit the cumin and paprika. When the shrimp turns pink on one side, turn it over and add $1/4$ cup minced fresh parsley leaves. Raise the heat slightly and cook until the shrimp are done, about 2 minutes more. Stir in 1 tablespoon freshly squeezed lemon juice, dry sherry, vinegar, or white wine if you like and cook another 30 seconds before garnishing with more parsley and serving.

Shrimp with Spicy Orange Flavor: Follow the directions for the Shrimp "Scampi" variation. Add 2 or more small dried hot red chiles and the roughly chopped peel of 1 orange along with the garlic. Add the juice of the orange along with the shrimp and spices. Substitute cilantro for the parsley if you like.

Spicy Grilled or Broiled Shrimp

Makes 4 servings

Time: 20 minutes, plus time to preheat the grill

Be forewarned: This is the kind of dish that makes people eat more than they should. Make extra; I always do.

1 large clove garlic
1 tablespoon coarse salt
$1/2$ teaspoon cayenne
1 teaspoon paprika
2 tablespoons olive oil
2 teaspoons freshly squeezed lemon juice
$1^{1}/2$ to 2 pounds shrimp, in the 20 to 30 per pound range, peeled, rinsed, and dried
Lemon wedges

1 Start a charcoal or gas grill or preheat the broiler; in any case, make the fire as hot as it will get and adjust the rack so that it is as close to the heat source as possible.

2 Mince the garlic with the salt; mix it with the cayenne and paprika, then make it into a paste with the olive oil and lemon juice. Smear the paste all over the shrimp. Grill or broil the shrimp, 2 to 3 minutes per side, turning once. Serve immediately or at room temperature, with lemon wedges.

Roast Shrimp with Tomatoes

Makes 4 servings

Time: 30 minutes

If you have nice, juicy tomatoes to moisten the bread crumbs, stick to these proportions. If your tomatoes are dry, cut back on the bread crumbs or increase the butter a little.

4 tablespoons ($1/2$ stick) butter, more or less, or use extra-virgin olive oil
$3/4$ cup plain bread crumbs, preferably fresh
$1/2$ cup minced fresh parsley leaves
1 teaspoon minced garlic
Salt and freshly ground black pepper to taste
$1^{1}/2$ to 2 pounds shrimp, in the 20 to 30 per pound range, peeled, rinsed, and dried
About 12 thick slices ripe tomato

1 Preheat the oven to 450°F. Melt about half the butter over medium heat in a large non-stick skillet, then toss in the bread crumbs, parsley, and garlic. Cook until the bread crumbs are nicely browned, stirring occasionally, and the mixture is fragrant. Turn off the heat and let it cool a bit, then season with salt and pepper.

2 Spread 1 teaspoon or so of the remaining butter around the bottom of 9 × 13-inch baking dish, then arrange the shrimp in the dish; sprinkle with salt and pepper. Cover with about half the bread crumb mixture, then arrange the tomatoes on top. Sprinkle with the remaining bread crumbs and dot with the remaining butter. Bake until the shrimp are pink and hot, 8 to 12 minutes, depending on the size of the shrimp.

Roast Shrimp with Orange and Rosemary

Makes 4 servings

Time: 20 minutes

A lightning-quick, less-is-more dish with a wonderful marriage of flavors.

3 tablespoons extra-virgin olive oil
1 teaspoon minced fresh rosemary leaves or
   $1/2$ teaspoon dried rosemary (tarragon is also nice)
$1^1/2$ to 2 pounds shrimp, in the 20 to 30 per pound range, peeled, rinsed, and dried
$1/2$ cup freshly squeezed orange juice
Zest of 1 orange, finely minced
Salt and freshly ground black pepper to taste

1. Preheat the oven to 450°F. When it is hot, warm 2 tablespoons of the olive oil in a 9 × 13-inch baking pan, then add the rosemary; return to the oven until the rosemary begins to sizzle.
2. Add the shrimp, then sprinkle with the orange juice and zest, the salt and pepper, and the remaining olive oil. Roast until the shrimp turns pink, about 10 minutes.

Curried Shrimp

Makes 4 to 6 servings

Time: 45 minutes

This is a good dish for a party, since you can make the sauce hours in advance, then add the shrimp and lemon juice at the last minute.

2 tablespoons peanut or vegetable oil
2 large onions, minced
1 tablespoon All-Purpose Curry Powder, store-bought curry powder, or other spice mixture (page 778)
$1/4$ teaspoon cayenne, or to taste
2 tablespoons minced cilantro leaves
1 pound small waxy red or white potatoes, peeled and halved
2 cups cored and chopped canned or fresh tomatoes, with their liquid
Salt to taste
1 to $1^1/2$ pounds shrimp, in the 20 to 30 per pound range, peeled, rinsed, dried, and cut into halves or thirds
2 tablespoons freshly squeezed lemon juice

1. Heat the oil over medium heat in a large skillet for 2 minutes. Add the onions and cook, stirring, until golden, about 10 minutes.
2. Add the curry powder, cayenne, and half the cilantro and stir. Add the potatoes, tomatoes, and salt, stir, cover, and cook over low heat, stirring occasionally, until the potatoes are tender, about 30 minutes.
3. Add the shrimp and lemon juice and cook, uncovered, until the shrimp turn pink, 3 to 5 minutes. Add the remaining cilantro and serve with white rice.

Stir-Fried Shrimp with Black Beans

Makes 4 servings

Time: 30 minutes

See Stir-Fried Chicken with Chinese Cabbage (page 383) for a basic stir-fry recipe, with loads of variations. Just substitute shrimp for the chicken; cooking time will be about the same. In this recipe, use the shrimp shells to make a quick, delicious stock.

1 to 1¹/₂ pounds shrimp, in the 20 to 30 per pound
  range
1 tablespoon fermented black beans (sold in Asian
  markets)
2 tablespoons dry sherry or white wine
1¹/₂ teaspoons sugar
2 tablespoons soy sauce
1 clove garlic, sliced, plus 1 tablespoon minced garlic
1 teaspoon salt
2 teaspoons dark sesame oil
1 pound bok choy or other cabbage, trimmed,
  washed, and dried
2 tablespoons peanut or vegetable oil
1 tablespoon peeled and minced or grated fresh
  ginger
¹/₄ cup minced scallions

① Peel the shrimp. Place the peels in a medium saucepan with 1 cup of water, turn the heat to high, and bring to a boil. Turn the heat to low, cover, and cook while you work on the rest of the recipe. Soak the black beans in the sherry.

② Marinate the shrimp in ¹/₂ teaspoon of the sugar, 1 tablespoon of the soy sauce, the sliced garlic, salt, and 1 teaspoon of the sesame oil while you assemble the other ingredients.

③ Separate the bok choy leaves from the stems; chop the stems into ¹/₂- to 1-inch pieces, and chop the leaves. Drain the shrimp peels, reserving ³/₄ cup of the broth.

④ Preheat a wok or large non-stick skillet over medium-high heat for 3 to 5 minutes. Add 1 tablespoon of peanut oil and raise heat to high. When it begins to smoke, add the minced garlic and, immediately thereafter, the shrimp and its marinade. Cook the shrimp for about 2 minutes, stirring occasionally. Spoon it out of the wok or skillet.

⑤ Put the remaining oil in the wok or skillet and, when it smokes, add the ginger, followed immediately by the bok choy stems. Cook, stirring, until the bok choy is lightly browned, 3 to 5 minutes, then add the

greens. Cook, stirring, for 1 minute, then add the shrimp stock and let it bubble away for a minute or two. Return the shrimp to the wok or skillet and stir; add the black beans and their liquid, the scallions, and the remaining sugar and soy sauce. Stir and cook for 1 minute. Turn off the heat, drizzle over the remaining sesame oil, and serve.

Shrimp with Cumin and Mint

Makes 4 servings

Time: 30 minutes

This currylike dish has a wonderful sauce, spiked with mint (you can also use cilantro), and made bright yellow with the addition of turmeric. To make shrimp stock from the peels, see Shrimp Stock (page 50).

2 tablespoons peanut or vegetable oil
1 large onion, chopped
1 large red or yellow bell pepper, stemmed, peeled
  if desired, seeded, and chopped
2 cloves garlic, smashed
Salt and freshly ground black pepper to taste
2 tablespoons minced fresh mint or cilantro leaves
  or 2 teaspoons dried mint
¹/₄ teaspoon cayenne
1 teaspoon ground cumin
1 teaspoon ground turmeric
¹/₂ cup dried unsweetened shredded or grated
  coconut
Juice of 1 lemon
1 cup shrimp, chicken, beef, or vegetable stock,
  or water (see "Soups" for stock recipes)
1 to 1¹/₂ pounds shrimp, in the 20 to 30 per pound
  range, peeled, rinsed, dried, and cut into halves
  or thirds
Minced fresh mint, cilantro, or parsley leaves for
  garnish

1 Heat the oil over medium heat in a large skillet for 2 minutes. Add the onion and red pepper and cook, stirring, until soft, about 5 minutes. Add the garlic, salt, and pepper and cook, stirring, 2 or 3 minutes more. Turn off the heat and let cool for a few minutes.

2 Place the mixture in a blender or food processor with the mint, cayenne, cumin, turmeric, coconut, lemon juice, and enough stock or water to make a thick liquid when blended. Blend until smooth.

3 Return to the pan, bring to a boil, and reduce the heat to low. Taste and adjust the seasonings as necessary. Add the shrimp and cook until pink, 3 to 5 minutes. Garnish and serve immediately, with white rice.

Shrimp "Marinara" with Pasta or Rice

Makes 4 servings

Time: 30 minutes

A tried-and-true dish, still a favorite in old-style Italian restaurants throughout the country. With fresh herbs, it's a revelation. Make plain white rice or pasta while you prepare this dish.

2 tablespoons olive oil

1 tablespoon minced garlic

4 cups cored and chopped canned or fresh tomatoes, with their liquid

1/2 cup chopped fresh basil leaves

1 teaspoon minced fresh oregano or marjoram leaves or 1/4 teaspoon dried oregano or marjoram

1/2 teaspoon freshly ground black pepper

Salt to taste

1 pound shrimp, in the 20 to 30 per pound range, peeled, rinsed, and dried

1 Heat the oil over medium-low heat for 1 minute. Add the garlic and cook, stirring once or twice, until golden, 3 or 4 minutes.

2 Add the tomatoes, raise the heat to medium-high, and let bubble, stirring occasionally, for about 10 minutes. Add half the basil, the oregano, pepper, and salt. Stir and taste for seasoning. Reduce the heat to medium and let simmer while you cook rice or pasta if you choose to do so.

3 When you're just about ready to eat, add the shrimp to the sauce; cook until the shrimp are firm and pink, about 5 minutes. Remove 3 or 4 shrimp from the sauce and set aside. Toss the sauce with pasta, or spoon it over rice; top with the remaining basil and the reserved shrimp, and serve.

Shrimp with Feta Cheese: This is better over rice than noodles. Step 1 remains the same. In Step 2, use 1 1/2 cups tomatoes and 1/2 cup dry white wine; omit the basil and use 2 tablespoons of minced fresh parsley leaves. Be careful in adding salt, because the feta cheese is quite salty. When the shrimp are done in Step 3, gently stir in 4 ounces of fresh feta cheese, cut into 1/2-inch cubes. Garnish with a little more parsley and serve immediately.

Shrimp and Beans

Makes 4 servings

Time: About 1 hour, largely unattended

These are the classic Tuscan beans with shrimp; but you can vary this dish easily by changing the spices or seafood and adding a vegetable or two. For more information about cooking beans, see The Basics of Cooking Beans, pages 502–505.

2 cups dried white beans: cannellini, navy, pea, Great Northern, washed and picked over (page 500)

20 fresh sage leaves or 1 tablespoon dried sage

Freshly ground black pepper to taste

About 1/2 teaspoon salt, or to taste

2 teaspoons minced garlic

1 pound shrimp, in the 20 to 30 per pound range, peeled, rinsed, dried, and cut into 3 or 4 pieces each

2 tablespoons extra-virgin olive oil

1 Place the beans in a large, deep pot with water to cover. Turn the heat to high and bring to a boil; skim the foam if necessary. Turn the heat down so the beans simmer; add the sage and pepper and cover loosely.

2 Cook, stirring occasionally, until the beans begin to soften, about 30 minutes; add about 1/2 teaspoon salt and some more pepper. Continue to cook until the beans are very tender, usually at least 1 hour; add additional water if necessary.

3 Drain the cooking liquid if necessary, then add the garlic, additional salt if necessary, and shrimp. Cook over low heat until the shrimp turn pink, 3 to 5 minutes. Drizzle with the olive oil and serve.

Pasta and Beans with Shrimp: Add 2 cups chopped fresh or canned tomatoes to the drained beans along with the garlic and salt. Simmer 10 minutes. Add the shrimp and about 1/2 pound cooked but quite firm penne or other pasta. Stir, add more water or pasta cooking liquid if necessary, and cook until the shrimp are done, about 3 to 5 minutes. Serve garnished with the olive oil and minced fresh parsley leaves.

Crayfish Boil, Louisiana-Style

Makes 2 or 3 servings

Time: 30 minutes, plus cooling time

You can make this more of a full meal by adding potatoes, corn, and/or whole small onions to the boil.

About 4 quarts water or Fast Fish Stock (page 49) or Shrimp Stock (page 50)

1 bay leaf

1 teaspoon dried thyme

Several black peppercorns

2 cloves garlic, crushed

Several coriander seeds

3 cloves

3 small dried hot red chiles

Salt to taste

3 pounds whole crayfish

Tabasco or other hot red pepper sauce

Lemon wedges

Freshly ground black pepper

1 Bring the liquid to a boil in a medium-to-large saucepan and add the bay leaf, thyme, peppercorns, garlic, coriander, cloves, chiles, and plenty of salt. Turn the heat to medium and cook for 10 minutes.

2 Add the crayfish. Cook for 5 minutes, then turn off the heat and let the crayfish cool in the liquid.

3 Remove the crayfish with a slotted spoon, sprinkle with more salt, and serve, passing hot sauce, lemon wedges, and black pepper at the table.

The Basics of Crab

Crabs of all types are among the most delicious and treasured crustaceans. All crabs have some things in common: They must be sold live, or cooked and frozen or refrigerated; they have sweet, white delicious meat; they can be cooked by simple boiling (even if they have been frozen); and they taste almost as good cold as hot. You can take frozen king crab legs, defrost them (slowly, in the refrigerator), serve them with any mayonnaise (page 761) or mustard sauce (page 764), and have an eating experience you couldn't duplicate if you worked for two hours.

Crabs do have differences, mostly in size and form:

Blue Crab: The familiar four- to six-inch blue crustacean. Often sold live, it's also picked from the shell, to be sold throughout the country, refrigerated or frozen. When sold as picked meat, "lump" means large pieces from the body, "flake" means smaller pieces, but "claw" is best. Fresh blue crabmeat is expensive, but incredibly convenient and wonderfully flavorful; with a squirt of lemon, it's celestial. Or toss it with some mild mayonnaise (page 761). Frozen, canned, or pasteurized "fresh" crabmeat are all decidedly inferior.

Dungeness Crab: This great-tasting Pacific crab, which runs from three to four pounds, is better compared to lobster than to the blue crab; it's that good and that meaty. It's almost always cooked and refrigerated (for local sales) or frozen (for shipping) immediately after the catch. It's sold whole and easy to eat. Rock crabs look like small Dungeness crabs, but are treated like blue crabs.

King Crab: The largest crab, which may weigh twenty-five pounds and measure six feet from tip to tip. This northwestern (mostly Alaskan) delicacy is not available fresh elsewhere in the country; the crabs are cooked, dismembered, and frozen. Sometimes the legs are split, which is nice, because it makes eating them so easy. But they're not difficult in any case. Two or three legs make a good serving.

Stone Crab: The recyclable crab of Florida; claws are broken off by fishermen, and the crab returned to the water, where it generates another limb (it's illegal to be in possession of whole crabs). It has a very hard shell, which is usually cracked with a small wooden mallet. Serve cold (they're usually sold cooked), with mustard sauce, page 764.

Soft-Shell Crab: Spring brings one of the best treats of all to fish counters: the live soft-shelled crab. This strange delight (everyone is at least a little squeamish when first biting into a whole crab) is nothing more than a plain old blue crab, caught just after it has molted—shed—its hard outer shell. Once out of the water the crabs will not form new shells. But they live only a couple of days, and are therefore either shipped immediately, by air, or cleaned and frozen. When you get a live soft crab home, you have three choices: Clean it (your fishmonger may do this for you) and eat it, clean it and refrigerate it (which will give you a day or two to think about it, but no longer than that), or clean it and freeze it. Though soft-shells freeze fairly well, this last option is a bit wasteful, since frozen soft crabs are available year-round. Figure two soft-shells per serving for average appetites, although eating three or four is not that difficult.

Note: Surimi, a processed blend of fish, sugar, and other ingredients, is sometimes made to look like crab (it's sold as "crabstick," or "imitation crab"). Unless the label *says* crabmeat—and unless it's expensive—it probably isn't.

Boiled Blue or Rock Crab

Makes 1 or 2 servings

Time: 10 minutes

Yes, you can eat a dozen blue crabs by yourself. And then some. Eating blue crabs is a laid-back, messy activity, rewarding only in the sense that it is delicious. Neither blue nor rock crabs require salt, lemon, or butter, but some people like them spicy. If you're one of them, see the variation.

6 to 12 live blue or rock crabs

1 Bring a large pot of water to a boil. Plunge the crabs in, one by one (use a tongs—when crabs don't try to pinch you they're probably dead).

2 Cook about 5 minutes. Drain in a colander and eat, or cool and eat later.

3 To eat, twist off the claws and break them open to pick and suck out the meat. Break off the apron, then pull off the top shell. Rub off the feather gills and break the body in two; then break it in two again. Go to work, picking and sucking that meat out of there and forgetting your manners entirely.

Spicy Crab Boil: To 1 gallon of salted water, add 2 roughly chopped onions; 2 roughly chopped celery stalks; the juice of 2 limes or $1/4$ cup vinegar; 1 tablespoon thyme leaves or 1 teaspoon dried thyme; 1 teaspoon ground allspice; 2 chiles or 1 teaspoon cayenne; 1 tablespoon paprika; and 1 teaspoon freshly ground black pepper. Simmer for 15 minutes before adding the crabs and finishing as above.

Grilled or Steamed King Crab Legs

Makes 4 servings

Time: 20 minutes, plus time to build a fire

King crab legs are delicious, whether grilled or steamed. You can cook them while they're still frozen; just allow a minute or two more time.

> 8 to 12 king crab legs
> Melted butter or lemon wedges

1 To grill, start a charcoal or gas fire; position the grill rack at least 4 inches from the heat source. To steam, bring 1 inch of salted water to boil in a large pot.

2 Grill, turning once, just until the shells are too hot to touch, 5 to 8 minutes (if the legs have been split, grill flesh side up so the juices do not spill out). Steam on a rack in the covered pot until hot, about 5 minutes. Serve immediately with butter or lemon wedges.

Crab Cakes

Makes 4 servings

Time: 15 minutes, plus refrigeration time

I like crab cakes that are mostly crab and seasonings, with a minimum of bread crumbs.

> 1 pound fresh lump crabmeat, picked over for cartilage
> 1 egg
> $1/4$ cup minced red bell pepper
> $1/2$ cup minced scallion
> $1/4$ cup Basic Mayonnaise (page 761), or use prepared mayonnaise
> 1 tablespoon Dijon mustard
> Salt and freshly ground black pepper to taste
> 2 tablespoons plain bread crumbs, or as needed
> About 1 cup flour for dredging
> 1 teaspoon curry powder (optional)
> 2 tablespoons peanut, olive, or vegetable oil
> 2 tablespoons butter (or use all oil)
> Lemon wedges and/or Real Tartar Sauce (page 762)

1 Mix together the crabmeat, egg, bell pepper, scallion, mayonnaise, mustard, salt, and pepper. Add sufficient bread crumbs to bind the mixture just enough to form into cakes; start with 2 tablespoons and use more if you need it.

2 Refrigerate the mixture until you're ready to cook (it will be easier to shape if you refrigerate it for 30 minutes or more, but it is ready to go when you finish mixing).

3 Season the flour with salt, pepper, and curry if you like. Preheat a large skillet, preferably non-stick, over medium-high heat for 2 or 3 minutes. Add the oil and butter and heat until the butter foam subsides. Shape the crabmeat mixture into four cakes, dredge each in the flour, and cook, adjusting the heat as necessary and turning once (very gently), until golden brown on both sides. Total cooking time will be about 10 minutes. Serve with lemon wedges.

Dungeness Crab Salad

Makes 2 servings

Time: 1 hour, with cooked defrosted Dungeness

Unless you live in the Northwest, you'll be buying your Dungeness crab cooked and frozen. If it's fresh—that is, alive—cook over boiling water for five to eight minutes, then chill.

    2 cooked Dungeness crabs, defrosted if frozen
    Any vinaigrette (page 91) or mayonnaise (page 761)
    About 4 cups torn mixed greens (washed and dried)

1 Crack all the Dungeness claw shells and break the body in half. Drizzle them with the vinaigrette and refrigerate an hour or so before eating, stirring occasionally.

2 Serve over the greens, which will catch not only the excess vinaigrette but the delicious juices from the crab.

Sautéed Soft-Shell Crabs, Version I

Makes 2 to 4 servings

Time: 20 minutes (with cleaned soft-shells)

Soft-shells spatter; if you don't want to mess up the kitchen, cover them for the first two minutes of cooking. They will not be as crisp, but they will still be delicious and you won't regret cooking them during the twenty minutes it will take you to clean up after the meal.

    4 tablespoons (1/2 stick) butter, olive oil, or a
        combination, plus more if needed
    4 soft-shell crabs, cleaned and dried thoroughly
    Flour for dredging
    1 egg lightly beaten with 1 tablespoon water
    Plain bread crumbs for dredging, seasoned with salt
        and freshly ground black pepper
    Lemon wedges, any vinaigrette (page 91),
        or Real Tartar Sauce (page 762)

1 Heat a large non-stick skillet over medium-high heat for 2 or 3 minutes.

2 Melt the butter in the skillet and, when the foam subsides, dredge a crab in flour, dip it in the egg, then dredge it in the bread crumbs, and place it in the skillet. Repeat the process (depending upon the size of your crabs, you may have to cook in two batches; add more fat if necessary).

3 Cook the crabs—covering the skillet if you like—until golden brown on one side, then turn and cook until golden brown on the other, about 4 minutes per side. Serve immediately, with lemon wedges.

Sautéed Soft-Shell Crabs, Version II

Makes 2 to 4 servings

Time: 20 minutes (with cleaned soft-shells)

A simpler recipe than above, but one which finishes with a quick sauce.

    Flour for dredging
    Salt and freshly ground black pepper to taste
    4 tablespoons peanut (preferred) or olive oil, or butter
    4 large soft-shell crabs, cleaned
    1/2 cup dry or slightly sweet white wine or water
    Dash cayenne
    Juice of 2 limes

1 Heat a large skillet over medium-high heat for 3 or 4 minutes. Season the flour with salt and pepper.

2 When the skillet is hot, add the oil. Dredge the crabs in the flour, add them to the pan, and raise the heat to high. Cook until golden, adjusting the heat as necessary and turning once, about 6 to 8 minutes total.

3 Remove the crabs and lower the heat to medium. Add the wine and cayenne and cook, stirring, for about 1 minute, or until most of the liquid is gone. Add the lime juice, stir to blend and heat through, and pour over the crabs.

Sautéed Soft-Shell Crabs with Shallots and Capers: Use olive oil or butter; otherwise, Steps 1 and 2 remain the same. After removing the crabs, add 1 additional tablespoon oil or butter, along with 2 tablespoons minced shallots. Cook, stirring, about 2 minutes over medium-high heat, then add the white wine (omit the cayenne). Cook until almost dry, stirring; add salt and pepper to taste, $1/4$ cup capers, drained of their vinegar, and $1/4$ cup minced fresh parsley leaves. Pour this sauce over the crabs and garnish with additional parsley. Serve with lemon wedges.

Grilled Soft-Shell Crabs

Makes 2 to 4 servings

Time: 10 minutes (with cleaned soft-shells), plus time to build a fire

This is a fuss-free way to make soft-shells.

3 tablespoons butter
Salt to taste
Juice of $1/2$ lemon
Tabasco or other hot red pepper sauce to taste
4 soft-shell crabs, cleaned and dried thoroughly
Minced parsley leaves for garnish
Lemon wedges

1 Start a charcoal or gas fire; don't make it too hot, and position the grill rack at least 4 inches from the heat source; soft-shells burn easily.

2 Melt the butter in a small saucepan and add salt, lemon juice, and hot sauce to taste. Grill the crabs, turning with tongs (if you use a fork you'll lose all the liquid) and brushing frequently with butter mixture; don't worry about burnt claw-tips—they're inevitable. Total cooking time will be 6 to 10 minutes; the crabs are done when they're bright red and firm; don't overcook. Garnish and serve, with lemon wedges.

The Basics of Lobster

For the most part, I steam or boil my lobsters. A good, fresh one, not overcooked, makes butter and everything else superfluous. But there are some buying tips you need to make sure you're getting a fresh one. As a friend who sells lobster for a living says, "Just because it's alive doesn't mean it's fresh." When you're buying lobster, lift each one (make sure its claws are pegged or banded); if it doesn't flip its tail and kick its legs, look for another.

In the summer, lobsters, like crabs, grow by discarding their old shells and growing new ones. But soft-shell lobsters ("shedders") have a smaller meat-to-shell ratio than hard-shells, and they fill with water as you cook them. Some people believe that soft-shells have sweeter meat, and, indeed, some are terrific, but I look for hard-shells; you can tell the difference with a little squeeze—soft shells will yield to pressure.

Then there's size. Lobsters grow slowly, and have been overfished for decades. Consequently, there are more "chickens" (one-pounders), eighths (one-and-an-eighth pounds), and quarters than there are larger lobsters. But, in my experience, two people sharing a three-pound lobster will get more meat of equally high quality than if each has his own pound-and-a-half lobster. There's less work, less waste, and more meat hidden in those out-of-the-way places.

Should you boil or steam? It doesn't matter much. If you're cooking one batch of lobsters—whatever fits in your pot—steam them; it's much easier, and, because the lobster absorbs less water, far less messy. But lobsters flavor the cooking water (you should consider saving it as broth), which in turn flavors the lobsters. So if you're cooking a bunch, boil them. And eat the last of the batch yourself. As for other cooking methods, grilling, stir-frying, roasting, and broiling are all good options.

To kill a lobster before cooking, as you do for any method other than steaming or boiling, use a thin, sturdy, pointed knife to poke a hole behind the lobster's eyes, right at the cross-hatch. It's also good to do this *after* boiling, then to drain out the water that's accumulated in the beast. As an added refinement, you might also crack the claws (with a nutcracker, small hammer, or the back of a chef's knife), and split the tail, before bringing the lobster to the table. All of this, along with eating "instructions," is illustrated on page 335.

There are actually very few parts of a lobster that you cannot eat. If you split the lobster for grilling, you can remove the head sac before cooking. You can also remove the tomalley (the green, liverlike organ) and the coral (the very dark red eggs, which turn bright red after cooking; found in females only) to use in sauces. Otherwise, just remove the head sac after boiling.

Finally, there is the spiny lobster, also called Florida lobster, rock lobster, or, in Florida, crawfish. These lobsters and their related species are available worldwide, and it is their tails which are frozen to become the ubiquitous "lobster tails." With no claws, these babies are far simpler to eat than northern lobsters. They're not bad at all, and can be used in any recipe for lobster, shrimp, or crayfish.

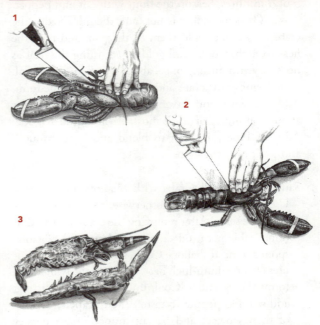

(Step 1) Before grilling or stir-frying, you can kill a lobster by parboiling it for a couple of minutes, or you can simply plunge a heavy knife right into the "crosshairs" behind the head. (Step 2) Cut up through the head and down through the tail. (Step 3) Your final product will look like this.

Basic Boiled or Steamed Lobster

Makes as many servings as desired

Time: 30 minutes or less

For each person, choose a lobster that weighs $1\frac{1}{2}$ pounds or more; a three-pound lobster is enough for two people.

1 In a large, covered pot (like one used for pasta), bring lots of water to a boil—or just 1 inch if you

choose to steam—and add salt, a couple of hand-fuls or so (if you have access to clean seawater, that's a nice touch, as is steaming atop a pile of fresh seaweed).

2 Plunge the lobster(s) into the pot, cover, and cook about 8 minutes for its first pound—from the time the water returns to the boil—and then an additional 3 or 4 minutes per pound thereafter. Thus a three-pounder should boil for 15 to 20 minutes. Lobster is done when the meat becomes opaque and firm, and the coral—which you only find in females—turns, well, coral-colored (it stays dark red until it is cooked). None of this does you any good if the lobster is whole, since you can't see or feel the meat or the coral. One assurance: It's difficult to

undercook a small lobster, if you use the timing guidelines above. If you're boiling a larger one, insert an instant-read thermometer into the tail meat by sliding it in between the underside of the body and the tail joint; lobster is done at 140°F.

3 Remove the lobsters, which will be bright red, and let them sit for 5 minutes or so before serving. If lobsters have been boiled, poke a hole in the cross-hatch right behind the eyes, and drain out the water. Eat. The traditional accompaniment is drawn butter, but lobster is rich enough without it. Try a squeeze of lemon. Steamed or boiled lobster is also great with Soy and Sesame Dipping Sauce or Marinade (page 776).

EATING LOBSTER

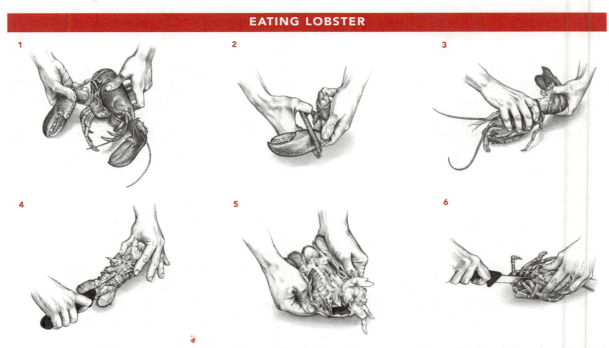

(Step 1) Twist the claws to remove them; they will come off easily. (Step 2) Use a nutcracker to split their shells and a pick to pull out the meat. (Step 3) Twist the lobster in half to separate the tail from the body. (Steps 4–5) Cut through the soft side of the tail and crack it open like a shrimp to remove the tail meat. (Step 6) Cut through the underside of the front part of the body; pick out the small bits of meat in there.

Grilled Lobster

Time: 30 minutes, plus time to preheat the grill

You can grill whole lobsters, but the timing is tricky. It's better to split them (page 334) and remove the inedible parts. They will then grill evenly and quickly. Another alternative is to remove the claws and tail and just grill them.

    4 lobsters, about 1½ pounds each
    Salt and freshly ground black pepper to taste
    Lemon quarters or melted butter

1 Start a charcoal fire or preheat a gas grill; the fire need not be super-hot. Set the grill rack at least 4 inches from the heat source.

2 Kill 4 lobsters as illustrated on page 334, cut them in half, and remove the head sac. You can leave the coral and tomalley in the body, or remove and reserve them for sauces.

3 Grill each lobster for about 5 minutes on its back to firm up the meat. Sprinkle it with salt and pepper, turn it over, and grill for another 5 minutes or so. The meat is done when it is firm and opaque. Serve with lemon quarters or melted butter.

Stir-Fried Lobster with Black Bean Sauce

Makes 4 to 6 servings

Time: 40 minutes

This recipe stretches three lobsters to serve several people, especially with side dishes. If you plan to serve it with rice (which you should), start the rice as soon as you assemble the ingredients. Once you prepare the lobsters as described below, you can use them in any stir-fry recipe.

    3 (1¼-pound) lobsters, or slightly larger
    1 tablespoon fermented black beans (sold in Asian
        markets)
    2 tablespoons dry sherry or white wine
    2 tablespoons peanut or vegetable oil
    1 teaspoon minced garlic
    1 teaspoon peeled and minced or grated fresh ginger
    ½ teaspoon cayenne, or to taste (optional)
    ½ cup chicken, fish, shrimp stock, or lobster-cooking
        water, or water (see "Soups" for stock recipes)
    1 tablespoon soy sauce
    1 cup chopped scallions, with some of the greens,
        or 1 cup chopped fresh chives
    1 teaspoon dark sesame oil

1 Assemble all the ingredients before killing the lobsters. Kill the lobsters as illustrated on page 334. Soak the black beans in the sherry.

2 Remove the claws and tails from lobsters. Reserve the bodies and the small legs for another use (or simmer them for 10 minutes or so and use this stock in this or other recipes). Cut the tails crosswise into 3 or 4 sections each, and separate the claws at the joints. Smack each of the claw pieces with a hammer or the back of a large knife to crack the shell in a couple of places. You will have a couple of dozen pieces altogether.

3 Heat a wok over high heat for 3 or 4 minutes. Add the peanut oil, then the garlic and ginger. Stir, then put in the lobster pieces. Stir and cook for a minute or two; add the cayenne if you're using it. Add the black beans with the sherry, the stock or water, and soy sauce; stir and cover. Cook until all the lobster pieces are bright red, about 5 minutes.

4 Uncover and, with the heat still on high, add almost all of the scallions (reserve a little for garnish). Stir and cook until nicely blended, a minute or so. Turn off the heat, drizzle the sesame oil on top, and garnish with the rest of the scallions before serving.

Broiled Lobster with Herb Stuffing

Makes 4 servings

Time: 30 minutes

This is "baked stuffed lobster" as you've never had it in restaurants, the crisp, seasoned bread crumbs providing a nice foil for the sweet lobster meat.

    4 lobsters, about 1¼ pounds each
    1 clove garlic, peeled
    1 cup fresh parsley leaves
    Salt and freshly ground black pepper to taste
    2 cup plain bread crumbs
    ¾ cup olive oil, plus more if needed
    2 tablespoons freshly squeezed lemon juice,
        plus more if needed

1 Kill the lobsters as illustrated on page 334; cut them in half, then remove the head sac. Remove and reserve the tomalley and coral (if any). Preheat the broiler and set the rack about 6 to 8 inches from the heat source.

2 In a food processor, combine the garlic, parsley, salt, pepper, bread crumbs, olive oil, lemon juice, and the tomalley and coral. Add a little additional olive oil or lemon juice if the mixture seems dry. Stuff the lobsters' body cavities with this mixture and broil until the tail meat is white and firm and the stuffing nicely browned, 5 to 10 minutes. (If the lobster is browning too quickly, either move it further from the heat source or turn off the broiler and turn the oven heat to 500°F to complete the cooking.)

The Basics of Octopus and Squid

Both of these cephalopods are increasingly popular, but mostly in restaurants. It's a shame; they're not hard to cook, they're inexpensive, and they're among the best-flavored fish.

Most octopus is cleaned and frozen at sea; defrost it in the refrigerator, or in cold water.

Nearly everyone will tell you that octopus must be "tenderized" before cooking, and nearly everyone has some bizarre method of doing so—dipping it into boiling water three times, kneading it with grated radish, or hurling it against a stand of rocks (or, more likely, the kitchen sink). The reality is that some octopuses are more tender than others, so I don't pretenderize; instead, I cook the fish until it is tender (revolutionary!), which sometimes takes quite a while.

Squid, in the form of fried calamari, has become ubiquitous in restaurants. Since frying it at home inevitably leads to a mess (nothing spatters quite so much), we can leave it there. But since squid is inexpensive, low in fat, easy to cook, and great to eat, you should try some of these recipes; I've been a squid fan for fifteen years and still love it.

Like shrimp, squid freezes well, and can be defrosted and refrozen with little loss in flavor or texture. Frozen squid, typically cleaned before freezing, is available in supermarkets all over the country, frequently for less than two dollars a pound. Fresh squid should be purple to white, not brown. As with all fish, the smell should be clean and sweet (spoiled squid smells particularly foul), and the skin should shine. To clean squid, see page 338.

The timing of cooking squid is a bit tricky and can be summed up like this: "Cook squid for two minutes or two hours." It's an oversimplification, but it points in the right direction: Over high heat, squid is usually done within three minutes. Cook it as you would pasta, and taste it every minute or so; the instant it loses its rawness, turn off the heat and serve. I give an example of a stir-fried squid recipe, but you can use squid in any of the stir-fries for chicken (pages 383–386); just be sure not to overcook it.

A whole, uncleaned squid.

In braised dishes, squid performs much more predictably. After thirty minutes to an hour of cooking, toughness is no longer a concern. But take care not to cook longer than necessary because, when the squid has lost all of its water (about two-thirds of its total weight), it can become quite dry.

A word about serving size   One-quarter to one-half pound of squid per person is sufficient for quickly cooked dishes. But shrinkage is so significant when you braise or stew squid that you should figure a good half-pound of raw squid per person in such recipes. In either case, if you begin with fresh, uncleaned squid, assume that twenty-five percent or more of the original weight will be lost in cleaning.

PREPARING SQUID

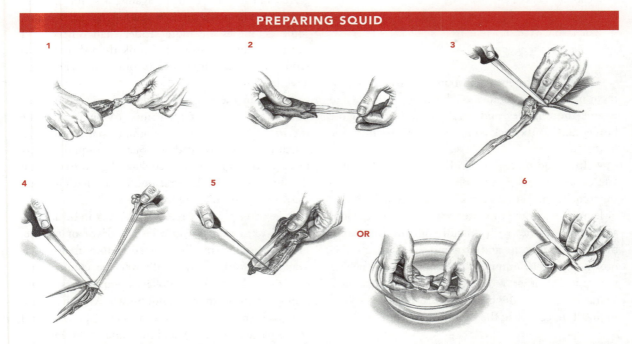

(Step 1) Pull off the tentacles and head; they'll come out in one piece. (Step 2) Reach inside the body, pull out the hard, plastic-like quill and discard. (Step 3) Cut the tentacles from the head and discard the head and the hard, ball-shaped "beak" inside it. (Step 4) You may remove any longish tentacles if you find them offensive, although they're perfectly edible. (Step 5) Peel off the skin, using a knife if necessary (your fingernails will likely be enough). Alternatively, submerge the squid in a bowl of water, which may make skinning it easier. (Step 6) To make squid rings, simply cut across the cleaned body.

Octopus with Tomatoes and Red Wine

Makes 4 servings

Time: 2 to 3 hours, largely unattended

I suggest you cook this in advance, even if it's just the afternoon of the day you plan to serve it because exact timing is difficult. This dish is great with Crispy Sautéed Potatoes with Rosemary (page 597) stirred into it at the last moment.

1 (2-to 3-pound) octopus, cleaned and rinsed
3 cloves garlic, lightly crushed, plus 1 tablespoon minced garlic
1 bay leaf
3 tablespoons extra-virgin olive oil
1 large onion, coarsely chopped
1 teaspoon fresh thyme leaves or $1/2$ teaspoon dried thyme
10 fennel seeds
3 tomatoes, cored and cut into chunks (canned are fine; drain them first)
2 cups strong red wine
Salt and freshly ground black pepper to taste
$1/2$ cup minced fennel, parsley, or basil leaves

1 In a large saucepan, combine the octopus, crushed garlic, bay leaf, and water to cover. Bring to a boil over high heat, turn the heat to medium, and simmer until the octopus is nearly tender, 1 hour or more (poke it with a sharp, thin-bladed knife; when the knife enters fairly easily, the octopus is ready). Drain the octopus in a colander, reserving the liquid.

2 Raise the heat to high and reduce the liquid until just about 1 cup remains, about 20 minutes.

3 Cut the octopus into bite-sized pieces. Heat the oil over medium-high heat in a large, deep skillet; cook the octopus, stirring, until it begins to brown, about 5 minutes. Add the onion and lower the heat to medium. Cook and stir until the onion softens a bit, 2 or 3 minutes.

4 Add the thyme, fennel seeds, and tomatoes and stir. Cook for 1 minute, then add the wine. Raise the heat to high and boil for 2 minutes. Add the reduced octopus stock; bring to a boil, then turn the heat to low. Add salt and pepper.

5 Cook until the liquid is reduced to a sauce (raise the heat if the octopus becomes very tender but too much liquid remains), about 20 minutes. Add the minced garlic, stir, and cook another 5 minutes. Add half the fennel, parsley, or basil leaves and stir. Garnish with the remaining herbs and serve.

Octopus with Rice: In Step 2, reduce the octopus cooking liquid to 3 cups rather than 1 (add water in the unlikely event that you don't have 3 cups). Use 2 cups of the liquid to cook 1 cup rice (see Basic Long-Grain Rice, page 198). When the octopus is cooked, serve it over the rice.

Grilled Octopus

Makes 4 servings

Time: $1^1/2$ hours or more, largely unattended

After simmering octopus until it is tender, you can grill it as below, or with Soy and Sesame Dipping Sauce or Marinade (page 776). This recipe can be prepared a day or two in advance up to Step 1; be sure to cool the octopus, wrap it well, and refrigerate it.

1 (2-to 3-pound) octopus, cleaned and rinsed
3 cloves garlic, lightly crushed
1 bay leaf
$1/2$ cup olive oil
2 tablespoons freshly squeezed lemon juice
1 tablespoon minced fresh oregano or marjoram leaves or 1 teaspoon dried oregano or marjoram

1 In a saucepan, combine the octopus, crushed garlic, bay leaf, and water to cover. Bring to a boil over high heat, turn the heat to medium, and simmer until the octopus is nearly tender, 1 hour or more (poke it with a sharp, thin-bladed knife; when the knife enters fairly easily, the octopus is ready). Drain the octopus; discard the liquid or reserve it for stock or risotto.

2 Cut the octopus into large pieces. Start a charcoal fire or gas grill; the rack should be about 4 inches from the heat source. Combine the olive oil, lemon juice, and herb. Brush the octopus with this mixture and grill them on all sides until they become slightly crisp. As they come off the grill, brush them with a little more of the oil and lemon juice mixture. Serve immediately, passing the remaining mixture at the table.

Stir-Fried Squid with Basil and Garlic

Makes 4 servings

Time: 15 minutes with cleaned squid

Make sure the accompanying rice is cooked before you begin to cook the squid; this Thai-style dish takes just a couple of minutes once you get started.

1 1/2 pounds cleaned squid, rinsed well

1/2 cup whole basil leaves, washed and dried

2 tablespoons peanut oil

1 tablespoon minced garlic

1/8 teaspoon crushed red pepper flakes, or to taste

1 teaspoon salt, or to taste

1 Dry the squid well, using cloth or paper towels. Cut vertically through the group of tentacles if it is large (page 338); otherwise, leave whole. Cut the squid bodies into rectangles, diamonds, or squares, with no dimension greater than 1 inch. The pieces should be fairly uniform in size.

2 If the leaves are large, chop into pieces about the same size as the squid. Mix together the squid and the basil. Heat a wok or large skillet over high heat.

3 Lower the heat to medium; add the peanut oil. Swirl it around and add the garlic. Stir once, then return the heat to high and add the squid-basil mixture. Stir and add the red pepper. Stir frequently until the squid becomes opaque, less than a minute. Begin tasting the squid and continue to taste until it is tender, between 1 and 3 minutes more. Add salt to taste. Turn off the heat and serve, over rice.

Braised Stuffed Squid

Makes 4 main-course servings

Time: 1 hour

Stuffed squid makes an impressive first course, which can easily be turned into a sauce for pasta. Since squid shrinks significantly during cooking, make sure not to overstuff it.

About 1/2 cup fresh bread crumbs

3 tablespoons olive oil, plus 1 teaspoon (part of this may be anchovy oil)

1/3 cup pine nuts or chopped walnuts

8 whole squid, with bodies about 8 inches long, cleaned, washed, and dried (about 1 1/2 pounds)

1 teaspoon minced garlic, plus 3 cloves garlic, peeled

6 anchovy fillets, minced

1/3 cup minced fresh parsley leaves

2 tablespoons freshly grated Parmesan cheese (optional)

1/3 cup dry white wine

Freshly ground black pepper to taste

Salt to taste

3 small dried hot red chiles

1 1/2 cups drained and chopped canned plum tomatoes

2 teaspoons minced fresh rosemary leaves or

1/2 teaspoon dried rosemary

1 Toast the bread crumbs in a heatproof skillet or dish in a 350°F oven for 8 to 10 minutes, just until darkened. Heat the teaspoon of olive oil in a small skillet over medium-low heat. Add the nuts. Cook, stirring occasionally, until lightly browned, 2 to 3 minutes. Put ¼ cup of the nuts in a bowl; save the remainder for garnish.

2 Chop the tentacles of the squid so that no piece is larger than a pea. Add them to the pine nuts, along with the minced garlic, half the anchovies, ¼ cup of the parsley, the Parmesan, wine, and 1 tablespoon of the olive oil. Stir to combine.

3 Add bread crumbs as needed to make a moist stuffing. Add pepper. Cook 1 teaspoon or so in a few drops of oil over medium heat. Taste and add salt, pepper, garlic, anchovy, or cheese if necessary.

4 Stuff the squid bodies with this mixture, using your fingers and a teaspoon. Each body should get about 2 teaspoons of the mixture; do not overstuff. Close the openings with 1 or 2 toothpicks (round ones are less likely to break than flat ones).

5 Over medium heat, heat the remaining 2 table-spoons of olive oil in a deep skillet large enough to hold all the squid in one layer (the squid will shrink). Add the chiles and peeled garlic cloves and stir occasionally until the garlic is brown. Remove the chiles and garlic and discard. Add the remaining anchovies and stir briefly. Add the stuffed squid and brown on both sides (raising the heat if necessary), about a minute per side.

6 Add the tomatoes and rosemary, reduce the heat to low, cover, and set a timer for 15 minutes. Don't worry if the mixture appears dry; the squid will throw off plenty of liquid. When the timer goes off, check to make sure no squid is sticking to the bottom of the pan, reduce heat a bit further, and re-cover.

7 Fifteen minutes later, remove the cover and stick a toothpick into one of the squid. It should penetrate easily (if not, re-cover and cook 10 more minutes). Remove the cover, raise the heat to medium, and reduce the sauce—with the squid still in the pan—for

about 10 minutes. Remove the squid from the pan and let it sit 5 minutes or so while you reduce the sauce for another 5 minutes, or until the sauce is thick.

8 To serve as a first course, slice each squid into ½-inch diagonals, top with a teaspoon or two of sauce, and garnish with the reserved pine nuts and parsley. Serve either 1 or 2 squid per person. To serve as a main course, toss the remaining sauce with 1 pound of cooked linguine or other pasta. Top each serving with several slices of stuffed squid, and garnish with pine nuts and parsley.

Poached Squid with Cilantro and Coconut

Makes 4 servings

Time: 40 minutes with cleaned squid

This is a lovely dish, yellow, red, and green; it looks great over rice. Cooking time varies with the squid's natural tenderness; five minutes is average, but it could take as few as two minutes or as many as ten. Again, I recommend frequent tasting, beginning as soon as the squid becomes opaque. If the squid begins to toughen, get it off the stove.

1½ pounds cleaned squid, rinsed well

1 cup dried unsweetened grated coconut

⅛ teaspoon saffron, measured after crumbling a few threads, or 1 teaspoon turmeric

2 cups boiling water

3 tablespoons peanut or vegetable oil

1 large onion, cut into ⅛-inch-thick slices

1 tablespoon peeled and minced or grated fresh ginger

1 teaspoon minced garlic

¼ teaspoon cayenne, or to taste

½ cup minced cilantro leaves

2 plum tomatoes, cored, halved, seeded, and cut into ¼-inch dice

Salt to taste

1 Cut the squid into diamonds, rectangles, or squares, no longer than 1 to 1$^{1}/_{2}$ inches.

2 Put the coconut and saffron in the container of a blender and pour the boiling water over them. Holding the top of the blender firmly closed with a folded towel, blend for 10 or 15 seconds. Let sit for 10 minutes or so, then pour the liquid through a fine strainer into a bowl, pressing on the coconut to extract as much cream as possible. There should be almost 2 cups.

3 Heat the oil in a large skillet over medium heat. Add the onion and cook, stirring, until slightly softened and translucent, about 5 minutes. Adjust the heat so the onion does not brown.

4 Add the ginger, garlic, and cayenne to the onion and cook over medium-low heat, stirring, for about 5 minutes. Add 1$^{1}/_{2}$ cups of the coconut cream and raise the heat to medium. Bring to a gentle boil, add a bit more than half of the cilantro, and cook, stirring occasionally, until the sauce is slightly reduced, 5 to 10 minutes.

5 Drain the squid of any accumulated liquid and add it, along with the tomatoes, to the sauce. Cook over medium heat, stirring occasionally. The mixture may look dry at first, but as the squid cooks it will release some liquid. Add a bit more coconut cream if the mixture remains dry.

6 Begin tasting the squid when it becomes opaque. Continue to taste frequently until it is tender, about 5 minutes. When done, add the remaining cilantro and season with salt. Turn out onto a large platter full of hot rice and serve immediately.

The Basics of Clams

Clams range from little ("littlenecks") to sea clams that weigh hundreds of pounds; they may be hard (littlenecks, cherrystones, or quahogs), or soft (steamers, razor clams, and other clams with fragile shells). The biggest and toughest are chopped into bits to be made into chowder. The choicest—essentially the smallest—are sold live, and are great raw, on the half-shell.

Most clams grow in tidal flats; the hard-shells in sandier bays and along beaches, the soft-shells in muddier areas. Both hard- and soft-shell clams can be found on East and West coasts, though most of the commercial production is from the East Coast. Hard-shells come in a wide range of colors—from white to slate gray to brown—and are, of course, quite hard. Soft-shells, which gape, are usually stark white and quite brittle.

Clams may be dug at any time of year, but since it is easier to dig in the summer months, they may be more plentiful and less expensive at that time. You can, of course, dig your own, once you check with the local regulators (or a good sporting goods shop, which can also sell you the appropriate rake or other tool) to see whether the beds are open and whether a license is required.

Commercially harvested clams (and other mollusks) are subject to a fairly strict inspection and, by law, all clams should be shipped with a certification tag. You can ask to see this when you buy clams if you are wary of the dealer. Eating raw clams may be risky; see the general discussion on food safety, page 276.

Buying clams is easy, since those in the shell must be alive. When hard-shells die, you can move their shell apart; otherwise, they're shut up pretty tight, and you cannot even slide their shells from side to side. Live soft-shells react visibly to your touch, retracting their necks and closing slightly (they are never closed all the way—hence the name "gapers"). Dead clams smell pretty bad, so it's unlikely you'll be fooled.

Never store clams in sealed plastic or under water; they'll die. Just keep them in a bowl in the refrigerator, where they will remain alive for several days.

Soft-shells usually contain large quantities of sand, and you must wash them well before cooking (soft-shells are never eaten raw). Hard-shells require little more than a cleaning of their shells. I use a stiff brush to scrub them under running water. To shuck them, see the illustrated steps below. Serve with lemon if you like; sauces are superfluous. Small hard-shells—under two inches across—are also nice lightly steamed, like mussels.

*To open a clam, you must use a blunt, fairly thick knife; there is a knife made specifically for this purpose (called, not surprisingly, a "clam knife"), and it's worth having for this chore. (**Step 1**) Hold the clam in your cupped hand, and wedge the edge of the knife into the clam's shell opposite the hinge. Once you get it in there the clam will give up all resistance. (**Step 2**) Run the knife along the shell and open up the clam. Try to keep as much juice inside the shell as you can. Detach the meat from the shell and serve.*

Grilled Hard-Shell Clams

Makes 4 appetizer servings

Time: 30 minutes, plus time to preheat the grill

This dish can be made in the oven, too, or with any mixture of clams, mussels, and oysters you like. For most people, the novelty of grilled mollusks—and their wonderful flavor—comes as a completely enjoyable surprise.

    30 to 40 hard-shell clams
    4 tablespoons (¹/₂ stick) butter
    Hot red pepper sauce to taste (optional)
    Freshly squeezed lemon juice to taste

1 Preheat a gas grill or start a charcoal fire (to make this dish in the oven, preheat to 500°F). Meanwhile, rinse the clams or mussels in several changes of water, until the water runs clear; drain. When the fire is hot, dump the clams onto the grill or place them in a basket and put the basket on the grill. (If you are using the oven, place the clams in a baking pan and slide it into the oven.)

2 Melt the butter in a small saucepan over low heat, add the hot sauce and the lemon juice, and let it sizzle for a couple of minutes over low heat.

3 As the clams open—some will take a minute or two, others several—remove them to a platter and move the more stubborn members to hotter parts of the fire. Try to keep the liquor in the shells of those that open, but don't be a fanatic about it; you're bound to lose some. When they're all cooked, drizzle the butter over them and bring to the table. Be careful: the hot shells can be damaging to careless lips. Use a small knife to open any clams that may have remained closed; as long as they were alive to begin with, they are perfectly safe.

Steamed Littlenecks with Butter and Herbs

Makes 4 appetizer servings

Time: 20 minutes

Be sure not to salt the broth until you taste it; clams can be quite salty.

    Roughly 4 pounds littlenecks, the smaller the better
    ¹/₂ cup dry white wine
    3 shallots, chopped
    Several sprigs fresh parsley
    Several sprigs fresh mint (optional)
    1 tablespoon minced chervil leaves (optional)
    4 tablespoons (¹/₂ stick) unsalted butter, softened

1 Rinse the clams in several changes of water, until the water runs clear; drain. Place them in a large pot with the wine, shallots, parsley, mint, and chervil. Cover the pot and cook over high heat, shaking occasionally, until the clams are open, 5 to 10 minutes.

2 Remove the clams to four bowls and reduce the sauce over high heat for about 10 minutes (if any of the clams did not open, leave them in the sauce while you reduce it—they will "pop" eventually). Lower the heat to medium and stir in the butter, a tablespoon at a time, until melted. Use a sieve lined with a paper towel to strain the sauce over the clams; serve.

Stir-Fried Littlenecks in Hot Sauce

Makes 4 servings

Time: 20 minutes

Use the smallest clams you can find for this dish, or substitute very well-washed mussels (see The Basics of Mussels, page 346) if you like. Since the recipe makes abundant sauce, you can increase the amount of clams by a pound or two and still have plenty of liquid. Serve this over rice.

3 pounds littleneck clams
2 tablespoons peanut or vegetable oil
1 tablespoon minced garlic
1 teaspoon peeled and minced or grated fresh ginger
1/2 cup chicken, fish, or vegetable stock, or water (see "Soups" for stock recipes)
1 tablespoon dry sherry or white wine
1 tablespoon soy sauce
1 teaspoon crushed red pepper flakes, or to taste
Freshly ground black pepper
Minced cilantro leaves for garnish

1 Rinse the clams in several changes of water, until the water runs clear; drain. Make rice—it will take longer than cooking the clams.

2 In a wok or large, deep pot, heat the oil over medium-high heat for a couple of minutes. Add the garlic and ginger and stir for 30 seconds or so. Add the clams, raise the heat to high, and stir. Add the stock or water and cook, stirring occasionally, until the clams begin to open, 3 to 5 minutes.

Fifteen Shellfish Dishes for Fish Haters

Most people like shellfish, but you can convert many of those who don't with these recipes.

1. Shrimp, My Way, page 324
2. Shrimp "Scampi," page 324
3. Shrimp with Spicy Orange Flavor, page 325
4. Spicy Grilled or Broiled Shrimp, page 325
5. Grilled or Steamed King Crab Legs, page 331
6. Dungeness Crab Salad, page 332
7. Crab Cakes, page 331
8. Sautéed Soft-Shell Crabs, any version, pages 332–333
9. Grilled Soft-Shell Crabs, page 333
10. Basic Boiled or Steamed Lobster, page 334
11. Grilled Lobster, page 336
12. Stir-Fried Lobster with Black Bean Sauce, page 336
13. Grilled Hard-Shell Clams, page 343
14. Curried Mussels, page 347
15. Grilled Scallops with Basil Stuffing, page 350

3 Add the sherry, soy sauce, crushed red pepper, and black pepper, lower the heat to medium, and continue to cook and stir until almost all the clams are open, a few minutes more. (Those clams that do not pop open can be easily opened at the table with a knife.) Garnish and serve, over white rice.

Baked Stuffed Clams

Makes 4 to 6 appetizer servings

Time: About 30 minutes

Like Linguine with Clams (page 146), this is one of those dishes that is far better at home than in restaurants.

12 hard-shell clams, each under 2 inches in diameter
1 tablespoon olive oil
1 tablespoon minced garlic
1 cup plain bread crumbs, preferably fresh
2 tablespoons minced fresh parsley leaves
Dash cayenne
Salt and freshly ground black pepper to taste
Freshly squeezed lemon juice if needed
Lemon wedges
Tabasco or other hot red pepper sauce to taste

1 Preheat the oven to 450°F. Shuck the clams, reserving half the shells and as much of the liquor as possible. (If you're not confident about shucking, steam the clams lightly, removing them the second their shells begin to open and preserving as much of their liquid as possible. You can also microwave, again removing them the second they begin opening.) Mince the clams (you can do this in a small food processor if you are careful; don't overprocess).

2 Heat the olive oil over medium heat in a medium skillet. Add the garlic and cook, stirring, just until it begins to color. Add the bread crumbs and cook,

stirring, until the mixture browns. Add the parsley, cayenne, salt, and pepper. Stir and taste for seasoning. Add the reserved liquor and, if the mixture seems dry (or simply if you want a moister, more acidic mixture), some lemon juice. Add the minced clam meat.

3 Stuff the shells with this mixture, place them on a baking sheet or roasting pan, and bake until lightly browned, 10 to 15 minutes. Serve hot or warm, with lemon wedges and Tabasco.

Basic Steamed Clams
"Steamers"

Makes 4 servings

Time: 15 minutes, longer if you have time

Sometimes, steamers are so sweet you'll swear you never had better seafood. In my experience, the best come from the North—Maine and the Maritime Provinces of Canada. For more elaborate recipes, see the variations under Basic Steamed Mussels (page 346).

4 to 6 pounds soft-shell clams ("steamers")
1/2 onion or several cloves garlic, lightly smashed
Several sprigs fresh parsley
1 cup white wine or water
Melted butter

1 Rinse the clams in a few changes of water, getting rid of the coarsest dirt. Then, if you have time, soak them for a few hours in cold salted (or sea) water to which a couple of handfuls of cornmeal have been added. Then rinse them again. If you don't have time, proceed.

2 Place the onion, parsley, and wine in a large, deep pot that has a lid over medium-high heat, along with the clams. Cover and turn the heat to high. Steam the clams, shaking the pot often until they open, 5 to 10 minutes.

3 Remove the clams with a slotted spoon; place them in a bowl. Use a sieve lined with a paper towel to strain the broth into another bowl. Serve immediately, with melted butter. Eat by removing each clam from its shell, then taking the black membrane off its "neck" or "foot," dipping it in the broth to clean it of any remaining sand, then into the butter.

The Basics of Mussels

Mussels are usually much less expensive than clams, and can be as heavenly as a good lobster. They come from everywhere, from Maine to New Zealand. In my opinion, they don't freeze well, but there are those who disagree and enjoy the frozen green-lipped mussels from New Zealand). I once preferred wild to cultivated mussels, but definite strides have been made in farm-raising mussels, so I don't much fuss about it.

The biggest hassle about mussels is cleaning them. If possible, start with clean mussels (farmed mussels are almost always cleaner than wild mussels) instead of muddy ones. If you have the time, let them sit in a pot under slowly running cold water for thirty minutes or more. Then wash the mussels carefully, discarding any with broken shells, those whose shells remain open after tapping them lightly, or those which seem unusually heavy (chances are they're filled with mud). As you clean them, pull or scrape off the "beard"—the weedy growth attached to the bottom of shell—from each one. Rinse thoroughly.

Most mussels have a "beard," a small amount of vegetative growth extending from their flat side. Pull or cut it off before cooking.

Some mussels contain pea crabs, pea-sized animals which live in a symbiotic relationship with the mussel. The crunchy little pea crabs are not only harmless, they are edible. Although no one seems to like them, there doesn't seem to be much that can be done about it.

Basic Steamed Mussels

Makes 4 servings

Time: About 15 minutes, plus cleaning time

When mussels are good—fat and sweet—one pound per person is just about right for a main course. A little bit of saffron added to the steaming liquid gives the broth a wondrous flavor. Serve with crusty bread to soak up the extra broth.

> 3 tablespoons extra-virgin olive oil
> 4 cloves garlic, smashed
> 1 medium onion, roughly sliced
> 1/2 cup dry white wine
> 1/2 cup roughly chopped fresh parsley leaves
> At least 4 pounds large mussels, well washed
>   (page 346)

1 In a large pot over medium heat, heat the oil, then add the garlic and onion and cook, stirring, just until the onion softens.

2 Add the wine, parsley, and mussels, cover the pot, and turn the heat to high. Steam, shaking the pot frequently, until the mussels open, about 8 to 10 minutes. Use a slotted spoon to put the mussels into a serving bowl; if you like, you can strain a little of the liquid over them.

Mussels with Cream: Follow the above recipe and place the mussels in a warm, covered bowl. Strain the cooking liquid through a sieve lined with a paper towel into a medium saucepan; bring it to a boil over medium-high heat. Add 1 teaspoon minced fresh tarragon leaves or $^1/_2$ teaspoon dried tarragon. Reduce the liquid to about $^1/_2$ cup, then turn the heat to low. Add 2 tablespoons butter, cut into bits. When it has melted, add 1 cup heavy cream or half-and-half. Heat but do not boil. Taste the sauce for seasoning (feel free to add a little more tarragon) and pour it over the mussels.

Mussels with Butter Sauce: Follow the basic recipe and keep the mussels warm. Strain the cooking liquid through a sieve lined with a paper towel into a medium saucepan and bring it to a boil over medium-high heat. Meanwhile, discard 1 shell of each mussel, and arrange the remaining shells, with the mussel meat, on a platter. Keep warm in a low oven while the liquid reduces. When the steaming liquid is reduced to about $^1/_4$ cup, add 3 tablespoons butter, cut into bits, and let it melt. Add 1 teaspoon minced garlic and $^1/_4$ cup minced fresh parsley leaves. Cook over medium heat for a minute or two. Check for salt, then drizzle the sauce over the mussel meats and serve.

Curried Mussels: Follow the basic recipe. Strain the cooking liquid through a sieve lined with a paper towel into a medium saucepan and bring it to a boil over medium-high heat; reduce it to $^1/_2$ cup. Meanwhile, shell the mussels and place them in a warm, covered bowl. In a small saucepan, melt 1 tablespoon butter over medium heat. Stir in 1 tablespoon each flour and curry powder, then turn the heat to low. Cook, stirring constantly, for a couple of minutes. Gradually add the reduced mussel cooking liquid to the flour and butter mixture, stirring constantly. When the mixture is smooth, add $^1/_2$ cup heavy cream, stirring all the while. Heat but do not boil. Taste the sauce for seasoning (feel free to add a little more curry) and stir in the mussels. Serve over rice.

The Basics of Oysters

The best oysters should be eaten raw; they can be cooked, of course, but they lose something in the translation. Nevertheless some—especially those from the Deep South—are better cooked.

Although oysters are perfectly safe year-round, they are really at their best in months whose names contain an "R," and, if you only want to eat the best oysters, in winter. At that time, few species are spawning, and the water in the best beds—the northernmost beds—is as cold as it gets before icy waters make harvesting difficult or impossible. And cold water means peak flavor.

There are four major species of oysters seen in the United States: the familiar Atlantic (*Crassostrea virginica*), known for its brininess and grown all along the East and Gulf coasts; the European (*Ostrea edulis*), a round, metallic-tasting, flat-shelled oyster grown in the Northwest and in a few spots in Maine; the Olympia (*Ostrea lurida*), the half-dollar-sized oyster that is indigenous to the Northwest and grown only there; and the Pacific (*Crassostrea gigas*), known for its wildly scalloped shell and fruity flavors.

Within each species, there are nicknames: The Atlantic is not only called the Eastern but is casually referred to by many of its place names, especially Bluepoint, Wellfleet, and Apalachicola; the European is known as the "flat" (*plat* in French), and also—incorrectly—as the Belon, a name that belongs to a small region in France; and the Pacific, which is also grown in Europe, is sometimes called a Portuguese ("Portugaise"), from a now-extinct species that once made up the majority of oysters grown in Europe.

Nomenclature is confusing but important, because each of the four species is markedly different from the others. Even within each species the differences between a northern and a southern oyster are amazing, because much of the distinctive flavor of a given oyster comes not only from its species but from its home. If you're eating oysters on the half-shell, learn to recognize your favorite (or do what I do—eat the best oyster you can find). I strongly believe that the best oysters come from the coldest waters, and usually opt for those from Long Island north on the East Coast, and from Puget Sound north on the West. If you're cooking oysters, the differences are not as important.

Buying and Serving Raw Oysters

Buying oysters for cooking is easy; you can use those that have been shucked, packaged, and marked with a "sell-by" date. But for oysters on the half-shell, you first have to determine which oyster you like (see above), and then make sure the shells are undamaged and shut tight. To clean them, just scrub the shells thoroughly with a not-too-stiff brush. There's never any sand inside.

Shucking is the truly difficult part; see below for illustrations, but also ask your fishmonger if he can do it for you. Keep them on a bed of crushed ice and eat them within a couple of hours.

To serve oysters on the half-shell, use any condiment you like. I prefer nothing at all (the great thing about

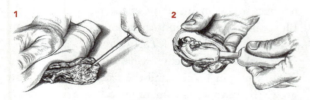

You can use an oyster knife, a can opener, or any sturdy (but preferably not too sharp) knife to open an oyster. The danger is in slipping, so protect your hand with a towel or glove. (Step 1) Place the oyster, cupped side down, on a flat surface and insert the knife into the hinge. Press and wiggle and twist that knife in there, until the oyster pops. Twist off the top shell, trying to keep as much juice inside as possible. (Step 2) Detach the meat from the shell and serve.

oysters is their intense flavor), or at most a squeeze of lemon. But many people, especially those accustomed to the large, dull-flavored oysters of the South, prefer freshly ground black pepper; Tabasco sauce; or shrimp cocktail sauce (see Shrimp Cocktail, page 324). Another possibility is a flavored vinegar called mignonette: Make this by combining a teaspoon coarsely ground black pepper, a tablespoon minced shallot, and a half cup good quality champagne or white wine vinegar.

Sautéed Oysters

Makes 4 appetizer servings or 2 main-course servings

Time: 30 minutes

Frying fish at home, as noted elsewhere, is not as much fun as, for example, having someone do it for you. But pan-fried oysters are terrific, and not as messy. This is a good recipe for preshucked oysters.

2 eggs
1/4 cup milk
Flour for dredging
Salt and freshly ground black pepper to taste
24 large shucked oysters, drained and dried
Plain bread crumbs for dredging
2 tablespoons olive or vegetable oil
2 tablespoons butter (or use all oil)
Lemon wedges

1 Beat the eggs lightly with the milk. Season the flour with salt and pepper. Dredge the oysters, one by one, in the flour, then dip in the egg mixture, then in the bread crumbs. Let them stand on waxed paper until you are ready to start cooking (you can refrigerate them for a few hours if you like).

2 Heat a large, deep skillet over medium-high heat for 2 or 3 minutes. Add the oil and butter. When the butter foam subsides, add the oysters, a few at a time.

Do not crowd; you may have to cook in batches (and use more butter and oil). Cook, turning once, until browned on both sides, about 5 or 6 minutes total. Serve immediately, with lemon wedges.

Sautéed Oysters with Wine-Shallot Sauce: Steps 1 and 2 remain the same. When you remove the oysters, keep them warm. Add $1/2$ cup dry white wine, 1 tablespoon minced shallots, and $1/2$ cup minced fresh parsley leaves to the skillet; cook over high heat, stirring, until the liquid is reduced by about half. Stir in a teaspoon or two of butter or extra-virgin olive oil. Drizzle over the oysters and serve. (Omit the lemon wedges.)

The Basics of Scallops

The creamy and almost translucent scallop offers the most complex flavors and enjoyable texture of any mollusk. It certainly is cooked in more ways than its cousins.

Scallops differ in another important way, too: Because their shells never close completely, scallops are usually shucked immediately after harvest (the relatively rare West Coast pink scallops are the exception; they're often steamed like mussels). Then, to prevent spoilage, the guts are removed and discarded. What remains is the massive muscle. Sometimes, the muscle is sold together with the reddish-orange roe, which is delicious. Once shucked, scallops are almost never eaten raw.

The best scallops, depending on your wealth and geographic orientation, are either bay scallops or sea scallops (I'm going to ignore pink scallops, which are almost never seen outside of the Northwest and are not even common there). The least desirable (and of course the least expensive), are the tiny calicos, not much bigger than pencil erasers and just as rubbery when overcooked.

Note that all scallops are sold with their tendon, a stark-white strip of gristle that attaches the muscle to the shell. It is often overlooked, and can be, especially with smaller scallops. But if you are cooking just a few scallops, or are making seviche, or have a little extra time, just strip it off with your fingers. This is an added refinement, far from essential but worthwhile. Here's how they break down:

Sea scallop: Harvested year-round in the North Atlantic, sea scallops range from mild to quite briny. They are best cooked so that their interior remains creamy. Some range to several ounces; most weigh one-half ounce or so.

Bay scallop: Caught in the winter months in a small area between Long Island and Cape Cod, these are the most expensive scallops. Cork-shaped and about the size of pretzel nuggets, they are slightly darker in color than other scallops. They're very expensive; if you're not paying at least twelve dollars a pound—and probably more—you're not buying real bay scallops. The farm-raised version from China is much less expensive but nowhere near as good.

Calico scallop: These are the little scallops that sell for four dollars a pound in supermarkets, referred to above as pencil erasers (they're actually a bit bigger than that). Found in warmer waters, off the Atlantic and Gulf coasts, and also in Central and South America, these are shucked by blasting the shells with a hit of steam. Of course this semi-cooks them as well, further contributing to their tendency to become overcooked. Calicos run to two or even three hundred per pound, although larger ones are also harvested (and are passed off as bays).

Many scallops are soaked in phosphates, which cause them to absorb water and lose flavor. Always buy scallops from someone you trust, and let him or her know that you want unsoaked (sometimes called "dry") scallops.

Scallop Seviche

Makes 6 to 8 appetizer servings

Time: About 2 hours

Citrus juice "cooks" the scallops, resulting in chemical changes nearly identical to those produced by heat. Any white-fleshed fish—fillets of flounder or sea bass are especially good—can be used to make seviche; just make sure it is unquestionably fresh.

> 1 pound bay or other scallops, perfectly fresh
> Juice of ¹/₂ lime
> Juice of ¹/₂ lemon
> Juice of ¹/₂ orange
> 2 scallions, minced
> 2 tablespoons minced cilantro leaves
> 1 teaspoon soy sauce (optional)
> 1 or 2 limes, quartered

1 Briefly rinse the scallops. Remove the tough stark white hinge that attaches the scallop to the shell. Leave tiny calico scallops whole; cut cork-shaped bay scallops in half; cut large sea scallops into slices.

2 Combine the scallops in a bowl with the citrus juice and scallions, cover, and refrigerate; stir occasionally, until they become opaque, about 2 hours. Sprinkle with cilantro and the optional soy sauce and serve with lime quarters.

Grilled Scallops

Makes 4 to 6 servings

Time: 30 minutes, plus time to preheat the grill

Add as many sturdy, quick-cooking fish to these skewers as you like: shrimp, grouper, lobster, or monkfish, for example.

> Juice of 1 lemon
> 2 tablespoons extra-virgin olive oil
> 1 teaspoon minced garlic
> 1 teaspoon salt
> ¹/₂ teaspoon freshly ground black pepper
> 2 pounds large sea scallops

1 Start a charcoal or wood fire or preheat a gas grill or broiler; the fire should be quite hot, and the rack as close to the heat source as you can get it.

2 Combine the lemon juice, oil, garlic, salt, and pepper, and toss with the scallops (do not marinate).

3 Skewer the scallops (through their equators rather than their axes, or they may break), or put them in a basket. Grill until brown, then turn and brown again. Total cooking time should be just about 5 minutes—stop cooking before the scallops' interior becomes opaque. Serve immediately.

Grilled Scallops with Basil Stuffing

Makes 4 servings

Time: 30 minutes, plus time to preheat the grill

This is among the most impressive and wonderful dishes I know; the hardest part is finding good sea scallops and fresh basil. Feel free to make it on the stove top if you don't want to grill: Just heat a large, deep skillet and brown the scallops on both sides, with only the oil that clings to them.

> ¹/₂ cup fresh basil leaves
> 1 clove garlic, peeled
> 1 teaspoon salt
> ¹/₄ teaspoon freshly ground black pepper
> ¹/₃ cup plus 1 tablespoon extra-virgin olive oil
> 1¹/₂ pounds or more large sea scallops
> Lemon wedges

1 Mince the basil, garlic, salt, and pepper together until very fine, almost a puree (you can do this in a food processor, but it really won't save you time or effort). Mix in a small bowl or cup with 1 tablespoon of the olive oil.

2 Make a deep horizontal slit in the side of each of the scallops, but don't cut all the way through. Fill each scallop with about 1/2 teaspoon of the basil mixture; close. Pour the remaining oil onto a plate or pan and turn the scallops in it. Let sit while you preheat a gas grill or start a charcoal fire; it should be very hot before grilling, with the rack about 4 inches from the heat source.

3 Place the scallops on the grill (don't pour the remaining oil over them, as it will catch fire), and grill 2 to 3 minutes per side, no more. Serve immediately, with lemon wedges.

Roasted Sea Scallops

Makes 4 servings

Time: 30 minutes

Sea scallops are absolutely essential for this dish; even bay scallops are likely to overcook.

1 medium tomato, peeled if you have time, cored, and roughly chopped
1 medium onion, minced
2 tablespoons minced fresh parsley leaves, plus more for garnish
1 teaspoon paprika
1 tablespoon extra-virgin olive oil
Salt and freshly ground black pepper to taste
1 1/2 pounds sea scallops

1 Preheat the oven to 450°F. Mix together all ingredients except the scallops and garnish in a baking dish just large enough to hold the scallops in one layer.

2 Bake until the juices begin to bubble, about 10 minutes. Mix in the scallops, return to the oven, and bake just until the scallops are opaque about halfway through, about 10 minutes more, depending on their size. Garnish and serve.

Sautéed Scallops

Makes 4 servings

Time: 15 minutes, more or less

To avoid overcooking, it's best to remove the scallops from the pan after an initial browning, then return them for a brief cooking period once the sauce is made.

2 tablespoons olive oil
1 teaspoon minced garlic
1 to 1 1/2 pounds scallops, preferably sea or bay
Salt and freshly ground black pepper to taste
Juice of 1 lemon
1 tablespoon minced fresh chives

1 Heat a large non-stick skillet over medium-high heat for 3 or 4 minutes; add the olive oil, garlic, and, 30 seconds later, the scallops, a few at a time. Turn them as they brown, allowing about 2 minutes per side (less for scallops under an inch across, somewhat more for those well over an inch). Season them with salt and pepper as they cook; remove them to a bowl as they finish.

2 Add the lemon juice to the liquid in the pan and cook over medium-high heat until the liquid is reduced to a glaze, 1 or 2 minutes. Return the scallops to the skillet, along with the chives, and stir to coat with the sauce and reheat, 1 to 2 minutes. Serve immediately.

Buttery Scallops: In Step 1, preheat the skillet for just 2 minutes; replace all or half the oil with butter. Don't brown the scallops; keep the heat at medium, and cook them on both sides until they are opaque. In Step 2, add 1 teaspoon minced fresh tarragon leaves or $^1/_2$ teaspoon dried tarragon, along with the lemon juice, salt, and pepper. Finish as above, stirring in 1 teaspoon of butter with the scallops (omit the chives) and garnish with minced chervil, tarragon (just a little), or parsley leaves.

Ginger Scallops: In Step 1, use peanut or vegetable oil. Add 1 tablespoon peeled and minced or grated fresh ginger with the garlic. Add 3 chopped scallions to the skillet with the scallops. In Step 2, use a mixture of 1 tablespoon soy sauce, 1 tablespoon dry sherry or white wine, and 2 tablespoons water, chicken, fish, or vegetable stock in place of the lemon juice. Finish with chives or some minced scallions, and add salt and pepper if necessary.

The Basics of Conch and Snails

These "univalve" mollusks—unlike the mollusks above, their shells do not open and close—come in various shapes and sizes, from the nearly foot-long whorled conch, treasured by beachcombers, to the tiny periwinkle. All are difficult to find in stores, largely unappreciated, and delicious.

You might see live conch (also called whelk) in the shell, but more often you will be offered a large (up to one-quarter pound) hunk of conch meat. This has been precooked, not quite to the point of tenderness, but enough so that cooking time is minimized (you can pound it to death to tenderize it, but cooking is easier, more reliable, and takes more time than energy). The only preparation necessary before cooking is cutting off the operculum, the shell-like covering that protects the meat. Fresh conch is prepared the same way, only the cooking time is longer. Conch remains one of the least expensive mollusks. It still sells for under three dollars a pound for meat only, which—compared to the meat of comparable seafood—is a steal. It's available year-round, and can be used in almost any clam-meat recipe, or in sauces, such as Penne with Tomato-Shrimp Sauce (page 147).

There are two kinds of snails you may find: The garden or field snails known as escargots, which are relatively large and almost always sold in cans, and the half-inch-long periwinkle, a black dot seen by the thousands at low tide on many northern beaches. Garden snails are cooked before canning; all you need do is reheat them in butter or oil scented with plenty of minced garlic.

Periwinkles are cooked like conch and, although they don't take quite as long to cook, the process takes a while. They are best soaked in fresh water to cover before cooking; see the recipe below.

Fresh Snails with Garlic Butter

Makes 4 appetizer servings

Time: About 90 minutes, largely unattended

You can make these without garlic butter, of course, or you can cook them, chill them, and serve them in Seafood Salad, Adriatic-Style, page 119. If you have canned escargots, simply heat them in the garlic butter over low heat and serve.

2 pounds fresh snails (periwinkles)

1 cup cornmeal

2 tablespoons white or red wine vinegar or rice vinegar

8 tablespoons (1 stick) butter

1 tablespoon minced garlic

Salt and freshly ground black pepper to taste

$^1/_2$ cup roughly chopped fresh parsley leaves

1 Place the snails in water to cover and mix in the cornmeal; soak for at least 30 minutes (1 hour is better), stirring occasionally. During this time, change the water once or twice (you don't need to add more cornmeal), mixing with your hands and rinsing as you do so.

2 Drain the snails and put them in a medium saucepan. Cover with fresh water and the vinegar and bring to a boil. Turn the heat to medium and cook for about 15 minutes. Remove a snail from the pot and, using a pin, try to pull the snail from its shell; if the operculum (the hard, shell-like disk at the end of the meat) falls off and the snail comes out easily, the snails are done. If not, continue cooking until all the snails are ready.

3 When the snails are almost cooked, cut the butter into chunks and melt it over medium-low heat in a small saucepan. Add the garlic and cook, stirring occasionally, for about 5 minutes, or just until the garlic loses its rawness. Season with salt and pepper and keep warm.

4 When the snails are done, drain them, then return them to the pot with a couple of tablespoons of the butter. Garnish and serve with pins or toothpicks to remove the snails, along with the garlic butter.

Poultry

Chicken has become the preferred meat of many Americans. Not surprising, since it—and other birds, like turkey—is low in fat, cooks quickly, and has mild flavor and tender texture.

That mild flavor offers both opportunities and challenges. Most supermarket chicken is more than mild—it's downright bland. Which leaves you in the same position you're in when you're cooking pasta: You must add flavor in the form of herbs, spices, aromatic vegetables, small amounts of other meats, or through a flavorful cooking medium, such as grilling.

That's the opportunity. Basic seasonings do wonderful things for chicken. Recipes can remain uncomplicated and still be quite delicious. Because chicken is essentially a blank slate, you have unlimited flavor options; and, as long as they're sensibly combined, the results will be just fine.

The Basics of Buying Chicken

The results will be even better if you're able to start with a high-quality chicken. And chicken has become so popular that many supermarkets now offer some choices: two budget chickens (a store brand and a commercial brand); one kosher chicken; and one premium, "natural," or free-range chicken. Each of these must be considered separately:

Store-brand and name-brand chickens There is no difference between these two; they're raised on the same farms by the same methods, just packaged differently. They are the least expensive chickens, but they also have least flavor and the softest texture. Furthermore, they raise some difficult issues about habitat, feed, and drug residues. However, they are the chickens that most people buy most of the time, so it pays to know how to take full advantage of them: They're best broiled, grilled, or cooked in fat, in each case with plenty of flavor added. They're not as good when cooked in liquid, because they dry out very, very quickly. For that same reason, it's important not to overcook them.

Kosher chickens   Now sold in many supermarkets throughout the country, this is a different breed of bird that is handled somewhat better. In addition, kosher chickens are salted before sale—part of the koshering process—which gives them tighter, meatier texture and more flavor. The disadvantages: Kosher chicken is often frozen (this does it little harm, but it means some planning is necessary), and it is sometimes twice as expensive as commercial chicken. Still, it can be cooked with a minimum of seasonings and still taste good, and its firm texture takes well to any kind of cooking. It wins almost every "taste-test" in which it is entered.

"Premium," "organic," and "free-range" chickens   These are poorly defined terms (in fact, as of this writing it is illegal to use the term "organic" in referring to chicken), and generalizations about birds carrying these labels are difficult to make. Some are tough and stringy but flavorful (making them excellent candidates for recipes like Chicken in a Pot, page 363); others are virtually indistinguishable from more mass-produced chickens; still others are wonderful. The chickens from Bell and Evans, Murray's, D'Artagnan, and Rocky have all been consistently good over the last few years.

Fresh versus frozen chicken   For years, much of the chicken that was sold as "fresh" had actually been shipped frozen. Although this practice has been discontinued, it served to point out one thing: Chicken freezes brilliantly. You can usually buy frozen birds (and, often, that's the only way organic or kosher chickens are sold) with confidence, but, more important, this means that you can buy as much chicken as you can store when it's on sale and freeze it yourself. Just remove it from the package, then wrap it tightly

in two layers of plastic, and place in the freezer, which should be as cold as you can make it. The quality will deteriorate, but very slowly; as long as you use the chicken within two months, it's unlikely you'll notice any difference. It's less expensive, of course, to buy whole birds and cut them up yourself. And, if you're storing a few chickens in the freezer, leaving them whole means that you have the option of cooking them in any form you want once they're defrosted. Cutting up a chicken, illustrated in detail on page 368, is a simple matter, and takes less than five minutes once you've had some practice.

About size   Years ago, chickens were labeled fryers, broilers, pullets, hens, and fowl, according to size, sex, and age. Now, you rarely see anything other than frying/broiling chickens (anything under four pounds or so) and roasting chickens (anything larger). "Fowl," also labeled "stewing chicken," is a large bird that is likely to be tough unless cooked in liquid; it should be quite flavorful in a dish such as Chicken in a Pot (page 363). But most commercial fowl is best used for stock.

The Basics of Cooking Chicken

Details about all the methods used in cooking chicken and other birds follow. There are, however, a couple of rules that apply across the board:

Don't undercook   The absolute safety of food can never be assured, and the mass production and wide distribution of it makes undercooking any food (even vegetables) somewhat risky. But chicken is a special case, because more than ten percent of many samples of birds contain salmonella (see page xv for more about this potentially harmful bacteria).

Salmonella is completely killed, however, by cooking chicken until it is fully done. You can reliably judge this in two ways: The easiest and surest is to use an instant-read thermometer; poke it into the breast in two or three places (don't touch the bone), then into the thigh (again, avoiding the bone) and, finally—if you're cooking a whole bird—into the joint between the thigh and lower leg. It should read 160°F to 165°F in all of these places (actually, the breast really tastes fine at a slightly lower temperature but should be cooked to at least one hundred and sixty degrees to kill bacteria). You can also check for doneness by making a small cut in any section, right down to the bone; the slightest tinge of pink is acceptable (the meat will finish cooking by the time you get it to the table), but you should see no red whatsoever. When the chicken is done, don't let it touch marinades or anything else that came into contact with it before cooking (unless, in the case of marinades, you boil them while you're cooking the chicken).

Don't overcook Yes, you want to make your chicken safe. But most chicken is delicate; once it is cooked, remove it from the heat. Overcooked chicken, no matter how wonderful to begin with, is dry and chewy.

The Basics of Roast Chicken

The "secret" of roast chicken is simple: Start with a good bird, time the cooking properly, and serve it promptly. The crisp skin and moist interior for which roast chicken is justly renown are fleeting qualities.

Because I prefer to roast smaller chickens, I don't usually stuff them. (This, of course, does not prevent you from using any of the stuffings in the turkey section of this chapter in your chicken. If you do, though, plan to increase the cooking time by about twenty-five percent, and use your instant-read thermometer.)

Trussing Trussing adds a step to a simple process without providing a great deal of benefit. But it does make it slightly easier to handle the bird—the wings and legs all stay in place—and makes the presentation somewhat more attractive. And, when birds are stuffed, trussing helps keep the stuffing in place. If you choose to truss your chicken before roasting it, see the illustrations below.

Roasting Racks and Pans You don't need a rack to roast chicken, but elevating the bird above the floor of the roasting pan helps to keep its skin crisp and prevents it from sticking. I favor heavy, V-shaped racks because they make it a little easier to turn the bird. By the way, vertical roasters and other gimmicky racks do not produce miracles.

An ordinary nine by thirteen-inch roasting pan is fine for most chickens; in fact, you want to use the *smallest* roasting pan that will comfortably hold your

TRUSSING CHICKEN

1

2

3
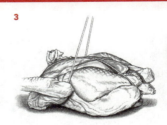
4
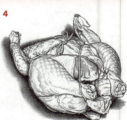

(Step 1) Use a piece of string about three feet long. Place the center of the string under the rear end of the bird and loop it around the ends of the legs. (Step 2) Cross the string over the top of the bird's breast. (Step 3) Loop the string under and around the wings. (Step 4) Tie a knot or a bow on top of the bird to join the ends of the string. Trim as necessary.

bird, so you can concentrate the juices and keep them from burning. But you'll need a larger pan if you want to add roast vegetables to the mix.

Technique I like to start chickens breast side down to shield them a bit from the initial intense heat of the oven, then finish them breast side up to complete the cooking and brown the breast. If, during the initial high-heat period, the pan juices begin to produce a great deal of smoke, just add a little water or wine (white or red, your choice) to the pan.

How to Render Chicken (or any other) Fat

Rendering fat takes time but almost no effort. To render a pound of chicken fat, for example, cut the fat into roughly one-half-inch pieces and place it in a medium skillet over low heat. Cook, stirring only occasionally, until there is nothing left but clear fat in which pieces of browned skin are sitting; this will take at least thirty minutes. About one-half cup of minced onion added during the second half of the rendering process is a nice touch. After the fat has cooled slightly, strain it. The bits of crispy skin and onion may be salted and eaten as a snack, or combined with other dishes. The fat itself will keep, refrigerated, for weeks.

Simple Roast Chicken

Makes 4 servings

Time: About 1 hour

We associate roast chicken with elegance, but it's also great weeknight food, since it takes just about an hour from start to finish. This method gives you a nicely browned exterior without drying out the breast meat, and it's easily varied (the variations I offer are a fraction of the possibilities). Use kosher or free-range chicken if at all possible.

1 whole (3- to 4-pound) chicken, trimmed of excess
    fat, then rinsed and patted dry with paper towels
3 tablespoons olive oil
2 teaspoons chopped fresh thyme, rosemary, marjoram,
    oregano, or sage leaves, or 1 teaspoon dried
Salt and freshly ground black pepper to taste
Chopped fresh herbs for garnish

1 Preheat the oven to 500°F.

2 Place the chicken, breast side down, on a rack in a roasting pan. Begin roasting. Mix together the olive oil, herb, salt, and pepper.

3 After the chicken has roasted for about 20 minutes, spoon some of the olive oil mixture over it, then turn the bird breast side up. Baste again, then again after 7 or 8 minutes; at this point the breast should be beginning to brown (if it hasn't, roast a few more minutes). Turn the heat down to 325°F, baste again, and roast until an instant-read thermometer inserted into the thickest part of the thigh reads 160° to 165°F. Total roasting time will be under an hour.

4 Before removing the chicken from the pan, tip the pan to let the juices from the bird's cavity flow into the pan (if they are red, cook another 5 minutes). Remove the bird to a platter and let it rest for about 5 minutes. While it is resting, pour the pan juices into a clear measuring cup, and pour or spoon off as much of the fat as you can. Reheat the juice, carve the bird (see illustrations on page 359), garnish, and serve with the pan juices.

Roast Chicken with Soy Sauce: Step 1 remains the same. In Step 2, replace the olive oil mixture with a combination of $1/4$ cup soy sauce; 2 tablespoons peanut (or vegetable) oil; 2 tablespoons honey; 1 teaspoon minced garlic; 1 teaspoon peeled and grated or minced fresh ginger or $1/2$ teaspoon ground ginger; and $1/4$ cup minced scallions. Steps 3 and 4 remain the same.

(Step 1) Cut straight down on either side of the breastbone, following the shape of the carcass. (Step 2) Continue to cut down toward the back until you reach the joints holding the thigh and wing to the carcass. (Step 3) Cut through those joints to free the entire half of the bird. (Step 4) Separate leg and breast sections by cutting through the skin that holds them together; hold the knife almost parallel to the cutting board, cut from the breast toward the leg, and you will easily find the right spot. (Step 5) Separate the wing from the breast if you like. (Step 6) Separate leg and thigh; the joint will offer little resistance once you find it.

Roast Chicken with Cumin, Honey, and Orange Juice: Step 1 remains the same. In Step 2, replace the olive oil mixture with a combination of 1 tablespoon olive oil; 2 tablespoons freshly squeezed orange juice; 2 tablespoons honey; 1 teaspoon minced garlic; 2 teaspoons ground cumin; and salt and pepper to taste. Steps 3 and 4 remain the same.

Roast Chicken with Roasted New Potatoes

Makes 4 servings

Time: About 1 hour

The cooking time for this bird is short, so use very small potatoes, under 1½ inches in diameter. Or cut larger potatoes into chunks.

6 tablespoons olive oil
1 tablespoon chopped fresh thyme, rosemary, marjoram, oregano, or sage leaves, or 2 teaspoons dried
Salt and freshly ground black pepper to taste
1 whole (3- to 4-pound) chicken, trimmed of excess fat, then rinsed and patted dry with paper towels
1½ to 2 pounds waxy red or white potatoes, the smaller the better, skins on and scrubbed
Chopped fresh herbs for garnish

1 Preheat the oven to 450°F.

2 Mix together the olive oil, herb, salt, and pepper. Place the chicken, breast side down, on a rack in a roasting pan. Toss half of the herb mixture with the potatoes and scatter them in the pan. Begin roasting.

3 After the chicken has roasted for about 20 minutes, spoon some of the olive oil mixture over it and the potatoes, then turn the bird breast side up. Shake the pan so the potatoes turn and cook evenly.

4 Shake the pan and baste the chicken again after 7 or 8 minutes; at this point the breast should be beginning to brown (if it isn't, roast a few more minutes). Turn the heat down to 325°F, baste again with the remaining olive mixture, and roast until an instant-read thermometer inserted into the thickest part of the thigh reads 160° to 165°F. Total roasting time will be 50 to 70 minutes.

5 Remove the chicken and taste a potato; if it isn't quite done, raise the heat to 425°F and roast while you rest and carve the chicken; it won't be long. Serve the chicken, garnished with herbs, with the potatoes scattered around it.

Roast Chicken with Roast Vegetables: When combining this roast with other vegetables, you must make sure that they are small enough to cook through in the relatively brief roasting time. (See Roasted Root Vegetables, page 616.) Start with about 2 pounds of any root or other winter vegetables—carrots, celery, parsnips, turnips, kohlrabi, white or sweet potatoes, winter squash, garlic, and so on—peel them (you need not peel individual garlic cloves) and make sure that no piece is greater than 1½ inches in diameter. Substitute the vegetables for the potatoes in the above recipe.

Roast Chicken with Herb Butter

Makes 4 servings

Time: About 1 hour

A slightly simplified version of a classic which preserves the most important elements: A crisp-skinned chicken smacking of butter and herbs. This recipe is one of the few in which substituting olive oil simply won't do; if you will not or cannot cook with butter, stick with Simple Roast Chicken (page 358).

8 tablespoons (1 stick) butter
1 tablespoon chopped fresh dill, tarragon, parsley, or chervil leaves, or a combination
Salt and freshly ground black pepper to taste
1 whole (3- to 4-pound) chicken, trimmed of excess fat, then rinsed and patted dry with paper towels
½ cup dry white wine or water, plus a little more if needed
1 clove garlic, lightly smashed (optional)
Minced fresh herbs for garnish

1 Preheat the oven to 450°F.

2 Using a fork, small food processor or blender, or potato masher, mash half the butter together with the herb(s), salt, and pepper. Loosen the skin of the chicken wherever you can, and spread some of this mixture between skin and meat, in the chicken cavity, and on top of the breast of the bird. Sprinkle the outside of the bird with more salt and pepper.

3 Put the remaining butter in a casserole or roasting pan and place the pan in the oven. When the butter has melted and its foam subsided, add the wine and the optional garlic. Place the chicken, breast side down, on a rack in the pan.

4 After the chicken has roasted for about 20 minutes, spoon some of the butter mixture over it, then turn the bird breast side up. (If, at any point, the pan juices are beginning to stick to the pan, add a little more liquid.) Baste again, then again after 7 or 8 minutes; at this point the breast should be beginning to brown (if it hasn't, roast a few more minutes). Turn the heat down to 325°F, baste again, and roast until an instant-read thermometer inserted into the thickest part of the thigh reads 160° to 165°F. Total roasting time will be under 1 hour.

There are many ways to roast a chicken, but these are the simplest variations on the basic recipe:

1. Use three tablespoons freshly squeezed lemon juice in addition to or in place of olive oil.
2. Use three tablespoons freshly squeezed lime juice in a soy sauce mix (as in the variation above), or with some minced jalapeño or crushed red pepper flakes and chopped cilantro leaves to taste, and a tablespoon or two of peanut oil.
3. Combine two tablespoons to one-third cup any mustard with two tablespoons honey and baste the chicken with this mixture during the final stages of roasting.
4. Place one-half cup white wine and two cloves crushed garlic in the bottom of the roasting pan; baste with this in addition to or in place of the olive oil mixture above.

5 Before removing the chicken from the pan, tip the pan to let the juices from the bird's cavity flow into the pan (if they are red, cook another 5 minutes). Remove the bird to a platter and let it rest for about 5 minutes before carving. Garnish with minced herbs and serve with the pan juices.

Roast Chicken with Herb Butter and Wine Sauce: Steps 1 through 4 remain the same. In Step 5, while the bird is resting, place the roasting pan on a burner over high heat. Add 1 cup dry white wine and cook, stirring and scraping the bottom of the pan to loosen any solids that have stuck there, until the liquid is reduced by about half. Add 1 tablespoon of the minced fresh herb you have been using (less if you used tarragon), stir again, and serve with the chicken.

Roast Chicken with Onions and Parsley

Makes 4 servings

Time: Just over 1 hour

A crisp, lovely bird with a smooth, bright sauce easy enough to make on a weeknight.

1 tablespoon freshly squeezed lemon juice
1 1/4 cups minced fresh parsley or chervil
1 teaspoon minced garlic
Salt and freshly ground black pepper to taste
1 whole (3- to 4-pound) chicken, trimmed of excess fat, then rinsed and patted dry with paper towels
3 tablespoons butter or olive oil
2 cups thinly sliced onions
1/2 cup chicken or vegetable stock or water (see "Soups" for stock recipes)

1 Preheat the oven to 500°F.
2 Mix together the lemon juice, 1/4 cup parsley, garlic, and some salt and pepper, and rub this mixture all over the chicken. Place the chicken, breast side down, on a rack in a roasting pan.
3 Begin roasting the chicken. Meanwhile, melt the butter or heat the olive oil in a medium skillet or saucepan over medium heat, then add the onions; cook, stirring occasionally, until softened, about 10 minutes. Stir in the remaining parsley and the stock.
4 After the chicken has roasted for about 20 minutes, spoon some of the onion mixture over it, then turn the bird breast side up. Top with more of the onion mixture, leaving some in the saucepan. Baste again after 7 or 8 minutes; at this point the breast

should be beginning to brown (if it hasn't, roast a few more minutes). Turn the heat down to 325°F, baste again, and roast until an instant-read thermometer inserted into the thickest part of the thigh reads 160° to 165°F. Total roasting time will be about an hour.

5 Remove the chicken from the oven and let it rest for about 5 minutes. Meanwhile, pour some or all of the pan juices into the saucepan with the remaining onion mixture and reheat. Carve the chicken and serve with the sauce.

Roast Chicken with Rice-and-Nut Stuffing

Makes 4 to 6 servings

Time: $1^1/_2$ hours

There are times you'll want to stuff a chicken for various reasons: to make it seem more festive, because the bird is big enough to carve, or just because you feel like it. Use this technique with any of the stuffings for turkey on pages 405–406. And see Simple Roast Capon, too (page 410); it's a splendid alternative to both chicken and turkey.

$^1/_2$ cup long-grain white rice (basmati is best)

4 tablespoons olive oil or butter

$^1/_4$ cup pine nuts or shelled pistachio nuts

2 tablespoons raisins or currants (optional)

Salt and freshly ground black pepper to taste

2 tablespoons freshly squeezed lemon juice

1 tablespoon minced fresh marjoram or oregano leaves or 1 teaspoon dried

1 whole $4^1/_2$- to 6-pound chicken, trimmed of excess fat, interior cavity carefully cleaned, rinsed and patted dry with paper towels

1 Bring a large pot of water to boil; salt it. Add the rice and simmer, stirring occasionally, until it is tender but not at all mushy, 8 to 10 minutes. Drain it, rinse it, and drain it again. Preheat the oven to 400°F.

2 Heat 2 tablespoons of the oil or butter in a large, deep skillet over medium heat for 2 minutes. Toss in the nuts and the raisins or currants, if you are using them, and stir for 1 minute. Add the rice and stir, seasoning with salt and pepper, while cooking for another minute; the rice need not get hot. Add the lemon juice and half the herb. (You may prepare the recipe in advance up to this point; refrigerate, well wrapped or in a covered container, for up to 2 days before proceeding.)

3 Stuff the chicken loosely with this mixture. Do not overstuff; if there's extra stuffing, just heat some up later and serve it on the side. Truss the chicken if you like (see illustrations, page 357; this will help keep the stuffing in the bird). Rub the chicken with 1 tablespoon of the remaining olive oil or butter and season it with salt and pepper. Place it on a rack in a roasting pan, breast side up, and put the pan in the oven.

4 Roast the chicken for at least $1^1/_4$ hours (depending on its size; a larger bird will take longer), basting with the remaining tablespoon of oil or butter about halfway through, and any pan juices that accumulate. The bird is done when an instant-read thermometer inserted into the thickest part of the thigh reads 160° to 165°F.

5 Remove the chicken from the oven and let it rest for about 5 minutes. Carve, garnish with the reserved herb, and serve with the stuffing and the pan juices.

Roast Stuffed Chicken with Roast Vegetables: If you're using a larger bird—5 or 6 pounds—you can roast vegetables using the same heat and cooking times as above. (At this relatively low temperature, vegetables will not become tender with a smaller bird, which will be cooked in $1^1/_4$ hours.) Use about 2 pounds of any root or other winter vegetables—carrots, celery, parsnips, turnips, kohlrabi, white or sweet potatoes, winter squash, garlic, and so on. Peel the vegetables (don't bother to peel individual garlic cloves) and make sure that no piece is greater than 1 1/2 inches in diameter, preferably smaller. When you remove the chicken in Step 5, taste a couple of the vegetables; if they are not quite done, raise the heat to 450°F and roast while you rest and carve the chicken; it won't be long.

Roast Stuffed Chicken with Pan Gravy: This is best when the chicken is cooked with butter. Steps 1 through 4 remain the same. In Step 5, while the bird is resting, place the roasting pan on a burner over high heat. Add 1 cup chicken or other stock and cook, stirring and scraping the bottom of the pan to loosen any solids that have stuck there, until the liquid is reduced by about 50 percent. Turn the heat to low. Add about 1 teaspoon of the minced fresh herb you have been using along with 1 tablespoon of butter; stir until the butter melts. Serve with the chicken.

Other Methods to Cook Whole Chicken

There is more than one way to cook a whole bird. In addition to roasting chickens, you can poach them in stock or other flavorful liquid (and cook them again afterward, to crisp them up a bit); grill them; even smoke them—see Tea-Smoked Duck (or Chicken), page 415. These methods give wonderful results.

Poached and Roasted Chicken with Soy Sauce

Makes 4 to 6 servings

Time: About 1 hour

This two-step process guarantees a bird with crisp skin. Strain and freeze or refrigerate the poaching sauce for reuse, adding fresh scallions, ginger, and garlic each time. See Roast Chicken with Soy Sauce (page 358) for a different approach with similar flavors.

1 cup soy sauce
3 cups water
3 tablespoons dry sherry
1 tablespoon sugar
1/2 cup chopped scallions
5 or 6 nickel-thick slices unpeeled fresh ginger
   or 1 tablespoon ground ginger
4 cloves garlic, smashed
1 star anise
1 whole (3- to 4-pound) chicken, trimmed of excess
   fat, then rinsed and patted dry with paper towels
1/4 cup minced scallions for garnish

1 Combine all ingredients except the chicken and minced scallions in a large pot; cover, turn the heat to high, and bring to a boil.

2 Place the chicken in the boiling liquid and continue to boil, covered, with the heat still on high, for 15 minutes.

3 Turn off the heat; let the chicken sit in the liquid, still covered, for 20 minutes more. (You may prepare the recipe in advance up to this point; refrigerate, well wrapped or in a covered container, for up to a day before proceeding.) Preheat the oven to 500°F.

4 Remove the chicken from the cooking liquid and place it on a rack in a roasting pan. Place in the oven and cook, undisturbed, until the chicken is deep brown, 15 to 20 minutes. Carve the chicken (page 359) and garnish with minced scallions. Serve hot or at room temperature. (Refrigerate if you will not be serving it within the hour.)

Chicken in a Pot

Makes 4 servings

Time: About 1 1/2 hours

The original one-pot dinner. Serve it one of two ways: as a stew with everything in the bowl; or as a plain broth with butter dumplings (page 74) and a dill or parsley garnish, followed by the chicken and vegetables on a platter.

Canned stock serves very nicely here, since its flavor is increased by the chicken and vegetables during the simmering time. If you don't have any stock at all, remove the chicken's backbone (page 365) and wing tips and simmer them along with the neck and gizzard in eight cups water for about thirty minutes before starting; fish them out before adding the other ingredients.

1 whole (3- to 4-pound) chicken, trimmed of excess
    fat, then rinsed and patted dry with paper towels
8 cups chicken stock (see headnote)
3 onions, quartered
2 large or 4 small-to-medium carrots, peeled and
    cut into chunks
2 leeks, split, trimmed, cleaned (page 580),
    and cut into 2-inch lengths
1 bay leaf
4 allspice berries
10 whole peppercorns
4 sprigs fresh thyme or 1 teaspoon dried thyme
Salt and freshly ground black pepper to taste
Minced fresh parsley or dill leaves for garnish

1 Put the chicken in a large pot with the stock, onions, carrots, and leeks. Bring to a boil over medium-high heat, then immediately reduce heat to medium-low. Skim foam from the surface if necessary.

2 Add the bay leaf, allspice, peppercorns, and thyme to the pot along with some salt and pepper. Simmer about 45 minutes, until the chicken and vegetables are nearly tender and the chicken is cooked through. With 15 minutes of cooking time remaining, preheat the oven to 200°F.

3 When the chicken is done, use a slotted spoon to remove it and the vegetables to an ovenproof platter and place the platter in the oven.

4 Raise the heat to high and boil the stock until it reduces by about 25 percent, 10 to 15 minutes.

5 Strain the stock into a large bowl or another large pot and adjust the seasoning as needed. Serve the soup as a first course, garnished with dill or parsley, followed by the chicken and vegetables, or cut up the chicken and serve in deep bowls with the broth and the vegetables. Garnish each serving with dill or parsley.

"Sour" Chicken in a Pot with Cabbage: In Step 2, add 4 cups chopped white, Savoy, or Napa cabbage to the pot 15 minutes after you add the herbs. After reducing and straining the liquid in Steps 4 and 5, beat together 1 cup heavy or light cream, 1 egg, and 2 tablespoons red or white wine vinegar. Add 1 cup of the hot stock to the cream mixture, and stir. Return this mixture to the pot and heat through; do not boil. Taste and adjust seasoning. You can also make this variation without the cream and egg—simply stir vinegar to taste into the stock.

Braised Whole Chicken with Tarragon
Makes 4 to 6 servings

Time: About 1 hour

I brown this bird first, in the oven; it's easy, and it deepens both the flavor and color of the finished dish.

2 tablespoons butter or olive oil
1 tablespoon chopped fresh tarragon leaves
    or 1 teaspoon dried tarragon
1 whole (3- to 4-pound) chicken, trimmed of excess
    fat, then rinsed and patted dry with paper towels
Salt and freshly ground black pepper to taste
1 teaspoon minced garlic
2 cups sliced onion or 24 pearl onions, peeled
1/4 cup red wine vinegar
1 cup dry red wine or water, plus more as needed
Minced fresh parsley leaves for garnish

1 Preheat the oven to 500°F.

2 Put the butter or oil in a large casserole or Dutch oven that can later be covered, and place the uncovered casserole in the oven. When the butter has melted (or the oil is hot), place a bit of the tarragon in the chicken's cavity. Put the chicken in the pot and roast it, breast up and undisturbed, until it is lightly browned, about 20 minutes, basting with the butter or oil once. Remove the casserole from the oven and season the chicken with salt and pepper.

3 Remove the chicken from the pot and set it aside. Place the pot on a burner and add the garlic and onion. Cook over medium-low heat until the vegetables soften, about 5 minutes.

4 Add the remaining tarragon, the vinegar, and the wine, and return the chicken to the pot, breast side up. Cover and simmer over low heat, checking occasionally to make sure the vegetables do not dry out (add a little more wine or water if necessary). When the chicken is done (an instant-read thermometer will measure at least 160°F), after 30 to 40 minutes, remove it from the pot and serve, garnished with the parsley and surrounded by the onions.

The Basics of Split Chicken

Split or butterflied (or, to use an antiquated term, "spitchcocked") chicken is another form of whole chicken (or almost whole: the backbone is usually removed). Split chicken has its advantages: It can be grilled or sautéed, and it cooks more quickly than truly whole chicken. In fact, it cooks nearly as quickly as cut-up chicken, and retains more of its juice. Split chicken is not always readily available in the supermarket, but the procedure is easy to do at home; follow the illustrations to the right. (You can also ask the supermarket butcher to do it for you.)

Any recipe can be adapted for split chicken; follow the guidelines outlined here and season the chicken any of the ways you would for sautéed, grilled, roasted, or broiled whole chicken or parts.

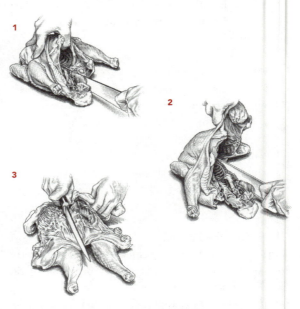

(Steps 1–2) To split a chicken: With the breast facing up, use a heavy knife to cut on either side of the backbone, cutting from front to rear. Once the backbone is removed, you will be able to lay the chicken out flat and flatten it on both sides. (Step 3) If you like, you can split the chicken into two halves.

Chicken Under a Brick
Pollo al Mattone
Makes 4 servings

Time: 45 minutes, plus optional marinating time

The great dish of Lucca, Italy, always made with the best olive oil available. I weight the chickens with a cast-iron pan and a couple of big rocks. The only problem is that handling the hot, heavy pan takes a steady, strong wrist, so use two hands. The effort is well worth it: This is the simplest and best method for producing a beautiful, crisp-skinned bird.

I specify rosemary here, which is delicious. But most herbs are equally wonderful: Try savory or dill (in similar quantity); parsley, basil, chervil, chives (use twice as much); or tarragon, marjoram, or thyme (use half as much).

1 whole (3- to 4-pound) chicken, trimmed of excess
   fat, then rinsed and patted dry with paper towels
1 tablespoon minced fresh rosemary leaves or
   1 teaspoon dried rosemary, plus 2 sprigs fresh
   rosemary (optional)
2 teaspoons salt
1 tablespoon coarsely chopped garlic
2 tablespoons extra-virgin olive oil
1 lemon, quartered

1 Follow the illustrations on page 365 to remove the backbone and split the chicken. Mix together the rosemary leaves, salt, garlic, and 1 tablespoon of the olive oil and rub this all over the chicken. Tuck some of it under the skin as well. Allow to marinate, if time permits, for up to a day, refrigerated.

2 When you are ready to cook, preheat the oven to 450°F. Preheat an large ovenproof skillet over medium-high heat for about 3 minutes. Press the rosemary sprigs if you are using them into the skin of the chicken. Put the remaining olive oil in the pan and wait a minute for it to heat up. Place the chicken in the pan, skin side down, along with any pieces of rosemary and garlic. Weight the chicken with another skillet or a flat pot cover and a couple of bricks or rocks. The basic idea is to flatten the chicken by applying a fair amount of weight evenly over its surface.

3 Cook over medium-high to high heat for 10 minutes; transfer, still weighted, to the oven. Roast for 15 minutes more. Take the chicken from the oven and remove the weight; turn the chicken over (it will now be skin side up) and roast 10 minutes more. To check for doneness, insert an instant-read thermometer into the thickest part of the thigh; it should read

160°F to 165°F. Serve hot or at room temperature (refrigerate if you will not be serving it within the hour), with lemon wedges.

Grilled or Broiled Split Chicken
Makes 4 servings

Time: 45 minutes, plus marinating time if desired, and time to preheat the grill

Basically the same ingredients as the above recipe, but with a different technique. It's not essential to weight the bird when you grill it, although it still helps the meat to brown evenly (it's impossible to weight it for broiling, of course). A couple of bricks or rocks, wrapped in aluminum foil, will do the trick.

1 whole (3- to 4-pound) chicken, trimmed of excess
   fat, then rinsed and patted dry with paper towels
1 tablespoon fresh minced rosemary leaves or
   1 teaspoon dried rosemary
2 teaspoons salt
1 tablespoon coarsely chopped garlic
2 tablespoons extra-virgin olive oil
1 lemon, quartered

1 Follow the illustrations on page 365 to remove the backbone and split the chicken. Mix together the rosemary leaves, salt, garlic, and 1 tablespoon of the olive oil and rub this all over the chicken. Tuck some of it under the skin as well. Marinate, if time permits, for up to a day, refrigerated.

2 When you are ready to cook, start a charcoal or wood fire or preheat a gas grill or broiler; the fire should be quite hot, but you should place the rack 5 or 6 inches from the heat source.

3 Grill (skin side down) or broil (skin side up), for 10 to 12 minutes, then baste with any remaining marinade and turn. Grill or broil another 12 to 15 minutes, baste and turn. Grill or broil until skin is crisp and bird is cooked through, about 10 minutes more. To check for doneness, insert an instant-read thermometer into the thickest part of the thigh; it should read 160°F to 165°F. Drizzle with the remaining olive oil and serve with lemon wedges.

Grilled or Broiled Split Chicken with Honey and Mustard: This is delicious, but you must watch it very carefully, because the honey makes it especially susceptible to burning. Combine $1/4$ cup Dijon or other good mustard and $1/4$ cup honey; add $1/2$ teaspoon minced fresh thyme or tarragon leaves (or $1/4$ teaspoon dried). Smear the chicken with this mixture and let it sit while you prepare the fire or preheat the broiler, or up to a couple of hours, refrigerated. Steps 2 and 3 remain the same. Serve hot or at room temperature, with lemon wedges.

Tandoori Chicken: Allow a day for marinating. In a blender or food processor, combine 1 medium onion; 2 cloves garlic; a $1/2$-inch piece of peeled ginger (or 1 teaspoon ground ginger); 1 tablespoon ground cumin; 1 teaspoon ground coriander; $1/4$ teaspoon cayenne, or to taste; 1 teaspoon salt; and 1 cup plain yogurt. Blend until smooth. Marinate the chicken in this mixture, refrigerated, for 12 to 24 hours, turning occasionally. Steps 2 and 3 remain the same. Serve hot.

The Basics of Chicken Parts

This, of course, is the way almost everyone buys bone-in chicken these days. Cut into eight pieces—two legs, two thighs, two breast halves, two wings, with the back usually discarded or saved for stock—it's undeniably convenient. See page 368 for illustrations showing how to cut up a bird by yourself.

Because breasts and legs cook at different rates it sometimes makes sense to cook them separately, serving the breasts at one meal and the legs at another. But it's also nice to give people a choice, and those who eat together regularly usually find some routine in divvying up the bird. In these recipes, I usually specify whole chickens, cut up. But in recipes such as the Browned-and-Braised Chicken Parts, where the chicken is cooked with liquid, dark meat is preferable to breasts (so much so that I specify thighs in a couple of recipes), because dark meat becomes more tender and remains juicy longer when cooked with liquid, whereas breasts easily become overcooked.

In any chicken recipe, care must be taken when cooking white and dark meat together, since white meat cooks so much faster. Sometimes, the thickness of a bone-in breast compensates for the difference, and everything finishes at about the same time. You can also increase the likelihood of this by starting the legs a little before the breasts, and by keeping them in the hottest part of the pan (usually the center, if you're cooking on top of the stove). In addition, it pays to cut the legs in two, right through the joint where thigh meets lower leg (see illustrations, page 368) to help them cook more quickly. In any case, keep an eye on things and remove the breasts as soon as they're done, even if the legs have a few minutes more to go. When measured with an instant-read thermometer, breasts are done at 160°F, thighs closer to 165°F.

Browned-and-Braised Chicken Parts

Most of these are fast, flavorful, one-pot chicken dinners, with vegetables and/or grains cooked in the chicken liquid. Traditionally, such recipes begin with an initial browning of the chicken, but I consider this step optional. It takes time and energy to create a crisp skin (it also messes up the stove), but when you add liquid and cover the pan to finish the cooking, the

There are more ways to cut a chicken into eight or ten pieces than you can imagine; this one has become my favorite.

(Step 1) Cut through the breast near, rather than through, the wing joint. This serves two purposes: It's easier (you don't have to locate the exact spot of the joint) and it gives you a much meatier wing at little sacrifice to the breast. (Step 2) Hold up one of the legs by its end and slice the skin between the breast and leg; it's easy to see. (Step 3) Find the joint where the thigh meets the carcass and cut through it. (Step 4) Pop the back off the breast; the carcass will break in half quite easily. (Step 5) Cut the back away from the breast. (Make sure to save the back, wing tips, and any other scraps for stock.) (Step 6) Cut the breast in half; what's illustrated here is cutting lengthwise, but you can cut across the breast as well. You can also cut it into three or four pieces instead of two. (Step 7) Find the joint connecting the leg and thigh and cut through it if you like. (Step 8) Find the joint connecting the wing sections and cut through it if you like. Cut off the wing tips (they have virtually no meat) and reserve for stock.

skin softens again, and many people take the skin off anyway. The initial browning adds flavor; but if you're in a hurry, or you're going to do away with the skin, skip it.

For these recipes, you need a very large (at least twelve inches), deep skillet, or a Dutch oven or casserole. It's important, especially if you are browning, that all the chicken fit comfortably in one layer.

Chicken, Provençal-Style

Makes 4 servings

Time: About 40 minutes

You can add eggplant and/or zucchini to this vegetable mixture if you like, or use boneless chicken meat. Feel free, too, to substitute another herb, or a combination of herbs, for the thyme. Remove the chicken skin if you choose to skip the browning.

2 tablespoons olive oil

About 1 cup all-purpose flour for dredging

Salt and freshly ground black pepper to taste

1 (3- to 4-pound) chicken, cut up, with each leg cut
   into 2 pieces (page 368), trimmed of excess fat,
   then rinsed and patted dry with paper towels

2 medium onions, chopped

2 anchovy fillets, minced (optional)

1 teaspoon minced garlic

2 cups cored and chopped tomatoes (canned are
   fine; don't bother to drain)

1/4 teaspoon cayenne (optional)

1/2 cup dry white wine, chicken or vegetable stock,
   or water (see "Soups" for stock recipes)

1 cup Niçoise or other good black olives

1/2 teaspoon fresh thyme leaves or 1/4 teaspoon
   dried thyme

Minced fresh parsley leaves for garnish

1 Heat the oil over medium-high heat in a large, deep skillet. Put the flour on a plate or in a shallow bowl and season it with salt and pepper. When the oil is hot (a pinch of flour will sizzle), dredge the chicken pieces in the flour (thighs first, followed by drumsticks, then finally breasts and wings), shaking off any excess. As you coat the chicken pieces, add them to the oil and brown on all sides. Regulate the heat so that the oil bubbles but is not so hot that it will burn the chicken. Season the pieces with salt and pepper as they brown. (You can skip this browning step if you like, as noted above; heat the oil and go directly to cooking the onions.)

2 When the chicken is nicely browned, remove it from the skillet and turn the heat to medium. Pour or spoon off all but a tablespoon of the oil. Add the onions and anchovies; cook over medium heat until the onions soften, about 5 minutes. Add the garlic, tomatoes, and cayenne, if desired, and raise the heat slightly. Cook until some of the tomato juice bubbles away, 1 to 2 minutes. Add the wine or other liquid and cook another 2 minutes.

3 Add the olives and the thyme, along with some salt (remember that the olives are salty) and pepper. Cook 1 minute; submerge the chicken in the sauce, cover, and cook over medium-low heat, turning the pieces every 5 minutes or so, until the chicken is cooked through, 20 to 30 minutes (longer if you skipped the browning step). Garnish and serve immediately, with rice or crusty bread.

Chicken with Onions: A simpler version of the above. In Step 2, double the amount of onions and omit anchovies, garlic, tomatoes, and cayenne. Include the wine as above. In Step 3, omit the olives but use the thyme. Proceed as above.

Chicken with Rice (Arroz con Pollo): In Step 2, cook the onions without anchovies as above; when they're soft, add 1 tablespoon minced garlic and 2 cups long-grain white rice; cook, stirring, until the rice is coated with oil. Omit tomatoes, cayenne, wine, olives, and thyme. Return the chicken to the pan with some salt and pepper. With the heat on medium, add 4 cups liquid—chicken, meat, or vegetable stock, or water, or a combination—and stir gently. Cover the pan, reduce the heat to medium-low, and cook, lowering the heat as necessary to maintain a very gentle simmer. Cook until all the water is absorbed and the chicken is cooked through, about 30 minutes. Adjust the seasonings as necessary, garnish, and serve.

Chicken in Red Wine Sauce

Makes 4 servings

Time: About 40 minutes

Dried porcini, red wine, and tomatoes make this classic, dark-sauced dish, sometimes called *coq au vin.*

1 ounce dried porcini mushrooms

2 tablespoons olive oil

About 1 cup all-purpose flour for dredging

Salt and freshly ground black pepper to taste

1 whole (3- to 4-pound) chicken, cut up, with each leg
    cut into two pieces (page 368), trimmed of excess
    fat, then rinsed and patted dry with paper towels

2 tablespoons butter, or more olive oil

1/2 pound white button mushrooms, trimmed
    and sliced

2 medium onions, chopped

1 teaspoon minced garlic

Salt and freshly ground black pepper to taste

1 sprig fresh thyme or 1/2 teaspoon dried thyme

1 bay leaf

1 cup dry red wine

1/4 cup minced fresh parsley leaves, plus more
    for garnish

1   Soak 1 ounce dried porcini mushrooms in hot water to cover while you proceed with the recipe.

2   Heat the oil over medium-high heat in a large, deep skillet, Dutch oven, or casserole. Put the flour on a plate or in a shallow bowl and season it with salt and pepper. When the oil is hot (a pinch of flour will sizzle), dredge the chicken pieces in the flour (thighs first, followed by drumsticks, then finally breasts and wings), shaking off any excess. As you coat the pieces, add them to the oil and brown on all sides. Regulate the heat so that the oil bubbles but is not so hot that it will burn the chicken. (You can skip this browning step if you like, as noted above; heat the oil and go directly to cooking the mushrooms.)

3   When the chicken is nicely browned, remove it from the skillet and turn the heat to medium. Pour off all the fat and add the butter or additional oil. A minute later, add the white mushrooms.

4   Cook, stirring, until the mushrooms begin to darken, about 5 minutes. Drain the porcini and reserve their liquid. Chop the mushrooms and add

them and a little of their liquid (pour carefully, or strain it first if it is gritty), along with the onions, garlic, salt, pepper, and thyme. Cook until the onions soften, about 5 minutes.

5   Add the bay leaf, wine, parsley, the remaining mushroom soaking liquid, and the chicken. Cover, turn the heat to low, and cook, turning the pieces every 5 minutes or so, until the chicken is cooked through, 20 to 30 minutes (longer if you skipped the browning step). Remove the cover. If the sauce is too watery, raise the heat to high and cook, stirring and scraping the bottom of the pan, until the liquid is reduced slightly. Adjust the seasoning if necessary, then garnish and serve.

Chicken with Indian Spices and Yogurt

Makes 4 servings

Time: About 45 minutes

4 tablespoons peanut or canola or other oil

About 1 cup all-purpose flour for dredging

Salt and freshly ground black pepper to taste

1 whole (3- to 4-pound) chicken, cut up (legs cut in
    two), trimmed of excess fat, then rinsed and patted
    dry with paper towels

2 medium onions, chopped

1 tablespoon minced garlic

1 tablespoon peeled and grated fresh ginger
    or 1 teaspoon ground ginger

1/2 teaspoon cayenne, or to taste

1 teaspoon ground cumin

1 teaspoon ground coriander

1 teaspoon ground cardamom

1/2 teaspoon ground turmeric

1/2 teaspoon ground cinnamon

2 cups plain yogurt

Minced cilantro leaves for garnish

1 Heat the oil over medium-high heat in a large, deep skillet, Dutch oven, or casserole. Put the flour on a plate or in a shallow bowl and season it with salt and pepper. When the oil is hot (a pinch of flour will sizzle), dredge the chicken pieces in the flour (thighs first, followed by drumsticks, then finally breasts and wings), shaking off any excess. As you coat the pieces, add them to the oil and brown on all sides. Regulate the heat so that the oil bubbles but is not so hot that it will burn the chicken. (You can skip this browning step if you like, as noted above; heat the oil and go directly to cooking the onions.)

2 When the chicken is nicely browned, remove it from the skillet and pour off all but a couple of table-spoons of the oil. Turn the heat to medium and add the onions, along with some salt and pepper. Cook, stirring, until they soften, about 5 minutes.

3 Add the garlic, ginger, and spices, along with an additional $1/2$ teaspoon of pepper. Cook with the onions, stirring, until very aromatic, 2 or 3 minutes. Stir in the yogurt, then add the chicken pieces. Cover and cook over medium-low heat, turning the pieces every 5 minutes or so, until the chicken is cooked through, 20 to 30 minutes (longer if you skipped the browning step).

4 Taste and adjust seasoning as needed. Garnish and serve.

Chicken with Clams

Makes 4 servings

Time: About 1 hour

An East-West dish that has become a classic since the first time I ate it, about twenty years ago. The clams add a delicious brininess to the braised chicken, so take it easy on the salt.

2 tablespoons olive oil

About 1 cup all-purpose flour for dredging

Salt and freshly ground black pepper to taste

1 whole (3- to 4-pound) chicken, cut up (legs cut in two), trimmed of excess fat, then rinsed and patted dry with paper towels

1 teaspoon minced garlic

1 medium carrot, peeled and diced

$1/2$ cup dry white wine or water

1 tablespoon peeled and minced fresh ginger, plus a little more for garnish

2 dozen littleneck clams, rinsed in several changes of water until water runs clear and drained (see The Basics of Clams, page 342)

$1/2$ cup minced scallions

1 Heat the oil over medium-high heat in a large, deep skillet, Dutch oven, or casserole. Put the flour on a plate or in a shallow bowl and season it with salt and pepper. When the oil is hot (a pinch of flour will sizzle), dredge the chicken pieces in the flour (thighs first, followed by drumsticks, then finally breasts and wings), shaking off any excess. As you coat the pieces, add them to the oil and brown on all sides. Regulate the heat so that the oil bubbles but is not so hot that it will burn the chicken. (You can skip this browning step if you like, as noted above; heat the oil and go directly to cooking the garlic and carrot.)

2 When the chicken is nicely browned, remove it from the skillet and turn the heat to medium. Pour or spoon off all but a couple of tablespoons of the oil. Add the garlic and carrot and cook, stirring, for about 5 minutes. Add the wine or water, 1 tablespoon ginger, and chicken. Season all with pepper, but hold off on additional salt because the clams are salty.

3 Cover, turn the heat to low, and cook, turning the pieces every 5 minutes or so, until the chicken is almost cooked through, 15 to 20 minutes (longer if you skipped the browning step). When the chicken is

almost done, add the clams. Re-cover and raise the heat to medium.

4 Cook until the clams open, about 10 minutes. Taste and adjust seasoning, then garnish with the scallions and remaining ginger and serve.

Chicken and Garlic Stew

Makes 4 servings

Time: About 1¼ hours, largely unattended

This is the now-classic "chicken with forty cloves of garlic." If you've never eaten stewed garlic, get ready for a treat: It's soft and mild-flavored. Note that it's not essential to peel the garlic; in fact, the skins keep the cloves intact. They are easily peeled with a knife and fork (or fingers) at the table. If you like, remove the chicken skin before you start cooking.

1 whole (3- to 4-pound) chicken, cut up (legs cut in
    two), trimmed of excess fat, then rinsed and patted
    dry with paper towels
2 tablespoons extra-virgin olive oil
At least 2 heads garlic, separated into cloves but
    not peeled
½ cup minced fresh parsley leaves, plus more for
    garnish
Salt and freshly ground black pepper to taste
½ teaspoon ground cinnamon or ¼ teaspoon
    ground allspice
½ cup white wine, chicken, meat, or vegetable stock,
    or water (see "Soups" for stock recipes)

1 Place the chicken, olive oil, garlic, parsley, salt, pepper, and cinnamon or allspice in the bottom of a large saucepan, casserole, or Dutch oven. Pour the liquid over all and mix together.

2 Turn the heat to medium-high and bring to a boil. Cover tightly and reduce the heat to low. Cook, undisturbed, for about an hour, until the chicken and garlic are very tender. Transfer to a deep platter, garnish with parsley, and serve, spreading the softened garlic cloves onto good crusty bread.

Chicken Thighs with Soy Sauce and Lemon

Makes 4 servings

Time: 30 to 40 minutes

This is a quick, easy, fresh-tasting dish that makes plenty of light sauce for plain white rice.

1 tablespoon peanut or other oil
2 pounds bone-in chicken thighs or mixed chicken
    parts, rinsed and patted dry with paper towels
1 teaspoon minced garlic
1 tablespoon minced or grated lemon zest
¼ teaspoon cayenne, or to taste
2 tablespoons soy sauce
1 teaspoon sugar
⅓ cup water
Juice of 1 lemon

1 Heat a large, deep skillet, preferably non-stick, over medium-high heat for 2 or 3 minutes. Add the oil to the skillet, swirl, and add the chicken. Brown quickly on both sides.

2 Turn off the heat and remove the chicken and all but 1 tablespoon of fat from the skillet. Let the pan cool for a minute or so, then turn the heat to medium and add the garlic. Cook, stirring, until it softens, a minute or two.

3 Add the remaining ingredients except for the lemon juice; stir. Return the chicken to the skillet and turn it once or twice in the liquid. Cover, reduce the heat to medium-low, and simmer, turning once or twice, until the chicken is done, 20 to 30 minutes.

(Step 1) To cut the leg-thigh piece in two, simply find the joint where they meet and cut through it with a sharp knife. You'll know when you've found it because the knife will not hit bone. (Step 2) To bone the thigh, cut the meat away from the thick center bone on the meat (non-skin) side. (Step 3) Continue to cut until the bone is nearly free. (Step 4) Cut the bone from the remaining meat and remove the skin.

④ Remove the chicken to a serving platter and stir the lemon juice into the broth. Pour some of the broth over the chicken and pass the rest at the table.

Chicken Thighs with Tomatoes and Olives

Makes 4 servings

Time: About 45 minutes

A simple Provençal-style dish. Use good quality oil-cured olives if possible.

1 tablespoon olive oil
2 pounds bone-in chicken thighs or mixed chicken parts, rinsed and patted dry with paper towels
1 cup chopped onion
1 teaspoon minced garlic
2 cups cored and chopped tomatoes (canned are fine; don't bother to drain)
½ cup dry white wine, chicken or vegetable stock, or water (see "Soups" for stock recipes)
1 cup small black olives, pitted
¼ cup minced fresh basil leaves, plus more for garnish
1 sprig fresh thyme or ½ teaspoon dried thyme
Salt and freshly ground black pepper to taste

① Heat a large skillet, preferably non-stick, over medium-high heat for 2 or 3 minutes. Add the oil to the skillet, swirl, and add the chicken. Brown the chicken thighs quickly on both sides.

② Remove the chicken, along with all but about 2 tablespoons of the fat. Turn the heat to medium and add the onion. Cook, stirring, about 5 minutes. Add the garlic and tomatoes. Raise the heat to medium-high and cook, stirring occasionally, until some of the tomato juice bubbles away, about 5 minutes. Add the wine, stock, or water and cook, stirring occasionally, another 5 minutes. Add the olives, basil, thyme, salt, and pepper. Cook 1 minute.

③ Return the chicken to the skillet and turn it once or twice in the liquid. Cover, reduce the heat to medium-low, and simmer, turning once or twice, until the chicken is done, 20 to 30 minutes.

④ Garnish and serve with crusty bread.

Roast Chicken Parts

Roast chicken parts do not make for the same striking presentation as a whole roast chicken but they do cook considerably faster. There's another advantage: More of the seasoning comes into direct contact with the chicken. This means that all seasonings—whether subtle or strong—have more impact.

Roast Chicken Parts with Herbs and Olive Oil

Makes 4 to 6 servings

Time: 40 minutes

You can use almost any mild green herb here, from parsley, basil, dill, or mint to more obscure herbs such as summer savory or burnet.

> ¹/₄ cup extra-virgin olive oil or butter
> 1 whole (3- to 4-pound) chicken, cut up (legs cut in two), trimmed of excess fat, then rinsed and patted dry with paper towels
> Salt and freshly ground black pepper to taste
> ¹/₂ cup any mild green herb or a combination of herbs

1 Preheat the oven to 450°F. When it is hot, put 1 tablespoon of the oil or butter in a roasting pan and place it in the oven—leave it there for about 1 minute, or until the oil is hot or the butter melts.

2 Add the chicken, skin side up, season with salt and pepper, and return the pan to the oven. Combine the herb and the remaining butter in the container of a small food processor and blend, or mince the herb and mix it with the oil or butter in a bowl.

3 After the chicken has cooked 15 minutes, spread about one quarter of the herb mixture over it, turn, add another quarter of the mixture, and roast another 10 minutes. Turn the chicken over again (now skin side up) and add another quarter of the herb mixture.

4 Cook until the chicken is done (you'll see clear juices if you make a small cut in the meat near the bone), a total of 30 to 40 minutes. Drizzle or spread with the remaining herb mixture and serve.

Roast Chicken Parts with Asian Seasonings: First, soak 2 tablespoons fermented black beans in water, sherry, or wine to cover. Step 1 remains the same (use peanut or other oil). In Step 2, mix together 1 tablespoon minced garlic, 2 minced scallions, 1 teaspoon peeled and minced fresh ginger, 2 tablespoons soy sauce, and 1 teaspoon sugar or honey. Drain the black beans and add them to this mixture; thin it to a paste, if necessary, with a little more soy sauce. Spread a little of this mixture all over the chicken and place the chicken in the roasting pan; return the pan to the oven. Proceed with Steps 3 and 4, using the soy-based mixture for basting in place of the herb mixture.

Four Simple Ideas for Roast Chicken Parts

Use any of these flavorings with the above recipe, or see Four Simple Ways to Flavor Roast Chicken, page 361:

1. Any compound butter, pages 768–770
2. Any flavored oil, pages 774–775
3. Any vinaigrette, pages 91–94
4. Basic Pesto (page 766), or other herb pastes

Broiled or Grilled Chicken Parts

As explained in The Basics of Grilling and Broiling on page 10, broiling and grilling have much in common. But although grilling has been all the rage for the past decade or so, broiling makes much more sense in all but the hottest weather. It's easier to adjust the distance from heat source to food with a broiler than with a grill, which means it's easier to limit flare-ups. This is especially true with chicken, which must cook for a while; as everyone who's tried grilling chicken knows, long grilling times give the fat plenty of opportunity to drip onto flames and set itself on fire.

If you're careful and attentive, however—which means not trying to do two or three other dishes that require steady attention—grilled chicken is not that challenging. And almost all grilled or broiled chicken dishes (the exceptions are those that contain butter) are as good at room temperature as they are hot, which means you can cook them at your leisure.

The easiest way to grill chicken is to start it off over relatively low, indirect heat. If you have a gas grill, turn the burners to high, and let the grill heat to 400°F or so. Then turn off one of the burners, place the chicken over this cooler part, and close the top of the grill. Walk away for ten or fifteen minutes, then turn the chicken; ignore it for a few minutes more. At this point, it will be partly cooked, some of the fat will have been rendered, and you can turn the heat up and brown the chicken for the last few minutes of cooking. You'll still have to keep an eye on the chicken, but you'll have minimized the likelihood of flare-ups and your attention can be minimized. (This is one of the great uses of a gas grill.)

You can follow the same procedure with a charcoal grill, as long as it has a cover: Build a fire as usual. When it's hot, bank the coals to one side of the grill and cook the chicken on the other side, exactly as described in the previous paragraph. After twenty to thirty minutes, spread out the coals and finish cooking the chicken over direct heat.

Of course you can also grill chicken over direct heat in an uncovered grill, whether wood, hardwood charcoal, briquettes, or gas. Don't build too hot a fire, and keep part of the grill cool—don't put any fuel under it at all—so you can move the pieces over to it should any of them cause flare-ups.

Broiled or Grilled Chicken with Pesto

Makes 4 servings

Time: 20 minutes, plus time to preheat the grill

This basic recipe begins with pesto. But as you can see, it is almost infinitely variable. I give a few options here, but you can broil or grill chicken with almost any compound butter (pages 768–770) or flavored oil

(page 774–775), or many of the other sauces in "Sauces, Salsas, and Spice Mixtures"; in my opinion, those that are based on olive oil or soy sauce are best.

> 1/2 to 1 cup Basic Pesto (page 766)
> 1 whole (3- to 4-pound) chicken, cut up (legs cut in
> two), trimmed of excess fat, then rinsed and patted
> dry with paper towels
> Salt and freshly ground black pepper to taste
> Lemon wedges

1 Start a charcoal or wood fire or preheat a gas grill or broiler. The fire should not be too hot, and the rack should be at least 6 inches from the heat source.

2 If you're broiling, spread a tablespoon or so of the pesto on a non-stick broiling or baking pan; place the chicken pieces on top and sprinkle them with salt and pepper. Spread a little more of the pesto on the chicken. If you're grilling, spread some of the pesto all over the chicken.

3 Broil or grill the chicken, turning and basting frequently with the pesto, until nicely browned all over and cooked through (the juices will run clear if you make a small cut in the meat near the bone), 20 to 30 minutes. Brush once more with the pesto and serve hot or at room temperature (refrigerate if you will not be serving it within the hour), with lemon wedges.

Broiled or Grilled Chicken with Mustard: Instead of the pesto, combine 1/2 cup good quality Dijon or coarse-grained mustard, 1 tablespoon freshly squeezed lemon juice, and salt and pepper to taste. If you're broiling, spread a tablespoon or so of olive oil on a baking sheet or broiling pan; if you're grilling, rub the chicken with some of the mustard mixture. In Step 3, baste with the mustard mixture. If you like, sprinkle some bread crumbs over the chicken during the final 2 or 3 minutes of broiling, taking care not to let them burn.

Broiled or Grilled Chicken with Lemon and Herbs:
This has the advantage of using no added fat. Omit the pesto. Loosen the skin of each piece of chicken (use a paring knife if necessary to separate skin from meat) and insert a bit of fresh herb—a leaf of sage, tarragon, or basil, or a few pieces of rosemary, chervil, or thyme—between the skin and the meat. Rub the chicken all over with freshly squeezed lemon juice and sprinkle it liberally with salt and pepper to taste. Cook as in Step 3, brushing with more lemon juice from time to time. Garnish with minced fresh herbs and serve with lemon wedges.

Broiled or Grilled Chicken with Cilantro and Lime:
Instead of the pesto, whisk together 3 tablespoons of peanut or other oil, 2 tablespoons minced cilantro leaves, 1 tablespoon freshly squeezed lime juice, 1 tablespoon minced shallot, $1/4$ teaspoon cayenne (or to taste), and salt and pepper to taste. Smear a little oil on a baking sheet and spread about a third of the cilantro mixture on the chicken. Cook as in Step 3, basting the chicken occasionally with the cilantro mixture. When the chicken is done, drizzle it with the remaining mixture and garnish with additional minced cilantro; serve with lime wedges.

Broiled or Grilled Chicken with Soy and Ginger:
Instead of the pesto, whisk together $1/4$ cup soy sauce, 1 tablespoon dark sesame oil, $1^1/2$ teaspoons rice or other light vinegar, $1/2$ teaspoon minced garlic, and 1 tablespoon peeled and grated fresh ginger (or 1 teaspoon ground ginger). Smear a little oil on a baking sheet and spoon about a third of the soy mixture on the chicken. Cook as in Step 3, basting

Twenty-Five Chicken Dishes Good Cold or at Room Temperature

Whether left-over or prepared in advance, many simple chicken dishes are great at room temperature or straight from the fridge. Some personal favorites:

1. Simple Roast Chicken, page 358
2. Chicken Under a Brick, page 365
3. Grilled or Broiled Split Chicken, page 366
4. Tandoori Chicken, page 367
5. Broiled or Grilled Chicken with Pesto, page 375
6. Broiled or Grilled Chicken with Mustard, page 375
7. Broiled or Grilled Chicken with Lemon and Herbs, page 376
8. Fried Chicken, page 378
9. Chili-Spiced Fried Chicken, page 378
10. Fried Chicken with Bay Leaves, page 378
11. Basic Grilled or Broiled Chicken Cutlets, page 380
12. Grilled or Broiled Chicken Cutlets with Honey and Cumin, page 380
13. Grilled or Broiled Chicken Cutlets with Cracked Pepper, page 381
14. Grilled or Broiled Chicken Cutlets with Mixed Spices, page 381
15. Fried Chicken Breasts, page 386
16. Basic Sautéed Chicken Cutlets, page 388
17. Chicken Cutlets with Seasoned Bread Crumbs, page 388
18. Extra-Crisp Chicken Cutlets, page 388
19. Spice-Coated Chicken Cutlets, page 388
20. Herbed Chicken Cutlets, page 389
21. Sesame-Coated Chicken Cutlets, page 389
22. Herb-Roasted Chicken Cutlets, page 393
23. Spicy Chicken Thigh Kebabs, page 397
24. Chicken Thigh Kebabs with Gentle Spices, page 398
25. Chicken Satay, page 399

the chicken occasionally with the soy mixture. When the chicken is done, drizzle it with the remaining mixture and garnish with 1 tablespoon sesame seeds that have been toasted until brown in the oven (5 to 10 minutes at 350°F), in a dry sauté pan (3 to 4 minutes, shaking the pan, over medium heat), or in a microwave (1 minute at high power; stir and cooking for 1 more minute if necessary).

Broiled or Grilled Chicken with Citrus Sauce: Instead of the pesto, combine the zest and juice of a lemon with the sections of another lemon (see page 634); the sections of an orange; and the sections of a grapefruit. Add $1/4$ cup olive oil, 1 teaspoon fresh thyme leaves (or $1/2$ teaspoon dried thyme), $1/2$ teaspoon minced garlic, 1 small onion, minced, and salt and pepper to taste. Warm gently, then broil or grill the chicken as in Step 3, using just a little olive oil to lubricate the pan and/or chicken as it cooks. Serve the chicken with the Citrus Sauce.

Chicken Adobo

Makes 4 servings

Time: About $1^1/4$ hours, plus time to preheat the grill

This Philippine classic has been called the best chicken dish in the world by a number of friends of mine. Like the Poached and Roasted Chicken with Soy Sauce on page 363, it is cooked in liquid first, then roasted. Here, however, the initial poaching sauce is reduced to become a sauce to pass at the table for both the chicken and white rice, the natural accompaniment to this dish.

You can make Chicken Adobo in two steps, first poaching and then broiling or grilling, refrigerating the chicken and the sauce in between. If you do this, skim the fat from the sauce before reheating.

1 cup soy sauce

$1/2$ cup white or rice vinegar

1 cup water

1 tablespoon chopped garlic

2 bay leaves

$1/2$ teaspoon freshly ground black pepper

1 whole (3- to 4-pound) chicken, cut up (legs cut in two), trimmed of excess fat, then rinsed and patted dry with paper towels; or use 2 pounds bone-in thighs

1 Combine the first six ingredients in a covered pot large enough to hold the chicken in one layer. Bring to a boil over high heat. Add the chicken; reduce the heat to medium-low and cook, covered, for about 30 minutes, turning once or twice. (You may prepare the recipe in advance up to this point; refrigerate the chicken, in the liquid, for up to a day before proceeding.)

2 Start a charcoal or wood fire or preheat a gas grill or broiler. The fire need not be too hot, but place the rack just 3 or 4 inches from the heat source.

3 Remove the chicken and dry it gently with paper towels. Boil the sauce over high heat until it is reduced to about 1 cup; discard bay leaves and keep the sauce warm. Meanwhile, grill or broil the chicken until brown and crisp, about 5 minutes per side. Serve the chicken with the sauce and white rice.

Fried Chicken Parts

Fried chicken isn't difficult, but it can be messy. I make two adjustments to make it a little less so: One, I use a minimum of oil (which still seems like a lot by today's standards). And two, I cover the skillet for the first few minutes, which reduces spattering substantially. Then I uncover the chicken to make sure it doesn't steam in its own juices, which would defeat the point of frying—namely, a super-crisp skin and moist interior.

There is a myth that olive oil is not good for frying; on the contrary, it adds a delicious flavor to most savory fried foods. Peanut oil is also great, as is lard, or a mixture of lard and butter. If cost is an issue, however, use the least expensive vegetable oil you can find, such as soy or canola; as long as the oil is clean its flavor will be neutral. You can re-use frying oil, too; cool and strain it after frying, then refrigerate in a covered container. Use it for frying (it's best to stick with the same or similar foods, because the oil will be flavored by its previous use) or for stir-frying or sautéing.

Chicken should be fried at about 350°F, but slightly higher temperatures, up to 375°F, will do no harm. Use a frying thermometer for accuracy; too-low temperatures will result in soggy chicken. As with any fried foods (see The Basics of Deep-Frying, page 13), the temperature will plunge as soon as you begin to add the chicken, so keep the heat as high as possible at first to enable the temperature to recover as quickly as possible. Don't crowd, either; if the chicken pieces touch each other, they won't brown at all.

Fried Chicken

Makes 4 to 6 servings

Time: About 30 minutes

Like all good fried chicken dishes, this one is fine at room temperature.

> Olive oil, peanut oil, lard, vegetable oil, or a
>   combination for frying
> 2 cups all-purpose flour
> 1 tablespoon coarse salt
> 1 teaspoon freshly ground black pepper
> 2 tablespoons ground cinnamon
> 1 whole (3- to 4-pound) chicken, cut up, trimmed of
>   excess fat, then rinsed and patted dry with paper
>   towels
> Lemon wedges (optional)

1 Heat about $1/2$ inch of the fat over medium-high heat in a deep-fryer, large, deep skillet, or broad saucepan that can later be covered. While it is heating, mix together the flour and seasonings in a plastic bag. Toss the chicken in the bag, 2 or 3 pieces at a time, until they are well coated with flour. Put them on a rack as you finish.

2 When the fat reaches 350°F, raise the heat to high and begin to slowly but steadily add the chicken pieces, skin side down, to the skillet (if you add them all at once, the temperature will plummet). When they have all been added, cover the skillet, reduce the heat to medium-high, and set a timer for 7 minutes. After 7 minutes, uncover the skillet, turn the chicken, and continue to cook, uncovered, for another 7 minutes.

3 Turn the chicken skin side down again and cook for about 5 minutes more, turning as necessary to ensure that both sides are golden brown.

4 As the chicken pieces finish cooking (the juices near the bone will run clear), remove them from the skillet and drain them on paper towels. Serve hot, warm, or at room temperature with lemon wedges, if desired.

Chili-Spiced Fried Chicken: Use peanut or vegetable oil. Season the flour with 2 tablespoons each chili powder and ground cumin, 2 teaspoons ground turmeric, $1/2$ teaspoon cayenne (optional), and salt and pepper; omit cinnamon. Proceed as above. Serve with lime wedges.

Fried Chicken with Bay Leaves: Use olive oil and heat it with 5 bay leaves; omit cinnamon. When the bay leaves begin to sizzle, toss a peeled garlic clove into the oil. Cook, moving the bay leaves and garlic around in the oil, for 3 to 5 minutes, until the garlic clove begins to brown. Remove the garlic and the bay leaves. Proceed as above. Serve with lemon wedges.

The Basics of Boneless Chicken Breasts

Boneless chicken breasts have become standard weeknight fare for many Americans—just think how often you visit a friend and see a package defrosting on the kitchen counter (although defrosting overnight in the refrigerator is safer). And no wonder: They can be cooked in minutes using any of a number of techniques: on top of the stove in a skillet or wok (they're ideal for stir-fries), on a grill, under a broiler, or in the oven. They can be cooked with little or no added fat. And they can take almost any seasoning. If there is a problem with them, it is that care must be taken not to overcook them or they will become tough and dry as jerky.

So use bold flavorings, marinate if there's time, and keep the cooking time very short, as little as six minutes for one-half-inch-thick boneless breasts. Generally, it's best to remove them from the heat when the inside is still a little pearly, rather than chalky-white. (It's not easy to use an instant-read thermometer on thin boneless breasts, but you can get an accurate reading by sliding the probe in from the end, rather than the top, and inserting it into the middle; breasts are done at 160°F.)

Note that you can easily make your own chicken cutlets by buying whole breasts, or whole chicken, and removing the meat (see below). It doesn't take long, especially once you get good at it, it leaves you with terrific bones for stock, and it's considerably cheaper. But, of course, it is not nearly as convenient as buying the breasts already boned and cut up, which is often the whole idea.

Grilled or Broiled Chicken Cutlets

You don't have to build a killer fire, or preheat your broiler for half an hour to cook chicken cutlets. But you should grill or broil them fairly close to the heat source, which will enable you to brown the outside of the chicken before the inside dries out and toughens.

Any of these recipes can be used for turkey cutlets as well as for chicken—or, for that matter, veal cutlets or thin-sliced pork. Most of them (especially those that add strong flavors) are also great with boneless thighs. You'll have to increase the cooking time somewhat, to around 6 to 8 minutes per side.

BONING CHICKEN BREAST

| 1 | 2 | 3 |

(Step 1) Use a sharp, thin-bladed knife (usually called a boning knife) and cut as close to the bone as you can on the breastbone (not rib) side. (Step 2) Continue to cut the meat away from the bone, keeping the knife blade just about parallel to the bone. (Step 3) When the meat is almost detached, make the final cut. Trim the boneless breast of any pieces of tendon and, if you like, remove the skin.

A note about terms A "chicken breast" is the whole breast, two sides joined by a breastbone. Thus a whole breast, boned and cut in half, produces two "fillets" or "cutlets," which can be made even thinner by slicing the cutlets in half.

Basic Grilled or Broiled Chicken Cutlets

Makes 4 servings

Time: 20 minutes, plus time to preheat the grill

Soy sauce makes a great non-fat basting liquid. If you prefer olive oil—which keeps the meat moister—see the first variation.

4 boneless, skinless chicken cutlets (2 breasts), 1 to
   1 1/2 pounds, rinsed and patted dry with paper towels
2 tablespoons soy sauce
Freshly ground black pepper to taste
1 tablespoon freshly squeezed lime juice
1 teaspoon dark sesame oil (optional)

1 Start a charcoal or wood fire or preheat a gas grill or broiler. The fire should not be too hot, but the rack should be fairly close to the heat source, 4 inches or less. If necessary, you can pound the chicken slices lightly between two pieces of waxed paper so that they are of uniform thickness.

2 Brush the chicken pieces with the soy sauce and sprinkle it with pepper. If you have time, let the chicken marinate in the refrigerator for 1 hour or more.

3 Grill or broil the chicken very quickly; it should take no more than 3 or 4 minutes per side. Sprinkle with lime juice and sesame oil; serve hot or at room temperature.

Grilled or Broiled Chicken Cutlets with Olive Oil:
Substitute olive oil for the soy sauce and freshly squeezed lemon juice for the lime juice. Season with salt as well as pepper. Omit the sesame oil.

Grilled or Broiled Chicken Cutlets with Honey and Cumin: Great on a bed of Cold Cooked Greens, Greek Style (page 97). In Step 2, rub the chicken breasts with 1 tablespoon olive oil (omit the soy sauce). Combine 2 tablespoons honey, 1 tablespoon dry sherry, white wine, freshly squeezed orange juice, or water, 1 tablespoon ground cumin, 1/2 teaspoon minced garlic, and salt and pepper to taste. Grill or broil the chicken as in Step 3, brushing once or twice with the honey-cumin mixture (omit the lime juice).

Grilled or Broiled Chicken Cutlets in Sweet Soy Marinade ("Chicken Teriyaki"): In Step 2, immerse the chicken in a combination of 1 teaspoon dark sesame oil, 1/4 cup soy sauce, 1 tablespoon peeled and finely minced or grated fresh ginger, 1/4 cup minced scallion, both green and white parts, 1 teaspoon minced garlic, 1 tablespoon dry sherry, white wine, or water, and 1 tablespoon honey or sugar. (Marinate in refrigerator for 1 hour, if possible.) Remove the chicken from the marinade and boil the marinade for 1 minute. Grill or broil the chicken as in Step 3, brushing frequently with the marinade (omit the lime juice). Garnish with more minced scallion and serve.

Grilled or Broiled Chicken Cutlets with Basil and Tomato: In Step 2, immerse the chicken breasts in a combination of 1 tablespoon olive oil, 1/2 cup chopped fresh basil leaves, 2 tablespoons freshly squeezed lemon juice, and salt and pepper to taste. While the grill is preheating, cut a ripe medium tomato (peeled and seeded if you like, page 609) into little cubes, about 1/4 inch on each side. Remove the chicken from the marinade and boil the marinade for 1 minute. Grill or broil the chicken as in Step 3, brushing frequently with the marinade. Serve, garnished with the tomato cubes, some minced basil, and a drizzle of olive oil.

Grilled or Broiled Chicken Cutlets with Ginger and Cilantro: A very low-fat recipe. In Step 2, combine 1 tablespoon olive oil, the juice of 1 lime, $1/2$ teaspoon minced garlic, 3 tablespoons minced cilantro leaves, 1 tablespoon peeled and minced fresh ginger, and salt and pepper to taste. Marinate if you have time, and grill or broil the chicken as in Step 3. Garnish with more minced cilantro and serve with lime wedges.

Grilled or Broiled Chicken Cutlets with Capers and Tomatoes: This recipe works well with thighs. In Step 2, rub the chicken breasts with 1 tablespoon olive oil. While the grill is preheating, heat 2 additional tablespoons of olive oil in a medium-to-large skillet over medium heat. Add 1 tablespoon minced garlic and cook, stirring, until it colors lightly. Add 2 tablespoons capers and cook for 15 seconds. Add 2 cups cored and chopped fresh or drained canned tomatoes and cook over medium-high heat until thick, about 10 minutes. Taste and add salt and pepper to taste, then cook 1 minute more. Keep warm while you grill or broil the chicken as in Step 3. Serve the chicken with the tomato sauce, garnished with minced fresh basil or parsley leaves.

Grilled or Broiled Chicken Cutlets with Cracked Pepper: Very low in fat. In Step 2, rub the chicken all over with a mixture of 2 tablespoons cracked or ground pepper (or use half pepper and half coriander seeds, a terrific combination); 1 tablespoon minced garlic; and 1 teaspoon coarse salt. Grill or broil the chicken as in Step 3. Garnish with minced fresh parsley or cilantro leaves and serve with lime wedges.

Grilled or Broiled Chicken Cutlets with Mixed Spices: Another low-fat, high-taste recipe. In Step 2, rub the chicken all over with a mixture of 1 tablespoon ground cumin, 1 teaspoon ground allspice, 1 teaspoon ground ginger, $1/2$ teaspoon ground cinnamon, $1/4$ teaspoon cayenne, and $1/8$ teaspoon freshly grated nutmeg. Or simply rub it with 2 tablespoons curry powder, five-spice powder, or any other spice mixture (pages 777–779). Grill or broil the chicken as in Step 3. Garnish with minced fresh parsley or cilantro leaves and serve with lime wedges.

Grilled or Broiled Chicken Cutlets with Herb Marinade: In Step 2, combine 1 tablespoon olive oil (using a blender or food processor) with 2 to 4 tablespoons mixed fresh herbs—parsley and chervil, basil, dill, tarragon, whatever you have on hand—and a clove of garlic. Immerse the chicken in this mixture while the grill is heating (an hour or so marinating time will do some good here, but it isn't necessary). Remove the chicken from the marinade and boil the marinade for 1 minute. Grill or broil the chicken as in Step 3, brushing frequently with the marinade. Garnish with more minced herbs and serve.

Grilled or Broiled Chicken Cutlets with Horseradish Sauce

Makes 4 servings

Time: 20 minutes if eaten immediately or up to 6 hours if marinated, plus time to preheat the grill

This is an escabeche-like dish, meaning that the meat is first cooked, then marinated. You can let it sit for a while, or eat it soon after you finish cooking.

4 boneless, skinless chicken cutlets (2 breasts), 1 to
    1 1/2 pounds, rinsed and patted dry with paper towels

1 tablespoon peanut or other oil

1 clove garlic, cut in half

Salt and freshly ground black pepper to taste

1/2 cup rice or other mild vinegar

2 tablespoons mirin (sweet rice wine; available in
    Asian markets) or 1 tablespoon honey mixed with
    1 tablespoon water

2 tablespoons soy sauce

1 tablespoon peeled and minced fresh ginger

1/2 to 1 teaspoon wasabi powder or 1 tablespoon
    prepared horseradish

1/4 cup minced scallion (green and white parts)

1 Start a charcoal or wood fire or preheat a gas grill or broiler; the rack should be as close to the heat source as possible. Rub the chicken with the oil, then with the cut sides of the garlic. Season with salt and pepper.

2 Grill or broil the chicken very quickly; about 3 to 4 minutes per side.

3 Remove the chicken and place it on a serving platter. Combine the remaining ingredients except the scallions in a small saucepan and simmer over medium-low heat for about 2 minutes. Pour this mixture over the chicken. Serve immediately or refrigerate for 1 to 6 hours. Serve cold or at room temperature, garnished with scallions.

Stir-Fried Chicken Breasts

In addition to the usual reasons for favoring chicken— it's cheap, easy-to-find, easy to handle, and low in fat—chicken breasts are ideal for stir-fries. You can cut the chicken in satisfyingly chewy chunks or slices and their pale color and mild flavor combine to showcase all but the lightest sauce beautifully.

As with other stir-fries (for general information about ingredients and techniques, see page 12),

certain adjustments must be made for the relative lack of power generated by home stoves. In restaurants, huge flames under deep woks allow cooks to sear meat and vegetables together. If you try that at home, you won't get much browning at all; the amount of food will overwhelm the heat your stove generates, and you'll end up braising rather than browning. To compensate, I sometimes parboil the vegetables, and I always stir-fry in batches, usually vegetables and meat or other protein separately, with some seasonings added during each batch. It's a little slower than would be ideal, but it still usually amounts to less than fifteen minutes in front of the stove.

Stir-frying is more of a series of techniques than a series of recipes. All the parts are interchangeable— protein, vegetables, and seasonings—so once you get the hang of it you can improvise more freely than with any other type of cooking.

All this is a long way of saying "substitute at will." For the chicken, any meat or meat substitute: boneless chicken thighs; slices of boneless pork or beef; shrimp, scallops, or other seafood; or frozen and/or pressed tofu are all brilliant in most of these recipes. For the seasonings, whatever you like. And for the vegetables, any other, as long as you take two things into account: One, starchy or root vegetables—potatoes, for example, or beets—do not work well in stir-fries (turnips and other cabbagey root vegetables are sometimes an exception) and two, you'll need to make careful adjustments in cooking times. Turnips, even cut small, take far longer to cook than broccoli, and spinach leaves far shorter than kale.

You can also vary the proportions in stir-fries. I specify twelve ounces of meat for four servings, which makes these light on meat, at least relative to the traditional American diet. But if you're looking to cut back on meat intake, they'll taste just as good with eight ounces (increase the amount of vegetables, however); if you want more chewiness, increase the meat to sixteen ounces or even a little more. If you do this,

I'd increase the seasonings slightly rather than cut back on the vegetables.

Finally, a word about thickening: In many Chinese restaurants (at least those in the United States), stir-fries are finished with a mixture of cornstarch and water that makes the sauce shiny and thick. I see this as an extra step that is not only unnecessary but is of debatable aesthetic value. Should you like to try it, I give directions in the master recipes here, but it is always optional.

Stir-Fried Chicken with Chinese Cabbage

Makes 4 servings, with rice

Time: 30 minutes

This is the simplest of stir-fries: You don't have to parboil the vegetables, as you do with many others. Napa cabbage shreds nicely and cooks quickly, but you can use bok choy (cut it small), ordinary green head cabbage, or Savoy cabbage.

2 tablespoons peanut or other oil

2 tablespoons minced garlic

1 tablespoon peeled and grated fresh ginger

1/4 cup chopped scallion (white and green parts), plus minced scallion greens for garnish

1 pound Napa cabbage, cored and shredded

12 ounces boneless, skinless chicken breast, rinsed and patted dry with paper towels, cut into 1/2- to 3/4-inch chunks

1 teaspoon sugar (optional)

2 tablespoons soy sauce

Salt and freshly ground black pepper to taste

1 tablespoon cornstarch (optional)

1/4 cup chicken or vegetable stock, or water (see "Soups" for stock recipes)

1 Heat a wok or large, deep skillet over medium-high heat for 3 to 4 minutes. Add half the oil, swirl it around, and immediately add half the garlic and ginger. Cook for 15 seconds, stirring, then add the 1/4 cup chopped scallion and the cabbage. Raise the heat to high and cook, stirring occasionally, until the cabbage scorches a little in places and becomes soft, 5 to 8 minutes. Turn the heat to medium and remove the cabbage.

2 Add the remaining oil to the pan, then the remaining garlic and ginger. Stir, then add the chicken. Raise the heat to high, stir the chicken once, then let it sit for 1 minute before stirring again. Cook, stirring occasionally, until the chicken has lost its pinkness, 3 to 5 minutes. Don't worry about the chicken cooking through; it will. And don't worry about the chicken bits that stick to the bottom; you'll get them later. Turn the heat down to medium.

3 Return the cabbage to the pan and toss once or twice. Add the sugar, if desired, and the soy sauce, and toss again. Season with salt and pepper. If using, combine the cornstarch with the stock or water and add to the pan. Otherwise, just add the liquid. Raise the heat to high and cook, stirring and scraping the bottom of the pan, until the liquid is reduced slightly and you've scraped up all the bits of chicken. If you've used cornstarch, the sauce will have thickened.

4 Garnish and serve immediately, scooping out some of the sauce with each portion of cabbage and chicken.

Stir-Fried Chicken with Orange Flavor: In Step 1, add 3 or more small whole dried red chiles (or 1/4 teaspoon or more crushed red chiles) and the chopped zest of an orange (see Lemon, page 634) with the garlic and ginger. Cook 1 cup sliced onion and 1 red bell pepper, seeded, stemmed, and sliced, in the seasonings in place of the cabbage, tossing until soft, about 5 minutes; hold off on adding the scallion. Remove the vegetables and proceed with Step 2 as above. In Step 3, add the scallion when you return the vegetables. Add 2 tablespoons freshly squeezed orange juice along with the soy sauce and reduce the amount of stock or water to 2 tablespoons. Garnish, if you like, with orange sections and minced scallion. Do not eat the chiles.

Stir-Fried Chicken with Broccoli or Cauliflower

Makes 4 servings, with rice

Time: 20 to 30 minutes

Here is a model recipe for making stir-fry with "hard" vegetables, those that must be parboiled before stir-frying. The extra step actually saves time—it's much faster to soften broccoli and like vegetables with a quick poaching than by stir-frying.

2 cups broccoli or cauliflower florets and stems,
    cut into bite-sized pieces
2 tablespoons peanut or other oil
2 tablespoons minced garlic
1 tablespoon peeled and grated fresh ginger
1 cup sliced onion
$1/2$ cup trimmed and chopped scallions, plus minced
    scallion greens for garnish
12 ounces boneless, skinless chicken breast,
    rinsed and patted dry with paper towels,
    cut into $1/2$- to $3/4$-inch chunks
1 teaspoon sugar (optional)
2 tablespoons soy sauce
Salt and freshly ground black pepper to taste
1 tablespoon hoisin sauce (optional; available at
    Asian markets)
$1/2$ cup toasted cashews (optional)
1 tablespoon cornstarch (optional)
$1/4$ cup chicken or vegetable stock, or water
    (see "Soups" for stock recipes)

1 Bring a medium pot of salted water to a boil; add the broccoli or cauliflower and cook for about 2 minutes, just long enough to remove the hardest crunch. Drain and plunge into cold water to stop the cooking; drain again.

2 Place a wok or large, deep skillet over high heat. Add half the oil, swirl it around, and immediately add half the garlic and ginger. Cook for 15 seconds, stirring, then add the onion and cook, stirring, for 2 minutes. Add the broccoli or cauliflower and $1/2$ cup chopped scallions and cook over high heat until the broccoli or cauliflower browns and becomes tender but not at all mushy, about 5 minutes.

3 Turn the heat to medium and remove the vegetables. Add the remaining oil to the pan, then the remaining garlic and ginger. Stir, then add the chicken. Raise the heat to high, stir the chicken once, then let it sit for 1 minute before stirring again. Cook, stirring occasionally, until the chicken has lost its pinkness, 3 to 5 minutes.

4 Return the vegetables to the pan and toss once or twice. Add the sugar, if desired, and the soy sauce, and toss again. Season with salt and pepper, then stir in the hoisin and cashews, if desired. If using, combine the cornstarch with the stock or water and add to the pan. Otherwise, just add the liquid. Raise the heat to high and cook, stirring and scraping the bottom of the pan, until the liquid is reduced slightly and you've scraped up all the bits of chicken. If you've used cornstarch, the sauce will have thickened.

5 Garnish and serve immediately, scooping out some of the sauce with each portion of meat and chicken.

Stir-Fried Chicken with Kale or Collards: In place of the broccoli or cauliflower, simmer 2 cups washed and trimmed kale or collard leaves and stems for about 2 minutes. Rinse under cold water, squeeze dry, and chop. Proceed as above.

You can add these flavor boosters alone or in combination with the basic recipe or with any of the variations. All are readily available at any Asian market and many supermarkets.

1. Add one tablespoon or more hoisin, plum, oyster, or ground bean sauce with the soy sauce.
2. Add one-quarter teaspoon or more Vietnamese or Chinese chile paste with garlic with the liquid.
3. Add one teaspoon dark sesame oil with the soy sauce.
4. Toss the chicken chunks with one tablespoon All-Purpose Curry Powder (page 778) or store-bought curry powder, or five-spice powder.
5. Toss in one-half to one cup raw or roasted cashews or peanuts when you return the vegetable to the pan.
6. Add one-half to one cup canned or Fresh Coconut Milk (page 291) along with the soy sauce. (Omit stock or water.)
7. Add one cup cored and chopped fresh tomatoes when you return the vegetable to the pan.
8. Replace half of the soy sauce with Asian fish sauce (*nuoc mam* or *nam pla*) or freshly squeezed lime juice or vinegar.
9. Add one cup mung bean sprouts when you return the vegetable to the pan.
10. Add one-half cup chopped shallots with the chicken.
11. Garnish with two tablespoons Toasted Sesame Seeds (page 776).
12. Use snow peas, mushrooms, or other quick-cooking vegetables, alone or in combination, in addition to or in place of the cabbage.

Stir-Fried Chicken with Basil and Chiles (Thai-Style): Omit Step 1. In Step 2, add 3 or more small whole dried red chiles (or $1/4$ teaspoon or more crushed red chiles) with the garlic and ginger. Cook 1 cup sliced onion in the seasonings in place of the broccoli or cauliflower, tossing until soft, about 5 minutes; hold off on adding the scallions. Remove the onion and proceed with Step 3 as above. In Step 4, add the scallions when you return the onion, along with 1 cup shredded fresh basil (or mint) leaves. Substitute Asian fish sauce (*nuoc mam* or *nam pla,* available at Asian markets) for soy sauce (or use half-and-half) if you like. Garnish with minced basil or scallions. Do not eat the chiles.

Stir-Fried Chicken with Chinese Mushrooms: First, soak about $1/4$ cup of Chinese fungi (such as tree ears) and $1/4$ cup dried shiitake ("black") mushrooms in warm water until soft, about 10 minutes. Drain and reserve the liquid. Trim them of any hard parts and cut into bits. Cook them with the broccoli or cauliflower (or use other vegetables), proceeding as above. Use the reserved liquid to replace some or all of the stock or water.

Stir-Fried Chicken with Spinach

Makes 4 servings, with rice

Time: 20 to 30 minutes

This is a wonderful combination of chicken, spinach, and sesame flavors.

2 tablespoons peanut or other oil

2 tablespoons minced garlic

1 tablespoon peeled and grated fresh ginger

1 cup sliced onion

12 ounces boneless, skinless chicken breast, rinsed
and patted dry with paper towels, cut into
$^1/_2$- to $^3/_4$-inch chunks

$^1/_4$ cup chopped scallion (white and green parts),
plus minced scallion greens for garnish

2 cups chopped spinach, trimmed, washed, and
well dried

1 teaspoon sugar (optional)

2 tablespoons soy sauce

Salt and freshly ground black pepper to taste

1 tablespoon cornstarch (optional)

$^1/_4$ cup chicken or vegetable stock, or water
(see "Soups" for stock recipes)

2 tablespoons Toasted Sesame Seeds (page 776)

1 tablespoon dark sesame oil

1 Heat a wok or large skillet over medium-high heat for 3 to 4 minutes. Add half the oil, swirl it around, and immediately add half the garlic and ginger. Cook for 15 seconds, stirring, then add the onion. Raise the heat to high and cook, stirring occasionally, until the onion becomes soft, about 5 minutes. Remove the onion.

2 Stir over high heat, add the remaining oil to the pan, then the remaining garlic and ginger. Stir, then add the chicken, stir again, then let it sit for 1 minute before stirring again. Cook, stirring occasionally, until the chicken has lost its pinkness, 3 to 5 minutes. Turn the heat down to medium.

3 Add the $^1/_4$ cup chopped scallion and the spinach to the pan and toss. Return the onion to the pan and add sugar, if desired, and the soy sauce, and toss again. When the spinach wilts, season with salt and pepper. If using, combine the cornstarch with the stock or water and add to the pan. Otherwise, just add the liquid. Raise the heat to high and cook, stirring

and scraping the bottom of the pan, until the liquid is reduced slightly and you've scraped up all the bits of chicken. If you've used cornstarch, the sauce will have thickened.

4 Garnish with the sesame seeds and minced scallion greens and drizzle with the sesame oil.

Stir-Fried Chicken with Black Beans: First, soak 2 tablespoons fermented black beans (available at Asian markets) in 2 tablespoons dry sherry or white wine. Add the black beans and their soaking liquid along with the soy sauce and 1 or 2 tablespoons of oyster sauce (optional; available at Asian markets). Finish as above, omitting the sesame seeds and oil.

Fried Chicken Breasts
Makes 4 servings

Time: 30 minutes, longer if you choose to
marinate

These do not feature the ultra-crisp coating of fast-food fried chicken nuggets, but a wonderful, crisp-tender coating that doesn't overwhelm the chicken. I think yogurt makes the best marinade here, but buttermilk is more traditional. Plain milk is an acceptable substitute.

If you like, season the marinade with hot sauce (such as Tabasco), or season the flour with cinnamon, allspice, thyme, cayenne, curry powder, chili powder, or other herbs or spices.

$1^1/_2$ pounds boneless, skinless chicken breast, rinsed
and patted dry with paper towels

$1^1/_2$ cups yogurt, buttermilk, or milk

Olive oil, peanut oil, lard, vegetable oil, or a
combination for frying

Flour for dredging

Salt and lots of freshly ground black pepper to taste

① Cut the chicken breasts into 2-inch strips. Marinate them in the yogurt or milk for at least as long as it takes to heat the fat; you can marinate for up to 24 hours, refrigerated.

② Heat at least 1 inch of the fat over medium-high heat in a deep-fryer or saucepan. Turn the oven to its lowest temperature. Season the flour with salt and pepper.

③ When the fat reaches 350°F, raise the heat to high and begin to dredge the chicken pieces in the flour, then place them in the fat. You may have to cook in batches of 3 or 4 pieces, but cooking time is minimal, 2 to 3 minutes (when the pieces are nicely browned, they're done). Drain on paper towels and, if necessary, keep warm in a 200°F oven.

Sautéed Chicken Cutlets

This is yet another basic chicken breast preparation that can rescue you on any given weeknight.

There are a couple of things to bear in mind before you begin cooking (for general information about sautéing, see The Basics of Sautéing, page 12). One, you must use a large enough skillet. For two chicken breasts (four cutlets), you need a large skillet. This may mean using a little more fat, but it will enable you to avoid overcrowding and make it easier to turn the meat.

When cooking, the skillet must be hot before you add the fat, and the fat must be hot before you add the meat (oil will shimmer and sizzle when you add a pinch of flour; the foam of butter will subside and it will begin to turn brown). This is not just to prevent sticking—a non-stick skillet will achieve that automatically—but to properly brown the meat. Too-cool temperatures, which can also result from adding too much meat to the pan too quickly, or from overcrowding, result in a soggy coating.

For the ideal crust, there must also be enough fat. If you want to follow these recipes using less fat, by all means do. They'll still be easy to cook and moist and tender. But you may experience scorching on some parts of the exterior, and a little mushiness on others. And don't expect a wonderfully crunchy crust; that is simply not possible unless the coating is in contact with the fat at all points during cooking. In summary, reducing the fat is less than ideal, but it's hardly tragic.

In addition, sautéing requires near-constant attention. Yes, you can answer the doorbell, but your station is the stove. For even browning, which means even crispness, you must tend to the food almost constantly.

The payoff, of course, is meat that is crisp on the outside and moist and tender on the inside. This does not happen by magic, although it does happen quickly—from the time you put the chicken in the pan until the time you remove it will be less than ten minutes. This is great, although, as always, you must take care not to overcook the chicken. Thin slices will cook in six minutes, thicker ones in ten, and most in about eight. When they're firm, or an instant-read thermometer reads 160°F (you'll have to slide it in from one end, lengthwise, to get an accurate reading), they're done. Get them out of the pan.

I like to set the oven at about 200°F as I begin this cooking process. If you choose to make a sauce, a warm oven will hold the chicken perfectly as you do so. But even if you do not, it gives you the option of moving those pieces that finish cooking a little more quickly than others, whether because they are thinner or closer to the center of the pan, to a place where they will stay hot and crisp until you need them. Don't abuse this procedure, though; I do not recommend holding the cooked cutlets in the oven for more than ten minutes or so.

Finally, about substitutions. In the not-too-distant past, creative chefs and cookbook authors "discovered" that boneless chicken breasts made a near-ideal substitute for far more expensive veal cutlets. Today, chicken is far more common than veal and carries neither the relatively high price tag nor the stigma of veal. However, you can substitute turkey, pork, or veal cutlets in any recipe.

Basic Sautéed Chicken Cutlets

Makes about 4 servings

Time: 20 minutes

This is among the simplest of recipes: It has no sauce and virtually no seasonings. But, given good chicken and care not to overcook, it is delicious.

> 4 boneless, skinless chicken cutlets (2 breasts), 1 to
>   1¹/₂ pounds, rinsed and patted dry with paper towels
> Salt and freshly ground black pepper to taste
> 1 cup all-purpose flour, plain bread crumbs,
>   or cornmeal
> 2 tablespoons olive oil
> 1 tablespoon butter (or use all olive oil)
> Lemon wedges
> Minced fresh parsley leaves for garnish (optional)

1 Heat a large skillet, preferably non-stick, over medium-high heat for 2 or 3 minutes. While it is heating, sprinkle the chicken breasts with salt and pepper and place the flour, bread crumbs, or cornmeal on a plate or in a shallow bowl.

2 Add the oil and butter, if any, to the skillet and swirl it around. When it is hot—a pinch of flour will sizzle—dredge a piece of the chicken in the coating, pressing it down a bit to coat evenly. Shake it a little so that excess coating falls off. Add the chicken piece to the pan, then move on to the next one. (Don't be tempted to dredge in advance and add all the pieces at once; the coating will become soggy, and the heat in the pan will drop too quickly.)

3 Cook the chicken, regulating the heat if necessary so that there is a good constant sizzle but no burning. After 2 minutes, rotate the chicken (do not flip) so that the outside edges are moved toward the center and vice versa. After 3 to 4 minutes, when the pieces are brown, turn them over.

4 Cook on the second side 3 to 4 minutes, until the chicken breasts are firm to the touch. If you are unsure whether they're done, cut into one with a thin-bladed knife; the center should be white (the barest trace of pink is okay, too—they will finish cooking on the way to the table). Serve with lemon wedges; garnish with parsley if you like.

Chicken Cutlets with Seasoned Bread Crumbs: For the coating, make your own bread crumbs: start with 3 or 4 slices of not-too-fresh bread (it can be quite stale). Whir them in a food processor with 1 clove of garlic and ¹/₂ cup fresh parsley leaves until fairly fine. Proceed as above.

Extra-Crisp Chicken Cutlets: Use seasoned bread crumbs (see previous variation) if possible. In Step 1, set up three bowls: one with all-purpose flour, one with a beaten egg, and one with the bread crumbs. In Step 2, when the fat is hot, dredge each piece of chicken first in the flour, as above, then in the egg, and finally in the bread crumbs, pressing to help them adhere. Proceed as above, lowering the heat a bit after the first minute or two in order to avoid burning the bread crumbs.

Chicken Parmigiana: Make Extra-Crisp Chicken Cutlets, above, cooking chicken just enough to brown it (don't worry about cooking it fully). Preheat the oven to 400°F. Spread about ¹/₂ cup of Basic Tomato Sauce (page 130) on the bottom of a 9-inch square baking dish. Place the cutlets on top of the sauce, and top with another cup of sauce. Sprinkle 1¹/₂ cups coarsely grated mozzarella over the sauce. Bake until the cheese melts and the sauce is hot, 10 to 15 minutes. Top with a tablespoon or two of minced parsley or oregano leaves and serve.

Spice-Coated Chicken Cutlets: Before coating the chicken, combine the flour or cornmeal with

1 tablespoon chili powder, curry powder, five-spice powder, or ground cumin. Proceed as above, using all oil (peanut or vegetable oil is best in this case) and garnishing with lime wedges rather than lemon.

Herbed Chicken Cutlets: Use the seasoned bread crumbs in the first variation recipe. While the chicken is cooking, heat 2 tablespoons extra-virgin olive oil, butter, or a combination in a small saucepan. Add 20 fresh sage leaves or 1 teaspoon dried sage; 3 or 4 sprigs fresh thyme or $1/2$ teaspoon dried thyme; 1 tablespoon fresh rosemary leaves or 1 teaspoon dried rosemary; or any other herb that appeals to you. (A crushed garlic clove or a tablespoon of minced shallot added to the oil along with the herb will do no harm.) Cook over medium-low heat until the herb sizzles. Turn off the heat. When the chicken is done, drizzle it with this herb-flavored oil or butter.

Sesame-Coated Chicken Cutlets: Use sesame seeds or ground nuts as the coating, instead of flour, cornmeal, or bread crumbs, pressing well to help them adhere. Proceed as above, using all oil (peanut or vegetable oil is best in this case), and cooking over slightly lower heat to avoid burning. (Increase the cooking time by 1 to 2 minutes.) Finish, if you like, with a drizzle of dark sesame oil, a sprinkling of lime, and a few minced cilantro leaves.

Sautéed Chicken Cutlets with Quick Sauce

Makes 4 servings

Time: 25 minutes

Spend an additional five minutes in front of the stove and you can make a flavorful sauce with which you can top not only the chicken breasts but rice, potatoes, or pasta. A combination of wine and stock is most commonly used for the sauce, but almost any liquid will do: all wine or stock, water, cream, diluted soy sauce, fruit juice, water . . . whatever. See the variations and don't be afraid to experiment.

This recipe begins with the same procedure as the preceding basic recipe. But feel free to start with any of the variations on the coating. And note the Twelve Simple Additions that follow this recipe and its variations.

4 boneless, skinless chicken cutlets (2 breasts), 1 to
   $1^1/2$ pounds, rinsed and patted dry with paper towels
Salt and freshly ground black pepper to taste
1 cup all-purpose flour, plain bread crumbs,
   or cornmeal
2 tablespoons olive oil
2 tablespoons butter (or use all olive oil)
$1/2$ cup dry white wine (or use all stock)
$1/2$ cup chicken or vegetable stock, or water
   (see "Soups" for stock recipes)
$1/4$ cup minced fresh parsley leaves, plus a little more
   for garnish

1 Heat a large skillet, preferably non-stick, over medium-high heat for 2 or 3 minutes. Preheat the oven to 200°F. Meanwhile, sprinkle the chicken breasts with salt and pepper and place the flour, bread crumbs, or cornmeal on a plate or in a shallow bowl.

2 Add the oil and half the butter, if you are using any, to the skillet and swirl it around. When it is hot—a pinch of flour will sizzle—dredge a piece of the chicken in the coating, pressing it down a bit so that the coating gets into the cracks and crevices. Shake it a little so that excess coating falls off. Add the chicken piece to the pan, then move on to the next one. (Don't be tempted to dredge in advance and add all the pieces at once; the coating will become soggy, and the heat in the pan will drop too quickly.)

3 Cook the chicken, regulating the heat if necessary so that there is a good constant sizzle but no burning. After 2 minutes, rotate the chicken (do not flip), so that the outside edges are moved toward the center and vice versa. After 3 to 4 minutes, when the pieces are browned, turn them over.

4 Cook on the second side about 3 minutes, until the chicken breasts are just firm to the touch. If you are unsure whether they're done, cut into one with a thin-bladed knife; the center should be white or slightly pink (since they will sit in the oven for 5 minutes, marginal undercooking is preferable to marginal overcooking). Remove the chicken to a platter and place it in the oven.

5 With the heat on medium-high, add the wine to the skillet. Let it bubble away, stirring and scraping the bottom of the pan, until it is reduced by about half, about 2 minutes. Add the stock or water and continue to cook, stirring, until the mixture has reduced somewhat again and become slightly thickened and a bit syrupy, another 2 or 3 minutes. (If you want just a little bit of sauce, cook longer; if you want more, cook a little less.) Add the remaining butter (or oil, if you are not using any butter) and swirl the pan around until the butter melts (if you are using olive oil, stir vigorously with the back side of a spoon). Add any juices that have accumulated around the cooked chicken, along with the $^1/_4$ cup of parsley. Stir; taste and adjust seasoning.

6 Spoon the sauce over the chicken, garnish with a bit more parsley, and serve.

Sautéed Chicken Cutlets with Cream Sauce: In Step 1, use flour for dredging. In Step 4, after removing the chicken, cook $^1/_2$ cup minced onion in the remaining fat over medium heat, stirring, until soft, about 5 minutes. Sprinkle with 1 teaspoon paprika as they cook. Raise the heat to medium-high and continue with the recipe. After you add the wine and stock and reduce the sauce, turn off the heat, wait 30 seconds, then stir in 1 cup heavy cream, sour cream, or yogurt. Turn the heat to low; reheat,

stirring, but do not boil (be especially careful if you use yogurt). Spoon some of this sauce over the chicken and garnish with minced parsley or a sprinkling of paprika. Pass the remaining sauce at the table.

Sautéed Chicken Cutlets with Ginger: In Step 1, use flour or cornmeal for dredging, combined with $^1/_2$ teaspoon or more of cayenne. In Step 2, use peanut oil, if possible. In Step 4, after removing the chicken, cook $^1/_2$ cup minced onion in the remaining fat over medium heat, stirring, until softened, 3 to 4 minutes. Stir in 1 tablespoon peeled and minced fresh ginger (or 1 teaspoon ground ginger), $^1/_8$ teaspoon freshly grated nutmeg, 1 teaspoon paprika, and $^1/_4$ teaspoon ground cinnamon. Omit the wine and increase stock to 1 cup. Omit the butter and parsley; instead, stir $^1/_4$ cup minced cilantro leaves and 1 tablespoon freshly squeezed lime juice into the sauce before spooning it over the chicken. Garnish with a little more minced cilantro and serve with lime wedges.

Twelve Simple Additions to Sautéed Chicken Cutlets with Quick Sauce

Use your judgment to combine these as you like.

1. Add one to two tablespoons capers along with the stock.
2. Add one teaspoon to two tablespoons of any fresh minced herb in place of the parsley; use minced chives, dill, basil, chervil, or cilantro for garnish.
3. Stir in one tablespoon balsamic or other good vinegar just before adding the butter or oil at the end.
4. Cook two tablespoons minced shallots, scallions, or onions, or one teaspoon minced garlic in the fat remaining in the pan for one minute, stirring,

just before adding the wine. Add one tablespoon minced anchovy if you like.

5. Add one tablespoon freshly squeezed lemon juice after swirling in the butter or oil at the end. Add one teaspoon to one tablespoon grated or minced lemon zest at the same time if you like.

6. Add one cup chopped fresh tomatoes (peeled and seeded if possible) just after reducing the stock.

7. Cook one-half cup chopped mushrooms in the fat remaining in the pan for one minute, stirring, just before adding the wine. Or use reconstituted dried mushrooms.

8. Stir in one teaspoon to one tablespoon Dijon or other mustard after swirling in the butter or oil at the end.

9. Replace the wine with one-quarter cup cream sherry or Madeira.

10. Increase the amount of butter in the final addition to as much as four tablespoons. The butter should be cold and cut into small bits, then incorporated a little at a time. (This is not an option with oil.)

11. Add two or three tablespoons pitted and chopped olives along with the stock.

12. Add one-half cup or more peeled, seeded, and diced tomato along with the stock.

Sautéed Chicken Cutlets with Lime Sauce

Makes 4 servings

Time: 25 minutes

This crisp chicken with a light, soy-based lime sauce might have been considered exotic a few years ago. Now it's fit fare for a weeknight.

4 boneless, skinless chicken cutlets (2 breasts), 1 to 1½ pounds, rinsed and patted dry with paper towels
Salt and freshly ground black pepper to taste
1 cup cornmeal
3 tablespoons peanut or other oil
1 lime, thinly sliced
1 teaspoon minced garlic
1 tablespoon minced shallot or onion
½ cup dry white wine or chicken or vegetable stock, or water (see "Soups" for stock recipes)
1 tablespoon soy sauce
Juice of 1 lime
Minced cilantro leaves for garnish

1. Heat a large skillet, preferably non-stick, over medium-high heat for 2 or 3 minutes. Preheat the oven to 200°F. Meanwhile, sprinkle the chicken breasts with salt and pepper and place the cornmeal on a plate or in a shallow bowl.

2. Add the oil to the skillet and swirl it around. When it is hot—a pinch of cornmeal will sizzle—dredge a piece of the chicken in the coating, pressing it down a bit so that the coating gets into the cracks and crevices. Shake it a little so that excess coating falls off. Add the chicken piece to the pan, then move on to the next one. (Don't be tempted to dredge in advance and add all the pieces at once; the coating will become soggy, and the heat in the pan will drop too quickly.)

3. Cook the chicken, regulating the heat if necessary so that there is a good constant sizzle but no burning. After 2 minutes, rotate the chicken (do not flip), so that the outside edges are moved toward the center and vice versa. After 3 or 4 minutes, when the pieces are brown, turn them over.

4. Cook on the second side about 3 minutes, until the chicken breasts are just firm to the touch. If you are unsure whether they're done, cut into one with a thin-bladed knife; the center should be white or slightly pink (since they will sit in the oven for

5 minutes, marginal undercooking is preferable to marginal overcooking). Remove the chicken, decorate with the lime slices, and place it in the oven.

5 With the heat on medium, add the garlic and shallot to the pan and cook, stirring, for 1 minute. Add the liquid and let it bubble away, stirring and scraping the bottom of the pan, for 1 minute.

6 Add the soy sauce and half the lime juice. Cook for 10 seconds, then spoon this sauce over the chicken. Drizzle with the remaining lime juice, garnish, and serve.

Crunchy Curried Chicken Breasts

Makes 4 servings

Time: 20 minutes

This quick batter, combined with shallow-frying in oil, yields an ultra-crisp crust. I like it spiked with curry powder, but you can use any spice blend. Alternatively, you can stir a handful of fresh herbs into the batter.

4 boneless, skinless chicken cutlets (2 breasts), 1 to
    1 1/2 pounds, rinsed and patted dry with paper towels
1 tablespoon white or wine vinegar
Salt to taste
1/2 teaspoon freshly ground black pepper
1 tablespoon curry powder or other spice mixture
    (pages 777–779)
1 cup all-purpose flour
1/2 cup warm water, plus more as needed
Peanut or vegetable oil as needed
Freshly squeezed lime juice or rice vinegar or other
    mild vinegar

1 Rub the chicken all over with the vinegar. Combine the salt, pepper, and curry powder and rub

this mixture into the chicken. In another bowl, mix the flour gradually with warm water, adding more water as necessary to make a paste the thickness of yogurt.

2 Heat a large skillet, preferably non-stick, over medium-high heat for 2 or 3 minutes. Add enough oil to the pan to reach a depth of about one-eighth of an inch. When the oil is hot (a pinch of flour will sizzle), dip each cutlet into the batter and place it in the skillet. Raise the heat to high and cook, regulating the heat if necessary so that there is a good constant sizzle but no burning. After 2 minutes, rotate the pieces (do not flip), so that the outside edges are moved toward the center and vice versa.

3 After 4 minutes, turn the pieces over. Cook until golden and crisp on each side, about 8 minutes total. Sprinkle with a little lime juice or vinegar and serve immediately.

Double Coconut Chicken Breasts

Makes 4 servings

Time: About 40 minutes

Ground coconut makes a flavorful and crunchy crust, but it burns easily, so be careful.

1 cup canned or Fresh Coconut Milk (page 291)
A few threads saffron or 1/2 teaspoon ground turmeric
About 1 1/2 cups dried unsweetened shredded coconut
3 tablespoons peanut or vegetable oil
4 boneless, skinless chicken cutlets (2 breasts), 1 to
    1 1/2 pounds, rinsed and patted dry with paper
    towels, and cut into 1-inch chunks
Salt and freshly ground black pepper to taste
1 tablespoon minced shallot
Minced fresh parsley or cilantro leaves for garnish

1 Warm the coconut milk (it will be warm already if you prepared it yourself) and add the saffron or turmeric to it. Let it sit, stirring once or twice, as the mixture cools.

2 Place the dried coconut in the workbowl of a food processor; process until the coconut pieces are about the size of grains of coarse salt. Put the ground coconut on a plate.

3 Heat a large skillet, preferably non-stick, over medium heat for 2 or 3 minutes.

4 Add 2 tablespoons of the oil to the skillet; dredge the chicken in the ground coconut and add a piece at a time to the skillet. Cook the chicken, turning frequently and seasoning it with salt and pepper, and adjusting the heat so it becomes nicely browned on all sides; total cooking time should be 6 to 8 minutes, no more. As the pieces finish, remove them to a plate.

5 When all the chicken is cooked, wipe out the skillet and return it to the stove over medium heat. Heat the remaining tablespoon of oil and add the minced shallot. Cook, stirring occasionally, until the shallot softens, 3 or 4 minutes. Add the coconut milk, raise the heat to medium-high, and bring the mixture to a boil, stirring frequently. Reduce the heat to medium and cook, stirring, until the mixture thickens slightly, 3 or 4 minutes. Add the chicken pieces to the sauce and heat for a minute or so. Check the seasoning and adjust if necessary. Garnish and serve.

Roasted Chicken Cutlets

Oven-roasting boneless chicken breasts is easy but a little risky: Because they are so thin and so low in fat, the danger of drying out is great. Therefore, it's important to roast them quickly, at high heat, and to include some liquid in the seasoning mix.

Herb-Roasted Chicken Cutlets

Makes 4 servings

Time: 30 minutes

Here the crust of the chicken combines with stock to make a simple sauce.

1 tablespoon minced fresh tarragon or summer
    savory, dill, parsley, or chervil leaves
1/4 cup minced fresh parsley leaves, plus a little more
    for garnish
1 cup all-purpose flour
Salt and freshly ground black pepper to taste
3 tablespoons butter, olive oil, or a combination
4 boneless, skinless chicken cutlets (2 breasts), 1 to
    1 1/2 pounds, rinsed and patted dry with paper towels
1 cup chicken or vegetable stock, or water, plus a little
    more if needed (see "Soups" for stock recipes)

1 Preheat the oven to 450°F. Mix together the herbs, flour, salt, and pepper. Heat a flame-proof baking dish over medium-high heat for 2 or 3 minutes, then add the butter and/or olive oil. When it is hot, dredge the chicken in the flour mixture, add it to the pan, and brown for a minute or so on each side. Add the stock or water and place the pan in the oven.

2 Roast the chicken, turning once or twice, until it is cooked through, about 6 to 10 minutes (if you are unsure whether the cutlets are done, cut into one with a thin-bladed knife; the center should be white or slightly pink). Remove the pan from the oven; transfer the chicken to a plate. If the juices remaining in the pan are thin, return the pan to the stove and cook over high heat for a minute or two to thicken them; if they're too thick, add a little more stock or water and cook over medium heat for a minute or two. Garnish the chicken and serve with some of the sauce spooned over it. Pass the remaining sauce.

Chicken Cutlets Roasted with Tomatoes

Makes 4 servings

Time: 40 minutes

I like to scent both the chicken and the sauce in this dish with a little bit of an assertive spice, such as cumin, coriander, or chili powder. You can, of course, eliminate the spice or substitute another.

> 1/4 cup minced fresh parsley or cilantro leaves, plus more for garnish
> 1 teaspoon minced garlic
> Pinch cayenne
> 1 tablespoon ground cumin
> 1/2 teaspoon ground coriander
> Salt and freshly ground black pepper to taste
> 4 boneless, skinless chicken cutlets (2 breasts), 1 to 1 1/2 pounds, rinsed and patted dry with paper towels
> 2 tablespoons olive oil
> 2 cups cored and chopped ripe (or canned) tomatoes, placed in a strainer for 5 minutes

1 Preheat the oven to 450°F. Mix together the parsley, garlic, cayenne, 1/2 tablespoon cumin, coriander, salt, and pepper (you can do this in a food processor and avoid mincing the garlic and parsley by hand; add 1 teaspoon of olive oil or water if needed to process). Rub the chicken all over with this mixture.

2 Mix the remaining 1/2 tablespoon cumin with the remaining olive oil, tomatoes, and some more salt and pepper; spread half of this mixture on the bottom of a roasting pan. Place the chicken on top and spread the remaining tomato mixture over it. Roast until the chicken is tender and cooked through, 15 to 20 minutes, basting once or twice with pan juices (if you are unsure whether they're done, cut into one with a thin-bladed knife; the center should be white or just slightly pink). Garnish and serve.

Poached Chicken Cutlets

Of all the techniques given for boneless chicken breasts, poaching is probably the most forgiving, since the chicken is cooked in liquid from start to finish. This gives you a little more latitude in timing, although severe overcooking will result in dry chicken in a wet sauce, so it's still best to strive for precision. All of these dishes create enough sauce to moisten a side dish of rice, noodles, polenta, potatoes, bread, or other starchy foods.

Chicken in Lemon Sauce

Makes 4 servings

Time: 30 minutes

A more-or-less traditional Provençal preparation, one that must be served with good bread, or at least a spoon for the sauce.

> 4 tablespoons (1/2 stick) butter or olive oil
> 2 leeks, washed well and diced, including some of the green part
> 1/2 cup dry white wine
> 1/2 cup chicken or vegetable stock, or water (see "Soups" for stock recipes)
> 1/2 teaspoon minced fresh thyme or tarragon leaves, or a good pinch dried thyme or tarragon
> 4 boneless, skinless chicken cutlets (2 breasts), 1 to 1 1/2 pounds, rinsed and patted dry with paper towels, and cut into 1- to 1 1/2-inch chunks
> 2 tablespoons freshly squeezed lemon juice
> Salt and freshly ground black pepper to taste
> Minced fresh parsley leaves for garnish

1 Melt 2 tablespoons of the butter or oil in a large skillet over medium heat. Add the leeks and cook, stirring, until softened, about 5 minutes. Add the wine, stock or water, and herb; bring to a boil and let bubble for a minute or two.

2 Add the chicken, turn the heat to medium-low, cover, and simmer until the meat is barely cooked through, 5 or 6 minutes. Remove the chicken with a slotted spoon and keep warm.

3 Turn the heat to high and cook the sauce rapidly, stirring occasionally, until just about $^3/_4$ cup remains; this will take 5 to 10 minutes. Lower the heat to medium-low, add the lemon juice, then stir in the remaining butter or oil, a bit at a time. If you're using oil, add it gradually, stirring vigorously with the back of a spoon as you do so.

4 Season with salt and pepper and return the chicken chunks to the sauce to heat through. Garnish and serve immediately.

Chicken in Ginger Sauce: Best over white rice. In Step 1, use peanut or vegetable oil. Substitute 1 teaspoon minced garlic and 3 tablespoons peeled and minced fresh ginger for the leeks and cook only 2 or 3 minutes. Reduce the wine to $^1/_4$ cup and omit the herb; add $^1/_4$ cup soy sauce after you have reduced the wine and stock. Steps 2 and 3 remain the same, but you need not reduce this sauce; simply adjust the seasoning after the chicken is cooked through and serve. Omit the lemon juice and garnish with minced cilantro instead of parsley.

Chicken and Fruit in Curry Sauce: Also best over white rice: In Step 1, use peanut or vegetable oil. Substitute 1 cup sliced onions for the leeks. When they're soft, add 2 tablespoons All-Purpose Curry Powder (page 778) or store-bought curry powder and stir for 1 minute; omit the wine, stock, and herb. In Step 2, add 2 cups peeled and chunked apples, bananas, papayas, or a mixture, along with 1 cup peeled, cored, and chopped tomatoes, with the chicken. Cook, covered, for 5 minutes as above, then remove the cover and raise the heat to medium-high; cook until the mixture thickens slightly, just another minute or two. Omit the lemon juice. Garnish with minced cilantro instead of parsley, then serve.

"Steamed" Chicken Cutlets

You can steam chicken directly over water, but I find that it becomes dry and flavorless. Better, in my opinion, is to steam the chicken, along with the flavorful juices of wine, tomato, oil, or stock, in a wrapped package, in the oven. This method—traditionally called cooking *en papillote*—is simple and foolproof. It's also impressive to serve individual packages at the table, using either parchment paper or aluminum foil to wrap the chicken and its seasonings. Easier still, if not quite as attractive, is to combine everything in a covered glass or ceramic casserole.

"Steamed" Chicken Cutlets with Tomatoes

Makes 6 servings

Time: 1 hour

The sole problem with wrapping food in packages is that if you open the packages and find that you've undercooked the food, you have to rewrap the packages to continue cooking. Two solutions: Cook everything in a covered dish so that you can check the chicken periodically, or cook long enough to ensure doneness, at the risk of overcooking. This is not as risky as it sounds, because you're cooking the chicken with liquid.

4 boneless, skinless chicken cutlets (2 breasts), 1 to
    1$^{1}/_{2}$ pounds, rinsed and patted dry with paper towels
6 thick slices ripe tomato
Salt and freshly ground black pepper to taste
12 fresh tarragon leaves or about $^{1}/_{2}$ teaspoon dried
    tarragon; or use basil, chervil, or dill
2 tablespoons olive oil, approximately
3 teaspoons freshly squeezed lime juice

1 Preheat the oven to 450°F. Tear off a 1-foot-square piece of aluminum foil (the more traditional parchment paper is, of course, acceptable). Place a chicken cutlet on the foil; top with a slice of a tomato, salt and pepper, tarragon, and a drizzle of oil and lime juice. Seal the package and repeat the process. Alternatively, layer all the ingredients neatly in a casserole with a cover. (You may prepare the recipe in advance up to this point; refrigerate for up to 4 hours before proceeding.)

2 Place all the packages in a large baking dish and bake for about 20 minutes; the chicken will be white and tender when finished. Serve closed packages, allowing each diner to open his or her own at the table.

"Steamed" Chicken Cutlets with Broccoli and Sun-Dried Tomatoes: Substitute a small piece of oil-cured sun-dried tomato and 2 or 3 small broccoli florets for the ripe tomato. Use marjoram, thyme, or oregano for the herb, and substitute freshly squeezed lemon juice for lime juice. Cook and serve as above.

"Steamed" Chicken Cutlets with Grated Vegetables: Mix together about $^{1}/_{2}$ cup each (3 cups total) of mixed grated vegetables, such as carrots, zucchini or summer squash, onion, potatoes, turnips, sweet potatoes, or winter squash, and use this as the first layer. Use the tomato if it is in season. Sprinkle a few drops of balsamic or other good vinegar over the top; omit the lime juice.

The Basics of Boneless Chicken Thighs

Increasingly, we are seeing boneless chicken thighs in the supermarket. But even when they're not available, boning a few chicken thighs takes just a few minutes. Boning thighs yourself (see page 373) is less expensive and, of course, gives you bones for stock. Don't worry about doing a perfect job of boning chicken thighs—you usually cut them into chunks before cooking anyway.

Rather than repeating many chicken breast recipes here, let me just say that there is not a single stir-fry or broil-or-grill recipe for boneless chicken breasts that won't work for boneless thighs as well. Some of those that work best:

Basic Grilled or Broiled Chicken Cutlets, and its
    variation, page 380
Stir-Fried Chicken with Chinese Cabbage, and its
    variations, page 383
Stir-Fried Chicken with Broccoli or Cauliflower,
    and its variations, page 384
Stir-Fried Chicken with Spinach, page 385

When making these adaptations remember that, generally speaking, thighs are a bit slower to cook. But because you'll usually be using smaller pieces, the timing balances out. As a rule of thumb, cook chunks of boneless thigh meat about as long as you'd cook whole boneless chicken breasts; cook them a little longer—just a minute or two—than you would chunks of breast meat.

Thighs, as you know, are dark meat—dense, rich, flavorful meat—and therefore best with Asian, North African, Indian, and Middle Eastern flavors and those of the south of France and Italy, such as vinegar, tomatoes, garlic, soy sauce, and strong spices. This jives well with the meat's sturdy texture as well, which makes it close to ideal for stir-frying and especially grilling. On the other hand, because thigh meat is dense, it pays to steer clear of very fatty sauces, especially those with a lot of butter and/or cream.

Sautéed Chicken Thighs with Soy Glaze

Makes 4 servings

Time: 30 minutes, plus time to marinate

This is a special stir-fry, one containing no vegetables but finishing with a thick, syrupy glaze. Most kids love it (it's pretty sweet). You don't have to marinate the meat here, but it does make a difference so I'd recommend it if you have the time.

- $1/2$ cup soy sauce
- $1/3$ cup water
- $1/4$ cup mirin (sweet rice wine; available in Asian markets) or 2 tablespoons honey and 2 additional tablespoons water
- 1 teaspoon peeled and minced fresh ginger or $1/2$ teaspoon ground ginger
- 1 to $1^1/_2$ pounds boneless chicken thighs (or start with about 2 pounds bone-in thighs and remove the bones, page 373), rinsed and patted dry with paper towels
- 1 tablespoon peanut or vegetable oil
- 2 teaspoons minced lemon zest (optional)

1 Combine the soy sauce, water, mirin, and ginger in a bowl. Prick the meat all over with a fork or skewer, then cut it into 1-inch or smaller chunks. If time allows, marinate the meat in the soy mixture in a casserole dish for 2 hours or overnight, refrigerated, stirring occasionally. (If you're cooking right away, don't bother combining the meat with the sauce.)

2 Heat a large skillet, preferably non-stick, over medium-high heat for 2 or 3 minutes. If you have marinated the chicken, remove it from the marinade with slotted spoon, leaving as much of the marinade behind as possible.

3 Add the oil to the skillet, wait 15 seconds, then add the chicken. Cook, stirring occasionally—not constantly—until the meat is browned all over, 8 to 10 minutes. Remove the meat from the pan and turn the heat to medium-low.

4 Put the soy mixture in the skillet and let it bubble for 1 to 2 minutes. Return the chicken to the skillet, turn the heat to high, and cook, stirring almost constantly, until the chicken is glazed with the sauce and almost all the liquid has evaporated. Remove the chicken to a serving dish and serve garnished, if you like, with the lemon zest.

Grilled or Broiled Chicken Thighs with Soy Glaze: Try to marinate for at least an hour or two. In Step 2, start a charcoal or wood fire or preheat a gas grill or broiler; the fire should be moderately hot. Remove the meat from the marinade with a slotted spoon and thread it onto skewers, alternating meat with thin slices of onion. Boil the sauce for 1 minute; reserve some for passing at the table. Grill or broil the skewers about 4 inches from the heat source, basting frequently with the sauce and turning the chicken every 2 or 3 minutes, until browned all over and cooked through (remove a piece and cut it in half to check), a total of 8 to 12 minutes. Give the meat one final baste and serve with the reserved sauce.

Spicy Chicken Thigh Kebabs

Makes 4 servings

Time: About 1 hour, plus marinating time if you have it and time to preheat the grill

Here is a recipe that will work beautifully with any medium-dark meat, not only chicken thighs, but cubed turkey thighs, pork, even sturdy fish such as swordfish or salmon.

1 to 1½ pounds boneless chicken thighs (or start with about 2 pounds bone-in thighs and remove the bones, page 373), rinsed and patted dry with paper towels

Minced zest and juice of 1 lime

1 tablespoon peanut oil or other oil

1 tablespoon soy sauce

2 tablespoons minced garlic

2 tablespoons minced cilantro leaves, plus a bit more for garnish

¼ teaspoon cayenne, or to taste

2 tablespoons natural peanut butter

Salt and lots of freshly ground black pepper to taste

1 Cut the chicken thighs into 1- to 1½-inch cubes. Mix it together with all other ingredients and marinate, if you have the time, in a large dish or bowl for 1 to 24 hours, refrigerated.

2 Start a charcoal or wood fire or preheat a gas grill or broiler; the fire should be moderately hot. Remove the chicken from the marinade and boil the marinade for 1 minute. Thread the meat onto skewers and grill or broil about 4 inches from the heat source, basting with the sauce and turning every 2 or 3 minutes, until browned all over and cooked through (remove a piece and cut it in half to check), a total of 8 to 12 minutes. Garnish and serve.

Chicken Thigh Kebabs in Yogurt-Cumin Sauce: In Step 1, replace the marinade with 1 cup yogurt; 1 medium onion, minced; 1 tablespoon minced garlic; the minced zest and juice of 1 lime; 1 table-spoon ground cumin; ¼ teaspoon cayenne, or to taste; ½ teaspoon ground coriander; 1 teaspoon paprika; and salt and pepper to taste. Proceed.

Chicken Thigh Kebabs with Cherry Tomatoes: A great summer dish. Consider the asparagus optional, although it is quite wonderful (use about 1 pound). In Step 1, replace the marinade with 3 tablespoons olive oil; the minced zest and juice of 1 lime; ½ cup minced fresh basil leaves; and salt and pepper to taste. Don't marinate for longer than 30 minutes. If you're using thick asparagus, peel it and parboil it for 2 to 4 minutes until it begins to become tender; drain and plunge into ice water to cool quickly; drain again; (skip this step if using thin asparagus). Skewer the asparagus, 15 to 20 cherry tomatoes, and the chicken, drained of its marinade, on separate skew-ers. Proceed as in Step 2, using the marinade to baste the asparagus and tomatoes as well as the chicken. Garnish with freshly minced basil.

Chicken Thigh Kebabs with Gentle Spices: In Step 1, replace the marinade with 1 teaspoon ground cardamom; 1 tablespoon minced garlic; 1 teaspoon ground allspice; ¼ teaspoon freshly grated nutmeg; 1 teaspoon ground turmeric; 1 teaspoon minced fresh thyme leaves or ½ teaspoon dried thyme; the minced zest and juice of 1 lime; salt and pepper to taste; and enough peanut or other oil to make this mixture into a thin paste. Proceed as in Step 2.

Chicken Thigh Kebabs with Citrus: In Step 1, replace the marinade with 2 tablespoons soy sauce; 1 tablespoon peanut or other oil; the minced zest and juice of 1 medium orange, 1 lemon, and 1 lime; 1 tablespoon peeled and minced fresh ginger; 1 table-spoon honey; 1 small onion, minced; and salt and pepper to taste. Proceed as in Step 2.

Chicken Thighs in Bitter Garlic Sauce

Makes 4 servings

Time: 40 minutes

Garlic takes on an entirely different character when it is cooked until dark brown: it becomes strong and bitter. Powerful as this flavor is, it is also readily enjoyable.

1 whole head garlic
1 small dried hot red chile
$1/4$ cup olive oil
2 cups cored and chopped fresh or drained canned tomatoes
Salt and freshly ground black pepper to taste
$1/2$ cup minced fresh parsley leaves
1 to $1^1/2$ pounds boneless chicken thighs (or start with about 2 pounds bone-in thighs and remove the bones, page 373), rinsed and patted dry with paper towels

1 Split the garlic into cloves; peel and slice into slivers. Place the garlic in a large skillet with the chile and oil over medium heat. Cook, stirring only occasionally, until the garlic begins to sizzle; then cook it carefully, until it is dark brown but not burnt, about 10 minutes. Turn off the heat and wait 3 minutes.

2 Cut up or crush the tomatoes and add them, along with any of their juice, to the garlic. Turn the heat to medium-high and cook about 10 minutes, or until the sauce is fairly thick; add salt, pepper, and half the parsley. Add the chicken pieces and cook over medium-low heat, covered and stirring occasionally, until the chicken is done, about 10 minutes. Serve immediately, garnished with the remaining parsley.

Chicken Satay

Makes 10 skewers, enough for 5 to 10 appetizer or 3 or 4 main-course servings

Time: 30 minutes to 24 hours, depending on marinating time, plus time to preheat the grill

When sliced thinly for satays, thighs are much less likely to dry out than breasts. They brown better, too.

1 pound boneless chicken thighs (or start with $1^1/2$ to 2 pounds bone-in thighs and remove the bones, page 373), rinsed and patted dry with paper towels
$1/4$ cup soy sauce
$1/4$ cup fish sauce (*nuoc mam* or *nam pla*, available at Asian markets), or use more soy sauce
$1/2$ cup water
1 teaspoon ground cumin
1 teaspoon ground coriander
1 tablespoon natural peanut butter or tahini (sesame paste)
1 teaspoon peeled and minced fresh ginger
1 tablespoon minced garlic
1 tablespoon sugar
1 tablespoon freshly squeezed lime or lemon juice or vinegar

1 Slice the chicken about $1/8$ inch thick (it's easier if you freeze it for 15 to 30 minutes first).

2 Mix together the remaining ingredients and stir in the chicken slices. Let sit until the fire is ready; or marinate up to 24 hours, refrigerated.

3 When you're ready to cook, start a charcoal or wood fire or preheat a gas grill or broiler; the fire should be quite hot and the rack as close to the heat source as possible. Thread the chicken onto skewers without crowding. Grill or broil until browned all over, a total of 5 to 8 minutes. While the meat is cooking, bring the marinade to a boil and reduce it slightly. Serve the skewers hot, using the marinade as a dipping sauce.

The Basics of Chicken Wings

In addition to the recipes I give here, there are literally dozens of recipes in this chapter that can be adapted for chicken wings. For example, you might try Broiled or Grilled Chicken with Pesto and its variations, page 375; Basic Grilled or Broiled Chicken Cutlets and its variations, page 380; or Grilled or Broiled Chicken Thighs with Soy Glaze, page 397.

For quicker cooking and neater eating, cut the wing in three before you start cooking (page 368). Freeze the wing tips for making chicken stock. Cook the two-boned middle section and drumstick-like upper wing together; usually the thicker drumstick section takes a minute or two longer to cook. You'll probably find that everyone at your table prefers one or the other, even if they don't yet know it.

I prefer broiling, or grilling, and stir-frying for chicken wings, and here's why: Broiling and grilling are fast and easy, and gives consistently good results. Stir-frying, while a bit trickier, is by far the easiest way to cook wings on top of the stove. Roasting saves you neither time nor much effort over broiling, and the results are usually not quite as good. Browning-and-braising, simmering, or any other method of cooking wings with liquid is not especially satisfying because the wings have a relatively large amount of skin and both the wings and cooking liquid become gummy.

Broiled or Grilled Chicken Wings

Makes 4 servings

Time: 30 minutes, plus time to preheat the grill

Of all the techniques you can use for cooking chicken wings, I like this one the best. It takes a little more attention than roasting, but brown, crispy wings are guaranteed. Cook them halfway through before adding the sauce to make sure it doesn't burn.

> 2 to 3 pounds chicken wings, rinsed and patted dry with paper towels, cut into 3 pieces (page 368), wing tips saved for stock
> 2 tablespoons extra-virgin olive oil

> Salt and freshly ground black pepper to taste
> 2 tablespoons freshly squeezed lemon juice
> 1 tablespoon minced fresh tarragon, chervil, or basil leaves

1 Start a charcoal or wood fire or preheat a gas grill or broiler. The fire should not be too hot, and the rack should be 4 to 6 inches from the heat source. Put the chicken pieces in a bowl, add 1 tablespoon of the olive oil and some salt and pepper, and toss to coat. Place the pieces in a roasting pan or on a rack in a roasting pan, or place them on the grill.

2 Cook, turning after 4 to 5 minutes, or when the first side is beginning to brown. Meanwhile, combine the remaining 1 tablespoon olive oil with the lemon juice and herb. After the second side is beginning to brown, brush the wings lightly with the olive oil mixture. Continue to cook, turning once or twice more, until nicely browned all over, about 15 to 20 minutes total. Give a final brush and serve.

Sesame-Broiled Chicken Wings: Step 1 remains the same; substitute peanut or vegetable oil for the olive oil. In Step 2, replace the basting mixture with $1/4$ cup soy sauce; 1 tablespoon honey; 1 teaspoon minced and peeled fresh ginger; 1 teaspoon minced garlic; 1 tablespoon Toasted Sesame Seeds (page 776); and 1 teaspoon dark sesame oil.

Stir-Fried Chicken Wings with Black Bean Sauce

Makes 4 servings

Time: 30 minutes

This illustrates the basic technique for stir-fried chicken wings; master this, then use it for any of the stir-fries on pages 383–386.

2 tablespoons fermented black beans

2 tablespoons dry sherry or white wine

1 tablespoon peanut or other oil

2 to 3 pounds chicken wings, rinsed and patted dry
    with paper towels, cut into 3 pieces (page 368),
    wing tips saved for stock

2 tablespoons minced garlic

1 tablespoon peeled and minced or grated fresh ginger

1/2 cup scallions (white and light green parts), cut into
    1- to 2-inch lengths, plus minced scallion greens
    for garnish

2 tablespoons soy sauce

Freshly ground black pepper to taste

Salt to taste (optional)

1 tablespoon cornstarch (optional)

1/4 cup chicken or vegetable stock, or water
    (see "Soups" for stock recipes)

1 Soak the black beans in the sherry or wine. Heat a wok or large, deep skillet over medium-high heat for 3 to 4 minutes. Add the oil, swirl it around, and immediately add the chicken wings. Raise the heat to high and cook stirring and tossing occasionally, until browned and cooked through, 10 to 12 minutes. Remove the chicken with a slotted spoon and reduce the heat to medium.

2 Add the garlic and ginger to the skillet and cook for 15 seconds, stirring. Add the scallions and cook 30 seconds, stirring, just until they begin to wilt. Return the chicken to the pan.

3 Add the soy sauce, toss, then taste and add some pepper and some salt if necessary. Add the black beans and their soaking liquid. If you're using cornstarch, blend it with the stock or water and add it to the pan. If you're not using cornstarch, simply add the stock or water. Raise the heat to high and cook, stirring and scraping the bottom of the pan, until the liquid is reduced slightly and you've scraped all the bits of chicken off the pan. (If you've used cornstarch, the sauce will have thickened.)

4 Garnish with the minced scallions and serve immediately.

The Basics of Whole Turkey

I know no one who prefers turkey to other birds, but you can't buck tradition, and the Thanksgiving feast is among the few national holidays that transcend all divisions (or at least most divisions: vegetarians have a hard time with it). Properly handled, a turkey can provide not just plentiful but good eating; however, it *is* a tricky bird to handle, especially given its size.

Buying Turkey

There are several kinds of turkeys out there, including standard, "wild," free-range, self-basting (such as Butterball), and kosher. My views on each:

Standard This often amazingly cheap bird is versatile and, well, standard. Until something better comes along—such as a consistently high-quality free-range bird—this is often the best bet.

"Wild" turkey True wild turkeys exist, of course, but you're not going to get one unless you or a friend shoot it yourself. The "wild" turkeys sold by mail-order houses and specialty stores are domesticated. They're quite expensive, not especially flavorful, and generally pretty tough. Try one out yourself before you commit to making it your Thanksgiving bird.

Free-range In theory, a better bird than the standard, but, in fact, wildly inconsistent and often outrageously expensive. Your best bet is to find a local source and, if it's good and reasonably priced, stick to it. But many free-range turkeys are tougher than the standard variety, and no more flavorful.

Self-basting This and other fat-injected turkeys are not terrible in concept—since turkey meat is inevitably dry, an internal load of fat makes some sense—but they are terrible in execution, since the ingredients used are little more than seasoned vegetable oil. Try not to overcook your turkey and baste it frequently and you'll do just as well with a standard bird.

Kosher Marginally better in flavor and texture than standard birds, at about twice the price. Usually sold frozen, although increasingly seen fresh at Thanksgiving. Worth a try.

Fresh versus Frozen Turkey

Although more and more turkey is sold fresh—even at times other than Thanksgiving—much is still frozen. Unless the turkey is of ultra-high quality, it doesn't make much difference. Frozen turkey is often put on sale at almost incomprehensibly low prices—thirty-nine cents a pound translates to less than four dollars for a ten-pound bird—and offers the convenience (as long as you have a large freezer) of having the bird whenever you want it.

Of course, if your turkey is frozen, you must defrost it before cooking, and even "small" turkeys don't defrost quickly. The easiest way to defrost a turkey is to let it sit in the refrigerator for two days before you plan to cook it. If you're in a hurry, defrost it by letting it sit in a sink or bowlful of cold water, changing the water occasionally; but you should still plan for it to take a whole day or more for a large bird.

Roasting Whole Turkey

I don't like to fuss with a Thanksgiving-sized turkey; even a small one is just too big to be turning every so often, the way you do chicken. So there are two options. The first is to roast the bird breast side up the whole time; this works well, because most turkey cooks for so long that it browns pretty much on its own. (If, toward the end of cooking, the bird is not as attractive as you'd like, turn the heat up to 400°F, or even a little higher.) This is fine as long as you're serving gravy; you'll need it, because the breast meat is almost guaranteed to be dry.

The alternative is to turn the bird once: Start it on its breast, and flip it over to its back for the final thirty to sixty minutes. This is not so bad with a "small" turkey of eight pounds or so, but it's nearly impossible with a fifteen-pounder, and that's the size many people roast on Thanksgiving. So, when dealing with a bigger bird, I skip turning entirely; I do, however, protect the breast with some aluminum foil for part of the cooking.

As you may have already found out, cooking a twenty-pound turkey is a lot of work, even assuming you have an oven large enough for it (many of us do not). If you have two ovens, you might consider roasting two smaller turkeys.

Timing Chart for Defrosting Large Birds

Weight	Defrosting Time (Refrigerated)	Defrosting Time (Cold Water)
6–8 pounds	18–24 hours	4–6 hours
10–12 pounds	24–36 hours	8–12 hours
14–18 pounds	36 hours+	12–16 hours
18 pounds+	48 hours or more	18 hours+

Timing Chart for Roasting Turkey and Other Large Birds

Weight	Roasting Time (Unstuffed)	Roasting Time (Stuffed)
6–8 pounds	2–2½ hours	2½–3 hours
10–12 pounds	3–3½ hours	4 hours+
14–18 pounds	3½–4 hours	5–6 hours
18 pounds+	4 hours+	6 hours+

Roast Turkey and Gravy, without Stuffing

Makes 4 servings

Time: $2^1/_2$ to 5 hours, depending on the size of the bird

Basting helps improve the color and especially the flavor of the skin, and it also adds a little moisture. If the bird is under ten pounds, roast it on its breast for the first hour, then flip it over for the second. If it's bigger than that, shield the breast with aluminum foil for the first couple of hours, then let it brown.

For cooking time, use the above chart or figure fifteen minutes per pound, the longer time for smaller birds. For example, an eight-pound bird will take about $2^1/_2$ hours; a sixteen-pound bird should take just about four hours. Timing varies considerably, however, based on the frequency of basting and how much heat your oven loses, the original temperature of the turkey, and other factors. Your best bet for determining doneness is an instant-read thermometer, which should read 165° to 170°F in the thickest part of the thigh before you remove the bird from the oven.

1 (8- to 20-pound) turkey, with giblets

1 whole onion, plus 1 to 2 cups chopped onions

1 whole carrot, unpeeled, halved if large, plus 1 to 2 cups peeled and chopped carrots

Stems from 1 bunch parsley

$^1/_2$ teaspoon salt

Freshly ground black pepper to taste

8 tablespoons (1 stick) butter, melted, or extra-virgin olive oil, approximately

$^1/_2$ to 1 cup chopped celery

About 1 cup chicken stock or water, plus more as needed (see "Soups" for stock recipes)

$^1/_4$ cup cornstarch mixed with $^1/_2$ cup cold water (per 3 cups gravy) (optional)

1 Make sure the turkey is thoroughly defrosted before starting. Preheat the oven to 350°F. Combine the turkey neck, wing tips, and gizzard (not the liver) in a medium saucepan. Add the whole onion, whole carrot, and parsley stems. Add water to cover, $^1/_2$ teaspoon salt, and a few grindings of pepper. Bring to a boil, turn the heat to low, and simmer, adding water as necessary to keep the meat and vegetables covered. Skim any foam that arises to the top of the pot; after 1 hour of simmering, turn off the heat, cover, and refrigerate if the turkey will cook for a great deal longer. Reheat when you get to Step 5.

2 Fit a large roasting pan with a V-shaped rack if you have one; otherwise use a flat rack. Brush the turkey with 1 tablespoon of the butter or oil and sprinkle it with salt and pepper. If you can handle the turkey easily, place it breast side down; if not, place it breast side up and cover it loosely with aluminum foil (remove the foil when about 1 hour of roasting time remains). Scatter the chopped onions, carrots, and celery around the turkey. Drizzle with 1 tablespoon of the butter or oil. Pour in about 1 cup of stock or water.

3 Roast, basting with a little additional butter or oil every 30 minutes and adding stock or water to the vegetables to keep them moist (better too wet than too dry in this case; you won't be eating them anyway). If you started the turkey with the breast down, flip it after an hour or so.

4 When the bird has about 1 hour of cooking to go (the internal temperature will be about 125°F), if the breast is not sufficiently browned (and it certainly won't be if you tented it with foil), turn the oven heat up to 400°F for the remaining cooking time. If at any time the bird appears to be browning too quickly, turn the heat back down (you can prop open the oven door for a couple of minutes to hasten the oven's cooling).

5 When the bird is done—an instant-read thermometer should read at least 165°F when inserted in mid-thigh—remove the bird to a platter but don't carve it until it has rested for at least 15 minutes. Reheat the giblet stock if necessary, then strain it into a bowl; then strain the vegetables that cooked with the bird into a larger bowl, pushing on them to extract as much liquid as possible. Combine these liquids. Mince the reserved liver.

6 Place the roasting pan over two burners on your stove, turn the heat to medium-high, and add 2 cups of the combined liquid and the reserved liver. Cook,

stirring and scraping the bottom of the pan, until the liquid is reduced slightly. If your bird is small, season the gravy to taste and serve. If it is large, add as much more stock (using hot water to stretch it if necessary) as you like. If you want thicker gravy, combine $1/4$ cup cornstarch with $1/2$ cup cold water (per 3 cups of gravy) and stir it into the gravy until thickened.

7 Carve the turkey (below) and serve with the gravy.

CARVING TURKEY

1

First, remove the leg-thigh section by cutting straight down between the leg and carcass, and through the joint holding the thigh to the carcass. Set aside for the moment.

2

At this point you have two options: Either cut thick slices of white meat from the breast, or remove the breast entirely from the carcass and slice it as you would a boneless roast.

3

Cut the wing from the carcass.

4

Carve the leg-thigh sections, repeat on the other side of the bird, and serve.

Roast Turkey with Stuffing: Select any of the stuffings on the following pages; plan to use about 3 to 4 cups for a small bird, 6 to 8 cups for a larger one. Just before roasting, stuff the bird (or consider cooking the stuffing in a separate roasting pan, using some of the giblet stock to moisten it) and truss it if you like (page 357), or simply close the rear vent with metal skewers to keep the stuffing from falling out. Increase roasting time by about 5 minutes per pound, still relying primarily on the thermometer. In the interests of simplicity, I roast stuffed birds breast side up the entire time, shielding the breast with aluminum foil until the bird is almost cooked.

Stuffing for Turkey and Other Poultry

I tend to be pretty conservative with almost all aspects of turkey-making for feasts (no cilantro here!), and that includes the stuffing. (When you're serving a dozen people or more, many of them kids, you don't want to slave over a fancy stuffing just to hear people say "ick.") So I keep stuffings simple and strive to make them one of the less challenging aspects of the meal. As you already know, *any* stuffing you make from scratch is going to be infinitely better than the instant kind most people are used to, so you're way ahead of the game.

I have two more thoughts about stuffing: Some is better cooked outside of the bird. If you want a moist, soft, juicy stuffing, pack it in there. But if you want a clean-flavored, crisp stuffing that can stand on its own as a side dish, consider cooking it on its own. (And, although this is not really a concern if you cook your birds thoroughly —the temperature of the stuffing needs to reach 165°F, just like the meat—the chances of harmful bacteria developing in the bird are greater if you cook the stuffing inside of it.)

The other thing: Don't skimp on the fat or the seasonings. Lean, underseasoned stuffing is little more than mushy bread.

My Favorite Bread Stuffing
Makes about 6 cups, enough for a 12-pound bird

Time: 20 minutes, plus baking time

Like almost everyone else, I have cut back on my use of butter in recent years. But this classic dressing, which is based on a wonderful recipe by James Beard, is so great that I refuse to compromise when I make it. I'd rather skip dessert than miss out on this yearly treat. Check out the variations if you prefer to use olive oil.

1/2 pound (2 sticks) butter
1 cup minced onion
1/2 cup pine nuts or chopped walnuts
6 to 8 cups fresh bread crumbs (page 239)
1 tablespoon minced fresh tarragon or sage leaves
   or 1 teaspoon dried crumbled tarragon or sage
Salt and freshly ground black pepper to taste
1/2 cup minced scallions
1/2 cup minced fresh parsley leaves

1 Melt the butter over medium heat in a large, deep skillet, Dutch oven, or casserole. Add the onion and cook, stirring, until it softens, about 5 minutes. Add the nuts and cook, stirring almost constantly, until they begin to brown, about 3 minutes.

2 Add the bread crumbs and the tarragon or sage and toss to mix. Turn the heat to low. Add the salt, pepper, and scallions. Toss again; taste and adjust seasoning if necessary. Add the parsley and stir. Turn off the heat. (You may prepare the recipe in advance up to this point; refrigerate, well wrapped or in a covered container, for up to a day before proceeding.)

3 Pack this into the turkey if you like, or simply put it in an ovenproof glass or enameled casserole and bake it with the turkey during the last 45 minutes of cooking.

Yes, cranberry sauce is traditional, but there are other side dishes even the kids will eat. I omit the obvious here, such as Baked Sweet Potatoes.

Bread Stuffing with Giblets and Fruit: Finely chop the gizzard, heart, and liver. In Step 1, add the giblets to the onion after it softens. Omit the nuts. In Step 2, add 2 teaspoons fresh thyme leaves (or 1 teaspoon dried), 1 finely crumbled bay leaf, 1 1/2 cups coarsely chopped pitted prunes, and 2 cups peeled and diced tart apples. Omit the tarragon and scallions and proceed as above. (If you make this recipe you will have to make stock for gravy from just the neck and wing tips.)

Bread Stuffing with Sage and Chestnuts: Start by boiling or roasting 3/4 to 1 pound chestnuts until they are tender (see Boiled, Grilled, or Roasted Chestnuts, page 561 for details). Shell, skin, and chop. Cook the onions as in Step 1, above. When they are soft, add the chestnuts and 1/2 cup dry white wine (omit nuts). Simmer for 5 minutes. In Step 2, use sage and just 2 tablespoons minced fresh parsley; proceed as above.

Bread Stuffing with Sausage: In Step 1, omit butter. Cook 1 pound sausage meat (you can squeeze the meat from links) in its own fat over medium heat until pinkish-gray. Spoon off the fat, then add the onion and cook until the onion softens, about 5 minutes. Omit the nuts. Add 1 tablespoon minced garlic, 1 teaspoon peeled and minced fresh ginger (or 1/2 teaspoon ground ginger), and 1 teaspoon ground cumin (optional). Omit tarragon or sage; proceed with Step 2.

Bread Stuffing with Mushrooms: In Step 1, use butter or olive oil and cook 1 cup trimmed and sliced white mushrooms along with the onion. If you have them, add 1 ounce soaked, drained, trimmed, and minced porcini mushrooms at the same time (page 582). Add 1 teaspoon minced garlic when the mushrooms have softened. Omit the nuts. Use sage or thyme (1 teaspoon fresh or 1/2 teaspoon dried) and proceed with Step 2 as on page 405.

The Basics of Turkey Parts

Much has been made of the new abundance of turkey parts in our supermarkets, but this has happened not because of any increased demand by consumers but because the turkey producers would prefer to operate year-round, rather than for six weeks. It's my belief that most of us would eat turkey less frequently than we would eat capon, a much tastier big bird, were it not for the traditions around Thanksgiving and Christmas.

There has been some good to come out of the turkey boom, however. Whole turkey breast is quite good roasted, either on or off the bone. Turkey thighs, while for my money not nearly as good as chicken thighs, make a nice change, and are reminiscent of pork when braised. And boneless turkey cutlets, again not as tender or tasty as a good chicken cutlet, are worth buying if the price is right. In addition to the recipes here, you can treat turkey cutlets exactly as you would chicken cutlets, using any of the recipes on pages 380–396.

Basic Roast Turkey Breast, on the Bone

Makes 8 or more servings

Time: About 1 hour

At three to six pounds, a turkey breast can feed a small party. It can also give plenty of leftovers for turkey sandwiches made with real turkey. And the roasting is a breeze. You can also use any of the variations for whole roast chicken on pages 358–363, adjusting cooking time accordingly.

1 (3- to 6-pound) turkey breast
About 3 tablespoons olive oil or melted butter
    for basting
Salt and freshly ground black pepper to taste

1 Preheat the oven to 450°F. Place the turkey on a rack in a roasting pan.

2 Brush the turkey with oil or butter and season it with salt and pepper. Place it in the oven. Roast for about 45 minutes, basting every 15 minutes or so, then begin checking every few minutes with an instant-read thermometer. The turkey is ready when the thermometer reads 160°F. Let the turkey rest for 5 to 10 minutes before carving and serving.

Roast Boneless Turkey Breast with Savoy Cabbage

Makes 8 or more servings

Time: About 1 hour

I love this dual method of cooking cabbage—half of it is sautéed, and half of it is roasted—which was developed by my friend, Chef Jean-Louis Gerin. The result is that some of the cabbage is tender, and some is crunchy, a nice combination that makes a great base for any poultry, from turkey to pheasant.

1 medium head Savoy or green cabbage,
    about 2 pounds
2 tablespoons plus 1 teaspoon extra-virgin olive oil
    or peanut oil
1 tablespoon peeled and minced fresh ginger
1 teaspoon minced garlic
Salt and freshly ground black pepper to taste
1 (3- to 6-pound) turkey breast, taken off the bone
    (page 379), or 2 filleted turkey breast halves,
    rinsed and patted dry with paper towels
1 tablespoon dark sesame oil
$^1/_2$ cup minced scallion greens for garnish

1 Preheat the oven to 450°F. Core and shred the cabbage, then chop coarsely. Divide in half, and chop one half a little more finely.

2 Heat the 2 tablespoons of oil over medium heat in a large skillet for 2 or 3 minutes. Add the coarsely chopped cabbage and cook, stirring occasionally, until softened, about 10 minutes. Add the ginger and garlic and continue to cook until the cabbage is slightly browned, another 5 minutes or so. Add salt and pepper; cover and keep warm.

3 While the cabbage is cooking, use the remaining 1 teaspoon oil to lightly grease the bottom of a baking dish slightly larger than the turkey. Cover the bottom of the dish with the finely chopped cabbage. Sprinkle with salt, then lay the turkey on top. Salt the turkey lightly. Roast for 25 to 30 minutes, until the turkey is almost done; it will be firm to the touch but not rubbery, white or very pale pink inside, and about 160°F on an instant-read thermometer.

4 Scatter the sautéed cabbage around the turkey and roast another 5 minutes. Slice the turkey and place it on a platter, surrounded by the cabbage. Sprinkle everything with sesame oil and scallions and serve.

Herb-Roasted Boneless Turkey Breast

Makes 8 or more servings

Time: About 1 hour

There's a small time savings in boning a turkey breast before you roast it, but there is another benefit that is even more significant: The bone and meat that cling to it, even from a small turkey breast, are hefty enough to make a great stock. In fact, in not much more time than it takes to make the breast, you can make the breast and a simple soup (turkey stock is great with butter dumplings; see Chicken Soup with Butter Dumplings, page 74).

3 tablespoons minced fresh herbs: tarragon, summer savory, dill, chervil, basil, fennel leaves, or a combination

1/2 cup minced fresh parsley leaves, plus a little more for garnish

Salt and freshly ground black pepper to taste

1 (3- to 6-pound) turkey breast, taken off the bone (page 379), or 2 filleted turkey breast halves

1 tablespoon softened butter or extra-virgin olive oil

1 cup chicken or vegetable stock, or water, plus a little more if needed (see "Soups" for stock recipes)

1 Preheat the oven to 450°F. Mix together the herbs (except the parsley for the garnish), salt, and pepper. Rub the turkey breasts all over with the fat.

2 Place the turkey in a baking dish, and put the baking dish in the oven. Add about 1/3 cup of stock or water to the bottom of the pan. Roast the turkey, basting every 10 minutes or so and adding more stock or water if necessary, until it is cooked through, about 30 minutes. (If you are unsure whether it's done, cut into it; the center should be white. An instant-read thermometer will show 160°F.)

3 Remove the turkey to a plate. Add the remaining liquid (or add an additional 1/2 cup if you've already used up all the liquid) and cook, stirring and scraping the bottom of the pan, until the liquid is reduced slightly. Slice the turkey and spoon the sauce over it (there will just be enough to give it a nice glaze). Garnish with parsley and serve.

Turkey Thighs Braised in Red Wine

Makes about 6 servings

Time: About 1 1/2 hours, plus marinating time

With their dark, rich meat and somewhat coarse texture, turkey thighs are reminiscent of pork. Substitute them for chicken parts or pork in any stewlike recipe.

3 tablespoons olive oil

2 to 3 pounds turkey thighs (4 to 6), skin removed if you like, rinsed and patted dry with paper towels

1 cup chopped onions

$^1/_2$ cup chopped carrots

1 celery stalk, chopped

2 teaspoons minced garlic

2 cups red wine

$^1/_4$ cup red wine vinegar or other vinegar

3 cloves or pinch ground cloves

3 juniper berries

1 bay leaf

1 section orange peel (optional)

Salt and freshly ground black pepper to taste

1 ounce dried porcini mushrooms or $^1/_2$ cup trimmed and sliced fresh shiitake ("black") mushrooms, stems removed (optional)

Stock or water as needed (see "Soups" for stock recipes)

Minced fresh parsley leaves for garnish

① Heat 2 tablespoons of the oil over medium-high heat in a Dutch oven or other heavy pot that can later be covered; brown the thighs on all sides. Remove the thighs and wipe out the pan.

② Reduce the heat to medium and add the remaining oil. A minute later, add the onion, carrot, celery, and garlic. Cook, stirring, until the vegetables soften, about 5 minutes.

③ Add the wine and raise the heat to medium-high. Bring to a boil and cook, stirring, for 1 minute. Add the vinegar, cloves, juniper berries, bay leaf, orange peel if using, salt, and pepper, and stir. Return the thighs to the pot, reduce the heat to low, and cover. The meat should cook slowly, with just a few bubbles arising from the liquid.

④ Prepare the mushrooms. If you're using porcini, soak them in hot water to cover until softened, about 10 minutes. Trim and chop them, reserving their liquid.

⑤ Turn the turkey every 15 minutes or so, and add a little stock or water if pan becomes dry. When the turkey is tender—usually about 45 minutes after covering—add the mushrooms and their reserved liquid if any.

⑥ Remove the turkey from the pot and keep it warm. Skim the fat from the surface of the remaining juice, raise the heat to high, and reduce the liquid by about half. Check for seasoning and spoon over the turkey. Garnish and serve.

The Basics of Ground Chicken and Turkey

Ground chicken and turkey are "new" meats, and can be used in any recipe calling for ground meat. Their advantage, presumably, is that they are lower in fat than their beefy cousins; if that's your concern, please read the label to make sure the fat content is five percent or less. If it is not, you can always use a food processor or meat grinder to grind your own chicken or turkey, using skinned breast or thigh meat, or a combination (or grind your own beef from very lean beef).

If you're using a food processor, cut the meat, which should be very cold—or even partially frozen—into chunks, then pulse in the machine until it reaches the texture you like. A very distinct advantage to grinding your own chicken or turkey (or other meat) is that you can add herbs, spices, or other seasonings during the final stages of processing, making your burgers that much more flavorful.

I would not use ground chicken or turkey to make actual burgers, because they absolutely must be cooked to the well-done stage, which means they would be horribly dry on a bun. Rather, I would substitute them for ground meat in those recipes in which the meat will be cooked to the well-done stage anyway such as Basic Meatballs (page 494), Basic Meat Loaf (page 495), chili (page 519), Meat Sauce, Bolognese-Style (Ragu) (page 150), lasagne (page 163), ravioli (page 160), and Pot Stickers or Steamed Dumplings (page 34).

The Basics of Capons, Cornish Hens, Poussins, and Guinea Hens

These birds may all be cooked using any chicken recipe, as long as you adjust for time. Since many of them are larger or smaller than chicken, this is important. But please remember: In other respects they may be treated as you would the more common chicken. So use them frequently, because, for the most part, they are more flavorful, especially when compared to store- and name-brand chickens.

Capon (castrated roosters) grow to be quite large, seven pounds or so, and are usually far more flavorful than the roasting chickens sold in supermarkets. They have another advantage, too: Their breast meat remains moist when cooked. But because capons are not very popular, you almost always find them frozen; many supermarkets have them tucked away, so ask. Defrost as you would turkey (page 402).

Cornish hens are tiny, just over one pound each. They serve one or two people each, and are great split before cooking. Poussins, which are essentially baby chickens, may be treated as Cornish hens.

Guinea hens are a variety of chicken, usually more flavorful. Buy them if you see them and roast them simply, as you would a good chicken.

To make stock from the trimmings of any bird Combine the neck, wing tips, gizzard, and any other scraps in a small saucepan, with water to cover. Add one small onion (don't bother to peel it), one carrot, and one stalk celery, along with a pinch of salt and a few peppercorns. Bring to a boil, turn the heat to low, cover partially, and cook for as few as thirty (if you're in a hurry) to as many as sixty minutes.

Simple Roast Capon
Makes at least 6 servings

Time: About 1½ hours

There's nothing better than a good roast chicken. But if you want a large bird, a simple roast capon is the best. The technique is almost the same as that for Simple Roast Chicken, and you can use any of the variations on pages 358–359.

3 tablespoons olive oil
2 teaspoons fresh thyme leaves, 1 teaspoon dried thyme, or any other potent green herb, such as rosemary, marjoram, oregano, or sage
Salt and freshly ground black pepper to taste
1 (6- to 7-pound) capon, trimmed of excess fat, then rinsed and patted dry with paper towels
Fresh herbs for garnish

1 Preheat the oven to 450°F.

2 Mix together the olive oil, thyme, salt, and pepper. Place the bird, backside up, on a rack in a roasting pan, and place the pan in the oven.

3 After the capon has roasted for about 30 minutes, spoon some of the olive oil mixture over it, then turn the bird breast side up. Baste again, then again after 10 or 12 minutes; at this point the breast should be beginning to brown (if it hasn't, roast a few more minutes).

4 Turn the heat down to 350°F, baste again, and roast until an instant-read thermometer inserted into the thickest part of the thigh reads 165°F. Total roasting time will be at least 1 hour 15 minutes.

5 Before removing the capon from the pan, tip it to let the juices from its cavity flow into the pan (if they are red, cook another 5 minutes). Remove the bird to a platter and let it rest for about 5 minutes. Carve, garnish, and serve with the pan juices.

Roast Capon with Bacon-Nut Stuffing

Makes at least 6 servings

Time: About 2 hours

You can use this stuffing with a roasting chicken, or with turkey, although chances are good you'll have to double or triple the quantities.

$^1/_2$ pound slab or sliced bacon

3 tablespoons butter or oil (optional)

3 cups chopped onions

1 teaspoon minced garlic

2 cups fresh bread crumbs (page 239)

$^1/_2$ cup pine nuts or chopped walnuts

$^1/_2$ cup dry white wine, chicken or vegetable stock, or water (see "Soups" for stock recipes)

1 teaspoon fresh thyme leaves or $^1/_2$ teaspoon dried thyme, plus several sprigs of fresh thyme if available

1 bay leaf

Salt and freshly ground black pepper to taste

1 (6- to 7-pound) capon, trimmed of excess fat, then rinsed and patted dry with paper towels

2 carrots, chopped

1 cup water or stock (see To Make Stock from the Trimmings of Any Bird, page 410)

1 If you are using slab bacon, cut it into $^1/_2$-inch cubes; if you're using sliced bacon, chop it coarsely. Cook the bacon in a medium skillet over medium heat, stirring or turning, until crisp. Drain, dry, and crumble; reserve the fat.

2 Heat 3 tablespoons of the bacon fat (or use butter or olive oil) over medium heat in a large, deep skillet. Cook 2 cups of the chopped onions, stirring, until softened, about 5 minutes. Add the garlic, bread crumbs, nuts, wine, thyme, bay leaf, and bacon, and remove from the heat. Season to taste with salt—you may not need any—and pepper.

3 Preheat the oven to 425°F. Fill the bird with the stuffing and truss it if you like (page 357) or simply close the rear vent with metal skewers to keep the stuffing from falling out. Set the bird on a rack in a roasting pan, brush it with a little of the bacon fat, some melted butter, or some olive oil, and sprinkle it with salt and pepper. Scatter the remaining onion, carrots, and thyme sprigs around the bird and place it in the oven.

4 Roast, basting every 10 minutes, first with butter or fat, then with pan juices. After 30 minutes, lower the heat to 350°F. Continue to baste every 15 minutes or so. The total cooking time will be $1^1/_2$ to 2 hours. When the bird is done, an instant-read thermometer inserted into the thigh will measure about 165°F, and the juices will run clear rather than pink.

5 Transfer the bird to a hot platter. Spoon off most of the fat from the pan and place it over one or two burners on your stove. Turn the heat to high, add the water or stock, bring to a boil, and cook, stirring and scraping the bottom of the pan, until the liquid is reduced slightly, about 2 minutes. Season to taste. Carve capon and serve with stuffing and gravy.

Grilled or Broiled Cornish Hens with Vinegar

Makes 2 to 4 servings

Time: About 40 minutes, plus time to preheat the grill

This light sauce is great with any grilled poultry, from chicken to squab. Good with rabbit, too. Once you split the hens, you can cook them according to any recipe for Grilled or Broiled Split Chicken (pages 366–367), adjusting the cooking time accordingly.

2 Cornish hens, about 1 pound each, rinsed and
    patted dry with paper towels
1 cup chicken, beef, or other stock (see To Make
    Stock from the Trimmings of Any Bird, page 410)
2 tablespoons any good vinegar
Salt and freshly ground black pepper to taste
Minced fresh parsley leaves for garnish

1   Start a wood or charcoal fire or preheat a gas grill or broiler; the fire should be moderately hot. Remove the backbone of the hens by cutting along their length on either side. Boil the stock in a small saucepan until reduced by about half; stir in the vinegar and some salt and pepper if necessary.

2   Grill or broil the hens 4 to 6 inches from the heat source, turning frequently so they brown but do not burn, and seasoning them with salt and pepper. Toward the end of their cooking time (which will be 20 to 30 minutes total, depending on the intensity of the heat), begin basting the hens with the vinegar sauce. When the hens are done, sprinkle them with the remaining sauce. Garnish and serve hot or at room temperature.

Cornish Hens and Sauerkraut

Makes 4 to 6 servings

Time: About 2 hours

This is an elegant dish, but a straightforward one. Steer clear of canned sauerkraut; instead, look for a bottled brand that contains no more than cabbage, salt, and water (natural foods stores usually have high-quality

sauerkraut). This preparation also works well with pheasant, chicken, and duck.

4 Cornish hens, about 1 pound each, rinsed and
    patted dry with paper towels
4 slices good bacon, diced (or substitute 3 tablespoons
    olive oil)
2 pounds sauerkraut
2 cloves
1 teaspoon juniper berries, crushed with the side
    of a knife
1 sprig fresh thyme or pinch dried thyme
1 bay leaf
1 cup white wine
Stock or water as needed (see To Make Stock from
    the Trimmings of Any Bird, page 410)
Salt and freshly ground black pepper to taste

1   Remove the backbone of the hens by cutting along their length on either side. Separate breast and leg quarters.

2   Cook the bacon over medium heat in a large, deep, ovenproof skillet, until it is crisp (or heat the olive oil until it shimmers). Remove the bacon with a slotted spoon and reserve. Add the hen pieces to the bacon fat or olive oil and brown them on all sides. While they are browning, rinse the sauerkraut in a colander and preheat the oven to 300°F.

3   When the bird is nicely browned, add the sauerkraut, cloves, juniper berries, thyme, bay leaf, and white wine to the skillet. Cook over medium heat until about half of the liquid has evaporated, about 10 minutes; move the skillet into the oven.

4   Bake for about 30 minutes, stirring occasionally and adding liquid as needed, until the legs are tender and the sauerkraut slightly browned. Remove the skillet from the oven, then remove the cloves and bay leaf; check for seasoning and serve.

The Basics of Duck and Goose

These two birds have a great deal in common: They're fatty—amazingly so, if you're used to chicken—which means they need to be treated differently from other birds. It also means they develop a beautifully crisp, dark skin.

Both birds have dark meat that is flavorful without being at all gamy. (I'm talking about domesticated ducks and geese, of course. Wild ones are quite gamy—but they're also hard to come by.) Finally, because they are water birds, they have a huge chest cavity and a bone structure that makes their size deceptive. If you've ever roasted a four- or five-pound duck and tried to serve six people with it, you know what I mean; there's really only enough meat on the bird to serve two or three. That's why duck is a good candidate for smoking; when it's done, you can cut it up and use it in stir-fries, where it lends its great flavor to other ingredients.

"Duck," by the way, usually means Peking duck, the kind found in every supermarket. It's usually sold "fresh" but in fact is shipped frozen and then thawed; truly fresh duck is rare. All duck has dark meat that is far richer than that of chicken.

Many cooks avoid duck because of its high fat content. But there are lots of methods that render the subcutaneous fat from duck and goose without drying the bird out. For a basic roast bird, I've gone back to the method my mother taught me: You prick the skin as the bird roasts. It's a bit of a nuisance, and sometimes makes a mess of the oven, but it works brilliantly. And, if you roast in an empty pan, you get a great deal of nice, clean fat that you can save (it keeps for weeks in the refrigerator, months in the freezer) for cooking other dishes in which you want a flavor boost.

For other recipes, I like to render the duck fat with an initial steaming. This method, which is Chinese in origin, is simple and effective, and results in a lean bird. After the initial steaming, you can treat the duck however you like: marinate it, broil it, grill it, even smoke it. The major disadvantage is that it is a two-step process. But it's easy and straightforward, and you can use it for goose as well.

Goose is nearly always sold frozen; you order it and thaw it yourself. The easiest way to thaw goose is to let it sit in the refrigerator for two days before you plan to cook it. If you're in a hurry, defrost it by letting it sit in cold water, changing the water occasionally; but you should still plan for it to take the better part of a day for a ten-pound bird.

Basic Roast Duck

Makes 2 to 4 servings

Time: About 1¼ hours

As I noted above, trying to stretch a duck to serve four is not an easy task, but it can be done if your co-eaters are not big on meat and you make a point of providing plenty of side dishes.

1 (4- to 5-pound) duck, excess fat removed, rinsed
    and patted dry with paper towels
Salt and freshly ground black pepper to taste
1 tablespoon soy sauce (optional)

1 Preheat the oven to 350°F. Prick the duck skin all over with a sharp fork, skewer, or thin-bladed knife; try not to hit the meat (the fat layer is usually about ¼ inch thick). Season the duck with salt and pepper and place it, breast side down, on a rack in a roasting pan.

2 Roast the duck for 15 minutes, prick the exposed skin again, then roast another 15 minutes. Brush with a little soy sauce, if desired, and then turn it breast side up. Prick again, brush with a little more soy sauce, then roast until the meat is done, about another 45 minutes; all juices, including those from the center vent, should run clear, and the leg bone should wiggle a little in its socket. When the bird is done, an instant-read thermometer inserted into the thigh will measure about 180°F. Raise the heat to 400°F for the last 10 minutes of cooking if the duck is not as brown as you'd like.

3 Carve the duck (page 359) and serve.

Roast Duck with Orange Sauce

Makes 4 servings

Time: About 1$\frac{1}{2}$ hours

An updated, not-too-sweet version of duck *à l'orange*.

1 (4- to 5-pound) duck, excess fat removed, rinsed and patted dry with paper towels
Salt and freshly ground black pepper to taste
1 medium onion, sliced
2 cloves garlic, lightly smashed
4 oranges
$\frac{1}{2}$ cup chicken or duck stock (see To Make Stock from the Trimmings of Any Bird, page 410)
$\frac{1}{2}$ cup dry white wine or water
1 tablespoon cornstarch mixed with 2 tablespoons water (optional)

1 Preheat the oven to 350°F. Prick the duck skin all over with a sharp fork, skewer, or thin-bladed knife; try not to hit the meat (the fat layer is usually about $\frac{1}{4}$ inch thick). Season the duck with salt and pepper and stuff it with the onion and garlic. Quarter one of the oranges and place it in the cavity too. Place the duck, breast side down, on a rack in a roasting pan.

2 Roast the duck for 15 minutes, prick the exposed skin again, then roast another 15 minutes. Turn it breast side up, prick again, then roast until the meat is done, about another 45 minutes; all juices, including those from the center vent, should run clear, and the leg bone should wiggle a little in its socket. When the bird is done, an instant-read thermometer inserted into the thigh will measure about 180°F. Raise the heat to 400°F for the last 10 minutes of cooking if the duck is not as brown as you'd like.

3 While the duck is cooking, remove the zest from one of the remaining oranges; juice the orange and reserve. Mince half the zest and reserve. Simmer the remaining zest in the stock for 2 minutes.

4 Peel the remaining 2 oranges and cut them into sections. When the duck is done, remove and discard the orange, onion, and garlic from the cavity and transfer the bird to a warm platter.

5 Drain all the fat from pan and place it on one or two burners on your stove. Turn the heat to high and add the wine or water; cook, stirring and scraping the bottom of the pan, until the liquid is reduced slightly. Strain the stock and add it to the pan along with the orange juice and sections; bring to a boil and cook, stirring, for 1 minute.

6 Carve the duck, spoon the sauce over it, garnish with the reserved zest, and serve. (If you want a thicker sauce, stir 1 tablespoon cornstarch mixed with 2 tablespoons water into it and cook, stirring, until thickened.)

Steamed and Roasted Duck

Makes 2 to 4 servings

Time: About 1$\frac{1}{2}$ hours

This method produces a crisp, delicious duck with very little fat. Feel free to steam the duck a day or two before you roast it.

1 (4- to 5-pound) duck, excess fat removed, rinsed
   and patted dry with paper towels
Salt and freshly ground black pepper to taste
2 tablespoons soy sauce
2 tablespoons honey
1 tablespoon peeled and minced or grated fresh
   ginger or 1 teaspoon ground ginger
1 teaspoon minced garlic
2 tablespoons sherry or white wine
2 tablespoons white wine or water

① Prick the duck skin all over with a sharp fork,
skewer, or thin-bladed knife; try not to hit the meat
(the fat layer is usually about $1/4$ inch thick). Place
1 to 2 inches of water in a pot fitted with a rack.
Place the duck on the rack, cover the pot, and turn the
heat to high. Steam for about 45 minutes, adding
boiling water if necessary.

② Remove the duck from the pot, place it on a
rack, and cool for at least 15 minutes (you can also
wrap it well and refrigerate until you're ready to cook,
for up to 24 hours.)

③ Preheat the oven to 375°F. Combine all remaining
ingredients in a saucepan and cook over low heat, stirring, until just shy of a boil. Place the duck, breast side
down, on a rack in a roasting pan. Baste with the sauce.

④ Roast the duck for 15 minutes, baste it, then
turn it breast side up. Raise the heat to 425°F. Baste
the bird again and roast it until the skin is crisp,
another 15 minutes or so. Carve and serve.

Tea-Smoked Duck (or Chicken)

Makes 2 main-course and up to 8 appetizer servings

Time: At least $1^1/_2$ hours

Like the preceding recipe, this begins with a quick
steaming. The smoking is easy, but don't try it unless
your kitchen is equipped with a decent exhaust fan.
This duck is incredibly delicious. If you can manage
not to eat the entire thing yourself, try cutting it up
and using it in stir-fries. This recipe will work with
chicken, too; you can skip the initial steaming step.

1 (4- to 5-pound) duck, excess fat removed, rinsed
   and patted dry with paper towels
$1/2$ cup soy sauce, plus 2 tablespoons
$1/2$ cup water
2 pieces star anise
1 cinnamon stick
$1/2$ cup raw long-grain white rice
1 cup strong black tea leaves (Lapsang souchong,
   which is smoky, is a good choice)
$1/2$ cup sugar
1 teaspoon dark sesame oil

① Prick the duck skin all over with a sharp fork,
skewer, or thin-bladed knife; try not to hit the meat
(the fat layer is usually about $1/4$ inch thick). Place the
$1/2$ cup of soy sauce, water, anise, and cinnamon in a
pot fitted with a rack (a cake rack usually works
nicely, but you won't be able to fit much water under
it, so be careful not to boil the pot dry). Place the duck
on the rack, cover the pot, and turn the heat to high.
Steam for about 45 minutes, adding boiling water if
necessary. Remove the duck; you can also wrap it well
and refrigerate, covered, for up to 2 days at this point.

② Line a large wok or heavy pot with heavy aluminum foil. Mix the rice, tea, and sugar in the wok.
Make a platform for the duck that is an inch or so
above the smoking mixture; use a cake or roasting
rack, or improvise with a crisscross of four chopsticks.
Place the duck, breast side up, on the platform. Cover
the wok very tightly with a cover or a double thickness
of aluminum foil or both; either must be an inch or
more above the top of the duck.

③ Turn heat to high. (Turn on any exhaust fans,
too!) Start timing when the mixture begins to smoke

(you will know because it will leak from somewhere; patch the leak if possible). After 10 minutes, turn the heat to medium. Smoke another 15 to 20 minutes. Turn off the heat, but do not remove the cover for another 15 minutes. The duck will be a deep mahogany color all over; remove from wok.

4 To avoid lingering smokiness in the kitchen, discard the smoking mixture and aluminum foil right away. Mix the remaining 2 tablespoons soy sauce and sesame oil and brush this mixture over the duck. Cut into pieces and serve at room temperature, or stir-fry with vegetables.

Indian-Spiced Duck with Lentils

Makes 4 servings

Time: 3 to 24 hours, largely unattended

Here's a dish in which one duck, because it is augmented by lentils, can legitimately serve four. Like the preceding recipes, it begins with steaming, this time over Indian spices.

1 (4- to 5-pound) duck, excess fat removed, rinsed
    and patted dry with paper towels
10 coriander seeds or 1 teaspoon ground coriander
2 teaspoons ground cardamom
2 tablespoons ground cumin
1 tablespoon minced garlic
1 tablespoon peeled and minced or grated fresh
    ginger
1/4 teaspoon cayenne, or to taste
1 tablespoon paprika
1 cup plain yogurt
1 cup green or orange lentils
1/2 teaspoon ground turmeric
3 cups water
Minced cilantro leaves for garnish

1 Prick the duck skin all over with a sharp fork, skewer, or thin-bladed knife; try not to hit the meat (the fat layer is usually about 1/4 inch thick). Place the coriander, half the ground cardamom, and half the ground cumin in a pot fitted with a rack (a cake rack usually works nicely, but you won't be able to fit much water under it, so be careful not to boil the pot dry). Add water to the base of the rack. Place the duck on the rack, cover the pot, and turn the heat to high. Steam for about 45 minutes, adding boiling water if necessary. Remove the duck, cool slightly, and cut it into serving pieces (page 368).

2 In a large bowl, mix the remaining cardamom and cumin together with the garlic, ginger, cayenne, paprika, and yogurt. Add the duck and marinate for at least 2 hours and up to 24 hours in the refrigerator.

3 Meanwhile, cook the lentils in a medium saucepan with the turmeric and water, stirring occasionally, until most of the water is absorbed and the lentils are tender, about 45 minutes. Mash some of the lentils with a potato masher or fork until the mixture has a somewhat creamy consistency.

4 About 30 minutes before serving, preheat the broiler and place the duck pieces, skin side down, on a broiling pan. Reheat the lentils. Broil the duck about 4 to 6 inches from the source of heat until browned; turn over and brown the other side. Spoon a serving of lentils onto a plate and top with a piece or two of duck. Garnish and serve.

Braised Duck with Turnips

Makes 4 servings

Time: About 1 1/2 hours

This is not a crisp-skin duck recipe, but one that makes the meat very tender. The turnips—or other root vegetable of your choice—are simmered in delicious duck drippings.

1 (4- to 5-pound) duck, excess fat removed, rinsed
   and patted dry with paper towels,
   and cut into serving pieces (page 368)
Salt and freshly ground black pepper to taste
1 teaspoon minced fresh thyme leaves or $1/2$ teaspoon
   dried thyme; or 1 tablespoon minced fresh chervil
   or summer savory leaves
1 bay leaf
2 pounds purple-topped turnips, peeled and cut into
   1-inch chunks
Minced fresh parsley leaves for garnish

1 Preheat the oven to 350°F. Prick the duck skin all over with a sharp fork, skewer, or thin-bladed knife; try not to hit the meat (the fat layer is usually about $1/4$ inch thick). In a large casserole dish that can later be covered, brown the duck on all sides over medium-high heat on top of the stove; you need no added fat to do this. Sprinkle with salt and pepper and prick the skin all over as it browns. Take your time and do a thorough job of browning, regulating the heat so that the duck does not burn. The process will take 15 to 20 minutes.

2 Drain the fat from the casserole dish, add the thyme and bay leaf, cover the casserole, put it in the oven, and roast for about 30 minutes.

3 Remove the casserole from the oven and carefully pour off most of the fat, add the turnips, cover the casserole, and return it to the oven. Stir and baste the turnips every 10 minutes or so until the duck is done, an additional 30 minutes or so (the juices will run clear, and the leg bone will wiggle a little in its socket). When the bird is done, an instant-read thermometer inserted into the thigh will measure about 180°F.

4 Carve the duck (page 359), garnish, and serve.

Basic Roast Goose
Makes 6 to 10 servings

Time: About 3 hours

Like duck, goose does not serve many people per pound. But the rich, dense meat is enormously satisfying, and the skin makes the effort worth it. If you plan on serving lots of people, figure about six servings; you can easily stretch it, though, with a few side dishes. One way to stretch the goose is to stuff it as you would a turkey, using any of the stuffings on pages 405–406 (stuffings with fruit are best here).

1 (8- to 10-pound) goose, excess fat removed, rinsed
   and patted dry with paper towels
Salt and freshly ground black pepper to taste

1 Preheat the oven to 350°F. Prick the goose skin all over with a sharp fork, skewer, or thin-bladed knife; try not to hit the meat (the fat layer is usually about $1/4$ inch thick). Season the goose with salt and pepper and place it, breast side down, on a rack in a roasting pan.

2 Put the roasting pan in the oven and roast the goose for 20 minutes, prick the exposed skin again, then roast another 20 minutes, or until it begins to brown. Then turn the goose breast side up, prick again, and baste with some of the accumulated pan juices (there will be plenty). Roast for another hour, pricking the skin and basting two or three times during that period.

3 Unless the goose is already very brown, raise the heat to 400°F and continue to roast until the meat is done, about another 30 minutes. At that point, all juices, including those from the center vent, should run clear, and the leg bone should wiggle a little in its socket. When the bird is done, an instant-read thermometer inserted into the thigh will measure about 180°F.

4 Carve (see page 359) and serve.

The Basics of Squab, Quail, and Pheasant

These birds need not be gamy to be distinctive, although that is undeniably part of their appeal to some. The amazing thing is how different in flavor they can be, even within species: Farm-raised pheasant are plump and mild-tasting, "free-range" birds are leaner and slightly gamy, and most truly wild specimens—which have darker skin, meat, and fat—have a slightly "off" aroma and a powerful flavor.

Squab, quail, and pheasant, the most common game birds, are sometimes sold fresh, but more often they're frozen. Tiny quail (you need two per serving) are available frozen in many supermarkets. Squab—the most delicious bird there is—can be ordered by any butcher; each bird weighs about a pound, and is so rich that it can legitimately serve two. Pheasant is fairly common, and is often sold in rural areas where it is raised; it can also be ordered. Pheasant have tough, muscular legs that require longer cooking than their breasts. The answer, quite frequently, is to cook the legs and breasts separately. In restaurants, that may mean "cooking the breast and tossing the rest." At home, it makes more sense to work with recipes that exploit the good flavors of the entire bird. Domesticated pheasant, the most common kind, are much like chickens, weighing in at two pounds and more.

Grilled Squab, Vietnamese-Style

Makes 4 to 8 servings

Time: About 1 hour, plus time to preheat the grill

This simple boning technique—in which the wing is left intact, protecting the breast against overcooking—can be used with any bird, including chicken. You can substitute quail (just split them in half), or even Cornish game hens, for squab; the results will be somewhat less flavorful but much less expensive.

> 4 squab, about 1 pound each, innards and excess fat removed, rinsed and patted dry with paper towels
> 1 tablespoon peanut or olive oil
> 1 teaspoon minced garlic
> 2 tablespoons minced shallots
> 2 teaspoons sugar
> 1/4 cup fish sauce or soy sauce
> 1 teaspoon dark sesame oil
> 1/2 teaspoon freshly ground black pepper

1 Place the bird on its back on a cutting board. Using a sharp boning knife, begin at the breastbone and, following the bone, cut straight down through the bird. Cut through the "shoulder" joint, where the wing meets the body. Using your hands, pop out the "hip" joint and separate the thigh from the body, then cut through the skin, meat, and tendons with the knife (see page 368). You will have a half bird; handle it gently, since the leg and breast quarters are held together by nothing more than skin. Repeat the process for the other half of the bird. Reserve or discard carcasses.

2 Mix together all the other ingredients and marinate the squab for up to 2 hours in the refrigerator (even a 20-minute bath is effective). Start a charcoal or wood fire or preheat a gas grill or broiler; the fire should be quite hot and the rack should be about 4 inches from the heat source. Grill the squab about 6 minutes per side, basting frequently and turning once. It is at its best when crisp outside and still fairly pink inside.

Wine-Braised Quail with Herbs

Makes 4 to 8 servings, depending on the number of side dishes

Time: Less than 1 hour

Quail is so small and lean that it inevitably dries out unless it's cooked with liquid. If you enjoy quail, use this recipe and any of the ingredients in the Browned-and-Braised Chicken Parts recipes on pages 367–373, adjusting the cooking time accordingly.

2 tablespoons olive oil, plus more if needed

About 1 cup all-purpose flour for dredging

8 quail, split in half (page 365), excess fat removed, rinsed and patted dry with paper towels

Salt and freshly ground black pepper to taste

1 cup dry white wine

2 ripe tomatoes (or use canned, drained), peeled, cored, seeded, and chopped

1 tablespoon minced fresh sage leaves or 1 teaspoon crumbled dried sage; or 1 teaspoon fresh thyme or rosemary leaves or 1/2 teaspoon dried thyme or rosemary

Minced fresh parsley leaves for garnish

① Heat the oil over medium-high heat in a large, deep skillet, Dutch oven, or casserole. Put the flour on a plate or in a shallow bowl. When the oil is hot (a pinch of flour will sizzle), dredge the quail halves lightly in the flour, shaking off any excess. Add them one at a time to the oil and brown on both sides; you will have to work in batches. Regulate the heat so that the oil bubbles but is not so hot that it will burn the quail. Season the pieces with salt and pepper as they brown and add additional oil if necessary.

② When all the quail are browned, remove them from the skillet. Turn the heat to medium and add the wine, tomatoes, and herb (except the parsley garnish); bring to a boil and let cook for a minute or two. Return the quail to the skillet, turn the heat to low, cover, and cook, turning the quail occasionally, until it is tender, 25 to 30 minutes.

③ Remove the birds to a warm platter. If the sauce is watery turn the heat to high and cook, stirring and scraping the bottom of the pan, until the liquid is reduced by about half. When it's done, pour it over the quail, garnish, and serve.

Thirteen Poultry Dishes You Can Reheat

Prepared in advance or simply left-over, most moist chicken dishes are fine reheated. Some of the best:

1. Chicken in a Pot, page 363
2. "Sour" Chicken in a Pot with Cabbage, page 364
3. Braised Whole Chicken with Tarragon, page 364
4. Chicken, Provençal-Style, page 368
5. Chicken with Onions, page 369
6. Chicken in Red Wine Sauce, page 369
7. Chicken and Garlic Stew, page 372
8. Chicken Thighs with Tomatoes and Olives, page 373
9. Turkey Thighs Braised in Red Wine, page 408
10. Indian-Spiced Duck with Lentils, page 416
11. Braised Duck with Turnips, page 416
12. Wine-Braised Quail with Herbs, page 419
13. Pheasant Stewed with Dried Fruits and Vinegar, page 420

Pheasant Stewed with Dried Fruits and Vinegar

Makes 2 to 4 servings

Time: About 1 hour

Pheasant is like an extreme version of chicken, with tough legs that must be cooked for considerably longer than tender breasts. This easy sweet-and-sour recipe takes that into account. Serve it on top of a bed of barley, orzo, or rice. Use any dried fruit you like here.

12 dried apricots

12 pitted prunes

2 tablespoons olive oil

1 (2- to 3-pound) pheasant, cut into serving pieces (page 368), rinsed and patted dry with paper towels

Salt and freshly ground black pepper to taste

1 cup sliced onion

1 teaspoon minced garlic

2 cups chicken, beef, pheasant stock (see To Make Stock from the Trimmings of Any Bird, page 410), or Vegetable Stock (page 50), or water

2 tablespoons sherry or good wine vinegar

Minced fresh parsley leaves for garnish

1 If the fruit is especially dry, soak it in warm water to cover for 10 to 20 minutes; if it's moist enough to eat, don't bother.

2 Heat a large, deep skillet or casserole over medium-high heat for 2 or 3 minutes. Add the olive oil and, 30 seconds later, begin browning the pheasant pieces. Turn them frequently and regulate the heat so that they do not burn. Season the pieces with salt and pepper as they cook. When they are nicely browned, remove to a plate.

3 Turn the heat to medium and add the onion to the pan; cook, stirring occasionally, for 2 or 3 minutes. Add the garlic and cook for 30 seconds more. Add the stock or water, fruit (drain it first, if necessary), and vinegar. Turn the heat to high and bring to a boil. Return the pheasant to the pan, turn the heat to low, and cover.

4 After 20 minutes, check the breast pieces; when they are done (cooked through but still tender), remove them to a warm plate; cover loosely with aluminum foil. Continue to cook the legs until tender, another 20 to 30 minutes.

5 If the sauce is watery, turn the heat to high and cook, stirring and scraping the bottom of the pan, until the liquid is reduced by about half. When done, return the breast pieces to the skillet and reheat them. Garnish and serve.

Meat

That Americans are eating less meat than we did twenty years ago is not news. Chicken is now the most popular animal protein, fish consumption has climbed steadily, and more Americans than ever call themselves vegetarians. Nevertheless, meat remains the centerpiece of many dinners, whether celebratory or quick. The reasons for this are the same as they always were: As a main course, meat is filling, requires relatively little work, is a relatively inexpensive and an excellent source of protein, and is a least common denominator—that is, most people like it and few reject it. In addition, eating meat remains festive.

Americans seem to be dealing with the health issues presented by the fat content of meat by downsizing the portion size, eating leaner meat, and by eating meat less frequently, at least at home. Bacon, for example, is no longer a given at breakfast, nor is a hamburger at lunch.

How much meat you eat is your business, but you should be aware that smaller portion sizes have had an impact on the estimated number of servings for the recipes in this chapter. In most of my recipes, I assume that a pound of meat serves three to four people rather than the two to three it did not long ago. Obviously, you can change proportions to more accurately reflect your personal style.

As for frequency, if we are eating less meat, we want to make the most of it. This jives perfectly with our overall desire to cook simply, and most of the recipes in this chapter are not only simple but easy. They're designed not to hide the flavor of the meat but to showcase it, even when the meat is not the sole major player, as in the case of stir-fries.

The fact that most meat is leaner than it was twenty and even ten years ago, however, presents cooks with a number of challenges. There was a time when you could throw a pork roast in the oven and cook it to death. The pork contained so much intra-muscular fat that its self-basting qualities provided a great deal of leeway; it took serious overcooking to really ruin a pork roast. Now much pork is too lean for long roasting, or even for grilling or pan-cooking. It must be cooked with liquid, or at the very least removed from the heat when it is short of well done.

In addition, our health concerns clash with our epicurean desires. (This was probably always the case; we just didn't realize it until this century, when food became abundant for a majority of the American population.) It's one thing to say "fat is bad for you," but it's another to codify this statement, as has been done with beef. Whereas once beef was labeled Prime, Choice, and Good—giving you a pretty clear sense which meat to buy, as long as you could afford it—it is now labeled Prime, Choice, and Select, a system that's confusing at best. The fact that Select beef is leaner than either Prime or Choice makes it more desirable in some instances and less desirable in others. Do you want the best-tasting steak? You want Prime. The lowest in fat? Select.

I suspect that as vegetables, grains, and the techniques for cooking them, continue to become increasingly available—from all over the world and throughout the year—our meat consumption may decline a little more. Not much, though, at least anytime soon. Many people will always crave meat. There is something primitive and animal-like in our desire to eat it, and I, for one, don't believe that's a desire that we're better off conquering—just moderating. In the near future, at least, most Americans will continue to eat meat regularly. But the more of a luxury meat becomes, the simpler the preparations should be: Elaborate sauces or stuffings are, for the most part, a thing of the past. They will not make a comeback.

The Basics of Cooking Meat

You can use just about every cooking technique that exists in preparing meat, with a couple of exceptions. It's unusual to boil or steam most meats. More often than not, even when meat is cooked in flavorful liquid, it tends to be a braise rather than a stew—that is, a dish with enough liquid to provide moisture but not so much to make a dish that is soupy.

Most meat tastes best when it's browned, because the process of browning creates literally hundreds of flavor compounds. You can brown by grilling, broiling, pan-grilling, roasting, or sautéing, usually with added fat. The first four of these techniques are not merely the initial process of a given recipe but the entire technique; that is, when you brown meat by grilling, broiling, pan-grilling or roasting, you usually finish cooking it that way also.

That is sometimes the case with sautéing too. But when you're braising or stewing meat (or poultry, for that matter), you frequently want to give it an initial browning to heighten flavors. There are two things you might want to note about this: First, this is a step that can be skipped. The initial browning is more noticeable in some final dishes than in others but, given that most braised recipes have several added flavors, it isn't always essential. This is heretical in fine cooking, and many food writers and chefs may call me idiotic for saying this, but if you're pressed for time, skip the browning step; it's unlikely that you'll be disappointed by the results (and if you are, well, you've learned something, and you can call me idiotic too). Don't get me wrong: I'm all for browning, but if it makes the difference between finding another recipe or proceeding without the browning step, I'll sometimes choose the latter, and I'm rarely sorry.

If you do choose to brown meat before proceeding with cooking, you should try the oven. It's easier to brown a large quantity of meat at high heat (450° to 500°F) in the oven than on top of the stove, and it is also far less messy. In addition, you can usually use less fat in the process. Once you try it, you'll probably become a convert.

The Basics of Beef

Cooking beef is often little more than combining the right cooking technique with the right cut. The more tender cuts—such as sirloin, tenderloin, and rib eye— are best grilled or roasted, and cooked rare. The tougher cuts—like chuck, round, and brisket—need to be broken down with long cooking and moist heat, and are better well done.

If you had a good butcher, it would be almost as simple as that. The problem is that there are few real butchers left. Supermarket meat managers fill out a form to order beef, and know far more about selling the animals than raising or even butchering them.

The meat arrives wrapped in plastic, broken down into secondary cuts, ready for final cutting (which is often done with a saw rather than a knife) and packaging. Where was the animal raised? What was it fed? How old was it? Was it fatty or lean? How much did it weigh? He doesn't know, and you'll never find out.

Sadly, buying beef in a supermarket is a bit of a crapshoot. In some supermarkets, you can buy Prime beef and, if you're looking for a good steak or roast, that is definitely the way to go, although there are times when high-quality Choice is preferable to not-so-great Prime. In some cities and even rural areas, you can still find a butcher, who can guide you in selecting the cut that best meets your plans; he may even hang beef for aging, improving both its flavor and its texture, something that is never done in a supermarket. Or, if you're energetic and have a large freezer, you can probably find someone locally who is raising a few cattle the old-fashioned way, and will sell you a side or a quarter after slaughter or, better still, after a little aging.

Most times, though, you'll buy a piece of beef in the supermarket within a day or two of cooking it. In

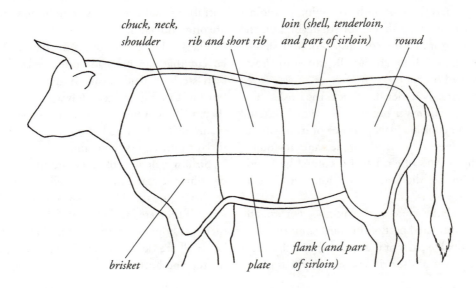

chuck, neck, shoulder

rib and short rib

loin (shell, tenderloin, and part of sirloin)

round

brisket

plate

flank (and part of sirloin)

this case, the most important decision you make will be in matching the cut to the technique. If you grill chuck (or any cut from the front quarter) or roast round, you will be disappointed. Similarly, braising good sirloin is not only a waste of money but will give less than ideal results.

Most beef is quite flavorful; one of the most expensive cuts, the tenderloin, is a notable exception. But some beef must be cooked with liquid, or sliced very thinly, in order to be chewable.

If a piece of beef is cut thinly, it can be called a steak; a thick piece can be called a roast or a pot roast. Unfortunately none of these terms guarantees tenderness or tastiness; we've all had "steaks" that were tough, or tasteless, or roasts that refused to soften even after hours of cooking. To guarantee the results you're looking for, you must buy the right cut.

Chuck   The neck/shoulder area, back to the fifth rib, is muscular and has lots of connective tissue, which means it is flavorful, but best suited to long, slow cooking. Cuts from the chuck are called shoulder roast (or steaks), arm roast (or steaks), blade, top blade, or underblade roast (or steaks), and eye roast. The steaks have good flavor, but they're tough, and do not taste as good as those from the rib, loin, or sirloin. Boneless chuck meat is suitable for stir-frying; much is ground. The front of the cow also produces shank and shin, both of which are usually cut into short lengths and used for soup.

Brisket   Directly under the chuck, the brisket has good flavor but will never become what you call tender; even if you cook the daylights out of it, it will be chewy. (This doesn't mean it's unpleasant; it's quite tasty, just chewy.) It's often used for corned beef and pastrami. In front of the brisket is the foreshank, good for stew or soup meat.

Rib   Behind the chuck, ribs number 6 through 12 (rib 13 is considered part of the loin) comprise one of the most valuable parts of the steer (ribs 10 through 12 are best). Rib steaks (or rib-eye steaks) are as good

as they come, and so are the cuts used for the famous *entrecôte* of France and *bistecca alla fiorentina* of Italy. Rib roasts are the best pieces of beef to roast dry; and short ribs—pieces of the long rib bones cut into sections—are wonderful for braising.

Plate   Behind the brisket and under the rib, this is even tougher and harder to cook than brisket; it's often cured to make pastrami, but is sometimes sold as steaks, which have good flavor but are very, very tough. Good for stew meat.

Loin, or Short Loin   Another highly valuable section directly behind the rib. Actually it's two sections: the top (shell) and the bottom (tenderloin). The tenderloin can be sold whole (and makes a great roast), or cut into filet mignon or *tournedos*; it's the most tender part of the steer, but not that flavorful, so steaks or roasts made from the tenderloin are much improved by sauces. The shell, which extends back to the sirloin, is where the most popular and some of the best steaks come from, especially New York strip— also called shell steaks, club steaks, or strip loin steaks. T-bone and porterhouse steaks, nearly identical, are part tenderloin (tender but not especially tasty) and part of the shell (not so tender, but much more flavorful). Delmonico steaks contain no tenderloin, and are often boneless.

Flank   Under the loin is the flank, a lean, muscular cut that can be made into steaks, labeled either skirt steak or flank steak. Both steaks are delicious, but must be thinly sliced (always across the grain) or they will be tough. Good for stir-frying and for "London broil," which simply means broiled steak, sliced thinly across the grain.

Sirloin   Behind the loin and the flank, the sirloin contains the rear end of the shell, which makes steaks of varying quality. They may simply be labeled "sirloin"; if they are labeled more fully, choose pin-bone, then flat-bone, then round-bone, and finally wedge-bone; all are decent, but pin-bone is best. It also has the top and bottom butt, or rump, which may be sold as boneless sirloin or other roasts (not as good as rib, but better than round) or steaks, such as rump steaks or Newport steaks.

Round The rear end of the cow, which is best used as ground meat, is often cut into steaks (top round, also called rump) and roasts (top or bottom round), which are almost always tough and never especially flavorful. Their one advantage: They are really lean. For pot-roasting, look to chuck. For oven-roasting or steaks, look to the rib, loin, or sirloin. Round meat is good, however, for stir-frying, as long as it is sliced thinly. From the rear end of the cow, too, comes "oxtail" (rarely, if ever, from ox anymore), which is cross-cut and used for soups or stews.

The Basics of Steaks

The old adage, "You can't ruin a good steak" is almost true. A "good" steak means the right cut and, given that, you can ruin it only by cooking it to a point of doneness that doesn't please you, or by overcooking it altogether. If you're unsure of your timing, aim to undercook by a wide margin, then use a thin-bladed knife to peek inside the meat and check for doneness; you can always throw the steak back on for a couple of minutes if it's too rare for you. You can also check steaks—especially thick ones—for doneness with an instant-read thermometer. Rare steaks will measure 120° to 125°F; medium-rare to medium measures from 130° to about 150°F; I'd consider anything above that well done.

There are three or four cuts of beef that are both tender and tasty enough to be cut as steaks and grilled or broiled without much further fuss. These are all from the loin or the rib sections. From the loin are cut strip steaks (also called shell, club, New York, or top loin), which are usually sold boneless and make the ideal individual steak. The loin also yields T-bone, or Porterhouse, a bone-in steak that contains mostly sirloin but also a bit of the tender but less flavorful

tenderloin; these are best cut thick to serve two or more people. Rib-eye steaks, the boneless center of the rib, are also very tender and very flavorful, and make good individual steaks. A trustworthy butcher can guide you to one or two obscure cuts of beef that also make good steaks, such as hanger or skirt steak, but it's unlikely that you will find them in a supermarket.

Steaks simply labeled "sirloin" and sold bone-in or bone-out, are riskier; some are better than others and generalizations are difficult. But they're usually quite flavorful, and the worst that can happen is that they are on the chewy side. This is also the case with flank steak, a delicious cut from between the loin and ribs, which is guaranteed to be chewy but flavorful. It's a good steak to marinate and grill, then cut into slices. Like some other cuts that are not ideal steaks—such as the pieces of very lean top round that are often sold as steak—it is also good cut into bits and stir-fried, or very quickly grilled or broiled, then sliced thin—which makes it "London broil."

A word about chuck: Despite the assurances of your supermarket meat manager, it's guaranteed to be very, very chewy if you cook it as a steak. Chuck is a great meat for grinding or cooking with liquid. Don't try to grill it.

Grilled Steak, American-Style

Makes 2 to 4 servings

Time: About 10 minutes, plus time to build the fire

Straightforward and simple. Start with the right steak (prime, if you can find it, is worth it in this instance) and don't overcook. This is one of those times where a gas grill simply will not do the trick; you need a blazing hot fire and no cover if you want your steak crisp and slightly charred on the outside and rare inside; use real hardwood charcoal if at all possible. In this single case, pan-grilling is closer to grilling than broiling, since most home broilers just don't get hot enough.

> 2 sirloin strip, rib-eye, or other steaks, 8 ounces each
>   and about 1 inch thick
> Salt and freshly ground black pepper to taste

1 Remove the steaks from the refrigerator and their packaging if you have not already done so. Build a medium-hot charcoal fire; you should not be able to hold your hand 3 inches above it for more than 2 or 3 seconds (see The Basics of Grilling and Broiling, page 10). The rack should be 3 or 4 inches from the top of the coals.

2 Dry the steaks with paper towels. Grill them without turning for 3 minutes (a little more if they're over an inch thick, a little less if they're thinner or you like steaks extremely rare). Turn, then grill for 3 minutes on the other side. Steaks will be rare to medium-rare.

3 Check for doneness. If you would like the steaks better done, move them away from the most intense heat and grill another minute or two longer per side; check again. When done, sprinkle with salt and pepper and serve.

Grilled Porterhouse (T-bone) Steak: These are best when very thick, 1¹/₂ inches or more, and weigh about 2 pounds, in which case they will easily serve 4 to 6 people. In Step 2, grill for 4 to 5 minutes per side, taking care not to burn the meat; the leaner tenderloin (the smaller of the two pieces on either side of the bone) is best very rare, so keep it toward the coolest part of the fire. Check for doneness, preferably with an instant-read thermometer and in both the sirloin and the tenderloin sections. If not done to your liking, move the steak to a cooler part of the grill and cook for another 2 to 3 minutes per side before checking again.

Broiled Steak: See The Basics of Grilling and Broiling, page 10, and remember that a broiler is little more than an upside-down grill. The major difference is that melting fat can build up in your broiling pan and catch fire, so it's best to broil on a rack. Turn the broiler to maximum, preheat it, and broil 3 to 4 inches from the heat source (any more, and you won't brown the steak; any less, and you'll burn it). Proceed as for grilling, with this exception: If your broiler heat is not intense enough to brown the steak well, don't turn it, but cook it the entire time on one side only. It will cook reasonably evenly, and should develop a nice crust on the top.

Pan-Grilled Steak: See Pan-Grilling, page 12. A terrific option for 1-inch-thick steaks (not much thicker, though), as long as you have a decent exhaust fan; otherwise, see the next option. Preheat a cast-iron or other sturdy skillet just large enough to hold the steaks over medium-high heat for 4 to 5 minutes; the pan should be really hot—in fact, it should be smoking. Sprinkle its surface with coarse salt and put in the steaks. Clouds of smoke will instantly appear; do not turn down the heat. The timing remains the same as for grilled steaks.

Pan-Grilled/Oven-Roasted Steak: An excellent alternative to grilling for homes without good exhaust systems. Turn the oven to its maximum temperature, at least 500°F, and set a rack in the lowest possible position (if you can place a skillet directly on the oven floor, so much the better). Preheat a cast-iron or other sturdy, ovenproof skillet large enough to hold the steaks over medium-high heat for 4 to 5 minutes; the pan should be really hot, just about smoking. Sprinkle its surface with coarse salt and put in the steaks. Immediately transfer the skillet to the oven (wearing a thick oven mitt to protect your hand); timing remains the same as for grilled steaks.

Bistro Steak: After cooking, top each steak with 1 teaspoon to 1 tablespoon of any compound butter (page 768). For example, try parsley butter mixed with a little garlic (with some minced anchovy, if you like).

Tuscan Steak: Drizzle some flavorful extra-virgin olive oil over the steak when it is done; top with freshly squeezed lemon juice to taste.

Grilled Marinated Flank Steak

Makes 4 to 8 servings

Time: About 1 hour, largely unattended,
plus time to preheat the grill

Flank steak is best for slicing; a marinade gives each slice more flavor. You can grill the whole piece, of course, but I like to grill half of it and leave the rest in its marinade, refrigerated, for a day or two. I use some for a salad and some for a stir-fry; see the variations, below.

Flank steak is also good without marinating: just coat it with All-Purpose Curry Powder (page 778), chili powder, or any other commercial or homemade spice rub before cooking.

After cooking, slice the meat against the "grain"—that is, across its natural striations.

4 tablespoons freshly squeezed lime juice
2 tablespoons soy sauce or fish sauce (*nuoc mam* or *nam pla*, available at Asian markets)
1 teaspoon minced garlic
1 teaspoon peeled and minced or grated fresh ginger or 1 teaspoon ground ginger
1 teaspoon sugar
Salt and freshly ground black pepper to taste
1 flank steak, 2 to 2$\frac{1}{2}$ pounds

① Combine all the seasonings in a shallow bowl or platter and marinate the steak in them for at least 30 minutes (if the marinating time is longer than an hour, refrigerate). Near the end of the marinating time, start a charcoal or wood fire or preheat a gas grill or broiler; make it very hot.

② Remove the meat from the marinade and dry well with paper towels. Grill or broil the steak about 4 inches from the heat source for 3 to 4 minutes per side, or until nicely browned. Move the meat to a cooler part of the grill (or lower the broiling rack) and cook for another 2 minutes per side. Check for doneness by touch, with a thin-bladed knife, or, preferably, with an instant-read thermometer (125°F is about right for rare to medium-rare).

③ Let rest for 5 minutes before cutting into thin slices, across the grain, using a sharp carving knife.

Salad with Grilled Marinated Flank Steak: Cut $\frac{1}{2}$ recipe of flank steak, cooked as above, into chunks. Toss with 6 cups of torn washed and dried mixed lettuces (a store-bought mesclun mixture is great), and top with some quartered ripe tomatoes and sliced cucumber. Mix together 6 tablespoons freshly squeezed lime juice, 1 tablespoon soy sauce, and 2 tablespoons peanut oil; add pepper, salt if necessary, and a dash of cayenne if you like. Taste and adjust seasoning. Drizzle over the salad and serve. (Makes 4 servings.)

Marinated Flank Steak for Stir-Fries: Reserve one quarter to one half of the flank steak while you marinate the rest. Freeze the reserved piece for 30 minutes. When you remove the larger piece of steak for grilling, slice the frozen portion as thinly as possible. Use the same liquid to marinate it for up to a day, then use in any stir-fry recipe (see, for example, Stir-Fried Beef with Onions, page 441).

Pan-Seared Steak with Red Wine Sauce

Steak au Poivre

Makes 4 servings

Time: 15 minutes

Few elegant, impressive dishes are as fast as this one. If you use tenderloin, you'll really need the sauce because the meat is so lean. If you use sirloin or rib-eye, the peppercorns and butter alone will be delicious (although the sauce won't hurt). For extra flavor, coat the steaks with the peppercorns an hour or so before cooking and let them sit at room temperature.

Decent red wine makes a difference here; zinfandel, for example, has a spicy fruitiness that complements the tarragon and shallots nicely. Use a skillet that will fit the steaks comfortably, without either crowding them (which will cause them to steam rather than brown) or leaving too much room, which will allow the butter to burn.

This recipe is easily varied; use any spice rub, or ground Szechwan peppercorns, in place of the black peppercorns. And see Eleven Ideas for Reduction Sauces, page 791.

4 tenderloin steaks (filet mignon or "tournedos"),
    4 to 6 ounces each, or use sirloin strip or rib-eye
Freshly ground black pepper, or a mixture of
    black pepper and crushed (see Step 2)
    allspice berries
3 tablespoons butter (preferred) or olive oil
1 tablespoon minced shallots
³/₄ cup zinfandel or other good red wine
2 sprigs fresh tarragon or ¹/₄ teaspoon dried
    tarragon, plus fresh sprigs for garnish (optional)
Salt to taste

1 Preheat a large skillet over medium heat for about 3 minutes; turn the oven to 200°F.

2 Sprinkle steaks liberally with pepper. For genuine steak au poivre, coarsely grind about 1 tablespoon of pepper and press into the meat. About 1 part ground allspice berries to 3 parts pepper lends an interesting dimension.

3 Put 2 tablespoons of the butter into the skillet; when the foam subsides, turn the heat to medium-high and put in the steaks. Cook the steaks for about 3 minutes per side for rare meat, a bit longer if you like it medium to well done. Undercook them a bit as they will continue to cook in the oven.

4 Remove the steaks to an ovenproof platter and place the platter in the oven. Over medium heat, add the remaining butter to the pan, along with the shallots. Stir until the shallots soften, about 1 minute.

5 Add the wine and the tarragon, raise the heat to high, and let most of the liquid bubble away. Pour any juices that have accumulated around the steaks into the sauce and add salt to taste. Spoon the sauce over the steaks and serve, garnished with additional tarragon if you like.

Chopped Steak with Wine Sauce: Use 1¹/₂ pounds freshly ground meat (see page 432). Shape the meat gently into 4 patties, incorporating 1 teaspoon salt and 1 teaspoon freshly ground black pepper. Omit exterior coating of pepper. Proceed as above.

The Basics of Roast Beef

Supermarkets will sell you almost anything as an oven roast, from chuck to round. But roasting, like grilling, must start with tender meat—dry cooking does very little to tenderize meat, especially if you like it rare. Which leaves you with four good choices for roasting:

Prime rib My favorite cut of beef for roasting; like leg of lamb, it's so big that if you cook the deepest center to rare you are also going to wind up with spots that are medium and those that are well done, pleasing everyone. And prime rib is so juicy that even well done (not overcooked, just well done) meat is tender and moist. If you want the best roast, make a special request for the small end (the twelfth through the seventh ribs) and ask the butcher—even a supermarket butcher can do this—to cut it to order for you, removing the short ribs; you want what's called a "short" roast. (You can cook those short ribs separately with any of the recipes on pages 433–434.) If you are serving four to six people, buy three or four ribs (higher numbers are better, so look for ribs twelve through ten, or nine); if you're serving more, add another rib for every two people, unless you want to serve gargantuan portions. I usually buy a three-rib roast for up to six people and have leftovers, but I believe in serving lots of side dishes when I make a roast so no one is tempted to eat a pound of meat. For rare meat, figure *about* fifteen to twenty minutes per pound roasting for any prime rib roast, regardless of the size, but see the recipe for details.

Boneless prime rib   You can get the meat taken off the bones by the butcher, or do it yourself (see illustrations, page 431), but the resulting roast will be neither as flavorful nor as much fun. Still, it will be a *lot* easier to carve. Be careful not to overcook; removing the bone decreases your margin of error.

Fillet of beef   This is the whole tenderloin, and a wonderfully tender roast it is, but not a super-flavorful one. Unlike prime rib, which requires no saucing whatsoever, you should make a sauce if you want a roast fillet. I don't think it's worth the expense, and would rather use fillet for sautéing or grilling, but this is inarguably easy and makes a beautiful presentation, so you may want to try it; directions and sauce suggestions follow. You can also grill a whole fillet; it won't take more than thirty minutes, but don't keep it over super-hot coals the entire time or the outside will burn. Rather, sear it over the hottest part of the fire, then move it a little to the side to finish cooking; cover the grill if possible after the initial sear.

Whole strip   This is the cut I recommend for the best steaks, but it can also be left whole. For roasts, it is boned (and called a "shell" as often as it is a "strip"). It's flavorful and expensive, but my second-favorite roast after prime rib. A whole roast weighs about ten pounds and will serve twenty people or more, depending on side dishes. You don't have to cook the whole strip, of course; I've roasted three-pound pieces with great success. This can easily be grilled too, in much the same way as the fillet.

A word about roasts and doneness: All beef is rare at 125°F (120°F for really rare); there are noticeable differences in meat color for each 5° difference in temperature. I'd never cook anything beyond 155°F, although some cooks suggest cooking roast beef to 170°F for well done. Large roasts will rise at least 5° in temperature between the time you remove them from the oven and the time you carve them, so bear that in mind as well. Remember, too, that cutting into a piece of meat to check its doneness is far from a sin; it's one of those things that everyone does but no one talks about. So if you're at all in doubt, cut into the middle or take a slice from the end. Your presentation will not be as beautiful but if the meat is perfectly cooked no one will care.

Prime Rib Roast for a Small Crowd

Makes about 6 servings

Time: About 1^1/$_2$ hours, largely unattended

See above for information about cuts. This is a simple roasting technique: high heat to sear the meat, lower heat to cook it through. If you want a really crisp exterior, turn the heat back to 450°F for a few minutes right at the end of cooking; this won't affect the internal temperature too much.

Leftover roast beef makes great hash; see Corned Beef (or Roast Beef) Hash, page 439.

1 (3-rib) roast, about 5 pounds, trimmed of excess
but not all fat
Salt and freshly ground black pepper to taste
1 or 2 cloves garlic (optional)
1 cup red wine, stock, or water (see "Soups"
for stock recipes)

1 Bring the meat to room temperature by removing it from the refrigerator at least an hour before cooking, preferably two. Preheat the oven to 450°F.

2 Place the meat, bone side down, in a large roasting pan. Season it with salt and pepper. If you like garlic, peel the cloves and cut them into tiny slivers; use a boning or paring knife to poke small holes in the meat and insert the garlic into them.

3 Place the roast in the oven and cook for 15 minutes, undisturbed. Turn the heat down to 350°F and continue to roast for about 1 hour; check in several places with a meat thermometer. When no spot checks in at under 125°F (120°F if you like your meat really rare and your guests are of the same mentality), the meat is rare; cook another 5 or 10 minutes if you like it better done, then check again, but in no case let the temperature of the meat go above 155°F.

4 Remove the meat from the oven (now's the time to cook Yorkshire pudding; see below, and cover the meat with foil to keep it warm). Pour off all but a few tablespoons of the fat and place the roasting pan over a burner set to high. Add the liquid and cook, stirring and scraping up any brown bits, until it is reduced by half. Slice the roast and serve, splashing a little of the sauce on the meat platter and passing the rest at the table.

Prime Rib for a Big Crowd: With bigger roasts, 5 ribs or more, make sure to allow plenty of time to let the meat reach room temperature. In Step 2, use more garlic if you like. In Step 3, increase initial browning time to 20 minutes. After that, cooking instructions remain the same, and cooking time will be only marginally longer, but be sure to use an instant-read thermometer in several different places to check the meat. Increase the liquid in Step 4 to at least 2 cups.

Prime Rib with Roasted Vegetables: If the roast is small, cut vegetables into 1-inch chunks; if it is large, you can leave them whole as long as they are not huge. Allow 1 medium peeled potato, 1 medium peeled carrot, 1 medium peeled onion, a couple of cloves of garlic (you don't have to peel these), and similar amounts of turnips, parsnips, and other root vegetables as you like (or just use potatoes). Scatter them around the roast at the beginning, and drizzle them with a little bit of olive oil. Roast with the meat; you don't need to baste, since the dripping fat will take care of that. Remove the vegetables and keep warm. If you like, brown them for a minute or two longer under the broiler while you prepare the reduction sauce, but watch them carefully to prevent burning.

Yorkshire Pudding: Essentially a large popover (see Popovers, page 253), this will serve at least 6; make 2 separate ones if you're going to serve 12 or more. The batter can be made ahead: Beat 3 eggs until foamy and light; add 1 cup milk and beat some more. Add salt to taste and 1 cup all-purpose flour; stir gently, only enough to combine ingredients. Refrigerate until 10 minutes before the roast is done. At that time, place a large cast-iron skillet or a 9-inch square baking pan in the oven to preheat. When you take the roast from the oven, put 3 tablespoons of its drippings into the pan, working carefully to avoid getting burned. Turn the heat to 450°F and put the pan back in the oven until your oven reaches that temperature. Carefully pour the batter into the pan. Bake 10 minutes, then lower the heat to 350°F and reverse the pan back to front once during cooking so the pudding browns evenly. Bake another 10 minutes, or slightly more, until the pudding is high and brown. Cut up and serve immediately, with the carved roast and its juices.

Boneless Prime Rib: Have the butcher tie it so that it is of roughly uniform thickness. Cook as above, using a meat thermometer to gauge doneness; total weight won't matter much since there is no bone and the roast is relatively thin. A 3-pound boneless roast is almost certain to be done in less than an hour, so plan accordingly and watch it carefully; a 5- or 6-pound roast won't take a whole lot longer.

For a bone-in prime rib, cut close to the bone, between the ribs, for the first slice.

Unless you want huge portions, the second slice is boneless.

Roast Tenderloin with Herbs
Makes at least 10 servings

Time: At least 1½ hours, largely unattended

A large piece of beef tenderloin makes a beautiful presentation.

½ cup extra-virgin olive oil

1 tablespoon balsamic or sherry vinegar

¼ cup roughly chopped fresh parsley, stems included

1 teaspoon fresh thyme leaves, or several thyme sprigs, or ½ teaspoon dried thyme

1 bay leaf

2 cloves garlic, lightly smashed

1 (5-pound) tenderloin, trimmed of fat

Salt and freshly ground black pepper to taste

Béarnaise Sauce (page 789), Walnut Oil Vinaigrette (page 92), or Anchovy-Caper Vinaigrette (page 93)

1 Combine the first six ingredients; marinate the meat in this mixture for an hour or more (refrigerated if longer than an hour). When you're ready to cook, preheat the oven to 450°F.

2 Remove the meat from the marinade and pat it dry. Roast for 20 minutes, then check with meat thermometer; when the meat measures 125°F in a couple of places (since the thickness doesn't vary much, there shouldn't be much change in temperature from one spot to another) it is medium-rare; remove the roast from the oven and season with salt and pepper.

3 Let the meat rest for about 5 minutes before carving; cut into thick (at least ½ inch) slices, and serve with one of the sauces suggested above, or the sauce of your choice.

Roast Sirloin Strip: You can use anything from a 3- to a 10-pound (whole) strip; here, the weight won't affect cooking time much, because there is no bone and the thickness is uniform. Cook exactly as above, beginning to check temperature after 45 or 50 minutes; marinating and saucing are unnecessary, but a reduction sauce (see The Basics of Reduction Sauces, page 790) made with parsley or chervil and red wine is quite nice.

The Basics of Burgers

Ground chuck—which generally corresponds to the "eighty percent lean" ground meat sold in supermarkets—makes the best burgers; the fat acts to keep it moist. Of course you can use more expensive round or sirloin as well, but beware that the leaner the burger the more important it is to serve it rare (fat keeps overcooked burgers somewhat juicy, but lean simply dries out).

Given concerns about the safety of store-ground meat—preground meat has been linked to contamination by the salmonella and E. coli bacteria—you might want to try grinding your own meat for burgers. It's easy: Buy a chuck roast, cut it into one- to two-inch cubes, and pulse a small batch—about one-half pound—at a time in the food processor (see The Basics of Appliances and Electric Gadgets, page 7). Make sure you don't pulverize the meat and it'll be wonderful. Freeze what you don't use immediately.

If you do buy pre-ground meat, most authorities now recommend that you cook it to well done—160°F—to kill the harmful bacteria. Do this once and you're likely to begin grinding your own meat, since well-done hamburgers are often too dry to eat.

The Basic Burger

Makes 4 servings

Time: 20 minutes, plus time to preheat the grill

Like steak, burgers need not be grilled; they're terrific made in a heavy skillet sprinkled with salt (see below for details). If you like cheeseburgers, add cheese as soon as you turn the meat.

1¼ to 1½ pounds ground chuck or sirloin,
   not too lean

1 teaspoon salt, plus more if you're pan-grilling

1 You want to handle the meat as little as possible to avoid compressing it; shape it lightly into 4 burgers, about 4 to 5 inches across, sprinkling with salt as you do so. Start a charcoal or wood fire or preheat a gas grill; if you're cooking on a stove top, preheat a large, heavy skillet (cast iron is best) over medium-high heat for 3 or 4 minutes; sprinkle its surface with coarse salt.

2 The fire should be quite hot; you should barely be able to hold your hand 3 or 4 inches over the rack. Put the burgers on the rack and grill about 3 minutes per side for very rare, and another minute per side for each increasing stage of doneness, but no more than 10 minutes total unless you like hockey pucks. Timing on the stove top is exactly the same.

3 Serve on buns, toast, or hard rolls, garnished as you like.

Eight Simple Ideas for Flavoring Burgers

Like any ground or chopped meat, burgers respond brilliantly to added seasonings. Try incorporating some of the following combinations during shaping, combining them at will and experimenting to find those you like best:

1. Two tablespoons minced fresh parsley, basil, chervil, or other herbs
2. One-fourth teaspoon or more minced garlic
3. One tablespoon minced anchovies
4. One teaspoon peeled and minced or grated fresh ginger, or ground ginger
5. One tablespoon soy, Worcestershire, steak, or other flavored sauce
6. One-fourth cup minced onion, shallot, or scallion
7. Tabasco or other hot sauce to taste (start with one-half teaspoon)
8. One teaspoon All-Purpose Curry Powder (page 778), chili powder, or other spice mixtures to taste

The Basics of Short Ribs

Most short ribs are simply the cut-off ends of the prime rib. (They may also be cut from a different part of the cow, but are treated the same.) You can grill or broil short ribs, and they are delicious; but make sure your teeth are strong and be prepared to exercise your jaw muscles. Because they're so tough, it's better to cook short ribs in liquid until they are *really* tender, practically mushy. Their great flavor will intensify any liquid surrounding them.

Short ribs cut the long way—called breast plate or flanken—are good braised with beans; take the meat off the bone before serving. These recipes can also be used for shank, or shin, and oxtail; cooking times will probably be longer.

Short Ribs Simmered with Potatoes and Mustard

Makes 4 servings

Time: About 2 hours, or overnight, largely unattended

The ideal way to cook this is to simmer the meat and vegetables one day, then separate them and refrigerate. The next day, you can skim the fat before finishing the dish. Or cook the whole thing in one session.

2 tablespoons any neutral vegetable or olive oil

3 pounds meaty short ribs, more or less

Salt and freshly ground black pepper to taste

2 cups minced onions

1 cup chicken, beef, or vegetable stock, or water (see "Soups" for stock recipes)

1 pound waxy red or white potatoes, peeled, cut in half if large

Dry red wine (optional)

2 tablespoons Dijon or other good mustard

Minced fresh parsley leaves for garnish

1 Heat the oil over medium-high heat in a Dutch oven or similar pot. Brown the short ribs well on all sides, seasoning them as they cook with salt and pepper. Regulate the heat so that the ribs do not burn. This process will take 20 minutes or so; don't rush it. (You can also do the initial browning in the oven: Preheat to 500°F and roast the ribs, turning once or twice, until brown all over; time will be about the same, 20 minutes.)

2 Remove the ribs to a plate, pour off all but 2 tablespoons of the fat, and turn the heat to medium.

3 Cook the onions over medium heat until soft, stirring occasionally, about 10 minutes; stir in the stock or water, salt, and pepper. Return the ribs to the pot, bring to a boil over medium-high heat, cover, and reduce the heat to low. Cook, stirring occasionally.

4 After 30 minutes, add the potatoes. Cook, turning the ribs in the stock every 15 minutes or so, and adding a little more liquid—stock, water, or dry red wine—if the mixture seems dry. The dish is done when the meat is very tender and almost falling off the bone, and the potatoes are soft, at least another 30 minutes. (At this point you may use a slotted spoon to remove the meat and vegetables to a platter and refrigerate them and the stock overnight. The next day, skim the fat from the stock, add the meat and vegetables back to it, and reheat.) Stir the mustard into the stew, taste and adjust seasonings, garnish, and serve.

Short Ribs with Horseradish: When the ribs are done (Step 4), remove them and the potatoes to a platter and keep warm. Turn the heat to high and reduce the cooking liquid to about 1 cup. Add 1 tablespoon wine vinegar and 2 tablespoons freshly grated or prepared horseradish, or to taste. Pour the sauce over the ribs, garnish with parsley, and serve hot.

Anise-Scented Short Ribs

Makes 4 servings

Time: 2 hours, or a little more, largely unattended

You can also make these with lamb shanks. If you do, it's definitely easier to use the oven for browning.

1 tablespoon peanut or neutral vegetable oil

3 pounds meaty short ribs, more or less

Freshly ground black pepper or Szechwan
  peppercorns to taste

1 medium-to-large onion, chopped

5 nickel-sized slices fresh ginger or 2 teaspoons
  ground ginger

3 cloves garlic, lightly crushed

5 whole star anise

1/4 cup soy sauce or fish sauce (*nuoc mam* or
  nam pla, available at Asian markets)

1 cup water

1 tablespoon rice or white wine vinegar

2 tablespoons sugar

2 medium carrots, peeled and cut into 1/4-inch-thick
  slices

Salt (optional)

① Heat the oil over medium-high heat in a Dutch oven or similar pot. Brown the short ribs well on all sides, seasoning them as they cook with pepper. Regulate the heat so that the ribs do not burn. This process will take 20 minutes or so; don't rush it. (You can also do the initial browning in the oven: Preheat to 500°F and roast the ribs, turning once or twice, until brown all over; time will be about the same, 20 minutes.)

② Remove the ribs with a slotted spoon and pour off most of the fat. Lower the heat to medium and cook the onion, stirring, until it begins to soften, about 5 minutes. Stir in the ginger and garlic and continue to cook for 2 minutes. Add all the remaining ingredients except the carrots and salt. Bring to a boil and return the ribs to the pot. Reduce the heat to low and cover. Cook gently, turning the ribs occasionally, for about 1 hour.

③ Add the carrots, re-cover the pot, and cook about 30 minutes more, or until the ribs are tender and the meat just about falling off the bone. Turn the oven to 200°F. With a slotted spoon, remove the ribs and the carrots to a platter and place in the oven. Discard any ginger pieces and the star anise. Turn the heat under the pot to high and reduce the liquid, stirring, until it is thick and syrupy, about 10 minutes. Taste and add salt or more soy sauce if necessary. Spoon the sauce over the ribs and serve with white rice.

The Basics of Beef Stews

I'd choose to call most meat dishes cooked with liquid braises rather than stews; the two factors defining a braise are that the meat is browned first and that it doesn't swim in the liquid. (Stews, in my opinion, contain more liquid, so you can turn any "braise" into a "stew" by adding more liquid.) Feel free to vary the liquid you use—it's usually only one of many seasonings. And don't be afraid to use water; the intensity may be somewhat diminished, but the meat will make its own stock as it cooks.

Chuck, brisket, round, and rump are all good cuts for braising, and even some sirloin cuts benefit from it. Cooking time varies from one cut to another (and, indeed, from one animal to another). Keep the heat low and allow plenty of time, testing every fifteen minutes or so after the first hour. If the dish is done ahead of schedule, don't worry about it: Let it cool and reheat it; it will only get better with time. If you plan ahead and make the dish long before serving, refrigerate it; if a thick layer of fat rises to the surface, skim some or all of it off with a spoon.

Classic Beef Stew

Makes 4 to 6 servings

Time: 1½ to 2 hours, largely unattended

Browning the beef before braising adds another dimension of flavor, but isn't absolutely necessary; see the following recipe, Garlicky Beef Daube. Try it both ways; skipping the browning step saves time and mess.

Note, too, that stewed beef can be spiced in many different ways; I offer a couple here, but you can also make a chili-like beef stew (add the seasonings from the recipe for Chili con Carne, page 520), a beef curry (see Lamb Curry, page 486), or a sweet, Thai-flavored stew (see Sweet Simmered Pork Chops, page 459). The substitutions are easy and work perfectly.

2 tablespoons canola or other neutral oil, or olive oil

1 clove garlic, lightly crushed, plus 1 tablespoon minced garlic

2 to 2½ pounds beef chuck or round, trimmed of surface fat and cut into 1- to 1½-inch cubes

Salt and freshly ground black pepper to taste

2 large or 3 medium onions, cut into eighths

3 tablespoons flour

3 cups chicken, beef, or vegetable stock, or water, or wine, or a combination (see "Soups" for stock recipes)

1 bay leaf

1 teaspoon fresh thyme leaves or ½ teaspoon dried thyme

4 medium-to-large potatoes, peeled and cut into 1-inch chunks

4 large carrots, peeled and cut into 1-inch chunks

1 cup fresh or frozen (thawed) peas

Minced fresh parsley leaves for garnish

1 Heat a large casserole or deep skillet that can later be covered over medium-high heat for 2 or 3 minutes; add the oil and the crushed garlic clove; cook, stirring, for 1 minute, then remove and discard the garlic. Add the meat chunks to the skillet a few at a time, turning to brown well on all sides. Do not crowd or they will not brown properly; cook them in batches if necessary. (You may find it easier to do the initial browning in the oven: Preheat to 500°F and roast the meat with 1 tablespoon of the oil and the garlic clove, shaking the pan to turn them once or twice, until brown all over. Remove the garlic clove before continuing.) Season the meat with salt and pepper as it cooks.

2 When the meat is brown, remove it with a slotted spoon. Pour or spoon off most of the fat and turn the heat to medium. Add the onions. Cook, stirring, until they soften, about 10 minutes. Add the flour and cook, stirring, for about 2 minutes. Add the stock or water or wine, bay leaf, thyme, and meat, and bring to a boil. Turn the heat to low and cover. Cook, undisturbed, for 30 minutes.

3 Uncover the pan; the mixture should be quite soupy (if it is not, add a little more liquid). Add the potatoes and carrots, turn the heat up for a minute or so to resume boiling, then lower the heat and cover again. Cook 30 to 60 minutes until the meat and vegetables are tender. Taste for seasoning and add more salt, pepper, and/or thyme if necessary. (If you are not planning to serve the stew immediately, remove the meat and vegetables with a slotted spoon and refrigerate them and the stock separately. Skim the fat from the stock before combining it with the meat and vegetables, reheating, and proceeding with the recipe from this point.)

4 Add the minced garlic and the peas; if you are pleased with the stew's consistency, continue to cook, covered, over low heat. If it is too soupy, remove the cover and raise the heat to high. In either case, cook an additional 5 minutes or so, until the peas have heated through and the garlic flavor has pervaded the stew. Garnish and serve.

Belgian Beef Stew with Beer (Carbonnade): Step 1 remains the same. In Step 2, omit the flour. Use

$1^1/_2$ cups good dark beer for the liquid. Omit the potatoes, carrots, peas, and minced garlic, but otherwise follow the above procedure. This is good finished with a tablespoon of Dijon mustard and served over buttered noodles or with plain boiled potatoes.

Spicy Braised Beef with Lime: In Step 1, use peanut oil if you have it. In Step 2, omit bay leaf and thyme and add 1 tablespoon minced garlic, 2 or 3 small dried hot red chiles (or to taste), and the minced peel of 1 lime; use only $1^1/_2$ cups of liquid. Do not add vegetables. When the meat is tender, finish the dish by adding additional minced garlic and the juice of 1 or 2 limes, to taste. Garnish with minced cilantro leaves.

Beef Stew with Bacon: In Step 1, cut $^1/_4$ pound of bacon (preferably slab) into small cubes and cook it over medium heat, stirring, until crisp. Remove with a slotted spoon and reserve. Proceed with the recipe, browning the meat in the bacon fat. Stir in the bacon cubes a minute before serving.

Beef Stew, Greek-Style: Step 1 remains the same. In Step 2, use 2 bay leaves and omit the thyme. Add 2 cloves, $^1/_2$ teaspoon ground cinnamon, and 1 (6-ounce) can tomato paste. In Step 3, add 20 peeled pearl onions (frozen are fine), each skewered with a toothpick through its equator (this holds them together), and $^1/_4$ cup red wine vinegar; in Step 4, omit the peas. Garnish with parsley.

Garlicky Beef Daube

Makes 4 to 6 servings

Time: $2^1/_2$ hours, or overnight, largely unattended

A fairly low-fat braise that tastes great. It's also easy, because there is no initial browning. Try this method with any of the variations from the preceding recipe.

8 cloves garlic
2 to 3 pounds beef chuck or round, trimmed of surface fat and cut into 1- to $1^1/_2$-inch cubes
1 large onion, coarsely chopped
1 large or 2 medium carrots, peeled and cut into $^1/_4$-inch-thick rounds
Salt and freshly ground black pepper to taste
1 tablespoon sherry or other vinegar
1 cup red wine or any stock (see "Soups" for stock recipes)
$^1/_2$ teaspoon minced fresh thyme leaves or pinch dried thyme
1 bay leaf
Minced fresh parsley leaves for garnish

① Peel and mince 6 of the garlic cloves. Combine them in a bowl or non-reactive saucepan with all the remaining ingredients except for the remaining garlic and the parsley. Stir, cover, and refrigerate, stirring occasionally, for 1 to 24 hours.

② Place the meat mixture in a large saucepan over medium heat. Bring to a boil, lower the heat, and cover. Simmer gently until the meat is tender, 1 to $1^1/_2$ hours. (The daube may be made in advance up to this point and stored, covered, in the refrigerator, for up to 2 days.) Uncover and boil the liquid to reduce it slightly if necessary.

③ Peel and mince the remaining garlic, add it to the daube, and simmer another 5 minutes. Sprinkle with the parsley and serve over rice, noodles, or with crusty bread.

The Basics of Pot Roasts

Here, chuck, rump, or brisket are best, although cuts of shank, or shin, or oxtails can also be used in any of these recipes. As with the stews in the previous section, cooking time will vary from one cut to another. Keep the heat very low and allow plenty of time, testing every fifteen minutes or so after the first hour.

Although some people believe it's impossible to overcook pot roasts, I'm not one of them; when the meat is tender, it is done. Hold it in the warm liquid for a while if you like (you can even slice it and let the slices rest in the gravy), but don't plan to hold it for too long. This is especially true for chuck and rump; brisket, which is laced throughout with fat, is the most forgiving of the cuts and can stand a little overcooking.

Basic Pot Roast

Makes 6 to 8 servings

Time: 2$\frac{1}{2}$ to 4 hours, largely unattended

Use low heat when simmering this meat, and don't cook it forever; pot roast need not be overcooked to be tender and delicious. If you have time—a day or more—try the Vinegar-Marinated Pot Roast, below; its flavor is quite special.

If you don't have extra time but want a different type of roast, rub the meat with one tablespoon of mild chili powder (add some cayenne if you like hot food) along with the bay leaf.

1 clove garlic

1 (3- to 4-pound) piece chuck or rump roast,
   tied if necessary

1 bay leaf

Salt and freshly ground black pepper to taste

2 tablespoons olive or peanut oil

2 cups chopped onions

1 cup peeled and chopped carrot

1 celery stalk, chopped

$\frac{1}{2}$ cup red wine or water

1 cup chicken, beef, or vegetable stock, or water
   (see "Soups" for stock recipes)

1 Peel the garlic clove and cut it into tiny slivers; insert the slivers into several spots around the roast,

poking holes with a thin-bladed knife. Crumble the bay leaf as finely as you can and mix it with the salt and pepper. Rub the meat all over with this mixture.

2 Heat the oil over medium-high heat in a Dutch oven or other heavy pot that can later be covered; brown the roast on all sides, taking your time. Adjust the heat so the meat browns but the fat does not burn. Remove the meat to a platter and add the vegetables to the Dutch oven. Cook them over medium-high heat, stirring frequently, until softened and somewhat browned, about 10 minutes.

3 Add the red wine, and cook, scraping the bottom of the pot with a wooden spoon, until the wine has just about evaporated. Add about half the stock or water, return the roast to the pot, and turn the heat down to very low.

4 Turn the meat every 15 minutes and cook until it is tender—a fork will pierce the meat without pushing too hard and the juices will run clear—about 1$\frac{1}{2}$ to 2$\frac{1}{2}$ hours, but possibly longer if your roast is higher than it is long (very thick roasts may require as long as 4 hours if you keep the heat extremely low). Add a little more stock if the roast appears to be drying out, an unlikely possibility (and a sign that your heat is too high). Do not overcook; when the meat is tender, it is done.

5 Remove the meat from the pot and keep it warm. Skim the fat from the surface of the remaining juice. Turn the heat to high and cook, stirring and scraping the bottom of the pan, until the liquid is thick and almost evaporated. Check for seasoning. Slice the meat and serve it with the pan juices.

Vinegar-Marinated Pot Roast (Sauerbraten): In a covered pot or other container (or a heavy plastic bag), marinate the meat in a mixture of 2 cups red wine (or water); $\frac{1}{2}$ cup red wine vinegar; 3 cloves (or a pinch of ground cloves); 5 juniper berries; 5 peppercorns; and half the onions, carrot, and celery. Refrigerate, turning occasionally, for 1 to 3 days.

Remove from the marinade and strain out the vegetables, reserving the liquid and discarding the vegetables. Dry the meat well and proceed as in Step 1, above. In Step 2, use the remaining fresh vegetables, augmenting them with more if you like. Use the reserved marinade in Step 3 in place of the red wine and stock, and proceed as above.

Braised Beef Brisket

Makes 10 or more servings

Time: About 3 hours, largely unattended

Brisket becomes reasonably tender as long as it is cooked for a long time, with plenty of moisture. My favorite seasonings for it are very, very basic: the taste of the meat itself, some spices, and onions simmered in butter; a little bit of tomato is also nice. I serve brisket made this way, over broad noodles. But brisket is also great seasoned with bolder spices, or with sweet fruits and vegetables; see the variations.

Two technical points: You can skip the initial browning if you're pressed for time or don't want to bother; the difference, in the end, will be minimal. And although it's tempting to "tear" brisket along the grain, it's better to slice it against the grain; use a very sharp carving knife and you can get beautiful, thin slices.

1 tablespoon vegetable or olive oil

1 whole beef brisket, about 5 pounds

Salt and lots of freshly ground pepper to taste

3 tablespoons butter (preferred) or more oil

2 cups minced onions

3 tablespoons tomato paste or 1 large ripe tomato, cored and chopped (peeled and seeded if you have time)

1 teaspoon minced garlic

3 cups chicken, beef, or vegetable stock, or water (see "Soups" for stock recipes)

1 Preheat the oven to 325°F (you can also cook this brisket on top of the stove if you like). If you choose to brown the brisket first, heat a large casserole or Dutch oven that can later be covered over medium-high heat for 2 or 3 minutes. Add the oil, swirl it around, then add the beef. Sear it for about 5 minutes on each side, or until it is nicely browned. Season it with salt and pepper and remove to a platter.

2 Wipe out the pan with paper towels and return it to the stove; turn the heat to medium and add the butter. When it foams, add the onions and cook, stirring, until they are golden and soft, at least 10 minutes. Add salt and pepper, then stir in the tomato paste and the garlic. Return the meat to the pan, add the stock or water, and cover.

3 Cook over low heat or in the oven, turning the meat about every 30 minutes, until tender, $2^{1}/_{2}$ to 3 hours. If the sauce seems too thin, allow the meat to rest on a platter for a few minutes while you boil the liquid down over high heat, scraping the bottom of a pan with a wooden spoon, until it thickens somewhat. Taste the sauce and add salt and/or pepper if needed. Slice the meat, return it to the sauce, and serve.

Spicy Beef Brisket: Before searing, rub the meat all over with a mixture of 1 teaspoon salt, 2 teaspoons sugar, 2 teaspoons ground cumin, 1 teaspoon ground black pepper, $^{1}/_{4}$ teaspoon cayenne (more if you like), $^{1}/_{2}$ teaspoon ground coriander, and 2 teaspoons paprika. In Step 1, increase the oil to 2 tablespoons. In Step 2, use 2 tablespoons oil in place of the butter, and cook the onions over medium-high heat, stirring, until they begin to brown, about 10 minutes. Proceed as above.

Sweet Beef Brisket with Garlic: Steps 1 and 2 remain unchanged. When the meat is somewhat tender but not quite done—after about $1^{1}/_{2}$ to 2 hours of braising—add to the pot 1 pound peeled and chunked sweet potatoes; 2 carrots, peeled and chunked;

$^1/_2$ cup dried apricots; $^1/_2$ cup dried pitted prunes (or other dried fruit); and 1 head of garlic, with most of the papery coating removed, cut in half horizontally. Continue to cook until all the fruits and vegetables are soft but not until they dissolve, 30 to 60 minutes. Serve, spreading the soft garlic on crusty bread.

Corned Beef

Makes 6 to 12 servings

Time: 3 hours, largely unattended

Corned beef is the beef equivalent of wet-cured ham, beef that has been steeped in a spicy brine for days or longer (or shorter, now that there are fast, chemically enhanced cures). Most corned beef is from the brisket, and that's the only kind you should buy. If you have a choice, buy the flat cut rather than the point cut; it's the better end.

Cooking corned beef is as close to a no-brainer as there is. It's difficult to overcook it, although it can be done, of course, so this is a good candidate for the crock-pot, if you have one. I think corned beef cooked without garlic lacks character but you can omit the garlic if you prefer. With mustard, pickles, and good bread, this makes a fine old-fashioned meal.

1 corned beef, 3 to 5 pounds
1 bay leaf
1 head garlic
3 cloves
10 peppercorns
5 allspice berries or pinch or two ground allspice
1 onion, whole

1 Put the corned beef in a large, heavy pot and cover with water. Add all the remaining ingredients. Bring to a boil and skim all the foam that rises to the surface.

2 Lower the heat so that the water bubbles occasionally rather than constantly. Cook turning every 30 minutes or so, for about 2 hours. Pierce with a thin-bladed knife, such as a boning knife; the meat will probably still be fairly tough, but it's time to begin checking.

3 Check every 15 minutes or so; when the corned beef allows the knife to pass into the middle without much resistance, it is ready. Drain; if you like, put the meat into a 300°F oven for 10 minutes to dry out the exterior a little. (Or wrap it carefully in tin foil and refrigerate for up to 2 days; reheat at 300°F for 30 minutes in the foil; unwrap and heat about 15 minutes more.) Slice (across the grain, as you would brisket), and serve.

New England Boiled Dinner (Corned Beef and Cabbage): In Step 2, after 2 hours of cooking, add the following per person: 1 medium peeled waxy red or white potato; 1 or 2 medium peeled carrots; 1 wedge of cabbage, pierced with a skewer or a couple of toothpicks to keep it from falling apart; and any other root vegetable you like, such as whole peeled onions, peeled turnips, or peeled parsnips. It's best to leave most vegetables whole, but if the meat appears to be nearly done you may cut them in half or quarters to hasten their cooking, especially if they are large. In any case, do not overcook the vegetables; when they are tender, remove them. In Step 3, place the drained meat and vegetables on a platter and let sit in a 300°F oven for 10 minutes before serving. Garnish with plenty of minced fresh parsley leaves.

Corned Beef (or Roast Beef) Hash: Toss together 2 cups cut-up leftover corned beef and 2 cups cut-up cold boiled potatoes, all cut into small cubes. Add 1 cup chopped onion and $^1/_2$ cup liquid—stock, tomato sauce, milk, cream, or gravy—enough to moisten the mixture but not so much as to make it soupy. Heat 3 tablespoons oil or butter in a heavy skillet, preferably non-stick, over medium-low heat. When the butter has melted or the oil begins to shimmer, put the hash in the pan and cook it, undisturbed, for about 10 minutes, or until a nice crust has formed. Turn the hash and brown the other side; or flip half of it over onto the other; or brown the top under a broiler. Serve. This can also be baked in a lightly greased, uncovered casserole at 350°F until brown on top. To make Red Flannel Hash, replace half the boiled potatoes with peeled cooked beets (page 541).

The Basics of Stir-Fried Beef

See The Basics of Stir-Frying on page 12. Remember that stir-frying is the most flexible of cooking techniques: You can vary the ingredients almost at will. For example, Spicy Beef with Basil is not only excellent with pork, but with pieces of tofu, shrimp, or squid; Beef with Ginger and Onions is equally good with tofu, chicken, or lamb. Conversely, you can substitute beef for the protein in many of the other stir-fries throughout the book.

Stir-Fried Spicy Beef with Basil

Makes 4 to 6 servings

Time: 15 minutes to 1 hour

Once you get this Thai-style dish set up, it's so quick to make that if you're serving it with rice, you should have the rice finished before you begin stir-frying. You can use round or chuck here, but the best cuts are flank or sirloin, which are more tender and equally tasty. Tenderloin, another possibility, will not give you as much flavor but will be supremely tender.

1½ pounds flank or sirloin steak, or other beef
½ cup loosely packed basil leaves
1 tablespoon peanut oil, plus 1 teaspoon (optional)
1½ tablespoons minced garlic
¼ teaspoon crushed red pepper flakes, or to taste
1 tablespoon soy sauce or fish sauce (*nuoc mam* or *nam pla*, available at Asian markets)
Juice of ½ lime

1 Slice the beef as thinly as you can, across the grain; it's easier if you freeze it for 15 to 30 minutes first. Cut the slices into bite-sized pieces.

2 Wash and dry the basil; if the leaves are large, chop them coarsely. If time permits, mix the beef, basil, and the teaspoon of peanut oil in a bowl. Cover and refrigerate for an hour or so (although far from essential, this helps the flavor of the basil permeate the meat).

3 When you are ready to cook, have all ingredients ready (including a serving dish and rice, if any). If you have not yet done so, mix together the beef and basil. Preheat a wok or a large skillet over high heat until it smokes, 3 or 4 minutes.

4 Lower the heat to medium and add the tablespoon of peanut oil to the wok. Swirl it around and add the garlic. Stir once or twice. As soon as the garlic begins to color—about 15 seconds—return the heat to high and add the beef-basil mixture. Stir quickly and add the red pepper. Stir frequently (but not constantly), just until meat loses its redness, a minute or two longer. Add soy sauce and lime juice, stir, turn off heat, and serve immediately, over rice.

Super-Spicy Beef with Orange Flavor: In Step 2, substitute the zest of 1 large orange for the basil. Mince about 1 tablespoon of the zest and leave the rest in large chunks. Combine this with the meat. In Step 4, add 10 to 30 small dried hot red chiles, or to taste, along with the garlic. Continue as above, adding some of the orange's juice along with the lime juice at the end. Serve immediately, over rice.

Stir-Fried Beef with Onions

Makes 4 servings

Time: 30 minutes

Onions, beef, and ginger are an almost holy combination; the synthesis is simply delicious. Again, flank and sirloin are the cuts of choice here.

³/₄ to 1 pound flank or sirloin steak, or other beef
Salt and freshly ground black pepper to taste
2 tablespoons peanut (preferred) or vegetable oil
2 large or 3 medium onions, thinly sliced
1 teaspoon minced garlic
1 tablespoon peeled and minced or grated fresh
    ginger, plus 1 teaspoon
¹/₂ cup stock or water (see "Soups" for stock recipes)
1 tablespoon hoisin sauce (available in Asian markets)
    or soy sauce

① Slice the beef as thinly as you can; it's easier if you freeze it for 15 to 30 minutes first. Cut the slices into bite-sized pieces. Season with salt and pepper and set aside.

② Heat a wok or large skillet over high heat until it smokes. Add 1 tablespoon of oil and the onions. Stir immediately, then stir every 30 seconds or so until the onions soften and begin to char slightly, 4 to 5 minutes. Season the onions with salt and pepper, then remove them; keep the heat high.

③ Add the remaining oil to the pan, then the garlic and 1 tablespoon of ginger; stir and immediately add the beef. Stir immediately, then stir every 20 seconds or so until it loses its color, just a minute or two longer; stir in the onions. Add the stock or water, the hoisin or soy, and the remaining ginger; let some of the liquid bubble away and serve immediately, over rice.

Stir-Fried Beef with Tomatoes and Black Beans: In Step 1, soak the sliced meat in 2 tablespoons soy sauce while you get everything else ready. At the same time, soak 1 tablespoon fermented black beans in 2 tablespoons dry sherry (or use stock, white wine, or water). Step 2 remains the same. In Step 3, add 3 or 4 scallions, including some of the green parts, cut into 1-inch lengths, along with the garlic and ginger. Add the beef and soy sauce, cook for 1 minute, then add 3 medium tomatoes, cored and roughly chopped (peel and seed the tomatoes if you like), then add the black beans and their liquid and the onions. Omit the stock and hoisin sauce. Stir, taste for salt and pepper, and serve immediately, over rice.

The Basics of Beef Kebabs

Most traditional kebabs are made with lamb (as on page 483), but you can make them with any meat you like (even ground meat—see page 432). But although most people not only tolerate but enjoy chewy steaks, nearly everyone prefers tender kebabs. The best choice, then, is to use tenderloin, which is available in almost all supermarkets. Tenderloin is perfect, for two reasons: First, it's the most tender beef there is, and second, it doesn't have that much flavor of its own to begin with, so it really needs the full-flavored treatments given here. Of course, there is a downside of tenderloin: It is expensive. To economize, use sirloin.

A couple of general comments about kebabs: You always have a choice between wood and metal skewers. Metal skewers require a higher initial investment, but last forever (or until you lose them) and do not burn. They become extremely hot and difficult to handle, and food sometimes slips on them, which can make turning a hassle. Wood skewers are inexpensive, but tend to burn (you can ameliorate this tendency slightly by soaking them for thirty minutes or so before use). They're easier to handle, and you don't have to wash them since you toss them out. The choice is yours.

You also have a choice when it comes to style of skewering. Although alternating pieces of meat and vegetables is undeniably attractive, since meat and vegetables may cook at different rates, and you don't want raw onions or overdone meat, it makes more sense to make separate skewers of each. If you do want to mix meat and veggies on the same skewer, cut the vegetables a little smaller, to make sure they're tender by the time the meat is cooked.

Grilled or Broiled Beef and Vegetable Kebabs

Makes 4 to 6 servings

Time: 45 minutes, plus time to preheat the grill

I like to serve this with Tomato-Onion Salsa (page 772), which takes just a couple of extra minutes to prepare. But it isn't necessary, especially if you use sirloin or other full-flavored beef in place of tenderloin.

1 tablespoon olive oil

2 tablespoons freshly squeezed lime or lemon juice or vinegar

1 tablespoon soy sauce

Salt and freshly ground black pepper to taste

2 tablespoons minced fresh parsley or cilantro leaves, 2 teaspoons minced fresh thyme or rosemary leaves, or 1 teaspoon dried herb of your choice

1 teaspoon minced garlic

6 medium onions, quartered

2 bell peppers, any color but green, stemmed, seeded, and cut into about 1½-inch chunks

12 medium button mushrooms, trimmed and cut in half

2 to 3 pounds beef tenderloin, cut into 1½- to 2-inch chunks

Minced fresh parsley or cilantro leaves for garnish

Tomato-Onion Salsa (page 772) (optional)

1 Start a charcoal or wood fire or preheat a gas grill or broiler; the fire should be quite hot and large.

2 Combine the first six ingredients in a small bowl. Arrange the vegetables and meat on separate skewers (the vegetables need a little more time to cook). Don't cram the stuff together, but leave a little space around each piece. Brush with most of the marinade and let sit while your fire is getting ready.

3 Start the vegetables first, cooking them on a relatively cool part of the grill. Brush them with a little of the marinade from time to time, and turn them, until they begin to brown and become tender. Then start the meat, on the hottest part of the fire; grill it for about 1 to 2 minutes per side, until each of the four sides browns. Do not overcook (cut a chunk in half after 5 minutes of cooking to judge its stage of doneness).

4 Give everything a final baste with the marinade if any remains, place the skewers on a platter, garnish, and serve. Remove the skewers at the table and pass the platter, with the salsa following.

Spice-Rubbed Beef Kebabs: In Step 2, omit marinade and instead make a paste of ½ cup minced onion, 1 teaspoon minced garlic, 1 teaspoon salt, 1 teaspoon freshly ground black pepper, 1 tablespoon All-Purpose Curry Powder, Garam Masala, chili powder, or other spice mixture (pages 777–779), 1 teaspoon paprika, and oil as needed. Spread this on the meat (if you would like to make vegetable skewers too, simply brush with olive oil) and grill as in Step 4. Serve with a sauce made by whisking together 1 cup plain yogurt, ¼ cup minced onion or scallion, 1 teaspoon ground ginger, ¼ cup minced cilantro or fresh mint leaves, 1 teaspoon ground cumin, and salt and pepper to taste (add cayenne, too, if you like). This dressing can be made well in advance, and can also be used as a dip for cucumber and other vegetables.

The Basics of Veal

Needless to say, veal is the subject of much debate. Old-guard chefs, food writers, and industry representatives continue to argue that the only way to obtain white, tender veal is to raise calves in crates in a borderline state of anemia. And they are right about one thing: Anemic, underdeveloped calves have exceedingly pale and tender meat. But tenderness is not a problem with any young animal; the primary determinant is age, not exercise. To me, "milk-fed" veal (which is in fact fed with a formula containing not only milk but antibiotics) is distinguished by its lack of color, undistinguished flavor, and fork-tenderness (which you might call mushiness). It's also distinguished by the singular cruelty of its production methods.

That's why I strive to find what the USDA calls "calf," also sold as "humanely raised" veal. There are differences: Calf is rosy pink rather than pinkish-grayish-white. Calf may be slightly chewier, although it's still quite tender. And calf is likely to have been raised in ways that I don't find objectionable. Some calves, in fact, roam with their mothers (I'd call that "milk-fed"). But one thing is for certain: "Humanely" or "naturally" raised veal, which is as difficult to define as "free-range" chicken, has a far lower chance of containing the residues of antibiotics and steroids that are at least occasionally found in crate-raised veal. Furthermore, it bears no more stigma than beef or pork, and usually somewhat less. Finally, it has more flavor.

Which leads to two questions: Where do you get "naturally" raised veal? And, should you buy supermarket "milk-fed" veal if it's all you can find?

I buy naturally raised veal where I can find it. I buy a few different cuts and toss them in my freezer. You can do the same thing in any major city, and many not-so-major ones. Look in large, natural foods–oriented supermarkets (such as Bread and Circus, Fresh Fields, and Mrs. Gooch's). There are also good mail-order sources.

As for the second question: It's your decision. But consumption of "milk-fed" veal has declined steadily for years, largely because of ongoing consumer dissatisfaction. Refusal to purchase it will eventually lead to a market in which "naturally raised" veal dominates.

Now that we're through with politics, we can address cooking. Regardless of the kind of veal you buy, it will be quite lean. Properly cooked, it will also be quite tender.

Those cuts of veal that are tender enough to be cooked with dry heat, primarily the chop and the rear leg, should not be overcooked. Medium—that is, with some pinkness but no redness in the interior—is how I prefer this veal, about 140°F on an instant-read thermometer. Stop cooking when the meat measures about 135°F, or a little more, and you'll hit it right.

Braised veal, including osso buco, veal breast, and the cut-up shoulder, neck, and pieces from the leg that are sold as stew, must be cooked until well done and tender. However, this often takes considerably less time than corresponding cuts of beef.

Shoulder Best for stew meat, and for roasts (blade roast, arm roast) cooked with liquid. Do not buy steaks (or chops) from this section (labeled arm or shoulder steaks, blade steak); they will be tough.

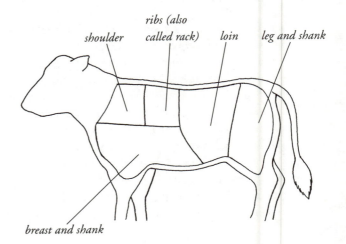

shoulder

ribs (also called rack)

loin

leg and shank

breast and shank

Breast   Usually sold whole (breast of veal), and can be cooked bone-in, or boned (in which case it is usually stuffed).

Shank   Great for Classic Osso Buco (page 450), or roasted whole.

Rib   Rib chops are superb. Veal rib roasts, which are manageable in size and quite nice (and are also called rack of veal), may be sold bone-in or -out; unfortunately, they are not seen very often.

Flank   Almost always ground.

Loin   Like the rib, wonderful for chops. Good roasts, also, especially the boneless (and expensive) saddle roast.

Sirloin   In veal, the sirloin is not that desirable an area. Chops, which are really steaks, are not as good as those from the rib or loin. Same with roasts.

Leg   Thin slices are cut for veal scallops, or cutlets (or scallopine). Rump or round roasts are neither tender nor flavorful, but roast veal leg—bone-in—is a treat.

Grilled or Broiled Veal Chop

Makes 4 servings

Time: 30 minutes, plus time to preheat the grill

There is nothing like a good veal chop, but the problem, as noted above, lies in getting good veal. This is a rare occurrence so you will want to keep things simple and savor the meat. My favorite veal chop is one rubbed lightly with good olive oil and scented with rosemary and a suspicion of garlic. It needs nothing else, but a bed of cooked vegetables or raw greens makes it a bit more elegant; see the variations.

Veal chops are best on the medium-rare-to-medium side; figure about eight to ten minutes' total cooking for a one-inch-thick chop (an instant-read thermometer should read 130°F or a little more).

4 veal loin chops, 6 to 10 ounces each
1 clove garlic, cut in half
3 tablespoons extra-virgin olive oil
1 tablespoon minced fresh rosemary leaves or
    1 teaspoon dried rosemary, crumbled
Salt and freshly ground black pepper to taste

1 Start a charcoal or wood fire or preheat a gas grill or broiler; the fire should be quite hot. As the fire heats, let the chops reach room temperature if you haven't already done so.

2 Rub the chops all over with the split garlic, then with 2 tablespoons of the olive oil. Mix together most of the rosemary along with some salt and pepper and rub this well into the chops.

3 Grill or broil the chops about 4 inches from the heat source for 5 minutes. Turn, grill or broil 4 minutes more, and check for doneness; the center should be fairly pink. Drizzle with the remaining olive oil, sprinkle with a tiny bit more rosemary, and serve.

Grilled Veal Chops on a Bed of Vegetables: Heat 2 tablespoons olive oil in a medium skillet over medium heat for 2 minutes. Cook 1 large chopped onion, stirring, until it begins to soften, 3 to 5 minutes; add 1 medium chopped zucchini or summer squash and cook, stirring, for 5 minutes. Add 2 large cored and chopped tomatoes and $1/2$ cup pitted good black olives and cook until the mixture is soft, about 10 minutes more. Add 1 teaspoon minced fresh rosemary, or minced marjoram or oregano leaves, or 1 tablespoon minced fresh parsley or basil leaves, or $1/2$ teaspoon dried marjoram or rosemary, and salt and pepper to taste. Keep warm while you grill the chops. Serve the chops on the vegetables.

Grilled Veal Chops on a Bed of Greens: Serve the chops over The Best and Simplest Green Salad (page 94), or any of its variations; drizzle lemon vinaigrette (page 92) over all.

Veal Cutlets, 1950s-Style

Makes 4 servings

Time: 30 minutes

Back in the 1950s and 1960s, before we "discovered" boneless chicken breasts, thin slices of veal cut from the leg—called cutlets, scallops, or scallopine—were the only thin, tender, boneless meat widely available. But veal was expensive, and remains so. Still, veal does have a different texture and flavor than chicken breasts, and good veal cutlets are still wonderful sautéed in olive oil and drenched in lemon juice. You can make any of the following recipes with thinly pounded chicken or turkey cutlets, or with any thin-sliced pork.

1¼ to 1½ pounds thinly sliced veal, from the leg
    (scallopine)
¼ cup olive oil, or a little more
Flour for dredging
Plain bread crumbs for dredging
2 eggs
Salt and freshly ground black pepper to taste
½ cup dry white wine
Juice of 1 lemon
Minced fresh parsley leaves for garnish
1 lemon, cut into quarters

① The cutlets should be less than ¼ inch thick; if they're not, pound them gently (I use a flat rolling pin, but you can use the back of a skillet or a wine bottle) between two sheets of waxed paper.

② Heat the olive oil in a large skillet over medium heat while you set out the flour and bread crumbs on plates and beat the eggs lightly in a small bowl. Season the flour liberally with salt and pepper. Set everything near the stove.

③ When the oil is good and hot (a pinch of flour will sizzle), dredge the cutlets, one at a time, in the flour, then dip in the egg, then dredge in the bread crumbs. Add them to the skillet as they're ready. Cook them over heat high enough to make the oil bubble; don't crowd. Cook in batches if necessary, adding additional oil as needed. Set the oven at 200°F.

④ Turn the cutlets as soon as they're browned, then cook the other side. The total cooking time should be 5 minutes or less. As each piece of veal is done, remove it to an ovenproof platter; place the platter in the oven.

⑤ When all the veal is finished, pour off the fat. Return the skillet to the stove and add the wine, over medium-high heat. Cook, stirring, until the wine is just about evaporated. Add the lemon juice, stir, and pour this sauce (there won't be more than a few tablespoons) over the veal. Garnish and serve, passing lemon quarters at the table.

Veal Cutlets with Rosemary and Parmesan: Here, you can skip the flour-and-egg treatment and dredge directly in the bread crumb–Parmesan mixture; the results will be very good. Combine ½ cup freshly grated Parmesan cheese, ½ cup plain bread crumbs, 1 tablespoon minced fresh rosemary leaves or 1 teaspoon dried rosemary, and some salt and pepper in a bowl. In Step 3, dredge in flour and egg if you like, or omit this step. In any case, finish by dredging the cutlets in the bread crumb–Parmesan mixture. Proceed as above, skipping Step 5 and serving the veal with lemon quarters as soon as it's cooked.

Veal Parmigiana: The classic Italian-American veal dish. Preheat the oven to 450°F, then proceed as in the master recipe, through Step 4, but undercook the cutlets slightly (less than 4 minutes per cutlet total cooking time). Place all the cutlets in a baking dish without overlapping (use two dishes if necessary). Top each with a spoonful or two of any tomato sauce you like (see pages 130–134) and then with a thin slice of mozzarella. Put the baking dish in the oven and cook just until the cheese melts, 5 to 10 minutes. Serve immediately.

Veal Stew with Tomatoes

Makes 4 servings

Time: About 1 hour

The odd cuts of veal from the shoulder or leg are frequently packaged and sold by supermarkets as "veal stew." The best way to cook this meat is by braising—in a covered skillet, with some liquid. The meat is flavorful, becomes tender more quickly than beef, and takes well to a number of different flavors, all using the same basic cooking techniques. It's best to brown the meat first for extra depth of flavor, but it is not essential; skip the browning step if you're pressed for time.

This veal stew and its variations have a lot of liquid—serve them with bread, rice, or noodles, whichever seems appropriate.

> 3 tablespoons olive oil or butter
> 1 1/2 to 2 pounds lean veal stew meat, cut into
>   1- to 1 1/2-inch chunks
> 1 cup diced onion
> 1 teaspoon minced garlic
> Salt and freshly ground black pepper to taste
> 1 cup white wine, meat or vegetable stock, or water
>   (see "Soups" for stock recipes)
> 2 cups cored and chopped tomatoes (canned are
>   fine; drain them first)
> 1 bay leaf
> 1 teaspoon minced fresh thyme or rosemary leaves
>   or 1/2 teaspoon dried thyme or crumbled rosemary
> 1 cup good pitted black olives (optional)

1 Place a large skillet, preferably non-stick, over medium-high heat for 2 or 3 minutes. Add 2 tablespoons of the olive oil or butter. A minute later, when

the butter foam subsides or the first wisps of smoke rise from the oil, brown the veal chunks, adding a few at a time, turning them to brown all over, and removing the pieces as they brown. Take your time and don't crowd the chunks or they will not brown properly.

2 Wipe out the pan, lower the heat to medium, add the remaining oil or butter, and cook the onion, stirring occasionally, until softened, 5 to 10 minutes. Add the garlic and cook 1 minute more. Add the salt and pepper and the wine, stock, or water, bring to a boil, and let cook for 1 minute.

3 Add the tomatoes, bay leaf, and thyme or rosemary, and bring to a simmer. Return the veal to the skillet, turn the heat to very low, cover, and cook, stirring every now and then, until the veal is tender, 45 minutes or more. Add the olives if you like. Taste and correct seasoning if necessary, then serve. (The recipe can be prepared a day or two in advance; cool, place in a covered container, and refrigerate; reheat in a saucepan before serving.)

Veal Stew with Caraway: Step 1 remains the same. In Step 2, cook 3 cups of thinly sliced onions over medium-low heat until soft, about 15 minutes. Omit garlic. Add salt, pepper, and wine as above. In Step 3, replace tomatoes, bay leaf, and thyme with 1 tablespoon caraway seeds and 1 tablespoon white wine or other vinegar. Cook as above, stirring occasionally and adding additional liquid if needed. (Do not add olives.)

Veal Stew with Sage: Step 1 remains the same. In Step 2, use 3 or 4 medium carrots, peeled and chopped and 1/2 cup chopped shallots, scallions, or onion; cook over medium heat until they begin to brown, about 5 minutes. Omit garlic. Add salt, pepper, and wine as above. In Step 3, replace tomatoes, bay leaf, and thyme with 20 fresh sage leaves, 1 teaspoon dried sage, or an equivalent amount of marjoram, rosemary, or savory. Proceed as above; do not add olives.

Veal Stew with Paprika: Serve over white rice. Step 1 remains the same. In Step 2, cook $^1/_2$ cup chopped celery with the onion and increase the garlic to 1 tablespoon. Sprinkle the cooked vegetables with 1 tablespoon paprika (or to taste). Add salt, pepper, and wine as above. Omit other ingredients and cook as above, stirring occasionally and adding additional liquid if needed. When the meat is tender, remove the cover and raise the heat to high; when the liquid is all but gone, turn the heat to a bare minimum and stir in 1 cup sour cream or plain yogurt, thinned with a tablespoon or two of milk. (If you make this in advance, add sour cream only after reheating.)

Veal Stew, Central Asian–Style: Great with bread or Basic Couscous (page 191). Step 1 remains the same. In Step 2, increase garlic to 2 tablespoons and add $^1/_2$ crushed red pepper flakes (or to taste). Cook over medium-high heat, until onion begins to brown. Add salt and at least 1 teaspoon freshly ground black pepper but omit wine. In Step 3, add tomatoes; omit herbs and olives. Add 3 tablespoons lemon juice. Cook as above, stirring occasionally and adding a little additional liquid if needed. (If you make this in advance, perk it up with a little additional lemon juice after reheating.)

Veal Stew with Chinese Flavors: Serve over white rice. Step 1 remains the same (do not use butter, and use peanut oil if you have it). In Step 2, increase garlic to 1 tablespoon and add 1 tablespoon peeled and minced fresh ginger at the same time. In Step 3, omit tomatoes and herbs but add 2 tablespoons soy sauce. Cook as above, stirring occasionally and adding additional liquid if needed. While the stew is simmering, cook $^1/_2$ pound fresh mushrooms, trimmed and roughly chopped, and $^1/_2$ pound snow peas, trimmed, in 1 tablespoon oil over medium-high heat until beginning to brown, 4 to 5 minutes.

When the meat is tender, add the vegetables, along with 1 teaspoon each minced garlic and ginger. Cook for 2 minutes, then drizzle 1 tablespoon dark sesame oil over all. (Do not make this variation in advance.)

Roast Veal Eye of Round with Shallot Sauce

Makes 4 servings

Time: 1 hour

Generally speaking, you have to go out of your way to find a piece of veal large enough to roast. Most supermarkets do not routinely carry them, and even a butcher may not have one on hand. But if you can find a cut for roasting, the results can be excellent. My favorite cut for a veal roast is the eye of the round, a super-lean piece of meat that roasts quickly, stays tender (as long as it is not overcooked), and has a subtle but distinct flavor. You may have to find a butcher to remove this long, slender cut from the middle of the leg for you, although it is occasionally seen in supermarkets. The loin, which can also be boned, is another good choice. You need some kind of sauce for either, and I suggest some slow-cooked shallots mixed with the pan juices.

1 veal eye of round, about 1$^1/_4$ pounds, or a boneless veal loin of similar size or slightly larger
3 tablespoons olive oil, plus one additional tablespoon if not using butter
Salt and freshly ground black pepper to taste
1 tablespoon fresh rosemary leaves
About 1 cup chicken, beef, or vegetable stock, or water (see "Soups" for stock recipes)
$^3/_4$ pound shallots, sliced thin (about 3 cups)
1 tablespoon sugar
1 cup dry white or red wine
1 tablespoon balsamic, sherry, or other flavorful vinegar
1 tablespoon butter (or see olive oil above)

1 Let the meat come to room temperature if time allows. Preheat the oven to 350°F. Rub the meat all over with 1 tablespoon olive oil, then sprinkle it liberally with salt and pepper. Rub it all over with the rosemary and place it on a rack in a roasting pan; put ¹/₂ cup stock in the bottom of the pan.

2 Roast the meat for 30 to 45 minutes, depending on its thickness, basting it occasionally with a few tablespoons of the pan juices and adding stock as necessary. When the meat is cooked to an internal temperature of about 130°F, remove it from the oven and let it rest on a carving board.

3 While the meat is roasting, add 2 tablespoons olive oil to a medium skillet over medium heat. Put in the shallots, turn the heat to medium-low, and cook, stirring, until tender, about 10 minutes. Stir in the sugar and cook, stirring, for 1 minute. Add half the wine, bring to a boil over medium-high heat, turn the heat back down to medium, and cook until most of the liquid evaporates, 10 minutes or so. Stir in the vinegar and turn off the heat.

4 After you remove the meat from the roasting pan, put the roasting pan over one or two burners set to high. Add the remaining wine (or use any remaining stock if you like) and cook, stirring and scraping up any bits of meat stuck to the bottom of the pan. Keep the heat high and cook until the liquid is all but evaporated, then stir in the butter or additional tablespoon of olive oil. Stir until the butter melts, about 20 seconds, then add the liquid and bits of solids to the shallot sauce, along with any juices that have accumulated around the meat. Slice the meat thinly, top it with bit of the sauce, and pass the rest at the table.

Braised Boneless Shoulder (or Leg or Rump) of Veal with Vegetables

Makes 8 to 12 servings

Time: 2 hours or more, largely unattended

For braising, a veal shoulder is the best choice; it usually has a bit of fat on it, and the flavor is excellent. This roast is delicious, and perfect for a family gathering; just be sure not to overcook it. As usual, you can skip the initial browning if you're really pressed for time, but here it really does contribute mightily to the flavor of the finished dish.

Braised veal makes especially fine leftovers, which can be served with a thin mayonnaise, the Italian tuna sauce (see the second variation below), or just as you would turkey.

3 to 5 tablespoons butter or olive oil
1 clove garlic, lightly smashed
1 (4- to 5-pound) veal roast, from the shoulder, leg, or rump, boned and tied (any butcher, including one in the supermarket, can do this for you)
Salt and freshly ground black pepper to taste
2 cups chopped onions
2 or 3 carrots, peeled and chopped
2 celery stalks, chopped
1 cup cored and chopped tomatoes, preferably fresh (drained first if canned)
1 teaspoon minced fresh marjoram, oregano, or thyme leaves or ¹/₂ teaspoon dried
1 bay leaf
¹/₂ cup chicken, beef, or vegetable stock, or water, plus more if needed (see "Soups" for stock recipes)
Minced fresh parsley leaves for garnish

1 Heat a large casserole or Dutch oven over medium-high heat for 2 or 3 minutes; add 3 tablespoons of the

butter or oil and, 1 minute later, the garlic clove; cook, stirring, for 1 minute, then remove and discard the garlic. Dry the meat well, season it with salt and pepper, and put it in the casserole, turning to brown well on all sides. Do not hurry; you'll need a few minutes per side for good browning. Regulate the heat so that the fat doesn't burn but sizzles steadily. (You may find it easier and less messy—if a bit more time-consuming—to do the initial browning in the oven: Preheat the oven to 450°F and roast the meat with the butter or oil and garlic clove, turning it occasionally, until brown all over. Remove the garlic clove before continuing.)

2 Remove the roast from the casserole. If the fat has burned, pour it out, wipe out the pan, and add 2 tablespoons more butter or olive oil. If not, simply continue. In either case, turn the heat to medium and add the onions, carrots, and celery. Cook, stirring occasionally, until softened but not browned (lower the heat if necessary), about 10 minutes. Add the tomatoes, herb, bay leaf, and salt and pepper and cook, stirring, until the tomatoes break down, 5 to 10 minutes.

3 Return the meat to the pot and pour about half the stock or water over it. Cover and turn the heat to very low. Cook, turning the meat occasionally and adding more liquid if necessary, until the meat is very tender, about $1^1/_2$ to 2 hours. Remove the meat to a platter and let it rest. If the sauce is very soupy, cook it over high heat, stirring and scraping the bottom of the pan, for a few minutes to reduce it somewhat; if it is dry (unlikely), add some more stock and boil it, stirring and scraping, for a minute or two longer. Slice the meat, spoon some of the vegetables and sauce over it, garnish, and serve. Pass the remaining sauce at the table.

Braised Veal in the Style of Venison: Note that you must start this at least a day in advance. In a 2- or 3-quart pot, bring to a boil 1 cup red wine vinegar, 1 cup red wine, 1 cup chopped onion, 1 bay leaf, 3 cloves, 10 black peppercorns, pinch of ground all-spice, and about 20 lightly crushed juniper berries. Cook 2 minutes, then cool. Marinate the veal in this mixture, turning occasionally, for 24 to 48 hours. Remove it when you're ready to cook (reserve the marinade, discarding the solids), then proceed with Step 1 of the recipe. Cook the vegetables as in Step 2, above, but omit the tomatoes. Proceed to Step 3, substituting the reserved marinade for the stock.

Vitello Tonnato (Veal with Tuna Sauce): Braise the veal exactly as in the original recipe. Remove it from its liquid and chill (or serve it, and make this recipe with leftovers). Make Anchovy Mayonnaise (page 762), with 6 or 8 anchovies. With the mayonnaise still in the blender or food processor, add 1 small clove garlic, peeled, and 3 tablespoons capers, with a little of their juice (if you have salted capers, soak them first). Process until smooth. Add 1 (6-ounce) can tuna (preferably Italian, packed in olive oil), drained if it was packed in water or soy oil, with its oil if packed in olive oil. Process until blended but not completely smooth. By hand, blend in enough olive oil to soften the mayonnaise and reduce it to a pourable consistency (you can also thin with cream, sour cream, or water). Slice the veal as thinly as possible and serve with the tuna sauce drizzled over it.

The Basics of Miscellaneous Veal Cuts

The large, ungainly, and often tough organs and odds and ends of full-grown beef are small, tender, manageable, and eminently desirable in veal. Cuts such as whole head, tongue, and brain are too much for many people to take, although beloved by many of those who try them. Liver, kidney, thymus gland (sweetbreads), and heart, however, are mild-flavored and easy to prepare and enjoy. The marrow-filled shank—often called osso buco, its Italian name—and relatively large, inexpensive breast, are two more "peasant" cuts that have become classy, and rightly so.

Classic Osso Buco
Braised Veal Shanks
Makes 4 servings

Time: About 2 hours, largely unattended

Literally, "bone with hole." And it's the holes in the bones, which contain the creamy, delicious marrow, that make this dish so wonderful. (Yes, the meat is good too.) So when you're buying veal shank for osso buco, make sure each piece contains a nice soft center (press to check); pieces from the hind shank are meatier than those from the foreshank.

Traditionally, osso buco is served following Risotto alla Milanese (page 208), which is not a bad idea. It's also served with Gremolada (recipe follows), a strong-flavored condiment that sometimes seems overkill to me. But it only takes a couple of minutes to make, so give it a try at least once.

The master recipe here is a rather "pure" osso buco, dominated by the flavors of veal and butter or oil. The variation is bolder, with a rich sauce that is absolutely a killer. Both are terrific.

4 large veal shanks, 8 to 12 ounces each

Flour for dredging

4 tablespoons (1/2 stick) butter, or a combination of
    butter and olive oil, or all olive oil

Salt and freshly ground black pepper to taste

1 cup chopped onion

1 celery stalk, chopped

2 medium carrots, peeled and chopped

1 or 2 sprigs fresh thyme or 1/2 teaspoon dried thyme

3/4 cup dry white wine

1 cup chicken, beef, or vegetable stock, or water
    (see "Soups" for stock recipes)

1 Preheat the oven to 350°F. For a somewhat more elegant presentation, tie the shanks around their circumference with a piece of kitchen twine to prevent the meat from falling off the bone (you don't need to do this). Select a large, ovenproof casserole that can later be covered, and place it over medium-high heat for 3 to 4 minutes.

2 Dry the shanks well and dredge them in the flour. When the casserole is hot (a pinch of flour will sizzle), add half the butter and/or oil. A minute later, add the shanks and brown them well on both sides, sprinkling them with salt and pepper as they cook. This will take a total of 10 to 15 minutes.

3 Remove the shanks to a plate and wipe out the casserole with a towel. Turn the heat to medium and add the remaining butter or oil. A minute later, add the vegetables and thyme. Cook, stirring occasionally, until soft, about 10 minutes, sprinkling with a little more salt and pepper. Add the wine, turn up the heat a bit, and let it bubble away for 1 minute.

4 Nestle the shanks among the vegetables and pour the stock or water over all. Cover and place in the oven. Cook for 1 1/2 to 2 hours, turning three or four times during the cooking, or until the meat is very tender and just about falling off the bone. Remove the meat to a warm platter and sprinkle it with Gremolada if you like. If the sauce is very soupy, cook it over high heat for a few minutes to reduce it somewhat, then pour it over the meat. Serve hot, with crusty bread, and spoons or dull knives for extracting the marrow.

Gremolada: Mix together 1 tablespoon minced lemon zest, 2 tablespoons minced fresh parsley leaves, and 1/4 to 1 teaspoon minced garlic. Remember that this will not be cooked, so take it easy on the garlic.

Osso Buco with Tomatoes, Garlic, and Anchovies: Steps 1 and 2 remain unchanged. In Step 3, before adding the vegetables and thyme, cook

1 tablespoon minced garlic and 3 minced anchovy fillets in the butter and/or oil, stirring until the anchovies break up. Add the vegetables and wine as above, then add 2 cups cored and chopped tomatoes (canned are fine; drain them first). Cook until the mixture becomes saucy. Add only $\frac{1}{2}$ cup of stock (the richer the better) and finish cooking as above.

Stuffed Veal Breast

Makes 4 to 6 servings

Time: About 3 hours, largely unattended

Veal breast is usually the cheapest cut of veal, and a delicious one. Unfortunately, the most common way to cook veal breast—with a pocket cut into it—makes the least sense. Unless you sew the pocket up with a needle and thread, a task for which few modern cooks have the patience, the stuffing inevitably leaks out and burns.

There are however, two ways to prepare veal breast that work beautifully. The first, which is simple, is to treat it just as you would veal shanks; use either of the osso buco recipes on page 450. To serve, you can either remove the bones, which come out easily after cooking, or just cut through the ribs and give one to each diner.

The second, presented here, is more complex and time-consuming but fabulous: Remove the bones (ask your butcher to do it), then stuff it, roll it up, and roast it in the oven. Sliced, it makes a beautiful presentation. I like to use leafy greens to stuff the meat, but you can use any stuffing in this book, or a personal favorite; just keep the quantity about the same.

1 pound fresh spinach, washed and trimmed
4 tablespoons ($\frac{1}{2}$ stick) butter, olive oil, or a
    combination
$\frac{1}{2}$ cup pine nuts
Salt and freshly ground black pepper to taste
$\frac{1}{4}$ cup freshly grated Parmesan cheese
Pinch freshly grated nutmeg
1 egg, lightly beaten
1 minced shallot, about 1 tablespoon
$\frac{1}{2}$ cup plain bread crumbs
$\frac{1}{2}$ cup minced fresh parsley leaves
1 boned breast of veal, $1\frac{1}{2}$ to 2 pounds after boning
    (at least 3 pounds with the bone)
$\frac{1}{2}$ cup dry white wine
1 cup chicken, beef, or vegetable stock, or water, plus a
    little more if needed (see "Soups" for stock recipes)

1. Preheat the oven to 350°F. Bring a large pot of water to the boil and put the spinach into it. Let it sit for 30 seconds, then take it out. Drain and, when it cools, squeeze the water from it and chop it.

2. Heat a large casserole or Dutch oven over medium heat for 2 or 3 minutes. Add 1 tablespoon of the butter or oil and, 1 minute later, the pine nuts. Cook, stirring, until they begin to brown. Add the spinach and toss to mix; season with some salt and pepper and scoop the mixture from the skillet. When the skillet cools, wipe it out with a towel.

3. Toss the spinach mixture with the Parmesan, nutmeg, egg, shallot, bread crumbs, and all but 2 tablespoons of the parsley. Taste it and add salt, pepper, and nutmeg as needed.

4. Lay the veal breast out flat and spread the stuffing mixture all over it, leaving a 1-inch border on all sides. Roll the meat up and tie it with string.

5. Reheat the skillet or casserole over medium-high heat for 2 or 3 minutes. Add the remaining butter or oil and, 1 minute later, begin to brown the roast on all side, turning as each side browns. Expect this to take 10 to 15 minutes. Regulate the heat so that, although the meat browns, the fat doesn't burn. Add the wine and, as it bubbles away, turn the meat so that each surface is moistened.

6 Add the stock or water and place the roast in the oven. Cook for $1^1/_2$ to 2 hours, turning the meat in the pan juices every 15 minutes and adding a little more liquid—stock or water—if needed. When the meat is tender—a thin-bladed knife will pierce it easily—place it on a platter and let it rest. If the pan liquid is soupy, reduce it a bit over high heat, scraping up any brown bits from the bottom. If it is dry, add a little liquid and place it over high heat, again scraping to incorporate any brown bits.

7 Cut the roll into 1-inch slices, douse with a little of the sauce, sprinkle with reserved parsley, and serve.

Sautéed Calf's Liver

Makes 3 to 4 servings

Time: 15 minutes

I'm sure that some people actually find the taste of liver unappealing, but my guess is that many more don't like it because they've only had it overcooked. Liver cooked medium-rare to medium is delicious, and as tender as any meat there is. If you want to serve it with bacon, cook the bacon first and use the bacon fat to cook the liver.

3 or 4 tablespoons butter, olive oil, or a combination
1 pound calf's liver, cut into $^1/_2$-inch-thick slices
Salt and freshly ground black pepper to taste
Flour for dredging
$^1/_2$ cup white wine or chicken or beef stock, optional
(see "Soups" for stock recipes)
1 tablespoon freshly squeezed lemon juice or
balsamic or sherry vinegar
Minced fresh parsley leaves for garnish
1 lemon, quartered

1 Preheat the oven to 200°F. Heat a large skillet over medium-high heat for 3 to 4 minutes.

2 Add 2 tablespoons of butter or oil and, when the butter's foam subsides or the first wisps of smoke arise from the oil, season with salt and pepper. Then dredge a slice of liver in the flour, shake off the excess, and put it in the skillet. Repeat until the pan is full but not crowded; the chances are you'll have to do this in two batches. As soon as a slice browns on one side (about 2 minutes), turn and brown the other side. Add additional butter or oil as needed, and keep the first slices warm in the oven as you finish the others.

3 When all the liver is done, you can simply garnish with parsley and serve with lemon or you can make a quick sauce: Turn the heat under the skillet to high and add the wine or stock. Cook, stirring all the while, until it is reduced by half. Add the lemon juice or vinegar and pour over the liver. Garnish with parsley and serve with lemon.

Sautéed Liver with Spices: In Step 2, use a minimum of flour, and spike it with:

- One tablespoon dry mustard. In Step 3, stir one tablespoon Dijon mustard into the reduction sauce along with the lemon juice or vinegar.
- One tablespoon curry powder. In Step 3, stir one-half cup sour cream or plain yogurt into the reduction sauce in place of the lemon juice or vinegar.
- One tablespoon five-spice powder. For cooking, use peanut oil if you have it, vegetable oil if you don't. In Step 3, stir one tablespoon soy sauce into the reduction in place of the lemon juice or vinegar.

Sautéed Liver with Onions: This takes a little longer; start the onions first. Peel and slice 5 or 6 medium onions; you want at least 4 cups of rings. Place them, dry, in a skillet, cover, and turn the heat to medium-low. Cook about 15 minutes, stirring every 5 minutes and re-covering, until the onions have given up their liquid and become dry. Uncover, add 3 tablespoons olive oil or butter, and cook over medium heat, stirring occasionally, until golden brown and tender, another 10 or 15 minutes. Cook the liver as above and serve, garnished with the onions.

Sautéed Liver with Apples: Here, the apples are cooked after the liver, so cook the liver just as you do in the master recipe and leave it in the oven. Don't make a reduction sauce, but add 2 tablespoons butter (much better than oil in this instance) to the skillet and cook 2 to 3 cups of peeled, cored, and sliced Granny Smith or other tart, crisp apples. Stir frequently until tender, about 7 or 8 minutes.

Broiled or Grilled Veal Heart

Makes 2 servings

Time: 20 minutes, plus time to marinate
   if you like, and time to preheat the grill

If you like dense, crisp-crusted, deep-flavored meat, heart is worth trying; it's probably the most under-rated cut there is. I like to deal with it almost as if it were a steak: grilled or broiled, with a minimum of seasoning, it's quick, wonderful, and best medium-rare.

   1 veal heart, about 1 pound
   1 tablespoon olive or peanut oil
   1 teaspoon any good vinegar
   1 tablespoon soy sauce
   Freshly ground black pepper to taste

   1 Start a charcoal or wood fire or preheat a gas grill or broiler; the fire should be quite hot.

   2 Trim the heart of as much external fat and connective tissue as you can. Split it in half and remove any veins; rinse and dry well. Mix together all remaining ingredients.

   3 You have two choices here: You can either brush the heart sections with the oil-vinegar mixture and start grilling, or let the meat sit in it, as a marinade, for 1 hour or so. Don't make any extra effort to marinate; it doesn't make that much difference.

   4 When you're ready to cook, grill or broil the heart, cut side up, about 3 or 4 inches from the heat source, for about 3 minutes. Baste, turn, and grill another 3 minutes. Baste, turn, and grill about 1 minute. The meat will be medium-rare and very juicy. Cook a little longer if you like, but don't overdo it.

Veal Kidneys with Sherry

Makes 2 servings

Time: About 30 minutes

Kidneys, especially those of veal, are a traditional light savory, served at breakfast or after dinner. They also make a fine meat at lunch or supper. Be careful not to overcook them.

   2 veal kidneys, about $1/2$ pound
   Salt and freshly ground black pepper to taste
   4 tablespoons ($1/2$ stick) butter (preferred) or oil
   Flour for dredging
   1 tablespoon minced shallot or scallion
   $1/2$ cup not-too-dry sherry, such as cream or oloroso
   Minced fresh parsley leaves for garnish

   1 Cut the kidneys into $1/2$- to $3/4$-inch-thick slices; trim off any hard parts. Season them well with salt and pepper. Preheat the oven to 200°F.

   2 Heat a large skillet over medium-high heat for 2 or 3 minutes. Add half the butter and, when the foam begins to subside, dredge the kidney slices, one at a time, in the flour, shake off the excess, and add them to the skillet. Raise the heat to high and cook them until browned on both sides, about 2 or 3 minutes per side, no more. Remove the kidney slices to an ovenproof plate and place in the oven.

3 Turn the heat under the skillet to medium-low and add the remaining butter. When it melts, add the shallot and cook, stirring, until it softens, about 2 minutes. Add the sherry and raise the heat to high. Cook, stirring and scraping the bottom of the pan, until the liquid has a syrupy quality. Return the kidney slices to the pan, garnish with parsley, and serve.

Sautéed Sweetbreads

Makes 4 servings

Time: 2 hours, somewhat unattended

Preparing sweetbreads is something of a nuisance (that's why many of their admirers eat them in restaurants, but few prepare them at home), but the reward is meat that is not only crisp on the outside but almost creamy inside. Make sure you are buying sweetbreads of veal, which weigh about a pound per pair (and are sold that way); beef sweetbreads are tough.

> About $1/2$ tablespoon salt
> 1 tablespoon any vinegar
> 2 pairs veal sweetbreads, about 2 pounds total
> 3 tablespoons butter or extra-virgin olive oil
> Flour for dredging
> Freshly ground black pepper to taste
> $1/2$ cup dry white wine
> Freshly squeezed lemon juice to taste
> Minced fresh parsley leaves for garnish

1 Set a pot of water, large enough to hold the sweetbreads, to boil. Add about $1/2$ tablespoon of salt

and the vinegar. When the water boils, add the sweetbreads and adjust the heat so that the pot boils but not furiously. Cook for 10 minutes.

2 Drain, then plunge the sweetbreads into a bowl of ice water, or run under cold water until cool. Pick off any bits of the membrane that are loose, but don't worry about it too much; they're quite tender. Dry the sweetbreads with paper towels and place them on a plate. Cover with another plate and a couple of pounds of weight—some cans, or a rock or two. Place in the refrigerator for about an hour, or up to a day.

3 When you're ready to cook, cut the sweetbreads into $1/2$-inch-thick slices. Place a large skillet over medium-high heat for 2 or 3 minutes; add the butter or oil. When the butter melts or the oil is hot, about 1 minute later, dredge the sweetbread slices in the flour, one at a time, shaking off excess flour.

4 Sauté the slices for about 2 or 3 minutes per side, or until golden brown and crisp, seasoning well with salt and pepper as they cook. When they're done, place them on a warm platter. Add the wine to the skillet and cook, stirring, for about 1 minute, until it is reduced to a tablespoon or two. Add a squeeze of lemon juice and pour over the sweetbreads; garnish and serve immediately.

The Basics of Pork

The last twenty years have been filled with change for pork: First, it was declared the enemy, the fattiest and least healthy of all meats. The response, on the part of pork producers, has been to reduce the fat in every cut, wherever possible, through genetics, through diet, and through butchering.

For pork lovers, there are aspects of this cure that have been worse than the disease. What we have now is a new animal. Much pork is so lean that it must be cooked quickly to keep it from drying out. This is especially true with chops and tenderloin, which were pretty lean to begin with. Fortunately, the fattier cuts of pork can still take a few hours to develop their best flavor, and will stay moist despite long cooking times.

Yet, if pork takes more care in cooking, it remains quite flavorful. And, next to poultry, it's the cheapest meat you can buy, still well under two dollars a pound for many cuts.

Many people wonder how they can cook pork quickly if it must be cooked well done. But for many cuts, super-well-done pork is a thing of the past. It's true that most people still prefer their pork to be served well done, but that doesn't mean you need to cook it until it is a dark gray 170°F (or worse: old cookbooks often recommend cooking pork to 185°F!). Pork tastes best when still on the pink side, at around 150°F. Since trichinae—which causes the dread trichinosis—is killed at 137°F, eating medium pork is widely considered safe, especially since there are more cases of trichinosis each year from wild boar than from farm-raised pork. (Other bacteria, including salmonella, may not be killed at this temperature; if this concerns you, cook pork to 160°F—well done—but note that you should be doing the same for beef and veal.)

It's not as difficult to buy the right cut of pork as it is of beef, but it's still worth knowing which end is up.

Shoulder Contains two major cuts, the Boston butt (in Boston, evidently, they did *not* know which end was up, since this is the shoulder) and the picnic ham (the front leg). The latter is, like ham, frequently cured. Both cuts are fatty and delicious, among the best parts of the pig to roast or cook in liquid because they remain moist and become tender. Hocks and "trotters" (feet) also come from the front legs.

Loin Behind the shoulder, this is the area from which the ultra-lean tenderloin is removed, as well as all loin roasts and chops, whether boneless or bone-in. There are several names commonly used for loin roasts: rib-end (from the shoulder end), loin- or rump-end (from the rear end), and center loin (or center-cut loin or center-cut rib). All are equally good, the rear end being a little leaner. All of these roasts may, of course, be cut into chops. Boneless center-cut loin is smoked to make Canadian bacon. Back ribs and country-style "ribs" (which are not ribs at all) are also cut from the loin.

Belly The cut that contains spareribs and bacon. Salted belly is salt pork; salted and smoked belly is bacon.

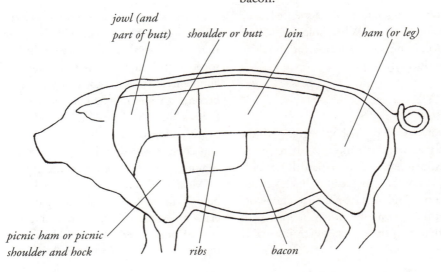

jowl (and part of butt) *shoulder or butt* *loin* *ham (or leg)*

picnic ham or picnic shoulder and hock *ribs* *bacon*

If you're looking for a dish to anchor your next cook-out, stop here:

Ham   The rear legs, almost always cured, sold whole, in pieces, or in slices. When sold fresh, ham can be cooked according to any recipe for shoulder, although it is considerably leaner.

The Basics of Pork Chops

As with most meat, a good pork chop begins with the right cut. What you want is center-cut loin chops, which have a distinct "eye" of meat (and little meat elsewhere). Avoid shoulder (also called blade) chops and loin-end chops. And make sure that chops are at least an inch thick—you'll be much happier with one thick chop than two thin ones, which invariably overcook.

As noted above, today's pork is so lean that small cuts like chops must be cooked with liquid, with one exception: I still like a grilled (or pan-grilled) pork chop, seasoned with little more than salt, olive oil, and lemon, although care must be taken not to overcook it, or it will become dry and tough. This method, with a variation, follows the reliably moist Sautéed Pork Chop, right, in which I brown the chops, add flavorings and liquid, and cook, covered and very slowly, for about fifteen minutes, until the pork is cooked through but not dry.

Most pork chop recipes—including all of those here—can be used for bone-in chicken parts, especially breast halves, whose cooked texture is not unlike that of pork. Since most chicken breasts are thicker than an inch, cooking time will be somewhat longer.

Sautéed Pork Chops, Eight Ways

Makes 4 servings

Time: 30 minutes

A straightforward, simple method that always gives good results, no matter what seasonings you add. Use center-cut loin chops if at all possible.

4 center-cut loin pork chops, about 1 inch thick, trimmed of excess fat

Salt and freshly ground black pepper to taste

2 tablespoons olive oil, plus more if not using butter

$^{1}/_{2}$ cup dry white wine

1 teaspoon minced garlic or 2 tablespoons minced shallot, onion, or scallion

$^{1}/_{2}$ cup chicken, beef, or vegetable stock, or water, plus more if needed (see "Soups" for stock recipes)

1 tablespoon butter (you can use more olive oil instead, especially if it's flavorful)

1 tablespoon freshly squeezed lemon juice or wine vinegar

Minced fresh parsley leaves for garnish

① Sprinkle the chops with salt and pepper. Place a large skillet over medium-high heat for 2 or 3 minutes. Add the 2 tablespoons olive oil; as soon as the first wisps of smoke rise from the oil, add the chops and turn the heat to high. Brown the chops on both sides, moving them around so they develop good color all over. The entire browning process should take no longer than 4 minutes, and preferably less.

② Reduce the heat to medium. Add the wine and the garlic and cook, turning the chops once or twice, until the wine is all but evaporated, about 3 minutes. Add $^{1}/_{2}$ cup of stock or water, turn the heat to low, and cover. Cook for 10 to 15 minutes, turning the chops once or twice, until the chops are tender but not dry. When done, they will be firm to the touch,

their juices will run just slightly pink and, when you cut into them (which you should do if you're at all unsure of their doneness), the color will be rosy at first glance but quickly turn pale.

③ Remove the chops to a platter. If the pan juices are very thin, cook, stirring and scraping the bottom of the pan, until the liquid is reduced slightly. If they are scarce (unlikely), add another $^{1}/_{2}$ cup of stock or water; cook, stirring and scraping the bottom of the pan, until the liquid is reduced slightly. Then stir in the butter or oil over medium heat; add the lemon juice, pour over the chops, garnish, and serve.

Pork Chops with Sherry-Garlic Sauce: Steps 1 and 2 remain the same. In Step 3, after removing the chops, add $^{1}/_{2}$ cup not-too-dry sherry (oloroso or amontillado) and cook, stirring and scraping the bottom of the pan, until the liquid is reduced slightly. Add 1 tablespoon olive oil and 1 tablespoon minced garlic and continue to cook until the liquid becomes syrupy. Omit butter. Stir in $^{1}/_{4}$ cup minced fresh parsley leaves and the juice of $^{1}/_{2}$ lemon. Taste for seasoning, pour over the chops, garnish and serve.

Pork Chops with Apples: Steps 1 and 2 remain the same. In Step 3, after removing the chops, cook 2 cups peeled, cored, and sliced apples in the remaining liquid, stirring and scraping the bottom of the pan as the apples cook and adding about $^{1}/_{2}$ cup more liquid (white wine or stock) if necessary. When the apple slices are soft, about 5 minutes, stir in 1 tablespoon lemon juice (omit butter), pour over the chops, garnish, and serve.

Pork Chops with Dried Fruit: Soak about 1 cup dried apricots, apples, or prunes, or a mixture, in water to cover while the pork chops cook. Add them, with some of their liquid, as you would the apples in the variation above.

Pork Chops with Vinegar: Step 1 remains the same. In Step 2, use $1/3$ cup balsamic or sherry vinegar in place of the stock. Step 3 remains the same; use stock if you need more liquid, and omit the lemon juice.

Pork Chops with Mustard: Steps 1 and 2 remain the same. In Step 3, stir in 1 tablespoon or more of Dijon mustard with the lemon juice (some capers are good here, too, as is a dash or two of Worcestershire sauce). Finish as above.

Pork Chops with Onions and Peppers: Steps 1 and 2 remain the same; undercook the chops slightly and preheat an oven to warm. In Step 3, after removing the chops, put them in the warm oven. Stir in 2 cups thinly sliced onions and 2 cups stemmed, seeded, and sliced peppers, any color but green. Stir, re-cover the pan, and cook for 5 minutes over medium heat. Remove the cover and cook, stirring, until the vegetables are softened and beginning to brown, about 5 more minutes. Moisten with $1/2$ cup stock, then cook until most of the stock is absorbed. Omit butter. Stir in 1 tablespoon of lemon juice or vinegar, taste and adjust seasoning, and serve over the chops. A teaspoon of minced fresh marjoram, oregano, or thyme leaves (or $1/2$ teaspoon of dried herb), or a tablespoon or two of minced fresh basil or parsley is good stirred into the vegetables just as they finish cooking.

Pork Chops with Butter, Chervil, and Shallots: Do the initial browning in half oil, half butter; otherwise, Steps 1 and 2 remain the same. In Step 3, after removing the chops, pour off all of the liquid and add 2 tablespoons of butter and $1/4$ cup minced shallots to the skillet. Cook over medium heat until the shallots soften, 3 or 4 minutes. Add $1/2$ cup stock or water and cook, stirring, until syrupy. Add $1/4$ cup minced fresh chervil or basil leaves, or 1 teaspoon minced fresh tarragon leaves, and stir. Add

1 tablespoon more butter, the lemon juice, and pour over the chops. Serve, garnished with a bit more of the minced fresh herb.

Grilled Pork Chops

Makes 4 servings

Time: 20 minutes, plus time to preheat the grill

Simple but, unless you get fatty, old-fashioned pork from a neighbor, likely to be on the dry side; still, I find these irresistible. The variation is especially wonderful, but you must plan ahead for it. See the second variation—Pan-Grilled Pork Chops—if you want to cook inside.

> 4 center-cut loin pork chops, about 1 inch thick, trimmed of excess fat
> 2 tablespoons best olive oil
> 1 tablespoon freshly squeezed lemon juice
> Salt and freshly ground black pepper to taste
> Lemon quarters

1 Start a charcoal or wood fire or preheat a gas grill; the fire should be moderately hot. As the fire heats, let the chops reach room temperature if you haven't already done so.

2 Dry the chops, then rub them with half the olive oil and the lemon juice. Sprinkle them liberally with salt and pepper.

3 Sear the chops over the hottest part of the fire for a minute or two per side, taking care not to let them burn. Then move them to a cooler part of the grill and cook, turning once or twice, until done, 10 to 20 minutes more (the timing depends on the heat of the fire, the thickness of the chops, and whether you cover the grill). The chops are done when they are firm to the touch, their juices run just slightly pink, and, when you cut into them (which you should do if you're at all unsure of their doneness), the color is rosy at first glance but quickly turns pale.

4 Brush the chops with a little more olive oil and serve with lemon quarters.

Herb-Marinated Grilled Pork Chops: Start these at least 2 hours and as long as 3 days before you plan to eat them. Dry the chops well. Mix together 1 teaspoon salt; 1 teaspoon dried sage or thyme (or 1 tablespoon minced fresh); $^1/_2$ teaspoon freshly ground black pepper; 1 bay leaf, finely broken up; and 1 teaspoon finely minced garlic, and rub them all over with this mixture. Cover or wrap the chops and let them sit at room temperature for up to 2 hours or refrigerated for up to 3 days. Grill as above, without olive oil. Serve with lemon quarters if you like.

Pan-Grilled Pork Chops: Turn the oven to its maximum temperature, at least 500°F, and set a rack in the lowest possible position. Preheat a cast-iron or other sturdy, ovenproof skillet just large enough to hold the chops over medium-high heat for 4 to 5 minutes; the pan should be really hot, just about smoking. Rub the chops with olive oil only, then place in the skillet. Immediately transfer the skillet to the oven; cook about 5 minutes per side. Season with salt, pepper, and freshly squeezed lemon juice and serve with lemon quarters.

Sweet Simmered Pork Chops

Makes 4 servings

Time: 20 minutes

There is no browning of the meat in this easy, Japanese-style dish. Still, the flavors are quite complex. Make plenty of rice for the sauce. If you are using a mild, natural soy sauce (such as that labeled "shoyu"), change the soy sauce to water ratio to one-half cup each.

$^1/_3$ cup soy sauce

$^2/_3$ cup water

$^1/_3$ cup dry sherry

$^1/_4$ cup mirin or 2 tablespoons honey thinned with a little water

2 tablespoons rice or white wine vinegar

5 or 6 thin slices peeled fresh ginger

3 or 4 cloves garlic, crushed

4 center-cut loin pork chops, about 1 inch thick, trimmed of excess fat

$^1/_2$ cup minced scallions or $^1/_4$ cup minced chives for garnish

1 In a large skillet with a cover, mix together all the ingredients except the pork and the scallions or chives. Bring to a boil over medium-high heat, turn the heat to medium-low, and simmer, uncovered, for about 5 minutes. Preheat the oven to 200°F.

2 Add the pork, cover, and simmer, turning occasionally, until the meat is just about cooked through, about 15 minutes.

3 Place the chops on an ovenproof platter and put the platter in the oven. Turn the heat under the skillet to high and reduce the sauce to 1 cup or a little less; remove the ginger slices if you like.

4 Spoon a little sauce over the chops, garnish with scallions or chives, and serve, passing the remaining sauce at the table.

The Basics of Pork Stir-Fries and Other Tidbits

Until recently, the rich tenderness of pork made it the ideal meat for stir-fries: You could brown small bits before they overcooked, because their high fat content kept the pieces moist and soft. Now, however, pork is more like chicken: Care must be taken when cooking smaller bits of it, whether in stir-fries or kebabs, and it should be removed the moment it is done.

When stir-frying, my solution is to cook the pork first at the highest heat possible, then remove it before cooking the remaining ingredients, adding it back only at the end of cooking to reheat briefly. With kebabs, I simply cut bigger pieces than I once did, turn them often, baste them with liquid if necessary, and be sure not to overcook.

Substitute thinly cut pork for any of the meats in the other stir-fries in this chapter and "Poultry," or add it to any vegetable stir-fry.

Stir-Fried Pork with Spinach

Makes 4 servings

Time: About 15 minutes

When they're in season, substitute any tender green—arugula, cress, chard, or dandelion are all good—for the spinach. And add a small handful of chopped basil at the last minute of you like.

A couple of other pointers about this basic stir-fry: If you like a strong garlic flavor, reserve one-half tablespoon of the garlic and stir it in at the end of the cooking, along with the soy sauce and lime juice. And if the mixture is drier than you like after you've added the soy sauce and lime juice, add one-quarter to one-half cup of water or any stock you have on hand; heat through and serve.

1 pound pork tenderloin, fresh ham, loin, or shoulder, trimmed of external fat
About 1 pound spinach, trimmed and well washed (page 604)
2 tablespoons peanut or other vegetable oil
1½ tablespoons minced garlic
1 tablespoon soy sauce
Juice of ½ lime
½ cup minced scallion or ¼ cup minced chives for garnish

1 Slice the pork as thinly as you can (it's easier if you freeze it for 15 to 30 minutes first). Cut the slices into bite-sized pieces, about the size of a quarter. Chop or tear the spinach coarsely.

2 When you're ready to cook, have all ingredients ready, including a serving dish and rice, if any. Preheat a wok or a large, heavy skillet over high heat until it begins to smoke. Immediately add half the peanut oil and the pork. Cook, stirring occasionally (*not* constantly), until the pork browns and loses all traces of pinkness, about 3 minutes. Use a slotted spoon to remove the pork to a bowl, and lower the heat to medium.

3 Add the remaining peanut oil to the wok. Swirl it around and add the garlic. Stir once or twice. As soon as garlic begins to color—about 15 seconds—return the heat to high and add the spinach. Stir frequently, just until the spinach wilts, a minute or two longer.

4 Add the pork and stir for 1 minute. Add the soy sauce and lime juice, stir, turn off the heat, garnish, and serve immediately.

Stir-Fried Pork with Sweet Onions: In Step 1, use 3 cups peeled and sliced onions in place of spinach. In Step 3, cook the onions with the garlic, stirring over medium-high heat until they soften and begin to brown, 7 to 10 minutes. Sprinkle them with 1 teaspoon of sugar, then proceed to Step 4.

Stir-Fried Pork with Snow Peas and Ginger: In Step 1, trim 2 cups of snow peas (or snap peas) in place of spinach. Step 2 remains the same. In Step 3, cook 2 tablespoons peeled and minced fresh ginger with the garlic, then add the snow peas, stirring over medium-high heat until they soften and begin to brown, about 5 minutes. In Step 4, add 1 teaspoon peeled and minced fresh ginger along with the soy sauce and lime juice.

Stir-Fried Pork with Hoisin and Sesame Oil: Execute Step 1 through Step 3 in the master recipe or any of the variations. In Step 4, stir 1 tablespoon hoisin sauce into the stir-fry along with the soy sauce; omit lime juice. Drizzle with 1 teaspoon dark sesame oil before serving.

Ten Simple Additions to Pork Stir-Fries

1. Add one-quarter teaspoon or more crushed red pepper flakes along with the garlic.
2. Use any combination of raw vegetables, cut into small pieces, and cook with the garlic.
3. Add one tablespoon of sugar to the pork as it cooks for added color, crispness, and sweetness.
4. Add two tablespoons whole or chopped peanuts or cashews along with the vegetables.
5. Add five-spice or All-Purpose Curry Powder (page 778) along with the pork.
6. Add one-half cup Fresh Coconut Milk (page 291) just at the end of cooking.
7. Add one teaspoon ground spices, especially Szechwan peppercorns, with the garlic.
8. Marinate pork in one-fourth cup of soy sauce mixed with one-fourth cup of water or wine and teaspoon of vinegar before stir-frying.
9. Use fish sauce (*nuoc mam* or *nam pla*, available in Asian markets) in place of soy sauce.
10. Add ground bean paste (about one tablespoon), plum sauce (about one tablespoon), or chile-garlic paste (about one-half teaspoon, or to taste) during the last minute of cooking.

West Indian Crispy Pork Bits

Makes 4 to 8 servings

Time: About 2 hours, plus marinating time if desired, largely unattended

West Indian to start with, yes, but as you can see from the variations here, there are many ways to season bits of pork before cooking them until they are brown; I find all of them irresistible. Here, it's best to use fattier cuts—from the shoulder or the butt, rather than the loin or ham—because you need fat to keep the meat moist as it cooks and absorbs spices.

The traditional way to make pork crisp is to cook it in a skillet over medium heat for a while, stirring occasionally. This works fine, but spattering is a problem. I've taken to letting the oven work its magic here, and believe that the results are equally good and the clean-up much less work. You can also grill them: Cut them a little larger—say, $1^1/_2$- to two-inch cubes—and put them on skewers. Grill them over direct but relatively low heat, turning frequently, until brown and crisp, about twenty minutes, taking care not to let them burn.

Marinating these for an hour, six hours, a day, or two days makes the flavor somewhat more intense, but is hardly necessary. If you serve these as a main course, make a quick pan sauce as directed in Step 3; if you'd like to serve them on toothpicks as an appetizer, don't bother. They're great at room temperature also.

$1^1/_2$ to 2 pounds boneless pork shoulder or butt, trimmed of most external fat, but with some left on
Salt and freshly ground black pepper to taste
1 tablespoon minced garlic
1 teaspoon ground allspice
$^1/_4$ teaspoon ground or freshly grated nutmeg
1 teaspoon fresh thyme leaves or $^1/_2$ teaspoon dried thyme
$^1/_2$ cup minced onion or scallion
1 tablespoon peanut, olive, or vegetable oil
$^1/_4$ cup freshly squeezed lime juice
$^1/_2$ cup any stock or water, optional (see "Soups" for stock recipes)

1 Cut the meat into 1-inch or larger cubes. Toss with all other ingredients except stock or water. Cover and marinate, refrigerated, for as long as you like (up to 2 days). Or cook right away.

2 Preheat the oven to 375°F. Place the meat in a roasting pan large enough to allow it to fit in one layer (it will shrink considerably, so a tight fit is okay). Roast for about 1 hour, shaking and stirring the meat occasionally, until the meat is brown and crisp on all sides. Remove meat with a slotted spoon. Serve hot or at room temperature, or proceed to the next step to make a quick sauce.

3 Pour off all but a tablespoon or two of the fat, leaving any solids and as much non-fatty liquid behind as possible. Place the pan on a burner over high heat, add $1/2$ cup stock or water, and cook, stirring and scraping the bottom of the pan, until the liquid is reduced by about half and all the solids are incorporated. Pour over the pork bits and serve.

"Jerk" Pork: Replace the thyme with 1 teaspoon ground coriander and add half (or more) of a stemmed, seeded, and minced Scotch bonnet chile to the marinade, or use any other chile pepper, cayenne, crushed red pepper flakes, or chili sauce to taste.

Pork Bits with Iberian Flavors: Eliminate from the marinade: the allspice, nutmeg, thyme, and lime juice. Add to the marinade: 1 tablespoon ground cumin, 2 teaspoons paprika, 1 tablespoon grated or minced lemon zest, and $1/4$ cup freshly squeezed lemon juice.

Pork Bits with Asian Flavors: Eliminate from the marinade: the allspice, nutmeg, thyme, and lime juice. Add to the marinade: 2 tablespoons peeled and minced or grated fresh ginger (or 1 tablespoon ground ginger), 2 tablespoons soy (or fish) sauce, and 1 tablespoon sugar.

Pork Bits with Mexican Flavors: Eliminate from the marinade: the allspice, nutmeg, and thyme. Add to the marinade: 1 teaspoon each ground cumin and chili powder (or use 2 teaspoons of either) and

1 tablespoon minced fresh oregano leaves (or 1 teaspoon dried oregano).

Pork Satay

Makes 10 skewers, about 5 servings

Time: 1 hour or less, plus time to preheat the grill

Satays are the easiest way to grill pork bits. Because you cut the pork into thin slices before grilling, the cooking process takes just five minutes or so, avoiding problems with burning. Cut the marinating time to five minutes if you are pressed for time.

1 pound pork tenderloin, fresh ham, loin, or shoulder, trimmed of external fat
$1/2$ cup soy sauce
$1/2$ cup water
1 teaspoon chili powder
1 tablespoon peanut butter or sesame (tahini)
1 teaspoon peeled and minced or grated fresh ginger
1 tablespoon minced garlic
1 tablespoon sugar
1 tablespoon freshly squeezed lime or lemon juice or vinegar

1 Slice the pork as thinly as you can (it's easier if you freeze it for 15 to 30 minutes first). Cut the slices into pieces, about $1^1/2$ inches in diameter. Just before you're ready to eat, start a charcoal or wood fire or preheat a gas grill or broiler; the fire should be quite hot.

2 Mix together the remaining ingredients and stir the pork into them. Let sit for a while or overnight, refrigerated.

3 When you're ready to cook, thread the pork onto skewers without crowding. Grill or broil until browned all over, a total of 5 to 8 minutes. While the meat is cooking, bring the marinade to a boil and reduce it slightly. Serve the skewers hot, using the marinade as a dipping sauce.

Sautéed Medallions of Pork with Lemon and Parsley

Makes 4 servings

Time: 15 minutes

You can follow any recipe for cutlets of veal (pages 445–446) or chicken (pages 380–382) for pork medallions. Like these other meats, medallions of pork are so thin that they cook through in the time it takes to brown them. Here's a basic recipe on which to build. Add a tablespoon or two of drained capers with the lemon juice if you like.

1 (1- to 1¼-pound) pork tenderloin,
¼ cup olive oil
Flour for dredging, liberally seasoned with salt
    and pepper
½ cup dry white wine
Juice of 1 lemon
1 lemon, quartered
Minced fresh parsley leaves for garnish

1 Cut the tenderloin into ½-inch-thick slices (it will be easier if you freeze the meat for about 30 minutes before cutting). Pound them gently (use a flat rolling pin, the back of a skillet, or a similar object) between two sheets of waxed paper to make them a bit thinner.
2 In a large skillet over medium heat, heat the olive oil; set the seasoned flour in a shallow bowl near the stove.
3 When the oil is good and hot (a pinch of flour will sizzle), dredge the medallions, one at a time, in the flour, then place them in the skillet. Cook them over heat high enough to make the oil bubble; don't crowd. Set the oven to 200°F.

4 Turn the pieces as soon as they're browned, then cook the other side; total cooking time should be 5 minutes or less, so adjust heat accordingly. As the meat is done, remove it to an ovenproof platter and place the platter in the oven.
5 When all the pork is finished, pour off the fat from the pan. Return the skillet to the stove and add the wine, over medium-high heat. Cook, stirring, until the wine is just about evaporated. Add the lemon juice, stir, and pour this sauce (there won't be more than a few tablespoons) over the meat. Garnish and serve, passing lemon quarters at the table.

Grilled or Broiled Pork Tenderloin with Mustard Curry

Makes 3 to 4 servings

Time: About 30 minutes, plus time to preheat
    the grill

Pork tenderloin is lower in fat than almost any other cut of meat. And, since the cut is slender and relatively small, cooking time is fast, so fast that you can grill or broil it. There is a trade-off, however: The tenderloin is not the most flavorful cut.

It's a good idea to double this recipe, because thinly sliced leftovers make sensational sandwiches.

2 tablespoons Dijon mustard
2 tablespoons All-Purpose Curry Powder (page 778),
    store-bought curry powder, Garam Masala
    (page 778), or other spice mixture, or to taste
Salt and freshly ground black pepper to taste
1¼ pounds pork tenderloin, in 1 piece
Fresh Fruit Chutney with Mustard and Curry
    (page 785), Corn and Tomato Relish (page 782),
    or bottled chutney

1 Start a charcoal or wood fire or preheat a gas grill or broiler; the rack should be 2 to 4 inches from the heat source and the fire should be quite hot.

2 Blend the mustard, curry, salt, and pepper in a small bowl, then rub the meat all over with this mixture. Grill or broil, turning to brown all sides, until almost cooked through but still slightly pink in the very center, about 10 to 15 minutes (the internal temperature at the very center should be no higher than 145°F when you remove it from the heat). Let the meat sit for 10 minutes before cutting into ¹/₂-inch-thick slices and serving with chutney or relish.

The Basics of Pork Roasts

The generally preferred cut of pork for oven-roasting is the loin. Many people prefer a boneless roast, which is certainly less work when it comes to carving. But leaving the bone in usually results in moister meat—the added bulk and protection of the bone gives you more flexibility in timing—and always results in more flavorful meat. So, although I'd just as soon not wrestle with the bone, I deal with it. And it's not that difficult, really, as long as the chine (bottom) bone is cut through in advance, preferably by your butcher.

There are other good cuts for roasting and, except for timing, three of them are interchangeable with the loin: the shoulder, the butt, and the (fresh) ham. These may be quite large, however (a whole ham can weigh in at thirty pounds or more), so it's likely you'll be cooking just a piece. The shoulder and the butt are fatty, which doesn't eliminate them as roasts (on the contrary), but makes it unwise to cook vegetables with them; they'll become too greasy. Like fresh ham, the shoulder is nice because proper roasting gives you crispy skin to munch on, one of the great pleasures of pork.

Then there is the pork tenderloin. This is so lean that it is best suited for cutting into medallions and sautéing, then finishing with a sauce, or grilling. But it can be roasted with good results, as long as the timing is quick and precise.

Finally, there is the crown roast of pork, two loin sections partially boned and tied together in the shape of a ring, or crown. Any butcher can put this together for you, and it perhaps the most impressive roast of all. If you're planning to serve a crowd of ten or more, consider it.

There is one major difference between pork roasts and those of other meat. Although almost no one cooks pork to the degree once thought necessary, it still is at its best when only a trace of rosiness remains in its center. This makes an instant-read thermometer almost essential. If you remove the roast when the thermometer reads 145°F (test it in two or three places to be sure) and let it rest for a few minutes before carving, its temperature will rise to 155°F, which will leave the very center just pinkish. If you prefer it really well done, roast it to 150°F; during its rest the temperature will rise to 160°F. Any cooking beyond that is unnecessary.

Roast Pork with Garlic and Rosemary
Makes 6 or more servings

Time: 1¹/₂ to 2 hours, largely unattended

The basic roast pork. Serve with very light side dishes; this is the kind of dish that drives you wild and makes you eat more than you want to. If you want a more garlicky flavor, cut a clove of garlic into tiny slivers and, using a thin-bladed knife, insert them into the roast all over. You can do this a day or two in advance; if you do, rub the roast all over with salt, too, and keep refrigerated, covered loosely with a towel or piece of waxed paper.

Salt and freshly ground black pepper to taste

2 tablespoons minced fresh rosemary leaves or
1 teaspoon dried rosemary

1/4 teaspoon cayenne (optional)

1 tablespoon sugar

1 teaspoon minced garlic

1 (3- to 4-pound) pork loin roast, bone-in,
or 1 (2- to 3-pound) boneless roast, or a
similar-size portion of fresh ham

1 1/2 cups dry white wine or stock, approximately
(see "Soups" for stock recipes)

1 tablespoon butter (optional)

① Preheat the oven to 450°F. Mix a liberal amount of salt and pepper together with the rosemary, cayenne, sugar, and garlic, and rub it all over the roast. Place the meat in a roasting pan (use a rack if the roast is boneless, but don't bother if the bone is still in) and put in the oven. Roast, undisturbed, for 15 minutes.

② Open the oven and pour about 1/2 cup of wine or stock over the roast; lower the heat to 325°F. Continue to roast, adding about 1/4 cup of liquid every 15 minutes or so. If the liquid accumulates on the bottom of the pan, use it to baste; if not, add more.

③ Start checking the roast after 1 1/4 hours of total cooking time (it's likely to take about 1 1/2 hours). When it is done—an instant-read thermometer will register 145° to 150°F—remove it to a warm platter. Put the roasting pan on the stove over one or two burners set to medium-high. If there is a great deal of liquid in it, reduce it to about 3/4 cup, scraping the bottom of the pan with a wooden spoon to release any brown bits that have accumulated. If the pan is dry, add 1 cup of liquid and follow the same process. When the sauce has reduced some, stir in the butter if you like, slice the roast, and serve it with the sauce.

Roast Pork with Sage and Potatoes

Makes 6 or more servings

Time: 1 1/2 to 2 hours, largely unattended

An authentic recipe from Naples, this is my absolute favorite. It's best with firm, waxy potatoes; if they're small enough, keep them whole.

2 tablespoons minced garlic

2 tablespoons minced fresh sage leaves or
2 teaspoons dried sage

Salt and freshly ground black pepper to taste

About 2 pounds potatoes, peeled and cut into
1-inch cubes

2 tablespoons olive oil, plus more as needed

1 (3- to 4-pound) pork loin roast, bone-in,
or 1 (2- to 3-pound) boneless roast, or a
similar size portion of fresh ham

① Preheat the oven to 425°F. Mix together the garlic, sage, salt, and pepper. Put the potatoes in a roasting pan that is also large enough to hold the pork, and toss them with a couple of tablespoons of olive oil and about 1 teaspoon of the garlic-sage mixture. Place the roasting pan in the oven while you prepare the pork.

② Using a thin-bladed knife and your fingers, make slits all over the pork and insert most of the remaining garlic-sage mixture. Spread the rest of it all over the outside of the roast, and nestle it among the potatoes. Pour a little more olive oil over the meat and place it in the oven.

③ Roast, undisturbed, for 30 minutes. Remove it from the oven, stir the potatoes (you will probably have to scrape some of them off the bottom of the pan), and baste the pork with a little of the pan juices. Lower the heat to 325°F and continue to cook, stirring the potatoes every 15 minutes or so. After 1 1/4 hours or so total cooking time, begin to check the meat (it's likely to take longer, but it's worth checking); when an instant-read thermometer registers 145° to 150°F, remove the meat to a warm platter.

4 While the meat rests for 10 to 15 minutes, turn the oven heat up to 450°F to make sure the potatoes are done and crisp (use your judgment; you can simply run them under the broiler if they just need a bit of browning, or keep the oven at 325°F if they're perfectly done). Carve the meat and serve with the potatoes.

Roast Pork with Dried Fruits

Makes 6 or more servings

Time: About 2 hours, largely unattended

There are three ways to stuff a pork loin with fruit: One is to remove the bone, lay the meat out flat, and lay the fruit onto it before rolling and tying it into a neat package. Another is to leave the bone in and make a hole straight through the meat; this is the method I prefer, and I give directions below. The third is to simply "stud" the meat with the fruit, poking holes with a knife and cramming it in there; that works well also.

$^1/_2$ cup pitted dried prunes
$^1/_2$ cup dried apricots (or use any combination of dried fruit and fresh apples and/or pears)
1 (4- to 5-pound) pork loin roast, bone-in
$^1/_2$ teaspoon ground cinnamon
Salt and freshly ground black pepper to taste
1 tablespoon sugar
1 teaspoon peeled and minced or grated fresh ginger, or ground ginger
$^1/_2$ cup white wine or apple cider, plus more as needed (optional)

1 Soak the prunes and apricots in hot water to cover while you prepare the pork. If you're using fresh fruit, peel, core, and cut into $^1/_2$-inch cubes. Preheat the oven to 425°F.

2 Using a sharp boning knife, poke two holes, dead center, in the eye of the meat. Now, using the knife, a clean dowel, the end of a wooden spoon, a sharpening steel, or some other like implement, force a hole all the way through the meat. Make it at least wide enough to put your thumb in.

3 When the fruit is tender but not mushy (change the water if it is not quite ready), drain it, reserving the liquid. Combine the fruit with the cinnamon and stuff this mixture into the roast, forcing it into the hole. Push it all the way to the center with your fingers, the implement you used to create the hole, or whatever else you can come up with.

4 Combine the salt, pepper, sugar, and ginger, and rub the meat all over with it. Put the meat in a roasting pan and pour about $^1/_2$ cup of the fruit-soaking liquid over it, or use white wine or cider. Roast, undisturbed, for 20 minutes. Lower the heat to 325°F and continue to cook, basting with pan juices or added liquid about every 15 minutes. After $1^1/_4$ hours or so total cooking time, begin to check the meat; when an instant-read thermometer registers 145° to 150°F, remove it to a warm platter. (When checking the temperature of the meat, be sure the thermometer is actually in the meat rather than in the fruit.)

5 Let the meat sit for 15 minutes. Meanwhile, put the roasting pan on the stove over one or two burners set to medium-high. If there is a great deal of liquid in it, reduce it to about $^1/_2$ cup, scraping the bottom of the pan with a wooden spoon to release any brown bits that have accumulated. If the pan is dry, add 1 cup of wine, cider, or fruit-soaking liquid and follow the same process. When the sauce has reduced some, slice the roast and serve it with the sauce.

Roast Pork with Dried Fruits and Apricot-Mustard Glaze: Steps 1 through 3 remain the same. In Step 4, when the meat is almost done (the internal temperature at about 125°F), mix together $1/4$ cup Dijon or other good mustard and $1/2$ cup apricot or peach jam. Brush or spoon this over the meat and continue to cook and finish as above, but with no further basting.

Roast Pork Shoulder, Puerto Rican–Style

Makes 6 to 10 servings

Time: At least 5 hours, largely unattended

This recipe, from the family of my friend Peter Blasini, is one of the great dishes of Puerto Rican cooking. It is almost as good left over and reheated as it is fresh, so I recommend opting for a large piece of meat. The shoulder is among the easiest roasts to cook; because it is quite fatty, it is essentially self-basting.

The seasoning here is adobo, an oregano-based spice mixture that can be purchased already made; this fresh version is vastly superior.

4 cloves garlic, peeled

1 medium onion, quartered

2 tablespoons fresh oregano leaves or 1 tablespoon dried oregano

1 tablespoon salt

2 teaspoons freshly ground black pepper

2 tablespoons peanut (preferred) or any other oil

2 tablespoons wine or cider vinegar

1 (4- to 7-pound) pork shoulder or portion of fresh ham, trimmed of excess but not all fat

1 Mix the first five ingredients together in a food processor, adding the oil in a drizzle and scraping down the sides as necessary (or mince them together on a cutting board). Blend in the vinegar.

2 Rub this mixture well into the pork, getting it into every nook and cranny you can find. Place the

meat on a rack and let sit, uncovered, for 1 to 24 hours; refrigerate if the weather is hot or the time is greater than 2 hours or so.

3 Preheat the oven to 350°F. Roast the pork for about 3 hours, turning every 30 minutes or so and basting with the pan juices, until it is well done and very tender, and the skin is crisp. (The internal temperature should be at least 150°F, but no more than 160°F.) Let the meat rest for 10 to 15 minutes before cutting it up; the meat should be so tender that cutting into uniform slices is almost impossible; rather, whack it up into chunks.

Crown Roast of Pork

Makes at least 10 or 12 servings

Time: About $2^{1}/_{2}$ hours, largely unattended

Like a turkey, a crown roast can be stuffed with just about anything. But since this meat is fairly heavy, I prefer to keep the stuffing on the light side, using bread crumbs and fruit. I prefer to cook the stuffing separately to allow it to crisp and limit the amount of fat it absorbs, but you can place it in the center of the crown if you like.

$1/2$ cup dried apricots

1 crown roast of pork, 14 to 16 ribs, about 7 pounds

Salt and freshly ground black pepper to taste

1 carrot, peeled and chopped

1 celery stalk, chopped

1 onion, cut into quarters, plus 1 cup minced onion

3 tablespoons olive oil

1 tablespoon minced garlic

2 teaspoons minced fresh tarragon leaves or $1/2$ teaspoon dried tarragon, crumbled

2 cups water or white wine, plus more as needed

$1/2$ pound (2 sticks) butter

4 cups plain bread crumbs, preferably fresh (page 239)

1. Preheat the oven to 450°F. Soak the apricots in hot water to cover. Sprinkle the roast with salt and pepper and place it on a rack in a roasting pan. Toss the carrot, celery, and quartered onion with 1 tablespoon of the olive oil and some salt and pepper and scatter them on the bottom of the pan.

2. Mix the remaining olive oil together with half the garlic and tarragon. Rub the roast all over with this mixture, making sure to spread a bit into all the crevices you find.

3. Roast the meat for 20 minutes, then turn the heat down to 325°F. Moisten the vegetables with about $1/2$ cup of liquid every 15 minutes, or whenever they look dry.

4. In a deep skillet or saucepan over medium heat, melt the butter. Add the minced onion and cook, stirring, until it is soft, about 5 minutes. Drain and chop the apricots and add them, then add the bread crumbs, remaining garlic and tarragon, salt, and pepper. Toss to combine. Put the stuffing in an 8-inch square or comparable baking dish in a 1- to 2-inch-thick layer and place in the oven. Cook the stuffing until it is crisp on top, then stir it up; repeat this process while you finish cooking the meat.

5. Total cooking time for the roast will be about 2 hours, or a little longer; its internal temperature (check it in several places), should be about 150°F. When it's ready, remove it to a cutting board and let it rest while you make the sauce. Lower the oven temperature to keep the stuffing warm (if the stuffing looks dry, baste it with some of the juices at the bottom of the roasting pan).

6. Pour or spoon off as much of the fat from the roasting pan as you can without losing the darker juices. Put the roasting pan on the stove over one or two burners set to medium-high. Add about $1/2$ cups of liquid and cook, stirring and scraping, until the liquid is reduced by about half. Remove the vegetables with a slotted spoon and press them into a strainer, adding any liquid you extract to the sauce.

7. Pile the stuffing into the center of the roast, then present the roast whole. Carve it, then serve with a bit of the stuffing, spooning a little of the sauce over it while passing the rest.

The Basics of Pork Stews and Braises

The best cuts for braising pork, the shoulder and the butt, have a fair amount of fat in them. This fat melts during the long, moist cooking process, and can be removed with a spoon at the end of cooking. Better still, cook the meat in advance and refrigerate it and its sauce separately; the fat will all rise to the top of the sauce, from which you can easily skim it. Then reheat the meat in the defatted sauce.

Boneless roasts are fine for braising; just make sure they are cut into evenly sized pieces or tied into a relatively uniform shape so that no part becomes overcooked at the expense of another. It is possible to overcook pork, even in liquid; the result is stringy meat (which, compared to other overcooked meat, is not altogether unpleasant). As with other braises, if you're pressed for time you can skip the browning step with little loss of flavor.

Braised Pork with Vinegar and Bay

Makes 4 to 6 servings

Time: About $1^{1}/_2$ hours, largely unattended

I like to serve this (and most other) braised pork dishes with mashed, boiled, or pan-browned potatoes. But it is also great with rice or crusty bread. The point is, whichever you prefer, you need something with which to salvage all the delicious cooking juices.

If you use pearl onions, skewer each one through its equator with a toothpick; this will keep them intact.

2 tablespoons olive oil

1 (2- to 3-pound) boneless roast of pork shoulder, butt, or other cut

Salt and freshly ground black pepper to taste

1 tablespoon minced garlic

2 cups sliced onions or 24 peeled pearl onions (frozen are fine)

6 bay leaves

$^1/_2$ cup red wine vinegar

$^1/_2$ cup dry red wine or water, plus $1^1/_2$ cups water, wine, or stock, if needed (see "Soups" for stock recipes)

Minced fresh parsley leaves for garnish

1 Heat a covered casserole or Dutch oven over medium-high heat for 2 or 3 minutes; add the oil and heat for another minute or so. Dry the meat and brown it on all sides, turning about every 3 to 4 minutes and regulating the heat so that the fat does not burn. As you turn it, season each side with salt and pepper.

2 Remove the pork, pour off most of the rendered fat, and turn the heat to medium-low. Add the garlic and onions (hold off if you're using pearl onions) and cook, stirring, until the vegetables soften, about 5 minutes. Add the bay leaves, vinegar, and $^1/_2$ cup wine; bring to a boil and let cook for 1 minute. Turn the heat to low and return the meat to the pot, along with the pearl onions if you're using them. Cover and cook over low heat, checking occasionally to make sure that the vegetables do not dry out.

3 When the meat is tender (a sharp, thin-bladed knife will pierce to the center without much resistance and an instant-read thermometer will read at least 150°F), about $1^1/_4$ hours later, remove it from the pot. Spoon off as much of the transparent fat as you can. If the sauce is very soupy, turn the heat to high and reduce it to about 1 cup, stirring and scraping any brown bits off the bottom of the pan and incorporating them into the sauce. If it's dry, add $1^1/_2$ cups

water, wine, or stock, and reduce by 50 percent over high heat.

4 Slice the pork and serve, garnished with the parsley and surrounded by the onion sauce.

Braised Pork with Horseradish Sauce: Step 1 remains the same. In Step 2, omit the bay leaves; reduce the vinegar to 1 tablespoon; add 1 teaspoon fresh thyme leaves or $^1/_2$ teaspoon dried thyme; substitute stock for the wine (water or wine is okay). In Step 4, stir $^1/_4$ cup freshly grated or 2 tablespoons prepared horseradish (or to taste) into the reduced sauce. Serve as above, passing more horseradish at the table.

Braised Pork with Beer and Juniper Berries: Step 1 remains the same. In Step 2, use only 1 bay leaf and omit the vinegar and wine; add 2 cups peeled and chopped carrots and 1 cup chopped celery along with the onions. Sprinkle the vegetables with 2 tablespoons flour, then return the pork to the pot. Add 1 bottle (12 ounces) good dark beer, bring to a boil, and turn the heat to low. Add 2 cloves, 1 teaspoon fresh thyme leaves or $^1/_2$ teaspoon dried thyme, and 10 juniper berries, crushed with the side of a knife. Steps 3 and 4 remain the same.

Spicy Pork with Cinnamon
Vindaloo Pork
Makes 6 servings

Time: About $1^1/_2$ hours, largely unattended

Like any "curry," this contains several spices. Although you can make it quite hot, the flavor of cinnamon is dominant—and wonderful. Don't be put off by the long ingredient list here; once you gather everything, the preparation work takes less than ten minutes.

4 tablespoons canola or other neutral oil

1 tablespoon minced garlic

1 tablespoon peeled and minced or grated fresh
    ginger

1 teaspoon ground coriander

Crushed red pepper flakes or cayenne to taste

Pinch ground cloves

1 teaspoon yellow or black mustard seeds (optional)

1 teaspoon ground cardamom

5 cinnamon sticks or 1 tablespoon ground cinnamon

1/2 teaspoon freshly ground black pepper

Salt to taste

2 pounds boneless pork, cut from butt or shoulder,
    excess fat removed and cut into 1 1/2- to 2-inch
    chunks

1/2 cup rice wine vinegar or other mild vinegar

1 Warm the oil over medium heat in a large skillet or casserole that can later be covered. After about 2 minutes, add the garlic, ginger, spices, and salt, stirring, for a minute or two, until the fragrances are released.

2 Add the pork and vinegar, stir, bring to a boil, and turn the heat to low. Cover and cook, stirring occasionally, until the pork is tender, at least 1 hour. Taste and add more red pepper, cinnamon, salt, or vinegar if necessary. (The recipe can be prepared a day or two in advance up to this point; cool, place in a covered container, and refrigerate.) Serve over white rice.

Sweet Pork with Spicy Soy Sauce

Makes 4 to 6 servings

Time: About 1 hour

This dish is great hot, but I also like to make it in advance, refrigerate and skim the fat, then slice the

meat and use it in one of three ways: reheated, in the sauce; cold, in sandwiches; or added to stir-fry or noodle dishes (especially the Quick Asian Noodle Soup with Pork, page 78). All of these preparations are lightning-quick.

1 fresh or dried hot chile, or to taste

2 pounds boneless pork, cut from the butt or
    shoulder, excess fat removed and cut into
    1 1/2- to 2-inch chunks

1/2 cup soy sauce or fish sauce (*nuoc mam* or
    nam pla, available at Asian markets)

2 tablespoons sugar

1 cup chicken, beef, or vegetable stock, or water
    (see "Soups" for stock recipes)

1 tablespoon minced garlic

1 cup thinly sliced onion

2 tablespoons freshly squeezed lime juice

Salt and lots of freshly ground black pepper to taste

1 If you are using a fresh chile, remove the stem and seeds and mince it. If you're using a dried one, simply crumble it. Then combine all ingredients, except for 1 tablespoon of lime juice and the salt and pepper, in a large pot with a cover. If you have the time, let the mixture sit, refrigerated, for up to a day. (If not, that's okay too.)

2 Bring to a boil over medium-high heat, turn the heat to a minimum and cook, covered, stirring every 10 minutes or so, until the pork is tender, less than 1 hour. (The recipe can be prepared a day or two in advance up to this point; cool, place in a covered container, and refrigerate.)

3 Remove the lid, raise the heat, and boil until the liquid is reduced to less than 1 cup. Taste, add plenty of pepper and some salt if necessary; taste again and adjust seasoning with more pepper, chile, or soy sauce. Sprinkle with the remaining lime juice and serve immediately or refrigerate and use as described above.

The Basics of Spareribs

To me, ribs are spareribs. Baby back ribs (which are from the loin) are good, but prohibitively expensive and often too lean. Country ribs are not ribs at all but a section of the loin cut into rib-like chops.

Spareribs are best cooked slowly, to render their fat and make them tender; this is the epitome of barbecuing (as opposed to grilling), which is difficult but not impossible at home. If you take the time for this, you'll get ribs with delicious meat that comes off the bone with just a little tug. I think this process is worth it. If you want to grill ribs—that is, throw them straight on the fire and cook them right through—you should probably use baby back ribs. But don't expect the deep flavor and incredible tenderness of real ribs.

Slow-Grilled Ribs with Chris's Great Rub

Makes 4 to 6 servings

Time: At least 3 hours, largely unattended, plus time to preheat the grill

You can make these faster and easier (see the first variation), but—at home at least—I don't think you can make them any better. This spice rub, my favorite with ribs, is based on one developed by my friends Chris Schlesinger and John Willoughby, authors of *The Thrill of the Grill* and other great cookbooks.

Some people parboil ribs before cooking, but I'm not wild about those results. I prefer to cook them slowly for a few hours with dry heat, then crisp them up at the end. You can do the first, slow cooking (to the point of browning them) up to a day in advance of the final blast. This is one instance when a gas grill is arguably as good as a charcoal fire; it's certainly easier.

About 3 cups hickory, oak, or other hardwood chips (optional but very nice)

1/2 tablespoon salt

1 tablespoon sugar

1/2 tablespoon ground cumin

1/2 tablespoon freshly ground black pepper

1/2 tablespoon chili powder

1 tablespoon paprika

About 4 pounds spareribs

1 Soak the wood chips in water to cover. Mix the salt and all the spices together and rub them well into the ribs. If you have a gas grill, preheat by using only one burner on medium heat for about 15 minutes. If you are using a charcoal or wood fire, bank it to one side of your grill and keep the fire as low as possible, starting with just enough coals to get heat, about fifteen briquettes or the equivalent in hardwood charcoal. Sprinkle a handful of wood chips onto the rack above the heat source, allowing them to fall directly onto the fire.

2 Place the ribs away from the heat source (over the unlit burner of a gas grill) and cover the grill. You want a very cool fire, under 300°F if possible (you should be able to hold your hand right over the area with the ribs are cooking with just a little discomfort). If you are using solid fuel, add a few lumps of charcoal or a few briquettes an hour, just enough to keep the fire going. Turn the ribs every half hour or so, adding more wood chips as needed.

3 Depending on the heat of your fire, after 2 to 6 hours the ribs will have lost much of their fat and developed an unquestionably cooked look. Just before you're ready to eat, raise the heat to high (or add a bunch more briquettes and wait awhile) and brown the ribs on both sides. Be very careful; they still should have enough fat on them to flare up and burn, ruining all your hard work in an instant (believe me, I've done it several times). Watch them constantly and move them frequently. Browning will take about 10 minutes.

4 Serve immediately, with or without Fast Barbecue Sauce (page 780).

Oven-"Grilled" Ribs: Faster, easier, and still real good: Preheat the oven to 300°F. Rub the ribs all over as above, and place in a roasting pan in one layer. Bake, pouring off accumulated fat every 30 minutes or so, for about 2 hours, or until the ribs are cooked (if you're in a hurry, cover the roasting pan with alu-

minum foil). When you're ready to eat, roast the ribs at 500°F for about 10 minutes, or run them under the broiler, watching carefully, until nicely browned.

Sweet Grilled Ribs: Use either oven or grill and omit the initial rub, simply sprinkling the ribs with salt and pepper. During the last half hour of slow cooking, begin basting the ribs with a mixture of 1 cup apricot or peach preserves or orange marmalade

---

Thirty-Seven Meat Dishes That Are As Good or Better the Next Day

Many inexpensive cuts of meat require long, slow cooking, and are in fact better when left to sit refrigerated for a day before reheating and serving. This practice also makes it easy to skim excess fat before serving, since it will rise to the top and congeal as the dish chills. Some good examples:

1. Short Ribs with Horseradish, page 433
2. Anise-Scented Short Ribs, page 434
3. Classic Beef Stew, page 435
4. Belgian Beef Stew with Beer (Carbonnade), page 435
5. Spicy Braised Beef with Lime, page 436
6. Beef Stew, Greek-Style, page 436
7. Garlicky Beef Daube, page 436
8. Basic Pot Roast, page 437
9. Vinegar-Marinated Pot Roast (Sauerbraten), page 437
10. Braised Beef Brisket, page 438
11. Spicy Beef Brisket, page 438
12. Veal Stew with Tomatoes, page 446
13. Veal Stew with Caraway, page 446
14. Veal Stew with Sage, page 446
15. Veal Stew with Paprika, page 447
16. Veal Stew, Central Asian–Style, page 447
17. Braised Boneless Shoulder (or Leg or Rump) of Veal with Vegetables, page 448
18. Braised Pork with Vinegar and Bay, page 468
19. Braised Pork with Horseradish Sauce, page 469
20. Braised Pork with Beer and Juniper Berries, page 469
21. Spicy Pork with Cinnamon (Vindaloo Pork), page 469
22. Sweet Pork with Spicy Soy Sauce, page 470
23. Lamb Stew with Potatoes (Irish Stew), page 484
24. Lamb Stew with Dill and Root Vegetables, page 485
25. Lamb Stew with Cabbage and Tomatoes, page 485
26. Lamb Stew with Lentils, page 485
27. Lamb Stew with Eggplant or Green Beans, page 485
28. Lamb Stew with Vinegar, page 486
29. Lamb Stew with White Beans, page 486
30. Lamb Stew with Cinnamon, page 486
31. Lamb Curry, page 486
32. Lamb Curry with Coconut Milk, page 487
33. Lamb Shanks with Tomatoes and Olives, page 488
34. Lamb Shanks with Onions and Apricots, page 488
35. Lamb Shanks with White Beans, page 488
36. Cassoulet, page 493
37. Marinated and Stewed Rabbit (Hasenpfeffer), page 497

whisked with 1 tablespoon Dijon mustard, 1 table-spoon vinegar, and 1 tablespoon ketchup or Worcestershire sauce. Brown as in Step 3, above, basting once or twice more and being extra careful to prevent burning.

Chinese Grilled Ribs: Use either oven or grill and omit the initial rub, simply sprinkling the ribs with salt and pepper. During the last half hour of slow-cooking, begin basting the ribs with a mixture of $^3/_4$ cup honey, $^1/_4$ cup hoisin sauce, 2 tablespoons sherry or white wine, and 1 tablespoon soy sauce. Brown as in Step 3, above, basting once or twice more and being extra careful to prevent burning.

The Basics of Pork Sausage

There's no way to put it delicately: The best sausage contains a good deal of fat, usually about a third as much as lean. There are poultry sausages and even sea-food sausages, but these attempts to make lean sausages are, in my opinion, complete flops. The original and best sausages are made from pork and are fatty, which means you can make them crisp on the outside while they remain moist on the inside. If you can't get pork fatback (plain, as opposed to salted, pork fat) to mix with lean meat, just buy a fatty-looking piece of pork shoulder and don't trim the excess fat; chances are you'll get good results.

If you like, you can cut the fat to a minimum of about twenty percent of total weight, but beyond that you will be looking at a hockey puck rather than a sausage (imagine a nearly all-lean hamburger cooked until well done, and you'll have a good sense of what I'm talking about). So add the fat or turn the page.

All sausages follow the same basic principle: Grind together pork, fat, and spices. You can stuff the meat into casings if you like, but it's far easier to cook patties. I use the food processor (see the Basics of Appliances and Electric Gadgets, page 7) but of course you can use an old-fashioned meat grinder for sausage-making.

Basic Breakfast Sausage
Makes about 2$^1/_2$ pounds

Time: 30 minutes, including cooking time

Breakfast sausages have the characteristic flavor of sage. They're almost as easy to make as hamburgers if you have the ingredients on hand. The variations below are just a couple of possibilities. Fatty ground pork can be combined with any spice mixture you like to make sausages.

2 pounds lean boneless pork
$^1/_2$ to $^3/_4$ pound fresh pork fatback (not salt pork)
1 teaspoon salt
$^1/_2$ teaspoon freshly ground black pepper
$^1/_8$ teaspoon freshly grated nutmeg
1 teaspoon minced fresh sage leaves or about
    $^1/_2$ teaspoon dried sage, crumbled

1 Cut the pork and fat into 1-inch cubes. Place about 2 cups of the mixture into the container of a food processor and mince in 1-second pulses until finely chopped. Take your time and be careful not to pulverize the meat. As you finish each batch, transfer it to a bowl.

2 Season with the spices; add a little water if the mixture seems very dry. If you have time, break off a small piece, shape it into a patty, and cook it in a small skillet over medium heat until brown on both sides and cooked through. Taste it and adjust seasonings if necessary.

3 This amount will make 8 large sausages, so you might want to freeze half if you're serving only 4 people (shape the sausage before freezing it). Shape into patties. Heat a large skillet over medium heat for 2 or

3 minutes, then add the patties. Let them cook, undisturbed, for about 5 minutes, then move them so they brown evenly. When one side is brown, turn to brown the other. Serve when nicely browned and cooked through, about 15 minutes total.

Garlic-Fennel Sausage: Step 1 remains the same. In Step 2, substitute 1 teaspoon or more minced garlic and 2 teaspoons fennel seeds for the nutmeg and sage; add $^1/_4$ to $^1/_2$ teaspoon cayenne if you like. Proceed as above.

Johnny Earles's Spicy Sausage: Step 1 remains the same. In Step 2, substitute $^1/_4$ cup minced fresh parsley leaves, 1 teaspoon minced garlic, 1 teaspoon ground coriander, 1 teaspoon ground cumin, $^1/_2$ teaspoon ground dried thyme, $^1/_4$ teaspoon ground cinnamon, and $^1/_4$ teaspoon cayenne for the sage (keep the nutmeg). Proceed as above.

Sautéed "Italian" Sausage with Peppers and Onions

Makes 4 servings

Time: About 30 minutes

There are two ways to proceed here: Cook the vegetables in olive oil first, then combine them with the sausage after browning, or cook the sausages first, then use the sausage fat to cook the vegetables. The first method cuts saturated fat, the second boosts flavor; it's your choice. I detail the first method here; to do the second, simply cook the sausage, as directed, leave the fat in the pan, and cook the vegetables in it.

Sausages cooked this way are fantastic between two thick slices of good bread, or inserted into a lengthwise-cut loaf of French or Italian bread. Strong mustard is the natural accompaniment.

2 cups sliced onions

3 tablespoons olive oil

2 bell peppers, any color but green, stemmed, peeled if desired, seeded, and cut into strips

Salt and freshly ground black pepper to taste

1 pound fresh link Italian sausage, sweet or hot

1 Place the onions in a large skillet, turn the heat to medium, cover the pan, and cook, undisturbed, for about 5 minutes, until the onions are dry and almost sticking to the pan. Remove the cover, add the oil, and stir. Cook for a minute or two longer, then add the peppers, salt, and pepper. Cook, stirring frequently, until the vegetables are tender and soft, about 10 more minutes. Remove the vegetables and keep warm.

2 Cook the sausage in the same pan over medium heat. Prick the sausage in a few places with a fork to allow excess fat to escape and turn the sausage frequently. Cook until nicely browned all over. Total cooking time will depend on the thickness of the sausages; the best way to determine doneness is to cut into one—when the barest trace of pink remains, they are done. Drain the sausages on a paper towel and serve with the peppers and onions.

Sausages and Mashed Potatoes (Bangers and Mash): Omit Step 1. Prepare Mashed Potatoes (page 596), and cook the sausage as in Step 2, above. Serve the sausages with the potatoes and some good strong mustard. If you like, make a pan gravy from the sausage fat and some stock, wine, or water: When the sausages have finished cooking, pour off all but 2 tablespoons of the fat. Over medium-high heat, add 1 cup of any stock (or water) to this and cook, stirring and scraping, until the liquid is reduced by half. Use this sauce for the potatoes.

Sausages and Beans: Omit Step 1. Prepare White Beans, Tuscan-Style (page 509) or Sautéed Beans and Tomatoes (page 511) and place in a large baking dish. Cook the sausage as in Step 2, above. Preheat the oven to 350°F and, when the sausages are nearly but not quite done, nestle them in the beans. Sprinkle with bread crumbs and bake until the crumbs brown, about 15 minutes (see page 239). Serve, drizzled with a little of the best olive oil you can lay your hands on.

Sautéed Sausages with Grapes

Makes 8 appetizer servings

Time: About 30 minutes

A traditional Roman combination in which the sweetness of the grapes is nicely offset by the garlic.

    2 tablespoons extra-virgin olive oil
    About 1 pound fresh, sweet, garlicky sausage
    2 cloves garlic, slivered
    About 1/2 pound seedless grapes
    Salt and freshly ground black pepper to taste

1 Place the oil in a large skillet, preferably non-stick, and turn the heat to medium-high. Add the sausage and cook it, turning from time to time, until it is nicely browned.

2 Remove the sausage from the skillet (don't worry about it being done) and cut it into bite-sized pieces. Return it to the skillet, over medium heat; cook, turning occasionally, until all sides of the sausage are nicely browned, about 5 more minutes.

3 Add the garlic and cook, stirring occasionally, for 3 or 4 minutes. Add the grapes and heat through. Check for salt and sprinkle liberally with pepper. Serve immediately.

The Basics of Ham

There are two basic hams: dry- and wet-cured. The first includes the world's great hams, from prosciutto to Virginia and other American country hams. In fact, most Western countries (indeed, most regions of most Western countries) have their own local ham, some smoked, some not, all cured with salt. Wet-cured ham includes just about everything else, from the sweet, smoked, Vermont-style mail-order hams to the chemically cured hams you find in your supermarket.

Dry-cured hams, for my money, are best raw or as an ingredient. They keep forever anyway (if mold appears, you just cut it away), and they're too big-flavored to subdue with glazes and eat in large quantities. Cut off a sliver and make a sandwich, use a few chunks in pasta sauces, place tiny pieces on crackers, cut paper-thin slices for fruit. Nevertheless, they can be cooked, especially for a crowd, and are delicious that way, although the procedure is both time- and labor-consuming.

Wet-cured hams are pretty much a no-brainer. You put them in the oven, heat them through, and eat them. The quality of the dish is entirely dependent on the quality of the cure. A good old-fashioned cure begins with a real brine of salt, water, and sugar, and concludes with a long period of smoking. A high-tech cure begins with a chemically augmented injected brine and ends with a douse of liquid smoke. You can taste the difference. Find a brand you like—mail order is usually your best bet—and stick to it. Most supermarket hams, including canned hams, are just a step above the heavily processed ham you buy at the deli counter.

Baked Country Ham

Makes 15 or more servings

Time: 36 hours, largely unattended

Plan to soak the ham from one morning to the next, then boil it, and let it cool in its liquid before skinning, glazing, and baking. This is a lot of work, but you'll be rewarded with the best cooked ham you've ever had.

1 (12- to 15-pound) Virginia or other country ham
6 cups assorted chopped aromatic vegetables and
    herbs or scraps—onions, carrots, parsnips, celery,
    and parsley, for example
1 tablespoon black peppercorns
Several allspice berries
2 tablespoons cider or other vinegar
4 cloves, plus additional cloves for scoring ham
    (optional)
1 cup orange marmalade or apricot or peach
    preserves
1 tablespoon Dijon mustard, or more to taste
2 cups or more dry apple cider or white wine (optional)

① If the ham is too big to fit in your biggest pot, saw off the shank. Any saw will do; just be patient. (Use the shank in soup; it will be wonderful.) Scrub the ham with a brush under running water, then soak it in cold water to cover for 24 hours, changing the water once or twice.

② Put the ham, vegetables, peppercorns, allspice, vinegar, and 4 cloves in the pot and cover with fresh water. Bring to a boil, lower the heat, and simmer for 2 hours. Cool in its liquid for at least another 2 hours.

③ Drain the ham, discarding the cooking liquid. Skin the ham, then score the fatty layer in a diamond pattern. Insert a clove into each diamond if you like.

④ About 1 hour before you're ready to serve, preheat the oven to 400°F. Place the ham on a rack in a roasting pan and, in a small saucepan, heat the marmalade or preserves over low heat until they thin slightly. Stir in 1 tablespoon or more of mustard. Spoon this mixture all over the ham and bake until the outer layer is crisp and brown, about 30 minutes. If you want pan juices with which to top the ham (not necessary—it will be fine with no more than good

mustard), add $1/2$ cup of cider or wine to the bottom of the pan at the beginning of roasting and whenever it threatens to become dry.

⑤ Remove the ham to a platter. To make pan juices, place the roasting pan on one or two burners over high heat. Add 1 cup of liquid to that already in the pan and cook, stirring and scraping, until the liquid has been reduced by about half and has thickened slightly. Carve the ham and serve with pan juices, mustard, or both.

Baked Wet-Cured Ham: Allow about 10 minutes per pound cooking time. Skip steps 1 and 2. Score and stud the ham the ham with cloves as in Step 3, if you like. Preheat the oven to 350°F and proceed as above.

The Basics of Cooking Bacon

Oh, let me count the ways: sautéing, roasting, broiling, microwaving . . . you have lots of choices, each with advantages. If you have slab bacon, really good bacon, you almost must choose sautéing, for the control and even browning it gives (as long as you're careful). For regular supermarket bacon, take your pick.

Figure three or four slices as a serving. Doneness is a matter of taste; I like bacon cooked but still chewy, but many people prefer it crisp, almost burned. Always drain on paper towels before eating, unless you are going to use the bacon in other dishes, in which case draining is usually unnecessary.

Sautéing You see what's going on, which is an advantage, and can regulate the heat accordingly. But it requires the most attention, and inevitably messes up the stove. Start the bacon in a large, deep skillet over medium-high heat. When it begins to sizzle, separate the slices if you haven't done so already and regulate the heat so that the slices brown evenly without burning, turning frequently. Total time will be ten to twenty minutes, longer for large quantities.

Microwaving   The best method for three to six slices, although the microwave will smell for days if you don't clean it thoroughly afterward (on the other hand, you might enjoy the aroma). Place the bacon on a triple layer of paper towels on a microwave-safe plate, and cover with a double layer of towels. Microwave on high for two minutes, then check; move the pieces around a little and continue to microwave for one-minute intervals until done. Total time will depend on the power of your microwave, but will be less than five minutes even in a small oven.

Roasting   Slow, but easy and reliable, especially for large quantities. Preheat the oven to 450°F. Place the bacon in a roasting pan large enough to hold it in one layer (this may be a very large pan) and slide it into the oven. Check after ten minutes; separate the slices if necessary. Continue to roast, turning occasionally, pouring off excess fat, and checking every five minutes or so; total time will be thirty minutes or so. If you like, brown under the broiler at the last minute.

Broiling   Pay close attention and this is fast and easy. Preheat the broiler; set the rack about six inches from the heat source. Place the bacon in a roasting pan large enough to hold it in one layer (this may be a very large pan) and slide it into the oven. Check after two minutes; separate the slices if necessary. Continue to broil, turning occasionally, and checking every minute or two; total time will be about ten minutes.

The Basics of Lamb

The most flavorful of all of our domesticated meats, lamb—like the best beef—needs little more than salt but can stand up to whatever flavors you add to it. Unlike beef, however, almost all lamb is this way, regardless of where you buy it and regardless of the cut.

In fact, thanks to an odd combination of factors, lamb is the closest to "natural" meat you can buy in the supermarket, which is at least in part why it has such intense flavor. Sheep are easy to raise and herd, and can graze where other animals cannot. (Goat is an exception, and its meat is similar.) Furthermore, demand for lamb has never been high, nor have prices, so producers have had little incentive to "rationalize" production—that is, to make it factory-like, as they have with beef and pork. As a result, I'm more comfortable buying lamb than any other meat in a supermarket.

Furthermore, because lamb is so small (a whole lamb usually weighs well under a hundred (and often half that) pounds, compared to several hundred for pig and close to half a ton for steer), many cuts contain several muscles, meaning you get a variety of different tastes and textures, an unusual pleasure.

Most lamb is best rare, but not quite as rare as beef. However, it also can be quite delicious medium, and even well done—it has the flavor and juiciness to handle it. What's wonderful about the leg of lamb, with or without the bone, is that its odd shape means that if the thick center is cooked to rare the thinner edges are well done. So, for once, you can satisfy everyone.

By far the smallest of the common meat animals, lamb allows us the luxury of eating whole shoulders and legs. Understanding the animal is simple:

Shoulder   Fatty and flavorful, wonderful for roasting and stewing. Good cut into chops as well. Meat from this area should always be cooked to the medium- to well-done stage.

Shank/Breast   Inexpensive shanks are wonderful braised; the breast is usually cut into riblets, and can be quite good.

Rib   Best known for the rack of lamb, this section can also be cut into rib chops. Always good cooked rare- to medium-rare.

Loin   This can be sold whole, as a saddle; it's a wonderful roast. Or it can be cut into loin chops, which are fine. It can also be boned and cut into medallions.

Leg   Sold whole or in halves; occasionally cubed for shish kebab, for which it is wonderful.

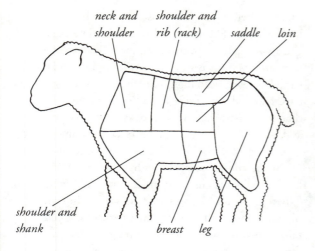

neck and shoulder | shoulder and rib (rack) | saddle | loin | shoulder and shank | breast | leg

The Basics of Lamb Chops

If you take a rack of lamb and cut it up, you get lamb rib chops, which are the most tender and least fatty. Loin chops are similar. Both rib and loin chops should be cooked rare to medium-rare. The far less expensive shoulder chops, however, are equally flavorful; you just have to discard a bit more gristle and fat and do a bit more chewing. In addition, they're better cooked a little longer, until just about medium.

Basic Grilled or Broiled Lamb Chops

Makes 4 servings

Time: 15 minutes, plus time to preheat the grill

Like a simple strip sirloin steak, the lamb chop is a terrific convenience food—filling, fast, and, even without additions, flavorful. If you can get butcher-like service at your meat counter, or visit a butcher, ask for double-rib chops, which are easier to cook to medium-rare, exactly how they should be. You can also pan-grill these in a skillet; see Pan-Grilled Steak, page 426.

4 double-rib or large shoulder chops or 8 rib or loin chops
Salt and freshly ground black pepper to taste
1 clove garlic (optional)
Lemon wedges

1 Start a charcoal or wood fire or preheat a gas grill or broiler; the fire should be moderately hot for double chops, very hot for single chops. Sprinkle the meat with salt and pepper. If you like, cut the clove of garlic in half and rub it over the meat.

2 Grill or broil the chops, 3 or 4 inches from the heat source, until they are nicely browned on both sides. If they are single chops, allow no more than 2 or 3 minutes per side. With double chops, there is a greater margin for error, but cooking time will most likely still be less than 10 minutes. Serve with lemon wedges.

Onion-Marinated Lamb Chops: Using the food processor or a hand grater, grate 1 medium onion. Place the onion and its juice in a bowl and toss with 1 tablespoon olive oil, 1 teaspoon ground cumin, 1 tablespoon minced cilantro leaves, and salt and pepper to taste. Spread this paste over the chops and marinate for an hour or more (refrigerate if marinating for longer than an hour). Scrape the marinade from the chops and grill or broil as in Step 2, above. Garnish with minced cilantro and serve with lime wedges.

Broiled or Grilled Lamb Chops, Italian-Style

Makes 4 servings

Time: 20 minutes, plus time to preheat the grill

Use shoulder chops for this recipe, and allow only one per person (they're much bigger). If you have the time, use half the herb mixture as a marinade, rubbing it into the chops and letting them sit for an hour or so. To vary the flavor, try mixing the parsley with small amounts of other herbs: one tablespoon of fresh basil, dill, or chervil, one teaspoon of fresh rosemary, sage, marjoram, oregano, or lavender, or a few pinches of any dried herb.

> 1 tablespoon olive oil
> 1 clove garlic, peeled
> 2 or more anchovy fillets
> 1/2 cup chopped fresh parsley leaves, plus more for garnish
> 1 tablespoon freshly squeezed lemon juice
> Freshly ground black pepper to taste
> 4 (3/4-inch-thick) shoulder lamb chops, trimmed of excess fat
> Lemon wedges

1 Unless you are marinating the chops, start a charcoal or wood fire or preheat a gas grill or broiler; the fire should be moderately hot and the rack about 4 inches from the heat source. Combine all the ingredients except the lamb, lemon wedges, and garnish in a food processor and puree. Rub the chops with half of this mixture; if you have the time marinate for an hour or so (start the grill or broiler at the appropriate time, of course).

2 Grill or broil the chops, basting frequently with the remaining herb mixture, until nicely browned on both sides, a total of 6 to 8 minutes. Garnish and serve with lemon wedges.

The Basics of Leg of Lamb

Leg of lamb is one of the great roasts for a crowd of six people or so—even with minimal seasoning, its flavor and juice power a meal. With lots of herbs and spices, it's the greatest, and the ideal excuse to break out that good bottle of red wine you've been hoarding. You can buy the leg with the shank, but it's a better buy without, because the shank doesn't take that well to roasting, and so adds a pound of not-great

meat to the price. It also necessitates a longer roasting pan, which you may not have. I'd go so far as to remove the shank myself, freezing it for a later occasion and one of the recipes on pages 488–490.

You can also buy half-legs of lamb; the butt half is preferable. Plan on cooking times for a three- to four-pound half-leg to be about two thirds of what they are for a whole leg.

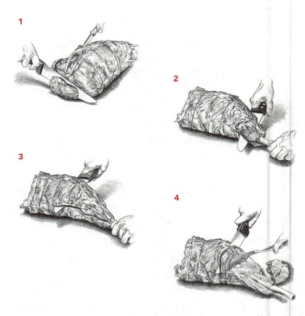

(Step 1) To carve a leg of lamb, take a slice or two off the thick end and set aside. (Steps 2–3) Make a long slice parallel to the cutting board as close to the bone as is possible. (Step 4) Cut thin slices from the top of the leg.

Basic Roast Leg of Lamb
Makes at least 6 servings

Time: About 1 1/2 hours, largely unattended

I would only make this most basic of leg of lamb recipes if some timid eaters were coming to dinner. Otherwise, see the wonderfully strong-flavored variations.

1 leg of lamb, about 5 to 7 pounds, preferably at room temperature

1 teaspoon salt

1 teaspoon freshly ground black pepper

2 pounds waxy red or white potatoes, peeled and cut into 1½-inch chunks

4 carrots, peeled and cut into 1½-inch chunks

2 onions, quartered

½ cup chicken, beef, or vegetable stock, or water, plus more as needed (see "Soups" for stock recipes)

1 Preheat the oven to 425°F. Remove as much of the surface fat as possible from the lamb; rub the meat all over with salt and pepper. Place it in a roasting pan and scatter the vegetables around it; moisten with ½ cup of the stock or water.

2 Roast the lamb for 30 minutes, then turn the heat down to 350°F. Check the vegetables; if they're dry, add another ½ cup of liquid. After about 1 hour of roasting, check the internal temperature of the lamb with an instant-read thermometer. Continue to check every 10 minutes, adding a little more liquid if necessary. When it reaches 130°F for medium-rare (125°F for very rare)—check it in several places—it is done (total cooking time will be less than 1½ hours). Let it rest for a few minutes before carving (see illustrations on page 479 for carving instructions). Serve with the vegetables and pan juices.

Roast Leg of Lamb with Garlic and Coriander Seeds: Include or omit the vegetables as you like. Mix the salt and pepper with 2 tablespoons of crushed coriander seeds (put them in a plastic bag and pound gently with a rolling pin, rubber mallet, or like object) and 1 teaspoon minced garlic. Use a thin-bladed knife to cut some small slits in the lamb and push a bit of the spices into them; rub the lamb all over with the remaining spices. If you have the time, let the lamb sit, for an hour or more (refrigerate if it

will be much longer). Roast as in Step 2, omitting liquid if you choose to omit the vegetables. This roast is better, in my opinion, closer to medium than to rare—about 135°F.

Roast Leg of Lamb with Provençal Flavors: Include or omit the vegetables as you like. Mix the salt and pepper with 1 tablespoon minced fresh rosemary leaves or 1 teaspoon dried rosemary; 1 tablespoon minced garlic; 3 or 4 anchovy fillets, minced (optional); and 2 tablespoons olive (or anchovy) oil. Use a thin-bladed knife to cut some small slits in the lamb and push a bit of the spices into them; rub the lamb all over with the remaining spices. If you have the time, let the lamb sit, for an hour or more (refrigerate if it will be longer). Roast as in Step 2, omitting liquid if you choose to omit the vegetables. When the meat is done, remove it to a warm platter. Spoon or pour off most of the accumulated fat from the roasting pan and place it on one or two burners set to medium-high. Add ½ cup red wine or stock and ½ cup water and cook, scraping the bottom of the pan with a wooden spoon to release any brown bits, until the liquid is reduced to ½ to ¾ cup. Carve the lamb and serve with the sauce; garnish with sprigs of rosemary if you have them.

Grilled Leg of Lamb

Makes at least 6 servings

Time: About 1½ hours, largely unattended, plus time to preheat the grill

It's easier and faster to grill butterflied leg of lamb (as you'll see in the recipes following this one), but grilling a whole leg is not only fun, it's impressive. Unless you're an expert, however, don't try it without a covered grill.

1 leg of lamb, about 5 to 7 pounds

1 teaspoon freshly ground black pepper

1 tablespoon salt

1 tablespoon minced garlic

1/2 cup minced mixed fresh herbs: parsley, dill, rosemary, thyme, etc. (optional), or 1 tablespoon ground or peeled and minced or grated fresh ginger

1/4 cup soy sauce

1 Start a charcoal or gas grill; if you're using charcoal, build an indirect fire (see The Basics of Grilling and Broiling, page 10). If you're using a gas grill, turn the heat to high on one side and low on the other. (Delay this step until you're just about ready to cook if you choose to marinate the meat.) Remove as much of the surface fat as possible from the lamb. Mix together all remaining ingredients. Cut some small slits in the lamb and push a bit of the spice mixture into them; rub the lamb all over with the remaining mixture. If you have the time, let the lamb sit, for an hour or more (refrigerate if it will be much longer).

2 When the grill is hot, brown the meat over the coals or high burner, turning it frequently and moving it away from the heat if it threatens to burn. When the lamb is nicely browned all over, move it to the coolest part of the grill and put on the cover.

3 Turn the meat occasionally and, after about an hour of total cooking (including the browning), begin to check with an instant-read thermometer. When it reads 125° to 130°F in a few places, the meat will be rare to medium-rare. Remove it from the grill and let rest for 10 minutes or so before carving; see page 479 for carving instructions.

BONING LEG OF LAMB

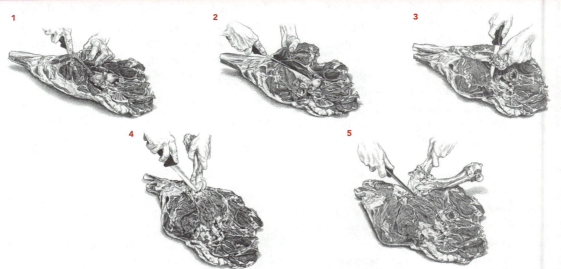

Like all boning jobs, this involves finding the bone and separating it from the meat; since the two adjoining bones in a leg of lamb are both large, it's really just a matter of patience.
(Steps 1–2). Turn the leg smooth side down and use a boning knife to cut on either side of the large bone, scraping off the meat.
(Step 3) When you can get under the bone, cut the meat away from there too. (Steps 4–5) Lift the bone up and find the point at which it meets the smaller bone; cut that one away as well.

Basic Grilled or Broiled Butterflied Leg of Lamb

Makes at least 6 servings

Time: About 40 minutes, plus time to preheat the grill

Although you can bone a leg of lamb yourself (page 481), butterflied leg is also sold in supermarkets. It's not cheap, but it's not outrageously expensive either, and it qualifies as a true luxury because it is delicious, tender, and easy to cook. I think it's especially great because of its uneven thickness. This means if you cook the thickest parts to rare you also get meat that is cooked to medium; and medium lamb, unlike medium beef, is moist and tender.

The variation suggests only one of many possibilities for spicing this lamb; you can also go with cumin mixed with a little honey and some minced orange peel; minced ginger and scallions mixed with soy sauce; Basic Pesto (page 766); or All-Purpose Curry Powder (or similar spice mixture, see page 778), moistened with a bit of yogurt.

If you find or create a larger boneless leg—sometimes they are up to six pounds—either cut off a piece and freeze it for a later use, or make the whole thing—but increase the other ingredients proportionally and plan to serve eight to twelve people.

1 (3- to 4-pound) butterflied leg of lamb
1 tablespoon olive oil
1 teaspoon minced garlic
1 tablespoon fresh rosemary leaves or 2 teaspoons dried rosemary
2 teaspoons fresh thyme leaves or 1 teaspoon dried thyme
Salt and freshly ground black pepper to taste
Minced fresh parsley leaves for garnish
Lemon wedges

1 Start a charcoal or wood fire or preheat a gas grill or broiler; the fire should be quite hot, and the rack should be at least 4 inches from the heat source. (Delay this step until you're just about ready to cook if you choose to marinate the meat.) Trim the lamb of any excess fat. Mix together the olive oil, garlic, rosemary, thyme, salt, and pepper; rub this mixture well into the lamb, making sure to get some into all the crevices. If you have the time, let the lamb sit, for an hour or more (refrigerate if it will be much longer).

2 Grill or broil the meat until it is nicely browned, even a little charred, on both sides, about 20 to 30 minutes, and the internal temperature at the thickest part is about 125°F; this will give you some lamb that is quite rare, as well as some that is nearly well done. Let rest for 5 minutes before slicing thinly, as you would a thick steak. Garnish, and serve with lemon wedges.

Butterflied Leg of Lamb with Provençal Spices: For the herbs in Step 1, substitute 1 teaspoon fresh or dried lavender, chopped; 1 teaspoon fresh or dried rosemary, chopped; $1/2$ teaspoon fennel seeds. Proceed as in Steps 1 and 2, above.

Grilled or Broiled Butterflied Lamb with Coconut Milk

Makes at least 6 servings

Time: About 40 minutes, plus time to preheat the grill

This is a slightly more elaborate preparation than the basic one preceding, but if you enjoy Asian spices you'll find the effort worth it. I like to intensify the color of the marinade with a little turmeric (or saffron, if I have some), but it isn't necessary because the flavor comes largely from the other ingredients. While you grill the lamb, you can simmer the marinade for a few minutes and use it as a sauce for the meat itself, or for some plain white rice.

If you find or create a larger boneless leg—sometimes they are up to six pounds—either cut off a piece and freeze it for a later use, or make the whole thing—but increase the other ingredients proportionally and plan to serve eight to twelve people.

1 butterflied leg of lamb, about 3 to 4 pounds
2 cups canned or Fresh Coconut Milk (page 291)
$1/2$ teaspoon ground turmeric or a few threads saffron
    (optional)
2 medium onions
1 tablespoon peeled and minced or grated fresh
    ginger or 1 teaspoon ground ginger
$1/4$ cup minced cilantro leaves, plus more for garnish
Salt and freshly ground black pepper to taste

1 Start a charcoal or wood fire or preheat a gas grill or broiler; the fire should be quite hot, and, in the broiler, the rack should be a good 6 inches from the heat source. (Delay this step until you're just about ready to cook if you choose to marinate the meat.) Trim the lamb of any excess fat.

2 In a blender, puree the coconut milk with the turmeric and one of the onions until it is smooth and evenly colored. Mince the remaining onion and add it to the coconut milk along with the ginger, $1/4$ cup minced cilantro, salt, and pepper. Cover the lamb with the coconut milk mixture and, if you have the time, let it marinate for 1 or 2 hours at room temperature, or for up to 24 hours in the refrigerator, turning it from time to time.

3 Remove the meat from the marinade and dry it with paper towels. Grill or broil the meat until it is nicely browned, even a little charred, on both sides, about 20 to 30 minutes, and the internal temperature at the thickest part is about 125°F; this will give you some lamb that is quite rare, as well as some that is nearly well done. Let rest for 5 minutes before slicing

thinly, as you would a thick steak. Garnish with minced cilantro and serve.

Grilled Skewered Lamb Chunks
Shish Kebab
Makes 4 to 6 servings

Time: 20 minutes, plus time to preheat the grill

Chunks of lamb shoulder make for moister shish kebab and more margin for error in cooking; pieces cut from the leg are leaner but easier to overcook and drier if cooked beyond the rare stage. But because it is leaner, the leg is easily cut into beautiful chunks that brown quickly without rendering a lot of fat, the cause of flare-ups on the grill. The choice is yours.

2 pounds boneless shoulder or leg of lamb, trimmed
    of all excess fat and cut into 2-inch chunks
3 bell peppers (any color but green), stemmed,
    peeled if desired, seeded, and cut into $1^1/2$-inch
    squares
1 large or 2 medium onions, quartered and separated
    into layers
About 16 cherry tomatoes (optional)
1 tablespoon olive oil
Salt and freshly ground black pepper to taste
$1/2$ cup freshly squeezed lemon juice
2 cloves garlic, roughly chopped
6 pita breads
Lemon wedges

1 Start a charcoal or wood fire or preheat a gas grill or broiler; the fire should be moderately hot, and, in the broiler, the rack should be a good 6 inches from the heat source.

2 Thread the lamb onto 3 skewers and the vegetables onto 3 others. (Although alternating pieces of meat and vegetables on the same skewer is attractive, meat and vegetables may cook at different rates, so it makes more sense to make separate skewers of each. If you do want to mix meat and veggies on the same skewer, cut the vegetables a little smaller, to make sure they're tender by the time the meat is cooked.)

3 Brush lightly with olive oil and season liberally with salt and pepper. Mix together the lemon juice and garlic and brush a little of this mixture onto the meat and vegetables.

4 Grill or broil, turning the skewers as each side browns and taking care to avoid flare-ups; total cooking time should be from 12 to 15 minutes for medium-rare meat. The meat will become slightly more done after you remove it from the grill, so take this into account. Brush frequently with the lemon-garlic mixture.

5 Serve each of the skewers with a bread (you can wrap the bread around the meat and vegetables to pull them from the skewer) and a couple of lemon wedges.

Shish Kebab with Rosemary: If you have them, use rosemary branches for skewers. In any case, add 1 tablespoon minced fresh rosemary leaves or 2 teaspoons dried rosemary, crumbled between your fingers, to the lemon-garlic mixture.

Marinated Shish Kebab: An hour or longer before cooking (up to a full day; refrigerate if more than 2 hours), marinate the lamb cubes in a mixture of 1 cup plain yogurt; 1 minced onion; 1 tablespoon ground cumin or $1/4$ cup minced fresh mint or $1/4$ cup minced fresh dill leaves; $1/4$ to $1/2$ teaspoon cayenne (optional); and 1 tablespoon freshly squeezed lemon juice. When you're ready to cook, remove the lamb from the marinade; do not brush with olive oil. Grill, brushing with reserved marinade. Serve, garnished with minced parsley, cilantro (if you used cumin), dill, or mint.

The Basics of Lamb Shoulder

The shoulder is another cut suitable for roasting, but because of its higher fat content it is not a good grilling cut. In fact, I think its fattiness makes the shoulder (and the nearby neck) best for cooking it with liquid. And, although some people braise lamb shoulder whole, I think it makes more sense to cut it up for a stew—this makes it much easier to discard excess fat, and to reduce the cooking time as well. Shoulders are sold whole or in pieces, with the bone in or out; boneless shoulders, obviously, are much easier to cut into chunks.

Wherever there is lamb—which includes a great deal of the world, sheep being readily adaptable to a variety of environments—there is lamb stew. I give as many variations as possible here, but there are only a few keys to remember if you want to experiment with your own spices and vegetable additions:

- Discard as much of the hard lamb fat as you can when trimming the meat.
- Start the vegetables after the lamb so they do not overcook and disintegrate.
- Cook any of the recipes that call for browning without that step if you're pressed for time.

Finally, if there is any way you can prepare the stew a day before eating it, do: the flavor will deepen, and you can skim excess fat from the surface. Lamb stew freezes perfectly, so don't worry about making it a week in advance, or about doubling these recipes.

Lamb Stew with Potatoes
Irish Stew
Makes 4 to 6 servings

Time: About 2 hours, largely unattended

The basic lamb stew combines potatoes, onions, meat, and water; browning is unnecessary. Nearly every other lamb stew is just a step away from this one. If you have a lot of parsley, add two cups of it, chopped, with the potatoes in Step 2.

> 3 pounds waxy red or white potatoes, peeled
> 2 pounds boneless lamb shoulder, trimmed of excess fat and cut into 2-inch cubes, or 3 to 4 pounds bone-in shoulder or neck, cut into roughly 2-inch chunks
> 3 cups sliced onions
> Salt and freshly ground black pepper to taste
> 2 to 3 cups liquid: any combination of water, red wine, chicken, beef, or vegetable stock, or lamb stock made from extra bones (see "Soups" for stock recipes)
> Minced fresh parsley leaves for garnish

1 Preheat the oven to 350°F (you can also cook this on the stove if you prefer). Cut the potatoes into $^1/_4$-inch-thick slices and set half of them aside in a bowl of cold salted water. In a large pot or casserole with a cover, combine the lamb, remaining potatoes, onions, salt, and pepper. Add about 2 cups of the liquid to the casserole.

2 Cover the pot, bring it almost to a boil over high heat, then either turn the heat to low or place the stew in the oven. Adjust the heat so the lamb bubbles gently. After the lamb has cooked for about 45 minutes, add the remaining potatoes and more liquid if the mixture seems dry or if you like your stew on the soupy side. Cook until the lamb is tender and the second batch of potatoes is tender but not mushy, another 30 to 60 minutes. Garnish and serve.

Lamb Stew with Dill and Root Vegetables: In Step 1, omit the potatoes and parsley and cut the amount of onions in half. In Step 2, add about 3 pounds of any combination of root vegetables—such as potatoes, carrots, turnips, and parsnips—all peeled and cut into 1- to 1$^1/_2$-inch chunks. Strip the feathery leaves from a bunch of dill and reserve; tie the stems together and place them in the stew. When the lamb is ready, remove the dill stems. Chop the remaining dill and add all but 1 tablespoon to the stew; stir once, taste for salt and pepper, add a little lemon juice, and taste again, adding more lemon juice if necessary. Garnish with the remaining dill and serve immediately.

Lamb Stew with Cabbage and Tomatoes: In Step 1, omit the potatoes and cut the amount of onions in half; add 4 cups cored and shredded Savoy or green head cabbage (see page 547), 1 cup peeled and chopped carrots, and 1 tablespoon minced garlic. Add 2 cups cored and chopped tomatoes (canned are fine) and 1 cup liquid (the canned tomato liquid is perfect). Cook as in Step 2, checking and adding more liquid if necessary after 45 minutes. Garnish with minced parsley before serving.

Lamb Stew with Lentils: In Step 1, omit the potatoes and cut the amount of onions in half; add 2 cups dried lentils, and 3 cups liquid. In Step 2, add 1 teaspoon minced garlic, $^1/_2$ cup peeled and minced carrots, $^1/_2$ cup minced celery, and 1 cup cored and chopped tomatoes (canned are fine; drain them first). Add more liquid if necessary and cook as above.

Lamb Stew with Eggplant or Green Beans: In Step 1, omit the potatoes; use 1 teaspoon fresh thyme leaves or $^1/_2$ teaspoon dried thyme. Peel, cube, and salt 3 cups of eggplant (see page 568), or trim and cut in half 3 cups of green beans. In Step 2, add 1 teaspoon minced garlic, the vegetable, and 1 cup cored and chopped tomatoes (canned are fine; drain them first). Add more liquid if necessary. Garnish with minced parsley before serving.

Lamb Stew with Vinegar

Makes 4 to 6 servings

Time: About 2 hours, largely unattended

Here are some lamb stews in which I recommend browning the meat. On the whole, they have more flavor than the preceding batch. Despite the large amount of garlic here, the flavor of this recipe is defined by the lamb, the thyme, and the vinegar. You may find it easier to brown the meat in the oven; see Step 1.

2 tablespoons olive oil
2 pounds boneless lamb shoulder, trimmed of excess fat
   and cut into 2-inch cubes, or 3 to 4 pounds bone-in
   shoulder or neck, cut into roughly 2-inch chunks
Salt and freshly ground black pepper to taste
1 cup chopped onion
1 head garlic, separated into cloves (peeling is not
   necessary)
1 bay leaf
Several sprigs fresh thyme, 1 1/2 teaspoons fresh
   thyme leaves, or about 1 teaspoon dried thyme
1/4 cup sherry vinegar (preferred) or red wine vinegar
1/2 cup dry red wine, stock, or water, or a little more
   (see "Soups" for stock recipes)
Minced fresh parsley leaves for garnish

1 Heat the olive oil over medium-high heat in a large, deep skillet or casserole that can later be covered. Add the lamb chunks a few at a time, removing them as they brown and seasoning with salt and pepper as they cook. When they are all nicely browned, return them all to the pan, lower the heat to medium, and add the onion. Cook, stirring, until the onion softens. (You can also do the initial browning in the oven: Preheat to 500°F and roast the lamb chunks and oil, turning once or twice, until brown all over; time will be about the same, 20 minutes. Move the casserole to the stove—carefully—and proceed as above.)

2 Add all of the remaining ingredients except the parsley and stir. Bring to a boil over medium-high heat, cover, reduce heat to low, and cook until the lamb is tender, at least 1 hour, stirring occasionally and checking after about 30 minutes to make certain that the mixture is not too dry. (The recipe can be prepared a day or two in advance up to this point; cool, place in a covered container, and refrigerate.) Garnish and serve hot. The garlic cloves will readily slip from their peels if they haven't done so already, and are wonderful eaten as is or spread on bread or toast.

Lamb Stew with White Beans: Step 1 remains the same. In Step 2, omit the garlic, thyme, and vinegar. Cook for 30 minutes, then stir in 4 to 6 cups Sautéed Beans and Tomatoes (page 511), slightly undercooked if possible (this won't be possible if you're using leftovers, but don't worry about it). Cook, stirring occasionally and scraping the bottom to make sure the beans do not burn; add a little liquid if necessary.

Lamb Stew with Cinnamon: In Step 2, omit the thyme and the vinegar. Use stock or water (not wine) and increase it to 1 cup; add 2 cloves, 1/2 teaspoon ground cinnamon, and 1 (6-ounce) can tomato paste. Blend well. After 30 minutes, add 20 peeled pearl onions (frozen are fine), each skewered with a toothpick, and 1 tablespoon red wine vinegar. Garnish with parsley and serve over rice or broad noodles.

Lamb Curry

Makes 4 to 6 servings

Time: About 1 1/2 hours, largely unattended

"Curry," which has come to mean almost any stew with almost any assortment of Indian spices, is no more difficult to produce than any other stew.

Ingredient lists are long but the process is simple and infinitely variable.

2 tablespoons peanut (preferred) or other
    vegetable oil
2 pounds boneless lamb shoulder, trimmed of excess
    fat and cut into 2-inch cubes, or 3 to 4 pounds
    bone-in shoulder or neck, cut into chunks
Salt and freshly ground black pepper to taste
2 cups thinly sliced onions, plus 1 cup chopped onion
1 tablespoon minced garlic
1 tablespoon peeled and minced or grated fresh
    ginger or 1 teaspoon ground ginger
2 tablespoons any curry powder or the All-Purpose
    Curry Powder or Garam Masala on page 778
$^1\!/_2$ teaspoon cayenne (optional)
$1^1\!/_2$ cups chicken, beef, or vegetable stock, or stock
    made from lamb bones, or water, plus more as
    needed (see "Soups" for stock recipes)
$^1\!/_2$ cup plain yogurt
Minced cilantro leaves for garnish

1 Heat the oil over medium-high heat in a large, deep skillet or casserole that can later be covered. Add the lamb chunks a few at a time and brown them on all sides (removing them as they brown), seasoning with salt and pepper as they cook. (You can also do the initial browning in the oven: Preheat to 500°F and roast the lamb chunks [you may omit the oil], turning once or twice, until brown all over; time will be about the same, 20 minutes.) Remove the lamb and remove and discard all but 2 tablespoons of fat. Cook the sliced onions over medium heat, stirring occasionally, until they are golden brown, 10 to 15 minutes.

2 Add the chopped onion, garlic, ginger, spice mixture, and cayenne, if you are using it. Stir and cook over medium heat for 3 or 4 minutes, until the chopped onion softens.

3 Return the lamb to the pot along with the stock or water. Bring to a boil, cover, turn the heat to low,

and simmer until the lamb is tender, at least 1 hour. Remove the cover and, if the mixture is soupy, turn the heat to high and reduce it a bit. (If it's dry, which is unlikely, add $^1\!/_2$ cup to 1 cup more liquid and cook 10 minutes before proceeding.) Taste and adjust seasoning. (The recipe can be prepared a day or two in advance up to this point; cool, place in a covered container, and refrigerate.) Stir in the yogurt, remove from the heat, and serve, garnished with cilantro.

Lamb Curry with Coconut Milk: In Step 1, pour off all the fat after the lamb is browned and cook the sliced onions in 3 tablespoons of butter. In Step 2, add 1 teaspoon ground turmeric (or several strands of saffron, crushed between your fingers) along with the other spices. In Step 3, substitute canned or Fresh Coconut Milk (page 291) for some or all of the stock; use more coconut milk in place of the yogurt.

The Basics of Lamb Shanks and Ribs

Lamb shanks are special because they're cheap and delicious; braise some on a cold winter night, open a bottle of red wine, and relax. Like most meats that take best to braising, they can be cooked in advance; up to a day or two if you refrigerate them, up to a week or two if you freeze them. Skim excess fat from the top before reheating.

You can braise lamb shanks on top of the stove or in the oven; I give examples of both methods here. Note, too, that lamb shanks take well to Chinese seasonings; try them in the recipe for Anise-Scented Short Ribs (page 434).

Like other ribs, those from lamb are good for grilling. But they will be tough (and are likely to burn to a crisp) unless you parboil them first. After that initial treatment, which is neither time-consuming nor difficult, you may treat them as you would any other ribs.

Lamb Shanks with Tomatoes and Olives

Makes 4 servings

Time: 2 hours or more, largely unattended

Good olives make this dish; I like a mixture of the big green kind from southern Italy and Calamatas or another flavorful black variety, but use what you can get.

- 1 tablespoon olive oil
- 4 lamb shanks, about 1 pound each
- Salt and freshly ground black pepper to taste
- 2 cups sliced onions
- 1 tablespoon minced garlic
- $1/2$ teaspoon fresh thyme leaves, a couple sprigs fresh thyme, or $1/2$ teaspoon dried thyme
- $1/2$ cup chicken, beef, or vegetable stock, or white or red wine, or water, or a combination (see "Soups" for stock recipes)
- 1 cup cored and chopped tomatoes (canned are fine; drain them first)
- $1 1/2$ cups assorted olives, pitted (page 26)
- Minced fresh basil or parsley leaves for garnish

1 Heat the oil over medium-high heat in a large, deep skillet or casserole that can later be covered. Add the shanks and brown on all sides, seasoning with salt and pepper as they cook. (You can also do the initial browning in the oven: Preheat to 500°F and roast the lamb shanks [you may omit the oil], turning once or twice, until brown all over; this will take a little longer but will be somewhat easier and much neater.) Remove the lamb and remove and discard all but 2 tablespoons of fat. Cook the onions over medium heat, stirring occasionally, until they soften and turn golden, about 10 minutes.

2 Add the garlic and thyme and cook another minute, then add the liquid(s), some salt and pepper, and the tomatoes; stir to blend. Return the lamb shanks to the pan, turn them once or twice, cover, and turn the heat to low.

3 Cook for 30 minutes, turn the shanks, and add the olives. Continue to cook for at least another hour, turning occasionally, until the shanks are very tender (a toothpick inserted into them will meet little resistance) and the meat is nearly falling from the bone. (The recipe can be prepared a day or two in advance up to this point; cool, place in a covered container, and refrigerate.) Garnish and serve.

Lamb Shanks with Onions and Apricots: Soak $1/2$ cup chopped dried apricots in $1/2$ cup port or other sweet wine. Step 1 remains the same. In Step 2, substitute $1/2$ teaspoon ground cinnamon for the thyme, omit the tomatoes, and stud each of the shanks with a clove before returning them to the pan. In Step 3, substitute the apricots and their liquid for the olives. Proceed as above, garnishing with parsley.

Lamb Shanks with White Beans

Makes 4 servings

Time: 2 hours or more, plus soaking time

Lamb and white beans is one of the most comforting combinations I know. This dish can easily serve eight people if no one is too determined to fill up on meat: Cook the lamb as directed here, then take it all off the bone and shred it, then stir it back into the beans. Then top with bread crumbs and run under the broiler until they brown lightly. The result: instant, if primitive, cassoulet.

1 pound dried white beans (pea, Great Northern,
    navy, etc.)

4 cloves garlic, crushed

1 cup cored and chopped tomatoes (canned are fine;
    drain them first)

1 bay leaf

1 tablespoon minced fresh sage leaves or 1 teaspoon
    dried sage; or 1 teaspoon fresh thyme leaves or
    $1/2$ teaspoon dried thyme

4 lamb shanks, $3/4$ to 1 pound each

Salt and freshly ground black pepper to taste

$1/2$ cup red wine or water

$1/2$ cup chicken, beef, or vegetable stock, or water
    (see "Soups" for stock recipes)

Minced fresh parsley or sage leaves or thyme sprigs
    for garnish

1 Place the beans in a large, deep pot with water to cover. Turn the heat to high and bring to a boil; skim the foam if necessary. Turn the heat down so the beans simmer, then add the garlic, tomatoes, bay leaf, and about a third of the herb. In 1 hour or more, when they are tender but not mushy, turn off the heat.

2 Meanwhile, preheat the oven to 350°F. Rub the lamb shanks with a third of the herb along with some salt and pepper, and place them in a roasting pan. Pour the wine and the stock or water around them and cover tightly with aluminum foil. Bake until the shanks are completely tender (a toothpick inserted into the meaty part will meet little resistance on its way in or out), about $1^1/2$ to 2 hours.

3 Remove the shanks to a plate, spoon off as much fat from the pan juices as is possible, and pour the remaining liquid into the still-warm beans. (Do not wash the roasting pan.) Simmer until most of the liquid is absorbed, 10 to 15 minutes; the beans should be quite soft. (The recipe can be prepared a day or two in advance up to this point; cool, place in a covered container, and refrigerate.)

4 Check the seasoning and spoon the beans into the roasting pan. Nestle the lamb shanks among them, sprinkle with the remaining sage, and return the pan to the oven, uncovered this time, for 15 minutes or so, or until hot. Garnish and serve.

Grilled or Broiled Lamb Ribs
Makes 4 servings

Time: 1 hour, plus time to preheat the grill

Many butchers and supermarkets cut up the breast (a not-common cut that you may braise using any shank recipe; cooking time will be somewhat less) and offer the pieces as lamb ribs. These little morsels make wonderful eating but take a two-step cooking process: They must be parboiled before grilling or broiling. If you skip the parboiling step, they'll be tough and virtually inedible.

If you find a whole breast, cut it into large sections and parboil it that way; then separate into ribs before grilling.

4 pounds lamb breast, whole or in riblets

Salt and freshly ground black pepper to taste

$1/2$ cup orange marmalade or maple syrup

$1/4$ cup Dijon mustard

1 tablespoon vinegar

1 teaspoon ground cumin

1 Bring a large pot of water to the boil; salt it. Put in the lamb and simmer for 30 minutes if riblets are already separate, 45 minutes if the breast is in large sections. Meanwhile, start a charcoal or wood fire or preheat a gas grill or broiler; the fire should be only moderately hot and the rack should be at least 4 inches from the heat source.

2 Drain the ribs and let them sit until they are cool enough to handle. Mix together all remaining ingredients. If necessary, cut the sections into individual ribs (just cut between them with a boning knife), and grill or broil them, basting frequently with the sauce. These burn very easily, so turn frequently and watch carefully. When they are brown and crisp all over—a matter of no more than 10 or at the most 15 minutes—remove from the grill and serve.

The Basics of Rack and Saddle of Lamb

These are the luxury (that is, expensive) cuts of lamb. They're delicious, and virtually foolproof if you take care not to overcook them. The traditional bread crumbs–garlic-parsley treatment for the rack—the front rib section—has never been bettered. You can use the same coating for the saddle (the rear rib section, also called the loin), although I prefer a simple brushing with oil and an herb (I use rosemary). Boned sections of rack or saddle, sometimes called boneless loin, can be cut into medallions, quickly cooked and served with a wine reduction; this is a wonderful dish to make for an intimate dinner for two.

Roast Saddle of Lamb

Makes 4 to 6 servings

Time: 25 minutes

You'll know a saddle when you see it (although take care that the butcher does not give you a baron, the saddle with both legs attached)—it's the part of the lamb you'd sit on. This is an odd cut: The cooking is nearly mindless, the presentation elegant, and the initial carving simple. But you should only eat a saddle in relaxed company, because you will ultimately start picking at the bones using your fingers (a small paring knife is helpful). If meat remains on the carcass, save

it; the next day, pop it in a 500°F oven until crisp, salt it liberally, and have it as a snack.

1 saddle of lamb, about 5 pounds
2 tablespoons olive oil
1 tablespoon fresh rosemary leaves or about
   1 teaspoon dried rosemary
1 clove garlic, peeled
Salt and freshly ground black pepper to taste

1 Preheat the oven to 500°F.

2 Cut any excess fat from the saddle. Using a knife, mortar and pestle, or food processor, make a paste of the olive oil, rosemary, garlic, salt, and pepper, and rub the lamb all over with this mixture. Place the saddle in a roasting pan, top side up.

3 Roast the lamb for 20 minutes and insert a meat thermometer straight in from one end into the meatiest part. If it reads 125°F or more, remove the lamb immediately. If it reads less, put the lamb back for 5 minutes, no more. Remove and let sit for 5 minutes. Carve by cutting straight down along the sides; bring the carved meat and the carcass to the table, along with a paring knife to aid in picking.

Roast Rack of Lamb with Persillade

Makes 4 servings

Time: 30 minutes

There are seven ribs per rack, and only a couple of bites per rib, so you'll need two racks for four people, although fourteen ribs could easily serve five in a pinch, and even six if there's plenty of other food and the crowd is not ravenous. (This is true despite the fact that many restaurants serve one rack per customer—way too much for most eaters.) Make sure the chine bone is removed so you can easily cut through the ribs to separate them at the table, but don't bother to ask to have the ribs "frenched" (the meat removed from the top of the bones); the crisp meat along the bones is one of the pleasures of a rack of lamb. You didn't want to use little frilly doilies on top of the bones anyway, did you?

2 racks of lamb, about 2 pounds each
2 tablespoons olive oil
Salt and freshly ground black pepper to taste
1 cup plain bread crumbs, preferably fresh (page 239)
$^1/_2$ cup minced fresh parsley leaves
1 teaspoon minced garlic

1 Preheat the oven to 500°F. Trim the lamb of excess fat, but leave a layer of fat over the meat. Cut about halfway down the bones between the chops; this allows the meat between them to become crisp.

2 Combine all remaining ingredients and rub over the meat side of the racks. Put them in a roasting pan and place in the oven; roast for 20 minutes, and insert a meat thermometer straight in from one end into the meatiest part. If it reads 125°F or more, remove the lamb immediately. If it reads less, put the lamb back for 5 minutes, no more. Remove and let sit for 5 minutes. Serve, separating the ribs by cutting down straight through them.

Lamb Medallions with Shallots, Tarragon, and Red Wine

Makes 2 servings

Time: 20 minutes

Ask the butcher to bone a rack of lamb for you, and don't let him discard the bones. Rather, use them for a simple lamb stock or just crisp them up in a very hot oven, sprinkle liberally with salt, and have them for a snack.

1 boneless rack of lamb (lamb loin), about $^1/_2$ pound
2 tablespoons butter (preferred) or olive oil
Salt and freshly ground black pepper to taste
1 tablespoon minced shallots
1 teaspoon minced fresh tarragon leaves or $^1/_4$ teaspoon dried tarragon
$^1/_2$ cup red wine

1 Cut the lamb into $^3/_4$-inch-thick rounds; there will be 6 or 8. Heat a large non-stick skillet over medium-high heat for 3 or 4 minutes. Heat the oven to 200°F.

2 Reserve 1 teaspoon of butter and add the rest to the pan; it should sizzle. Swirl the pan so the butter melts quickly and coats the pan evenly. Add the lamb medallions; sprinkle with salt and pepper and cook until brown on both sides, a total of 4 to 5 minutes. Turn the heat to low, remove the lamb to an oven-proof plate, and place in the oven.

3 Add the shallots to the pan. Cook, stirring, until the shallots are softened, about 2 minutes. Add the tarragon and wine, raise the heat to medium-high, and cook, stirring, until reduced by about half, about 5 minutes. Stir in the remaining butter. If any juices have seeped out of the lamb, add them to the pan, then spoon or pour the sauce over the lamb and serve.

The Basics of Ground Lamb

Lamb makes wonderful ground meat—incredibly flavorful and reasonably lean. You can grind it yourself from any cut, or just buy it in the supermarket. The two recipes below are more or less traditional uses for ground lamb, but you can use it in place of ground beef in most recipes.

Lamburgers with Smoked Mozzarella

Makes 4 servings

Time: 30 minutes, plus time to preheat the grill

Broil these, grill them, or pan-grill them. Any way you cook them, the outside will become crisp, the mozzarella will melt, and the inside will stay pink. A good way to wean kids from McDonald's.

Coarse salt (optional)
1/4 pound smoked mozzarella
1 pound ground lamb, or a little more
Salt and freshly ground black pepper to taste

1 Start a charcoal or wood fire or preheat a gas grill or broiler; the fire should be moderately hot. Or heat a large skillet over medium-high heat for 3 or 4 minutes before you start cooking, then sprinkle it with coarse salt.

2 Cut the cheese into 4 pieces and form the meat into patties around each one; season with salt and pepper.

3 Grill, broil, or pan-grill, 2 to 4 inches from the heat source, for about 3 or 4 minutes per side, or until the outside feels very firm. If you like your meat on the well-done side, move the burgers to a lower heat and cook an additional minute or two longer per side.

Lamb Patties with Bulgur

Kibbe

Makes 4 to 8 servings

Time: About 30 minutes, plus time to preheat the grill

Kibbe (or kibbeh, pronounced kibbey) is an important Middle Eastern (primarily Lebanese) dish that is

made in a variety of forms, including raw and stuffed. This is a basic kibbe, a simple combination of ground lamb and cracked wheat (bulgur) that has wonderful flavor; serve it with a salad, or in a pita bread with raw vegetables, with Tahini Dressing (page 770) or Cucumber-Yogurt Dip with Mint (page 771).

1 cup fine-grind (Number One) or medium-grind
   (Number Two) bulgur (available in Middle Eastern
   or natural foods stores; see page 185)
2 cups boiling water
1 large or 2 medium onions
1 pound lean ground lamb
Salt and freshly ground black pepper to taste
1 tablespoon ground cumin
Pinch ground allspice
1/4 teaspoon ground cinnamon
Minced fresh parsley, mint, or cilantro leaves
   for garnish

1 While you prepare the other ingredients, soak the bulgur in a bowl with boiling water for about 15 to 20 minutes for fine grind, 20 to 25 for medium grind. It will absorb most or all of the water; drain it if it does not. Start a charcoal or wood fire or preheat a gas grill or broiler; the fire should be quite hot, and the rack 3 to 4 inches from the heat source. (You can also sauté kibbe: Just before cooking, heat a large skillet over medium-high heat for 3 or 4 minutes, then add 2 tablespoons of butter or oil before adding the patties.)

2 Meanwhile, quarter the onion(s) and put them in a food processor; turn on the machine and puree. Add the lamb, salt, and spices, then pulse to blend. Add the drained bulgur and pulse a few more times. Try not to overprocess.

3 Remove the mixture and shape into 8 patties. Grill, broil, or sauté, turning occasionally. Kibbe are cooked to well done but not dry; total cooking time will be 10 to 12 minutes. Garnish and serve.

Baked Kibbe as an Appetizer: Preheat the oven to 375°F. Spread the kibbe mixture in an 8-inch square baking pan and score the top in a diamond pattern. Place a pine nut on each section and bake for about 20 minutes, or until cooked through and brown at the edges. Let cool for 5 minutes, then cut through the score marks. Garnish with parsley or cilantro and serve sections hot or at room temperature.

The Basics of Mixed Meats

We tend to cook meats individually not because they're best that way but because they're more convenient that way. But combining several meats in the same dish produces a variety of flavors and textures that you cannot get otherwise. Thus cassoulet (which can contain poultry as well as meat) is the paragon of stews, and meat loaf or meatballs made with two meats are far better than those made with one. Yet somehow many Americans have slipped into the habit of making meatballs and meat loaf primarily of beef, this despite the fact that many supermarkets pack different kinds of ground meat together in a "meat loaf" mix.

There's no need to cook ground meat mixtures in ball-like shapes or loaves; you can make them into patties and serve them on rolls, as you would hamburgers; or you can shape them into steaks and grill them. The point is that most of the mixtures have the same ingredients; it's only the cooking that varies.

Cassoulet

Makes at least 12 servings

Time: 2¹/₂ hours, largely unattended

You can spend all day (and all your money) making cassoulet, but what this classic dish boils down to is a pile of mixed meats combined in a stew with beans.

(One could argue, in fact, that franks and beans, or pork and beans, is a form of cassoulet.) Here's a fairly basic cassoulet that is grand enough for any company; you can make it well in advance, then reheat it in the oven for about 30 minutes before adding the bread crumb–parsley mixture and browning.

1¹/₂ pounds white beans (pea, navy, Great Northern, etc.)

Chicken, beef, or vegetable stock, water, or a mixture, as needed (see "Soups" for stock recipes)

4 cloves garlic, crushed

1 medium-large onion, chopped

2 carrots, peeled and chopped

2 cups cored and chopped tomatoes (canned are fine; drain them first)

1 clove

3 or 4 sprigs fresh thyme, 1 teaspoon fresh thyme leaves, or ¹/₂ teaspoon dried thyme

2 bay leaves

¹/₄ pound slab bacon or salt pork, in 1 piece

1 pound garlic (Italian) sausage

2 pounds pork shoulder or butt

2 pounds boneless shoulder or leg of lamb, trimmed of excess fat

Salt and freshly ground black pepper to taste

1 cup red wine or water

1 tablespoon minced garlic

1¹/₂ cups plain bread crumbs

1¹/₄ cups minced fresh parsley leaves

1 Place the beans in a large Dutch oven or casserole with water to cover. Turn the heat to high and bring to a boil; skim the foam if necessary. Turn the heat down so the beans simmer, then add the crushed garlic, onion, carrots, and tomatoes. Tie the clove, thyme, and bay leaves in a cheesecloth bag or place them in a tea ball, and cook along with the beans, stirring occasionally. In 1 hour or more, when the beans are tender but not mushy, turn off the heat.

2 As the beans are cooking, cook the bacon or salt pork in boiling water to cover for 2 minutes. Dice the meat and add it to the beans. Preheat the oven to 450°F.

3 Cut the garlic sausage, pork, and lamb into 1¹/₂-inch chunks. Place in a roasting pan and sprinkle liberally with salt and pepper. Roast, shaking the pan occasionally, until the meats are very well browned, about 30 minutes. Remove the meat and turn the oven to 350°F.

4 When the beans are tender and the meat is done, stir the meat into the beans, discarding the fat if you like. Turn the heat to medium-low and keep the mixture hot. Put the roasting pan over medium-high heat and add the wine or water; cook, stirring and scraping to loosen any brown bits that have stuck to the bottom of the pan, then add this liquid to the stew. (The recipe can be prepared a day or two in advance up to this point; cool, place in a covered container, and refrigerate.)

5 Taste the stew for salt and pepper and add some if necessary. Stir in the garlic. Combine the bread crumbs and 1 cup of the parsley and spread this mixture over the stew. Bake for 15 to 20 minutes, or until the bread crumbs have browned nicely. Garnish with the remaining parsley and serve.

Basic Meatballs

Makes 6 to 8 servings

Time: 45 minutes to 1¹/₂ hours

You need not cook meatballs in a skillet. Instead, try roasting them (omit the butter or oil) in a 375°F oven, shaking occasionally, until they are nicely browned, twenty to thirty minutes. Then pour off any excess fat and finish as in Steps 3 and 4, below.

The cream addition is not essential, but it is a pleasant and very traditional touch (if you're looking

to cut the fat, see the lean variation below). Serve these with crusty bread, noodles, or rice.

Note: For Spaghetti and Meatballs, see page 152.

¹/₂ cup plain bread crumbs
¹/₂ cup milk or cream
2 tablespoons butter or olive or vegetable oil
¹/₂ cup minced onion
2 pounds mixed ground meats: beef, veal, lamb, and/or pork
Salt and freshly ground black pepper to taste
¹/₂ cup minced fresh parsley leaves
1 egg, lightly beaten
Pinch ground allspice or cinnamon
1 tablespoon flour
1 cup chicken, beef, or vegetable stock, or water (see "Soups" for stock recipes)
1 cup half-and-half or cream (optional)
Minced fresh parsley leaves for garnish

1 Soak the bread crumbs in the milk until the milk is absorbed, about 5 minutes. Melt 1 tablespoon butter in a small skillet over medium heat. Cook the onion in it, stirring, until it is softened, 4 to 5 minutes. Remove from the heat.

2 Mix together the bread crumbs, onion, meat, salt, pepper, parsley, egg, and allspice or cinnamon. Shape into meatballs 1¹/₂ inches in diameter. Melt the remaining butter in a large, deep skillet over medium heat. Add the meatballs (you may have to do this in batches; if so, it may be easier to use the oven; see the note above) and cook, shaking gently every couple of minutes. Adjust the heat so that the meatballs brown but the fat does not burn, and cook until they are brown all over. Cook until an instant-read thermometer inserted into the center of a meatball reads 160°F.

3 Remove the meatballs to a platter and keep warm while you prepare the sauce: Pour off all but a tablespoon or two of the fat, then stir in the flour and cook, stirring, for about a minute. Over medium-high heat, add the stock or water and cook, stirring, until the liquid is reduced by about half. (If you choose not to use the cream, pour this sauce over the meatballs and serve.)

4 Stir in the cream, reduce the heat to medium-low, and cook, stirring, for about 2 minutes, until the sauce is smooth, golden brown, and slightly thickened. Pour over the meatballs, garnish, and serve.

Leaner Meatballs: Omit bread crumbs, milk, and egg; increase onion and parsley to 1 cup each. Grill, broil, or bake at 400°F until done, 15 minutes or less. Serve without sauce.

Spiced or Herbed Meatballs: To either the master recipe or the lean variation, add 1 tablespoon ground cumin or curry or chili powder; or add 1 tablespoon minced fresh mint leaves, $1/4$ teaspoon ground cinnamon, and $1/8$ teaspoon ground allspice; or substitute fresh dill, chervil, or chives for some or all of the parsley.

Basic Meat Loaf

Makes 6 to 8 servings

Time: About 1 hour, largely unattended

There are two basic differences between meatballs and meat loaf: The shape (you knew that) and the cooking time—meat loaf takes longer. Other than that, the recipes are essentially interchangeable.

I like free-form meat loaf more than the kind cooked in a loaf pan, for a couple of reasons—it browns on three sides rather than just one, and the fat can run off, rather than become trapped between pan and meat. It's easy to shape meat loaf by hand, and it will retain virtually any shape you give it.

$1/2$ cup plain bread crumbs, preferably fresh (page 239)

$1/2$ cup milk

2 pounds mixed ground meats: beef, veal, lamb, and/or pork

1 egg, lightly beaten

$1/2$ cup freshly grated Parmesan cheese

$1/4$ cup minced fresh parsley leaves

$1/2$ teaspoon minced garlic

1 small onion, minced

1 small carrot, peeled and minced

1 teaspoon minced fresh sage leaves or pinch crumbled dried sage leaves

Salt and freshly ground black pepper to taste

3 slices bacon (optional) (but good, especially if meat is very lean)

1 Preheat the oven to 350°F. Soak the bread crumbs in the milk until the milk is absorbed, about 5 minutes.

2 Mix together all ingredients except bacon. Shape the meat into a loaf in a baking pan; top with bacon if you like. Bake 45 to 60 minutes, basting occasionally with rendered pan juices. When done, meat loaf will be lightly browned and firm, and an instant-read thermometer inserted into the center of a meat loaf reads 160°F.

Meat Loaf with Spinach: Bring a large pot of water to a boil; salt it. Trim and wash a 10-ounce package of fresh spinach (page 604); cook it in the boiling water for 30 seconds, then remove it. Drain and cool it, then chop it finely, seasoning with salt, pepper, and a grating of nutmeg. In Step 1, increase bread crumbs to 1 cup. In Step 2, integrate the chopped spinach into the meat loaf, substituting a grating of nutmeg for the sage. Cook as above.

The Basics of Game Meats

Although game is most accurately defined as meat that has been hunted rather than farm-raised, the word has come to mean almost any meat or poultry that we are not accustomed to eating. Thus rabbit, which is raised in a manner similar to chicken and can be found in the freezer compartment of most supermarkets (and the fresh meat department of many), is lumped into the same category as rattlesnake or camel, two animals that are readily available by mail but are hardly common.

What you can say about game is that most of it is leaner than domesticated meat, and most of it has fairly strong flavor. Not surprisingly, the game that has become most popular, and most common, is the mildest. This includes venison, which may be any one of several varieties of deer (some elk is also sold as venison); rabbit, which "tastes like chicken"—in some instances it has better flavor, but it can easily become unpalatably dry—and can be treated as such; and buffalo, or, as it is called more properly, bison. Bison has a mild, beefy flavor that, objectively speaking, makes beef itself seem a little on the "gamy" side. You can cook bison exactly as you would beef; keep it rare, though, because it dries out quickly.

Roast Leg of Venison

Makes 8 to 10 servings

Time: About 2 hours, longer if you choose to marinate, largely unattended

You don't see venison in supermarkets: You either hunt it or get it from a friend who hunts it (probably the most common method). You can also order it, through a butcher or by mail, but it's expensive and, unless you have a vicious craving for it, not worth the money. Should you come across any elk, reindeer, or moose, you can use these recipes for them.

You can roast a leg of venison, which usually weighs about six pounds, exactly as you would a leg of lamb. But if it is from a wild deer, you may choose to marinate it first. This marinade is also good with venison rump or chunks. After letting the meat sit in the marinade for a day or two, strain out the vegetables, and replace them with fresh vegetables, then stew the whole thing—meat, marinade liquid, and vegetables—together until the meat is tender.

2 cups red wine

$^1/_2$ cup red wine vinegar

20 juniper berries

4 bay leaves

5 cloves

5 cloves garlic, lightly smashed

20 peppercorns

1 large onion, chopped

2 celery stalks, chopped

2 carrots, peeled and chopped

1 (6- to 8-pound) leg of venison

Salt and freshly ground black pepper to taste

1 Combine the first ten ingredients in a large plastic bag or other waterproof container large enough to hold the venison. Add the meat and seal so that it is surrounded by liquid (or plan to turn and baste it from time to time). Marinate, refrigerated, for 24 to 72 hours.

2 Preheat the oven to 450°F. Remove the meat and dry it. Strain the liquid and discard the solids. Season the meat with salt and pepper and place it on a rack in a roasting pan. Roast for 30 minutes, basting once with the reserved marinade. Turn the heat to 350°F.

3 Continue to roast the meat, basting every 15 minutes or so with the reserved marinade and/or pan juices, for about another hour, until its temperature, taken with an instant-read thermometer, is about 135°F in the thickest spot.

4 Remove the roast from the oven and let it rest. Carve as you would a leg of lamb (page 479).

Marinated and Stewed Rabbit

Hasenpfeffer

Makes 3 to 4 servings

Time: 1¹/₂ hours, plus marinating time, largely unattended

Not only does domesticated rabbit "taste like chicken," it's difficult to taste the difference. Rabbit has finer, drier meat, and a different bone structure, but the distinctions pretty much end there. So, if you buy rabbit parts in the supermarket, treat them exactly as you would chicken, taking care not to overcook.

If, however, you get your hands on a wild rabbit, or hare, or a rabbit raised by a farmer, use this recipe, which highlights the gamier flavor of wild meat. Note the addition of chocolate, which is not only traditional but brilliant. This is nice served over Basic Polenta (made with 5 cups of water, page 187).

2 cups good red wine

¹/₂ cup red wine vinegar

1 carrot, peeled and roughly chopped

1 onion, roughly chopped, plus 2 cups minced onion

1 rabbit or hare, about 3 pounds, cut into 8 serving pieces (as you would chicken)

Several sprigs fresh parsley or thyme

Salt and freshly ground black pepper to taste

4 thick slices good bacon

1 cup peeled and diced carrot

1 cup diced celery

¹/₂ pound wild or button mushrooms, or 1 ounce dried porcini, soaked in water to soften, drained (reserve the soaking liquid), and mixed with ¹/₂ pound button mushrooms

Flour for dredging

1 ounce unsweetened chocolate, grated or chopped

① Mix together the wine, vinegar, and chopped carrot and onion in a bowl large enough to hold the rabbit. Tie together the parsley or thyme, or put in a cheesecloth sack or tea ball. Add the herb to the marinade with the rabbit, and add some salt and pepper. Marinate in the refrigerator, turning the rabbit pieces occasionally, for 12 to 24 hours. Strain the marinade, reserving it, and dry the rabbit pieces.

② Cut the bacon into bits and render it over medium-low heat in a Dutch oven or large, deep skillet. When it has given up much of its fat and is becoming nice and crisp, remove it with a slotted spoon and set it aside; add the 2 cups minced onions, carrot, and celery. Cook, stirring, still over medium-low heat; chop the mushrooms and add them too. When the vegetables are soft, about 10 minutes later, remove them with a slotted spoon and set aside with the bacon.

③ Turn the heat to medium-high, dredge the rabbit pieces in the flour, and brown them in the fat that remains in the pan. Season them with salt and pepper as they brown. When they are browned, lower the heat and return the vegetables and bacon to the skillet; stir, then add the reserved marinade and mushroom-soaking liquid, if any. Raise the heat a bit, bring to a boil, stir, then add the chocolate, some salt, and plenty of pepper.

④ Lower the heat even further, cover, and cook until the rabbit is tender and the sauce thick, about 1 hour. If the sauce is too thin, remove the meat to a warm oven and reduce the sauce over high heat, stirring almost constantly, until it is of a pleasant thickness. Remove the herbs, check and correct seasoning, and serve immediately, with buttered noodles, rice, or crusty bread.

Beans

Beans—a generic term used for beans, peas, split peas, lentils, and other dried legumes—may never be chic, but they have become standard fare in the last ten years, and that's a real change. Or perhaps a reversion to the way things once were: In the nineteenth century, before the mass production of meat and poultry, beans were a primary source of protein for many Americans. The widespread availability of so many types of animal protein changed that, but the slow move away from complete dependence on meat has begun to move the pendulum in the other direction.

Beans, generally speaking, are a low-fat, no-cholesterol, low-calorie (less than one hundred fifty calories per four-ounce serving) source of high-quality protein. No, you cannot obtain all your nutritional requirements from beans, but you can come pretty close, and a diet that contains grains, plenty of vegetables—and, for most people, some dairy and/or meat—completes the picture.

Beans boast of three other important assets: For one thing, they're cheap. Although "designer" and heirloom beans—those lesser-known varieties that are not grown in large quantities—can run up to five dollars a pound, most beans fall into the seventy-nine-cents-a-pound range.

Second, beans are easily stored and almost never go bad. Because they are dried, their shelf life is more or less unlimited. (Still, it makes sense to find fresh dried beans, those from the most recent harvest: They're likely to contain more nutrients, and they certainly cook more quickly.)

Finally, there's a lot you can do with beans. As a simple side dish, with olive oil, lemon juice, butter, or herbs, they bring variety to the winter table, when good fresh vegetables are hard to find. As part of a stew, with or without meat, they offer a level of heartiness that no vegetable provides. And cooked with fresh vegetables in quick, simple ways, they bring both body and earthy flavor to dishes that otherwise would have neither.

Although there are literally hundreds of varieties of dried beans, virtually all of them can be treated in the same way. Since there are some misconceptions about storing and cooking beans, I'll cover the basics before looking at the individual types and categories.

The Basics of Buying and Preparing Beans

They're almost always dried, but there is still a difference between fresh and stale. Your best shot at buying fresh beans is to go to a place where there is a fair amount of turnover—a natural foods store, for example, or a Latin market. Even supermarkets sell a lot of beans these days, so you might start there. But if it seems to you that the beans you buy take longer to cook than you might expect given my guidelines, try buying them elsewhere.

Generally, beans should look consistent, and have deep, somewhat glossy color; faded, dry-looking beans are likely to be older, and those that are starting to wrinkle are not worth buying. Avoid a given batch, too, if it contains a high percentage of cracked or broken beans.

Store beans in covered containers or thick plastic bags in a dry place. I make a policy of finishing all the beans I've accumulated during the course of the year each summer, so that I know that I don't keep any longer than a year. Since most beans are harvested late in summer, the new crop is available in stores in the fall; and since newer beans taste better, cook faster, and contain more nutrients, it's worth "updating." It's rare, though, to see beans actually go bad. They just take

longer and longer to cook, and lose a little flavor and a little of their nutrients with each passing month.

Beans are cleaned by machines, which do a good job. Still, spend a minute or two sorting through them just before soaking or cooking: Put the beans in a pot and fill it with water, then swish the whole thing around while looking into the pot. Remove any beans that are discolored, shriveled, or broken (if there's a high percentage of these, buy different beans next time) and, obviously, remove any pebbles or other stray matter. Then dump the beans into a colander and rinse for a minute or so.

Preparing Beans: Here the myths proliferate. The three big ones, all untrue:

1. You must soak beans before cooking.
2. You must not add salt during cooking.
3. You must not add acid during cooking.

The first is the most egregious, and the most harmful, because it has given millions of people the impression that beans must be prepared well in advance. *Although soaking speeds cooking, it does not do so significantly.* If you soak most beans overnight, you will shave fifteen to thirty minutes off the cooking time. If that's important to you, by all means soak. Or, if you happen to think about it, soak. There is one real advantage to soaking, especially in hot water, and I'll get to that in a minute.

But please don't let the fact that you didn't plan to cook beans until the last minute stop you from cooking them at all. With a pressure cooker (see page 507), you can move beans from pantry to table in a half hour or so. Even without pressure cooking, many beans can simmer away on a back burner, with only an occasional stir, and soften completely in as little as an hour (far less for lentils and split peas).

It's also been said, forever, that salting beans during cooking prevents them from softening. But the only difference I note in cooking two identical pots of beans, side by side, one with salt and one without, is that one is salty and one is not. And adding salt after beans are cooked does not give beans the same flavor as adding salt during cooking. My recommendation: Salt beans as you would any other food, during cooking. If you want to be safe, salt them halfway through cooking, after they have begun to tenderize. But do not wait until they are done to add salt.

Similarly, acid is said to slow bean cooking time (and, conversely, alkaline substances such as baking soda are said to speed it). In fact, baking soda helps to break down the skin of beans, and acid helps to keep skins intact. If you're looking for a mushy bean dish, in which the individual beans begin to lose definition, you might indeed add a pinch or two of baking soda to the pot. If, however, you like well-defined, individual beans, include a teaspoonful of vinegar or lemon juice in the water. I don't include acid unless I want its flavor.

Plain Talk about Beans and Gas

Okay, beans give many people gas. So, however, may meat, or fruit, or—quite certainly—cauliflower. Most digestive gas is caused by compounds that are not broken down in the stomach, but pass on to the large intestine more or less intact. Thus they are never completely digested.

Beans contain these kinds of compounds, a group of carbohydrates called oligosaccharides. In many people, oligosaccharides are not digested in the stomach. When digestion does take place, in the large intestine, gas is a by-product. There are four ways to approach this problem:

1. Ignore it.
2. Eat beans more often; you'll develop a tolerance. Many vegetarians, who rely on beans much more heavily than do omnivores, have no problems with beans and gas.
3. Cook beans with Beano, a commercially available product (usually sold in the bean department, where else?), which contains an enzyme that breaks up the oligosaccharides.
4. Soak, but soak the right way. It's true that I don't think that soaking is really worth it for the savings in time (although, as I said, it does no harm), but there is a series of soaking techniques that decrease the amount of oligosaccharides in beans. These are the steps to follow:

- Rinse and pick over the beans, as described above.
- Place the beans in a pot and cover them with water; about twelve cups water per pound of beans.
- Bring to a boil, cook for two minutes, then turn off the heat.
- Soak from one to twenty-four hours (refrigerated for longer periods, or in a very warm kitchen).
- Rinse the beans and cook as usual in fresh water.

This process does the trick for many people.

Freezing Home-Cooked Beans versus Buying Canned Beans

This brings us to the all-important issue of freezing and canning beans. It's inarguable that, soaked or not, cooking beans takes longer than cooking most other foods. And, especially since most of us eat beans as a side dish, a one- to $1^1/_2$-hour cooking time (not to mention the added time and inconvenience of soaking, should you choose to) reduces the appeal of cooking beans on a regular basis.

There are, however, two solutions to this problem. The first is to buy canned beans. Canned beans are precooked and take no work whatsoever: You open the can, drain and rinse the beans, and proceed. Elapsed time: a minute. But canned beans have several disadvantages:

- Although still quite inexpensive, they are much more expensive than dried beans.
- They give you no control over texture. Although many people like the extremely soft texture of canned beans, they come that way and that way only. Should you want less tender beans—a likely eventuality at some point, especially if you want to combine mostly cooked beans with other ingredients—you're out of luck. (Canned organic beans, such as those sold in natural foods stores and some supermarkets, are not always overcooked quite so badly. But they're usually much more expensive.)
- They range in quality from decent taste, to no taste (you'd be hard put to tell a canned black bean from a canned white bean with your eyes closed), to a decidedly "tinny" taste.

The second solution (my preference, as you've already guessed) is to freeze cooked beans. Instead of cooking a cup of dried beans—usually enough for a side dish for four—cook a couple of cups, or more. Then freeze the remainder in individual containers, in the bean cooking liquid. Defrost in the refrigerator or microwave and proceed. Frozen beans keep perfectly for months and months.

The Basics of Cooking Beans

In some ways, this is the simplest part of the discussion. Beans are always cooked in liquid, and that liquid is usually water. (It's worth mentioning that beans cooked in meat or vegetable stock are especially delicious and take no more work.) A couple of general suggestions: Cover the beans with water, but don't drown them in it—it's easier to add more water than to boil it out. And, although you can stir beans as they cook, don't do so aggressively as the end of the cooking time nears, or you'll break them up. Mix them with a large spoon, scooping gently from the bottom, with a motion similar to that used for folding egg whites.

A word about amounts   Most beans double or triple their bulk during cooking; that is, a cup of dried beans yields at least two cups of cooked beans. As a side dish, you'd figure one-half to one full cup of cooked beans per person; as a main dish, somewhat more. All of this depends, of course, on the other food being served and the individual eaters. I generally like to make $1^1/_2$ to two cups of dried beans for four people; that is, I figure three to six cups of cooked beans. But if you have precooked beans, please don't let my quantities dissuade you; if I ask for six cups of cooked beans and you only have four, make the recipe anyway, by all means. Just reduce the seasonings slightly.

Sprouting beans   You'll find full instructions for sprouting on page 524.

The Bean Lexicon

Are beans interchangeable in recipes? Yes and no. Beans look different from one another, and they have different flavors and textures, but they all react pretty similarly in the pot. If you cook black-eyed peas in place of pea beans, or vice versa, you'll have a dish with somewhat different flavors and quite different textures; but it will still be a good dish. Generally, it's very safe to substitute white beans for other white beans, and red for red. Other than that, I'd try to stick to the beans recommended in each recipe, unless you're familiar enough with beans to know that you want to make a given substitution.

Adzuki

Appearance   Small (one-quarter inch long or so), oval, maroon; very pretty.

Use   An Asian bean usually made into flour, or sprouted, or used in desserts. Its slightly sweet flavor makes it an odd choice for a dinner bean.

Cooking time   Forty-five minutes or less.

Appaloosa

Appearance   Speckled red or black and white, rather long (up to an inch), thin ovals.

Use   Roughly interchangeable with pinto, pink, and kidney beans.

Cooking time   About forty-five minutes.

Black (Turtle bean)

Appearance   Medium-sized (up to one-half inch long), round to almost square, deep black with a white line and interior.

Use   Multipurpose, among the most valuable and best-tasting beans. Especially good in soup.

Cooking time   Can be quite long, up to two hours, but usually one hour or less. Good candidate for the pressure cooker.

Black-Eyed Pea (Cow pea)

Appearance   Ivory in color, with a black spot; kidney-shaped and small, no more than one-half inch long.

Use   Southern dishes, often with meat; Hoppin' John (page 515).

Cooking time   Twenty (these are often very fresh) to forty-five minutes.

Cannellini

Appearance   Looks like a white kidney bean, which it is sometimes called.

Use   As for other white beans.

Cooking time   Up to one hour.

Chickpea (Garbanzo)

Appearance   Deep beige, round, but with lumps and lines; one-fourth to one-half inch in diameter.

Use   With pasta, in casseroles and salads, by itself.

Cooking time   Often as long as two hours, sometimes less. Good candidate for the pressure cooker.

Cranberry (Borlotti)

Appearance   Medium-size (about one-half inch long), dark tannish-pink with brown dappling.

Use   In pasta, soup, or salads, or as a more flavorful replacement for pinto beans.

Cooking time   Usually less than one hour.

Fava (Broad bean)

Appearance   Usually quite large, over an inch long, although there are smaller varieties; flat kidney shape akin to that of lima.

Use   Often eaten fresh (see The Basics of Buying and Preparing Beans, page 500); dried beans are great mashed or pureed (page 510). Always buy split dried beans, which will cook faster and eliminate the need for skinning.

Cooking time   If skinned, thirty minutes or less; if not, about one hour (skins should be removed before eating).

Flageolet

Appearance   Medium in size (about one-half inch long), kidney-shaped, and a lovely pale green. These are kidney beans harvested before maturity.

Use   Quick-cooking and very fresh-tasting, these are best treated simply. The classic treatment (see

Flageolets, French-Style, page 509), which is delicious, features cream and herbs.

Cooking time   Thirty to sixty minutes.

Great Northern

Appearance   Large (up to an inch long), oval, and white. One of the most common white beans.

Use   All-purpose.

Cooking time   Usually one hour or so.

Haricot

Haricot is a generic term for all New World beans, which includes almost everything: kidney, pinto, navy, pea, Great Northern, anasazi, cannellini, flageolets, appaloosa, and more.

Appearance   Varies widely; this category includes most of the dried beans found in the supermarket.

Use   Any and all; some of the more popular varieties are detailed elsewhere in this chapter.

Cooking time   Thirty to forty-five minutes for small beans, forty-five to sixty minutes for larger ones. Older beans take longer.

Kidney

Appearance   Reddish brown, up to an inch long, kidney-shaped.

Use   Chili, beans and rice, puree, refried beans, baked beans—virtually all-purpose.

Cooking time   Usually a good hour, and sometimes more.

Lentil

Appearance   There are three major kinds: common green (or brown), which are round disks about one-eighth inch in diameter; red, which are smaller, bright orange, quick-cooking, and have a tendency to fall apart; and French (not always from France), or Le Puy, a tiny, dark-green French variety, which takes the longest to cook and has the best flavor.

Use   In salads, soups, the Indian dish known as dal (see Split Peas, Mung Beans, or Lentils with Curry, page 524), and simple side dishes. Very useful.

Cooking time   From twenty minutes (red) to forty minutes (Le Puy). Rarely longer.

Lima (Butter)

Appearance   Pale green, kidney-shaped, large (over an inch long in some cases); "baby" limas are smaller and cook more quickly.

Use   Usually eaten fresh. Can be used in many bean dishes calling for white beans.

Cooking time   Usually about one hour. These produce a lot of foam, and skins float off; skim frequently. Not a good candidate for the pressure cooker.

Mung

Appearance   Tiny (about one-eighth inch in diameter), round, and either green or, if peeled, yellow.

Use   Used to make bean-thread noodles, and great for sprouting (page 524); sometimes used in the Indian dish known as dal (see Split Peas, Mung Beans, or Lentils with Curry, page 524).

Cooking time   Whole, about one hour. Peeled, about thirty minutes.

Navy (Pea bean)

Appearance   Small round bean, white, about one-fourth inch in diameter.

Use   The most basic of white beans. Great for puree, baked beans, and simple uses. Mild-flavored.

Cooking time   About forty-five minutes.

Pea (Split pea)

Appearance   Whole, like dried green peas (which is what they are). More commonly split, in which case they may be green or yellow; there is little difference between the two.

Use   For soup (see Simplest Split Pea Soup, page 65), in place of lentils, or in the Indian dish known as dal (see Split Peas, Mung Beans, or Lentils with Curry, page 524).

Cooking time   Usually about thirty minutes. Easily overcooked.

Pigeon Pea (Gandule)

Appearance   Tan and nearly round, with one side flattened; about one-fourth inch in diameter.

Use   Classic bean for beans and rice in much of the Caribbean.

Cooking time   One hour or more; skins are tough.

Pink (Red)

Appearance   Its name tells you its color. A small, slightly ovate bean essentially interchangeable with the pinto.

Use   Beans and rice, refried beans, puree, chili.

Cooking time   About forty-five minutes.

Pinto

Appearance   From beige to rust, usually mottled; about one-half inch long, oval-shaped.

Use   Beans and rice, refried beans, puree, chili.

Cooking time   About forty-five minutes.

Soybean

Appearance   Round, under one-half inch in diameter, and usually yellowish, but may be other colors.

Use   Not a prime cooking bean, but used to make tofu, for which you'll find recipes on pages 526–527.

Cooking time   Less than one hour.

Basic Beans

Time: 30 minutes to 2 hours, largely unattended

It's best to precook beans whenever you can because, unfortunately, precise timing is nearly impossible. A small white bean from a recent harvest may cook twice as fast—may be done in thirty minutes, in fact—as one that's been sitting on your shelf for more than a year and may in fact be two years old. So allow enough time unless you've cooked beans from the same batch before and can predict cooking time. Beans store well, in their own liquid, in the refrigerator or freezer, and reheat perfectly on stove top, in the oven, or in a microwave.

Any quantity dried beans, washed and picked over (see
   The Basics of Buying and Preparing Beans, page 500)
Salt to taste

1   Place the beans in a large pot with water to cover. Turn the heat to high and bring to a boil; skim the foam if necessary. Turn the heat down so the beans simmer. Cover loosely.

2   Cook, stirring occasionally, until the beans begin to become tender; add about 1 teaspoon salt per $1/2$ pound of beans, or to taste.

3   Continue to cook, stirring gently, until the beans are as tender as you like; add additional water if necessary. Drain and serve, or use in other recipes, or store covered, in their cooking liquid, in the refrigerator (3 days) or freezer (3 months).

Slightly Faster Beans: You can speed the cooking process a little bit by thinking ahead. Soak the beans for at least 6 hours in water to cover, drain, then cook in fresh water. Or boil the beans for 2 minutes in water to cover, then soak them for 2 hours in that water, drain, then cook in fresh water. Either of these techniques usually reduces cooking time by 25 to 50 percent, or 15 to 30 minutes.

The Basics of Pressure Cookers

New-model pressure cookers are easy to use and completely safe. They are not cheap, especially if you buy a large, heavy duty model—which can run upward of one hundred dollars—but a good one will last a lifetime. If you make a lot of soups, stews, whole grains, and/or beans, and you feel that you never have enough time, you should consider buying one. (Many people who live above five thousand feet find a pressure cooker especially useful, because the lower ambient air pressure decreases the temperature at which water boils and therefore increases cooking times.)

However, do not expect miracles. Most pressure-cooker advocates will tell you that by raising the pressure and therefore the boiling point of water (to about 250°F), pressure cooking cuts cooking times by two-thirds.

That has not been my experience. Browning time, or time spent sautéing aromatic vegetables such as onions, remains exactly the same. Estimates of pressure cooking times frequently dismiss the time it takes to bring the pot "up to pressure"—often as long as fifteen minutes. And time is needed to release the pressure as well. So although it's true that the pressure cooker is only operating under pressure for about five minutes to prepare white rice, the whole process takes more than twice that long. Given that it only takes twenty minutes with normal cookware, I'd say that this is an instance when the pressure cooker isn't worth it.

However, there are at least three instances in which it may be, and if you begin to use the pressure cooker regularly you may find more. Consider the pressure cooker when you are cooking:

- **Beans:** See Pressure-Cooked Beans, on the next page. I don't like canned beans much, but I don't always have precooked beans in the freezer, and there's not always time to make them the normal way. The pressure cooker takes care of most beans, without presoaking, in fifteen to twenty minutes—not bad. You can use virtually any recipe using dried beans in the pressure cooker; just don't fill the pot more than half full, because very "foamy" beans can clog the relief valve.
- **Whole grains:** See Pressure-Cooked Tough Grains, page 181. Most people don't cook brown rice, whole barley, wheat, or rye, that often, but if you do, you'll think the pressure cooker is a godsend.
- **Soups and stews:** I don't find the pressure cooker worth it for most soups and stews, because—as I said earlier—the preparation time and initial browning of meat or sautéing of vegetables remains the same, and after that all you're doing is simmering anyway; the cooking itself is largely unattended. With the pressure cooker, the cooking goes faster, but you have to pay much more attention, especially if you want some control over the texture of the finished dish. If you overcook in a pressure cooker, you may wind up with mush, and to check the progress of anything, you must first reduce the pressure. If it isn't done, you must relock the lid and then bring the pot back up to pressure.

Having said all of that, almost any soup or stew can be made in the pressure cooker, with cooking times of about half that of normal (again, this discounts initial browning and bringing the pot up to pressure). So a two-hour pot roast will take about one hour to cook under pressure.

General guidelines for using the pressure cooker:

- Sauté vegetables or brown meats in the pressure cooker, using it as you would any other pot, before adding liquid.
- When making a soup, stew, or other dish that combines tough meat with vegetables, you must cook in two stages. First deal with the meat, cooking it under pressure until it is nearly done. Then add the vegetables during the final five to ten minutes of cooking; if you add them at the beginning they will turn to mush before the meat is tender.
- Generally, you'll reduce the amount of liquid used in conventional recipes, because there is little evaporation. But every pressure cooker has a minimum amount of liquid needed in order to create the proper amount of pressure. For this and other details particular to the pressure cooker you're using, refer to the owner's manual (most of these are pretty good).

Pressure-Cooked Beans

Makes 4 servings

Time: About 30 minutes

There are three disadvantages to cooking beans in a pressure cooker:

1. As with all pressure cooking, the timing is imprecise; this means you must open the device and check the progress, usually two or three times.
2. Pressure-cooked beans sometimes disintegrate completely. This is great if you're making soup, but it isn't always desirable.

3. Some beans, especially limas, chickpeas, and favas, create a great deal of foam when cooked. If they're crowded into a pressure cooker, this foam can jam the valve and cause problems. As long as you don't fill the pressure cooker more than half full, you need not worry about this.

None of these problems can take away from the fact that you cannot beat the pressure cooker for speed; it's really the only way to cook most dried beans in less than an hour, and usually in less than half that time, presoaked or not.

Don't bother to use the pressure cooker for very fast-cooking beans, such as lentils or split peas, which are done in about five minutes and may be overdone in six. Usually, you'll have the thirty to forty minutes it takes to cook these conventionally.

1½ cups dried beans, any type except lentils or split peas, washed and picked over (see The Basics of Buying and Preparing Beans, page 500)
6 cups water, plus more if necessary
1 tablespoon any oil
1 teaspoon salt

1 Combine all ingredients in a pressure cooker and lock on the lid. Turn the heat to high.

2 Bring to high pressure, then adjust the heat so that it is just high enough to maintain pressure. Cook 10 to 25 minutes (the shorter time for small or quite fresh beans, the longer for larger or very dry beans).

3 Cool the pressure cooker by running cold water over the top. When the pressure is down, carefully remove the top and taste a bean. If it is done, store the beans in their liquid or drain and serve, or use in any recipe for cooked beans. If the beans are tender but not quite soft, add more water if necessary, and cook without the lid for a few minutes. If they are not yet tender, repeat Steps 1 and 2, cooking for 5 to 10 minutes at a time.

Buttered Beans

Makes 4 servings

Time: 15 minutes with precooked beans

Once cooked, beans are easy to dress up. You can, of course, simply reheat them with no further adornment. But more delicate beans, such as navy beans, are best reheated with some butter and parsley (or pureed, as in the following recipe).

2 tablespoons butter, or to taste
About 4 cups drained cooked or canned navy
  or other white beans

½ cup bean cooking liquid, or chicken, beef,
  or vegetable stock, or water (see "Soups"
  for stock recipes)
Salt and freshly ground black pepper to taste
Minced fresh parsley leaves for garnish

1 Place the butter in a large skillet and turn the heat to medium. When the butter melts, turn the heat up to medium-high and add the beans and the liquid.

2 Cook, stirring, for about 5 minutes. Mash some of the beans with a fork or potato masher if you would like a creamier mixture. Season with salt and pepper, garnish, and serve.

Beans with Olive Oil: Best with pink, red, black, or other dark beans. Use olive oil in Step 1. When it is hot, add 1 tablespoon slivered garlic or ½ cup minced onion or scallion. Cook, stirring, over medium-low heat until tender but not brown, 5 to 8 minutes. Add the beans and the liquid and finish as above.

Eight Simple Additions to Basic Beans

Different beans take different flavorings, but you can use all of these suggestions with almost any dried bean.

1. Cook with bay leaf, a couple of cloves, some peppercorns, thyme sprigs, parsley leaves and/or stems, chili powder, or other herbs and spices. Be sure to remove the bay leaf before serving.
2. Cook an unpeeled onion, a carrot, a celery stalk, and/or three or four cloves of garlic.
3. Reheat with soy, Worcestershire, or Tabasco sauce, or with a tablespoon or two of miso thinned with hot bean cooking liquid.
4. Reheat with onions or other aromatic vegetables.
5. Reheat with chopped leafy greens, such as kale or collards.
6. Cook in chicken, beef, or vegetable stock, or reheat in stock (see "Soups" for stock recipes).
7. Add peeled, seeded, and chopped tomatoes as you reheat.
8. Cook a few slices of diced bacon (or pancetta) until crisp; remove, then reheat the beans in the rendered bacon fat. Garnish with the bacon.

White Bean Puree

Makes 4 servings

Time: 10 minutes with precooked beans

Not only a fine substitute for mashed potatoes, but an unexpected, even elegant side dish for any braised meat.

About 3 cups drained cooked or canned navy or
  other white beans
1 cup bean cooking liquid, or chicken, beef,
  or vegetable stock, or water (see "Soups"
  for stock recipes)
3 tablespoons butter
Salt and freshly ground black pepper to taste
Minced fresh parsley leaves for garnish

1 Puree the beans by putting them through a food mill or using a blender; add as much liquid as you need to make a smooth but not watery puree.

2 Place in a microwave-proof dish or medium non-stick saucepan along with the butter. Heat gently until the butter melts and the beans are hot; season with salt and pepper.

3 Garnish and serve very hot.

Pureed Beans with Cream: Cook the beans with a sprig of fresh summer savory or chervil, or a teaspoon of dried. Puree them with about $1/2$ cup heavy cream instead of bean cooking liquid or stock. Reheat very gently, using only 1 tablespoon butter. Garnish as above.

Garlicky Pureed Beans: Puree the beans, while still hot, with 1 teaspoon minced garlic and a few fresh rosemary leaves, or $1/2$ teaspoon dried rosemary. Reheat with butter or olive oil. Garnish as above.

White Beans, Tuscan-Style

Makes 4 servings

Time: 1 to 2 hours, largely unattended

The classic, simple, and always delicious beans of Tuscany. Great olive oil makes a big difference here. Add some cooked sausage and sautéed red bell peppers to make this into a simple main course.

> About $1/2$ pound dried white beans: cannellini, navy, Great Northern, etc., washed and picked over (see The Basics of Buying and Preparing Beans, page 500)
> 20 fresh sage leaves or 1 tablespoon dried sage
> Salt and freshly ground black pepper to taste
> 2 teaspoons minced garlic
> 2 tablespoons extra-virgin olive oil

1 Place the beans in a pot with water to cover. Turn the heat to high and bring to a boil. Add the sage; adjust the heat so the beans simmer. Cover loosely.

2 Cook, stirring occasionally, until the beans begin to soften; add about $1/2$ teaspoon salt and some pepper. Continue to cook until the beans are very tender; add additional water if the beans dry out.

3 Drain the cooking liquid if necessary, then add the garlic, along with some more salt and pepper if necessary. Stir in the olive oil and serve.

Flageolets, French-Style

Makes 4 servings

Time: 1 to 2 hours, largely unattended

A luxury preparation for a luxury bean. If you can get your hands on some crème fraîche (or make your own, page 671), it will be even better.

> $1/2$ pound dried flageolets, washed and picked over (see The Basics of Buying and Preparing Beans, page 500)
> 1 medium onion, unpeeled
> 1 bay leaf
> 1 clove
> 1 carrot, peeled and cut into chunks
> 4 sprigs fresh thyme or $1/2$ teaspoon dried thyme
> Salt and freshly ground black pepper to taste
> 2 tablespoons butter
> 1 tablespoon minced shallot
> 1 cup heavy cream, preferably not ultra-pasteurized
> Minced fresh parsley leaves for garnish

1 Place the beans in a large pot with water to cover. Turn the heat to high and bring to a boil.

2 Cut a slit in the onion and insert the bay leaf; insert the clove into the onion as well and put the onion in the pot. Add the carrot and thyme. Turn the heat down so the beans simmer. Cover loosely.

3 When the beans begin to soften, after about 30 minutes, season with salt and pepper. Continue to cook, stirring occasionally, until the beans are tender but still intact, about 45 minutes; add additional water if necessary.

4 Drain the beans and discard the onion and carrot. Place the butter and shallot in a deep skillet large enough to hold the beans. Turn the heat to medium and cook, stirring occasionally, until the shallot softens, about 5 minutes. Add the cream and the beans and continue to cook, stirring, until the beans are hot and have absorbed some of the cream, about 10 minutes. Check the seasoning, garnish, and serve.

Beans and Greens

Makes 4 servings

Time: 1 to 2 hours, largely unattended

Best with white beans, whether small or large. Cook them until they are just about falling apart; these should be very creamy.

$^1\!/_2$ pound dried white beans, washed and picked over (see The Basics of Buying and Preparing Beans, page 500)

1 medium onion, unpeeled

1 bay leaf

1 clove

Salt and freshly ground black pepper to taste

$1^1\!/_2$ pounds dark greens, such as kale, collards, mustard, or broccoli raab, well washed and roughly chopped

1 tablespoon minced garlic

4 teaspoons extra-virgin olive oil

1 Place the beans in a large pot with water to cover. Turn the heat to high and bring to a boil.

2 Cut a slit in the onion and insert the bay leaf; insert the clove into the onion as well and put the onion in the pot. Turn the heat down so the beans simmer. Cover loosely.

3 When the beans begin to soften, after about 30 minutes, season with salt and pepper. Continue to cook, stirring occasionally, until the beans are tender but still intact, about 1 hour; add additional water if necessary.

4 Add the greens to the pot and continue to cook until they are tender, 10 to 30 minutes, depending on the thickness of the stems. If you want a soupy mixture, add more water.

5 Remove the onion. Season the stew with additional salt and pepper. About 3 minutes before serving, add the garlic and stir. Spoon the beans and greens into individual bowls and drizzle with olive oil (or see the variation, below). Serve immediately.

Beans and Greens Gratin: Cook as above. When you're done, stir in 1 tablespoon olive oil and spread the mixture in a lightly oiled baking dish. Preheat the broiler. Top the mixture with 1 cup bread crumbs (preferably fresh, page 239). Drizzle with more olive oil to taste. Run under the broiler, about 4 to 6 inches from the heat source, until lightly browned, about 5 minutes. Serve hot or at room temperature.

Mashed Favas with Greens

Makes 4 servings

Time: About 1 hour

A Mediterranean classic that takes a little work but is worth it. Even better if you add about one-half cup minced prosciutto, prosciutto rind, or pancetta to the beans as they cook.

½ pound dried, peeled, and split fava beans, washed
and picked over (see The Basics of Buying and
Preparing Beans, page 500)
Salt and freshly ground black pepper to taste
1 pound greens, such as dandelion, escarole,
collards, kale, spinach, or mustard, well washed
⅓ cup olive oil
1 teaspoon minced garlic

1 Place the beans in a large pot with water to
cover. Turn the heat to high and bring to a boil.

2 Turn the heat down so the beans simmer. Cover
loosely. When the beans begin to soften, after about
30 minutes, season with salt and pepper. Continue to
cook, stirring occasionally, until the beans are very
soft, about 1 hour; add additional water if necessary.

3 Meanwhile, cook the greens in boiling salted
water to cover until tender; depending on the green,
this will take from 1 minute (spinach) to 20 or
30 minutes (collards).

4 When the greens are done, drain them and,
when they are cool enough to handle, squeeze them
dry. Chop them coarsely.

5 Place half the oil in a large skillet and turn the
heat to medium-low. Add the garlic and cook, stirring
occasionally, just until it colors, about 5 minutes. Toss
in the greens and stir to combine.

6 When the favas are done, drain them. Mash
them with a potato masher or wooden spoon, or put
them through a ricer or food mill.

7 Combine the favas and greens. Adjust seasoning,
then drizzle with the remaining olive oil and serve.

Sautéed Beans and Tomatoes

Makes 4 servings

Time: 20 minutes with precooked beans

An elegant side dish which is even better if you use
chicken stock to cook the dried beans.

2 tablespoons butter (preferred) or extra-virgin olive oil
1 tablespoon minced shallot or scallion
1 teaspoon fresh thyme leaves or ½ teaspoon
dried thyme
2 cups peeled, seeded, and diced tomatoes (canned
are fine; drain them first)
4 cups drained cooked or canned white beans
½ cup chicken, beef, or vegetable stock, juice from
canned tomatoes, or water (see "Soups" for stock
recipes)
Salt and freshly ground black pepper to taste

1 Place the butter or oil in a large, deep skillet and
turn the heat to medium. A minute later, add the shallot and cook, stirring, until it softens, 3 to 5 minutes.
Add the thyme and cook for about 30 seconds.

2 Add the tomatoes and cook, stirring occasionally,
until they break up and become "saucy," about 10 minutes. Then add the beans and stock and turn the heat
to medium-high. Cook, stirring, until the mixture is
hot and creamy, about 5 minutes. Season and serve.

Twice-Cooked ("Refried") Beans with Cumin

Makes 4 servings

Time: 20 minutes with precooked beans

The traditional medium for frying beans is lard, and
with good reason; it's delicious. But you can also make
wonderful refried beans with oil.

¼ cup canola or other neutral oil
1 cup chopped onion
1 tablespoon ground cumin, plus more if desired
3 to 4 cups drained cooked or canned kidney or
other red beans
Salt and freshly ground black pepper to taste
¼ teaspoon cayenne, plus more if desired

1 Place the oil in a large skillet, preferably non-stick, and turn the heat to medium. When the oil is hot, add the onion and cook, stirring, until it is golden brown, about 10 minutes.

2 Add the cumin and cook, stirring, 1 minute more. Add the beans and mash with a large fork or potato masher. Continue to cook and mash, stirring, until the beans are more or less broken up (some remaining chunks are fine).

3 Season with salt and pepper, add the cayenne and more cumin if you like, and serve.

Traditional Refried Beans: Substitute $^1/_2$ cup lard for the oil and reserve the onion and cumin. Add the beans to the hot lard. When they are nicely mashed, stir in the onion and cumin and cook for 5 minutes more, stirring frequently. Season as above and serve.

Black Beans with Cumin or Chili

Makes 4 to 8 servings

Time: $1^1/_2$ to 2 hours, largely unattended

Earthy, full-flavored black beans are at their best when highly seasoned. Remember that older black beans can take forever to cook (or so it seems).

1 pound black beans, washed and picked over (see The
  Basics of Buying and Preparing Beans, page 500)
2 bay leaves
4 cloves garlic
2 tablespoons ground cumin or chili powder
A few sprigs thyme or $^1/_2$ teaspoon dried thyme
Salt and freshly ground black pepper to taste
1 medium onion, minced

1 Place the beans in a large pot with water to cover. Turn the heat to high and bring to a boil.

2 Add the bay leaves; crush and peel 2 garlic cloves and add them too. Add the cumin or chili powder and thyme. Turn the heat down so the beans simmer and cover loosely.

3 When the beans begin to soften, season with salt and pepper. Continue to cook, stirring occasionally, until the beans are very tender, at least 1 hour; add additional water if necessary.

4 Mince the remaining garlic and add it to the pot along with the onion. Cook 5 to 10 minutes longer and season with additional salt, pepper, and cumin or chili powder. Remove and discard the bay leaves. Serve with rice.

Bean and Tomato Casserole

Makes 4 to 6 servings

Time: 30 minutes with precooked beans

This is suitable as a main course. To make it even more so, add other vegetables, such as potatoes or cut-up greens; adjust the cooking time accordingly.

1 tablespoon chili powder, plus more to taste
  if desired
6 cups drained cooked or canned beans, any type
  or a mixture
Salt and freshly ground black pepper to taste
2 tablespoons minced fresh savory, marjoram, or
  oregano leaves or about 20 fresh basil leaves, torn
4 medium-large tomatoes, sliced
2 large onions, sliced
1 cup grated Jack or Cheddar cheese

1 Preheat the oven to 400°F. Stir the chili powder into the beans; taste and add more if you like.

2 In a baking dish or casserole, place a layer of beans; season with salt and pepper, and sprinkle with a little of the herb. Add a layer of tomatoes, one of onions, and a sprinkling of cheese. Repeat until all the ingredients are used up, finishing with a fairly thick layer of cheese.

3 Bake until the casserole is hot and the cheese melted and bubbly, about 20 minutes. Serve hot.

Bean Casserole with Hominy and Tortillas: Substitute 2 cups cooked hominy (use canned, or see Basic Hominy, page 193) for 2 cups of the beans. Integrate a layer of corn tortillas into the mixture; place 1 or 2 tortillas on top of the bean-hominy mixture before topping with tomatoes, onions, and cheese. Bake as above.

Red Beans with Meat

Makes 6 to 8 servings

Time: About 2 hours, largely unattended

Don't turn this into a bean-flavored meat dish, because it should be the other way around; the meat is the seasoning.

2 cups kidney, pinto, or other beans, washed and picked over

1 or 2 meaty smoked ham hock(s), 1 chunk of bacon or salt pork, or 1 meaty ham bone

1/2 pound sweet Italian or spicy Cajun sausage

1 large onion, chopped

1 bell pepper, stemmed, seeded, and chopped

1 tablespoon minced garlic

4 or 5 sprigs thyme or 1 teaspoon dried thyme

2 bay leaves

1/4 teaspoon ground allspice

1 cup chopped tomatoes (canned are fine; don't bother to drain)

Salt and freshly ground black pepper to taste

Minced fresh parsley or cilantro leaves for garnish

Tabasco sauce (optional)

1 Place the beans in a large pot with water to cover. Turn the heat to high and bring to a boil; skim the foam if necessary. Add the ham hock(s) and turn the heat down so the beans simmer. Cover loosely and stir very occasionally; add additional water if necessary.

2 Place the sausage in a large skillet and turn the heat to medium. Cook, turning occasionally and pricking the sausage a few times to release its fat. When the sausage is nicely browned, remove it; don't worry about whether it is done. Cut it into small chunks.

3 Cook the onion, pepper, and garlic in the sausage fat, stirring frequently, until the pepper is softened, about 10 minutes. Remove with a slotted spoon. Return the sausage to the skillet and cook, turning occasionally, until the chunks are browned all over. Return the vegetables to the pan, along with the thyme, bay leaves, allspice, and tomatoes. Turn the heat to medium-low and cook, stirring, until the tomatoes break up, 10 to 15 minutes.

4 When the meat in the beans is very soft, remove it. When it is cool enough to handle, chop all the meat and return it to the pot, along with the sausage and vegetable mixture. Cook, until the beans are very tender. Remove and discard the bay leaves. Taste and add salt and pepper if necessary. Garnish and serve, passing Tabasco or other hot sauce at the table.

Vegetarian Red Beans: Obviously, omit the meat. Start the beans as above. Double the amounts of onion and pepper and add 2 chopped celery stalks. Cook the garlic and vegetables over medium heat in 2 tablespoons olive or other oil until softened, about 10 minutes. Add the thyme, bay leaves, allspice; or use 1 tablespoon chili powder, or to taste. Then add 2 cups chopped tomatoes and cook as above. Pour this mixture into the beans and adjust the seasoning as necessary. Garnish and serve, passing Tabasco at the table.

Black Beans with Crisp Pork and Orange

Makes 8 servings

Time: About 30 minutes with precooked beans

This is a liberal adaptation of the Brazilian feijoada, in which black beans are simmered with loads of meat—beef tongue and brisket, pork sausage, and pig's feet, plus—usually—a little salt pork thrown in for good measure. That dish, noble as it is, just doesn't appeal to that many people. This one, however, is more moderate, simpler, and equally tasty. If you are looking for a dish that is more "meat with beans" than "beans with meat," see Cassoulet, page 493.

8 cups drained cooked or canned black beans
2 cups bean cooking liquid, or chicken, beef, or veg-
    etable stock, or water (see "Soups" for stock recipes)
1 tablespoon ground cumin
Salt and freshly ground black pepper to taste
1 orange, well washed
1 pound Italian or other sausage, cut into 1-inch chunks
1 pound or more not-too-lean boneless pork (preferably
    from the shoulder), cut into 1-inch chunks
2 large onions, chopped
2 bell peppers, preferably red or yellow, stemmed,
    peeled if desired, seeded, and chopped
2 tablespoons minced garlic
1 cup dry red wine
$1/2$ cup orange juice, preferably freshly squeezed
Minced cilantro or fresh parsley leaves for garnish

1 Warm the beans in a large pot with the liquid; add the cumin, salt, and pepper. Peel the orange. Add the peel to the beans and section the flesh; set aside.

2 Turn the heat to medium under a large skillet. A minute later, add the sausage. Cook, turning occasionally, until browned on all sides; don't worry about it cooking through. Add to the beans.

3 Cook the pork bits in the same skillet, turning occasionally, until browned on all sides. Add to the beans.

4 Pour off all but about 3 tablespoons fat from the skillet. Add the onions and peppers and cook over medium heat, stirring occasionally, until the peppers soften, 8 to 10 minutes. Add the garlic and cook, stirring, 1 minute more. Add to the beans.

5 Turn the heat to high and add the red wine to the skillet. Cook, stirring and scraping to loosen any brown bits stuck to the bottom of the pan, until the wine is reduced by about half, about 5 minutes. Add to the beans, along with the orange juice. Taste the beans and season as necessary. Serve with rice, garnished with the reserved orange and some cilantro.

Black-Eyed Peas, Southern-Style

Makes 4 servings

Time: At least 2 hours, largely unattended

In the South, these beans are traditionally served on New Year's Day, for good luck. (The ham hock brings wealth, the greens health.) If you like, just add some chopped collards to the pot, right from the start. In this dish the greens are traditionally cooked until very soft—"to death," as some of my southern friends say.

2 cups black-eyed or pigeon peas, washed and
    picked over (see The Basics of Buying and
    Preparing Beans, page 500)
3 or 4 meaty smoked ham hocks or a meaty ham
    bone
2 large onions, chopped
Salt and freshly ground black pepper to taste
About $1/2$ teaspoon freshly ground black pepper
Red or white wine vinegar to taste
Tabasco sauce (optional)

1 Place the peas in a large pot with water to cover. Turn the heat to high and bring to a boil; skim the foam if necessary. Add the ham hocks, onions, and about $1/2$ teaspoon pepper. Turn the heat down so the beans simmer. Cover loosely and stir very occasionally; add additional water if necessary.

2 When the meat in the beans is very soft—at least an hour and a half later—remove it. When it is cool enough to handle, chop all the meat and return it to the pot, along with some salt if necessary.

3 Continue to cook until the beans are very tender. Drain if necessary and season with salt, pepper, vinegar, and Tabasco or other hot sauce. Serve hot or at room temperature.

The Basics of Rice and Beans

Rice and beans are one of the most important of all culinary marriages. They are cheap, they provide good protein and plenty of carbohydrates, and they don't take a lot of work to make them delicious. You don't need a recipe: Take any well-seasoned bean dish and serve it with any well-prepared rice. But here are a few examples of slightly more elaborate, traditional preparations.

Moors and Christians
Black Beans and Rice, Spanish-Style
Makes 4 to 6 servings

Time: 30 minutes with precooked beans

The Muslim Moors ruled devoutly Christian Spain for seven centuries; what else should the world's best-known bicolor dish be called?

2 tablespoons extra-virgin olive oil
1 medium onion, finely chopped
1 red or yellow bell pepper, stemmed, peeled if desired, and chopped
Salt and freshly ground black pepper to taste
1 tablespoon minced garlic
3 cups drained cooked or canned black beans
1 cup chopped tomatoes (canned are fine; don't bother to drain), optional
1 cup bean cooking liquid, or chicken, beef, or vegetable stock, or water (see "Soups" for stock recipes)
$1/2$ cup minced fresh parsley leaves
Rice Pilaf (page 202), or any of its variations

1 Place the oil in a large, deep skillet and turn the heat to medium. A minute later, add the onion and bell pepper. Season with salt and pepper and cook, stirring, until the pepper is soft, 8 to 10 minutes. Stir in the garlic, the beans, the optional tomatoes, and the liquid.

2 Turn the heat to medium-high and cook, stirring, until the beans are hot and most of the liquid is evaporated, 10 to 20 minutes. Stir in most of the parsley.

3 Arrange the pilaf on a platter, in a ring if you like. Spoon the beans over the rice or into the center of the ring, or pass them separately. Garnish with the remaining parsley and serve.

Hoppin' John
Makes 4 to 6 servings

Time: $1^1/2$ to 2 hours, largely unattended

Bacon, peas, and rice—southern staples—comprise Hoppin' John, our best indigenous rice and bean dish.

1 cup black-eyed or other dried peas, washed and
    picked over (see The Basics of Buying and
    Preparing Beans, page 500)
1/4 pound slab bacon or 1 smoked ham hock
1 large onion, chopped
1 (4-inch) sprig fresh rosemary, 2 sprigs fresh thyme,
    or 1/2 teaspoon dried rosemary or thyme
Salt and freshly ground black pepper to taste
1 1/2 cups long-grain rice

1 Place the peas in a medium pot with the bacon
or ham hock, onion, herb, and water to cover by at
least 2 inches. Bring to a boil over medium-high heat.

2 Turn the heat down to medium and cook, skim-
ming any foam that arises, until the peas are tender,
1 to 1 1/2 hours. Remove the meat and reduce the
liquid to about 3 cups; as the liquid is reducing, cut
the meat into chunks, removing extremely fatty pieces
if you like. Return it to the pot.

3 Taste the cooking liquid and add salt and more
pepper if needed. Remove the rosemary or thyme sprigs,
if used. Stir in the rice and cook, covered, until the rice
is done and the liquid is absorbed, 15 to 20 minutes.
This can sit for 15 to 20 minutes before serving.

Red Beans and Rice

Makes 4 to 6 servings

Time: About 30 minutes with precooked beans

You can make this with or without meat. But please
use coconut milk—it makes a difference.

3 cups Red Beans with Meat (page 513) or
    Vegetarian Red Beans (page 513)
1 1/2 cups long-grain rice
3 cups canned or Fresh Coconut Milk (page 291), warmed
Salt and freshly ground black pepper to taste
Minced fresh parsley leaves for garnish

1 Place the beans in a saucepan that can hold at
least double their bulk comfortably. Turn the heat to
medium-low and warm gently. If there is a great deal
of liquid in the beans, cook them, stirring frequently,
until they are moist but not swimming in liquid.

2 Add the rice and the coconut milk to the beans.
Cover and turn the heat to low. Cook for about
20 minutes, or until the rice is tender and the liquid
is absorbed. If necessary, uncover and raise the heat to
medium-high; cook, stirring, until the liquid is
absorbed. Season with salt and pepper, garnish, and
serve.

Lentils and Rice with Caramelized Onions

Makes 4 servings

Time: About 45 minutes

This Middle Eastern staple is one of my favorite lunch
dishes, a vegetarian one-pot meal that is easy, highly
seasoned, and a nice break from sandwiches and pasta.
Omit the caramelized onions if you like, but you
should try them at least once; they are a sensational
garnish.

3 tablespoons olive oil
1 medium onion, chopped, plus 1 large or 2 medium
    onions, halved and sliced
1 teaspoon minced garlic
1 teaspoon ground cumin
Salt and freshly ground black pepper to taste
2 cups lentils, washed and picked over (see The
    Basics of Buying and Preparing Beans, page 500)
About 6 cups chicken, beef, or vegetable stock, or
    water, warmed (see "Soups" for stock recipes)
1 cup long- or short-grain rice
Minced fresh parsley leaves for garnish

1. Place 1 tablespoon of the oil in a large, deep saucepan and turn the heat to medium. A minute later, add the chopped onion and cook until it begins to become tender, about 5 minutes. Add the garlic, cumin, salt, and pepper, and cook 3 minutes more. Add the lentils, stir, and add about 4 cups liquid.

2. Cook, stirring occasionally, until the lentils begin to soften, about 20 minutes. Add enough of the remaining stock or water so that the lentils are covered by about an inch of liquid. Stir in the rice. Cover and turn the heat to low.

3. Meanwhile, place the remaining oil in a medium skillet and turn the heat to medium-high. Cook the onion slices, stirring frequently, until they are dark brown but not burned, about 15 minutes. Scoop out the onions and let them drain on paper towels while you finish cooking the lentils and rice.

4. Check the rice and lentils after 20 minutes. When both are tender and the liquid is absorbed, the dish is ready. If the lentils and rice are not tender, add more liquid, cover, and cook for a few more minutes. If, on the contrary, the rice and lentils are soft and there is much liquid remaining, raise the heat a bit and cook, uncovered, stirring, until it evaporates.

5. Serve the rice and lentils, garnished with the caramelized onions and parsley.

Warm Lentils with Bacon

Makes 4 servings

Time: About 45 minutes

This dish is largely dependent on bacon for its flavor, so use the best you can find. It's also good with kidney or other red beans; cook them as in Basic Beans (page 505) until nearly tender, then drain before adding them to the onion mixture.

1 tablespoon olive or other oil
1/4 pound slab bacon, more or less, cut into small cubes
1 medium onion, chopped
1 carrot, peeled and diced
1 teaspoon minced garlic
3 to 4 cups chicken, beef, or vegetable stock, or water; or use 1/2 water and 1/2 red wine (see "Soups" for stock recipes)
2 cups lentils, washed and picked over (see The Basics of Buying and Preparing Beans, page 500)
Salt and freshly ground black pepper to taste
1 bay leaf
2 or 3 sprigs fresh thyme or 1/2 teaspoon dried thyme
About 1 teaspoon red wine vinegar, or to taste
Minced fresh parsley leaves for garnish

1. Place the oil in a medium saucepan and turn the heat to medium. Cook the bacon in the oil, stirring occasionally, until nicely browned, about 10 minutes. Remove the bacon with a slotted spoon and set aside, leaving the fat in the pot.

2. Cook the onion and carrot in the rendered fat over medium heat until the onion softens, about 5 minutes. Stir in the garlic and cook for 1 minute. Add 3 cups of liquid and bring to a boil over medium-high heat. Stir in the lentils, salt and pepper, and the bay leaf and thyme.

3. Cover partially and cook over medium-low heat, stirring occasionally, until the lentils are nice and tender, 30 minutes or more; add additional liquid as needed, but don't let the mixture become too soupy.

4. When the lentils are soft, raise the heat and boil off any excess liquid if necessary. Stir in about 1 teaspoon vinegar; taste and add more if necessary. Remove and discard bay leaf. Stir in the reserved bacon just before serving, then garnish and serve.

Baked Beans

Makes 4 servings

Time: At least 4 hours, largely unattended

These are traditional baked beans and as such are fairly minimalist. But changes are easily made; see Five Simple Ideas for Baked Beans, below.

1 pound navy, pea, or other white beans
$^1/_2$ pound salt pork or salty slab bacon (optional)
$^1/_2$ cup molasses, or to taste
2 teaspoons ground mustard or 2 tablespoons
    prepared mustard, or to taste
Salt and freshly ground black pepper to taste

1 Cook the beans as in Basic Beans (page 505), but only until they begin to become tender, about 30 minutes.

2 Preheat the oven to 300°F. Cube or slice the salt pork or bacon and place it in the bottom of a bean pot or other deep-sided ovenproof covered pot, such as a Dutch oven. Drain the beans, then mix them with the molasses and mustard. Pour them over the meat. Gently add enough boiling water to cover the beans by about an inch.

3 Bake, uncovered, for about 3 hours, checking occasionally and adding more water if necessary. At the end of 3 hours, taste and adjust seasoning; you may add more salt, sweetener, or mustard.

4 When the beans are very tender, scoop the meat up from the bottom and lay it on top of the beans; raise the heat to 400°. Cook until the pork browns a bit and the beans are very bubbly, about 10 minutes. (You may repeat this process several times, scooping the meat to the top and browning it; each repetition darkens the color of the dish and adds flavor.) Serve hot.

Vegetarian Baked Beans: Substitute 2 tablespoons butter or neutral oil (such as canola) and 1 large or 2 medium onions, quartered, for the meat. Add 2 cups peeled, seeded, and chopped tomatoes (canned are fine; don't bother to drain) along with the molasses and mustard. Cook as above.

Five Simple Ideas for Baked Beans

1. Add ketchup (essentially another sweetener, since it is mostly corn syrup) to taste or substitute sugar or maple syrup (or a combination) for the molasses.
2. Add Worcestershire, soy, or Tabasco sauce to taste.
3. Add an onion or two, quartered, and/or a few chunks of peeled carrots.
4. Substitute sausage, cut into chunks, for the salt pork or bacon.
5. Use pinto, kidney, or lima beans.

Roasted Chickpeas

Makes 4 servings

Time: Less than 30 minutes with precooked chickpeas

When you cook chickpeas—either on top of the stove or in the oven—they become crisp outside and tender inside. These are not only a great side dish, but a wonderful finger food.

3 tablespoons olive or other oil
2 cups well-drained cooked or canned chickpeas
1 tablespoon minced garlic
Salt and freshly ground black pepper to taste

1 Preheat the oven to 400°F. Place the oil in a large ovenproof skillet or roasting pan large enough to hold the chickpeas in one layer and turn the heat to medium.

2 A minute later, add the chickpeas, garlic, salt, and pepper. Shake the pan so that all the chickpeas are well coated with oil and are sitting in one layer. Place the skillet or pan in the oven.

3 Cook, shaking the pan occasionally, until the chickpeas begin to brown, about 15 or 20 minutes. Remove from the oven and cool slightly. If desired, sprinkle with chili powder, All-Purpose Curry Powder (page 778), or other spice mixture (page 777); or with more salt and pepper; or simply with a little extra-virgin olive oil and some freshly squeezed lemon juice. Serve hot or at room temperature.

Stewed Chickpeas with Chicken

Makes 4 servings

Time: About 45 minutes with precooked chickpeas

You can make this dish without the chicken—chickpeas with seasoned tomatoes are wonderful by themselves—or substitute vegetables for it, as in the variation.

4 cups drained cooked or canned chickpeas
2 cups bean cooking liquid, or chicken, beef, or vegetable stock, or water (see "Soups" for stock recipes)
Salt and freshly ground black pepper to taste
1 tablespoon canola or other neutral oil
2 to 3 pounds chicken parts, preferably leg-thigh pieces separated at the joint, rinsed and well dried, skin removed if desired
1 large onion, chopped
1 celery stalk, chopped
1 carrot, peeled and chopped
1 tablespoon minced garlic
1 teaspoon peeled and minced fresh ginger
$^1/_2$ teaspoon ground coriander
1 teaspoon ground cumin
2 cups peeled, seeded, and chopped tomatoes (canned are fine; don't bother to drain)
Minced cilantro or fresh parsley leaves for garnish

1 Preheat the oven to 400°F. Warm the beans in a large pot with the liquid; add salt and pepper. Turn the heat so that the mixture bubbles very slowly.

2 Place the oil in a large, deep skillet and turn the heat to medium-high. Brown the chicken well on all sides for a total of about 15 minutes; season with salt and pepper, transfer the chicken to a roasting pan, and place in the oven.

3 Pour off all but 3 tablespoons of the fat remaining in the skillet. Turn the heat to medium and add the onion, celery, and carrot. Cook, stirring occasionally, until the vegetables are softened, about 10 minutes. Add the garlic, ginger, coriander, cumin, and tomatoes, and cook for 5 minutes more, stirring occasionally and scraping the bottom of the pan to loosen any brown bits. Add the mixture to the simmering beans.

4 When the chicken has cooked for about 15 minutes, check for doneness (the juices will run clear if you make a small cut in the meat near the bone). When it is ready, remove it from the oven. When the vegetables are tender, place the chickpeas and the vegetables on a large, deep platter; top with the chicken, garnish, and serve.

Stewed Chickpeas with Vegetables: Omit the chicken. In Step 2, sauté 3 cups cubed, salted eggplant (page 568) or zucchini in 4 tablespoons of olive oil, until tender, 15 to 30 minutes. Remove and proceed to Step 3. Combine chickpeas and their seasonings with the eggplant and/or zucchini and roast for about 10 minutes, or until the mixture is bubbly and its top begins to brown. Garnish and serve.

Chili non Carne

Makes 4 servings

Time: About 2 hours, largely unattended

Chili can be quite simple, or more complicated. Although some chili purists insist that chili should be made with meat and no beans, I like bean-based chili. All chili contains chili powder or, even more basic, a combination of ground chiles, cumin, and oregano.

> 2 cups pinto, kidney, or other beans, washed and picked over (see The Basics of Buying and Preparing Beans, page 500)
> 1 whole onion, unpeeled, plus 1 small onion, minced
> Salt and freshly ground black pepper to taste
> 1 cup bean cooking liquid or chicken, beef, or vegetable stock, or water (see "Soups" for stock recipes)
> 1 fresh or dried hot chile, seeded, stemmed, and minced, or to taste (optional)
> 1 teaspoon ground cumin, or to taste (optional)
> 1 teaspoon minced fresh oregano leaves or $1/2$ teaspoon dried oregano (optional)
> 1 tablespoon chili powder (optional), if you prefer it to the combination of pepper, cumin, and oregano above
> 1 tablespoon minced garlic
> Minced cilantro leaves for garnish

1. Place the beans in a large pot with water to cover. Turn the heat to high and bring to a boil; skim the foam if necessary. Add the whole onion. Turn the heat down so the beans simmer and cover loosely.

2. When the beans begin to soften, season with salt and pepper. Continue to cook, stirring occasionally, until the beans are quite tender but still intact, 1 to 2 hours; add additional water if necessary.

3. Drain the beans, reserving the cooking liquid if you choose to use it. Discard the onion and add all the remaining ingredients except cilantro. Turn the heat to medium and bring to a boil. Cover and turn the heat to low.

4. Cook, stirring occasionally and adding more liquid if necessary, until the beans are very tender and the flavors have mellowed, about 15 minutes. Adjust seasoning as necessary and garnish with cilantro. Serve

with rice, crackers, or tortilla chips, and bottled hot sauce, such as Tabasco.

Chili with Tomatoes: Substitute 2 cups peeled, seeded, and chopped tomatoes (canned are fine; don't bother to drain) for the bean or other liquid. Add $1/4$ teaspoon ground cinnamon with the other spices. Cook carefully, adding a little bit more liquid if needed. Top with freshly grated Cheddar or jack cheese if you like.

Chili con Carne: While the beans are cooking, place 1 tablespoon canola or other neutral oil in a large skillet and turn the heat to medium. Add 1 pound hand-chopped or ground beef, pork, turkey, or chicken and cook, stirring, until the meat has lost its color. Season the meat with salt, pepper, and about 2 teaspoons chili powder, or to taste. Stir it into the beans along with the other ingredients. This variation can be combined with Chili with Tomatoes (the variation above) if you like.

The Basics of Bean Cakes

Pureed beans form the basis of cakes, fritters, croquettes, and other like items wherever beans are eaten. It makes sense, since mashed or pureed beans have almost the same texture as the batters used to make croquettes containing other items. Furthermore, they brown perfectly when subjected to oil. Make sure that any beans you use in making bean cakes are very well cooked; they should be so soft they almost puree themselves. Since flavor is not much of an issue here—you add so many flavorings to most croquette-like cakes—this is the perfect place for canned beans.

If you don't want to pan-fry bean cakes, there is an alternative: Heat the oven to 400°F. Shape the croquettes as in the following recipes and place them on a lightly oiled, non-stick baking sheet. Roast until lightly browned and cooked through, turning once, for a total of about twenty minutes. They will be lighter in flavor and somewhat more delicate than the pan-fried variety—not at all bad.

Simple Bean Croquettes

Makes 4 servings

Time: 20 minutes with precooked beans

The most basic of all bean cakes. Vary the seasoning as you like.

2 cups drained cooked or canned white or other
    beans, with a few tablespoons bean cooking liquid
    reserved (see Step 1)
$^1/_2$ cup minced onion
$^1/_4$ cup minced fresh parsley leaves
1 egg, lightly beaten
Salt and freshly ground black pepper to taste
About $^1/_2$ cup coarse cornmeal or bread crumbs
Peanut or other oil or bacon drippings as needed

1 If you want to serve the croquettes hot, preheat the oven to 200°F. Mash the beans by putting them through a food mill or into a blender or food processor. Use a little bean cooking liquid (or other liquid, such as water or stock) if the beans are too dry to mash. Do not puree; it's nice to leave a few bean chunks in this mixture.

2 Combine the beans with the onion, parsley, egg, salt, and pepper. Add cornmeal or bread crumbs by the tablespoon until you've made a batter that is barely stiff enough to handle. You want to be able to shape it with your hands without it sticking, but it should be quite fragile or the cakes will be dry.

3 Cover the bottom of a large, deep skillet with about $^1/_8$ inch of oil or bacon drippings; turn the heat to medium. Shape one fourth of the bean mixture

into a hamburger-shaped cake and place in the skillet. Repeat with the remaining batter.

4 Cook the croquettes until nicely browned on both sides, adjusting the heat so that they brown evenly without burning before turning, 3 to 5 minutes per side. Keep warm in the oven until ready to serve—for up to 30 minutes—or serve at room temperature.

Bean Croquettes with Southwestern Flavors: Substitute cilantro for the parsley. Add to the mix: $^1/_2$ teaspoon minced garlic; 1 jalapeño or other fresh hot or dried pepper, stemmed, seeded, and minced; 1 teaspoon ground cumin; 1 tablespoon tomato paste; $^1/_4$ cup minced red or yellow bell pepper; and 1 tablespoon freshly squeezed lime juice. Make sure to add enough cornmeal (better than bread crumbs, in this case) to the mix to compensate for the added liquids.

Bean Croquettes with Asian Flavors: Substitute scallion for the onion and cilantro for the parsley. Add to the mix: $^1/_2$ teaspoon minced garlic; 1 teaspoon peeled and minced ginger; 1 tablespoon soy sauce or fish sauce (*nuoc mam* or *nam pla,* available at Asian markets); 1 teaspoon finely ground Szechwan peppercorns (optional).

Four Simple Ways to Use Bean Croquettes

1. Use as a veggie burger: Place on a roll with lettuce, tomato, and dressing.
2. Use as a breakfast side dish in place of potatoes or meat.
3. Use as a main course at dinner, with any sauce you like, such as Basic Pesto (page 766), Tomato-Onion Salsa (page 772), Skordalia (page 763), or Rouille (page 761).
4. Use as an hors d'oeuvre: Shape into small ovals and serve with aioli (page 761) or Spicy Yogurt Sauce (page 772).

Bean-and-Corn Pancakes

Makes 4 servings

Time: 30 minutes with precooked beans

This amount will serve as a main course; for a side dish, halve the amounts. I like these with cumin, but you can use whatever suits your mood, from basil or parsley to chili or curry powder. Serve with sour cream or yogurt, or with a dish that has some good juices in it. And try adding about one-half cup corn kernels (frozen are fine; thaw them first) to the batter.

> 2 cups drained cooked or canned white or other
>   beans, with a few tablespoons cooking liquid
>   reserved (see Step 1)
> 1³/₄ cups coarse cornmeal
> Salt and freshly ground black pepper to taste
> 2 teaspoons baking powder
> 2 teaspoons ground cumin, or to taste
> ¹/₄ teaspoon cayenne, or to taste
> About 1¹/₂ cups milk, or chicken, beef, or vegetable
>   stock, or water (see "Soups" for stock recipes)
> 1 egg, lightly beaten
> Peanut or other oil as needed

1 If you want to serve the pancakes hot, preheat the oven to 200°F. Puree the beans by putting them through a food mill or into a blender or food processor. Use a little bean cooking liquid or some of the milk or stock if the beans are too dry to puree.

2 Combine the dry ingredients in a large bowl and mix well.

3 Stir half the milk into the dry ingredients; add the beans and mix well. Then stir in the egg and enough of the milk to make a thick, pancake-like batter (you should be able to spoon it, not pour it).

4 Put enough oil into a large skillet (preferably non-stick) to film the bottom; place it on the stove and turn the heat to medium-high. A minute later,

start dropping heaping tablespoonfuls of the batter into the skillet; do not crowd. Adjust the heat so that the cakes brown evenly on the bottom before turning; total cooking time, per cake, will be about 5 minutes. Keep warm in the oven until ready to serve—for up to 30 minutes—or serve at room temperature.

Indian-Style Split Pea Fritters

Makes 4 to 8 appetizer servings

Time: 3 to 4 hours, mostly soaking time

A recipe I learned from Julie Sahni. If you remember to soak the split peas (you can do it before you leave for work—longer soaking times, within reason, are not a problem), these are fast to make, and incredibly delicious. Their outside is crisp, but the interior flavors remain fresh and bright. I like to cook these in plenty of oil, in a wok or in a large, deep saucepan, but if you prefer, you can shape them into cakes and cook them in just enough oil to film the bottom of a non-stick skillet. In that case, cook them according to Step 4 of Bean-and-Corn Pancakes, above.

> 1 cup yellow (preferred) or green split peas, washed
>   and picked over (see The Basics of Buying and
>   Preparing Beans, page 500)
> Peanut or other oil as needed
> 1 jalapeño or other hot fresh or dried chile, stemmed,
>   seeded, and minced, or to taste
> 1¹/₂-inch piece ginger, peeled and roughly chopped
> 1 small clove garlic, crushed
> ¹/₂ cup cilantro (some stems are okay)
> 1 teaspoon ground coriander
> 1 teaspoon ground cumin
> ¹/₂ teaspoon ground fenugreek
> ¹/₂ cup minced onion
> Salt and freshly ground black pepper to taste
> 1 to 2 tablespoons flour, if necessary
> Lime wedges

① Soak the split peas in water to cover for at least 3 hours. Drain but leave them wet. Place the vegetable oil, to a depth of at least 3 inches, in a wok or large, deep saucepan over medium-high heat. Let it heat while you prepare the fritters; it should reach a temperature of 365° to 375°F. Preheat the oven to 200°F.

② Place the drained peas in the container of a food processor with the chile, ginger, garlic, cilantro, coriander, cumin, and fenugreek. Process until the mixture is a coarse puree—not perfectly smooth, but with no whole peas remaining. Add a couple of tablespoons of water if necessary to help the machine with its work.

③ Stir in the onion and salt and pepper. Taste the mixture and adjust the seasoning if necessary. The mixture should be fairly loose; add a little water if it is quite thick, or a tablespoon or two of flour if it is soupy.

④ Drop the mixture by the heaping tablespoon into the oil; do not crowd. Cook until lightly browned and crisp, turning if necessary; total cooking time will be about 3 or 4 minutes. Drain on paper towels and keep warm in the oven while you finish cooking.

⑤ Serve hot or at room temperature, with lime wedges.

Falafel

Makes 4 servings

Time: At least 2 hours, largely unattended

This traditional chickpea or fava bean fritter of the Middle East is not unlike the Indian-style fritters above (although it is, as you can see, quite a bit more garlicky). If you use peeled, split fava beans—my preference—twelve to twenty-four hours of soaking will soften them enough so that precooking is unnecessary. Chickpeas, of course, must be cooked. Serve these hot or at room temperature, with lime wedges or Tahini Dressing (page 770). Or serve them in pita bread with chopped lettuce, tomato, cucumber, and Tahini Dressing.

2 cups peeled, split fava beans or chickpeas
8 to 10 cloves garlic, crushed
1 medium onion, quartered
1 teaspoon ground coriander
1 tablespoon ground cumin
$^1/_4$ teaspoon cayenne, or to taste
$^1/_2$ cup cilantro (some stems are okay)
$^1/_2$ cup fresh parsley (some stems are okay)
Salt and freshly ground black pepper to taste
1 teaspoon baking powder
Peanut or other oil as needed

① If you're using fava beans, soak them for 12 to 24 hours in water to cover, or cook until very tender, about 45 minutes. If you're using chickpeas, cook them according to the recipe for Basic Beans, page 505. Rinse them in several changes of water to remove as many skins as possible, then drain.

② Place the drained beans in the container of a food processor with the garlic, onion, coriander, cumin, cayenne, cilantro, and parsley. Puree until very smooth, adding a couple of tablespoons of water if necessary to help the machine with its work.

③ Taste and adjust seasoning if necessary; add salt and pepper. Cover and let rest, refrigerated, for at least 30 minutes and up to 24 hours. Shape into balls 1 inch in diameter or into small flat cakes, about 2 inches wide and $^1/_2$ to $^3/_4$ inch thick. Refrigerate while you heat the oil.

④ Place the oil in a wok or large, deep saucepan, to a depth of at least 3 inches, and turn the heat to medium-high.

⑤ When the oil reaches 350° to 365°F, fry the falafel in it without crowding. Turn as necessary, and cook until they are quite brown, 2 to 4 minutes.

Split Peas, Mung Beans, or Lentils with Curry

Dal

Makes 4 servings

Time: 30 minutes to 1 hour

Red lentils and split peas become soft quickly, so the cooking time here is minimal. It's a wonderful winter side dish—or even a main course, with rice—when good fresh vegetables are scarce. Although this basic recipe is fine, the more interesting variation doesn't take much longer.

1 1/2 cups yellow (preferred) or green split peas, or yellow mung beans, or red lentils, washed and picked over (see The Basics of Buying and Preparing Beans, page 500)
4 cups chicken, beef, or vegetable stock, or water, plus more if needed (see "Soups" for stock recipes)
Salt and freshly ground black pepper to taste
1 tablespoon All-Purpose Curry Powder (page 778)
Minced cilantro leaves for garnish

1 Combine the peas, mung beans, or lentils, liquid, curry powder, salt, and pepper in a medium saucepan and bring to a boil over medium-high heat. Turn the heat to medium-low, cover partially, and cook gently, stirring occasionally, until the split peas, mung beans, or lentils are soft and beginning to turn to mush, at least 30 minutes; add additional liquid if necessary. The mixture should be moist but not soupy.

2 Taste and adjust seasoning if necessary. Serve over white rice (preferably basmati), and garnish.

Split Peas, Mung Beans, or Lentils with Mixed Spices: Omit the curry powder. Add to the mix: 1/4 teaspoon cayenne, or to taste; 1 pinch ground cloves; 1 pinch ground cinnamon; 1/4 teaspoon ground cardamom; 1/2 teaspoon ground coriander; 1/2 teaspoon ground cumin; 1/2 teaspoon freshly ground black pepper. Cook as above. When the peas or lentils are nearly done, heat 2 tablespoons butter or peanut (or other) oil in a small skillet over medium-low heat. Add 1 tablespoon each minced garlic and ginger and cook, stirring occasionally, until they soften, 5 to 8 minutes. Stir this mixture into the peas or lentils, garnish with minced cilantro, and serve.

Sprouts

Makes about 2 cups

Time: 1 week, largely unattended

Note that I don't say "bean" sprouts. Mung bean sprouts are very common, but so are alfalfa and radish sprouts, which are from seeds. In fact, you can sprout almost anything that will grow in soil: beans, whole grains, or seeds. Most common, in addition to those already mentioned, are wheat sprouts, lentil sprouts, and soybean sprouts, but herb sprouts—dill, fennel, or basil, for example—are just as easy, and really delicious. You can also combine sprouts of different types in the same container.

1/2 cup mung beans or other beans, seeds, or whole grains

1 Place the beans in a quart jar, such as a mayonnaise jar. Rinse once with water and drain, then cover with water and let soak for 6 to 12 hours. During that time, find something you can use to loosely cover the jar, such as cheesecloth, an old (clean) piece of screen, or a very coarse napkin.

2 Drain. Rinse the seeds and drain them again; prop the jar up so that it is on its side with the mouth tilted down. Shield from the light.

3 Continue rinsing and draining, at least twice a day but preferably three or four times. After a few days, you'll see that the seeds have sprouted. When the sprouts are the length you want them (generally, the bigger the seed, the longer the sprout), rinse one more time and expose to the light for a few hours; this will turn the sprouts green.

4 Store in the refrigerator and eat within a few days.

The Basics of Tofu (Bean Curd)

You can eat tofu, a mild-tasting cheese-like substance made from soybeans, simply dressed with soy sauce. Or cut it up and add it to soups, or puree it and use it as a no-cholesterol addition to sauces and salad dressings.

You can also cook tofu, a venerable meat substitute, and it can be quite good if handled well. Even though most tofu is packaged (in a small tub filled with water, then wrapped in plastic), it's best to use it as soon as you buy it. If you don't use it all at once, place the remainder in a plastic or glass container, cover it with fresh water, and seal tightly. Change the water daily.

Tofu is usually sold as being one of four textures; these are relative rather than absolute terms, but worth noting:

Silken: Best for soups, to puree for use in sauces, or to fry as in Creamy Fried Tofu, page 527.
Soft: As soft as silken but also can be pressed, frozen, or marinated and cooked on its own.
Firm: Good for stir-fries; can be marinated, pressed, or frozen.
Extra-firm: Best for stir-fries.

Twenty-Three Main Course Bean Dishes

With cornbread (or any bread) and salad, almost any bean dish can serve as a main course. But the following seem especially satisfying:

1. Beans and Greens, page 510
2. Beans and Greens Gratin, page 510
3. Black Beans with Cumin or Chili, page 512
4. Bean and Tomato Casserole, page 512
5. Bean Casserole with Hominy and Tortillas, page 513
6. Red Beans with Meat, page 513
7. Vegetarian Red Beans, page 513
8. Black Beans with Crisp Pork and Orange, page 514
9. Red Beans and Rice, page 516
10. Lentils and Rice with Caramelized Onions, page 516
11. Baked Beans, page 518
12. Vegetarian Baked Beans, page 518
13. Stewed Chickpeas with Chicken, page 519
14. Stewed Chickpeas with Vegetables, page 519
15. Chili non Carne, page 519
16. Chili with Tomatoes, page 520
17. Chili con Carne, page 520
18. Simple Bean Croquettes, page 521
19. Bean Croquettes with Southwestern Flavors, page 521
20. Bean Croquettes with Asian Flavors, page 521
21. Bean-and-Corn Pancakes, page 522
22. Stir-Fried Tofu with Scallions, page 526
23. Spicy Tofu with Ground Pork, page 526

Unless you're pureeing or freezing tofu, you should drain it on paper towels for at least a few minutes to remove excess moisture before cooking. You can change the texture of tofu by pressing or freezing it. Pressing makes tofu firmer; freezing makes it porous and downright chewy, a good texture for stir-fries or marinating.

To press tofu   Cut a brick of tofu in half through its equator. Place each half on a cutting board and prop the board up so that its lower end is at the edge of a sink. Top with another cutting board or similar flat, clean object. Weight the top board with a skillet, a couple of books, whatever. Let sit for thirty to sixty minutes, then drain on paper towels.

To freeze tofu   Freeze tofu by throwing the whole package in the freezer, where it will keep for months. About one hour before you need it, cover it with hot water—change the water once if necessary—to defrost it (it will have darkened in color), then drain and press it briefly. Marinate or cut into cubes and use right away.

Stir-Fried Tofu with Scallions
Makes 4 servings

Time: 20 minutes

A quick and simple stir-fry, best with pressed tofu. Serve with white rice.

1 pound firm or extra-firm tofu, cut into 1-inch cubes

2 tablespoons peanut (preferred) or other oil

1 cup cut-up scallions, cut into 1-inch pieces, the darkest green parts minced and reserved for garnish

1/2 cup chicken, beef, or vegetable stock, or water (see "Soups" for stock recipes)

2 tablespoons soy sauce

Salt and freshly ground black pepper to taste

1 Place the tofu on paper towels to drain some of its moisture while you prepare the other ingredients. Let it sit for up to 1 hour or press the tofu or use frozen tofu (page 526).

2 Place the oil in a wok or large, deep skillet, preferably non-stick, and turn the heat to medium-high. A minute later, add the scallions; cook, stirring, until they soften, a minute or two.

3 Add the tofu and turn the heat to medium. Cook, stirring only occasionally, until the tofu is heated through. Add the stock and cook until it is reduced by about half, a minute or so, then add the soy sauce and turn off the heat.

4 Taste and add salt and pepper if you like. Garnish with the reserved minced scallions and serve.

Spicy Tofu with Ground Pork
Makes 4 servings

Time: 30 minutes

A slightly more complex stir-fry, but a significantly more rewarding one.

1 pound firm or extra-firm tofu, cut into 1-inch cubes

1 tablespoon peanut oil

1/2- to 3/4-pound ground or minced pork

1 tablespoon minced garlic

1 teaspoon crushed red pepper flakes, or to taste

1 teaspoon peeled and minced ginger

1 teaspoon coarsely ground Szechwan peppercorns

1/2 cup cut-up scallions, cut into 1-inch pieces, the darkest green parts minced and reserved for garnish

1/2 cup chicken, beef, or vegetable stock, or water (see "Soups" for stock recipes)

2 tablespoons soy sauce or fish sauce (*nuoc mam* or *nam pla*, available at Asian markets)

Salt and freshly ground black pepper to taste

1 Place the tofu on paper towels to drain some of its moisture while you prepare the other ingredients. Let the tofu sit for up to an hour or press the tofu or use frozen tofu (page 526).

2 Place the oil in a wok or large, deep skillet, preferably non-stick, and turn the heat to medium-high. A minute later, add the pork. Cook, stirring frequently and breaking up any lumps, until it loses its color, about 5 minutes. Remove with a slotted spoon.

3 Add the garlic, red pepper, ginger, Szechwan peppercorns, and scallions and raise the heat to high. Cook, stirring, until the scallions begin to become limp, about 1 minute. Turn the heat to medium and add the tofu.

4 Cook, stirring only occasionally, until the tofu is heated through. Add the stock and turn the heat back to high. Cook until the stock is reduced by about half, a minute or so, then add the soy sauce and the pork. Cook, stirring, for 1 minute. Taste and add salt and pepper or other seasoning if you like. Garnish and serve, over white rice.

Creamy Fried Tofu

Makes 4 servings

Time: About 30 minutes

This delicate batter produces a deliciously crisp exterior, while the quick frying process leaves the tender interior of tofu intact. If you're looking to convert a tofu-hater, look no further. Serve this with Soy and Sesame Dipping Sauce or Marinade (page 776) or with lemon wedges or vinegar.

1 pound soft or silken tofu, cut into 1-inch or slightly larger cubes

Peanut or other oil for frying

2 cups all-purpose flour

1 teaspoon salt

$1/2$ teaspoon freshly ground black pepper

1 egg yolk, lightly beaten

1 Place the tofu on paper towels, then place another layer of paper towels on top of it. Change the towels if necessary; you want the tofu to be quite dry. You can let the tofu rest on the towels for up to 1 hour.

2 When you're ready to cook, place the oil in a wok or large, deep saucepan, to a depth of at least 3 inches, and turn the heat to medium-high.

3 Add 1 teaspoon salt and $1/2$ teaspoon pepper to 1 cup of the flour and place it on a plate. In a bowl, mix the egg yolk with 1 cup ice water (combine water and ice in a bowl for 1 minute, then measure the water). Add the remaining flour and stir lightly, just until blended; don't worry about remaining lumps—it's better not to overmix.

4 When the oil reaches 350°F, dredge the tofu pieces, one at a time, in the flour. Shake off the excess, dip them in the batter, and fry. Do not crowd; you may cook in batches if necessary. Stir occasionally (large pieces may need to be turned individually) and cook until golden brown. If pieces of batter separate and float to the top of the cooking oil, strain them out as you cook.

5 Drain the tofu on paper towels. Serve hot.

Vegetables

The size of the typical supermarket produce section has grown by a factor of about four in the past fifteen years. Where there was once spinach, there are now kale, bok choy, and half a dozen other greens for cooking; where there were all-purpose potatoes, there are now Yukon gold, little red, long white, and several more; on any given day the choices are staggering.

Many people find this overwhelming, but the truth of the matter is that cooking vegetables is simple. Of course, you need to identify the vegetable, and know the general rules for preparing it. But once you've done that, there's not much more you need to do to put a nicely finished vegetable dish on the table.

The great thing about vegetables is that although they are very, very distinctive—it would be much easier to mistake beef for lamb than it would be to mistake zucchini for broccoli—most of them can be handled in very similar ways. Few vegetables cannot be simmered or steamed to tenderness and then lightly dressed, with something as simple as lemon juice, vinaigrette, or that old standby, butter. And few vegetables cannot be cooked in a little olive oil, either over high heat so that they become crisp, or with some liquid, covered, over lower heat, so that they become meltingly tender.

The Basics of Cooking Vegetables

Generally speaking, there is not a single "ideal" way to prepare a given vegetable—it depends largely on matters of taste—but, with each vegetable, there are some techniques that are better suited than others. Vegetables usually must be tenderized if they are to be considered cooked, and there are different ways to accomplish this. To some extent, the correct cooking technique depends upon shape. You would not use a sauté pan to cook a whole potato, or a whole head of broccoli; but cut either into small bits and the skillet becomes a fine alternative to boiling or steaming. And there are other factors that determine the best cooking method for a given vegetable. Broccoli, for example, should not be roasted dry; its relatively low moisture content would assure that the result was tough unless extraordinary measures were taken. A baking potato, however, contains enough moisture of its own to be cooked with dry heat.

To help you with your cooking experiments, I list the best cooking methods for each vegetable. This doesn't necessarily mean that other techniques will not work at all, but that these methods will give the most consistent results with a minimum of fuss. You *could* roast that broccoli if you wanted to, but it would require its own recipe, and the game would not be worth the candle. You can, however, cook any of the vegetables here, without hassle, using the basic techniques I recommend.

For the most part, the recipes here are both simple and easy; this chapter reviews all the common vegetables and describes how to cook them. Most of us still use vegetables as accompaniments to other, more filling foods—such as meats, fish, pasta, and other grains—and that's the focus here. This is not, strictly speaking, a vegetarian chapter, but only a handful of the recipes contain meat, and, similarly, only a few of them have more than a tablespoon or two of added fat.

Note that although there are preparations here that can be used as sauces, there are many more recipes for vegetable-based sauces in other chapters. And note

that there are no raw vegetables here: Vegetables that are used solely or predominantly in salads—from lettuce to jicama to sea vegetables—are described in that chapter (pages 83–123). Finally, you'll see that throughout this chapter I offer suggestions for other recipes in which you can use the given vegetable under discussion. In many of these adaptations you will have to make allowances for the different cooking times of each vegetable; use your experience and your judgment to determine the correct timing.

The Basics of Buying Vegetables

If you buy super-fresh, super-high-quality vegetables, you can give them the minimalist treatment and they'll be singing with flavor. Unfortunately, few of us have access to great vegetables, especially in the winter months. But even then, simple treatments work well.

Although they may seem obvious to veteran cooks, there are some general rules for buying vegetables. These are:

- Never buy a vegetable with obvious damage—bruises, exceptionally soft spots, holes, and so on.
- Look for vegetables that are firm.
- Look for lots of green, or whatever the primary color of the vegetable happens to be (purple for eggplant, red for tomato); brown (and yellow, to some extent) is, generally speaking, a color you want to avoid.

It pays to wash almost every vegetable before you go any further (the exceptions, such as onions—which are peeled—are obvious). A soft brush is very useful for potatoes you don't want to peel, cucumbers with little spines, and other tasks. Greens and other vegetables should be washed in this manner:

1. Place them in a salad spinner (or a colander inside a large pot).
2. Fill it with water.
3. Swish the veggies around.
4. Lift the colander out of the water.
5. Drain the water.
6. Repeat as necessary until the water contains no traces of sand.

Note: Illustrations demonstrating peeling, slicing, dicing, and otherwise preparing vegetables are on this page and page 533. Specific instructions, as needed, accompany each vegetable.

The Basics of Steaming Vegetables

You can simmer almost any vegetable by immersing it in enough boiling water to cover it, and, in most cases, that's the easiest way to cook them. But most vegetables can also be steamed, and steaming has its advantages: It's quicker (you don't have to wait for a large pot of water to boil), and the vegetable has less of a chance of becoming waterlogged. There are disadvantages, too—steaming eventually leads to a burnt pot for almost everyone, because it may take only a five-minute absence from the kitchen for the pot to boil dry. And, since steaming is done under a cover, it's a little more difficult to track the progress of the vegetable.

Should you decide to steam, you can use a special pot designed for steaming, or the common and convenient basket of interlocking metal leaves that will convert almost any saucepan into a steamer. Or, you can simply arrange four chopsticks, or an upside-down ramekin, to build a little platform on the bottom of a pot; if necessary, you can steam your vegetables on a heatproof plate resting on this platform.

Preparing vegetables involves almost all aspects of knife handling—chopping, dicing, mincing, julienne, and more. The vast majority of tasks can be accomplished with just a chef's knife, a paring knife, and a cutting board. A peeler will also come in handy from time to time.

USING A MANDOLINE

Japanese mandolines are inexpensive and incredibly useful. You can make perfectly thin slices of almost any vegetable in seconds—just watch your fingers.

This technique will not work for every vegetable, such as those with super-high water content like zucchini and eggplant. But it can be used with the vast majority, and has very real advantages. It allows you to prepare the vegetable so that it can be brought to the table within five minutes, and it can be brought to that point as long as a day or two in advance. This means that you can start and finish the vegetable as you're bringing other dishes to the table, or just before. Of course, this method is also applicable to "leftover" simmered or steamed vegetables; just make sure to rinse them with boiling water to remove any prior seasoning, if necessary.

The process is simple:

1. Prepare the vegetable for cooking.

2. Steam or simmer individual vegetables it in salted boiling water to cover until it is tender.

3. Drain it, then drop it into ice-cold water.

4. Drain it again.

5. Set aside or cover and refrigerate for a day or two.

When you're ready to eat:

1. Turn the heat under a skillet to medium. Add enough butter or olive oil—usually a tablespoon or two—to cover the bottom of the skillet. (Alternatively, bring a pot of water to a boil.)

2. Add the vegetables to the pan, turn the heat to medium-high, and cook, stirring, until hot, just a couple of minutes (or submerge in the boiling water until hot, a minute or so). Season and serve.

Four Quick Ideas for Precooked Vegetables

As you become increasingly comfortable with cooking vegetables, you'll realize that the above technique allows you to finish the vegetable in both simple and complex ways. See the specific vegetables for more ideas.

1. Add minced onion, shallot, or garlic to the butter or oil. Cook for about a minute before adding the main vegetable.

2. Add herbs or spices to the vegetable as it heats. Parsley is always appropriate, but most fresh herbs combine nicely with simply cooked vegetables. Ginger, curry powder (page 778), dried red chiles, and other spices can all add their characteristic flavors to a variety of vegetables.

3. Sauce the vegetable with béchamel or one of its variations (page 787), or top it with grated Parmesan or other cheese, then run it under the broiler—carefully, so as not to burn the top—until hot.

4. Dress the hot vegetable with any vinaigrette (page 91), compound butter (page 768), or flavored oil (page 775).

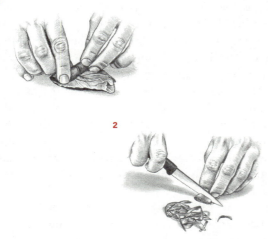

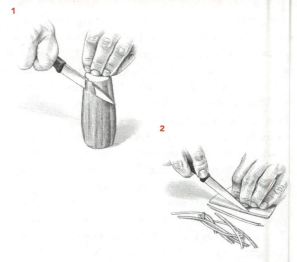

*This works for large leaves, such as kale, as well as smaller ones, like basil. (**Step 1**) Roll the leaf up from bottom to top. (**Step 2**) Cut slices of the leaf off from top to bottom.*

*(**Step 1**) To julienne any vegetable, cut a piece off each end so it will stand straight. Then cut thin slices using a knife or a mandoline (see page 531). (**Step 2**) Cut the thin slices into matchsticks. If you want tiny cubes, stack the matchsticks and cut across them.*

Artichokes

This domesticated thistle is a neat package of flavor. Usually boiled or steamed—steaming is preferable, because artichokes can become quite waterlogged—small specimens can be sautéed, deep-fried, roasted, or even grilled. (True "baby" artichokes, which unfortunately are relatively uncommon in this country, can be handled differently, for they have little or no "choke," the central cluster of nascent leaves that gets its name from the nasty feeling that one of them will give you should you make the mistake of swallowing it.)

Artichoke hearts, or bottoms, are the bottom and innermost part of the vegetable, with outer leaves and choke either removed or, in the case of baby artichokes, absent altogether. Although eating the meat

on the leaves of a whole artichoke is fun, getting to the incomparably delicious heart is what it's all about. Thus some recipes begin with trimming off the leaves and cooking just the heart.

Nevertheless, eating a whole artichoke is a worthwhile experience. The flavor of the leaves is every bit as good as that of the heart; there's just less meat on them. Start by preparing the artichoke as described in Basic Steamed Artichokes, page 535. Drain, then place on a plate with melted butter, vinaigrette, mayonnaise, freshly squeezed lemon juice, or just some salt in a nearby dipping bowl. Peel off the leaves one at a time; dip each one, then scrape the meat off the fleshy end with your front teeth. When you reach the tender internal cone of leaves, remove it as a group and eat as much of it as you can. You will have exposed the choke, a cluster of needle-like leaves that you definitely do not want to eat. (The choke presents no danger, but as soon as you mistakenly eat a piece you will carefully avoid it forever.) Use the side of a fork or dull knife to scrape away the choke, and trim around the bottom if necessary. What remains are the heart and bottom, both of which can be eaten with no further fuss.

Buying and storing Artichokes are in season year-round, most plentiful and cheapest in the spring. Size is irrelevant; any artichoke can be delicious, although large specimens are sometimes woody, so make sure big artichokes feel heavy for their size. Freshness, however, is important: A good artichoke will feel plump and squeak (really) when you squeeze it; the outer leaves will snap off crisply. Store, refrigerated, in the vegetable bin. Use as soon as possible.

Canned (or, more frequently, bottled) or frozen artichoke hearts are worth eating, but do not believe for a moment that they have the flavor of fresh.

Preparing I like to cut the pointed tips from artichoke leaves before cooking, but this is entirely optional; use a scissors or heavy knife to do this. Then use a paring knife to peel around the base and cut off the bottom one-quarter inch. Break off the roughest and darkest layers of exterior leaves. If you want to remove the choke before cooking, you can either cut the artichoke into quarters and scrape it out (this is the easy way, but obviously it means you can't cook the artichokes whole), or pry open the central petals with your fingers and scrape out the choke with a spoon. This is not difficult, and you will get the hang of it right away, but it does take some time.

Artichokes contain an enzyme that makes them discolor as soon as they're cut and cooked; if this bothers you—it doesn't affect the flavor—drop them into a mixture of one tablespoon of lemon juice or vinegar per cup of water as you prepare them, and add a splash of vinegar or lemon juice to the cooking water. It's also best to use non-aluminum knives and cooking utensils when working with artichokes.

Best cooking methods Steaming, sautéing, braising, all of which are described on pages 535–536. The hearts are best sautéed in butter or olive oil (slice them first), deep-fried with a coating of flour (see Fried Okra, page 585), or lightly steamed, then chilled for use in salads.

When is it done? For whole artichokes: When outer leaves pull off easily, taste one. If the meat comes off easily and is tender, the artichoke is done. For cleaned artichoke bottoms: When very tender; pierce with a skewer or thin-bladed knife to check, then taste to be sure.

TRIMMING ARTICHOKES, VERSION I

(Step 1) Use scissors or a sharp knife to cut the pointed tips from the tops of an artichoke. *(Step 2)* Cut the artichoke in half. *(Step 3)* Cut the artichoke into quarters. *(Step 4)* Scrape the fuzzy choke out from each of the quarters.

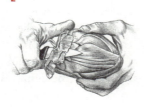

(Step 1) Peel off tough outer leaves. *(Step 2)* Trim around the bottom of the artichoke. *(Step 3)* If you only want to cook the bottom, cut off the top half of the leaves. *(Step 4)* Then scoop out the choke. If you want to leave the artichoke whole but remove the choke, leave it whole and force the top leaves open, then use a long spoon to scrape out the choke.

Basic Steamed Artichokes

Makes 4 servings

Time: 45 minutes

Artichokes can be simmered in water to cover but they tend to become a bit soggy. It's best to steam them; just make sure that the pot doesn't boil dry.

> 4 large or 12 very small artichokes
> Several sprigs fresh tarragon or thyme (optional)
> Salt and freshly ground black pepper to taste

1 With a scissors or large knife, trim the top ¹/₂ inch or so from the artichokes. Using a paring knife, peel around the base and cut off the bottom ¹/₄ inch. Break off the roughest of the exterior leaves.

2 Place bottom up in a steamer, adding herbs if you like. Cover and cook 20 to 40 minutes. Sample an outer leaf; when it pulls away easily and its meat is tender, the artichokes are done.

3 Drain them upside down for a minute or two longer before serving hot; store upside down if you plan to serve them later. Serve hot with melted butter, at room temperature with vinaigrette, or cold with mayonnaise. Or serve at any temperature with lemon and/or salt.

Sautéed Artichoke Hearts

Makes 4 servings

Time: 40 minutes

If you have very small ("baby") artichokes, you need not remove the choke. But cleaning four large artichokes won't take you more than ten minutes. You can use canned or jarred artichoke hearts, but the flavor will not be the same; rinse them gently first.

> 4 large or 12 very small artichokes
> 4 tablespoons (¹/₂ stick) butter or extra-virgin olive oil
> 1 clove garlic, lightly smashed (optional)
> Flour for dredging
> Salt and freshly ground black pepper to taste
> Minced fresh parsley leaves for garnish
> Lemon wedges

1 If you are using large artichokes, cut them into halves or quarters; remove the leaves and the choke, and trim the bottom. If the artichokes are very small, simply peel off all the leaves and trim the bottom; you can ignore the choke. Drop them into boiling salted water to cover, lower the heat, and simmer just until tender, from as little as 6 minutes for little ones to as long as 20 for larger ones. Plunge immediately into ice water.

2 Drain and dry the hearts. (You may prepare the recipe in advance up to this point; refrigerate, in a covered container, for up to 2 days before proceeding.) Place the butter or oil in a large, deep skillet; turn the heat to medium-high. When the butter foam subsides or the oil is hot, add the garlic if you like, then dredge each heart lightly in flour. Shake off the excess; place in the skillet. Cook, turning once or twice. Season with salt and pepper, until nicely browned all over, about 10 minutes.

3 Serve hot, garnished with parsley and accompanied by lemon wedges.

Curried Artichoke Hearts: Add about 1 teaspoon All-Purpose Curry Powder (page 778), or to taste, to the butter as it is melting (if you use oil, use peanut or other oil if possible). Proceed as above.

Braised Quartered Artichokes with Tarragon

Makes 4 servings

Time: 30 minutes

No precooking necessary; just clean the artichokes, cook them in hot oil for a few minutes, then finish with liquid. Substitute any herb you like for the tarragon (chervil is especially nice), or use chopped tomatoes in place of the stock.

4 large or 12 very small artichokes
3 tablespoons olive oil
1 tablespoon minced garlic
1 tablespoon minced fresh tarragon leaves or
   1 teaspoon dried tarragon
1 cup chicken, beef, or vegetable stock, or water
   (see "Soups" for stock recipes)
Salt and freshly ground black pepper to taste
1 tablespoon freshly squeezed lemon juice
Minced fresh parsley leaves for garnish

1 If you are using large artichokes, cut them into halves or quarters; remove the leaves and the choke, and trim the bottom. If the artichokes are very small, simply peel off all the leaves and trim the bottom; you can ignore the choke.

2 Heat the oil and garlic together in large, deep skillet over medium heat, just until the garlic begins to color, about 5 minutes. Add the artichokes and cook, stirring occasionally, for about 5 minutes. Add the tarragon and stock or water, bring to a boil, and cover; turn the heat to medium-low. Cook for about 10 minutes, then turn the artichokes. Check for tenderness every 5 minutes or so; total cooking time will be 15 to 30 minutes.

3 When the artichokes are tender, season with salt and pepper. If there is too much liquid, raise the heat to high for a few minutes and reduce it a bit.

4 Just before serving, sprinkle with lemon juice and garnish.

Asparagus

Spears rising from the earth in early spring, year after year—no wonder asparagus is the favorite of so many home gardeners. These days, we can buy it year-round (it's always spring somewhere), but the best asparagus is local asparagus, sold from February in the South through May or even June in the North.

Classically, asparagus is steamed, but it doesn't much matter how you cook the stalks, as long as you leave them just a little crisp—not so crisp that they crunch when you bite them, but not so soggy that they begin to fall apart. Some people eat asparagus with a knife and fork, but using your fingers is considered polite, even among sticklers.

Buying and storing Any color asparagus is good; we usually see green, but white and purple are common in Europe and occasionally make it to our markets. Size is a matter of debate; some people prefer super-thin stalks, which need not be peeled, a distinct advantage. But big, fat stalks are great to eat, too. My recommendation: Take what you get. Don't buy shriveled spears, or damaged ones; and don't buy canned or frozen asparagus. Store, wrapped loosely in plastic, in the refrigerator. Use as soon as possible.

Preparing Snap off the bottom of each stem; it will naturally break (more or less) where the woody part ends and tender part begins. Unless the asparagus are pencil-thin (or unless you're pressed for time), it's best, although not essential, to peel them from the base up to the beginning of the flower.

Best cooking methods Steaming is basic, but you can cook asparagus, especially thin ones, any way you like.

Asparagus can also be baked in sauce; see Baked Chard in Béchamel, page 559.

When is it done? Asparagus are done when you can easily insert a skewer or thin-bladed knife into the thickest part of the stalk. Undercooked asparagus are crisp; overcooked asparagus are mushy.

PREPARING ASPARAGUS

Snap off the bottom of each stalk; they will usually separate naturally right where the woody part ends.

All but the thinnest asparagus are best when peeled.

Basic Simmered, Steamed, or Microwaved Asparagus

Makes 4 servings

Time: 15 minutes

If the asparagus are pencil-thin, don't bother to peel them.

> 1½ to 2 pounds asparagus, trimmed and peeled (see opposite)
> Salt

1 To simmer the asparagus, lay them down in a skillet that can hold the spears without crowding, cover with salted water, cover the skillet, and turn the heat to high. Cook just until the thick part of the stalks can be pierced with a knife.

2 To steam the asparagus, stand them up in a pot with an inch of salted water on the bottom (it's nice, but hardly essential, to tie them in a bundle first). Cover and turn the heat to high. Cook just until the thick part of the stalks can be pierced with a knife.

3 To microwave the asparagus, lay them in a microwave-proof plate or shallow bowl with about 2 tablespoons of salted water; cover with a lid or plastic wrap. Microwave on high for 3 minutes, shake the container, and continue to microwave at 1-minute intervals, just until the thick part of the stalks can be pierced with a knife.

Eleven Quick Ideas for Cooked Asparagus

Once cooked by any of the above methods, asparagus can simply be drained and served in any of the following ways. Or you can drain it, drop it into a bowl of ice water to stop the cooking, drain again, place in a covered container, and refrigerate for up to two days. Then cook it according to the directions for Precooked Vegetables in Butter or Oil (page 532). Finish it, if you like, with:

1. Melted butter (butter cooked *just* to the point of browning is wonderful on asparagus)
2. Freshly squeezed lemon juice or balsamic or sherry vinegar
3. Extra-virgin olive oil
4. Any vinaigrette (pages 91–94)
5. Lemon butter (page 770)
6. Hollandaise Sauce (page 790)
7. Basic Mayonnaise (page 761)
8. A hefty topping of Sautéed Mushrooms (page 585)
9. A garnish of minced Hard-Boiled Egg (page 733), toasted bread crumbs (page 239), or minced roasted red bell pepper (see Marinated Roasted, Grilled, or Broiled Peppers, page 593)
10. Fresh herbs, especially tarragon and chervil. Or try reheating asparagus in butter or oil to which some curry powder has been added and cooked for thirty seconds or so
11. Thinly sliced prosciutto or other good ham; wrap the cooked room-temperature or cold spears in the meat

Roasted, Broiled, or Grilled Asparagus
Makes 4 servings

Time: 30 minutes, plus time to preheat the grill

If you're grilling or roasting meat or fish, it's easy to cook the asparagus the same way. And they're great when browned.

1½ to 2 pounds asparagus, trimmed and peeled (page 537)
1 to 2 tablespoons extra-virgin olive oil
Salt to taste
Lemon wedges

1. Preheat the oven to 450°F, preheat the broiler or a gas grill, or start a charcoal or wood fire. If you're roasting or broiling, place the asparagus in a roasting pan and drizzle with a tablespoon or two of oil; sprinkle with salt. If you're grilling, brush the asparagus with oil and sprinkle with salt. Place the asparagus in the oven, under the broiler, or on the grill.

2. Roast or grill, turning the spears once or twice, just until the thick part of the stalks can be pierced with a knife, 10 to 15 minutes. Broiling time will be shorter, 5 to 10 minutes total. Serve immediately, with lemon wedges.

Asparagus with Parmesan
Makes 4 servings

Time: 30 minutes

Butter and Parmesan are always a great combination. If you don't want to use butter, just eliminate it; the cheese alone will flavor the asparagus nicely.

1½ to 2 pounds asparagus, trimmed and peeled (page 537)
2 to 4 tablespoons butter, plus some for greasing the pan
Salt and freshly ground black pepper to taste
About 1 cup freshly grated Parmesan cheese

1. Simmer, steam, or microwave the asparagus (see Basic Simmered, Steamed, or Microwaved Asparagus, page 537); undercook it a little bit. Drain and plunge it into ice water, then drain and dry. (You may prepare the recipe in advance up to this point; refrigerate, well wrapped or in a covered container, for up to 2 days before proceeding.) Preheat the oven to 450°F.

2. Butter a casserole or baking pan, then place the asparagus in it. Dot with as much or as little butter as

you like and sprinkle with salt and pepper. Scatter about two-thirds of the cheese over the asparagus and bake until the cheese is just beginning to turn light brown, 10 to 15 minutes. Sprinkle with the remaining Parmesan and serve.

Crisp-Cooked Asparagus

Makes 4 servings

Time: 30 minutes

Do not use pencil-thin asparagus for this recipe; you want a total of twenty to twenty-five fairly thick stalks.

1 to 2 pounds asparagus, trimmed and peeled (page 537)
4 tablespoons ($^1/_2$ stick) butter or olive oil, or a combination
Flour for dredging
2 eggs, lightly beaten in a bowl
Plain bread crumbs
Lemon wedges

1 Simmer, steam, or microwave the asparagus (see Basic Simmered, Steamed or Microwaved Asparagus, page 537); undercook it a little bit. Drain and plunge it into ice water, then drain and dry. (You may prepare the recipe in advance up to this point; refrigerate, well wrapped or in a covered container, for up to 2 days before proceeding.)

2 Heat the butter and/or oil in a large skillet over medium-high heat. When the butter foam subsides or the oil is hot, dredge each stalk lightly in the flour, dip it in the eggs, then dredge in the bread crumbs. Place in the pan. Repeat, turning the stalks as they brown and removing them as they finish. Cook in batches if necessary, keeping the finished stalks warm in a 200°F oven.

3 Serve hot, with lemon wedges.

Stir-Fried Asparagus, Three Ways

Makes 4 servings

Time: 20 minutes

Each of these variations is a tiny more elaborate than the basic recipe. If you precook the asparagus in advance, the final preparation will take just three or four minutes.

1$^1/_2$ to 2 pounds asparagus, trimmed and peeled (page 537), then cut into 2-inch lengths
2 tablespoons peanut oil (preferred) or other oil
Salt to taste

1 Simmer, steam, or microwave the asparagus (see Basic Simmered, Steamed, or Microwaved Asparagus, page 537); undercook it a little bit. Drain and plunge it into ice water, then drain and dry. (You may prepare the recipe in advance up to this point; refrigerate, well wrapped or in a covered container, for up to 2 days before proceeding.)

2 When you're ready to cook, preheat a wok or large skillet over high heat for 3 or 4 minutes. Add the oil, wait a few seconds, then add the asparagus. Cook, stirring, with the heat on high, for 2 or 3 minutes, until the asparagus is dry, hot, and beginning to brown. Sprinkle with salt and serve.

Stir-Fried Asparagus with Soy: In Step 2, substitute 1 tablespoon soy sauce for the salt. Finish, if you like, with 1 teaspoon dark sesame oil. Stir and serve.

Stir-Fried Asparagus with Garlic: In Step 2, add 1 tablespoon minced garlic along with the asparagus. (You can also add 1 teaspoon crushed red pepper flakes, or to taste, at the same time.) Add $^1/_2$ cup chicken, beef, or vegetable stock, or water, along with the salt. Cook until most of the liquid evaporates, about 2 minutes. Add 2 tablespoons oyster or hoisin sauce, stir, and serve.

Avocado

A fruit we treat as a vegetable, the avocado is native to Central or South America (the name is a bastardization of the Aztec *ahuacatl*), but is now grown in Florida, California, and other warm places. The avocado is the exception to the rule that fruit is virtually fat-free. On the contrary, it's loaded with fat—about thirty percent—although none of it is saturated. It is also unusual in that, unlike most other fruits, it contains insignificant amounts of sugar and acid.

On the other hand, it is incomparable, spreadable like butter, creamy, and mild-tasting. Once it was served with sugar; I think it is at its best spread on bread and sprinkled with salt and freshly squeezed lemon juice. You can halve it and serve it like a melon, or fill it with shrimp salad, or serve it with a wedge of lime or lemon and a spoon. It's also wonderful on sandwiches, and is moist enough to allow you to do away with mayonnaise. Some salad dressings incorporate avocado, but its flavor is too subtle to stand up to the onslaught of many other ingredients; eat it alone and enjoy it. Or make Guacamole, page 22.

Buying and storing   You can buy avocados hard, and they will ripen quite nicely on your kitchen counter (do not refrigerate). Don't buy them if they're mushy or have bruises, and by all means handle them very gently. There are several varieties; all are good.

Preparing   Cut in half from pole to pole. If you want to store half, wrap it with the pit intact and refrigerate it with the pit to keep it from turning brown.

Best cooking methods   Best raw, avocado can be pureed and stirred into sauces and soups, but its subtle flavor is often lost.

When is it done?   It needs no cooking.

Bamboo Shoots

These are emerging bamboo plants, used extensively in stir-fries, especially in restaurants. They are sold canned in this country (although the increasing use of fast-growing bamboo as a "living fence" may change that someday). If you wish to include them in stir-fry dishes, add them toward the end of cooking; browning does nothing for their flavor and removes their distinctive crunch.

Beets

Beets would be used more if their juice didn't stain your counter and hands, although care in handling and cooking (see Beets Baked in Foil, page 541) can eliminate most problems. This root is delicious—some varieties are sweet enough to be used to make sugar—and quite simple to prepare. And unlike most vegetables, beets can and freeze pretty well, making them even more convenient.

Buying and storing   Beets grow spring through fall, but are available pretty much year-round. Size doesn't matter—large beets are easier to handle, and only rarely become woody. Don't buy them if they're mushy. One good indication of freshness is the presence of greens, which can be cooked separately like chard (page 558). To store, remove all but an inch of the greens (use them immediately), and place the roots in a plastic bag in the refrigerator. They keep for weeks.

Preparing   Scrub well before cooking, but leave an inch or so of the green tops on to minimize bleeding.

Best cooking methods   Baking beets in foil minimizes staining, and you can store the beets for days after cooking, removing the foil only when you're ready to recook or use cold. Many beet recipes call for some form of precooking, followed by a quick recooking with flavorings; but beets can also be shredded and cooked, as in Beet Roesti with Rosemary (page 542). Quick Pickled Beets (page 106) are also great.

When is it done? When you can easily pierce a beet with a skewer or thin-bladed knife, it's done. Slight overcooking is usually preferable to undercooking.

Other recipes in which you can use beets:

Quick-Braised Carrots with Butter, page 553 (cooking time will be longer with beets)

Mashed Potatoes, page 596 (best with half potatoes, half beets)

Pureed Parsnips, page 590 (best with half parsnips, half beets)

Beet Greens are nearly indistinguishable from Chard (page 557), and can be used in any chard and most spinach recipes.

Beets Baked in Foil

Makes 4 servings

Time: About 1 hour

This is the single best method for cooking beets. It's the easiest, least messy, and allows you to store the beets, without even handling them, until you want to eat them. At that point you unwrap and peel them, then slice them and heat in butter or oil, pickle them (see Quick Pickled Beets, page 106), or serve them cold with dressing (page 100). Since large beets will take much longer to cook than small ones, try to buy beets that are roughly equal in size. Alternatively, remove beets one by one from the oven as they become tender.

4 large or 8 medium beets, about 1½ to 2 pounds, with about 1 inch of their tops still on

1 Preheat the oven to 400°F. Wash the beets well. Wrap them individually in foil and place them on a baking sheet or roasting pan.

2 Cook, undisturbed, for 45 minutes to 1½ hours, until a thin-bladed knife pierces one with little resistance (they may cook at different rates; remove each one when it is done). If you want to serve them right away, peel, then serve hot with butter, any vinaigrette (pages 91–94), or freshly squeezed lemon juice. Or remove, cool, and refrigerate until ready to peel and use.

Simmered, Steamed, or Microwaved Beets

Makes 4 servings

Time: About 45 minutes

These methods are not as convenient as baking beets in foil, nor do they allow the beets to retain as much flavor, but they are a bit faster.

4 large or 8 medium beets, about 1½ to 2 pounds, with about 1 inch of their tops still on

1 To simmer the beets, bring a large pot of water to a boil; salt it. Place the beets in the water, cover the pot, and turn the heat to medium-low. Simmer until the beets can be pierced with a thin-bladed knife, about 30 to 45 minutes. Drain and drop into ice water; drain and peel.

2 To steam the beets, place them in a steamer above an inch or two of salted water. Cover and cook about 30 to 45 minutes, until they can be pierced with a thin-bladed knife. Drain and drop into ice water; drain and peel.

3 To microwave the beets, place them in a microwave-proof plate or shallow bowl with about 2 tablespoons of salted water; cover with a lid or plastic

wrap. Microwave on high for 6 minutes, shake the container, and continue to microwave at 2-minute intervals, just until they can be pierced with a thin-bladed knife. Drain and drop into ice water; drain and peel.

4　Serve hot beets with butter, any vinaigrette (pages 91–94), or freshly squeezed lemon juice, or see the recipes below.

Beet Roesti with Rosemary

Makes 4 servings

Time: 20 minutes

An almost unbelievably sweet and wonderful side dish. The sugar in the beets caramelizes, and the flavors of the rosemary, beets, and butter meld beautifully. With thanks to Michael Romano, the brilliant chef at New York's Union Square Café, who shared this recipe with me almost ten years ago.

1 to 1 1/2 pounds beets
1 teaspoon coarsely chopped fresh rosemary
1 teaspoon salt
1/4 cup flour
2 tablespoons butter

1　Trim the beets and peel them as you would potatoes; grate them in a food processor or by hand. Begin preheating a medium to large non-stick skillet over medium heat.

2　Toss the grated beets in a bowl with the rosemary and salt, then add about half the flour; toss well, add the rest of the flour, then toss again.

3　Place the butter in the skillet and heat until it begins to turn nut-brown. Scrape the beet mixture into the skillet, shape it into a nice circle, and press it down with a spatula. Turn the heat to medium-high and cook, shaking the pan occasionally, until the bottom of the beet cake is nicely crisp, 6 to 8 minutes.

Slide the cake out onto a plate, top with another plate, invert the two plates, and slide the cake back into the pan. Continue to cook, adjusting the heat if necessary, until the second side is browned. Cut into wedges and serve immediately.

Beets in Butter

Makes 4 servings

Time: 15 minutes with precooked beets

You can use either of these methods with canned beets as well. Beets take well to a number of different herbs, especially when cooked in butter or other neutral oil. Try snipped dill or chives, minced tarragon, or chopped parsley, chervil, or mint, to taste.

2 tablespoons butter (or use oil)
4 to 8 beets, cooked by any of the above methods, peeled, and sliced or cut into chunks
Salt and freshly ground black pepper to taste
Minced fresh chives or parsley leaves for garnish

Place the butter or oil in a large, deep skillet over medium-high heat. When the butter foam subsides or the oil is hot, add the beets. Cook, stirring, until hot, about 5 minutes. Season with salt and pepper, garnish, and serve.

Beets in Vinaigrette: Use oil for cooking the beets. When they're hot, drizzle them with any vinaigrette (pages 91–94), or this mixture:

1/4 cup minced shallots, scallions, or chives
2 tablespoons minced fresh parsley leaves
Salt and freshly ground black pepper to taste
2 tablespoons good wine, balsamic or sherry vinegar, or to taste
2 tablespoons extra-virgin olive oil

Boniato, or Batata

A popular tuber in both Latin America and Asia, frequently found here. It tastes like a cross between white and sweet potatoes, and can be treated like either; I suppose you might say it has more flavor than the first and less than the second, but see for yourself. Try especially baking, exactly as you would a white potato, making sure it is cooked all the way through, or peeling and boiling, always covered with water to prevent discoloration, and serving immediately.

Broccoli and Broccoli Raab

Like its close relative, the cauliflower (the "broccoflower" makes the connection obvious, as do long-stalked cauliflowers and big-flowered broccoli), broccoli is a member of the masive cabbage family. In fact, although they look different, broccoli and cauliflower are also essentially interchangeable in recipes.

In a generation, broccoli has gone from a much despised vegetable—few besides the Italians who brought it to this country actually ate it—to a featured staple in supermarkets. Not surprisingly: It keeps well, is nutrition- and flavor-packed, and takes little in the way of preparation. It's good raw or lightly or fully cooked.

Broccoli raab, or rape, is more bitter and has more stems and leaves than head broccoli, which is mostly flowers. It's delicious, and can be used in any broccoli recipe.

Buying and storing Broccoli grows best in cool weather; it's shipped nationwide from western states throughout the winter, and should be available from local sources all over the country—with the exception of the Sun Belt—from April through November or even later. Fresh broccoli is vastly superior to frozen and, since it's available year-round, should always be your choice. Look for tight heads, with no yellowing. Store in a loose plastic bag in the vegetable bin, and cook as quickly as you can.

Preparing Strip the stalk of leaves, if any (these can be cooked along with the tops and eaten, if you like). Remove the bottom inch of the stalk, or wherever it has dried out. Peel the tough outer skin of the broccoli stalk as best you can without going crazy; a paring knife or vegetable peeler work equally well. (To peel with a paring knife, hold the broccoli upside down; grasp a bit of the skin right at the bottom, between the paring knife and your thumb. Pull down to remove a strip of the skin.) If you like, cut the stalk into equal-length pieces and break the head into florets.

Best cooking methods Simmering, steaming, or microwaving all work fine; broccoli is good when precooked by one of these methods and then reheated. Stir-frying and braising are also good methods; there are recipes for all of these methods here. Regardless of the method, it often makes sense to cook the stalks longer than the florets; just start them a minute or two earlier. Broccoli also makes a good soup (see Cream of Broccoli, page 62), and pasta dish; see Pasta with Cauliflower or Broccoli, page 134.

When is it done? It's a matter of taste. When bright green, broccoli is still crisp and quite chewy, and some people like it that way. Cook it another couple of minutes and it becomes tender; overcook it and it becomes mushy and begins to fall apart. Try cooking until a skewer or thin-bladed knife can easily pierce the stalk.

Other recipes in which you can use broccoli:
Any cauliflower recipe (pages 554–556), usually with reduced cooking times.
Asparagus with Parmesan, page 538
Crisp-Cooked Asparagus, page 539
Cabbage Braised with Onions, page 549 (cooking time will be shorter for broccoli)
Chard with Garlic, Pine Nuts, and Currants, page 558 (don't chop the broccoli too finely)

Other recipes in which you can use broccoli raab:
Collards or Kale with Double Garlic, page 562
Collards or Kale, Brazilian-Style, page 563

Basic Simmered, Steamed, or Microwaved Broccoli or Broccoli Raab

Makes 4 servings

Time: 20 minutes

The thick stalks of broccoli are always worth peeling (page 543) and it usually makes sense to start cooking them a minute or two before the much more tender florets.

> 1 to 1¹/₂ pounds broccoli (or broccoli raab), trimmed and cut up (page 543)

1 To simmer the broccoli, bring a large pot of water to a boil; salt it. Place the stalk sections in the water and cook for 2 minutes. Add the florets and continue to cook for 2 to 6 minutes longer, until the pieces are bright green and tender.

2 To steam the broccoli, place the stalk sections in a steamer above an inch or two of salted water. Cover and cook about 2 minutes. Add the florets and continue to cook for 2 to 6 minutes longer, until the pieces are bright green and tender.

3 To microwave the broccoli, place the stalk sections on a microwave-proof plate or in a shallow bowl with about 2 tablespoons of salted water; cover with a lid or plastic wrap. Microwave on high for 2 minutes; shake the container and add the florets. Continue to microwave on high for 1-minute intervals, shaking and checking the broccoli, until it is bright green and tender.

4 Serve hot broccoli with butter, lemon butter (page 770), hollandaise (page 790), vinaigrette (page 91), or freshly squeezed lemon juice. Or drain it, drop it into a bowl of ice water to stop the cooking, drain again, place in a covered container, and refrigerate for up to 2 days. Then follow the directions for Precooked Vegetables in Butter or Oil (page 532).

Braised Broccoli with Garlic and Wine

Makes 4 servings

Time: 30 minutes

A Roman preparation, great at room temperature.

> 3 tablespoons olive oil
> 3 anchovies, minced (optional)
> 1 teaspoon minced garlic
> About 1¹/₂ pounds broccoli, trimmed and cut up (page 543)
> 1 cup dry white wine
> Salt and freshly ground black pepper to taste

1 Place the oil in a large, deep skillet that can later be covered and turn the heat to medium. Add the anchovies and the garlic and cook, stirring occasionally, until the anchovies begin to break up and the garlic begins to color, 3 to 5 minutes.

2 Add the broccoli and cook, stirring, for 3 or 4 minutes. Add the wine and let it bubble away for a minute or two. Cover, turn the heat to medium-low, and cook for 2 or 3 minutes.

3 Uncover, return the heat to medium, and cook until most of the wine has evaporated and the broccoli is tender, about 5 minutes more. Season to taste (you will not need much salt) and serve hot or at room temperature.

Stir-Fried Broccoli

Makes 4 servings

Time: 30 minutes

You need not precook the broccoli for these stir-fries, but if you have leftover or extra simmered or steamed broccoli (see Basic Simmered, Steamed, or Microwaved Broccoli or Broccoli Raab, page 544), by all means use them. Just keep the cooking time to a minimum, no longer than it takes to heat the broccoli through.

> About 1½ pounds broccoli, trimmed (page 543)
> 2 tablespoons peanut (preferred) or other oil
> Salt to taste
> 1 teaspoon sugar
> 1 cup chicken, beef, or vegetable stock, or water
>   (see "Soups" for stock recipes)

1 Cut the stalks of the broccoli into thin slices. Separate the florets into small sections.

2 Place the oil in a wok or large, deep skillet over medium-high heat. Two or three minutes later, add the broccoli, raise the heat to high and cook, stirring, until it become bright green and glossy and begin to brown, about 5 minutes.

3 Add the salt, sugar, and stock or water. Stir and continue to cook until almost all of the liquid evaporates and the broccoli is tender, about 5 minutes more. Serve immediately.

Stir-Fried Broccoli with Chinese Mushrooms: In Step 1, soak about ¼ cup dried shiitake ("black") mushrooms in 1 cup hot water until tender; drain them (reserving liquid), trim them, and cut them up. In Step 2, add the mushrooms along with the broccoli. In Step 3, add 1 teaspoon minced garlic and 1 teaspoon peeled and minced fresh ginger along with the salt and sugar. Stir for 15 seconds before adding the strained mushroom soaking liquid and 1 tablespoon of soy sauce.

Broccoli Raab with Sausage and Grapes

Makes 4 servings

Time: About 30 minutes

This is more of a main course than a side dish. Without the grapes, and thinned with a little water or stock, it can serve as a sauce for pasta. Substitute regular broccoli if you like.

> About 1½ pounds broccoli raab, trimmed and cut up
>   (page 543)
> About 1 pound sweet, garlicky sausage
> 2 cloves garlic, slivered
> About ½ pound seedless grapes
> Salt and freshly ground black pepper to taste

1 Simmer, steam, or microwave (see Basic Simmered, Steamed, or Microwaved Broccoli or Broccoli Raab, page 544) the broccoli raab for about 3 minutes, until it is bright green and beginning to become tender. Drain and plunge it into ice water for a few moments. (You may prepare the recipe in advance up to this point; refrigerate, well wrapped or in a covered container, for up to 2 days before proceeding.)

2 Cook the sausage over medium heat in a large, deep skillet, pricking it with a fork or thin-bladed knife a few times, and turning from time to time until it is nicely browned.

3 Remove the sausage from the skillet (don't worry about it being done) and cut it into bite-sized pieces. Return it to the skillet, over medium heat; cook, turning occasionally, until all sides of the sausage are nicely browned, about 5 more minutes.

4 Squeeze the excess liquid from the broccoli raab and chop it coarsely. Add it to the skillet along with the garlic and cook, stirring occasionally, for 3 or 4 minutes. Add the grapes and heat through. Check for salt and sprinkle liberally with pepper. Serve immediately.

Brussels Sprouts

Brussels sprouts look like miniature cabbages, and that's what they are. Like cabbage, they must not be overcooked, or they become soggy and strong-flavored. But bought well and handled simply, they can be wonderful.

Buying and storing   The smaller the better is a good rule. Reject any with yellow leaves, loose leaves, or those that are soft or not tightly packed. Generally, Brussels sprouts are a winter vegetable, found from September or October through early spring.

Preparing   Remove the stem and any loose leaves. Some people suggest cutting an "x" in the root bottom to ensure even cooking, but I haven't found that it matters much.

Best cooking methods   Simmering followed, if you like, by reheating in butter or oil or other reheating methods; braising. Brussels sprouts are also good finished with crumbled crisp-cooked bacon or toasted bread crumbs, page 239.

When is it done?   When just tender enough to be easily pierced by a skewer or a thin-bladed knife. Do not overcook.

Other recipes in which you can use Brussels sprouts:

Asparagus with Parmesan, page 538
Cardoons and Onions Cooked in Cream, page 551
   (don't precook Brussels sprouts)
Cabbage Braised with Onions, page 549
Braised Endive, Escarole, or Radicchio with
   Prosciutto, page 572

Braised Fennel with Onions and Vinegar,
   page 573
Turnips in Mustard Sauce, page 612

Simmered Brussels Sprouts
Makes 4 servings

Time: 20 minutes

This is the best way to cook Brussels sprouts. Steaming and microwaving are also fine, but you must keep a close watch on them to avoid overcooking. To vary this recipe, top the sprouts with one-quarter cup freshly grated Parmesan just before serving.

1 to 1¹⁄₂ pounds Brussels sprouts, trimmed
   (see opposite)
2 tablespoons butter or extra-virgin olive oil
1 clove garlic, smashed (optional)
1 tablespoon plain bread crumbs
1 tablespoon freshly squeezed lemon juice
1 tablespoon minced fresh parsley leaves
Salt and freshly ground black pepper to taste

1 Bring a large pot of water to the boil; salt it. Add the Brussels sprouts and, keeping the heat high, boil them just until tender, about 10 minutes; do not overcook. Drain and refresh in cold water. (You may prepare the recipe in advance up to this point; refrigerate, well wrapped or in a covered container, for up to 2 days before proceeding.)

2 Place the butter or oil in a large, deep skillet over medium heat; add the garlic. When the butter foam subsides or the oil is hot, add the sprouts and the bread crumbs. Stir until hot, about 3 minutes.

3 Remove the garlic, toss the sprouts with the lemon juice and parsley, season to taste, and serve.

Cabbage

There are countless varieties of cabbage, and although they're all good, some are better than others. The best head cabbage is Savoy, the light green variety with crinkled leaves; if you can't find it, the standard tight, smooth, light green cabbage will do. Napa (also spelled Nappa) cabbage, also called Chinese cabbage, is a good romaine-like variety, terrific for raw salads and coleslaw. For stir-fries, there is nothing better than bok choy, whose stems turn almost creamy after cooking.

If you think you hate cabbage, as so many people do, try eating it raw (you don't hate coleslaw, do you?), or in stir-fries. Many of the nasty things people say about cabbage result from overcooking it; cabbage, like many other brassicas, becomes waterlogged and strong-flavored when cooked too long. But keep the cooking time within reason, and you'll be rewarded with a crisp, bright-flavored vegetable.

Buying and storing   Cabbage is a year-round vegetable, widely shipped and found locally when the weather is cool. Large cabbages are fine to eat, but do you really want a four-pound vegetable? Unless you're making coleslaw for a crowd, or a winter's worth of sauerkraut, probably not. Reject any cabbages with yellow leaves, loose leaves, or those which are soft or not tightly packed. Forget about canned or frozen cabbage; there's no reason to buy it.

As for sauerkraut, look for a variety with few preservatives, packed in glass or plastic; canned sauerkraut often tastes of metal.

Preparing   All head cabbage, regardless of color, as well as Napa cabbage, should be cored before cooking or shredding. First remove a couple of layers of the outer leaves. Then use a thin-bladed knife to cut a cone-shaped section out of the core, making the wide end of the cone a circle about one-half inch wider than the core itself. To shred head cabbage, just cut the cabbage into quarters (or eighths, if it is large), and cross-cut thinly; it will shred itself. To shred Napa cabbage, just cross-cut; no quartering is necessary.

To prepare bok choy, wash, then remove any damaged leaves. Chop or otherwise prepare as you like, discarding the root end and the inch or so above it.

Best cooking methods   Braising, stir-frying, and sautéing; you'll find examples of all below. Simmering is also fine, but not for hours in the old "corned-beef-and-cabbage" style. Rather, separate the cabbage into leaves and plunge it into lots of boiling salted water until tender, three to five minutes. Then drain and serve, simply salted, or drain and reheat according to

CORING AND SHREDDING CABBAGE

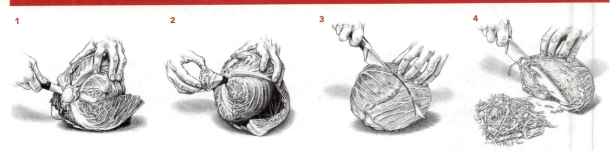

(Steps 1–2) The easiest way to core a head cabbage is to cut a small cone-shaped section from the bottom, then remove it. *(Step 3)* To shred head cabbage, first cut it into manageable pieces. *(Step 4)* Cut thin sections across the head; they'll naturally fall into shreds. (You can also use a mandoline for this; see page 531). If the shreds are too long, just cut across them.

Precooked Vegetables in Butter or Oil (page 532). Make sure to try Fresh Napa Kimchi (page 108) as well.

When is it done?   When crisp-tender to soft, but not mushy.

Other recipes in which you can use cabbage:
Collards or Kale with Double Garlic, page 562
Broccoli Raab with Sausage and Grapes, page 545
Braised Broccoli with Garlic and Wine, page 544

Braised Cabbage with Wine and Nutmeg

Makes 4 servings

Time: Less than 30 minutes

You can braise any cabbage, red, white, bok choy, Savoy—they'll all be great. You can also vary the spices as you like (cloves are great) but nutmeg is especially lovely.

2 tablespoons olive oil or butter
1 head cabbage, preferably Savoy, about 1¹/₂
    pounds, cored and shredded (page 547)
Salt and freshly ground black pepper to taste
¹/₂ cup white wine
1 teaspoon brown sugar
¹/₄ teaspoon freshly grated nutmeg

1   Place the olive oil or butter in a large, deep skillet that can later be covered, over medium heat. Add the cabbage and stir until it begins to brown, about 5 minutes.

2   Add salt and pepper, then the wine; let the wine bubble away for a few moments, then add the sugar and nutmeg. Cover and simmer until tender, about 15 minutes. Check the seasoning and serve.

Cabbage Cooked with Apples

Makes 4 servings

Time: About 45 minutes

Relatively long, slow cooking allows the cabbage to become tender and absorb all the sweetness of the apples, which virtually dissolve.

2 tablespoons butter
2 pounds Savoy or other cabbage, trimmed and
    shredded (page 547)
1 to 1¹/₂ pounds sweet apples, peeled, cored, and
    cut into chunks
3 cloves
¹/₂ cup chicken or vegetable stock, or not-too-dry
    white wine, apple cider, or water, plus more if
    needed (see "Soups" for stock recipes)
2 tablespoons apricot or raspberry jam or currant jelly
Salt and freshly ground black pepper to taste
1 tablespoon freshly squeezed lemon juice or cider
    vinegar

1   Melt the butter over medium heat in a large, deep skillet, saucepan, or casserole. Add the cabbage, apples, and cloves and cook, stirring, until the cabbage is glossy, about 3 minutes.

2   Add the liquid, turn the heat to medium-low, cover, and cook, stirring occasionally, for 30 minutes or more, until the cabbage is tender and the apples have fallen apart. If the mixture dries out, add a little more liquid.

3   Stir in the jam or jelly and season with salt and pepper. Add the lemon juice or vinegar a few drops at a time, tasting after each addition, until the sweetness of the cabbage and apples is balanced by a nice hint of acidity. Discard cloves and serve.

Gingered Cabbage

Makes 4 servings

Time: 30 minutes

Cabbage and ginger, generally thought of as a Chinese combination, are equally good cooked in a more Western style.

2 tablespoons peanut (preferred) or other oil
1 head cabbage, preferably Savoy, about 1½ pounds, cored, shredded, and chopped (page 547)
1 tablespoon minced garlic
Salt and freshly ground black pepper to taste
1 tablespoon peeled and minced or grated fresh ginger
Juice of 1 lime
Minced fresh parsley or cilantro leaves for garnish

1 Place the oil in a large, deep skillet over medium-high heat; wait 2 minutes, then add the cabbage. Cook, stirring occasionally, for 5 to 10 minutes.

2 When the cabbage is limp but not mushy, add the garlic, salt, and pepper, and cook another 2 minutes, stirring.

3 Add the ginger and cook another minute. Drizzle with the lime juice, garnish, and serve.

Sauerkraut with Juniper Berries

Makes 4 to 6 servings

Time: 40 minutes

If possible, use sauerkraut without preservatives; it's sold in bulk in specialty stores or in jars in some natural foods stores. Substitute caraway seeds for the juniper berries if you like.

2 tablespoons butter (preferred) or any light oil
1 onion, sliced
1½ to 2 pounds sauerkraut, rinsed
1 bay leaf
1 tablespoon juniper berries, lightly crushed with the side of a knife, or caraway seeds
1 cup chicken, beef, or vegetable stock, or not-too-dry white wine (see "Soups" for stock recipes)

1 Place the butter or oil in a large, deep skillet over medium heat. When the butter melts or the oil is hot, add the onion and toss until it begins to wilt, about 3 minutes.

2 Add the remaining ingredients, stir, and cook until some of the wine bubbles away, 1 to 2 minutes. Cover, lower the heat, and cook until the sauerkraut is tender, about 30 minutes. Discard bay leaf and serve hot or warm.

Cabbage Braised with Onions

Makes 4 servings

Time: About 1 hour

Slow-cooked onions add sweetness to this dish, and the touch of cayenne makes it wonderfully spicy.

2 cups sliced onions
3 tablespoons butter or olive oil
3 tablespoons tomato paste
¼ teaspoon cayenne, or to taste
½ cup water
1½ to 2 pounds Savoy or other white cabbage, cored and shredded (page 547)
Salt and freshly ground black pepper to taste

1 Place the onions in a large, deep skillet or casserole over medium-low heat. Cover and cook, stirring every 5 minutes, until the onions have given up their liquid and are almost sticking to the pan. Add the butter or oil, raise the heat to medium-high, and cook for 5 to 10 minutes, until the onion browns nicely.

2 Add the tomato paste, cayenne, water, and cabbage. Stir, then cover. Cook for about 30 minutes, stirring occasionally, until the cabbage is tender but not mushy. Season with salt and pepper and serve.

Stir-Fried Cabbage

Makes 4 servings

Time: 20 minutes

Cabbage is also good using the variations given for Stir-Fried Asparagus, Three Ways (page 539) and Stir-Fried Broccoli (page 545). Although bok choy is the best cabbage to stir-fry, you can use other varieties if you like.

> 2 tablespoons peanut (preferred) or other oil
> 1 tablespoon minced garlic
> 1 tablespoon peeled and minced fresh ginger
> $^1/_2$ cup cut-up scallions, cut into 1-inch lengths, plus minced scallions for garnish
> 2 pounds bok choy, cut into 1-inch sections, or other cabbage, cored and shredded (page 547)
> 1 cup chicken, beef, or vegetable stock, or white wine or water (see "Soups" for stock recipes)
> 1 tablespoon soy sauce
> Salt and freshly ground black pepper to taste
> Minced chives for garnish

1 Heat a wok or large, deep skillet over medium-high heat for 3 or 4 minutes. Add the oil and, almost immediately, the garlic, ginger, and $^1/_2$ cup cut-up scallions. Cook, stirring, for about 15 seconds, then add the cabbage and turn the heat to high.

2 Cook, stirring almost constantly, for 3 minutes, then add the liquid. Cook, stirring, until it evaporates and the cabbage is tender, about 5 minutes more. Add the soy sauce and turn off the heat. Season with salt and pepper if necessary, garnish, and serve.

Calabaza, or West Indian Pumpkin

A pumpkin-like winter squash, usually sold in slices or hunks in markets catering to Central and South Americans. Quite frequently better than pumpkin (page 600) when cooked in the same ways.

Cardoon

This relative of the artichoke is rarely seen in stores, but I think it soon will be. For now, you'll have to look for it at farmers' markets. You strip the leaves and cook and eat the stems, and they're delicious—which is why they're popular in Italy, France, and South America, and with gardeners and some chefs.

Buying and storing You're not going to have much choice, but look for firm stems and dark green leaves. Store, loosely wrapped in plastic, in the vegetable bin, and use as soon as possible.

Preparing Strip the stems of leaves and discard them. Chop the stems into two-inch lengths.

Best cooking methods Cardoons are almost always simmered or steamed before further cooking.

When is it done? When tender enough to easily pierce with a skewer or thin-bladed knife.

Other recipes in which you can use cardoons:
Asparagus with Parmesan, page 538
Crisp-Cooked Asparagus, page 539
Braised Broccoli with Garlic and Wine, page 544
Baked Chard in Béchamel, page 559
Braised Fennel with Onions and Vinegar, page 573

Basic Simmered or Steamed Cardoons

Makes 4 servings

Time: 15 minutes

After you have cooked cardoons this way, you can serve them with butter, freshly squeezed lemon juice, hollandaise, or any other sauce, use them in Bagna Cauda (page 26), or in the following recipe. Or substitute them for the asparagus in Asparagus with Parmesan (page 538).

1½ to 2 pounds cardoons, stripped of their leaves

1 To simmer the cardoons, bring a large pot of water to a boil; salt it. Cut the cardoon stalks into 2-inch lengths and place them in the water; turn the heat to medium and simmer until the stalks are just tender enough to pierce with a thin-bladed knife, about 10 minutes. Drain and serve immediately, or plunge into an ice-water bath and drain.

2 To steam the cardoons, place them in a steamer above an inch or two of salted water. Cover and cook 10 to 15 minutes, until they can be pierced with a thin-bladed knife. Drain and serve immediately, or plunge into an ice-water bath and drain.

Cardoons and Onions Cooked in Cream

Makes 4 servings

Time: 20 minutes with precooked cardoons, 35 minutes from scratch

This preparation gives good results not only with cardoons but with celery, Brussels sprouts, and other vegetables. Feel free to use frozen pearl onions in this dish; it's not even necessary to thaw them first.

2 tablespoons butter
1 recipe Basic Simmered or Steamed Cardoons (see opposite), drained well
20 pearl onions, peeled
1 cup heavy or light cream or half-and-half
Freshly grated nutmeg to taste
Salt and freshly ground black pepper to taste

1 Place the butter in a medium saucepan or casserole and turn the heat to medium-low. When it melts, add the cardoons and the onions. Cook, stirring, until the vegetables are coated with butter, just a minute or two.

2 Add the cream and bring the mixture to a boil over medium-high heat. Turn the heat back down to medium-low; simmer, stirring occasionally, until most of the cream is absorbed, about 20 minutes.

3 Mix a couple of gratings of nutmeg into the vegetables; taste and adjust seasoning with salt, pepper, and/or more nutmeg.

Carrots

It's likely there's a bag of carrots sitting in your refrigerator right now. You might peel them and eat them raw, or include them in soups or stews, all of which are excellent uses. But—although you might not know it from the sadly overcooked carrots of yesteryear—carrots are a terrific cooked vegetable. In fact, cooking often transforms the slightly bitter taste raw carrots frequently have into a distinctive sweetness.

Buying and storing   Carrots with tops are a treat, but carrots keep so well that even bagged carrots are usually quite good. Officially, the season is late summer through early winter, but carrots are readily available year-round. Don't buy them if they're flabby or growing new leaves.

Preparing   Among the easiest vegetables to prepare. Peel with a vegetable peeler (make long strokes), then trim off both ends (see illustration on page 552).

(Step 1) To dice a carrot, cut it in half lengthwise, then into quarters or, if necessary, smaller sections. *(Step 2)* Cut across the sections, as small as you like.

Best cooking methods Steaming, simmering, braising.

When is it done? When tender but not soft. Taste and you'll know.

Other recipes in which you can use carrots:
Stir-Fried Asparagus, Three Ways, page 539
Gingered Cabbage, page 549 (use precooked carrots)
Stir-Fried Cauliflower with Ginger and Oyster Sauce, page 555
Slow-Cooked Green Beans, page 577 (cut the carrots into ¹/₂-inch slices before cooking)
Mashed Potatoes, page 596 (or mix mashed potatoes and carrots)
Potato Pancakes, Version I, page 598 (or, again, use a mixture)

Pureed Parsnips, page 590
Pureed Butternut Squash with Ginger, page 613
Braised Butternut or Other Winter Squash with Garlic, page 614
Roasted Root Vegetables, page 615

Basic Simmered or Steamed Carrots

Makes 4 servings

Time: About 30 minutes

The only reason, really, to cook carrots this way is to use them in other recipes. For carrots as a side dish, you're much better off using the next recipe, which is just as easy and far more flavorful.

1 pound carrots, peeled and cut into chunks, slices, or julienne

1 To simmer the carrots, bring a large pot of water to a boil; salt it. Place the carrot pieces in the water; turn the heat to medium and simmer until they are tender, about 3 minutes for julienned carrots, up to 30 minutes for carrot chunks.

2 To steam the carrots, place them in a steamer above an inch or two of salted water. Cover and cook until they are tender, about 3 minutes for julienned carrots, up to 30 minutes for carrot chunks.

3 Serve hot carrots with butter, extra-virgin olive oil, and/or freshly squeezed lemon juice; season with salt and pepper and garnish with parsley if you like. Or drain, drop into a bowl of ice water to stop the cooking, drain again, place in a covered container, and refrigerate for up to 2 days. Then cook according to the directions for Precooked Vegetables in Butter or Oil (page 532).

Quick-Braised Carrots with Butter

Makes 4 servings

Time: About 20 minutes

Best with butter, but still delicious when made with oil. Even better is to cut back on the oil (as below) and use it as a neutral cooking medium rather than as a flavor enhancer. Simply cooked carrots are good spiked with spices. In addition to ginger (see the variation), try ground cardamom, cinnamon, cumin, or coriander.

> 1 pound carrots, peeled and cut into ¼-inch-thick slices
> 2 tablespoons butter or 1 tablespoon canola or other neutral oil
> ¼ cup water
> 1 teaspoon sugar or 1 tablespoon maple syrup
> Salt and freshly ground black pepper to taste
> Minced fresh parsley, mint, chervil, or cilantro leaves for garnish

❶ Place the carrots, butter or oil, water, sugar, salt, and pepper in a medium saucepan over high heat; bring to a boil and cover. Turn the heat to medium-low and cook for 5 minutes.

❷ Uncover and raise the heat a bit. Cook, stirring occasionally, until the liquid has evaporated and the carrots are cooking in butter or oil. Lower the heat and continue to cook, stirring occasionally, until tender, a couple of minutes longer.

❸ Taste and adjust the seasoning if necessary, then garnish and serve.

Quick-Braised Carrots with Orange and Ginger: In Step 1, substitute ¼ cup orange juice (preferably freshly squeezed) and 1 tablespoon minced orange zest for the water. In Step 2, add 1 tablespoon peeled and minced fresh ginger to the saucepan after removing the cover. Step 3 remains the same.

Cauliflower

Cauliflower is a member of the cabbage family (its name means "cabbage flower"). Closely related to broccoli (and virtually interchangeable in recipes), it is usually white but also may be green or purple. (The flower, or curd, is white when it is shielded from the sun by its leaves, called blanching; otherwise it darkens. The differences in color are cosmetic.) A good, fresh, garden-grown cauliflower is among the most delicious vegetables, and a real treat. But supermarket cauliflowers in good shape can be very good, good enough to eat raw or lightly cooked and barely dressed.

Buying and storing The first rule is no brown spots, which indicate an old cauliflower likely to have lost most of its flavor. The best bet is cauliflower with its leaves still wrapped around the flower, one that looks as if it just came out of the ground. Plastic-wrapped cauliflower should be creamy white, the leaves fresh and crisp-looking. Frozen cauliflower is acceptable, but never delicious.

PREPARING CAULIFLOWER

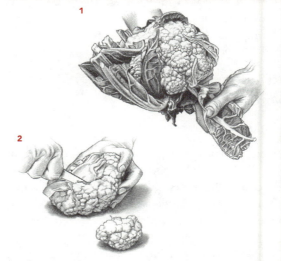

First, remove all outer leaves. You can cook the head whole or cut it into florets.

Preparing   Remove outer leaves. With a small knife, scrape off any brown or black spots. You can cook cauliflower whole or separate it into florets before cooking. To separate into florets, begin at the base of the head and cut florets from the core, one after the other. The florets may in turn be broken or cut into smaller pieces if you like.

Best cooking methods   Steaming, braising, simmering (plunge whole cauliflower or florets into boiling water, but be careful not to overcook), or microwaving (cut into florets and microwave as you would broccoli, page 544) are all good, as is stir-frying; examples of all follow. Cauliflower is also good with pasta; see Pasta with Cauliflower or Broccoli, page 134.

When is it done?   When just tender enough to pierce with a skewer or thin-bladed knife. Overcooking is not as disastrous as it is with other members of the cabbage family, but, naturally, it's not desirable.

Other recipes in which you can use cauliflower:
Any broccoli recipe (pages 544–546)
Asparagus with Parmesan, page 538
Curried Eggplant with Potatoes, page 570 (in place of the eggplant)
Turnips in Mustard Sauce, page 612

Basic Steamed Cauliflower

Makes 4 servings

Time: About 30 minutes

You can speed the cooking of cauliflower by cutting it up before cooking; but because it crumbles easily, you'll lose some of it in the process. It's best to allow enough time to cook the vegetable whole. Steaming is better than simmering, which can leave cauliflower waterlogged.

1 head cauliflower, about 1 1/2 pounds, trimmed of green parts (see illustration, page 553)
Minced fresh parsley leaves for garnish

①   Place the cauliflower in a steamer above an inch or two of salted water. Cover and cook until it is just tender enough to be pierced to the core with a thin-bladed knife, no longer (because of its relatively large mass, cauliflower retains quite a bit of heat after cooking, so it should still be ever-so-slightly chewy when you remove it from the steamer). Total cooking time will be 12 to 25 minutes, depending on the size of the head.

②   Serve hot cauliflower with butter, extra-virgin olive oil, and/or lemon juice; garnish with parsley. Or drain, drop into a bowl of ice water to stop the cooking, drain again, place in a covered container, and refrigerate for up to 2 days. Then break into florets and cook according to the directions for Precooked Vegetables in Butter or Oil (page 532).

Cauliflower with Garlic and Anchovies

Makes 4 servings

Time: 15 minutes with precooked cauliflower, about 30 minutes with raw

In a dish like this, the garlic and anchovies mellow somewhat and combine to produce a highly flavorful sauce.

1 recipe Basic Steamed Cauliflower (see opposite), slightly underdone
4 tablespoons extra-virgin olive oil
2 to 10 anchovy fillets, to taste, chopped
1 tablespoon minced garlic
1 teaspoon crushed red pepper flakes, or to taste (optional)
Minced fresh parsley leaves for garnish

①   Break or cut the cauliflower into florets 1 1/2 inches across or less.

②   Combine the oil, anchovies, garlic, and crushed red pepper in a large, deep skillet and turn the heat to medium-low. Cook, stirring occasionally, until the anchovies begin to break up and the garlic begins to color, about 5 minutes.

3 Add the cauliflower and raise the heat to medium-high. Continue to cook, stirring, for about 5 minutes more, until the cauliflower is coated with oil and heated through. Garnish and serve.

Stir-Fried Cauliflower with Ginger and Oyster Sauce

Makes 4 servings

Time: 30 minutes

Add some pieces of boneless chicken to the mix just before the cauliflower if you'd like to make this dish more substantial. Best served over rice.

1 recipe Basic Steamed Cauliflower (page 554), slightly underdone
2 tablespoons soy sauce
1/4 teaspoon sugar
2 tablespoons peanut (preferred) or other oil
1 tablespoon peeled and minced or grated fresh ginger
1 teaspoon minced garlic
2 scallions, minced
1/2 cup chicken or vegetable stock, or water (see "Soups" for stock recipes)
2 tablespoons oyster sauce
1 tablespoon cornstarch (optional)
2 tablespoons water (optional)

1 Break or cut the cauliflower into florets 1 1/2 inches across or less; mix it in a small bowl with 1 tablespoon soy sauce and the sugar.

2 Place the oil in a wok or large, deep skillet and turn the heat to high. When it starts smoking, add the ginger and garlic; cook, stirring, for about 15 seconds. Add the cauliflower and scallions and stir.

3 Cook for about 2 minutes, then add the stock or water, oyster sauce, and remaining soy sauce. Cook for 1 minute. For a thicker sauce, mix the cornstarch with 2 tablespoons of water and stir it in. Cook, stirring, until thickened, just a minute longer. Serve immediately.

Braised Cauliflower with Curry and Tomatoes

Makes 4 servings

Time: 30 minutes

The meatiness of cauliflower makes it perfect for curries. Sample it frequently as it cooks, not only so that you can adjust the flavor but so that you can stop the cooking just as it becomes tender. If you like, substitute about one tablespoon of All-Purpose Curry Powder (page 778) (or Garam Masala, page 778) for the dried spices. And feel free to add other vegetables to the mix. Serve with rice or Rice Pilaf (page 202).

2 tablespoons butter, peanut oil, or other oil
1 teaspoon minced garlic
1 teaspoon peeled and minced or grated fresh ginger
1 teaspoon salt
1 teaspoon freshly ground black pepper
1/2 teaspoon ground turmeric
1/4 teaspoon cayenne, or to taste
1/2 teaspoon ground cinnamon
Pinch freshly grated nutmeg
1 teaspoon ground coriander
1 teaspoon ground cumin
1 head cauliflower, about 1 1/2 pounds, trimmed of green parts and broken into florets (page 554)
1 cup cored, seeded, and chopped tomatoes (canned are fine; don't bother to drain)
1/2 cup water
1 1/2 cups fresh or thawed frozen peas (optional)
Minced cilantro leaves for garnish

1 Place the butter or oil in a large, deep skillet and turn the heat to medium. When the butter melts or the oil is hot, add the garlic and ginger. Cook, stirring, until the garlic begins to color, about 5 minutes.

2 Add the salt and all the spices and cook, stirring, for 30 seconds, or until the spices release their aromas. Add the cauliflower, tomatoes, and water. Stir, cover, and turn the heat to medium-low. Cook, checking and stirring every 3 or 4 minutes, until the cauliflower is almost tender, about 10 minutes.

3 Add the peas and adjust the seasoning. Cook until the cauliflower is tender, then garnish and serve.

Celery and Celeriac

These days, celery is usually eaten raw or in soups or stews. But cooking mellows the taste and texture of celery, yielding a distinctive and enjoyable vegetable.

Celeriac, or celery root, is a type of celery grown for its root. The large knob, which could be mistaken for jicama, is usually eaten raw, in salads. But it is wonderful in purees, especially with potatoes.

Buying and storing Buy celery, preferably with its leaves, unwrapped, crisp, and bright pale green. If trimmed and packed in plastic, make sure there are no signs of softness, wilting, or yellowing. Celery keeps very well, wrapped in plastic, for a couple of weeks. Celeriac should be hard and firm, with no soft spots; relatively smoothed-skinned specimens are easier to peel. As with most root vegetables, celeriac keeps for a long time, but its flavor is most intense when it is firm and crisp; don't wait until it becomes flabby to eat it.

Preparing Trim leaves from celery before cooking, but reserve them for garnishes or soups and stews. (You can dry them in a low oven if you like, after which they'll keep forever.) Remove the bottom core. You can "string" celery as you do rhubarb (see illustration, page 645) before cooking, but unless the celery is old and tough it is not necessary. Celeriac must be peeled before using; use a sharp knife rather than a vegetable peeler, and acknowledge from the outset that you will lose a good portion of the flesh. You might drop the celeriac into acidulated water (one tablespoon lemon juice or vinegar per cup of water) to keep it from discoloring.

Best cooking methods Celery: braising, hands down. Celeriac, simmered or pureed, or made into croquettes.

When is it done? Celery, when good and tender; taste a piece. Celeriac, when soft.

Other recipes in which you can use celery:
Asparagus with Parmesan, page 538
Cardoons and Onions Cooked in Cream, page 551 (substitute for cardoons, but don't precook it).
Baked Chard in Béchamel, page 559 (don't precook celery)
Braised Fennel with Onions and Vinegar, page 573 (substitute celery for the fennel)
Turnips in Mustard Sauce, page 612

Other recipes in which you can use celeriac:
Potato Croquettes, page 597 (or make croquettes with Celeriac and Potato Puree, page 557)

Basic Braised Celery

Makes 4 servings

Time: 30 minutes

Cooking celery mellows its flavor and improves its texture.

1½ pounds celery, more or less, trimmed
2 tablespoons butter or olive oil
Salt and freshly ground black pepper to taste
1 tablespoon flour
1 cup chicken, beef, or vegetable stock, or water (see "Soups" for stock recipes)
Minced fresh parsley or dill leaves for garnish

1 Cut the celery into pieces about 2 inches long. Melt the butter or heat the olive oil in a large, deep skillet over medium heat.

2 Cook the celery in the butter or oil, stirring, for about 2 minutes. Season with salt and pepper and sprinkle with the flour. Cook, stirring, for about 2 minutes more.

3 Add the stock or water and stir; bring to a boil, then turn the heat to low. Cover and cook until the celery is very tender, 10 to 15 minutes. Uncover; if the mixture is watery, turn the heat to high and boil off some of the liquid. When the mixture has a saucy texture, garnish and serve.

Braised Celery with Tomatoes, Olives, and Capers: In Step 2, cook 2 tablespoons minced onion or shallots with the celery. When you uncover the skillet in Step 3, add 1 tablespoon drained capers, $^1/_2$ cup pitted and chopped black olives, and 1 cup cored, seeded, and chopped tomatoes (canned are fine; drain first). Cook, stirring, for about 3 minutes, then garnish and serve.

Braised Celery with Buttered Almonds: Use butter in Step 1. While the celery is cooking, lightly brown $^1/_2$ cup blanched, slivered almonds in 2 tablespoons butter. Proceed as above, and when the celery is done, toss it with the buttered almonds and serve.

Celeriac and Potato Puree

Makes 4 servings

Time: 40 minutes

These celery-flavored mashed potatoes make a welcome addition to any meal that features meats cooked in liquid. You can hold this puree over very low heat or let it cool and microwave it just before serving.

1 pound celeriac (2 small knobs or 1 large one), peeled (page 556)
1 pound baking potatoes, such as Idaho or Russet, peeled
Salt
3 tablespoons butter
$^1/_2$ cup milk or cream, warmed
Freshly ground black pepper to taste
Minced fresh parsley leaves for garnish

1 Cut the celeriac and potatoes into roughly equal-sized pieces, 1 or 2 inches in diameter. Place in a pot with water to cover; add a handful of salt. Bring to a boil and cook until both potatoes and celeriac are tender, about 15 minutes.

2 Drain the vegetables well and rinse out the pot. (You may prepare the recipe in advance up to this point; refrigerate, well wrapped or in a covered container, for up to 2 days before proceeding.) Put the vegetables through a food mill placed over the pot, or mash them with a large fork or potato masher. Add the butter and, gradually, the milk, beating with a wooden spoon. When the mixture is smooth, season it with salt and pepper and serve, keep warm, or allow to cool for reheating later. Garnish before serving.

Chard, or Swiss Chard

Essentially a beet grown for leaves rather than roots, chard has a thick midrib which is white, pink, or brilliant red; the leaves are sometimes ruffled and are deep green, green with rich scarlet veins, or dark reddish-purple. Chard has a distinctive, acid-sweet flavor that makes it unlike any other vegetable; most people like the taste. It is a fine green on its own, but, like spinach, it is often cooked in omelets, pies, and other dishes.

Buying and storing Chard is available year-round (it's easy to grow, and tolerates a wide range of temperatures). Chard stems are delicate; look for those that are unbruised. There is thick- and thin-stemmed chard. If you prefer the leaves, look for the latter (red chard is almost always thin-stemmed); if it's the stalks you're after, the former. Red chard is arguably sweeter than green chard. Store, very loosely wrapped, in the vegetable bin, and use as soon as possible.

Preparing   Wash it well. If the stems are very thick, strip the leaves from them before proceeding so you can cook the stems a few minutes longer.

Best cooking methods   Simmering or steaming; it makes sense to cook thicker stems for a little longer than the leaves. If the stems are thin, throw everything in together. Slender-stemmed chard may also be steamed like spinach (see Basic Boiled, Steamed, or Microwaved Spinach, page 604), with the water that clings to its leaves. Take care when cooking red chard with other foods; its color will bleed.

When is it done?   When wilted and tender.

Other recipes in which you can use Swiss chard:
Asparagus with Parmesan (stalks only), page 538
Cardoons and Onions Cooked in Cream, page 551
   (use fat chard stems only; don't precook).
Dandelion Greens with Bacon, page 96 (use leaves
   and thin stems only).

Basic Simmered Chard
Makes 4 servings

Time: 20 minutes

Depending on the variety of chard you have, it may be very leafy or very stemmy; in either case, it makes sense to cook the relatively tough stems longer than the tender leaves, and simmering is the best method for this.

2 pounds Swiss chard, washed and trimmed (see opposite), leaves and stems separated, all roughly chopped

1 Bring a large pot of water to a boil; salt it. Cook the stems until they are almost tender, about 5 minutes. Add the chopped leaves. Continue to cook until both stems and leaves are quite tender, another couple of minutes.

2 Drain and serve hot chard with butter, extra-virgin olive oil, and/or vinegar. Or drain it, drop it into a bowl of ice water to stop the cooking, drain again, place in a covered container, and refrigerate for up to 2 days. Then cook it according to the directions for Precooked Vegetables in Butter or Oil (page 532).

Chard with Garlic, Pine Nuts, and Currants
Makes 4 servings

Time: 20 minutes

This sweet dish, which is also great when made with spinach, is wonderful as an accompaniment to savory meats. Or thin it with a little more olive oil and some of the chard cooking water to make a good pasta sauce.

2 tablespoons olive oil
1 tablespoon minced garlic
1/2 cup pine nuts
1 recipe Basic Simmered Chard (page 558), cooled,
   squeezed dry, and chopped
1/2 cup currants (preferred) or raisins, soaked in warm
   water for about 10 minutes, drained
Salt and freshly ground black pepper to taste

1 Place the oil and garlic in a large, deep skillet over medium-low heat. Cook until the garlic begins to color, about 5 minutes.

2 Add the pine nuts and cook another minute, stirring, then add the chard, currants, and salt and pepper; cook, stirring, for about 2 minutes. Serve hot or at room temperature.

Baked Chard in Béchamel

Makes 4 servings

Time: About 40 minutes

This is a great recipe if you have chard that is mostly stems; use the leaves as you would spinach, in a different recipe, or toss them in a salad.

    1 tablespoon butter
    1 tablespoon flour
    Salt to taste
    1 cup whole milk, warmed
    Freshly ground black pepper to taste
    Pinch freshly grated nutmeg
    $1/4$ teaspoon cayenne
    Stalks taken from 2 pounds very stemmy green chard,
        cooked as in Basic Simmered Chard (page 558)
        and drained well
    $1/2$ cup plain bread crumbs

1 Preheat the oven to 375°F.

2 Melt the butter in a small saucepan; add the flour and a bit of salt and cook over medium heat, stirring constantly, for about a minute. Add the milk a little at a time, whisking after each addition until the mixture is smooth. Cook over medium-low heat, stirring, until the mixture thickens slightly, 3 to 5 minutes. Add the pepper, nutmeg and cayenne.

3 Place the chard in a small ovenproof dish and pour the sauce over it. Top with bread crumbs and bake until the mixture is hot and the bread crumbs are lightly browned, 12 to 15 minutes. Serve immediately.

Chayote

Much like a summer squash—it's closely related—the chayote, or cho-cho, has only one large seed, and vaguely resembles an avocado. Treat it as you would zucchini or other summer squash—that is, quite gently.

Buying and storing Since most chayotes are imported, there really is no season for them, although they tend to be most common in winter. Chayotes should be not only firm but downright hard. Reject any with soft spots. Size doesn't matter much; smaller chayotes are a bit more tender, but the large ones become soft with cooking. Store in the vegetable bin—unlike summer squash, they'll keep for weeks.

Preparing Peel the skin under running water. Cut in half, remove the pit (it's edible in very small chayotes; cook it along with the pulp).

Best cooking methods Baking, steaming, or gently sautéing, as below. Treat chayote as you would zucchini (page 606) and you will never go far wrong.

When is it done? When tender, which takes a little longer than you think. Stop cooking when a skewer or thin-bladed knife easily pierces the flesh.

Basic Baked, Steamed, or Sautéed Chayote

Makes 4 servings

Time: 20 to 30 minutes

No matter how you cook chayote, you must keep the heat fairly gentle. Butter and plenty of pepper—with some vinegar or lemon juice if you like—are the best accompaniments.

2 chayotes, peeled, pits removed, cut into quarters

1 clove garlic, smashed (optional)

2 tablespoons butter

Salt and freshly ground black pepper to taste

1 teaspoon red or white wine vinegar or freshly
   squeezed lemon juice

Minced fresh parsley or dill leaves for garnish

1 To bake the chayote, preheat the oven to 350°F. Place the quartered chayote along with the optional garlic clove in a casserole or baking dish just large enough to fit it and dot with butter. Sprinkle generously with salt and pepper, then cover with a lid or aluminum foil. Bake until tender enough to be readily pierced with a thin-bladed knife, about 30 minutes. Place on a serving plate; drizzle with the pan juices and vinegar or lemon juice; garnish and serve.

2 To steam the chayote, place it in a steamer above an inch or two of salted water. Cover and cook until it is just tender enough to be pierced to the core with a thin-bladed knife, about 20 minutes. While it is cooking, heat the optional garlic and the butter in a small saucepan over medium heat. When the chayote is done, add the salt and pepper and vinegar or lemon juice to the butter. Place the chayote on a serving plate, drizzle with the butter, garnish, and serve.

3 To sauté the chayote, place the optional garlic clove and butter in a medium skillet; turn the heat to medium. When the butter melts, add the chayote and cook, turning occasionally, until the chayote is tender, about 15 minutes. Do not let it brown. Just before serving, sprinkle with salt and pepper and vinegar or freshly squeezed lemon juice, then garnish.

Chestnuts

Chestnuts are cooked much like vegetables, so I have included them here. We must get our chestnuts from Europe, thanks to the great chestnut blight early in this century, which killed nearly all the specimens of our native American chestnut. As a result, chestnuts are more expensive than they might be otherwise, and are not used as much in cooking as they once were. Still, they help make autumn cooking special.

Buying and storing In much of Europe, chestnuts fall to the ground through September and October, so the best season is definitely autumn. Buy heavy, big, full, unblemished nuts; they dry out as they age, and begin to rattle around in their shells. Their shelf life is not as long as you might think—just a week or two; refrigeration is neither necessary nor helpful.

Preparing Chestnuts must be precooked and their shells and skins removed. The easiest way to precook is to make a shallow cut on the flat end, using a sharp paring knife. Then simmer in water to cover or bake at about 350°F until the shells curl and can be peeled off. You must also remove the inner skin as

Before cooking a chestnut, score the flat side with a sharp knife, making an "x."

After cooking, remove both outer shell and inner skin.

well, using a paring knife. (See recipe, below.) If the process becomes difficult, reheat the chestnuts in the water.

Best cooking methods   Boiling, grilling, or roasting, all of which can be done just as simmering; see below. Cooked, shelled, and skinned nuts are good mashed with butter, just like potatoes, or braised with other vegetables or meats, or gently sautéed.

When is it done?   They're ready to eat when the shell is easily removed, or they can be cooked a little longer if you want to puree them.

Other recipes in which you can use chestnuts (always after precooking and peeling):
Precooked Vegetables in Butter or Oil, page 532
Quick-Braised Carrots with Butter, page 553
Pureed Parsnips, page 590
Mashed Potatoes, page 596

Boiled, Grilled, or Roasted Chestnuts

Makes 1 pound, 4 to 6 servings

Time: About 30 minutes, plus time to preheat the grill

Boil chestnuts only if you are going to use them in another recipe afterward. For eating chestnuts out of hand, roast them in the oven or grill them over hot coals.

1 pound chestnuts, flat side cut (page 560)

1   To boil: Place in a pot with lightly salted water to cover and bring to a boil. Turn off the heat after 3 or 4 minutes. Remove a few chestnuts from the water at a time and use a sharp knife to cut off the outer and inner skins. Use the chestnuts in other recipes, or reheat according to the directions for Precooked Vegetables in Butter or Oil (page 532).

2   To grill or roast: Start a charcoal or wood fire, or preheat a gas grill, or turn the oven to 450°F. Place the chestnuts directly on the grill, or on a sheet of aluminum foil with holes poked in it, or on a baking sheet. Grill (preferably with the cover down) or roast, turning occasionally, until you can remove the shells easily, about 15 minutes. Eat warm, out of hand.

Collards and Kale

The large, dark green, almost leathery leaves of collards have long been a southern favorite, in part because of their heat tolerance. But like kale—to which they are intimately related and with which they are always interchangeable—collards are at their sweetest when grown in cool weather. In fact, collards are known for their cold-hardiness, and can be harvested even in the snow.

There's only one trick to cooking collards and kale: Make sure you cook them long enough to soften the stems. Undercooked stems are unpleasantly tough and chewy. (One sure way to prevent this is to avoid collards with stems more than one-eighth inch thick.)

Buying and storing   Look for dark-green color and firm unwilted leaves. Young leaves with stems no thicker than a pencil will be easier to clean, less wasteful, and will cook more quickly. They will also have a better texture when cooked. Collards are sold year-round, but are best in the late fall. These are sturdy greens that keep well, especially if you wrap them in plastic. They are unlikely to rot, but will begin to turn yellow after a few days; try to use them before that happens.

Preparing   If the stems are thick, strip the leaves, chop the stems, and start cooking them a couple of minutes before the leaves. To easily cut the leaves, roll them up, then cut across the roll (page 562).

You may remove the stems if they are very thick (or simply cook them a little longer than the leaves). Cut on either side of them, at an angle.

The easiest way to chop large leaves is to roll them up and cut across the log (see chiffonade, page 533.)

Best cooking methods Steaming; boiling; stir-frying. Good in soup, too (see White Bean Soup with Greens and Rice, page 64).

When is it done? When the stems are tender enough to easily pierce with a skewer or thin-bladed knife.

Other recipes in which you can use collards or kale:
Gingered Cabbage, page 549 (shred the collards or
 kale as you would cabbage)
Dandelion Greens with Bacon, page 96

Basic Boiled Collards or Kale

Makes 4 servings

Time: 20 to 30 minutes

1 to 1¹/₂ pounds collards, kale, or other dark green,
 well washed

1 Bring a large pot of water to a boil; salt it. Meanwhile, if the collard stems are more than ¹/₈ inch thick, separate them from the greens. Roughly chop both stems and greens.

2 If the stems are thick, place them in the water first. After 5 minutes, add the leaves. Cook until the stems are tender enough to pierce with a thin-bladed knife, from 5 to 15 minutes depending on their thickness.

3 Drain and serve immediately, or plunge into an ice-water bath and drain. Reheat according to the directions for Precooked Vegetables in Butter or Oil (page 532).

4 Serve hot greens with butter, extra-virgin olive oil, and/or lemon juice or vinegar.

Collards or Kale with Double Garlic

Makes 4 servings

Time: 15 minutes

The first measure of garlic mellows as it cooks with the greens; it's the second teaspoon that gives the dish a real kick. Substitute minced ginger for the second addition of garlic if you like.

1 pound collards, kale, or broccoli raab, with stems
 under ¹/₄ inch thick, well washed
¹/₄ cup olive oil
¹/₄ cup thinly sliced garlic, about 5 or 6 cloves, plus
 1 teaspoon minced garlic, or more to taste
¹/₂ teaspoon crushed red pepper flakes, or to taste
Salt and freshly ground black pepper to taste
¹/₂ cup chicken, beef, or vegetable stock, or water
 (see "Soups" for stock recipes)
Lemon wedges

1 Coarsely chop the stems and leaves of the collards.

2 Place the olive oil in a large, deep saucepan. Add the sliced garlic, pepper flakes, salt, and black pepper and cook over medium-high heat for about 1 minute.

3 Add the collards and the stock or water. Cover and cook over medium-high heat for approximately 5 minutes, or until the greens are wilted and just tender but still a little firm.

4 Uncover the greens and continue to cook, stirring, over medium-high heat, until the liquid has all but evaporated and the greens are quite tender. Taste for seasoning and add red or black pepper and salt as needed; add the remaining minced garlic, cook for 1 minute more, and serve, with lemon wedges.

Collards or Kale with Capers: In Step 2, reduce the garlic by half and eliminate the pepper flakes. In Step 3, after the greens wilt, stir in 2 tablespoons of drained capers. In Step 4, eliminate the second addition of garlic. Drizzle with red or white wine vinegar and omit the lemon wedges.

Collards or Kale, Brazilian-Style

Makes 4 servings

Time: 15 minutes

It's best to find relatively small greens for this dish, which cooks far too quickly to soften tough stems.

1½ pounds young kale or collards, or other dark green, washed (page 561) and very well dried

3 tablespoons olive or peanut oil

1 tablespoon minced garlic

Salt and freshly ground black pepper to taste

¼ to ⅓ cup freshly squeezed lemon juice or red or white wine vinegar

1 Chop the greens into fairly small pieces; no dimension should be more than 2 inches.

2 Meanwhile, heat a 12-inch skillet or wok over high heat until smoking. Add the oil to the skillet, let sit for a few seconds, then toss in the greens and the garlic.

3 Cook over high heat, stirring almost constantly, until the greens wilt and begin to brown, 3 to 8 minutes (depending largely on the power of your burner).

4 Season with salt and pepper and add a little lemon juice or vinegar. Taste, adjust seasoning, and serve immediately.

Corn

We love corn—our only indigenous grain, eaten as a fresh vegetable—at least in the summer months when we can eat it off the cob—a grain (see The Basics of Hominy, or Pozole, page 192), and a meal (see The Basics of Cornmeal, page 187). But we don't make as much use out of it as they do in Mexico and other countries, where cornmeal is used as often as we use flour.

The old adage about fresh corn—start the water boiling, pick it, and cook it—will still give you the best quality corn on the cob. But the new breeds of corn retain their sweetness incredibly well, sometimes for several days.

Buying and storing   The color and shape of corn kernels on fresh-picked corn is the subject of great debate. My preference tends to ears that are pale, even white in color, and very young—I like to nibble on the cob. But plenty of people like deep-yellow corn, and prefer big ears to little ones. Although new varieties of corn retain their freshness well, generally speaking you're still better off buying corn at a farmstand than at a supermarket, if you have the option. Refrigerate corn, still in its husk; it will not go bad, but will decline in sweetness as it ages.

The "silk" must always be removed from corn before cooking. You can remove the husk, or simply peel it back and take out the silk, then fold the husk back over the corn. This works well for grilling; for steaming or boiling, remove the husk entirely.

Use a sharp knife to scrape kernels from the cob.

Frozen corn, while not to be compared to fresh corn on the cob, is a good product for cooking.

Preparing   Shuck corn just before cooking it. You can also scrape the kernels from the cob with a knife (above).

Best cooking methods   Steaming, roasting, grilling. You can also stir-fry corn kernels; follow the recipe for Quick Stir-Fried Snow Peas or Sugar Snap Peas (page 591). And relish and salsa made with corn (see Corn and Tomato Relish, page 782) are a real treat.

When is it done?   When it's hot; there's no point in cooking it any further.

Basic Steamed Corn
Makes 4 servings

Time: 20 minutes or less

Keep corn cool, shuck it at the last minute, cook it just long enough to heat it up, and you'll get the most out of it. There is no reason at all to boil corn: Steaming does a perfect job, and you need not bother to bring a huge quantity of water to the boil.

8 ears fresh corn, shucked (opposite)
Salt and freshly ground black pepper to taste
Butter (optional)

1 Place the corn in a pot with an inch or two of salted water; it's okay if some of the corn sits in the water and some above it. Cover and cook over high heat until it is just hot, 10 minutes or less (if the water is already boiling when you add the corn, or if you have a powerful stove, the cooking time could be as little as 3 minutes).

2 Serve the corn with salt, pepper, and butter.

Grilled or Roasted Corn
Makes 4 servings

Time: 20 minutes, plus time to preheat the grill

Although steamed corn is standard, grilled corn is the ultimate. Slightly charred kernels are both lovely and crispy-sweet.

8 ears fresh corn
Salt and freshly ground black pepper to taste
Butter (optional)

1 Start a charcoal or wood fire, or preheat a gas grill, or turn the oven to 450°F. Peel back the husks of the corn and remove the inner silks (page 564). Smooth the husks back in place, but don't worry about them completely covering the kernels. Or, if you prefer, shuck the corn entirely.

2 Grill or roast the corn, turning occasionally. With husks on, timing will be 15 to 20 minutes on the grill, 20 to 30 minutes in the oven. With husks off, less than half those times. When some of the kernels char a bit and others are lightly browned, the corn is done. Serve with salt, pepper, and butter.

Corn Fritters

Makes 4 servings

Time: 30 minutes

You want corn fritters in which the flavor of corn, rather than that of batter, dominates. That's why this recipe is based on cornmeal, and has a good deal of kernels combined with just enough batter to hold the whole thing together. Fritters are easy to fry because they barely spatter at all.

Vegetable oil as needed

3/4 cup cornmeal, the fresher the better

1/2 cup all-purpose flour

2 teaspoons baking powder

Salt and freshly ground black pepper to taste

1/2 teaspoon sugar

3/4 cup milk, plus more if needed

1 egg

2 cups freshly scraped or thawed frozen corn kernels (page 564)

1 Place the vegetable oil, to a depth of at least 3 inches, in a deep saucepan over medium-high heat. Let it heat while you prepare the fritters; it should reach a temperature of 365° to 375°F. Preheat the oven to 200°F.

2 Combine the dry ingredients in a large bowl. Beat together the milk and egg, then pour them into the dry ingredients, adding a few tablespoons more milk if necessary to make a thick but smooth batter. Stir in the corn.

3 Drop the fritters by the quarter-cup or large spoonful into the hot oil. Raise the heat to maintain a fairly consistent temperature. Cook the fritters in batches, turning once, until nicely browned on all sides, a total of about 4 or 5 minutes per batch. Drain the fritters, then eat them as they are done, or keep them warm in the oven until they are all done.

4 Serve the fritters with maple syrup (as is traditional), or with Salsa Cruda or other salsa (page 773), or with an aioli or other mayonnaise (page 761).

Cucumbers

A vegetable that is rarely cooked but ought to be—at least occasionally. Cucumbers are so mild-flavored that they are easily overwhelmed, so it's best to treat them gently. It's also best to remove the seeds from most cucumbers before cooking; small cucumbers from the garden or long "English" cucumbers are usually firmer and contain fewer seeds.

Buying and storing   Buy the firmest cucumbers you can find, preferably without wax (which is essentially a preservative that prolongs shelf life). Length does not matter so much, but narrower cucumbers generally contain fewer seeds. Store, unwrapped, in the vegetable bin, for up to a week, but use as soon as possible.

Preparing   Peel all waxed cucumbers before cooking; do not peel those that have not been waxed. Cut the cucumber in half lengthwise and use a spoon to remove the seeds if there are a lot of them (page 566). And consider salting to remove excess water (see Cucumbers in Butter and Cream, page 566).

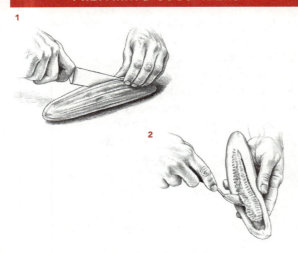

Thick cucumbers should always be seeded.

(Step 1) First cut the cucumber in half the long way. (Step 2) Then scrape out the seeds with a spoon.

Best cooking methods   Sautéing over high heat can also give good results. Pickling, for either short-term use or long-term storage (page 105), is probably the most common treatment.

When is it done?   When heated through; cucumbers will fall apart if overcooked.

Cucumbers in Butter and Cream

Makes 4 servings

Time: 20 to 40 minutes

Cucumbers fall apart if they are overcooked, so cook them only until heated through. Do not use soft, watery cucumbers for this or any other cooked dish.

About 1 pound cucumbers
1 tablespoon salt (if cucumbers are not firm)
2 tablespoons butter
$^1/_2$ cup chopped onion
Freshly ground black pepper to taste
$^1/_2$ cup sweet (heavy) cream, or sour cream, or yogurt
Lots of freshly snipped dill

1   Peel the cucumbers if waxed. Cut them in half lengthwise and scoop out the seeds with a spoon (see opposite). Cut them into $^3/_4$-inch chunks. If the cucumbers are not super-firm, place the chunks in a colander and sprinkle them with 1 tablespoon of salt. Shake to distribute the salt and let them drain for about 20 minutes. Rinse and dry. If the cucumbers are already firm, proceed with the recipe.

2   Place the butter in a medium to large skillet over medium heat. When it melts, add the onion and cook, stirring occasionally, until the onion softens, about 5 minutes. Do not let the onion brown. Add the cucumbers and cook, stirring, for about 5 minutes, until the cucumbers are just tender. Add pepper and, if you did not salt the cucumbers earlier, some salt.

3   Turn the heat to low, then stir in the cream or yogurt and a good handful of dill. Stir until well blended, then serve, garnished with more dill.

Crisp Sautéed Cucumbers with Lemon

Makes 4 servings

Time: 20 to 40 minutes

A surprising dish that gardeners will appreciate, especially in August, when they are frequently overrun by cucumbers.

About 1 pound cucumbers

1 tablespoon salt (if cucumbers are not firm)

1 lemon

2 tablespoons butter or peanut, olive, or other oil

At least 2 cups all-purpose flour for dredging

Salt and freshly ground black pepper to taste

Minced fresh parsley leaves for garnish

1 Peel the cucumbers if waxed. Cut them in half lengthwise and scoop out the seeds with a spoon (page 566). Cut them into $3/4$-inch chunks. If the cucumbers are not super-firm, place the chunks in a colander and sprinkle them with 1 tablespoon of salt. Shake to distribute the salt and let them drain for about 20 minutes. Rinse and dry. If the cucumbers are already firm, proceed with the recipe.

2 Remove a few strips of zest from the lemon with a zester or vegetable peeler; mince enough to measure 1 teaspoon. Cut the lemon in half through its equator and section it as you would an orange (page 638). Set the zest and sections aside.

3 Place the butter or oil in a large skillet over medium-high heat. Place about 2 cups of flour in a plastic or paper bag and, when the butter melts or the oil is hot, put a few chunks of cucumber at a time in the bag. Shake well, then add them to the skillet. Repeat until all the cucumbers are used up.

4 Cook over medium-high heat, stirring and turning occasionally, for about 10 minutes, until the exteriors of the cucumbers are crisp and the interiors are tender enough to be easily pierced with a thin-bladed knife. Add the lemon zest and sections, along with salt and pepper, and cook for 1 minute more.

5 Garnish and serve.

Dandelion

Dandelions greens are among the most nutritious foods known, containing more protein, fiber, calcium, and potassium than any other green; they're also loaded with beta-carotene. They are so popular in Europe that several different varieties there have been cultivated—those with big crowns, with thicker leaves, and so on. But we are lucky to find any in the supermarket, although they are becoming more common.

If you're picking wild dandelions, pick them as early as possible in the spring and, of course, from a place where no sprays have been used.

Buying and storing   The smaller the better. Leaves longer than six inches are almost certainly quite bitter when raw. If you can get part of the crown—the white part at the base of the leaves—so much the better.

Preparing   Wash very well to eliminate sand.

Best cooking methods   Steaming or sautéing (see The Basics of Steaming Vegetables, page 531).

When is it done?   When wilted and tender.

Other recipes in which you can use dandelions:
Any spinach recipe (pages 604–605)
Collards or Kale with Double Garlic, page 562
Collards or Kale, Brazilian-Style, page 563
Dandelion Greens with Bacon, page 96

Eggplant

The eggplant is certainly underappreciated when compared to its relatives, the tomato and the potato. But it does have its fans, especially among cooks who have become familiar with South European and East Asian cuisines, where it plays a large role. Few vegetables are as meaty as eggplant, and few can contribute so much to a meal.

Eggplant come in all sizes and colors. My favorite is the small lavender variety, usually sold in Asian markets but sometimes in Italian ones as well. White eggplant is also visually striking, although I've found no taste or texture advantage associated with this variety. The more common deep purple, nearly black eggplant, makes fine eating, as long as the individual specimen is a good one.

Buying and storing   Eggplant must be firm; like cucumber, the length is not so important, but the width is. Long, narrow eggplant tend to contain few seeds. Big, fleshy eggplant usually contain more seeds and become softer more readily. Store eggplant in the refrigerator, and use it as soon as you can; although the outside will not look much different, the inside will become soft and bitter within a few days.

Preparing   Eggplant need not be peeled unless the skin is very thick, or, of course, unless you prefer to do so. It's usually worth salting larger eggplant, a process which draws out excess moisture and a certain amount of bitterness along with it. Trim off the ends, then cut it into slices (you can cut long slices or crosswise ones) from one-half to one inch thick. Or cut it into chunks. Sprinkle both sides of the slices (or all sides of the chunks) liberally with coarse salt, then let drain in a colander for at least half an hour, or up to two hours. Rinse and squeeze dry between paper or cloth towels.

Best cooking methods   Many, especially grilling, broiling, roasting, and sautéing, all of which you'll find below. The eggplant dip known as Baba Ghanoush (page 23) is wonderful.

When is it done?   When tender and almost creamy.

Other recipes in which you can use eggplant:
Braised Cauliflower with Curry and Tomatoes, page 555
Summer Squash or Zucchini Pancakes, page 606

Grilled or Broiled Eggplant Slices

Makes 4 servings

Time: 20 minutes, plus time to preheat the grill and salt the eggplant

This is the simplest way to prepare eggplant, and it makes a delicious side dish.

1 medium-to-large eggplant (1 to 1$\frac{1}{2}$ pounds)
1 teaspoon minced garlic (optional)
4 to 6 tablespoons olive oil
Salt and freshly ground black pepper to taste
Minced fresh parsley leaves for garnish

① Peel the eggplant if the skin is thick or the eggplant is less than perfectly firm. Cut it into $\frac{1}{2}$-inch-thick slices and salt it if you like (see opposite). Start a charcoal or wood fire or preheat a gas grill or broiler; the rack should be 4 to 6 inches from the heat source.

② Stir the optional garlic into the olive oil, then brush one side of the eggplant slices with the oil. Place, oiled side down, on a baking sheet or directly on the grill. Sprinkle with salt (if you salted the eggplant, hold off) and pepper, then brush with more oil.

③ Broil or grill until browned on both sides, turning once or twice and brushing with more oil if the eggplant looks dry. Serve hot or at room temperature, garnished with parsley.

Grilled or Broiled Eggplant Slices with Miso Dressing: Use canola or other neutral oil in place of olive oil, and omit the garlic. Broil or grill the eggplant, and serve with a dressing made by mixing together 4 tablespoons miso; 1 teaspoon sugar; 1 tablespoon mirin (or $\frac{1}{2}$ tablespoon honey, thinned with water); and rice or other mild vinegar to taste.

Sautéed Eggplant

Makes 4 servings

Time: About 30 minutes, longer if you choose to salt the eggplant

It takes a while to cook eggplant on top of the stove, but the result is creamy, flavorful cubes that are like no other vegetable.

2 medium or 1 large eggplant (1^1/$_2$ to 2 pounds total)
Salt (optional)
^{1}/$_3$ cup olive oil, more or less
2 teaspoons minced garlic
Freshly ground black pepper to taste
Minced fresh parsley leaves for garnish

1 Peel the eggplant if the skin is thick or the eggplant is less than perfectly firm (page 568). Cut it into ^{1}/$_2$-inch cubes and salt it if you like (page 568).

2 Place the olive oil and all but ^{1}/$_2$ teaspoon of the garlic in a large, deep skillet, preferably non-stick, over medium heat. Two minutes later, add the eggplant. Stir and toss almost constantly until, after 5 or 10 minutes, the eggplant begins to release some of the oil it has absorbed.

3 Continue cooking, stirring frequently, until the eggplant is very tender, about 30 minutes (this can vary greatly). About 5 minutes before it is done, add the remaining garlic.

4 Season with pepper and additional salt if necessary; garnish and serve.

Twenty-Six Vegetable Dishes That Will Make Converts

Most vegetable haters are simply vegetable lovers who haven't yet realized it; these dishes can move the process along. They may not all work on the first try—most are solid, strong-flavored preparations—but they are real winners. (I omit the obvious crowd-pleasers, such as French Fries.)

1. Asparagus with Parmesan, page 538
2. Beets in Butter, page 542
3. Beet Roesti with Rosemary, page 542
4. Stir-Fried Broccoli, page 545
5. Cabbage Cooked with Apples, page 548
6. Quick-Braised Carrots with Orange and Ginger, page 553
7. Cauliflower with Garlic and Anchovies, page 554
8. Braised Cauliflower with Curry and Tomatoes, page 555
9. Grilled or Broiled Eggplant Slices with Miso Dressing, page 568
10. Curried Eggplant with Potatoes, page 570
11. Eggplant Parmesan, page 571
12. Leeks au Gratin, page 581
13. Sautéed Mushrooms with Garlic, page 584
14. Caramelized Small Onions or Shallots, page 588
15. Cooked Onions and Apples, page 588
16. Pureed Parsnips, page 590
17. Marinated Roasted, Grilled, or Broiled Peppers, page 593
18. Braised Pumpkin, Japanese-Style, page 601
19. Sushi-Style Spinach, page 605
20. Crisp-Cooked Sunchokes, page 607
21. Pureed Turnips, page 612
22. Braised Butternut or Other Winter Squash with Garlic, page 614
23. Roasted Root Vegetables, page 615
24. Roasted Vegetables, Catalonian-Style, page 616
25. Oven-Baked Ratatouille (Tian of Vegetables), page 616
26. Grilled Mixed Vegetables, page 617

Curried Eggplant with Potatoes

Makes 6 to 8 servings

Time: About 1 hour, longer if you choose to salt the eggplant

Butter makes this dish altogether heavenly, although you can substitute oil if you like. Feel free to add more vegetables to the mix.

2 medium-to-large eggplant (2 to 3 pounds total)
Salt (optional)
1 tablespoon canola or other neutral oil
1 teaspoon mustard seeds
$1/2$ teaspoon cayenne
$1/2$ teaspoon ground turmeric
2 teaspoons ground coriander
1 teaspoon ground cumin
1 tablespoon peeled and minced fresh ginger
2 tablespoons sliced garlic
4 tablespoons ($1/2$ stick) butter
3 large tomatoes, cored, peeled, seeded, and chopped (canned are fine; don't bother to drain)
3 large potatoes, any kind, peeled and cut into $1/2$-inch cubes
Freshly ground black pepper to taste
About 1 cup water, or more if needed
2 tablespoons freshly squeezed lime juice
Minced cilantro leaves for garnish

1 Peel the eggplant if the skin is thick or the eggplant is less than perfectly firm (page 568). Cut it into $1/2$-inch cubes and salt it if you like (page 568).

2 Combine the oil and mustard seeds in a large, deep skillet or casserole. Turn the heat to medium and cook until the seeds begin to pop, about 2 minutes. Add the remaining spices, the ginger, the garlic, and the butter and cook, stirring occasionally, until the ginger and garlic soften, about 5 minutes.

3 Add the tomatoes, potatoes, eggplant, salt, and pepper, and about a cup of water. Turn the heat to medium-low and cover; cook, stirring once or twice, for about 30 minutes.

4 Remove the cover and turn the heat to medium; add more water if the mixture is dry. Cook, stirring occasionally, until both the eggplant and potatoes are very tender, about 15 minutes longer. Stir in the lime juice and adjust the seasoning to your taste. Garnish and serve.

Roasted Eggplant with Garlic and Parsley

Makes 4 servings

Time: About 45 minutes, longer if you choose to salt the eggplant

This is a very garlicky, creamy dish.

2 medium or 1 large eggplant ($1 1/2$ to 2 pounds total)
Salt (optional)
3 tablespoons olive oil
2 teaspoons minced garlic
$1/2$ cup minced fresh parsley leaves, plus more for garnish
Freshly ground black pepper to taste

1 Peel the eggplant if the skin is thick or the eggplant is less than perfectly firm (page 568). Cut it into 1-inch-thick slices and salt it if you like (page 568).

2 Preheat the oven to 400°F. Brush a baking sheet with 1 tablespoon of the oil. Cut several slits on one side of each of the eggplant slices and lay them on the baking sheet, cut side up. Mix together the remaining oil, the garlic, the $1/2$ cup minced parsley, and some black pepper. Spread this mixture on the eggplant slices, pushing it into the slits.

3 Bake until the eggplant is soft, 40 minutes or more. Garnish and serve hot or at room temperature.

Eggplant Parmesan
Makes 6 servings

Time: About 1 hour, longer if you choose to salt the eggplant

To save both time and effort, you can use broiled eggplant slices (page 568) in this dish, omitting the sautéing of the eggplant. In Parma (where we must suppose this dish originated), no one would dream of using mozzarella here, and you should try it that way at least once.

2 medium-to-large eggplant (2 to 3 pounds total)
Salt (optional)
Olive oil as needed
Flour for dredging
Freshly ground black pepper to taste
2 cups Basic Tomato Sauce (page 130)
$^1/_2$ pound grated mozzarella cheese, about 2 cups
    (optional)
1 cup freshly grated Parmesan cheese, plus more if
    you omit the mozzarella
About 30 fresh basil leaves

1 Peel the eggplant if the skin is thick or the eggplant is less than perfectly firm (page 568). Cut it into $^1/_2$-inch-thick slices and salt it if you like (page 568).

2 When you're ready to cook, preheat the oven to 350°F. Place about 3 tablespoons of olive oil in a large skillet and turn the heat to medium. When the oil is hot (a pinch of flour will sizzle), dredge the eggplant slices, one at a time, in the flour, shaking off the excess. Place in the pan, but do not crowd; you will have to cook in batches. Cook for 3 or 4 minutes on each side, until nicely browned, then drain on paper towels. Add some pepper to the slices as they cook, as well as some salt if you did not salt the eggplant. Add more oil to the skillet as needed.

3 Lightly oil a baking dish, then spoon a little of the tomato sauce into it. Top with a layer of eggplant, then a thin layer of each of the cheeses, and finally a few basil leaves. Repeat until all the ingredients are used up, reserving some of the basil for garnish. End with a sprinkling of Parmesan.

4 Bake for 20 to 30 minutes, or until the dish is bubbling hot. Mince the remaining basil and sprinkle over the top. Serve hot or at room temperature.

Endive, Escarole, and Radicchio

A confusing group of vegetables that includes the tight little oval that is Belgian endive, the small red head that is radicchio, and the lettuce-like head that is generally called escarole. They are all chicory, or closely related to chicory; the differences are more in form and cultivation (Belgian endive is the leaves grown from the chicory root, but in the dark—which keeps it nearly white) than in flavor or handling. Since they're all quite bitter, firm, and fleshy, they're as good cooked as they are raw.

Buying and storing   All chicories, including Belgian endive, are crops of the late fall and winter, and can be found when other interesting salad greens are scarce. Buy firm, fleshy specimens, and store, lightly wrapped, in the vegetable bin. Belgian endive is considered best if it is nearly white; it turns green when exposed to light, and becomes a little more bitter. All of these keep better than most salad greens—up to a week—but are still best when used as soon as possible.

Preparing   Trim, clean, and wash as you would any lettuce.

Best cooking methods   Grilling (brush with olive oil first), braising, sautéing (as you would collards or other sturdy greens). All of these greens, of course, can be part of a good salad (see pages 84–85).

When is it done?   When crisp-tender; if you let them cook until they are completely tender, mushiness is the inevitable result.

Other recipes in which you can use these vegetables:

Chard with Garlic, Pine Nuts, and Currants, page 558

Braised Fennel with Onions and Vinegar, page 573

Grilled Mixed Vegetables, page 617

Braised Endive, Escarole, or Radicchio with Prosciutto

Makes 4 servings

Time: About 1 hour

Endive, with its neat little shape, is perfect for braising, but escarole and radicchio taste just as good.

1 tablespoon olive oil

4 Belgian endives, trimmed at the base, damaged leaves removed, or about 1 pound of escarole or radicchio, cleaned and roughly chopped

¼ cup minced prosciutto or other dry-cured ham

½ cup chicken, beef, or vegetable stock, or water (see "Soups" for stock recipes)

Salt and freshly ground black pepper to taste

1 teaspoon freshly squeezed lemon juice or white wine vinegar

1   Heat the olive oil over medium heat in a medium to large non-stick skillet that can later be covered.

Add the endives and cook, turning once or twice, until they begin to brown.

2   Add the ham, stock or water, salt, and pepper. Cover and cook over the lowest possible heat, turning occasionally, until very tender, about 45 minutes. Uncover and turn the heat up a bit to evaporate any remaining liquid.

3   Drizzle with lemon juice or vinegar and serve.

Fennel

I vividly remember my first taste of "licorice celery," as we used to call it. There it was, sitting on a plate of antipasto, looking innocent, like a piece of celery—that first taste was a revelation, and I've never stopped loving to munch on it. But it took another twenty years before I learned how wonderful fennel was when cooked.

Buying and storing   You're primarily interested in the bulb, not the stalks (although both the stalks and the feathery leaves can be used as seasoning, and the stalks make a wonderful platform for grilled foods; just put them directly on the grate and grill on top of them). It should be tight and greenish white, with little or no browning or shriveled parts. Store fennel, loosely wrapped, in the vegetable bin, for up to a week—but use it as soon as you can.

Preparing   Trim the feathery fronds and hollow stalks; use them for seasoning or discard. Trim off the hard bottom and cut vertical slices through the bulb. Or cut in half, dig out the core, and cut into thin strips for sautéing, braising, salads, or roasting (but not grilling, where you need larger pieces).

Best cooking methods   Braising, which brings out its flavor and gives it the texture of cooked celery; roasting (it's good in Roasted Root Vegetables, page 615), baking, sautéing, or grilling. Fennel is also wonderful raw, in salads (see Beet and Fennel Salad, page 100).

(Step 1) Trim the hard, hollow stalks from the top of the bulb. Save the feathery fronds for garnish if you like. (Step 2) Cut a thin slice from one side of the fennel. (Steps 3–4) Stand the bulb on its side and cut through it vertically. Or cut it horizontally.

When is it done? When tender enough to easily pierce with a skewer or thin-bladed knife.

Other recipes in which you can use fennel:
Asparagus with Parmesan, page 538
Braised Broccoli with Garlic and Wine, page 544
Cardoons and Onions Cooked in Cream, page 551
(don't precook fennel)
Cauliflower with Garlic and Anchovies, page 554
(don't precook fennel)
Braised Endive, Escarole, or Radicchio with Prosciutto, page 572
Grilled Mixed Vegetables, page 617

Braised Fennel with Onions and Vinegar

Makes 4 servings

Time: About 30 minutes

This makes a fine pasta sauce, thinned with a little of the pasta cooking water.

¹⁄₄ cup olive oil
1 cup chopped onion
1 tablespoon minced garlic
2 bulbs (about 1¹⁄₂ pounds) fennel, trimmed and thinly sliced (see above)
¹⁄₂ cup chicken or vegetable stock, or dry white wine, or water (see "Soups" for stock recipes)
Salt and freshly ground black pepper to taste
1 tablespoon minced fresh marjoram or oregano leaves or 1 teaspoon dried marjoram or oregano
1 tablespoon sherry, balsamic, or other flavorful vinegar

1 Place the oil in a medium skillet or casserole that can later be covered and turn the heat to medium. Add the onion and cook, stirring, until it softens, about 5 minutes.

2 Add the garlic and fennel and cook, stirring occasionally, for about 5 minutes.

3 Add the liquid, salt, and pepper and cover; turn the heat to medium-low. Cook until the fennel is just about tender, another 5 to 10 minutes, then uncover. If the mixture is very wet, raise the heat a bit to evaporate most but not all of the liquid.

4 Stir in the herb and the vinegar, taste and adjust seasoning, and serve.

Fennel Baked with Stock and Parmesan

Makes 4 servings

Time: About 1 hour

Steamed or boiled fennel has little appeal, but if you undercook it slightly and finish it in the oven with good-flavored stock and Parmesan, it's quite wonderful.

1 or 2 bulbs (about 1½ pounds) fennel, trimmed (page 573) and cut in half

3 tablespoons butter

Salt and freshly ground black pepper to taste

1 cup chicken, beef, or vegetable stock, warmed (see "Soups" for stock recipes)

½ to 1 cup freshly grated Parmesan cheese

1 Preheat the oven to 400°F. Bring a pot of water to a boil; salt it. Place the fennel halves in the pot and cook until nearly tender, about 10 minutes. Remove and plunge into a bowl of ice water. Remove and drain. (You may also steam the fennel over an inch of boiling water; keep a close eye on it to avoid overcooking.)

2 Slice the fennel thinly. Use some of the butter to grease the inside of a smallish baking dish. Place the fennel in the dish, sprinkle with salt and pepper, and pour in the stock. Top the fennel with the remaining butter and sprinkle generously with the Parmesan. Bake, undisturbed, until most of the stock is absorbed and the dish is nicely browned, about 30 minutes.

Fiddlehead

A young, barely emerged, tightly coiled (hence the name) fern, available only in spring, and locally—they will not ship. Better as a wild food picked your-self than a supermarket item. If you find them, or buy them, simmer or steam as you would asparagus, then reheat in butter or dress with vinaigrette.

Garlic

Garlic, known as the "stinking rose," is not only one of the most important seasonings; it is among the best-tasting cooked vegetables. Slowly sautéed or stewed garlic has a sweet flavor and an aroma that fills the kitchen like nothing else. You'll find garlic in countless recipes in this book, but here are a few that feature garlic and little more.

Buying and storing Avoid those little boxes of garlic heads; buy it loose instead. Look for hard bulbs that have not sprouted and where each clove is firm. Size is not important, nor is skin color. Store garlic at room temperature in a dark dry spot where it is

MINCING GARLIC

There are many techniques to mince garlic, but the easiest is to peel, crush, and then chop (or thinly slice) the cloves.

Then use a rocking motion of the knife to cut across the pieces repeatedly; the knife must be sharp.

exposed to air; when it becomes soft, discard it. Sprouts are more bitter than the cloves from which they erupt, but are treasured by some cooks; there's no reason not to try them.

Preparing When preparing garlic as a vegetable, you need not peel it first; the meaty cloves will slip from their skins after cooking. You can, of course, peel it if you like: To ease the chore of peeling several cloves, simmer the garlic in water to cover for thirty seconds (see Garlic Simmered in Oil and Vinegar, page 576), or toast it in a dry pan over medium heat, shaking the pan frequently, for about five minutes. Either of these treatments will loosen the skin and make it easy to slip out the cloves.

Best cooking methods Roasting, simmering in oil.

When is it done? When very, very tender, almost mushy. The cloves will easily squeeze out of their skins.

PEELING GARLIC

If you're peeling more than a few cloves, drop them in boiling water for a few seconds and the peels will slip right off. To peel without parboiling, crush the cloves lightly with the side of a large knife.

The peels will come off easily.

Garlic Bruschetta
Makes 2 servings

Time: 10 minutes

This is sheer heaven in summer, with some tomatoes and basil on top.

> About 1 head roasted or simmered garlic, with its oil, from either of the preceding recipes
> Olive oil, if needed
> 4 slices good bread, preferably cut from a large round loaf
> Salt if needed
> Minced fresh parsley or basil leaves or chopped tomatoes for garnish

1 Preheat the broiler and adjust the rack so that it is at least 4 inches from the heat source. Mash the roasted or simmered garlic with its oil, adding additional oil if necessary to make a thick paste.

2 Broil the bread on one side until nicely browned. Turn it over and broil it for a minute or two on the other side. Spread this second side with the garlic puree; sprinkle with additional olive oil and salt if you like. Broil until hot and lightly browned, taking care not to burn. Garnish and serve.

Roasted Garlic
Makes 2 heads

Time: About 1 hour

Roasted or simmered garlic is a wonderful condiment for bread or salads, and a great ingredient for any dish in which you want to add a lovely, mellow, but distinctively garlicky flavor.

2 whole heads garlic

1/4 cup water

Salt

1 tablespoon extra-virgin olive oil

1 Heat the oven to 375°F. Without breaking the heads apart, remove as much of the papery coating from them as you can.

2 Place the garlic and water in a small baking dish; sprinkle with salt and drizzle with the olive oil. Cover with aluminum foil and bake, basting with the oil-and-water mixture after about 30 minutes. Bake until the garlic is soft (you'll be able to pierce it easily with a thin-bladed knife), about 1 hour total.

Faster Roasted Garlic: Break the heads into individual cloves, but do not peel them. Spread them on a baking sheet, sprinkle with salt, and drizzle with oil. Bake, shaking the pan occasionally, until tender, about 30 minutes.

Garlic Simmered in Oil and Vinegar

Makes 2 heads

Time: About 30 minutes

The addition of vinegar gives this unusual preparation a nice sweet-and-sour, syrupy quality. Add the garlic to salsas (page 772), spread it on Bruschetta (page 265), or toss it into other vegetable dishes during the last minute of cooking. Use the wonderful oil in vinaigrettes or pasta dishes.

2 heads garlic

1/2 cup extra-virgin olive oil

1/4 cup balsamic, sherry, or other full-flavored vinegar

1/2 teaspoon salt

1 Break the garlic heads into individual cloves and peel them. (The easiest way to do this is to drop them into boiling water for about 30 seconds; remove and peel the skins off from the root end up; the whole process will take you about 5 minutes.)

2 Place the cloves in a saucepan over medium-low heat with the other ingredients.

3 Cook until tender, regulating the heat so the cloves don't burn, 30 to 45 minutes. The vinegar will glaze the garlic and evaporate. When there is only oil left in the pan, and the garlic cloves are very soft, they are done. Strain and store separately in the refrigerator; use the garlic within a few days, the oil within 2 weeks.

Green Beans

Green beans may be one of any number of beans that are eaten fresh, such as the string bean, the thin haricot vert (common in France), the yard-long bean (originally from China, now grown here also), the wax or yellow bean (obviously not green at all), and the romano, a gardening favorite. All can be eaten raw, briefly cooked—so that they remain crunchy—or cooked to complete tenderness. I include lima beans here, the only fresh bean routinely shelled in this country. (Fresh or frozen soybeans, sold in pods, may be cooked as green beans, but are shell beans; shuck after cooking, or at the table.)

Buying and storing   Sold year-round, beans are at their best in summer, when they're most likely to be local. Although beans appear to keep well—they don't shrivel or rot very quickly—they lose their best flavor almost as fast as tomatoes. Buy beans that snap rather than fold when you bend them in half, and avoid any with browning or other obvious signs of spoilage. Store, loosely wrapped in plastic, in the vegetable bin, and use as soon as possible, preferably within a day.

Preparing   You can leave beans whole, simply snapping off the stem end, or cut them to any length you like.

Best cooking methods You name it—steaming, simmering, microwaving, stir-frying, sautéing, roasting, braising.

When is it done? Your choice: Crisp-tender and still crunchy, or cooked to melting tenderness.

Other recipes in which you can use green beans:
Asparagus with Parmesan, page 538
Stir-Fried Asparagus, Three Ways, page 539
Stir-Fried Broccoli, page 545
Gingered Cabbage, page 549 (don't shred the green beans, but prolong the cooking time as necessary)
Cabbage Braised with Onions, page 549
Cauliflower with Garlic and Anchovies, page 554 (don't precook green beans)
Stir-Fried Cauliflower with Ginger and Oyster Sauce, page 555 (don't precook green beans)
Braised Cauliflower with Curry and Tomatoes, page 555
Collards or Kale with Double Garlic, page 562
Curried Eggplant with Potatoes, page 570
Braised Endive, Escarole, or Radicchio with Prosciutto, page 572
Braised Fennel with Onions and Vinegar, page 573
Quick Stir-Fried Snow Peas or Sugar Snap Peas, page 591

Basic Simmered, Steamed, or Microwaved Green Beans

Makes 4 servings

Time: About 20 minutes

Fresh, crisp green beans can be just terrific when simply steamed or simmered and minimally dressed. But supermarket green beans, which are rarely of the highest quality, benefit mightily from being finished in butter; see Precooked Vegetables in Butter or Oil (page 532).

About 1½ pounds green beans, the smaller the better, washed and trimmed (page 576)

1 To simmer the beans, bring a large pot of water to a boil; salt it. Place them in the water and cook for about 4 minutes, or until they are bright green and as tender as you like them (it's easiest to tell when they're done by tasting one).

2 To steam the beans, place them in a steamer above an inch or two of salted water. Cover and cook from 4 to 6 minutes, until the pieces are bright green and as tender as you like them.

3 To microwave the beans, place them in a microwave-proof plate or shallow bowl with about 2 tablespoons of salted water; cover with a lid or plastic wrap. Microwave on high for 2 minutes; shake the container and continue to microwave on high for 1-minute intervals, shaking and checking the beans until they are bright green and as tender as you like them.

4 Serve hot beans with butter, lemon butter (page 770), vinaigrette (page 91), or freshly squeezed lemon juice. Or drain them, drop into a bowl of ice water to stop the cooking, drain again, place in a covered container, and refrigerate for up to 2 days. Then cook according to the directions for Precooked Vegetables in Butter or Oil (page 532).

Slow-Cooked Green Beans

Makes 4 servings

Time: About 1 hour

An adaptation of a Greek recipe found in Paula Wolfert's *Cooking of the Eastern Mediterranean*. Although "overcooking" vegetables is out of favor, these are meltingly tender and delicious.

About 1½ pounds green beans, the smaller the better, washed and trimmed (page 576)

¼ cup extra-virgin olive oil, plus more for sprinkling

1 cup minced onion

1 cup cored, peeled, seeded, and chopped tomatoes (canned are fine; drain them first)

½ cup water, plus more if needed

Salt and freshly ground black pepper to taste

Freshly squeezed lemon juice to taste, plus a few drops for sprinkling

1 tablespoon minced garlic

¼ cup chopped scallion

1 teaspoon crushed red pepper flakes, plus more if necessary

1 tablespoon sugar

2 tablespoons soy sauce

Salt to taste

1 teaspoon hot sesame oil (optional)

1 Combine all ingredients in a large saucepan and bring to a boil. Cover tightly and cook over medium-low heat for 1 hour, checking every 15 minutes and adding a few tablespoons of water if necessary. Longer cooking, up to 1 hour longer, will not hurt a bit.

2 When the beans are very tender and all the liquid is absorbed, they are ready. (You may prepare the recipe in advance up to this point; refrigerate, well wrapped or in a covered container, for up to 2 days before proceeding.) Serve hot or at room temperature, sprinkled with a little more oil and a few more drops of lemon juice.

"Dry-Fried" String Beans, Chinese-Style

Makes 4 servings

Time: About 30 minutes

This unusual dish begins with deep-frying and finishes with stir-frying. It's worth the work. Eliminate the pork if you like—the beans will still be sensational.

Vegetable oil for deep frying

1½ to 2 pounds green beans, the smaller the better, washed, trimmed (page 576), and very well dried

¼ to ⅓ pound minced or ground pork (or substitute ground beef, chicken, or turkey)

1 Place oil to a depth of 2 or 3 inches in a wok or very deep skillet; turn the heat to high and bring the oil's temperature to about 375°F. Add the beans all at once, and cook, stirring occasionally, until they begin to brown, about 6 minutes. Remove them with a slotted spoon and drain in a colander.

2 Wait a few minutes for the oil to cool a bit, then pour off all but 2 tablespoons of it (refrigerate and reserve it for making this dish again, or for other stir-fries). Turn the heat to high and place the pork in the pan; cook, stirring almost constantly, until the lumps break up and the color turns from pink to gray.

3 Add the garlic, scallion, and red pepper flakes and cook for 30 seconds, stirring. Add the beans and cook, stirring, for about 2 minutes. Add the sugar and soy sauce, stir, and turn off the heat. Taste and add salt and more hot pepper flakes if necessary. Sprinkle with sesame oil and serve.

Steamed Fresh or Frozen Lima Beans

Makes 4 servings

Time: 10 to 15 minutes

Fresh limas are a treat, but almost all of the crop is frozen or canned. The canned variety is hopelessly soft, but frozen beans can be quite good as long as they are not overcooked. You can treat fresh fava beans (page 503) in the same fashion.

1 pound shelled fresh or frozen (and at least partially
    thawed) lima beans
About ¹/₂ cup water
Salt and freshly ground black pepper to taste
1 tablespoon butter, plus 1 tablespoon more if desired

1 Place the limas in a small, tightly covered saucepan with about ¹/₂ cup of water. Add a good pinch of salt, some pepper, and the butter. Turn the heat to medium-high.

2 Cook for about 10 minutes (half that time for frozen beans), or until the limas are tender but not mushy. Remove the cover and boil off any excess liquid. Add another pat of butter if you like and serve.

Steamed Limas in Cream: After boiling off excess liquid (Step 2), turn the heat to low and add ¹/₂ cup heavy cream and a tiny grating of nutmeg (eliminate the extra butter). Cook, stirring occasionally, for 3 to 4 minutes, until the beans have absorbed some of the cream and the sauce is thick. Garnish with minced parsley or chervil and serve.

Succotash: After boiling off excess liquid (Step 2), turn the heat to low and add 1 to 2 cups freshly scraped corn kernels (eliminate the extra butter). Stir, cook for about 2 minutes, and add ¹/₂ cup heavy cream and a pinch of cayenne, or to taste. Cook, stirring occasionally, for 3 to 4 minutes, until the beans have absorbed some of the cream and the sauce is thick. Garnish with minced parsley or chervil and serve.

Kale

Kale and collards are essentially interchangeable, the only difference being that kale's curly leaves may require more thorough washing. See page 561.

Kohlrabi

The "cabbage-turnip," aptly named since although it is strictly speaking a cabbage, it is always treated exactly as if it were a turnip. Use it in turnip recipes.

Buying and storing   Not too big—golf-ball-size is probably best, or a little larger. Any bigger and you run the risk of buying a very woody vegetable. Store in the vegetable bin for up to a week.

Preparing   Small specimens need not be peeled.
Best cooking methods   See Turnips (page 611).
When is it done?   See Turnips (page 611).

Leeks

A member of the onion family that deserves (and generally gets) special recognition and treatment. The flavor of leeks, relatively speaking, is subtle and sweet, and their color is delightful. Unfortunately, they are almost always expensive and, because onions are generally quite cheap and a good substitute, they are not as popular as they would be otherwise.

Buying and storing   Big, plump leeks are wonderful. You're going to trim a lot of the green part off when you clean them, so make sure there's plenty of white, especially if you're buying by the pound. There should be no browning or drying, except perhaps on the ends of the outermost green leaves. Store, loosely wrapped in plastic, in the refrigerator; they will keep for months (literally), although they're best when used much sooner than that. In many climates, it takes a year and a half to grow good leeks (they're planted one spring and harvested the fall of the following year), so they are at their best from late summer to late autumn.

Preparing   Leeks must be very well washed before use; they almost always contain a great deal of sand. Trim off the root end and trim any hard green leaves. Make a long vertical slit through the center of the leek, starting about one inch from the root end and

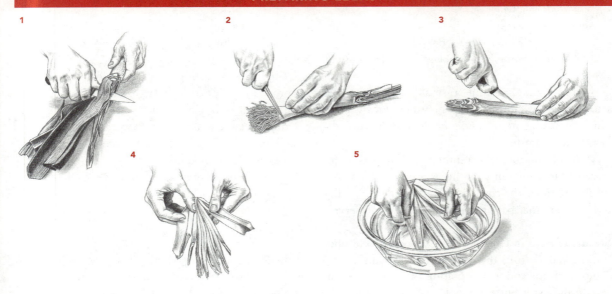

(Step 1) Always remove the tough green leaves from leeks. (Step 2) Cut off the root end. (Step 3) Slice the leek almost in half, just about to the root end. (Steps 4–5) Fan out the leaves and rinse either under cold running water or in a bowl.

cutting all the way to the green end (leaving the root end intact helps keep the leek from falling into pieces when you wash it.) Wash well, making sure to get the sand out from between the layers.

Best cooking methods   Braising, steaming, grilling, roasting.

When is it done?   When very tender, past the point where a thin-bladed knife pierces them easily. Leeks may be stringy and tough when undercooked.

Other recipes in which you can use leeks:
Asparagus with Parmesan, page 538
Pureed Parsnips, page 590
Turnips in Mustard Sauce, page 612
Roasted Root Vegetables, page 615

Leeks Braised in Butter or Oil
Makes 4 servings

Time: 30 minutes

Leeks and butter are a traditional combination. But extra-virgin olive oil also complements leeks beautifully.

4 tablespoons (1/2 stick) butter or extra-virgin olive oil
4 leeks, trimmed and cleaned (see above), cut into
    4-inch sections
Salt and freshly ground black pepper to taste
1/2 cup chicken or vegetable stock, or water (see
    "Soups" for stock recipes)
A few sprigs fresh parsley or thyme
About 1 tablespoon freshly squeezed lemon juice,
    or to taste, plus more for sprinkling

1 Place the butter or oil in a skillet or saucepan large enough to fit the leeks in one layer. Turn the heat to medium. When the butter melts or the oil is hot, add the leeks; sprinkle them with salt and pepper and cook, turning once or twice, for about 5 minutes.

2 Add the stock or water and the herb and bring to a boil. Turn the heat to low, cover, and cook until the leeks are tender, about 20 minutes. Uncover; if the leeks are swimming in liquid, raise the heat a bit and boil some of it away, but allow it to remain moist.

3 Sprinkle about 1 tablespoon of lemon juice over the leeks, then taste and adjust seasoning. Serve hot, at room temperature, or cold, sprinkled with a little more lemon juice.

Leeks au Gratin: Cook leeks as above, using an oven-proof skillet. In Step 3, omit the lemon juice; sprinkle the leeks with about 1 cup of grated Emmenthal (Swiss) or Parmesan cheese and run under the broiler until brown, just 3 or 4 minutes.

Grilled Leeks Vinaigrette
Makes 4 servings

Time: 20 to 30 minutes, plus time to preheat the grill

If the leeks are very thin, sandwich them in a grilling basket and turn them all at once. This is also a good way to prepare scallions.

About 2 pounds leeks, trimmed and cleaned
  (page 580)
Extra-virgin olive oil
Salt and freshly ground black pepper to taste

1 Start a charcoal or wood fire or preheat a gas grill; the fire should be quite hot.

2 Brush the leeks lightly with olive oil and sprinkle with salt and pepper. If they are thick, place them directly on the grill; if not, sandwich them in a grilling basket, then place on the grill.

3 Grill, turning occasionally, until nicely browned all over and very tender, 5 to 15 minutes, depending on their thickness. Serve with any vinaigrette or compound butter (page 768) or flavored oil (page 775).

Steamed Leeks with Tarragon
Makes 4 servings

Time: 20 minutes

This dish is also good with about one pound of spinach steamed along with the leeks.

4 leeks, trimmed and cleaned (page 580), cut into
  1-inch sections
1 teaspoon minced fresh tarragon leaves or
  $1/_2$ teaspoon dried tarragon
2 or 3 tablespoons extra-virgin olive oil
1 or 2 tablespoons freshly squeezed lemon juice
Salt and freshly ground black pepper to taste

1 Place the leeks and tarragon in a steamer over about 1 inch of boiling water; steam until the leeks are tender, 10 minutes or more. Transfer the leeks to a platter.

2 Whisk the olive oil with some of the lemon juice, add salt and pepper to taste, and see whether you want to add more lemon juice. Drizzle over the leeks and serve.

Malanga, or Yautia

A tuber sold in all Latin American markets and some supermarkets, often confused with taro (which it is not). Raw, it has the texture of jicama, but it is not eaten raw. It is best boiled, fried, or included in stews—in short, treated exactly like a potato. Buy very firm, crisp specimens, and don't count on keeping them too long. Peel and trim before cooking.

Mustard and Turnip Greens

Wash these often-sandy greens very well before cooking, and treat them as you would broccoli raab, collards, or kale. They are strong-flavored, widely available, and very inexpensive.

Mushrooms

The mysterious fruits of the woods have become downright trendy. And although many of the "new" mushrooms are generally referred to as "wild" mushrooms, what has happened is that many kinds of mushrooms are now under cultivation and therefore routinely sold in supermarkets. No matter; they are better than the traditionally domesticated button mushrooms regardless of what you call them.

Although different types of mushrooms sport distinctive flavors and textures, they can be used interchangeably (with the exception of the slender enoki, which is little more than a garnish anyway). But better than substituting one for another is combining them: A dish that features oyster mushrooms, shiitakes, and the common button mushroom—and these are sold almost all the time in most supermarkets—is much more exciting than a dish containing one alone. And, if you add a couple of reconstituted dried porcini or morels, you crank the flavor up another notch.

A quick primer to the most common mushrooms, in rough order of desirability:

Porcini (Cèpes): Meaty and spectacular. Increasingly seen fresh in this country, but still not commonly, they are always available dried, and worth keeping in your pantry. Buy from a reputable dealer in quantities of at least an ounce at a time; the small packages of one-eighth ounce for three dollars are among the world's greatest rip-offs.

Morel: Fine-flavored and odd-textured. Found wild all over the North, and sometimes in a large enough quantity to make it to stores (although rarely supermarkets). Sold dried, and worth having.

Chanterelle: Wild and domesticated, a good, fleshy mushroom with subtle flavor.

Shiitake: The best domesticated mushroom, now sold in most supermarkets. Great flavor. Also sold dried (the Chinese black mushroom is shiitake and is usually very inexpensive). The stem is too tough to be eaten; discard or use it in stocks.

Oyster: Wild and domesticated, a good choice in supermarkets.

Cremini/Portobello: The second is merely a giant version of the first. Both are domesticated brown mushrooms, and have much better flavor than button mushrooms. Portobellos are wonderful grilled.

Button: The common white-to-tan cultivated mushroom. Much improved when cooked with some reconstituted dried porcini, or with some fresh shiitakes.

Enoki: A slender Asian mushroom, sold in small packages. Use raw or lightly cooked as a garnish.

Buying and storing Don't buy drying, damaged, shriveled up, or slimy mushrooms and you'll be fine. It's better to sort through bins to buy them in bulk than to buy prepackaged mushrooms. Dried mushrooms keep almost forever, so there's rarely a problem in buying them, although you want to make sure you actually get dried porcini when you pay for dried porcini (which usually sell for upward of one hundred dollars a pound). Store fresh mushrooms, loosely wrapped in waxed paper (not plastic), in the refrigerator bin; amazingly, given their fragility, they often keep upward of a week.

Preparing Rinse mushrooms as lightly as you can (they absorb water like a sponge if they sit in it), but make sure to get dirt out of hidden crevices; with some mushrooms, it's easier to trim them first. Cut off any hard or dried-out spots—usually just the end of the stem. The stems of most mushrooms are perfectly edible, but those of shiitake should be discarded or reserved for stock. Clean the stems well, cut them in half if they're large (as are those of portobellos), and cook them with the caps. Or, reserve the stems for stock or duxelles (see next recipe).

To reconstitute dried mushrooms Soak in hot water to cover for ten or fifteen minutes, or until soft. Change the water if they are not softening quickly enough, but reserve the soaking water for use in sauces, stocks, and stews (strain it first; it's often sandy). Trim the hard parts from the mushrooms and use as you would fresh.

Best cooking methods Sautéing and grilling. Wonderful in soup (see Mushroom Soup, page 56) and omelets (see Mushroom Omelet, page 738). You can also simmer or steam mushrooms for about five minutes, which will firm them up a bit; then dress them with olive oil and freshly squeezed lemon juice; or slice them, raw, and serve with olive oil, freshly squeezed lemon juice, and thinly sliced Parmesan.

When is it done? When tender.

Other recipes in which you can use mushrooms:
Quick Stir-Fried Snow Peas or Sugar Snap Peas, page 591
Stuffed Mushrooms, page 31

Duxelles
Makes a little more than 1 cup

Time: About 30 minutes

What a revelation duxelles are for people who rummage through supermarket bargain shelves! If you take less-than-perfect but still halfway decent mushrooms—or the stems of top-quality mushrooms—and cook them gently with butter and shallots, you have a brilliant seasoning for soups, stews, omelets, or toast, or a great ingredient for stuffing almost anything. Duxelles keep, refrigerated, for about a week, and freeze well.

3 tablespoons butter or extra-virgin olive oil
$1/4$ cup minced shallots, scallions, or onion
About 1 pound mushrooms, preferably an assortment, or mushrooms stems, cleaned, trimmed (see opposite), and minced; mix in some reconstituted dried mushrooms for extra flavor if you like
Salt and freshly ground black pepper to taste
$1/4$ cup minced fresh parsley leaves

1   Place the butter in a large, deep skillet and turn the heat to medium. Just as the foam begins to subside, stir in the shallots. Cook, stirring occasionally, until they soften, 3 to 5 minutes.

2   Stir in the mushrooms. Cook, stirring, until they have given up most of their liquid, about 10 minutes. Turn the heat to low and continue to cook, stirring, until almost all the liquid has evaporated. Season well, then stir in the parsley. Use immediately or refrigerate.

Grilled Portobello Mushrooms

Makes 4 servings

Time: About 20 minutes, plus time to preheat the grill

You can grill just the caps of portobellos if you like, or cut them down the middle and grill cap and stem together; make sure the stem is washed well.

¹⁄₃ cup extra-virgin olive oil
1 tablespoon minced shallot, scallion, or onion
Salt and freshly ground black pepper to taste
4 large portobello mushrooms, trimmed (page 583) and cut in half right down the middle
Minced fresh parsley or chervil leaves for garnish

1 Start a charcoal or wood fire or preheat a gas grill or broiler; the fire should be quite hot and the rack about 4 inches from the heat source. Mix together the olive oil, shallot, salt, and pepper and brush the mushrooms all over with about half of this mixture.

2 Grill or broil the mushrooms with the tops of their caps away from the heat until they begin to brown, 5 to 8 minutes. Brush with the remaining oil and turn. Grill until tender and nicely browned all over, 5 to 10 minutes more. Garnish and serve.

Sautéed Mushrooms with Garlic

Makes 4 servings

Time: About 20 minutes

These are best served at room temperature. Stir in some other herbs—such as chives, chervil, and/or tarragon—and a teaspoon or two of good vinegar along with the parsley if you like.

¹⁄₂ cup extra-virgin olive oil
About 1 pound mushrooms, preferably an assortment, cleaned, trimmed (page 583), and sliced; mix in some reconstituted dried mushrooms for extra flavor if you like
Salt and freshly ground black pepper to taste
¹⁄₄ cup dry white wine
1 teaspoon minced garlic
2 tablespoons chopped fresh parsley leaves

1 Place the olive oil in a large, deep skillet over medium heat. When it is hot, add the mushrooms, then some salt and pepper. Cook, stirring occasionally, until tender, 10 to 15 minutes.

2 Add the wine and let it bubble away for just 1 minute or so longer. Turn the heat to low. Add the garlic and parsley, stir, and cook for 1 minute. Turn off the heat and allow the mushrooms to sit in this mixture for 1 hour or so before serving.

Okra

Many northerners have never come to appreciate okra. It *is* an unusual vegetable, in that it produces an odd, thick liquid (useful in thickening stews) when it cooks for a long time. But it has good flavor and is wonderful fried.

Buying and storing   The smaller the better; don't buy okra when it's over two or three inches long. Pods should be firm and not at all mushy and, of course, undamaged. The season is summer, but you may find okra through the fall.

Preparing   Easy: Rinse, then cut off the stem end.

Best cooking methods   Frying, gently stewing.

When is it done?   When tender; overcooking makes okra slimy.

Other recipes in which you can use okra (always minimize cooking time):

Fried Okra

Makes 4 servings

Time: 30 minutes

The flour-and-egg treatment is optional here; you can simply toss okra with cornmeal and fry it. The first method gives a thicker crust, the second a lighter one.

Vegetable oil for deep frying
About 1½ pounds okra, trimmed
Flour for dredging (optional)
2 eggs, lightly beaten in a bowl (optional)
Cornmeal for dredging (optional)
Salt and freshly ground black pepper to taste
Lemon wedges

1 Place the vegetable oil to a depth of at least 2 inches in a large, deep saucepan over medium-high heat. Let it heat while you prepare the okra; it should reach a temperature of 365° to 375°F. Preheat the oven to 200°F.

2 If you choose to use the flour and eggs, place the flour in a paper or plastic bag. Place the cornmeal in a bowl. Toss the okra with the flour, then dip in the egg, then toss in the cornmeal. Or simply toss in the cornmeal. Fry the okra without crowding; it's likely you will need to do this in batches. Brown the okra nicely—it will take just 3 or 4 minutes—and drain on paper towels.

3 Keep the okra warm in the oven until it is all done, then sprinkle with salt and pepper and serve with lemon wedges.

Okra, Corn, and Tomato Stew

Makes 4 servings

Time: 45 minutes

This traditional summer dish is popular throughout the South. Although cilantro is not the usual garnish, it works beautifully.

2 tablespoons canola or other neutral oil
1 large onion, chopped
1 red or yellow bell pepper, stemmed, peeled if
desired, seeded, and chopped
Salt and freshly ground black pepper to taste
3 ripe tomatoes, cored, peeled, seeded, and
chopped
1 cup okra, trimmed and cut into small pieces
1 tablespoon chili powder, or to taste
2 cups freshly scraped corn kernels (page 564)
Minced cilantro or fresh parsley leaves for garnish

1 Place a large, deep skillet or casserole over medium heat. Add the oil and, 1 minute later, the onion and pepper. Sprinkle with salt and pepper and cook, stirring occasionally, until the pepper is fairly tender, about 10 minutes.

2 Add the tomatoes, okra, and chili powder, turn the heat to low, and stir. Cover and cook, stirring once or twice, for about 10 minutes, or until the okra is tender.

3 Uncover and stir in the corn. If the mixture is very liquid, raise the heat to medium and cook with the cover off for 5 minutes, stirring frequently. If the mixture is fairly dry, cover and cook over low heat for 5 minutes. Garnish and serve.

Onion

In most of its forms, a kitchen staple that we take for granted (the leek and relatively mild, still fairly pricey shallot are exceptions). Although some are sweeter than others, this difference doesn't matter as much in cooking as it does when eating onions raw; for cooking purposes, onions are pretty much interchangeable.

Bermuda, Spanish, and other large onions are on the mild side, and they're easier to handle—it's less hassle to peel and chop one large onion than two small ones—and so are a good choice for daily use. But the standard "yellow" onion, the one sold in mesh sacks year-round, is more common and a fine choice. Vidalia and other "sweet" onions, among the first crops of spring, are touted as being so mild they can be eaten like an apple. For most of us, they are not; use them as you would any onion. Because of their relatively high sugar content, they do not store as well as thicker-skinned onions.

Buying and storing   "New" onions, with their bright green stems and glossy bulbs, should be bought and cooked immediately—they're very fresh and fragile (and are a good substitute for leeks). Scallions, too, cannot be stored for long. Shallots, small and brown- or purple-skinned, will keep for months in the refrigerator.

Yellow, white, Bermuda, Spanish, pearl, red (don't cook these—their color will sadly change the color of everything else in the pot), and other onions will keep for weeks without refrigeration. Buy hard onions, with no trace of sprouting (or, of course, rotting), and store them in a dark, cool, preferably airy place. Once you peel an onion (or a shallot), wrap it tightly in plastic and refrigerate. Frozen peeled pearl onions are so convenient that their mild flavor can be forgiven.

Preparing   If you have a lot of onions to peel, drop them into boiling water for thirty seconds to one

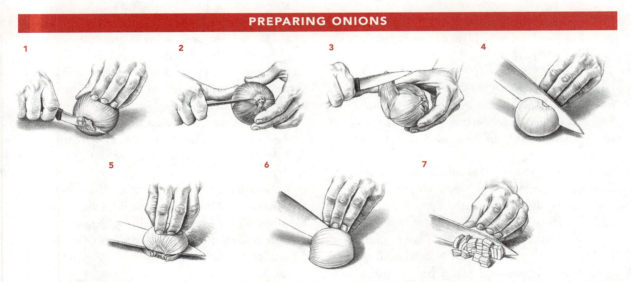

PREPARING ONIONS

(Step 1) Cut off both ends of the onion. (Steps 2–3) Then make a small slit in the skin, just one layer down. The peel will come off easily. (Step 4) Cut the onion in half. (Step 5) Make two or three cuts parallel to the cutting board into the vegetable; don't cut all the way through. (Step 6) Now make several cuts down through the top of the vegetable. Again leave the vegetable intact at one end. (Step 7) Cut across the vegetable to create a dice.

minute, then rinse in cold water; remove the root end and the skins will slip off easily. To peel just a couple of onions, cut a thin slice off both ends, then make a shallow cut from one end to the other, just through the skin and top layer of flesh; peel off both together.

You can wear goggles when chopping or slicing onions (page 586) if you find yourself crying easily, but a very sharp knife solves most problems by quickly and cleanly cutting through the flesh without spraying as much of the offending substance into the air as does a slow, dull knife. (This substance, called lachrimator, combines with the moisture in your eyes to form a weak solution of sulfuric acid. No wonder it burns!)

Best cooking methods As a vegetable, baking and grilling. Leave the root end on onions you will cook whole; they'll stay together better. Whole small pearl onions can be sautéed; sliced large onions can be battered and fried. Be sure to try Linguine with Slow-Cooked Onions (page 137). And always include onions (and/or shallots) in Roasted Root Vegetables (page 615).

When is it done? When very tender but not quite falling apart.

Grilled Spanish Onions

Makes 4 servings

Time: 20 minutes, plus time to preheat the grill

Don't bother to peel onions when grilling; the peel helps them keep their shape, and comes off easily after cooking.

4 medium-to-large Spanish or Bermuda onions, well
    washed and dried
Extra-virgin olive oil
Salt and freshly ground black pepper to taste

1 Start a charcoal or wood fire or preheat a gas grill. Cut the root and flower end from each onion so that it will sit flat on the grill. Then cut each onion in half, through its equator.

2 Brush the top and bottom with olive oil and sprinkle with salt and pepper. Grill, turning once or twice, until nicely browned on both sides and tender throughout, about 15 minutes. Serve.

Baked Spanish Onions

Makes 4 servings

Time: 1 to 1$\frac{1}{2}$ hours

Baked onions have more flavor than baked potatoes, but remain a product of what you put on them. I like to serve them with a variety of toppings: butter, sour cream, crumbled bacon, freshly grated Parmesan, crumbled Gorgonzola, or mixed fresh herbs, for example.

4 medium-to-large Spanish or Bermuda onions,
    peeled, leaving root end intact (page 586)
4 teaspoons butter or extra-virgin olive oil, or more if
    you like
Salt and freshly ground black pepper to taste

1 Preheat oven to 375°F.

2 Cut a deep "x" in the top (flower end) of each onion. Place each onion on a square of foil, dot with butter, sprinkle with salt and pepper, and wrap tightly. Place the onions in a baking dish.

3 Bake for 1 hour, or until very tender (a thin-bladed knife will pierce the foil and the center of the onion with very little resistance). Spread onions open and serve with toppings.

Cooked Onions and Apples

Makes 4 servings

Time: 30 minutes

A great fall or winter dish to serve with pork.

3 cups peeled and sliced onions (page 586)
2 tablespoons lard, bacon drippings, butter, or olive oil
3 cups peeled, cored, and sliced firm apples, such as Granny Smiths
Pinch ground allspice, mace, or cinnamon
Sugar, if needed
Salt and freshly ground black pepper to taste
Minced fresh parsley leaves for garnish

1 Place the onions in a large, deep skillet over medium heat and cover. Cook for 10 minutes, stirring once or twice, until they are dry and almost sticking to the pan. Stir in the fat.

2 Add the apples and spice. Turn the heat to low, cover, and cook, stirring occasionally, until the apples begin to soften, about 10 minutes.

3 Uncover and taste; add sugar if the apples have not contributed enough sweetness. Season with salt and pepper, turn the heat to medium, and cook until the apples are completely tender but not mushy, a few minutes more. Garnish and serve.

Fried Onion Rings

Makes 4 servings

Time: 30 minutes

These are vastly superior to the battered or breaded onion rings served in most restaurants. Eat them as you make them; they do not hold well in an oven.

Vegetable oil for deep-frying
4 Bermuda, Spanish, or other very large onions, peeled (page 586)
3 cups flour, or flour mixed half and half with cornmeal
Salt and freshly ground black pepper to taste

1 Place the vegetable oil, to a depth of at least 2 inches, in a large, deep saucepan over medium-high heat. Let it heat while you prepare the onions; the oil should reach a temperature of 365° to 375°F.

2 Slice the onions thinly and separate them into rings; a food processor equipped with the slicing disk works well for this.

3 Place the flour in a plastic or paper bag and toss in a handful of rings at a time. Shake the bag, then shake the rings to remove excess flour and drop them in the oil. Cook them without crowding, stirring once or twice, until golden brown, about 4 minutes. When done, lift the onions from the oil with a slotted spoon, drain on paper towels, season, and serve immediately.

Caramelized Small Onions or Shallots

Makes 4 servings

Time: 20 minutes

You can use tiny pearl onions for this (even the frozen, peeled ones are fine), or small yellow onions. None should be over an inch or so in diameter.

3 tablespoons butter or extra-virgin olive oil
12 to 24 very small onions or shallots, peeled (page 589)
2 tablespoons sugar
1 teaspoon fresh thyme leaves (optional)
1 cup chicken, beef, or vegetable stock, or white wine, or water (see "Soups" for stock recipes)
1 tablespoon balsamic, sherry, or other vinegar

The technique for mincing any round or oval root vegetable is essentially the same. These illustrations use a shallot to demonstrate.

(Step 1) First peel the shallot, then cut it in half from top to bottom. (Step 2) Place one half, cut side down, on your cutting board. Make two or three cuts parallel to the cutting board into the vegetable; don't cut all the way through. (Step 3) Now make as many cuts as are practical down through the top of the vegetable. Again, leave the vegetable intact at one end. (Step 4) Cut across the vegetable to mince.

1 Place the butter in a medium skillet and turn the heat to medium. When it melts, add the onions and cook, stirring, until the onions begin to brown all over, about 10 minutes.

2 Sprinkle with sugar (and thyme if you like), and stir. Add the liquid and raise the heat to medium-high. Cook, stirring frequently, until the onions are glazed and the liquid almost completely evaporated, about 5 minutes.

3 Stir in the vinegar and continue to cook until the onions are syrupy, another minute or two. Serve hot or at room temperature.

Parsnips

Talk about underrated—the parsnip is probably the best vegetable that never gets eaten. Sweeter than even carrots, easy to prepare, parsnips have great shelf life; you can store them like carrots, for weeks or even months. Their highest and best use is pureed, but they are also wonderful mixed with other vegetables in a roasting pan or cooked in any way you would carrots.

Buying and storing The best season is fall, but you can usually find parsnips year-round. You want relatively small ones, four to six per pound, because real large parsnips (they can weigh a pound each) may have a woody core that must be removed. Avoid soft or flabby specimens.

Preparing Treat as you would a carrot. If the parsnip is large (more than one inch thick at its broad end), you must remove its woody core: cut the thinner portion off and set it aside. Cut the thick portion in half and dig out the core with the end of a vegetable peeler, a paring knife, or a sharp spoon; the procedure is neither difficult nor time-consuming.

Best cooking methods Pureed parsnips are wonderful, but you can use parsnips in any cooked carrot recipe.

When is it done? When tender enough to easily pierce with a thin-bladed knife or skewer. Overcooking makes parsnips mushy.

Other recipes in which you can use parsnips:
Any carrot recipe, pages 552–553
Roasted Root Vegetables, page 615

Pureed Parsnips

Makes 4 servings

Time: 30 minutes

Parsnips can be combined with soft-cooked potatoes, turnips, or carrots before pureeing, but their own flavor is heavenly. Because they have a tendency to become waterlogged, it's best to steam or microwave parsnips rather than boil them.

About 1¹/₂ pounds parsnips, peeled, cored if necessary (page 589), cut into chunks

Salt and freshly ground black pepper to taste

2 tablespoons butter

2 tablespoons cream, milk, or reserved parsnip cooking water, as needed

¹/₄ cup minced fresh parsley leaves, plus more for garnish

1 To steam the parsnips, place them in a steamer above an inch or two of salted water. Cover and cook about 15 minutes, or until they can be easily pierced with a thin-bladed knife. Drain.

2 To microwave the parsnips, place them in a microwave-proof plate or shallow bowl with about 2 tablespoons of salted water; cover with a lid or plastic wrap. Microwave on high for 6 minutes, shake the container, and continue to microwave at 2-minute intervals, until the parsnips can be easily pierced with a thin-bladed knife. Drain.

3 Place the parsnips in the container of a food processor along with salt, pepper, and butter. Puree, adding the liquid of your choice through the feed tube, until the mixture is smooth and creamy but not too thin. (You may prepare the recipe in advance up to this point; refrigerate, well wrapped or in a covered container, for up to 2 days before proceeding.) Place in a bowl or small saucepan.

4 Stir in the ¹/₄ cup parsley, then taste and adjust seasoning. Reheat over very low heat, stirring almost constantly, or in the microwave. Garnish and serve.

Peas

The pea world has changed greatly twice in the last fifty years. The first change occurred when no one had enough time (or thought they didn't) to sit with a stack of peas in their lap and shell enough for dinner; that brought us canned (ugh) and frozen (acceptable but not close to fresh) peas. Now, most people who do buy peas in the pod shell them and eat them out of hand, as a snack—which is a great idea.

The second change came with the popularity of edible-pod peas, such as the Chinese snow pea (also called mange-tout, or "eat all"), which has an edible pod and tiny peas inside, and the newly developed sugar snap, or snap pea, an edible pod that also contains peas of some size. Both give you great pea flavor without the hassle of shelling.

Buying and storing   For peas to shell, open a pod or two in the store; they should be full of medium-sized peas. Real big peas can be tough, so taste a couple; if you want to keep eating, buy them. If the peas are large and tough, they will need to be cooked before eating. Snow and snap peas should be bright green and undamaged; taste one before buying. It should be crisp and sweet. Store all peas, loosely wrapped in plastic, in the vegetable bin. But use them quickly; their sweetness is fleeting.

Preparing   With the flat end of the pea down, grasp the tip of the flower end and pull down, removing the string along the bottom of the pea.

Best cooking methods   Steaming, quick-braising in butter, stir-frying. Peas are almost always a welcome addition to risotto (pages 208–211).

Always remove the little string from peas before cooking.

When is it done? As soon as they are hot and bright green, usually less than five minutes.

Other recipes in which you can use peas:
Stir-Fried Asparagus, Three Ways, page 539 (edible-podded peas only)
Stir-Fried Broccoli, page 545 (edible-podded peas only)
Stir-Fried Cauliflower with Ginger and Oyster Sauce, page 555 (edible-podded peas only)
Pureed Parsnips, page 590 (peas only)

Buttered Peas

Makes 4 servings

Time: 15 minutes

It's tough to shell enough fresh peas to cook in any quantity, since the temptation to eat while you shell is overwhelming. But should you have two cups or so (you need at least $1^1/_2$ pounds of unshelled peas in pods), cook them this way, which is also the best way to cook frozen peas.

2 cups shelled or frozen peas
1 to 2 tablespoons butter
Salt and freshly ground black pepper to taste
2 tablespoons minced fresh mint, basil, chervil, or parsley leaves (optional)

1 Bring a small pot of water to the boil over high heat; salt it. Place the peas in it, with the heat still on high, and cook for 2 to 3 minutes, no more—just until the peas are bright green and tender.

2 Drain the peas. Place the butter in a medium-to-large skillet and turn the heat to medium. When the butter melts, turn the heat to low and cook the peas, salt and pepper, and optional herb in it for 2 or 3 minutes, shaking the skillet occasionally, just until the peas are hot and coated with butter.

Quick Stir-Fried Snow Peas or Sugar Snap Peas

Makes 4 servings

Time: 10 minutes

There's nothing to this, but if your peas are fresh, it's sensational.

2 tablespoons peanut, canola, or other oil
About $1^1/_2$ pounds snow or sugar snap peas, washed and trimmed (page 590)
2 tablespoons soy sauce
1 teaspoon dark sesame oil (optional)

1 Place the oil in a large, deep skillet or wok and turn the heat to high. When the oil begins to smoke, toss in the peas and cook, stirring almost constantly, until they are glossy, bright green and begin to show a few brown spots, about 5 minutes.

2 Turn off the heat and remove to a platter. Drizzle with soy sauce and sesame oil, if you like, and serve.

Peppers

Here we're talking about sweet, or bell peppers (as opposed to hot, which it's best to call chiles to avoid confusion). When it comes to sweet peppers, color is far more important than shape. Actually, there's only one color that really matters: green. Green peppers may be "mature," but they are not ripe, at least not if ripeness implies the peak of flavor. Where a green pepper is sharp, almost acrid, and likely as not to cause indigestion, the same pepper picked a week or two later, when red, yellow, or orange, will have mellowed considerably. Of course red peppers are usually more expensive than green, and not always available, so there are times when we have to settle. But there is no question which pepper is preferable. Note: Purple peppers are green peppers in disguise; the purple color fades to muddy green as they cook, and the flavor is usually bitter.

Buying and storing   Yellow and orange peppers seem to be mellowest, but they're usually expensive, so red is the common first choice, green a distant last. Avoid peppers with soft spots or bruises, or those that feel very full—since you buy them by weight, there's no need to pay for lots of seeds. Store peppers, unwrapped, in the vegetable bin, for a week or so.

Preparing   Peppers should always be cored and stemmed before cooking unless, of course, you're roasting or grilling them whole. If you plan to cut the peppers into strips, or dice them, just start by cutting them in half; remove the cap and seed mass with your fingers. Alternatively, you can cut a circle around the cap and pull it off, along with most of the seeds; rinse out the remaining seeds. Peppers can also be peeled with a vegetable peeler, an added refinement that doesn't take long and removes an element of bitterness.

Best cooking methods   Roasting, grilling, broiling, sautéing.

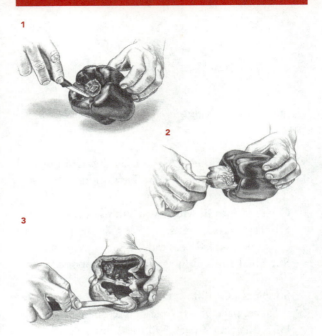

(Step 1) To core a pepper, first cut around the stem. (Step 2) Then pull the core out; rinse to remove remaining seeds. (Step 3) Alternatively, cut the pepper in half, break out the core, and scrape out the seeds.

When is it done?   When roasting or grilling, blackened and collapsed. In a pan, when very tender and soft; taste one.

Other recipes in which you can use peppers:
Stir-Fried Asparagus, Three Ways, page 539 (do not precook peppers)
Stir-Fried Broccoli, page 545
Gingered Cabbage, page 549
Cabbage Braised with Onions, page 549
Collards or Kale with Double Garlic, page 562
Quick Stir-Fried Snow Peas or Sugar Snap Peas, page 591

Marinated Roasted, Grilled, or Broiled Peppers

Makes 4 servings

Time: About 1 hour, plus marinating time and time to preheat the grill

There are many techniques for "roasting" peppers; all work. These are the three easiest and neatest.

4 red or yellow bell peppers, rinsed
1/4 cup extra-virgin olive oil
1 clove garlic, crushed
1 tablespoon balsamic, sherry, or other flavorful vinegar
Salt and freshly ground black pepper to taste
Minced fresh basil, oregano, or parsley leaves for garnish

1 To roast the peppers, preheat the oven to 500°F. Put the peppers in a roasting pan and place in the oven, with the rack set near the top. Roast, shaking the pan frequently, until the peppers shrivel and collapse, 30 to 40 minutes. Proceed to Step 4.

2 To grill, start a charcoal or wood fire or preheat a gas grill; the fire should be quite hot. Place the peppers on the grill (cover the grill if possible) and cook, turning occasionally, and taking care not to let the peppers burn too badly (some blackening is not only okay, it's desirable), until the peppers collapse, 10 to 20 minutes total. Proceed to Step 4.

3 To broil the peppers, preheat the broiler. Place the peppers in a roasting pan and set under the broiler, about 4 inches from the heat source. Broil, turning as each side browns and taking care not to let the peppers burn too badly (some blackening is not only okay, it's desirable), until the peppers shrivel and collapse, 10 to 20 minutes total. Proceed to Step 4.

4 Place the hot peppers in a bowl and cover with plastic wrap. Let cool, then peel, discarding skins, seeds, and stems.

5 Combine the oil, garlic, vinegar, salt, and pepper and marinate the peppers in this mixture, from 1 to 24 hours. Serve at room temperature, garnished with minced herb.

Corn-Stuffed Peppers with Spicy Tomato Sauce

Makes 4 servings

Time: About 1 hour

Use leftover grains for this dish if you can, but use fresh corn if possible.

1 1/2 cups cooked white or brown rice, barley, or quinoa
1 medium onion, minced
1/2 cup diced fresh mushrooms
2 cups cored, peeled, seeded, and diced tomatoes (canned are fine; drain them first)
1 1/2 cups corn kernels, preferably fresh
1 egg, lightly beaten
Salt and freshly ground black pepper to taste
4 red or yellow peppers, caps removed and center hollowed out (page 592)
2 tablespoons peanut or olive oil
2 cloves garlic, crushed
2 small dried hot red chiles
1 tablespoon cumin (seeds or ground)
1 tablespoon soy or Worcestershire sauce, or to taste
2 teaspoons sugar, or to taste
Dry white wine, if needed
Minced fresh chives or parsley leaves for garnish

1 Preheat the oven to 375°F. Combine the grain, onion, mushrooms, half the tomatoes, corn, egg, salt, and pepper. Pack this mixture into the peppers. Place the peppers in a roasting pan with 1/2 inch of water and bake for 45 minutes, or until the peppers are tender.

2 Meanwhile, make the sauce: Place the oil in a large, deep skillet over medium-high heat. Add the garlic and red chiles and cook, stirring, until the garlic is golden; scoop out the garlic and chiles and discard. Add the cumin and stir. Add the remaining tomatoes, crushing them with a fork or spoon. Bring to a boil, turn the heat to medium-low, and add the soy sauce. Simmer gently for 10 minutes, then taste and add sugar as necessary; season with salt and pepper. Thin with a little wine if necessary. Puree in a blender and keep warm.

3 Serve the peppers with a little of the sauce spooned over, garnished with chives or parsley. Pass the remaining sauce at the table.

Simple Sautéed Peppers

Makes 4 servings

Time: About 30 minutes

You may add a cup or more of sliced onion to this, right from the beginning.

> 2 tablespoons extra-virgin olive oil
> 3 or 4 red or yellow bell peppers, stemmed, peeled if desired, seeded, and cut into thin strips (page 592)
> Salt and freshly ground black pepper to taste
> 2 teaspoons balsamic, sherry, or other good vinegar
> 1 teaspoon fresh thyme leaves or ¹/₂ teaspoon dried thyme, or ¹/₄ cup chopped fresh parsley or basil leaves

1 Place the oil in a large, deep skillet and turn the heat to medium-high; 1 minute later, add the peppers.

2 Cook, stirring occasionally, until the peppers are lightly browned and very tender, at least 15 minutes. Season with salt and pepper; if you're using thyme, add it now.

3 Stir in the vinegar and turn the heat to low; cook another 2 minutes. If you're using parsley or basil, stir it in. Adjust the seasoning and serve.

Plantains

The plantain looks similar to the banana but is usually somewhat larger and is never found in bunches. It's also always cooked, whether it is green, greenish yellow, yellow, yellow and black, or so black that the uninitiated would toss it into the trash without a moment's thought. During the ripening process, which takes between several days and a couple of weeks at room temperature, plantains become sweeter and sweeter. Unlike dessert bananas, however, they retain their firm texture almost to the end. Even black plantains can be cut into chunks and sautéed; in fact, that is the best way to cook them.

Buying and storing   You can buy plantains in any Latino store, but also in many supermarkets. If possible, buy several green ones at a time; this allows you to cook a few when they're green, then wait a few days and cook some when they're riper. If you develop a preference for green bananas, just keep them in the refrigerator; ripening can be retarded for weeks with no loss of quality.

Preparing   Don't try to peel any but the ripest plantains as you would a banana. Instead, begin by cutting off both tips of the plantain; then cut the plantain into a few sections (page 595). Make three vertical slits in the skin of each section, then peel each piece of the skin off. Trim any remaining skin from the plantain with a paring knife.

Best cooking methods   Sautéing, braising, or stewing with meats.

When is it done?   Ripe plantains are done when they are nicely browned all over.

Other recipes in which you can use plantains:

Pureed Parsnips, page 590 (plantains must be yellow-ripe)

Mashed Potatoes, page 596 (plantains must be yellow-ripe)

Plantain Chips, page 27

Sautéed Ripe Plantains

Maduros

Makes 4 servings

Time: 20 minutes

Two cautions about making these plantains, the traditional and ideal accompaniment to Chicken with Rice (Arroz con Pollo), page 369. One, don't use plantains unless they are black, far riper than any banana you'd consider eating. And two, keep the heat moderate to low or the high sugar content of the plantains will cause them to burn.

2 ripe plantains, almost completely black, peeled (see below)

3 to 4 tablespoons neutral oil such as canola or butter, or a combination

Salt to taste

Lime wedges

① Cut the plantain pieces in half, lengthwise. Place the oil in a large skillet over medium heat. When it's hot, add the plantains and turn the heat to medium-low.

② Cook, turning frequently and adjusting the heat so as not to burn the plantains (the riper they are, the more sugar they contain, and the more likely to burn). They are done when golden brown and tender, 10 minutes or less.

③ Sprinkle with salt and serve with lime wedges.

Potatoes

What can be said about this most substantial and popular of all vegetables? It is a New World native that took centuries to become popular in Europe (where it was long believed to be poisonous) and didn't really catch on here until the mid-nineteenth century. It's incredibly cheap, often still available for ten cents a pound. And it is fun to cook and eat, even more so if you pay attention to the kinds of potatoes you buy and use them in the manner to which they are best suited. Potatoes take dozens of distinct forms, and fall into three categories in the kitchen:

Starchy potatoes, often called Idaho or Russet, make the best baked and mashed potatoes and good

PREPARING PLANTAINS

(Step 1) Plantains are unusual, and must be peeled this way. First, cut off both ends and discard. (Step 2) Cut the plantain into several chunks. (Step 3) Make three shallow, vertical slits in each chunk. (Step 4) Remove the peel in pieces. If any parts of the peel cling to the flesh, remove them with a paring knife.

French fries. In this book, I call these "baking potatoes, such as Idaho or Russet."

All-purpose potatoes, often called Eastern, have a moderate amount of starch, still too much to make great boiled potatoes. But they make good mashed potatoes and decent French fries and baked potatoes. I don't specifically call for all-purpose potatoes in this book. You can use them in most recipes, with good if not ideal results. The Yukon gold potatoes now becoming widely available are the closest thing to a true "all-purpose."

Low-starch potatoes, sometimes called "new" potatoes (although any potato can be new, since in this instance it means freshly dug), may be red- or white-skinned, are usually thin-skinned, and are sometimes quite "waxy." They make the best boiling potatoes, are great roasted, and are decent for other uses. In this book, I call these "waxy red or white potatoes."

Buying and storing Fresh potatoes are dug in spring through fall, but potatoes are stored and sold year-round. Smooth, nicely shaped potatoes are easier to peel and clean. Small potatoes are easier to boil and grill—their interior cooks before their exterior burns or turns to mush, which is what often happens when you try to boil or grill larger potatoes. But peeling small potatoes is a tiresome task. The solution is to keep more than one kind of potato in the house.

All potatoes should be quite firm when you buy them. Look out for damaged potatoes, those with mold or soft spots, those that are flabby, those with sprouts, or those with green spots. Store potatoes in a dark place and a cool one, but not in the refrigerator (low-starch potatoes can be refrigerated, however). Don't buy more than you can use in a month or two unless you have a cool, dark, and reasonably dry cellar.

Preparing Wash. Peel if necessary, removing "eyes," dark-brown spots, or traces of green. If the potato is largely green or has rot, discard it.

Best cooking methods All.

When is it done? For starchy potatoes, when mealy. For low-starch potatoes, when tender.

Other recipes in which you can use potatoes:
Turnips in Mustard Sauce, page 612
Braised Butternut or Other Winter Squash with Garlic, page 614
Roasted Root Vegetables, page 615

Mashed Potatoes
Makes 4 servings

Time: About 40 minutes

So much fuss has been made about mashed potatoes in recent years that you'd think they were difficult to make; nothing could be further from the truth. If you like your mashed potatoes lumpy, mash them with a fork or potato masher; if you like them creamy, use a food mill or ricer. And if you like them with the peel, just scrub them well before cooking.

2 pounds baking potatoes, such as Idaho or Russet, peeled and cut into quarters
3 tablespoons butter
3/4 cup milk, gently warmed
Salt and freshly ground black pepper to taste

1 Boil the potatoes in a pot with salted water to cover, until soft; this will take about 30 minutes. Do not overcook or poke them too often to check doneness, or they will absorb too much water.

2 When the potatoes are done, drain them, then mash them well or put them through a food mill. Return them to the pot over very low heat and stir in the butter and—gradually—the milk, beating with a wooden spoon until smooth and creamy. Season with salt and pepper as necessary. Serve immediately, keep warm, or reheat in a microwave.

Potato Croquettes

Makes 4 to 6 servings

Time: At least 1 hour

Crisp, creamy, old-fashioned.

> 1¹/₂ pounds baking potatoes, such as Idaho
>   or Russet, prepared as for Mashed Potatoes
>   (page 596) but without the butter
> 2 eggs
> Pinch freshly grated nutmeg
> 2 tablespoons minced fresh parsley leaves, plus more
>   for garnish
> ¹/₂ cup freshly grated Parmesan cheese
> Salt and freshly ground black pepper to taste
> Flour as needed
> Olive oil or butter as needed
> Plain bread crumbs for dredging

1 Combine the potatoes, eggs, nutmeg, 2 table-spoons parsley, Parmesan, salt, and pepper. Add enough flour (you may not need any) to allow the potatoes to hold their shape; mold into hamburger-shaped cakes. If time allows, refrigerate for 1 hour.

2 Place the oil or butter in a large, deep skillet and turn the heat to medium-high. When the butter melts or the oil becomes hot, dredge the cakes in bread crumbs and place in the pan.

3 Cook until brown on one side, about 5 minutes. Turn and brown the other side. Garnish and serve hot or at room temperature.

Baked Potatoes

Makes 4 servings

Time: 1¹/₂ hours

If you're in a hurry, you can crank up the oven to 450°F and cut the cooking time to under an hour, but the potato will not be quite as pleasantly mealy, and the skin not as pleasantly chewy. Don't, however, resort to the microwave unless you want a potato that is closer to steamed than baked.

> 4 large baking potatoes, such as Idaho or Russet,
>   well scrubbed and trimmed

1 Preheat the oven to 350°F. Use a skewer or a thin-bladed knife to poke a hole or two in each pota-to. Place them in the oven and bake for about 1¹/₄ hours, or until you can easily poke a thin-bladed knife into them.

2 Serve immediately, with salt, pepper, butter, sour cream, and chives, or other toppings.

Crispy Sautéed Potatoes with Rosemary

Makes 4 servings

Time: 45 minutes

Roasted Root Vegetables (page 615) will also give you crisp potatoes, but these are faster, simpler, and even crisper.

> 1¹/₂ to 2 pounds waxy red or white potatoes, peeled
>   and cut into ¹/₂-inch to 1-inch cubes
> ¹/₄ cup olive oil, more or less
> 2 teaspoons chopped fresh rosemary leaves or ¹/₂
>   teaspoon dried rosemary
> 1 teaspoon minced garlic
> Salt and freshly ground black pepper to taste

1 Place the potatoes in a pot of salted water, bring to a boil, and simmer until nearly tender, 10 to 15 minutes. Drain well.

2 Heat the oil over medium-high heat in a 12-inch non-stick skillet for 3 or 4 minutes. You can use more oil (for crisper potatoes) or less (for less fat). Add the potatoes and cook, tossing and stirring from time to time (not constantly), until they are nicely browned all over, 10 to 20 minutes. Add the rosemary and garlic and continue to cook for 5 more minutes, stirring frequently. Adjust seasoning and serve.

Potato Pancakes, Version I

Makes 6 servings

Time: About 40 minutes

These are the traditional latkes, served in many Jewish households during Hanukkah. They are excellent with any meat served with gravy, or with applesauce or sour cream.

About 2 pounds baking potatoes, such as Idaho or
   Russet, peeled
1 medium onion
2 eggs
Salt and freshly ground black pepper to taste
2 tablespoons plain bread crumbs or matzo meal
Canola or other neutral oil as needed

1 Grate the potatoes by hand or with the grating disk of a food processor. Drain in a colander or strainer; grate the onion. Preheat the oven to 200°F.

2 In a large bowl, beat the eggs with the salt, pepper, and bread crumbs or matzo meal; stir in the potatoes and onion.

3 Place a $1/8$-inch layer of oil in a large, deep skillet and turn the heat to medium. When the oil is hot, drop the potato batter into it by the quarter-cup or large spoon. Cook until browned on both sides, about 10 minutes per pancake. Drain pancakes on paper towels and keep warm in the oven until all of them are finished. Serve hot, with sour cream or applesauce.

Potato Pancakes, Version II

Makes 6 servings

Time: 20 to 40 minutes

These are simpler and "purer" pancakes. The batter is also good made into one large pancake.

About 2 pounds baking potatoes, such as Idaho or
   Russet, peeled
1 teaspoon salt
3 tablespoons any oil or butter

1 Grate the potatoes by hand or with the grating disk of a food processor; drain very briefly, pressing lightly. Mix in salt.

2 Heat the oil or butter over medium heat, preferably in a large, seasoned cast-iron or non-stick skillet. Drop potatoes in by large spoonfuls, flattening the pancakes with the back of the spoon. Don't try to turn them until they're brown and crisp on the first side. Turn and continue cooking until brown and crisp on the second side, about 6 to 8 minutes total. Or put the whole batch of potatoes in the pan at once; when the underside is brown (it will take 10 to 15 minutes), slide the pancake out onto a plate. Cover with another plate, then invert the two plates. Return to the pan, uncooked side down, and finish cooking. Serve hot or at room temperature.

Boiled New Potatoes

Makes 4 servings

Time: 40 minutes or less

One of the great joys of early summer is a simple dish of boiled new potatoes and butter; mint, in season at the same time, adds a pleasant kick. Follow this same general procedure for boiled potatoes of any size.

About 2 pounds waxy red or white potatoes, the
    smaller the better, skins on and scrubbed
Several fresh mint leaves (optional)
Butter (optional)
Minced mint or parsley for garnish (optional)

1 Place the potatoes in a pot with salted water to cover; turn the heat to high and bring to a boil. Add the mint if you like and turn the heat down to medium. Cook at a gentle boil until the potatoes are nice and tender, about 20 to 40 minutes depending on their size.

2 Drain the potatoes and return them to the pot over the lowest heat possible. Add the butter if you like and cook, shaking the pan occasionally, until all traces of moisture have disappeared, about 5 minutes. Garnish and serve hot.

Lemon Potatoes: Substitute 3 tablespoons olive oil for the butter. Just before serving, toss with the minced zest and juice of 1 lemon. Garnish with minced parsley or oregano.

French Fries
Makes 4 servings

Time: 40 minutes

Making French fries at home is neither difficult nor especially messy. And these are likely to be the best fries you've ever had.

4 large or 6 medium baking potatoes, such as Idaho
    or Russet, peeled
Vegetable oil as needed
Salt to taste

1 Cut the potatoes into any shape you like. Rinse in a few changes of water, then soak in ice water while you heat the oil.

2 Place the vegetable oil to a depth of at least 3 inches in a large, deep saucepan over medium-high heat. Heat it to a temperature of 325°F.

3 Drain the potatoes and dry them well; drop them, a handful at a time, into the oil. After the first addition, turn the heat to high. Once they are all in, turn the heat to medium. Fry the potatoes in one batch, stirring occasionally, for about 10 minutes, or until the majority of them have begun to brown. Turn the heat to low (or turn it off if you're going to wait to fry them again) and drain the potatoes on paper towels or a paper bag; they will be pale and soggy. If you like, you can allow them to rest here for up to 1 hour before proceeding.

4 Raise the heat to high and bring the oil to 375°F. Put the potatoes back in the oil and cook, stirring now and then, until brown and crisp, just a couple of minutes. Drain on paper towels or paper bags, season with salt, and serve immediately.

Five Flavorings for French Fries
If you are bored with ketchup and repelled by mayonnaise (the most frequently used condiment for fries in Europe), you might try any of the following. To thoroughly coat fries with a dry condiment such as chili powder, toss them together in a paper bag while the fries are still hot.

1. Spicy mustard
2. Chili powder
3. Five-spice powder
4. Malt or other vinegar
5. Three kinds of ground pepper: black, Szechwan, and a pinch of cayenne

Pumpkin

Bigger than other winter squashes, but not much different in other respects; we treat it differently, I think, only because of Halloween. In any case, it has many more uses than as an ingredient in pie.

Buying and storing   Unless you want a jack-o'-lantern, buy small pumpkins—three pounds is big enough. Avoid those with soft spots. Store at room temperature or refrigerate, for up to a month.

Preparing   Use a cleaver or very large knife to split the pumpkin in half or cut wedges. Scoop out the seeds and strings and discard (or make Fiery Pumpkin Seeds, page 17). To peel, use a paring knife, and don't fret if you take a fair amount of the flesh with the skin; it's unavoidable.

Best cooking methods   Baking, braising.

When is it done?   When very tender but not quite mushy.

Other recipes in which you can use pumpkin:
Pureed Parsnips, page 590
Mashed Potatoes, page 596
Pureed Butternut Squash with Ginger, page 613
Braised Butternut or Other Winter Squash with
    Garlic, page 614

Baked Pumpkin Slices

Makes 4 to 6 servings

Time: About 1 hour

An easy and flavorful preparation.

1 (2- to 3-pound) pumpkin
1 tablespoon canola or other neutral oil
2 tablespoons freshly squeezed lemon juice
1 tablespoon soy sauce
1 tablespoon brown sugar
$1/2$ teaspoon ground cinnamon
$1/2$ teaspoon ground ginger

① Preheat the oven to 325°F. Cut the pumpkin, from top to bottom, into 1- to $1^1/2$-inch-thick slices.

Discard seeds and strings, and spread slices on a lightly oiled baking sheet.

② Combine the remaining oil with the rest of the ingredients and brush a bit of this mixture onto the pumpkin. Bake for about 25 minutes, then brush again. Turn, brush again, and bake until done, an additional 20 to 30 minutes.

③ Run the slices very briefly under the broiler to brown them if you like. Serve.

Oven-Braised Sweet-and-Sour Pumpkin

Makes 6 to 8 servings

Time: About 1 hour

This is a creamy pumpkin dish, great served with spicy grilled meat or chicken.

2 tablespoons minced fresh mint leaves or 1 table-
    spoon dried mint
1 (3-pound) pumpkin, peeled, seeded, and cut into
    1-inch cubes
$1/4$ cup water, more or less
1 medium onion, chopped
3 tablespoons mild cider or rice wine vinegar
2 tablespoons brown sugar
Salt and freshly ground black pepper to taste

① Preheat the oven to 350°F.

② If you have fresh mint, reserve a bit of the mint for garnish, then combine all ingredients in a 2-inch-deep baking dish or casserole. Toss to mix, cover (use aluminum foil if necessary), and bake for 30 minutes.

③ Remove from the oven and uncover. If the mixture seems dry, add a little more water, re-cover, and return to oven. If it seems watery, return, uncovered, to oven. Continue to bake until pumpkin is tender, another 15 to 30 minutes. Taste for seasoning, garnish with the remaining mint, and serve.

Braised Pumpkin, Japanese-Style: In Step 2, use a mixture of $1/4$ cup water; 2 tablespoons soy sauce; 2 tablespoons brown sugar, maple syrup, or honey; and 2 tablespoons sake or white wine instead of the ingredients above.

Radishes

Crisp radishes are the first root vegetable of spring, and a sure sign for gardeners that there are more good things to come. Most of us take radishes for granted, since they sit in supermarkets year-round, waiting for us to do little more than trim them and toss them into salads. But cooked radishes, which are not unlike turnips, can be quite delicious.

It's worth noting that there are radishes beyond the familiar round red ones. Daikon, a long white radish, is milder, and is frequently grated as a garnish for Japanese dishes; it may also be pickled or dipped in soy sauce. Black radishes are super-hot, and wonderful peeled, grated, salted, and eaten with good buttered bread.

Buying and storing   If you can buy radishes with their greens, so much the better. In any case, they should be firm, fairly smooth, and undamaged. Large radishes may be woody. Wrap loosely in plastic, store in the vegetable bin, and use as soon as possible, before they become soft (which can happen in as little as a week).

Preparing   Just trim; you can peel them if you like (black radishes should always be peeled).

Best cooking methods   Braising in butter. The best fresh radishes are ideal served with good bread, butter, and salt.

When is it done?   When crisp-tender to fully tender but not mushy.

Another recipe in which you can use radishes: Turnips in Mustard Sauce, page 612

Butter-Braised Radishes
Makes 4 servings

Time: 20 minutes

Yes, you can cook radishes—and they're good.

> 2 tablespoons butter
> 1 tablespoon canola or other neutral oil
> 1 pound radishes, more or less, trimmed (see opposite)
> Salt and freshly ground black pepper to taste
> $1/4$ cup chicken, beef, or vegetable stock, or white wine (see "Soups" for stock recipes)
> 1 tablespoon balsamic or other vinegar
> 1 teaspoon sugar
> Minced fresh parsley leaves for garnish

1   Combine the butter and oil in a medium to large skillet that can later be covered; turn the heat to medium. When the butter melts, add the radishes and cook, stirring, until they are coated with butter, just a minute or two longer. Season with salt and pepper.

2   Add the remaining ingredients, except the garnish, stir, and cover. Turn the heat to low and cook until the radishes are barely tender, about 5 minutes.

3   Uncover and raise the heat to medium-high. Cook, stirring, until the radishes are glazed and the liquid is syrupy, another few minutes. Taste and adjust seasoning, garnish, and serve.

Rutabaga, or Swede

A root vegetable that is not a turnip but is treated like one, the rutabaga is larger and somewhat coarser in texture than its cousin. Unless you are a devotee, you will probably find that you like the white-fleshed turnip (page 611) more than the orange-fleshed rutabaga. However, rutabaga stores well in the refrigerator and can be used in any turnip recipe.

Salsify, or Oyster Plant

A root that, theoretically at least, tastes like an oyster (personally, I don't get it). Grayish or black (in which case it is called scorzonera) on the outside, pearly white on the inside, salsify should be peeled—drop into acidulated water to prevent discoloration, as you would artichoke—and cooked like carrots, parsnips, or potatoes.

Sea Vegetables (Seaweed)

Sea vegetables—the respectful term used to refer to the nutrition-packed plants commonly called "seaweed"—were undoubtedly among the first foods humans ate. Everywhere there is a fertile ocean there is evidence of a history of people foraging for sea vegetables. And sea vegetables remain a traditional food for both humans and animals in northern Europe, Russia, throughout the Arctic, and even in the high Andes. But until quite recently, the use of sea vegetables in this country was limited to a few ethnic groups and adherents of macrobiotic diets.

Now, however, sea vegetables are more widely available than ever (although still not exactly popular). They may not be as varied as "land" vegetables, but neither are they all dark and stringy or green and leafy. They vary by color, shape, texture, and flavor and can be used in salads, as a condiment, or on their own. To take them one at a time:

Nori (laver) The omnipresent sushi wrapper (see Sushi Rolls, page 200), nori can also be dry-roasted (in the oven or run, quickly and carefully, over an open flame), crumbled, and used as a condiment for soups or rice dishes, or added to any stir-fry.

Kelp (kombu) This is the largest sea vegetable, growing up to 1,500 feet long (compare this to the tallest land plant, the Douglas fir, which is a mere 400 feet). Kelp is an integral part of Dashi (page 168), the vegetarian stock that is one of the principal ingredients of Japanese cooking. Not often eaten on its own, kelp enhances the flavor and nutritional content of beans, soups, grains, and almost any other slow-simmered food.

Arame and hiziki Dark, almost black, thin, and wiry, these are both mild-tasting (hiziki is somewhat stronger). Soak in water before using—they will double in size—then add to salads, soups, or stews, sauté or braise with other ingredients.

Alaria and wakame These close relatives are pale green, almost transparent, are best used in soups (cook for at least 20 minutes for best taste and texture), cooked with grains, or, after a brief soaking, in salads.

Dulse Dulse is a lovely brick red with a mild sweet flavor. Even dried, it remains soft and pliable, and can be eaten out of hand as a snack (a practice which remains common in parts of Ireland); it can also be pan-toasted and served like chips (as it was in New England taverns through the 1920s), and is good in sandwiches and salads after a brief rinse; it softens so quickly that actual soaking is unnecessary. It can also be included in chowders or other soups, where it cooks in five minutes or less.

Most sea vegetables (there are many types; several are detailed above) are very high in protein—nearly 34 percent for nori, around 20 percent for most others—which means they compare favorably to almost any other "high-protein" food. Sea vegetables are also high in vitamins A, B, C, and E, and are among the few non-meat sources of B_{12}. The biggest advantage of sea vegetables, however, is in their super mineral

Vegetables are not always best prepared at the last minute; many do fine when allowed to sit for an hour or two before eating, and some actually benefit from a little resting time.

1. Basic Steamed Artichokes, page 535
2. Braised Quartered Artichokes with Tarragon, page 536
3. Basic Simmered, Steamed, or Microwaved Asparagus, page 537
4. Roasted, Broiled, or Grilled Asparagus, page 538
5. Beets in Vinaigrette, page 542
6. Basic Simmered, Steamed, or Microwaved Broccoli or Broccoli Raab, page 544
7. Basic Steamed Cauliflower, page 554
8. Cauliflower with Garlic and Anchovies, page 554
9. Braised Cauliflower with Curry and Tomatoes, page 555
10. Chard with Garlic, Pine Nuts, and Currants, page 558
11. Collards or Kale with Double Garlic, page 562
12. Curried Eggplant with Potatoes, page 570
13. Braised Endive, Escarole, or Radicchio with Prosciutto, page 572
14. Garlic Simmered in Oil and Vinegar, page 576
15. Basic Simmered, Steamed, or Microwaved Green Beans, page 577
16. Leeks Braised in Butter or Oil, page 580
17. Steamed Leeks with Tarragon, page 581
18. Grilled Leeks Vinaigrette, page 581
19. Baked Spanish Onions, page 587
20. Grilled Spanish Onions, page 587
21. Caramelized Small Onions or Shallots, page 588
22. Marinated Roasted, Grilled, or Broiled Peppers, page 593
23. Oven-Braised Sweet-and-Sour Pumpkin, page 600
24. Braised Pumpkin, Japanese-Style, page 601
25. Basic Boiled, Steamed, or Microwaved Spinach, page 604
26. Sushi-Style Spinach, page 605
27. Roasted Root Vegetables, page 615
28. Roasted Vegetables, Catalonian-Style, page 616
29. Grilled Mixed Vegetables, page 617

content: Most provide significant amounts of potassium, magnesium, phosphorous, iron, iodine (difficult to obtain from natural sources) other important minerals, and trace elements (rapidly disappearing from land vegetables due to soil depletion).

Buying and storing   Unless you gather your own, sea vegetables are sold dried, in plastic or cellophane packages, in natural foods stores, some supermarkets and specialty stores, and by mail. They keep indefinitely.

Preparing   See detail above; most must be soaked before use. Best cooking methods: Nori (laver) is used without cooking, or toasted very lightly over an open flame. Most other seaweed must be soaked in warm water until tender before use; this usually takes just a few minutes. Once reconstituted, sea vegetables need not be cooked at all, but they can be included in soups, stews, grain dishes, and so on.

When is it done?   When tender.

Spaghetti Squash

A winter squash that is different: Baked or steamed until done (cook whole, not cut in half, piercing the skin a few times with a skewer or thin-bladed knife), using the same methods as for winter squash (page 613). Then cut in half to reveal the flesh, which resembles a mass of spaghetti-like strands. Scrape this out of the skin, then toss the strands with any sauce or, more simply, with butter, salt, and pepper; or treat as you would grated summer squash or zucchini (page 606), sautéing it or making it into pancakes. The flavor is incredibly bland, especially compared to the best winter squashes; but it is a pleasant novelty.

Spinach

Neither ultimate body-builder (Popeye needed protein and carbs, too) nor most-despised vegetable (Brussels sprouts get worse press), spinach is among the first cooking greens of spring. Many people think of spinach as a year-round vegetable, and, indeed, it is grown through the winter in California and elsewhere and is always in good supply.

Reliable as it is, however, the large, relatively tough, super-crinkly leaves of packaged spinach cannot compare with the tender, flat-leafed variety grown by local farmers and gardeners. When it is young, with stems one-eighth inch in diameter or less, it wilts in a flash and requires almost no trimming. (In fact, in such plants, the stems meet in a pink-tinged crown, which can be cut from the leaves, washed well, cooked separately—for three or four minutes, instead of the one or two needed for the leaves—and topped with freshly squeezed lemon juice, vinaigrette, soy sauce, or any other light dressing.)

Buying and storing   Spinach leaves must be plump; any wilting or yellowing is a bad sign. Store it, loosely wrapped in plastic, in the vegetable bin, but use it as fast as you can. It will keep for a few days. Sold year-round, in season locally in cool but not cold or hot weather.

Preparing   Wash well, in several changes of water; it's sandy. Remove very thick stems, but leave thinner ones on; they'll be fine. Don't chop before cooking, or you'll lose too many little pieces to the cooking water.

Best cooking methods   Quick simmering (drop into boiling water, then remove). Or steaming or sautéing. In any case, don't overcook. Leftover spinach makes an ideal omelet filling (see Baked Eggs with Spinach, page 737).

When is it done?   As soon as it wilts.

Other recipes in which you can use spinach:
Gingered Cabbage, page 549 (cooking time will be significantly shorter for spinach)
Chard with Garlic, Pine Nuts, and Currants, page 558
Collards or Kale with Double Garlic, page 562
Collards or Kale, Brazilian-Style, page 563
Dandelion Greens with Bacon, page 96

Note: Since spinach is frequently packed in ten-ounce bags, I give that as an alternative in these recipes; but if you are buying it in bulk, for four people, you're better off with one pound.

Basic Boiled, Steamed, or Microwaved Spinach
Makes 4 servings

Time: 20 minutes

I prefer to boil spinach; it takes less than a minute from the time the spinach hits the water until it is done. But you can also steam or microwave it successfully.

10 to 16 ounces spinach, trimmed and well washed (see opposite)

1 To boil the spinach, bring a large pot of water to a boil; salt it. Place the spinach in the water and cook for about 1 minute, or until it is bright green and tender.

2 To steam the spinach, place it in covered saucepan with about a tablespoon of water (or with the water that clings to its leaves after washing). Cook about 4 minutes, until the spinach is bright green and tender.

3 To microwave the spinach, place in a microwave-proof plate or shallow bowl with just the water that clings to its leaves after washing; add salt and cover with a lid or plastic wrap. Microwave on high for 1 minute, shake the container, and continue to microwave at 1-minute intervals, just until it wilts.

4 Serve hot spinach with butter. Or drain it, drop it into a bowl of ice water to stop the cooking, drain again, place in a covered container, and refrigerate for up to 2 days. Then cook it according to the directions for Precooked Vegetables in Butter or Oil (page 532).

Creamed Spinach: Cool the cooked spinach; squeeze excess moisture from it and chop it. Place $1/2$ cup cream in a small saucepan, turn the heat to medium, and cook for 5 minutes. Turn the heat to low and add the spinach, 2 tablespoons of butter, a pinch of freshly grated nutmeg, salt, and pepper. Simmer, stirring occasionally, until the mixture is creamy and very soft, about 10 minutes. Serve hot.

Sushi-Style Spinach: Cool the cooked spinach; squeeze excess moisture from it and chop it. Sprinkle the spinach with a little salt and 1 tablespoon of soy sauce. Shape it into a 1-inch-thick log (if you have a bamboo sushi-rolling mat, use this to achieve a perfect shape). Cut the log into 1-inch-long slices; dip both ends of each slice into some Toasted Sesame Seeds (page 776) and arrange on a plate. Drizzle with a few drops of dark sesame oil. Serve immediately or refrigerate.

Eleven Quick Toppings for Simply Cooked Spinach

Spinach is so flavorful it doesn't need much. But there are flavorings beyond butter. Try any of these, alone or in combination:

1. Extra-virgin olive oil
2. Freshly squeezed lemon or lime juice
3. Soy sauce
4. Worcestershire sauce
5. Fish Dipping Sauce (page 776)
6. Any vinaigrette (pages 91–94) or flavored oil (page 775)
7. Toasted Sesame Seeds (page 776)
8. Toasted bread crumbs (page 239)
9. Vinegar, especially balsamic, rice, or sherry
10. A sprinkling of dark sesame oil
11. A pat of any compound butter (page 768)

Summer Squash and Zucchini

The fastest growing of summer fruits, treated as a vegetable in our kitchens. Caught young, they can be firm and flavorful, but they quickly become watery. This makes them not difficult to cook, but difficult to cook well. The "secret" is in finding very firm specimens and, if necessary, salting them (as you would cucumber, page 565) first.

Buying and storing There are many varieties, including yellow summer squash and the ubiquitous green zucchini, but the same rules hold for all: Buy the firmest specimens you can find, which will usually—though not always—be the smallest. If they're at all soft, dented, or bruised, move on. Store in the vegetable bin, but use as fast as you can, certainly within a couple of days.

Preparing   If the squash is at all flabby, salt as you would cucumber, page 565.

Best cooking methods   Sautéing (especially after salting, see below); grilling (see Grilled Mixed Vegetables, page 617), roasting (as for Roasted Eggplant with Garlic and Parsley, page 570); if the zucchini are small, cut them in half lengthwise rather than into disks; in any case, zucchini will take less time than eggplant).

When is it done?   When tender; cooked too long it will fall apart.

Other recipes in which you can use summer squash or zucchini:

Crisp Sautéed Cucumbers with Lemon, page 566
Quick Stir-Fried Snow Peas or Sugar Snap Peas, page 591

Sautéed Summer Squash or Zucchini

Makes 4 servings

Time: 15 to 45 minutes

Salting grated summer squash enables you to brown it quickly, but it isn't essential.

About 2 pounds summer squash or zucchini,
    the smaller the better
1 tablespoon salt (optional)
3 to 4 tablespoons olive or other oil
Freshly ground black pepper to taste
1 clove garlic, smashed (optional)
Minced fresh mint, parsley, or basil leaves for garnish

1 Coarsely grate the squash by hand or with the grating disk of a food processor. If time allows, place grated squash in a colander and salt it liberally—use 1 tablespoon or more of salt. Toss to blend and let drain

for at least 30 minutes. Rinse quickly and dry by wringing in a towel.

2 When you're ready to cook, place the oil in a large non-stick skillet and turn the heat to medium-high; add the garlic if you choose to do so. When the oil is hot, toss the squash in the oil, sprinkle with pepper, and raise the heat to high. Cook, stirring frequently, until the squash is browned, about 10 minutes. Garnish and serve hot.

Summer Squash or Zucchini Pancakes

Makes 4 servings

Time: At least 30 minutes

A bit of work, but a wonderful use for zucchini. If you make four thick patties, they will be moist and tender; eight thin patties will be dry and crisp.

About 2 pounds summer squash or zucchini, the
    smaller the better
1 egg, lightly beaten
1/2 cup minced onion
1/4 cup flour or plain bread crumbs, more or less,
    plus more for dredging
1/2 cup freshly grated Parmesan cheese
Salt and freshly ground black pepper to taste
1/4 cup minced fresh basil or parsley leaves
4 tablespoons olive or other oil
Lemon wedges

1 Finely grate the squash by hand or with the grating disk of a food processor. Combine it with the egg, onion, flour or bread crumbs, Parmesan, salt, pepper, and herb. Add more flour or bread crumbs if necessary to make a mixture capable of holding its shape.

2 Shape into 4 to 8 burger-shaped patties. If time allows, refrigerate for 1 hour to allow them to firm up.

3 When you're ready to cook, place the oil in a large skillet and turn the heat to medium-high. When the oil is hot, dredge the cakes in flour or bread crumbs and place in the skillet (if you've made 8, do this in two batches). Cook, turning once, until nicely browned on both sides, about 15 minutes. Serve with lemon wedges.

Summer Squash or Zucchini Rounds Cooked in Butter

Makes 4 servings

Time: 20 minutes

A simple, fresh-tasting use for zucchini.

> About 2 pounds summer squash or zucchini, the
>   smaller the better
> 3 tablespoons butter
> Salt and freshly ground black pepper to taste
> 1 tablespoon honey
> 3 or 4 tablespoons minced fresh mint leaves

1 Cut the squash into $1/4$-inch-thick slices. Place the butter in a large skillet and turn the heat to medium-high. When its foam subsides, add the squash and sprinkle with salt and pepper.

2 Raise the heat to high and cook, stirring occasionally, until the squash becomes tender and begins to brown, about 15 minutes. Stir in the honey and mint, check the seasoning, and serve.

Sunchokes or Jerusalem Artichokes

They're not artichokes, but the root of a perennial sunflower, also called topinambours. Whatever you call them, they're the knobby little tubers that look like ginger and have a mild, delicious flavor and such a high sugar content that they brown beautifully in the pan. (This sugar can also cause mild gastric distress, in the form of flatulence, in some people. You'll know if you're one of them. If parboiling, as below, doesn't help, you may want to avoid them.) They can be eaten raw, but are best cooked.

Buying and storing Buy firm, not flabby specimens. Those that are smooth will be easiest to wash and/or peel. Store, wrapped in plastic, in the vegetable bin; they'll keep well for weeks.

Preparing Some people peel sunchokes; I just wash them well.

Best cooking methods Sautéing, preferably after a brief simmering.

When is it done? When quite tender; taste one.

Crisp-Cooked Sunchokes

Makes 4 servings

Time: About 30 minutes

It isn't essential to parboil sunchokes before sautéing them, but it speeds the process.

> About $1^1/2$ pounds sunchokes, well scrubbed
> 3 tablespoons extra-virgin olive oil
> Salt and freshly ground black pepper to taste
> Minced fresh parsley leaves for garnish
> Lemon wedges

1 Bring a large pot of water to a boil; salt it. Add the sunchokes in descending order of size: largest first, followed by somewhat smaller ones a minute or so later, and so on. Cook just until they lose their crispness; poke them with a skewer or thin-bladed knife and you'll be able to tell. Don't overcook or they will become mushy. Remove them as they finish (they almost never all become tender at once) and plunge them into ice water. The chokes will take between 2 and 10 minutes to become tender, depending on their size.

2 Place the oil in a large, deep skillet and turn the heat to medium. Cut the sunchokes into about $1/4$-inch slices and place in the oil. Cook, stirring and turning occasionally, until the chokes are nicely browned on both sides, about 20 minutes. Season with salt and pepper as they cook. Garnish and serve hot, with lemon wedges.

Broiled Sunchokes with Parmesan: After parboiling in Step 1, grease a baking dish with olive oil, then lay the sunchokes in it; drizzle with more olive oil(you won't need 3 tablespoons), sprinkle with salt and pepper, and top with $1/2$ cup freshly grated Parmesan cheese. Roast at 450°F for 10 minutes, then run under the broiler for a minute or two longer to brown. Garnish and serve, with lemon wedges if you like.

Sweet Potatoes

Not yams which—popular nomenclature to the contrary—are a different tuber. These are the familiar bright orange-fleshed tubers (more exotic varieties have rose, purple, yellow, or white flesh) of fall and winter. Brilliant baked, they are also good handled in many of the same ways you would treat white potatoes and winter squash—fried, mashed, or roasted.

Buying and storing Like potatoes—firm, undamaged tubers. Store, like potatoes, in the dark, in a cool place, but not for as long—just a couple of weeks.

Preparing Peel if necessary.

Best cooking methods Baking, by far. Cooking in liquid is also good.

When is it done? When very tender and mealy.

Other recipes in which you can use sweet potatoes:
Mashed Potatoes, page 596
Potato Pancakes, Version I, page 598
Oven-Braised Sweet-and-Sour Pumpkin, page 600
Pureed Butternut Squash with Ginger, page 613
Braised Butternut or Other Winter Squash with Garlic, page 614

Baked Sweet Potatoes
Makes 4 servings

Time: About 1 hour

You must bake sweet potatoes in a baking pan, because they tend to drip their syrupy juice, which clings to everything.

4 sweet potatoes
Butter

1 Preheat the oven to 425°F. Line a baking pan with aluminum foil and place the potatoes in it.

2 Pierce each of the potatoes a few times with a skewer or thin-bladed knife. Bake, shaking the pan once or twice, for about 1 hour, or until the potatoes are very soft and tender. Serve with butter.

Microwaved or Simmered Sweet Potatoes
Makes 4 servings

Time: About 20 minutes

This also works perfectly for any winter squash. If you like your sweetness balanced with some acidity, be sure to add a little lemon juice to this mix.

2 pounds sweet potatoes, peeled and cut into chunks
2 tablespoons butter or canola or other neutral oil
2 tablespoons maple syrup or brown sugar
1 tablespoon freshly squeezed lemon juice (optional)
Salt and freshly ground black pepper to taste

1 To microwave, combine all ingredients with 2 tablespoons of water in a microwave-proof plate or shallow bowl; cover with a lid or plastic wrap. Microwave on high for 3 minutes, shake the container, and continue to microwave at 2-minute intervals, until the sweet potatoes are very tender. Serve hot.

2 To simmer, combine all ingredients with $1/3$ cup of water in a covered saucepan, turn the heat to medium, and bring to a boil. Turn the heat to low and cook, stirring every 5 minutes or so and adding a little additional water if necessary, until the sweet potatoes are very tender, 20 to 30 minutes. Serve hot.

Taro

The most flavorful of the "new" tubers sold in many supermarkets and many Latin American and Asian markets. Treat it as a potato—its flavor is actually better than that of most potatoes—but do not overcook or it will become dry. I have had success with boiling, frying, and sautéing.

Tomatoes

Another of our more popular vegetables (actually a fruit), about which volumes have been written. Canned tomatoes are great for sauces, obviously, but the fresh tomato season is very, very short—from spring in the South to mid-fall in the North. Tomatoes will not grow in much of the South when the weather is hot; they will not ripen at all in some areas of the North except in very long, hot summers, and, when ripe, they ship terribly (despite what the supermarkets and bioengineers think). Nor do unripe tomatoes taken from the vine ever become truly delicious. So enjoy them when they're here, and pass them by at other times.

Buying and storing Good tomatoes are soft, and deep red in color. (There are exceptions: some green near the stem is fine; there are also orange and yellow varieties, and even varieties with stripes. And in many parts of the world, including northern Italy, they're often used in salads when still on the green side.) They should be undamaged, of course, and will yield to light pressure. Good tomatoes aren't necessarily great tomatoes, but you can only determine that by tasting them. Note that plum tomatoes, which are best for making sauce, are never as luscious as good round tomatoes but because they ship well may often be your best choice in the supermarket. Store all tomatoes at room temperature and use them as soon as you can.

Preparing To core tomatoes, cut a cone right around the core and remove it. To seed, cut the tomato in half through its equator, and squeeze and shake out the seeds (you may want to do this over a strainer in order to save the liquid). To peel, cut a small "x" in the flower (smooth, non-stem) end of the tomato and drop into boiling water for ten to thirty seconds, until the skin loosens. Plunge into ice water and peel off the skin.

Best cooking methods Sautéing, grilling or broiling, roasting. Probably ninety percent of cooked tomatoes are used for sauce; see the Pasta chapter.

When is it done? When tender but not quite collapsed; tomatoes will dissolve into sauce if overcooked.

(Step 1) First, core the tomato. Cut a wedge right around the core and remove it. (Step 2) Then peel the tomato. Cut a small "x" in the flower (non-stem) end. Drop it into boiling water until the skin begins to loosen, usually less than thirty seconds. (Step 3) Remove the peels with a paring knife. (Step 4) Finish by seeding the tomato. The easiest way to remove seeds is to simply cut the tomato in half through its equator, then squeeze and shake out the seeds. Do this over a bowl if you wish to strain and reserve the juice.

Pan-Fried Green and/or Red Tomatoes

Makes 4 servings

Time: 20 minutes

Tomatoes make a wonderful side dish when cooked; they must not be too ripe, however, or they will liquefy.

3 tablespoons extra-virgin olive oil, or more
2 or 3 large green, reddish-greenish, or greenish-red
  tomatoes, cored (page 609) and cut croswise into
  $1/2$-inch-thick slices
Plain bread crumbs or flour for dredging
Salt and freshly ground black pepper to taste

1   Place the olive oil in a large, deep skillet and turn the heat to medium-high. When it is hot, dredge the tomato slices, one at a time, in the bread crumbs or flour and add them to the skillet.

2   Cook, adding a little more olive oil if needed to keep the slices sizzling and seasoning with salt and pepper as they cook. Turn when the first side is golden brown, then cook the other side; total cooking time will be less than 10 minutes. Handle gently and serve hot or at room temperature.

Grilled, Broiled, or Roasted Red Tomatoes

Makes 4 servings

Time: 20 minutes, plus time to preheat the grill

You can roast or broil perfectly ripe tomatoes, but they should be a little on the green side for grilling or they will fall apart.

2 large or 4 medium tomatoes, cored, cut in half, and
  seeds shaken out (page 609)
Extra-virgin olive oil
Salt and freshly ground black pepper to taste
Fresh minced herbs for garnish: parsley, basil, chervil,
  oregano, marjoram, or a mixture

1   Start a charcoal or wood fire, or preheat a gas grill or broiler—the rack should be at least 4 inches from the heat source—or turn the oven to 450°F.

2   Rub the tomato halves lightly with oil, then sprinkle with salt and pepper. Place them directly on the grill, cut side down; or place them in a broiling or roasting pan, cut side up, under the broiler or in the oven.

3 Grill until lightly charred, just a few minutes, then turn and continue to grill until softened, about 10 minutes total. In the broiler, turning is not necessary; just adjust the distance from the heat source so the tomatoes soften a bit before they begin to burn. In the oven, turning is not necessary either; just roast until they begin to shrivel, about 15 minutes. Garnish and serve hot, or set aside and serve at room temperature.

Oven-Dried Tomatoes

Makes 24 pieces

Time: Several hours, largely unattended

This method will work to dry many fruits and vegetables, but unless you live in the Southwest, forget sun-drying. Fortunately, the oven does a great job, as long as you don't forget about them. Season the tomatoes as they cook by using more olive oil or adding a variety of fresh herbs or crushed garlic. Use the tomatoes as a garnish with lightly sauced fish or chicken dishes, or—more likely, at least in my house—eat them like candy.

12 just-ripe plum tomatoes
2 tablespoons extra-virgin olive oil
Salt

1 Peel the tomatoes as directed on pages 609–610. Cut them in half and scoop out the seeds. Line a baking sheet with aluminum foil and turn the oven to 175°F, or a little higher.

2 Brush the foil with some of the olive oil and arrange the tomatoes, cut side down. Sprinkle lightly with salt and the remaining oil. Place in the oven and forget about them for 2 hours.

3 Turn the sheet back to front and see how the tomatoes are doing. You have several choices about determining doneness. If you just want to intensify the tomato flavor and use them immediately, they're

done when still soft but somewhat shriveled, 2 to 3 hours total. If you want to keep them for a few days, they're done when they're shriveled and mostly dry, at least 4 hours total (wrap and refrigerate). If you want to keep them for weeks, they're done when they're dark, shriveled, and dry, 6 or more hours total (wrap and refrigerate, or store in a jar in the pantry).

Turnips

Members of the cabbage family eaten for roots rather than greens (although the greens can be cooked like kale, collards, or broccoli raab), turnips were traditionally poor people's food, because they are easy to grow and keep for a long time.

But small turnips, especially the white or white-and-purple kind, are delicious and tender—even the orange-fleshed rutabaga, technically not a turnip, is good when handled well. Puree them or braise them and they are mild-flavored and enjoyable.

Buying and storing   Turnips should be firm, not at all soft, and, of course, undamaged. They should also be small; those larger than two inches in diameter may be woody. Store them, lightly wrapped in plastic, in the vegetable bin; they'll keep for weeks.

Preparing   Peel. Most white turnips can be peeled with a vegetable peeler; rutabagas have tougher skin, and must be tackled with a paring knife.

Best cooking methods   Simmering in liquid, or roasting with other vegetables.

When is it done?   When cooked in liquid, until tender but not waterlogged. Roasted, until very soft.

Other recipes in which you can use turnips:
Quick-Braised Carrots with Butter, page 553
Curried Eggplant with Potatoes, page 570
Crispy Sautéed Potatoes with Rosemary, page 597
Boiled New Potatoes, page 598
Roasted Root Vegetables, page 615

Turnips in Mustard Sauce

Makes 4 servings

Time: 30 to 40 minutes

This rich, warm, wintry dish has a classic feel to it, and is great with any roast.

> 1 tablespoon extra-virgin olive oil
> About 3 pounds white turnips, rutabaga, or a combination, peeled and quartered
> Salt and freshly ground black pepper to taste
> 1 cup chicken, beef, or vegetable stock (see "Soups" for stock recipes)
> 2 teaspoons cornstarch
> 3 tablespoons Dijon mustard
> ¼ cup chopped fresh parsley leaves for garnish

1 Place the oil in a large, deep skillet that can later be covered and turn the heat to medium. A minute later, add the turnips, salt, and pepper and cook, stirring occasionally, until the turnips begin to brown, about 10 minutes.

2 Add the stock, cover, and simmer until the turnips are tender, 10 to 15 minutes.

3 Remove the turnips to a serving bowl with a slotted spoon; keep warm. Mix the cornstarch into the mustard and stir the mixture into the pan juices. Cook over low heat until lightly thickened, a minute or two longer. Pour the sauce over the turnips, garnish, and serve.

Pureed Turnips

Makes 4 servings

Time: About 40 minutes

Turnip puree is deliciously sweet but can be a little on the thin side. Adding one medium potato for every three turnips makes a thicker, creamier, and more substantial puree.

> About 1½ pounds turnips, preferably the purple-tinged variety, peeled and cut into chunks
> 1 or 2 medium potatoes, peeled and cut into chunks
> 2 tablespoons butter or extra-virgin olive oil, plus more if desired
> Salt and freshly ground black pepper to taste
> Minced fresh parsley leaves for garnish

1 Bring a large pot of water to a boil; salt it. Add the turnips and potatoes and turn the heat to medium, so that the mixture is bubbling gently. Cook until the turnips and potatoes are very tender, 20 to 30 minutes.

2 Drain the turnips and potatoes well and place in the container of a food processor, or pass through a food mill or ricer. Add the butter or oil and process or mix until smooth. Taste and adjust seasoning; add more butter or oil as well as salt and pepper if you like. (You may prepare the recipe in advance up to this point; refrigerate, well wrapped or in a covered container, for up to 2 days before proceeding.)

3 Reheat over low heat or in a microwave. Garnish and serve.

Winter Squash

These are long-keeping squashes that have much in common with pumpkin and sweet potato: yellow to orange flesh, usually quite sweet and creamy when cooked. The most difficult thing about winter squash is peeling it—even the smooth-skinned varieties, such as butternut, can defeat many peelers. (Use a paring knife and be careful.) For acorn and other bumpy squash, you have no choice but to cook with the skin still on.

Buying and storing   This is easy: Winter squash should be firm, with no soft spots or obvious damage. It's in season from late summer through winter, although it keeps so well that there are almost always some for sale. Store as you would potatoes, in a cool, dry place, but not in the refrigerator. Use within a month.

Preparing   Use a cleaver or very large knife to split the squash in half. Scoop out the seeds and strings and discard (or bake the seeds as you would Fiery Pumpkin Seeds, page 17). Peeling butternut squash is fairly easy, as long as you have a sturdy vegetable peeler or a paring knife. Peeling acorn and other odd-shaped squash is virtually impossible, so don't try.

Best cooking methods   Steaming, microwaving, roasting, braising.

When is it done?   When very tender. If you're cooking with liquid, make sure it doesn't become waterlogged. If you're roasting or sautéing, it's difficult to overcook.

Other recipes in which you can use winter squash:
Crispy Sautéed Potatoes with Rosemary, page 597
Baked Pumpkin Slices, page 600
Fiery Pumpkin Seeds, page 17
Oven-Braised Sweet-and-Sour Pumpkin, page 600
Roasted Root Vegetables, page 615

Pureed Butternut Squash with Ginger

Makes 4 servings

Time: About 20 minutes

Because it is so porous, winter squash absorbs water readily; thus it's better to cook it above water rather than in it.

1½ pounds butternut or other winter squash, peeled (see opposite) and cut into chunks
2 tablespoons butter
1 to 2 teaspoons peeled and roughly chopped fresh ginger or 1 teaspoon ground ginger, or to taste
Salt and freshly ground black pepper to taste
1 teaspoon brown sugar, or to taste (optional)

1   Place the squash in a steamer above about 1 inch of salted water. Cover and cook until the squash is very tender, about 20 minutes. To microwave, place the squash and 2 tablespoons of water in a microwave-proof plate or shallow bowl; cover with a lid or plastic wrap. Microwave on high for 3 minutes, shake the container, and continue to microwave at 2-minute intervals, until the squash is very tender.

2   While it is still hot, place the squash in the container of a food processor with the butter and ginger; process until smooth. Taste and add salt, pepper, and brown sugar if you like. (You may prepare the recipe in advance up to this point; refrigerate, well wrapped or in a covered container, for up to 2 days before proceeding.)

3   Reheat over low heat or in a microwave and serve.

Six Quick Flavorings for Pureed Squash
Try any of the following, alone or in combination:

1. A seeded jalapeño or other chile
2. A small handful of fresh herbs, including parsley, cilantro, mint, and sage
3. Maple syrup or honey in place of brown sugar
4. Olive oil in place of butter
5. Other ground spices in place of ginger, including cardamom, cinnamon, mace, and nutmeg
6. Curry powder or other spice mixtures, page 778

Roasting Hard-to-Peel Winter Squash

Makes 4 servings

Time: About 1 hour

Generally, it's best to roast squash according to the directions for Roasted Root Vegetables, page 615. But some squash is so difficult to peel that you're better off simply roasting it with the skin on. Here are three ways to do it:

1 (2- to 3-pound) acorn or other winter squash, or 2 smaller ones, washed
2 tablespoons butter or olive oil, more or less
Salt and freshly ground black pepper to taste
Maple syrup or brown sugar (optional)
1 clove garlic, cut (optional)

Preheat the oven to 400°F.

Option 1: Cut the squash(es) in half and scrape out the strings and seeds (page 613). In each half, put some butter, salt, pepper, and sweetener, if desired. Place on a baking sheet, open side up, and bake until tender, about 1 hour. Serve.

Option 2: Cut the squash(es) in half and scrape out the strings and seeds (page 613). Sprinkle each half with salt and pepper, and rub with a little garlic if you like. Brush a baking sheet with olive oil and place the squash, open side down, on the sheet. Bake until tender, about 1 hour. Serve.

Option 3: Cut the squash(es) in large slices, each about 1 inch thick. Place them on a lightly greased baking sheet and sprinkle with salt and pepper. Dot with butter or brush with olive oil. Bake until tender, 30 to 45 minutes.

Braised Butternut or Other Winter Squash with Garlic

Makes 4 servings

Time: About 30 minutes

One of those dishes whose wonderful flavor belies its simplicity.

2 tablespoons olive oil
1 tablespoon minced garlic
1½ pounds butternut or other winter squash, peeled (page 613) and cut into ½- to 1-inch cubes
¼ cup chicken, beef, or vegetable stock, or water (see "Soups" for stock recipes)
Salt and freshly ground black pepper to taste
Minced fresh parsley leaves for garnish

1 Place the olive oil and garlic in a large, deep skillet and turn the heat to medium. When the garlic begins to color, add the squash, stock or water, salt, and pepper. Bring to a boil, cover, and turn the heat to low. Cook, stirring once or twice, until the squash is tender, about 15 minutes.

2 Uncover the pan and turn the heat to medium-high. Cook, shaking the pan occasionally and stirring somewhat less often, until all the liquid is evaporated and the squash has begun to brown, 5 to 10 minutes. Turn the heat to low and cook until the squash is as browned and crisp as you like.

3 Taste and adjust seasoning, garnish, and serve.

Yam, or Name

The true yam, and it is not a sweet potato (although, since there are hundreds of species, some are similar). Very bland and, when cooked, very, very dry. It can be fried as chips, but is more often used in meaty stews that contain plenty of liquid, wherever you'd use potatoes.

Yuca, or Cassava, or Manioc

This is the root from which tapioca is made. Think of how much liquid tapioca absorbs when you cook it. Now you know why yuca is always, always served with plenty of liquid. You can bake it like a potato, roast it like a plantain, grate it and make fritters (like Potato Pancakes, Version I, page 598) or even puddings. But always plan to serve it with liquid.

The Basics of Mixed Vegetable Dishes

Combining vegetables can turn a simple side dish into a dramatic one, or even into a main course. And it usually isn't much more work to cook several more vegetables at once, as long as you choose those that have the same characteristics. In roasting, for example, you want to choose vegetables that will soften all at about the same time; it doesn't matter whether this time is long or short, just whether it's about the same for everything you're cooking. In grilling, on the other hand, you usually want to use soft, moist vegetables that will cook quickly, before their exterior burns. (Alternatively, you can use harder vegetables, even potatoes, if you parboil them to near doneness before beginning.) For braising, choose vegetables that will become very soft and give off liquid, to make a vegetable stew.

Cut vegetables that take about the same amount of time to cook into same-size pieces. To minimize differences in natural cooking times—eggplant, for example, always cooks more slowly than zucchini—make larger chunks of fast-cooking vegetables, smaller ones of slow cookers.

Roasted Root Vegetables

Makes 4 servings

Time: 1 hour or more

This may be the dish that best defines contemporary cooking: It's low in fat, high in flavor, gets lots of vegetables into you, is easy—and it's roasted. You can combine almost any vegetables you want, but I think carrots, onions, and garlic (unpeeled—you peel each clove before you eat it) are essential to the mix. Experiment and see what you like.

4 tablespoons extra-virgin olive oil, butter, or a mixture
1½ to 2 pounds mixed root vegetables, such as carrots, potatoes, sweet potatoes, parsnips, turnips, shallots (leave whole), and onions, peeled and cut into 1½- to 2-inch chunks
Several sprigs fresh thyme or about 1 tablespoon fresh rosemary leaves (optional)
Salt and freshly ground black pepper to taste
1 head garlic, broken into cloves
Minced fresh parsley leaves for garnish

1 Preheat the oven to 425°F. Place the olive oil or butter in a large roasting pan on top of the stove and turn the heat to low. When the butter melts or the oil is hot, add all the vegetables (except the garlic), along with the thyme or rosemary. Sprinkle them with salt and pepper and cook them briefly, shaking and stirring so that everything is coated with oil or butter. Place the pan in the oven.

2 Cook for 30 minutes, opening the oven and shaking the pan once or twice during that period. Add the garlic and stir the vegetables up; at this point they should be starting to brown. If they are not, raise the oven temperature to 450°F.

3 Continue to cook, stirring and shaking every 10 minutes or so, until the vegetables are tender and

nicely browned, at least another half hour. If the vegetables soften before they brown, just run them under the broiler for a minute or two. If they brown before they soften, add a few tablespoons of water to the pan and turn the heat down to 350°F.

④ Garnish and serve hot or at room temperature.

Roasted Vegetables, Catalonian-Style

Makes 4 servings

Time: About 45 minutes

Here is a good basic recipe for roasting the vegetables of late summer; it's best served at room temperature.

3 bell peppers, red, yellow, orange, or any combination, stemmed, halved, and seeded

2 small zucchini, about $1/2$ pound total, ends cuts off

4 tiny eggplant, or 2 small ones, about 1 pound total, ends cut off

1 large ripe tomato, cored

2 small artichokes, cut into quarters, the choke removed (page 535) (optional)

1 large onion, quartered

3 tablespoons olive oil

1 tablespoon sherry or other good vinegar

① Preheat the oven to 450°F. Toss the vegetables with 2 tablespoons of the olive oil. Place them in a large roasting pan and cook, shaking the pan occasionally, until they are quite soft, 30 to 45 minutes. Remove from the oven.

② When the vegetables are cool enough to handle, remove the skin from the tomato and peppers. Cut the peppers, zucchini, and eggplant into strips, and mix with the other vegetables; the tomato will fall apart during this process. Drizzle with the sherry vinegar and remaining tablespoon of olive oil.

Oven-Baked Ratatouille

Tian of Vegetables

Makes 4 servings

Time: About $1^1/4$ hours

This is another mixture of soft vegetables, gently baked in layers until very tender. If you have good olive oil and fresh herbs, this will be sensational.

10 cloves garlic

2 large onions, thinly sliced

2 large eggplant, about 2 pounds total, sliced $1/2$-inch thick and salted if time allows (page 568)

4 red or yellow bell peppers, stemmed, peeled if desired, seeded, and sliced into 3 or 4 pieces each

4 ripe red tomatoes, cored, skins and seeds removed (page 610), and cut into thick slices

1 teaspoon fresh thyme, rosemary, or savory leaves

Salt and freshly ground black pepper to taste

2 tablespoons minced fresh parsley, basil, or chervil leaves for garnish

$1/2$ cup extra-virgin olive oil

① Preheat the oven to 350°F.

② Either of these techniques will make the garlic easier to peel: Drop it into boiling water; leave it there for 30 seconds, then remove it. Or toast it in a dry skillet over medium heat, shaking frequently, for 3 or 4 minutes. Peel and cut each clove in half.

③ In a casserole, make a layer of onion, followed by one of eggplant, peppers, tomatoes, herbs, salt, pepper, and garlic cloves. Repeat. Drizzle the ratatouille with the olive oil and place in the oven. Bake for about an hour, pressing down on the vegetables occasionally, until they are all completely tender. Garnish and serve, hot or at room temperature.

Grilled Mixed Vegetables

Makes 4 to 6 servings

Time: 45 minutes, plus time to preheat the grill

This is a "for instance" recipe. You can grill almost any vegetable, as long as you slice it into one-half-inch-thick (or slightly thinner) slices. Soft vegetables, such as zucchini, can be made thicker. Very hard vegetables, such as potatoes (always use waxy red or white potatoes for grilling), are best parboiled until nearly tender before grilling.

1 Spanish or other large onion
2 red or yellow bell peppers, stemmed, halved, and seeded
1 eggplant, cut into ¹/₂-inch-thick slices and salted (page 568) if time allows
1 zucchini, cut lengthwise into ¹/₂-inch-thick slices
Extra-virgin olive oil as needed
Salt and freshly ground black pepper to taste
Minced parsley leaves for garnish

1 Start a charcoal or wood fire or preheat a gas grill. Cut the root and flower end from the onion so that it will sit flat on the grill. Then cut it in half, through its equator. Prepare the other vegetables.

2 Brush all the vegetables liberally with olive oil and sprinkle with salt and pepper. Grill, turning once or twice, until nicely browned on both sides and tender throughout, about 15 minutes. Drizzle with a little more olive oil if you like, garnish, and serve hot or at room temperature.

Fruits

Like vegetables, fruit has greatly increased its presence in the typical supermarket compared to just ten years ago. In apple season, there may be six or eight varieties; the same is true of plums. There are fruits we never heard of, and many we still don't know what to do with. You could eat a different fruit every day for a month.

Not all of this is good news. Almost all food, of course, is better when bought close to its source, but this is especially true of fruit. When you buy a peach from Chile in January, you're not only buying a peach that was picked unripe and has traveled thousands of miles under refrigeration over a period of at least a week, you're also buying one that was bred to tolerate such mistreatment. To compare such a peach to one plucked ripe from a tree in August is to compare costume jewelry to the crown jewels—at a glance, the imitator may look like the original, but it bears no resemblance under close inspection.

This is a long way of saying that the best fruit is grown locally. In other words, eat oranges in January and peaches in July and you'll be eating good fruit. Eat them where they're grown and you'll be eating great fruit.

Of course this isn't always possible. There are times when we must settle for what we can get, and treat it as well as we are able. To do that, it pays to know the characteristics of each fruit. For example, although you can buy a hard peach with the certainty that it will ripen on your counter—not to perfection, but to a good state of edibility—you cannot do the same for a pineapple; all it will do on your counter is rot.

Similarly, it is worth knowing how to cook fruit. While most people would agree that many fruits are at their best eaten out of hand, this is true only for fruit of the best quality. Out of season or unripe fruit almost always benefits from cooking, and certain fruits—apples and bananas, for example—are so common that there always comes a point at which a change of form is desirable.

Most fruits can be cooked, and you'll find not only fruit-specific recipes here, but many recipes that will work for a number of fruits, and some that work for combinations. Many fruits can be substituted for others in certain recipes, so, when appropriate, I've included other recipes in the descriptions of each fruit (this refers only to dessert recipes, whether within this chapter or in one of the following dessert chapters; for savory recipes using fruit, see Index).

The Basics of Ripening Fruit

To quote Harold McGee, author of *On Food and Cooking* (Scribner's, 1984), "Ripening is a sudden, rapid, and drastic change in the life of the fruit, which merges into its death." This perfectly summarizes the fleeting moments of ripeness, during which fruit is at its peak—in fact, the only point at which it is fit to eat. We have all seen a peach go from too-hard-to-eat in the morning to too-moldy-to-eat at night; sometime during the day, that peach was ripe, and we missed that moment.

Some fruits (pineapple, for example, and some melons), barely ripen once removed from the vine—it isn't worth buying these unless they are already ripe. Most, however, continue to ripen, although in some instances refrigeration can retard that ripening. In many instances, ripening can also be hastened. Most ripening fruit gives off ethylene, a naturally occurring gas, as it ripens. And, as it happens, this ethylene induces further ripening. If you trap the ethylene near the fruit, or place another source of ethylene next to it, the fruit will ripen more quickly.

To trap a fruit's naturally occurring ethylene, place it in a sealed paper bag (plastic bags also hasten ripening but, by depriving the fruit of oxygen, hasten rot as well). To move the process along even more, place it in a bag with a banana, which gives off more ethylene than most other fruits. To really ripen fruit quickly, some fruit distributors spray it with ethylene—but don't try this at home.

Apple

Arguably the most important of all fruits, at least in the United States and much of western Europe, apples are also among the most plentiful. There are literally thousands of varieties, including many heirlooms that we sadly miss when we buy our fruit in the supermarket. The best time and place to buy apples, of course, is in the fall, near an orchard. Buying apples for eating is easy: Choose any that tastes good. If you're buying apples for cooking, and you're choosing among unfamiliar varieties, save softer specimens for recipes in which you want the apples to fall apart—like apple sauce—and firmer ones for those where it's important that they hold their shape, such as baked apples.

These are the most important and widely seen varieties:

Braeburn: A pleasant older apple that has made a comeback; very sweet, which makes it good for cooking.

Cortland: Better-tasting then McIntosh, with similar texture. Good all-purpose apple.

Empire: Cross between Red Delicious and McIntosh; better than the first, not as good as the second, but stores better than either, so popular in winter. Decent flavor, can be mushy.

Fuji (or Matsu or Crispin): Decent eating apple, but nothing special.

Golden Delicious: Excellent eating apple: crisp with full flavor.

Granny Smith: Relative newcomer to the States, discovered in Australia. Very popular because it holds up well. Super-crisp but mildly tart; its flavor is not unlike a Macoun.

Ida Red (also Paula Red): Large, sweet, and great for baking.

Jonagold: Very similar to Golden Delicious, with even better flavor. Hard to find, though.

McIntosh: Sweet, crisp when very fresh, becomes mushy quickly. Excellent for sauce, good all-purpose.

Macoun: The New England favorite. Super-crisp, not especially sweet. Good eating during its very short season.

Red Delicious: Sweet but rarely complex flavor, and usually inferior texture. Nice-looking, which in part explains its popularity.

Rome: Great flavor, soft texture. Best for sauce and pies.

Buying and storing Firmness is key; mushy apples are fit only for cooking. Although apples store well, they are best when fresh from the tree, which means late summer through the first hard frost. But apples can be kept in your refrigerator (or garage, if it's cool), for weeks, especially if they're "keeping" apples like Empires. Wholesalers keep apples in reduced-oxygen storage, where they remain in reasonably decent shape for months. But watch out: When they are removed from these special storage conditions, they deteriorate rapidly, so use winter apples quickly.

Preparing (See illustrations.) Everyone has a favorite technique for peeling apples. Start at the stem or flower end and working in latitudinal strips; a U-shaped peeler is best.

For coring, you have several options. You can remove the core and leave the apple whole by digging into the stem end with a sturdy melon baller and removing it; this leaves the blossom end intact, a nice presentation for baked apples. Or you can buy a slicer-corer, which will cut the apple into six or eight slices around the core in one swift motion. Finally, you can quarter the apple and dig out each piece of the core with a paring knife.

Apples brown quickly once peeled; drop them into acidulated water (one part lemon juice to about ten parts water) or white wine, or toss with lemon juice, to prevent this.

You can core an apple either of two ways. For baked apples, use a melon baller and dig into the flower (non-stem) end, taking out a little at a time until the core has been removed.

For other uses, simply cut the apple in quarters and remove the core with a melon baller or a paring knife.

Other recipes in which you can use apples:

Blueberry Cobbler, page 630
Pears Poached with Red Wine, page 642
Pear Clafouti, page 642 (cut the apples into eighths or rings)
Fruit or Berry Ice Cream, page 667
Raspberry, Strawberry, or other Fruit Sauce, page 672

Apple Dumplings

Makes 6 servings

Time: About 1 1/4 hours

This old-fashioned dessert, which is essentially apples wrapped in very rich pastry, deserves more attention.

6 medium apples, preferably Cortland or Ida or
    Paula Red

2 1/2 cups (about 11 1/2 ounces) all-purpose flour,
    plus more as needed

Pinch salt

1/2 pound (2 sticks) cold unsalted butter, cut into
    pieces

Cold water as needed

1/2 cup brown sugar

1/2 teaspoon ground cinnamon

1 teaspoon grated or minced orange or lemon zest
    (optional)

1 egg white, lightly beaten

White sugar for sprinkling

1 Peel and core the apples, leaving a bit of the flower (not stem) end of the core intact (see illustrations on page 621).

2 Combine the flour and salt in the container of a food processor; add 1 1/2 sticks of the butter and process until blended. Add cold water 1 tablespoon at a time, pulsing only until the dough forms a ball. Wrap the ball in plastic and chill for 30 minutes, or up to a day, if time allows. (To mix the ingredients by hand, soften the butter slightly, toss together the dry ingredients, then work in the butter with your fingertips, a pastry blender, or a fork.)

3 Meanwhile, cream the remaining butter with the brown sugar, cinnamon, and fruit zest; spoon one sixth of this mixture into the cavity of each apple.

4 Preheat the oven to 375°F. Use as much flour as is necessary to roll the dough into a rectangle about 12 × 18 inches. Place the apples equidistant from one another on the dough, open side up. Cut the dough into 6 squares. Wet the edges of each square with a little cold water, then seal the dough by pulling each of the corners in turn onto the top of the apple; stretch the dough slightly to enclose the apple if necessary. Brush the pastry with egg white and sprinkle with sugar.

5 Place the apples on a baking sheet and bake until the pastry is brown and the apples tender, about 30 minutes. Let rest for at least 15 minutes, then serve warm or at room temperature.

Apple Pandowdy

Makes 6 to 8 servings

Time: About 1 1/2 hours

This classic dessert uses a sweetened pie crust for the topping. Traditionally, some of the crust is incorporated into the fruit about halfway through the baking, a nice touch.

6 cups peeled, cored, sliced apples or other fruit,
    washed and dried if necessary

Sugar to taste, plus about 2 tablespoons sugar

Butter for greasing the pan

1 recipe Sweetened, Enriched Pie Crust, well chilled,
    page 685

1 tablespoon milk

1/2 teaspoon ground cinnamon

1. Preheat the oven to 375°F. Toss the fruit with sugar, and spread it in a lightly buttered 8-inch square or 9-inch round baking pan.

2. Roll out the dough according to the directions on page 685, and lay it over the fruit. Tuck the edges under the sides of the fruit. Brush the top of the dough with milk; mix about 2 tablespoons sugar with the cinnamon and sprinkle it over the top.

3. Bake about 30 minutes, until the crust is golden. If you like, score the crust in a diamond pattern and use a spatula to press it partway down into the fruit. Bake until the crust is browned, a total of 45 minutes or more. Serve from the pan or invert onto a plate.

Apple Crisp
Makes 6 to 8 servings

Time: About 1 hour

Although there are a dozen or more kinds of baked fruit desserts with crusts (or other toppings) on top, they all have as their goal a simple topping that usually does not require rolling and complements the fruit with contrasting flavors and textures. You can top fruit with almost any pastry before baking, but if I had to pick a favorite it would be the crisp, because I love the way its sweet, crunchy granola–like topping works with fruit, especially soft, tart fruit such as blueberries, or apples spiked with lemon.

You can make this crisp with apples, pears, stone fruits, berries, or a combination; in any case, start with six cups of fruit, somewhere between two and three pounds. If you use more watery fruits, such as berries, toss them with a tablespoon or two of flour or cornstarch before cooking. If you use very tart fruits, such as rhubarb, increase the sugar.

6 cups peeled, cored, sliced apples or other fruit

1 teaspoon ground cinnamon

Juice of 1/2 lemon

2/3 cup brown sugar, or to taste

5 tablespoons cold unsalted butter, cut into bits, plus butter for greasing the pan

1/2 cup rolled oats

1/2 cup all-purpose flour

1/4 cup shredded unsweetened coconut (optional)

1/4 cup chopped nuts (optional)

Dash salt

1. Preheat the oven to 400°F. Toss the fruit with half the cinnamon, the lemon juice, and 1 tablespoon of the sugar, and spread it in a lightly buttered 8-inch square or 9-inch round baking pan.

2. Combine all the other ingredients—including the remaining cinnamon and sugar—in the container of a food processor and pulse a few times, then process a few seconds more until everything is well incorporated but not uniform. (To mix the ingredients by hand, soften the butter slightly, toss together the dry ingredients, then work in the butter with your fingertips, a pastry blender, or a fork.)

3. Spread the topping over the apples and bake 30 to 40 minutes, until the topping is browned and the apples are tender. Serve hot, warm, or at room temperature.

Baked Apples
Makes 4 servings

Time: About 1 hour

A simple and healthy dessert, especially if you keep the cream to a minimum. Here's the basic recipe; note that suggestions for making it more complicated follow.

4 large round apples, preferably Cortland or Ida or
    Paula Red
About 1 cup water, sweet white wine, or apple juice
About 8 teaspoons sugar

1 Preheat the oven to 350°F.

2 Core the apples (see illustrations on page 621) and peel the top half of each, leaving the stem end intact. Place in a baking dish with about ¹/₂ inch of liquid on the bottom. Put about 1 teaspoon of sugar in the cavities of each apple, and sprinkle another teaspoon or so of sugar on top.

3 Bake open end up, uncovered, until the apples are very tender, about an hour. Cool and serve warm, or at room temperature, or refrigerate (it's best to bring the apples back to room temperature before serving). Best served with sweet or sour cream or yogurt.

Five Simple Ideas for Baked Apples

1. Mix the sugar with one teaspoon or more ground cinnamon and/or other spices.
2. Cream the sugar with two tablespoons unsalted butter before adding it.
3. Substitute maple syrup, honey, or brown sugar for the white sugar.
4. Add about one-half cup chopped nuts, shredded coconut, raisins, and/or chopped figs or dates to sugar for filling.
5. Fill cavities of apples with jam about ten minutes before the end of cooking.

Apple Brown Betty

Makes 4 to 6 servings

Time: At least 45 minutes

This traditional dessert is a good way to use stale bread, but it's even better with leftover pound cake, biscuits, or other pastry. Decrease the amount of sugar if you use sweet baked goods in place of bread. Use apples that will soften as they cook, such as Rome or McIntosh.

4 cups cubed day-old bread, cake, or biscuits,
    cut into ¹/₄- to ¹/₂-inch cubes
4 cups peeled, cored, and sliced baking apples
    (about 4 to 6 medium-to-large apples)
Juice of ¹/₂ lemon
¹/₄ cup brown sugar
¹/₂ cup white sugar
1 teaspoon ground cinnamon, or more to taste
¹/₄ teaspoon freshly grated nutmeg
Pinch ground cloves
Pinch ground allspice, or more to taste
8 tablespoons (1 stick) unsalted butter

1 Preheat the oven to 300°F. Place the bread on a baking sheet and put the sheet in the oven. Bake until very lightly browned, about 10 minutes, shaking the sheet once or twice during baking. Meanwhile, prepare the apples and toss them with the lemon juice. Melt the butter in small saucepan over low heat.

2 When the bread is done, turn the oven heat to 375°F. Toss the bread with the sugars, spices, and half the butter. On the bottom of an 8- or 9-inch square baking pan, or an oval gratin dish, place about one third of the bread. Top with half the apples. Repeat, then finish with a layer of bread. Drizzle the remaining butter over all.

3 Bake for at least 30 minutes, or until the liquid in the dish is bubbly and the top is nicely browned. Serve warm with fresh cream, whipped cream (page 671), Crème Fraîche (page 671), Swedish cream (see Strawberries with Swedish Cream, page 647), or ice cream. Apple Brown Betty also may be prepared several hours in advance and reheated at 300°F for about 15 minutes.

Sautéed Apples

Makes 4 servings

Time: 30 minutes

You can cook apples with no sugar at all (in fact, they're wonderful with onions), and serve them as a side dish, or you can make them into this dessert, which is sort of a Tarte Tatin without the crust. Serve as is or with a scoop of vanilla ice cream or dollop of whipped cream (page 671) or Crème Fraîche (page 671).

4 tablespoons (½ stick) unsalted butter
About 1½ pounds firm crisp apples, such as
    Golden Delicious, peeled, cored, and cut into 8
    or 10 pieces each
½ cup white or brown sugar
½ teaspoon ground cinnamon

1 Place the butter in a large, deep skillet and turn the heat to medium. When the butter melts, add the apples and stir; turn the heat to low, cover, and cook for 10 minutes.

2 Add the sugar and cinnamon and raise the heat to medium. Cook, stirring frequently, until the apples are tender and glazed, another 10 minutes or so. Serve hot or warm.

Apricot

The Armenian apple (Prunus armeniaca), as the Greeks called it, probably came from further East—most likely China. Good specimens are among the most luxurious of fruits when ripe. They're sweet and tart, with a silken skin and internal texture that rivals that of the peach. But good specimens are also among the scarcest for those of us without our own trees or access to farmers' markets in areas where they are grown. Apricots grow best in places with cold winters and hot summers, but most easily in warmer climates, so most of the world's supply comes from California and the eastern Mediterranean.

Fortunately, apricots can be preserved, and the dried apricot should be a staple of every household. Those dried without sulfur dioxide have better flavor.

Buying and storing When fresh, the color should be deep orange. But that is only half the battle; an apricot should be tender and juicy, and, usually, they are neither. Even an imperfect apricot can be worth eating, but once you've had a good one you'll be spoiled for life. For dried apricots, try several sources—including Asian markets and natural foods stores—to find one you like. Then buy it in quantity; they keep for a year or more.

Preparing Apricot kernels—you reach them by cracking the pit—are very similar to almonds; roast them before eating. The fruit itself is among the easiest to pit, and can be peeled, if you like, by plunging it into boiling water for about ten seconds, after which the peel will slip off. Dried fruit can be stewed or soaked to soften.

Other recipes in which you can use fresh apricots:
Apple Brown Betty (best combined with berries
    unless the apricots are very juicy), page 624
Raspberry Gratin, page 628
Peaches with Fresh Blueberry Sauce, page 639
Poached Peaches with Red Wine and Spices, page
    640
Pears Sautéed in Butter, page 641
Pear Clafouti, page 642
Plums Poached in Orange Sauce, page 645
Strawberries with Swedish Cream, page 647
Summer Fruit Compote, page 649
Fruit Mousse with Gelatin, page 649
Blueberry Cobbler, page 630
Peach and Other Stone Fruit Pies, page 689

Another recipe in which you can use dried apricots: Macerated Dried Fruits with Cinnamon, page 650

Apricot Custard

Makes 4 to 6 servings

Time: About 1 hour

Not a true custard, but a creamy, sweet, and rich dessert with a lovely color.

1 cup dried apricots or 1¹/₂ cups peeled, pitted, and
    sliced fresh apricots (6 to 8)
¹/₂ cup sugar, more or less
Pinch salt
1 to 2 tablespoons lemon juice, or to taste
2 eggs, separated, plus 2 egg whites

1 If you're using dried apricots, cook them in water just to cover for 10 to 15 minutes, or until very tender; drain, reserving a little of the cooking liquid. Place the apricots in a blender or food processor and puree; if the dried apricots need a little liquid to become a puree, add some of the reserved cooking liquid. (The recipe can be prepared a day or two in advance up to this point; cool, place in a covered container, and refrigerate.)

2 Preheat the oven to 325°F. Combine the apricot puree with sugar to taste; add a pinch of salt and a tablespoon or two of lemon juice, or to taste.

3 Beat the egg yolks until lightened, just a minute or two, and stir them into the apricots. Whip the whites until they hold soft peaks, and stir about a quarter of them into the puree to lighten it. Then gently but thoroughly fold in the remaining whites.

4 Pour the mixture into a 6-cup soufflé dish or other ceramic baking dish, or into 6 (4-ounce) custard cups. Place the dish or cups in a large baking pan and pour hot water in, to within about 1 inch of the top of the dish or cups. Bake until the mixture just sets— it should wobble just a little in the middle—about 25 to 30 minutes for the cups, 30 to 40 minutes if you're baking in a dish. Serve warm, at room temperature, or cold, preferably with a little heavy cream drizzled on top of the custard.

Banana

Next to the apple, the banana is our most common and useful fruit, and probably the most widely eaten fruit in the world. We don't cook it much, which is unfortunate, because even sweet, or dessert bananas— as the common yellow banana is called by those who have become familiar with the plantain, page 594— make great, and quite simple, desserts.

There are four hundred varieties of bananas, but until recently we were only offered one. Now you might see red bananas, little yellow bananas, or other oddities from time to time; all are worth sampling.

Buying and storing Bananas may be bought green or ripe; although personal tastes vary, they are generally considered to be at their peak when deep yellow and spotted with brown, with no traces of green remaining.

Other recipes in which you can use bananas:
Apple Brown Betty, page 624 (bananas are best
    mixed with other fruits, such as berries)
Raspberry Gratin, page 628
Ambrosia, page 638
Strawberries with Swedish Cream, page 647
Summer Fruit Compote, page 649
Grilled Fruit Skewers with Ginger Syrup, page 650
Winter Fruit Compote, page 651
Fruit Fritters, page 651
Banana-Strawberry Cream Tart, page 697
Coconut Cream Pie or Banana Cream Pie,
    page 691

Sautéed Bananas

Makes 4 servings

Time: 15 minutes

A fast and easy dessert, and one for which you will almost always have the ingredients on hand.

> 4 bananas, ripe but not too soft
> 3 tablespoons unsalted butter
> Flour for dredging
> 2 tablespoons sugar, plus more to pass at the table
> Freshly squeezed lemon juice

❶ Peel the bananas, cut them in half crosswise, then lengthwise, so that each banana has been made into 4 pieces. Place the butter in a large, deep skillet over medium-high heat.

❷ Dredge the banana pieces lightly in the flour, shaking them to remove the excess. When the butter foam subsides, add the pieces to the skillet. Cook, turning frequently, until they are golden and beginning to brown, about 10 minutes. Sprinkle with the 2 tablespoons sugar and cook 1 minute more.

❸ Serve, passing additional sugar and lemon juice.

Broiled Bananas

Makes 4 servings

Time: 10 minutes

Prepare green bananas this way and sprinkle them with salt and lemon juice; they make a fine side dish.

> 1 tablespoon unsalted butter, softened, plus some for greasing the dish
> 4 bananas, ripe but not too soft
> 2 tablespoons sugar
> Freshly squeezed lemon juice as needed

❶ Preheat the broiler; lightly grease a large baking dish. Peel the bananas, cut them in half lengthwise, and arrange them in the dish. Dot with the 1 tablespoon butter and sprinkle with the sugar.

❷ Broil about 6 inches from the heat source, until lightly browned, 5 to 10 minutes. Serve hot, sprinkled with lemon juice.

Blackberries and Raspberries

There are hundreds of types of berries, not only black and red, but orange, yellow, or almost white—cloudberry (which grows north of the Arctic Circle), loganberry, boysenberry, dewberry, and more—but all are treated more or less the same. Some, typically those that are red or yellow, are far more fragile than others; black ones are usually sturdier. (Technically, a raspberry leaves its inner core behind when picked; the core comes along when you pick a blackberry.)

Buying and storing   All are extremely expensive in the market, largely because they are so perishable. Fortunately, almost the entire northern half of the country has some growing wild at one time or another in the summer, and most people have a favorite berry patch for picking. When you buy, be sure to look carefully for mold, which is quite common in store-bought berries, and for those that are simply rotten or falling apart. When you get them home, don't store; eat.

Preparing   Wash and dry very gently if at all; I do not wash wild berries as long as I'm sure of the source.

Other recipes in which you can use blackberries and raspberries:
Apple Brown Betty, page 624 (substitute berries for about half the apples)
Blueberry Cobbler, page 630
Strawberries with Swedish Cream, page 647
Summer Fruit Compote, page 649

Raspberry Fool

Makes 4 to 6 servings

Time: 20 minutes

A perfect treatment for raspberries, which require no cooking at all to be tender. But a fool can be made with any fruit: Just toss with whipped cream (page 671) and sugar to taste.

2 to 3 cups raspberries
¹/₂ cup superfine or confectioners' sugar, plus 1 table-
    spoon sugar, plus more if needed
1 cup heavy cream, preferably not ultra-pasteurized

1 Puree about one-third of the raspberries in a blender with ¹/₄ cup sugar. Force the puree through a sieve to remove seeds. Taste; the puree should be quite sweet. If it is not, add a little more sugar.

2 Toss the remaining berries with ¹/₄ cup sugar. Beat the cream with 1 tablespoon sugar, until it holds soft peaks. Beat in the raspberry puree, then fold in the sugared berries. Taste and add more sugar if necessary. Serve immediately or refrigerate for up to an hour.

Raspberry Gratin

Makes 4 servings

Time: 2 hours, largely unattended

This delicious gratin—fruit robed in a sweet custard—is fabulous with blueberries, raspberries, strawberries, or a mixture, or with any tender fruit you like—even bananas.

1 cup milk
¹/₂ teaspoon ground cinnamon
1 egg, plus 1 egg yolk
Pinch salt
¹/₂ cup sugar
¹/₄ cup all-purpose flour
³/₄ cup heavy cream
3 cups berries, picked over, washed, hulled if neces-
    sary, and dried, or other sliced fruit

1 Place the milk and cinnamon in a small saucepan and turn the heat to medium. When steam rises from the milk, remove it from the heat.

2 Meanwhile, beat the egg and yolk with the salt until light and foamy. Combine the sugar and flour and beat about half of the mixture into the eggs; add about half the milk and beat again. Add the remaining sugar-flour mixture, beat, then the remaining milk.

3 Place the mixture in a small saucepan and turn the heat to medium-low. Cook, stirring almost constantly, until the mixture begins to boil; it will thicken almost immediately. Remove the custard from the heat and continue to stir for a minute or so longer. Cover well and chill thoroughly, at least 1 hour and up to 12 hours.

4 About 20 minutes before you want to eat the dessert, preheat the broiler. Stir about ¹/₄ cup of the cream into the custard to lighten it. Whip the remaining cream until it holds soft peaks (page 671). Fold the cream gently into the custard.

5 Place the fruit on the bottom of an 8- to 10-inch-long gratin dish or an attractive 8-inch square baking dish. Pour the cream mixture over the top and shake the pan a little to distribute it among the berries or fruit. Broil about 4 to 6 inches from the heat until lightly browned on top, about 10 minutes. Serve immediately.

Gratin with Swedish Cream: Faster and easier. Combine the fruit with $1^1/_2$ cups Swedish cream (see Strawberries with Swedish Cream, page 647) and broil as above.

Summer Pudding

Makes 4 to 6 servings

Time: 20 minutes, plus chilling time

Not unlike Tiramisu (page 663) in concept and consistency, and equally wonderful. Keep all the berries whole, except for strawberries, which should be sliced.

    4 cups mixed berries: whole blackberries, raspberries,
       blueberries, currants, and strawberries; the rasp-
       berries held aside
    About 1 cup water
    $1/_2$ cup sugar, or more as needed
    Unsalted butter as needed
    6 to 8 slices good white bread, crusts removed

1 In a large saucepan, combine all the berries except the raspberries with about 1 cup of water and the $1/_2$ cup sugar; turn the heat to medium. Cook, stirring occasionally, until the berries fall apart, 10 to 15 minutes. Stir in the raspberries. Taste and add more sugar if needed; pass through a sieve to remove seeds and skins.

2 Meanwhile, butter the bread and the bottom and sides of an 8-cup soufflé, gratin, or other dish; sprinkle lightly with sugar. Put half the bread in the bottom of the dish. Cover with half the berry mixture, then repeat the layers.

3 Cover with a plate that fits into the dish, and weight the plate so it presses down on the mixture. Refrigerate for several hours or overnight. Unmold if you like, or serve straight from the dish, preferably with whipped cream (page 671).

Blueberry

More closely related to the cranberry than to the raspberry, the blueberry (as well as bilberry, huckleberry, and like berries) is distinctively different from both, and not just for its color. Unlike the cranberry, it is sweet enough to eat raw, whole, and out of hand. Unlike the raspberry, it is sturdy enough to store, and it even freezes well. With its relatively high sugar and acid content, it is the closest thing to an all-purpose berry, native to North America and adored by indigenous people and colonizers for centuries.

Buying and storing When overripe, blueberries sometimes turn to mush and sometimes dry up; avoid either. You want firm, plump berries. Size has little impact on flavor; don't fall for the "tiny berries are best" line. The best berries taste best, and you can always sample one or two before buying.

Preparing Pick over and remove stems.

Other recipes in which you can use blueberries:
Apple Crisp, page 623
Apple Pandowdy, page 622
Raspberry Gratin, page 628
Raspberry Fool, page 628
Summer Pudding, page 629
Peaches with Fresh Blueberry Sauce, page 639
Strawberries with Swedish Cream, page 647
Strawberry Shortcakes, page 647 (great mixed with
   strawberries)

Blueberry Cobbler

Makes 6 to 8 servings

Time: About 1 hour

My friend John Willoughby found this recipe in a southern boardinghouse about ten years ago. I've since made it dozens of times, and it's always been a hit. I love this with blueberries, but you can make it with any fruit you like.

> 4 to 6 cups blueberries or other fruit, washed and
>   well dried
> 1 cup sugar, or to taste
> 8 tablespoons (1 stick) cold unsalted butter,
>   cut into bits, plus some for greasing the pan
> ½ cup all-purpose flour
> ½ teaspoon baking powder
> Pinch salt
> 1 egg
> ½ teaspoon vanilla extract

1 Preheat the oven to 375°F. Toss the fruit with half the sugar, and spread it in a lightly buttered 8-inch square or 9-inch round baking pan.

2 Combine the flour, baking powder, salt, and ½ cup sugar in the container of a food processor and pulse once or twice. Add the butter and process for 10 seconds, until the mixture is well blended. By hand, beat in the egg and vanilla.

3 Drop this mixture onto the fruit by tablespoonfuls; do not spread it out. Bake until golden yellow and just starting to brown, 35 to 45 minutes. Serve immediately.

Carambola (Star Fruit)

One of the recent tropical imports, now grown in Florida and found in most supermarkets. It has yellow, near-translucent skin (which is tough but edible), and slices take the shape of a star. Best eaten raw. Also takes well to grilling; see Grilled Fruit Skewers with Ginger Syrup (page 650).

Cherimoya (Custard Apple)

A native American fruit, now grown in California, with lumpy greenish-brown skin and a creamy white interior studded by watermelon-like seeds. At its best, it is creamy, sweet, and flavorful, but it's difficult to find prime specimens. Eat with a spoon.

Cherry

Sadly, I think most of us have missed out on the really good cherries; this is the fruit of romance, of fairs, of paradise. Yet none of the cherries we are able to buy come close. Yes, there's an occasional one or two in the batch that makes us pause and think, "Oh. Now I remember why I love these." But these days the fact is that a bowl of cherries is a lot like life—fairly mundane, with some high spots.

There are two kinds of cherries, the sweet eating cherries with which we are all familiar, and the more acidic "sour" cherries, sold fresh only during the absolute peak of the season—and then usually at farmstands more often than supermarkets—but far better for pies and cooking. Each of these major categories is divided into dozens of varieties, of course, but only those us of with orchards, or at least access them, will have the opportunity to know the difference among them. Mostly we see Bing cherries, a dark-red variety.

Buying and storing   The season is short, even in the supermarket. I see people picking out cherries as if they were peaches—one at a time, looking for those that are firm and dark—but most of us grab handfuls. Steer clear unless the majority look sound. Store in the refrigerator, but they won't last long, nor should they.

Preparing   Remove stems and pit; cherry-pitting gadgets (which can also be used for olives) are good if you're going to pit a large number. Wash and dry.

Other recipes in which you can use cherries:
Apple Pandowdy, page 622
Raspberry Gratin, page 628
Pear Clafouti, page 642
Summer Fruit Compote, page 649
Fruit or Berry Ice Cream, page 667
Soft Fruit Sorbet, page 669
Raspberry, Strawberry, or Other Fruit Sauce, page 672
Cherry Pie, page 690

Stewed Cherries

Makes 4 to 6 servings

Time: About 30 minutes

A simple treat, not unlike cherry pie without the crust. Best with sour cherries.

2 pounds cherries, preferably sour
1 cup water
About $1/2$ cup sugar, or more to taste
$1/4$ teaspoon ground cinnamon (optional)
1 tablespoon freshly squeezed lemon juice, if using sweet cherries, or to taste
1 teaspoon minced lemon zest (optional)

1 Pit the cherries and combine them with 1 cup water in a medium saucepan; turn the heat to medium-high and cook, stirring occasionally, until the cherries are very tender, about 20 minutes.

2 Stir in the sugar and the cinnamon if you are using it; taste and add more sugar, lemon juice, or lemon zest if you like. Cool, then chill and serve the cherries cold, with their juice.

Cherries Jubilee: A favorite of kids. Omit the cinnamon, lemon juice, and lemon zest. Proceed as above, making the stew quite sweet. Dole out 4 to 6 servings of vanilla or other ice cream. Add $1/4$ cup brandy to the cherries while still warm; carefully touch with a match, then spoon the flaming mixture over the ice cream and serve.

Cranberry

There are several species of cranberry—the lingonberry of Scandinavia is one—but we're most accustomed to the one that is native to North America, and it's a good one: large, tart, and a terrific keeper. In fact, cranberries are the only berries that can be kept through the winter, which made them extremely valuable to Native Americans and to the colonizers as well.

Cranberries are also among the only berries that cannot be eaten out of hand—they are simply too hard and too tart. (There are a few species that are exceptions, but they never make it to our markets.) They are almost always cooked and, if not, chopped to make a relish. You can also add a handful of cranberries to many other cooked fruit dishes, such as Apple Brown Betty (page 624), Sautéed Bananas (page 627), or Rhubarb Compote with Dates (page 646).

Buying and storing   Berries should be firm and whole; you can freeze them almost indefinitely, or store them in the refrigerator for weeks. Incredibly, it doesn't make much difference.

Preparing   Nothing to it: Pick over, wash, and, if necessary, dry.

Currant

Tiny, grape-like berries which may be red (usually), black (frequently), or white (sometimes). They are often dried like raisins, or made into the liqueur cassis (the French word for black currant), but are good to eat fresh, too. They are delicious and powerful; combine them with other fruits , such as pears, apples, other berries, in pies and other desserts.

Buying and storing   Like grapes—they should be firm and intact. Currants are not especially fragile, but should be used within a few days.

Preparing   Make sure to remove *all* the stems. Pick over, wash and, if necessary, dry.

Other recipes in which you can use currants:
Summer Pudding, page 629
Summer Fruit Compote, page 649

Date

A staple of the eastern Mediterranean and western Asia, underappreciated here, the date is borne prolifically on palm trees that often grow one hundred feet tall and die only when they fall over from their inability to support their own height. Few fruits are as intensely sweet. Fresh dates, which we unfortunately see only rarely (although, I'm pleased to report, with gradually increasing frequency), are a revelation.

Dried or fresh, dates may be eaten out of hand, minced and used in baked goods (see Date-Nut Bread, page 248), or added to braised meats as you would raisins or apricots. Both fresh and dried dates are wonderful with the pit removed and replaced with a tiny bit of cream cheese.

Buying and storing   Fresh, you rarely have a choice; buy them if they are unbruised, moist, and affordable. Deglet Noor is the variety you'll most often see dried, and it's a good one. As with most dried fruit, it's worth looking for organic specimens in a natural foods store.

Other recipes in which you can use dates:
Rhubarb Compote with Dates, page 646
Macerated Dried Fruits with Cinnamon, page 650

Fig

Unlike the date, the fig has begun to make routine appearances in its fresh form. In those places where it grows easily—throughout the Mediterranean, and in California and the Southwest—it is cheap and plentiful. In supermarkets elsewhere, it is expensive and only rarely of good quality. A good, fresh fig, however, is sheer delight.

Fresh figs are little used in cooking, but are lovely added to meat or poultry stews. Dried figs are wonderful poached or macerated. Both are great eaten out of hand.

Buying and storing   Fresh figs, which may be dark purple or pale green, are very fragile, and are best bought as close to the tree as possible. In the supermarket, they should be quite soft (if they are not ripe they will not be sweet) but not at all damaged; that's a tough combination to find. But given that they cost as much as a dollar each, and you can easily eat several at a sitting, it pays to be careful; an unripe fig is a disappointment. Dried figs are better bought in bulk then prepackaged; they should be moist and tender.

Preparing   Wash and eat fresh ones. Dried figs may be soaked or stewed as any dried fruit.

Other recipes in which you can use figs:
Broiled Grapefruit, page 633 (cut fresh figs in half and broil with a little sugar, flesh side up; omit butter)
Macerated Dried Fruits with Cinnamon, page 650

Grape

Best known for its ability to produce the world's greatest alcoholic beverage, the grape has become a year-round staple of the supermarket. Newer varieties ship so well, that even those grown in our winter, from the Southern Hemisphere, are inexpensive and worth eating. Older varieties, especially those grown in locally in season, are certainly more flavorful. These seeded grapes make a fine, leisurely after-dinner snack, chilled and rinsed, or in a bowl of ice water in hot weather.

Raisins, as everyone knows, are dried grapes. Again, some varieties are more interesting than others; these days, most are made from Thompson seedless (also the most widely grown table grape), but you can find others in natural foods or specialty stores.

Buying and storing   Taste one. Grapes should be sweet, but also have enough acidity to be interesting. Obviously, avoid those that are shriveled or damaged.

Preparing   Pick over and rinse clean.

Other recipes in which you can use grapes:
Summer Fruit Compote, page 649
Winter Fruit Compote, page 651
Strawberry Tart with Pastry Cream (best mixed with other fruit), page 697

Grapefruit

West Indian in origin, now widely grown in Florida (which produces the best), California, and elsewhere. Each year, it seems, breeding techniques make grapefruit sweeter and sweeter; and seeds are long a thing of the past in new hybrids. Pomelo (or shaddock) and ugli (aptly if cruelly named) are similar and may be treated as grapefruit.

Like oranges, most grapefruit are made into juice, and the rest are eaten simply, out of hand or with a spoon. Still, grapefruit has its uses in cooking, and makes a terrific sorbet.

Buying and storing   Generally, pink grapefruit is sweeter, not always an advantage. Buy heavy, undamaged fruit and store in the refrigerator unless you will be eating the fruit within a couple of days.

Preparing   In addition to the common method involving a grapefruit knife, you can peel and separate a grapefruit as you would an orange; this is especially useful with smaller specimens.

Other recipes in which you can use grapefruit:
Winter Fruit Compote, page 651
Ambrosia, page 638
Lemon, Lime, or Grapefruit Sorbet, page 670

Broiled Grapefruit

Makes 2 to 4 servings

Time: 15 minutes

Substitute brown sugar or honey for the sugar if you like, or try sprinkling the top with shredded coconut and/or very finely minced fresh or crystallized ginger.

    2 large grapefruit, cut in half and sectioned
    1 tablespoon melted unsalted butter (optional)
    4 teaspoons sugar, or to taste

1   Preheat the broiler and set the rack 4 to 6 inches from the heat source.

2   Brush the grapefruit with butter if you like, and sprinkle with sugar. Place on a roasting pan and put under the broiler. Broil, rotating the pan once, until the top is hot and bubbly, 5 to 10 minutes. Serve hot.

Kiwi

A relative newcomer to our shores, the kiwi is originally from China but comes to us from New Zealand. It is now widely grown in all moderate climates, and some varieties will even survive as far north as New England. Its unusual and starkly green color has made it a popular garnish, but it is also a decent-tasting fruit, inexpensive, widely available, and easy to eat. Add kiwi to fruit salad, or poach it in a light syrup.

Buying and storing   Truly ripe kiwi are quite tender, but like many other fruits, they are shipped unripe. You can ripen them at home, or buy them tender but not mushy. Store at room temperature and eat when ripe.

Preparing   Cut in half and scoop out the flesh, as you would a little melon, or peel and slice the fruit.

Another recipe in which you can use kiwi:
Winter Fruit Compote (add toward the end of the marinating period), page 651

Kumquat

The most unusual of citrus fruits (well, in fact, it isn't a citrus, but it looks and acts like one), with a thin peel that is sweeter than the flesh. Wonderful poached, or chopped raw.

Buying and storing   Buy firm, unblemished fruits; store in the refrigerator.

Preparing   Wash, dry, and slice or quarter; remove and discard seeds and the small amount of flesh; use the skin and juice.

Lemon

The most useful of all fruits in European cooking (the lime being the most useful in Asian and tropical cooking), the lemon adds mild, flavorful acid to dishes in a way that nothing else can, not even the finest vinegar. It is among the most important condiments; squeeze it on raw or cooked vegetables, on meats, poultry, fish, on raw fruit, in desserts. If you always keep a lemon or two in the kitchen, you'll wind up using it daily; the simplest low-fat dish always is grilled, broiled, or roasted anything with fresh lemon.

Buying and storing   Buy firm thin-skinned lemons whenever possible. Thick-skinned lemons, and hard ones, have less juice; mushy lemons are over the hill. Store in the refrigerator, but bring to room temperature before using. (The best way to do this is to buy six or ten lemons at once, and keep one or two on the counter.) Meyer lemons, widely available in California (which grows more lemons than anyplace else) but not elsewhere, are the most flavorful.

Preparing   Cut into halves, quarters, wedges, or slices, and remove the pits with the point of a knife. Or cut into halves and juice.

There are two ways to zest a lemon. The first is to use a nifty little gadget called a lemon zester (see The Basics of Miscellaneous Tools, page 5), which removes the zest (the yellow part of the peel, which is what you want) in long, thin strips; you can then mince these if you like. The alternative is to use a vegetable peeler or paring knife to remove the peel in long ribbons. Since this inevitably brings part of the bitter white pith with it, to do a perfect job you should then lie the strips down on a cutting board and scrape the white part off with a paring knife.

Other recipes in which you can use lemon:
Lemon, Lime, or Grapefruit Sorbet, page 670
Lemon, Orange, or Grand Marnier Soufflé, page 675
Lemon Meringue Pie, page 691
Gabrielle's Lemon Squares, page 718
Lemon Pound Cake, page 723
Lemon Cheesecake with Sour Cream Topping, page 728

Lemon Curd

Makes about 2 cups

Time: About 30 minutes

Lemon curd is a wonderful and traditional spread for toast or crackers, but can also be used as the basis for a fruit gratin, such as the one on page 628.

> 3 lemons
> 8 tablespoons (1 stick) unsalted butter
> 1 cup sugar
> 1 teaspoon peeled and very finely minced fresh ginger (optional)
> 3 eggs

① Zest the lemons and mince the zests; juice the lemons. Combine the zest and juice with the butter and sugar and place in a small saucepan over very low heat or in the top of a double boiler over simmering water.

② Cook, stirring occasionally, until the sugar dissolves. Add the ginger if you like. Beat the eggs and add them to the mixture; make sure the heat is very low.

③ Cook, stirring constantly, until the mixture thickens, about 10 minutes; do not let the mixture boil or the eggs will curdle. Cool slightly, then pour into custard cups, small bowls, or jars; cool, then refrigerate.

Lime

If the lemon did not exist, we would rely supremely on the lime, which has a stronger and less fragrant nature; some call it harsher. Its juice is excellent, and can be used instead of lemons in almost every instance. But lime has one advantage over lemon: It takes better to very strong flavors. Thus lime juice mixed plain with minced garlic or chiles is a terrific condiment, as long as your food can stand up to it. Key limes, are small, hard, quite flavorful, and not especially common.

Buying and storing Buy firm, thin-skinned limes; store in the refrigerator.

Preparing To extract the most juice from a lime, cut it in thirds through its axis, then squeeze by hand. To zest, see Lemon.

Other recipes in which you can use lime:
Lemon Curd, page 635
Lemon, Lime, or Grapefruit Sorbet, page 670
Key Lime Pie, page 692

Mango

There are dozens of varieties of this tropical Asian fruit, a relatively recent arrival to our markets but now found everywhere throughout the year. In Asia, the mango is eaten both ripe and unripe—that is, sweet and tart. Unripe, it is great cooked, or in dishes such as Fresh Fruit Chutney with Mustard and Curry (page 785). When soft and ripe, it is lovely in salsas, or eaten neat or, even better, with a squeeze of lime. There are two ways to eat a mango: sucking at the skin and pit, or removing the flesh with a knife. Most of us stick with the first until we learn the second, which is illustrated on page 636.

Buying and storing Color is irrelevant—good mangoes may be green, orange, yellow, or red. Texture, however, is important. If you want your mango sweet, it must be soft. Bought at any stage, however, the mango will ripen on your counter. Just make sure to eat it before it rots.

Preparing See illustrations, below. There are at least three ways to remove the flesh from a mango. If you're just going to eat it, cut it into wedges, and attack both pit and each of the pieces; it's a mess, but a worthwhile one. For a neater, more economical job, trim a piece off the bottom end. Stand the fruit on a cutting board, trim off the skin with a sharp paring knife, then slice fruit from around the pit. Or see version II, below.

Other recipes in which you can use mangoes:
Fruit Mousse with Gelatin, page 649
Soft Fruit Sorbet, page 669
Granita, page 670
Raspberry, Strawberry, or Other Fruit Sauce, page 672.

SKINNING AND SEEDING MANGO, VERSION I

(Step 1) There are two ways to get the meat out of a mango. The first way begins with peeling, using a normal vegetable peeler. (Step 2) Then cut the mango in half, doing the best you can to cut around the pit. (Step 3) Finally, chop the mango with a knife.

SKINNING AND SEEDING MANGO, VERSION II

(Step 1) Alternatively, begin by cutting the mango in half, doing the best you can to cut around the pit. (Step 2) Score the flesh with a paring knife. (Step 3) Turn the mango half "inside out" and the flesh is easily removed.

Melon

There are three kinds of melons (plus the watermelon, page 648, a different species entirely). Small melons with ridged skin, such as the charentais, are more popular in Europe than here; they are excellent, and we will see more of them. Those with a meshed rind, like the cantaloupe (sometimes called a muskmelon), are most common here. Those with smooth rind, like the honeydew, are also popular. All melons fall into one of these categories, and may have flesh that runs the gamut from pale pinkish-orange to deep green; since melons can be crossbred with no trouble (and indeed do so themselves all the time), it's probably anyone's guess how many types there are.

All are good when fully ripe, but there's the rub. Finding a ripe melon is not easy, and melons do not ripen well once they're off the vine. So it's up to you to sort through a pile of two hundred at the supermarket, or find a good farmstand where they are grown. There's no sure way to tell if a melon is ripe (really ripe melons slip off their vines, but chances are you won't have the opportunity to find that out). There are, however, some keys: First, smell it; an appetizing smell is a good sign. Next, shake it; loose seeds are a decent indication of ripeness. Finally, squeeze the ends, especially the end opposite the stem; it should be fairly tender, almost soft.

Buying and storing   If you've just bought a ripe melon, there's no need to store it: Eat it. But if you've bought an unripe melon, store it at room temperature and eat it when you deem it to be ripe (a crap shoot at best). Do not refrigerate until it's open, unless you think it is becoming overripe.

Preparing   Cut the melon in half, then scrape out the seeds. Cut into slices and remove the slices from the rind with a paring knife, or use a melon baller to scoop out sections of the halves.

Although chilled melon is the norm, it lacks the flavor of melon served at room temperature; try it.

And try a squeeze of lemon or lime, even on perfectly ripe melon. You may consider it an improvement.

Other recipes in which you can use melons:
Soft Fruit Sorbet, page 669
Granita, page 670

Orange

Oranges were once such a treat that they were given as Christmas presents, like treasures. Now we're spoiled, and no more so than by the omnipresence of presqueezed orange juice, a decent enough product, but one which barely compares to the real thing.

We tend to think of oranges as juice oranges, such as Temple—full of pits and juice, but brilliantly flavored—or eating oranges, such as navel, which have no pits and are easy to peel. But there are also bitter (Seville) oranges, used primarily for marmalade and not often seen in this country; blood oranges, with striking red flesh and low acidity, and now in supermarkets every winter; and other varieties. Except for Seville oranges, most make for tastier out-of-hand eating than the navel. But they are a bit more hassle.

Buying and storing   Like all citrus, oranges keep well. Color is not as important as we've been led to believe; there's no problem with greenish oranges. Just make sure they're firm and undamaged. Store in the refrigerator, but keep a couple at room temperature for instant eating.

Preparing   See illustrations, page 638. Oranges are easiest to eat when cut into eighths rather than quarters. To peel, cut four longitudinal slits from pole to pole, through the skin but not into the flesh. Peel each of these off.

To zest an orange, see Lemon.

Other recipes in which you can use oranges:
Winter Fruit Compote, page 651

(Step 1) Before beginning to peel and segment citrus, cut a slice off both ends of the fruit so that it stands straight. (Step 2) Cut as closely to the pulp of the fruit as possible, removing the skin in long strips. (Step 3) To segment citrus, use a paring knife to cut between the sections, leaving the membrane behind. (Or simply segment as you would a grapefruit.)

Lemon, Lime, or Grapefruit Sorbet, page 670
Lemon, Orange, or Grand Marnier Soufflé, page 675
Orange-Almond Cake, page 722

Ambrosia

Makes 4 servings

Time: 20 minutes

A traditional, simple, and worthwhile dessert.

4 oranges
2 bananas, peeled and sliced
1 cup shredded unsweetened coconut
Sugar to taste (optional)

1 Peel and section or thinly slice 3 of the oranges (page 638); remove the pits. Juice the remaining orange.

2 In a bowl, make layers of oranges, bananas, coconut, and, if you like, sugar. Drizzle with the orange juice and let sit for a few minutes before serving.

Papaya

A spectacular-looking supremely exotic orange-fleshed, melon-like fruit, best split down the middle, black seeds removed (they are edible, so crunch away if you prefer), and served with lime juice—typically for breakfast. Some weigh ten pounds, but most are about the size of a mango, with which the papaya is sometimes confused, although only by us North Americans.

Papaya contains an enzyme, called papain, that tenderizes meat and is extracted for use in commercial preparations.

Buying and storing   Papaya will ripen at room temperature, so you can buy firm specimens; eat when soft.

Preparing   Cut in half, remove seeds, and eat.

Other recipes in which you can use papaya:
Fruit Mousse with Gelatin, page 649
Soft Fruit Sorbet, page 669

Passion Fruit

Purplish-brown on the outside, filled with (edible) pits and orange flesh inside, the passion fruit does not inspire passion until one eats it. Unadulterated, it is tart and hard to take. I like to strain the flesh and use the juice in Soft Fruit Sorbet (page 669).

Peach and Nectarine

Similar fruits, one with a fuzzy skin, one with smooth (no, the nectarine is not a cross between peach and plum). I claim peach as my favorite summer eating fruit and, once the season finally gets going, go way out of my way to avoid buying them at supermarkets in order to find the best varieties at local orchards. And, yes, fuzz is important; what other fruit offers you texture so close to soft skin? The peach is not only delicious, it can be downright erotic. Nectarines, good as they are, are not in the same league.

There are many varieties of peaches, of different colors; white peaches, actually a very pale yellow, are among the best. All fall neatly into one of two categories: freestone or clingstone, determined by how stubbornly the flesh clings to the pit.

Buying and storing Tree-ripened peaches are best, but peaches do ripen at room temperature, and quickly. Keep an eye on them, because they frequently go from hard to rotten in a day. If you can buy ripe peaches, so much the better; if not, buy specimens that are close to ripeness. And don't buy too many at once, unless you're planning to cook with them; they usually all ripen at the same time.

Preparation Wash, peel if you like, and eat. To pit, cut in half from pole to pole; twist the halves, which will either come completely free of the pit (freestone) or leave a fair amount of flesh on the pit (clingstone). To peel, drop into boiling water for ten to thirty seconds, just until the skin loosens; plunge into a bowl of ice water; remove the peel with your fingers and/or a paring knife.

Other recipes in which you can use peaches and nectarines:

Peaches with Fresh Blueberry Sauce

Makes 4 servings

Time: 15 minutes

Most of the work in this minimalist dessert is in finding the best peaches and blueberries available.

4 large ripe peaches
1 pint blueberries, picked over and washed briefly
1½ teaspoons minced or grated lemon zest
¼ teaspoon ground cinnamon
Sugar or honey to taste
Fresh mint leaves for garnish

1 Bring a pot of water to the boil; dip the peaches in, one or two at a time, for a few seconds, long enough for their skins to loosen, 10 to 30 seconds. Peel, pit, and slice them.

2 Puree the blueberries in a blender or food processor. Add the lemon zest, cinnamon, and as much sweetener as needed.

3 Spoon the sauce over the middle of four dessert plates; arrange the peach slices over the sauce. Garnish and serve.

Poached Peaches with Red Wine and Spices

Makes 4 servings

Time: About 1 hour, largely unattended

An austere but delicious and unusual dessert; you can make it more luxurious by adding a topping of sweetened whipped cream (page 671) and/or Raspberry, Strawberry, or Other Fruit Sauce (page 672).

About 1¹/₂ pounds just-ripe peaches, plums,
    nectarines, or other soft fruit
1¹/₂ cups fruity red wine, preferably Pinot Noir
    (Burgundy) or Beaujolais
¹/₂ cup sugar
¹/₂ cinnamon stick
15 allspice berries, 3 star anise, or 5 juniper berries

1 Bring a pot of water to the boil; dip the peaches in, one or two at a time, for 10 to 30 seconds, long enough for their skins to loosen. Peel and pit them.

2 Cut the peaches into halves or slices. In a medium saucepan, bring the wine, sugar, and spices to a boil; reduce to about a cup (this will take about 10 minutes). Pour over the fruit and let cool to room temperature.

3 Remove the cinnamon stick and other spice. Serve immediately or chill with wine syrup.

Mary Willoughby's Broiled Peaches

Makes 4 servings

Time: 20 minutes or less

In the words of John—Mary's son—"these are good when you cook them so long that the edges are black." I like them a little less done than that, but use your judgment. Best, for obvious reasons, with freestone peaches.

4 peaches, washed
4 teaspoons unsalted butter
4 teaspoons honey

1 Preheat the broiler; the rack should be about 4 inches from the heat source.

2 Cut the peaches in half and remove the pits. Set each one on its "back" and fill the cavities with a dot of butter and a spoonful of honey. Broil until the edges just begin to brown, or a little longer. Serve hot or warm.

Pear

Like the apple, there are countless varieties of pears and, like the apple, some are better than others. Unlike the apple, however, catching a pear at the peak of its ripeness is a trick, so a perfectly ripe but less-than-prime variety like the Anjou is preferable to an unripe Comice—even though a perfect Comice is a near-perfect fruit.

Although this may sound a little prissy, I assure you that most of us—by all means myself included—know next to nothing about pear varieties. As Jane Grigson, the late great food writer, wrote about her husband Geoffrey, "[He] remembers being taken by his mother to the Midlands before the First World

War, and visiting house after house where pears were produced from back garden trees, as a special treat. They were sampled and compared as knowledgeably and thoughtfully as wine at a tasting." Compare this to shopping for pears at a supermarket, or even a farmstand.

It pays to distinguish among pear varieties, even though we're usually offered only the first two or three listed here. But should you see any of the remaining ones, this may help:

Anjou: Our most common pear, green to greenish red, and broad. Texture can be quite good, if a little gritty; flavor is never spectacular. Good for poaching.

Bartlett: Green with red, an early pear which ripens in summer. Rarely first-rate.

Bosc: The narrow yellow-to-brown pear. More aromatic than the Anjou, with equally good texture.

Comice: Short, green tending toward brown. The best pear commercially available, very fragrant, with fantastic texture.

Packham: Green, usually with no other colors. Imported in mid-winter from Chile, South Africa, and New Zealand. Generally unexceptional.

Seckel: Small yellow-to-brown pear with great, spicy flavor. Texture is not the best, but always worth biting into.

Buying and storing   Pears do ripen on the kitchen counter, so there's little or no reason to eat unripe pears just because that's all the supermarket sells. A pear is ripe when the "shoulders" feel quite tender and the body yields to soft pressure. All of this refers to European pears (originally from the Caucasus); there are Asian pears as well, meant to be eaten crisp; but these are closer to a Golden Delicious apple than to other pears.

Preparing   Peel a pear with a vegetable peeler. You can core it by cutting it into quarters and scooping out the core with a paring knife, but it's easier to cut the pear in half, then dig out each half of the core with a melon baller; if you like, you can also dig out the core from the blossom end with a melon baller, leaving the pear intact. (The latter method is best when you're going to poach the pear.)

Other recipes in which you can use pears:
Apple Dumplings, page 622 (the pears should be slightly underripe)
Apple Crisp, page 623
Apple Pandowdy, page 622
Apple Brown Betty, page 624
Mary Willoughby's Broiled Peaches, page 640
Winter Fruit Compote, page 651
Apple-Pear Pie, page 688
Simplest Apple Tart, page 696

Pears Sautéed in Butter

Makes 4 servings

Time: 20 minutes

A wonderful warm dessert, served with ice cream (especially spiked with cinnamon), whipped cream (page 671), sour cream, Swedish cream (see Strawberries with Swedish Cream, page 647), Vanilla Custard Sauce (page 673), or on its own. Pears should be just short of perfectly ripe.

4 tablespoons (1/2 stick) unsalted butter
4 pears, peeled, cored, and sliced
1/4 cup sugar, or more
2 tablespoons port or pear brandy

1 Place half the butter in a large, deep skillet and turn the heat to medium-high. When the butter foam

subsides, add the pears and cook, sprinkling with the sugar and turning occasionally, until they begin to brown, about 10 minutes.

2 Add the port or brandy and cook, stirring gently, until the mixture becomes saucy, just a minute or two longer. Add the remaining butter, turn the heat to low, and cook until the butter melts and coats the pears. Serve immediately.

Pears Poached in Red Wine

Makes 4 servings

Time: Overnight, largely unattended

A light, simple, and classic dessert. Use not-quite-fully-ripe Bosc pears if at all possible.

4 Bosc pears, ripe but not mushy

1^1/$_2$ cups water

1^1/$_2$ cups red wine

^{3}/$_4$ cup sugar

1 lemon, sliced

1 cinnamon stick

1 Peel the pears; use a melon baller to remove the core from the blossom end, but leave the stem on.

2 In a medium saucepan, bring the water, wine, and sugar to a boil. Turn the heat to medium-low and add the lemon, cinnamon stick, and pears. Cover the pan and simmer until the pears are very tender, at least 20 minutes.

3 Remove the pears to a bowl and continue to cook the sauce, over medium-high heat, until it reduces by about half and becomes syrupy. Strain the syrup over the pears and refrigerate overnight.

4 Serve the chilled pears whole, with a little of the syrup poured over them.

Pear Clafouti

Makes 4 to 6 servings

Time: 1 hour

This traditional French dessert is essentially a large, sweet pancake baked with fruit. It is among the best desserts you can make at the last minute. Put it in the oven when you sit down to dinner and you can eat it for dessert.

1 tablespoon unsalted butter, more or less, for greasing the pan

^{1}/$_2$ cup sugar, plus some for dusting the pan

About 4 pears, peeled, halved, and cored

3 eggs

^{1}/$_3$ cup all-purpose flour

^{3}/$_4$ cup heavy cream or plain yogurt

^{3}/$_4$ cup milk

1 teaspoon vanilla extract

Pinch salt

Confectioners' sugar

1 Preheat the oven to 350°F. Butter a gratin dish, about 9 × 5 × 2 inches deep, or a 10-inch round deep pie plate or porcelain dish; sprinkle it with sugar, then invert to remove the excess. Lay the pears in one layer in the dish.

2 Beat the eggs until foamy. Add the ^{1}/$_2$ cup of sugar and beat with a whisk or electric mixer until foamy and fairly thick.

3 Add the flour and continue to beat until thick and smooth. Add the cream, milk, vanilla, and salt.

4 Pour the batter over the pears. Bake for about 20 minutes, or until the clafouti is nicely browned on top and a knife inserted into it comes out clean. Sift some confectioners' sugar over it and serve warm or at room temperature.

Baked Pears

Makes 4 servings

Time: About 1 hour

As with baked apples, there are lots of options here. I give my favorite; see the recipe for Baked Apples (page 623), for alternative suggestions.

4 pears, peeled, halved, and cored
4 teaspoons unsalted butter
4 teaspoons brown sugar
1 teaspoon freshly squeezed lemon juice

1 Preheat the oven to 350°F. Place the pears, cavities up, in a baking pan filmed with a little water.

2 Fill the cavities with a dot each of butter and sugar. Cover the pan and bake until very soft, about 30 minutes. Sprinkle lightly with lemon juice and serve warm or at room temperature.

Persimmon

The most common persimmon, the heart-shaped Hachiya variety, is the orange, smooth-skinned fruit that is torturously tart when unripe, but sweet and delicious when finally ready—by which time you're convinced it's turned to mush. (There is no such thing as an overripe persimmon.) When they gain a translucent, shiny glow, they'll be juicy and sweet, with an interior like firm jelly. Simply lop off the top and eat the insides with a spoon or quite messily, out of hand.

The harder-to-find Fuyu variety, which looks more like an orange tomato, is edible when not fully ripe—you can eat it when it's soft, or even before then.

Buying and storing   Generally, the softer the better. Dark color is a good sign.

Preparation   It's all in the ripening, which can take up to a month. Ripen on the counter or in a

paper bag. You can eat the peel if it tastes good; if not, scoop out the flesh with a spoon.

Pineapple

There's a reason most pineapple is canned: The fruit barely ripens after picking, and the journey from Costa Rica or Hawaii to the mainland U.S. markets is a long one. This means that fruit must be picked underripe so that it isn't rotten by the time you buy it. Which means, in turn, that buying a hard pineapple and allowing it to sit on the kitchen counter in hopes of its ripening is not a good idea.

Buying and storing   My supermarket usually sells two types of pineapples: relatively inexpensive, almost always unripe ones that have been shipped by boat, and rather expensive but ripe ones that have been shipped by plane. (It seems that in the short span of time between originally writing these words and editing them just before publication there has been an increase in the number of inexpensive ripe pineapples in the supermarket. This may be explained by a decrease in the cost of air freight.) I go for the latter, and recommend that you do too. Eat as soon as possible.

Preparing   See illustrations on the following page. There are a few ways to dismember a pineapple: For either one, first cut off the spiky top. Then, with a chef's knife peel around the perimeter and remove all of the spiny skin, and use a paring knife to dig out any eyes. At that point, cut the pineapple crosswise into round slices or top to bottom into halves or quarters, and cut out the woody core. Alternatively, cut straight down from top to bottom with a chef's knife to cut the pineapple in half; then cut each half in half again to make quarters. Use a smaller knife to cut off the woody core portion from each quarter, and then use a grapefruit or paring knife to separate the flesh from the skin by cutting between the two; cut the quarter into slices and serve.

(Step 1) Cut the top of the pineapple off about an inch below the flower. (Step 2) Slice off the stem end as well. (Step 3) Cut the pineapple into quarters. (Step 4) Use a grapefruit knife to separate the fruit from the rind, and a paring knife to dig out any "eyes." Remove the core (the hard edge where the fruit comes to a point), slice, and serve.

Other recipes in which you can use pineapple:
Broiled Bananas, page 627
Grilled Fruit Skewers with Ginger Syrup, page 650

Plum and Prune

A good plum is, like a good peach, the near-perfect summer fruit: You can eat a dozen of them. But a good plum is hard to find. Usually, we must buy unripe fruit and let it sit on the counter where, we hope, we can catch it at the peak of ripeness, before it begins to turn. Fortunately, plums do ripen quickly and reliably at room temperature, so the process is short and reasonably predictable.

There are dozens of varieties of plums, of many shades. One shade we do not see enough of is green. Although my favorite plums have always had dark-red interiors, there are parts of the world where only green plums are considered worth eating. My response to that is to try every plum I see, and to always hope to see more. Don't ignore the small, dark purple-skinned, yellow-fleshed Italian ("prune") plums that come very late in the season; they are delicious and

wonderful for cooking, especially in crisps, betties, and the like.

Buying and storing   Black, red, green, purple, orange—they're all good. Ripe plums are quite soft, and plums can become very ripe before they begin to turn rotten; try not to eat them underripe, unless you like sour fruit. Store them on the kitchen counter, at room temperature, and they will usually ripen within a couple of days. You can also refrigerate plums; it will slow down the ripening process but not stop it. Prunes, like other dried fruit, are best bought in bulk at a natural foods store.

Preparing   Plums can be skinned for cooking: Drop them into boiling water for about ten seconds, or until the skins loosen, then peel them off with a paring knife.

Other recipes in which you can use plums:
Apple Crisp, page 623
Apple Brown Betty, page 624
Apple Pandowdy, page 622
Poached Peaches with Red Wine and Spices, page 640
Summer Fruit Compote, page 649
Peach and Other Stone Fruit Pies, page 689

Plums Poached in Orange Sauce

Makes 4 servings

Time: 20 minutes, plus time to cool

You will thank yourself if you take the extra effort required to use fresh orange juice here.

1 cup orange juice, preferably freshly squeezed
1 tablespoon freshly squeezed lemon juice
1 teaspoon grated or minced lemon zest
$^1/_2$ cup honey
8 to 12 ripe unbruised plums, peaches, pears,
    nectarines, or other soft fruit, halved and pitted

① Combine the fruit juices, lemon zest, and honey in a medium saucepan and turn the heat to medium. Bring to a simmer and add plums.

② Cover the pan and turn the heat as low as possible. Simmer gently, turning the plums once or twice, until they are tender but still whole, 5 to 10 minutes, depending on their size and their ripeness.

③ Remove plums to a platter and turn the heat to medium-high; reduce the liquid by about half. Pour the syrup over the plums, cool, and serve chilled.

Pomegranate

Certainly among the strangest and most cumbersome of the fruits we eat, a labyrinth of seeds wrapped in fruit buried in a mass of inedible flesh surrounded by a tough skin. To "eat," you suck on or chew the seeds, which have delightful, sweet-tart flavor. This is a lot of work, so even admirers of the pomegranate actually eat the fruit only occasionally. The best way to enjoy its flavor is by purchasing pomegranate molasses, available at Middle Eastern stores.

Buying and storing   We don't get the best pomegranates, I'm sure, so you don't have much choice: You buy them and you eat them. They seem to keep well, but there's no reason not to eat them immediately.

Rhubarb

There are indeed some very real limits to what can be done with rhubarb. The stems of this vegetable—and it *is* actually a vegetable, despite a 1947 court ruling proclaiming it a fruit—are the only edible part. The roots have been used for a couple of thousand years in Europe and Asia as a purgative; the leaves contain poisonous levels of oxalic acid. And the flavor is strong: plain-stewed rhubarb, without sweeteners or seasonings, is not pleasant-tasting. Thus the common uses for rhubarb begin with poaching in a light sugar syrup or stewing with other fruits. And those remain the best way to use it.

Buying and storing   It should be firm, like celery, not limp. Store in the refrigerator but use as soon as possible; it does not improve with age.

Preparing   See illustrations, below. Although it's not entirely necessary, rhubarb is best if you "string" it—grab one end between a paring knife and your thumb and pull straight down to remove the celery-like strings that run lengthwise through each stalk. Remember that rhubarb leaves are poisonous.

Rhubarb is usually best when its "strings" are removed. Simply grasp the end of the fruit between your thumb and a paring knife and pull the strings down the length of the stalk.

You can substitute rhubarb for up to half of the strawberries in pies, cobblers, or crisps, but increase amount of sweetener by about a third.

Another recipe in which you can use rhubarb:
Strawberry, Rhubarb, or Strawberry-Rhubarb Pie, page 689

Rhubarb Compote with Dates

Makes 4 servings

Time: 20 minutes

This is an unusual rhubarb recipe in that the sweetener comes not from sugar but from dates; you can, of course, sweeten it further if you wish.

1 to 1½ pounds rhubarb, strings removed and chopped
1 cup minced pitted dates (you may substitute raisins)
Juice and grated or minced zest of 1 large orange
3 cloves
Sugar, honey, or maple syrup (optional)

1 Combine the first four ingredients in a saucepan just large enough to hold them; add boiling water to cover.

2 Simmer until rhubarb and dates are tender, about 15 minutes; discard the cloves and add additional sweetener if necessary. Serve warm or at room temperature.

Strawberry

Good strawberries, like so many fruits, do not travel well. I'm sure Florida strawberries taste delicious in Florida; same with those from California. But neither of them taste like a good strawberry where I live, and I'm not sure that some of them don't taste like a raw potato. The strawberries grown at the farm a few miles from here are pretty good, but even those are selected by the farmer for hardiness and disease resistance, not for flavor. Those grown in people's gardens—or those that grow wild—are true strawberries. And if you've picked good strawberries yourself, or stumbled upon a hillside covered with the distinctive red blanket of wild strawberries, you know what all the fuss is about.

It's funny, though. As heavenly as strawberries are, they're not the best fruit for cooking. Eaten plain, yes. Eaten with cream, the ultimate. Used in shortcake or jam, of course. But there's little more to them than that. They are just too fragile, and too precious, to mess about with.

Buying and storing Taste one. If it tastes like cotton, buy asparagus instead; it's a better way to celebrate spring. If it tastes good, buy only as many as you will eat (or turn into jam) in the next twenty-four hours. Do not refrigerate. In season, California strawberries seem to be consistently better than those from elsewhere.

Preparing See illustration, below. Pick off the leaves with your fingers, or cut them off with a paring knife, or use a paring knife or small melon baller to dig out the stem and small core (which is not all that distasteful, but is relatively tough) at the same time. Wash and dry.

To prepare strawberries, first remove the leaves, then cut a cone-shaped wedge with a paring knife to remove the top of the core. A small melon baller also does this job nicely.

Other recipes in which you can use strawberries:

Strawberry Shortcakes

Makes 12 shortcakes, enough for 12 people

Time: About 40 minutes from scratch, less with already-made biscuits

These are real strawberry shortcakes—buttery biscuits with strawberries and cream.

    1 recipe Drop ("Emergency") Biscuits (page 252) or
       Cream Scones (page 252), with 2 tablespoons
       sugar added to the dry ingredients
    2 pints (1 quart) ripe strawberries
    2 tablespoons sugar
    2 cups heavy cream, preferably not ultra-pasteurized
    1/2 teaspoon vanilla extract

1 Make the biscuits and bake them. Let them cool on a rack when they're done; you don't want to eat them hot.

2 Meanwhile, wash, hull, and slice the strawberries. Toss them with 1 tablespoon of sugar and let sit while you whip the cream.

3 Whip the cream until it holds soft peaks, then whip 1 minute more, incorporating the remaining sugar and the vanilla.

4 Split the biscuits and fill them with cream and strawberries. Serve immediately.

Strawberries with Swedish Cream

Makes 4 to 6 servings

Time: 10 minutes

Swedish cream, a mixture of sour and fresh cream, is akin to Crème Fraîche (page 671), but quicker to make. It's a wonderful and simple garnish for fruit.

    1 cup heavy cream
    1/2 cup sour cream
    Sugar or honey to taste
    1 tablespoon Grand Marnier, Amaretto, or other
       liqueur (optional)
    1 quart strawberries, washed, hulled, and left whole

1 Whip the sweet cream until it holds soft peaks, then fold it into the sour cream; add sugar to taste and liqueur if you like.

2 Place the berries in four to six bowls or stemmed glasses and top with the cream.

Strawberries with Balsamic Vinegar

Makes 4 to 6 servings

Time: 10 minutes

In the area in which *aceto balsamico* originated, drizzling the real stuff over berries is common. A tiny sprinkling of black pepper is quite nice here, too.

1 quart strawberries, washed, hulled, and sliced

1/4 cup sugar, or more to taste

1 tablespoon high-quality balsamic vinegar, or more
   to taste

About 1/8] teaspoon freshly ground black pepper

1 Toss the strawberries with the 1/4 cup sugar and let sit for 10 minutes.

2 Sprinkle with the vinegar; taste and add more sugar or vinegar if necessary. Sprinkle with the pepper and serve.

Tangerine

What we call tangerines are called mandarins elsewhere in the world; all that matters is that they're loose-skinned oranges. The best is the clementine, the small, flattened, seedless fruit that is easier to peel, has less pith, and is sweeter than all other tangerines. It is a relative newcomer to our markets, but one that has quickly put all other tangerines in second place. Perhaps even more than the banana and the apple, the clementine is the ideal snack fruit.

Tangerine juice is also delicious, and makes a wonderful sorbet. But the delicate flavor of tangerines never survives cooking, so there are few cooked recipes for them worth considering.

Buying and storing   The thin skin should actually be a little loose; obviously, there should be no bruises or unusually soft spots. Store at room temperature for a few days, or refrigerated for longer than that. Eat at room temperature.

Preparing   To zest a tangerine, see Lemon.

Other recipes in which you can use tangerines:
Ambrosia, page 638
Winter Fruit Compote, page 651

Watermelon

A hot-weather melon that is more popular in the United States than most, if not all, other places. Some varieties are better than others, and certainly the new seedless types are welcome. And, unlike many new fruit hybrids, they're no less flavorful than their parents. Perhaps that's because watermelon doesn't have much flavor to begin with; it's a simple, very wet taste, refreshing when the watermelon is cold and the weather is hot, and nice to eat when you are so stuffed that you can't possible consider anything else. Uncookable, but not bad when made into Granita (page 670; it needs no added water). The rinds are traditionally pickled. Finally, try watermelon combined with salty cheese, such as goat cheese or feta; it makes a nice salad.

Buying and storing   Do you really need a thirty-pound watermelon? Okay, then buy it. But plan on serving it at room temperature, because you probably can't fit it in your refrigerator. Consider slices or chunks, refrigerate, and eat within a few days; watermelon keeps pretty well, even after it has been cut open.

Mixed Fruit Recipes

Many fruits, fresh or dried, can be combined in a fruit salad, soup, compote, and so on. It isn't as if it usually doesn't matter at all what combinations of fruits you use, but it doesn't matter much. Most seasonal fruits go pretty well together, and some fruit, such as bananas or berries, fit in everywhere. Apples, less than perfectly ripe pears, and citrus should be used sparingly, or at least carefully, because their textures are tough and tend to overwhelm those of more delicate fruits.

About dried fruit   Apricots, pears, apples, plums (prunes), grapes (raisins), peaches, and more, all can be and are dried. Drying, when done well, removes the water and leaves both intense flavor and sugar behind. The result is an ultra-sweet fruit that makes a great snack. It can also be used as an ingredient in many breads and cakes, and in granola. Or it can be macerated or stewed, after which it can be eaten on its own or combined with fresh fruit. The best dried fruit is bought in bulk, rather than plastic packages. It's worth going to a natural foods store and looking for high-quality, even organic, dried fruit; the flavor is usually superior.

Summer Fruit Compote

Makes 4 to 6 servings

Time: 20 minutes

A quick fruit compote that is a delicious way to make a variety of fruit into something grand.

1/2 cup sugar, plus more if needed

1/2 cup water

1/4 cup minced fresh mint leaves

About 1 1/2 pounds mixed ripe fruit: berries, peeled and pitted peaches, peeled bananas, pitted plums or cherries, etc.

Pinch salt

1 teaspoon vanilla extract

A few tablespoons freshly squeezed lemon juice, plus more if needed

① Mix the sugar, water, and mint in a small saucepan and turn the heat to medium. Bring to a boil, stir to dissolve the sugar, and cool. Strain and set aside.

② Puree about half the fruit; cut the rest into bite-sized pieces or slices if necessary; mix the puree with the remaining fruit. Add the salt, vanilla, sugar syrup,

and a few tablespoons of lemon juice. Taste and add more lemon juice or sugar as needed. Serve immediately or refrigerate for a couple of hours before serving.

Fruit Mousse with Gelatin

Makes 8 to 10 servings

Time: About 30 minutes, plus time to chill

The gelatin is not absolutely essential here, so leave it out if you're a vegetarian. But it gives this creamy mixture a nice, stiff body.

2 cups any soft fruit, such as berries, peaches, mangoes, papayas, or cherries, measured after pitting, peeling, etc.

1/3 cup sugar, or to taste

1 lemon, halved

1 (3- to 4-inch) cinnamon stick

1/3 cup water, plus 1/4 cup, plus a little more if needed

1 envelope unflavored gelatin

2 cups whipping or heavy cream, preferably not ultra-pasteurized

1/3 cup confectioners' sugar

1 tablespoon cassis or orange-flavored liqueur (optional)

① Place the fruit, sugar, lemon, cinnamon stick, and 1/3 cup water in a medium saucepan over medium-low heat. Bring to a gentle boil and simmer about 10 minutes, until the mixture is mostly liquid and the fruit is soft. Put through a medium-fine strainer, pushing to extract as much juice as possible. There should be about 2 cups; add a bit more water if necessary. Cool the liquid (if you are in a hurry, put it in a container, and place the container in a bath of ice water, then stir). Taste and add a little more sugar if necessary.

2 Put the ¼ cup of water in a small saucepan and sprinkle the gelatin onto it; let stand until the gelatin softens, about 5 minutes. Meanwhile, whip the cream; when it is almost stiff, add the confectioners' sugar and finish whipping. Cook the gelatin mixture over low heat, stirring, until the gelatin dissolves, about 5 minutes; add it to the fruit juice, stirring constantly. Carefully fold together the fruit juice, cassis or liqueur, and whipped cream, then pile the mixture into individual serving dishes. Chill until set, about 2 hours.

Macerated Dried Fruits with Cinnamon

Makes 6 to 8 servings

Time: 3 to 24 hours, depending on the fruit

This is a great treat in the dead of winter, when you're hungry for a variety of good fruit. Serve with yogurt or fresh or sour cream if you like.

2 pounds assorted dried fruit: apricots, pears, peaches, prunes, raisins, etc.
½ pound blanched almonds, halved or slivered (optional)
2 cups orange juice, preferably freshly squeezed, or water
1 teaspoon ground cinnamon

1 Mix all ingredients together; add enough water to cover the fruit by an inch or two. If your house is cool, simply cover and put aside; if it is warm, refrigerate.

2 Stir every few hours and serve when fruit is tender. Or, when fruit is tender, drain it, cover, and refrigerate.

Stewed Dried Fruit: Place ingredients in saucepan with enough water to cover. Turn the heat to medium-high and, when the water boils, turn it to low. Cook, adding additional water if necessary, until the fruit is tender, 20 to 30 minutes. Taste the syrup and add a little sugar if needed. Flavor with cinnamon, freshly squeezed lemon juice, rose water, or orange blossom water.

Grilled Fruit Skewers with Ginger Syrup

Makes 6 servings

Time: 20 to 30 minutes

This dessert is perfect for a summer meal of grilled food; make sure your grill is perfectly clean. With thanks to Johnny Earles.

1 cup sugar
1 cup water
¼ cup peeled and thinly sliced fresh ginger
2 not overly ripe bananas
2 apples, pears, carambolas, or other fairly firm fruit
1 small pineapple
1 ripe but not-too-soft papaya

1 Combine the first three ingredients in a saucepan over medium heat. Bring to a boil and simmer for 3 minutes. Remove from heat, cool to room temperature, and strain. (Refrigerate if you're not using this right away; it'll keep for at least a week.)

2 Do not peel the bananas; cut them into 2-inch-long chunks and make a small slit in the peel to facilitate peeling at the table. Cut the apples, pears, or carambolas into ¾-inch-thick slices. Peel and core the pineapple (see page 644); cut it into 2-inch chunks. Peel the papaya, cut it in half, discard the seeds, and cut it into 2-inch chunks.

3 Put the fruit on 6 skewers and brush it lightly with the ginger syrup. Grill over fairly high heat until lightly browned, about 2 minutes per side. Brush again with the ginger syrup and serve warm or at room temperature.

Winter Fruit Compote

Makes 6 to 8 servings

Time: About 30 minutes

The ideal low-fat dessert when you don't want to cook but have some fruit in the house. The only requirement is patience: There's a lot of peeling and cutting here. This is a somewhat arbitrary combination, but it will get you started; substitute freely, and serve with yogurt or sour cream if you like.

1 cup seedless grapes, cut in half, or 1/2 cup raisins
1/2 cup orange juice, preferably freshly squeezed, or pineapple juice
1 grapefruit
2 oranges
2 tangerines or clementines
2 bananas
1 apple
1 pear
2 tablespoons freshly squeezed lemon juice, or to taste
Confectioners' or superfine sugar (optional)

1 If you're using raisins, soak them in the orange juice while you prepare the other fruit. Peel the citrus fruits, removing as much of the white pith as possible, and cut into chunks. Peel and cut up the bananas. Peel, core, and cut up the apple and pear.

2 Combine all the fruits with the orange and lemon juice; taste and add sugar if necessary. Serve, or refrigerate, covered, for several hours.

Fruit Fritters

Makes 8 servings

Time: 30 minutes

In fritters, the fruit doesn't cook much. By the time the batter is crisp, the fruit is indeed hot, but it will not soften if it was hard to begin with, so make sure the fruit is ripe. You can use any frying batter and any fruit you like to make fritters. Bananas are my favorite, but strawberries, peaches, apricots, apples, and pears are all fine. Even dried fruit works; before cooking, soak it in flavorful liquid, such as a mixture of port and cinnamon, to reconstitute.

Vegetable oil for deep-frying
1 cup all-purpose flour
Pinch salt
1/2 teaspoon baking powder
1 tablespoon sugar
1 cup milk
2 eggs, separated
About 24 pieces fruit, such as whole strawberries or banana chunks
Confectioners' sugar for dusting
Freshly squeezed lemon juice to taste

1 Put enough oil to come to a depth of at least 3 inches in a large, deep saucepan. The broader the saucepan, the more of these you can cook at once, but the more oil you will use. Turn the heat to medium-high; you want the temperature to be at about 375°F when you start cooking.

2 Combine the flour, salt, baking powder, and sugar in a bowl and stir to combine. Mix together the milk and egg yolks. Beat the egg whites until they hold soft peaks; the peaks should droop a bit when you remove the beaters.

3 Stir the milk-yolk mixture into the dry ingredients, then gently but thoroughly fold in the whites.

Dip the fruit pieces into the batter, then fry them until the coating turns golden brown. Drain briefly on paper towels or paper bags, dust with confectioners' sugar, and sprinkle with lemon juice. Serve immediately.

The Basics of Jam

Any fruit can be cooked with sugar to make jam. And, if you don't care about whether jam gels—if you use it mostly to sweeten yogurt, for example, or for sauces—the best jam involves nothing more than cooking fruit with sugar to taste, adding a little lemon juice to balance the flavors, and refrigerating or freezing. This is the best-tasting product, and the one that most closely resembles the flavor of the fruit that jam-making attempts to preserve. If you have a freezer with room in it, I suggest you try Low-Sugar Jam, on the next page, or the variation, in which the fruit is gelled with apple.

But if you like the idea of preserving your fruit in jars, and you want to have fruit jam that is reliably thick and gooey, you need to add more sugar. Sugar not only acts as a thickener, it acts as an antibacterial agent, which allows you to pour the preserves into sterilized jars (easily done), cap them, and store them without refrigeration for long periods. None of the recipes here call for liquid pectin, but if you want to make absolutely certain that your jams gel firmly, add 1 teaspoon of liquid pectin (such as Certo) per cup of fruit.

You can determine in advance whether your fruit will gel: When it has cooked down to a mush, place 1 teaspoonful on a cold plate (freeze the plate for 10 minutes first, or dip it in ice water; dry it before proceeding). Place the plate in the refrigerator, and look at it in 2 minutes; if the jam has gelled, you're all set. If it hasn't, cook a little longer, adding a little liquid pectin if you like. Or use an instant-read thermometer: At 224°F, all jam will gel.

Traditional Jam

Makes about 3 pints

Time: About 40 minutes

Sterilizing jars for jam is not a big deal, but there are some rules:

- Clean jars before sterilizing.
- Place jars in boiling water to cover by at least 2 inches for at least 10 minutes to sterilize.
- Dip all utensils in boiling water before using them to handle jars.
- Replace lids each year (rings to hold the lids on may be reused).
- Do not place hot jars on cold surfaces.
- Make sure jars are nearly full before sealing, but leave $1/4$ inch between the top of the jar and the top of the jam.
- Cool to room temperature before refrigerating or storing.

Refrigeration, while theoretically not necessary, is still a good idea for homemade jam; or store jars in a pantry or garage that remains cool but does not freeze. If any jam has mold on it when you open the jar, you must (regretfully) discard it without a second thought.

6 cups berries or pitted, peeled, and roughly
   chopped stone fruit, such as peaches, plums, or
   nectarines
3 to 4 cups sugar
1 to 4 tablespoons freshly squeezed lemon juice
3 to 6 teaspoons liquid pectin (optional)

1 Place all the fruit in a large saucepan and crush lightly with a fork or potato masher. Add 3 cups of sugar and 1 tablespoon lemon juice. Turn the heat to medium-high.

2 Cook, stirring almost constantly, until the sugar dissolves and the mixture liquefies. Taste and add more lemon juice if necessary.

3 Turn the heat to low and cook, stirring occasionally, until the fruit has broken down and the mixture is thick, about 30 minutes. Test for gelling (see The Basics of Jam, above); return to the heat and add more sugar or liquid pectin if necessary.

4 While the jam is cooking, prepare the jars as detailed above. When the jam is done, spoon it into the hot jars and seal.

Low-Sugar Jam

Makes about 3 pints

Time: About 30 minutes

This fresh-tasting jam may or may not gel, depending on the fruit you use, but it is definitely not safe for room-temperature storage. Freeze cooled jam for up to 1 year in tightly sealed containers or resealable plastic bags. Or refrigerate and use within a couple of weeks. For thicker jam, see the variation.

> 6 cups berries or pitted, peeled, and roughly chopped stone fruit, such as peaches, plums, or nectarines
> $1^1/_2$ to 2 cups sugar, more or less
> 2 teaspoons freshly squeezed lemon juice, or to taste

1 Place all the fruit in a large saucepan and crush lightly with a fork or potato masher. Add $1^1/_2$ cups of sugar and the lemon juice. Turn the heat to medium-high.

2 Cook, stirring almost constantly, until the sugar dissolves and the mixture liquefies. Taste and add more sugar if necessary; you may want 2 cups or more, total.

3 Turn the heat to low and cook, stirring occasionally, until the fruit has broken down and the mixture is thick, 15 to 30 minutes. Taste and add more sugar or lemon juice if necessary, then cool and refrigerate (use within a few days) or freeze.

Low-Sugar Jam with Apple: The addition of apple and a little more sugar guarantees jam that gels without noticeably affecting its fresh flavor. This jam should also be stored in the freezer or refrigerated and used within a week or two. Use 4 cups berries or stone fruit and 2 cups peeled, cored, and minced apple. Use full 2 cups sugar and proceed as above, cooking until the apple virtually dissolves, about 30 minutes. Test for gelling (see The Basics of Jam, above) and return to the heat if necessary.

Desserts

Many home cooks limit themselves to flour-based desserts, like cakes, cookies, pies, and tarts. But there is, of course, a wonderful universe of desserts that contain little or no flour at all, mostly soft, smooth combinations of dairy or fruit and flavorings—puddings, ice creams, sorbets, soufflés, and so on. Also covered in this chapter are dessert sauces, which can enhance many simple desserts, and some *very* simple candies—which need no further explanation, and no special talents.

For the most part, all of these desserts are easily made, and you'll almost always have the ingredients to make them on hand. The sole exception to that is probably cream, a substance once common in American homes but now often banished for health reasons. There *are* plenty of desserts here that do not contain cream; but if you want rich, luxurious, traditional American desserts, you will be cooking with cream. There are many ways to get around that; quite often, a simple substitution of milk will do the trick, with some sacrifice in flavor and, especially, texture. But my feeling is this: there are desserts that are decent without cream and dreamy with—make them with, or turn to one of the fine desserts that isn't based on cream at all.

For The Basics of Butter, see pages 681–682; for The Basics of Eggs, see page 731. For more information on cream, see page 684.

The Basics of Custards and Puddings

Gently cooked eggs not only thicken other ingredients, they gain a silken texture unmatched by anything else.

And there's no trick to it, except to remember that overcooked eggs are essentially scrambled eggs. You must cook eggs at relatively low heat, and just until they thicken, in order to make them smooth and uniform. When you're cooking on top of the stove—as you will with most soft custards—this isn't so much of a problem: Don't "shock" the eggs by plunging them into boiling hot liquids, and don't cook them past the point where they thicken, and they will not curdle.

Removing custards and other egg-thickened desserts from the oven is trickier: By the time a custard appears to be set, it's almost always overcooked. You must make a leap of faith and remove it from the oven while the center is still wobbly. When you get the timing down, you'll be making brilliant custards.

Although it is not always essential, it also helps to cook your custards in a water bath: Just put the baking dish or individual custard cups in a larger baking pan (a roasting pan often works well) and pour hot water at least halfway up the height of the custard. By moderating the temperature around the custard, the water bath (also called a *bain-marie*) makes for more even cooking.

Old-Fashioned Baked Custard
Pots de Crème
Makes 4 to 6 servings

Time: About 45 minutes

This all-American custard is easy to make and incredibly filling. You will be sneaking leftovers at midnight and breakfast, especially if you make it with good, farm-fresh eggs and cream. Substitute one teaspoon vanilla extract for the cinnamon and nutmeg if you like.

2 cups heavy cream, light cream, or milk, or a mixture
1/2 teaspoon ground cinnamon
1/2 teaspoon freshly grated nutmeg
2 eggs, plus 2 yolks
Pinch salt
1/2 cup sugar (more if you like things very sweet)

1 Place the cream in a small saucepan with the cinnamon and half the nutmeg and turn the heat to medium. Cook just until it begins to steam.

2 Use a whisk or electric mixer to beat the eggs and yolks with the salt and sugar until pale yellow and fairly thick. Preheat the oven to 300°F and set a kettle of water to boil.

3 Add the cream gradually to the egg mixture, stirring constantly. Pour the mixture into a large bowl or six 4- to 6-ounce custard cups and top with the remaining nutmeg. Place the bowl or cups in a baking pan and pour hot water in, to within about 1 inch of the top of the bowl or cups. Bake until the mixture is not quite set—it should wobble just a little in the middle—about 30 minutes for the cups, longer if you're baking in a bowl. Use your judgment; cream sets up faster than milk. Serve warm, at room temperature, or cold, within a day.

Flan (Crème Caramel): Here, a layer of caramel is placed on the bottom of the custard before baking. Place 1 cup sugar and 1/4 cup water in a small, non-aluminum saucepan. Turn heat to low and cook, stirring occasionally, until the sugar liquefies, turns clear, then golden brown, about 15 minutes. Remove from the heat and immediately pour the caramel into the bottom of a large bowl or six custard cups. Make the custard exactly as above, pouring it into the prepared bowl or cups and baking as above. Cool on a rack, then chill or serve. To remove, dip the bowl or cups in boiling water for about 15 seconds, then invert onto a plate or plates.

Although most of the desserts in this chapter are quick to make, some have a more festive feel than others. A list of those most people will find impressive:

Chocolate Custard: A richer custard than Chocolate Pudding (page 659), but no more difficult to make. Substitute 1 teaspoon vanilla for the cinnamon and nutmeg. Heat 1 ounce chopped bittersweet chocolate in a double boiler or in a very small saucepan over very low heat, stirring almost constantly, until it melts; cool slightly. Proceed as above, stirring the chocolate into the eggs before the cream. You can use 2 ounces of chocolate for an even more intense flavor.

Lemon Custard: You need more eggs to compensate for the added liquid, and more sugar to compensate for the tartness here; as a result, this will serve 6 easily. Step 1 remains the same. In Step 2, increase the yolks to 4, the whole eggs to 3, and the sugar to $3/4$ cup. Add $1/2$ cup strained lemon juice and 1 tablespoon very finely minced lemon zest to the mixture. Proceed as above.

Six Simple Ideas for Baked Custards

1. Add minced crystallized ginger, a tablespoon or two, just before baking.
2. Add dried shredded coconut, sweetened or unsweetened, one-quarter cup or more, just before baking.
3. Add minced or grated orange zest, about one teaspoon, just before baking.
4. Add raspberries or other fruit, placed on the bottom underneath the custard, a tablespoon or two per serving.
5. Substitute one teaspoon vanilla extract for the cinnamon and nutmeg, or infuse one three-inch piece of vanilla bean with the cream or milk (see Crème Brûlée, below for details).
6. Infuse warm cream or milk with one-half cup coarsely ground coffee; let stand ten minutes and strain before proceeding.

Crème Brûlée

Makes 4 to 6 servings

Time: Several hours, largely unattended

"Burnt cream," a rich custard topped with a hard sugar crust. It's rare to succeed in making that crust on the first try, so practice once or twice before serving it to people you want to impress. Most home cooks are forced to resort to the broiler for the final step, but every chef knows that the easy way is to use a propane torch; if you have one in the garage or basement, try it. Make the custard in one bowl until you're good at it, so you don't have to repeat the caramelization process four or six times.

Crème brûlée is a subtly flavored dessert, so I think it's worth infusing a vanilla bean for it; but you can use extract, of course.

1 vanilla bean or 1 teaspoon vanilla extract

2¹/₂ cups heavy cream, light cream, or milk, or a mixture

6 egg yolks

1 cup sugar

1 Preheat the oven to 300°F. If you're using a vanilla bean, split it in half, lengthwise, and scrape the seeds into the cream. Put the pod in the cream, too.

2 Heat the cream in a small saucepan with the vanilla until steam rises. Cover the pan, turn off the heat, and let steep for 10 to 15 minutes. If you're using vanilla extract, just heat the cream and proceed.

3 Use a whisk or electric mixer to beat the yolks and ¹/₂ cup sugar together until pale yellow and fairly thick. Remove the vanilla bean from the cream and slowly add the cream to the yolks, stirring all the while. If you're using vanilla extract, add it now.

4 Pour the custard into a 1-quart ovenproof glass, porcelain, pottery, or enameled baking dish or into four individual 4- to 6-ounce cups or ramekins. Set the dish or the cups in a baking pan and pour hot water in, to within about 1 inch of the top of the dish or cups. Bake until the mixture just sets—it should wobble a little in the middle—about 25 to 30 minutes for the cups, longer if you're baking in a dish. Use your judgment; cream sets up faster than milk.

5 Remove the custard from the oven, cool, then cover with plastic wrap and chill. (The recipe can be prepared a day or two in advance up to this point; make sure it is wrapped well so it does not pick up other flavors in the refrigerator.) Just before you're ready to serve, place a rack as close to the broiler as the height of your dish or cups will allow and turn on the broiler. Sprinkle the top of the custard evenly with the remaining ¹/₂ cup sugar. Broil, watching carefully and turning the dish or cups as necessary; when the sugar bubbles and browns, it is ready. Let sit for a few minutes before serving. To brown the top with a propane torch, simply heat it with the flame until the sugar bubbles and browns; it's foolproof, easy, and fast.

Vanilla Pudding
Makes 4 to 6 servings

Time: About 20 minutes, plus time to chill

This is a soft, stove-top pudding, not much more difficult to produce than the packaged "instant" variety.

¹/₂ cup sugar

3 tablespoons cornstarch

Pinch salt

3 eggs

2¹/₂ cups half-and-half or whole milk or 2¹/₄ cups low-fat milk mixed with ¹/₄ cup cream

2 tablespoons unsalted butter, softened

1 vanilla bean or 1 teaspoon vanilla extract

1 In a small saucepan, combine the sugar with the cornstarch and salt. Mix together the eggs and half-and-half.

2 If you're using a vanilla bean, split it and scrape out the seeds; stir them into the half-and-half mixture (reserve the bean itself to make vanilla sugar; see The Basics of Sugar, page 682).

3 Stir the egg and half-and-half mixture into the sugar-cornstarch mixture over medium heat; whisk to eliminate lumps, then stir almost constantly until the mixture thickens, about 10 minutes. Stir in the butter and vanilla extract, if you're using it.

4 Pour the pudding into one large or four to six small bowls. Place plastic wrap directly on top of the pudding to prevent the formation of a "skin," or do not cover if you like skin. Refrigerate until chilled, and serve within a day, with whipped cream if you like (page 671).

Blancmange: Without eggs or butter, this is a relatively low-fat pudding. Omit the eggs; increase the cornstarch to 5 tablespoons. Heat the half-and-half and add it very gradually to the cornstarch mixture, stirring constantly. After the mixture thickens, reduce the heat to very low and continue to cook, stirring, for at least 10 minutes more. Finish as above, omitting the butter if you like.

Chocolate Pudding: This can be made with either the Vanilla Pudding recipe or the Blancmange variation. Heat 2 ounces chopped unsweetened chocolate in a double boiler or in a very small saucepan over very low heat, stirring almost constantly, until it melts. Stir into the thickened cornstarch mixture.

Butterscotch Pudding: This also can be made with the Vanilla Pudding recipe or Blancmange variation. Just substitute brown sugar for the white sugar.

Tembleque
Coconut Blancmange
Makes 8 servings

Time: About 40 minutes, plus time to chill

This foolproof Puerto Rican pudding, made with extra-rich coconut milk, is guaranteed to drive coconut-lovers wild. If you prefer, make the pudding using half milk and half canned coconut milk.

4 cups milk or half-and-half, or a little more
2 cups dried unsweetened grated coconut,
   plus 2 tablespoons
$1/3$ cup cornstarch
Dash salt
$1/2$ cup sugar
$1/2$ teaspoon ground cinnamon or 1 tablespoon
   orange blossom water

1 Place $3^1/2$ cups of the milk in saucepan and turn the heat to medium; cook, stirring occasionally, until small bubbles appear on the sides. Combine in a bowl with the 2 cups of coconut and stir to blend; cover

and let rest for 20 minutes. Place in a blender (in batches if necessary) and whiz for 10 or 20 seconds. Put through a strainer, pressing to extract as much liquid as possible. Measure the resulting liquid, then add enough milk to make a total of $3^1/2$ cups.

2 Whisk the cornstarch with $1/2$ cup milk. Place the coconut milk in a heavy medium saucepan over medium-low heat and gradually whisk the cornstarch mixture into it. Stir in the salt and sugar. Raise the heat to medium-high and cook, stirring constantly, until the mixture thickens; lower the heat and continue to cook, still stirring, for another 5 minutes. Stir in the cinnamon or orange water and turn off the heat.

3 Pour into eight rinsed and not dried custard cups or into a large bowl or soufflé dish that has been rinsed and not dried. Cool, then chill. (The recipe can be prepared a day or two in advance up to this point; cool, wrap well, and refrigerate.) Just before serving, toast the remaining 2 tablespoons of coconut in a small dry skillet over medium heat, shaking and stirring until it browns; garnish the tembleque with this toasted coconut and serve.

Panna Cotta
Makes 6 servings

Time: About 30 minutes, plus time to chill

An Italian eggless custard, thickened with gelatin and flavored with nothing but vanilla.

1 cup milk
1 ($1/4$ ounce) package unflavored gelatin
1 vanilla bean
2 cups heavy cream
$1/2$ cup sugar
An assortment of berries, or raspberry sauce
   (see Raspberry, Strawberry, or Other Fruit Sauce,
   page 672) (optional)

1 Place $^1/_2$ cup of the milk in a medium saucepan and sprinkle the gelatin over it; let sit for 5 minutes. Turn the heat to low and cook, stirring, until the gelatin dissolves completely.

2 Cut the vanilla bean in half, lengthwise. Scrape out seeds; add both seeds and pod to the pot, along with the remaining milk, cream, and sugar. Cook over medium heat, stirring, until steam arises from the pot. Turn off the heat, cover, and let steep for 15 to 30 minutes.

3 Remove the vanilla pod and pour the mixture into six custard cups. Chill until set. Serve in the cups, or dip the cups in hot water for about 10 seconds each, then invert onto plates. Serve, the same day you make it, with berries or sauce if you like.

Indian Pudding

Makes about 8 servings

Time: At least 3 hours, largely unattended

Indian pudding—a favorite of the early English colonists—can be served warm, in which case it is very soft, or chilled, at which point it can be sliced. Either way, it's best served with heavy or ice cream.

4 cups milk

$^1/_2$ cup molasses

$^1/_4$ cup sugar

$^1/_2$ cup cornmeal

1 teaspoon ground cinnamon

$^1/_2$ teaspoon ground ginger

$^1/_4$ teaspoon ground nutmeg

$^1/_4$ teaspoon ground allspice

$^1/_2$ teaspoon salt

2 tablespoons unsalted butter, plus some for greasing the dish

1 Place $3^1/_2$ cups of the milk in a medium saucepan and turn the heat to medium. Stir in the

molasses and sugar and, when they are incorporated, turn the heat to low. Preheat the oven to 300°F.

2 Slowly sprinkle the cornmeal over the warm milk mixture, stirring or whisking all the while; break up any lumps that form. When the mixture thickens— this will take 10 minutes or more—stir in all the remaining ingredients, except the remaining milk, and turn off the heat.

3 Grease an 8- or 9-inch square baking dish or similar-sized gratin dish and turn the warm mixture into it; top with the remaining $^1/_2$ cup milk; do not stir. Bake $2^1/_2$ to 3 hours, or until the pudding is set. Serve warm, cold, or at room temperature; wrapped well and refrigerated, this keeps for several days.

Chocolate Mousse

Makes 6 servings

Time: 20 minutes, plus time to chill

Once thought of as the most elegant of desserts, this ultra-rich chocolate pudding is still a real winner. It's blazing quick to make—I've prepared it after dinner and still served it before my guests left—which I do early. Once the chocolate is melted, the cooking is over; the mousse just sits until it sets up.

You can spike chocolate mousse with rum, coffee, or other flavorings, but I like it simple—it's the intensity of chocolate that makes it special.

Note that this recipe contains a raw egg; please see The Basics of Eggs, page 731.

2 tablespoons unsalted butter

4 ounces bittersweet or semisweet chocolate, chopped

3 eggs, separated

$^1/_4$ cup sugar

$^1/_2$ cup heavy cream

$^1/_2$ teaspoon vanilla extract

1 Use a double boiler or a small saucepan over low heat to melt the butter and chocolate together. Just before the chocolate finishes melting, remove it from the stove and beat with a wooden spoon until smooth.

2 Transfer the chocolate mixture to a bowl and beat in the egg yolks with a whisk. Refrigerate.

3 Beat the egg whites with half the sugar until they hold stiff peaks but are not dry. Set aside. Beat the cream with the remaining sugar and vanilla until it holds soft peaks.

4 Stir a couple of spoonfuls of the whites into the chocolate mixture to lighten it a bit, then fold in the remaining whites thoroughly but gently. Fold in the cream and refrigerate until chilled. If you are in a hurry, divide the mousse among six cups; it will chill much faster. Serve within a day or two of making.

Lemon Mousse

Makes at least 6 servings

Time: About 30 minutes, plus time to chill

A refreshing cold mousse that contains cream and eggs but is stabilized by gelatin, which makes it virtually foolproof. Use any citrus you like in place of the lemon, adjusting the amount of sugar accordingly. To make a "mousse" with other fruit, such as berries, see Raspberry Fool, page 628.

Note that this recipe contains a raw egg; please see The Basics of Eggs, page 731.

1 (¼ ounce) package unflavored gelatin
½ cup freshly squeezed lemon juice
4 eggs
1 tablespoon grated or minced lemon zest
½ cup sugar
1 cup heavy cream
Whipped cream (page 671), mint or lemon verbena
    leaves, berries, or toasted almonds for garnish

1 In a small saucepan, sprinkle the gelatin over the lemon juice and let sit while you proceed to Step 2.

2 Beat the eggs, lemon zest, and sugar with a whisk or electric mixer until lemon-colored and slightly thickened.

3 Warm the gelatin mixture over low heat, stirring occasionally, until the gelatin dissolves, just a minute or two. Cool for 1 minute, then stir into the egg mixture.

4 Working quickly (you don't want the gelatin to set up prematurely), whip the cream until it holds soft peaks, then stir thoroughly into the egg mixture.

5 Refrigerate, stirring occasionally for the first hour or two, until well chilled. Garnish and serve the same day.

Tapioca Pudding

Makes 4 servings

Time: About 20 minutes, plus time to chill

Tapioca is somewhere between rice and cornstarch when it comes to pudding—it acts as a neutral thickener, like cornstarch, but it gives a distinctive texture, like rice. Some people don't like the texture, but others find it heavenly.

⅓ cup quick-cooking tapioca
½ cup sugar
Pinch salt
2 cups milk
2 eggs, separated
1½ teaspoons vanilla extract

1 Combine the tapioca, sugar, salt, and milk in a small saucepan and turn the heat to medium. Cook, stirring, until the tapioca becomes transparent, about 5 minutes. Remove from the heat, cool for a minute or two, then beat in the egg yolks. Cool the mixture for a few more minutes before proceeding.

2 Beat the egg whites until they hold soft peaks; fold them gently into the yolk mixture along with the vanilla. Spoon into individual serving cups and serve, or chill before serving; this keeps well for up to 2 days. Serve with whipped cream (page 671) if you like.

Coconut-Tapioca Pudding: Substitute Fresh Coconut Milk (page 291), or use canned coconut milk, for all or part of the milk.

Bread Pudding

Makes 6 servings

Time: About 1 hour, largely unattended

A dessert that, deservedly, has made a resurgence in the nineties. There are few ways to use leftover bread that equal this.

    3 cups milk
    4 tablespoons (1/2 stick) unsalted butter, plus some
       for greasing the pan
    1 1/2 teaspoons ground cinnamon
    1/2 cup sugar plus 1 tablespoon
    Pinch salt
    8 slices white bread, crusts removed if they are
       very thick
    3 eggs

1 Preheat the oven to 350°F. Over low heat in a small saucepan, warm the milk, butter, 1 teaspoon cinnamon, 1/2 cup sugar, and salt, just until the butter melts. Meanwhile, butter a 1 1/2-quart or 8-inch square baking dish (glass is nice), and cut or tear the bread into bite-sized pieces; they need not be too small.

2 Place the bread in the baking dish and pour the hot milk over it. Let it sit for a few minutes, occasionally submerging any pieces of bread that rise to the top. Beat the eggs briefly and stir them into the bread mixture. Mix together the remaining sugar and cinnamon and sprinkle over the top. Set the baking dish in a larger baking pan and pour hot water in, to within about an inch of the top of the dish.

3 Bake 45 minutes to 1 hour, or until a thin-bladed knife inserted in the center comes out clean, or nearly so; the center should be just a little wobbly. Run under the broiler for about 30 seconds if you like, to brown the top a bit. Serve warm or cold, with or without sweetened whipped cream (page 671). This keeps well for 2 days or more, covered and refrigerated.

Chocolate Bread Pudding: In Step 1, melt 2 ounces chopped bittersweet chocolate with the butter and milk. Proceed as above.

Apple-Raisin Bread Pudding: Step 1 remains the same. In Step 2, add 1 cup peeled, grated, and drained apples and 1/4 cup or more raisins to the mixture along with the eggs. Proceed as above.

Rice Pudding

Makes 8 servings

Time: 40 minutes

This simple, no-egg rice pudding is sweet and easy.

    2 cups water
    1 cup long- or short-grain rice
    Dash salt
    2 cups milk
    3/4 cup sugar, or more to taste
    1 teaspoon ground cinnamon or cardamom

1 Bring the water to a boil in a medium saucepan; stir in the rice and the salt. Cover and cook over low heat until almost all the water is absorbed, about 20 minutes.

2 Uncover, pour in the milk and cook, stirring frequently, until about half the milk is absorbed. Stir in the sugar and spices and continue to cook until the rice is very soft and the milk absorbed. About halfway through cooking, taste and add more sugar if necessary.

3 Spoon into custard cups and serve warm or cold, garnished with whipped cream (page 671) if you like. This keeps well for 2 days or more, covered and refrigerated.

Six Simple Ideas for Rice Pudding

1. Add one-quarter cup or more raisins, or snipped dates, figs, or other dried fruit about halfway through the cooking.
2. Use Fresh Coconut Milk (page 291), or canned coconut milk, in place of some or all of the milk.
3. Add one teaspoon of vanilla extract or orange blossom or rose water at the end of cooking.
4. Finish as you would Crème Brûlée, page 657, with a crust of burnt sugar.
5. Add one teaspoon minced lemon or orange zest in place of spices.
6. Garnish with a sprinkling of toasted sliced almonds or other nuts.

Tiramisu

Makes 4 servings

Time: At least 4 hours, largely unattended

Literally "pick-me-up," tiramisu is the trendy nineties' version of the classic English trifle, from which it varies little. One version of tiramisu is made with mascarpone cheese, a thick sweet cheese that can be difficult to find. Another relies on a good custard, which is easy to put together and works just as well.

$^1/_2$ cup sugar

$1^1/_2$ tablespoons cornstarch

Pinch salt

2 cups milk

3 eggs

1 tablespoon unsalted butter

1 teaspoon vanilla extract

About 2 cups broken or torn-up leftover Sponge Cake (page 726), or any yellow cake, ladyfingers, or even biscotti

1 cup strong cold coffee, preferably espresso

Unsweetened cocoa powder as needed

1 In a small saucepan, combine the sugar with the cornstarch and salt. Mix together the milk and eggs. Stir the milk-egg mixture into the sugar-cornstarch mixture over medium heat; at first, whisk occasionally to eliminate lumps. Then stir almost constantly until the mixture boils and thickens, about 10 minutes. Stir in the butter and vanilla extract. Cool, then lay plastic wrap onto the surface of the custard and refrigerate for at least 1 hour.

2 When the custard is cool, prepare the cake (or cookies) by dividing half of it among four dessert bowls. Sprinkle with about half the espresso and dust with a little cocoa powder. Spoon half the custard over it.

3 Top with the remaining cake, then repeat the process, finishing with a dusting of cocoa powder. Chill until set, at least 1 hour (and probably longer) and serve cold. This keeps well for a day or more, covered and refrigerated.

The Basics of Ice Cream and Frozen Yogurt

The best ice cream is little more than frozen custard. It's an eggy custard, because eggs lend smoothness. Even though the best "premium" store-bought ice creams are custard-based, the simplest of homemade custard ice creams will amaze you, because they are so much better. For this reason: *despite the fact that it is stored in the freezer, ice cream is best when it's fresh.*

In fact, ice cream is at its peak when it comes straight from the machine, at which point its temperature is just below freezing; once it is stored at 0°F (the temperature of most home freezers), it is never quite as good again. To be sure, it is still wonderful stuff; but be certain to warm it slightly before serving, by letting it rest for about thirty minutes in the refrigerator or fifteen minutes on the counter.

Custard ice cream is usually called French ice cream. You can also make ice cream without eggs, or with very few eggs, and all cream "iced" cream. This is called Philadelphia-style (or sometimes, New York–style) ice cream and, because it contains fewer ingredients and requires no cooking at all, is easier to produce. It has a super-creamy mouth feel that not everyone enjoys, but you should try making it the next time you can get your hands on some really good cream, just so you can judge for yourself. Philadelphia-style ice cream makes a wonderful base for fruit-flavored ice creams.

While I am not an adherent of buying every appliance available, I do recommend that you buy an ice cream machine. The chances are you will not make ice cream regularly, but there will always be a few times a year when the idea becomes irresistible, and it's worth it to have a machine for those occasions. Like most kitchen appliances, they're fairly easy to find at tag sales, because someone is always giving up on the idea. The best are the one-quart-plus capacity machines with built-in refrigeration units; they weigh about fifty pounds, cost at least four hundred dollars, and do all the thinking for you. But the thirty-dollar hand-cranked machines, in which you prefreeze a sleeve that fits into a container with a crank, work brilliantly. Old-fashioned ice cream makers that require rock salt and plenty of ice also work well; now you're talking about a project, not a recipe.

Frozen yogurt, a relative newcomer to the dessert world, is best when it remains true to its origins—which is to say that it should be slightly sour. The frozen yogurt served in most ice cream shops is soft ice cream by another name. The recipe here will give you a fresh-but-tangy yogurt that can be flavored in the same way as ice cream.

Basic French Vanilla Ice Cream
Makes about 1 quart

Time: About 30 minutes, plus time to chill and churn

One of the two ice cream recipes from which all others are derived. You can reduce the number of yolks to four or even three if you like, and still produce quite a rich ice cream. It will not be the ultimate, however.

1 vanilla bean or 2 teaspoons vanilla extract
2 cups half-and-half or milk
$1/2$ to $3/4$ cup sugar
6 egg yolks
1 cup heavy cream, or more milk or half-and-half

1 If you're using a vanilla bean, split it in half and scrape out the seeds (reserve the bean itself for vanilla sugar; see The Basics of Sugar, page 682). Combine the seeds with the half-and-half and $1/4$ cup sugar in a small saucepan. Heat, stirring occasionally, until steam arises from the milk; remove from the heat.

2 Using a whisk or electric mixer, beat $1/4$ cup sugar with the egg yolks until light yellow and thick, 2 to 4 minutes. Beat $1/2$ cup hot half-and-half into this, then gradually stir this mixture into the saucepan with the remaining half-and-half. Cook over medium-low heat, stirring almost constantly, until the mixture

These can be made with any of the three basic recipes (Basic French Vanilla Ice Cream, Basic Philadelphia Vanilla Ice Cream, or Basic Vanilla Frozen Yogurt); omit the vanilla unless noted below.

Maple-Nut Ice Cream: Substitute $3/4$ cup maple syrup for the sugar. Stir 1 cup chopped (not ground) nuts into the ice cream before freezing. Walnuts and pecans may be used with their skins; almonds should be blanched and peeled; peanuts or pistachios should be unsalted. Nuts may be toasted lightly in a dry skillet before adding.

Chocolate Chip, M&M, Rocky Road, or other chunky ice cream: Ice cream is a thick custard that can support a great deal of solid ingredients, but don't push it. One cup of any solid ingredient, or combination of ingredients, stirred into the mixture just before freezing, gives you a fairly normal amount of chips or chunks in the ice cream. Two cups is overkill. Use your judgment.

Butterscotch Ice Cream: Use the vanilla if you like. Melt 2 tablespoons butter in a saucepan, then add $1/4$ cup sugar (in addition to the sugar called for in the basic recipe). Cook over medium-low heat, stirring almost constantly, until nicely browned. Add the cream or milk to this mixture and proceed as in the basic recipe, using a whisk if necessary to blend the mixture thoroughly.

Chocolate or Butterscotch Swirl Ice Cream: Use the vanilla and make the ice cream normally. When it is frozen, transfer it to a large, shallow bowl or baking pan. Top it with $1/3$ cup or more of Chocolate Sauce (page 672) or Butterscotch Sauce (page 672), cooled to lukewarm (or warmed slightly if chilled). Use a spoon or rubber spatula to swirl the sauce through the ice cream, then transfer to the freezer.

Coffee Ice Cream: In a small saucepan, heat 1 cup milk with $1/2$ cup coarsely ground coffee until the milk steams. Turn off the heat, then cover and let sit for 15 to 30 minutes. Strain and use the milk as part of the liquid component.

---

reaches 175 to 180°F, or is slightly thickened; do not boil. (There will be a thick coating on the back of a spoon, one that will hold the outline of your finger after you pass it through.)

③ Strain the custard into a glass or plastic bowl and stir in the cream. Taste and, if more sugar is needed, stir it in while the mixture is still hot. Add vanilla extract if you're using it. Chill to 40°F (you can hasten this process by setting the bowl in a large bowl filled with a mixture of ice and water; stir occasionally), then churn in an ice cream maker according to the manufacturer's directions. Serve immediately or freeze; use within 2 days, "warming" in the refrigerator for about 30 minutes before serving.

Basic Philadelphia Vanilla Ice Cream

Makes about 1 quart

Time: About 10 minutes, plus time to chill and churn

Since this doesn't require making a custard, it's even easier, and provides a great base for flavored ice creams. But it may require some hunting around; top-quality cream that has not been ultra-pasteurized is essential if you want this to be really great.

Philadelphia ice cream is traditionally made with no eggs at all, but the addition of just one smoothes it significantly. Note that it is raw, however, and see The Basics of Eggs, page 731.

> 1 vanilla bean or 2 teaspoons vanilla extract
> 4 cups heavy cream or heavy cream mixed with
>   light cream (or half-and-half), preferably not
>   ultra-pasteurized
> $^3/_4$ cup sugar, preferably superfine
> 1 egg (optional)
> Pinch salt

① If you're using a vanilla bean, split it in half and scrape out the seeds (reserve the bean itself for vanilla sugar; see The Basics of Sugar, page 682).

② Combine all ingredients and stir until the sugar is dissolved. Churn in an ice cream maker according to the manufacturer's directions. Serve immediately or freeze; use within 2 days, "warming" in the refrigerator for about 30 minutes before serving.

Basic Vanilla Frozen Yogurt

Makes about 1 quart

Time: About 45 minutes, plus time to chill
and churn

You can make pretty good frozen yogurt with gelatin, but it has a gummy quality. Better is this compromise, which gives you the tang of yogurt with the fine texture of custard-based ice cream. Needless to say, the better the yogurt, the better-tasting the results. Low-fat yogurt will work fairly well; non-fat yogurt will give you a thin, sour product; and full-fat yogurt is best.

> 1 vanilla bean or 2 teaspoons vanilla extract
> $1^1/_2$ cups milk or half-and-half
> $^3/_4$ cup sugar, less if you like fairly tangy frozen yogurt
> 4 egg yolks
> 2 cups plain yogurt

① If you're using a vanilla bean, split it in half and scrape out the seeds (reserve the bean itself for vanilla sugar; see The Basics of Sugar, page 682). Combine the seeds with the milk and half the sugar in a medium saucepan. Heat, stirring occasionally, until steam arises from the milk; remove from the heat.

② Using a whisk or electric mixer, beat the remaining sugar with the egg yolks until light yellow and thick, 2 to 4 minutes. Beat $^1/_2$ cup hot milk into this, then gradually stir this mixture into the saucepan with the remaining milk. Cook over medium-low heat, stirring almost constantly, until the mixture reaches 175 to 180°F, or is slightly thickened; do not boil. (There will be a thick coating on the back of a spoon, one that will hold the outline of your finger after you pass it through.)

③ Strain the custard into a glass or plastic bowl and cool to room temperature (you can hasten this process by setting the bowl in a large bowl filled with a mixture of ice and water; stir occasionally). Stir in the yogurt and the vanilla extract if you're using it.

④ Chill to 40°F (again, use a large bowl filled with a mixture of ice and water to hasten cooling if you like), then churn in an ice cream maker according to the manufacturer's directions. Serve immediately or freeze; use within 2 days, "warming" in the refrigerator for about 30 minutes before serving.

HANDLING VANILLA BEANS

(Step 1) To use a vanilla bean, split it in half the long way. (Step 2) Scrape out the seeds. Reserve the pod for vanilla sugar; see The Basics of Sugar, page 682.

Chocolate Ice Cream

Makes about 1 quart

Time: About 30 minutes, plus time to chill and churn

You can add three to six ounces of chocolate to ice cream, using all semisweet, all bittersweet, or a combination. A little unsweetened (about ten percent of the total) is also nice, if you like. Generally, you'll only need one-half cup of sugar; the vanilla is optional—you don't need it, but it won't hurt either.

2 cups half-and-half or milk
5 ounces bittersweet or semisweet chocolate, chopped (or use chocolate chips)
$^1/_2$ ounce unsweetened chocolate, chopped (optional)
$^1/_2$ cup sugar, or more to taste
6 egg yolks
1 cup heavy cream, or more milk or half-and-half
1 teaspoon vanilla extract

1 Combine the half-and-half, chocolate, and $^1/_4$ cup sugar in a medium saucepan. Heat, stirring occasionally, until steam arises from the milk and the chocolate melts; remove from the heat.

2 Using a whisk or electric mixer, beat $^1/_4$ cup sugar with the egg yolks until light yellow and thick, 2 to 4 minutes. Beat $^1/_2$ cup hot half-and-half into this, then gradually stir this mixture into the saucepan with the remaining half-and-half. Cook over medium-low heat, stirring almost constantly, until the mixture reaches 175 to 180°F, or is slightly thickened; do not boil. (There will be a thick coating on the back of a spoon, one that will hold the outline of your finger after you pass it through.)

3 Strain the custard into a glass or plastic bowl and stir in the cream. Taste and, if more sugar is needed, stir it in while the mixture is still hot. Chill to 40°F (you can hasten this process by setting the bowl in a large bowl filled with a mixture of ice and water; stir occasionally), stir in the vanilla, then churn in an ice cream maker according to the manufacturer's directions. Serve immediately or freeze; use within 2 days, "warming" in the refrigerator for about 30 minutes before serving.

Fruit or Berry Ice Cream

Makes about 1 quart

Time: About 30 minutes, plus time to chill and churn

Philadelphia-style ice cream "supports" fruit better than does French-style ice cream. To adapt to French ice cream, reduce the amount of fruit by half and stir it into the custard before freezing. Note that this recipe contains a raw egg; see The Basics of Eggs, page 731.

3 cups washed and pitted, skinned, and/or cored (if necessary) fruit or berries, or a combination, chopped, if necessary, into $^1/_2$-inch pieces
$^1/_2$ cup sugar, preferably superfine, plus more to taste
Freshly squeezed lemon juice if necessary
3 cups heavy cream, or heavy cream mixed with light cream
1 egg (optional)

1 Place the fruit—except for raspberries—in a medium skillet, sprinkle lightly with sugar, and turn the heat to medium. Cook, stirring, until the fruit is tender, from 2 or 3 minutes for strawberries to 10 minutes for apples. (For raspberries, just toss with sugar.) Taste and add more sugar or lemon juice—by the $^1/_2$ teaspoon—to balance the flavors if necessary.

2 When the fruit is perfectly delicious, mix together the cream, $^1/_2$ cup sugar, and the egg. At this point you can either combine the fruit and cream, chill to 40°F, and freeze together, or freeze the cream separately until it is very nearly frozen, then add the chilled fruit. The first method is more likely to pulverize the fruit and distribute it throughout the ice cream, leaving small or no chunks; the second will give you less well-distributed, more readily identifiable chunks of fruit. The choice is yours.

Coconut Ice Cream

Makes about 1 quart

Time: About 30 minutes, plus time to chill and churn

A basic, fairly rich ice cream recipe enhanced not only by the addition of shredded coconut but of coconut milk.

2 cups cream, milk, or half-and-half

$1/2$ cup sugar

6 egg yolks

$1/2$ cup dried unsweetened shredded coconut, toasted in a dry skillet until lightly browned if you like

1 cup canned or Fresh Coconut Milk (page 291)

1 Place the cream and $1/4$ cup sugar in a heavy medium saucepan. Heat, stirring occasionally, until steam arises from the cream.

2 Using a whisk or electric mixer, beat $1/4$ cup sugar with the egg yolks until light yellow and thick, 2 to 4 minutes. Beat $1/2$ cup hot cream into this, then gradually stir this mixture into the saucepan with the remaining cream. Cook over medium-low heat, stirring almost constantly, until the mixture reaches 175 to 180°F, or is slightly thickened; do not boil. (There will be a thick coating on the back of a spoon, one that will hold the outline of your finger after you pass it through.)

3 Stir in the coconut and coconut milk. Pour into a covered container. Chill to 40°F (you can hasten this process by setting the bowl in a large bowl filled with a mixture of ice and water; stir occasionally), then churn in an ice cream maker according to the manufacturer's directions. Serve immediately or freeze; use within 2 days, "warming" in the refrigerator for about 30 minutes before serving.

Milk Shakes, Malteds, and Frappes

Makes 1 (12-ounce) drink

Time: 3 minutes

A milk shake might be milk, shaken up, with or without flavorings—if that's how it was when you were

---

Six Simple Ideas for Ice Cream

1. Add spices, such as ground cinnamon or ginger, in place of the vanilla. Start with one teaspoon, taste before freezing, and add more if necessary.

2. Add peanut butter, about four tablespoons per batch, stirred in before freezing (the churning will distribute it evenly).

3. Replace the vanilla with almond extract, especially for nut ice creams.

4. Replace the vanilla with peppermint extract.

5. Add one-half cup or more chopped, minced, or crushed candy—peanut brittle, peppermint candy, Mounds bars, Heath bars, or crystallized ginger, for example—to the mixture before freezing. Substitute almond or peppermint extract for the vanilla if appropriate.

6. Add one-half cup or more crumbled Oreos, brownies, gingersnaps, or other cookies.

growing up. For most people, it's synonymous with a frappe: milk, syrup, and ice cream. To make a malted, you add a tablespoon or more of malt powder—no longer sold in many supermarkets, unfortunately—to the mix. Don't overprocess; shakes should be thick and ice cold. For extra richness, add an egg or about half of a banana, preferably frozen.

1 cup milk

1 scoop ice cream

2 tablespoons chocolate or other syrup, or to taste

1 tablespoon malt powder, or to taste (optional)

Combine all ingredients in a blender and whiz just until combined.

Sorbet (Sherbet) and Granitas

There are a few ways to make sorbet, one of which contains milk. But the best thing about sorbets—and granitas, their close cousins, which can be made in a home freezer without an ice cream machine—is the purity of flavor. Generally, there are three or four ingredients: sugar, water, and one or two flavorings. There is no fat, and nothing to obscure the essence of the main ingredients. Fruit sorbets can be incredible; so can one made from chocolate.

For years, I wondered why restaurants had such creamy sorbets, while mine were hard and granular. The key is to serve them fresh, as soon after making as possible. The best restaurants, in fact, allow any sorbet they have not served to thaw overnight, then refreeze it the following day. This works fine at home, too, but don't try it for more than a day or two.

Bitter Chocolate Sorbet

Makes 4 servings

Time: 10 minutes, plus time to chill and churn

The biggest bang for your buck in the dessert world. There is no work involved here—assuming you have an electric ice cream machine, of course—and few ingredients. But the results are spectacular. Serve straight from the machine, or within an hour or two of making, if at all possible.

If you want a really bitter sorbet, cut the sugar back to $^1/_2$ cup; if you want one that is sweeter, use a full cup.

$^3/_4$ cup sugar

$^3/_4$ cup unsweetened cocoa powder

About 2 cups hot water

$^1/_2$ teaspoon vanilla extract

1 Mix together the sugar and cocoa then, stirring constantly, add enough hot water to make a thick paste. Add the remaining hot water and stir or whisk until smooth. Add the vanilla.

2 Refrigerate until cool, then churn in an ice cream maker according to the manufacturer's directions.

Soft Fruit Sorbet

Makes 4 servings

Time: 20 minutes, plus time to churn and chill

There are two keys to making good fruit sorbets. One is to taste, taste, taste before freezing—each batch of fruit (even the same fruit) has a different level of sweetness, and the amount of sugar and lemon juice will always vary. The other is to eat them as soon as possible after freezing; the ideal soft, creamy consistency doesn't last long. I recommend running your ice cream machine while you're eating dinner, so the sorbet doesn't wait too long before you eat it.

> 2 cups any soft ripe fruit: cherries, berries, mangoes, melons, etc., picked over, pitted, peeled, washed, and/or dried, as necessary
> About 1 cup superfine sugar (if you don't have superfine sugar, see the variation)
> About 1 tablespoon freshly squeezed lemon juice

1 Puree the fruit in a blender with most of the sugar and a bit of lemon juice. Taste and add more of either if necessary.

2 If you have used raspberries or blackberries, put the puree through a sieve to remove the seeds.

3 Refrigerate until cool, then churn in an ice cream maker according to the manufacturer's directions.

Sugar Syrup Sorbet: If you don't have superfine sugar, or you just want to make the process easier, begin by making a sugar syrup: Combine 2 cups sugar and 1 cup water and bring to a boil; stir until the sugar dissolves. This can be refrigerated indefinitely and added to fruit—start with about $1/2$ cup of syrup, and adjust to taste—just before pureeing.

Five Simple Ideas for Fruit Sorbets

1. Add one teaspoon or more minced citrus zest to any mixture.
2. Combine fruits.
3. Add one tablespoon or more flavored liqueurs such as Amaretto, triple sec, and so on.
4. Add one-eighth teaspoon (or to taste) ground black pepper or chili powder.
5. Add about one cup milk or light cream, right before freezing—this makes for a somewhat creamier texture.

Lemon, Lime, or Grapefruit Sorbets
Makes 4 servings

Time: 30 minutes (less if you've made sugar syrup in advance), plus time to churn and chill

Despite the high percentage of sugar, these are still lip-smackingly tart. To make orange sorbet, reduce the amount of sugar syrup to one cup before tasting.

> 2 cups sugar
> 1 cup water
> $1^1/2$ cups freshly squeezed lemon, lime, or grapefruit juice
> 1 tablespoon minced or grated lemon or lime zest

1 Combine the sugar and water in a small-to-medium saucepan and bring to a boil; stir until the sugar dissolves. Cool (to hasten cooling, place the syrup in a bowl, and place the bowl in another bowl filled with a mixture of ice and water).

2 Combine about $1^1/2$ cups sugar syrup with the citrus juice. Taste and add more syrup if necessary. Stir in the zest.

3 Refrigerate until cool if necessary, then churn in an ice cream maker according to the manufacturer's directions.

Granita
Makes 4 servings

Time: About 2 hours

Don't expect smooth texture from a granita; that's not what it is about. These are crushed ice desserts, super-refreshing but hardly elegant. Note that granitas have no shelf life whatsoever: They must be eaten within a few hours of making them.

2 cups any soft ripe fruit: cherries, berries, mangoes, melons, etc., picked over, pitted, peeled, washed, and/or dried, as necessary; or 2 cups liquid, such as fruit juice, coffee, or coconut milk

Superfine sugar or sugar syrup (see Sugar Syrup Sorbet, page 670) to taste

Freshly squeezed lemon juice or lemon zest to taste (optional)

1 If you're using fruit, puree it in a blender; if you have used raspberries or blackberries, put the puree through a sieve to remove the seeds.

2 Add enough sugar or sugar syrup to make a nicely sweet blend. Spike with lemon juice or zest if you like.

3 Pour into a shallow glass or ceramic pan and freeze for about 2 hours, stirring to break up the crystals every 30 minutes. The ideal granita is slushy, with ice crystals in a solution of frozen liquid. If the granita becomes too hard, pulse it (do not puree) in a food processor before serving.

The Basics of Dessert Sauces

For some reason, homemade dessert sauces have fallen from fashion, even though packaged sauces are rarely more than sugar (or high-fructose corn syrup) and artificial ingredients. Yet even store-bought ice cream or pound cake can be transformed into an elegant dessert by the addition of a real sauce. None of these takes more than a few minutes to prepare, and all are made from simple, readily available—and need I mention pure?—ingredients.

How to Make Whipped Cream

The first dessert "sauce" to consider is whipped cream. There are four rules to follow in making whipped cream:

1. Use the purest cream you can find (see page 684).
2. Make sure the cream is very cold—whip it straight from the refrigerator.
3. Although it isn't essential, it helps to chill the bowl and beater as well.
4. Don't overwhip.

What is overwhipped cream? Cream that looks like the whipped cream you probably grew up with—Reddi Whip, for example. When homemade whipped cream stands up like a soft ice cream cone, it's overwhipped. For most purposes (exceptions are noted in individual recipes), stop as soon as the cream barely holds a soft peak; for a dessert topping, you can whip it even less—it's nice that way, too.

To beat, use a whisk, or an eggbeater, or an electric mixer; but be careful of the tendency of powerful electric mixers to overwhip; you may wind up with butter, or something close to it.

Sweeten the whipped cream when it is about halfway done, using about one tablespoon of granulated sugar per cup, or to taste. You can also make whipped cream a little tangier by whipping in, from the beginning, one tablespoon or more of sour cream per cup. This produces something akin to Crème Fraîche (see below).

Finally, you can store whipped cream, covered and refrigerated, for several hours. If it separates, beat it a little to pull it back together. But considering how easy it is to whip cream, it's best to do it at the last minute if at all possible.

Crème Fraîche

Makes 1 cup

Time: At least 12 to 36 hours, largely unattended

Somewhere between fresh and sour cream, crème fraîche is ubiquitous in France, where it is served—sometimes lightly whipped, with a bit of sugar—as a tangy complement to sweet desserts. You might also try Swedish cream; see Strawberries with Swedish Cream, page 647.

1 cup heavy cream
1 teaspoon buttermilk

1　In a very small saucepan over very low heat (or use the microwave), heat the cream to body temperature, not over 100°F. Stir in the buttermilk.

2　Keep in a warm place, at least 75°F, until thickened, 12 to 36 hours. If your house is cool, immerse the container containing the cream in a larger one filled with warm water; change the water periodically.

3　When the mixture thickens slightly, stir, cover, and refrigerate. Crème fraîche will keep well for about a week, becoming tangier as time passes.

Butterscotch Sauce

Makes about 1¹/₂ cups

Time: 10 minutes

Good butterscotch is like a good butter cookie—easy to make, simple tasting, and very rich.

³/₄ cup heavy cream
6 tablespoons (³/₄ stick) unsalted butter, cut into pieces
³/₄ cup brown sugar
Pinch salt

1　Combine the cream and butter in a small saucepan and cook over medium-low heat, stirring occasionally, until the butter melts.

2　Stir in the sugar and salt and cook, stirring frequently, until the mixture is thick and shiny, 5 to 10 minutes. Taste and add more sugar if you like. Use right away, or refrigerate, well covered, for up to 1 week and rewarm before using.

Chocolate Sauce

Makes about 1¹/₂ cups

Time: 15 minutes

This is a rich chocolate sauce, more substantial than syrup. Note the Hot Fudge variation.

4 ounces semisweet or bittersweet chocolate, chopped
4 tablespoons (¹/₂ stick) unsalted butter
¹/₄ cup sugar
Pinch salt
¹/₄ cup water
1 teaspoon vanilla extract

1　Combine all ingredients except vanilla in a small saucepan over very low heat. Cook, stirring, until the chocolate melts and the mixture is smooth.

2　Add the vanilla and serve immediately, or keep warm over hot water until ready to serve, or refrigerate for up to a week and rewarm before using.

Hot Fudge Sauce: This is chewy and fudgy when you put it on top of ice cream. After the ingredients are combined, add ¹/₃ cup corn syrup to the mixture. Bring to a boil, turn the heat to low, and cook for 5 to 10 minutes, until thick and shiny. Add vanilla and serve hot. Or store up to a week and reheat very gently (a double boiler is best) before serving.

Raspberry, Strawberry, or Other Fruit Sauce

Makes about 2 cups

Time: 5 to 10 minutes

There are two ways to make fruit sauces (actually, there are dozens; these are the two I like best). The first, which is no work at all, gives you pure, straightforward flavor, and a very saucy consistency; it works well with soft fruits and berries. The second, which yields chunky fruit in a thick sauce, is more luxurious, and is also great with apples and pears. Take your pick.

Method 1

2 cups any berries or other soft ripe fruit: peaches,
    cherries, nectarines, mangoes, etc., picked over,
    pitted, peeled, washed, and/or dried, as necessary
Confectioners' sugar to taste
A little orange juice, freshly squeezed lemon juice,
    or fruity white wine (optional)

1 Puree the fruit in a blender; if you have used raspberries or blackberries, put the puree through a sieve to remove the seeds.

2 Combine with confectioners' sugar to taste. If necessary, thin with a little water, or use orange juice, lemon juice, or fruity white wine. Use immediately or refrigerate for a day or two.

Method 2

$1/2$ cup water
$1/2$ cup sugar
3 tablespoons unsalted butter
2 cups berries or other ripe fruit: apples, pears,
    bananas, peaches, cherries, nectarines, berries,
    mangoes, melons, etc., picked over, pitted,
    peeled, washed, and/or dried, as necessary

1 Combine the water, sugar, and butter in a medium heavy-bottomed saucepan and cook over medium-high heat, shaking and stirring, until the mixture is thick and syrupy but not browned.

2 Toss in the fruit and cook over low heat until the fruit begins to break up and release its juices, about 2 minutes for berries, longer for other fruit (some fruits, such as apples, may also require the addition of a little more water). Serve warm or at room temperature. This sauce keeps well, refrigerated, for up to a week.

Blueberry Sauce
Makes 4 servings

Time: 20 minutes

Halfway between a sauce and a syrup, this is great on pancakes, pound cake, or cheesecake, in which case the lemon juice should be kept to a minimum. But it is also appropriate with grilled lamb or other meats, as long as you add more lemon juice (or vinegar).

2 cups blueberries, picked over and washed
1 tablespoon cornstarch mixed with 1 tablespoon water
$1/2$ cup water
$1/2$ cup sugar, or to taste
Freshly squeezed lemon juice to taste

1 Combine the first four ingredients in a small-to-medium saucepan and turn the heat to medium. Cook, stirring, until the liquid is thick and the blueberries soft, about 10 minutes.

2 Taste and add lemon juice and more sugar if needed. Thin with a little more water if necessary, and serve immediately or refrigerate for up to a week.

Vanilla Custard Sauce
Crème Anglaise
Makes about 2 cups

Time: 15 to 30 minutes

A fine sauce for plain cakes, fruit, or any time you want a sweet sauce for dessert.

1 vanilla bean or 1 teaspoon vanilla extract
2 cups milk
3 egg yolks, or 2 whole eggs
$1/2$ cup sugar

1 If you're using the vanilla bean, heat the milk and the bean together in a small saucepan until the milk steams. Cover and let sit for 15 minutes. Remove the bean (you can rinse it off, wrap it in foil, and use it again if you like). If you're not using the bean, just heat the milk.

2 Use an electric mixer or whisk to beat the egg yolks or eggs and sugar together until pale yellow and thick. Slow add the hot milk, stirring all the while.

3 Return the mixture to the saucepan and cook over very low heat, stirring, until it reaches 175° to 180°F, or is slightly thickened; do not boil. (There will be a thick coating on the back of a spoon, one that will hold the outline of your finger after you pass it through.) Remove from the heat and pour into a bowl (if the mixture seems at all lumpy, strain it into the bowl); stir in the vanilla extract if using. Cool, then cover and refrigerate until ready to use, up to a day; or use right away.

Sabayon or Zabaglione

Makes about 2 cups

Time: 20 minutes

Sabayon is usually eaten warm, within minutes of making it. But it can also be refrigerated and served cold, or spooned over fruit—berries, for example— and run under the broiler. Sabayon can also be made with whole eggs (see the variation).

4 egg yolks

$^1/_3$ cup sugar, plus 1 tablespoon

$^1/_2$ cup any sweet spirits: Marsala wine, sweet sherry, or any dessert wine or liqueur

$^1/_2$ cup heavy cream

1 Place the egg yolks in the top of a double boiler (or in a medium saucepan, if you swear to stand next to the stove the entire time, whisking) with $^1/_3$ cup sugar and the spirits. Turn on the heat and whisk constantly until thick. Keep beating; eventually—it will take about 10 minutes total—the mixture will become light and frothy. Turn off the heat.

2 Immediately beat the cream with the remaining sugar until it holds soft peaks (page 671). Fold the cream into the beaten yolks and serve immediately, while still warm, or refrigerate.

Whole Egg Sabayon: Step 1 remains the same. In Step 2, omit the cream and beat 2 egg whites and the sugar until they hold soft peaks; fold the mixture into the beaten yolks and serve.

The Basics of Dessert Soufflés

There are three kinds of dessert soufflés: those, like savory soufflés, that are based on a white sauce; those whose support is derived entirely from beaten egg whites; and those that are frozen. Here is one of each. See The Basics of Eggs, Revisted, page 683, for information on beating egg whites as well as recipes for savory soufflés.

Vanilla or Chocolate Soufflé

Makes 4 to 6 servings

Time: About 1 hour, largely unattended

If you undercook this soufflé slightly, it will remain moist in the middle and need no sauce. If you cook it until it is completely dry, serve it with Vanilla Custard Sauce (Crème Anglaise) (page 673), whipped cream (page 671), or any light sauce. You can prepare the soufflé, through Step 3, hours in advance. Refrigerate the sauce. About an hour before you're ready to serve the soufflé, bring the sauce and the whites to room temperature. Beat the whites as you preheat the oven, and finish the soufflé.

3 tablespoons unsalted butter, plus 1 teaspoon
    for greasing the soufflé dish
$1/3$ cup sugar, plus some for dusting the soufflé dish
1 cup milk
3 tablespoons flour
2 ounces bittersweet or semisweet chocolate,
    chopped, or $1^1/2$ teaspoons vanilla extract
4 eggs, separated
Pinch salt
Confectioners' sugar for dusting

1 Use 1 teaspoon of butter to grease a 2-quart soufflé dish or other deep baking dish, such as a Corningware-type dish. (If you want to make individual soufflés, use a little more butter and grease four $1^1/2$- to 2-cup ramekins.) Sprinkle the dish with sugar and invert it to remove excess sugar. Set aside and preheat the oven to 350°F.

2 Warm the milk in a small saucepan over low heat with the $1/3$ cup sugar. In a small saucepan, heat the 3 tablespoons butter over medium-low heat. When the foam begins to subside, stir in the flour. Turn the heat to low and cook, stirring almost constantly, until the flour-butter mixture darkens, about 3 minutes.

3 Stir in the milk, a little bit at a time, using a whisk. It will be quite thick; stir in the chocolate if you are using it and remove from the heat. Let cool for 5 minutes. Beat the egg yolks and stir them in. Add the vanilla if you are using it. (The recipe can be prepared a few hours in advance up to this point; cool, wrap well, and refrigerate.)

4 Beat the egg whites with the salt until very stiff but still glossy. Stir a good spoonful of them thoroughly into the sauce to lighten it, then fold in the remaining whites, using a rubber spatula or your hand. Transfer to the prepared soufflé mold and bake until the center is set, or nearly so, 30 to 40 minutes (15 to 25 minutes for individual soufflés). Dust with confectioners' sugar and serve immediately.

Lemon, Orange, or Grand Marnier Soufflé
Makes 4 to 6 servings

Time: About 45 minutes

When you make soufflés without the basic white sauce, they are extremely light and delicate. They're also quite simple and, although you may not believe it, reliable.

About 1 teaspoon unsalted butter
1 cup sugar, plus some for dusting the soufflé dish
6 eggs, separated
1 tablespoon minced or grated lemon or orange zest
$1/4$ cup freshly squeezed lemon or orange juice or
    Grand Marnier or other orange-flavored liqueur
Pinch salt

1 Use the teaspoon of butter to grease a 2-quart soufflé dish or other deep baking dish, such as a Corningware-type dish. (If you want to make individual soufflés, use a little more butter and grease four $1^1/2$- to 2-cup ramekins.) Sprinkle the dish with sugar and invert it to remove excess sugar. Set aside and preheat the oven to 350°F.

2 Whisk the egg yolks with $3/4$ cup of the sugar until light and very thick; the mixture will fall in a ribbon from the ends of the beaters when it is ready. Beat in the flavorings and set aside.

3 Beat the egg whites with the salt until they hold soft peaks; continue to beat, adding the remaining $1/4$ cup sugar gradually, until they are very stiff but still glossy. Stir a good spoonful of them thoroughly into the egg yolk mixture to lighten it, then fold in the remaining whites, using a rubber spatula or your hand. Transfer to the prepared soufflé mold and bake until the center is nearly set, 25 to 35 minutes (15 to 25 minutes for individual soufflés). Serve immediately.

Frozen Berry Soufflé

Makes 6 servings

Time: About 30 minutes, plus time to freeze

Not a true soufflé, strictly speaking, but a very easy one, and one which can be prepared as much as a day in advance.

> 3 cups any berries, picked over, well washed, and dried
> 1 tablespoon freshly squeezed lemon juice
> 3 eggs, separated
> 1 cup sugar
> 2 cups heavy cream

1 Puree the berries with the lemon juice and pass through a strainer to remove seeds.

2 Whisk the egg yolks with $^3/_4$ cup sugar until light and very thick, 5 to 10 minutes (it's worth it to use a standing mixer here if you have one); the mixture will fall in a ribbon from the ends of the beaters when it is ready. Combine the yolks with the berries.

3 Beat the egg whites until they hold soft peaks; continue to beat, adding the remaining $^1/_4$ cup sugar gradually, until they are very stiff but still glossy. Stir a good spoonful of them thoroughly into the berry mixture to lighten it, then fold in the remaining whites, using a rubber spatula or your hand.

4 Whip the cream until it holds soft peaks. Fold it very gently into the egg mixture. Turn into a $1^1/_2$- to 2-quart serving dish, or smaller individual dishes, and freeze for several hours.

The Basics of Sweet Crepes

The differences between savory and sweet crepes are few and clear: sweet crepes have a little sugar in the batter, they are typically folded rather than rolled (traditional, but not essential), and, quite naturally, their fillings are sweet. See page 750 for more information about cooking crepes as well as recipes for savory versions.

Crepes Suzette

Makes 15 to 20 crepes, enough for 4 to 6

Time: About 30 minutes

Crepes can be made well in advance, stacked, and refrigerated, even frozen. Bring them back to room temperature before proceeding.

> 1 cup (about $4^1/_2$ ounces) all-purpose flour
> Pinch salt
> $^1/_4$ cup sugar, plus 1 tablespoon
> $1^1/_4$ cups milk
> 2 eggs
> 2 tablespoons melted and cooled unsalted butter or canola or other neutral oil, plus 4 tablespoons ($^1/_2$ stick) unsalted butter and butter or oil as needed for cooking
> 1 teaspoon grated or minced lemon zest
> 1 tablespoon grated or minced orange zest
> $^1/_2$ cup freshly squeezed orange juice
> 2 tablespoons Grand Marnier or other orange-flavored liqueur

1 Combine the flour, salt, 1 tablespoon sugar, and milk and beat until smooth (you can do this in a blender if you like, but do not overblend). Beat in the eggs and stir in the 2 tablespoons melted butter or oil and the lemon zest. If time allows, refrigerate for 1 hour and beat again.

2 Place a small skillet, preferably one that is non-stick and has shallow sides, over medium heat. When a drop of water skitters across the surface before evaporating, add ¹/₂ teaspoon butter. Ladle about a tablespoon of batter into the skillet and swirl it around so that it forms a thin layer on the bottom of the pan. Pour excess batter back into the bowl.

3 The batter will dry before your eyes; when the top is no longer liquid, about a minute, turn the crepe and cook the other side for 15 to 30 seconds. The crepe should brown only very slightly and not become at all crisp. Fold the finished crepes into quarters and set aside. Repeat the process, adding butter to the skillet and adjusting the heat as needed.

4 Combine the remaining 4 tablespoons butter with the remaining ¹/₄ cup sugar in a large skillet over low heat. Cook, stirring, until melted, then stir in the orange zest and juice. Quickly turn the folded crepes gently in this sauce, a couple at a time. Finish the sauce by adding the Grand Marnier and allowing it to warm for a few seconds; ignite it with a match if you like. Pour the sauce over the crepes and serve.

Chocolate Crepes: In making the crepe batter, omit the sugar and lemon zest; add 1 teaspoon vanilla extract. After chilling in Step 1, melt 1 ounce bittersweet or semisweet chocolate over very low heat with 1 teaspoon butter. Remove from the heat before the chocolate is completely melted, then stir until smooth. Cool for about 10 minutes, then thoroughly blend with the crepe batter. Cook as above, then serve with the Suzette sauce, or with any chocolate or fruit sauce.

The Basics of Simple Candies

Candy-making can be one of the great challenges of the kitchen. But there are simple candies that are rewarding and easy. Fudge, one of the first dishes many people teach to their kids, immediately comes to mind. But there are others—some more suited to sophisticated palates—and they are just as rewarding.

If you're going to tackle candy-making, even the simple kind, it's worth buying a candy thermometer, one which concentrates on the range between 230°F and 300°F where sugar works its crystalline magic. You can judge the stage of cooked sugar by dropping a bit of it into a glass of cold water (and I've noted how to do that in individual recipes), but the thermometer is far easier and more reliable.

Fudge
Makes about 1¹/₂ pounds

Time: About 30 minutes, plus resting time

Like so many things, the best fudge is made with simple ingredients. Here, the two that matter most are top-quality chocolate and fresh cream, preferably not ultra-pasteurized.

2 tablespoons unsalted butter, plus some for
    greasing the pan
4 ounces unsweetened chocolate, chopped
1 cup heavy cream
2 cups sugar
Pinch salt
1 teaspoon vanilla extract
¹/₂ to 1 cup chopped (not minced) walnuts or pecans
    (optional)

1 Let the butter come to room temperature while you work; grease a 9-inch square baking pan.

2 Combine the chocolate and cream in a medium saucepan over low heat. Cook, stirring constantly, until well blended and smooth. Add the sugar and salt, still over low heat, and cook, stirring, until the mixture boils.

3 Stop stirring and cook until the mixture measures 236°F (a small piece of it will form a soft ball when dropped into a glass of cold water, but the thermometer is an easier and surer test).

4 Immediately remove from the heat. Add the butter, but do not beat. When the mixture is just lukewarm, add the vanilla and beat vigorously with a wooden spoon until the mixture is smooth and has lost its sheen. Add the nuts if you like. Scrape into the prepared pan. When the mixture has hardened, cut into squares. Wrap well and refrigerate; fudge keeps for weeks, but is best eaten fresh.

Caramels

Makes more than 1 pound

Time: About 20 minutes, plus time to cool

Creamy and dreamy, caramels keep for weeks.

  4 tablespoons (1/2 stick) unsalted butter, plus some
    for greasing the pan
  1 1/2 cups heavy cream
  2 cups sugar
  1/2 cup light corn syrup
  Pinch salt
  1 1/2 teaspoons vanilla extract

1 Grease a 9-inch square baking pan.

2 Combine all ingredients except vanilla in a small saucepan and turn the heat to low. Cook, stirring constantly, until the sugar dissolves, then cook, stirring only occasionally, until the mixture measures 245°F (a small piece of it will form a firm ball when dropped into a glass of cold water, but the thermometer is an easier and surer test).

3 Stir in the vanilla and pour into the prepared pan. When the mixture has cooled to room temperature, remove the block of caramel from the pan and use a sharp knife to cut it into small squares. Wrap each square in waxed paper or plastic wrap. These keep for weeks, but are best eaten fresh.

Chocolate Caramels: Chop 4 ounces unsweetened chocolate. Add it along with the other ingredients and take even more care to stir almost constantly until the sugar dissolves. You can omit the butter if you like; these will be plenty rich without it.

Chocolate Truffles

Makes about 2 dozen

Time: About 2 hours, largely unattended

If you like your chocolate sweet, add the optional sugar here; but these truffles are plenty sweet without it. They're also best eaten the same day they're made.

  8 ounces semisweet or bittersweet chocolate
  2 tablespoons water
  2 tablespoons unsalted butter
  3/4 cup heavy cream
  2 tablespoons confectioners' sugar (optional)
  Unsweetened cocoa powder

1 In a small saucepan over low heat, melt the chocolate with the water, stirring occasionally, until smooth, then add the butter a bit at a time, stirring to blend after each addition.

2 Gradually add the cream, stirring after each addition until the mixture is smooth. Taste and stir in some or all of the sugar if you like. Refrigerate until cool and stiff, about an hour.

3 Sift some cocoa powder onto a plate (alternatively, you can grind 1/2 cup toasted skinned almonds in a blender or spice mill with 1/4 cup confectioners' sugar and use that). Line another plate with waxed paper. Use two spoons or your hands to make small balls out of the chocolate mixture, and roll them in the powder. Place on the waxed paper and serve immediately, or refrigerate for up to a day or two.

Peanut Brittle
Makes about 1 pound

Time: About 20 minutes, plus time to cool

If you've never made peanut brittle, you will not believe how simple it is.

Unsalted butter for greasing the pan
2 cups sugar
2 cups roasted peanuts, salted or unsalted, your choice
Pinch salt if you're using unsalted peanuts

1 Use the butter to grease a baking sheet, preferably one with a low rim.

2 Place the sugar in a large, heavy skillet and turn the heat to low. Cook, stirring occasionally, until the sugar turns liquid. Then stir constantly until it turns golden but not brown.

3 Stir in the peanuts and the salt if you're using it and immediately pour the mixture onto the greased baking sheet. Cool, then break into pieces. (If you like, you can score the brittle with a knife when it has solidified slightly but not yet turned hard; that way, it will break into even squares.) Store in a covered container for as long as you like.

Candied Nuts
Makes 1 pound

Time: 30 minutes, plus time to cool

The same as those sold on street corners and at circuses, without the red food coloring. Wear a long-sleeved shirt and oven mitts for Step 3 to prevent accidental burns.

1 cup sugar
1/2 cup water
2 cups shelled peanuts or other nuts, unsalted

1 Combine sugar and water in a small saucepan, preferably one with a pouring spout. Cook, stirring, until the mixture boils. Then stop stirring and cook until the temperature reaches 236°F (a small piece of it will form a soft ball when dropped into a glass of cold water, but the thermometer is an easier and surer test).

2 While the sugar is cooking, warm the nuts over the lowest possible heat in a medium saucepan. When the syrup is ready, place a heat diffuser (such as that used for keeping coffee warm) under the nuts if you have one, or hold the nuts an inch or two above the flame; they should be barely warming.

3 Drizzle the syrup over the nuts, shaking the pan (the one with the nuts in it) constantly—or, if you have a third hand nearby, stirring occasionally—until all the syrup is absorbed and the nuts are coated. Cool on waxed paper and eat within a day or so.

Candied Orange or Lemon Peel
Makes at least 4 dozen pieces

Time: About 1 hour, plus time to dry

These are sweet and very sour, to me the perfect way to end a large meal. You can omit the corn syrup, but its flavor does not interfere and it helps keep the peel moist.

4 thick-skinned oranges or lemons
2 cups sugar, plus more for rolling
2 tablespoons corn syrup

1 Score the skin of the fruit with a paring knife and remove it (reserve the fruit for another use). In a medium saucepan, cover the peels with cold water and bring to a boil over high heat; turn the heat down, then simmer until tender, 5 to 10 minutes. Drain, reserving 1 cup of the water.

2 Scrape off the white material from the inside of the peels, then use a scissors or knife to cut the peels into long strips.

3 Combine the sugar, corn syrup, and reserved liquid in the saucepan and bring to a boil over medium heat. Cook until the mixture measures 236°F (a small piece of it will form a soft ball when dropped into a glass of cold water, but the thermometer is an easier and surer test). Return the peels to the saucepan and cook over low heat until most of the syrup has been absorbed, about 10 minutes. Cool the peels in the syrup.

4 When the peels are cool enough to handle, remove them with a tongs, drain briefly, and roll them in sugar. Shake to remove excess sugar, then dry on a rack for a few hours. Store, wrapped in waxed paper or an airtight container for up to a few days.

Candied Grapefruit Peel: You have to take a little extra care to make sure to purge the bitterness from these. Peel as above (2 grapefruits are usually plenty). Boil in cold water to cover; drain. Repeat this procedure two more times. Trim and cook the peels as above, mixing the sugar with fresh water.

Chocolate Candies
Makes a little more than 1 pound

Time: About 30 minutes, plus time to cool

The easiest chocolates you can make, definitely worth the effort.

> 1½ cups sugar
> 1 cup heavy cream
> 4 ounces unsweetened chocolate, chopped
> 2 tablespoons unsalted butter
> 1½ teaspoons vanilla extract or 1 teaspoon mint
> extract, or to taste

1 Combine the sugar, cream, and chocolate in a small saucepan and turn the heat to low. Cook, stirring constantly, until the mixture comes to a boil, then continue to cook, stirring only occasionally, until the temperature reaches 236°F (a small piece of it will form a soft ball when dropped into a glass of cold water, but the thermometer is an easier and surer test).

2 Stir in the butter, then cool to lukewarm and stir in the vanilla and beat until smooth, thick, and no longer shiny.

3 Drop teaspoonfuls onto waxed paper; shape or decorate with pieces of nuts or candied fruit if you like. Cool before eating, and eat within a day or two.

Pies, Tarts, and Pastries

These are crisp- and tender-crusted desserts, for the most part made of simple, common ingredients with simple, easily mastered techniques. You start with flour and water, add fat—usually in the form of butter—and all that's left is flavoring, filling, and technique.

And although technique for much pastry-making must be learned, it is literally child's play. If you can roll out a Play-Doh pie, you can make a real one. In fact, it is most often ingredients that are the downfall in pastry-making. As with any simple food, the quality of pastry is determined by very few things.

The Basics of Butter

The first consideration is butter. Simply put, butter combines two qualities not found in most other fats:

good flavor and the ability to hold air when beaten. Hydrogenated fats, such as Crisco (vegetable shortening) or margarine, are even better at holding air. But—although you will find them as pie crust ingredients in many, many cookbooks, even good ones—their flavor is neutral at best and foul at worst; I strongly recommend against using them. Nor should you be misled into believing that margarine or shortening is "better" for you than butter; most studies indicate that hydrogenated fats have no health advantages over butter or even lard. Indeed, the process of hydrogenating fat causes trans fatty acids to form, which have been proven to be harmful to humans.

Some oils, such as olive or nut oils, have good flavor but lack delicacy and add no loft to the pastry (still, olive oil pastries can be quite good). The flavor of pure lard, once not only appreciated but craved, has fallen out of favor for two reasons: It's perceived as unhealthy (in reality, it is no worse for you than butter, Crisco, or margarine) and its quality is not as good as it once was, so its flavor has suffered. (If you can get good lard, and using it appeals to you, combine one part lard with three parts butter for the best pie crust you ever tasted.)

For all of those reasons, I recommend you use butter almost exclusively in baking. My feeling is that if you want pastry, you must be willing to eat good fat. If you're avoiding fat, turn to "Fruits," where there are plenty of low- and no-fat desserts.

About salted butter: Salt is incorporated into butter largely as a preservative, which means that salted butter may sit around longer than unsalted (sweet) butter before it is sold. Since butter freezes well, and since salt is an ingredient you can add any time, I buy sweet butter. If you do buy salted butter, to eliminate the addition of salt entirely from most sweet baked goods; there's almost always enough salt in the butter to compensate.

The Basics of Flour, Revisited

Please see The Basics of White Flour and The Basics of Non-White Flour (pages 219–220) in "Breads" for more about flour.

There are essentially two types of flour used in pastry-making: cake flour and all-purpose flour. Cake flour, which is lower in protein, can help give a cake or cookie a tender, delicate crumb. In any recipe in which you are *not* looking for structure and toughness (as in bread, obviously, but also as in puff pastry), some percentage of cake flour is useful.

But all-purpose flour—which contains a combination of low-protein cake flour and high-protein bread flour—will work in every recipe in this and other chapters. Even when I specify cake flour, which is rare,

you can use all-purpose flour if that's all you have. (For absolutely best results when you don't have cake flour, use seven-eighth cup all-purpose flour and one-eighth cup cornstarch.)

Flour should be stored in a dry place, but, more important, it should be replaced every six months or so if you don't use it up. Flour is cheap—a five-pound bag of good-quality flour is always under two dollars, and frequently much less—and its quality deteriorates over time. If you bake a lot, you'll be replacing your flour every week or two. But if you don't, buy fresh flour before you tackle that all-important project.

About sifting Today's all-purpose flour is so uniform and so fine that unless you live in such a humid environment that your flour actually clumps up sifting is unnecessary. There are exceptions, but mostly they occur when you want to add flour as gradually and gently as possible to an existing batter, as in Angel Food Cake (page 725).

The Basics of Sugar

Like flour, white sugar is cheap and ubiquitous. It is also the most useful sweetener there is. Confectioners' sugar, which is powdered, is best in those recipes that will not be cooked at all, such as frostings, because it dissolves better than regular granulated sugar; it's also good, of course, sprinkled over finished baked goods. (You can also use superfine sugar in place of regular granulated sugar; it also dissolves more easily, although not as well as confectioners' sugar.)

Brown sugar is white sugar with molasses. Unless otherwise specified, use either light or dark brown sugar in recipes throughout the book. If you run out of it, combine one tablespoon molasses with every cup of white sugar, and you'll get the same effect. To keep brown sugar from hardening, put it in a plastic bag, put the plastic bag in a tightly sealed container, and put the container in the refrigerator.

To make vanilla sugar, place one vanilla bean into a jar filled with two cups of sugar, and seal tightly. Keep a jar going all the time, adding any vanilla pods from which you have scraped the seeds, or a whole vanilla bean from time to time (you can use the vanilla bean in any recipe as you normally would). Use vanilla sugar in any pastry in which you are planning to use vanilla for a more intense flavor.

The Basics of Eggs, Revisited

Please see The Basics of Eggs, page 731, in "Eggs, Breakfast, and Brunch Dishes" for more about eggs.

Large eggs are standard in baking, but extra-large eggs are not much bigger and can be substituted freely. Fresh eggs are of course best, and even better if they're from a nearby farm.

It's easiest to separate eggs when they're cold, but it's easiest to beat whites when they're at room temperature. So if you think of it, separate your eggs an hour or so before you begin to bake, return the yolks to the refrigerator (covered, so they don't pick up any stray odors), and leave the whites out. Alternatively, you can warm egg whites by placing the bowl containing them in a larger bowl of hot water, stirring gently, or holding it over a low heat for a few moments.

How to beat egg whites   To beat egg whites, you can use a wire whisk, or an eggbeater, or an electric mixer; a little bit of cream of tartar, which is acidic, helps them to hold their shape, but well-beaten eggs are quite good at doing that themselves. When you beat eggs, *do not overdo it.* Usually, you want them to hold soft, not stiff peaks, those that will droop a little when you remove the beaters. They should still be shiny and moist when you finish. Whites that do hold stiff peaks—useful for meringue—are on the verge of becoming overbeaten; stop immediately.

The Basics of Chocolate

People make a big fuss about chocolate, but in fact it's harder to find good eating chocolate than good cooking chocolate. There are several reasons for this, chief among them being that baking chocolate is a simpler, more straightforward product than eating chocolate. It's also worth noting that baking chocolate is never eaten by itself (it's inedibly bitter), so its flavor is never judged directly.

The baking chocolate sold in supermarkets is consistent and quite decent; it is, of course, unsweetened. Sweetened chocolate used in baking may be labeled semisweet or bittersweet; both are fairly sweet and you can use them interchangeably. Unsweetened cocoa powder is lower in fat than hard chocolate, and is useful in many recipes. The difference between regular cocoa and "Dutch process" cocoa is not significant.

Much has been made of the proper way to melt chocolate, but a great deal of that fuss is important only to people who use chocolate for dipping, glazing, and making fancy candies. Chocolate used in those situations must be "tempered"—heated and cooled in such a way that it will behave properly.

Melting chocolate that will be incorporated into batters or doughs for desserts is another matter entirely. Here, the only thing to remember is that chocolate cannot withstand high or even moderate heat. It should be warmed gently, over very low heat or, even better, in a double boiler over hot (not boiling) water. It helps to chop the chocolate first, so that it melts more evenly, reducing the risk of burning it. Use a chef's knife and a clean cutting board, keep the point of the knife in contact with the board, and chop slowly with a steady up-and-down motion. Alternatively, you can grate chocolate on the coarse side of a box grater.

When melting, it's helpful to add a tablespoon or two of water to the mixture, again to moderate the effect of the heat. Stir frequently, keep the heat very low, and you'll have no trouble. You can also melt chocolate in the microwave, and it does a decent job of it: Place in a covered container and microwave on medium, checking every minute and stirring once the chocolate starts to melt. If you burn chocolate—it will become unappealingly grainy instead of smooth—throw it out and start again. Use lower heat the next time.

About Cream and Vanilla

Cream   Good cream is not ultra-pasteurized; you can taste the difference in a flash. If you are making a dessert that is dependent on cream, go out of your way to find fresh, real cream. Most natural foods stores carry it, some supermarkets carry it, and any real dairy farm can give you some.

Vanilla   Whole vanilla beans need not be used in all recipes. Although there are indeed times when the subtle flavor of the bean can have a profound impact on a recipe, in most cases good-quality vanilla extract is perfect. Make sure the extract you buy contains alcohol and vanilla only, and not vanillin, an artificial ingredient made from wood.

The Basics of Pie Crusts

As you can tell from the discussion beginning on page 681, I believe pie crusts should rely solely on butter for fat. But if you prefer an even crisper crust, and you don't mind the flavor of shortening, add one part shortening for three parts butter (that is, if a recipe calls for eight tablespoons of butter, use six of butter and two of shortening).

I mix pie crusts (and many other doughs and batters) in the food processor, which is fast and reliable, as long as you don't overprocess. If you want to mix fat and flour by hand, cut cold butter into bits and rub it and the flour very quickly between your fingers, picking it up, rubbing it, and dropping it. If the mixture begins to feel greasy, refrigerate it for a few minutes before proceeding. I find this easier and more reliable than cutting the butter into the flour with a fork, two knives, or a pastry blender, but you can use any of those techniques if you prefer. In all crust-making, the goal is to surround bits of fat with flour; any way that happens is fine—the food processor is unquestionably the easiest.

In many instances, it pays to precook ("blind" bake) pie crusts before filling them (see Prebaked Flaky Pie Crust, page 686). This practice ensures that the crust cooks thoroughly, which produces the best flavor and color, and also controls shrinking, a problem with many crusts. The practice is easy: You press the crust firmly into the pie pan to anchor it, then refrigerate or freeze it for a short while; firming up the butter this way helps the crust hold its shape during the first few minutes of baking.

When you're ready to bake, you prick the crust all over with a fork, cover it with a double layer of foil (buttered on one side, to prevent sticking), and weight the foil with pie weights (available at any kitchen supply store), dried beans or rice (which can be reused for this purpose), or a pot or skillet that fits well. The initial baking is about twelve minutes, after which you remove the weight and foil and bake an additional fifteen minutes or so, or until the crust is nicely colored (the baking time is longer for those pies whose filling requires no additional baking).

Blind baking is not an option for double-crusted pies, of course, which generally means that the bottom crusts of these are not as crisp. Although I like the look of double-crusted pies, I generally prefer open pies and tarts. Double crusts make sense when the pie is massive and you want it to keep well, or if you are trying to get as many calories as possible into your diet via the pie—not a goal for too many people I know.

Whenever you bake a filled pie, it makes sense to place the pie plate on a baking sheet. Not only does this prevent spills from falling to the bottom of your oven and burning, it aids in the browning of the bottom crust.

Flaky Pie Crust

For any single-crust pie, 8 to 10 inches in diameter

Time: About 45 minutes, including resting time

I like to add a little sugar to any pie shell that will contain a sweet filling, which essentially means any dessert pie shell. Many crusts are bland and tasteless, and sugar changes that. In addition, it aids in browning. I also add a scant amount of flour initially, which gives you the leeway to add flour liberally during rolling.

1^1/$_8$ cups (about 5 ounces) all-purpose flour,
    plus some for dusting work surface
^{1}/$_2$ teaspoon salt
1 teaspoon sugar
8 tablespoons (1 stick) cold unsalted butter,
    cut into about 8 pieces
About 3 tablespoons ice water, plus more if necessary

1 Combine the flour, salt, and sugar in the container of a food processor; pulse once or twice. Add the butter and turn on the machine; process until the butter and flour are blended and the mixture looks like cornmeal, about 10 seconds.

2 Place the mixture in a bowl and sprinkle 3 tablespoons of water over it. Use a wooden spoon or a rubber spatula to gradually gather the mixture into a ball; if the mixture seems dry, add another ^{1}/$_2$ tablespoon ice water. When you can make the mixture into a ball with your hands, do so. Wrap in plastic, flatten into a small disk, and freeze the dough for 10 minutes (or refrigerate for 30 minutes); this will ease rolling. (You can also refrigerate the dough for a day or two, or freeze it almost indefinitely.)

3 You can roll the dough between two sheets of plastic wrap, usually quite successfully; sprinkle both sides of it with a little more flour, then proceed. Or sprinkle a countertop or large board with flour. Unwrap the dough and place it on the work surface; sprinkle its top with flour. If the dough is hard, let it rest for a few minutes; it should give a little when you press your fingers into it.

4 Roll with light pressure, from the center out. (If the dough seems very sticky at first, add flour liberally; but if it becomes sticky only after you roll it for a few minutes, return it to the refrigerator for 10 minutes before proceeding.) Continue to roll, adding small amounts of flour as necessary, rotating the dough occasionally, and turning it over once or twice during the process. (Use ragged edges of dough to repair any tears, adding a drop of water while you press the patch into place.) When the dough is about 10 inches in diameter (it will be less than ^{1}/$_4$ inch thick), place your pie plate upside down over it to check the size.

5 Move the dough into the pie plate by draping it over the rolling pin or by folding it into quarters, then moving it into the plate and unfolding it. When the dough is in the plate, press it firmly into the bottom, sides, and junction of bottom and sides. Trim the excess dough to about ^{1}/$_2$ inch all around, then tuck it under itself around the edge of the plate. Decorate the edges with a fork or your fingers, using any of the methods illustrated on page 686. Freeze the dough for 10 minutes (or refrigerate it for 30 minutes).

6 When you're ready to bake, prick it all over with a fork.

Sweetened, Enriched Pie Crust: Use this whenever you want a more flavorful crust; it's similar to the standard crust for the tarts on pages 695. Follow the above procedure, using 2 tablespoons sugar and 1 egg yolk, adding the yolk along with the water.

Generous Pie Shell for a 10-Inch or Larger Pie, or a Deep-Dish Pie: Increase flour to 1¹/₂ cups, salt to ³/₄ teaspoon, sugar to 1¹/₂ teaspoons, butter to 10 tablespoons, water to 4 tablespoons.

Pie Shell for a Two-Crust Pie: Increase flour to 2¹/₄ cups, salt to 1 teaspoon, sugar to 2 teaspoons, butter to 16 tablespoons, water to 6 tablespoons.

You can flute the edges of a pie crust in a variety of different ways. Three of the easiest are:

Pinch the dough between the side of your forefinger and your thumb.

Press a knuckle from one side into the space made by your thumb and forefinger on the other.

Simply press down with the tines of a fork along the edges of the dough.

Prebaked Flaky Pie Crust

For any single-crust pie, 8 to 10 inches in diameter

Time: About 30 minutes

As discussed in The Basics of Pie Crusts, prebaking—or "blind" baking, as it is sometimes called—is the solution to soggy, misshapen crusts.

> 1 recipe Flaky Pie Crust (page 685), refrigerated or frozen and pricked all over with a fork at ¹/₂-inch intervals
> Unsalted butter as needed

1 Preheat the oven to 425°F.

2 Tear off a piece of foil large enough to fit over the entire crust when folded in half; fold it. Smear butter on one side of the foil, then press it into the crust. Weight the foil with a pile of dried beans or rice (these can be reused for this same purpose), pie weights, or a tight-fitting skillet or saucepan—anything that will sit flat on the surface.

3 Bake 12 minutes. Remove from the oven, reduce the heat to 350°F, and carefully remove the weight and foil.

4 Bake another 10 to 15 minutes, or until the crust is a beautiful shade of brown. Remove and cool on a rack.

Graham Cracker Crust

For any single-crust pie, 8 to 10 inches in diameter

Time: 20 minutes

Graham cracker crusts, good for cream or meringue pies and cheesecakes, are often prebaked. You can use roughly these same proportions and techniques for any cookie crumb crust—such as vanilla wafers, chocolate cookies, or ginger snaps—although if the cookies contain a great deal of fat you'll want to reduce the amount of butter. If you need a larger crust, simply increase the ingredients proportionally.

To crumble graham crackers, place them in a heavy plastic bag and seal, then roll over the bag as many times as necessary with a rolling pin. Alternatively, break the crackers into the container of a food processor and process until crumbly. (Or buy graham cracker crumbs.)

6 tablespoons unsalted butter
6 ounces broken graham crackers, about 1¹/₂ cups
3 tablespoons sugar

1 Gently melt the butter in a small saucepan.

2 Combine sugar with graham cracker crumbs in a bowl or food processor. Slowly add the butter, stirring or processing until well blended. Press the crumbs into the bottom and sides of a 9-inch pie plate.

3 To prebake, heat the oven to 350°F. Bake the crust for 8 to 10 minutes, just until it begins to brown. Cool on a rack before filling; the crust will harden as it cools.

The Basics of Fruit Pies

Fruit pies are a joy of summer and autumn, and to sully their flavor with huge amounts of sweetener or their texture by overthickening is a sin. I keep thickener to a minimum—there's nothing wrong with a little fruit juice on the plate, is there?—and I taste as I sweeten to use just the right amount of sugar. Some blueberries, which can be quite tart, will take relatively large amounts of sugar, but perfectly ripe peaches or pears need very little.

A note about frozen fruit It's not widely known that the quality of frozen fruit has improved greatly in recent years. I'm not writing of fruit packed in syrup, but of IQF (individually quick frozen) fruit that is

packed in plastic bags with no added ingredients. It can be quite good, although it tends to become watery as it thaws. If you increase both sugar and thickener a little when using it, this frozen fruit can make your winter desserts a reminder of the past summer. Do not thaw or wash frozen fruit before using, unless it was packed in large pieces, such as peach halves, in which case it should be at least partially defrosted and then sliced.

Traditional Apple Pie
Makes about 8 servings

Time: About 1¹/₂ hours, plus cooling time

I usually don't thicken the filling for a simple apple pie, but if you want to make sure the juices don't run, add 1¹/₂ tablespoons cornstarch or two tablespoons instant tapioca when you toss the apples with the spices. I also keep spices to a minimum, since I'd rather taste the apples; you could safely double their quantity if you like a spicy pie, and add a pinch of allspice and/or cloves if you like.

¹/₄ cup brown sugar
¹/₄ cup white sugar, or more if you would like a very sweet pie, plus a little for the top of the pie
¹/₂ teaspoon ground cinnamon
¹/₈ teaspoon freshly grated nutmeg
Pinch salt
5 or 6 Cortland, McIntosh, or other good cooking apples
1 tablespoon freshly squeezed lemon juice
1¹/₂ tablespoons cornstarch or 2 tablespoons instant tapioca (optional)
1 recipe Pie Shell for a Two-Crust Pie (page 686), bottom crust fitted into a 9-inch pie pan, top crust transferred to a rimless baking sheet, both refrigerated
2 tablespoons unsalted butter, cut into bits
Milk as needed

1 Toss together the sugars, spices, and salt. Peel and core the apples and cut them into $^1/_2$- to $^3/_4$-inch-thick slices. Toss the apples and lemon juice with the dry ingredients, adding the cornstarch or tapioca if you want a less runny pie.

2 Pile the apples into the rolled-out bottom crust, making the pile a little higher in the center than at the sides. Dot with butter. Cover with the top crust. Decorate the edges with a fork or your fingers, using any of the methods illustrated on page 686. Refrigerate while you preheat the oven to 450°F.

3 Place the pie on a cookie sheet and brush the top lightly with milk; sprinkle with sugar. Use a sharp paring knife to cut two or three 2-inch-long vent holes in the top crust; this will allow steam to escape. Place in the oven and bake for 10 minutes. Reduce the heat to 350°F and bake another 40 to 50 minutes, or until the pie is golden brown. Do not underbake. Cool on a rack before serving warm or at room temperature.

Apple-Pear Pie: Add 1 tablespoon peeled and minced fresh ginger or 1 teaspoon ground ginger to the mixture of dry ingredients. Use half apples and half pears. Add 2 tablespoons cornstarch or 3 tablespoons instant tapioca to the mixture if you want a less runny pie.

Dutch Apple Pie: Add 2 tablespoons cornstarch or 3 tablespoons instant tapioca to the mixture. Proceed as above, making sure to cut a large vent hole in the center of the top crust. About 30 minutes into the baking time, pour $^1/_2$ cup heavy cream into the vent hole and finish baking as above.

Deep-Dish Apple Pie with Streusel Topping: Use a Generous Pie Shell for a 10-Inch or Larger Pie, or Deep-Dish Pie (page 686). Increase all filling ingredients by one third. Fill the pie as above. Cream together (you can use the food processor for this) 8 tablespoons (1 stick) butter and $^1/_2$ cup brown sugar. Stir in $^1/_2$ cup chopped walnuts or pecans, 1 tablespoon freshly squeezed lemon juice, $^1/_2$ teaspoon ground cinnamon (or to taste) and just enough flour to make the mixture crumbly, $^1/_2$ cup or less. Strew this mixture over the top of the apples. Bake at 375°F for 45 to 60 minutes, or until the center of the pie is bubbly and the streusel mixture and bottom crust are nicely browned.

Six Easy Additions to Apple Pie

1. Chopped nuts, one-half to one cup
2. Any appealing spice, generally in small amounts, such as minced fresh or crystallized ginger, allspice, or cloves
3. Bourbon or rum sprinkled over the top, about two tablespoons
4. Cranberries, left whole, about one cup (increase the amount of sugar slightly)
5. Pitted stone fruit, such as plums or cherries, cut up, or whole raspberries or blackberries, one cup or more (reduce the amount of apples accordingly)
6. Dried fruit, such as raisins or dried cranberries, one-half to one cup

Blueberry and Other Berry Pies

Makes about 8 servings

Time: About $1^1/_2$ hours, plus cooling time

There are variations on this standard, but it is the model for all berry pies. Again, I like to minimize the spices and other flavorings, emphasizing the flavor of the berries. Like apple pie, berry pies can be made with a streusel topping (page 688).

5 cups blueberries, picked over, briefly rinsed, and lightly dried (see "A note about frozen fruit," page 687)

1/2 to 1 cup sugar, depending on your taste and the sweetness of the berries, plus a little for the top of the pie

2 tablespoons cornstarch or 3 tablespoons instant tapioca

Pinch salt

1/4 teaspoon ground cinnamon

Pinch ground allspice or nutmeg

1 tablespoon freshly squeezed lemon juice

1 teaspoon minced lemon zest (optional)

1 recipe Pie Shell for a Two-Crust Pie (page 686), bottom crust fitted into a 9-inch pie pan, top crust transferred to a rimless baking sheet, both refrigerated

2 tablespoons unsalted butter, cut into bits

Milk as needed

1 Gently toss the blueberries with the sugar, thickener, salt, and spices. Stir in the lemon juice and optional zest and pile into the rolled-out shell, making the pile a little higher in the center than at the sides. Dot with butter. Cover with the top crust. Decorate the edges with a fork or your fingers, using any of the methods illustrated on page 686. Refrigerate while you preheat the oven to 450°F.

2 Place the pie on a baking sheet and brush the top lightly with milk; sprinkle with sugar. Use a sharp paring knife to cut two or three 2-inch-long vent holes in the top crust; this will allow steam to escape. Place in the oven and bake for 10 minutes. Reduce the heat to 350°F and bake another 40 to 50 minutes, or until the pie is golden brown. Do not underbake. Cool on a rack before serving warm or at room temperature.

Blackberry or Raspberry Pie: Combine these berries with each other, or with blueberries. Be gentle in washing and drying the fragile berries, and increase the amount of either thickener by 1 tablespoon.

Strawberry, Rhubarb, or Strawberry-Rhubarb Pie: Use a total of 5 cups of fruit, in any combination you like. String rhubarb, then cut it into 1-inch pieces. Hull strawberries; slice in half or leave whole. If using rhubarb, use at least 1 cup of sugar. Use 3 tablespoons of cornstarch or 4 tablespoons of instant tapioca for thickener. Omit the lemon juice and zest.

Peach and Other Stone Fruit Pies

Makes about 8 servings

Time: About 1 1/2 hours

A rather lemony peach pie with a streusel topping is absolutely delicious; to make this, simply follow the directions for Deep-Dish Apple Pie with Streusel Topping (page 688). The classic two-crusted peach (or cherry, apricot, plum, what-have-you) pie is the main recipe. Please: Use perfectly ripe fruit if at all possible.

About 2 pounds peaches, or a little more (6 to 10 peaches, depending on their size)

1 tablespoon freshly squeezed lemon juice

About 1/2 cup sugar, more if the peaches are not quite ripe, plus a little for the top of the pie

1/4 teaspoon ground cinnamon or 1/2 teaspoon almond extract

1/8 teaspoon freshly grated nutmeg or ground allspice, if you use cinnamon

1 1/2 tablespoons cornstarch or 2 tablespoons instant tapioca

1 recipe Pie Shell for a Two-Crust Pie (page 686), bottom crust fitted into a 9-inch pie pan, top crust transferred to a rimless baking sheet, both refrigerated

2 tablespoons unsalted butter, cut into bits

Milk as needed

1 Peel the peaches: Bring a pot of water to the boil and drop the peaches into it, a couple at a time, for 10 to 30 seconds, or until the skins loosen. Plunge into a bowl of ice water. Slip the peels off, using a paring knife to ease the process. Pit, slice, and toss with the lemon juice.

2 Mix together the dry ingredients (including the almond extract, if you're using it), and toss the peaches with this mixture. Pile into the rolled-out shell, making the pile a little higher in the center than at the sides. Dot with butter. Cover with the top crust. Decorate the edges with a fork or your fingers, using any of the methods illustrated on page 686. Refrigerate while you preheat the oven to 450°F.

3 Place the pie on a baking sheet and brush the top lightly with milk; sprinkle with sugar. Use a sharp paring knife to cut two or three 2-inch-long vent holes in the top crust; this will allow steam to escape.

4 Place in the oven and bake for 10 minutes. Reduce the heat to 350°F and bake another 40 to 50 minutes, or until the pie is golden brown. Do not underbake. Cool on a rack before serving warm or at room temperature.

Peach-and-Raisin Pie: Add ¹/₂ to 1 cup raisins to the mixture of peaches or other fruit.

Peach-and-Berry Pie: Add 1 cup berries (blueberries are best) to the mixture of peaches or other fruit.

Peach-and-Ginger Pie: Add 1 tablespoon minced fresh ginger (or 1 teaspoon ground ginger) to the mixture (do not combine with almond extract; use cinnamon and nutmeg).

Nectarine Pie: Substitute nectarines for peaches.

Plum Pie: Use the small prune (Italian) plums that come into season in early autumn.

Cherry Pie: Sour cherries are best for pie. Substitute 4 to 5 cups pitted sour cherries for the peaches; omit the lemon juice unless you're using sweet cherries. Proceed as above. If you use canned cherries, drain them well and increase the thickener by 1 tablespoon.

Cream Pie

Makes about 8 servings

Time: About 1¹/₂ hours

Master this one basic recipe and you can make all the cream pies you've dreamed of. Egg yolks, used without their whites, are traditional and wonderful when making cream filling. This has led, to topping cream pies with meringue. But cream pies are also wonderful topped with whipped cream. If this is what you'd prefer to do, see the whole egg variation (Cream-Topped Cream Pie), below.

Note that though they're called cream pies, milk is the chosen liquid. But use whole milk if at all possible. If you have only low-fat milk, substitute one-quarter cup of cream for one-quarter cup of the milk, if possible; incongruous, yes, but it will make for a better pie.

1 Flaky Pie Crust (page 685), or Graham Cracker Crust (page 686)

³/₄ cup sugar

2 tablespoons cornstarch

Pinch salt

3 or 4 eggs, separated

2¹/₂ cups whole milk or 2¹/₄ cups low-fat milk mixed with ¹/₄ cup cream

1 vanilla bean or 2 teaspoons vanilla extract

2 tablespoons unsalted butter, softened

Pinch cream of tartar

¹/₄ cup confectioners' sugar

1 Prebake the crust (see Prebaked Flaky Pie Crust, page 686),and start the filling while the crust is in the oven. When the crust is done, leave the oven at 350°F and cool the crust slightly on a rack.

2 In a small saucepan, combine the sugar with the cornstarch and salt. Mix together the egg yolks and milk. If you're using a vanilla bean, split it and scrape out the seeds; stir them into the milk mixture (reserve the bean itself to make vanilla sugar; see The Basics of Sugar, page 682). Stir the milk-egg mixture into the sugar-cornstarch mixture over medium heat; at first, whisk occasionally to eliminate lumps. Then stir almost constantly until the mixture boils and thickens, about 10 minutes. Stir in the butter (and vanilla extract, if you're using it) and set aside.

3 Make the meringue: Beat the egg whites with a pinch of salt and cream of tartar, until foamy. Keep beating, gradually adding the confectioners' sugar, until the mixture is shiny and holds fairly stiff peaks.

4 Place the pie plate on a baking sheet. Pour the warm filling into the warm crust. Cover with the meringue, making sure the meringue comes in contact with the edges of the crust. Note that the meringue will hold its shape, so you can decorate it if you like. Bake until the meringue is lightly browned, 10 to 15 minutes. Cool on a rack, then refrigerate; serve cool.

Coconut Cream Pie: Toast 1 cup dried sweetened or unsweetened shredded coconut by placing it in a dry skillet over very low heat and cooking, shaking almost constantly, until it begins to brown. Remove from the pan immediately. Stir this coconut into the thickened cream filling. Top the meringue with another $1/2$ cup untoasted coconut.

Banana Cream Pie: Stir 1 cup thinly sliced banana into the thickened cream filling before pouring it into the pie shell.

Chocolate Cream Pie: Add 2 ounces chopped or grated bittersweet or semisweet chocolate to the milk mixture as it cooks.

Cream-Topped Cream Pie: Prebake the crust (see Prebaked Flaky Pie Crust, page 686) until it is nice and brown, a total of about 35 minutes. Substitute 2 whole eggs for the yolks and proceed as above. After pouring the cream into the prebaked shell, cover directly with plastic wrap (this will prevent a skin from forming) and refrigerate until cool. Just before serving, beat 1 cup heavy cream (preferably not ultra-pasteurized) with 2 tablespoons confectioners' sugar and $1/2$ teaspoon vanilla or almond extract, or brandy or rum, until the cream holds stiff peaks. Spoon over the pie and serve.

Lemon Meringue Pie

Makes about 8 servings

Time: About $1^1/2$ hours

Not quite a cream pie, lemon meringue is little more than lemon flavor made solid, topped by a light cloud of sweet meringue.

1 Flaky Pie Crust (page 685) or 1 Graham Cracker Crust (page 686)

1 cup sugar

$1/3$ cup cornstarch

Pinch salt

2 cups boiling water

3 or 4 eggs, separated

2 tablespoons unsalted butter, softened

2 teaspoons grated or minced lemon zest

6 tablespoons freshly squeezed lemon juice

Pinch cream of tartar

$1/4$ cup confectioners' sugar

1 Prebake the crust (see Prebaked Flaky Pie Crust, page 686), and start the filling while the crust is in the oven. When the crust is done, leave the oven at 350°F and cool the crust slightly on a rack.

2 In a small saucepan, combine the sugar, cornstarch, salt, and boiling water and cook, stirring frequently, until smooth and thick, 10 to 15 minutes. While it is cooking, beat the egg yolks until smooth. When the cornstarch mixture is thick turn off the heat, then stir about $1/2$ cup of it into the egg yolks. Immediately stir the egg yolk mixture into the cornstarch mixture until thick and well blended. Return to low heat, add the butter, and cook, stirring, until smooth and hot, about 5 minutes. Stir in the lemon zest and juice, mix well, and turn off the heat.

3 Make the meringue: Beat the egg whites with a pinch of salt and cream of tartar, until foamy. Keep beating, gradually adding the confectioners' sugar, until the mixture is shiny and holds stiff peaks.

4 Place the pie plate on a baking sheet. Pour the warm filling into the warm crust. Cover with the meringue, making sure the meringue comes in contact with the edges of the crust. Note that the meringue will hold its shape, so you can decorate it if you like. Bake at 350°F until the meringue is lightly browned, 10 to 15 minutes. Cool on a rack, then refrigerate; serve cool.

Key Lime Pie

Makes about 8 servings

Time: About $1^1/2$ hours, plus time to cool

Key Lime Pie may be topped with meringue (as it is here), or with cream. If you'd prefer the latter, make adaptations according to the variation on page 691, Cream-Topped Cream Pie. If you have key limes—chances are you will not—by all means use them; but normal limes are fine.

1 Flaky Pie Crust (page 685) or 1 Graham Cracker Crust (page 686)
4 eggs, separated
1 (14-ounce) can sweetened condensed milk
$1/3$ cup freshly squeezed lime juice
Pinch salt
Pinch cream of tartar
$1/4$ cup confectioners' sugar

1 Prebake the crust (see Prebaked Flaky Pie Crust, page 686), and start the filling while the crust is in the oven. When the crust is done, leave the oven at 350°F and cool the crust slightly on a rack.

2 Beat the egg yolks just until combined. Beat in the condensed milk, then the lime juice, a little at a time; the mixture will thicken. Place the pie plate on a baking sheet. Pour the filling into the warm crust and bake until the filling is just firm, 10 to 15 minutes. Remove and cool on a rack for about 10 minutes.

3 Make the meringue: Beat the egg whites with salt and cream of tartar, until foamy. Keep beating, gradually adding the confectioners' sugar, until the mixture is shiny and holds fairly stiff peaks.

4 Cover the pie with the meringue, making sure the meringue comes in contact with the edges of the crust. Note that the meringue will hold its shape, so you can decorate it if you like. Bake until the meringue is lightly browned, 10 to 15 minutes. Cool on a rack, then refrigerate; serve cool.

Custard Pie

Makes about 8 servings

Time: About $1^1/2$ hours

Essentially cream pies without added thickener, custard pies are a little trickier to make. But the game is worth the candle: At its best, a custard pie is silky smooth, creaminess with just enough substance to hold together. In order to keep your crust from getting soggy and your custard from overcooking, bake the crust (pastry crust is definitely preferably to graham cracker here) while you prepare the custard, then combine both while hot. And remove the pie from the oven before it solidifies completely.

1 Flaky Pie Crust (page 685)

2 1/2 cups half-and-half, light cream, or whole milk

4 eggs

1/2 cup sugar

1 teaspoon vanilla extract

1/4 teaspoon freshly grated nutmeg

Pinch salt

1/2 teaspoon ground cinnamon

1 Prebake the crust (see Prebaked Flaky Pie Crust, page 686), and start the filling while the crust is in the oven. When the crust is done, turn the oven to 325°F.

2 Combine the half-and-half with the eggs in a bowl and beat until well blended. Add the remaining ingredients except for the cinnamon. Transfer to a medium saucepan and warm over medium-low heat until hot to the touch; do not boil.

3 Place the pie plate on a baking sheet. Pour the egg mixture into the still-hot crust and sprinkle with the cinnamon. Bake about 30 minutes, until the mixture shakes like Jell-O but is still quite moist. Cool on a rack and serve warm or at room temperature.

Nutty Custard Pie: To make a crisp, nutty pie, increase the sugar to 3/4 cup and add 1 cup ground blanched almonds to the liquid. Substitute 1/2 teaspoon almond extract for the vanilla if you like.

Coconut Custard Pie: See the directions for Coconut Cream Pie (page 691).

Twenty-Four Pies and Tarts That Are Killers with Ice Cream

If you're looking for a blow-out dessert, just combine any of these pies or tarts with a scoop of Basic French Vanilla Ice Cream (page 664) or any other ice cream.

1. Traditional Apple Pie, page 687
2. Apple-Pear Pie, page 688
3. Dutch Apple Pie, page 688
4. Deep-Dish Apple Pie with Streusel Topping, page 688
5. Blueberry and Other Berry Pies, page 688
6. Blackberry or Raspberry Pie, page 689
7. Strawberry, Rhubarb, or Strawberry-Rhubarb Pie, page 689
8. Peach and Other Stone Fruit Pies, page 689
9. Peach-and-Raisin Pie, page 690
10. Peach-and-Berry Pie, page 690
11. Peach-and-Ginger Pie, page 690
12. Nectarine Pie, page 690
13. Plum Pie, page 690
14. Cherry Pie, page 690
15. Pumpkin Pie, page 694
16. Pecan Pie, page 694
17. Chocolate Pecan Pie, page 694
18. Simplest Apple Tart, page 696
19. Apple-Almond Tart, page 696
20. Two-Apple Tart, page 696
21. Simple Berry Tart, page 698
22. Frangipane Tart, page 698
23. Free-Form Tart with Fruit, page 699
24. Caramelized Apple Tart (Tarte Tatin), page 700

Pecan Pie

Makes about 8 servings

Time: About 1¹/₂ hours

There are two types of pecan pies, one of which contains not only sugar but corn syrup. I don't like this version—not only is it too sweet, if you taste corn syrup by itself you'll never cook with it again. The other thickens the sugar with eggs—in other words, it's a custard pie, loaded with pecans. What could be better than that? Toast the pecans first for best flavor.

1 Flaky Pie Crust (page 685)

2 cups shelled pecans

5 eggs

1 cup white sugar

¹/₂ cup brown sugar

Pinch salt

6 tablespoons (³/₄ stick) butter, melted

1 tablespoon vanilla extract

1 Prebake the crust (see Prebaked Flaky Pie Crust, page 686), and place the pecans on a baking sheet and bake (you can do this before the oven reaches 425°F), shaking and stirring, for about 5 minutes, or until the pecans are hot. Cool the pecans; coarsely chop half of them and leave the other half intact.

2 Start the filling while the crust is in the oven. When the crust is done, turn the oven to 375°F.

3 Beat the eggs well, until they are foamy. Beat in the sugars, salt, and butter. While the crust is baking, warm this mixture in a medium saucepan over medium-low heat, stirring occasionally, until it is hot to the touch; do not boil. Stir in the vanilla extract and the pecans.

4 Place the pie plate on a baking sheet. Pour this mixture into the still-hot crust and bake 30 to 40 minutes, until the mixture shakes like Jell-O but is still quite moist. Cool on a rack and serve warm or at room temperature.

Chocolate Pecan Pie: Steps 1 and 2 remain the same. Before beginning Step 3, melt 2 ounces semisweet chocolate with 3 tablespoons of butter until smooth. Let cool while you beat the eggs, sugars, and salt (omit the remaining butter). Combine the chocolate and egg mixtures and warm gently as in Step 3 above, then proceed as above.

Pumpkin Pie

Makes about 8 servings

Time: About 1¹/₂ hours

A variation on Custard Pie (page 692), with lots of added spice and, of course, pumpkin. Substitute cooked, pureed, and strained winter squash, sweet potatoes, or white beans for the pumpkin if you like.

1 Flaky Pie Crust (page 685)

3 eggs

³/₄ cup sugar

¹/₂ teaspoon ground cinnamon

¹/₈ teaspoon freshly grated nutmeg

¹/₂ teaspoon ground ginger

Pinch ground cloves

Pinch salt

2 cups canned or fresh pumpkin puree or cooked

2 cups half-and-half, light cream, or whole milk

1 Prebake the crust (see Prebaked Flaky Pie Crust, page 686), and start the filling while the crust is in the oven. When the crust is done, turn the oven to 375°F.

2 Beat the eggs with the sugar, then add the spices and salt. Stir in the pumpkin puree and then the half-and-half. While the crust is baking, warm this mixture in a medium saucepan over medium-low heat, stirring occasionally, until it is hot to the touch; do not boil.

3 Place the pie plate on a baking sheet. Pour this mixture into the still-hot crust and bake 30 to 40 minutes, until the mixture shakes like Jell-O but is still quite moist. Cool on a rack and serve warm or at room temperature.

The Basics of Tarts

Tarts are European-style pies, open-faced, made with a rich, sweet crust (not unlike Sweetened, Enriched Pie Crust, page 685) and filled with fruit, pastry cream, and/or nuts. The typical fillings are a little more complex than those used in American pies, but still quite easy. Almost any tart can be made richer by adding pastry cream as a base, and almost anyone can be made leaner by removing the pastry cream.

Not surprisingly, you bake tarts in a tart pan instead of a pie pan. The difference is shape—in tarts, the sides of the crust are perpendicular to the bottom, as in a cake pan. These straight sides give tart pans an advantage: They are often made with perfectly flat bottoms and removable sides; when the tart is done, you can lift out the bottom and place the beautiful tart on a serving dish. This makes presentation lovely and cutting extremely easy. For these reasons, I recommend using two-piece tart pans.

Fruit tarts are often glazed with strained jam, which is then heated and thinned with liqueur or other flavorful liquid. I sometimes skip this step, because it is largely cosmetic—the tart is already flavorful and sweet enough—but it's a nice touch, and easily done. Try it once and decide for yourself.

Rich Tart Crust

Makes enough for a generous 10-inch tart

Time: 10 minutes

Egg yolks and a little extra butter enrich this crust, giving it more flavor and body than a typical pie crust.

In fact, it's like a great big cookie. For directions on mixing the dough by hand, see The Basics of Pie Crusts (page 684).

1½ cups (about 7 ounces) all-purpose flour,
    plus more as needed
½ teaspoon salt
2 tablespoons sugar
10 tablespoons (1¼ sticks) cold unsalted butter,
    cut into about 10 pieces
2 egg yolks, plus more as needed
3 tablespoons ice water, plus 1 tablespoon if needed

1 Combine the flour, salt, and sugar in the container of a food processor; pulse once or twice. Add the butter and turn on the machine; process until the butter and flour are blended and the mixture looks like cornmeal, about 10 seconds. Add the egg yolks and process another few seconds.

2 Place the mixture in a bowl and sprinkle 3 tablespoons of water over it. Use a wooden spoon or a rubber spatula to gradually gather the mixture into a ball; if the mixture is dry, add another tablespoon of ice water. When you can make the mixture into a ball with your hands, do so. Wrap in plastic, flatten into a small disk, and freeze the dough for 10 minutes (or refrigerate for 30 minutes); this will ease rolling. (You can also refrigerate the dough for a day or two, or freeze it almost indefinitely.)

3 You can roll the dough between two sheets of plastic wrap, usually quite successfully; sprinkle both sides of it with a little more flour, then proceed. Or sprinkle a countertop or large board with flour. Unwrap the dough and place it on the work surface; sprinkle its top with flour. If the dough is hard, let it rest for a few minutes; it should give a little when you press your fingers into it.

4 Roll with light pressure, from the center out. If the dough seems very sticky at first, add a little flour; but if it becomes sticky while you're rolling, return it to the refrigerator for 10 minutes before proceeding. Continue to roll, adding flour as necessary, rotating the dough occasionally, and turning it over once or twice. (Use ragged edges of dough to repair any tears, adding a drop of water while you press the patch into place.) When the diameter of the dough is about 2 inches greater than that of your tart pan, move the dough into the pan by draping it over the rolling pin or by folding it into quarters, then unfolding it into the pan. When the dough is in the pan, press it firmly into the bottom, sides, and junction of bottom and sides. Save scraps to patch holes, or just bake them as small, simple cookies.

5 Before filling, freeze the dough for 20 minutes (or refrigerate it for 1 hour).

Simplest Apple Tart

Makes about 8 servings

Time: About 1¹/₂ hours

This is a quick, crisp tart, in which delicious shell and straightforward filling share center stage. You can make this same tart with pears (make sure they're ripe), peaches, or nectarines (peel stone fruits first; see Peach and Other Stone Fruit Pies, page 689).

1 recipe Rich Tart Crust, well chilled (page 695)

2 to 3 pounds tart apples, such as McIntosh

1 tablespoon freshly squeezed lemon juice

2 tablespoons sugar

¹/₂ teaspoon ground cinnamon

1 tablespoon unsalted butter

¹/₃ cup strained raspberry, apricot, or currant preserves (optional)

1 tablespoon water or any liqueur (optional)

1 Preheat the oven to 425°F. Prick the crust all over with a fork. Line it with tin foil and weight the bottom with a pile of dried beans, rice (these can be reused for this same purpose), or other weights that will sit flat on the surface; a smaller pie plate works well too. Bake 15 minutes, or until the shell is no longer raw but still quite pale. Remove from the oven, reduce the heat to 375°F, and carefully remove the weight and foil. Set the shell aside to cool.

2 Peel and core the apples, then cut them into thin slices (about ¹/₈ inch thick); use a mandoline if you have one. Toss them with the lemon juice so they don't brown. Arrange the apple slices in concentric circles in the tart shell, with the circles overlapping. Sprinkle with sugar and cinnamon, then dot with butter. Place the tart pan on a baking sheet and bake until the apples are quite soft (a thin-bladed knife will pierce them easily) but still hold their shape, about 40 minutes. Cool on a rack for about 20 minutes before glazing if desired; serve at room temperature.

3 To glaze: While the tart is cooling, warm strained preserves with 1 tablespoon water or any liqueur in a very small saucepan over medium-low heat, until thinned. Brush the top of the tart with this mixture.

Apple-Almond Tart: Toast ³/₄ cup blanched almonds while you preheat the oven for the tart shell: Place them on a baking sheet and bake (you can do this before the oven reaches 425°F), shaking, for 5 to 10 minutes, or just until they begin to brown. Cool, then place them in a food processor and grind them finely (stop processing before they turn into a paste). Toss with ¹/₄ teaspoon ground cinnamon and 1 tablespoon sugar, then spread them on the bottom of the prebaked tart shell before topping with the apples and proceeding as above.

Two-Apple Tart: You'll need about twice as many apples for this tart. Prepare half of them as above. Peel, core, and coarsely chop the other half, then cook them over low heat, partially covered and stirring occasionally, with 1 tablespoon freshly squeezed lemon juice, 1 teaspoon grated or minced lemon zest, and $1/4$ cup water, until soft but still holding their shape, about 15 minutes. Add sugar to taste, about $1/2$ cup. Cool, then spread this on the bottom of the prebaked tart shell before topping with the uncooked apples and proceeding as above.

Strawberry Tart with Pastry Cream

Makes about 8 servings

Time: About $1^1/2$ hours

Classic pastry cream is almost identical to the filling used in Cream Pie (page 690). It's a delicious base for any fruit, but especially fresh berries. Although these tarts are elegant, they are actually easier than many pies, because everything is prepared separately and then assembled: You bake the crust, fill it with cream, top with berries, glaze if you like, and serve. You can use any berries or other peeled and sliced soft fruit for this tart.

1 recipe Rich Tart Crust, well chilled (page 695)

$2/3$ cup sugar

2 tablespoons all-purpose flour

2 tablespoons cornstarch

Pinch salt

2 eggs, or 3 or 4 yolks

2 cups light cream, half-and-half, or whole milk

1 vanilla bean or 2 teaspoons vanilla extract

2 tablespoons unsalted butter, softened

2 to 3 cups strawberries, hulled, lightly washed, and well dried

$1/2$ cup strained raspberry, apricot, or currant preserves (optional)

1 tablespoon water or any liqueur (optional)

1 Preheat the oven to 425°F. Prick the crust all over with a fork. Line it with tin foil and weight the bottom with a pile of dried beans, rice (these can be reused for this same purpose), or other weights that will sit flat on the surface. Bake 12 minutes. Remove from the oven, reduce the heat to 350°F, and carefully remove the weight and foil. Bake another 10 to 15 minutes, or until the crust is a beautiful shade of brown. Remove and cool on a rack. (You can start the filling while the crust is baking if you like.)

2 In a small saucepan, combine the sugar with the flour, cornstarch, and salt. Mix together the eggs or yolks and cream. If you're using a vanilla bean, split it and scrape out the seeds; stir them into the cream mixture (reserve the bean itself to make vanilla sugar; see The Basics of Sugar, page 682). Stir the cream-egg mixture into the sugar-cornstarch mixture over medium heat; at first, whisk occasionally to eliminate lumps. Then stir almost constantly until the mixture boils and thickens, about 10 minutes. Continue to cook until the mixture coats the back of a spoon; when you draw your finger through this coating, the resulting line will hold its shape. Stir in the butter (and vanilla extract, if you're using it) and set aside. Cool the pastry cream for a few minutes, then proceed or refrigerate, topped directly with plastic wrap to prevent a skin from forming.

3 To assemble the tart, spread a layer of pastry cream on the bottom of the shell; you may not need all of it. Arrange the strawberries, hulled side down, on the cream, packing in as many as you can. If you'd like to glaze the tart, warm the strained preserves with 1 tablespoon water or any liqueur in a very small saucepan over medium-low heat, until thinned. Brush the top of the strawberries with this mixture and refrigerate until ready to serve.

Banana-Strawberry Cream Tart: Peel and thinly slice 2 or 3 bananas; toss them with 1 tablespoon freshly squeezed lemon juice and 1 tablespoon brown sugar. Arrange them on the cooled tart shell, then top with the pastry cream. Proceed with Step 3 as above.

Seven Simple Ideas for Fruit Tarts

1. Place a layer of about one cup toasted, coarsely chopped nuts, such as almonds or pecans, beneath the pastry cream.

2. Flavor the pastry cream with about one teaspoon ground cinnamon.

3. Stir about one tablespoon of brandy or flavored brandy—such as Grand Marnier or poire William—into the pastry cream.

4. Mix berries or other fruit at will—half strawberries, half blueberries, for example, are very nice.

5. Use pitted, peeled, and thinly sliced peaches, nectarines, or apricots in place of the berries; especially good with Frangipane Tart (see opposite).

6. Use cored, peeled, and thinly sliced apples or pears in place of the berries, and frangipane (see Frangipane Tart, opposite) in place of pastry cream. Make sure the slices are very thin (about $1/8$ inch) or they will not cook through.

7. Brush cooled, baked tart shell with a little melted semisweet, bittersweet, or white chocolate and then fill as desired. Especially good with pastry cream since chocolate will help keep crust from becoming soggy.

Simple Berry Tart

Makes about 8 servings

Time: About $1^1/_2$ hours

This is half the work, and contains far less fat, than the above recipe; use any berries you like.

1 recipe Rich Tart Crust, well chilled (page 695)

$1/_2$ cup sugar

$1/_4$ cup cornstarch

3 cups strawberries, raspberries, blackberries, and/or blueberries, picked over, stemmed, and hulled if necessary

① Preheat the oven to 425°F. Prick the crust all over with a fork. Line it with tin foil and weight the bottom with a pile of dried beans, rice (these can be reused for this same purpose), or other weights that will sit flat on the surface. Bake 15 minutes, or until the shell is no longer raw but is still quite pale. Remove from the oven, reduce the heat to 350°F, and carefully remove the weight and foil.

② Rub together the sugar and cornstarch with your fingers until well combined. Toss with about 2 cups of the berries; crush some of the berries with a fork or potato masher to help dissolve the sugar. Pile the berries into the tart crust, then top with the remaining berries, left whole (or halved, if they are large strawberries for example).

③ Bake for about 30 minutes, or until the fruit mixture is bubbly. Cool, then serve warm or at room temperature, alone or with ice cream or whipped cream (page 671).

Frangipane Tart

Makes about 8 servings

Time: About $1^1/_2$ hours

This tart, with a delicious almond filling, is great not only with berries but also with thinly sliced pears or apples.

1 recipe Rich Tart Crust, well chilled (page 695)

1 cup roughly chopped or sliced almonds

6 tablespoons ($3/_4$ stick) unsalted butter

$1/_3$ cup sugar

1 egg

3 cups strawberries, raspberries, blackberries, and/or blueberries, picked over, stemmed, and hulled if necessary, or peeled, cored, and thinly sliced apples or ripe pears

1 tablespoon freshly squeezed lemon juice

1. Preheat the oven to 425°F. Prick the crust all over with a fork. Line it with tin foil and weight the bottom with a pile of dried beans, rice (these can be reused for this same purpose), or other weights that will sit flat on the surface. Bake 15 minutes, or until the shell is no longer raw but is still quite pale. Remove from the oven, reduce the heat to 375°F, and carefully remove the weight and foil.

2. Combine the almonds, 4 tablespoons of the butter, and sugar in the bowl of a standing mixer. Beat for about 2 minutes, until the almonds are crushed and the ingredients well combined, scraping down the sides as necessary. Beat in the egg.

3. Spread the frangipane on the bottom of the shell. Arrange the fruit in the tart. Melt the remaining butter and stir in the lemon juice; brush fruit with this mixture. Bake until the frangipane is golden brown and the fruit is bubbling, 30 to 40 minutes. Cool, then serve warm or at room temperature, along or with ice cream or whipped cream (page 671).

Free-Form Tart with Fruit

Makes about 8 servings

Time: About 45 minutes

The simplest of all tarts, essentially a sweet pizza. Even including time for making the dough, you can whip one of these up in less than an hour. Best served with ice cream.

1 recipe Sweetened, Enriched Pie Crust (page 685), not yet rolled out

2 cups raspberries or other berries, picked over, washed, and dried

2 tablespoons unsalted butter, melted

2 tablespoons confectioners' sugar

1. Preheat the oven to 425°F. Roll the crust out and place it directly on a baking sheet. One of the beauties of this tart is that the crust need not be perfectly round, or any special size; just roll it out to a very rough 9- or 10-inch circle.

2. Cover the round with the fruit, leaving about a 1 1/2-inch border all around. Fold up the edges of the crust around the fruit, pinching them together. Don't try to cover all of the fruit, just the outer rim of it.

3. Brush the exposed dough with most of the butter, and brush a little onto the fruit as well. Bake until the crust is golden brown and the fruit bubbly, 20 to 30 minutes.

4. Remove from the oven and cool on a rack; serve warm, dusted with confectioners' sugar.

Seven Simple Ideas for Free-Form Tarts

1. Use pitted, peeled, and sliced soft fruit (peaches, plums, nectarines, mangoes, etc.).

2. Use peeled, cored, and very thinly sliced (one-eighth inch or less) apples or pears.

3. Place a layer of crushed almonds or walnuts (or frangipane; see Frangipane Tart, page 698) under the fruit.

4. Brush the fruit with a combination of two tablespoons honey and one tablespoon melted butter.

5. Toss the fruit with one teaspoon or more ground cinnamon before placing it on the crust.

6. Sprinkle with a mixture of one-half teaspoon ground cinnamon and two tablespoons sugar (or just plain sugar) after brushing with butter. Omit confectioners' sugar.

7. Toss fruit with one teaspoon or more minced crystallized ginger.

Caramelized Apple Tart

Tarte Tatin

Makes about 8 servings

Time: About 1 hour

There is nothing better than tarte tatin but, to be at its best, it should be made almost at the last minute. The ideal is to prepare it just before serving the meal and bake it while you're eating.

> 6 Granny Smith or any other tart, hard apple
> Juice of 1/2 lemon
> 8 tablespoons (1 stick) butter, cut into pieces
> 3/4 cup sugar
> 1 recipe Rich Tart Crust, chilled but not yet rolled out (page 695)

1 Preheat the oven to 400°F.

2 Peel, core, and quarter the apples; toss with the lemon juice. Press the butter into the bottom and sides of a medium, heavy, ovenproof skillet (cast iron is good). Sprinkle the butter with the sugar. Press the apple slices into the sugar, arranging them in concentric circles and making certain to pack them in tightly; they will shrink considerably during cooking.

3 Place the pan over medium-high heat. Cook for 15 to 20 minutes, or until the butter-sugar mixture has turned a very deep, dark brown. While it is cooking, roll out the pastry. When the apples are ready, remove the pan from the heat. Lay the pastry on top of the apples, bringing the dough to the edges of the pan to seal it. Prick the dough with a fork and bake about 20 minutes, or until the pastry is golden brown.

4 Remove the tart from oven and let it sit for 5 minutes. Shake the hot pan to loosen the apples stuck to the bottom of the skillet. Invert the whole tart onto a large serving dish, taking care not to burn yourself (the juices are hot). Serve immediately or at room temperature.

Linzer Torte

Makes about 8 servings

Time: About 1 1/2 hours

Despite its name, this is a tart not a torte (that is, a cake). The most interesting thing about it is that the flavor (and the work) is almost all in the crust; the filling is nothing more than jam. Linzer torte is traditionally made with a lattice topping; if your tart is on

---

MAKING A LATTICE TOP

(Step 1) Begin by rolling out a piece of dough a couple of inches longer than the pie plate, and five or six inches wide. Cut ten 1/2-inch strips. *(Step 2)* Weave the strips over the top of the pie. *(Step 3)* Continue to weave, bending back the strips laid in one direction in order to add strips in the other. *(Step 4)* When the weaving is completed, press the edges into the crust and trim.

the small side, you will have enough dough to do so (see the preceding page for illustrations).

1 cup blanched almonds

1½ cups (about 7 ounces) all-purpose flour

Pinch salt

½ cup sugar

¼ teaspoon ground cinnamon

Pinch ground cloves

12 tablespoons (1½ sticks) cold butter, cut into pieces

1 teaspoon grated or minced lemon zest

2 egg yolks

1 teaspoon ice water if needed

About 1½ cups raspberry jam, the best you can find

Freshly squeezed lemon juice (optional)

Confectioners' sugar for dusting

1 Preheat the oven to 400°F.

2 Toast the blanched almonds: Place them on a baking sheet and bake, shaking and stirring occasionally, for 5 to 10 minutes, or just until they begin to brown. Turn the oven to 425°F.

3 Cool the almonds, then place them in the container of a food processor and grind them finely; stop processing before they turn into a paste. Add the remaining dry ingredients and pulse once or twice to blend. Add the butter and lemon zest and turn on the machine; process until the mixture is crumbly, about 10 seconds.

4 Remove the dough from the food processor and use a wooden spoon or a rubber spatula to blend in the egg yolks; gradually gather the mixture into a ball. (If the mixture is too dry, add 1 teaspoon ice water.) Wrap the ball in plastic or waxed paper, flatten into a small disk, and freeze the dough for 10 minutes (or refrigerate for 30 minutes).

5 Roll out about two-thirds of the dough, keeping the remainder wrapped in plastic. Place the dough in an 8- or 9-inch tart pan. Prick the crust all over with a fork. Bake 12 minutes, or just until it begins to darken. Remove and cool on a rack; turn the oven to 350°F.

6 Taste the jam; if it is too sweet, cut it with a little lemon juice. When the shell is cool, spread on the jam. Make a lattice (page 700) with the reserved dough, and place it on top of the jam. Bake for about 40 minutes, or until the crust is brown and the jam is very hot. Remove and sprinkle with a little confectioners' sugar. Cool on a rack, and serve at room temperature.

The Basics of Puff and Choux Pastries

Of all the pastries that exist, puff pastry is the best: a literally countless number of thin, crisp layers of pastry, each separated by a film of butter. The butter keeps the layers from sticking together, and the steam escaping from the dough during baking causes them to rise, just enough to make each distinctive.

There are really only three rules to follow in making puff pastry:

1. Take your time (this is a long, drawn-out process).
2. If at any step in the process the butter feels oily to you, refrigerate the dough for thirty minutes.
3. Don't try it on a hot day unless your kitchen is air-conditioned; you'll never keep the butter cold enough.

The dough should always be "doughy," never oily or so hard it will be difficult to roll. Remember the goal—layers of flour separated by butter—and take it slow. I succeeded in making puff pastry on my first try, and so will you. When you're done, you'll be ready to make the best apple turnovers, Napoleons, and tart, pie, or quiche crusts you've ever tasted.

It's worth mentioning that some frozen puff pastry is not at all bad (check the ingredients: they should be mostly flour and butter).

Choux, or cream-puff pastry, is another story entirely, a miraculous dough that can be prepared by a child. There are no secrets here, just a few minutes of hard work which result in a pastry shell that can be filled with anything creamy.

Puff Pastry

Enough for about 4 dozen small pastries

Time: All day, largely unattended

This makes a lot, but the dough freezes perfectly, as long as it is well wrapped, for weeks and even months.

> 4 cups (about 18 ounces) all-purpose flour, plus some
> for dusting work surface
> 1 pound (4 sticks) unsalted cold butter
> 2 teaspoons salt
> About 1/2 cup ice water

1 Place 3 cups of the flour in the container of a food processor. Cut about 1/2 stick of the butter into cubes and add to the flour. Pulse several times until the butter and flour are combined. (Alternatively, rub the butter into the flour with your fingers.) Place the mixture in a bowl and add about 1/3 cup of the ice water; use a wooden spoon or a rubber spatula to gradually gather the mixture into a ball, adding additional water if necessary. Knead on a lightly floured surface until smooth, about 2 minutes; then wrap in plastic wrap and chill.

2 Meanwhile, use a mixer (one with a paddle or dough hook works best) to cream the remaining butter with the remaining flour. When it is well combined, soft and smooth, shape into a disk, wrap in plastic, and refrigerate for about 30 minutes, or until cold but still malleable.

3 Remove the dough from the refrigerator, place it on a lightly floured surface, and roll out to a rectangle about 8 × 16 inches; it should be about 1/4 inch thick. Remove the butter from the refrigerator, place it on a lightly floured surface, and roll it out to a rectangle about 4 × 8 inches. Brush excess flour from the butter disk and place it in the center of the dough; fold over all four corners of the dough, in a cloverleaf shape, to completely enclose the butter. Sprinkle the dough with flour, wrap, and refrigerate for at least 15 minutes, possibly longer. Again, you want the butter to be firm but not hard, the dough to be pliable.

4 Remove the dough from the refrigerator, place it on a lightly floured surface, and gently roll it out again, to a rectangle about 8 × 16 inches. Be careful not to roll the edges thinner than the rest of the dough. Use flour as necessary and take your time. Brush off excess flour, then bring each of the short ends of the rectangle together in the middle; roll lightly, then fold in half—as if closing a book. Dust with a little flour, then wrap and refrigerate for about 30 minutes.

5 Repeat Step 4 at least two and preferably four more times; the more you do it, the lighter and finer your pastry. Chill at least 1 hour before proceeding with the following recipes.

Palmiers, Arcs, or Other Puff Pastry Cookies

Makes about 50

Time: About 1 hour

Here are two suggestions for shaping puff pastry into cookies; as you'll see, they're fast and easy once you've taken the time to make puff pastry. Be liberal with the sugar, since the pastry itself is not sweetened. Use half of a puff pastry recipe if you prefer; the remainder will freeze well. See the illustrations for making palmiers on the next page.

(Step 1) To shape palmiers, first roll out a sheet of puff pastry dough until it is about $1/4$-inch thick; sprinkle liberally with sugar as you work. (Step 2) Fold each long end of the dough to the middle. (Step 3) Fold the dough in half. (Step 4) Fold it in half again. (Step 5) Roll gently to seal, but do not press too hard. (Step 6) Cut $1/2$-inch slices from the roll and bake, cut side up.

1 recipe Puff Pastry, (page 702)
Sugar as needed

1 Use sugar to coat a work surface. Cut the pastry in half and roll it out, sprinkling with sugar as you work, until it is less than $1/4$ inch thick. To make arcs, roll up the dough as you would a carpet. To make palmiers, fold each of the short ends in about a quarter of the way to the middle. Then fold again. Wrap and refrigerate for about 30 minutes.

2 Preheat the oven to 350°F. Slice the roll(s) into $1/4$-inch-thick slices, sprinkle with a little more sugar, and place on an ungreased baking sheet. Bake for about 30 minutes, or until golden brown, turning the cookies once after about 20 minutes.

Apple Turnovers

Makes about 12 small turnovers

Time: About 1 hour

If you've never had a real apple turnover, one made with puff pastry, you are in for a treat. The shattering, buttery crust contrasted with the sweet, soft apple filling is nothing short of a revelation.

4 tart apples, peeled and cored
1 tablespoon freshly squeezed lemon juice
1 tablespoon cornstarch
1 teaspoon minced or grated lemon zest, or more to taste
1 teaspoon ground cinnamon, or more to taste
$1/2$ cup sugar, or more to taste, plus more for dusting work surface and for sprinkling
$1/2$ recipe Puff Pastry, page 702

1 Grate the apples in a food processor or on the coarse side of a box grater. Toss them with the lemon juice immediately. Add cornstarch, lemon zest, cinnamon, and $1/2$ cup sugar, or to taste. Taste and add more lemon zest or cinnamon if you like.

2 Use sugar to coat a work surface. Cut the pastry in half and roll it out, sprinkling with sugar as you work, until the dough is less than $1/4$ inch thick. Cut 4-inch squares of puff pastry (there will be leftovers and ragged ends; use the trimmings to make cookies). Sprinkle lightly with sugar.

3 Put 2 tablespoons of the apple filling in the center of each square; brush the edges of the pastry very lightly with water, then fold over the corners to form a triangle. Seal gently with your fingers, then slash the top of the turnover with a razor blade once or twice so steam can escape. Place turnovers on ungreased baking sheet and chill while you preheat the oven (or longer, up to several hours).

4 Preheat the oven to 350°F. Brush the tops of the turnovers with a little water and sprinkle with sugar. Bake for about 40 minutes, or until the turnovers are golden brown. Serve warm or at room temperature.

Fruit or Jam Turnovers: You can fill turnovers with any fruit filling, but it should be thick and have some binding, such as cornstarch, tapioca, or flour, as do the fillings for the fruit pies on pages 687–690. Jam also makes a good turnover, but because it is so sweet, it's best to make the turnovers smaller and use less filling: Make 3-inch squares, and dot with 1 teaspoon of jam before folding over.

Cream Puff Pastry
Choux Pastry
Makes enough for at least 2 dozen pastries

Time: 15 minutes

One of the great miracles of cooking, cream puff pastry expands to at least three times its size, leaving a gaping hole in the middle that is perfect for filling. Thus it is the basis for cream puffs, éclairs, and a number of savory foods such as Gougères (page 29). It is not only less time-consuming than puff pastry, it takes almost no time, and even less skill. Try it once and it'll become a part of your repertoire forever.

1 cup water
8 tablespoons (1 stick) unsalted butter
Pinch salt
1 cup (about 4$1/2$ ounces) all-purpose flour
4 eggs

1 Combine the water, butter, and salt in a medium saucepan; turn the heat to medium-high and bring to a boil. Cook, stirring, until the butter melts, just a minute or two. Add the flour all at once and cook, stirring constantly, until the dough holds together in a ball, 5 minutes or less.

2 Add the eggs one at a time, beating hard after each addition (this is a little bit of work; feel free to use an electric mixer). Stop beating when the mixture is glossy.

3 Bake immediately according to one of the following recipes, or cover and refrigerate for up to 2 days before using.

Cream Puffs

Makes 2 dozen large or 3 or 4 dozen small

Time: About 1 hour

You can make these large or small. If you want to get really fancy, pipe them from a pastry tube fitted with a one-half-inch star tip or equivalent; two spoons work nearly as well.

    1 recipe Cream Puff Pastry, (page 704)
    2 cups sweetened whipped cream (page 671)

1 Preheat the oven to 400°F.

2 Pipe mounds of the cream puff pastry onto a lightly buttered baking sheet; or use two spoons to form mounds about an inch wide and a little bit higher than that. Bake for about 40 minutes, until very puffy, golden brown, and hollow-sounding when tapped. Prick each with a skewer once or twice to allow steam to escape, then cool to room temperature.

3 Use a pastry tube to pipe the filling into each cream puff, or simply cut off a top cap from each, load it up with whipped cream (or use pastry cream; see Strawberry Tart with Pastry Cream, page 697), and replace the cap. Serve immediately, or the puffs will become soggy.

Éclairs: Use a #7 tip on a pastry bag to pipe 4- to 6-inch-long fingers of cream puff pastry onto lightly greased sheets, or shape with spoons, handling as little as possible. Bake as above. Poke a hole in one end of each éclair and pipe in the filling, or simply cut a slit along the top and spoon in the filling. Top with a sauce made by melting together 1 cup milk and 1 cup semisweet chocolate chips or chopped pieces.

Cookies, Brownies, and Cakes

Cookies and brownies are our most commonly made desserts, not only because they have the right combination of flavor and texture but because they are incomparably easy to prepare. The first of a batch of cookies or brownies can be coming out of the oven half an hour after the inspiration hits you, and by then cleanup is done as well.

Cakes are another story entirely. On the basic side, they are essentially extra-sweet, extra-eggy quick breads. But they can become as complex as anything, with several different preparations needed before assembly. I steer clear of elaborate cakes here—those with a couple of layers, butter cream filling, and glossy icing are as adventurous as I care to get.

Most of the ingredients that go into cookies and cakes are covered in detail elsewhere, either in "Bread" or in "Pies, Tarts, and Pastries." But it's worth touching on a couple of finer points.

The first of these is leavening. There are three ways to cause any pastry to rise:

1. By whisking eggs or egg whites, you incorporate air into them making them so sturdy that they can support other ingredients—such as flour and fat—during the baking process. This is essentially a mechanical process.
2. By using yeast, a living organism which generates gas as a by-product of its consumption of carbohydrates. Combine yeast, liquid, and flour, and you get bubbles, which are in turn trapped by the flour-liquid mixture, causing the dough to rise.
3. By combining baking soda, or its derivative baking powder, with liquid, heat, and/or acidic ingredients. This causes a chemical reaction which produces gas.

Yeast is sometimes used in making cake-like desserts—especially coffee cakes, such as the one on page 241—but it is time-consuming, and its distinctive flavor is not always welcome in desserts. So, for the most part, we leaven desserts using eggs or baking soda or powder.

The second ingredient worth mentioning is fat. It's tempting to say, "In cookies and cakes, there is not fat worth considering other than butter. Period." But the fact is that olive oil can make a good cookie or cake (see Orange-Almond Cake, page 722), although it's a different animal. The real simple statement I prefer is, "If you're going to bake, steer clear of margarine and shortening." Neither is as good-tasting as butter (and neither is any less harmful to your body).

The Basics of Baking Soda and Baking Powder

Most superior desserts are leavened with eggs, but many high-quality baked goods rely upon chemical leaveners—baking powder and/or baking soda. Used judiciously, there is nothing wrong with this.

Baking soda—sodium bicarbonate—is a good leavener in those pastries that contain acid. You can, therefore, use it freely whenever you're baking with buttermilk, sour cream, or yogurt, and I usually do. (Even recipes using sweet milk can be adapted. If, for example, a recipe calls for two teaspoons baking powder and one cup sweet milk, for example, use one-half teaspoon baking soda and one cup buttermilk.)

If there is little or no acid in a recipe and you want to use baking soda (or you've run out of baking powder), mix 1 teaspoon baking soda and 2 teaspoons cream of tartar. This works because cream of tartar is acidic, and eliminates the need for additional acid in the batter. You can use this as a replacement for commercial baking powder—on a one-for-one basis—but you must work quickly once you combine wet and dry ingredients.

Why? Because this homemade baking powder is a single-action baking powder, one which begins to do its work the instant it is combined with liquid. Commercial baking powders are double-action; part of them begins to work when exposed to liquid, but another part works only when exposed to heat. You can see this: Little bubbles form between the time you combine ingredients and move the batter to the pan, but the batter continues to rise in the oven.

Commercial baking powder, therefore, is more effective than the homemade kind. But it isn't necessarily more desirable, because it has a distinctive flavor. (This is especially true of those containing aluminum. The only national brand I know of that contains no aluminum is Rumford, and it's worth looking for.) It also becomes less effective over time; you should replace your baking powder, regardless of whether it's used up, at least once a year, and preferably more often than that.

How to Cream Butter

When you combine butter and flour in a food processor, as you do for pie crusts, the butter can be—in fact, *should be*—ice cold. But when you cream butter for cookies or cakes, you use an electric mixer (or a fork), and the butter is much easier to work if it is slightly softened. If you plan ahead by an hour or so, this presents no problems. If, however, you decide to make cookies or a cake on the spur of the moment, you will want to soften the butter more quickly. To do that, cut the butter into small cubes (say, sixteen cubes for a stick of butter, easily accomplished), or microwave on the lowest power for ten-second intervals, removing the butter well before it actually begins to melt.

On Sifting Dry Ingredients

Flour, once an inconsistent product, is now so fine that sifting is usually unnecessary. Nor is it necessary when mixing flour with other dry ingredients, such as sugar, salt, or baking powder, although it's worth whisking those ingredients together with a fork or whisk just to eliminate any lumps that might exist. When you do need to sift—to put a layer of flour on the bottom of a pan, or in delicate recipes such as Angel Food Cake (page 725), put the flour through an old-fashioned sifter, or simply pass through a not-too-fine sieve.

The Basics of Cookies

There are basically two types of cookies: drop cookies and refrigerator cookies. Here are the differences:

Drop cookies are usually made just before baking. In fact, they can (and should) be made as the oven is preheating. They are soft, buttery, sweet, and, because they have height, perfect for containing other ingredients. (The chocolate chip is the paradigm of drop cookies.) To adjust any drop cookie recipe to your personal taste, remember this: Butter makes cookies tender, flour makes them cakey, shorter cooking times (within reason, of course) produce chewier cookies, and longer ones make them crispier.

Refrigerator cookies—also called rolled cookies, because they can be rolled out and cut with a lightly floured cookie cutter (or that old standby, a glass)—must be made in advance. This can be an advantage, because you can make the dough days ahead and bake them whenever you get the urge (it's a disadvantage when you don't have the dough but you want cookies, like right now). You can also freeze the dough, and need not defrost it before baking, as long as you're happy to slice it instead of rolling and cutting it into shapes.

On baking cookies   Most ovens have hot spots, and it usually doesn't matter much. But with cookies, it can make a difference—the cookies in the back of the oven, for example, or those on the bottom rack, may brown much faster than those in front. The solution to this is simple: Halfway through the estimated baking time, turn the baking sheets back to front; if you're cooking more than one sheet at the same time, rotate them top to bottom as well.

On storing cookies   Cookies rarely go stale, because no one can resist them; store them lightly covered, at room temperature, and they do fine. But

---

Thirteen Cookies and Bars That Are Fun to Make with Kids

Kids love to eat cookies, obviously, but they like to make them too. Here are some that are easy enough to allow the single-digit set to participate. And don't forget Golden Cupcakes or Chocolate Cupcakes (pages 724–725).

they can be frozen successfully if you like; just make sure they're covered or wrapped very tightly to protect them from unwanted flavors. Often, however, it's better to freeze the finished batter, especially with refrigerator cookies—wrap the log in a couple of layers of plastic and freeze. You can then slice directly from the freezer (thirty minutes of thawing will make that job a little easier) and bake.

Butter Drop Cookies

Makes 2 to 3 dozen

Time: About 30 minutes

Handle this batter gently; good butter cookies are tender, and overworking the batter will develop the gluten in the flour and make them tough.

2 cups (9 ounces) all-purpose flour
$1/2$ teaspoon baking powder
Pinch salt
8 tablespoons (1 stick) unsalted butter, softened if combining by hand or mixer, chilled if using a food processor, plus some for greasing the baking sheets
$3/4$ cup sugar
1 teaspoon vanilla extract
1 egg
$1/4$ cup milk, plus more if needed

1 Preheat the oven to 375°F.

2 To combine the ingredients by hand, mix the flour, baking powder, and salt together in a small bowl. Cream the butter with a fork, then mash in the sugar until well blended. Stir in the vanilla and the egg, then about half the flour mixture. Add the milk, then the remaining flour, then a little more milk, if necessary, to make a soft batter that can be dropped from a spoon.

To combine the ingredients with an electric mixer, combine the flour, baking powder, and salt together in a small bowl. Place the butter and sugar in the mixing bowl and beat on low speed until well blended and creamy. Add the vanilla and the egg and beat on low speed until well combined. Add about half the flour mixture, beat for a moment, then add the milk. Beat for about 10 seconds, then add the remaining flour and a little more milk, if necessary, to make a soft batter that can be dropped from a spoon.

To make the batter in a food processor, place all the dry ingredients in the processor and pulse once or twice to combine. Cut the chilled butter into bits, add to the machine, and process for about 10 seconds, until butter and flour are well blended. Add the vanilla, egg, and milk and pulse just enough to blend. If more milk is needed to make a soft batter than can be dropped from a spoon, add it by hand.

3 Drop rounded teaspoons of the batter onto buttered baking sheets and bake for about 10 minutes, or until the edges are browned. Let each sheet sit on a rack for 2 minutes before removing the cookies with a spatula and cooling them on a rack. Store in a covered container at room temperature for no more than a day or two.

Chocolate Drop Cookies: A combination of unsweetened and sweetened chocolate is good here, but you can use all sweetened if you prefer (if you use all unsweetened, increase the sugar to 1 cup). Increase the milk very slightly, to about $1/3$ cup. Melt 1 ounce each semisweet and unsweetened chocolate and add to the mixture after combining wet and dry ingredients.

Sour Cream or Sugar Drop Cookies: The use of sour cream not only gives you a tangy taste but lets you use baking soda, whose flavor is less obtrusive than that of baking powder. And these may be dropped, or refrigerated for about 1 hour, then rolled into

1. To make butter nut cookies, add one-half cup chopped nuts to the finished batter.
2. To make coconut cookies, add one cup dried unsweetened coconut to the finished batter.
3. To make butterscotch cookies, use two-thirds cup brown sugar in place of the white sugar.
4. To make orange or lemon cookies, add one tablespoon grated or minced orange or lemon zest to the finished batter; omit the vanilla. Add two tablespoons poppy seeds as well, if you like.
5. To make raisin cookies, add up to one-half cup raisins or chopped dried fruit to the finished batter.
6. To make ginger cookies, add two tablespoons or more chopped crystallized ginger to the finished batter.
7. To make cinnamon cookies, dust the cookies with a mixture of two tablespoons white sugar and one teaspoon ground cinnamon just before baking.
8. To make spice cookies, stir one teaspoon ground spice, especially ginger, cardamom, or cinnamon, into the finished batter.

walnut-sized balls before baking. Substitute 1 teaspoon baking soda for the all of the baking powder. Substitute sour cream for the milk; you will need about $1/2$ cup. To make sugar cookies, roll the dough balls in sugar, or sprinkle drop cookies with sugar halfway through baking.

Olive Oil Drop Cookies: The simplest variation is to do nothing more than substitute light olive oil (not extra-virgin oil, whose flavor may dominate) for the butter; increase the flour by $1/2$ cup. But you also can make a delicious, not-too-sweet olive oil cookie

this way: Increase the flour by $1/4$ cup; decrease the sugar to $1/2$ cup. Add $1/4$ teaspoon freshly ground black pepper and 1 teaspoon finely minced fresh rosemary leaves (or $1/2$ teaspoon crushed dried rosemary) with other dry ingredients. Substitute red wine for the milk and bake as above. When done, sprinkle very lightly with confectioners' sugar. For slightly crunchier, more flavorful cookies, substitute $1/2$ cup cornmeal for the same amount of flour in this variation.

Classic Chocolate Chip Cookies

Makes 3 to 4 dozen

Time: About 30 minutes

This simple drop cookie recipe makes a typically chewy chocolate chip cookie, one with a little height. Add two tablespoons milk or water to the batter if you want a flatter, crisper cookie.

$1/2$ pound (2 sticks) unsalted butter, softened
$3/4$ cup white sugar
$3/4$ cup brown sugar
2 eggs
2 cups (9 ounces) all-purpose flour
$1/2$ teaspoon baking soda
$1/2$ teaspoon salt
1 teaspoon vanilla extract
2 cups chocolate chips

1 Preheat the oven to 375°F.
2 Use an electric mixer to cream together the butter and sugars; add the eggs one at a time and beat until well blended.
3 Combine the flour, baking soda, and salt in a bowl and add them to the batter by hand, stirring to blend. Stir in the vanilla and then the chocolate chips.

Drop by teaspoons or tablespoons onto ungreased baking sheets and bake until lightly browned, about 10 minutes. Cool for about 2 minutes on the sheets before using a spatula to transfer the cookies to a rack to finish cooling. Store in a covered container at room temperature for no more than a day or two.

Oatmeal Cookies

Makes 3 to 4 dozen

Time: About 30 minutes

These can be made with raisins, chopped dried fruit (cranberries and cherries are good), chocolate chips, or coconut—the batter can handle up to $1^1/2$ cups of any of these, or a combination. Stir them into the batter along with the dry ingredients.

8 tablespoons (1 stick) unsalted butter, softened
$1/2$ cup white sugar
$1/2$ cup brown sugar
2 eggs
$1^1/2$ cups (about 7 ounces) all-purpose flour
2 cups rolled oats (not the instant kind)
$1/2$ teaspoon ground cinnamon
Pinch salt
2 teaspoons baking powder
$1/2$ cup milk
$1/2$ teaspoon vanilla or almond extract

1 Preheat the oven to 375°F.
2 Use an electric mixer to cream together the butter and sugars; add the eggs one at a time and beat until well blended.
3 Combine the flour, oats, cinnamon, salt, and baking powder in a bowl. Alternating with the milk, add the dry ingredients to the batter by hand, a little a time, stirring to blend. Stir in the vanilla or almond

extract. Drop by teaspoons or tablespoons onto ungreased baking sheets and bake until lightly browned, 12 to 15 minutes. Cool for about 2 minutes on the sheets before using a spatula to transfer the cookies to a rack to finish cooling. Store in a covered container at room temperature for no more than a day or two.

Lacy Oatmeal Cookies: Melt the butter and combine it with the sugars, oats, and salt; beat in the eggs. Omit the flour, baking powder, milk, and vanilla; add the cinnamon if you like. Bake at 350°F on greased baking sheets for 8 to 10 minutes; let rest a minute before removing with a thin-bladed spatula. Cool on a rack.

Refrigerator (Rolled) Cookies

Makes at least 3 dozen

Time: 30 minutes, plus time to chill

These are ideal for cookie-cutter cookies because refrigerating a stiff cookie dough makes it easy to roll out. That doesn't mean you must do so; the alternative is to shape the dough into logs and slice it thinly before baking. Generally, rolled cookies are more crumbly and less chewy than drop cookies. But if you want them on the chewy side, underbake them just a little bit, removing them from the oven while the center is still a little soft.

I like the flavor and texture of cookies that are very dense and rich in butter—not unlike shortbread—but there are alternatives; see below.

To glaze cookies, drizzle or spread them with a mixture of one cup confectioners' sugar and just enough milk or cream to make a thin paste—about one-third cup. Or decorate before baking with sprinkles or other tiny candies.

½ pound (2 sticks) unsalted butter, softened,
   plus some for greasing the baking sheets
1 cup sugar
1 egg
3 cups (about 14 ounces) all-purpose flour,
   plus some for dusting the work surface
Pinch salt
1 teaspoon baking powder
1 tablespoon milk
1 teaspoon vanilla extract

1   Use an electric mixer to cream the butter and sugar together until light; beat in the egg.

2   Combine the flour, salt, and baking powder in a bowl. Mix the dry ingredients into the butter-sugar mixture, adding a little milk at a time as necessary. Stir in the vanilla.

3   Shape the dough into a disk (for rolled cookies) or a log (for sliced cookies), and refrigerate for at least 2 hours, or as long as 2 days (or wrap very well, and freeze indefinitely).

4   Preheat the oven to 400°F. Cut the dough disk in half. Lightly flour a work surface and a rolling pin and roll gently until about ⅛ inch thick, adding flour as necessary and turning the dough to prevent sticking. Cut with any cookie cutter. (To slice, simply cut slices from the log, about ⅛ inch thick.)

5   Bake on lightly greased baking sheets until the edges are lightly brown and the center set, 6 to 10 minutes. Let rest on the sheets for a minute or two before removing with a spatula and cooling on a rack. Store in a covered container at room temperature for no more than a day or two.

Lighter Rolled Cookies: In Step 1, add ½ cup additional white (or brown) sugar and beat 2 eggs into creamed butter and sugar. In Step 2, add ½ teaspoon baking soda to the dry ingredients (including the baking powder); add ¼ cup of milk to the batter along with the flour mixture.

Nine Simple Ideas for Rolled Cookies

1. Stir one tablespoon grated lemon or orange zest into the flour mixture before combining with the butter-sugar mixture (omit the vanilla). Add two tablespoons poppy seeds as well, if you like.

2. Add one cup dried unsweetened coconut to the butter-sugar mixture, alternating with the flour.

3. Add one cup chopped walnuts, pecans, almonds, or hazelnuts to the batter along with the vanilla. Or add one-half cup nuts and one-half cup raisins.

4. Add one teaspoon ground ginger to the flour mixture; for a super-ginger flavor, add one-quarter cup minced crystallized ginger to the butter-sugar mixture.

5. Replace some or all of the white sugar with brown sugar.

6. Add one-half cup raisins or chopped dried fruit to the dough.

7. Dust cookies with mixture of two tablespoons white sugar and one teaspoon ground cinnamon just before baking.

8. Stir one teaspoon ground spice, especially ginger, cardamom, or cinnamon, into the dough.

9. Replace vanilla extract with one-half teaspoon amount of almond extract. Use in combination with chopped nuts if you like.

Fancier Rolled Cookies: After rolling and cutting (or slicing), top each cookie with a pecan, walnut, or other nut; a raisin or other piece of dried fruit; an M&M or other small candy; some sprinkles; or any other decoration you like. Or glaze the baked and cooled cookies with chocolate, using the glaze in number 4 of Seven Simple Ideas for Biscotti (page 716).

Peanut Butter Cookies: In Step 1, cream ½ to ¾ cup peanut butter with the butter-sugar mixture. You can use smooth or crunchy peanut butter, as you like. You can also add about $1/2$ cup chopped peanuts (try those with salt for an interesting change), along with the vanilla, in Step 2.

Aunt Big's Gingersnaps

Makes 4 to 5 dozen

Time: About 40 minutes, plus time to chill

These are super-crisp gingersnaps, the kind that stick in your teeth, and are savory enough to eat in place of dinner. "The dough is also great undercooked," says my friend Sally, who is Aunt Big's niece.

$1/2$ pound (2 sticks) unsalted butter, softened
1 cup sugar
1 cup molasses
1 heaping teaspoon baking soda
2 tablespoons hot water
$3^1/2$ cups (about 1 pound) all-purpose flour
1 heaping tablespoon ground ginger
1 tablespoon ground cinnamon
Pinch salt

1 Use an electric mixer to cream the butter, sugar, and molasses until smooth. Mix the baking soda with 2 tablespoons hot water and beat into this mixture.

2 Mix together the flour, spices, and salt in a bowl; stir them into the butter mixture and beat well. Shape into 2 long rolls, wrap in waxed paper, and refrigerate several hours or overnight.

3 Preheat the oven to 350°F. Slice the cookies as thinly as you can, place on ungreased baking sheets, and bake about 10 minutes, watching carefully to prevent burning. Remove from sheet when still warm and cool on a rack. Store in a covered container at room temperature for several days.

Gingerbread Men: Remove the refrigerated dough from the refrigerator about 15 minutes before beginning to work; preheat the oven. When the dough is slightly softened, roll it out as thinly as possible; hand-cut if you're brave, or use a gingerbread man cutter. Bake as above, then cool. Decorate, if you like, with small candies and a glaze made from confectioners' sugar thinned with milk. Store in a covered container at room temperature for up to several days.

Molasses-Spice Cookies: Add $1/2$ teaspoon freshly grated nutmeg, $1/8$ teaspoon ground cloves, and $1/4$ teaspoon ground allspice along with the ginger.

Shortbread

Makes $1^1/2$ to $2^1/2$ dozen

Time: About 20 minutes, plus time to chill

"Short," meaning with lots of butter—and therefore very tender (cornstarch makes them even more so) and *very* yummy. You can cut these, put them on a baking sheet, cover them, and freeze them for days before baking, straight from the freezer. Or just chill them for half an hour or so and then slice and bake.

$1/2$ pound (2 sticks) unsalted butter, softened
$3/4$ cup sugar
1 egg yolk
$1^1/2$ cups (about 7 ounces) all-purpose flour
$1/2$ cup cornstarch
Pinch salt

1 Use an electric mixer to combine the butter and sugar; mix on low speed, just until combined, 30 seconds or so. Still on low speed, beat in the egg yolk, then the flour, cornstarch, and salt, until the mixture barely holds together; this will take a few minutes.

2 There are two ways to shape the dough and both require chilling. If you want to make real shapes, form the dough into a rough ball or disk, wrap in plastic, and freeze or refrigerate for at least 30 minutes, or until fairly firm. Roll it out on a lightly floured board until it is ¼ inch thick. Cut into any shapes you like, then place the cookies on a baking sheet. They will not spread much, so you can put them pretty close together. Chill for 1 hour, or freeze for as long as you want. (Once they're frozen, you can take them off the sheets and store them in a plastic bag for several days if you like.)

Alternatively, shape the dough into a round, triangular, or rectangular log and refrigerate or freeze until firm, about 30 minutes. (You can also store the log, frozen.) Slice ¼ inch thick, place on a sheet, and bake.

3 Preheat the oven to 275°F. Bake the shortbreads for about 30 minutes, or until just firm but still quite tender and not at all brown. Remove from the oven, let cool for a minute, and then gently remove from the sheet with a spatula. Store on a plate, uncovered, for no more than a day.

Five Simple Ideas for Shortbread

You can combine these ideas if you like.

1. Add two tablespoons minced orange or lemon zest to the dough. For more flavor, decrease the butter by two tablespoons; replace it with two tablespoons freshly squeezed orange or lemon juice.
2. Add one-half cup toasted/finely ground pecans, hazelnuts, almonds, or walnuts to the dough.
3. Add one teaspoon ground cinnamon or ginger to the dough.
4. Add about one teaspoon finely minced rosemary, thyme, or lavender.
5. Add one teaspoon vanilla or almond extract (especially good with nuts).

Meringues
Makes 4 to 5 dozen

Time: 2 hours or more, largely unattended

Light, sweet, and low in fat, meringues are the perfect use for leftover egg whites. They are best made in dry weather. If your oven is small, use two egg whites and one-half cup sugar; you want to bake all the meringues at once. If you like, omit the nuts and coconut and stir about one cup chocolate chips into the batter before baking.

½ cup pecans or walnuts
3 egg whites, at room temperature
¾ cup superfine sugar
½ teaspoon vanilla extract
1 cup dried unsweetened shredded coconut

1 Preheat the oven to its lowest setting, preferably about 150°F. Line two baking sheets with parchment paper.

2 Toast the pecans in a dry skillet over medium heat, shaking the pan occasionally, just until they begin to brown. Cool and chop; do not mince or grind.

3 Use an electric mixer to beat the egg whites until foamy; then add the sugar, a bit at a time, until the mixture is stiff and dry, the whites no longer shiny. Gently fold in the vanilla, nuts, and coconut.

4 You can pipe the meringue mixture through a pastry bag onto the baking sheets, or shape it with two spoons into small ovals. Bake in the oven at least 2 hours (assuming you are baking at 150°F), or until the meringues are dry but not brown; they will still be tender. If they are still quite moist, bake another hour. If, after 3 hours, they are still not done, turn off the oven and let them sit in there, undisturbed, for another hour or two. Cool, then serve. Meringues will keep well in an airtight container at room temperature if the humidity is low, but should be eaten more or less immediately otherwise.

Biscotti

Makes 3 to 4 dozen

Time: About 1¼ hours

Biscotti can be made with no butter at all, which makes them extra crunchy. Butter, however, adds tenderness and flavor, and I prefer them that way.

4 tablespoons (½ stick) unsalted butter, softened, plus more for greasing the baking sheets
¾ cup sugar
2 eggs
½ teaspoon vanilla or almond extract
2¼ cups (about 10 ounces) all-purpose flour, plus more for dusting the baking sheets
2 teaspoons baking powder
Pinch salt

1 Preheat the oven to 375°F. Use an electric mixer to cream together the butter and the sugar until light and fluffy; beat in the eggs, one at a time, then the vanilla or almond extract.

2 Mix the flour, baking powder, and salt in a bowl, and add it to the batter a little at a time.

3 Butter two baking sheets and dust them with flour; invert the sheets and tap them to remove excess flour. Divide the dough in half and shape each half into a 2-inch-wide log. Place each log onto one of the baking sheets.

4 Bake until the loaves are golden and beginning to crack on top, about 30 minutes; remove the logs from the oven. Lower the oven temperature to 250 degrees.

5 When the loaves are cool enough to handle, cut each on the diagonal into ½-inch-thick slices, using a serrated knife. Place the slices on the sheets, return to the oven, and leave them there until they dry out, about 15 to 20 minutes; turn once. Cool on wire racks. These will keep in an airtight container for several days.

Seven Simple Ideas for Biscotti

Use these ideas alone or in combination:

1. Add one teaspoon ground fennel or anise seeds, or one teaspoon ground cinnamon, to the dry ingredients.
2. Stir one cup slivered blanched almonds; toasted and chopped hazelnuts; whole pine nuts; or other chopped nuts into the prepared dough before baking.
3. Mix one teaspoon minced lemon zest or orange zest into the dry ingredients.
4. Melt eight ounces semisweet chocolate with three tablespoons unsalted butter. Spread this mixture onto one side of the biscotti when they are done. Cool on rack until chocolate coating is firm.
5. Stir about one-quarter cup minced crystallized ginger into the dry ingredients.
6. Mix about one-half cup dried fruit, such as raisins, cherries, or cranberries, into the dough before baking.
7. Mix about three-quarter cup chocolate chips into the dough before baking.

Coconut Macaroons

Makes about 2 dozen

Time: About 45 minutes, plus time to chill

Almond macaroons may be standard, but coconut ones are better, faster, and easier. Note that they contain no butter, egg yolks, or cream, and can be assembled in no time flat.

3/4 cup sugar

2 1/2 cups shredded unsweetened coconut

2 egg whites

1 teaspoon vanilla extract

Pinch salt

①　Preheat the oven to 350°F. Combine all ingredient in a large bowl and mix well with a rubber spatula or your hands.

②　Use a non-stick baking sheet, or line a baking sheet with parchment paper. Wet your hands and make small piles of the mixture, each 1 to 2 tablespoons, about an inch apart. Bake until light brown, about 15 minutes. Remove the baking sheet and cool on a rack for at least 30 minutes before eating. These keep well in a covered container for up to 3 days.

The Basics of Brownies and Bars

Brownie and bar doughs are virtually identical to cookie dough (in fact, you can take any drop cookie dough and bake it in brownie form). The major difference is that brownies and bars never become crisp (unless, of course, you overcook them mightily). If you like very soft brownies, remove them from the oven when the center first sets; a toothpick inserted into the middle will still bring a few crumbs out with it, although it will not actually be wet.

Brownies
Makes 1 to 2 dozen

Time: 30 to 40 minutes

My kids have taught me two things about making brownies: One, they're better without nuts than with (obviously a matter of taste, but mine has changed). Two, if you line the baking pan with lightly greased aluminum foil, you reduce cleanup time by fifty percent; not bad. These are chewy and dense, dominated by chocolate and nothing else. If you like cakier brownies, add one-half teaspoon baking powder to the flour.

2 ounces unsweetened chocolate, roughly chopped

8 tablespoons (1 stick) unsalted butter, softened, plus a little for the greasing pan

1 cup sugar

2 eggs

1/2 cup all-purpose flour

Pinch salt

1/2 teaspoon vanilla extract

①　Preheat the oven to 350°F. Grease an 8-inch square baking pan, or line it with aluminum foil and grease the foil.

②　Combine the chocolate and butter in a small saucepan over very low heat, stirring occasionally. When the chocolate is just about melted, remove from the heat and continue to stir until the mixture is smooth.

③　Transfer the mixture to a bowl and stir in the sugar. Then beat in the eggs, one at a time. Gently stir in the flour, salt, and vanilla. Pour and scrape into the prepared pan and bake 20 to 25 minutes, or until just barely set in the middle. It's better to underbake brownies than to overbake them. Cool on a rack before cutting. Store, covered and at room temperature, for no more than a day.

1. Add one-half to one cup chopped nuts to the batter; toast the nuts first for even better flavor.
2. Add one-half to one cup chocolate chips to the batter.
3. Use one-half teaspoon almond or mint extract in addition to or in place of the vanilla.
4. Add one-half cup mashed bananas to the batter.
5. Add one-quarter cup bourbon, scotch, or other whisky to the batter; increase the flour by one tablespoon.
6. Add two tablespoons instant espresso powder with the vanilla.
7. Stir one-half cup dried fruit, especially dried cherries, into the prepared batter.
8. Top with Vanilla Butter Cream Frosting or Chocolate Butter Cream Frosting (pages 727–728).

Butterscotch Brownies

Blondies

Makes 1 to 2 dozen

Time: 30 to 40 minutes

Maybe you're allergic to chocolate, or don't like it, or are out of it. Maybe you just feel like a change. These will fix you right up. Add one cup of chocolate chips to the batter if you want to hedge a little; nuts, or any of the other ideas above, are also good.

8 tablespoons (1 stick) unsalted butter, softened, plus a little for greasing the pan
1 cup brown sugar
1 egg
1 teaspoon vanilla extract or $1/2$ teaspoon almond extract
Pinch salt
1 cup ($4^1/2$ ounces) all-purpose flour

1. Preheat the oven to 350°F. Grease an 8-inch square baking pan, or line it with aluminum foil and grease the foil.
2. Melt the butter over low heat. Transfer to a bowl and use an electric mixer to beat in the sugar until very smooth, then beat in the egg and vanilla, stirring down the sides of the bowl every now and then.
3. Add the salt, then gently stir in the flour. Pour into the prepared pan and bake 20 to 25 minutes, or until just barely set in the middle. It's better to underbake brownies than to overbake them. Cool on a rack before cutting. Store, covered and at room temperature, for no more than a day.

Gabrielle's Lemon Squares

Makes 1 to 2 dozen squares

Time: About 1 hour

These two-step squares are sweet-tart and moist.

8 tablespoons (1 stick) unsalted butter, softened, plus a little for greasing the pan
$1^1/4$ cups sugar
1 cup all purpose flour, plus 2 tablespoons (about 5 ounces)
2 eggs
2 tablespoons freshly squeezed lemon juice
$1/2$ teaspoon baking soda
Grated or minced zest of 1 lemon
Confectioners' sugar

1. Preheat the oven to 350°F. Grease an 8-inch square baking pan.
2. Use an electric mixer to cream the butter with the $1/4$ cup of sugar. Stir in the cup of flour. This mixture will be quite dry; press into the greased pan and bake for 15 minutes, no longer. Remove from the oven and cool slightly.

③ Beat together the eggs, lemon juice, baking soda, remaining sugar and flour, and lemon zest. Pour over the crust and bake until firm on the edges but still a little soft in the middle, another 20 minutes. Cool, then sprinkle with confectioners' sugar. Cut into squares and serve. Store, covered and refrigerated, for up to 2 days.

Cream Cheese Brownies

Makes 16

Time: About 1 hour

The richest, densest, most luxurious brownies I know—sort of like very heavy chocolate cheesecake.

4 ounces German sweet chocolate or semisweet chocolate, roughly chopped

5 tablespoons unsalted butter, softened, plus some for greasing the pan

4 ounces cream cheese

1 cup sugar

3 eggs

1 cup plus 1 tablespoon (about 4$^1/_2$ ounces) all-purpose flour

$^1/_2$ teaspoon freshly squeezed lemon juice

1$^1/_2$ teaspoons vanilla extract

$^1/_2$ teaspoon baking powder

Pinch salt

$^1/_2$ cup chopped walnuts (optional)

$^1/_2$ teaspoon almond extract

① Preheat the oven to 350°F. Grease a 9-inch square baking pan.

② Combine the chocolate and 3 tablespoons of the butter in a small saucepan over very low heat, stirring occasionally. When the chocolate is just about melted, remove from the heat and continue to stir until the mixture is smooth.

③ Use a fork or electric mixer to cream the remaining butter with the cream cheese and $^1/_4$ cup of the sugar. Beat in one of the eggs. Stir in the tablespoon of flour, lemon juice, and $^1/_2$ teaspoon of the vanilla.

④ In a separate bowl, use an electric mixer to beat the remaining eggs until thick; gradually add the remaining sugar and beat until quite thick (when you remove the mixer from the eggs, a ribbon of egg will fall from the beaters).

⑤ In a separate bowl, mix together the baking powder, salt, and remaining flour. Gently stir into the beaten egg mixture. Add the chocolate mixture, nuts if using, almond extract, and remaining vanilla. Spread half the chocolate mixture in the bottom of the baking pan; top with the cream cheese mixture, then the remaining chocolate mixture. Swirl through all with a rubber spatula to create a marbled effect. Bake 25 to 30 minutes, or until just barely set in the middle. Cool on a rack before cutting. Store, covered and refrigerated, for no more than a day.

The Basics of Cakes

Some cakes are so elaborate that they take all day to make; I, for one, do not have time for these. The result can be gorgeous (once you've practiced for a few years), but no better-tasting than a simple cake. I leave these complicated creations to professionals.

But the other end of the spectrum is even more distasteful. This is the standard American cake, which is more likely to begin in a box than in a refrigerator. Many cakes, especially those made from mixes, are merely high, good-looking, overly sweet things that taste of sugar and little else. They are no more than a symbol of a real cake, good-looking and impressive until you put a piece in your mouth.

A good cake is meltingly tender, tasting of butter, eggs, and simple seasonings such as chocolate, vanilla, or lemon, sweet but not overly so, good-looking in its

None of the cakes in this chapter are difficult to make, but some make a nicer presentation than others. Some cakes that will wow your guests:

classic simplicity and regal stature. The cakes here meet those standards.

Because no cake is truly simple—even the easiest have a dozen ingredients, and may require several procedures before baking—it's difficult to argue that a single ingredient is of paramount importance. But cakes have a way of showcasing off-flavors: If an ingredient is stale (or worse, rancid), or even second-rate, that flavor will somehow pop to the fore. Use high-quality butter, eggs, chocolate, nuts, and extracts for the best cakes.

Use the right bakeware, too: The difference between an eight-inch and a nine-inch cake pan is nearly twenty square inches—that's a large distance over which to spread a batter. If you plan to do a lot of cake baking, you'll need three each eight- and nine-inch layer pans, a ten-inch springform pan (the kind with the removable rim), and a nine-inch tube pan, at least. You'll also want to buy a standing mixer or at the very least a handheld electric mixer if you don't have one already; the vigorous action of food processors is great for bread, where you want to develop the gluten and toughen the dough, but disastrous for cakes, where a tender crumb is the goal.

Note that cakes with icing can hold for a day, if covered, but no cake—iced or not—is ever as tender and moist as it is the day you make it.

As discussed in The Basics of White Flour (page 219), cakes have more tender texture when made with cake flour, although all-purpose flour is usually a good substitute. (Even better than all-purpose flour, though, is all-purpose flour mixed with cornstarch— seven-eighths cup flour to one-eighth cup cornstarch for every cup of flour needed.) When you try cake flour, or the cornstarch solution, you will notice the difference and stick with it.

When baking cakes, be sure to butter the entire pan, and flour it lightly as well: Smear the butter all over, dust with flour, then tap out the excess flour. To be doubly sure you don't leave part of the delicate batter behind, it pays, too, to line the pan with parchment or waxed paper.

Finally, as with cookies, when you're baking cakes, rotate the pan(s) so that different sections cook in different parts of the oven for equal times.

Single-Layer Butter Cake

Makes at least 8 servings

Time: About 1 hour

This is my favorite "plain" cake, a purebred of all the essential ingredients in the right proportions. It can be served plain, with a little confectioners' sugar, or with some fruit salad. Or you can split, fill, and top it with whipped cream (page 671), jam, or any icing.

12 tablespoons (1 1/2 sticks) unsalted butter, softened, plus butter for greasing the pan and paper

Flour for dusting the pan

1 1/4 cups sugar

6 eggs

1/2 pound blanched almonds

Grated or minced zest of 1 lemon or orange, or more if you like

1 Preheat the oven to 350°F. Butter the bottom and sides of a 2-inch-deep 10-inch layer or spring-form pan; cover the bottom with a circle of waxed or parchment paper, butter the paper, and sift flour over the whole pan; invert to remove the excess flour.

2 Use an electric mixer to cream the butter and 1/4 cup of the sugar. Separate 3 of the eggs and reserve the whites. Beat in the yolks one at a time, until the mixture is light in color.

3 Grind the nuts in a food processor until they are the consistency of meal. Mix them with 3/4 cup of the sugar and the lemon zest. Beat in 3 whole eggs, one at a time, blending well.

4 Beat the egg whites; when they are foamy, gradually beat in the remaining 1/4 cup sugar, until the mixture holds a soft peak. Combine the butter and nut mixtures and stir. Gently fold in the beaten egg whites and pour into the pan.

5 Bake for about 30 minutes, or until a toothpick inserted into the center of the cake comes out clean. Let cool for 10 minutes, then unmold. This keeps fairly well for a day or two, wrapped in waxed paper.

Sand Cake

Makes at least 8 servings

Time: About 1 1/4 hours

A buttery northern European specialty whose name derives from its delightfully crumbly texture.

1/2 pound (2 sticks) unsalted butter, softened, plus a little more for greasing the pan

1/2 cup fresh bread crumbs

1 3/4 cups (about 8 ounces) all-purpose flour

1/4 cup cornstarch

2 teaspoons baking powder

1/4 teaspoon salt

2 teaspoons ground cardamom

1/2 teaspoon ground ginger

1/2 teaspoon ground cinnamon

1/4 teaspoon ground nutmeg

1 cup sugar

4 eggs

1 teaspoon vanilla extract

1 Preheat the oven to 350°F. Butter the bottom, sides, and cone of an 8- or 9-inch tube pan and sprinkle with bread crumbs; invert pan over the sink to remove excess crumbs.

2 Sift together the flour, cornstarch, baking powder, salt, and spices and set aside. Use an electric mixer to cream the butter with the sugar until light and fluffy, 5 minutes or so. Add the eggs one at a time, beating until well blended. Add the vanilla and beat another 30 seconds.

3 Add the dry ingredients all at once; mix by hand only until they are well incorporated. Pour and scrape the batter into the prepared pan. Bake 45 minutes before checking; the cake is done when it is golden brown and a toothpick inserted in its center comes out clean.

4 Remove the cake from the oven and let it rest for a couple of minutes. Run a knife between cake and pan, cover the pan with a rack, and invert the rack and pan. Cool before serving, plain, with whipped cream (page 671), or sprinkled with confectioners' sugar. Store, covered with waxed paper and at room temperature, for no more than a day.

Quick Coffee Cake

Makes at least 8 servings

Time: About 1 hour

See also Yeasted Coffee Cake (page 241). Since this enriched biscuit batter is leavened with baking powder, it's much faster.

8 tablespoons (1 stick) cold unsalted butter,
   plus some for greasing the pan
2 cups all-purpose flour, plus 3 tablespoons
   (about 10 ounces)
1 1/4 cups sugar
2 teaspoons ground cinnamon
1 cup chopped walnuts or pecans
2 teaspoons baking powder
1/2 teaspoon salt
1 egg
3/4 cup milk

1 Preheat the oven to 375°F. Grease a 9-inch square baking pan. Combine 3 tablespoons of flour, 3/4 cup of sugar, 1 teaspoon of cinnamon, and 3 tablespoons of butter with the nuts. Set aside.

2 Combine remaining 2 cups of flour, the baking powder, salt, and the remaining 1/2 cup of sugar, 1 teaspoon of cinnamon, and 5 tablespoons of the butter, cut into bits, in a bowl (you can use an electric mixer for this; use low speed). Mix well with a fork until all of the flour is coated with some of the butter.

3 Still on low speed, beat the egg into the butter-flour mixture, then the milk until blended. Pour half the batter into the prepared pan and sprinkle over it about half the streusel mixture. Add the remaining batter, then the remaining streusel. Bake for about 30 minutes, or until a toothpick inserted in the center comes out clean. Cool on a rack for at least 15 minutes before cutting. Best served warm, but not bad a day or two later, reheated.

Orange-Almond Cake

Makes at least 8 servings

Time: About 1 hour

This cake is low in saturated fat but not flavor.

1/2 cup light olive oil (do not use extra-virgin oil),
   plus some for greasing the pan
1 1/4 cups sugar
2 eggs
3/4 cup blanched slivered almonds
2 1/2 cups (about 12 ounces) all-purpose flour
1/2 teaspoon ground cinnamon
1 1/2 teaspoons baking powder
1/4 teaspoon salt
1/2 cup orange juice, preferably freshly squeezed,
   plus 1/3 cup additional orange juice for the glaze
   (optional)
Grated or minced zest of 1 orange
1/3 cup confectioners' sugar for the glaze (optional)

1 Preheat the oven to 350°F. Brush the bottom, sides, and cone of an 8- or 9-inch tube pan with olive oil.

2 Use an electric mixer to combine the olive oil and sugar, then add the eggs and beat until thick and fluffy, 5 to 7 minutes. Grind 1/2 cup of the almonds until fine. Mix them with the flour, cinnamon, baking powder, and salt.

3 Stir a portion of the flour mixture into the egg mixture, then add a little of the orange juice. Repeat, stirring after each addition, until well blended. Stir in the orange zest, then turn the batter into the tube pan; sprinkle with the remaining slivered almonds.

4 Bake for 35 minutes or until a toothpick inserted in the center comes out clean. Cool on a rack for 15 minutes in the pan, then invert onto a rack and remove the pan. Cut carefully around the sides of the cake and remove. Cool for 10 minutes before turning right side up onto another rack.

5 To glaze, stir together the orange juice and confectioners' sugar until smooth and spoon over the top of the cake. Let cool completely before cutting. Store for up to a day at room temperature, covered with waxed paper.

Pound Cake

Makes at least 8 servings

Time: About 1¹/₂ hours

Really, this should be called "half-pound" cake, because the proportions are about half of the classic, which makes two loaves, or one huge one. The idea is the same: roughly equal amounts (by weight) of flour, eggs, butter, and sugar. It remains a delight, especially toasted with butter or varied as suggested below. It's worth using cake flour here for extra tenderness, but if you don't have it all-purpose flour will give you fine results.

¹/₂ pound (2 sticks) unsalted butter, softened,
    plus some for greasing the pan
2 cups (9 ounces) cake or all-purpose flour
1 teaspoon baking powder
Pinch salt
¹/₂ teaspoon freshly grated nutmeg
    (optional but very nice)
1 cup sugar
5 eggs, separated
2 teaspoons vanilla extract

1 Preheat the oven to 350°F. Butter a 9 × 5-inch loaf pan. Combine the flour, baking powder, salt, and nutmeg in a bowl and set aside.

2 Use an electric mixer to cream the butter until it is smooth. Add about half the sugar and beat until it is well blended, then add the remaining sugar. Beat until the mixture is light in color and fluffy in texture,
scraping down the sides of the mixing bowl if necessary. Beat in the egg yolks, one at a time.

3 Mix in the dry ingredients by hand just until smooth; do not overmix, and do not beat. Add the vanilla and stir until blended. Beat the egg whites until they hold soft peaks; fold them in gently but thoroughly.

4 Turn into the loaf pan and bake for about 1¹/₄ hours, or until a toothpick inserted into the top comes out clean. Let the cake rest in the pan for 5 minutes before inverting onto a rack. Remove the pan, then turn the cake right side up. Cool before slicing. Store at room temperature, covered with waxed paper, for a day or two; you can gain a couple more days by wrapping in plastic, but at some loss of texture.

Marble Cake: Before adding the egg whites in Step 3, combine 3 tablespoons unsweetened cocoa powder with 5 tablespoons sugar and blend this mixture with about 1 cup of the batter. Fold the beaten egg whites into the remaining batter. Place half the batter in the bottom of the loaf pan; top with the chocolate mixture, then with the remaining batter. Use a knife or spatula to swirl the mixtures together and bake as above.

Lemon Pound Cake: You can do this with orange as well. Omit the vanilla and add 1 teaspoon grated or minced lemon zest and 1 tablespoon lemon juice in its place.

Lemon-Poppy Seed Cake: Follow the above variation, folding in ¹/₄ cup poppy seeds along with the egg whites.

Spice Pound Cake: Add ¹/₂ teaspoon ground ginger, ¹/₄ teaspoon ground allspice, and ¹/₈ teaspoon ground cloves to the dry ingredients. If you like, substitute 1 tablespoon bourbon for the vanilla.

Golden Layer Cake

Makes at least 10 servings

Time: About 1 hour

This tender, delicate cake takes either white or chocolate frosting beautifully, and can be given the subtle flavor of vanilla or the bolder flavor of orange. It also makes wonderful cupcakes—see the variation.

- 10 tablespoons (1¼ sticks) unsalted butter, softened, plus some for greasing the pans and the paper
- 2 cups (about 9 ounces) cake or all-purpose flour, plus some for dusting the pans
- 1¼ cups sugar
- 4 eggs or 8 yolks
- 1 teaspoon vanilla extract or 1 tablespoon grated or minced orange zest
- ¼ teaspoon almond extract
- 2½ teaspoons baking powder
- ¼ teaspoon salt
- ¾ cup milk

1 Preheat the oven to 350°F. Butter the bottom and sides of two (9-inch) or three (8-inch) layer cake pans; cover the bottom with a circle of waxed or parchment paper, butter the paper, and sift flour over the pans; invert to remove the excess flour.

2 Use an electric mixer to cream the butter until smooth, then gradually add the sugar. Beat until light, 3 or 4 minutes. Beat in the eggs or yolks, one at a time, then the vanilla or orange zest and the almond extract. Combine the flour, baking powder, and salt; add to the egg mixture by hand, a little at a time, alternating with the milk. Stir just until smooth.

3 Turn the batter into the pans and bake for about 25 minutes, or until a toothpick inserted into the center of the cakes comes out clean. Cool on a rack for 5 minutes, then invert onto a rack and complete cooling. Finish with one of the icings on pages 727–728.

Store, covered with waxed paper and at room temperature, for no more than a day.

Golden Cupcakes: Liberally butter two muffin tins. Place cupcake papers in each of the compartments; fill almost to the brim. Bake at 350°F for 20 to 25 minutes. Cool on a rack, then use any icing on pages 727–728 to top the cupcakes while still in the tins. Remove and serve in the papers.

Coconut Layer Cake: Stir ½ cup dried sweetened shredded coconut into the batter along with the dry ingredients and the milk. Use Vanilla Butter Cream Frosting (page 727). After frosting the bottom layer, sprinkle the frosting with ½ cup dried sweetened shredded coconut. After frosting the assembled cake, press another 2 cups or more of sweetened shredded coconut onto the top and sides.

Chocolate Layer Cake

Makes at least 10 servings

Time: About 1 hour

This is the basic, simple layer cake, not much more difficult than a mix but far more delicious.

- 8 tablespoons (1 stick) unsalted butter, softened, plus some for greasing the pans and the paper
- 2 cups (9 ounces) cake or all-purpose flour, plus some for dusting the pans
- 3 ounces unsweetened chocolate, roughly chopped
- 1 cup sugar
- 2 eggs, separated
- 1 teaspoon vanilla extract
- 2 teaspoons baking powder
- ½ teaspoon baking soda
- ½ teaspoon salt
- 1¼ cups milk

1 Preheat the oven to 350°F. Butter the bottom and sides of two (9-inch) layer cake pans; cover the bottom with a circle of waxed or parchment paper, butter the paper, and sift flour over the pans; invert to remove the excess flour.

2 Melt the chocolate in a small saucepan or double boiler. If over a saucepan, cook over very low heat, stirring occasionally; if in a double boiler, cook over hot (not boiling) water, stirring occasionally. When the chocolate is just about melted, remove from the heat and continue to stir until the mixture is smooth.

3 Use an electric mixer to cream the butter until smooth, then gradually add the sugar. Beat until light and fluffy, 3 or 4 minutes. Beat in the egg yolks, one at a time, then the vanilla, and finally the chocolate. Mix together the flour, baking powder, baking soda, and salt in a bowl and add them to the chocolate mixture by hand, a little at a time, alternating with the milk. Stir until smooth, no longer.

4 Beat the egg whites until they hold soft peaks. Use your hand or a rubber spatula to fold them gently but thoroughly into the batter. Turn it into the cake pans and bake for about 30 minutes, or until a toothpick inserted into the center of the cakes comes out clean. Cool on a rack for 5 minutes, then invert onto a rack and complete cooling. Finish with one of the icings on pages 727–728. Store, covered with waxed paper and at room temperature, for no more than a day.

Chocolate Cupcakes: Use this batter, and see Golden Cupcakes, page 724, for directions.

Devil's Food Cake: The tang and richness of sour cream and the absence of baking powder makes this special. Substitute 1 cup sour cream or buttermilk for the sweet milk; omit the baking powder and increase the soda to 1 1/2 teaspoons. Baking time will be a few minutes less.

Angel Food Cake
Makes at least 10 servings

Time: About 1 1/2 hours, plus time to cool

Light and wonderful, with virtually no fat and a lovely crust whose flavor can't be beat. Serve with any fruit sauces (see Raspberry, Strawberry, or Other Fruit Sauce, page 672), Chocolate Sauce (page 672), or simply with some sliced fruit tossed with a little sugar.

1 cup (about 4 1/2 ounces) cake flour, sifted
    (do not use all-purpose flour)
1 1/2 cups sugar
9 egg whites
1/4 teaspoon salt
1 teaspoon cream of tartar
1 teaspoon vanilla extract
1/2 teaspoon almond extract

1 Preheat the oven to 325°F.

2 Sift together the flour and 1/2 cup of the sugar. Repeat.

3 Beat the egg whites until foamy. Add the salt and cream of tartar and continue to beat until they hold soft peaks; the tops of the whites should droop a little bit when you remove the beaters. Beat in the remaining sugar and vanilla and almond extracts and continue to beat until the peaks become a little stiffer.

4 Gradually and gently fold in the flour mixture, using a rubber spatula or your hand. Turn the batter into an ungreased 9- or 10-inch tube pan (not one with ridged sides) and bake 45 minutes to 1 hour, until the cake is firm, resilient, and nicely browned.

5 Invert the cake onto a rack and let cool for about an hour. Cut carefully around the sides of the cake and remove. Cool completely before slicing with a serrated knife or pulling apart with two forks. Angel Food Cake is best the day it is made; it becomes stale quickly (although it is wonderful toasted).

Chocolate Angel Food Cake: In Step 2, substitute ¹/₄ cup unsweetened cocoa powder for ¹/₄ cup of the flour. (To marble the cake, make two batters, one with all flour and one with ¹/₈ cup cocoa substituted for ¹/₈ cup flour. Add the batters alternately to the tube pan, and swirl together with a knife or spatula before baking.)

Sponge Cake
Makes at least 10 servings

Time: About 1¹/₂ hours, plus time to cool

Sponge cake, like angel food cake, contains no butter. Unlike its lightweight cousin, however, it does contain egg yolks—lots of them. This makes it yellow and rich. I like light sponge cake, so I separate the eggs; if you like a denser cake, don't bother. Serve plain, with ice or whipped cream (page 671), or any fruit sauce (see Raspberry, Strawberry, or Other Fruit Sauce, page 672).

1 cup (4¹/₂ ounces) cake or all-purpose flour

¹/₄ teaspoon salt

5 eggs, separated

1 cup sugar

2 teaspoons grated or minced orange or lemon zest

1 tablespoon freshly squeezed lemon juice or
   2 tablespoons freshly squeezed orange juice

1 Preheat the oven to 350°F. Mix the flour and salt together.

2 Use an electric mixer to beat the egg yolks until very thick and light, about 5 minutes. Gradually add half the sugar and beat another 5 minutes or so. The mixture should be thick and light-colored. Beat in the zest and juice.

3 Beat the egg whites until they hold soft peaks; the tops of the whites should droop a little bit when you remove the beaters. Gradually add the remaining sugar and continue to beat until the peaks become a little stiffer.

4 Use a rubber spatula or your hand to gently but thoroughly fold the egg whites into the yolk mixture. Sift the flour-salt mixture into this batter, a little at a time, gently but thoroughly folding it in after each addition. Turn the batter into an ungreased 9- or 10-inch tube pan (not one with ridged sides) and bake 40 to 50 minutes, until the cake is firm, resilient, and nicely browned.

5 Invert the cake onto a rack and let cool thoroughly, about an hour. Cut carefully around the sides of the cake and remove. Cool completely before slicing and eat within a day.

Death-by-Chocolate Torte
Makes at least 10 servings

Time: About 3 hours, largely unattended

This is the kind of thing that restaurants would have you believe is magic. On the contrary, there are only two challenges here: assembling the ingredients, and clearing out enough time.

8 tablespoons (1 stick) unsalted butter, softened,
   plus some for greasing the pan and the paper

1 cup (about 4¹/₂ ounces) all-purpose flour, plus some
   for dusting the pan

3 ounces unsweetened chocolate

¹/₂ cup water

7 eggs

1 cup plus 2 tablespoons sugar

2 teaspoons vanilla extract

Pinch salt

2 tablespoons unsweetened cocoa powder

1 Preheat the oven to 350°F. Butter the bottom and sides of a 9-inch layer cake pan; cover the bottom with a circle of waxed or parchment paper, butter the paper, and sift a little flour over the whole pan; invert to remove the excess flour.

2 Melt the 3 ounces of chocolate with the water over low heat; cool. Use an electric mixer to beat five of the eggs until light; gradually add 1 cup of the sugar, continuing to beat until the mixture is very thick. Gently stir in half the flour, then the chocolate mixture, then the remaining flour, and finally half of the vanilla and a pinch of salt. Turn into the prepared cake pan and bake 40 to 50 minutes, until the cake is firm and a toothpick inserted in the center comes out dry, or nearly so. Cool for 5 minutes before turning out onto a rack.

3 To make the butter cream, place 2 egg yolks (reserve the whites for another use, or discard) in the container of a blender. Add the remaining sugar, remaining vanilla, and the cocoa. Turn on the blender and add the butter, a little bit at a time. When the butter is blended in, chill to a spreading consistency.

4 When the cake is completely cool, use a serrated knife to carefully split it in half horizontally. Spread the bottom layer with chilled butter cream, then put the top layer in place. Chill for an hour or so, then make Dark Chocolate Glaze, below. Use a lightly oiled spatula to spread the glaze over the top and sides of the torte. Serve small slices, with whipped cream (page 671) if you like. Because of its dense texture, this cake keeps better than most; you can cover and refrigerate it for up to a couple of days—it will remain a treat.

Dark Chocolate Glaze

Makes enough to cover 1 (9-inch) layer cake

Time: 10 minutes

If you fill your cake with jam or butter cream (as in the Death-by-Chocolate Torte, page 726), and you love dark chocolate, this is the perfect finish for your cake. It's bittersweet and rich, very intense, but you don't use that much; it isn't a filling, just a glaze. Apply it while it's hot, with an oiled spatula, on a chilled cake; it will solidify perfectly and almost instantly.

³/₄ cup top-quality unsweetened cocoa powder
¹/₂ cup heavy cream
6 tablespoons (³/₄ stick) unsalted butter, cut into bits
³/₄ cup confectioners' sugar
Tiny pinch salt
¹/₂ teaspoon vanilla extract

1 Mix together the cocoa, cream, butter, confectioners' sugar, and salt in a small saucepan. Cook over low heat until combined and thickened, 5 to 10 minutes.

2 Stir in the vanilla and use immediately.

Vanilla Butter Cream Frosting

Makes enough frosting and filling for 1 (9-inch) layer cake, or 2 dozen cupcakes

Time: 10 minutes

The simplest and best frosting you can make. Cream is better than milk here, but you can use milk if you like.

8 tablespoons (1 stick) unsalted butter, softened
4 cups confectioners' sugar
6 tablespoons cream or milk, plus a little more if needed
2 teaspoons vanilla extract

1 Use a fork or electric mixer to cream the butter. Gradually work in the sugar, alternating with the cream and beating well after each addition.

2 Stir in the vanilla. If the frosting is too thick to spread, add a little more cream, a teaspoon at a time. If it is too thin (unlikely, but possible, especially after the addition of lemon or orange juice as in the variation below), refrigerate; it will thicken as the butter hardens.

Chocolate Butter Cream Frosting: Add 2 ounces melted and cooled unsweetened chocolate to the mixture after adding about half of the sugar.

Mocha Butter Cream Frosting: Add 1 ounce melted and cooled unsweetened chocolate to the mixture after adding about half the sugar. Substitute 2 tablespoons very strong coffee (espresso is best) for 2 tablespoons of the cream or milk.

Lemon or Orange Frosting: This is very good made with half butter and half cream cheese, but can also be made with all butter. Omit cream. Reduce vanilla to 1 teaspoon. Thin mixture with 1 large egg yolk (note that this egg will not be cooked; see The Basics of Eggs, page 731) and 1 teaspoon freshly squeezed lemon juice or 1 tablespoon freshly squeezed orange juice or undiluted orange juice concentrate. Stir in 1 teaspoon grated or minced lemon zest or 1 tablespoon grated or minced orange zest.

Lemon Cheesecake with Sour Cream Topping

Makes at least 12 servings

Time: About 1¹/₂ hours

Most veteran cooks have their favorite cheesecake, and this is mine. It's relatively low in sugar, and the lemon provides balance. You can skip the sour cream topping if you feel that enough is enough.

Unsalted butter for greasing the pan
1 double recipe Graham Cracker Crust (page 686)
4 eggs, separated
24 ounces (3 [8-ounce] packages) cream cheese
Grated zest and juice of 1 lemon
1 cup sugar, plus 1 tablespoon (optional)
1 tablespoon all-purpose flour
2 cups sour cream (optional)
1 teaspoon vanilla extract (optional)

1 Liberally butter a 9- or 10-inch springform pan, then press the crust into its bottom. Preheat the oven to 325°F.

2 Use an electric mixer to beat the egg yolks until light; add the cheese, lemon zest and juice, and 1 cup of the sugar and beat until smooth. Stir in the flour.

3 Beat the egg whites until they hold soft peaks; use a rubber spatula or your hand to fold them into the yolk-cheese mixture gently but thoroughly. Turn the batter into the prepared pan and place the pan in a baking pan large enough to hold it comfortably. Add warm water to the baking pan, so that it comes to within an inch of the top of the springform pan (see the information about water baths on page 655). Transfer carefully to the oven and bake until the cake is just set and very lightly browned, about an hour. Turn the oven up to 450°F if you're making the sour cream topping.

4 Remove the cake from the oven and cool completely if not adding the sour cream topping. If you're making the topping, combine the sour cream with the vanilla and the optional 1 tablespoon sugar and spread on the top of the cake. Return it to the oven for 10 minutes, without the water bath; turn off the oven and let the cake cool for 30 minutes before removing it. Cool on a rack, cover with plastic wrap, then refrigerate until well chilled before slicing and serving. This will keep in good shape for several days.

Ricotta Cheesecake: This is somewhat lighter (and far lower in calories, especially if you use part-skim ricotta): Substitute $1^1/_2$ pounds fresh ricotta for the cream cheese. Beat it in an electric mixer until lightened, then add the yolks. Increase the sugar to $1^1/_4$ cups; the flour remains the same. Substitute 1 teaspoon orange zest for the lemon zest, and use 1 additional teaspoon vanilla in place of the lemon juice. You can omit or include the sour cream topping, as you like. Bake as above.

Eggs, Breakfast, and Brunch Dishes

The archetypal "American" breakfast, a direct descendant of the typical English breakfast, is considered elaborate—not to mention overly fatty—by many standards. Even if that were not the case, most breakfasts usually are simple and quick, ranging from Pop-Tarts to dried cereal, to some crusty bread, left over from dinner, toasted and served with butter or jam or cheese, along with a piece of fruit.

Still, there is no denying that a luxurious breakfast of eggs, pancakes, or something even more complex, along with breakfast meat, is a treat that many people look forward to all week. And the preparation of it need not be especially time-consuming.

Given that ingredients for most breakfasts are limited, and that many are covered in depth in other chapters of this book, it's important to devote some space to that all-important ingredient that is not given much attention elsewhere: The Egg.

The Basics of Eggs

No other ingredient has the power to transform itself or other dishes as does the egg, perhaps the most important food in our kitchen. There is not a chapter in this book in which you won't find the egg playing a leading or supporting role, and many of our favorite foods—not just breakfasts, of course, but desserts and baked goods of all types—would be unrecognizable without the egg. The egg is also a nutritional miracle, containing all nine essential amino acids and a host of vitamins.

Yet the egg has been vilified from a health standpoint, first because of its high cholesterol content, then because of salmonella contamination. Both of these concerns are worth addressing.

Although the cholesterol content of eggs has been cut from nearly three hundred milligrams to just over two hundred, the number is still relatively high. At the same time, concerns about dietary cholesterol in general have declined. There is serious question about just how much your cholesterol intake affects your cholesterol level, since your body manufactures cholesterol. (Furthermore, although this is not the place for this discussion, there are legitimate questions about the issue of the link between cholesterol and heart disease.) More important, it seems, is your overall intake of saturated fat. If your cholesterol level is considered high, and you've been advised by a physician to keep away from high-cholesterol foods, I am not in a position to tell you to enjoy all the egg yolks you want. But I eat a few eggs a week with a fairly clear conscience.

However, if egg intake concerns you, there is a simple measure you can take to make almost any egg-based dish with less fat and cholesterol: Substitute some egg whites for some whole eggs, in a proportion of about two to one. For example, instead of using four eggs in a given recipe, use three eggs and two whites, or two eggs and four whites.

As for salmonella and eggs: Recent statistics indicate that a small number of eggs (about one in ten thousand, or fewer) may contain the salmonella bacteria. If this bacteria multiplies—unlikely in refrigerated, uncracked eggs—and you eat the egg raw, (as you would in mayonnaise) or undercooked (as you would in many eggs cooked for breakfast), you might become ill, suffering intestinal problems that are as bad as the flu. The very young, very old, or those with compromised immune systems may have even worse problems, and should avoid recipes with raw or undercooked eggs. But the general population should consider eggs safe, and eat them without fear, especially if they have been handled properly.

One last word about eggs: If you live anywhere near a functioning farm, you should go out of your way to buy freshly laid eggs from free-range hens. They are unquestionably more flavorful than store-bought eggs, and the brighter, deeper yellow yolk alone makes it worth the trip.

A note about egg size   Large eggs weigh twenty-four ounces per dozen, or about two ounces each; extra-large eggs weigh twenty-seven ounces per dozen, or about 2.25 ounces each. They may be substituted freely for each other in these or any other recipes, with the possible exception of those baking recipes that use more than six eggs, in which case you should always use large eggs.

Cooking Eggs

Health cautions aside, eggs are usually best when cooked fairly slowly—the omelet is a kind of exception—and never until they are completely hard. Scrambled eggs, cooked over low heat for about thirty minutes, become creamy and custard-like, a texture that is impossible to achieve over high heat. And even fried eggs, which must be started over high heat, benefit from a quick reduction of heat to low; this prevents the bottom part of the yolk from become hard-cooked. Other than that, there are no major concerns in cooking eggs, and few foods provide as much pleasure with so little work.

A final word: Most of us grew up eating eggs cooked in butter, an undeniable delight. But eggs cooked in extra-virgin olive oil, or with an absolute minimum of fat (as in boiled eggs, or eggs cooked in a nonstick skillet) are also delicious. Don't miss out on egg-eating just because you've given up on butter. On the other hand, please don't sully the flavor of eggs with that of margarine; use olive oil or skip the fat entirely.

Boiled Eggs

There are two keys to successfully boiling an egg. The first is to poke a tiny hole in the broad end of the egg, using a pin or a needle. This provides an outlet for the pressure created by the swelling and hardening white and virtually eliminates cracked shells. The second is to use medium-to-low heat, which keeps the egg from bouncing around in the saucepan and helps prevent overcooking. All that's left is the timing.

Soft-Boiled Egg

Makes 1 serving per egg

Time: Less than 10 minutes

Don't crowd the saucepan; there must be water circulating around each egg. And, if you're cooking more than one egg at a time, extend the cooking time to the longer end of the range (four minutes, in this case).

1 Use a pin or needle to poke a hole in the broad end of each egg. Place each egg on a spoon, ladle, skimmer, or other tool and lower it into a small saucepan of gently boiling water.

2 Cook for 3 to 4 minutes, the lower time if you want the yolk completely runny and the white not quite set, the latter if you want the white very soft but set.

3 Run the egg very briefly under cold water, crack the shell, and scoop out the egg.

Medium-Boiled Egg

Makes 1 serving per egg

Time: About 10 minutes

These eggs make wonderful substitutes for poached eggs, and can even be reheated after shelling by dipping them quickly—no more than thirty seconds—into a saucepan of simmering water.

1 Use a pin or needle to poke a hole in the broad end of each egg. Place each egg on a spoon, ladle, skimmer, or other tool and lower it into a small saucepan of gently boiling water; do not crowd.

2 Cook for 5 to 6 minutes; the shorter time guarantees a cooked but runny yolk, but there may be some undercooked white. With the longer time, the white will be fully cooked, but some of the yolk may have hardened. Try it both ways and see which you prefer.

3 To remove the shell, plunge into cold running water for about 30 seconds, then crack and peel gently, as you would a hard-boiled egg.

Hard-Boiled Egg

Makes 1 serving per egg

Time: About 15 minutes

Much better when ever so slightly undercooked, so the yolk is on the creamy side.

1 Use a pin or needle to poke a hole in the broad end of each egg. Place each egg on a spoon, ladle, skimmer, or other tool and lower it into a small saucepan of gently boiling water; do not crowd.

2 Cook for 10 to 15 minutes; the shorter time guarantees a fully cooked white, and leaves some of the yolk a little underdone, which I prefer. Any time longer than 12 minutes will give you the standard hard-boiled egg (if you want to be doubly sure the egg is cooked through, increase the time to 15 minutes).

3 To remove the shell, plunge into cold running water for 30 seconds (if you want to eat the egg while hot) to 2 minutes (if you want to make shell removal as easy as possible and don't care whether the egg cools off). Remove the peel gently.

Poached Eggs

Makes 2 servings

Time: 10 minutes

Producing a perfect-looking poached egg takes practice. If you just want a poached egg to place on a piece of toast or corned beef hash for your morning breakfast, this hardly matters—a few ragged edges aren't going to ruin your day. But if you want your poached eggs to look attractive, cook them in advance, then trim off the ragged edges and reheat them by dipping them into a saucepan of simmering water for thirty seconds. Remember, though, that shelled medium-boiled eggs can be substituted for poached eggs in any recipe, and are much easier to make.

1 teaspoon salt
1 teaspoon white vinegar
2 eggs

1 Bring about an inch of water to a boil in a deep, small skillet, add the salt and vinegar, and lower the heat to the point where it barely bubbles. One at a time, break the eggs into a shallow bowl and slip them into the water. At this point, cover the skillet or begin to spoon the water over the tops of the eggs.

2 Cook 3 to 5 minutes, just until the white is set and the yolk has filmed over. Remove with a slotted spoon. If you are eating the eggs right away, place them directly on the toast, corned beef hash, or what have you. If you are reserving them for another use, drain them on paper towels. Poached eggs are delicate, but they can be handled as long as you are careful.

Eggs Benedict for Four: First, poach 8 eggs, 2 to 4 at a time, as described above, taking care not to overcook them (or use medium-boiled eggs). Trim if you like. Then make Hollandaise Sauce (page 790), and keep it warm. Toast 4 English muffins and cover each with a thin slice of pan-fried or broiled ham. Reheat the eggs for 30 seconds in gently boiling water, and place one on top of each piece of ham. Top with a spoonful of Hollandaise.

Eggs with Cheese Sauce for Four: First, poach 8 eggs, 2 to 4 at a time, as described above, taking care not to overcook them (or use medium-boiled eggs). Trim if you like. Make Mornay (Cheese) Sauce (page 787), using Parmesan or other strong-flavored cheese. Place the eggs on slices of toast or English muffins, then top with a bit of the sauce. Run under a broiler for about 30 seconds, or just until the sauce colors lightly.

Fried Eggs

Makes 2 servings

Time: 10 minutes

Fried eggs can be tough and rubbery or nearly as delicate as poached eggs. The key to keeping the whites tender and the yolk undercooked is low heat. Follow these instructions carefully once or twice and you'll never have trouble making fried eggs again. You can use the smaller amount of butter listed here with only a minor sacrifice in flavor.

1 teaspoon to 1 tablespoon butter
2 eggs
Salt and freshly ground black pepper to taste

1 Place a medium skillet, preferably non-stick, over medium heat for about 1 minute. Add the butter and swirl it around the pan. When its foam subsides, about a minute later, crack the eggs into the skillet. As soon as the whites lose their translucence—this only takes a minute—turn the heat to low and season with salt and pepper.

2 Cook until the whites are completely firm; the last place for this to happen is just around the yolk. If the egg has set up high, rather than spread out thin, there are two techniques to encourage it to finish cooking: The first is to cut right through the uncooked parts with a small knife; this allows some of the still-liquid white to sink through the cooked white and hit the surface of the pan, where it will cook immediately. The second is to cover the skillet for a minute or two longer to encourage the white to finish cooking. When the eggs are cooked, remove them from the pan and eat immediately.

Six Simple Ideas for Fried Eggs

1. Substitute extra-virgin olive oil for the butter.
2. As the butter or oil heats, season it with a few leaves of fresh herbs or a smashed clove of garlic.
3. Cook bacon in the skillet, then use its rendered fat to fry the eggs.
4. As the white sets, use a butter knife to fold its edges over the yolk, making a little package and further protecting the yolk from overcooking.
5. Add Worcestershire sauce or other liquid seasoning such as soy or hot sauce to the white before it sets.
6. Cook one-half-inch-thick tomato slices alongside the eggs (increase the amount of butter slightly).

Weekday Morning Scrambled Eggs

Makes 2 servings

Time: 10 minutes

The best scrambled eggs take time (see the next recipe), but you can make good scrambled eggs in a hurry as long as you do not overcook them. Adding a little extra liquid helps prevent overcooking (if that liquid is cream, of course, it also lends a luxurious texture).

> 1 tablespoon butter or olive oil
> 4 eggs
> Salt and freshly ground black pepper to taste
> 1 to 2 tablespoons milk, cream, or water (optional)

1 Place a medium skillet, preferably non-stick, over medium heat for about a minute. Add the butter and swirl it around the pan. Meanwhile, crack the eggs into a bowl and beat them, just until the yolks and whites are combined. Season with salt and pepper and beat in milk, cream, or water if you like.

2 Add the eggs to the skillet and turn the heat to medium-low. Cook, stirring, frequently, just until the eggs have lost their runny quality, 2 to 4 minutes; do not overcook. Serve immediately.

Scrambled Eggs with Cheese or Salsa: Try using cheese and salsa together to make huevos rancheros. As the eggs begin to set, stir in $^1/_2$ cup grated cheese and/or $^1/_2$ cup prepared salsa (page 782). Proceed as above.

Scrambled Eggs with Onion: You can also double the amount of onion here and cook it slowly until it is very tender; or combine onion and minced red bell pepper. Begin by cooking $^1/_2$ cup minced onion in 1 tablespoon butter over medium-low heat. Cook until the onion is translucent but not brown, about 5 minutes. Add the eggs, raise the heat to medium, and proceed as above.

Scrambled Eggs with Spinach: Add $^1/_2$ teaspoon minced garlic along with the spinach. Take $^1/_2$ cup cooked spinach and press all the liquid from it; chop it finely. Cook it in 1 tablespoon butter over medium heat for 1 minute. Proceed as above.

Best Scrambled Eggs

Makes 2 servings

Time: 40 minutes

A Sunday morning indulgence, these take time, cream, butter, tarragon, and—the really hard part—a great deal of patience. With thanks to James Beard.

2 to 4 tablespoons butter
5 eggs
Salt and freshly ground black pepper to taste
1 teaspoon minced fresh tarragon leaves or
   $1/4$ teaspoon dried tarragon
2 tablespoons cream

1 Place a medium skillet, preferably non-stick, over medium heat for about 1 minute. Add the butter and swirl it around the pan. After the butter melts, but before it foams, turn the heat to low.

2 Beat the eggs with the remaining ingredients and pour into the skillet. Cook over low heat, stirring occasionally with a wooden spoon. At first nothing will happen; after 10 minutes or so, the eggs will begin to form curds. Do not lose patience: Keep stirring, breaking up the curds as they form, until the mixture is a mass of soft curds. This will take 30 minutes or more. Serve immediately, with lots of toast.

Twelve Simple Additions to Scrambled Eggs

As in making an omelet (page 738) or frittata (page 741), you can add almost anything you want to the beaten uncooked eggs before scrambling. Try any of these with either Weekday Morning Scrambled Eggs or Best Scrambled Eggs (see above):

1. Minced pickled jalapeños to taste
2. Sautéed mushrooms or other cooked vegetables, cut into small dice, about one-half cup
3. Diced cooked shrimp or other seafood, about one-half cup
4. Chopped fresh herbs, one teaspoon (stronger herbs) to one tablespoon (milder ones). For scrambled eggs aux fines herbes, add about one-half teaspoon tarragon, one teaspoon chervil, and one tablespoon each parsley and chives, all chopped
5. Sour cream, cream cheese (cut into bits), or goat cheese, about one-third cup
6. Minced smoked salmon or other fish, about one-half cup
7. Chili, or any cooked beans, about one-half cup
8. Chopped salami or other smoked meats, about one-half cup
9. Peeled, seeded, and diced tomatoes, up to one cup; or one-quarter cup reconstituted sun-dried tomatoes (or, even better, one-half cup Oven-Dried Tomatoes, page 611)
10. Tabasco, Worcestershire, or other prepared sauces to taste
11. Minced scallions, up to one-half cup
12. Chopped roasted red peppers (see Marinated Roasted, Grilled, or Broiled Peppers, page 593), up to one-half cup

Baked (Shirred) Eggs

Makes 1 or 2 servings

Time: 20 to 30 minutes

It amazes me that shirred eggs have fallen from favor: There is something so luxurious about them and, although they take a little time, they are delicious. Furthermore, it's easy to make them in quantity—it doesn't take much longer than this to make a dozen. Top these with bread crumbs, grated cheese, minced parsley—or a combination—before baking if you like.

Butter as needed

Cream (optional)

2 eggs

Salt and freshly ground black pepper to taste

1 Preheat the oven to 375°F. Butter two custard cups or small ramekins. If you like, place a couple of teaspoons of cream in the bottom of each (a nice touch). Break 1 egg into each of the cups, then place the cups on a baking sheet.

2 Bake for 10 to 15 minutes, or until the eggs are just set and the whites solidified. Because of the heat retained by the cups, these will continue to cook after you remove them from the oven, so it's best to undercook them slightly. Season to taste and serve.

Baked Eggs with Tomato: Substitute olive oil for butter if you like; omit the cream. Before adding the eggs to each cup, place a tablespoon or two of chopped fresh tomato (or a slice of tomato, if your cups are broad or tomatoes small) in the bottom. Top with minced parsley. Add the eggs and bake as above.

Baked Eggs with Spinach

Eggs "Florentine"

Makes 4 servings

Time: About 45 minutes

A great use for leftover spinach if you have it.

2 pounds fresh spinach, washed and trimmed
   according to the directions on page 604

3 tablespoons butter or olive oil

8 eggs

Salt and freshly ground black pepper to taste

1/2 cup freshly grated Parmesan cheese

1/2 cup plain bread crumbs

1 Preheat the oven to 350°F.

2 Bring a large pot of water to a boil; salt it. Place the spinach in the water and cook for about a minute, or until it is bright green and tender. Drain well. When it is cool enough to handle, squeeze the moisture from it and chop.

3 Place the butter or oil in a 9 × 13-inch baking pan and put the pan in the oven. When the butter melts or the oil is hot, toss the spinach in the pan, stirring to coat with the fat. Spread the spinach out and use the back of a spoon to make 8 little nests in the spinach. Crack 1 egg into each. Top with salt, pepper, cheese, and bread crumbs.

4 Bake for 15 to 20 minutes, or until the eggs are just set and the whites solidified. Scoop out some spinach with each egg and serve on toast or toasted English muffins.

Baked Eggs with Onions and Cheese

Makes 4 to 8 servings

Time: About 1 hour

A nice dish for a small crowd. You can cook the onions several hours in advance if you like.

4 tablespoons (1/2 stick) butter or olive oil

4 cups sliced onions

1 cup plain bread crumbs

2 cups grated Cheddar cheese

8 eggs

Salt and freshly ground black pepper to taste

1 Preheat the oven to 350°F.

2 Place the butter or oil in a large skillet over medium heat. Two minutes later, add the onions and cook, stirring occasionally, until they are very soft and tender but not browned, about 15 minutes. Spread

the onions over the bottom of a 9 × 13-inch baking pan, or other similar-sized baking dish.

3   Top with half the bread crumbs and half the cheese. Use the back of a spoon to make 8 little nests in the mixture and crack 1 egg into each. Top with salt, pepper, and the remaining bread crumbs and cheese.

4   Bake for 15 to 20 minutes, or until the eggs are just set and the whites solidified. Serve with toast.

The Basics of Omelets

Non-stick skillets changed omelet making from a skill that needed to be developed to a virtual no-brainer. Just make sure the butter (or oil) is hot before adding the eggs, and keep the heat fairly high. It may seem at first glance that this recipe for omelets goes against the rule of cooking eggs over low heat, but when you watch an omelet cook, you realize that much of the egg mixture is protected against the heat by the thin layer of egg that is in direct contact with the bottom of the skillet. So, in a way, it too cooks gently and remains tender.

Basic Omelet

Makes 2 servings

Time: 10 minutes

Master this technique and you'll never be without a quick lunch or supper again. The butter (or oil, if you prefer) is an integral part of the flavor of this creation; don't skimp unless you must.

2 tablespoons plus 1 teaspoon butter (you can use
    less with a non-stick pan, or substitute extra-virgin
    olive oil)
4 or 5 eggs
2 tablespoons milk or cream
Salt and freshly ground black pepper to taste

1   Place the 2 tablespoons butter in a medium-to-large skillet, preferably non-stick, and turn the heat to medium-high. Beat together the eggs and milk or cream, just until blended; add salt and pepper to taste.

2   When the butter melts, swirl it around the pan until its foam subsides, then pour in the egg mixture. Cook undisturbed for about 30 seconds, then use a fork or thin-bladed spatula to push the edges of the eggs toward the center. As you do this, tip the pan to allow the uncooked eggs in the center to reach the perimeter.

3   Repeat until the omelet is still moist but no longer runny, a total of about 3 minutes. If you prefer, you can even stop cooking a little sooner, when there are still some runny eggs in the center; most of this will cook from the heat retained by the eggs, and you'll have a moister omelet.

4   Use a large spatula to fold the omelet in half or in thirds and place it on a plate. Rub the top of the omelet with the remaining teaspoon of butter and serve.

Mushroom Omelet: Before cooking the omelet, sauté 1 cup minced mushrooms in 2 tablespoons butter or oil in a small skillet over medium-high heat until softened, about 10 minutes. Sprinkle with salt and pepper and finish with 1 tablespoon of cream (optional). Make the omelet, keeping the mushrooms warm. Place the mushrooms across one side of the egg mixture just before it is completely set. Fold the other side over and finish as above.

Spanish Omelet: Before cooking the omelet, melt 1 tablespoon butter in a small saucepan over medium heat. Add 2 tablespoons minced scallion or onion and cook for 30 seconds. Stir in 1 cup chopped tomatoes and cook for about 2 minutes. Season with salt and pepper and keep warm. Make the omelet, placing the filling across one side of the egg mixture just before it is completely set. Fold the other side over and finish as above.

You can fill an omelet with almost anything you like. Generally, place the filling across one side of the egg mixture just before it is completely set. Cooked fillings, such as vegetables or sauces, should be warm; raw fillings, such as cheese, should be grated finely, so they melt or at least heat up quickly.

Use these fillings alone or in combination, but don't exceed about one cup of filling for an omelet this size.

1. Grated cheese
2. Any cooked and diced vegetable (leftovers are fine, whether steamed, boiled, or sautéed; rinse with boiling water before using if necessary to remove unwanted flavors)
3. Peeled, seeded, and diced tomatoes
4. Cottage cheese or goat cheese (or Herbed Goat Cheese, page 24)
5. Minced ham, crisp-cooked bacon, sausage meat, or other chopped meat
6. Marmalade, jam, or jelly (sprinkle the top of the omelet with a little sugar before serving if you like)
7. Minced fresh herbs, preferably a combination of two tablespoons parsley, one tablespoon each chervil and chives, and one-half teaspoon tarragon (all chopped), but you can adjust this according to taste
8. Fruit, such as peeled and grated apples, briefly cooked with butter, sugar, and cinnamon
9. Cream cheese and smoked salmon, about one-quarter cup each, cut into bits
10. Cooked seafood, such as shrimp, scallops, or crabmeat, shredded or minced
11. Minced red bell pepper, or roasted red pepper (see Marinated Roasted, Grilled, or Broiled Peppers, page 593)
12. Gently sautéed sliced or chopped onion, about one-half cup (measured after cooking)

Western Omelet: More like a frittata (page 740), but nevertheless an American tradition. In Step 2, when the butter melts, add to it 2 tablespoons each minced bell pepper (preferably red), onion, and ham. Cook for 2 minutes, stirring, before adding the eggs and proceeding as above.

Baked Sweet Omelet

Makes 2 to 4 servings

Time: About 30 minutes

A cross between an omelet and a frittata, this light omelet looks bigger than it really is. It's wonderful served with jam and sour cream or yogurt.

4 eggs
½ cup milk
1 tablespoon flour
Pinch salt
2 tablespoons sugar
2 tablespoons butter

1. Preheat the oven to 350°F.
2. Separate the eggs. Beat the yolks with the milk, flour, pinch of salt, and sugar. Beat the whites until stiff but not dry.
3. Place a large ovenproof skillet, preferably nonstick, over medium heat and add the butter. When it melts, gently fold the egg whites into the yolk mixture. Pour into the skillet and cook for 2 minutes, then transfer to the oven. Bake until puffy and browned on top, 10 to 20 minutes.

To separate eggs, break the egg with the back of a knife or on the side of a small bowl.

The easiest way to separate eggs is to use the shell halves, moving the yolk back or forth once or twice so that the white falls into a bowl. Be careful, however, not to allow any of the yolk to mix in with the whites or they will not rise fully during beating.

Spanish Potato Omelet (Tortilla)

Makes at least 4 servings

Time: 45 minutes

This is really more like a frittata. Not bad at breakfast, but perfect for a late dinner or anytime snack.

$1/3$ cup extra-virgin olive oil

1 pound waxy red or white potatoes, peeled and cut into $1/8$-inch-thick slices

Salt and freshly ground black pepper to taste

1 large onion, sliced

1 red bell pepper, stemmed, peeled if desired, seeded, and sliced

1 teaspoon minced garlic

6 eggs

$1/2$ cup minced fresh parsley leaves

1 Place about half the olive oil in a large ovenproof skillet, preferably non-stick, and turn the heat to medium. Add the potato slices and season liberally with salt and pepper. Cook, turning gently from time to time, until they soften, about 20 minutes. Remove with a slotted spoon.

2 Add the remaining oil to the pan, followed by the onion and red pepper, and cook, stirring occasionally, until nice and soft, about 10 minutes. Add the garlic and cook another 2 minutes. Preheat the oven to 375°F.

3 Return the potatoes to the skillet and turn the heat to medium-low. Continue to cook, turning with a spatula, for about 5 more minutes. Beat the eggs with the parsley.

4 Turn the heat to low and pour the eggs over the potatoes. Shake the pan to distribute the eggs evenly and cook, undisturbed, for about 5 minutes. Transfer to the oven and bake until the mixture is set, about 10 minutes more. Remove the pan and cool to room temperature before cutting into chunks or wedges; serve.

The Basics of Frittate

The classic Italian egg pie, the frittata is an attractive dish that requires no fancy rolling or split-second timing, so it can be made perfectly on the first try. And because it incorporates a substantial amount of filling—usually vegetables or carbohydrates—into just a few eggs, the frittata elicits less guilt than an omelet for those concerned with such things. (For lower cholesterol, make a frittata with four egg whites and three whole eggs in place of the whole eggs in the recipe.)

Much of the preparation for most frittate can be done in advance; the open-faced omelets also make good use of leftovers. Finally, frittate taste just as good at room temperature as they do hot; cut them into small wedges and serve as a snack or hors d'oeuvre.

Basic Frittata

Makes 4 servings

Time: About 30 minutes

The basic frittata is very much like the basic omelet, but even easier to master. The variations may be used singly or in combination, but they all spring from this single recipe.

    2 tablespoons butter or olive oil
    5 or 6 eggs
    ½ cup freshly grated Parmesan or other cheese
    Salt and freshly ground black pepper to taste
    Minced fresh parsley leaves for garnish

1. Preheat the oven to 350°F.
2. Place the butter or oil in a medium-to-large ovenproof skillet, preferably non-stick, and turn the heat to medium. While it's heating, beat together the eggs, cheese, salt, and pepper. When the butter melts or the oil is hot, pour the eggs into the skillet and turn the heat to medium-low. Cook, undisturbed, for about 10 minutes, or until the bottom of the frittata is firm.
3. Transfer the skillet to the oven. Bake, checking every 5 minutes or so, just until the top of the frittata is no longer runny, 10 to 20 minutes more. (To speed things up, turn on the broiler, but be very careful not to overcook.) Garnish and serve hot or at room temperature.

Vegetable Frittata: Stir about 1 cup cooked and roughly chopped broccoli, asparagus, spinach, chard, or kale into the egg mixture just before turning it into the skillet. Proceed as above.

Onion Frittata: Before beginning, sauté about 1 cup chopped onion in 1 tablespoon butter or oil until soft but not browned, 5 to 10 minutes. Cool slightly, then stir into the egg mixture just before turning it into the skillet. Proceed as above.

Herb Frittata: Mince about 1 cup of fresh herbs—chervil, parsley, dill, or basil should make up the bulk of them, but others such as tarragon, oregano, marjoram, or chives may be added in smaller quantities—and stir them into the egg mixture just before turning it into the skillet. Proceed as above, garnishing with whatever fresh herb you like.

Nine Ideas for Additions to Frittate

Almost anything you find appetizing can be used in a frittata; the basic proportions are one to two cups filling for every four or five eggs. Again, these may be used alone or in combination:

1. Chopped, steamed spinach or chard, mixed with a dash of lemon and nutmeg or sautéed, with minced garlic, in olive oil
2. Crisp bacon mixed with pan-fried apple and onion slices
3. Minced salami, cooked sausage, ham, cooked or smoked fish
4. Sautéed onion, fresh tomato, and basil
5. Sautéed potatoes and onions
6. Grated, salted, and quickly cooked zucchini (page 606)
7. Sautéed mushrooms
8. Peeled, seeded, and diced tomato, or Oven-Dried Tomatoes, page 611
9. Goat cheese (or Herbed Goat Cheese, page 24)

The Basics of Soufflés

Few dishes have intimidated so many people for so long as the soufflé, yet the fact is that soufflés are not difficult. If you beat the egg whites thoroughly and integrate them into the batter carefully, the battle is won. You can hold the soufflé, refrigerated, for fifteen or even thirty minutes before baking, and all you need do is serve the soufflé the moment you remove it from the oven, when it is in its glory—a light, fluffy mound of beautifully browned eggs and flavorings.

All you need know about beating egg whites is that those at room temperature will gain a little more volume, but not so much to make you abandon the project should your eggs be cold (also, cold eggs are easier to separate, so you must take that into account). The slightest amount of fat will keep the eggs from gaining volume, so make sure your bowl is completely free of oil residues and that no yolk taints the whites. (The easiest way to remove a bit of yolk from the whites is to use a half eggshell to scoop it out.)

Beat the whites by hand, using a whisk, or with a handheld or standing beater or mixer. Adding a pinch of salt or cream of tartar stabilizes the mixture. And stop beating as soon as the whites hold a soft peak, one that droops a bit.

Recipes for dessert soufflés are on page 674.

Cheese Soufflé
Makes 4 to 6 servings

Time: About 1 hour

Obviously, the type of cheese you use in a soufflé is the determining factor in its flavor. I almost always include some freshly grated Parmesan, because it complements everything else. Along with it, you can use anything, from mild Cheddar or Jack to sharp Gorgonzola or Roquefort—whatever you like.

4 tablespoons (1/2 stick) butter, plus 1 teaspoon
1/4 cup flour
1 1/2 cups milk, warmed until hot to the touch
6 eggs, separated
Salt and freshly ground black pepper to taste
Dash cayenne or 1/2 teaspoon dry mustard
1/2 cup freshly grated Parmesan cheese
1/2 cup grated or crumbled Cheddar, Jack, Roquefort,
    Emmenthal, and/or other cheese
Pinch cream of tartar (optional)

1 Preheat the oven to 400°F. Use the teaspoon of butter to grease a 2-quart soufflé dish or other deep baking dish, such as a Corningware–type dish. If you want to make individual soufflés, use a little more butter and grease four 1 1/2- to 2-cup ramekins.

2 Place a medium saucepan over medium heat and add the remaining butter. When it foams, add the flour and turn the heat to medium-low. Cook, stirring, until the mixture darkens a bit, about 3 minutes. Whisk in the milk a little at a time to avoid lumps, then cook until the mixture is thick, just a minute or two longer.

(Step 1) To fold whites, first lighten the mixture by stirring a couple of spoonfuls of the beaten whites into it. (Step 2) Then gently fold the rest of the egg whites in, scooping under the mixture and smoothing over the top. You can use a rubber spatula or your hand, which works equally well.

3 Turn off the heat and stir in the egg yolks, salt, pepper, cayenne or mustard, and cheese(s). Beat the egg whites with a pinch of salt or cream of tartar, just until they hold soft peaks. Stir a couple of spoonfuls of the beaten whites into the batter, then very gently—and not overly thoroughly—fold in the remaining whites, using a rubber spatula or, better still, your hand. Be as gentle as possible.

4 Turn the batter into the prepared dish(es) and bake until the soufflé has risen and is browned on top, about 15 to 40 minutes (the lower timing is for smaller, individual soufflés; a single soufflé will take 30 minutes or more). Use a thin skewer to check the interior; if it is still quite wet, bake another 5 minutes. If it is just a bit moist, the soufflé is done. Serve immediately.

Spinach Soufflé: You can use any cooked, drained, and chopped or pureed vegetable here, but spinach is the classic. In Step 3, add 2 tablespoons minced onion and 1 cup cooked, drained, and chopped spinach to the batter, along with the Parmesan cheese; omit the other cheese. Proceed as above.

Ham and Cheese Soufflé: You can use ground cooked chicken or turkey, or crumbled cooked bacon instead of ham if you like. In Step 3, add 3/4 cup cooked minced or ground ham along with the cheese(s).

Tomato Soufflé: Puree 1 cup of Basic Tomato Sauce (page 130), or any other tomato sauce, and use it to replace 1 cup of the milk in Step 2. Stir in 1/2 cup fresh, torn basil leaves along with the cheese(s).

The Basic of Quiches

A quiche is a savory open-faced pie, made with an unsweetened pie or tart crust or—if you want to get fancy—puff pastry and relying on cheese or a custard to bind other solid ingredients. It can be served as part of a meal, serving four to eight. And it can be prepared up to a day ahead of time and reheated at the last moment or served at room temperature.

The doughs for quiches are best made with butter, but can also be made with olive oil. The flavor will be excellent, the texture not so great, but if you are off butter, you'll probably think the trade-off worthwhile. Bear in mind that these are savory crusts, and so can be flavored in any way you like: Add one teaspoon of minced garlic to the crust, or one teaspoon to one tablespoon of any herb that you're using in the filling, for example. Cornmeal substituted for about one-quarter of the flour also makes for a nice change, adding crunch and flavor.

Like any custard, the filling should be cooked gently so it becomes creamy rather than hard. For this reason, and to keep the crusts crisp, crusts are precooked at high temperature, then filled and returned to the oven at lower temperature.

Basic Cheese Quiche

Makes 4 to 8 servings

Time: About 1 1/2 hours

A few tablespoons of pureed Roasted Garlic (page 575) added to this makes it even more delicious.

1 recipe Generous Pie Shell (page 686), made without sugar, or Rich Tart Crust (page 695), made without sugar, in a 10-inch tart pan or 9-inch deep dish pie pan, and chilled

6 eggs, at room temperature

2 cups grated Emmenthal, Gruyère, Cantal, Cheddar, or other flavorful cheese

2 cups cream, half-and-half, or milk, gently heated just until warm

1/2 teaspoon salt

1/4 teaspoon cayenne

1 Preheat the oven to 425°F. Prick the crust all over with a fork. Line it with tin foil and weight the bottom with a pile of dried beans, rice (these can be reused for this same purpose), or other weights that will sit flat on the surface. Bake 12 minutes. Remove from the oven and carefully remove the weight and foil; turn the oven to 325°F.

2 Combine eggs, cheese, liquid, and seasonings and beat until well blended.

3 Place the baked crust on a baking sheet. Pour the egg mixture into the crust, right to the top. Carefully transfer the baking sheet to the oven and bake 30 to 40 minutes, until the mixture is set but is still moist; it should still jiggle just a little in the middle. Cool on a rack and serve warm or at room temperature.

Onion Quiche

Makes 4 to 8 servings

Time: About 1½ hours

Any dish that highlights the sweetness of cooked onions is a good one, and this gives them center stage.

    1 recipe Generous Pie Shell (page 686), made
        without sugar, or Rich Tart Crust (page 695),
        made without sugar, in a 10-inch tart pan or
        9-inch deep dish pie pan, and chilled
    4 tablespoons (½ stick) butter or olive oil
    6 cups thinly sliced onions
    Salt and freshly ground black pepper to taste
    1 teaspoon fresh thyme leaves or ½ teaspoon
        dried thyme
    6 eggs, at room temperature
    2 cups cream, half-and-half, or milk, gently heated
        just until warm

1 Preheat the oven to 425°F. Prick the crust all over with a fork. Line it with tin foil and weight the bottom with a pile of dried beans, rice (these can be reused for this same purpose), or other weights that will sit flat on the surface. Bake 12 minutes. Remove from the oven and carefully remove the weights and foil; turn the oven to 325°F.

2 Meanwhile, place the butter or oil in a large, deep skillet and turn the heat to medium; when the butter melts or the oil is hot, add the onions, salt, and pepper. Turn the heat to medium-high and cook, stirring frequently, until the onions are very soft and golden brown, at least 20 minutes. Add the thyme, stir, and turn off the heat.

3 Beat the eggs with the liquid and stir in the onions. Place the baked crust on a baking sheet. Pour the egg mixture into the crust, right to the top. Carefully transfer the baking sheet to the oven and bake 30 to 40 minutes, until the mixture is set but is still moist; it should still jiggle just a little in the middle. Cool on a rack and serve warm or at room temperature.

Onion Quiche with Bacon: You can make this variation with the Basic Cheese Quiche as well (just cook the bacon and discard the fat), but I like it better with onions. Omit the butter or oil. Cook 8 to 12 slices of good bacon in its own fat until nice and crisp. Remove the bacon with a slotted spoon and cook the onions in the bacon fat, stirring, until very tender, 10 to 15 minutes. Mix with the eggs. Place the bacon in the crust, pour the egg-onion mixture over it, and proceed as above.

The Basics of Waffles

A good waffle is super-crisp outside and creamy inside. (When was the last time you had one that fit that description?) Which means that the important thing about waffles is not so much what you put in them or on them, but how you make them and how quickly you serve them.

Eggs are among the best foundations for light dinners or late-night suppers. Among my favorite heartier breakfast and brunch dishes to serve at night:

1. Scrambled Eggs with Spinach, page 735
2. Baked Eggs with Tomato, page 737
3. Baked Eggs with Spinach (Eggs "Florentine"), page 737
4. Baked Eggs with Onions and Cheese, page 737
5. Any omelet, pages 738–740
6. Any frittata, pages 740–741
7. Any soufflé, pages 742–743
8. Any quiche, pages 743–744
9. Overnight Waffles or Quick and Easy Waffles, with some of the heartier additions, pages 745–747
10. Filled Savory Crepes, page 751
11. Cheese Blintzes, page 752
12. Welsh Rarebit (or Rabbit), page 754

There are essentially three options for waffle batter: A raised yeast batter, by far the most time-consuming (you start it the night before), is the best. Butter-laden waffles made with buttermilk, yogurt, or sour cream are a close second. And simple, pancake-like waffles are also definitely worth eating, especially when you're out of other ingredients. Once prepared, all three batters are treated the same. A few guidelines:

- The iron should be hot. Most have indicator lights. Preheat yours until the light goes off.
- The iron should be clean and lightly oiled. Even some non-stick irons aren't non-stick. If your first waffle sticks next time try brushing or spraying the iron lightly with oil before turning it on. When it's preheated, open it for a minute to let any oily smoke escape, close it until it becomes hot again, then start cooking.
- Don't underbake the waffle. After pouring (or spreading) the batter onto the iron, close the top and walk away for at least two minutes. Gently pull up on the top of the iron. If there is resistance, give it another minute or two longer; the waffle isn't ready. (Note: the indicator light on many waffle irons goes on when they are still a bit underdone. For a crisper waffle, wait an extra minute or so after the light has gone on.)

- Eat waffles immediately. You can keep them warm on a rack in a 200°F oven for five minutes, but not much longer. I serve them as they come from the iron, for waffles are delicate creatures.
- If you think of it, melt the butter and gently warm the maple syrup before serving.

Overnight Waffles

Makes 4 to 6 servings

Time: 8 hours, or more, largely unattended

Super-crisp outside, light and tender inside, with the complex flavor of yeast-risen batter, these are the best waffles you can make, and they're no more work than any other waffle; you just have to think ahead.

1/2 teaspoon instant yeast
2 cups all-purpose flour
1 tablespoon sugar
1/2 teaspoon salt
2 cups milk
8 tablespoons (1 stick) butter, melted and cooled
1/2 teaspoon vanilla extract (optional)
Canola or other neutral oil for brushing on waffle iron
2 eggs

1 Before going to bed, combine the dry ingredients and stir in the milk, then the butter and vanilla. The mixture will be loose. Cover with plastic wrap and set aside overnight at room temperature.

2 Brush the waffle iron lightly with oil and preheat it. Separate the eggs and stir the yolks into the batter. Beat the whites until they hold soft peaks. Stir them gently into the batter.

3 Spread a ladleful or so of batter onto the waffle iron and bake until the waffle is done, usually 3 to 5 minutes, depending on your iron. Serve immediately or keep warm for a few minutes in a low oven.

Rich Buttermilk Waffles
Makes 4 to 6 servings

Time: 10 minutes, plus time to bake

The best waffles you can make at the last minute, with a sour tang that sets off maple syrup beautifully.

2 cups all-purpose flour
$1/2$ teaspoon salt
2 tablespoons sugar
$1 1/2$ teaspoons baking soda
$1 3/4$ cups buttermilk (see Note) or $1 1/2$ cups sour
  cream or plain yogurt thinned with $1/4$ cup milk
2 eggs, separated
4 tablespoons ($1/2$ stick) butter, melted and cooled
$1/2$ teaspoon vanilla extract (optional)
Canola or other neutral oil for brushing on waffle iron

1 Combine the dry ingredients. Mix together the buttermilk, sour cream, or yogurt and the egg yolks. Stir in the butter and vanilla (if you are using it).

2 Brush the waffle iron lightly with oil and preheat it. Stir the wet into the dry ingredients. Beat the egg whites with the whisk or electric mixer until they hold soft peaks. Stir them gently into the batter.

3 Spread a ladleful or so of batter onto the waffle iron and bake until the waffle is done, usually 3 to 5 minutes, depending on your iron. Serve immediately or keep warm for a few minutes in a low oven.

Note: For the buttermilk, you can substitute $1 3/4$ cups of milk, at room temperature, mixed with 2 tablespoons white vinegar, and left to clabber for 10 minutes.

Quick and Easy Waffles
Makes 4 to 6 servings

Time: 10 minutes, plus time to bake

The basic waffle, still a treat. If you have the time, separate the eggs and beat the whites as in the previous two recipes.

Canola or other neutral oil for brushing on waffle iron
2 cups all-purpose flour
$1/2$ teaspoon salt
2 tablespoons sugar
3 teaspoons baking powder
$1 1/2$ cups milk
2 eggs
4 tablespoons ($1/2$ stick) butter, melted and cooled
1 teaspoon vanilla extract (optional)

1 Brush the waffle iron lightly with oil and preheat it.

2 Combine the dry ingredients. Mix together the milk and eggs. Stir in the butter and vanilla (if you are using it). Stir the wet into the dry ingredients. If the mixture seems too thick to pour, add a little more milk.

3 Spread a ladleful or so of batter onto the waffle iron and bake until the waffle is done, usually 3 to 5 minutes, depending on your iron. Serve immediately or keep warm for a few minutes in a low oven.

Eleven Quick Variations for Waffles

You can make these changes to any of the three recipes above.

1. Substitute one cup cornmeal for one cup flour. (If you make Quick and Easy Waffles, it's really worth separating the eggs and beating the whites in this instance.)
2. Lay two or three strips of bacon over the batter after spreading on the waffle iron and before closing the lid in any of the above recipes. The bacon will cook along with the waffles; cooking time may be a minute or two longer.
3. Stir one cup chopped (not minced) nuts, Crunchy Granola (page 756), or shredded sweetened or unsweetened coconut into the batter.
4. Add minced or grated orange or lemon zest, about two teaspoons per batch of batter.
5. Add grated mild cheese, such as Cheddar or Jack, about one cup per batch of batter.
6. Substitute whole wheat, rye, or other flour for up to half of the white flour.
7. Substitute up to one-half cup molasses for one-half cup milk (excellent with cornmeal).
8. Add freshly minced or ground ginger, up to two teaspoons per batch of batter.
9. Add ground cinnamon, up to two teaspoons per batch of batter.
10. Add fresh fruit such as blueberries, raspberries, or other fruit cut into one-quarter- to one-half-inch dice to the batter.
11. Serve waffles topped with ice cream, whipped cream, and/or fresh fruit.

The Basics of Pancakes

Unlike waffles, which are delicate and fairly temperamental, you can bind almost anything with flour and egg and cook it on a griddle. Here we're talking about breakfast pancakes and the best, usually reserved for weekends, are moist, delicate creatures, made with beaten egg whites or cottage cheese—something to lighten them up. The simplest breakfast pancakes contain few ingredients, take less time to prepare than it does to preheat a griddle or skillet, and are a weekday staple. Leftover batter can be kept, covered and refrigerated, for several days.

Pancakes are best hot, and adding cold butter and maple syrup does them no good. If you think of it, melt the butter and gently warm the maple syrup (I use the microwave for both) before serving.

Basic Pancakes

Makes 4 to 6 servings

Time: 20 minutes

Americans must have been sadly alienated from the kitchen for pancake mixes to ever have gained a foothold in the market, for these are ridiculously easy to make.

2 cups all-purpose flour
1 tablespoon baking powder
$1/2$ teaspoon salt
1 tablespoon sugar
1 or 2 eggs
$1^1/2$ to 2 cups milk
2 tablespoons melted and cooled butter (optional), plus unmelted butter for cooking, or use oil

1 Preheat a griddle or large skillet over medium-low heat while you make the batter.

2 Mix together the dry ingredients. Beat the egg(s) into $1^1/2$ cups of the milk, then stir in the 2 tablespoons melted cooled butter (if you are using it). Gently stir this into the dry ingredients, mixing only enough to moisten the flour; don't worry about a few

lumps. If the batter seems thick, add a little more milk.

3 If your skillet or griddle is non-stick, you can cook the pancakes without any butter. Otherwise, use a teaspoon or two of butter or oil each time you add batter. When the butter foam subsides or the oil shimmers, ladle batter onto the griddle or skillet, making any size pancakes you like. Adjust the heat as necessary; usually, the first batch will require higher heat than subsequent batches. The idea is to brown the bottom in 2 to 4 minutes, without burning it. Flip when the pancakes are cooked on the bottom; they won't hold together well until they're ready.

4 Cook until the second side is lightly browned and serve, or hold on an overproof plate in a 200°F oven for up to 15 minutes.

Light and Fluffy Pancakes
Makes 4 servings

Time: 20 minutes

These are ethereal, clouds of egg made into cakes; they also develop a very nice crust. Add more sugar if you'd like them sweet.

1 cup milk

4 eggs, separated

1 cup all-purpose flour

Dash salt

1 tablespoon sugar

1 1/2 teaspoons baking powder

Butter or canola or other neutral oil as needed

Pancake Variations

Use any of these variations with either Basic or Light and Fluffy Pancakes.

Polenta Pancakes: Slowly add 1/2 cup cornmeal to 1 cup boiling water and cook over low heat, stirring, until smooth and well blended, about 3 minutes; cool. Make either of the above batters and stir in the cornmeal mush (before adding the beaten egg whites in the second recipe). You might also substitute molasses for the sugar in this variation, with excellent results.

Blueberry Pancakes: Blueberries, about 1 cup, should be the last ingredient you add. If they are fresh, pick them over and wash and drain them well before adding. If they are frozen, add them without defrosting. Cook more slowly than you would other pancakes, because they have a tendency to burn.

Banana Pancakes: Really, really great, and a fine use for overripe bananas. Make any pancake batter as usual.

After beginning to cook each batch, simply place a few rounds of 1/4-inch-thick slices of banana directly onto the surface of the cooking batter; press them into each cake a little bit. Turn carefully and cook a little more slowly than you would other pancakes, but be sure to cook through.

Buttermilk, Sour Milk, or Yogurt Pancakes: Substitute any of these for the milk in Basic or Light and Fluffy Pancakes; use 1/2 teaspoon baking soda in place of the baking powder and proceed as above. If necessary (as it probably will be with sour cream or thick yogurt), thin the batter with a little milk.

Buckwheat Cakes: Substitute buckwheat flour for the white flour, cup for cup. Double the amount of sugar and increase the amount of milk or other liquid by 1/4 cup if necessary (buckwheat is "thirstier" than white flour). Cook as above.

1 Preheat a griddle or large skillet over medium-low heat while you make the batter.

2 Beat together the milk and egg yolks. Mix the dry ingredients. Beat the egg whites with a whisk or electric mixer until stiff but not dry.

3 Combine the dry ingredients and milk-yolk mixture, stirring to blend. Gently fold in the beaten egg whites; they should remain somewhat distinct in the batter.

4 Add about 1 teaspoon of butter or oil to the griddle or skillet and, when it is hot, add the batter by the heaping tablespoon, making sure to include some of the egg whites in each spoonful. Cook until lightly browned on the bottom, 3 to 5 minutes, then turn and cook until the second side is brown. Serve, or hold in a 200°F oven for up to 15 minutes.

Sourdough Pancakes

Makes 3 to 4 servings

Time: 1½ hours, largely unattended

You need sourdough to make these, but if you have it they're quite simple. Good with one-half cup buckwheat flour substituted for one-half cup white flour.

1 cup sourdough starter (see Sourdough Bread, page 226)
1 cup all-purpose flour
½ to 1 cup milk
¼ teaspoon salt
1 tablespoon sugar
½ teaspoon baking powder
1 egg
Butter or canola or other neutral oil as needed

1 Combine the starter, flour, and enough milk as needed to make a medium-thin batter (the amount of milk will depend on the thickness of your sourdough. Let sit for about an hour.

2 Preheat a griddle or large skillet over medium-low heat while you finish the batter. Stir in the salt, sugar, and baking powder. Beat in the egg.

3 Add about 1 teaspoon of butter or oil to the griddle or skillet and, when it is hot, add the batter by the heaping tablespoon. Cook until lightly browned on the bottom, 3 to 5 minutes, then turn and cook until the second side is brown. Serve, or hold in a 200°F oven for up to 15 minutes.

Eight Other Ideas for Pancakes

1. Use the batter for Overnight Waffles, page 745.
2. Add chocolate chips as the pancakes are cooking (see Banana Pancakes, above).
3. Add grated peeled apples or pears, crushed drained pineapple, or any other fruit, pitted, peeled, and chopped (or drained and chopped if canned), as you would blueberries. Or add peeled and sliced fresh fruit (or lightly cooked, for hard fruit such as apples) as you would bananas.
4. Add one tablespoon or more of freshly squeezed lemon juice to the batter, using baking soda (one-half teaspoon per cup of flour) in place of baking powder. Add a little lemon rind as well if you like the flavor.
5. Spoon the batter over pieces of cooked bacon.
6. Use orange juice in place of milk; add one teaspoon grated or minced orange zest to the batter.
7. Sprinkle ground cinnamon, ginger, cloves, and/or allspice over the batter as it cooks. Be sparing.
8. Substitute one-half cup cornmeal or other grains or cereals, such as oats, rice, or cream of wheat, for one-half cup of the flour.

Cottage Cheese and Sour Cream Pancakes

Makes 3 to 4 servings

Time: 20 minutes

These are a different creation entirely, light, rich, and creamy, with just enough flour to hold the liquid ingredients together.

> 1 cup cottage cheese
> 1 cup sour cream or plain yogurt
> 3 eggs, separated
> 1/4 teaspoon baking soda
> 1 cup all-purpose flour
> Dash salt
> 1 tablespoon sugar
> Butter or canola or other neutral oil as needed

1 Preheat a griddle or large skillet over medium-low heat while you make the batter.

2 Beat together the cottage cheese, sour cream or yogurt, and egg yolks. Combine the dry ingredients. Beat the egg whites until stiff but not dry.

3 Stir the flour mixture into the cottage cheese mixture, blending well but not beating. Gently fold in the beaten egg whites; they should remain somewhat distinct in the batter.

4 Add about 1 teaspoon of butter or oil to the griddle or skillet and, when it is hot, add the batter by the heaping tablespoon, making sure to include some of the egg whites in each spoonful. Cook until lightly browned on the bottom, 3 to 5 minutes, then turn and cook until the second side is brown. Serve immediately; these will not hold.

The Basics of Crepes and Blintzes

Crepes are French; blintzes are East European. Aside from the fact that the traditional fillings are not the same, they are very similar. Both are thin pancakes, made with just a couple of tablespoons of watery batter.

A crepe pan, useful for making blintzes as well, can be any shallow, heavy skillet with a six- to eight-inch base. A long handle is helpful, since the way to make the crepes or blintzes is to put in a little more batter than you need, swirl it around the bottom of the pan, then pour the excess—that which does not dry immediately on contact with the pan—back into the bowl.

Crepes can be rolled or folded (in France, sweet crepes are typically rolled, savory ones folded), and blintzes are almost always folded. With any amount of filling over one tablespoon or so, you're better off folding: Put the filling on the bottom third of the pancake, fold the bottom lip over to cover it, then fold in both sides. Make a final turn and you're done.

Crepes

Makes 12 to 16 crepes, enough for 4 to 8 servings

Time: About 30 minutes

Crepes can be served with a sweet topping or rolled around a variety of sweet or savory fillings. If you will be filling them with something sweet, add a tablespoon of sugar to the batter.

> 1 cup all-purpose flour
> Pinch salt
> 1 1/4 cups milk
> 2 eggs
> 2 tablespoons melted and cooled butter or canola or other neutral oil, plus more (unmelted) for cooking

1 Combine the flour, salt, and milk and beat until smooth (you can do this in a blender if you like, but do not overblend). Beat or blend in the eggs and stir in the melted and cooled butter or oil. If time allows, refrigerate for an hour and beat again.

2 Place a small non-stick skillet with shallow sides, over medium heat. When a drop of water skitters across the surface before evaporating, add ¹/₂ teaspoon of butter. Ladle about 1 tablespoon of batter into the skillet and swirl it around so that it forms a thin layer on the bottom of the pan. Pour excess batter back into the bowl or blender container.

3 The batter will dry before your eyes; when the top is no longer liquid, less than a minute, turn the crepe and cook the other side for about 15 seconds. The crepe should brown only very slightly and not become at all crisp. Repeat the process, adding butter to the skillet (if you use a non-stick skillet you won't need any at all) and adjusting the heat as needed. Stack the finished crepes on a plate; you will usually reheat them before serving.

Light, Simple Crepes: These are a great breakfast treat. Separate the eggs. Add the yolks to the batter as above, then beat the whites until stiff but not dry; gently fold them into the batter. Cook the crepes as above; they will be thicker. As they finish, do not stack, but sprinkle them each with about 1 teaspoon sugar (or to taste) and ¹/₈ teaspoon ground cinnamon. Run under a preheated broiler until the sugar melts, about 1 minute. Serve immediately, with butter or freshly squeezed lemon juice.

Filled Sweet Crepes: As you finish cooking each crepe, place 1 to 2 tablespoons of filling in the center, then fold it into quarters. When they are all done, arrange them on a greased (preferably with butter) ovenproof platter. Dot with butter and sprinkle with sugar and cinnamon (optional). Heat in a 400°F oven for 10 minutes, then serve.

Filled Savory Crepes: These are essentially eggy tortillas. As you finish cooking each crepe, place about 2 tablespoons of filling in the center and fold them up. Arrange them on a greased ovenproof platter. Sprinkle with lemon juice, butter, grated Parmesan or other cheese, Béchamel (Milk) Sauce (page 787), or other toppings. Heat in a 400°F oven for 10 minutes, then serve.

Spoon some filling across the lower third of the crepe.

Lift the bottom edge and roll it up.

A filled crepe.

Five Filling Ideas for Sweet Crepes

1. Any jam, marmalade, preserves, or jelly
2. Any peeled, seeded (or pitted, or cored) fresh fruit, cooked briefly with sugar to taste, some butter if you like, and a little rum or cinnamon
3. Cream cheese, Yogurt Cheese (page 757), or sour cream, or a mixture sweetened with sugar to taste
4. Sweetened butter to which you have added seasonings such as cinnamon, rum, or minced orange zest

5. A mixture of one-half cup sugar, one teaspoon cinnamon, three tablespoons butter, and one-half cup chopped walnuts, pecans, or almonds, or another streusel-like mixture

Five Filling Ideas for Savory Crepes

1. Cooked, drained, and chopped green vegetables, reheated in butter or oil as per the directions on page 532 (don't bother to chop vegetables whose shape is naturally suited to crepes, such as asparagus spears)
2. Any thick stew of meat, chicken, or fish.
3. Cooked spiced beans, or beans and rice
4. Thin slice of ham and grated cheese
5. Sautéed mushrooms and/or onions

Cheese Blintzes

Makes 4 servings

Time: About 1 hour

This close relative of the crepe uses just about the same batter (it's a little eggier), but is usually sautéed in butter for the final heating. Traditional fillings are well-seasoned mashed potatoes, any cooked fruit, or the cheese filling given below. Blintzes are somewhat sturdier than crepes and usually contain more filling.

3/4 cup all-purpose flour

Salt as needed

1 cup milk

3 eggs

2 tablespoons melted and cooled butter or canola or other neutral oil, plus more (unmelted) for cooking

1 1/2 cups cottage cheese, drained if very moist

1/2 cup sour cream or thick plain yogurt

1 tablespoon sugar, or to taste

1 teaspoon ground cinnamon, or to taste

1 Combine the flour, a pinch of salt, and the milk and beat until smooth (you can do this in a blender if you like, but do not overblend). Beat in the eggs and stir in the 2 tablespoons melted and cooled butter or oil. If time allows, refrigerate for an hour and beat again.

2 Place a small skillet, preferably one that is non-stick and has shallow sides, over medium heat. When a drop of water skitters across the surface before evaporating, add 1/2 teaspoon of butter. Ladle about 1 tablespoon of batter into the skillet and swirl it around so that it forms a thin layer on the bottom of the pan. Pour excess batter back into the bowl or blender container.

3 The batter will dry before your eyes; when the top is no longer liquid, about a minute, turn the blintz and cook the other side for 15 to 30 seconds. The blintz should not brown at all, nor should it become at all crisp. Repeat the process, adding butter to the skillet (if you use a non-stick skillet you won't need any at all) and adjusting the heat as needed.

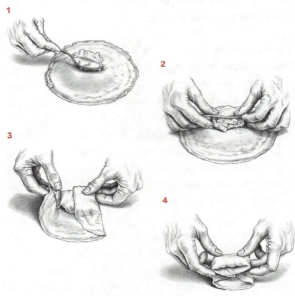

(Step 1) Spoon some filling about a third of the way from the bottom of the blintz. (Step 2) Fold the bottom third over the filling. (Step 3) Fold in the sides. (Step 4) Roll from the bottom up.

Stack the finished blintzes on a plate; you will usually reheat them before serving.

④ Combine the cottage cheese, sour cream, another pinch of salt, sugar, and cinnamon, and place about 2 tablespoons of filling in the bottom third of each blintz. Fold the bottom up over the filling, then tuck in the sides, then roll up. When they are all done, you have two choices:

- Arrange them on a greased (preferably with butter) ovenproof platter. Dot with butter and sprinkle with sugar and cinnamon (optional). Heat in a preheated 400°F oven for 10 minutes, then serve.
- Sauté several at a time in 1 or 2 tablespoons butter until brown and crisp on both sides, a total of about 5 minutes.

The Basics of Toast

You know how to make toast, of course, but there are some fine points worth considering, and some variations worth preserving. White bread, the soft, packaged kind, makes lousy toast—it browns nicely but becomes soft almost immediately. Toast should have crunch; it's best made with slightly stale bread, good bread—the kind you cut with a knife. And it's best made under a broiler, where you can watch it and control the heat. Turn it frequently and watch it carefully, until evenly browned and quite dry.

Pulled Bread

Makes 4 servings

Time: 10 to 20 minutes

An informal and altogether delightful way to make toast. The uneven surfaces of pulled bread give you peaks of dry crispness and valleys of moist tenderness.

About 1 baguette or other slightly stale,
    crusty bread
Butter and/or jam

① Preheat the oven to 450°F, or start the broiler. Pull the bread apart with your hands; the uneven sizes and shapes of the bread are what makes pulled bread fun. Put on a baking sheet.

② Place in the oven or under the broiler. If you bake, you can ignore the bread for about 10 minutes, then turn it when it begins to brown. If you broil, watch carefully and turn the pieces as they brown. Pulled bread is done when some of the points are beginning to char and the bread is toasted all over.

③ Serve immediately, with butter and/or jam.

Cinnamon Toast for One

Makes 1 serving

Time: 5 minutes

Yes, you can make cinnamon toast in a toaster, but this way, which is on the old-fashioned side, is so much better that I doubt you'll ever return to the more common method.

2 slices top-quality white bread
Butter
1/2 teaspoon sugar, or to taste
1/2 teaspoon ground cinnamon, or to taste

① Using a broiler or toaster oven, toast the bread lightly on one side. Turn it over and spread liberally with butter, then sprinkle with sugar and cinnamon.

② Return to the broiler and toast until the butter, cinnamon, and sugar all melt together and the bread is nicely browned. Serve immediately.

Milk Toast for One

Makes 1 serving

Time: 5 minutes

This old-fashioned dish, served like breakfast cereal, requires good, crusty, preferably stale bread made into toast, and whole milk. Given those two things (and a sprinkling of sugar, if you ask me), it's the paradigm of comfort food.

> 2 slices crusty white bread
> 1/2 cup milk
> 2 teaspoons butter
> Pinch salt (optional)
> 1/2 teaspoon sugar or to taste

1 Toast the bread and heat the milk just to the boiling point.

2 Spread the bread with butter and sprinkle it with salt (if you used salted butter, do not) and sugar. Place in a bowl and pour the milk over it. Let sit for a minute, then dig in.

French Toast

Makes 4 servings

Time: 20 minutes

French toast (in French, *pain perdu,* or lost bread) originated as a way to use stale bread, and it is still a fine way to soften and freshen a hard, crusty loaf. But most people now make it with packaged white bread, which, although it almost never gets stale, does make decent French toast, because it absorbs so much liquid. (For the best French toast, use Brioche, page 232, or Challah, page 231.) You can make this mixture eggier by using less milk; you can also adjust it as you cook, adding more milk or another egg if you find

you need it. If you like very mushy French toast, and tend to soak the bread in the batter rather than dip it, you will need more batter than this.

> 2 eggs
> 1 cup milk
> Dash salt
> 1 tablespoon sugar (optional)
> 1 teaspoon vanilla extract or ground cinnamon
>   (optional)
> Butter or canola or other neutral oil as needed
> 8 slices bread

1 Preheat a large griddle or skillet over medium-low heat while you prepare the liquid mixture.

2 Beat the eggs lightly in a broad bowl and stir in the milk, salt, and optional ingredients (if you are using them).

3 Add about 1 teaspoon of butter or oil to the griddle or skillet and, when it is hot, dip each slice of bread in turn in the batter and place it on the griddle. Cook until nicely browned on each side, turning as necessary (you may find that you can raise the heat a bit). Serve, or hold in a 200°F oven for up to 30 minutes.

Crispy French Toast: There are two ways to give French toast a bit of a crust. The first is to stir 1/2 cup flour into the batter. The second is to dip the bread in the batter, then dredge it in sweetened bread crumbs or crushed cornflakes. In either case, cook as above.

Welsh Rarebit (or Rabbit)

Makes 2 to 4 servings

Time: About 20 minutes

This antecedent of nachos—essentially a spicy white sauce laced with good cheese and served with toast—is the classic late-night supper or morning-after breakfast.

Once you have the basics down, you can vary this to your taste. It is best with well-aged farmhouse Cheddar or other fairly hard British cheeses, but it's also good with Emmenthal, Gruyère, or any full-flavored cheese that melts well.

2 tablespoons butter
2 tablespoons flour
1 cup milk
Salt and freshly ground black pepper to taste
Pinch cayenne or ½ teaspoon mustard, or to taste
Worcestershire sauce to taste
At least 2 cups (about ½ pound) grated cheese
4 to 8 slices bread or 2 to 4 split English muffins, toasted and buttered

1 Place a medium saucepan over medium heat and add the butter. When it foams, add the flour and turn the heat to medium-low. Cook, stirring, until the mixture darkens a bit, about 3 minutes. Whisk in the milk a little at a time to avoid lumps, then cook until the mixture is thick, just a minute or two longer.

2 Turn the heat to low and season well, stirring (and tasting) frequently. Then stir in the cheese and continue to cook until the mixture is smooth, another minute. Taste and adjust seasoning, then spoon over toast and serve.

Four Ideas for Welsh Rarebit

1. Substitute beer, tomato juice, or pureed tomato sauce for the milk.
2. Stir in one-half cup well-seasoned cooked beans (puree them if you like) along with the cheese.
3. Stir in one-half cup peeled, cored, seeded, and minced tomatoes along with the cheese.
4. Cool the rarebit, then use it as a sandwich spread (it's like chic Cheez Whiz). Good bread spread with rarebit and sprinkled with chopped onion and capers is wonderful.

The Basics of Breakfast Cereals

Although cooked cereals are sometimes known by the rather unattractive name of gruel, they remain breakfast staples, and they should. Whole or partially milled grains are filling and nutritious. They are also incredibly flavorful on their own (given that they rarely contain any seasonings), although they are almost always improved by the addition of butter and/or sweetener.

Buy your grains, if possible, in bulk at a natural foods store, where they are liable to be fresher (and certainly cheaper) than the packaged stuff sold at the supermarket. And see "Grains" for methods of cooking other grains, which can be readily adapted as breakfast cereals by the mere addition of sweetener.

Granola, a relatively recent addition to the American larder, is a mixture of barely cooked grains laced with nuts and sweeteners. It's easy to make at home, and usually far better than anything you can buy in a store.

Grits
Makes 2 to 4 servings

Time: 20 minutes

The difference between grits and cornmeal? Not much. Which means the difference between cooked grits (cooked ground hominy, a form of dried corn) and polenta (cooked ground corn) is not much either. But grits are southern, and served at breakfast, with butter, whereas polenta is Italian, and served at dinner, with butter and sauce (or at least cheese).

2 cups water
½ cup quick-cooking grits
Freshly ground black pepper to taste
1 tablespoon butter, or more

1 Place the water in a small saucepan and bring it to a boil over medium-high heat. Turn the heat to low and slowly stir or whisk in the grits. Beat with a wire whisk to eliminate lumps.

2 Turn the heat down to a minimum and cover the saucepan. Cook, stirring once or twice, until all the water is absorbed and the grits are creamy, 5 to 10 minutes. Season with pepper, stir in some butter, and serve.

Scrapple: Cook a double recipe of grits as above (you can use cornmeal if you like). When the grits are just about done, stir in 1 to 2 cups minced cooked bacon or sausage meat, along with 1 tablespoon of minced fresh sage (or 1 teaspoon of dried crumbled sage). Continue to cook until the mixture is thick. Pack it into a small, greased loaf pan, cover with plastic wrap, and refrigerate overnight. At breakfast time, cut into 1/2-inch-thick slices and pan-fry the slices in butter, oil, or bacon fat until browned and crisp on both sides.

Oatmeal

Makes 2 servings

Time: 15 minutes

Why people buy instant oatmeal I'll never know. Buy rolled oats in bulk (and keep them in the refrigerator or freezer; rolled oats are perishable). They take all of fifteen minutes, largely unattended, to cook. I like oatmeal fairly creamy, so I use this proportion; if you prefer it thicker, use a bit less water.

2 1/4 cups water
Dash salt
1 cup rolled oats
Butter to taste (optional)
Salt, sweetener (such as maple syrup, sugar, or honey), and/or milk or cream as desired

1 Combine the water, salt, and oats in a small saucepan and turn the heat to high. When the water boils, turn the heat to low and cook, stirring, until the water is just absorbed, about 5 minutes. Add butter if desired, cover the pan, and turn off the heat.

2 Five minutes later, uncover the pan and stir. Add other ingredients as desired and serve.

Crunchy Granola

Makes about 8 cups

Time: 30 minutes

The contents and proportions of granola are governed more by individual taste than most other foods. If you hate coconut, omit it; if you like it, add more. Same with the nuts, which can be any kind you like. If you like lots of little nuts and seeds, add more. If you like lots of dried fruit, add more. And so on. Experiment with spices, too: Small amounts (one-quarter teaspoon) of nutmeg and/or cardamom can make granola seem downright mysterious.

6 cups rolled oats (not quick-cooking or instant)
2 cups mixed nuts and seeds: a combination of sunflower seeds, chopped walnuts, pecans, almonds, cashews, sesame seeds, etc.
1 cup dried unsweetened shredded coconut
1 teaspoon ground cinnamon, or to taste
Dash salt
1/2 to 1 cup honey or maple syrup, or to taste
1 cup raisins or chopped dried fruit

1 Preheat the oven to 300°F.

2 Place a 9 × 13-inch baking pan over medium-low heat (place the pan over two burners if it's convenient). Add the oats and cook, stirring occasionally, until they begin to change color and become fragrant, 3 to 5 minutes.

3 Add the nuts and seeds and continue to cook, stirring frequently, for 2 minutes. Add the coconut and cook, stirring, for 2 minutes more. Add the cinnamon, salt, and sweetener, stir, and place in the oven. Bake for 20 minutes, stirring once or twice during that period.

4 Add the dried fruit, stir, and cool on a rack, continuing to stir once in a while until the granola reaches room temperature. Transfer to a sealed container and store in the refrigerator; it will keep indefinitely.

Yogurt

Makes 1 quart

Time: Overnight, or longer, largely unattended

Yogurt (and cheese, for that matter) is a traditional way of preserving milk. It has remained popular because it tastes good, and because of its reputed health-giving properties. Although almost no one using this book will have a cow, and even fewer will have the problem of preserving that cow's milk production, there is a certain pleasure in making your own yogurt, especially because it is usually much sweeter-tasting than the store-bought kind.

Whole milk makes the best yogurt, but you can use any milk you like, even reconstituted nonfat dry milk, too; mix it about twice as thick as the package indicates.

1 quart milk
$^1/_2$ cup natural plain yogurt ("with active cultures")

1 Place the milk in a small-to-medium saucepan and bring just to the boil; turn off the heat and cool to 110° to 115°F.

2 Whisk the milk and yogurt together. Place in a yogurt maker, a prewarmed thermos, or a preheated bowl wrapped in a towel or blanket and set in a warm place. The idea is to keep the mixture at about 100°F.

3 Do not disturb the mixture at all for at least 6 hours. Then carefully check by tilting the container to see whether the milk has become yogurt. If not, leave alone for another 6 hours. When the yogurt is done, refrigerate and use within 1 week.

Yogurt Cheese: You can make this with store-bought yogurt as well. Instead of refrigerating the yogurt, place it in a jelly bag or several layers of cheesecloth and suspend it over the sink or a large bowl. Let drain for at least 6 hours, preferably longer, until the yogurt has a cream cheese–like consistency. Use exactly as you would cream cheese.

Three Important but Miscellaneous Breakfast Dishes Found Elsewhere

For some, breakfast is not complete without potatoes and sausage.

1. For Home Fried Potatoes, I suggest you make Crispy Sautéed Potatoes with Rosemary, page 597, omitting the garlic and rosemary and substituting butter for the olive oil if you like.
2. For Hash Browns, try Potato Pancakes, Version II (page 598), made as one big cake. Cook it slowly so the inside becomes tender before the outside burns.
3. For Basic Breakfast Sausage, see page 473.

Sauces, Salsas, and Spice Mixtures

Sauces for savory foods (you'll find dessert sauces on pages 671–674) may be assertive or very mild, thick or thin, emulsified or not, bound with eggs or flour or not. They may take two minutes to make, or twenty (these days, few take longer than that). They generally serve to moisten food, to enhance it, to complement it; or they may be the most interesting aspect of a given dish. In any case, a good sauce is a light dressing, simply made, to finish a dish in which the whole is greater than the sum of its parts. (There was a time that sauces were used to disguise spoiled food, but fortunately we no longer routinely cook with spoiled food.)

Although most cuisines use them, we associate sauces primarily with France. (Italian sauces, for the most part, are used on pasta and polenta and are largely discussed in those chapters, although the brilliantly versatile pesto is covered here.) It was the French who codified complicated sauce-making, and whose sauces became the standards of "fancy" cooking. But once-common French sauces, such as brown sauce or hollandaise, both of which became classic American sauces, are no longer made with the frequency they once were. Still, many French sauces are certainly worth knowing. The selection in this chapter includes those I consider most valuable, such as mayonnaise and beurre blanc, and those I use only rarely, but which are too important to omit, such as hollandaise.

Sauces have changed. We may use stock, but it is no longer the foundation of most worthwhile sauces. We are not as concerned with obtaining deep brown color as were the cooks of earlier generations, who would resort to food coloring (as do most commercial sauce manufacturers) if all else failed. Nor are we as concerned with thickness; a sauce that has been thickened with flour—or even the more reliable cornstarch—has no better flavor than one that has not. (If it's a creamy texture you're after, consider eggs or cream. Yes, they add calories, but they also add flavor.)

Like any preparation, a sauce is no better than the most basic ingredients that go into it. If you combine vegetable oil and water in a blender you'll get a creamy-looking white substance that can be seasoned with anything and used as a sauce. But all you've got is vegetable oil, water, and seasonings—why not add the seasonings directly to the cooked food and leave out the superfluous ingredients?

It was that kind of thinking, I believe, that led to the spirit behind the sauces that finish many contemporary dishes. Today, most sauces are light and simple, beginning with clean, up-front flavors and building on them. A basic "sauce" might be a sprinkling of freshly squeezed lemon juice or vinegar. You might choose to combine that acid with oil, to give it body, smoothness, more flavor, and balance. You might add fresh herbs, or minced aromatics, to boost the flavor. You might also emulsify the combination, so that it gains a pleasing creaminess. Each of these refinements adds complexity, texture, and even elegance to your basic flavor. But that basic flavor is still what the sauce is about, and in most cases you still will have spent no more than ten minutes in preparation.

Similarly, a basic sauce might be a few spoonfuls of a well-made stock added to pan juices with an herb or two and finished in an instant, or smoothed even further with a little butter or olive oil.

It makes sense to divide sauces into two groups: those that are made separately from the dish with which they'll be used, and those that are based directly on it. The first is by far the larger category: It includes vinaigrettes (pages 90–94), mayonnaise, pesto, ketchup, chutneys, salsas, hollandaise, béchamel, tomato-based sauces (pages 130–134), even apple or cranberry sauce—anything that is made independently.

Many of these are classics from France and elsewhere, and are unquestionably useful, especially for those foods such as starches cooked in water (like pasta), or grilled food, in which there are no pan juices.

Then there are reduction sauces, which build on the pan juices that naturally result from stove-top cooking or oven-roasting of meat, poultry, fish, or sometimes vegetables. The making of reduction sauces (page 790) is a simple art, and one with which every home cook should become familiar. A good reduction exploits the natural flavors of the dish, those that are already there and which would otherwise be discarded. And it can be made in minutes, with little extra effort and whatever ingredients are on hand—although stock is often preferable, wonderful reductions can be made with milk, cream, juice, even water.

Most experienced cooks find both types of from-scratch sauce-making simple and rewarding. A sautéed chicken breast takes on splendor when graced with a reduction sauce, and a tuna sandwich or a slab of cold roast beef with *real* mayonnaise is a revelation.

The Basics of Mayonnaise

From the moment you make your first batch of mayonnaise, it will become a staple. The production process takes five minutes in blender or food processor, and the result is far superior to the store-bought stuff; you don't need much of it for flavor, and there's almost no limit to what you can do with it. You'll probably still keep bottled mayo in the fridge—there are times you won't want to bother to make a batch of fresh mayo for a sandwich—but you'll use it a lot less often.

Mayonnaise, as you may know, is an emulsion of egg, oil, and liquid. You can use egg yolks only, for a more beautiful color, but I usually use a whole egg, which works perfectly. Mayonnaise can be stored, refrigerated, for a week or even a little longer.

Although some people complain that it "breaks"—separates into its component ingredients—after a day or two in the refrigerator, you won't have that problem if you make it with a food processor.

As long as you have an egg, you can use any oil and other liquid you want to make mayonnaise. Extra-virgin olive oil alone makes a strong-flavored mayonnaise, which is a great base for aioli (see the variation), a wonderful dip, and a fine sauce for raw or cooked vegetables. But it's a little strong for other uses, so try mayonnaise made with half extra-virgin olive oil and half neutral oil, such as canola, corn, or grapeseed, which is perfect for sandwiches and traditional chicken, tuna, and egg salads; using all-neutral oil makes a mayonnaise not unlike the better store-bought varieties. In any case, make sure the oil is fresh: Rancidity that you might not detect when cooking will leap to the fore in a raw sauce like this one.

I think the best liquid for mayonnaise is lemon juice, because it adds such good flavor; lime juice is nearly as good. Vinegar is also fine, but unless it is very mild, such as rice vinegar, it should be diluted half and half with water, or its flavor will dominate.

The major problem with homemade mayonnaise is that it contains raw egg (see the discussion of eggs and food safety in The Basics of Eggs on page 731). If this concerns you, simply substitute the equivalent amount of Egg Beaters or other pasteurized egg product and proceed with the recipe, or try Harold McGee's "Safe" Mayonnaise, given as a variation below.

Basic Mayonnaise

Makes 1 cup

Time: 10 minutes

With the food processor or blender you can make perfect mayonnaise the first time you try it. Remember, however, you need a total of two tablespoons of liquid for the emulsion to work. If you don't have lemon juice, which is the perfect liquid, use half vinegar and half water; if you use all vinegar its flavor will dominate.

1 egg or egg yolk
Dash cayenne
$^1/_2$ teaspoon dry mustard
Salt and freshly ground black pepper to taste
2 tablespoons freshly squeezed lemon juice, or white wine, or Champagne or other vinegar mixed half and half with water
1 cup extra-virgin olive oil, or canola or other neutral oil, or a combination, or more if needed

1 Combine the egg, cayenne, mustard, salt, pepper, lemon juice, and $^1/_4$ cup of the oil in the container of a blender or food processor; turn on the machine and, with the machine running, add the oil in a thin, steady stream.

2 After you've added about half of the oil, the mixture will thicken; you can then begin adding the oil a bit faster. You can add up to $1^1/_2$ cups of oil and still have a pleasant, yellow (or pale yellow, if you included the egg white) mayonnaise. If the mixture is thicker than you'd like, add a little warm water, with the machine still running, or stir in a little cream or sour cream by hand. Check the seasoning and serve or store in the refrigerator for up to a week.

Aioli, or Garlic Mayonnaise: Serve with fish, or as a dip for vegetables, or as a sauce for any simple cooked food. Add 1 to 4 whole peeled cloves of garlic at the beginning. If you like, add a small (no larger than 1 inch thick in any direction) boiled and peeled potato to the mixture at the start for extra body. Thin as necessary with cream, stock, or water.

Rouille: Frequently served with fish stews, where it is often dolloped onto garlic toasts or croutons. Add $^1/_2$ cup roasted, peeled, and seeded red bell pepper (or used bottled "pimento"), cayenne to taste, and 2 cloves garlic, all at the beginning. As in Aioli (see above), a small boiled and peeled potato may be added. Thin as necessary with stock or water.

Real Tartar Sauce: Stir ¹/₄ cup of minced sour pickles (preferably cornichons) and 1 tablespoon minced shallots or scallions into finished mayonnaise. Add prepared horseradish to taste.

Anchovy Mayonnaise: Add 2 or 3 anchovy fillets to the initial mix. Use the oil from the anchovies to replace part of the olive or other oil.

Herb Mayonnaise: Add ¹/₄ cup or more of fresh herbs to the basic recipe, at the beginning. Start with parsley or chives, but experiment with dill, tarragon (smaller amounts, or mixed with parsley), basil, and so on. If you want rather green mayonnaise, start with the herb of your choice, and add at least ¹/₄ cup parsley to the mix.

"Safe" Mayonnaise: Harold McGee developed this technique for his excellent book *The Curious Cook* (North Point Press, 1990). It takes some practice, because all microwaves are different, but it does heat the egg sufficiently to kill any bacteria without causing coagulation. Place the yolk in a 2-cup measure or glass bowl and whisk until smooth. Beat in 1 tablespoon freshly squeezed lemon juice and 1 tablespoon water. Beat again and wash the whisk with soap (or break out another whisk). Cover the bowl with a plate and microwave on high; watch carefully. After 10 to 30 seconds (depending on the strength of your oven), the yolk will begin to shake; count to 5, remove the bowl, and whisk. Repeat the cooking, again counting to 5 when the mixture heaves, and beating with a clean whisk. Cover and let sit 1 minute, then place the bowl in a bowl of cold water and beat—again with a clean whisk—

until cool. Proceed as for any other mayonnaise, using no more than one-quarter olive or unrefined oil; more than that and the mixture will not emulsify as it normally does. (Use refined oil such as canola for the balance.)

Handmade Mayonnaise: This gains a certain creaminess that machine-made mayonnaise doesn't have, but I don't think it's worth the trouble. You may disagree: Start as above, but combine the ingredients in a bowl. Add the oil about a teaspoon at a time, while beating with a wire whisk, until the mixture becomes thick (if it becomes too thick to handle, add a few drops of water or freshly squeezed lemon juice). Then beat in the remaining oil about a tablespoon at a time; taste and adjust seasoning, or thin if necessary.

Ten Other Ways to Flavor Mayonnaise

1. Use lime juice or flavored vinegar (dilute vinegar with water) for the liquid.
2. Add chili powder, curry powder, or other spices or spice blends to the mix; start with about a teaspoon per cup of oil, and add more to taste.
3. Add prepared horseradish (at least one teaspoon) or wasabi powder (one-half teaspoon or more) at the end; taste and adjust seasoning.
4. Use Dijon or other prepared mustard in place of dry mustard.
5. Add one teaspoon or more of grated lemon zest.
6. Stir in one-half cup cored, peeled, seeded, and minced tomato and/or roasted red bell pepper (or canned "pimento").
7. Season the mayonnaise with Worcestershire or other prepared sauces.
8. Stir in one-half cup minced scallion, shallot, or mild onion.
9. Add one teaspoon or more of peeled and minced fresh ginger and one tablespoon or more of

minced cilantro leaves; use freshly squeezed lime juice for the liquid.

10. Stir in one-half cup toasted and chopped almonds, walnuts, or pecans.

Russian Dressing

Makes about 1 cup

Time: 10 minutes

This is better as a sandwich topping than a salad dressing, I think. It's best, of course, when made with fresh mayonnaise.

1/2 cup mayonnaise
1/4 cup ketchup
1 tablespoon red or white wine vinegar or freshly squeezed lemon juice
1 tablespoon minced onion
Dash dry mustard
Salt and freshly ground black pepper to taste

1. Combine all ingredients in a small bowl and beat with a fork.

2. Taste and adjust seasoning. If it is too thin, add a bit more mayonnaise; if it is too thick, add more vinegar, lemon juice, or ketchup. This keeps as well as mayonnaise: a week or more in the refrigerator.

Skordalia

Eggless Greek Mayonnaise

Makes about 2 cups

Time: 15 minutes

The Greek version of aioli is thickened with bread and enhanced by the addition of nuts. Serve with hot or cold vegetables or grilled, fried, or cold fish.

3 slices good white bread, hard crusts removed
1/2 cup walnuts or blanched almonds
2 to 6 cloves garlic, peeled
Salt and freshly ground black pepper to taste
2 tablespoons freshly squeezed lemon juice or vinegar
1 cup extra-virgin olive oil
Fast Fish Stock (page 49) or chicken stock mixed with water, or water as needed (see "Soups" for stock recipes)

1. Soak the bread in warm water for a few minutes to soften. Squeeze out the water, then put the bread in the container of a blender or small food processor with the nuts, garlic, salt, pepper, and lemon juice.

2. Turn on the machine and, while it is running, add the oil in a thin, steady stream. If the sauce becomes too thick, thin with a teaspoon or more of stock or water. Correct seasonings and serve. This does not hold as long as an egg-based mayonnaise; it's best to make it just before serving, and use it all at once.

Cold Mustard Sauce

Makes about 1 cup

Time: 10 minutes

A thin, highly seasoned mayonnaise-like sauce created for gravlax but useful as a sauce for any smoked fish or chilled, cooked vegetables.

1 egg or egg yolk
4 tablespoons Dijon mustard
1/2 teaspoon confectioners' sugar
1/2 teaspoon salt
1/2 teaspoon finely ground pepper (preferably white)
2 tablespoons dry white wine
1 teaspoon mild vinegar, such as rice vinegar
1/2 cup canola or other neutral oil
3 tablespoons minced fresh dill leaves

1 Place the first seven ingredients in a small food processor or blender and turn the machine on. With the machine running, add the oil in a steady stream and continue to blend until the mixture has thickened.

2 Stir in the dill by hand. If the sauce is too thick, thin with a little cream or warm water. Store, refrigerated, for up to a week in the refrigerator.

The Basics of Mustards

It's nearly impossible for the home cook to exactly replicate the classic mustards, such as Dijon, Moutarde de Meaux, or even the all-American spicy brown. Fortunately, however, you can make a range of good mustard with little effort. You can buy powder or seeds, which can in turn be crushed or ground into powder; or you can use a mixture. There are three kinds of seeds: yellow, which are the mildest; brown, which are more flavorful; and black, which are quite sharp.

Mustard, especially mustard powder, is hot and irritating. Take care not to get any into your eyes or on other sensitive body parts, and wash your hands thoroughly after you're done mixing.

Smooth, English-Style Mustard

Makes ¹/₂ cup

Time: 5 minutes

It's difficult to grind seeds fine enough to use them in this super-sharp mustard, which resembles both Coleman's (the standard English mustard) and the mustard often placed on tables in Chinese restaurants. You can use this mustard immediately, but the flavor will be quite harsh. Its quality will peak at about one week, and intensity will begin to decline after that. If you use it more quickly, double the recipe.

¹/₂ cup yellow mustard seed powder
1 teaspoon salt
1 tablespoon flour
Water, white wine, or beer as needed

1 Combine the first three ingredients in a small bowl. Whisk in the liquid, a little bit at a time, until the mixture is smooth and creamy. Let sit for at least 30 minutes before using.

2 Store in the refrigerator, covered, until ready to use.

Wasabi: Here's how to make the paste served universally with sushi: Substitute wasabi powder (available at all Asian markets) for the yellow mustard seed powder and omit the flour. Use water to thin. Make sure to wash your hands thoroughly after mixing.

Sweet Herb Mustard: Add 1 teaspoon minced fresh tarragon, chervil, thyme, or other herb leaves, 1 tablespoon minced chives, and 1 teaspoon confectioners' sugar to the mix. Taste and add more herbs if you like.

Grainy, French-Style Mustard

Makes 1 cup

Time: 5 minutes, plus at least 1 day for maturing

This is best made with brown seeds, but you can use brown mixed with yellow and even a little black.

1 cup mustard seeds, brown, yellow, or a combination
White or rice vinegar as needed
¹/₄ cup yellow mustard seed powder
1 teaspoon salt
¹/₄ cup water, more or less
Water, white wine, or beer as needed

1. Place the mustard seeds in a coffee or spice grinder and process, but not too finely. You want the seeds to retain some crunch. Stir in enough vinegar to make a thick paste. Set aside.

2. Combine the mustard powder with the salt. Stir in enough water to make a thick paste.

3. Mix the two pastes together and add enough water, white wine, or beer to make a smooth, pasty consistency (you won't need much). Store in the refrigerator, covered, until ready to use. This mustard will keep for several weeks.

Simple Hot Mustard

Makes 2 tablespoons

Time: 2 minutes, plus resting time

This is best if you let it sit for about thirty minutes before using. It is very, very hot; drizzle it lightly over cooked or raw foods, or add it to vinaigrettes or mayonnaise when you want an extra kick.

1 tablespoon dry mustard
1 tablespoon warm water
1 teaspoon sugar
Dash salt

Mix all ingredients in a bowl and let rest for 30 minutes. Use within a day.

The Basics of Pesto

A traditional method of preserving herbs (especially basil) in oil, pesto has become a staple, to the point where it's sold in supermarkets and offered on fast-food pizza. You can make a big deal out of pesto (purists insist on using a mortar and pestle), or you can put it together simply in a food processor or blender. I make quarts of it at summer's end (it keeps in the refrigerator for weeks and the freezer for months), and I like to keep the ingredients few and the process quick. These proportions will work for any amount of basil; you're only limited by your supply of basil and patience.

To take the key ingredients in turn:

The Basil The fresher the better, of course. There are different varieties of basil, with slightly different flavors, but the ordinary large-leafed green kind is perfectly suitable. Use leaves and the smallest of stems only; large stems will not puree, and furthermore tend to be bitter. Flowers, however, may be included. Wash the basil well; dry it in a salad spinner. Other herbs may be substituted, as you will see from the recipes. In every case, discard stems and wash leaves.

The Oil Extra-virgin olive oil is best but if you're making a large batch and wish to economize, mix extra-virgin oil with pure olive oil, or with a neutral oil such as canola or grapeseed.

The Nuts Traditionally pine nuts, which are delicious, especially if you toast them first, but expensive. Walnuts lend a distinctive bite that is not at all unpleasant, and which many people prefer.

The Cheese Genuine Parmigiano-Reggiano (its name is stenciled on the rind) is best, of course, but you may substitute other hard cheeses if you like— Grana Padano, asiago, Pecorino Romano, or the "Parmesan" made in Argentina or other countries are all acceptable. Cheese should be considered optional in pesto, and is completely inappropriate in pesto-like blends made with herbs such as cilantro.

The Garlic To taste, please. Recipes that call unconditionally for two to four cloves of raw garlic do not take into account that many dishes are completely overwhelmed by the flavor, and that many people find large quantities of raw garlic offensive.

A note about freezing If you want to freeze your pesto, do so without the cheese. The cheese suffers from freezing, and not every use of pesto is best with cheese. To help the pesto retain its bright green color, drizzle a layer of olive oil over the top once you have put it in the container.

Finally: Pesto makes a great-tasting pasta sauce, but it tends to be dry. To avoid this, thin the pesto with pasta-cooking water, tomato sauce, stock, olive oil, or a combination, before dressing the pasta.

Basic Pesto
Makes about 1 cup

Time: 5 minutes

You can make pesto thick or thin, according to your taste. Keep adding oil until you like the texture.

    2 loosely packed cups fresh basil leaves, big stems
        discarded, rinsed, and dried
    Salt to taste
    $1/2$ to 2 cloves garlic, crushed
    2 tablespoons pine nuts or walnuts, lightly toasted in
        a dry skillet
    $1/2$ cup extra-virgin olive oil, or more
    $1/2$ cup freshly grated Parmesan or other hard cheese
        (optional)

1 Combine the basil, salt, garlic, nuts, and about half the oil in a food processor or blender.

2 Process, stopping to scrape down the sides of the container occasionally, and adding the rest of the oil gradually. Add additional oil if you prefer a thinner mixture. Store in the refrigerator for a week or two, or in the freezer for several months (see "A note about freezing," above). Stir in the Parmesan by hand just before serving.

Pesto with Butter: For really special pesto, stir in 2 tablespoons softened butter just before tossing with lean foods such as pasta.

Minimalist Pesto: Combine basil, garlic, salt, and $1/4$ cup oil and process. Use warm water for thinning.

Cilantro "Pesto"
Makes about 1 cup

Time: 10 minutes

This is different from traditional (basil) pesto, not only in flavor but in texture; it's made with less oil and is far less creamy.

    1 clove garlic, crushed
    1 cup loosely packed cilantro leaves
    3 tablespoons peanut (preferred) or olive oil
    Juice of 1 lime
    Salt and freshly ground black pepper to taste

1 Place all ingredients in a food processor or blender.

2 Process until creamy, adding a little water if necessary to help the machine do its work. You can store this for a few days, but the flavor weakens with time.

Cilantro Pesto, Thai-Style: This is powerful stuff; use it to season soups or other sauces. Blend $1/2$ cup cilantro leaves with 1 tablespoon minced garlic, $1/4$ teaspoon freshly ground black pepper, and $1/2$ teaspoon salt; use just enough peanut oil (or water) to allow the blade to come into contact with the other ingredients.

Arugula "Pesto"
Makes about 1 cup

Time: 15 minutes

A thin paste with the distinctive flavor of arugula. I like to use it with grilled chicken or shrimp.

2 cups arugula, well washed and dried

1 clove garlic, crushed

2 tablespoons walnuts or pine nuts, lightly toasted in a dry skillet

Salt and freshly ground black pepper to taste

$^3/_4$ cup olive oil, more or less

1 Remove any tough stems from the arugula. Place it in a food processor or blender with the garlic, nuts, salt, and about $^1/_4$ teaspoon pepper.

2 Add $^1/_4$ cup olive oil and pulse a few times. With the motor running, add additional olive oil to make a creamy sauce, stopping the machine occasionally to scrape down the sides if necessary. Use within a day.

Mint "Pesto"

Makes about 1 cup

Time: 15 minutes

Mint pesto makes a refreshing sauce for pasta; it is also great with grilled vegetables, or with lamb.

2 cups loosely packed fresh mint leaves, well washed and dried

$^1/_2$ clove garlic, crushed (optional)

$^1/_4$ cup pine nuts or walnuts, lightly toasted in a dry skillet

2 tablespoons freshly squeezed lemon juice

Salt and freshly ground black pepper to taste

$^3/_4$ cup canola or other neutral oil

1 Place the mint in a food processor or blender with the garlic, nuts, lemon juice, salt, and $^1/_4$ teaspoon pepper.

2 Add $^1/_4$ cup oil and pulse a few times. With the motor running, add additional oil to make a creamy sauce, stopping the machine occasionally to scrape down the sides if necessary. Use within a day.

Parsley "Pesto"

Makes about 1 cup

Time: 15 minutes

This is a great sauce for any broiled or grilled chicken or fish. Try it, too, with shiitake ("black") or other mushrooms that have been browned in oil or butter.

2 cups loosely packed parsley leaves, well washed and dried

1 large clove garlic, crushed

Zest and juice of 1 medium lemon

$^1/_4$ cup pine nuts or walnuts, lightly toasted in a dry skillet

Salt and freshly ground black pepper to taste

$^3/_4$ cup extra-virgin olive oil

1 Place the parsley in a food processor or blender with the garlic, lemon zest and juice, nuts, salt, and $^1/_4$ teaspoon pepper.

2 Add $^1/_4$ cup oil and pulse a few times. With the motor running, add additional olive oil to make a creamy sauce, stopping the machine occasionally to scrape down the sides if necessary. This stores as well as pesto made with basil.

The Basics of Compound Butters

Once compound butters were a staple of every restaurant kitchen; they were used to finish sauces. And, indeed, if you stir compound butter into a reduction sauce (see The Basics of Reduction Sauces, page 790), you may take up the practice yourself.

But compound butters are great on their own. And if you have one or more on hand (they freeze perfectly), or the ability to make one (they take no time), you can jazz up just about any grilled or broiled food with no work at all. To refrigerate compound butters, roll into a log (wrap in plastic first to reduce mess), then wrap tightly in plastic and use within a day or two (the butter will keep much longer than that, but the seasoning will lose power quickly). For longer keeping, wrap tightly in plastic and freeze; the seasoning will retain flavor longer, but will gradually fade, so try to use the butter within a month of making it.

To use compound butter, just put a teaspoon to a tablespoon on any hot food. It's fine if the butter is cold—the heat of the food will melt it—but it should not be frozen. Room temperature butter is also fine, of course.

All of these can be made in a small food processor, but it's just as easy to cream the butter with a fork. The technique is almost always the same: Puree or mince the flavoring, then mash with the butter.

Anchovy Butter

Makes 4 to 8 servings

Time: 10 minutes

Use on grilled meat or fish, or on steamed vegetables. Canned anchovies are better than the salted variety for this purpose.

3 anchovy fillets, drained
4 tablespoons (1/2 stick) butter, at room temperature
1 teaspoon freshly squeezed lemon juice

Mince the anchovy fillets. Cream the butter with a fork, then add the fillets and lemon juice. Cover or wrap and refrigerate or freeze until needed.

Herb Butter

Makes 4 to 8 servings

Time: 10 minutes

All-purpose herb butters are appropriate wherever you would use the herb: on noodles or rice, steamed vegetables, grilled or roasted meat, poultry, or fish. Some herbs are stronger than others, so vary the amount based on the individual herb.

2 tablespoons mixed or single herbs: parsley, chervil, tarragon, chives, dill, sage, rosemary, cilantro, etc.
4 tablespoons (1/2 stick) butter, at room temperature
Salt to taste
Freshly ground black pepper to taste (optional)
Juice of 1/2 lemon (optional)

Mince the herbs and use a fork to cream them with the butter; add salt as needed and pepper if you like. Add lemon to taste if you like. Cover or wrap and refrigerate or freeze until needed.

Mustard Butter

Makes 4 to 8 servings

Time: 10 minutes

Use any kind of mustard you like; for a real hot butter, add dry mustard or wasabi (Japanese dried horseradish, available in Asian food stores) to taste. Wonderful on crackers served with tuna, crab, shrimp, or other seafood salads; or on any grilled food.

1 tablespoon Dijon mustard
4 tablespoons (1/2 stick) butter, at room temperature
Salt and freshly ground black pepper to taste

Use a fork to cream the mustard and butter together; add salt and pepper. Cover or wrap and refrigerate or freeze until needed.

Horseradish or Wasabi Butter

Makes 4 to 8 servings

Time: 10 minutes

A hot butter that is at its best on full-flavored grilled foods, especially steak, chicken, or swordfish or tuna.

4 tablespoons (¹/₂ stick) butter, at room temperature
1 tablespoon prepared horseradish, drained, or
  1 teaspoon wasabi (Japanese dried horseradish, available at Asian markets), or to taste

Use a fork to cream the butter and horseradish or wasabi together. Cover or wrap and refrigerate or freeze until needed.

Garlic Butter

Makes 4 to 8 servings

Time: 10 minutes

Essential. Make this once, and it will become a friend forever. Use it on broiled or grilled fish or meats, on baked potatoes, rice, barley, or other grains, or on noodles.

1 tablespoon butter
1 teaspoon minced garlic
4 tablespoons (¹/₂ stick) butter, at room temperature
Salt and freshly ground black pepper to taste
Freshly squeezed lemon juice to taste

❶ Melt 1 tablespoon butter in a small saucepan over low heat; add the garlic and cook just until the garlic softens, 2 or 3 minutes. Let cool.
❷ Cream with softened butter; add salt, pepper, and lemon juice.

Ginger-Garlic Butter: Add 1 teaspoon peeled and minced fresh ginger to cooking garlic just before it is done cooking; add a few drops of soy sauce with the lemon juice.

Jalapeño Butter

Makes 4 to 8 servings

Time: 10 minutes

Make this as hot as you like, and serve it on food that can stand the heat, mostly grilled, broiled, or roasted meats.

4 tablespoons (¹/₂ stick) butter, at room temperature
Salt and freshly ground black pepper to taste
Juice of ¹/₂ lemon
2 jalapeños or other small fresh chiles, stemmed, seeded, and minced, or to taste

Use a fork to cream all ingredients together. Cover or wrap and refrigerate or freeze until needed.

Ginger Butter

Makes 4 to 8 servings

Time: 10 minutes

Terrific on grilled fish of any type, but especially mahi-mahi, tuna, swordfish, and other full-flavored fish.

4 tablespoons ($^1/_2$ stick) butter, at room temperature
Salt and freshly ground black pepper to taste
Juice of $^1/_2$ lemon
1 ($^1/_2$-inch) piece fresh ginger, peeled and minced,
    or more

Use a fork to cream all ingredients together. Cover or wrap and refrigerate or freeze until needed.

Balsamic Butter

Makes 4 to 8 servings

Time: 10 minutes

A gentle butter that goes well with baked or sautéed fish dishes, grilled mild fish, or steamed vegetables.

4 tablespoons ($^1/_2$ stick) butter, at room temperature
Salt and freshly ground black pepper to taste
1 tablespoon minced shallot
1 tablespoon balsamic vinegar

Use a fork to cream all ingredients together. Cover or wrap and refrigerate or freeze until needed.

Lime or Lemon Butter

Makes 4 to 8 servings

Time: 10 minutes

You can also make this butter with orange or other citrus fruit. Great on fish or poultry, cooked any way, or on vegetables.

4 tablespoons ($^1/_2$ stick) butter, at room temperature
Salt and freshly ground black pepper to taste
1 teaspoon minced lemon or lime zest
1 tablespoon freshly squeezed lemon or lime juice

Use a fork to cream all ingredients together. Cover or wrap and refrigerate or freeze until needed.

Uncooked Sauces, Salsas, and Dips

These have little in common except that they are easy, flavorful, and uncooked, or nearly so: A few have cooked ingredients, but their simplicity makes them appropriate here nevertheless.

Tahini Dressing

Makes about 2 cups

Time: 10 minutes

A creamy dressing based on tahini, or ground sesame seed paste. Use on salads or sandwiches, or combine in a food processor with cooked chickpeas to make instant hummus.

1 clove garlic, peeled
1 teaspoon salt
1 cup tahini
1 teaspoon paprika or ground cumin
$^1/_4$ cup freshly squeezed lemon juice, or to taste
$^1/_2$ cup water, more or less

1 Use a mortar and pestle or small food processor to combine the garlic and salt. Add the tahini and the spice; the mixture will be very thick.

2 Add the lemon juice, followed by enough water to achieve a creamy consistency, thin enough to pour.

3 Taste and adjust seasonings. Use within a day.

Yogurt-Avocado Dressing

Makes about 1¹/₂ cups

Time: 10 minutes

Creamy, rich, pale green, and very mild. A nice dressing for cut-up raw vegetables.

1 large avocado, halved, pitted, and flesh scooped
    out to produce about 1 cup pulp
¹/₄ cup freshly squeezed lemon juice, plus more
    if needed
¹/₄ cup freshly squeezed orange juice
1 teaspoon grated lemon peel
1 tablespoon minced shallot or onion
¹/₂ cup plain yogurt, more or less
Salt and freshly ground black pepper to taste

1 Remove the pulp from the avocado and place it in the container of a blender or food processor. Add the juices and puree.

2 Add the lemon peel, shallot or onion, yogurt, salt, and pepper and blend again. Taste and adjust consistency and acidity by adding more lemon juice if needed. Taste and adjust seasonings if necessary. This sauce does not keep well; use as soon as possible.

Quick Blue Cheese Dressing

Makes about 1 cup

Time: 5 minutes

This is a sharp, creamy sauce. Add one-quarter teaspoon or so of minced garlic if you want to make it even more pungent. Great as a dip as well as a salad dressing.

¹/₂ cup crumbled Roquefort or other blue cheese,
    such as Stilton, Maytag blue, or Gorgonzola
¹/₂ cup sour cream or plain yogurt
Freshly squeezed lemon juice as needed
Salt and freshly ground black pepper to taste

1 Combine the cheese and sour cream or yogurt in a small bowl, mashing with a fork; the mixture should remain somewhat lumpy.

2 Add enough lemon juice to give a creamy consistency. Add salt if necessary and a bit of pepper. This sauce keeps fairly well, refrigerated, for a few days.

Cucumber-Yogurt Dip with Mint

Makes about 2 cups

Time: 10 minutes

A quickly made, low-fat sauce that is good for dipping vegetables or passing with grilled foods, especially lamb. Good when made with parsley or dill, too.

1 medium cucumber, peeled if desired
Salt and freshly ground black pepper to taste
1 cup plain yogurt
2 teaspoons minced onion, shallot, or scallion
1 tablespoon olive oil
3 tablespoons minced fresh mint leaves

1 Cut the cucumber in half lengthwise and scoop out the seeds. Chop it into ¹/₂-inch dice and combine it with all remaining ingredients.

2 Check seasoning and serve, or refrigerate until ready to use, but use within a few hours.

Spicy Yogurt Sauce

Makes about 1 cup

Time: 5 minutes

This dressing, a variation of the standard Indian raita, can be made in advance. Use it as a dip for vegetables or a sauce for grilled meats. Use half yogurt and half sour cream if you'd like a richer sauce.

> 1 cup plain yogurt
> 1/4 cup minced onion or scallion
> 1 teaspoon peeled and minced fresh ginger
>   or ground ginger
> 1/4 cup minced cilantro leaves
> 1 teaspoon ground cumin
> Salt and freshly ground black pepper to taste
> Cayenne to taste (optional)

Whisk all ingredients together; taste and adjust seasoning as necessary. This sauce keeps well, but its flavor degrades quickly, so it's best to use it within a day.

Homemade Horseradish

Makes about 1 cup

Time: 10 minutes, plus time to rest

Thanks to the food processor, horseradish is easy to prepare. But it really clears out the sinuses, so be careful. If you're planning to process large quantities, consider goggles and gloves—really.

> 1 (1-foot-long) horseradish root
> 1/2 cup white or rice wine vinegar
> Salt to taste

① Peel the horseradish with a sturdy vegetable peeler or paring knife and cut it into chunks. Place in the container of a food processor with about half the vinegar. Put the cover on and turn on the machine.

② Process, stopping the machine and scraping the mixture down as needed, until finely minced. (Do not try this with a blender; it will not work. The only alternative is to grate the horseradish by hand.) Taste and add more vinegar and salt as necessary. Store in the refrigerator. Horseradish will keep indefinitely, but will become increasingly mild.

Tomato-Onion Salsa

Makes about 1 cup

Time: 10 minutes

This pureed salsa is good as a sauce for chilled food, such as leftover grilled chicken.

> 1 medium onion, peeled
> 2 medium tomatoes, cored, peeled, and seeded
> 1 teaspoon paprika or 1/4 to 1/2 teaspoon cayenne
> 1 clove garlic, peeled
> 1 tablespoon any good vinegar, plus more to taste
> 1 teaspoon salt, or to taste
> 1 teaspoon sugar
> 1 tablespoon freshly squeezed lemon juice,
>   or to taste

① Quarter the onion and tomatoes and whiz them in a food processor or blender with all the other ingredients except the lemon juice.

② Taste and add more salt and paprika or cayenne if needed along with the lemon juice or vinegar to taste. Serve or refrigerate for up to a day or two before serving.

Pico de Gallo

Makes 2 cups

Time: At least 1 hour, largely unattended

The classic raw tomato salsa, great with chips, grilled meat, fish, or chicken, or, of course, fajitas.

2 cups cored, peeled, seeded, and coarsely chopped
   tomatoes
1 cup minced chopped scallions (preferred), onion,
   or a combination
1/2 teaspoon minced garlic
2 tablespoons freshly squeezed lime juice
Salt and freshly ground black pepper to taste
2 stemmed and minced jalapeño or hot red chiles,
   or to taste, or cayenne or crushed red pepper
   flakes to taste
1/2 cup minced cilantro leaves

1 Combine the first six ingredients, then taste and see whether you want to add more salt, pepper, or chiles. Stir in about half the cilantro, then set aside for 1 hour, or cover and refrigerate for up to a day.

2 Taste and adjust seasoning, garnish with remaining cilantro, and serve.

Sicilian Pesto, or Salsa Cruda

Makes 1 cup

Time: At least 1 hour, largely unattended

This chunky sauce is fine for spooning over grilled meats at the table. It is also a super-fast, flavorful pasta sauce. If you use cilantro in place of basil, it makes a good dip for taco chips.

1 cup cored, peeled, and seeded very ripe tomatoes
   (canned are fine; drain them first)
1 teaspoon balsamic vinegar
1 tablespoon olive oil
Salt and freshly ground black pepper to taste
1 clove garlic, smashed
4 tablespoons minced fresh basil leaves

1 Place all ingredients in a broad-bottomed bowl and mash well, using a fork or potato masher (do not puree).

2 Let rest at room temperature for an hour or two, and remove garlic before serving. You can refrigerate this for a day; serve at room temperature.

Green Tomato Salsa

Makes about 2 cups

Time: 10 minutes

A late fall salsa, useful when you're wondering what to do with those green tomatoes.

1 cup cored and finely chopped green tomatoes
   (or tomatillos)
2 tablespoons minced cilantro leaves
1 tablespoon freshly squeezed lime juice
1/2 teaspoon sugar, or to taste
1/2 teaspoon minced garlic
Salt and freshly ground black pepper to taste
Cayenne or crushed red pepper flakes to taste

Mix all ingredients, taste, and correct seasoning. Serve immediately, or refrigerate for up to a week.

Note: For another salsa recipe, see also Mild Tomato Salsa, page 782.

Red Pepper Relish

Makes 4 servings

Time: 1 hour

A great relish for almost anything grilled, but especially chicken or fish. Wonderful with a teaspoon or two of ground cumin added.

    4 red bell peppers
    1 tablespoon olive oil
    1 teaspoon balsamic vinegar
    1/4 teaspoon minced garlic
    Salt and freshly ground black pepper to taste

1 Roast the peppers as directed in Marinated Roasted, Grilled, or Broiled Peppers, page 593. As soon as they are cool enough to handle, peel the skins and remove the seeds.

2 Chop the flesh coarsely and mix with the olive oil, balsamic vinegar, garlic, and salt and pepper to taste. Serve immediately or refrigerate for a day or two and serve at room temperature.

Homemade Mild Chile Paste

Makes about 1 cup

Time: 10 minutes

It's easy to buy fiery hot chile paste, but more difficult to find a mild variety. If you grow your own ancho, poblano, or other relatively mild chiles, or buy dried ones, you may want to make your own chile paste, which you can then conveniently add to anything you are cooking. This keeps for a couple of months in the refrigerator, and can be stirred into stews, used as a marinade or basting sauce for grilled meat, combined with cooked rice or other grains, and more. The same

procedure may be used with hot chiles. Also, feel free to add garlic, cumin, or other seasonings to the mix.

    2 or 3 large mild chiles, fresh or dried
    Hot water as needed
    1/2 teaspoon salt

1 If the chiles are fresh, remove the stems and seeds and chop roughly. If they are dried, bake them in a 300°F oven for 5 minutes, until they begin to swell; discard the stems and seeds.

2 Puree in a blender, gradually adding enough water to make a paste. Add salt, stir, and store in a covered container.

Jack Bishop's Chile Oil

Makes about 1/2 cup

Time: 15 minutes

A medium-hot sauce that is super for basting anything you are grilling, especially vegetables. My friend Jack tucks a bit of this between corn husk and kernels before grilling corn.

    1 dried ancho or other not overly hot chile
    2 teaspoons salt
    1/4 cup corn, peanut, olive, or vegetable oil

1 Toast the chile on the grill or under the broiler for 1 minute. Turn and grill chile for another minute, until it is soft and fragrant; keep an eye on it so that it does not burn.

2 Remove the chile and cool, then cut off and discard the stem. Place the chile and its seeds in a spice grinder and pulverize into a fine powder. Combine the powder with salt and stir it into the oil. You can refrigerate this indefinitely.

Garlic Oil

Makes 1 cup

Time: 5 minutes plus 2 hours waiting time

Use good olive oil for this and you'll have a delicious dressing for steamed vegetables or fish, or anything grilled. Keep it refrigerated (bring back to room temperature before serving) and use it within a week.

1 cup olive oil
6 cloves garlic, peeled and sliced
$^1/_2$ teaspoon salt

❶ Warm the olive oil very gently in a small saucepan over low heat, until it is about body temperature.
❷ Add the garlic and salt, stir, and let sit at room temperature about two hours, until the flavors meld. Strain and use immediately or refrigerate in a sealed container.

Ginger Oil: The procedure is the same: Use 20 nickel-sized pieces of ginger in place of the garlic; don't bother to peel the ginger.

Chile Oil: Use peanut oil if you have it. Heat the oil over medium heat until it is fragrant. Turn off the heat and toss in 10 to 20 dried red chiles and 1 teaspoon ground paprika (mostly for color). Let sit until cool, then strain.

Achiote Oil

Makes about a cup

Time: 20 minutes

Made with annatto, a small, hard triangular seed, this oil lends a deep yellow color and pleasant flavor to anything it touches (including your clothes!). I like to make it without the chile, because its flavor is pretty mild. Use for sautéing pilaf-style rice dishes, plantains (see Sautéed Ripe Plantains, page 595), or any foods that you want to give a nice yellow-orange color.

1 cup olive or vegetable oil
$^1/_2$ cup annatto seeds
1 dried chile, crumbled (optional)
1 bay leaf

❶ Combine all ingredients in a small saucepan and turn the heat to low. Bring to a gentle boil.
❷ Simmer for about 10 minutes, then strain through a fine strainer or cheesecloth into a jar. Keeps indefinitely in the refrigerator.

Herb or Spice Oil

Makes 1 cup

Time: 10 minutes

It's great to have a little flavored oil on hand to drizzle over vegetables, fresh mozzarella, soup, or grilled bread. Don't make too much of this at once—its flavor is volatile. Store it covered in the refrigerator.

1 cup olive oil
$^1/_2$ cup any minced fresh herb: parsley, sage,
    rosemary, thyme, cilantro, marjoram, etc.,
    or a combination, *or*
$^1/_2$ cup any ground spice: pepper, curry, coriander,
    ginger, cumin, etc., or a combination

❶ Place the oil and the herb or spices in a heavy skillet and turn the heat to medium. When the herb begins to sizzle, count to ten and turn off the heat; let cool.
❷ Strain into a jar or other container, seal, and refrigerate.

Lemon-Tabasco Dipping Sauce

Makes ¹/₂ cup

Time: 5 minutes

Simple, but the cleanest, most refreshing sauce to serve with fried fish or vegetables. Take it easy on the hot sauce, and leave the bottle on the table so heat freaks can get their fill. You can also mix this with olive oil or melted butter and use it as a basting sauce.

¹/₂ cup freshly squeezed lemon juice

Tabasco sauce to taste

Salt and freshly ground black pepper to taste

Combine all ingredients. Taste and adjust seasoning. Use within 1 hour.

Soy and Sesame Dipping Sauce or Marinade

Makes about ¹/₂ cup

Time: 10 minutes

A basic recipe that is almost infinitely variable; all versions make terrific marinades.

1 tablespoon Toasted Sesame Seeds (see right)

¹/₄ cup soy sauce

1 tablespoon dark sesame oil

1¹/₂ teaspoons rice or other light vinegar

¹/₂ teaspoon minced garlic

1 tablespoon peeled and minced fresh ginger
   or 1 teaspoon ground ginger

¹/₂ teaspoon sugar

Combine all the ingredients and stir briefly to blend. Taste; if the mixture is too strongly flavored (which it

may be, if your soy sauce is strong), add water, a teaspoon at a time, until the flavor mellows. Use within 1 hour.

Soy-Citrus Dipping Sauce: Omit sesame oil and vinegar. Add 1 teaspoon minced lemon, lime, or orange zest. Mix together all ingredients, then add freshly squeezed citrus juice until the flavor is balanced. Good with some Dijon mustard stirred in.

Fiery Peanut Sauce: Omit sesame seeds and oil. Add 2 tablespoons finely chopped peanuts and 1 tablespoon stemmed, seeded, and minced fresh hot chiles, such as pequíns or jalapeños. Taste and add more chiles if you like.

Sweet-and-Sour Sauce: Omit sesame seeds and oil. Increase sugar to 2 tablespoons; increase vinegar to 2 tablespoons. Cook briefly over low heat, stirring, to dissolve the sugar. Taste and add more vinegar if necessary. Cool before serving, or use warm as a basting sauce. You can make this hot-and-sour sauce by adding cayenne to taste.

Fish Dipping Sauce: Omit sesame seeds and oil. Substitute 1 tablespoon or more fish sauce (*nuoc mam* or *nam pla,* available at any Asian market) for an equal amount of soy sauce. Good with minced hot chiles stirred in.

Toasted Sesame Seeds

Makes ¹/₂ cup

Time: 10 minutes

Sesame seeds are almost always toasted before use; it brings out much more of their flavor. This same technique is useful for pine nuts, walnuts, almonds, and so on. Sesame seeds are best toasted just before using, but they will retain their fragrance for a few days if you wrap them tightly and refrigerate.

1/2 cup sesame seeds

1 Place the seeds in a dry skillet just large enough to contain them in one layer and turn the heat to medium.

2 Cook, shaking the pan frequently, until the seeds darken in color and begin to pop, 5 to 10 minutes. Cool slightly before using.

Cranberry Relish with Orange and Ginger

Makes about 1 quart

Time: 10 minutes

Quite tart, easily the equal of Traditional Cranberry Sauce (page 783), and even better on sandwiches of leftover turkey. The food processor makes quick work of this. Stir in one-half cup of raisins and/or chopped walnuts or pecans at the end if you like.

1 large navel or other orange
4 cups (about 1 pound) fresh cranberries, picked over and washed, or frozen cranberries
1/2 cup sugar, or more to taste
1 teaspoon peeled and minced or grated fresh ginger, or to taste

1 Use a vegetable peeler or paring knife to remove the entire zest of the orange; set aside. Remove the thick white pith. Separate the orange into sections and remove the white pithy parts.

2 Combine the orange flesh, zest, cranberries, and sugar in the container of a food processor. Turn on the machine and process until the mixture is chunky. Stir in the ginger and additional sugar if needed. This can

be served right away, but is best if it sits for at least 30 minutes to allow the flavors to marry. It stores well, refrigerated, for a few days.

Mango-Onion Relish

Makes about 1 1/2 cups

Time: 10 minutes

A thin sauce that is superb on almost anything, but is especially good with grilled tuna or chicken legs.

2 mangoes
1/2 cup diced red onion
Juice of 2 limes
2 tablespoons minced cilantro leaves
Salt and freshly ground black pepper to taste

1 Peel and pit the mangoes. Chop their flesh and combine it with the onion, lime juice, and cilantro; season with salt and pepper.

2 Serve immediately or refrigerate for a day or two and serve at room temperature.

The Basics of Spice Mixtures

Many cuisines have standby spice mixtures that are added to many foods as they cook. Curry powder, probably the best known of these, is also the best to make at home, because store-bought curry powder invariably contains a great deal of turmeric, a spice that turns food yellow but does little else except add bitterness. Most other spice mixtures are best made on the spot, but there are a couple of others it pays to make in advance.

Whenever you make a spice mixture, it makes sense to grind your own spices if at all possible. First combine the whole spices (break cinnamon sticks into pieces; crush nutmeg into chunks; remove cardamom seeds from their pods; etc.) in a dry skillet and toast over medium-high heat until they become aromatic, a minute or two. Then whiz the spices together in a coffee or spice grinder. It's best to have a separate grinder for this purpose, but you can use your coffee grinder if you clean it by grinding rice to a powder after removing the spices; the rice powder will remove all (or at least most) of the seasonings when you dump it out.

Fragrant Curry Powder

Makes about ¹/₂ cup

Time: 10 minutes

This is a sweeter, spicier (but not hotter) curry than All-Purpose Curry Powder (see next recipe).

¹/₄ teaspoon nutmeg pieces
¹/₂ teaspoon black peppercorns
3 cloves
1 teaspoon cardamom seeds
1 (2-inch) piece cinnamon stick
1 teaspoon fennel seeds
1 teaspoon fenugreek seeds
2 tablespoons cumin seeds
4 tablespoons coriander seeds
1 tablespoon ground ginger
2 tablespoons ground turmeric

Toast and grind the first nine spices. Mix them with the ginger and turmeric. Store in a tightly sealed jar for several months.

All-Purpose Curry Powder

Makes about ¹/₂ cup

Time: 10 minutes

A perfect standby, good for any time you want an intense spicy flavor boost. To make it a hot curry powder, add one-half teaspoon or more ground cayenne.

1 teaspoon black peppercorns
3 tablespoons cumin seeds
4 tablespoons coriander seeds
1 tablespoon ground ginger
2 tablespoons ground turmeric

Toast and grind the first three spices. Mix them with the ginger and turmeric. Store in a tightly sealed jar for several months.

Garam Masala

Makes about ¹/₂ cup

Time: 10 minutes

A fairly mild, almost sweet curry. Add one-quarter teaspoon of saffron if you have it.

¹/₄ teaspoon nutmeg pieces
1 (3-inch) piece cinnamon stick
3 cloves
1 tablespoon black peppercorns
3 tablespoons coriander seeds
2 teaspoons cardamom seeds

Toast and grind all spices together. Store in a tightly sealed jar for several months.

Pickling Spice

Makes about 1 cup

Time: 10 minutes

Add some of this any time you pickle vegetables, or—in small amounts—to braised dishes when you don't have time to season carefully. Try to use whole spices so you can break the large ones up and leave the small ones whole, or nearly so.

2 (3- to 4-inch) cinnamon sticks
10 bay leaves
2 small dried red hot chiles
5 star anise
4 tablespoons mustard seeds
2 tablespoons ground ginger
2 tablespoons allspice berries
2 teaspoons cloves
2 tablespoons black peppercorns
2 tablespoons coriander seeds
2 teaspoons cardamom seeds
2 tablespoons dill seeds

1 Break the cinnamon stick, bay leaves, chiles, and star anise into pieces.

2 Roughly chop all the other ingredients, leaving most of the seeds whole.

3 Combine and store in a tightly sealed jar for several months.

Recado Rojo

Puerto Rican–Style Seasoning Paste

Makes ¹/₄ cup

Time: 10 minutes

Use this paste for roast, braised, or grilled meats. Add ¹/₂ teaspoon or more of cayenne if you want it hot.

1 teaspoon black peppercorns
1 teaspoon dried oregano
4 cloves
¹/₂ teaspoon cumin seeds
1 (1-inch) piece cinnamon stick
1 teaspoon coriander seeds
1 teaspoon salt
5 cloves garlic, peeled
2 tablespoons cider vinegar
1¹/₂ teaspoons all-purpose flour

1 Combine all ingredients except the vinegar and flour and grind as finely as possible.

2 Mix in the vinegar and flour to form a paste; cover and let stand several hours or overnight before using. You can refrigerate this for up to a few days before using it.

Lightly Cooked Sauces

These need cooking, whether to thicken them, tame their strong flavors, or meld their seasonings. They're usually—though not necessarily—served warm.

Ketchup

Makes 2 quarts

Time: About 2 hours

Ketchup, as you'll see from the recipes, is closely related to chutney and, as such, can be varied as you like. Store-bought ketchup is much sweeter than this, but you can double or triple the amount of sugar here if you want to approximate that flavor. Even then, this will be far more complex thanks to the addition of real vegetables and seasonings.

1 tablespoon olive or other oil

12 cups cored and halved tomatoes

2 red bell peppers, stemmed, seeded, and roughly
    chopped

2 medium onions, roughly chopped

4 cloves garlic, peeled

1 celery stalk, roughly chopped

1 tablespoon salt

1/2 cup sugar

1/2 teaspoon cayenne, or to taste

1 tablespoon paprika

2 teaspoons mustard powder

1 teaspoon ground cloves

1 (3- to 4-inch) cinnamon stick

1 to 2 cups cider or wine vinegar

1 Place olive oil in a large saucepan and turn the heat to medium-high. Add the tomatoes, peppers, onions, garlic, and celery, and cook, stirring, until the tomatoes have broken down and all the vegetables are soft, 20 to 30 minutes.

2 Put the mixture through a food mill. Discard the skins and seeds, and return the pulp and liquid to the saucepan, along with the salt, sugar, cayenne, paprika, and mustard. Place the cloves and cinnamon stick in a cheesecloth bag or tea ball and add it to the mix. Cook over medium-high heat, stirring frequently, until the mixture is thick, 30 minutes to 1 hour.

3 Add 1 cup vinegar and cook again until just a little less thick than bottled ketchup (it will thicken more after you're done), about 30 minutes. Taste and add the remaining vinegar if the mixture is not tart enough. Refrigerate for up to 2 weeks, or freeze indefinitely.

Chili Sauce: In Step 2, add 2 tablespoons ground cumin, or to taste; add 1 teaspoon crushed red pepper flakes, or increase the amount of cayenne to taste. In Step 3, use up to 3 cups of vinegar. Refrigerate or freeze as above.

Fast Barbecue Sauce
Makes about 2 cups

Time: 20 minutes

This must be heated just long enough to take the edge off the onion and garlic; you can do it in the microwave if you prefer. Use this sauce to baste meat or chicken as you grill it, but don't begin to apply it until the cooking is almost done, or it will burn.

2 cups ketchup

1 tablespoon Worcestershire or soy sauce

1 tablespoon chili powder, or to taste

1/2 cup dry red wine or water

1/4 cup wine or rice vinegar

1/2 cup minced onion

1 teaspoon minced garlic

Salt and freshly ground black pepper to taste

Combine all ingredients in a small saucepan. Cook over medium-low heat, stirring, for about 10 minutes. Taste; adjust seasoning as necessary. Refrigerate, for up to a week.

Citrus Sauce
Makes about 1 cup

Time: 20 minutes

A light, tangy sauce that is ideal over grilled fish and also good with chicken breasts.

1 lemon

1 orange

1 grapefruit

1 teaspoon extra-virgin olive oil

1 teaspoon fresh thyme leaves or 1/2 teaspoon
    dried thyme

1 teaspoon minced garlic

1/4 cup minced onion
Salt and freshly ground black pepper to taste
1/2 cup white wine

1 Zest the lemon and mince the zest; section the lemon, orange, and grapefruit as you would a grapefruit half for eating.

2 Mix together the oil, thyme, garlic, onion, salt, pepper, and wine in a small saucepan. Bring to a boil over medium heat, then turn the heat to low and cook until reduced by about half, 10 minutes or so.

3 Stir in the fruit and the zest, and cook for 15 seconds. Use immediately, passing at the table.

Anchovy Sauce

Makes about 1/2 cup

Time: 20 minutes

A strong-flavored sauce that can be used hot or cold on fish or chicken. Great on grilled food.

1 tablespoon minced garlic
6 or 8 anchovy fillets, minced, with 2 tablespoons
    or more of the anchovy oil reserved
1/2 cup mild vinegar, such as white wine or rice
1 tomato, cored and chopped (canned is fine;
    drain it first)
Salt and freshly ground black pepper to taste

1 Combine the garlic and the anchovy oil in a small saucepan and turn the heat to medium-low. Cook just until the garlic begins to color, about 5 minutes.

2 Add the anchovies and stir; cook for 1 minute over low heat. Add the vinegar, raise the heat to medium, and cook for 5 minutes, stirring.

3 Add the tomato and cook until the sauce separates, about 10 minutes. Season, place in a bowl, and whisk with a fork before serving. Use within a day.

Lime Sauce

Makes about 1/2 cup

Time: 10 minutes

The fragrance of this lightly cooked sauce is irresistible. Use it to top grilled chicken breasts or fish just before serving.

1 teaspoon peanut or canola or other oil
1 clove garlic, minced
1 teaspoon peeled and minced fresh ginger
2 scallions, minced
1/2 cup white wine
2 tablespoons soy sauce
Juice of 2 limes
Salt, if needed

1 Place the oil in a medium non-stick skillet over high heat for 1 minute. Add the garlic, ginger, and scallions, turn the heat to medium, and cook about 30 seconds, stirring.

2 Add the wine and let it bubble away for another 30 seconds or so. Add the soy sauce and half the lime juice and cook a few more seconds. Add the remaining lime juice and salt to taste; use immediately.

Tomato-Dill Sauce

Makes about 2 cups

Time: 30 minutes

This is great with roasted meats. Spoon a bit of it over the meat when it is nearly done, or just serve it at the table.

1/3 cup minced shallots
1/4 cup extra-virgin olive oil
2 cups cored, peeled, seeded, and chopped
    tomatoes (canned are fine; drain them first)

Salt and freshly ground black pepper to taste

3 tablespoons snipped fresh dill leaves

$^1/_2$ cup plain yogurt or sour cream (optional)

1 Combine the shallots and olive oil in a medium skillet and turn the heat to low. Cook until softened, not browned, about 10 minutes.

2 Add the tomatoes, raise the heat to medium, and cook, stirring frequently, until the mixture becomes "saucy," about 10 minutes.

3 Add salt and pepper, then the dill. Add the optional yogurt or sour cream and serve. Use within a day.

Corn and Tomato Relish

Makes about 1 cup

Time: 10 minutes

A quintessential summer sauce with a bit of bite. Pass it at the table with red meats and chicken.

1 teaspoon olive oil

4 ears corn, husked and stripped of their kernels

2 large luscious red tomatoes, cored and roughly chopped

1 teaspoon ground cumin, or to taste

$^1/_4$ teaspoon cayenne, or to taste

Salt and freshly ground black pepper to taste

1 Place the oil in a medium non-stick skillet over high heat and heat for 2 minutes. Add the corn and sauté until lightly browned, a minute or two.

2 Turn the heat to medium, add the tomatoes and the spices, and cook 30 seconds more; turn off the heat.

3 Season with salt and pepper. Serve immediately or refrigerate for a day or two and serve at room temperature.

Mild Tomato Salsa

Makes about 4 cups

Time: About 1 hour

This is a pureed, all-purpose sauce, richly flavored with vegetables and mild poblano chiles.

$^1/_4$ cup olive oil

1 cup chopped onion

1 cup minced celery

1 cup minced carrot

2 fresh poblano or other relatively mild chiles, stemmed, seeded, and chopped

2 tablespoons chopped garlic

$^1/_4$ cup red wine or water

2 pounds tomatoes (canned are fine; drain them first), cored, peeled, seeded, and chopped

1 teaspoon chopped fresh tarragon leaves or $^1/_4$ teaspoon dried tarragon

Salt to taste

$^1/_4$ teaspoon freshly ground black pepper

1 Place the oil in a large skillet over medium-high heat. A minute later, add the onion, celery, carrot, chiles, and garlic; cook, stirring, until the vegetables soften a bit, about 5 minutes. Add the red wine and tomatoes, cover, turn the heat to low, and simmer for 30 minutes, stirring occasionally.

2 Cool the mixture slightly, then puree it in a blender or food processor. Return the sauce to the pot and cook over medium-high heat, uncovered. Stir frequently to prevent burning, and cook until the sauce is reduced by about half, about 15 minutes from the time it returns to the boil. Add the tarragon, salt, and pepper, and cook for a few more minutes over low heat. Taste and correct seasonings, then serve hot or at room temperature. This sauce keeps well for up to a week.

Sherried Garlic Sauce with Nectarines

Makes about 1 cup

Time: 30 minutes

Mellowed garlic mixed with fruit is not only wonderful on grilled fish and poultry, but on rice and vegetables. Pass it at the table so everyone can drizzle his or her own.

10 cloves garlic
$1/2$ cup sherry vinegar
1 teaspoon olive oil
Salt to taste
$1/4$ cup dry (fino) sherry
2 very ripe nectarines or peaches, peeled, pitted, and coarsely chopped
Juice of 1 lime

① Peel the garlic (crush it lightly to make peeling easier). Place it in a small saucepan with vinegar and olive oil; bring to a boil and cook over medium-low heat until almost all of the liquid has evaporated, about 20 minutes.

② Salt lightly and add the sherry; bring to a boil and simmer for 3 minutes, until once again the mixture is almost dry.

③ Place the nectarines in a bowl with the lime juice and crush lightly with a fork. Chop the sherried garlic and stir it in, along with any of its juices. Serve or store in the refrigerator for a day or two; serve at room temperature.

Applesauce

Makes about 2 quarts

Time: About 1 hour

This is the easiest and best way to make applesauce; you get all the flavor of the skins, and lots of their color, too. If you don't have a food mill, now's the time to buy one. (If you don't, you must peel and core the apples before beginning.) If you're making applesauce in late summer, add some raspberries to the pot; they'll intensify both the flavor and color.

Now here's the best thing to do about applesauce: Buy the biggest pot that will fit on your stove: twenty, forty, or sixty quarts. Buy enough apples to fill the pot. Follow this recipe. Freeze the applesauce in pint or quart containers and defrost as necessary.

Finally, don't forget that applesauce is good to eat warm, and that it makes a great companion to savory foods, especially roast meats.

5 pounds apples, preferably a mixture of varieties, washed
Sugar if necessary

① Cut the apples in half or, if they're very large, in quarters. Don't bother to peel or core them. Dump them into a pot with about $1/2$ inch of water on the bottom. Cover the pot and turn the heat to medium.

② When the water begins to boil, uncover the pot. Cook, stirring occasionally and lowering the heat if the mixture threatens to burn on the bottom, until the apples break down and become mushy, at least 30 minutes. Let sit until cool enough to handle. Taste the mixture and add sugar if necessary; usually it is not.

③ Pass the mixture through a food mill, discarding the solids that stay behind. Freeze or refrigerate.

Traditional Cranberry Sauce

Makes about 1 quart

Time: 20 minutes, plus time to chill

Most cranberry sauce is too sweet, but that's traditional, and it has this advantage: The sauce will gel upon cooling. If you want to make a less-sweet sauce, by all means do, but expect it to be runnier (a better solution is to make Cranberry Relish with Orange and Ginger, page 777). If you want a very firm sauce, make the variation.

> 4 cups (about 1 pound) fresh cranberries, picked over and washed, or frozen cranberries
> 1 1/2 cups sugar
> 2 cups water

1 Combine all ingredients in a medium saucepan and turn the heat to medium-low. Cover and cook, stirring occasionally, until the berries are broken, 10 to 15 minutes.

2 Transfer to a bowl; cool, then chill until ready to serve. This keeps well, refrigerated, for up to a week.

Firm Cranberry Sauce or Cranberry Jelly: Increase sugar to 2 cups. For Firm Cranberry Sauce, proceed as above. For jelly, cook 5 minutes longer, stirring frequently. Pass through a sieve into a mold, bowl, or jelly jars and cool, then chill until firm. Slice to serve.

The Basics of Chutneys

Chutney is savory jam—fruit cooked with sweetener, spices, and other seasonings, such as onion or garlic. The goal, which is easily accomplished, is to create a savory accompaniment to strong-tasting foods—from highly seasoned grilled meat dishes to strongly flavored braised ones. There are several things worth pointing out about chutney. First of all, it doesn't pay to use delicate or expensive fruit; raspberries, for example, get lost in the shuffle. The fruit contributes texture more than anything else, so it's best to make chutney with firm fruit—green mangoes (which are not sweet) are classic, but you can use underripe bananas, peaches or other stone fruit, apples, green tomatoes (or barely ripe red ones, or a mixture), or—

and this is my favorite—dried fruit, such as apricots, figs, raisins, peaches, dates, or a combination. You'll see how easy it is once you make your first batch.

Because you're not attempting to preserve the flavor of the season when you make chutney—if you were, you wouldn't be adding pepper, onion, and so on—there's no reason to add tons of sugar as a preservative, nor is there any good reason to make more chutney than you need for a few days. Make a small batch of about two cups at a time—and it'll be gone one or two meals later. It's better to see chutney as a spur-of-the-moment accompaniment, almost like a salsa, than as a long-term project.

Finally, chutney is subject to wild improvisations. You cannot go wrong (well, almost). I give a couple of examples here but, as I said, as soon as you get started you'll pick up the "system" and readily be on your own.

Dried Apricot Chutney with Star Anise

Makes about 2 cups

Time: 20 minutes

If you learn only one chutney, this should be it, because as long as you have dried fruit in the house, you're in business.

> 1/4 cup any vinegar
> 1/2 cup water
> 1/4 cup sugar, honey, or other sweetener
> Salt
> 1/4 teaspoon freshly ground black pepper
> 1 small dried hot red chile, or to taste
> 3 star anise
> 1 tablespoon peeled and minced fresh ginger or 2 teaspoons ground ginger
> 1/2 cup minced onion
> 20 dried apricots, cut into 4 or 8 pieces each

1 Combine all ingredients except the apricots in a small saucepan and turn the heat to medium. Bring to a boil, stirring occasionally, then lower the heat and cook for 5 minutes.

2 Add the apricots and continue to cook until all but a tiny bit of the liquid is gone. If the mixture is not "jammy," or the apricots not quite tender, add a little more water and cook some more. Taste and adjust seasoning as necessary; you may add more of anything you like. Use within a few days and serve hot, warm, or at room temperature.

Fresh Fruit Chutney with Mustard and Curry

Makes about 2 cups

Time: 20 minutes

Use any mixture of stone fruit you like here.

8 pieces stone fruit, preferably a combination of
    peaches, nectarines, and plums
¼ cup raisins
½ cup orange or pineapple juice
¼ cup any vinegar
¼ cup sugar, honey, or other sweetener
½ cup minced onion
½ cup stemmed, seeded, and minced red bell
    pepper
1 small dried hot red chile, or to taste
1 tablespoon yellow mustard seeds
1 tablespoon All-Purpose Curry Powder (page 778)
    or store-bought curry powder

1 Peel the fruit by dipping each piece in boiling water until the skin loosens, about 30 seconds; then remove it with a paring knife. Pit and chop the fruit.

2 Combine all the remaining ingredients in a medium saucepan and turn the heat to medium.

Bring to a boil, stirring occasionally, then lower the heat and cook for 5 minutes.

3 Add the chopped fruit and continue to cook until all but a tiny bit of the liquid is gone. If the mixture is not "jammy," or the fruit is not quite tender, add a little water and continue to cook. Taste and adjust seasoning as necessary; you may add more of anything you like. Use within 2 days; serve hot, warm, or at room temperature.

Vegetable Chutney with Garlic

Makes about 4 cups

Time: 30 minutes

More of a hearty, spicy side dish than the chutneys above, this still qualifies—in my book at least—because it is sweet and jammy.

Salt to taste
2 cups peeled and roughly chopped carrots
2 cups shredded green head cabbage or Napa
    cabbage or chopped bok choy
¼ cup peanut or other oil
¼ cup roughly chopped garlic
¼ cup minced onion
½ cup stemmed, seeded, and minced red bell
    pepper
1 tablespoon peeled and minced fresh ginger
1 tablespoon All-Purpose Curry Powder (page 778)
    or store-bought curry powder
¼ teaspoon freshly ground black pepper
½ cup any vinegar
½ cup water, or more if needed
¼ cup sugar, honey, or other sweetener
Minced fresh mint, parsley, or cilantro leaves
    for garnish.

1 Bring a pot of water to the boil and salt it; cook the carrots until they are nearly tender, 5 to 10 minutes. Remove the carrots with a slotted spoon and cook the cabbage in the same water, just until it loses its crunch, 3 to 5 minutes. Remove the cabbage with a slotted spoon.

2 Meanwhile, place the oil in a broad saucepan or large, deep skillet and turn the heat to medium-low. Add the garlic, onion, red pepper, and ginger and cook, stirring, until the onion is translucent, about 5 minutes. Add the curry powder and cook, stirring, for 2 minutes. Add the pepper, vinegar, water, salt, and sweetener and turn the heat to medium. Bring to a boil and cook, stirring occasionally, for about 5 minutes.

3 Add the carrots and cabbage and cook until the vegetables are very tender, 15 minutes or more. If more water is needed, add it. Taste and adjust seasoning. Use within 2 days, and serve hot, warm, or at room temperature. Garnish just before serving.

The Basics of Traditional Cooked French and American Sauces

These include the classic flour-thickened sauces, cream sauces, and butter sauces. There are literally scores of variations on these sauces, but I've stuck to what I believe are the most important. Although many of these sauces have fallen out of fashion, there are times when you'll find them useful: A simple brown sauce is still good with meat loaf, Mornay sauce is essential for real macaroni and cheese, curry sauce transforms a plain sautéed chicken breast, and so on.

But remember: A stock-based sauce is only as good as the stock you use. One of the reasons so few people admire classic sauces is that many of the ones they've

tried have been built on a foundation of less-than-ideal or even artificial ingredients. I would make a brown sauce only if I knew it was going to complement the meat I was planning to serve it with, not just hide it under a shiny liquid blanket.

Butter needs no introduction. If you must steer clear of it for health reasons, skip the butter sauces below. But if you are willing to eat dairy for dessert, you might consider butter for sauce-making; butter sauces are luxuries that are often worth the fat intake.

Basic Brown Sauce

Makes about 1 cup

Time: 10 to 20 minutes

Brown sauce begins with the best homemade stock. But a decent pan gravy can be made with canned stock, with milk, with wine or vermouth, or even with water, as you'll see in the variations. If you want really dark sauce, cook the flour-butter mixture longer, and add dark, rich stock.

> 1½ tablespoons butter
> 1½ tablespoons flour
> 1 to 1½ cups chicken, beef, or vegetable stock, warmed (see "Soups" for stock recipes)
> Salt and freshly ground black pepper to taste

1 In a small saucepan, heat the butter over medium-low heat. When the foam begins to subside, stir in the flour. Turn the heat to low and cook, stirring with a wire whisk almost constantly, until the flour-butter mixture darkens, at least 3 minutes. You can cook it longer if you would like a darker color and slightly more complex flavor.

2 Stir in the liquid, a little bit at a time, still using the whisk. When about a cup of the liquid has been stirred in, the mixture will be fairly thick. Add more stock, a little at a time, until the consistency is just a little thinner than you like, then cook, still over low heat, until the mixture is the thickness you want.

3 Season to taste and serve immediately or keep warm over gently simmering water for up to an hour, stirring occasionally.

White Sauce: Use chicken or veal stock, and cook the flour-butter mixture for just a minute or so.

Velouté (Fish) Sauce: Use fish or lobster stock.

Béchamel (Milk) Sauce: Use milk in place of stock. Cook very gently.

Cream Sauce: Reduce the flour to 1 tablespoon and use cream in place of stock. Cook gently.

Mornay (Cheese) Sauce: Begin with Béchamel or Cream Sauce. Add $1/2$ to 1 cup grated Emmenthal (Swiss), Gruyère, or other good cheese to the mixture after it has thickened.

Curry Sauce: Add 1 tablespoon store-bought curry powder or All-Purpose Curry Powder (page 778), or to taste, along with the flour.

Ten Simple Additions to Basic Sauces

Not every addition below is appropriate for every variation above, so I give some guidance. But feel free to experiment.

1. Cook one tablespoon minced shallots in the butter until softened before adding the flour. Especially good with Brown Sauce (see above).
2. Cook one or two tablespoons pine nuts or other chopped nuts in the butter until lightly browned before adding the flour. Good with Brown, White, Cream, and Curry sauces (see above).

3. Whisk in one tablespoon or more prepared mustard during the last minute of cooking. Always appropriate.
4. Season to taste with lemon or vinegar during the last minute of cooking. Always appropriate.
5. Stir in one tablespoon or more capers during the last minute of cooking. Best with Brown and Velouté sauces (see above).
6. Use mushroom-soaking liquid for part of the stock, and add one or two tablespoons minced reconstituted dried mushrooms during the last minute of cooking. Always appropriate.
7. Stir in any minced fresh or dried herbs you like during the last minute of cooking. Always appropriate.
8. Stir in one tablespoon or more prepared horse-radish during the last minute of cooking. Always appropriate.
9. Add Worcestershire, soy, or fish sauce (*nuoc mam* or *nam pla,* available at Asian markets) to taste during the last minute of cooking. Use your judgment.
10. Add about a tablespoon tomato paste about a minute before removing the sauce from the heat. Best with Béchamel or White sauces (see above).

Onion Sauce

Soubise

Makes 2 to 3 cups

Time: About 1 hour

The technique here is much the same as for Basic Brown Sauce, above, but it takes longer to make because the onions must brown slowly. Properly made, this has all the flavor of the best onion soup. It is a killer sauce for old-fashioned grilled or broiled steaks or chops, but it is also capable of turning plain white rice into a meal.

4 very large onions, thinly sliced (about 6 cups)

3 tablespoons butter

½ cup dry white wine

3 tablespoons flour

2 to 3 cups chicken, beef, or vegetable stock, or
    water, warmed (see "Soups" for stock recipes)

Salt and freshly ground black pepper to taste

1 Place the onions in a large, deep skillet and turn the heat to medium-low. Cover the skillet and cook, stirring occasionally, until the onions are dry and almost sticking to the pan, about 15 minutes. Uncover and add the butter.

2 Turn the heat to medium and cook, stirring occasionally, until the onions are deep brown, about 20 minutes more. Stir in the wine and let it bubble away for a minute or two. Stir in the flour and turn the heat back to medium-low. Cook, stirring frequently, for about 5 minutes.

3 Add about a cup of the stock and stir; the mixture will thicken quickly. Continue to add the stock, about ½ cup at a time, stirring after each addition, until the mixture is just a little thinner than you'd like it to be. Season to taste and continue to cook and stir until the mixture is the thickness you want. Serve immediately.

Mushroom Sauce: Reduce the onions by half. After Step 1, stir in 1 cup trimmed and chopped fresh mushrooms or 2 ounces reconstituted and chopped dried mushrooms (save their soaking liquid to add to the stock) and proceed as above.

Three Simple Butter Sauces

It doesn't take much more than butter to make a sauce, but you have to cook it long enough to brown a few of the milk solids it contains; this browning heightens flavor. In general, it's better to use unsalted butter so you can control the salt level.

Brown Butter
Makes ¼ cup

Time: 10 minutes

A far more dignified treatment for steamed vegetables than a pat of cold butter.

4 tablespoons (½ stick) butter

Place the butter in a small saucepan and turn the heat to medium-low. Cook, shaking the pan every now and then, until the butter melts and then turns from yellow to pale brown, about 5 minutes. Use immediately.

Black Butter
Makes ¼ cup

Time: 10 minutes

The classic sauce for skate is delicious over any poached or grilled fish, and also over fried foods. The optional capers are often a great touch.

4 tablespoons (½ stick) butter

2 tablespoons white wine, Champagne, or other
    vinegar

1 tablespoon drained capers (optional)

Minced fresh parsley leaves for garnish

1 Place the butter in a small saucepan and turn the heat to medium-low. Cook, shaking the pan every now and then, until the butter turns from yellow to medium brown, about 7 minutes.

2 Drizzle the butter over whatever food you're serving. Turn the heat to medium and "rinse" the pan with the vinegar, shaking and letting about half the vinegar evaporate; this will take less than 1 minute.

Stir in the capers if you like, then drizzle this mixture over the food. Garnish with parsley before serving.

Parsley Butter

Makes ¹/₄ cup

Time: 10 minutes

About as simple a sauce as you can make, and it is wonderful on plain grilled fish. Substitute any delicate herb for the parsley if you like—dill or chervil are especially fine.

4 tablespoons (¹/₂ stick) butter
1 tablespoon minced shallot
1 tablespoon good wine vinegar or freshly squeezed
  lemon juice, plus 1 teaspoon if needed
Salt and freshly ground black pepper to taste
2 tablespoons minced fresh parsley leaves

1 Place the butter in a small saucepan and turn the heat to medium-low. When it melts, add the shallot and cook until softened, 3 to 5 minutes.

2 Stir in the tablespoon of vinegar or lemon juice, along with some salt and pepper, and cook for 1 minute. Add the parsley and taste. Add the remaining teaspoon of vinegar or lemon juice if necessary, and serve immediately.

Three More Complicated (But Not Difficult) Butter Sauces

Here, the butter is cooked and combined with flavorings and, in the case of Béarnaise and Hollandaise (see below), egg yolks. The most challenging is Buerre Blanc, which is not thickened with eggs and takes near-constant attention. But even that can be mastered the first time around.

Béarnaise Sauce

Makes about 1 cup

Time: 20 minutes

Yes, béarnaise is overkill, but this old-fashioned sauce has such good flavor it deserves to be made every now and then. And béarnaise, which is best with grilled beef or fish, is not at all difficult. In addition to the variation below, you can spike béarnaise with many other seasonings: a dollop of Dijon mustard or horseradish, one-half teaspoon of finely minced raw garlic, one tablespoon of chopped capers, or minced fresh herbs—especially tarragon, chervil, or parsley—to taste.

1 tablespoon minced shallot
2 teaspoons minced fresh tarragon leaves or
  ¹/₂ teaspoon dried tarragon
Salt and freshly ground black pepper to taste
¹/₃ cup white wine or other vinegar
2 egg yolks
1 tablespoon water
8 tablespoons (1 stick) butter, cut into pieces
Freshly squeezed lemon juice, if needed

1 In a small saucepan, combine the shallot, most of the tarragon, the salt, pepper, and vinegar, and turn the heat to medium-low. Cook until all but about 2 tablespoons of the vinegar has evaporated. Cool.

2 Beat the egg yolks with the water and stir into the vinegar mixture. Return to the stove over low heat and beat continuously with a wire whisk until thick, about 5 minutes.

3 With the heat as low as possible, use a wooden spoon to stir in the butter a bit at a time. Add the remaining tarragon and taste; add salt and pepper if necessary and, if the taste is not quite sharp enough, a bit of lemon juice. If the sauce is too thick, stir in hot water, a teaspoon at a time. Serve immediately.

Béarnaise Sauce with Tomato (Choron Sauce): Stir $1/2$ cup or more pureed tomato sauce (such as Basic Tomato Sauce, page 130) into the finished béarnaise. Or combine $1/4$ cup tomato paste with $1/4$ cup cream and stir that in.

Hollandaise Sauce

Makes about 1 cup

Time: 10 minutes

Once a challenging sauce to make, hollandaise became a breeze with the invention of the blender; there's little reason to make it any other way. Note that hollandaise and mayonnaise are very similar; only the fats differ. If you like, stir one teaspoon or more of minced fresh herbs—especially tarragon or dill—into the sauce after making it.

8 tablespoons (1 stick) butter
3 egg yolks
$1/2$ teaspoon salt
Pinch dry mustard or cayenne
1 tablespoon freshly squeezed lemon juice,
    or more to taste

1 Melt the butter in a small saucepan over low heat or in the microwave; do not let it brown.

2 Combine all the other ingredients in the blender and turn on the machine. Drizzle in the butter. The mixture will thicken. Taste and add more lemon juice or other seasonings if necessary. Transfer to a container and serve or keep warm by placing the hollandaise in a bowl and nesting the bowl in a bowl filled with very hot water, stirring occasionally, for up to 30 minutes.

Beurre Blanc

Makes about $1/2$ cup

Time: 10 minutes

This light, easy sauce, popularized during the 1980s, is essentially béarnaise without egg, and is brilliant over any simply cooked fish or vegetable. Make sure the butter is cold.

2 tablespoons minced shallots
$1/3$ cup white wine or rice vinegar
$1/3$ cup dry white wine
Salt and freshly ground black pepper to taste
8 tablespoons (1 stick) cold butter, cut into bits

1 Combine the first four ingredients in a small saucepan and turn the heat to medium. Cook, stirring occasionally, until reduced to a couple of tablespoons, about 5 minutes. Cool for 2 minutes.

2 Turn the heat as low as possible and whisk in the butter, a bit at a time. As each piece is incorporated, add the next. When the sauce is creamy and smooth, and all the butter is incorporated, you're done. Serve immediately; this sauce will not keep.

The Basics of Reduction Sauces

The straightforward drill for reduction sauces can be described quickly, and executed almost as fast.

1. Remove the meat, chicken, fish, or vegetables from your roasting or sauté pan.
2. Add twice as much water or other liquid—such as wine or vermouth, milk or cream, or stock—as you would like sauce.
3. Turn the heat to high (if you're working with a large roasting pan, set it over two burners).

4. Stir, scraping the bottom of the pan to release any solids left from cooking, until the liquid is reduced in quantity by about half.

5. Stir in some softened butter (or any appropriate compound butter, pages 768–770), olive oil (preferably extra-virgin), or cream if you like.

6. Serve.

Every reduction sauce is a variation on these simple steps. Some are thickened by adding flour before the liquid, or a cornstarch mixture after the reduction; most are more heavily seasoned. But basically, that's about it.

Here are the two basic reductions—one thickened, one not—with plenty of ideas for more.

Eleven Other Ideas for Basic Reduction Sauce

1. Add one-half cup or more of minced aromatic vegetables—onion, shallots, mushrooms, celery, carrot, or a combination—to the fat remaining in the pan before adding the wine. Cook, stirring, until soft, then add liquid.

2. Substitute heavy cream for half or all of the stock.

3. Substitute sherry, Madeira, port, or vermouth for the wine. All are more assertive.

4. Add minced herbs or ground spices at the beginning or the end of the sauce-making process. Those added at the beginning will become better incorporated, those at the end will retain more of their flavor. Add them twice if you like.

5. Add chopped anchovies or olives along with the shallot.

6. Add 1 tablespoon or more of freshly squeezed lemon juice or vinegar at the end of cooking, tasting as you add.

7. Add chopped or crushed tomatoes or tomato sauce in place of or in addition to some of the stock.

8. Add one tablespoon or more of marmalade or jam, whisked in at the end of cooking; especially good with broiled meats.

9. Add reconstituted dried mushrooms along with shallot or onion at the beginning of the sauce-making. Use the mushroom-soaking liquid to replace some of the broth.

10. Use fruit juice—especially orange or tomato—in place of some of the stock or water.

11. Add prepared Dijon or grainy mustard, along with some cream if you like, in place of or in addition to the optional butter.

Basic Reduction Sauce or Pan Gravy

Makes ¹/₂ cup

Time: 10 minutes

All of this takes place after cooking, in the same skillet or roasting pan in which you cooked whatever it is you're dressing. Keep your food warm in a low oven if necessary while you prepare the sauce. Or just add the food back to the pan with the finished sauce and heat through for a minute or so.

1 tablespoon minced shallot or onion
¹/₂ cup dry white (for fish, poultry, or vegetables) or red (for red meats) wine
¹/₂ cup chicken, beef, or vegetable stock, or water, warmed (see "Soups" for stock recipes)
2 tablespoons softened butter (optional)
Salt and freshly ground black pepper to taste
A few drops of freshly squeezed lemon juice or vinegar (optional)
Minced fresh parsley leaves for garnish

1 Pour off all but 1 or 2 tablespoons of the cooking fat (if there are dark, non-fatty juices in the skillet or roasting pan leave them in there). Turn the heat under the skillet or pan to medium-high and add the shallot and the wine. Cook, stirring and scraping,

until most of the wine has evaporated, the shallot is soft, and the bottom of the pan is clean.

2 Add the stock and repeat; when there is just under $1/2$ cup of liquid, turn off the heat. Add the butter, a little at a time, stirring well after each addition to incorporate it. Taste and season if necessary with salt, pepper, and/or lemon juice or vinegar.

3 Spoon this sauce over the meat, garnish, and serve.

Asian Sauce: Cook 1 tablespoon each minced garlic, ginger, and scallions (in place of shallot) until soft before adding the wine. Proceed as above, omitting butter. Stir in 1 tablespoon soy or fish sauce (or Worcestershire sauce), and finish with a few drops of freshly squeezed lime juice. Garnish with minced cilantro leaves.

Mushroom Sauce: Before adding the wine, cook $1/2$ cup chopped wild or domestic mushrooms along with 2 tablespoons shallots, until soft. Proceed as above. Best with $1/4$ cup or more of heavy cream added at the last minute.

Lemon-Caper Sauce: Add 1 tablespoon or more minced capers along with the shallot and wine. Finish with freshly squeezed lemon juice to taste, at least 1 tablespoon.

Thickened Reduction Sauce or Pan Gravy

Makes 2 cups

Time: 20 minutes

This is the standard gravy for turkey or meat loaf. Many cooks thicken by sprinkling one tablespoon

or more of flour onto the pan juices before adding liquid. The following method is easier, faster, and never produces lumps. Stir in one-quarter cup or more of heavy cream just before serving if you want a creamier, richer-tasting sauce.

1 cup dry white wine
$1/2$ cup chopped onion
3 cups plus 3 or 4 tablespoons chicken, beef, or vegetable stock, or water, warmed (see "Soups" for stock recipes)
$1/2$ cup minced giblet or other meat, or more (optional)
2 tablespoons cornstarch, or a bit more
Salt and freshly ground black pepper to taste

1 Spoon off all but 1 or 2 tablespoons of the cooking fat (if there are dark, non-fatty juices in the skillet or roasting pans leave them in there). Add the wine and onion and turn the heat to high. Cook, stirring and scraping, until most of the wine has evaporated, the onion is soft, and the bottom of the pan is clean, about 5 minutes.

2 Add the 3 cups of stock or water and continue to cook, stirring, until reduced by about half, 5 to 10 minutes. If you have any solids—such as minced giblets—now is the time to add them. Combine the remaining stock with the cornstarch and turn the heat to low. Stir the cornstarch mixture into the liquid; it will begin to thicken almost immediately.

3 Cook, stirring, for about 5 minutes; season to taste. If the sauce is not as thick as you'd like, combine another tablespoon of cornstarch with 1 tablespoon of water or stock and add to the mixture. Cook another 5 minutes and serve.

Beverages

Too often, we take beverages for granted. We buy the same coffee our mothers did; we drink milk without judging its flavor; we create mixed drinks with packaged powders. But beverages make up an important part of our daily intake of food, and it's a shame not to put the same amount of thought and effort into making them delicious as we do into the food we chew.

The good news is that it isn't difficult to make top-notch drinks; mostly, it's about buying good ingredients and assembling them from scratch. And if you've never had real hot chocolate, for example, or a whiskey sour made without mix, you're in for a treat.

The most important ingredient in many beverages is water. If your tap water tastes so bad that you feel it necessary to buy bottled water, you ought to use that same bottled water for making coffee, tea, and any other water-based beverage (arguably, the same holds true for cooking, but that gets expensive in a hurry). Of course there are other important ingredients in beverages: coffee, tea, liquor, fruit. And all of these should be the best quality you can find. But good coffee beans won't do you much good if your water is bad.

The Basics of Coffee

All coffee is grown in the tropics and, although some regions grow better coffee than others, those differences are of concern only to true enthusiasts. For the rest of us, there is one distinction that is extremely important, and that involves not the beans' place of origin but their type.

There are two kinds of coffee beans, arabica and robusta. Arabica is what you usually get if you buy coffee by the pound from a reputable dealer. Robusta, or at best a blend of robusta and arabica, is what you get when you buy preground coffee in cans. Since arabica is widely acknowledged to be the superior coffee, it pays to buy coffee from a specialist.

All coffee is roasted (the beans are green until then), and there are many levels of roasts. But they boil down to just two or three: American, or breakfast roast, which is the lightest; and French and Italian roasts, which are considerably darker. (There is no specified distinction between French and Italian roasts; sometimes French is darker, sometimes Italian.) American roast is most commonly used for American-style coffee, but a little French or Italian roast blended in adds flavor and body, and people who like very strong coffee often use all dark beans for American-style coffee. For espresso, you must use French or Italian roast, beans with a shiny, dark, oily surface.

The next question is grinding. Once, grinding coffee was part of a daily routine; now, obviously, it's possible to have any coffee, even that of the highest quality, preground at purchase. While pregrinding is not ideal, if you drink a lot of coffee—say, half a pound a week—and you're not a stickler for the ultra-highest quality, and you store the coffee in a tight container (don't refrigerate ground coffee), it's really not going to make much of a difference.

But if you want the best coffee, you'll grind it yourself. If you are a fanatic, buy a coffee mill to do the grinding; these cost a minimum of forty dollars, and usually quite a bit more. Inexpensive grinders begin at ten dollars and do a good enough job for all but the most dedicated drinkers. For espresso, grind the coffee as finely as you can. For drip coffee, the grind should still be fine, but not super-fine. For plunger or percolator coffee, keep the grind fairly coarse.

Store coffee beans in the refrigerator if you buy a pound at a time, in the freezer if you buy more, or if you use coffee only occasionally.

The Basics of Coffee Makers

Finally, there is the method. For espresso or cappuccino, you need an electric machine, or a metal stove-top espresso maker; there is no other choice (see below). But there are plenty of choices for American-style coffee, and here are the best in order of my preference.

- **Drip maker:** Placing finely ground coffee in a paper, cloth, or fine metal mesh filter and pouring water through it is easy and reliable; it's now the most common method as well. Flavor and intensity are controlled by the amount of coffee used (at least 1½ level tablespoons per eight-ounce cup, or to taste) and the fineness of the grind. Most electric coffee machines are drip makers too. There are also metal pots that drip water through the coffee, but these are difficult to keep clean and often leave a metallic taste.
- **Plungers:** Water is poured over grounds in a cylindrical container, then the floating grounds are forced to the bottom by a plunger with a fine screen. Easy to make and very reliable; flavor and intensity are controlled by the amount of coffee used (at least 1½ level tablespoons per eight-ounce cup, or to taste), the fineness of the grind (slightly coarse is better in this case, because the plunger is not as efficient as the filter at removing grinds), and the length of time you allow the water and coffee to remain in contact with one another, usually just a couple of minutes. One caution: Many people find that coffee made in plungers is not hot enough. If you have this problem, fill the plunger pot with boiling or very hot tap water while you are grinding the coffee. Empty the warmed pot just before adding the coffee and water.
- **Percolators:** This once-popular method makes boiled coffee, which lacks the fine flavor of the

two methods already mentioned. But it remains the best way to make coffee for a crowd, which is why you still see so many percolators at big home parties. Use a fairly coarse ground, keep perking time relatively short—about five minutes is usually right—and turn off the heat when done perking. If your crowd is small—say, fewer than twenty people—you might be better off making a couple of batches of drip coffee and keeping it hot in thermoses; it will certainly taste better.

All coffee deteriorates quickly after brewing. Keeping it hot on a hot plate (as do electric machines), by continual simmering (as do electric percolators), or even by placing it in a warm water bath (probably the best method) will all produce bitterness, usually within thirty minutes. The best way to keep coffee hot is to brew it, then pour it into a heated thermos. This will retain good quality for several hours, although the quality will become noticeably inferior with each passing hour. The best coffee is freshly made coffee, and even not-great coffee, freshly made, is better than the best coffee an hour old.

By the way, the same rules hold for decaf as for regular coffee. Buy water-processed decaf if possible. And avoid instant coffee altogether, unless you enjoy its distinctive flavor.

The Basics of Espresso Machines

In Italy, where most people drink only espresso-based drinks, coffee is made at home in a simple stove-top coffeemaker called a *moka*, which makes second-rate espresso by any standards. But of course, in Italy, most coffee is consumed in the ubiquitous bars, where it is cheap and almost invariably good.

How to Make Espresso and Cappuccino

The rules for making espresso are simple:

1. Make sure the machine is hot; many have thermostats, and so can be left on for hours at a time.
2. Grind the coffee as finely as you can, to a powder if possible.
3. Preheat your cup and the filter holder by running them under hot water.
4. Pack the coffee into the filter, and tamp it down tightly.
5. Insert the filter into the filter holder and use the machine according to the manufacturer's directions.
6. For cappuccino, make sure the milk is not just hot but foamy.

Although espresso and cappuccino are becoming more common here, they're still expensive and hard to find outside of the downtown areas of most cities. As a result, many aficionados have turned to home-brewing of espresso and cappuccino and, in turn, the prices of some quite decent machines have come down, to the point where you can hope to buy a fairly reliable machine with an electric pump that can produce decent espresso and cappuccino for less than two hundred dollars. Unfortunately, it's difficult to recommend brand names in a market that is changing rapidly, and I have found no store that will allow you to "try before you buy" (which would be ideal), so you will have to rely on the recommendations of magazines such as *Consumer Reports* and *Cook's Illustrated*.

If, however, you live in a family in which more than one person drinks espresso or cappuccino, and you rely on them for most of your coffee drinking, and intend to do so for many years to come, you should seriously consider buying one of the more expensive machines with the sturdier and more reliable hand pump. These, unfortunately, usually cost in excess of four hundred dollars, but I bought one used (for one hundred and fifty dollars, a stroke of luck) twenty years ago, and have made literally ten thousand or more cups of espresso in it; although I've had a few maintenance bills, there is no way one of the less-expensive machines is ever going to duplicate this performance.

The Basics of Coffee Drinks

Most coffee drinkers drink so much coffee that they forget it's easy to make it special, and the producers of instant flavored coffees would have you believe that there is some kind of trick to spicing coffee. In fact, most of the coffees which we consider "special" are daily beverages in their cultures of origin.

In addition to these variations, you can spike any coffee with cinnamon, cardamom, cocoa powder, vanilla, or any spice that suits your taste.

Café au Lait, or Caffè Latte   If you have an electric espresso machine or milk steamer, steam a large quantity of milk and mix it, half-and-half (or whatever proportion you like) with fresh coffee. If you do not have an espresso machine, cook the milk in a small saucepan until tiny bubbles appear on its sides.

Viennese Coffee   Whip heavy cream, sweetened to taste (a tablespoon per cup is about right), until it holds soft peaks. Use this to top coffee.

Turkish Coffee   Combine equal amounts of coffee and sugar; about a tablespoon each per cup. Add one-half cup water per serving. Bring to a boil in a very small saucepan, then remove from the heat for a moment. Repeat twice more. Serve by pouring the liquid into espresso cups, leaving as much of the dregs behind as possible. Drink the liquid only, leaving the dregs in the cups.

Iced Coffee   Brewed coffee stores fairly well in the refrigerator, so you can make this in advance,

although it is still best fresh. Make very strong coffee (at least two tablespoons coffee per cup) and pour it over plenty of ice. If the coffee is hot, it should be exceptionally strong, as it will melt a lot of ice. Place a metal knife or spoon in the glass with the ice to keep the glass from cracking from the heat of the coffee.

Foamy Iced Coffee   Combine one cup coffee, a teaspoon or more of sugar, and cream or milk to taste, and about one-half cup crushed ice in a blender. Whiz until foamy and serve. This is even better with a little chocolate syrup added to the mix.

The Basics of Tea

As with coffee, a tiny effort can bring great benefits when buying tea. Tea sold in tea bags is not quite uniformly bad, but only because some are worse than others. To have good tea—whether black, green, or herbal—it pays to buy product in bulk and brew it in a teapot or tea ball. For the most part, you cannot even buy high-quality tea in a supermarket, but it is widely available. The best is often purchased by mail.

There are many, many kinds of tea; these are the three most important in this country:

Green Tea   Unfermented tea, usually from China or Japan. Light in flavor and color, it can be quite refreshing.

Black Tea   The same tea, fermented to gain flavor and color. The best are from the Darjeeling and Assam regions of Indian and Keemun from China. But there are dozens from all over Asia (and some from Africa, especially Kenya), and many are good. Some are flavored: Lapsang souchang, for example, is smoked; jasmine tea (usually only lightly fermented, and sometimes green), is scented with jasmine; black currant and other fruit teas are scented with extracts of the named fruit; Earl Grey tea is spiked with bergamot, a powerful extract.

Herb Tea Everything else, which is quite a lot: dried leaves, roots, and/or flowers; spices (such as cardamom and ginger); fresh savory herbs such as sage or thyme; and even fruits—dried orange peel, for example—can all be added to the mix, or used individually. Mint and chamomile are the most common herb teas, but tea is brewed from almost every non-poisonous plant somewhere, and often health-giving or ailment-curing properties are attributed to it. Virtually no herbal teas contain caffeine.

Brewing Tea

All tea is made in the same way, with minor variations: Heat a teapot by allowing very hot water to sit in it for a minute or so. Bring water to a boil in a kettle and remove it from the heat. Drain the teapot, and add one rounded teaspoon of tea for each cup, plus an extra teaspoon for the pot. Pour the boiled water into the teapot and cover. Brew for three to five minutes. The amount of tea used and the time of brewing are both completely dependent on the type and form of tea, and on your taste. In black teas, whole leaf teas require more tea—usually one heaping teaspoon per cup, or more—and take longer to brew. Processed teas, however, may need one scant teaspoon per cup and be done in a minute. Use your judgment; these are easy differences to learn. For herb teas, you may wind up using as much as one tablespoon per cup.

If you are only brewing one cup, and don't want to make a pot, use a tea ball or a small strainer, and at least 1¹/₂ teaspoons of tea. Preheat the cup if possible and brew as above.

To make iced tea Like coffee, tea stores fairly well in the refrigerator, so you can make this in advance. Make double-strength tea and pour it over plenty of ice. If the tea is hot, it should be exceptionally strong, as it will melt a lot of ice. Place a metal knife or spoon in the glass with the ice to keep the glass from cracking from the heat of the tea. To premake sweetened tea, stir sugar to taste into hot tea and then pour over ice or store in the refrigerator. Iced tea may also be made by steeping plenty of tea in cold water for several hours; this results in a brew that will not cloud over ice.

Hot Chocolate

Makes 4 servings

Time: 10 minutes

To make hot chocolate for one, use eight ounces milk, 1¹/₂ tablespoons cocoa, and two tablespoons sugar, or to taste. A tiny bit of vanilla extract, added at the last moment, is a welcome addition here; or you may prefer a little mint.

4 cups whole, reduced-fat, or skim milk
¹/₄ cup powdered cocoa, such as Hershey's
 (or use 2 squares of unsweetened baking
 chocolate, chopped)
¹/₄ cup sugar, or to taste
Pinch salt

1 Pour the milk into a blender, then add the other ingredients, and turn the machine on; let run for 10 seconds or so. Alternatively, blend the dry ingredients with about ¹/₂ cup of the milk over very low heat in a small saucepan, stirring until smooth. Stir in the rest of the milk, beating with a fork or wire whisk.

2 Heat the mixture over medium-low heat (or in a microwave), stirring occasionally, until hot. Pour into cups and serve.

Mocha Hot Chocolate: Substitute freshly brewed coffee for half or more of the milk.

Mexican Hot Chocolate: The easiest way to make this is to chop one of the 3-ounce chunks of cinnamon-flavored Mexican chocolate (sold in many Latino and all Mexican-American markets) and combine it in a medium saucepan with about 3 cups of milk. Then cook over medium-low heat, stirring with a wire whisk, until the chocolate dissolves. Or for a close second, add about $1/2$ teaspoon ground cinnamon, or to taste, to each serving of Hot Chocolate (see above). You can mix the cinnamon with the cocoa powder, or add it to the finished hot chocolate.

The Basics of Fresh Fruit Shakes and Punches

Sitting on your kitchen counter is a tool that can turn any soft fruit into a great drink in moments: the blender. There are a handful of sample recipes on the following pages, but first, some general suggestions that will allow you to make great fruit drinks without any recipes at all.

- Use soft, ripe fruit. Slightly overripe fruit is usually fine; rotten fruit is not.
- If you use berries—especially raspberries and blackberries, but even strawberries—you may want to remove the seeds first. To do so, mash the berries in a bowl and then place them in a mesh strainer or sieve and press them with a wooden spoon or spatula to separate out the seeds.
- Sweeten with sugar only to taste; bananas, for example, can sweeten other fruit enough so that sugar isn't needed at all. Use Sugar Syrup if possible: You can make it in five minutes—see the recipe, below—and it keeps forever in the refrigerator. Alternatively, you may use honey, maple syrup, or any other sweetener.

- Add some crushed ice if you like (or ice cubes, if your blender is powerful enough), for extra chill and body.
- Use a squeeze of lemon or lime to balance the sweetness and add complexity.
- For many fruits, you'll need some added liquid as well: Use orange, apple, grape, or pineapple juice, or milk, or water (sparkling water adds a nice touch).
- Taste after blending; it's never too late to adjust the flavors.
- Double, triple, or quadruple any of these recipes to serve a crowd. You can almost always stretch them even further by adding sparkling water, not-too-sweet sodas (such as ginger ale), iced tea, orange, pineapple, apple, or grape juice, milk, and/or crushed ice. Always adjust the sweetener, and check to see if a little freshly squeezed lemon juice would balance the mix.

Sugar Syrup

Makes about 2 cups

Time: 10 minutes

The easiest all-purpose sweetener for any cold drink, because it dissolves instantly. Make it in any quantity you like.

2 cups water
2 cups sugar

1 Combine in a small saucepan and turn the heat to medium.

2 Cook, stirring occasionally, until the sugar is completely dissolved. Store in the refrigerator.

Soft Fruit Shake

Makes 2 servings

Time: 5 minutes

Use this and the following recipes as the bases for improvisation.

2 cups cut-up mixed soft fruit: melons, skinned
   peaches, oranges, bananas, etc.
1 tablespoon freshly squeezed lemon juice,
   plus more if necessary
Sugar (preferably Sugar Syrup, page 798) to taste
1/2 cup crushed ice

Combine all ingredients in a blender and whiz until smooth. Taste and adjust seasoning by adding more lemon juice or Sugar Syrup if necessary.

Rich Berry Shake

Makes 4 to 6 servings

Time: 10 minutes

An ice cream shake without the ice cream. (For shakes with ice cream, see Milk Shakes, Malteds, and Frappes, page 668.) Use one-quarter light cream or half-and-half for extra richness.

4 cups strawberries or other berries, cleaned
6 cups milk or a mixture of milk and cream
   (see headnote)
Sugar (preferably Sugar Syrup, page 798) to taste
Freshly squeezed lemon juice or vanilla extract to taste

1 Puree the berries in a blender and put through a sieve if necessary to remove seeds.

2 Combine all ingredients in a blender and whiz until smooth. You may need to do this in batches; simply divide the ingredients in half and recombine them for a moment before proceeding to the next step.

3 Taste and adjust seasoning by adding more lemon juice, vanilla extract, or Sugar Syrup if necessary.

Rich Orange Milkshake

Makes 4 servings

Time: 10 minutes

Like the recipe above, this is as flavorful as an ice cream milkshake but not quite as rich.

4 cups orange juice or a mixture or orange and
   grapefruit juice, preferably freshly squeezed
1 cup milk or half-and-half
1 cup water
1 teaspoon vanilla or 1/2 teaspoon almond extract,
   plus more if necessary
Sugar (preferably Sugar Syrup, page 798), to taste
1 cup crushed ice

1 Combine all ingredients in a blender and whiz until smooth.

2 Taste and adjust seasoning by adding more vanilla or Sugar Syrup if necessary.

Banana-Yogurt Shake

Makes 2 servings

Time: 5 minutes

When your bananas become overripe (it happens, doesn't it?), peel them and wrap them in plastic wrap; freeze. Use them to make this great early morning drink.

1 frozen banana
1 cup orange juice, preferably freshly squeezed
1 cup plain or vanilla yogurt

Combine all ingredients in a blender and whiz until smooth.

Banana-Vanilla Shake

Makes 2 servings

Time: 5 minutes

Instead of vanilla, you can use a grating of nutmeg and a little cinnamon here.

1 ripe banana (frozen is okay)
1 cup milk
1/2 cup crushed ice
Sugar (preferably Sugar Syrup, page 798) to taste
1/2 teaspoon vanilla extract, plus more if necessary
    (or see headnote)

1 Combine all ingredients in a blender and whiz until smooth.

2 Taste and adjust seasoning by adding more vanilla or Sugar Syrup if necessary.

Pineapple-Berry Punch

Makes 4 to 6 servings

Time: 10 minutes

Canned pineapple juice is a convenient and good-tasting product; here, it contributes to an exotic punch that is easily varied.

1/2 cup or more fresh strawberries or other berries, cleaned
4 cups canned pineapple juice
1/2 cup freshly squeezed orange juice
Several thin slices fresh orange
1/2 cup freshly squeezed lemon juice, plus more if necessary
Sugar (preferably Sugar Syrup, page 798) to taste
1 cup crushed ice (optional)
1 cup cored and cut-up fresh pineapple

1 Puree the berries and put through a sieve if necessary to remove seeds.

2 Combine all ingredients in a blender and whiz until smooth. You may need to do this in batches; simply divide the ingredients in half and recombine them for a moment before proceeding to the next step.

3 Taste and adjust seasoning by adding more lemon juice or Sugar Syrup if necessary.

Lemonade or Limeade

Makes 4 servings

Time: 5 minutes

Real, fresh lemonade is a taste from the past that deserves a home in the present. Incomparable, and not at all bad when hot. Also great mixed half and half with iced tea.

3 cups water
1 cup freshly squeezed lemon or lime juice
1/2 cup sugar (preferably Sugar Syrup, page 798),
    plus more to taste

Combine the water and lemon or lime juice with 1/2 cup Sugar Syrup and taste. You will need more Sugar Syrup, but add it slowly. The drink should be mouth-puckeringly tart.

Orangeade: Substitute freshly squeezed orange juice for the lemon or lime juice, but add $1/4$ cup freshly squeezed lemon juice to the mix. You will need less sugar.

Raspberry-Ade: This is great with a little mint pureed with the raspberries, and a sprig or two of mint used as a garnish. Roughly puree a cup or more raspberries and put through a sieve to remove the seeds. Stir into lemonade and adjust sweetness as necessary.

Grape-Lime Rickey

Makes 4 servings

Time: 5 minutes

Adding soda to sweet juices makes a quick and easy drink. If the juice is sweet, add lemon or lime and use seltzer; if it's tart, add ginger ale or other not-too-sweet soda.

> 2 cups grape juice
> Juice of 2 limes
> 2 cups seltzer
> 1 lime, quartered

Mix the grape juice and the lime juice together in a large pitcher; add seltzer. Fill tall glasses with ice and pour in the liquid; garnish with lime wedges.

The Basics of Classic Mixed Drinks

There are drinks whose name tells you how to make them—gin and tonic, for example. There are those, like the Screwdriver, that everyone seems to know by the time he or she is old enough to consume alcohol.

And there are those, like the Sea Breeze—vodka mixed with cranberry and grapefruit juice—that people make without knowing their name. But many classic mixed drinks confuse everyone but the people who drink them routinely and the bartenders who make them daily. Here, then, are recipes for the important classics and more modern "blenderized" drinks. Since liquor keeps indefinitely, it will become immediately clear that you only need stock a few common ingredients to be able to make most of these—without mix, I might add—at a moment's notice.

The process is made even easier if you have on hand superfine sugar or Sugar Syrup (page 798), either of which dissolve even in the coldest liquids. Generally use twice as much Sugar Syrup to substitute for sugar, but it pays to add it to taste until you gain experience.

Many mixed drinks can be made without alcohol: Bloody Mary becomes Virgin Mary, Tequila Sunrise becomes Tequila Sunset, and so on. You might want to increase other flavorings to make up for the lost punch.

For many of these, I give recipes for four servings; just divide by four to make individual drinks.

Black Russian

Makes 4 servings

Time: 5 minutes

Note the simple variations on this coffee-flavored drink.

> $1/2$ cup (4 ounces) vodka
> $1/4$ cup (2 ounces) coffee-flavored liqueur, such as Kahlúa

Mix together and serve in cocktail glasses, over ice.

Sombrero: Substitute milk for the vodka.

White Russian: Add cream, half-and-half, or milk to taste.

Bloody Mary
Makes 4 servings

Time: 5 minutes

A good Bloody Mary can only be made to your taste. This is how I like mine.

3 cups tomato juice
3/4 cup (6 ounces) vodka
Several drops Tabasco or other hot sauce
1 teaspoon Worcestershire sauce, or to taste
1 teaspoon prepared horseradish, more if it is not strong, or to taste
Salt and freshly ground black pepper to taste
1 lemon, cut into quarters
1 celery stalk, trimmed and cut in half the long way, then cut in half the short way, for garnish (optional)

1. Combine the first six ingredients and adjust balance as necessary.
2. Fill four tall glasses with ice and add the liquid. Squeeze some of the juice from each lemon quarter into each glass, then drop the lemon quarter in. Garnish and serve.

Champagne Cocktail
Makes 1 serving

Time: 2 minutes

The most elegant cocktail there is. Naturally, it's best made with top-quality Champagne, but it also happens to be a good way to disguise the flaws of sparkling wines that are less than the best. Bitters—the most popular brand is Angostura—is a concentrated mixture of alcohol, herbs, and spices, which packs a powerful flavor; it can be omitted from many drinks, but is nearly essential here.

1 small square sugar cube (the kind that measure about 1/2 × 1/2 inch, not the larger rectangular ones)
Tiny dash bitters
3 to 4 ounces chilled Champagne

1. Place the sugar in the bottom of a champagne flute and add the bitters.
2. Fill with chilled Champagne and serve.

Frozen Daiquiri
Makes 4 servings

Time: 10 minutes

Frozen Daiquiris have taken over from the traditional kind, which, as "straight-up" drinks, are stronger.

3/4 cup (6 ounces) rum
1 tablespoon superfine sugar or 2 tablespoons Sugar Syrup (page 798), or to taste
1/4 cup freshly squeezed lime juice
1 cup crushed ice, or more to taste

1. Combine all ingredients in a blender and whiz until creamy.
2. Pour into cocktail glasses and serve.

Traditional Daiquiri: Use the above ingredients, but make as you would a Martini (page 804).

Strawberry Daiquiri: Add 1 cup cleaned, hulled, and roughly chopped strawberries to the blender with the other ingredients.

Gin or Vodka Gimlet

Makes 4 servings

Time: 5 minutes

This can be made with gin (somewhat more traditional) or vodka (currently more popular). If you like slightly sweet drinks, add the Sugar Syrup. Make these like Martinis (page 804), or serve on the rocks.

$^3/_4$ cup (6 ounces) gin or vodka
$^3/_8$ cup freshly squeezed lime juice
Sugar Syrup (page 798) to taste (optional)
4 lime wedges for garnish

1 Combine the gin or vodka, lime juice, and Sugar Syrup in a shaker or pitcher with plenty of ice and shake or stir to combine and chill. (Or, if you want gimlets on the rocks, just combine the liquids and pour over ice.)

2 Strain into cocktail glasses, garnish, and serve.

Irish Coffee

Makes 4 servings

Time: 5 minutes

Every European country has a history of spiking coffee for an added boost (in Italy, it's called "correcting" the coffee). Here, Irish Coffee is typically made with bar coffee that has sat on a hot-plate for two hours. When you make it at home with freshly brewed coffee, it's quite wonderful.

$^3/_4$ cup (6 ounces) Irish whiskey, or use bourbon, brandy, Scotch, rye, etc.
About 3 cups freshly brewed coffee
1 tablespoon sugar, or to taste
Whipped cream (optional)

1 Divide the whiskey among four mugs and add coffee to within $^1/_2$ inch of the top. Add sugar to taste.

2 Top with whipped cream if you like and serve.

Mint Julep

Makes 4 servings

Time: 5 minutes

The traditional, refeshing, and potent drink of the Kentucky Derby, and a long-standing Southern favorite.

$^1/_4$ cup fresh mint leaves, plus 4 sprigs for garnish
1 cup (8 ounces) bourbon
1 tablespoon superfine sugar or 2 tablespoons Sugar Syrup (page 798), or to taste

1 Crush the mint leaves with a mortar and pestle or the blunt end of a large knife. Distribute it among four tall, narrow glasses and fill the glasses with ice.

2 Divide the bourbon among the glasses, sweeten to taste, garnish, and serve.

Manhattan

Makes 4 servings

Time: 2 minutes

Like a Martini with rye and more significant amounts of vermouth. Some people also add a dash of bitters. The traditional garnish is a maraschino cherry; I prefer a tiny twist of lemon, but this is heresy.

$^3/_4$ cup (6 ounces) rye or blended whiskey (such as Canadian Club)
$^3/_8$ cup (3 ounces) sweet vermouth
1 dash bitters, or to taste (optional)
4 maraschino cherries for garnish

1 Combine the liquids in a shaker or pitcher with plenty of ice and shake or stir to combine and chill. (Or, if you want Manhattans on the rocks, just combine the liquids and strain over fresh ice.)

2 Strain into cocktail glasses, garnish, and serve.

Rob Roy: Substitute Scotch for the whiskey or rye.

Margarita
Makes 4 servings

Time: 10 minutes

If you choose to salt the rims, this is a bit more work than most other mixed drinks. But it's easy enough.

1 lime, quartered
Coarse salt
³/₄ cup (6 ounces) tequila
Scant ¹/₄ cup (2 ounces) orange liqueur,
    such as Cointreau
4 tablespoons freshly squeezed lime juice

1 Squeeze each lime quarter over its respective glass, then rub the rim with the lime. Dip the rim into a bowl of coarse salt to coat it. Drop the lime into the glass.

2 Combine the tequila, liqueur, and lime juice in a shaker or pitcher with plenty of ice and shake or stir to combine and chill. (Or, if you want Margaritas on the rocks, just combine the liquids and strain over fresh ice.)

3 Strain into the prepared glasses and serve.

Frozen Margarita: Typically made on the sweet side. Add 1 tablespoon superfine sugar, or 2 tablespoons Sugar Syrup (page 798), or to taste, to the mix. Combine all ingredients in a blender with 1 cup or more of crushed ice and whiz until creamy. Pour into prepared glasses and serve.

Martini
Makes 4 servings

Time: 5 minutes

Some rules: Even a "not-dry" Martini contains very little vermouth. When people ask for a "very dry" Martini, they essentially mean a glass of gin, with a drop—literally—of vermouth added. This recipe makes a "normal" martini. Martinis are traditionally served in a classic triangular glass, straight up; you can also serve them on the rocks.

1 tablespoon dry vermouth
³/₄ cup (6 ounces) gin
4 green olives or twists of lemon peel for garnish

1 Combine the vermouth and gin in a shaker or pitcher with plenty of ice and shake or stir to combine and chill. (Or, if you want Martinis on the rocks, just combine the liquids and pour over ice.)

2 Strain into Martini or other cocktail glasses, garnish, and serve.

Gibson: Serve with a pickled pearl onion in place of the olive.

Vodka Martini: Substitute vodka for gin.

Old-Fashioned
Makes 4 servings

Time: 5 minutes

Another traditionally strong drink, tempered by sugar and a splash of sparkling or still water, which should be added to each glass individually.

1 cup (8 ounces) blended whiskey (such as Canadian Club), or Scotch, bourbon, or rye
2 teaspoons superfine sugar or 1 tablespoon Sugar Syrup (page 798)
Several dashes bitters
Water, still or sparkling
4 twists lemon or orange peel for garnish

1 Combine the first three ingredients and add more sugar or bitters if necessary. Pour into cocktail glasses filled with ice (or serve at room temperature).

2 Add a bit of still or sparkling water to each glass, according to taste. Garnish and serve.

Piña Colada

Makes 4 servings

Time: 10 minutes

Once shaken or stirred, Piña Coladas are now almost always made in a blender with crushed ice. I don't think this drink needs sugar, but so many bars make extra-sweet Piña Coladas that you may find this too dry without it.

³/₄ cup (6 ounces) rum
1¹/₂ cups pineapple juice
³/₄ cup canned or Fresh Coconut Milk (page 291)
1 tablespoon superfine sugar or 2 tablespoons Sugar Syrup (page 798), or to taste (optional)
1 cup crushed ice

1 Combine all ingredients in a blender and whiz until creamy. Taste and add more sugar syrup or sugar if necessary.

2 Pour into cocktail glasses and serve.

Screwdriver

Makes 4 servings

Time: 5 minutes

A delicious cliché, especially with freshly squeezed orange juice.

³/₄ cup (6 ounces) vodka
3 cups orange juice, or to taste

Mix together and serve in tall glasses, over ice.

Sea Breeze

Makes 4 servings

Time: 5 minutes

Tart and refreshing.

³/₄ cup (6 ounces) vodka
1¹/₂ cups grapefruit juice, or to taste
1¹/₂ cups cranberry juice, or to taste
Lime wedges for garnish

1 Mix together the vodka and about half the grapefruit juice. Add half the cranberry juice.

2 Taste and add more of either or both juices. Garnish and serve.

Side Car

Makes 4 servings

Time: 5 minutes

This can also be made with tequila, with the rim dipped in sugar instead of salt (see Margarita).

¾ cup (6 ounces) brandy
¼ cup (2 ounces) orange liqueur, such as Cointreau
¼ cup (2 ounces) freshly squeezed lemon or
    lime juice
Maraschino cherries and orange slices for garnish

1 Combine the brandy, liqueur, and lemon or lime juice in a shaker or pitcher with plenty of ice and shake or stir to combine and chill. (Or, if you want Side Cars on the rocks, just combine the liquids and pour over ice.)

2 Strain into cocktail glasses, garnish, and serve.

Tequila Sunrise
Makes 4 servings

Time: 2 minutes

Essentially, a Screwdriver with tequila instead of vodka.

1 cup (8 ounces) tequila
Orange juice as needed
Grenadine (optional)

1 Divide the tequila among four tall, ice-filled glasses.

2 Fill each with orange juice and add a splash of grenadine for color if you like.

Tom Collins
Makes 4 servings

Time: 5 minutes

A mild, sweet drink—which explains why it was my favorite in my youth. To make a Vodka Collins…well, you can figure it out.

¾ cup (6 ounces) gin
1 tablespoon superfine sugar or 2 tablespoons Sugar
    Syrup (page 798), or to taste
3 tablespoons freshly squeezed lemon juice
1 tablespoon freshly squeezed lime juice
2 to 3 cups sparkling water
Lemon or lime wedges for garnish

1 Combine the first four ingredients and stir until mixed. Pour into tall glasses filled with ice.

2 Fill the glasses to the top with sparkling water, garnish, and serve.

Whiskey Sour
Makes 4 servings

Time: 5 minutes

One of the precursors of today's frozen, blended drinks, this can be made in a blender but is still best shaken. You can use any liquor, from vodka to bourbon, to make a sour.

¾ cup (6 ounces) whiskey, any kind, or other spirits
1 tablespoon superfine sugar or 2 tablespoons Sugar
    Syrup (page 798), or to taste
¼ cup freshly squeezed lemon juice
Lemon twists for garnish

1 Combine the whiskey, sugar, and lemon juice in a shaker; add ice and shake.

2 Strain into cocktail glasses or pour with ice into cocktail glasses to serve on the rocks, garnish, and serve.

A Few Odd Drinks

These are not exactly cocktails, as are the drinks above, but are (usually) alcoholic drinks served at other times of day.

Sangria

Makes 12 or more servings

Time: 15 minutes

There is no "real" sangria recipe. Basically, you combine red wine with stronger alcohol (if you like), and plenty of fruit, some of which should be citrus. Here's one interpretation.

> 2 bottles (750 milliliters each) dry red wine
> 1 cup (8 ounces) rum or orange-flavored liqueur, such as Cointreau
> 1 orange, sliced
> 1 lemon, sliced
> 1 cup sliced fruit such as peaches (canned is acceptable), or more if desired
> Soda water or club soda (optional)

1. Mix together the first five ingredients.
2. Add soda water to taste if desired and serve in a pitcher.

Hot Buttered Rum

Makes 1 serving

The grown-up equivalent of hot cocoa—perfect when you're chilled to the bone. Add a pinch of ground cloves, cinnamon, and/or nutmeg if you like.

> 1 cup water
> 1 teaspoon butter
> 1 teaspoon sugar, or to taste
> 3 tablespoons (1½ ounces) rum

1. Bring 1 cup of water to a boil.
2. Place the remaining ingredients in a mug and pour boiling water over them. Stir and serve.

Mulled Wine or Cider

Makes 4 to 6 servings

Time: 15 minutes

Do not boil the wine; just warm it gently.

> 1 bottle (750 milliliters) dry red wine or cider
> 1 lemon, sliced
> 1 orange, sliced, plus several orange slices reserved for garnish
> ¼ teaspoon freshly grated nutmeg, or to taste
> 2 cloves
> 1 (3-inch) piece cinnamon stick or ½ teaspoon ground cinnamon
> Sugar to taste (optional)

1. Combine the first six ingredients in a medium saucepan; turn the heat to medium-low. Cook, stirring occasionally, until quite hot to the touch but not boiling. Add sugar if needed and stir to dissolve.
2. Strain out the solids and serve, garnished with fresh orange slices.

Egg Nog

Makes 4 servings

Time: 10 minutes

Real egg nog is a super-treat, with or without rum.

 3 eggs, separated
 2 tablespoons sugar, or to taste
 1/2 teaspoon vanilla extract
 3 cups milk or half-and-half
 1/2 cup rum (optional), or more if desired
 Freshly grated nutmeg to taste

1 Beat the yolks with the sugar until well blended. Stir in the vanilla and the milk or half-and-half and rum if desired.

2 Beat the egg whites and fold them in thoroughly. (You need not be too gentle; they should lighten the drink but not be discernible.) Top with grated nutmeg and serve.

Menus

Breakfasts
Weekday Breakfasts

Family Weekday Breakfast
    Weekday Morning Scrambled Eggs
    Onion Bagels
    Café au Lait

Summer Weekday Breakfast
    Quick and Easy Waffles
    Summer Fruit Compote
    Banana-Yogurt Shake

Winter Weekday Breakfast
    Oatmeal
    Macerated Dried Fruits with Cinnamon
    coffee or tea

Weekday Breakfast for One
    Cinnamon Toast for One
    orange juice
    Mexican Hot Chocolate

Weekday Wake-Up-Late Breakfast
    Crunchy Granola
    Broiled Grapefruit
    coffee or tea

Weekend Breakfasts

Reading-the-Sunday-Paper Breakfast
    Vegetable Frittata
    Rhubarb Compote with Dates
    English Muffins
    coffee or tea

Summer Weekend Breakfast
    Polenta Pancakes
    Peaches with Fresh Blueberry Sauce
    grapefruit juice
    coffee or tea

Winter Weekend Breakfast
    Welsh Rarebit (or Rabbit)
    Basic Breakfast Sausage
    Baked Pears
    tomato juice
    coffee or tea

A Baked Weekend Breakfast
    Baked Eggs with Tomato
    Yogurt or Buttermilk Biscuits
    fresh fruit
    coffee or tea

Sweet and Tangy Weekend Breakfast
    Baked Sweet Omelet
    Cranberry Nut Bread
    grapefruit juice
    Café au Lait

Brunches
Sit-Down Brunches

Classic Sit-Down Brunch
    Onion Quiche
    Yeasted Coffee Cake
    Broiled Bananas
    juice
    coffee and tea

Adult Sit-Down Brunch
    Herb Frittata
    Buckwheat Cakes
    Baked Apples
    Bloody Marys
    juice
    coffee and tea

Rich Sit-Down Brunch
    Ham and Cheese Soufflé
    Sour Cream or Yogurt Muffins
    Rich Berry Shake
    coffee and tea

Family Sit-Down Brunch
    Baked Eggs with Spinach
    Filled Sweet Crepes
    Nut Bread
    coffee and tea

Southern-Style Sit-Down Brunch
    Mint Juleps
    Roasted Buttered Nuts
    Simplest Cheese Straws
    Chicken in a Pot
    Fried Okra
    Steamed Fresh or Frozen Lima Beans
    Hush Puppies
    Pecan Pie

Indian-Style Sit-Down Brunch
 Indian-Spiced Duck with Lentils
 Indian-Style Split Pea Fritters
 Curried Rice Noodles with Vegetables
 Basic Steamed Cauliflower
 Coconut-Tapioca Pudding

Buffet Brunches

Open House Buffet Brunch
 Spanish Potato Omelet (Tortilla)
 Banana-Nut Muffins
 Spice Muffins
 Grilled Fruit Skewers with Ginger Syrup
 Pineapple-Berry Punch
 coffee and tea

Morning after Buffet Brunch
 Onion Frittata
 Cinnamon Rolls
 Blueberry Cobbler
 juice
 coffee and tea

Summer Buffet Brunch
 Basic Cheese Quiche
 Bagels Topped with Sesame Seeds, Poppy Seeds,
  Coarse Salt, etc.
 Zucchini or Pumpkin Bread
 Plums Poached in Orange Sauce
 Foamy Iced Coffee
 Iced Tea

New York–Style Buffet Brunch
 Bagels Topped with Sesame Seeds, Poppy Seeds,
  Coarse Salt, etc.
 Raisin Bagels
 Onion Bagels
 Cream Cheese Spread
 Gravlax
 tomato slices
 onion slices
 coffee and tea

Tex-Mex Buffet Brunch
 Bean Casserole with Hominy and Tortillas
 Corn Bread
 Coconut Rice
 Bloody Marys
 juice
 coffee and tea

Southern-Style Buffet Brunch
 Hoppin' John
 Flash-Cooked Hominy with Kale or Collards
 Poached Peaches with Red Wine and Spices
 coffee and tea

Italian-Style Buffet Brunch
 Marinated Mozzarella
 Peppers and Anchovies
 Spaghetti alla Carbonara
 Panzanella
 Ricotta Cheesecake
 espresso and cappuccino

Lunches

Light Lunches

Home Alone Lunch
  Potato Soup with Sorrel
  Carrot Salad with Cumin
  Whole Grain Bread
  Aunt Big's Gingersnaps

Italian Country-Style Light Lunch
  Minestrone
  Red and Green Salad
  Herb and Onion Bread
  Olive Oil Drop Cookies
  espresso

Sophisticated Italian-Style Light Lunch
  Garlic Soup with Rice or Orzo and Peas
  Eggplant Salad, Italian-Style
  Sourdough Bread
  Soft Fruit Sorbet
  espresso

Vegetarian Italian-Style Light Lunch
  White Bean Dip
  Caponata with Raisins and Pine Nuts
  Easiest and Best French Bread
  Basic Vanilla Frozen Yogurt

Japanese-Style Light Lunch
  Miso Soup
  Seaweed and Cucumber Salad
  Stir-Fried Broccoli
  Basic Short- or Medium-Grain Rice, Version II
  fresh fruit

Middle Eastern-Style Light Lunch
  Hummus
  Lentil Soup
  Pita Bread
  fresh fruit

Light Seafood Lunch
  Lower-Fat Clam or Fish Chowder
  Crackers
  Braised Quartered Artichokes with Tarragon
  Meringues

Light Continental Lunch
  Salade Niçoise
  Fastest Yeast Bread
  Biscotti

Greek-Style Light Lunch
  Egg-Lemon Soup
  Simple Greek Salad
  Whole Grain Flatbread
  Lighter Rolled Cookies

Israeli-Style Light Lunch
  Borscht
  Gefilte Fish
  Couscous Salad with Mint and Parsley
  Challah
  fresh fruit

Lunches to Pack

Classic Deli Lunch
    Reuben
    Kosher Pickles, the Right Way
    Brownies

Everyday Bag Lunch
    Chicken Breast Sandwich with Spinach
    Spicy Coleslaw
    Classic Chocolate Chip Cookies

Brown Bag Lunch for School
    Tuna Without Mayo
    celery sticks
    Marble Cake

Offbeat Bag Lunch
    Curried Pork Tenderloin Sandwich with
      Chutney and Arugula
    Cabbage and Carrot Salad
    Cream Cheese Brownies

Packed-in-Containers Bag Lunch
    Jicama and Orange Salad
    White Bean Salad
    Onion-Rye Bread
    Molasses-Spice Cookies

Lunch to Take to a Sick Friend
    Beef and Vegetable Soup
    Raisin or Nut-and-Raisin Bread
    Cream Cheese Spread
    Quick Coffee Cake

Picnic Lunches

Middle Eastern-Style Bag Lunch
    Mixed Veggie Sandwich with Tahini Dressing
    Chickpeas with Lemon
    Coconut Macaroons

Updated Classic Picnic
    Lemonade or Limeade
    Chicken Salad with Olive Oil and Chives
    Endives, Scallions, and Mint with Yogurt Dressing
    Classic American Potato Salad
    Apple-Pear Pie
    Gabrielle's Lemon Squares

Spicy Picnic
    Pineapple-Berry Punch
    Spiced Melon Balls
    Curried Chicken Salad
    Spicy Coleslaw
    Potato Salad with Double Mustard Dressing
    Gingerbread Men

Elegant Picnic
    Chicken or Duck Salad with Walnuts
    Cress and Barley Salad with Dill Vinaigrette
    Sorrel Salad with Hard-Cooked Eggs
    Simple Berry Tart
    Iced Tea

Offbeat Picnic
    Raspberry-Ade
    Salmon Salad with Beans
    Watercress and Sesame Salad
    Brioche
    Ambrosia

Hearty Picnic
Hard-Boiled Eggs
Chicken Salad with Cabbage and Mint
Mussel and Potato Salad
Arugula and Blue Cheese Salad
Deep-Dish Apple Pie with Streusel Topping
Ice Coffee

Early Fall Picnic
Beef Salad with Mint
Arborio Rice Salad with Peas
Orange, Onion, and Rosemary Salad
Spice Pound Cake

Sit-Down Lunches

Sit-Down Lunch with Children
Thick Chicken Soup with Rice or Noodles
Green Salad with Tomatoes
Chicken Cutlets with Seasoned Bread Crumbs
Quick-Braised Carrots with Butter
Parker House Rolls
Chocolate Drop Cookies
Orangeade

Summer Sit-Down Lunch
Grape-Lime Rickey and Other Sparkling Fruit
    Drinks
Summer Fruit Soup
Wild Greens Salad
Chicken in Lemon Sauce
Asparagus with Parmesan
Strawberry, Rhubarb, or Strawberry-Rhubarb
    Pie

Winter Sit-Down Lunch
Kale and Potato Soup
Caesar Salad
Veal Cutlets with Rosemary and Parmesan
Caramelized Small Onions
Beets in Vinaigrette
Chocolate Pudding

Classic Italian Sunday Lunch
Marinated Olives
Fettuccine with Spinach, Butter, and Cream
Roast Chicken with Onions and Parsley
Basic Simmered Chard
Crispy Sautéed Potatoes with Rosemary
Easiest and Best French Bread
Watercress and Endive Salad
Panna Cotta
espresso

French Seafood Sit-Down Lunch
Black Olive Paste
Easiest and Best French Bread
Pasta with Provençal Seafood Sauce
Whiting or Other Small Whole Fish Baked in
    White Wine
Sautéed Summer Squash or Zucchini
Beet and Fennel Salad
Bitter Chocolate Sorbet

Hearty French Sit-Down Lunch
Garlicky Beef Daube
Easiest and Best French Bread
Simmered Brussels Sprouts
Baked Chard in Béchamel
Mesclun with Goat Cheese and Croutons
Old-Fashioned Baked Custard

Chinese-Style Sit-Down Lunch
Pot Stickers or Steamed Dumplings
Fried Rice with Greens
Stir-Fried Shrimp with Black Beans
Super-Spicy Beef with Orange Flavor
"Dry-Fried" String Beans, Chinese-Style
fresh fruit

Indian-Style Sit-Down Lunch
Cumin-Scented Rice
Tandoori Chicken
Braised Cauliflower with Curry and Tomatoes
Indian Potato-Stuffed Flatbreads
Coconut Ice Cream

Mexican-Style Sit-Down Lunch
Cheese Quesadillas
Chicken with Rice
Twice-Cooked ("Refried") Beans with Cumin
Basic Baked, Steamed, or Sautéed Chayote
Wheat Flour Tortillas
Flan

Southern-Style Sit-Down Lunch
Fried Chicken
Okra, Corn, and Tomato Stew
Dandelion Greens with Bacon
Lighter, Richer Corn Bread
Apple Pandowdy

Mother's Day Lunch
Prosciutto and Melon
Broiled Fillets with Mustard and Herbs
Pilaf with Onions, Raisins, and Pine Nuts
Braised Fennel with Onions and Vinegar
Linzer Torte

Father's Day Lunch
Stuffed Mushrooms
Roast Leg of Lamb with Garlic and Coriander
  Seeds
Potato Croquettes
Turnips in Mustard Sauce
Coconut Custard Pie

Birthday Party—10 Years Old
Grape-Lime Rickey and other Sparkling Fruit
  Drinks
Basic Meatballs
Baked Sweet Potatoes
Fried Onion Rings
Chocolate Layer Cake
Butterscotch Ice Cream

Birthday Party—20 Years Old
Sangria
Beef-Filled Samosas
Chicken and Garlic Stew
Basic Polenta (any version)
Collards or Kale, Brazilian-Style
Baked Spanish Onions
Coconut Layer Cake

Birthday Party—30 Years Old
Vodka Martinis
Pakoras
Grilled or Broiled Cornish Hens with Vinegar
Brown Rice with Lentils and Apricots
Braised Cabbage with Wine and Nutmeg
Basic Simmered, Steamed, or Microwaved
  Broccoli or Broccoli Raab
Angel Food Cake

Buffet Lunches

Birthday Party—40 Years Old
Whiskey Sours
Phyllo Triangles with Cheese
Roast Cod with Potatoes, Onions, and Olive Oil
Rice with Fresh Herbs
White Beans, Tuscan-Style
Sautéed Eggplant
Pears Sautéed in Butter

Birthday Party—Stopped Counting
Old-Fashioneds
Simplest Cheese Straws
Risotto with Vegetables
Flageolets, French-Style
Cardoons and Onions Cooked in Cream
Braised Endive, Escarole, or Radicchio with
   Proscuitto
Winter Fruit Compote

Feed-a-Cold Lunch
Pasta and Bean Soup
Tuna Melt
Pureed Butternut Squash with Ginger
Chocolate Custard

Starve-a-Fever Lunch
Chicken Soup with Rice or Noodles
Crackers
Tapioca Pudding

Elegant Buffet Lunch
Champagne Cocktails
Iced Tea
Cold Poached Salmon with Lime-Ginger Sauce
Tender Greens with Peanuts and Tomatoes
Shrimp Salad, Mediterranean-Style
Sourdough Bread
Strawberries with Balsamic Vinegar

Seafood-Lovers' Buffet Lunch
Smoked Salmon or Trout Dip
Crackers
Shrimp Cocktail
Marinated Fresh Anchovies
Scallop Seviche
Crisp Sautéed Cucumbers with Lemon
Popovers
Lemon-Poppy Seed Cake

Vegetarian Buffet Lunch
Horseradish Dip
Roasted Eggplant Dip
Mashed Favas with Greens
Curried Bulgur with Nuts, Carrots, and Raisins
Vegetarian Lasagne
Baked Apples

Indian-Style Buffet Lunch
Lentil-Filled Samosas
Chicken with Indian Spices and Yogurt
Split Peas, Mung Beans, or Lentils with Curry
Pilaf with Indian Spices
Orange-Almond Cake

Dinners

Indoor Dinners

Winter Family Dinner
Stewed Chickpeas with Chicken
yellow rice
Roasted Root Vegetables
Simplest Apple Tart

Spring Family Dinner
Pasta and Beans with Shrimp
Basic Simmered or Steamed Carrots
Beets Baked in Foil
Brownies

Fall Family Dinner
Basic Meat Loaf
Bulgur with Spinach
Basic Simmered, Steamed, or Microwaved
    Green Beans
Peanut Butter Cookies

Summer Family Dinner
Grilled Chicken Salad
Tomato, Mozzarella, and Basil Salad
Sourdough Bread
Raspberry Gratin

Casual Dinner Party
Baked Ziti with Radicchio and Gorgonzola
Chicken Cutlets Roasted with Tomatoes
Broccoli Raab with Sausage and Grapes
Steamed Leeks with Tarragon
Frozen Berry Soufflé

Elegant Dinner Party
Herbed Goat Cheese
Crackers
Mushroom Spread for Toast
Waldorf Salad
Wine-Braised Quail with Herbs
Celeriac and Potato Puree
Chard with Garlic, Pine Nuts, and Currants
Wild Rice with White Rice
Death-by-Chocolate Torte
Lemon Cheesecake with Sour Cream Topping

Self-Serve Soup Party
Creamy Watercress, Spinach, or Sorrel Soup
Chicken Soup with Cabbage and Thin Noodles
White Bean Soup with Ham
White Pizza
Whole Grain Bread
Sourdough Bread
Golden Layer Cake *with* Chocolate Butter
    Cream Frosting

International Pizza Party
Cheese Quesadillas
Pissaladière
White Pizza with Clams
Baked Pizza with Tomato Sauce and Mozzarella
Pear Clafouti

Casual Dinner with Friends
Bruschetta with Roasted or Simmered Garlic
Pasta with Saffron-Cauliflower Sauce
Grilled, Broiled, or Roasted Red Tomatoes
Bruschetta
Rice Pudding

Dinner for Unexpected Guests
Lightning-Quick Fish Soup
The Best and Simplest Green Salad
Sautéed Cod or Other Fish Steaks in Green
    Sauce
Basic Braised Celery
Drop ("Emergency") Biscuits
Apple Crisp

Impressing-the-Boss Dinner
Plum Tomato Tart with Pesto
Pear and Gorgonzola Salad
Grilled Veal Chops on a Bed of Greens
Beet Roesti with Rosemary
Dinner Rolls
Lemon Mousse

Celebrating-Your-Raise Dinner
Broiled Lobster with Herb Stuffing
Braised Celery with Buttered Almonds
Roasted Eggplant with Garlic and Parsley
Strawberry Tart with Pastry Cream

"Italian" Dinner, Circa 1950
Linguine with Fresh Tomato Sauce and
    Parmesan
Veal "Parmigiana"
Garlic Bruschetta
Basic Boiled, Steamed, or Microwaved Spinach
Green Salad with Tomatoes
Sabayon or Zabaglione

Contemporary "Italian" Dinner
Bagna Cauda
Risotto with Pesto
Chicken Under a Brick
Cauliflower with Garlic and Anchovies
Tomato, Mozzarella, and Basil Salad
Granita
espresso

Chinese Banquet Dinner
Lighter, Steamed Wontons
Scallion Pancakes
Tea-Smoked Duck (or Chicken)
Stir-Fried Pork with Snow Peas and Ginger
Crispy Sea Bass or Other Small Whole Fish
    with Garlic-Ginger Sauce
Stir-Fried Asparagus with Garlic
Stir-Fried Cauliflower with Ginger and Oyster
    Sauce
Stir-Fried Cabbage
Shrimp or Pork Fried Rice with Peas
Basic Short-Grain Rice
oranges
pineapple

Cool Weather Japanese-Style Dinner
Vegetable or Fish Tempura
Crispy Skin Salmon with Gingery Greens
Cabbage and Carrot Salad
Braised Pumpkin, Japanese-Style
Basic Medium-Grain Rice
Pears Poached in Red Wine

Warm Weather Japanese-Style Dinner

Japanese Noodles with Shiitakes and Sesame
Ginger Scallops
Sushi-Style Spinach
Miso-Cured Vegetables
Basic Medium-Grain Rice
Plums Poached in Orange Sauce

Mexican-Style Dinner

Empanadas Filled with Beans and Mushrooms
Bean Burritos with Meat
Corn-Stuffed Peppers with Spicy Tomato Sauce
Sautéed Ripe Plantains
Lemon Custard

Southern-Style Dinner

"Oven-Fried" Catfish or Other Fillets
Basic Boiled Collards or Kale
Mashed Potatoes
Sweet Potato Biscuits
Peach and other Stone Fruit Pie

Southwestern-Style Dinner

Pan-Grilled Pork Chops
Bean Croquettes with Southwestern Flavors
Simple Sautéed Peppers
Bacon Corn Bread
Indian Pudding

Open-the-Package Dinner

Red Snapper or Other Fillets in Packages
Beets Baked in Foil
Corn-Stuffed Peppers with Spicy Tomato Sauce
Apple Turnovers

Vegetarian Feast

Marinated Olives
Baba Ghanoush
Vegetarian Red Beans
Brown Rice with Cashews and Herbs
Crisp-Cooked Asparagus
Grilled or Broiled Eggplant Slices with Miso
   Dressing
Summer Squash or Zucchini Pancakes
Focaccia
Chocolate Angel Food Cake

Light Dinner Before the Theater

Linguine with Fresh Herbs
Fennel Baked with Stock and Parmesan
Cold Cooked Greens, Greek-Style
Coffee Ice Cream

Comfort Food Dinner

Baked Macaroni and Cheese
Creamed Spinach
Quick Whole Wheat and Molasses Bread
Vanilla Pudding

Rent-a-Video-and-Relax Dinner

Mushroom-Barley Soup
White Pizza with Caramelized Onions and
   Vinegar
Braised Broccoli with Garlic and Wine
Sautéed Apples
Basic French Vanilla Ice Cream

Outdoor Dinners

Clambake
Basic Steamed Clams
Grilled or Roasted Corn
Baked Potatoes
Summer Squash or Zucchini Rounds Cooked in
  Butter
Chocolate Chip Ice Cream
Maple-Nut Ice Cream

Barbecue
The Basic Burgers
Grilled or Broiled Split Chicken with Honey
  and Mustard
Quick Pickled Vegetables
Grilled or Roasted Corn
The Best and Simplest Green Salad
Chocolate or Butterscotch Swirl Ice Cream
Chocolate Sauce

American Dinner from the Grill
Grilled Marinated Flank Steak OR
Grilled Mesclun-Stuffed Tuna or Swordfish Steaks
Grilled Mixed Vegetables
Wild Greens Salad
Strawberry Shortcakes

Italian-Style Dinner from the Grill
Broiled or Grilled Lamb Chops, Italian-Style
Grilled or Broiled Chicken Cutlets with Basil
  and Tomato
Grilled or Broiled Eggplant Slices
Watercress and Endive Salad
Lemon, Lime, or Grapefruit Sorbet
espresso

Indian-Style Dinner from the Grill
Chicken Satay
Grilled or Broiled Butterflied Lamb with
  Coconut Milk
Curried Eggplant with Potatoes
Coconut Ice Cream

Dinner-on-a-Stick from the Grill
Grilled or Broiled Beef and Vegetable Kebabs
Chicken Satay
Carrot Salad with Cumin
Grilled Fruit Skewers with Ginger Syrup

Dinner at the Beach House
Fried Chile-Spiced Clam Salad
Grilled Shrimp and Tomato Salad
Skewers of Swordfish, Tuna, or Other Steaks
  with Rosemary
Roasted, Broiled, or Grilled Asparagus
Rice Pilaf
Summer Pudding

Summer Dinner Party on the Patio
Minced Vegetable Dip
Anchovy Spread
Crackers
Roasted Gazpacho
Arugula and Blue Cheese Salad
Herb-Marinated Grilled Pork Chops
Grilled Leeks Vinaigrette
Pureed Parsnips
Basic Simmered, Steamed, or Microwaved
  Asparagus *with* Herb Butter
Peach-and-Berry Pie

Too-Hot-to-Move Dinner on the Porch
  Carpaccio
  Cold Cucumber and Dill Soup
  Vitello Tonnato
  Basic Steamed Artichokes
  Lemon Rice
  Strawberries with Swedish Cream

Special Occasion Dinners

Intimate New Year's Eve Dinner
  Champagne Cocktails
  Parmesan Spread for Toast
  Spaghetti with Eggplant
  Pan-Grilled Salmon Fillets with Lentils
  Braised Butternut or Other Winter Squash with
    Garlic
  Dinner Rolls
  Caramelized Apple Tart
  Chocolate Truffles

New Year's Eve Blowout Dinner
  Champagne Cocktails
  Gougères
  Cold Noodles with Sesame or Peanut Sauce
  Prime Rib for a Big Crowd
  Roasted Vegetables, Catalonian-Style
  Butter-Braised Radishes
  Frangipane Tart
  Candied Grapefruit Peel
  Hot Buttered Rum

Superbowl Dinner
  Real Buttered Popcorn
  Bean Dip for Tortilla Chips
  Guacamole
  Fried Tortilla Chips
  Fried Wontons or Egg Rolls
  Chili con Carne
  Basic Medium-Grain Rice
  Slow-Cooked Green Beans
  Marinated Roasted, Grilled, or Broiled Peppers
  Lemon Meringue Pie

Valentine's Day Dinner
  Pureed Tomato Soup
  Salmon Fillets in Red Wine
  Warm Lentils with Bacon
  Simmered, Steamed, or Microwaved Beets
  Couscous with Raisins and Pine Nuts
  Cherry Pie
  Chocolate Candies

Mardi Gras Dinner
  Sombreros
  Crab or Shrimp Spread
  Real Onion Dip
  Crackers
  Spicy Deep-Fried Catfish
  Corn Fritters
  Black Bean Salad
  Shrimp Jambalaya
  Crème Brulée

Passover Dinner
   Horseradish Dip
   matzo
   Chicken Soup with Matzo Balls
   Sweet Beef Brisket with Garlic
   Watercress and Endive Salad
   Basic Steamed Cauliflower
   Quick-Braised Carrots with Orange and Ginger
   Stewed Cherries

Easter Dinner
   Deviled (Stuffed) Eggs
   Roasted Pepper and Garlic Spread
   Crackers
   Mesclun with Goat Cheese and Croutons
   Baked Country Ham
   Sautéed Artichoke Hearts
   Grilled Spanish Onions
   Dinner Rolls
   Chocolate Crepes

Saint Patrick's Day
   Potato Soup with Leeks
   New England Boiled Dinner
   Cooked Onions and Apples
   Fastest Yeast Bread
   Bread Pudding

Chinese New Year Dinner
   Rice Paper Spring Rolls
   Stir-Fried Pork with Hoisin and Sesame Oil
   Stir-Fried Lobster with Black Bean Sauce
   Stir-Fried Tofu with Scallions
   Eggplant Salad with Sesame Dressing
   Quick Stir-Fried Snow Peas or Sugar Snap Peas
   Crisp Pan-Fried Noodle Cake
   Stir-Fried Brown Rice with Vegetables and Soy
   fresh fruit

Cinco de Mayo Dinner
   Frozen Margaritas
   Empanadas Filled with Beans and Mushrooms
   Chicken Adobo
   Coconut Rice with Chipotles
   Collards or Kale with Double Garlic
   Sautéed Bananas

Memorial Day Dinner
   Lamburgers with Smoked Mozzarella
   Tabbouleh
   Oven-Baked Ratatouille
   Lemon Pound Cake

Fourth of July Dinner
   Sweet Blueberry Soup with Yogurt
   Broiled or Grilled Chicken Wings
   Slow-Grilled Ribs with Chris's Great Rub
   Basic Steamed Corn
   Grilled, Broiled, or Roasted Red Tomatoes
   Traditional Apple Pie

Labor Day Dinner
Grilled Swordfish, Tuna, or Other Steaks with
    Corn and Tomato Relish
Garlicky Pureed Beans
Pan-Fried Green and/or Red Tomatoes
Quinoa "Pilaf"
Summer Pudding

First Day of School Dinner
Roast Chicken with Roasted New Potatoes
Leeks au Gratin
Sautéed Mushrooms with Garlic
Kasha with Golden Brown Onions
Oatmeal Cookies

World Series Dinner
Bruschetta with Tomatoes and Basil
Roast Pork with Dried Fruits
Basic Boiled, Steamed, or Microwaved Spinach
Sauerkraut with Juniper Berries
Apple Brown Betty

Columbus Day Dinner
Fritto Misto
Linguine with Clams
Red and Green Salad
Grilled Portobello Mushrooms
Roasted Garlic
Sourdough Bread
Apple-Raisin Bread Pudding

Halloween Dinner
Simplest Split Pea Soup
Sesame-Coated Chicken Cutlets
Oven-Braised Sweet-and-Sour Pumpkin
Fudge
Mulled Wine or Cider

Thanksgiving Dinner
Roast Turkey and Gravy, without Stuffing
Bread Stuffing with Sage and Chestnuts
Creamed Spinach
Mashed Potatoes
Succotash
Buttered Peas
Pumpkin Pie

Hanukkah Dinner
Roast Chicken with Rice-and-Nut Stuffing
Potato Pancakes (any version)
Cabbage Cooked with Apples
Quick-Braised Carrots with Butter
Two-Apple Tart
Peanut Brittle
Candied Nuts

Christmas Dinner
Wild Greens Salad
Basic Roast Goose
Bread Stuffing with Mushrooms
Pureed Turnips
Baked Pumpkin Slices
Broiled, Grilled, or Roasted Chestnuts
Lemon, Orange, or Grand Marnier Soufflé
Candied Orange or Lemon Peel
Egg Nog

In-Between Meals

Afternoon Teas

Child's Birthday Dinner
Roast Chicken Parts with Herbs and Olive Oil
Basic Simmered or Steamed Carrots
French Fries
Golden or Chocolate Cupcakes *with* Mocha
    Butter Cream Frosting

Adult's Birthday Dinner
Spicy Lentil Soup
Sicilian Onion Pizza
Skate with Brown Butter
Broiled Sunchokes with Parmesan
Duxelles
Key Lime Pie

Sabbath Eve Dinner
Endives, Scallions, and Mint with Yogurt
    Dressing
Broiled or Grilled Chicken with Lemon and
    Herbs
Leeks Braised in Butter or Oil
Basic Simmered, Steamed, or Microwaved
    Broccoli or Broccoli Raab *with* Lime or
    Lemon Butter
Challah
Lemon Pound Cake

Savory Tea
Simplest Cheese Straws
Deviled (Stuffed) Eggs
Salmon Sandwich with Cress and Juniper
tea

Sweet Tea
Lacy Oatmeal Cookies
Sour Cream Drop Cookies
Cream Scones
Coconut Macaroons
Sponge Cake
tea

Summer Tea
Roasted Buttered Nuts
Crab or Shrimp Spread
Cream Crackers
Orange-Nut Bread
Cheese Biscuits
Iced Tea

Winter Tea
Roasted Pepper and Garlic Spread
Herbed Sandwich Bread
Spinach-Cheese Triangles
Butter Drop Cookies
Refrigerator (Rolled) Cookies
tea

Cocktail Parties

High Society Cocktail Party
  Spiced Buttered Nuts
  Pastry Cheese Straws
  Eggs Stuffed with Spinach
  Anchovy Spread
  Crackers
  Manhattans
  Rob Roys

Tropical Cocktail Party
  Plantain Chips
  Potato-Filled Samosas
  Feta Cheese Dip
  Minced Vegetable Dip
  Pita Bread
  Piña Coladas
  Frozen Daiquiris

Round-Up-Your-Closest-Friends Cocktail Party
  Real Onion Dip
  Guacamole
  Goat Cheese–Stuffed Figs
  Whole Grain Flatbread
  Crackers
  Margaritas
  Sangria

Cocktail Party in Your First Apartment
  Sautéed Buttered Nuts
  Bean Dip for Tortilla Chips
  Baked Tortilla Chips
  Quick Marinated Mushrooms
  Screwdrivers
  Sea Breezes

Celebration Cocktail Party
  Herb-Stuffed Eggs
  Taramasalata
  Stuffed Grape Leaves
  Crackers
  Phyllo Triangles with Greens
  Gin or Vodka Gimlets
  Martinis

Miscellaneous

Sweet Snacks

- Mocha Hot Chocolate
- Rich Orange Milkshake
- Caramel Rolls
- Sweet and Rich Muffins
- Orange-Date Rolls
- Shortbread
- Milk Toast for One

Savory Snacks

- Grilled Cheese, Simple and Complex
- Marinated Olives *and* Crackers
- Baked White Pizza with Potatoes
- Onion Pan Bread
- Savory Muffins
- Quick Pickled Vegetables, Asian-Style
- Fattoush

Good Candidates to Bring to a Pot Luck

- Pastitsio
- Classic Lasagne, Bolognese-Style
- Bean and Tomato Casserole
- Chili non Carne
- Beans and Greens Gratin

Good Candidates for a Bake Sale Donation

- Carrot Bread
- Savory Muffins
- Coffee Cake Muffins
- Butterscotch Brownies
- Fancier Rolled Cookies
- Peanut Brittle

Good Courses for a Progressive Dinner Party

Soups
- Onion Soup
- Vichyssoise
- Corn, Tomato, and Zucchini Soup with Basil
- Shrimp Soup with Cumin
- Basic Red Gazpacho

Salads
- Arugula and Blue Cheese Salad
- Caesar Salad
- Beet and Fennel Salad
- Orange, Onion, and Rosemary Salad
- Seafood Salad, Adriatic-Style

Entrées
- Cod or Other Thick Fillets in Neapolitan Tomato Sauce
- Braised Whole Chicken with Tarragon
- Roast Duck with Orange Sauce
- Roast Pork Shoulder, Puerto Rican-Style
- Roast Rack of Lamb with Persillade

Desserts
- Death-by-Chocolate Torte
- Chocolate Mousse
- Pecan Pie
- Apple-Almond Tart
- Raspberry Fool

Quick Recipes

Recipes that Require Thirty Minutes or Less to Prepare

Twenty years ago, if you could cook a dish in under an hour it was considered fast. Now that's on the long side, and people strive to put something together in twenty minutes. The foods on this list don't always meet that goal, but many do, and the others come close.

With both this list and the following, I have had to make some judgment calls and some assumptions. When a preparation time is given as "thirty minutes," it always means **roughly** thirty minutes; so if it is a stir-fry, or some equally easy and uncomplicated dish, I put it in this list. If it is a baked dish, or something with a few different components, I've bumped it up to

the "Sixty Minutes or Less" list. (I made similar judgments with that list; if a dish takes roughly sixty minutes but needs to be cooked until tender, I usually omitted it.) Grilled foods make it onto both lists even though preheating a grill can sometimes take three-quarters of an hour; you can always plan a little ahead, or use the broiler. And so on.

As for assumptions, there are many dishes including beans, for example, that are quick to prepare as long as you have cooked (or canned) beans; so I've included them here although, obviously, if you have to cook beans from scratch they don't fit in the time parameters.

In short, like all lists these are imperfect. But they'll certainly steer you towards the fastest recipes in the book.

Appetizers

Sautéed Buttered Nuts
Spiced Buttered Nuts
Real Buttered Popcorn
Simplest Cheese Straws
Pastry Cheese Straws
Marinated Olives
Deviled (Stuffed) Eggs
Anchovied Eggs
Herb-Stuffed Eggs
Eggs Stuffed with Spinach
Spiced Melon Balls
Minced Vegetable Dip
Horseradish Dip
Real Onion Dip
Smoked Salmon or Trout Dip
Bean Dip for Tortilla Chips
Feta Cheese Dip
Taramasalata (Greek Fish Roe Dip)
Guacamole
Hummus
White Bean Dip
Cream Cheese Spread
Roasted Pepper and Garlic Spread
Anchovy Spread
Crab or Shrimp Spread
Herbed Goat Cheese
Goat Cheese–Stuffed Figs
Mushroom Spread for Toast
Parmesan Toasts
Black Olive Paste (Tapenade)
Bagna Cauda (Warm Anchovy Dip)
Fried Tortilla Chips
Baked Tortilla Chips
Plantain Chips
Prosciutto and Melon
Quick Marinated Mushrooms
Stuffed Mushrooms
Peppers and Anchovies
Wrappers for Wontons or Egg Rolls
Rice Paper Spring Rolls
Cheese Quesadillas

Soups

Vastly Improved Canned Chicken Broth
Vastly Improved Chicken Broth, Chinese-Style
Egg Drop Soup
Fast Fish Stock
Shrimp Stock
"Boiled Water" (Garlic Soup) note it should be
    indexed and x-refed with this parenthetical
    addition in all instances
Roasted Garlic Soup
Garlic Soup with Spinach and Tomatoes
Garlic Soup with Rice or Orzo and Peas
Lime and Garlic Soup
Miso Soup
Miso Soup with Spinach and Mushrooms
Kale and Potato Soup
Kale Soup with Soy and Lime
Simple Potato Soup with Carrots
Potato Soup with Leeks
Pureed Potato Soup with Leeks
Potato Soup with Sorrel
Mushroom Soup
Cream of Mushroom Soup
Tomato Soup, Three Ways
Cream of Tomato Soup
Corn, Tomato, and Zucchini Soup with Basil
Creamy Watercress, Spinach, or Sorrel Soup
Watercress Soup with Potatoes
Cream of Broccoli—or Any Vegetable—Soup
Egg and Herb Soup
Spinach and Egg Soup
Black Bean Soup
No-Holds-Barred Clam or Fish Chowder
Lightning-Quick Fish Soup
Chicken Soup with Rice or Noodles
Thick Chicken Soup with Rice or Noodles

Chicken Soup with Butter Dumplings
Chicken Soup with Passatelli
Chicken Soup with Tortellini and Watercress
Egg-Lemon Soup (Avgolemono)
Chicken Soup with Cabbage and Thin Noodles
Garlic Croutons
Herb Croutons

Salads

Basic Vinaigrette
Walnut Oil Vinaigrette
Lemon or Lime Vinaigrette
Lemon- or Lime-Thyme Vinaigrette
Lemon- or Lime-Dill Vinaigrette
Lemon- or Lime-Tarragon Vinaigrette
Lemon- or Lime-Onion Vinaigrette
Orange Vinaigrette
Nutty Vinaigrette
Anchovy-Caper Vinaigrette
Vinaigrette in the Style of Mayonnaise
Creamy Vinaigrette
The Best and Simplest Green Salad
Simple Greek Salad
Green Salad with Tomatoes
Wild Greens Salad
Watercress and Endive Salad
Arugula and Blue Cheese Salad
Cabbage and Carrot Salad
Caesar Salad
Chicken Caesar Salad
Mesclun with Goat Cheese and Croutons
Dandelion Greens with Bacon
Cold Cooked Greens, Greek-Style
Sorrel Salad with Hard-Cooked Eggs
Endives, Scallions, and Mint with Yogurt
  Dressing
Tender Greens with Peanuts and Tomatoes
Red and Green Salad
Watercress and Sesame Salad

Carrot Salad with Cumin
Tomato, Mozzarella, and Basil
Jicama and Orange Salad
Orange, Onion, and Rosemary Salad
Spicy Coleslaw
Waldorf Salad
Pear and Gorgonzola Salad
Seaweed and Cucumber Salad
Black Bean Salad
White Bean Salad
Fattoush (Lebanese Bread Salad)
Panzanella (Italian Bread Salad)
Couscous Salad with Mint and Parsley
Cress and Barley Salad with Dill Vinaigrette
Curried Chicken Salad
Chicken Salad with Cabbage and Mint
Chicken or Duck Salad with Walnuts
Beef Salad with Mint
Warm Salad of Scallops and Tender Greens
Shrimp Salad, Mediterranean-Style
Fried Chile-Spiced Clam Salad

Pasta

Basic Tomato Sauce
Buttery Tomato Sauce
Aromatic Tomato Sauce
Tomato Sauce with Wine
Thickened Tomato Sauce
Tomato Sauce with Bay Leaves
Tomato Sauce with Herbs
Pureed Tomato Sauce
Pink Tomato Sauce
Mozzarella Tomato Sauce
Puttanesca Sauce
Tuna Sauce
Fiery Tomato Sauce
Mushroom Sauce
Linguine with Fresh Tomato Sauce and Parmesan
Elegant Fresh Tomato Sauce

Garlicky Fresh Tomato Sauce
Fresh Tomato Sauce with Olive Oil
Lower-Fat Fresh Tomato Sauce
Fresh Tomato Sauce with Pesto
Penne Arrabbiata
Pasta with Onion and Bacon
   (Linguine all'Amatriciana)
Pasta with Whole Cloves of Garlic
   (Maccheroni alla San Giovanniello)
Pasta with Raw Tomato Sauce
   (Linguine con Salsa Cruda)
Pasta "Primavera"
Pasta with Butter, Sage, and Parmesan
Pasta with Olive Oil and Sage
Pasta with Butter, Eggs, Cream, and Parmesan
   (Fettuccine Alfredo)
Spaghetti alla Carbonara
Spaghetti with Zucchini and Eggs
Orzo "Risotto"
Ziti with Creamy Gorgonzola Sauce
Fettuccine with Spinach, Butter, and Cream
Penne with Ricotta, Parmesan, and Peas
Linguine with Garlic and Oil
Linguine with Chickpeas
Linguine with Anchovies and Walnuts
Linguine with Fresh Herbs
Pasta with Porcini
Spaghetti with Pesto
Linguine with Clams
Clams with Pesto and Pasta
Linguine with Scallops
Ricotta-and-Spinach Filling for Fresh Pasta
Cheese Filling for Fresh Pasta
Stronger Cheese Filling
Eggless Cheese Filling
Dashi
"Secondary" Dashi:
Japanese Noodles with Stock
Japanese Noodles with Miso
Japanese Noodles with Egg

Japanese Noodles with Chicken, Vegetables,
   Fish, or Meat
Cold Soba Noodles with Mushrooms
Chinese Egg Noodles in Stock
Stir-Fried Chinese Noodles with Vegetables
Stir-Fried Noodles with Meat or Shrimp
Stir-Fried Noodles with Stir-Fried Vegetables
Crisp Pan-Fried Noodle Cake
Cold Noodles with Sesame or Peanut Sauce
Quick Rice Noodles with Charred Onions and
   Cilantro

Grains

Simple Precooked Grains
Precooked Grains with Butter or Oil
Precooked Grains with Garlic or Onions
Precooked Grains with Mushrooms
Precooked Grains with Toasted Spice
Precooked Grains with Toasted Nuts or Seeds
Precooked Grains with Pesto
Basic Bulgur
Curried Bulgur with Nuts, Carrots,
   and Raisins
Bulgur Pilaf with Vermicelli
Basic Polenta, Version I
Basic Polenta, Version III
Hush Puppies
Basic Couscous
Couscous with Raisins and Pine Nuts
Flash-Cooked Hominy with Kale or Collards
Basic Kasha
Kasha with Golden Brown Onions
Basic Millet
Basic Quinoa
Quinoa "Pilaf"
Quinoa Stuffing with Bacon and Nuts
Basic Long-Grain Rice
Basic Short- or Medium-Grain Rice, Version I
Basic Short- or Medium-Grain Rice, Version III

Rice Pilaf
Pilaf with Onions, Raisins, and Pine Nuts
Pilaf with Wine and Tomatoes
Pilaf with Spinach
Pilaf with Indian Spices ("Biryani")
Coconut Rice
Coconut Rice with Beans
Coconut Rice with Chipotles
Cumin-Scented Rice
Rice with Fresh Herbs
Rice with Pesto or Herb Oil
Fried Rice with Egg
Shrimp or Pork Fried Rice with Peas
Fried Rice with Greens

Breads

Crackers
Cream Crackers
Yogurt or Buttermilk Biscuits
Baking Powder Biscuits
Cheese Biscuits
Drop ("Emergency") Biscuits
Sweet Potato Biscuits
Cream Scones
Pizza
Bruschetta
Bruschetta with Roasted or Simmered Garlic
Bruschetta with Tomatoes and Basil
Grilled Cheese, Simple and Complex
Tuna Melt
Reuben
Cuban Sandwich
Tuna without Mayo
Gert's Pepper and Onion Sandwich
Chicken Breast Sandwich with Spinach
Salmon Sandwich with Cress and Juniper
Pita with Ground Lamb and Zucchini
Bean Burritos
Bean Burritos with Meat

Fish

Broiled Flatfish or Other White Fillets
Broiled Fillets with Mustard and Herbs
Broiled Fillets with Garlic-Parsley Sauce
Broiled Fillets with Tomato Salsa
Broiled Fillets with Dill Butter
Broiled Fillets with Sweet Soy
Sautéed Flatfish or Other White Fillets
Sautéed Fillets with Capers
Sautéed Fillets with Curry and Lime
Sautéed Fillets with Soy Sauce
Sautéed Fillets with Sesame Crust
Extra-Crisp Red Snapper or Other Fillets with
    Butter-Toasted Pecans
Extra-Crisp Red Snapper or Other Fillets with
    Apples
"Oven-Fried" Catfish or Other Fillets
Deep-Fried Catfish or Other Fillets
Spicy Deep-Fried Catfish
Poached Catfish or Other Fillets in Ginger Sauce
Broiled Cod or Other Thick White Fillets
Broiled Fillet with Flavored Bread Crumbs
Broiled Fillet with White Wine and Herbs
Broiled Fillet with Tomatoes and Olives
Broiled Fillet with Pesto
Broiled Fillet with Pureed Parsley
Sautéed Cod or Other Thick White Fillets
Extra-Crisp Sautéed Cod or Other Thick White
    Fillets
Sautéed Cod or Other Thick White Fillets with
    Spicy Garlic Sauce
Sautéed Cod or Other Thick White Fillets with
    Raisins and Pine Nuts
Red Snapper or Other Thick White Fillets,
    Provençal-Style
Grilled Swordfish, Tuna, or Other Steaks with
    Mustard Sauce
Herb-Rubbed Grilled Swordfish, Tuna, or Other
    Steaks
Grilled Mesclun-Stuffed Tuna or Swordfish Steaks

Sautéed Cod or Other Fish Steaks
Sautéed Cod or Other Fish Steaks in Green Sauce
Sautéed Cod or Other Fish Steaks with Dill and
  Scallions
Halibut or Other Steaks Simmered in Soy Broth
Basic Grilled or Broiled Salmon Steaks
Pan-Grilled Salmon Fillets with Lemon
Pan-Grilled Salmon Fillets with Sesame Oil
  Drizzle
Pan-Grilled Salmon Fillets with Lentils
Salmon Roasted in Butter
Salmon Roasted with Herbs
Salmon Roasted with Buttered Almonds
Salmon Fillets in Red Wine
Salmon Croquettes
Sautéed Trout
Sautéed Trout with Bacon
Sautéed Trout with Almonds (Trout Amandine)
Broiled Bluefish or Mackerel Fillets with Lime
  Mustard
Broiled Bluefish or Mackerel Fillets with Vinegar
  and Mint
Broiled Bluefish or Mackerel Fillets with Herbs
Broiled Bluefish or Mackerel Fillets with Tomato,
  Ginger, and Garlic
Simmered Bluefish or Mackerel Fillets
Whiting or Other Small Whole Fish Baked in
  White Wine
Pan-Fried Croaker or Other Small Whole Fish
Crispy Sea Bass or Other Small Whole Fish with
  Garlic-Ginger Sauce
Simmered Flounder or other Flatfish
Steamed Black Sea Bass or Other Small Whole
  Fish with Black Beans
Shad Roe
Skate with Brown Butter
"Grilled" Sardines
Sautéed Smelts with Herb Butter
Shrimp Cocktail
Shrimp, My Way

Shrimp "Scampi"
Shrimp with Spicy Orange Flavor
Spicy Grilled or Broiled Shrimp
Roast Shrimp with Tomatoes
Roast Shrimp with Orange and Rosemary
Shrimp "Marinara" with Pasta or Rice
Shrimp with Feta Cheese
Boiled Blue or Rock Crab
Grilled or Steamed King Crab Legs
Dungeness Crab Salad
Sautéed Soft-Shell Crabs, Version I
Sautéed Soft-Shell Crabs, Version II
Grilled Soft-Shell Crabs
Basic Boiled or Steamed Lobster
Stir-Fried Squid with Basil and Garlic
Grilled Hard-Shell Clams
Stir-Fried Littlenecks in Hot Sauce
Steamed Littlenecks with Butter and Herbs
Basic Steamed Clams ("Steamers")
Sautéed Oysters
Grilled Scallops
Roasted Sea Scallops
Sautéed Scallops
Buttery Scallops
Ginger Scallops

Poultry

Broiled or Grilled Chicken with Pesto
Broiled or Grilled Chicken with Mustard
Broiled or Grilled Chicken with Lemon and
  Herbs
Broiled or Grilled Chicken with Cilantro and
  Lime
Broiled or Grilled Chicken with Soy and Ginger
Broiled or Grilled Chicken with Citrus Sauce
Basic Grilled or Broiled Chicken Cutlets
Grilled or Broiled Chicken Cutlets with Olive Oil
Grilled or Broiled Chicken Cutlets with Honey
  and Cumin

Grilled or Broiled Chicken Cutlets in Sweet Soy
Marinade ("Chicken Teriyaki")
Grilled or Broiled Chicken Cutlets with Basil
and Tomato
Grilled or Broiled Chicken Cutlets with
Ginger and Cilantro
Grilled or Broiled Chicken Cutlets with
Capers and Tomatoes
Grilled or Broiled Chicken Cutlets with
Cracked Pepper
Grilled or Broiled Chicken Cutlets with
Mixed Spices
Grilled or Broiled Chicken Cutlets with
Herb Marinade
Grilled or Broiled Chicken Cutlets with
Horseradish Sauce
Stir-Fried Chicken with Chinese Cabbage
Stir-Fried Chicken with Orange Flavor
Stir-Fried Chicken with Broccoli or
Cauliflower
Stir-Fried Chicken with Kale or Collards
Stir-Fried Chicken with Basil and Chiles
(Thai-Style)
Stir-Fried Chicken with Chinese Mushrooms
Stir-Fried Chicken with Spinach
Basic Sautéed Chicken Cutlets
Chicken Cutlets with Seasoned Bread Crumbs
Extra-Crisp Chicken Cutlets
Spice-Coated Chicken Cutlets
Herbed Chicken Cutlets
Sesame-Coated Chicken Cutlets
Sautéed Chicken Cutlets with Quick Sauce
Sautéed Chicken Cutlets with Cream Sauce
Sautéed Chicken Cutlets with Ginger
Sautéed Chicken Cutlets with Lime Sauce
Crunchy Curried Chicken Breasts
Herb-Roasted Chicken Cutlets
Chicken in Lemon Sauce
Chicken in Ginger Sauce
Chicken and Fruit in Curry Sauce

Broiled or Grilled Chicken Wings
Sesame-Broiled Chicken Wings
Stir-Fried Chicken Wings with Black Bean Sauce

Meat

Grilled Steak, American-Style
Grilled Porterhouse (T-bone) Steak
Broiled Steak
Pan-Grilled Steak
Pan-Grilled/Oven-Roasted Steak
Bistro Steak
Tuscan Steak
Pan-Seared Steak with Red Wine Sauce
Chopped Steak with Wine Sauce
The Basic Burger
Corned Beef (or Roast Beef) Hash
Stir-Fried Spicy Beef with Basil
Super-Spicy Beef with Orange Flavor
Stir-Fried Beef with Onions
Stir-Fried Beef with Tomatoes and Black Beans
Grilled or Broiled Veal Chop
Grilled Veal Chops on a Bed of Greens
Veal Cutlets, 1950s-Style
Veal Cutlets with Rosemary and Parmesan
Sautéed Calf's Liver
Sautéed Liver with Onions
Sautéed Liver with Apples
Broiled or Grilled Veal Heart
Veal Kidneys with Sherry
Sautéed Pork Chops, Seven Ways
Pork Chops with Sherry-Garlic Sauce
Pork Chops with Apples
Pork Chops with Vinegar
Pork Chops with Mustard
Pork Chops with Butter, Chervil, and Shallots
Grilled Pork Chops
Pan-Grilled Pork Chops
Sweet Simmered Pork Chops
Stir-Fried Pork with Spinach

Stir-Fried Pork with Sweet Onions
Stir-Fried Pork with Snow Peas and Ginger
Stir-Fried Pork with Hoisin and Sesame Oil
Sautéed Medallions of Pork with Lemon
    and Parsley
Sautéed "Italian" Sausage with Peppers
    and Onions
Sausages and Mashed Potatoes
    (Bangers and Mash)
Sautéed Sausages with Grapes
Basic Grilled or Broiled Lamb Chops
Broiled or Grilled Lamb Chops, Italian-Style
Roast Saddle of Lamb
Roast Rack of Lamb with Persillade
Lamb Medallions with Shallots, Tarragon,
    and Red Wine
Lamburgers with Smoked Mozzarella
Lamb Patties with Bulgur (Kibbe)

Beans

Pressure-Cooked Beans
Buttered Beans
Beans with Olive Oil
White Bean Puree
Pureed Beans with Cream
Garlicky Pureed Beans
Sautéed Beans and Tomatoes
Twice-Cooked ("Refried") Beans with Cumin
Bean and Tomato Casserole
Moors and Christians (Black Beans and Rice,
    Spanish-Style)
Red Beans and Rice
Roasted Chickpeas
Simple Bean Croquettes
Bean Croquettes with Southwestern Flavors
Bean Croquettes with Asian Flavors
Bean-and-Corn Pancakes
Stir-Fried Tofu with Scallions
Spicy Tofu with Ground Pork

Vegetables

Basic Simmered, Steamed, or Microwaved
    Asparagus
Roasted, Broiled, or Grilled Asparagus
Asparagus with Parmesan
Stir-Fried Asparagus, Three Ways
Stir-Fried Asparagus with Soy
Stir-Fried Asparagus with Garlic
Crisp-Cooked Asparagus
Beets in Butter
Beets in Vinaigrette
Beet Roesti with Rosemary
Basic Simmered, Steamed, or Microwaved
    Broccoli or Broccoli Raab
Braised Broccoli with Garlic and Wine
Simmered Brussels Sprouts
Braised Cabbage with Wine and Nutmeg
Gingered Cabbage
Stir-Fried Cabbage
Basic Simmered or Steamed Cardoons
Basic Simmered or Steamed Carrots
Quick-Braised Carrots with Butter
Quick-Braised Carrots with Orange and Ginger
Basic Steamed Cauliflower
Cauliflower with Garlic and Anchovies
Stir-Fried Cauliflower with Ginger and
    Oyster Sauce
Braised Cauliflower with Curry and Tomatoes
Basic Braised Celery
Basic Simmered Chard
Chard with Garlic, Pine Nuts, and Currants
Basic Baked, Steamed, or Sautéed Chayote
Basic Boiled Collards or Kale
Collards or Kale with Double Garlic
Collards or Kale with Capers
Collards or Kale, Brazilian-Style
Basic Steamed Corn
Grilled or Roasted Corn
Grilled or Broiled Eggplant Slices
Sautéed Eggplant

Braised Fennel with Onions and Vinegar
Garlic Simmered in Oil and Vinegar
Garlic Bruschetta
Basic Simmered, Steamed, or Microwaved
  Green Beans
Steamed Fresh or Frozen Lima Beans
Steamed Limas in Cream
Succotash
Leeks Braised in Butter or Oil
Steamed Leeks with Tarragon
Grilled Leeks Vinaigrette
Sautéed Mushrooms with Garlic
Grilled Portobello Mushrooms
Grilled Spanish Onions
Caramelized Small Onions or Shallots
Pureed Parsnips
Buttered Peas
Quick Stir-Fried Snow Peas or Sugar Snap Peas
Simple Sautéed Peppers
Sautéed Ripe Plantains (Maduros)
Butter-Braised Radishes
Basic Boiled, Steamed, or Microwaved Spinach
Creamed Spinach
Sushi-Style Spinach
Summer Squash or Zucchini Rounds Cooked
  in Butter
Crisp-Cooked Sunchokes
Broiled Sunchokes with Parmesan
Microwaved or Simmered Sweet Potatoes
Pan-Fried Green and/or Red Tomatoes
Grilled, Broiled, or Roasted Red Tomatoes
Pureed Butternut Squash with Ginger
Braised Butternut or Other Winter Squash
  with Garlic

Fruit

Sautéed Apples
Broiled Bananas

Sautéed Bananas
Raspberry Fool
Stewed Cherries
Broiled Grapefruit
Ambrosia
Peaches with Fresh Blueberry Sauce
Mary Willoughby's Broiled Peaches
Pears Sautéed in Butter
Rhubarb Compote with Dates
Strawberries with Swedish Cream
Strawberries with Balsamic Vinegar
Summer Fruit Compote
Grilled Fruit Skewers with Ginger Syrup

Desserts

Milk Shakes, Malteds, and Frappes
Butterscotch Sauce
Chocolate Sauce
Hot Fudge Sauce
Raspberry, Strawberry, or Other Fruit Sauce
Blueberry Sauce
Vanilla Custard Sauce or Crème Anglaise
Sabayon or Zabaglione

Pies

Graham Cracker Crust
Rich Tart Crust
Cream Puff Pastry (Choux Pastry)

Cookies

Dark Chocolate Glaze
Vanilla Butter Cream Frosting
Chocolate Butter Cream Frosting
Mocha Butter Cream Frosting
Lemon or Orange Frosting

Eggs

Soft-Boiled Egg
Medium-Boiled Egg
Hard-Boiled Egg
Poached Eggs
Fried Eggs
Weekday Morning Scrambled Eggs
Scrambled Eggs with Cheese or Salsa
Scrambled Eggs with Onion
Scrambled Eggs with Spinach
Basic Omelet
Spanish Omelet
Western Omelet
Rich Buttermilk Waffles
Quick and Easy Waffles
Basic Pancakes
Light and Fluffy Pancakes
Blueberry Pancakes
Banana Pancakes
Buttermilk, Sour Milk, or Yogurt Pancakes
Buckwheat Cakes
Cottage Cheese and Sour Cream Pancakes
Crepes
Light, Simple Crepes
Pulled Bread
Cinnamon Toast for One
Milk Toast for One
French Toast
Welsh Rarebit (or Rabbit)
Grits
Oatmeal

Sauces

Basic Mayonnaise
Aioli, or Garlic Mayonnaise
Rouille
Real Tartar Sauce
Anchovy Mayonnaise
Herb Mayonnaise

"Safe" Mayonnaise
Handmade Mayonnaise
Russian Dressing
Skordalia (Eggless Greek Mayonnaise)
Cold Mustard Sauce
Smooth, English-Style Mustard
Wasabi
Sweet Herb Mustard
Basic Pesto
Pesto with Butter
Minimalist Pesto
Cilantro "Pesto"
Cilantro Pesto, Thai-Style
Arugula "Pesto"
Mint "Pesto"
Parsley "Pesto"
Anchovy Butter
Herb Butter
Mustard Butter
Horseradish or Wasabi Butter
Garlic Butter
Ginger-Garlic Butter
Jalapeño Butter
Ginger Butter
Balsamic Butter
Lime or Lemon Butter
Tahini Dressing
Yogurt-Avocado Dressing
Quick Blue Cheese Dressing
Cucumber-Yogurt Dip with Mint
Spicy Yogurt Sauce
Homemade Horseradish
Tomato-Onion Salsa
Green Tomato Salsa
Homemade Mild Chile Paste
Jack Bishop's Chile Oil
Lemon-Tabasco Dipping Sauce
Soy and Sesame Dipping Sauce or Marinade,
    with Variations
Soy-Citrus Dipping Sauce

Fiery Peanut Sauce
Sweet-and-Sour Sauce
Fish Dipping Sauce
Toasted Sesame Seeds
Simple Hot Mustard
Mango-Onion Relish
Cranberry Relish with Orange and Ginger
All-Purpose Curry Powder
Fragrant Curry Powder
Garam Masala
Pickling Spice
Recado Rojo (Puerto-Rican-Style Seasoning Paste)
Fast Barbecue Sauce
Citrus Sauce
Lime Sauce
Anchovy Sauce
Corn and Tomato Relish
Basic Technique for Brown Sauce, with Variations
White Sauce
Velouté (Fish) Sauce
Béchamel (Milk) Sauce
Cream Sauce
Mornay (Cheese) Sauce
Curry Sauce
Brown Butter
Black Butter
Parsley Butter
Béarnaise Sauce
Beurre Blanc
Hollandaise Sauce
Basic Reduction Sauce or Pan Gravy
Asian Sauce
Mushroom Sauce
Lemon-Caper Sauce
Thickened Reduction Sauce or Pan Gravy

Beverages

Hot Chocolate
Mocha Hot Chocolate

Mexican Hot Chocolate
Sugar Syrup
Soft Fruit Shake
Rich Berry Shake
Banana-Yogurt Shake
Banana-Vanilla Shake
Rich Orange Milkshake
Pineapple-Berry Punch
Lemonade or Limeade
Grape-Lime Rickey
Black Russian
White Russian
Sombrero
Bloody Mary
Champagne Cocktail
Frozen Daiquiri
Traditional Daiquiri
Strawberry Daiquiri
Gin on Vodka Gimlet
Irish Coffee
Mint Julep
Manhattan
Rob Roy
Margarita
Frozen Margarita
Martini
Gibson
Vodka Martini
Old-Fashioned
Piña Colada
Screwdriver
Sea Breeze
Side Car
Tequila Sunrise
Tom Collins
Whiskey Sour
Sangria
Hot Buttered Rum
Mulled Wine or Cider
Egg Nog

Recipes that Require Sixty Minutes or Less to Prepare

Appetizers

Roasted Eggplant Dip
Gougères
Vegetable or Fish Tempura
Pakoras
Fritto Misto
Fried Wontons or Egg Rolls
Lighter, Steamed Wontons
Pot Stickers or Steamed Dumplings
Empanadas Filled with Beans and
    Mushrooms

Soups

Quickest Chicken Stock
Flavorful Fish and Vegetable Stock
Onion Soup
Cabbage Soup, Three Ways
Mushroom-Barley Soup
Pureed Tomato Soup
Minestrone
Creamy Pumpkin or Winter Squash Soup,
    Version I
Creamy Pumpkin or Winter Squash Soup,
    Version II
Lentil Soup
Spicy Lentil Soup
Pasta and Bean Soup (Pasta e Fagioli)
Lower-Fat Clam or Fish Chowder
Shrimp Soup with Cumin
One-Hour Bouillabaisse
Cotriade
Twice-Cooked Chicken Stock
Hot-and-Sour Soup
Hanoi Noodle Soup
Quick Asian Noodle Soup with Pork

Basic Red Gazpacho
Cold Cucumber and Dill Soup
Summer Fruit Soup
Sweet Blueberry Soup with Yogurt
Cherry Soup
Low-Fat Baked Croutons

Salads

Eggplant Salad, Italian-Style
Caponata with Raisins and Pine Nuts
Eggplant Salad with Sesame Dressing
Potato Salad with Double Mustard Dressing
Classic American Potato Salad
Quick Pickled Vegetables
Quick Pickled Vegetables, Asian-Style
Quick Pickled Cabbage
Tabbouleh
Grilled Chicken Salad
Chicken Salad with Olive Oil and Chives
Chef's Salad
Grilled Shrimp and Tomato Salad
Mussel and Potato Salad
Salade Niçoise

Pasta

Pasta with Cauliflower or Broccoli
Pasta with Cauliflower, Anchovies, and Hot Red
    Pepper
Garlicky Pasta with Broccoli Raab
Pasta with Cauliflower and Sausage
Pasta with Saffron-Cauliflower Sauce
Pasta with Radicchio, Pine Nuts, and Raisins
Linguine with Slow-Cooked Onions
Pasta with Lentils
Baked Ziti with Radicchio and Gorgonzola
Penne with Tomato-Shrimp Sauce
Pasta Sauce with Squid
Pasta Sauce with Scungilli (Conch)

Pasta Sauce with Seafood
Mussels, Portuguese-Style, over Pasta
Spaghetti and Meatballs
Spaghetti with Sausage
Baked Macaroni and Cheese
Kasha Varnishkes
Traditional Egg Pasta Dough
Hot Water Dough
Semolina Dough
Whole Wheat Dough
Spinach Pasta
Red Pasta
Peppery Pasta
Saffron Pasta
Herb Pasta
Spinach-and-Fish or Shrimp Filling for
   Fresh Pasta
Classic Lasagne, Bolognese-Style
Vegetarian Lasagne
Classic Lasagne, Italian-American-Style
Curried Rice Noodles with Vegetables
Curried Rice Noodles with Ground Meat
Curried Rice Noodles with Fresh Shrimp
Curried Rice Noodles with Cabbage and
   Mushrooms
Pad Thai
Broad Rice Noodles with Chiles, Pork, and Basil
Rice Noodles with Coconut Milk
Rice Noodles, Vegetarian-Style

Grains

Pressure-Cooked Tough Grains
Basic Barley
Barley, Pilaf-Style
Barley "Risotto" with Mushrooms
Bulgur with Spinach
Polenta "Pizza"
Basic Short- or Medium-Grain Rice, Version II
Sushi Rice

Rice, Mexican-Style (Arroz Blanco)
Cumin-Scented Rice with Shrimp
Short-Grain Rice with Chives
Risotto alla Milanese
Risotto with Spinach
Risotto with Parsley and Basil
Risotto with Tomatoes
Risotto with Dried Mushrooms
Risotto with Mushrooms, Garlic, and Anchovies
Risotto with Vegetables
Risotto with Meat
Shrimp Jambalaya
Basic Brown Rice
Brown Rice with Cashews and Herbs
Basic Wild Rice
Wild Rice with Curried Nuts
Wild Rice with White Rice
Wild Rice with Vegetables and Dried Mushrooms

Breads

Corn Bread
Bacon Corn Bread
Corn and Bean Bread
Onion Pan Bread
Irish Soda Bread
Banana Bread
Quick Whole Wheat and Molasses Bread
Nut Bread
Raisin or Nut-and-Raisin Bread
Date-Nut Bread
Orange-Nut Bread
Apple Bread
Apple-Nut Bread
Carrot Bread
Zucchini or Pumpkin Bread
Basic Muffins
Banana-Nut Muffins
Bran Muffins
Blueberry or Cranberry Muffins

Spice Muffins
Sour Cream or Yogurt Muffins
Coffee Cake Muffins
Savory Muffins
Sweet and Rich Muffins
Popovers
Any of the pizza recipes
Pan Bagna with Chicken Breast
Roasted Eggplant Sandwich with Tomato-Garlic
   Sauce
Mixed Veggie Sandwich with Tahini Dressing
Curried Pork Tenderloin Sandwich with Chutney
   and Arugula
Fajitas

Fish

Crisp Rockfish or Other Fillets on Mashed
   Potatoes
Red Snapper or Other Fillets in Packages
Red Snapper in Packages with Spinach
Red Snapper in Packages with Tomato and Herbs
Red Snapper in Packages with Carrots and
   Zucchini
Grilled Striped Bass or Other Fillets
Roast Cod or Other Thick White Fillets with
   Potatoes
Roast Cod with Potatoes, Onions, and Olive Oil
Roast Cod with Herbs
Cod or Other Thick White Fillets Poached in
   Tomato Sauce
Cod or Other Thick White Fillets in Neapolitan
   Tomato Sauce
Cod or Other Thick White Fillets with
   Winter Vegetables
Grouper or Other Thick White Fillets in
   Yellow Curry
Basic Grilled Swordfish, Tuna, or Other Steaks
Grilled Swordfish, Tuna, or Other Steaks with
   Corn and Tomato Relish

Skewers of Swordfish, Tuna, or Other Steaks
Skewers of Swordfish, Tuna, or Other Steaks
   with Rosemary
Monkfish or Other Steaks Roasted with Herbs
Monkfish or Other Steaks Roasted with Fennel
Poached Halibut or Other Steaks with Vegetables
Poached Halibut or Other Steaks with Vegetables
   and Mustard Sauce
Crispy Skin Salmon with Gingery Greens
Cold Poached Salmon with Lime-Ginger Sauce
Bluefish or Mackerel with Roasted Summer
   Vegetables
Grilled or Broiled Red Snapper or Other Large
   Whole Fish
Braised Whole Grouper or Other Large Whole
   Fish with Hot-and-Sour Sauce
Stir-Fried Shrimp with Black Beans
Curried Shrimp
Shrimp with Cumin and Mint
Shrimp and Beans
Pasta and Beans with Shrimp
Crayfish Boil, Louisiana-Style
Crab Cakes
Grilled Lobster
Stir-Fried Lobster with Black Bean Sauce
Broiled Lobster with Herb Stuffing
Poached Squid with Cilantro and Coconut
Baked Stuffed Clams
Basic Steamed Mussels
Mussels with Cream
Mussels with Butter Sauce
Curried Mussels
Grilled Scallops with Basil Stuffing

Poultry

Simple Roast Chicken
Roast Chicken with Soy Sauce
Roast Chicken with Cumin, Honey, and
   Orange Juice

Roast Chicken with Herb Butter
Poached and Roasted Chicken with Soy Sauce
Braised Whole Chicken with Tarragon
Chicken Under a Brick
Grilled or Broiled Split Chicken
Grilled or Broiled Split Chicken with Honey
   and Mustard
Chicken, Provençal-Style
Chicken with Onions
Chicken with Rice (Arroz con Pollo)
Chicken in Red Wine Sauce
Chicken with Clams
Chicken with Indian Spices and Yogurt
Chicken Thighs with Soy Sauce and Lemon
Chicken Thighs with Tomatoes and Olives
Roast Chicken Parts with Herbs and Olive Oil
Roast Chicken Parts with Asian Seasonings
Fried Chicken
Chili-Spiced Fried Chicken
Fried Chicken with Bay Leaves
Fried Chicken Breasts
Chicken Parmigiana
Double Coconut Chicken Breasts
Chicken Cutlets Roasted with Tomatoes
"Steamed" Chicken Cutlets with Tomatoes
"Steamed" Chicken Cutlets with Broccoli and
   Sun-Dried Tomatoes
"Steamed" Chicken Cutlets with Grated
   Vegetables
Chicken Thighs in Bitter Garlic Sauce
Chicken Satay
Grilled or Broiled Cornish Hens with Vinegar
Wine-Braised Quail with Herbs

Meat

Grilled Marinated Flank Steak
Salad with Grilled Marinated Flank Steak
Grilled or Broiled Beef and Vegetable Kebabs
Spice-Rubbed Beef Kebabs

Grilled Veal Chops on a Bed of Vegetables
Veal "Parmigiana"
Pork Chops with Onions and Peppers
Pork Satay
Grilled or Broiled Pork Tenderloin with
   Mustard Curry
Basic Breakfast Sausage
Garlic-Fennel Sausage
Johnny Earles's Spicy Sausage
Basic Grilled or Broiled Butterflied Leg of Lamb
Butterflied Leg of Lamb with Provençal Spices
Grilled or Broiled Butterflied Lamb with
   Coconut Milk
Grilled Skewered Lamb Chunks (Shish Kebab)
Shish Kebab with Rosemary
Baked Kibbe as an Appetizer
Basic Meat Loaf

Beans

Black Beans with Crisp Pork and Orange
Lentils and Rice with Caramelized Onions
Warm Lentils with Bacon
Stewed Chickpeas with Chicken
Split Peas, Mung Beans, or Lentils with
   Curry (Dal)
Creamy Fried Tofu

Vegetables

Basic Steamed Artichokes
Sautéed Artichoke Hearts
Braised Quartered Artichokes with Tarragon
Simmered, Steamed, or Microwaved Beets
Stir-Fried Broccoli
Stir-Fried Broccoli with Chinese Mushrooms
Broccoli Raab with Sausage and Grapes
Cabbage Cooked with Apples
Cabbage Braised with Onions
Sauerkraut with Juniper Berries

Cardoons and Onions Cooked in Cream
Celeriac and Potato Puree
Baked Chard in Béchamel
Boiled, Grilled, or Roasted Chestnuts
Corn Fritters
Cucumbers in Butter and Cream
Crisp Sautéed Cucumbers with Lemon
Roasted Eggplant with Garlic and Parsley
Braised Endive, Escarole, or Radicchio with
    Prosciutto
Fennel Baked with Stock and Parmesan
Faster Roasted Garlic
"Dry-Fried" String Beans, Chinese-Style
Slow-Cooked Green Beans
Duxelles
Fried Okra
Okra, Corn, and Tomato Stew
Cooked Onions and Apples
Fried Onion Rings
Marinated Roasted, Grilled, or Broiled Peppers
Mashed Potatoes
Crispy Sautéed Potatoes with Rosemary
Potato Pancakes, Version I
Potato Pancakes, Version II
Boiled New Potatoes
French Fries
Baked Pumpkin Slices
Oven-Braised Sweet-and-Sour Pumpkin
Sautéed Summer Squash or Zucchini
Summer Squash or Zucchini Pancakes
Pureed Turnips
Turnips in Mustard Sauce
Roasted Vegetables, Catalonian-Style
Grilled Mixed Vegetables

Fruit

Baked Apples
Apple Brown Betty
Summer Pudding

Lemon Curd
Poached Peaches with Red Wine and Spices
Baked Pears
Strawberry Shortcakes
Fruit Fritters

Desserts

Vanilla Pudding
Blancmange
Chocolate Pudding
Panna Cotta
Chocolate Mousse
Lemon Mousse
Tapioca Pudding
Coconut-Tapioca Pudding
Bread Pudding
Old-Fashioned Baked Custard, or Pots de Crème
Flan (Crème Caramel)
Chocolate Custard
Lemon Custard
Rice Pudding
Basic Philadelphia Vanilla Ice Cream
Bitter Chocolate Sorbet
Soft Fruit Sorbet
Vanilla or Chocolate Soufflé
Lemon, Orange, or Grand Marnier Soufflé
Crepes Suzette
Chocolate Crepes
Fudge
Caramels
Chocolate Caramels
Peanut Brittle
Chocolate Candies
Pies:
Flaky Pie Crust
Sweetened, Enriched Pie Crust
Generous Pie Shell for a 10-Inch or Larger Pie,
    or a Deep-Dish Pie
Free-Form Tart with Fruit

Caramelized Apple Tart (Tarte Tatin)
Palmiers, Arcs, or Other Puff Pastry
  Cookies
Apple Turnovers
Fruit or Jam Turnovers
Cream Puffs
éclairs

Cookies

Butter Drop Cookies
Chocolate Drop Cookies
Sour Cream Drop Cookies
Olive Oil Drop Cookies
Classic Chocolate Chip Cookies
Oatmeal Cookies
Lacy Oatmeal Cookies
Brownies
Butterscotch Brownies (Blondies)
Quick Coffee Cake
Single-Layer Butter Cake
Orange-Almond Cake

Eggs

Eggs Benedict for Four
Eggs with Cheese Sauce for Four
Best Scrambled Eggs
Baked (Shirred) Eggs

Baked Eggs with Tomato
Baked Eggs with Spinach (Eggs "Florentine")
Baked Eggs with Onions and Cheese
Baked Sweet Omelet
Spanish Potato Omelet (Tortilla)
Basic Frittata
Vegetable Frittata
Onion Frittata
Herb Frittata
Cheese Soufflé
Spinach Soufflé
Ham and Cheese Soufflé
Tomato Soufflé
Polenta Pancakes
Filled Sweet Crepes
Crunchy Granola

Sauces

Red Pepper Relish
Tomato-Dill Sauce
Mild Tomato Salsa
Sherried Garlic Sauce with Nectarines
Traditional Cranberry Sauce
Vegetable Chutney with Garlic
Dried Apricot Chutney with Star Anise
Fresh Fruit Chutney with Mustard and Curry
Onion (Soubise) Sauce
Mushroom Sauce

Glossary

adjust seasoning: To "adjust seasoning," taste what you're cooking just before serving, and salt, pepper, or add other seasoning to suit your taste. Remember that it's always easier to add seasoning than to compensate for too much.

adobo: The only consistent ingredient in this Caribbean spice mixture is oregano; most everything else varies from cook to cook. Sometimes it's a dry seasoning to be shaken onto meat or seafood; I prefer to create an *adobo* paste that can be rubbed into every nook and cranny. Not to be confused with the classic Philippine dish, Chicken Adobo (see my version, page 377), which coincidentally shares the name "Adobo."

adzuki bean: A small (one-quarter inch long or so), oval, maroon dried bean. This is an Asian bean usually made into flour, or sprouted, or used in desserts. Its slightly sweet flavor makes it an odd choice for a dinner bean.

aioli: This Provençal specialty is simply garlic-laced mayonnaise. It's traditionally strong-flavored, but you can decide how much garlic you want to use; there are times when half a clove is plenty.

al dente: Pasta should be cooked until it is firm to the bite, or *al dente,* from the Italian phrase "to the tooth." As discussed on page 127, you should taste pasta as it cooks, aiming for pasta that is tender but not mushy, firm but never hard, chewy but not crunchy. Pasta cooked al dente might seem undercooked to those of us who grew up eating mushy spaghetti and meatballs, but it will provide the optimum consistency for whatever sauce you choose.

Remember, too, that pasta will cook a little from its retained heat as you drain and sauce it.

all-purpose flour: Like all white flours, this is milled from the inner part of the wheat kernel and containing neither the germ (the sprouting inner part) nor the bran (the outer coating). It's a combination of hard (high-protein, or bread) and soft (low-protein, or cake or pastry) flours, and is suitable for most purposes. Avoid bleached flour if possible.

allspice: A pungent dried seed pod from an evergreen tree, with a flavor of cinnamon, nutmeg, and cloves—hence the name. Also called Jamaican pepper (in Jamaica it's called pimento), because it looks like a big peppercorn and the best is grown on that island.

almond extract: This intense flavoring is made from bitter-almond oil, usually combined with ethyl alcohol. It will keep indefinitely if stored in a cool, dark place.

ancho chile: This relatively mild dried chile pepper is a deep reddish brown. In its fresh green state, it's known as a poblano.

anchovies: Small, silvery fish that are usually cured with salt. Many are then tightly packed with oil in flat two-ounce tins, but salt-cured anchovies are also available. These should be rinsed, and may need to be filleted before using.

anise seed: Greenish-brown, comma-shaped spice with a sweet licorice flavor and a bit of heat. Anise seeds and star anise do not come from the same plant, although their flavors are similar.

apricots: Fresh apricots are only readily available in June and July, and their quality is always questionable. Luckily for us, they dry brilliantly. Sulfur dioxide is frequently used to preserve their color, but you can find apricots dried without sulfur dioxide if you prefer.

Arborio rice: This short-grain rice, grown in the north of Italy has a high starch content, which lends the Italian classic risotto its unusual creamy texture. The grains are almost as fat as they are long. Similar varieties are grown in Spain, and any short-grain rice can be substituted in a pinch.

aromatic: A vegetable, herb, or spice that gives food a lively fragrance and flavor. In classic cooking, a reference to "aromatics" most often means onion, carrot, and celery.

artichoke: A thistle, whose sharp outer leaves and central choke must be removed before you can eat the meat on the leaves and the incomparably delicious heart. Tender "baby" artichokes don't have chokes and can be eaten whole. Canned, bottled, or frozen artichoke hearts are worth eating, but do not believe for a moment that they have the flavor of fresh.

arugula: Arugula is the most strangely flavored of all the greens, possessing a distinctive hot muddiness that may be an acquired taste—but an easily acquired one. Younger, smaller arugula is milder; old arugula may be assaultively hot.

asiago: This hard Italian cheese has a rich nutty flavor. It's made from whole or part-skim cow's milk, and comes in small wheels. It's among the best substitutes for Parmigiano-Reggiano.

asparagus: Asparagus is good thick or thin (super-thin stalks need not be peeled) and in any color; we usually see green, but white and purple occasionally make it to our markets. These days we can buy it year-round, but the best asparagus is local asparagus, sold from February in the South through May or even June in the North. Some recipes call for the tips only, but the stalks can be steamed separately or added to an omelet.

aux fines herbes: A French term applied to a dish to which a combination of delicate fresh herbs (usually tarragon, chervil, parsley, and chives) have been added.

avocado: A fruit we treat as a vegetable, the avocado is native to Central or South America, but is now widely grown in Florida, California, and many other warm places. It should be quite soft before opening and eating; a ripe avocado with a squirt of lemon and a dash of salt is one of the great simple treats.

baba ghanoush: This Middle Eastern specialty is a mixture of roasted eggplant, tahini (sesame paste), olive oil, lemon juice, and garlic, served as either a dip or spread. Traditionally garnished with pomegranate seeds and mint, my version (page 23) incorporates the more readily available pine nuts, with fresh parsley on top.

bacon (slab): This is bacon in a chunk—you must slice it by hand (and may want to remove the rind first). Often the only way to find top-quality bacon.

baguette: A long, narrow loaf of French bread, usually with a crispy brown crust and a soft, but chewy interior. Special "baguette" pans are not necessary to make this bread (see my recipe, page 224).

bake: To cook food in an oven, which supplies free-circulating dry heat. It's important to preheat the oven and to know the actual temperature, especially when baking breads or pastries. Because oven gauges are surprisingly inaccurate (electric ovens tend to be better than gas, but neither is reliable), buy an oven thermometer and use it. I use the term "bake" mostly for bread and desserts; savory food is more often "roasted," at high temperatures.

baking potato: This term refers to Idaho and russet potatoes—the big potatoes with rough, brown skin and numerous eyes. These potatoes are low in moisture and high in starch, which makes them ideal for baking, because they have a wonderfully mealy texture. They also make good mashed potatoes and French fries.

baking powder: A derivative of baking soda, baking powder is a double-action leavener, activated when it's mixed with liquid, and further stimulated when exposed to heat. Most commercial baking powders have a distinctive flavor that comes from aluminum and other additives. For a functional homemade baking powder without this odd flavor, you can combine cream of tartar with baking soda (see my instructions on page 708).

baking sheet: Good baking sheets (also called cookie sheets) are thick, and the best are insulated. But a careful eye during baking can compensate for cheap aluminum baking sheets, and those are what I use. Non-stick baking sheets make life easier.

baking soda: Shorthand for sodium bicarbonate, baking soda is a good leavener in those pastries that contain acid, which stimulates a chemical reaction that produces gas—making your baked good rise. Use baking soda freely whenever you're baking with buttermilk, sour cream, or yogurt. If there is little to no acid in your recipe, you should use baking powder, which already has acid in it.

baking (pizza) stone: It's best to bake pizza and bread directly on a hot surface, and a baking stone gives you just that. It preheats while your oven does so your pizzas cook more evenly and your bread crusts are crisper. Just leave it on the bottom rack of your oven; you may need to replace it every couple of years.

balsamic vinegar: Once you've tasted this sweet but pungent vinegar, you'll always have a bottle at the ready. Unique to the area around Modena, Italy, it's made from the juice of white Trebbiano grapes, and gets its dark color and intense flavor from aging in barrels of various woods and graduating sizes. High-quality balsamic vinegars are aged ten years or more and can be quite expensive, and cheap, mass-produced versions are not as good as sherry vinegar, which is relatively inexpensive. Medium-quality balsamic vinegar, aged three years or so and costing about ten dollars a bottle, is a luxury that's worth it—use it by the teaspoonful and it will last for ages.

bamboo shoot: The young growth of a certain edible bamboo plant. Although fresh shoots, tender and ivory-colored, occasionally turn up in Asian markets, don't hold your breath. The canned ones are tasteless but provide decent crunch; you'll find them in Asian markets and many supermarkets.

barbecue: Don't confuse barbecuing with grilling. Grilling is food is cooked over high, direct heat; barbecuing is a long, slow method, usually involving indirect cooking with smoke. (See page 10 for more about grilling.) Usually, barbecued food is basted with a spicy sauce.

barley: A wonderful substitute for rice in side dishes and probably the best grain for soup-making; easy to cook and delicious. You can try whole barley, but I've found it never becomes truly tender, no matter how long you cook it (see Pressure-Cooked Tough Grains, page 181), so I recommend "pearled" barley instead. This has the tough outer coating removed, cooks relatively quickly, and retains a pleasant chewiness.

basil: A staple of Mediterranean cooking and now among the most popular herbs in America, especially in the summer. It must be fresh—dried basil is virtually useless—but fortunately is increasingly sold that way, year-round, in most supermarkets. It does not keep well; refrigerate, wrapped in damp paper towels and covered with a plastic bag for a few days, or standing in a glass of water, covered with a plastic bag (change the water every two days).

basmati rice: This aromatic long-grain rice has a perfumy, nut-like flavor and aroma. The kernels are incomparably long and slender. White basmati rice is most common, but you can also find brown (whole-grain) basmati rice at most health food stores.

baste: To spoon, brush, or drizzle food with butter, sauce, pan juice or other liquid as it cooks. Although it does add flavor to the exterior of food, basting's ability to keep food moist is largely overrated. You can use a bulb baster if you have one, but a spoon or brush will do.

batter: A semiliquid mixture made of flour, a leavening agent (such as eggs or baking powder), and a liquid. Batter can be spooned or poured; dough is thicker and must be molded by hand.

bay leaf: This pungent, woodsy herb comes from the evergreen bay laurel tree, native to the Mediterranean and usually sold dry. Bay is rarely available fresh, but can be grown as a house plant (and kept outside in summer or year-round in milder climates). If used whole, bay leaves may be removed from the dish before serving, although this isn't essential.

bean sauce: This soybean condiment is a useful essential ingredient in stir-fries. It is labeled either "whole bean sauce" or "ground bean sauce," which tends to be saltier. Available at Asian markets and at some supermarkets.

bean sprouts: Edible sprouts can be produced from a variety of seeds and beans, from the mung and alfalfa to lentil, radish, and even broccoli. For the greatest degree of crispness, mung bean sprouts should be eaten raw. They are firm enough to cook, but to avoid wilting, they shouldn't be sautéed or stir-fried for more than thirty seconds. Sprouts should be kept in the refrigerator in the ventilated container or plastic bag in which they're sold, and used within a few days.

beat: To mix ingredients rapidly until they are well blended.

béchamel sauce: A basic French white sauce, made by stirring milk into a mixture of butter and flour that has been slowly cooked over low heat. (See page 787 for my recipe.)

beef fillet (filet mignon): This tender but expensive boneless cut of meat comes from the small end of the tenderloin. It should be cooked quickly by grilling or sautéing; I recommend saucing it, too, because it is among the least flavorful pieces of meat.

beet: This root vegetable grows spring through fall, but it's available pretty much year-round. Large or small beets are equally good, although it's easier to bake them evenly if they're roughly the same size. A dependable indication of freshness is the presence of crisp, bright greens, which can be cooked separately like chard. Just be sure to remove all but an inch of the greens before storing the roots in a plastic bag in the refrigerator.

bell peppers: Also known as sweet peppers, bell peppers are "mature" when they turn bright green, but they are not yet ripe; their flavor is sharp, even acrid at this point. The same peppers picked a week or two later will have turned red, yellow, or orange, and their flavor will have mellowed considerably. Yellow and orange peppers are the most mellow, but they're usually expensive, so red is the common first choice. Avoid green if you have other options. (Note that purple peppers are just green ones in disguise.)

Bermuda onion: This big, sweet, ivory-colored onion truly does come from Bermuda. A sweet, crisp topping for sandwiches, this onion is also a good choice for everyday cooking; after all, it's easier to peel and chop one large onion than two small ones. However, Bermudas have a shorter shelf life than your basic yellow onion, and may cost more off-season (April to June is peak time for Bermudas).

biscotti: These crisp Italian cookies, which look a little like toasted slices of French bread, are baked twice: First you bake the dough in a loaf, then you slice the loaf and bake the slices. Not unlike zwieback.

bisque: A thick, luxurious soup made of pureed seafood and cream, but there are other options. See page 68.

black (turtle) bean: This multipurpose dried bean is medium-sized (up to one-half inch long), round to almost square, and deep black with a white line and interior. Among the most valuable and best-tasting of beans, it is especially good in soup, with rice, in salads, and pureed. It's a good candidate for the pressure cooker, as the cooking time can be quite long (up to two hours).

blackberries and raspberries: There are hundreds of types of black and red berries (some are orange, yellow, or almost white), but all are treated more or less the same. (Technically, a raspberry leaves its inner core behind when picked; the core comes along when you pick a blackberry). These highly perishable berries are extremely expensive in the market, of course, but almost the entire northern half of the country has some growing wild at one point or another in the summer, so pick for yourself if you can.

black pepper: Green, white, and black peppercorns all come from the berries of the *Piper nigrum* plant; black peppercorns are the strongest of the three varieties. Preground black pepper is sold cracked and coarsely or finely ground, but it looses its flavor quickly and should be stored in a cool dark place for no more than three months. Freshly ground black pepper is always best. If you don't have a pepper mill, you can use a rolling pin, mallet, or mortar and pestle to crush the peppercorns.

blancmange: A simple stove-top pudding made with milk, sugar, and vanilla, thickened with cornstarch. A variation on my Vanilla Pudding recipe (page 658)—minus the eggs and butter—it is relatively low in fat.

blender: If you are going to cook regularly, you will want a blender. You can get by without one, but if you make a lot of soups and want to make them creamy, this is the tool. It's also great for any blended drink (most food processors leak if loaded up with liquid) and for coconut milk. The new handheld immersion blenders are terrific for pureeing soup right in the pot.

blind bake: To precook pie crusts before filling them to ensure that they cook thoroughly, and to control shrinking. For instructions, see page 686.

blueberry: More closely related to the cranberry than to the raspberry, the blueberry (and bilberry, huckleberry, and like berries) is distinctively different from both. Unlike the cranberry, it is sweet enough to eat raw, whole, and out of hand. Unlike the raspberry, it is sturdy enough to store, and it even freezes well. With its relatively high sugar and acid content, it's the closet thing to an all-purpose berry.

blue cheese: The blue (or green) veins in blue cheese are created by flavor-producing molds injected (or occurring naturally) during the curing process. Roquefort, blue d'Avergne, Stilton, Gorgonzola, and Maytag blue are some of the best varieties. All blue cheeses smell strong, but some varieties are actually quite mild-flavored.

boil: The term not only means heating liquid until bubbles break the surface, but applies to cooking food in boiling liquid. Temperatures can be controlled not only by raising and lowering the heat of the burner, but by partially covering the pot. Actual boiling—with bubbles rapidly appearing—is useful for pasta, potatoes, and many vegetables. Most food is cooked at a simmer—a few bubbles breaking the surface, not real rapidly.

bok choy: This cabbage looks like a bunch of oversized white celery stalks with big flat green leaves. Bok choy has a mild flavor that's great raw in salads. It's also the best cabbage for stir-fries; the stems turn almost creamy after cooking. To prepare it, wash, then remove any damaged leaves and discard the stem end and the inch or so above it. Bok choy is available at most supermarkets, year-round.

boniato: Also called batata, this is a popular tuber in both Latin America and Asia, frequently found here. It tastes like a cross between white and sweet potatoes, and can be treated like either. Especially try baking them, exactly as you would a white potato, making sure it is cooked all the way through, or peeling and boiling, always covered with water to prevent discoloration, and serving immediately.

boning knife: This thin-bladed knife is very useful, not only for boning but also for piercing meat as it cooks to judge doneness.

bonito flakes: The dried flakes of a dark, full-flavored fish, used in the Japanese soup stock dashi (see page 168), which is among the simplest stocks you can make. Bonito flakes are available in Asian markets.

Boston lettuce: Part of the butterhead family, this simple lettuce sports soft but fairly well-defined heads with lots of loose outer leaves. The bland tenderness mingles nicely with some bitter loose leaf and super-crisp romaine.

boule: A ball-shaped loaf of bread that's baked without a pan in the oven.

braise: To cook food, first by browning it in a little fat, then by adding liquid to the pan, covering it, and finishing the cooking over moist, low heat. I often make the browning step optional; although it most definitely adds flavor, it's an additional step that won't make or break the dish. (For more on braising, see page 14.)

bread crumbs: There are two kinds of bread crumbs: fresh and dry. They should not be used interchangeably. Fresh crumbs can be made in a food processor or blender. Dried bread crumbs are lightly browned and may be plain or flavored. They can be bought or made from good quality stale bread (see page 239 for my recipe).

brioche: A light yeast bread made with lots of butter and eggs.

broccoli raab: Broccoli raab, or rape, is more bitter, and has more stems and leaves than head broccoli, which has more florets. It can be found from fall to spring in markets with specialty produce sections, and can be used in any broccoli recipe. (For recipes, see page 544.)

broil: To cook food directly under the heat source, with the aim of producing a crisp crust while cooking the interior to the desired degree of doneness. (Grilling is identical to broiling, except the food is above the heat source.) Generally, the best foods to broil are less than one inch thick; the thicker the food, the greater distance it should be from the heat source. (For more about broiling and broilers, see pages 10–11.)

broth: Closely related to stock, this is the basis of almost all soups. (I call the basic ingredient "stock" and the enhanced, nearly-ready-to-serve soup "broth.") It is made by cooking vegetables, meat, or fish in water, then straining and defatting the resulting stock.

brown: To cook food quickly in order to "brown" the outside, while keeping the interior moist. Browning is usually done in a hot skillet on top of the stove, but a very hot oven, broiler, or grill will work well also.

brown sugar: Brown sugar is simply white sugar combined with molasses. Dark brown sugar has lots of molasses; light brown sugar contains less. To recreate brown sugar, add two tablespoons molasses to one cup white sugar.

Brussels sprouts: Brussels sprouts look like miniature cabbages, and that's what they are. Like cabbage, they must not be overcooked, or they become soggy and strong-flavored. But chosen well and handled simply, they can be wonderful. The smaller the better is a good rule. Reject any sprouts with yellow leaves, loose leaves, or those that are soft or not tightly packed. Generally, Brussels sprouts are a winter vegetable, found from September or October on.

bulgur: Bulgur is not just cracked wheat; it is soft wheat that has been steamed, hulled, dried, and then cracked. A traditional grain of the Middle East, it's best-known use is in tabbouleh (for my recipe, see page 112). Bulgur is quick-cooking, in fact, you don't even cook some bulgur, you just soak it. (For more about buying and preparing bulgur, see page 185.)

butter: Butter is generally labeled either salted or sweet (unsalted); since salt is incorporated largely as a preservative and can be added anytime, I buy only sweet butter.

buttermilk: Once upon a time this was the milk remaining in the churn after the butter had been removed. Today, all commercial buttermilk is produced by adding a culture to whole or skimmed milk, which gives it the thicker texture and slightly tangy flavor associated with buttermilk.

button mushroom: This is the standard, white, cultivated mushroom. Better raw than cooked, button mushrooms also work well in concert with "wild mushrooms," which are more intensely flavored, but also more expensive.

cabbage: There are countless varieties of cabbage. The best is Savoy, the light green variety with crinkled leaves; if you can't find it, the standard tight smooth, light green cabbage will do. Napa cabbage, also called Chinese cabbage, is a good romaine-like variety, terrific for raw salads and coleslaw. For stir-fries, there is nothing better than bok choy. Cabbage is a year-round vegetable; reject any cabbages with yellow leaves, loose leaves, or those which are soft or not tightly packed.

calabaza: This pumpkin-like winter squash, usually sold in slices or hunks in markets catering to Central and South Americans. Also known as West Indian pumpkin, calabaza is quite frequently better than pumpkin when cooked in the same way.

calamata olives: Purple-black Greek olives of generally high quality. Also spelled *kalamata olives.*

canapé: Dainty pieces of bread (toasted or untoasted) topped with a garnish or spread. This is finger food—usually served as appetizers with cocktails.

canola oil: This neutral oil is your best choice for cooking because it is inexpensive, extremely low in saturated fats, has a high burning point, and does not detract from the flavor of the food with which it's combined. I use it for deep frying and the occasional sauce or dressing in which I want another flavor to dominate.

caramelize: To slowly dissolve sugar (granulated or brown) in water, then heat the resulting syrup until it turns caramel-brown. Caramelized sugar is sometimes called *burnt sugar.*

carambola (star fruit): This is one of the most recent tropical imports, now grown in Florida and found in most supermarkets. It has yellow, near-translucent skin (which is tough but edible), and slices take the shape of a star. Best eaten raw, but it also takes well to grilling.

caraway seeds: These tiny, curved, brown seeds come from a plant in the parsley family. They are aromatic, with a warm, nutty flavor.

cardamom: A native to India, cardamom is a member of the ginger family and one of the most flowery-sweet of all spices. It can be purchased either in the pod or ground, but commercially ground cardamom quickly loses its flavor. Each pod contains a dozen or so of the bumpy seeds, which can be used whole or ground with a mortar and pestle.

cardoon: This relative of the artichoke is rarely seen in stores, but its popular in Italy, France, and South America, and I think it will catch on here soon too. For now, you'll have to look for cardoons at farmers' markets; they should have firm stems and dark green leaves. To prepare, you strip the leaves and cook and eat the stems. They're done when tender enough to easily pierce with a skewer or thin-bladed knife.

carpaccio: An Italian appetizer made largely from thin shavings of raw beef fillet (filet mignon).

casserole: A casserole may be any deep, ovenproof vessel, usually used to cook food slowly. Dutch ovens are similar.

catfish: Popular white-fleshed fish with a medium-firm texture. Farm-raised catfish—widely available in supermarkets and fish stores—don't have the muddy taste that distinguish their wild counterparts. Look for fresh catfish with white rather than grayish flesh. Delicious oven-fried, stir-fried, sautéed, and roasted.

cayenne: Cayenne pepper is used to describe almost any hot, finely ground red chile pepper, but it was named after several tropical varieties that originated in Cayenne in French Guiana. The spice industry is gradually phasing out the term altogether in favor of the more generic "red pepper."

celeriac: A type of celery grown for its root, it is also known as celery root. The large knob—which could be mistaken for jicama—is usually eaten raw in salads, but it's delicious in purees, especially with potates. Celeriac must be peeled before using. (See page 556 for more on celeriac.)

chanterelle: Available both wild and domesticated, this is a good, fleshy mushroom with subtle flavor.

chard: Essentially beets grown for leaves rather than roots, chard has a thick white, pink, or red midrib and leaves that vary from deep green to green with scarlet veins. Chard has a distinctive, acid-sweet flavor. (For more about chard, see page 557.)

chayote: Much like summer squash—it's closely related—the chayote, or cho-cho, has only one large seed, and vaguely resembles the avocado. Treat it as you would zucchini or other summer squash—that is, quite gently. Cut in half, remove the pit (it's edible in very small chayotes), and peel the skin under running water. Since most chayotes are imported, they're available year-round, although most commonly in winter. Chayotes should be not just firm, but downright hard. Store in the vegetable bin—they'll keep for weeks.

cheesecloth: Essentially cotton gauze that doesn't fall apart when it gets wet and won't flavor the food it touches. Especially useful for straining liquids when you want to remove even the tiny particles that flow through a fine strainer.

cherimoya (custard apple): A native American fruit, now grown in California, with lumpy greenish-brown skin and a creamy white interior studded by watermelon-like seeds. At its best, this fruit is creamy, sweet, and flavorful, but it's difficult to find prime specimens. Eat with a spoon.

cherry: There are two kinds of cherries, the familiar sweet ("bing") cherries and the more acidic "sour" cherries, which you can only find occasionally, usually at farmstands or off trees. Sour cherries are far better than sweet for pies and cooking, so be on the look out for them—peak season is June.

chervil: The most delicate of fresh herbs, almost never sold in stores because its shelf-life is so short. Great anise-basil flavor. Dried chervil is a near-useless substitute.

chestnut: Mealy but delicious nut, almost always imported and usually found in autumn. Peeling its hard, dark brown shell and bitter inner skin takes some effort (see my instructions, page 560), but it's worth it.

chickpeas: Also called garbanzo beans, chickpeas are nutty-tasting, relatively large legumes that may take as long as two hours to cook; consider using a pressure cooker (see page 507 for recipe).

chicories: These are sharp crunchy greens (closely related to endives) that vary wildly in appearance, but much less so in taste and texture. Tight-headed, bright red radicchio; long, green, leafy radicchio; lettuce-looking escarole; and lacy frilly frisée are all crunchy and feature a stark bitterness tamed by cooking or smoothed by olive oil. In general, the flavor, texture, and versatility of this group of greens are unmatched.

chile paste: Sometimes labeled "chili-garlic paste," this hot condiment is made with chiles, salt, and garlic. It's available in Asian markets and many supermarkets, and will keep almost indefinitely if refrigerated.

chili powder: Chile powder may be ground-up chiles, or it's a seasoning mixture of garlic, onion, cumin, oregano, coriander, cloves, and/or other spices.

Chinese cabbages: These cabbages have oblong heads with thin, juicy, flavorful leaves—as compared to the round-headed common cabbage with thick, mild leaves. The Chinese cabbage found most commonly in the market is Napa cabbage, which is a pale green, romaine-like variety, terrific for raw salads and coleslaw. Mild, celery-shaped bok choy is another variety of Chinese cabbage.

chipotle chile: Smoked, dried jalapeños with a distinctive flavor, usually very hot. When dried, soak before using. Also sold canned in sauce (called adobo).

chives: An onion-like herb with a relatively mild flavor. Snip chives with scissors close to serving time so they retain their crispness.

chocolate: Unsweetened chocolate, also sold as bitter or baking chocolate, is simply unadulterated chocolate. Bittersweet, semisweet, extra-bittersweet, and sweet cooking chocolates result from the addition of cocoa butter, sugar, vanilla, and chocolate liquor (bittersweet contains at least thirty-five percent chocolate liquor; semisweet and sweet contain between fifteen and thirty percent). Although bittersweet and semisweet chocolate can be interchanged in some recipes, I highly recommend sticking to the recipe's suggestion.

chop: To cut food into pieces, ranging in size from one-quarter- to one-half-inch or so (finely chopped) to somewhat larger than that (coarsely or roughly chopped). Very fine chopping is called mincing.

choux pastry: Call it choux paste, pâte à choux or cream puff pastry, this is a miraculous dough that can be prepared by a child. Flour, butter, and water are cooked on the stove top before the pastry is shaped, baked until fluffy, then filled with anything creamy that you please.

chutney: A savory jam that ranges from chunky to smooth and mild to hot, made to serve with strong-tasting foods, from highly seasoned grilled meat dishes to strongly flavored braises.

cider vinegar: Fruity vinegar made from fermented apple cider.

cilantro: The leaves of the coriander plant, also called Chinese parsley. Although this herb is widely used in many cuisines, it has a distinctive flavor—some say it tastes soapy—that may take getting used to. Refrigerate up to a week in a glass of water (change it every two days) with a plastic bag over the leaves.

cinnamon: This sweet-hot spice comes from the inner bark of a tropical evergreen tree, which when spread out on the ground curls into long cigar-like rolls. These rolls of bark are cut into short lengths to make cinnamon sticks or ground for powdered cinnamon.

cleaver: Used mostly by Chinese cooks and butchers, a cleaver is like a small kitchen ax. A handy item but hardly an essential one.

cloud ear/tree ear: Thin, brownish-black mushrooms with a subtle, woodsy taste; a good addition to stir-fries. Available in dried form in Asian markets and many supermarkets, they become ear-shaped and five times as big when soaked in warm water. Tree ears are the larger variety; an albino type is called silver ears. Might be sold under the name "wood ear mushrooms."

clove: From the Latin word *clavus,* meaning "nail," this pungent and sweet spice is sold whole or ground, and is used in both sweet and savory dishes.

cocoa powder: From the cocoa bean, cocoa powder provides the basis for hot chocolate and is used in many baked goods. Dutch cocoa is cocoa that has been treated with alkali, which makes the cocoa more soluble and neutralizes its natural acidity.

coconut: This fruit of the coconut palm has several layers. A deep tan husk encases a hard, dark brown, hairy shell. Beneath the shell is a thin, brown skin, under which lies a layer of creamy coconut meat that surrounds a milky, sweet, opaque juice. Coconut meat is available sweetened or unsweetened, shredded or flaked, moist or frozen.

coconut milk: This is actually an infusion made by combining grated coconut meat with boiling water, and simmering until foamy. Then the liquid is strained through a cheesecloth, squeezing as much liquid as possible from the meat. The meat can then be boiled with more water, and the resultant second batch of coconut milk is much thinner.

cod: Most commonly sold as skinless fillets, this ever-popular mild-tasting, snow-white fish has lean flesh with a big flake. Some substitutes include haddock, hake, and pollock. Note that scrod is a market term for cod, not a separate species.

cognac: A fine brandy produced in and around the town of Cognac in western France.

colander: A metal or plastic bowl-shaped container with a perforated bottom for draining and straining food. You might eventually want to buy a fine-meshed strainer, but a colander is your basic, all-purpose one.

collard greens: Dark, leafy green in the cabbage family, closely related to kale. Parboil or sauté for best flavor.

compote: Simply fruit—fresh, dried, or canned—that has been cooked slowly in a sugary syrup.

compound butter: Butter creamed with herbs, spices, garlic, wine, or whatever you wish. Perfect for finishing sauces or jazzing up just about any grilled or broiled food.

conch: These "univalve" mollusks (their shells do not open and close) can be as large as a foot long. You might see live conch (also called whelk) in the shell, but more often you will be offered a large (up to one-quarter pound) chunk of conch meat. This has been precooked, not quite to tenderness; the only preparation before cooking is cutting off the operculum, the shell-like covering that protects the meat.

confectioners' sugar: This powdered sugar is best in those recipes that will not be cooked at all, such as frostings, because it dissolves better than regular granulated sugar; it's also good sprinkled on top of baked goods.

core: To remove the center or core of a fruit. The core might be woody and tough, as in apples, or contain small seeds, as in tomatoes. Use a paring knife or apple corer.

coriander: The small, tan, nutty-tasting seeds (actually the dried, ripe fruit) of the herb cilantro, or Chinese parsley; used as a spice.

corned beef: Brined beef, usually from the brisket; if you have a choice, buy the flank cut rather than the point cut.

cornichon: Crisp little pickles, intensely sour, traditionally paired with pâtés.

cornstarch: This is one of the most useful thickening agents in the kitchen, with twice the thickening power of flour. Mix it with a small amount of cold water or other liquid before stirring it into other foods.

corn syrup: This thick, sweet syrup, made from processed cornstarch, comes in both light and dark versions. I rarely use it.

Cortland apple: This is a good all-purpose cooking apple, juicy and sweet-tart, with crisp, creamy white flesh and smooth, shiny red skin.

couscous: We treat couscous like a grain, although it's actually pasta of North African origin. Traditional methods of cooking are fairly complicated. For a more simple method, see page 191; it may not be ideal, but it will make a good and reliable side dish for weeknight cooking. Serve couscous with any moist stew or other dish with plenty of gravy. It doesn't have much flavor on its own.

crab: Has wonderfully succulent, deliciously sweet flesh. Can be served cold or hot. Comes in various sizes and forms: blue crab often has red claw tips, is usually sold live (but can also be picked from shell, then refrigerated or frozen), and is convenient and wonderful with a squirt of lemon or tossed with mayonnaise; Dungeness crab is exceptionally meaty and delicious, almost always cooked and refrigerated or frozen; king crab, the largest crab, is available only in the Northwest; stone crab is a recyclable

Floridian crab (fishermen break off claws, then throw the crab back in the water, where it generates another limb). Soft-shell crab is basically a blue crab caught after it has shed its hard outer shell.

cranberry: There are several species of cranberries, but we're most accustomed to the large, tart ones that are native to North America. Too hard and tart to eat out of hand, cranberries must be cooked or chopped to make a relish. Fresh, they can be stored in the refrigerator for weeks; or they can be frozen for months.

cranberry bean: Known in Italy as *borlotti,* these cream-colored beans with red streaks turn pinkish brown when cooked. They have a nice nutty flavor, and can be substituted for red or white beans in many recipes.

cream: To beat an ingredient, usually a fat such as butter or margarine, alone or with sugar until softened and well blended.

cream cheese: This tangy, smooth, spreadable cheese is as delicious in dips, frostings, and all kinds of desserts as it is spread on bagels. Lower-fat versions are available, but the texture is more gummy than creamy.

cream of tartar: An acidic, fine white powder that can be used to make baking powder.

crème fraîche: Between fresh and sour cream in texture and taste, this dairy product is slightly more tart. It is usually served lightly whipped with sugar as a complement to sweet desserts.

cremini: This domesticated brown mushroom has much better flavor than button mushrooms.

crepe: These thin French pancakes can be served with a sweet topping for breakfast or dessert, or rolled around a variety of sweet or savory fillings. A crepe pan, also useful for making blintzes, can be any shallow, heavy skillet with a six-inch base. A long handle is helpful as you swirl the batter, but not crucial. Crepes can be made well in advance, stacked, and refrigerated, even frozen. Bring back to room temperature before proceeding. See page 750 for my recipe.

croquette: Essentially a hamburger made with things other than ground meat, usually but not necessary breaded before cooking.

croutons: Nothing more than crisped bits or whole slices of bread. They may be dried in the oven with no seasonings at all, or cooked in oil or butter, with or without garlic and/or herbs. See page 82 for some recipes to get you started.

crystallized ginger: Crystallized ginger is candied ginger; it's been cooked in a sugar syrup and coated with a coarse sugar. Available in Asian markets and specialty food shops.

cumin: Available whole or ground, cumin lends its distinct, aromatic and somewhat bitter taste to foods. Great in curries, soups, stews, and vegetable dishes.

currant: Tiny, tart, grape-like berries are red, black, or white when fresh. More frequently, recipes call for dried currants— which are actually not currants at all, but the dried, seedless zante grape. In cooking, dried currants are most often used in baked goods; you can usually substitute raisins in a pinch, but remember that they contain (and absorb) more moisture.

curry powder: Widely used in Indian cooking, curry powder is actually a blend of up to twenty spices;

tumeric gives it its characteristic yellow color. Curry powder quickly loses its pungency, so store it, airtight, for no longer than two months.

custard: Like pudding, custard is a thick, creamy mixture of milk, sugar, and flavorings. Custard is thickened with eggs, pudding with cornstarch or flour. Remove custard from the oven while the center is still slightly wobbly; once it appears set, it's almost always overcooked.

cutlet: A tender, thin, boneless cut of meat; it could be part of a chicken or turkey breast, or veal, lamb, or pork, usually taken from the leg.

daikon radish: This large (sometimes foot-long), pure white, carrot-shaped radish is milder than the familiar red radishes. Frequently grated raw as a garnish for Japanese dishes, it may also be dipped in soy sauce, pickled, or cooked with other vegetables and spices.

dandelion: A strong-tasting green that is among the most vitamin-packed foods on the planet; when young it's relatively mild, but when it matures, it's the most bitter of all greens. Grows like a weed (you probably think it is one!) and rarely costs more than a dollar a pound. Wash and dry thoroughly before cooking.

dash: An approximate term of measurement for seasoning meaning little more than a sprinkle of the specified ingredient, as in "a dash of salt." Start with a tiny amount, and add more until the flavor of the dish suits your tastes.

date: The brown, oval-shaped staple of the eastern Mediterranean and western Asia. Intensely sweet; Deglet Noor is a good, and common, dried brand. Fresh dates are increasingly available.

daube: A classic French stew or pot roast is made with beef, red wine, vegetables, and seasonings. It's slowly braised for several hours in a covered dish.

deep fry: To cook food in hot fat deep enough to cover the food being fried. The fat should be around 350 to 375 degrees: if it's not hot enough, too much fat will be absorbed, but if it's too hot, the food will burn. (A frying thermometer or electric deep-fryer will help regulate.) Use plenty of oil; dry the food well with paper towels before deep frying; and add the food in small increments to keep the temperature from dropping too much.

deglaze: A quick and easy way to make a reduction sauce. After sautéing meat or other food, remove it from the pan and add a small amount of liquid to the flavorful bits left in the pan; heat and stir until the liquid is reduced to the desired consistency. You can deglaze with water, lemon juice, vinegar, wine, stock, juice, cream, or a combination.

dice: To cut food into small (one-eighth to one-quarter inch) cubes of equal size.

Dijon mustard: Originally from Dijon, France, this mustard is made from brown mustard seeds, white wine, grape juice, and seasonings. Ranges from mild to hot.

dill: Feathery herb with a delicate caraway taste. Best fresh, although dried dill has some flavor. Best raw, too—it loses intensity quickly when heated, although stems may be cooked in stews for a good flavor. An attractive garnish. Dill seeds can also be eaten; they are small, flat, and oval, with a similar caraway flavor.

dogfish: Also known as cape shark. Fillets are longer, more narrow, and sturdier than those of any other white-fleshed fish. Can be substituted in recipes that call for more tender fillets. Delicious broiled, and ideal for sautéing—flesh doesn't break easily. The fish most frequently used in England's fish and chips.

double boiler: A duo of pots used to warm or cook heat-sensitive foods, like custards and chocolate. The lower pot holds water, which heats the ingredients in the upper pot that sits inside it. You may need a double boiler arrangement at some point, but the chances are good you can rig one up by setting one pot on top of another; the fit need not be perfect.

dough: Dough is a mixture of flour, liquid, and usually a leavening agent (such as eggs or yeast), which is stiff but pliable. The primary difference between dough and batter is the consistency: Dough is thicker and must be molded by hand, while batter is semiliquid, thus spooned or poured.

dredge: To lightly coat food for frying, usually with flour, cornmeal, or bread crumbs.

dry-sauté: Dry-sautéing, or pan-grilling as it is also called, is cooking food over high heat with no oil at all. Non-stick pans make this possible. You can also dry-sauté sturdy food with even surfaces (such as steaks) in a well-seasoned cast-iron skillet.

dumpling: A small mound of dough usually pan-fried, deep-fried, or cooked in a liquid mixture, such as broth or stew. (See pages 34–35.)

Dutch oven: This big sturdy pot with a tightly fitting lid is used for moist cooking, such as braising or stewing. A six- to eight- quart Dutch oven—or covered casserole of the same size—is a near-necessity for most cooks.

eggplant: Good grilled, broiled, roasted, and sautéed, this relative of the tomato is mild-tasting and great-textured. Eggplant comes in all sizes and colors: my favorite is the small lavender variety, usually found in Asian markets. The more common deep purple variety makes fine eating; look for long narrow eggplants (which contain fewer seeds). Refrigerate and use within a few days.

egg roll: Usually served as an appetizer, this small, deep-fried Chinese pastry is filled with minced or shredded vegetables and often meat. Egg roll skins are available in Asian markets and many supermarkets.

electric mixer: If you bake a lot, you will want both a powerful standing mixer and a small, handheld mixer. If you bake only occasionally, you'll want one or the other. (If you never bake, a hand mixer or eggbeater would still come in handy for beating the occasional egg white or heavy cream.) In addition to beaters, standing mixers frequently come with dough hooks, wire whisks, and other special attachments.

Emmental cheese: Named for Switzerland's Emmental valley, this mellow, sweet but nutty cheese is the best Swiss cheese you can buy. It has big holes and a natural, light-brown rind.

empanada: These flaky turnovers are a Latin American specialty. Meat and vegetables are the most traditional filling, but you can stuff them with almost anything. Lard makes the flakiest crust, but you can substitute vegetable oil with fine results.

emulsion: A mixture of two or more liquids that don't easily combine, such as oil and vinegar. Should you decide to emulsify vinaigrette (it isn't crucial, but it does have nice texture), you can use a food processor or blender to make an emulsion that's stable for hours. You can also whisk the oil, vinegar, and seasonings, or shake them vigorously in a jar to create a short-lived but perfectly acceptable emulsion.

endive: Closely related to and often confused with chicory, endive comes in two main varieties: Belgian and curly. Belgian endive is creamy white and oblong with pale yellow tips; it's grown completely in the dark to prevent it from turning green. Curly endive has prickly dark green leaves and a pleasantly bitter flavor.

enoki: A slender Asian mushroom sold in small packages; good raw in salads or cooked as a garnish. To use, just trim off the spongy base and separate the strands.

espresso: This dark, strong coffee is made from French or Italian roast—beans with a shiny, dark oily surface.

fava bean: Also called broad beans, favas are quite large, often over an inch long, with a flat, kidney shape akin to that of a lima. Often eaten fresh, but dried ones are great mashed or pureed. Always buy split dried beans, which will cook faster and eliminate the need to remove the tough skin.

fennel: Fennel is a crisp, aromatic vegetable with a licorice flavor and celery-like texture. The bulb is delicious raw in salads (and good cooked), and the feathery fronds can be used as seasoning.

fennel seeds: These oval, greenish seeds come from a bulbless variety of fennel. Available whole or ground, they have a slight licorice flavor and fragrance. As with most seeds, store them in an opaque container for no more than six months.

fenugreek: Widely used in Indian cooking, fenugreek seeds come ground and whole; the whole seeds are yellow and flat. They are bitter, so use sparingly.

fermented black beans: This pungent Chinese specialty consists of small black soybeans preserved in salt and sold in covered jars or plastic bags. Fermented black beans are available in Asian markets, sometimes under the name "salty black beans." They will keep indefinitely.

feta cheese: A classic white Greek cheese, usually made with sheep's milk. It's crumbly, and has a tangy flavor.

fiddlehead: A barely emerged, tightly coiled (hence the name) fern, available only in spring, and locally—they will not ship. Fiddleheads are better as a wild food picked yourself than a supermarket item. If you find them, or buy them, simmer or steam as you would asparagus, then reheat in butter or dress with vinaigrette.

fig: Readily available dried, the fig has begun to make routine appearances here in its fresh form. In those places where it grows easily—throughout the Mediterranean, and in California and the Southwest—it is cheap and plentiful. Fresh figs have soft flesh with many tiny, edible seeds, and range from purple to green.

fillet: A boneless piece of meat, chicken, or fish.

fish sauce: Salty brown sauce made from fermented fish, usually anchovies. Sold as either *nuoc mam* (Vietnamese) or *nam pla* (Thai) in Asian markets and supermarkets with good oriental sections. An acquired taste but a fabulous flavor.

five-spice powder: Made from five ground spices—cinnamon, clove, fennel seed, star anise, and Szechwan peppercorns—this pungent spice mixture is common in Chinese dishes. Prepackaged versions are available in Asian markets and many supermarkets.

flageolet: These immature kidney beans harvested before maturity are medium in size (about one-half inch long), kidney shaped, and a lovely pale green. Quick-cooking and very fresh-tasting, flageolets are best treated simply. The classic treatment (page 509) features cream and herbs.

flatfish: Includes flounders, flukes, sole, dabs, and plaices. Distinguished by their eyes (on the top of their head), and swimming style (on their side). Have thin, fine-grained flesh; all can be used interchangeably. Cook flatfish quickly—even undercook, as they finish cooking between stove and table.

fold: To incorporate a light, fluffy mixture, such as beaten egg white, into a heavier mixture by gently lifting from underneath with a rubber spatula, spoon, or hand.

food mill: A food mill is like a mechanical sieve; it has a hand-turned blade that forces food through fine holes at the bottom, leaving skin and seeds behind. It's essential if you want to make applesauce or pureed tomato sauce, but you can live without it if neither of those matter to you.

food processor: The most important electric tool in the kitchen, a food processor can grate massive amounts of almost anything in seconds; make bread and pie dough in an instant; grind meat, and puree and slice vegetables. Small ones are valuable, but a large model that can handle at least six cups of batter or dough is best.

frangipane: A candy-like filling, usually flavored with ground almonds, used in pastries, tarts, and cakes.

free-range chicken or turkey: In theory, these birds are much better than the standard. They're fed differently, given fewer drugs, and have more room to roam. However, the quality is inconsistent and the price often outrageously expensive. Your best bet is to find a good local source and stick to it.

frittata: The Italian version of an omelet, served open-faced.

fritter: A deep-fried morsel, which may be a chunk of food dipped in batter (as an apple fritter) or a batter into which bits of food have been folded (as a corn fritter).

galangal: Similar to ginger, but woodier. To use, mince it very, very finely.

garam masala: An Indian spice blend that varies from cook to cook but almost always includes cardamom, cinnamon, cloves, coriander, black peppercorns, and/or other spices. My version (page 778) is mild and sweet but more black pepper or some added cayenne can quickly alter that.

garlic: Garlic, known as the stinking rose, is not only one of the most important seasonings; it is among the best-tasting cooked vegetables. Slowly sautéed or stewed, garlic has a sweet flavor and an aroma that fills the kitchen like nothing else (for recipes, see page 575). Buy garlic loose. Look for hard bulbs that have not sprouted and where each clove is firm. Size is not important, nor is skin color. Store garlic at room temperature in a dark, dry spot where it is exposed to air; when it becomes soft, discard it. Sprouts are more bitter than the cloves, but are treasured by some cooks; there's no reason not to try then.

garnish: You can garnish for appearance, flavor, or both. A sprig of parsley next to a sautéed chicken breast does little. A small handful of parsley sprinkled over that same meat adds great flavor and lends color contrast. I use many garnishes, but they're almost always primarily for flavor; good looks are secondary. Garnishes are almost always optional.

gelatin: This thickening agent (made from pure protein) is odorless, tasteless, and colorless, but when dissolved in hot water and then cooled, it forms a jelly that thickens whatever food it's been added to.

giblets: The cleaned gizzard, liver, and heart (sometimes the neck, too) of poultry, generally used to flavor gravy.

ginger: Often called a root, ginger is actually a tropical rhizome that's commonplace in many Asian cuisines. Fresh ginger is knobby and has a tough skin that must be peeled away to get to the fragrant, spicy flesh underneath. Dried ground ginger is not a substitute for fresh, but is useful in many sweet and savory dishes, including gingerbread and curries. For a recipe for homemade pickled ginger to serve with your sushi, see page 107.

glaze: To coat food with a thin liquid, such as egg wash or chocolate topping, that will be smooth and shiny after setting.

goat cheese: Also packaged as "chèvre," goat's milk cheese is pure white with a distinctive tart flavor. It can range from creamy and moist to dry and semi-firm, and is packaged in a wide variety of shapes, from cylinders to discs.

Granny Smith apple: A tart, hard green apple with super-crisp flesh that holds up well during baking.

granulated sugar: This is your basic, refined "white sugar," for daily use and most baking.

grape leaves: Often used in Greek and Middle Eastern recipes to wrap food for cooking. Look for fresh grape leaves, which are not that hard to find in most parts of the country. The bottled ones have little flavor.

grate: To reduce firm or hard food to small particles or shreds in a food processor or by rubbing it against a grater. Graters come in several shapes and sizes; a small, handheld device will do for grating Parmesan onto pasta; for grating potatoes and the like, you need a food processor or a sturdy box grater.

gravy: Gravy is simply a sauce made from meat juices. It's usually diluted with water, milk, wine, or stock, and thickened with flour or cornstarch. See The Basics of Reduction Sauces, page 790.

green and red leaf lettuce: These basic salad greens are distinctive, pleasantly bitter loose leaf, bunching, or cutting lettuces. If loose leaf, they should be used quickly, as they won't keep for more than a few days, even when stored in a plastic bag.

green beans: These may be one of any number of beans that are eaten fresh, such as the string bean, the thin haricot vert, the yard-long bean, the wax or yellow bean, and the romano. All can be eaten raw, briefly cooked—so that they remain crunchy—or cooked to complete tenderness. Buy beans that snap rather than fold when you bend them in half.

greens: To buy greens—broccoli raab, kale, mustard or turnip greens, spinach, collards, chard, dandelions, escarole, and so on—look for bright, crisp, firm leaves with no wilting, dry, or yellowing leaves. If you don't plan on preparing greens right away, store them loosely in a zip-locked plastic bag, making sure that all loose air is released from the bag.

grill: To cook on a rack over direct heat. Unlike barbecuing, grilling creates a seared crust. Almost any food that can be broiled can also be grilled.

grind: To use a food processor, chopper, grinder, or mortar and pestle to break solid food down into small pieces. Food can be ground coarsely, finely, or somewhere in-between.

ground beef: Simply beef that has been finely chopped, ground beef is sold fresh or frozen. These days, ground beef has some health risks associated with it, and the USDA is recommending that it be cooked to well done (165°F).

grouper: There are hundreds of types of this excellent all-purpose fish with delicious, meaty, lobster-like texture. Has white, tender, mildly flavored flesh that pulls off the bones easily. Fillets are great for grilling and deep-frying. Can also be "kebabed."

guacamole: A simple Mexican specialty made with mashed avocados flavored with lemon or lime juice, and sometimes with garlic, chile pepper, cilantro, and/or scallion or red onion. I like to include chunks of seeded and cored tomatoes too, but only if they are perfectly ripe.

half-and-half: This combination of equal parts cream and milk cannot be whipped, and has between ten and fifteen percent milk fat. Although it can be substituted for cream in some recipes, it is mostly used on cereal and in coffee.

ham hock: Cut from the hog's lower leg, often smoked or cured. Great in bean soups and other slow-cooked soups and stews, where they lend rich, smoky flavors.

haricot: A generic term for all New World beans, which includes almost everything: kidney, pinto, navy, pea, Great Northern, anasazi, cannellini, flageolets, appaloosa, and more.

hash: From the French *hacher,* which means "to chop," hash is a dish of chopped meat, usually roast beef or corned beef, combined with vegetables and seasonings and sautéed until lightly browned. It is frequently served with a sauce or gravy.

hazelnuts: Also called filberts, hazelnuts are rich, sweet nuts that are often ground or roasted in pastries, cookies, and other desserts. To remove the skin, toast the nuts in a baking pan at 350°F, stirring occasionally, until the hulls loosen and the nuts are lightly browned; then rub the nuts in a towel.

hoisin sauce: Brownish-red, sweet and spicy sauce, made from soybeans, garlic, chile pepper, and assorted spices. Can be thought of as Chinese ketchup, although it's usually added to stir-fries during the last couple of minutes of cooking. Sold in cans or jars; store in a tightly sealed jar in the fridge.

hollandaise sauce: Rich, creamy, emulsified sauce similar to mayonnaise but made with butter instead of oil and always served hot. Very lemony.

hominy: A traditional Native American food (also known as pozole or posole), hominy is dried field corn kernels with the hull and germ removed. Hominy is perfectly fine canned and ready-to-eat, but I prefer the dried version, as reconstituting and cooking it intensifies the flavor. When ground, hominy is called grits.

honey: The original and all-natural sweetener. If honey develops crystals, place the opened jar in a pan of hot water over low heat until the crystals disappear, or place in the microwave for thirty seconds.

horseradish: Long, coarse-looking root whose intense heat nearly vanishes during cooking. Fresh horseradish is simply grated; "prepared" horseradish is combined with vinegar and sold in jars (red horseradish is colored with beet juice). A good condiment.

huevos rancheros: A Mexican dish of fried eggs served atop a tortilla and covered with tomato sauce.

hull: To remove the outer covering, or pull out the stem and leafy top portion, of berries, especially strawberries.

hummus: Thick Middle Eastern puree of mashed chickpeas seasoned with tahini (sesame paste), garlic, lemon juice, and other varying spices. Great dip and sandwich spread.

infuse: To extract flavor from an ingredient, such as herbs or tea leaves, by slowly steeping in a hot liquid.

Italian sausage: This pork sausage is available in two forms—hot (spiced with hot red peppers) and sweet—and is usually seasoned with garlic. A perennially popular pizza topping that can also add punch to pasta sauces.

Jalapeño pepper: A plump, two-inch long chile that may be dark green or red; widely available and usually quite hot, When dried and smoked, a jalapeño is called a chipotle.

jam: Thick syrupy mixture of fruit and sugar.

jambalaya: The Cajun-Creole version of paella, most often associated with New Orleans cuisine. Usually made with rice, pork, sausage, ham, shellfish, and various seasonings.

jicama: Light brown tropical root vegetable with crisp, crunchy flesh and a nutty, slightly sweet flavor. Pronounced HICK-a-mah. Good raw or cooked.

julienne: To cut solid food, usually vegetables, into slender strips of equal length. The thin strips are also called matchsticks.

juniper berries: Strong, piney, and slightly sweet berries from an evergreen tree. Most often used in making gin, the berries are good in marinades for poultry, game, and fish, or added to sauerkraut and pâtès. Sold as a bottled spice in most supermarkets.

kale: Flavorful curly-leafed green, widely available. Collards and kale can be substituted for one another.

kasha: Toasted, hulled and crushed buckwheat groats (seeds) with a mildly nutty taste. The crushed grain must be cooked lightly and carefully, as it easily turns to mush.

kebabs/kabobs: Small chunks of meat, fish, or shellfish—usually marinated—arranged on skewers and grilled over hot coals. Vegetables such as onions, tomatoes, and mushrooms are often cooked with the meat.

kelp: Also known as kombu, this is a dark brown or gray, strong-flavored sea vegetable that has been dried in the sun. Important in making Japanese dashi, a basic stock, kelp is sold in health food stores and Asian specialty stores.

key limes: Small, yellow-green limes that are tarter in flavor than the more common Persian limes. They are most famous for their role in key lime pie, the tangy, custard pie made with a meringue topping. Often hard to find.

kidney bean: This reddish brown dried bean is up to an inch long and, naturally, kidney-shaped. Virtually all-purpose, kidney beans are delicious whether they are baked, or as a puree; a tasty part of dishes such as chili, beans and rice, and refried beans. They take a good hour to cook, and sometimes more.

kimchi/kimchee: The fiery cabbage-based staple of Korea, heavily seasoned with garlic and chile.

kiwi: A relative newcomer to our shores, the kiwi is originally from China, but is now widely grown in all moderate climates. Its unusual and starkly green color has made it a popular garnish, but it is a decent-tasting fruit, inexpensive, widely available, and easy to eat. Add kiwi to fruit salad, or poach it in a light syrup.

knead: To mix pliable dough (usually bread dough) with your hands, electric mixer, or food processor in order to develop gluten, which makes dough elastic.

kohlrabi: A bulbous member of the cabbage family that resembles a turnip in appearance and flavor, and can be treated as such.

kosher salt: Coarse-grained salt that is easy to handle; keep a container near the stove and use it while you cook.

kumquat: The most unusual of citrus fruits (well, in fact, it isn't a citrus, but it looks and acts like one), with a thin peel that is sweeter than the flesh. Wonderful poached, or chopped raw in relish. Look for firm, unblemished fruits and store them in the refrigerator.

lard: Pork fat, rendered and clarified, with a firm texture and good flavor. Lard has fallen out of favor, but is great in pie crusts and good for frying (especially beans).

lattice topping: A topping consisting of strips of dough crisscrossed atop a pie.

leavening agent: An ingredient that causes dough or batter to rise, lightening its texture and increasing its volume, such as beaten eggs or egg whites, baking powder, baking soda, and yeast.

leeks: These members of the onion family look like big, fat scallions, and are delicious cooked. Look for leeks with lots of white, and wash them well; they're almost always sandy.

lemon: The most useful of all fruits in European cooking (the lime being the most useful in Asian and tropical cooking), the lemon adds mild, flavorful acid to dishes in a way that nothing else can—not even the finest vinegar. If you always keep a lemon or two in the kitchen, you'll wind up using it daily—a squeeze of fresh lemon juice can almost always used in the simplest, delicious, low-fat dish (grilled, broiled, or roasted). Lemon zest (the yellow part of the peel) is infinitely useful too; for instructions on how to zest a lemon, see page 634.

lemon verbena: Fragrant, sweet, lemony herb that makes a good tea and adds delicate flavor to custards and similar desserts.

lentils: Flat and round, lentils are the fastest cooking of all dried beans. The three major varieties are Le Puy, the most intensely flavored lentil; common green or brown lentils; and yellow or red lentils, which are popular in Indian cooking—particular dal.

lima beans: Flat, green-tinged beans (called butter beans in the South), which can be parboiled and buttered or used in stews and soups. Fresh are better than frozen, but frozen are acceptable.

lime: If the lemon did not exist, we would relay supremely on the lime, which has a stronger and less fragrant nature; some call it harsher. Its juice can be used instead of lemons in almost every instance. But lime has one advantage over lemon: It takes better to very strong flavors. To extract the juice from a lime, cut it in thirds through its axis, then squeeze by hand. To zest, see lemon instructions on page 634.

liqueur: Sweet alcoholic beverages flavored with fruits, herbs, or spices, usually served after dinner. Some, such as Amaretto and Grand Marnier, are useful as flavorings in desserts.

littleneck clams: There are essentially two types of clams: the softshell (or steamer) and the hardshell (or quahog). Littlenecks are the smallest of the hardshells.

lobster: The most crucial part of preparing lobster is in the purchase. Be sure to choose a freshly caught, lively one—one that flips its tail and legs about in and out of the water, and one with a rock-hard shell if possible. Cook and serve simply.

mace: The outer covering of nutmeg, reddish-orange and lacy. Used as nutmeg or cinnamon, with mild nutmeg-y flavor.

mahi-mahi: Contrary to popular belief, mahi-mahi is not a mammalian dolphin. A warm-water fish with dark meat that turns brown after cooking. With its good flavor and texture, mahi-mahi is a great alternative to swordfish. Great for grilling, and when cooked with many other flavorful ingredients.

mako shark: Fairly inexpensive fish with ivory-pink flesh that resembles swordfish in color and texture (but not in appearance). Be sure to smell shark when purchasing; never buy shark that has the slightest whiff of ammonia. Perfect for marinating, grilling, and cooking with spicy flavors. Other available shark includes dusky, black-tip, silky, lemon, bull, tiger, or hammerhead shark.

malanga: A tuber sold in all Latin American markets and some supermarkets; you might find it under the name "yautia." Raw, it has the texture of jicama, but it is not eaten raw. It's best boiled, fried, or included in stews—in short, treated exactly as a potato. Buy very firm, crisp specimens, and don't count on keeping them too long. Peel and trim before cooking.

mandoline: The original food processor, and still highly useful, the mandoline is the easiest way to cut thin slices of vegetables.

mango: Oblong tropical fruit of which there are some two hundred varieties. We usually eat them ripe, as a fruit or in salsa. Green mangoes, however, make great salads and chutneys.

maple syrup: Sap from the sugar-maple tree that has been boiled down until thick and sweet. Pure maple syrup is in a different universe than "pancake syrup," which is essentially colored corn syrup.

margarine: Vegetable oil made hard through a process called hydrogenation, margarine tastes lousy and is bad for you. Note that "shortening" is essentially white margarine. Stick with oil and butter as your primary cooking, baking, and eating fats.

marinate: To soak meat, vegetables, or fish in seasoned liquid. Adds flavor but, contrary to conventional "wisdom," does little to tenderize.

marjoram: Like oregano, but better, and not bad dried.

mash: To crush a food, such as avocados or cooked potatoes or beans, into a smooth mixture.

matzo meal: The ground version of unleavened bread. Interchangeable with cracker meal and a good substitute for bread crumbs.

melon: There are three kinds of melons (aside from watermelon, page 648, a different species entirely). Small melons with ridged skin, such as the charentais, more common in Europe; those with a meshed rind, such as the cantaloupe; and those with a smooth rind, like the honeydew. All of them are good when fully ripe, but finding a ripe melon is not easy, and they do not ripen well once they're off the vine. Here are some keys: First, smell it; an appetizing smell is a good sign. Next, shake it; loose seeds are a decent indication of ripeness. Finally, squeeze the ends, especially the one opposite the stem; it should be fairly tender, almost soft.

melt: To transform solids into liquids, usually using slow heat. The microwave is great for melting chocolate and butter.

meringue: Egg whites, combined with sugar, beaten until stiff and then baked as cookies or pie topping; crisp on the outside and light and fluffy within.

mesclun: A word used to describe a mixture of a dozen or more wild and cultivated greens, herbs, and edible flowers. Unless you're a gardener, you have no choice about what is included in a mesclun mix, but a good one will contain greens of various textures and flavors—including sweet, spicy, and bitter greens, and at least a smattering of herbs. Relatively speaking, it costs a fortune, but one-half pound will serve four.

mince: To cut solid food into very fine pieces.

mint: This highly recognizable herb adds its cool, refreshing taste to teas, desserts, and lamb dishes. The two most common varieties are peppermint and spearmint; better fresh, but decent dried.

monkfish: Known as the poor man's lobster, because of its extremely firm, meaty texture. Highly versatile, it can be poached, roasted, sautéed, or grilled. When purchasing, ask the fishmonger to remove any membrane that remains on the fillet; otherwise, cut it and peel it off before cooking.

morel: This fine-flavored and oddly-textured mushroom is found wild all over the North, and sometimes in large enough quantity to make it to stores (although rarely supermarkets). It's more readily available dried, and worth having in your pantry. (See page 583 for instructions for reconstituting dried mushrooms.)

mung bean: This tiny (about one-eighth inch in diameter), dried round bean is green or, if peeled, yellow. Used to make bean-thread noodles, and great for sprouting (page 524), mung beans are sometimes used in the Indian dish *dal* (page 524). They take about an hour to cook if they're whole, and about thirty minutes if peeled.

mussels: Much less expensive than clams, and almost as delicious as lobster. Look for clean, not muddy, mussels, and put them in a pot under slowly running cold water for thirty minutes or more. Wash carefully and toss out any broken shells, then scrape off beard. When steaming mussels, add a bit of saffron for a heavenly flavor.

mustard seed: The mustard plant seed is most often available in its brown version, which is the most flavorful. Black mustard seeds are sharper and more pungent, while the yellow or white seeds are the mildest.

nori: Also known as laver, these thin sheets of dried seaweed are mild-flavored and easy to like. Primarily used for wrapping sushi, but you can toast them to crisp them up, then crumble into salads or over cooked dishes such as grains.

nutmeg: Nutty, complex spice mostly in baking (but great with spinach). Use very sparingly.

ocean perch: A variety of West Coast rockfish, ocean perch are cheap, widely available, mildly flavored, pink-fleshed fillets. Ideal for use in any recipe that calls for white-fleshed fish. Generally quite tender; look for fresh, salty-smelling fillets.

okra: Many northerners have never come to appreciate okra. It is an unusual vegetable, in that it produces an odd, thick liquid (useful in thickening stews) when cooked for a long time. But it has good flavor and is wonderful fried. Okra should be small; don't buy it when it's over two or three inches long. Pods should be firm, undamaged, and not at all mushy. Its best season is summer, but you may find okra through the fall.

olive oil: There are two kinds of olive oil worth buying. The best is extra-virgin oil, which comes from the first, cold pressing of olives, and ranges from reasonably priced to very expensive. "Pure" olive oil is also decent—it may be extra-virgin oils that didn't make the grade, or, more often, oils extracted from the pulp left after making extra-virgin oils. Olive oil is the only real all-purpose oil.

orange roughy: Ocean perch–like fish from New Zealand. Often substituted for cod. Can be used in any recipe calling for white-fleshed fish.

oregano: A member of the mint family often associated with Italian cooking, but also popular in Greece and Mexico. Marjoram is similar and usually better.

oyster: Four major species in the United States are: Atlantic, found along the East and Gulf coasts; the European, a flat-shelled, round oyster of the Northwest and Maine; the Olympia, the half-dollar–sized oyster grown in the Northwest; and the fruit-flavored Pacific oyster, known for its wildly scalloped shell. See page 348 for illustrations on how to shuck oysters or, if possible, ask the fishmonger to shuck them for you. The best oysters should be eaten raw, but some taste divine when cooked. For oysters on the half-shell, use just a hint of lemon, or Tabasco, black pepper, or shrimp cocktail sauce.

oyster mushroom: A fan-shaped, wild mushroom with a grayish cap, cultivated in small clusters. Available in Asian markets and specialty produce stores.

papaya: A wonderful orange-fleshed, melon-like fruit, best split down the middle, black seeds removed (they are edible, so crunch away if you prefer), and served with lime juice—typically for breakfast. Some weigh ten pounds, but most are about the size of a mango. Papaya will ripen at room temperature, so you can buy firm specimens; eat when soft.

paprika: Ground dried red peppers, may be hot or sweet, and best when Hungarian in origin.

parboil/blanch: To parboil, or blanch, you partially cook food, usually vegetables, in boiling water to cover. This method keeps vegetables bright, while partially tenderizing them (see page 532, Precooked Vegetables in Butter or Oil, for details).

parchment paper: Grease-resistant paper good for lining baking sheets.

paring knife: Thin, sharp knife with a three- to four-inch blade. Essential kitchen tool.

Parmesan: Made from cow's milk, this nutty-sweet dry cheese is the best for grating (and good for eating out of hand). The only real parmesan is Parmigiano-Reggiano; the others are all imitations.

parsley: Whether curly or flat-leafed, this herb is indispensable in cooking and garnishing—its fresh flavor makes a super last-minute addition to countless savory dishes. Flat-leafed parsley has slightly better flavor.

parsnip: Root vegetable that looks like a white carrot. Great in soups and stews, and fine when pureed.

passion fruit: Purplish-brown on the outside, filled with (edible) pits and orange flesh inside, the passion fruit does not inspire passion until one eats it. Unadulterated, it is tart and hard to take. The best use is to strain the flesh and use the juice in Soft Fruit Sorbet (page 669).

pastry bag: A cone-shaped, open-ended bag that's worth owning if you do much baking. The small end is fitted with decorative tips of various sizes and patterns; dough, frosting, filling, or whipped cream is put in the large end.

pastry blender: A device of curving, sharp wires used to cut butter or other of fat into flour, usually for a pie crust. Not essential.

peanut oil: This flavorful oil borders on all-purpose. Its flavor, though distinctive, is not overpowering, and it is a great oil for cooking (especially highly spiced foods and Asian dishes in which olive oil is out of place), as well as for the occasional salad dressing. I use it for some sautéing and all stir-frying.

pearl onions: Tiny, marble-sized onions that are a pain to peel but make a good side dish or addition to soups or stews. Frozen ones are easier to deal with, if less flavorful.

Pecorino Romano: Hard grating cheese made from sheep's milk with a nutty, earthy flavor. Perfect on some pasta dishes and delicious eaten plain.

pectin: Found naturally in fruits and vegetables, gelatin- like pectin is used as a thickener in jellies and jams. Available in liquid and dry forms.

Pequín chile: Small red pepper with a lot of heat. Great in salsas.

persillade: A combination of garlic and chopped parsley usually added to dishes just before cooking is complete. Nice combined with bread crumbs as a crust.

persimmon: The brilliant orange, smooth-skinned fruit that is torturously tart when unripe, but sweet and delicious when finally ready—by which time you're convinced they've turned to mush. Unlike most other fruits, there is not such thing as an over-ripe persimmon. When they gain a translucent, shiny glow, they'll be juicy and sweet. Simply lop off the top and eat the insides with a spoon, or eat it, quite messily, out of hand.

pesto: Basil, pine nuts, garlic, olive oil, and Parmigiano-Reggiano cheese, although the mixture can vary. Great pasta sauce and all-purpose condiment.

phyllo dough: Papery-thin sheets of pastry dough used in many sweet and savory Greek dishes, which can be found in the frozen foods section of most supermarkets.

pickle: To preserve food in a vinegar or brine mixture. The process need not be a long one; see page 105.

pilaf: Rice-based dish in which the rice is cooked in hot oil or butter before simmering in liquid.

pimentos: A name used for roasted red peppers that have been canned or bottled in liquid. Look for brands without preservatives.

pinch: A very small amount, so-called because it can be held between the thumb tip and the forefinger.

pineapple: Buy perfectly ripe pineapples or none at all. The single best indicator of ripeness is fragrance—a good pineapple has an irresistibly enticing smell.

pine nuts: Also pignoli nuts, these small, pellet-shaped nuts from the pine cone have a wonderfully sweet, rich flavor. The Southwestern pignons are similar.

pinto bean: From beige to rust and usually mottled, this bean is about one-half inch long and oval-shaped. Pinto beans make wonderful refried beans; they are also good for beans and rice, chili, or served as a puree.

pipe: To squeeze a paste-like mixture (usually frosting) through a pastry bag.

pit: Or "stone." To remove the pit or seed from a fruit or olive.

pizza peel: A flat, broad sheet of wood or metal with a handle, also called a baker's peel. Allows you to slide breads and pizzas easily onto a stone.

plantain: The cooking banana, which can be used green, yellow, or black, and is terrific sautéed, braised, or stewed.

plum sauce: An Asian sweet-and-sour sauce made from plums, apricots, sugar, and other seasonings. Sold in jars or cans; store in a tightly covered container in the refrigerator.

plum tomatoes: These oval-shaped tomatoes have wonderful flavor, although they are never as luscious as a good round tomato. They are the best sauce tomatoes, because their flesh is quite thick.

poach: To cook by submerging food in a very gently boiling liquid.

poblano chile: Dark green, relatively mild chile known as ancho when dried.

polenta: Fluffy combination of cornmeal and water, successfully prepared by a variety of methods. Best served sauced or allowed to harden, sliced, and grilled.

pomegranate: The pomegranate is among the strangest and most cumbersome of the fruits we eat—a labyrinth of seeds wrapped in fruit buried in a mass of inedible flesh surrounded by a tough skin. To "eat," you suck on or chew the seeds, which are edible, but not especially pleasant. Were it not for the delightful, sweet-tart flavor of the fruit, not one would bother. The best way to enjoy this flavor is by purchasing pomegranate molasses, available in Middle Eastern stores.

poppy seeds: Tiny bluish-black seeds from the poppy flower that provide crunch and sweetness in cookies and other baked goods.

porcini: Also called cèpes, these meaty, large-topped mushrooms are simply the best. Although they are most frequently sold dried, it's becoming easier to find them fresh; they're expensive but a real treat.

portobello mushrooms: Enormous version of cremini with robust flavor. Delicious when grilled or broiled, good sautéed.

preserves: Fruits or vegetables, whole or chopped, simmered in a sugary syrup.

pressure cooker: Handy fast-cooking pot whose tight seal allows internal pressure to build, raising the temperature. Best for stews and soups, this is a useful but not essential piece of equipment.

prosciutto: This salt-cured, air-dried ham is best used as a seasoning or cut into paper-thin slices as an appetizer; great with melon, figs, or hunks of Parmesan cheese.

prune: Dried plum, best when purchased in bulk.

pudding: Like custards, thick, creamy mixtures of milk, sugar, and flavorings. Custards are thickened with eggs, puddings with cornstarch or flour.

puff pastry: Layers upon layers of pastry dough, each separated by a film of butter. Time-consuming but easy to make.

pulp: The succulent flesh of a fruit.

pulverize: To break a food down to powder by crushing or grinding.

puree: To finely blend and mash a food to a smooth, lump-free consistency. You can puree foods in a blender, food processor, or food mill.

quesadilla: Essentially a flour tortilla filled with cheese and perhaps beans, meat, salsa, or vegetables, a quesadilla is usually pan-fried or cooked under a broiler.

quiche: A savory, egg-based pie baked in a flaky crust; one of the great picnic dishes, also a fine lunch or appetizer.

quinoa: Sweet, light-yellow grain from South America.

radicchio: Peppery, crunchy, and bitter—like all member of the chicory clan—radicchio usually has bright red leaves and a tight head.

ragu: Meaty, slow-cooked tomato sauce, ideal with lasagne, ravioli, and any other fresh pasta. Make a large batch and freeze it for later use.

ramekins: Individual, ovenproof baking dishes made of ceramic, porcelain, or glass and used in the preparation of custards and other miniature sweet or savory dishes.

ravioli: Little pasta pillows filled with cheese, meat, vegetable(s), or other filling.

reconstitute: To bring a dried, dehydrated food back to its original consistency by adding a liquid.

red beans: These are medium-sized, dark red beans akin to kidneys and pintos.

red pepper flakes: The dried flakes of the red hot chile pepper.

reduce: To cook a liquid, usually a sauce or stock, over high heat, thereby decreasing its volume and intensifying its flavor.

reduction sauce: A sauce that uses as its base the pan juices that are created from stove-top cooking or oven-roasting meat, fish, poultry, or vegetables. Reduction sauces can be made easily and quickly.

render: To cook a food over low heat until it releases its fat.

rhubarb: A celery-like vegetable we treat as a fruit (in fact a court case once decided that it was a fruit). Never eat the leaves of a rhubarb, which contain poisonous levels of oxalic acid.

rice: Long-grain rice (including basmati rice) cooks in firm, dry kernels; short-grain, or medium-grain, rice cooks up moist and slightly sticky, as its outer layer absorbs more liquid than long-grain rice.

rice noodles: Common in Southeast Asia, we can find these dried in supermarkets and Asian markets. Can be served after soaking in hot water, but best when soaked and then boiled quickly.

rice paper: An edible paper made from rice and used to wrap dumplings, Vietnamese summer rolls, and other Asian foods.

ricer: A plunger-operated utensil that is the best tool for making mashed potatoes. Hardly essential, but a real pleasure.

rice vinegar: Delicately flavored vinegar with lower acidity than many other commercial vinegars, which makes it fine option for vinaigrette. Sold in many supermarkets and all Asian stores.

ricotta: Rich, fresh, moist cheese that may be made with whole or skim milk.

risotto: The classic creamy rice dish of northern Italy, usually made with Arborio rice.

roasting: This form of cooking uses indirect, dry, and usually high heat. Roasting should crisp up the exterior of foods while allowing the interior to cook relatively slowly. Liquids that result from roasting make great sauces.

roasting pan: I recommend purchasing a 8 × 12- or 9 × 13-inch metal or ceramic pan, which will come in handy for broiling meat, roasting chicken, making macaroni and cheese, and even baking breads or brownies. Stay away from uncoated aluminum.

rockfish: Wonderful, firm, white- and sweet-fleshed fish that is the West Coast equivalent of red snapper. Tasty and highly versatile, although not sturdy enough to grill, they can be considered all-purpose fish.

roe: A word used to refer to either a female fish's eggs or male fish's milt, or sperm. Exquisite roe can come from carp, mackerel, or herring, but Americans seems to focus on the roe of shad. Roe should smell fresh and be firm. Caviar is the salted roe of sturgeon.

rolling pin: Straight rolling pins, without ball bearings, are lighter and easier to handle than the more familiar type. Rolling pins come in handy for crushing bread crumbs and other foods.

romaine (cos) lettuce: This lettuce has long, narrow leaves, crunchy ribs, and a slight tang. Also called cos lettuce because of its origin on the Aegean island of Cos.

rosemary: Fragrant, piney herb. Fresh is best, but dried is quite good. Mince or crush the needles before adding to food.

rouille: A chile- and garlic-laced mayonnaise served most often with bouillabaisse.

Russian dressing: Better on sandwiches than salads, and best when made with fresh mayonnaise. But in its heart a simple mixture of mayo and ketchup.

rutabaga: A root vegetable that is not a turnip, but is treated like one, the rutabaga (also sold under the name "swede") is larger and somewhat coarser in texture than its cousin. Unless you are a devotee, you will probably find that you like the white-fleshed turnip more than the orange-fleshed rutabaga. However, rutabaga stores well in the refrigerator and can be used in any turnip recipe.

sabayon: Also known as zabaglione, a luscious dessert containing egg yolks, wine, cream, and sugar. It can be enjoyed by itself or served as a sauce for other desserts. Delicious when eaten warm, sabayon can also be refrigerated and served cold.

saffron: Fragrant, thread-like, hand-picked stigmas from the crocus. Adds super color and good mild but bitter flavor to many dishes. Highly expensive. The best thing to do is invest in an ounce (around fifty dollars)—stored in a tightly sealed opaque container in your pantry, it will last you ten years or more.

sage: Silver-green, fuzzy leaves with distinctive flavor (if you've eaten breakfast sausage, you know sage). Fresh is best, but dried can be quite good; crumble before adding.

sake: Japanese wine made from fermented rice.

salad spinner: A manual tool that is wonderfully helpful in draining excess moisture from freshly washed greens. Good investment.

salmon: One of the most popular finfish, rich, oily (it's beneficial oil), and highly flavorful. Easy to cook—in any number of ways (salmon can be poached, steamed, grilled, or broiled).There are many varieties to choose from, and purchasing salmon can be very confusing. Many markets sell "Norwegian" salmon as if it were a distinct species; but it is actually Atlantic salmon (and Atlantic salmon is now grown in the Pacific Northwest, northern Europe, Chile, and any other place where there is cold, protected seawater). There are five species of wild Pacific salmon: king (or Chinook) and sockeye, which are leaner than Atlantic salmon, and equally as flavorful; coho (silver); and chum (keta). I recommend purchasing the lean and rich king or sockeye salmon, or any succulent Atlantic salmon.

salsa: The Spanish (and Italian) word for "sauce," salsa usually refers to cooked or fresh combinations of fruits and/or vegetables. The most popular salsa is the refreshing Latino mixture of tomatoes and chile peppers.

salsify: Also called an oyster plant, because it, at least theoretically, tastes like an oyster (personally, I don't get it). Grayish or black (in which case it is called *scorzonera*) on the outside and pearly white on the inside, this root should be peeled and dropped into acidulated water to prevent discoloration, as you would artichoke, and cooked like carrots, parsnips, or potatoes.

salt cod: Expensive and relatively uncommon fish. Fish cakes made with salt cod are the best. Remove the center bone (if it has one), cut the meat into large pieces, and soak overnight (change the water at least four times). Cook fish before using in fish cakes.

samosa: An Indian fried dumpling of dough surrounding vegetables, meat, or both. Though typically deep-fried, samosas can be baked.

sardine: Small, silvery fish with rich, tasty dark flesh. Enormously popular in Europe as an appetizer.

Fresh sardines should be iced immediately after catching and eaten as soon as possible. Great broiled.

satay: Marinated meat, chicken, or fish on skewers, usually seasoned or served with a peanut sauce.

saturated fat: Mainly derived from animals, although some vegetable fats are also highly saturated. A good clue that a fat is saturated is that it is solid at room temperature.

saucepan: You need at least three—small, medium, and large. Stainless steel is your best bet, but aluminum and cast-iron with a porcelain coating are also good choices. Never use uncoated aluminum, as the metal will react with acidic ingredients.

sauerkraut: Meaning "sour cabbage," in German, it is shredded and pickled cabbage. Use sauerkraut without preservatives, and avoid canned sauerkraut, which often assumes the taste of metal.

sauté: French for "jump," sauté means to cook food in fat or butter until nicely browned. Best for thin cuts.

savory: Rosemary-like herb that works well with beans, meat, fish, and eggs. Winter and summer savory are interchangeable in recipes, and dried savory is quite decent.

scallion: Actually a green onion, a scallion is an immature onion with a white base (not yet a bulb) and long green leaves. Both parts of scallion are edible.

scallop: A great mollusk with creamy texture and subtle but distinctive flavor. True bay scallops and sea scallops are the best.

score: To cut shallow lines, diamonds, or triangles in meat, fish, or bread. Scoring aids in the tenderizing process, but it is also done simply for decorative purposes.

scungille: *See* Conch.

sea bass: This small, firm-fleshed species is one of the best fish to cook whole. The black sea bass of the North Atlantic is the most commonly seen species. Ideal for broiling, roasting, frying, or steaming, and perfect for pan-frying. Look for clean and sweet-smelling fish.

sear: To cook meat quickly over intense heat, usually in a skillet, on a grill, in an oven, or under a broiler, so as to form a crust.

season: To add flavor to foods—in the form of salt, pepper, herbs, spices, vinegar, etc.—so that their taste is improved.

sea vegetables: A rich source of iodine and an important food source in many oriental cultures. Sea vegetables such as dulse, hijiki, and arame can be soaked briefly in water, squeezed dry, and cut up for salad. Laver (or nori) is what you use to make sushi.

semolina flour: Delicately flavored flour made from coarsely ground durum wheat; primarily used to make pasta.

serrated knife: A knife with sharp, saw-like notches, best for slicing bread.

sesame oil: This oil pressed from sesame seeds has a slightly nutty flavor, making it a good cooking oil (especially in stir-fries) and tasty in some salads as well. Sesame oil is a mainstay of Chinese cookery.

Comes in two varieties, light and dark. Dark is always preferable (and it's what I always use).

sesame seeds: Flat, tiny, tan, and lightly sweet. When toasted, sesame seeds assume a nuttier, crunchy taste, making them great on breads, cookies, and pastries.

seviche: A popular dish in Latin-American cookery, seviche is raw fish marinated in citrus. The acid in the citrus "cooks" the fish, usually scallops, red snapper, or sole.

shallots: One of the finest and mildest flavored members of the onion family, finally widely available and useful in a wide range of dishes.

sherry vinegar: This recent addition to American markets is a good wine vinegar that is better than inexpensive balsamic vinegar. I love it in salads, and also as a marinade for grilled and broiled dishes.

shiitake: The best domesticated mushroom, with a rich, distinctive, smoky flavor, increasingly sold fresh in supermarkets. (It's also sold dried.) Do not eat the stem, but reserve it for stocks.

shortbread: A rich, buttery, tender, yet also crisp, cookie. One of the best.

shortening: Although good at holding air, shortening has either little or bad flavor—I recommend you stick with butter for baking.

short ribs: The cut-off ends of the prime rib, which should be cooked in liquid until quite tender—mushy, even.

shred: To slice food into very narrow strips, using a grater, food processor, or knife.

shrimp: America's most popular shellfish, the best shrimp is, of course, freshly caught and fairly local. Most shrimp is frozen, however, and is still quite good.

shuck: To peel off or remove the shell from oysters or clams, or the husk from an ear of corn.

sieve: Also called a strainer, the sieve has a mesh or perforated bottom, and is used for straining liquids or sifting.

sifter: When flour or sugar is passed through this old-fashioned mesh-bottomed kitchen tool, lumps are removed. These days, sifting is rarely necessary.

simmer: To cook in gently bubbling liquid.

skate: Relative of the shark, skate is fairly inexpensive, as it isn't widely used in the United States. Its unusual structure makes it easy to eat—just lift the meat off the central cartilage and you are left with a perfect fillet. When purchasing, look for sweet-smelling skate with no trace of an ammonia smell; never buy skate with the inedible skin on—it's very difficult to remove. Skate is usually poached before it is cooked in other ways; it can be sautéed, deep-fried, or broiled.

skewers: Thin wood or metal rods used for kebabs and other grilling. Also good for testing doneness of meat or fish.

skillet: Also called a frying pan, a skillet has a flat bottom, and slightly curved, shallow sides. Although copper is best and cast-iron very good, I prefer to use heavy-duty aluminum skillets with a non-stick coating, as they are light, cheap, and do a good job.

slice: To cut, into long, flat pieces.

snow peas: Edible-pod peas with soft, green pods and tiny peas.

soba noodles: Buckwheat noodles, brown, flat, and usually served in broth.

sorbet: Water, sugar, and flavorings, usually fresh fruit, frozen in an ice-cream machine. Best eaten immediately after making.

sorrel: Somewhere between an herb and a green, sorrel has a sour, lemony flavor. Great in soups.

soufflé: From the French for "breath," a fluffy, airy dish that can be savory or sweet. Soufflés rise as they bake, forming a top hat–like shape, and most should be served immediately.

soufflé mold: Also called a soufflé dish, this special dish is ovenproof and has straight sides to encourage the soufflé's rising.

sour cream: Cultured cream that gets its tanginess from lactic acid. Note that there's a big difference between sour cream and spoiled cream.

sourdough bread: Tangy bread made with a natural starter. Although the initial process is time-consuming, preparing and baking sourdough bread can become simple and easy.

soybean: Soybeans are round, under one-half inch in diameter, and usually yellowish, although they may be other colors. Not a prime cooking bean, soybeans are used to make a host of soy products, including that venerable meat substitute, tofu, for which you'll find recipes on pages 526–527.

soy sauce: This all-important Asian cooking ingredient is made from fermented soybeans, wheat (sometimes), water, and salt. Great as a marinade, in sauces and soups, and as a flavoring in meat, fish, and vegetable dishes.

spaghetti squash: The flesh of this squash resembles a mass of spaghetti-like strands. It's incredibly bland compared to the best winter squashes, but it is a pleasant novelty. Bake or steam it until done (cook whole, not cut in half, piercing the skin a few times with a skewer or thin-bladed knife). Cut it in half, scrape the flesh out of the skin, and toss the strands with any sauce or, more simply, with butter, salt, and pepper; or treat as you would grated summer squash or zucchini, sautéing it or making it into pancakes.

Spanish onions: Like Bermuda onions, these are large, relatively mild, easy to handle, and keep well for weeks. Good for baking.

spareribs: The long cut of meat from the lower breastbone of the hog. Spareribs are best cooked slowly, so that their fat can be rendered and they can become tender.

spatula: Made of rubber, metal, or plastic, the spatula is a flexible flat blade with a handle. Essential for turning foods (metal), scraping bowls and pans (rubber or plastic), and folding (rubber).

spinach: The best spinach is, of course, fresh, and should have crisp, robustly green leaves. Always wash well in several changes of water, and remove the extra-thick stems.

spice grinder: Basically a coffee grinder with another name. Useful.

split peas: Green or yellow, and mealy when cooked. Good soup base.

springform pan: This round baking pan has high, straight, removable sides, which allows cakes (especially cheesecake) to be removed easily.

spring rolls: Chinese pastries that are stuffed with vegetables and sometimes meat, then deep-fried.

squid: This cephalopod has become popular in the United States, as long as you call it calamari. Fresh squid should be purple to white—avoid any squid with brown coloring—and smell sweet and clean. Squid freezes well, and loses little flavor during defrosting and refreezing.

star anise: Aromatic spice that gets its name from the star-shaped pod that holds its seeds. Star anise, an ingredient in Chinese five-spice powder, is available in some supermarkets and Asian specialty markets.

steam: To cook a food in a closed vessel over (not in) simmering liquid, usually water. Food is placed in a steamer insert, which may be metal, bamboo, or a homemade creation.

steamer insert: A collapsible aluminum basket-like utensil used for steaming vegetables and other foods.

steep: To soak (usually tea bags) in boiling water for a few minutes. Steeping releases flavors into water.

stew: To gradually cook food—usually meats or vegetables—in liquid in a tightly covered pan or pot.

stir-fry: Quite similar to sautéing in that food is cooked over intense heat with just a little bit of fat, stir-frying starts with cut-up food and therefore proceeds faster. The keys to stir-frying are making sure that all of your ingredients are prepared and close to hand, and using very high heat.

stock: This intensely flavored broth is the resultant juice achieved after simmering seasoned meat, poultry, vegetables, or fish in water. Stock is strained before use.

stockpot: A large pot, usually of at least sixteen quarts, used primarily for making stock or broth.

stone fruits: As probably seems obvious, stone fruits are simply fruits with a stone, such as peach or plum.

strain: To remove particles from a liquid by pouring it through a cheesecloth or sieve.

striped bass: Firm-textured fish with meaty, pinkish flesh. When wild, striped bass are highly flavorful. Now being farm-raised in California. Can be substituted in recipes that call for cod or other milder fish, and some stronger fish, too. Easy to grill.

streusel: A delicious topping of sugar, butter, flour, and other spices that adds flavor and crunch to crumb cakes, coffee cakes, and some muffins.

stuffing: A well-seasoned mixture of bread, spices, vegetables, and usually meat that is "stuffed" inside the cavity of poultry or meat.

sugar snaps: Also called snap peas, these flavorful pea-filled pods are newly developed (introduced in 1979). Sugar snaps are deliciously crisp, with crunchy pods and sweet peas.

summer squash: These light, fleshy squashes of the late summer are available in many varieties—but most notably zucchini and yellow squash. Choose squash that is very firm.

sunchokes: Also called Jerusalem artichokes, sunchokes are the knobby roots of a perennial sunflower. They resemble ginger in appearance and have a subtle, delicious flavor. Their high sugar content enables them to brown well when fried or roasted.

sun-dried tomatoes: When a tomato is dried in the sun (or, more likely these days, the oven), the end result is a shriveled, intensely flavored tomato. They are usually packed in olive oil or packaged dried (when dried, soak them in hot water to reconstitute).

sunflower seeds: Seeds of the bright and beautiful sunflower, these can be roasted or dried in or out of their shells. They can be added to many sweet and savory dishes, including salads, baked goods, and granola.

superfine sugar: This finely granulated sugar is good in meringues and cold drinks; it dissolves quickly and easily.

sweetened condensed milk: Milk that has been evaporated to about a half of its volume and has sugar added. Sticky and sweet.

sweet potato: Contrary to popular belief, the sweet potato is different from the yam. Sweet potatoes are bright with orange flesh, though some varieties have yellow, white, or even purple flesh.

swordfish: Highly popular fish, wonderful on the grill. When buying, look for bright flesh with tight swirls; should smell good. Skin is inedible.

Szechwan peppercorns: Mildly hot spice from the prickly ash tree; brings a sharp, distinctive taste to foods. Szechwan peppercorns are usually toasted before they are ground, which brings out their intense flavor.

Tabasco: A brand-name hot sauce that is essentially chile peppers combined with salt and vinegar.

tahini: Creamy paste of toasted sesame seeds, originally from the Middle East. Best in hummus or made into a sauce with yogurt.

tangerine: What we call tangerines are called mandarins elsewhere in the world; all that matters is that they're loose-skinned oranges that make an ideal snack fruit. The best is the clementine—the small, flattened, seedless fruit that is easier to peel, has less pith, and is sweeter than all other tangerines.

tapioca: This is a starchy ingredient derived from the cassava plant. Tapioca puddings and custards are made with pearl tapioca, which serves as a thickening agent.

taro: The most flavorful of the "new" tubers sold in many supermarkets and many Latin American and Asian markets. Treat as a potato—its flavor is actually better than that of most potatoes—but do not overcook or it will become dry. I have had success with boiling, frying, and sautéing.

tarragon: This licorice-flavored herb is featured often in French cookery, mostly with chicken or shellfish, or in salad dressings and mayonnaise. Fresh is better than dried, but dried is useful. Use sparingly—it's strong stuff.

tart: A sweet- or savory-filled baked pastry with no top crust.

tarte Tatin: Upside-down apple tart with a sugar-and-butter caramelized topping. Best when served immediately after cooking.

tea ball: This perforated metal ball holds leaves or spices and is immersed in boiling water to make tea. Useful for bundling herbs in a stock or sauce; it can be removed easily after cooking.

Tempura: Japanese-style batter-dipped food; very light. Tempura should be served immediately and accompanied by soy sauce.

thermometer: Everyone should have an instant-read thermometer, which can help you judge doneness better than anything else. Frying thermometers and oven thermometers can also be quite handy.

thyme: The essential herb of France, thyme is pungent and somewhat minty. Thyme is used in sausages, stuffings, poultry dishes, stews, roasts, and more. Fresh sprigs are best, but dried thyme has decent flavor.

toast: To brown food by baking or placing under direct heat.

tofu: Also called bean curd, a bland, cheese- or custard-like food made from soybeans. Since tofu assumes the flavor of almost any food that it is cooked with, it can be prepared with almost any variety of different ingredients.

tomatillos: Firm, yellow-green tomatoes that are a staple in Mexican cooking. Great in salsas.

tomatoes: As you know, better from a garden than a supermarket. Off-season, plum tomatoes are a better bet than round ones. Canned tomatoes are often a good option.

tortellini: Small pasta pockets stuffed with cheese, meat, or vegetables.

tortilla: Thin, round bread made of corn or wheat flour; can be baked or fried.

toss: To quickly mix together ingredients, usually for a salad or pasta dish, with a large spoon and fork.

tube pan: This circular pan has a hollow center and is used for baking angel cake, sponge cake, and other cakes. The tube in the center encourages uniform baking.

tuna: An excellent steak fish (and the most popular canned fish), with tender, flaky, and highly flavorful flesh; the best substitute for a good steak, especially when cooked rare. Look for bluefin, but settle for yellowfin.

turmeric: Usually sold ground, and added primarily for its intense yellow color. It's what makes yellow mustard yellow.

turnip: A root vegetable with a sharp flavor that mellows and sweetens when cooked.

turnovers: Pastries filled with a savory or sweet mixture, then baked or deep-fried.

unsaturated fats: Mainly come from plants and are liquid (oil) in form. Largely polyunsaturated fats include corn oil, soybean oil, sunflower oil, and sesame oil. Largely monounsaturated fats, which may lower blood cholesterol levels, include olive oil, canola oil, and peanut oil.

vanilla: Vanilla comes in two forms: vanilla beans, long thin pods that are the fruit of an orchid plant native to Mexico, and vanilla extract, which is made by processing vanilla beans in an alcohol-water solution. There are times when the subtle flavor of whole vanilla beans can have a profound effect on a recipe; in most cases, good quality vanilla extract is perfect. Make sure the extract you buy contains alcohol and vanilla only, and not vanillin, an artificial ingredient made from wood. The label should say "pure vanilla extract"—avoid labels that say "imitation vanilla flavor" or some variation.

vinaigrette: Simply acid and oil, combined; every other addition is up for grabs. The acid may be freshly squeezed citrus juice, usually lemon or lime, or vinegar—the best you can find. The acidic ingredient is the most basic flavor of a vinaigrette, so it should be delicious. Oil can add to a vinaigrette or it may be nothing more than a carrier of other flavors. (For more about vinaigrettes, see page 90).

walnut or hazelnut oil: These highly flavorful oils should (almost) never be used for cooking, but are wonderful in salad dressing and drizzled over cooked foods. Always refrigerate, as nut oils go rancid more quickly than other oils.

wasabi: The Japanese version of horseradish, this root is used to make the fiery green condiment served with sushi and sashimi (see page 764 for my recipe.) It's available in all Asian markets in both powder and paste form; I recommend the powdered wasabi, but note that it deteriorates quickly once opened.

water bath: Also called a bain-marie, this is a technique for cooking delicate dishes like custards and sauces without breaking or curdling them. Just put the baking dish or individual custard cups in a larger baking pan (a roasting pan often works well) and pour hot water at least halfway up the height of the custard. By moderating the temperature around the custard, the water bath makes for more even cooking. It can also be used to keep cooked foods warm.

water chestnut: The tuber of a water plant known as the Chinese sedge, which has a crisp, nutty texture. Although water chestnuts are sometimes available fresh in Asian markets, canned water chestnuts retain the crunchy, juicy texture of fresh ones and are readily available in most supermarkets.

watercress: A member of the mustard family, this crisp, leafy green has a piquant, peppery flavor. Watercress is usually about a dollar a bunch, or more, but you don't need a lot for impact. Buy and use quickly, or risk rotting. Or, if you want to store for more than a couple of days, dunk the stem ends in a glass half-filled with water and wrap the whole thing, glass and all, in a plastic bag. Refrigerate. (For more about watercress and other potent greens, see page 85.)

waxy red or white potatoes: Sometimes sold as "new potatoes" when they are small, these are low-starch potatoes with thin red or white skins. They make the best boiling potatoes, are great roasted, and are decent for other uses. (For more about potato varieties, see page 595.)

weakfish: Has a mouth that is easily torn by fishing hooks—hence its name. This unusual fish with delicate flesh flakes easily, making it quite difficult to handle. Has soft white to rosy flesh. Delicious.

whip: To beat rapidly, by hand or with a whisk or electric mixer, to add air and increase volume. Egg whites or cream are common ingredients that are whipped.

whisk: This metal utensil has a series of looped wires that make lumps disappear as if by magic. You need at least one medium-sized stiff one for keeping sauces smooth, but if you beat cream, egg whites, and so on electronically, you may not need more than that.

whole wheat flour: White flour has had the germ and the bran removed; whole wheat flour contains both. It is nutritionally superior and has a stronger flavor that not everyone likes. The ground germ contains oil, which can grow rancid and bitter, so I recommend buying only as much as you plan to use in the following month or so. Store whole wheat flour in the freezer, if you have room (you need not defrost before using).

wine vinegar: Wine vinegar can be made from either red or white wine. It may be made by the traditional "Orleans method"—that is aging in barrels. But most reasonably priced wine vinegar is made by more efficient methods; it can be quite decent as long as it contains only wine. Good raspberry, tarragon, or other flavored vinegars usually begin with high-quality wine vinegar.

winter squash: These long-keeping squashes have much in common with pumpkin and sweet potato: yellow to orange flesh, usually quite sweet and creamy when cooked. Peel smooth-skinned varieties, like butternut, with a paring knife. For acorn and other bumpy squash, you have no choice but to cook with the skin still on. Winter squash is available almost year-round, although late summer through winter is its season. Look for firm squash with no soft spots or obvious damage, and store as you would potatoes, in a cool, dry place, but not within the refrigerator. Use within a month.

wok: A round-bottomed pan popular in Asian cooking. Preferably, woks are made of rolled steel, which provides excellent heat control. Traditionally, stir-fries are prepared in woks, but there is no reason for the home cook to follow this tradition. In fact, the design of the wok is not well suited to most home ranges; a large, deep-sided skillet, with sloping sides is best. These are sometimes sold as woks with handles, or, as discussed in the skillet section (page 2), in one of the hybridized "sauté pans" with deep, round sides—sort of a combination sauté pan/saucepan.

wontons: Like Chinese ravioli, these small dumplings are filled with meat, seafood, vegetables, or a combination. They may be boiled, steamed, or deep-fried, and served with dipping sauce. Wonton skins can be bought prepackaged in Asian markets and many supermarkets, or, if you're enterprising, see my recipe for wonton/egg roll skins (page 32).

Worcestershire sauce: First bottled in Worcestershire, England, this dark spicy condiment usually includes garlic, soy sauce, tamarind, onions, molasses, lime, anchovies, vinegar, and other seasonings. It's commonly used to season meat, gravy, soup—and the ever popular Bloody Mary.

yam: The true yam, also called *name*, is not the same as a sweet potato (although, since there are hundreds of species, some are similar). It's very bland and, when cooked, very, very dry. It can be fried as chips, but is more often used in meaty stews that contain plenty of liquid, wherever you'd use potatoes.

yeast: A living organism that generates gas as a by product of its consumption of carbohydrates. Combine yeast, liquid, and flour, and you get bubbles, which are in turn trapped by the flour-liquid mixture, causing the dough to rise.

yogurt: Available in standard, low-fat, and nonfat varieties, yogurt is made from milk, skim milk, and/or cream that's been fermented with a (friendly) culture or bacteria.

yuca: Also known as cassava or manioc, this is the root from which tapioca is made. Think of how much liquid tapioca absorbs when you cook it, and you will know why yuca is always served with plenty of liquid. You can bake it like a potato, roast it like a plantain, grate it, and make fritters or even puddings, but it must always be served with liquid.

zest: The outermost colored peel of lemons, oranges, and other citrus fruits. Employing a special utensil called a zester is the easiest way to remove it (see instructions, page 634), but not the only way. You can use a vegetable peeler or paring knife to remove the peel in long ribbons. Since this inevitably brings part of the bitter white pith with it, to do a perfect job you should then lie the strips down on a cutting board and scrape the white part off with a paring knife.

zucchini: The fastest growing of summer fruits, treated as a vegetable in our kitchens, zucchini can be firm and flavorful, but they quickly become watery. This makes them not difficult to cook, but difficult to cook well. The secret is in finding very firm specimens (pass up any that are soft, dented, or bruised) and, if necessary, salting them as you would cucumber (see Step 1 of recipe on page 566). If the yellow summer squash is firmer, substitute that. (For more about zucchini, see page 605.)

Fifty Cookbooks I'd Rather Not Live Without

In the preceding pages I've tried to give a broad survey of simple cooking with an international flair — the kind of cooking I like best. But every topic I touched upon can be gone into with a great deal more depth, and perhaps you're interested in doing that. Or perhaps you'd just like to see an approach to basic cooking that's different from mine.

For whatever reason, it's unlikely that this is the last cookbook you'll ever buy. What follows here is a list of books that I've found more-or-less indispensable over the last thirty years. You won't need most of them, but you'll probably want some, and of the thousands of books I've worked with, these are among the most valuable. They're not necessarily my favorite reference works, or the most literary cookbooks, or the trendiest; they're just the ones in which I believe you'll find the most useful recipes and techniques. (This was not an easy list to assemble, and it's a very personal one, created with apologies to any deserving friends and colleagues I may have omitted.)

Almost all are in print; those that are not may be found on remainder tables or in secondhand bookshops. Only a few are truly obscure, and I recommend those only because no popular book has yet surfaced to take their places.

By Technique

Microwave Gourmet, Barbara Kafka (Morrow, 1987). This answers every question you have about the mysterious appliance we love to hate. Roasting book is another Kafka must-have.

The Thrill of the Grill, Chris Schlesinger and John Willoughby (Morrow, 1990).

> Grilling and barbecuing defined and taken as far as you'll ever need to go. Written with humor and intelligence, as are all of their books.

How to Bake, Nick Malgieri (HarperCollins, 1995).

> Not only desserts, but all of baking. Nick's technique is perfect, and he makes the complex simple.

Desserts, Nancy Silverton (Harper & Row, 1986).

> Do-able but classy desserts from the California pastry master.

The Simple Art of Perfect Baking, Flo Braker (Morrow, 1985).

> The best all-around survey of fancy baked goods. Flo makes it all possible.

The Cake Bible, Rose Levy Beranbaum (Morrow, 1988).

> The title says it all.

Classic Home Desserts, Richard Sax (Chapters, 1994).

> The crowning glory of a great cookbook writer, and the best compilation of American desserts to date.

Sweet Times, Dorie Greenspan (Morrow, 1991).

> Simple desserts that not only work but impress.

By Region

Biscuits, Spoonbread, and Sweet Potato Pie, Bill Neal (Knopf, 1990).

> Southern baking explained; this is accessible, delicious, and authentic food.

Jasper White's Cooking from New England (Harper & Row, 1989).

> Way beyond boiled dinner, this is New England cooking for today. A classic.

The Taste of Country Cooking, Edna Lewis (Knopf, 1976).

> Down-home American food at its best. Lewis' *In Pursuit of Flavor* is another winner.

The Art of Mexican Cooking, Diana Kennedy (Bantam, 1989).

> Kennedy has wit and good taste; she makes a complex cuisine understandable.

The Art of South American Cooking, Felipe Rojas-Lombardi (HarperCollins, 1991).

> Unfortunately, the only serious book on the subject to date. Fortunately, it's damned good.

The Old World Kitchen, Elizabeth Luard (Bantam, 1987).

> A survey of European peasant cooking, and a real treasure. Look for it.

The Foods and Wines of Spain, Penelope Casas (Knopf, 1982).

> Easy-to-cook, full-flavored food.

Catalan Cuisine, Coleman Andrews (Atheneum, 1988).

> Andrews' book took an obscure cuisine and made it user-friendly.

Larousse Gastronomique, 1998 Edition (Crown).

> French cooking—and plenty else—defined, with solid classic recipes. Serious but don't let it intimidate you; it's reasonably accessible.

French Cooking in Ten Minutes, Edouard de Pomiane (North Point Press, 1994).

> Originally published in 1930, this book is part joke, part brilliance. You will absorb enough from it in one hour to make it worth your while. (Thanks, Barbara.)

The Cooking of Southwest France, Paula Wolfert
(Harper & Row, 1983).
>My favorite of Wolfert's books, all of which
>(Couscous, Mediterranean, World of Food, and
>more) are worth having.

Bistro Cooking, Patricia Wells (Workman, 1989).
>Not-too-fancy French restaurant food from *the*
>American in Paris.

French Farmhouse Cookbook, Susan Herrmann
Loomis (Workman, 1996).
>The best book about French home cooking written
>in English in this decade.

Italian Food, Elizabeth David
(Harper & Row, 1954).
>Incredibly, almost a half-century after it was writ-
>ten, this is fresh and vibrant. Any book by David is
>worth owning.

The Splendid Table, Lynne Rossetto Kasper
(Morrow, 1993).
>Italy's haute cuisine explained in depth.

Essentials of Classic Italian Cooking, Marcella Hazan
(Knopf, 1995).
>Her work from the '70s, repackaged and updated,
>and in many ways the only Italian cookbook you'll
>ever need. Nearly perfect.

The Complete Italian Vegetarian Cookbook,
Jack Bishop (Chapters, 1997).
>For light dinners, quick meals and, obviously, veg-
>etarians. Jack and I are from the same school—if
>you like my food, you'll like his.

A Book of Middle Eastern Food, Claudia Roden
(Knopf, 1968).
>The definitive work, not topped in 30 years.

The Flavor of Asia, Reynaldo Alejandro
(Beaufort, 1984).
>A slender volume you'll have trouble finding, but
>a sound introduction to a continent of great
>cooking.

The Cuisines of Asia, Jennifer Brennan
(St. Martin's, 1984).
>A flawed but serious survey; nothing better exists.

Real Thai, Nancie McDermott (Chronicle, 1992).
>A primer for anyone who wants to begin to take
>Thai cooking seriously.

Classic Indian Cooking, Julie Sahni (Morrow, 1980).
>The best introduction to Indian cooking. Her
>Classic Indian Vegetarian and Grain Cooking, is
>also worth having.

The Modern Art of Chinese Cooking, Barbara Tropp
(Morrow, 1982).
>By far the best contemporary work on the
>subject—complete, understandable, fresh-flavored,
>and hip.

Japanese Cooking, A Simple Art, Shizuo Tsuji
(Kodansha, 1980).
>Not as accessible as it might be, this remains the
>clearest introduction to Japanese cooking that
>exists, with a good deal of depth.

By Food

Splendid Soups, James Peterson (Bantam 1993).
>All of Jim's work is good, and this is as detailed as
>you could wish.

Fish: The Complete Guide to Buying and Cooking,
Mark Bittman (Macmillan, 1994).
>Excuse my immodesty. Informal and informative.

Jane Grigson's Fruit Book (Atheneum, 1982).
Like everything Grigson wrote, literate and brilliantly researched. Her Vegetable book is also a classic.

Bernard Clayton's New Complete Book of Breads (Simon & Schuster, 1987).
The bread bible. Use it in conjunction with Charlie Van Over's techniques for the entire world of bread baking.

The Best Bread Ever, Charles Van Over (Broadway, 1997).
Bread-baking modernized, by the man who makes it easy.

Flatbreads and Flavors, Jeffrey Alford and Naomi Duguid (Morrow, 1995).
An international cookbook that goes way beyond bread. Loads of fun, with much that is unusual.

General

La Varenne Pratique, Anne Willan (Dorling Kindersley, 1989).
Don't let the title put you off—this wonderfully photographed gem is an unsurpassed basic reference, and the recipes are solid.

The New James Beard (Knopf, 1981).
The best compilation by the dean of American cooking, and a joy to read.

The Way to Cook, Julia Child (Knopf, 1989).
America's own at the top of her game. A must-have.

The Dean & Deluca Cookbook, David Rosengarten (Random House, 1996).
International cooking for the 90s—simple and straightforward.

The Joy of Cooking, Rombauer/Becker (Scribner, 1975/1997).
Whether classic old version or recent revision, the best-selling cookbook of all time.

Pleasures of the Good Earth, Ed Giobbi (Knopf, 1991).
Great ideas for gardeners and cooks from a brilliant gardener, cook, and artist.

The New Making of a Cook, Madeleine Kamman (Morrow, 1997).
Kamman has spent a lifetime not only cooking but thinking, and it shows. A brilliant, careful work.

Chef's Books that Work for Home Cooks

Cucina Simpatica, Johanne Killeen and George Germon (HarperCollins, 1991).
This book offers trendy food that is not restaurant food and that works well at home.

Cooking with Daniel Boulud (Random House, 1993).
Incredibly written when Boulud was at Le Cirque. Here, the style is just right. A gem.

The Cuisine of Fredy Girardet (Morrow, 1982).
Simple, do-able, and incredibly delicious recipes from the man many consider the greatest chef of our era.

Home Cooking with a French Accent, Michel Richard (Morrow, 1993).
Richard is a great chef with a rare sense of humor; the combination is irresistible, and the food wonderfully accessible.

Jean-Georges: Cooking at Home with a Four-Star Chef, Jean-Georges Vongerichten and Mark Bittman (Broadway, 1998).
The master of Franco-Asian cooking, interpreted by yours truly. Check it out.

Mail-Order Sources

Almost every ingredient in this book is available at your local supermarket and nearly every piece of equipment at your local cookware supply store. If you live in a remote area, or are curious to see what's available beyond your area, these mail-order sources—my favorites—will be helpful.

General Ingredients

Zingerman's
422 Detroit Street
Ann Arbor, MI 48104
888-636-8162 or 313-769-1625

Balducci's
95 Sherwood Avenue
Farmingdale, NY 11735
800-BALDUCCI

Dean & Deluca
P.O. Box 20810
Wichita, KS 67208
800-221-7714

Cheese

The Mozzarella Company
2944 Elm Street
Dallas, TX 75226
800-798-2954 or 214-741-4072

Spices and Dried Herbs

Penzy's Spice House
P.O. Box 933
Muskego, WI 53150-9920
414-574-0277

Herbs

The Herb Farm
32804 Issaquah-Fall City Road
Fall City, WA 98024
800-866-HERB

Beans, Seeds, Chiles, and Corn

Seeds of Change
P.O. Box 15700
Santa Fe, NM 87506
888-762-7333

Game and Poultry

D'Artagnan
280 Wilson
Newark, NJ 07105
973-344-0565

Dried Fruits, Native Nuts, and Preserves

American Spoon Foods
P.O. Box 566
1668 Clarion Avenue
Petoskey, MI 49770
800-222-5886 or 616-347-9030

Mexican Ingredients

Kitchen Market
218 Eighth Avenue
New York, NY 10011
212-243-4433

The CMC Company
P.O. Box 322
Avalon, NJ 08202
800-CMC-2780

Asian Ingredients

Anzen Oriental Foods and Imports
736 NE Martin Luther King Jr. Boulevard
Portland, OR 97232
(503) 233-5111

The Oriental Pantry
423 Great Road
Acton, MA 01720
800-828-0368 or 978-264-4576

Turkish & Middle Eastern Ingredients

Sultan's Delight
P.O. Box 090302
Brooklyn, NY 11209
800-852-5046

Greater Galilee Gourmet
2118 Wilshire Boulevard
Suite 829
Santa Monica, CA 90403
800-290-1391 or 310-459-9120

Southwestern Ingredients

Coyote Cafe General Store
132 West Water Street
Santa Fe, NM 87501
800-866-HOWL or 505-982-2454

Baking Ingredients

King Arthur Flour Baker's Catalog
P.O. Box 876
Norwich, VT 05055
800-827-6836

Organic Ingredients (especially grains)
Gold Mine Natural Food Company
3419 Hancock St.
San Diego, CA 92110
800-475-FOOD

Walnut Acres
Walnut Acre Road
Penns Creek, PA 17862
800-433-3998

Coteau Connoisseur
Route 2
Box 182C Dakota Avenue
Luverne, MN 56156
507-283-2338

Equipment
Bridge Kitchenware
214 East 52 Street
New York, NY 10022
800-274-3435 or 212-838-1901

Williams-Sonoma
P.O. Box 7456
San Francisco, CA 94120
800-541-2233

The Chef's Catalog
P.O. Box 620048
Dallas, TX 75262
800-338-3232

Sur La Table
Catalog Division
1765 Sixth Avenue South
Seattle, WA 98134
800-243-0852 or 206-448-2244

Cookbooks
Jessica's Biscuit
Box 301
Newtonville, MA 02160
800-878-4264 or 617-965-0530

List of Illustrations

Index

Halibut steaks simmered in soy
       broth, 298
Ham. *See also* Prosciutto
    baked country, 475
    baked wet-cured, 476
    basics of, 456, 475
    and cheese soufflé, 743
    split pea soup with carrots and, 65
    white bean soup with, 64
Hamburgers. *See* Beef, burgers
Handmade mayonnaise, 762
Hanoi noodle soup, 78
Hard-boiled egg, 733
Haricots, basics of, 504
Hasenpfeffer (marinated and stewed
       rabbit), 497
Hash, corned beef (or roast beef),
       439
Hazelnut oil, about, 88
Hazelnuts, in nutty vinaigrette, 93
Heart, veal, broiled or grilled, 453
Heat, basics of, 10
Herb(-s, -ed). *See also specific herbs*
    bluefish or mackerel fillets with,
       broiled, 309
    brown rice with cashews and, 213
    butter, 768
       roast chicken with, 360
       sautéed smelts with, 322
       and wine sauce, roast chicken
           with, 361
    chicken cutlets, 389
    chicken with lemon and, broiled
       or grilled, 376
    cod or other thick white fillet
       with, roast, 288
    cod or other thick white fillet
       with white wine and,
       broiled, 286
    croutons, 82
    and egg soup, 61
    flatfish or other white fillets with
       mustard and, broiled, 278
    frittata, 741
    goat cheese, 24
    linguine with fresh, 145
    littlenecks with butter and,
       steamed, 343

marinade, chicken cutlets with,
       grilled or broiled, 381
-marinated grilled pork chops,
       459
mayonnaise, 762
meatballs, 495
monkfish or other steaks roasted
       with, 296
mustard, sweet, 764
oil, 775
    rice with, 207
and onion bread, 225
pasta, 159
quail with herbs, wine-braised,
       419
red snapper or other fillets in
       packages with tomato and,
       284
rice, 205
rice with fresh, 206
roast chicken parts with olive oil
       and, 374
-roasted boneless turkey breast,
       408
-roasted chicken cutlets, 393
-rubbed grilled swordfish, tuna,
       or other steaks, 294
salmon roasted with, 305
sandwich bread, 229
-stuffed eggs, 19
stuffing, broiled lobster with, 337
tea, 797
tenderloin with, roast, 431
tomato sauce with, 131
whiting or other small whole fish
       baked with shallots and, 316
Hiziki, about, 602
Hoisin, pork with sesame oil and,
       stir-fried, 460
Hollandaise sauce, 790
Homemade horseradish, 772
Homemade mild chile paste, 774
Hominy (pozole)
    basic, 193
    basics of, 192–93
    bean casserole with tortillas and,
       513
    creamed, 193

flash-cooked, with kale or
       collards, 193
Honey
    chicken cutlets with cumin and,
       grilled or broiled, 380
    roast chicken with cumin, orange
       juice, and, 359
    split chicken with mustard and,
       grilled or broiled, 367
Honeydew balls, spiced, 20
Hoppin' John, 515
Horseradish
    butter, 769
    dip, 21
    homemade, 772
    sauce
       braised pork with, 469
       chicken cutlets with, grilled or
           broiled, 381
    short ribs with, 433
Hot-and-sour sauce, braised whole
       grouper or other large whole
       fish with, 316
Hot-and-sour soup, 76
Hot buttered rum, 807
Hot chocolate, 797
    Mexican, 798
    mocha, 797
Hot cross buns, 242
Hot fudge sauce, 672
Hot red pepper, pasta with cauli-
       flower, anchovies, and, 135
Hot sauce, stir-fried littlenecks in,
       344
Hot water dough for pasta, 157
Hummus, 23
Hush puppies, 190

Iceberg lettuce, about, 84
Ice cream
    basics of, 663–64
    butterscotch, 665
       swirl, 665
    chocolate, 667
       swirl, 665
    chocolate chip, M&M, Rocky
       Road, or other chunky, 665
    coconut, 668

Quick stir-fried snow peas or sugar snap peas, 591

Quinoa
  basic, 195
  basics of, 195
  "pilaf," 196
  stuffing with bacon, 196

Rabbit, marinated and stewed (Hasenpfeffer), 497

Racks, metal, 6

Radicchio
  about, 84, 85, 571–72
  baked ziti with Gorgonzola and, 143
  pasta with pine nuts, raisins, and, 136
  with prosciutto, braised, 572
  in red and green salad, 99

Radishes
  about, 601
  butter-braised, 601

Ragu (meat sauce, Bolognese-style), 150

Raisin(s)
  about, 633
  bagels, 236
  bread, 248
    nut-and-, 248
  caponata with pine nuts and, 102
  couscous with pine nuts and, 192
  curried bulgur with nuts, carrots, and, 186
  pasta with radicchio, pine nuts, and, 136
  pie, peach-and-, 690
  pilaf with onions, pine nuts, and, 202
  sautéed cod or other thick white fillets with pine nuts and, 289

Raspberry(-ies)
  about, 627–28
  -ade, 801
  fool, 628
  gratin, 628
    with Swedish cream, 629
  pie, 689
  sauce, 672

Ratatouille, oven-baked (tian of vegetables), 616

Ravioli
  to make, 160
  meat filling for, 159

Raw tomato sauce, pasta with, 133

Razor blade, 221

Real buttered popcorn, 16

Real onion dip, 21

Real tartar sauce, 762

Reamer, citrus, 6

Recado rojo (Puerto Rican-style seasoning paste), 779

Red and green salad, 99

Red beans
  with meat, 513
  and rice, 516
  vegetarian, 513

Red bell pepper, roasted, and garlic spread, 24

Red gazpacho, basic, 79

Red pasta, 158

Red pepper relish, 774

Red snapper
  about, 312
  extra-crisp
    with apples, 281
    with butter-toasted pecans, 280
  in packages (en papillote), 284
    with carrots and zucchini, 284
    with spinach, 284
    with tomato and herbs, 284
  Provençal-style, 290
  whole
    grilled or broiled, 313
    roasted, 314
    roasted, with tomatoes and bread crumbs, 315

Reducing stock, 43

Reduction sauces. See Sauce(s), reduction

Red wine
  lamb medallions with shallots, tarragon, and, 491
  octopus with tomatoes and, 339
  pears poached in, 642
  poached peaches with spices and, 640
  salmon fillets in, 305

sauce
  chicken in, 369
  chopped steak with, 428
  pan-seared steak with (steak au poivre), 428

Refried beans
  with cumin, 511
  traditional, 512

Refrigerator (rolled) cookies, 712
  gingerbread men, 714
  gingersnaps, Aunt Big's, 714
  to glaze, 712
  lighter, 713
  molasses-spice, 714
  peanut butter, 713
  simple ideas for, 713

Relish
  corn and tomato, 782
  corn and tomato, grilled swordfish, tuna, or other steaks with, 294
  cranberry, with orange and ginger, 777
  mango-onion, 777
  red pepper, 774

Rendering fat, 358

Reuben sandwich, 268

Rhubarb
  about, 645–46
  compote with dates, 646
  pie, 689
    -strawberry, 689
  to prepare, 645

Ribs. See also Short ribs; Spareribs
  beef, and cinnamon, pasta sauce with, 151
  lamb, grilled or broiled, 489

Rice, 197–215. See also Risotto
Arborio. See also Risotto
  about, 198
  salad with peas, 114
basics of, 197
and beans
  basics of, 515
  lentils and rice with caramelized onions, 516

Doneness Temperatures

Use an instant-read thermometer for the best possible accuracy; always measure with the probe in the thickest part of the meat, not touching any bone (ideally, measure in more than one place). When you gain experience in cooking, you'll be able to judge doneness by look and feel.

Beef
- 125°F = Rare
- 130–135°F = Medium-rare
- 135–140°F = Medium
- 140–150°F = Medium-well
- 155°F + = Well-done

Pork
- 137°F = Temperature at which trichinosis is killed
- 150°F = slightly pink but moist
- 160°F = Well-done (and probably dry)

Chicken
- 160°F = Breast is done
- 165°F = Thigh is done

Lamb
- 125°F = Very rare
- 130°F = Rare
- 135°F = Medium-rare
- 140°F = Medium
- 150°F = Medium-well
- 160°F + = Well-done

USDA–Recommended Internal Temperatures

The recommended internal temperatures given in this book for meats and poultry are based on producing the best-tasting food, and are in line with traditional levels of doneness. The United States Department of Agriculture (USDA), however, generally recommends higher temperatures, which reduces the potential danger of contracting illness caused by bacteria.

Beef, Veal, and Lamb
- Ground meat (hamburger, etc.) 160°F

Roasts, Steaks, and Chops
- 145°F = Medium-rare
- 160°F = Medium
- 170°F = Well-done

Pork (all cuts including ground)
- 160°F = Medium
- 170°F = Well-done

Poultry
- Ground chicken and turkey: 165°F
- Whole chicken and turkey: 180°F
- Stuffing: 165°F
- Poultry Breasts: 170°F
- Poultry Thighs: Cook until juices run clear
- Egg Dishes: 160°F